The Cambridge Handbook of Discourse Studies

Discourse studies, which encompasses the ways in which language is used in texts and contexts, is a fast-moving and increasingly diverse field. With contributions from leading and upcoming scholars from across the world, and covering cutting-edge research, this handbook offers an up-to-date survey of discourse studies. It is organized according to perspectives and areas of engagement, with each chapter providing an overview of the historical development of its topic, the main current issues, debates and synergies, and future directions. The handbook presents new perspectives on well-established themes such as narrative, conversation-analytic and cognitive approaches to discourse, while also embracing a range of up-to-the-minute topics from post-humanism to digital surveillance, recent methodological orientations such as linguistic landscapes and multimodal discourse analysis, and new fields of engagement such as discourses on race, religion and money.

ANNA DE FINA is Professor of Italian Language and Linguistics at Georgetown University.

ALEXANDRA GEORGAKOPOULOU is Professor of Discourse Analysis and Sociolinguistics at King's College London.

Together they have co-authored *Analyzing Narrative* (2012) and co-edited *The Handbook of Narrative Analysis* (2015).

CAMBRIDGE HANDBOOKS IN LANGUAGE AND LINGUISTICS

Genuinely broad in scope, each handbook in this series provides a complete state-of-the-field overview of a major sub-discipline within language study and research. Grouped into broad thematic areas, the chapters in each volume encompass the most important issues and topics within each subject, offering a coherent picture of the latest theories and findings. Together, the volumes will build into an integrated overview of the discipline in its entirety.

Published Titles

The Cambridge Handbook of Phonology, edited by Paul de Lacy
The Cambridge Handbook of Linguistic Code-Switching, edited by Barbara E. Bullock and Almeida Jacqueline Toribio
The Cambridge Handbook of Child Language, Second Edition, edited by Edith L. Bavin and Letitia Naigles
The Cambridge Handbook of Endangered Languages, edited by Peter K. Austin and Julia Sallabank
The Cambridge Handbook of Sociolinguistics, edited by Rajend Mesthrie
The Cambridge Handbook of Pragmatics, edited by Keith Allan and Kasia M. Jaszczolt
The Cambridge Handbook of Language Policy, edited by Bernard Spolsky
The Cambridge Handbook of Second Language Acquisition, edited by Julia Herschensohn and Martha Young-Scholten
The Cambridge Handbook of Biolinguistics, edited by Cedric Boeckx and Kleanthes K. Grohmann
The Cambridge Handbook of Generative Syntax, edited by Marcel den Dikken
The Cambridge Handbook of Communication Disorders, edited by Louise Cummings
The Cambridge Handbook of Stylistics, edited by Peter Stockwell and Sara Whiteley
The Cambridge Handbook of Linguistic Anthropology, edited by N. J. Enfield, Paul Kockelman and Jack Sidnell
The Cambridge Handbook of English Corpus Linguistics, edited by Douglas Biber and Randi Reppen
The Cambridge Handbook of Bilingual Processing, edited by John W. Schwieter
The Cambridge Handbook of Learner Corpus Research, edited by Sylviane Granger, Gaëtanelle Gilquin and Fanny Meunier
The Cambridge Handbook of Linguistic Multicompetence, edited by Li Wei and Vivian Cook
The Cambridge Handbook of English Historical Linguistics, edited by Merja Kytö and Päivi Pahta
The Cambridge Handbook of Formal Semantics, edited by Maria Aloni and Paul Dekker
The Cambridge Handbook of Morphology, edited by Andrew Hippisley and Greg Stump
The Cambridge Handbook of Historical Syntax, edited by Adam Ledgeway and Ian Roberts
The Cambridge Handbook of Linguistic Typology, edited by Alexandra Y. Aikhenvald and R. M. W. Dixon
The Cambridge Handbook of Areal Linguistics, edited by Raymond Hickey
The Cambridge Handbook of Cognitive Linguistics, edited by Barbara Dancygier
The Cambridge Handbook of Japanese Linguistics, edited by Yoko Hasegawa

The Cambridge Handbook of Spanish Linguistics, edited by Kimberly L. Geeslin

The Cambridge Handbook of Bilingualism, edited by Annick De Houwer and Lourdes Ortega

The Cambridge Handbook of Systemic Functional Linguistics, edited by Geoff Thompson, Wendy L. Bowcher, Lise Fontaine and David Schönthal

The Cambridge Handbook of African Linguistics, edited by H. Ekkehard Wolff

The Cambridge Handbook of Language Learning, edited by John W. Schwieter and Alessandro Benati

The Cambridge Handbook of Germanic Linguistics, edited by Michael T. Putnam and B. Richard Page

The Cambridge Handbook of World Englishes, edited by Daniel Schreier, Marianne Hundt and Edgar W. Schneider

The Cambridge Handbook of Intercultural Communication, edited by Guido Rings and Sebastian Rasinger

The Cambridge Handbook of Discourse Studies, edited by Anna De Fina and Alexandra Georgakopoulou

The Cambridge Handbook of Discourse Studies

Edited by
Anna De Fina
Georgetown University
Alexandra Georgakopoulou
King's College London

CAMBRIDGE
UNIVERSITY PRESS

University Printing House, Cambridge CB2 8BS, United Kingdom

One Liberty Plaza, 20th Floor, New York, NY 10006, USA

477 Williamstown Road, Port Melbourne, VIC 3207, Australia

314–321, 3rd Floor, Plot 3, Splendor Forum, Jasola District Centre,
New Delhi – 110025, India

79 Anson Road, #06-04/06, Singapore 079906

Cambridge University Press is part of the University of Cambridge.

It furthers the University's mission by disseminating knowledge in the pursuit of education, learning, and research at the highest international levels of excellence.

www.cambridge.org
Information on this title: www.cambridge.org/9781108425148
DOI: 10.1017/9781108348195

© Cambridge University Press 2020

This publication is in copyright. Subject to statutory exception
and to the provisions of relevant collective licensing agreements,
no reproduction of any part may take place without the written
permission of Cambridge University Press.

First published 2020

Printed in the United Kingdom by TJ International Ltd, Padstow Cornwall

A catalogue record for this publication is available from the British Library.

Library of Congress Cataloging-in-Publication Data
Names: De Fina, Anna, editor. | Georgakopoulou, Alexandra, editor.
Title: The Cambridge handbook of discourse studies / edited by Anna De Fina, Georgetown University, Washington DC ; Alexandra Georgakopoulou, King's College, London.
Description: Cambridge ; New York : Cambridge University Press, 2020. | Series: Cambridge handbooks in language and linguistics | Includes bibliographical references and index.
Identifiers: LCCN 2020009238 (print) | LCCN 2020009239 (ebook) | ISBN 9781108425148 (hardback) | ISBN 9781108348195 (ebook)
Subjects: LCSH: Discourse analysis. | Discourse analysis – Methodology.
Classification: LCC P302 .C327 2020 (print) | LCC P302 (ebook) | DDC 401/.41–dc23
LC record available at https://lccn.loc.gov/2020009238
LC ebook record available at https://lccn.loc.gov/2020009239

ISBN 978-1-108-42514-8 Hardback

Cambridge University Press has no responsibility for the persistence or accuracy of URLs for external or third-party internet websites referred to in this publication and does not guarantee that any content on such websites is, or will remain, accurate or appropriate.

Contents

List of Figures	page x
List of Tables	xii
List of Contributors	xiii
Preface	xxiii

Part I: (Con)Textualizing Discourses 1
    Introduction 1
  1 Registers, Styles, Indexicality   *Robert Moore* 9
  2 Situating Discourse Analysis in Ethnographic
     and Sociopolitical Context   *Jennifer Roth-Gordon* . . . 32
  3 Context and Its Complications   *Jan Blommaert (with Laura
     Smits and Noura Yacoubi)* 52
  4 Historicity, Interdiscursivity and Intertextuality in Discourse
     Studies   *Branca Falabella Fabricio and Luiz Paulo Moita-Lopes* . . . 70
  5 Rethinking Narrative: Tellers, Tales and Identities
     in Contemporary Worlds   *Anna De Fina and Alexandra
     Georgakopoulou* 91

Part II: Perspectives and Modes of Analysis 115
    Introduction 115
  6 Sequence Organization: Understanding What Drives
     Talk   *Emily Hofstetter* 121
  7 Doing Micro-Analysis of Discourse: The Case of Ageing
     and Wellbeing   *Rachel Heinrichsmeier* 143
  8 Corpus-Assisted Discourse Studies   *Clyde Ancarno* . . . 165
  9 Cognitive Linguistic and Experimental Methods
     in Critical Discourse Studies   *Christopher Hart* 186
  10 Metaphor, Metonymy and Framing in Discourse
      Zsófia Demjén and Elena Semino 213

11 Poststructuralist Discourse Studies: From Structure
    to Practice   *Johannes Angermuller*   235

Part III: Discourse Materialities and Embodiment   255
    Introduction   255
12 Multimodality   *Sabine Tan, Kay O'Halloran and Peter Wignell*   263
13 Sign Theory and the Materiality of Discourse   *Jack Sidnell*   282
14 Discourse and the Linguistic Landscape   *Philip Seargeant
    and Korina Giaxoglou*   306
15 Discourse, Emotions and Embodiment   *Brigitta Busch*   327
16 Posthumanism and Its Implications for Discourse
    Studies   *Gavin Lamb and Christina Higgins*   350

Part IV: (Trans)Locations and Intersections   371
    Introduction   371
17 Transnationalism, Globalization and Superdiversity
    Zane Goebel   377
18 Translanguaging and Momentarity in Social Interaction
    Tong King Lee and Li Wei   394
19 Intersectionality, Affect and Discourse   *Kristine Køhler
    Mortensen and Tommaso M. Milani*   417
20 Expanding Academic Discourses: Diverse Englishes, Modalities
    and Spatial Repertoires   *Brooke R. Schreiber, Mohammad Naseh
    Nasrollahi Shahri and Suresh Canagarajah*   437

Part V: Ethics, Inequality and Inclusion   457
    Introduction   457
21 Ethics and the Study of Discourse   *Martyn Hammersley*   465
22 Migrants, Citizenship and Language Rights   *Lionel Wee*   487
23 Diversity and Inclusion in Education
    Yi-Ju Lai and Kendall A. King   505
24 Discourse and Racialization   *Virginia Zavala
    and Michele Back*   527
25 Discourse and Narrative in Legal Settings: The Political
    Asylum Process   *Amy Shuman and Carol Bohmer*   547
26 Discourse and Religion in Educational Practice
    Vally Lytra   571

Part VI: Discourses, Publics and Mediatization   593
    Introduction   593
27 The Critical Analysis of Genre and Social Action
    Anders Björkvall   601
28 Rhetorics, Discourse and Populist Politics   *Markus Rheindorf*   622

29 The Discourses of Money and the Economy *Annabelle Mooney* 644
30 Corporate Discourse *Sylvia Jaworska* 666
31 Mediatized Communication and Linguistic Reflexivity
    in Contemporary Public and Political Life *Cedric Deschrijver* 687
32 Discourse Analysis and Digital Surveillance *Rodney H. Jones* 708

Index 732

Figures

8.1	Concordances for the word cat (*MOP animals corpus*): keyword in context (KWIC) view	page 168
9.1a	Free motion schema	190
9.1b	Force-dynamic schema	191
9.2a	One-tailed action schema	192
9.2b	Force-dynamic schema	192
9.3	Two-tailed action schema	192
9.4a	Restricted viewing frame	197
9.4b	Expanded viewing frame	197
9.5	Schematization and spatial point of view in transitive versus reciprocal verb constructions	199
9.6	Sentence-image matching task (Hart 2019)	204
9.7	Image stimuli (Hart 2019)	206
13.1	Two representations of "the speech circuit" (Saussure 1959: 11, 12)	284
13.2	Object as correspondence-preserving projection (Kockelman 2005: 236, 242)	291
13.3	Osho's signature, 1976 version (left), from the will (right)	296
13.4	Diana and Carla, 1	297
13.5	Diana and Carla, 2	299
13.6	Language and interaction as disembodied heads à la Saussure (left) and as fully embodied participation à la Goodwin (right)	300
15.1	Bodies and affects as conceived in discourse, deployed in interaction and lived by subjects; "embodiment" standing for enactment (in interaction), incarnation (of discursively established positions) or incorporation (of lived experience)	344
18.1	Translanguaging sign (1): Watermelons	400
18.2	Translanguaging sign (2): Pineapples	401
18.3	"Our Story" page, *Kongish Daily*	403
18.4	A Singlish poster (image courtesy of Andrea Lau)	405

19.1	*One in Nine*, Joburg Pride 2012	429
27.1	*Code of Ethics*, Connecticut Department of Correction	603
27.2	Strategy 2016–2018 of the Food Safety Authority of Ireland (FSAI)	605
32.1	Quiz prompt from Nametest.com	709

Tables

8.1	Top twenty keywords for a corpus of newspaper articles about animals (reference corpus: *SiBol/Port corpus*)	page 170
8.2	Top twenty collocates for the word cat in the *MOP animals corpus*	171
8.3	Top twenty fourgrams for the *MOP animals corpus*	172
9.1	Construal operations, cognitive systems and discursive strategies	189
11.1	Three conjunctures of poststructuralism (Angermuller 2015: 19)	238

Contributors

Clyde Ancarno is Lecturer of Applied Linguistics at King's College London. She is interested in corpus-assisted discourse studies (CADS), particularly how these can be used across disciplinary boundaries to explore textual data.

Johannes Angermuller is Professor of Discourse, Languages and Applied Linguistics at Open University and has been director of the ERC DISCONEX and INTAC projects at Warwick University and the School for Advanced Studies in the Social Sciences (EHESS, Paris) since 2012. After obtaining a PhD at University of Paris-Est and Otto-von-Guericke University in 2003, he was a junior professor in the sociology of higher education at Mainz University. He has published widely in the field of discourse studies, including *Poststructuralist Discourse Analysis: Subjectivity in Enunciative Pragmatics* (Palgrave Macmillan, 2014) and *Why There Is No Poststructuralism in France: The Making of an Intellectual Generation* (Bloomsbury, 2015), which have been translated into French, German, Portuguese, Spanish and Turkish.

Michele Back is Associate Professor, World Languages Education, at the University of Connecticut and studies the intersection of multilingualism, race and ethnicity in educational and naturalistic contexts. Her works include *Transcultural Performance: Negotiating Globalized Indigenous Identities* (Palgrave, 2015) and *Racialization and Language: Interdisciplinary Perspectives from Peru* (coedited with V. Zavala; Routledge, 2019).

Anders Björkvall is Professor of Swedish at Örebro University. He is active in the fields of multimodal discourse analysis, social semiotics, genre analysis, and literacy and learning. His latest publications include "Material Sign-Making in Diverse Contexts: 'Upcycled' Artefacts as Refracting Global/Local Discourses" (with A. Archer; in *Making Signs, Translanguaging Ethnographies: Exploring Urban, Rural and Educational Spaces*, ed. by E. Adami and A. Sherris, Multilingual Matters, 2019),

"Keeping the Discussion among Civil Servants Alive: 'Platform of Values' as an Emerging Genre within the Public Sector in Sweden" (with C. Nyström Höög; *Scandinavian Journal of Public Administration*, 2018) and "Legitimation of Value Practices, Value Texts, and Core Values at Public Authorities" (with C. Nyström Höög; *Discourse & Communication*, 2019).

Jan Blommaert is Professor of Language, Culture and Globalization at Tilburg University and holds appointments at Ghent University and the University of the Western Cape. Publications include *Discourse: A Critical Introduction* (Cambridge University Press, 2005), *Grassroots Literacy* (Routledge, 2008), *The Sociolinguistics of Globalization* (Cambridge University Press, 2010) and *Durkheim and the Internet* (Bloomsbury, 2018).

Carol Bohmer is a lawyer and sociologist, a visiting scholar in the Government Department at Dartmouth College and a teaching fellow at King's College London. She has worked in the area of law and society, examining the way legal and social institutions interact, with particular emphasis on the role of gender in law. Her current research interests are in the field of immigration and asylum. She is coauthor with Amy Shuman of *Rejecting Refugees: Political Asylum in the 21st Century* (Routledge, 2007) and *Political Asylum Deceptions: The Culture of Suspicion* (Palgrave Macmillan, 2018).

Brigitta Busch is an applied linguist. In 2009 she was granted a Berta-Karlik research professorship by the University of Vienna. She has also been working for many years as an expert for the Council of Europe.

Suresh Canagarajah is Edwin Erle Sparks Professor in Applied Linguistics and English at Penn State University. His current research focuses on the academic communication of international STEM scholars.

Anna De Fina is Professor of Italian Language and Linguistics in the Italian department and affiliated faculty with the Linguistics department at Georgetown University. Her interests and publications focus on identity, narrative, discourse and migration, and superdiversity. Her books include *Identity in Narrative: A Study of Immigrant Discourse* (John Benjamins, 2003), *Analyzing Narratives* (with A. Georgakopoulou; Cambridge University Press, 2012) and the coedited volumes *Discourse and Identity* (with D. Schiffrin and M. Bamberg; Cambridge University Press, 2006) and *Storytelling in the Digital World* (with S. Perrino; John Benjamins, 2019).

Zsófia Demjén is Associate Professor of Applied Linguistics at the UCL Centre for Applied Linguistics, editor of *Applying Linguistics in Illness and Healthcare Contexts* (Bloomsbury, 2020). Her research interests include health communication, metaphor and the intersections of language, mind and health(care). She is author of *Sylvia Plath and the Language of Affective States: Written Discourse and the Experience of Depression* (Bloomsbury, 2015), coauthor of *Metaphor, Cancer and the End of Life: A Corpus-Based Study* (with E. Semino, A. Hardie, S. Payne and P. Rayson; Routledge,

2018) and coeditor of *The Routledge Handbook of Metaphor and Language* (with E. Semino; Routledge, 2017).

Cedric Deschrijver earned his PhD at King's College London, investigating metalanguage and shifting indexical links surrounding economic/financial terms in online debates. He is currently employed at Hong Kong Shue Yan University, and uses methods of linguistic-pragmatics discourse analysis to investigate the metapragmatics of online economics discourse and the metapragmatic labels surrounding media discourse (for example, "fake news" and "conspiracy theory").

Branca Falabella Fabricio is an associate professor at the Federal University of Rio de Janeiro, working in the Interdisciplinary Program of Applied Linguistics. She is also a researcher of the Brazilian National Research Council (CNPq). Her research interests are related to identity practices in changing institutional contexts, with a special focus on text trajectories and potential identity effects, leading to subtle rearrangements.

Alexandra Georgakopoulou is Professor of Discourse Analysis and Sociolinguistics at King's College London. She has developed small stories research, a paradigm for studying identities in everyday life stories. Her latest study of small stories on social media has been carried out within the ERC project "Life-Writing of the Moment: The Sharing and Updating Self on Social Media" (www.ego-media.org). Her latest book is entitled *Quantified Storytelling: A Narrative Analysis of Metrics on Social Media* (with S. Iversen and C. Stage; Palgrave, 2000).

Korina Giaxoglou is a lecturer in English language and applied linguistics at Open University. Her research focuses on the circulation of stories and affect in "traditional" and contemporary sharing practices. She has been investigating digital mourning as small stories linked to specific types of affective positioning in her research monograph *A Narrative Approach to Social Media Mourning. Small Stories and Affective Positioning* (Routledge, 2020).

Zane Goebel is an associate professor at the University of Queensland, where he teaches Indonesian and applied linguistics. Goebel works on language and social relations in Indonesia. He has published three monographs in this area: *Language, Migration, and Identity: Neighborhood Talk in Indonesia* (Cambridge University Press, 2010), *Language and Superdiversity: Indonesians Knowledging at Home and Abroad* (Oxford University Press, 2015) and *Global Leadership Talk: Constructing Good Governance in Indonesia* (Oxford University Press, 2020). He has also edited a number of collections, including *Rapport and the Discursive Co-construction of Social Relations in Fieldwork Settings* (Mouton de Gruyter, 2019), *Contact Talk: The Discursive Organization of Contact and Boundaries* (with D. Cole and H. Manns; Routledge, 2019) and *Reimagining Rapport* (Oxford University Press, forthcoming).

Martyn Hammersley is Emeritus Professor of Educational and Social Research at Open University. He has researched into the sociology of education and the sociology of the media; however, much of his work is concerned with the methodological issues surrounding social enquiry. His books include *The Dilemma of Qualitative Method* (Routledge, 1989), *What's Wrong with Ethnography?* (Routledge, 1992), *The Politics of Social Research* (Sage, 1995), *Reading Ethnographic Research* (Longman/Routledge, 1997), *Questioning Qualitative Inquiry* (Sage, 2008), *The Limits of Social Science* (Sage, 2014), *The Radicalism of Ethnomethodology* (Manchester University Press, 2018) and *Ethnography: Principles in Practice* (with P. Atkinson; 4th ed., Routledge, 2019).

Christopher Hart is Professor of Linguistics at Lancaster University. His research investigates the link between language, cognition and social action in political contexts of communication. He is author of *Critical Discourse Analysis and Cognitive Science: New Perspectives on Immigration Discourse* (Palgrave, 2010) and *Discourse, Grammar and Ideology: Functional and Cognitive Perspectives* (Bloomsbury, 2014). He is editor of *Cognitive Linguistic Approaches to Text and Discourse: From Poetics to Politics* (Edinburgh University Press, 2019) and coeditor of *Discourse of Disorder: Riots, Strikes and Protests in the Media* (with D. Kelsey; Edinburgh University Press, 2018).

Rachel Heinrichsmeier is a visiting research fellow at King's College London. Her research focuses on identity construction in interaction, particularly older age, gender and institutional identities, and combines a conversation analytic-informed discourse analysis with ethnographic methods. Her monograph, *Ageing Identities and Women's Everyday Talk in a Hair Salon*, was published by Routledge in Spring 2020.

Christina Higgins is a professor at the University of Hawaii in the Department of Second Language Studies. She is a sociolinguist who researches multilingualism from a discursive perspective. Much of her research has been in post-colonial contexts, including Tanzania and Hawaii, where she has examined the expression of different world views in public health communication, linguistic hybridity in everyday conversation and in the media, language learning and identity among transnationals, the dynamic nature of heritage among new speakers of Hawaiian and the shifting value of languages in their linguistic landscapes. She currently serves as coeditor of *Applied Linguistics*.

Emily Hofstetter is a postdoctoral researcher at Linköping University, examining how the body and voice are connected in interaction. Her past work has included several applied projects, examining service interactions in different settings.

Sylvia Jaworska is an associate professor in applied linguistics in the Department of English Language and Applied Linguistics at the University of Reading. Her main research is in the area of discourse analysis and corpus linguistics, and the application of both methods to studying media, health and business communication. She has published widely on discourse in these domains in *Applied Linguistics*, *Discourse & Society*, *Language in Society*, the *International Journal of Business Communication* and *Discourse, Context & Media*.

Rodney H. Jones is Professor of Sociolinguistics and Head of the Department of English Language and Applied Linguistics at the University of Reading. His recent books include *Discourse and Digital Practices* (Routledge, 2015), *Spoken Discourse* (Bloomsbury, 2016) and *A Sociolinguistics of Surveillance* (Oxford University Press, forthcoming).

Kendall A. King is Professor of Second Language Education at the University of Minnesota, where she teaches and researches sociolinguistics and language policy. She earned her PhD at the University of Pennsylvania and previously worked at New York University, Georgetown University and Stockholm University. She has written widely on indigenous language revitalization, bilingual child development and the language policies that shape student experiences. She is 2020–2021 president of the American Association of Applied Linguistics.

Yi-Ju Lai will earn her PhD degree in second language education from the University of Minnesota in 2020. Her research addresses multilingual populations' language socialization into academic discourse communities. Lai's work has appeared in *International Journal of Bilingual Education and Bilingualism* and the *Journal of Sociolinguistics*. Her current project examines the dialogic nature of language socialization in science fields, focusing on how disciplinary knowledge and ideologies, mediated through the use of language and multimodality, are constructed between international graduate instructors and undergraduate students.

Gavin Lamb recently received his PhD in second language studies from the University of Hawaii. His publications and research are in the areas of interactional sociolinguistics, multimodal discourse analysis, the sociolinguistics of multilingualism in Hawaii and ecolinguistics. His main research uses ethnographic discourse analysis to examine the forms of intercultural communication that arise in human entanglements with threatened species and places, with a focus on the linguistic, sociocultural and ethical dimensions shaping wildlife conservation and ecotourism contexts. He is currently a postdoctoral researcher in the Department of Language and Communication Studies at the University of Jyväskylä.

Tong King Lee is Associate Professor of Translation at the University of Hong Kong, NAATI-Certified Translator (Australia) and Chartered Linguist (Chartered Institute of Linguists, UK). He is the author of Translation and Translanguaging (2019, with M Baynham), Applied Translation Studies (2018), Experimental Chinese Literature (2015), and Translating the Multilingual City (2013).

Li Wei is Chair of Applied Linguistics at the UCL Institute of Education, University College London (UCL), UK. His research interests cover different aspects of bilingualism and multilingualism. He is Editor of the International Journal of Bilingual Education and Bilingualism and Applied Linguistics Review. His book Translanguaging: Language, Bilingualism and Education, jointly authored with Ofelia Garcia, won the 2015 British Association of Applied Linguistics Book Prize. He is a Fellow of the Academy of Social Sciences, UK.

Vally Lytra is Reader in Languages in Education in the Department of Educational Studies at Goldsmiths, University of London. Her research, practice and community engagement focus on bilingualism and biliteracy in homes, schools and communities that have experienced diverse migration flows. Her current ethnographic work explores how school leaders, teachers, parents and adult language learners involved in more established and more recent forms of Greek language education abroad are reconfiguring the Greek schools' mission, curricula and pedagogy.

Tommaso M. Milani is Full Professor of Multilingualism at the University of Gothenburg. His main areas of expertise include language policy, language ideology, (multimodal) critical discourse analysis and language, gender and sexuality. He has written extensively on these topics in international journals such as the *Journal of Sociolinguistics*, *Discourse & Society* and *Language in Society*. Among his most recent publications are the edited collections *Language and Masculinities* (Routledge, 2017) and *Queering Language, Gender and Sexuality* (Equinox, 2018). He is currently coeditor of the journal *Gender and Language* (with C. Caldas-Coulthard).

Luiz Paulo Moita-Lopes is a Full Professor of Applied Linguistics at the Federal University of Rio de Janeiro and a researcher of the CNPq. His most recent publications are *Global Portuguese: Linguistic Ideologies in Late Modernity* (Routledge, 2015/2018) and the coedited *Meaning Making in the Periphery* (with M. Baynham; Aila Review 30; John Benjamins, 2017).

Annabelle Mooney is Professor of Language and Society at the University of Roehampton. Her most recent publications include the coedited *The Language of Money and Debt* (with E. Sifaki; Palgrave, 2017) and *The Language of Money: Proverbs and Practices* (Routledge, 2018).

Robert Moore is a senior lecturer in educational linguistics at the Graduate School of Education, University of Pennsylvania. He has conducted fieldwork on Native North American languages and contributed essays on topics ranging from language endangerment and the politics of accent in Irish English to multilingualism policy in the EU and the semiotics of brands and branding.

Kristine Køhler Mortensen is a postdoctoral fellow at the University of Gothenburg. She completed her PhD at the University of Copenhagen in 2015, investigating online dating and how participants construct and negotiate desire through email, chat and personal profiles. She also studied language variation and social media practices among Danish youth with a focus on Snapchat in the project "Dialect in the

Periphery." She is currently leading a project funded by the Independent Research Fund Denmark on the introduction of compulsory education in "Danish sexual morals" for newly arrived migrants. Her work has been published in *Discourse Studies, Discourse, Context & Media, Gender and Language* and the *Journal of Language and Sexuality*. Among her latest publications is the coedited collection *Sociale medier og sprog: Analystiske tilgange* (with A. Candefors Stæhr; Samfunds litteratur, 2018).

Mohammad Naseh Nasrollahi Shahri is an Assistant Professor in the Department of Linguistics and Asian/Middle Eastern Languages at San Diego State University. His research lies in academic discourse, qualitative research methods, semiotics and linguistic anthropology.

Kay O'Halloran is Head of Department and Communication & Media Chair in the School of the Arts at the University of Liverpool. Prior to this, she led the Multimodal Analysis Group at Curtin University and was Director of the Multimodal Analysis Lab in the Interactive & Digital Media Institute at the National University of Singapore. Professor O'Halloran has a background in mathematics, multimodal discourse analysis and linguistics. She has extensive experience in establishing and leading interdisciplinary research teams to develop and make widely available new digital tools and techniques for analyzing images, videos and 360 videos. She is currently developing mixed methods approaches to combine multimodal analysis, data mining and visualization for big data analytics in areas including online extremism and political rhetoric.

Markus Rheindorf is an applied linguist and currently Senior Researcher at the Department of Linguistics, Vienna University. He specializes in critical discourse studies, genre analysis and argumentation. His research interests include political discourse, populism, nationalism, the construction of national identity as well as academic literacies. He recently published *Revisiting the Toolbox of Discourse Studies: New Trajectories in Methodology, Open Data, and Visualization* (Palgrave Macmillan, 2019).

Jennifer Roth-Gordon is Associate Professor of Anthropology at the University of Arizona, teaching courses in cultural and linguistic anthropology. She published *Race and the Brazilian Body: Blackness, Whiteness, and Everyday Language in Rio de Janeiro* (University of California Press, 2016).

Brooke R. Schreiber is an assistant professor of English at Baruch College, City University of New York. Her research focuses on second language writing pedagogy in ESL and EFL settings, including translingual approaches to writing pedagogy.

Philip Seargeant is Senior Lecturer in Applied Linguistics at Open University. He has authored several books on topics ranging from English around the world and language and social media to language and creativity. His most recent book is *The Emoji Revolution: How Technology is Shaping the Future of Communication* (Cambridge University Press, 2019).

Elena Semino is Professor of Linguistics and Verbal Art in the Department of Linguistics and English Language at Lancaster University and Director of the ESRC Centre for Corpus Approaches to Social Science. She holds a visiting professorship at the University of Fuzhou. She specializes in health communication, medical humanities, corpus linguistics, stylistics, and metaphor theory and analysis. She has (co)authored over eighty publications, including *Metaphor in Discourse* (Cambridge University Press, 2008) and *Metaphor, Cancer and the End of Life: A Corpus-Based Study* (with Z. Demjén, A. Hardie, S. Payne and P. Rayson; Routledge, 2018).

Amy Shuman is Professor of Folklore and Narrative in the Department of English at Ohio State University. She is coauthor, with Carol Bohmer, of *Rejecting Refugees: Political Asylum in the 21st Century* (Routledge, 2007) and *Political Asylum Deceptions: The Culture of Suspicion* (Palgrave Macmillan, 2018) and coeditor of *Technologies of Suspicion and the Ethics of Obligation in Political Asylum* (with B. M. Haas; Ohio University Press, 2019). Among other awards, she is the recipient of a Guggenheim Fellowship and a Fellowship at the Hebrew University Institute of Advanced Studies.

Jack Sidnell is a linguistic anthropologist and a professor of anthropology and linguistics at the University of Toronto, where he earned his PhD. He has conducted ethnographic research in the Caribbean and in Vietnam and made scholarly contributions to conversation analysis, linguistic pragmatics, sociolinguistics and linguistic anthropology. He is (co)author of three books and (co)editor of several more including *The Cambridge Handbook of Linguistic Anthropology* (with N. J. Enfield and P. Kockelman; Cambridge University Press, 2014).

Laura Smits completed her MA in online culture studies at Tilburg University.

Sabine Tan is a member of the Multimodal Analysis Group and a Senior Research Fellow in the School of Education, Faculty of Humanities, at Curtin University. She has a background in critical multimodal discourse analysis, social semiotics and visual communication, and has applied multidisciplinary perspectives to analyze institutional discourses involving traditional and new media. She has worked on interdisciplinary projects involving the development of interactive software for the multimodal analysis of images, videos and 360 videos for research and educational purposes, and contributed to the development of multimodal approaches to big data analytics in the fields of online terrorism, political discourse and 360 video.

Lionel Wee is Provost's Chair Professor in the Department of English Language & Literature at the National University of Singapore. He works on language policy, world Englishes and general issues in sociolinguistics and pragmatics. His latest book is *The Singlish Controversy* (Cambridge University Press, 2018).

Peter Wignell is a member of the Multimodal Analysis Group; formerly, he was a Senior Research Fellow in the School of Education, Faculty of Humanities, at Curtin University. His background is in systemic functional linguistics, discourse analysis and multimodal analysis, and his research has been both theoretical and applied. For example, his work on the role of language in the construction of specialized knowledge systems has informed literacy theory and pedagogy. Recent research on the application of a systemic functional multimodal analysis approach to violent extremist discourse and political discourse has led to publication in a diverse range of applications such as brand semiotics, performance studies and translation.

Noura Yacoubi completed her MA in online culture studies at Tilburg University and is currently pursuing a master's program in philosophy.

Virginia Zavala is Professor of Sociolinguistics at The Pontificia Universidad Católica del Perú, where she addresses issues surrounding language and education with a focus on the Andes, from an ethnographic and discourse analytic perspective. Her latest books are *Qichwasimirayku: Batallas por el quechua* (coauthored with L. Mujica, G. Córdova and W. Ardito; PUCP, 2014) and *Racismo y Lenguaje* (coedited with M. Back; PUCP, 2017).

Preface

Discourse analysis is nowadays a broad and cross-disciplinary field of studies and scholars seem to be unanimous in describing it as too difficult to delimit. Indeed, discourse analytic studies have surged not only within fields that have in common an interest in language use, such as linguistic anthropology, pragmatics, ethnography and media and communication studies, but also in a wide range of disciplines such as anthropology, history, psychology, literary studies, philosophy and sociology, to mention but a few. In turn, there is a diversity of theoretical and methodological perspectives. It is symptomatic of this diversity and the complexity of the field that definitions of discourse abound and diverge in their fundamental scope: from minimalist, language-based views such as the description of discourse as "language above the sentence or above the clause" (Stubbs 1993: 12), or as "utterances" (Schiffrin 1994: 39), to text-centered definitions as well as connections of discourse with the social world in its characterizations as "a type of social practice" (Fairclough 1992: 28). With the above in mind, our aim with this handbook has not been to superimpose either artificial boundaries or some kind of coherence on a heterogeneous field but, instead, to offer readers a panorama of current areas of engagement and cross-fertilization. In turn, our decision to opt for "discourse studies" in the title as opposed to "discourse analysis" reflects our wish to avoid identification with a traditional linguistic focus on "discourse" as a method of analyzing language-in-text. Such a disciplinary focus has often meant that emphasis is placed on specific approaches seen as foundational in the development of the field (for example, speech act theory, systemic-functional grammar, text-linguistics, etc.) at the expense of acknowledging that traditional ways of segmenting and labeling "discourse analyses" have diminishing resonance or relevance in the face of emergent research areas and new methodological combinations (for example, corpus-based critical discourse analysis).

In light of the above, the remit and organization of this handbook have stemmed from our belief that long-standing differentiations within the field in terms of traditional schools of thought and approaches (for example, conversation analysis, critical discourse analysis, pragmatics, systemic functional grammar, text-linguistics) or in terms of different methodological orientations (experimental, ethnographic, quantitative, qualitative, etc.) do not do justice to its evolution, its porous boundaries or indeed the synergies and intersections that have developed in the last two decades. As we hope to show, discourse analytic studies have experienced a productive merging of interests amongst different perspectives and trends, on the one hand, and, on the other hand, an exponential growth in works that draw on and bring together traditionally distinctive and separate approaches. For example, critical discourse analysis is often merged and combined with ethnographic approaches and corpus linguistics (for example, see Chapter 4 by Fabricio and Moita-Lopes, Chapter 9 by Hart and Chapter 27 by Björkvall) in ways that would have been unthinkable in the past; discourse studies in digital environments combine qualitative perspectives with big data analysis (see, for example, Chapter 5 by De Fina and Georgakopoulou and Chapter 8 by Ancarno); and multimodal approaches to data have been adopted within a variety of discourse analytic frameworks such as conversation analysis and translanguaging (for example, see Chapter 12 by Tan, O'Halloran and Wignell and Chapter 18 by Tong King Lee and Li Wei). New approaches such as linguistic landscapes or the analysis of digital surveillance also combine qualitative and quantitative methodologies (see, for example, Chapter 14 by Seargeant and Giaxoglou and Chapter 32 by Jones). At the same time, new theoretical and analytical challenges have emerged in the last two decades, not least as a result of the increased mediatization of social life. This has made apparent the need for well-established approaches to rethink, reconceptualize and update assumptions long held by discourse analysts. Examples of these are the recent attempts to develop a conversation analysis fit for online environments or the growth of journals and publications dealing with discourse and semiotic practices in digital environments. These attempts are often framed within the turn to materiality and posthumanist approaches to discourse (see Part III) that problematize and destabilize conventional definitions of discourse and the role of language in them. Awareness of the importance of mobility in contemporary societies has also impacted on how discourse analysts think about the ways in which communicative events are organized, communities are formed and function, and identities are expressed and negotiated, bringing to light the importance of different types of connection at a variety of scales (see Part IV). Connectivity and the ubiquitous merging of texts with other semiotic systems and embodied activities have pushed the boundaries of discourse analysis even further. In addition, the study of discourse as a means of reproducing or challenging social inequalities and its pivotal role in issues of social justice, inclusion and diversity, rather than being a concern in the interdisciplinary "margins" of the area, has become inherent to many of the topics under study, rendering previous distinctions between "critical" and "descriptive" discourse analyses problematic (see Part V).

Our aim has been to register and contribute to trends such as those just mentioned and, in the process, to reflect on the impact of rapid social and technological changes on the study of discourse and the redrawing of disciplinary boundaries. In this sense, this handbook does not aim at being comprehensive; rather, it is intended to be representative of twenty-first-century concerns of discourse studies. Besides giving space to new trends in discourse analysis, we have also ensured inclusion of approaches that are brought together by a focus on discourse practices and the study of concrete contexts, thus paying special attention to orientations focused on participants and their own ways of organizing discursive events and activities. We highlight the main trends and ideas that run through this vast production of research in discourse studies in the introductions to the handbook's parts.

The handbook is divided into six parts: Part I, *(Con)Textualizing Discourses*, is composed of chapters that provide critical presentations and discussions of some key ways in which different types of context have been theorized and incorporated into discourse studies, whilst problematizing and updating certain long-standing assumptions that are lacking in explanatory power in the era of digital media and globalization. Part II, *Perspectives and Modes of Analysis*, is devoted to questions regarding methodologies, data and units of analysis seen from different traditions, from conversation analysis to poststructuralism. In Part III, *Discourse Materialities and Embodiment*, the focus is on the relationships amongst discourse, embodiment and the material world. Contributors reflect on the implications of incorporating the environment, material objects and the body into the analysis of communication. Part IV, *(Trans)Locations and Intersections*, is concerned with the manifold ways in which mobility has impacted on methods of analysis and theorizations about identities and language practices in discourse studies. Part V, *Ethics, Inequality and Inclusion*, discusses justice and (in)equality issues from different perspectives in a variety of institutional domains. In Part VI, *Discourse, Publics and Mediatization*, contributors bring to the fore the impact of different kinds of discourse on public life in areas such as politics, the private and public sector, and digital communication.

This handbook would not have been possible without our contributors sharing our vision about an inclusive, interdisciplinary field of discourse studies: their chapters have in our view pushed boundaries beyond our expectations. We also gratefully acknowledge the support of Andrew Winnard, our commissioning editor, who was very convincing about the need for this handbook. Many of our ideas about what might work as part of such a collection, what should be included and in what spirit have been shaped by our long-standing engagement with the field as teachers of BA and MA modules, supervisors of PhD students and with colleagues within the Centre for Language, Discourse and Communication at King's College London and the Initiative for Multilingual Studies, the Italian department and the Linguistics department at Georgetown University. You are too many to mention by name, so please forgive a collective but heartfelt thank you! Finally, our thanks go to Jeremy Wegner and Dr. Anda Drasovean for their valuable editorial assistance in the early and the final stages of this handbook, respectively.

References

Fairclough, N. (1989). *Language and Power*. London: Longman.
Schiffrin, D. (1994). *Approaches to Discourse*. Cambridge, MA: Blackwell Publishers.
Stubbs, M. (1983). *Discourse Analysis*. Chicago, IL: University of Chicago Press.

Part I

(Con)Textualizing Discourses

Introduction

We open the handbook with a section devoted to contextualization in discourse. The choice of the term "contextualization" over "context" is not casual; indeed, the chapters focus on the processual nature of achieving understanding among participants in communicative events and on the multilayered interconnections that they create among different levels of meaning, rather than attempting to define context a priori. In that sense, the work presented in Part I does not aim to be representative of the many different ways of construing context that characterize various branches of discourse studies; rather, it aims to showcase views of context that, albeit stemming from within different traditions and representing applications to diversified domains of interest, also fundamentally converge on a practice-based, interactionally oriented focus on discourse and communication. Before we delve into the themes and issues raised in the chapters, we want to highlight some of the ways in which these contemporary orientations to context connect to, and at the same time diverge from, scholarly work that has developed nuanced and process-oriented understandings of context in the past within disciplines such as ethnography of speaking, interactional sociolinguistics and anthropological linguistics.

Let us start by noting that the definition of context is one of the most complex and controversial issues in discourse studies and that profound differences exist in the ways in which this construct is operationalized within the different orientations represented in the discipline. As rightly noted by De Saint Georges (2013: 920), different views of context are often the hallmark of orientations to the analysis of discourse. Thus, for many critical discourse analysts context is a mental representation (Van Dijk 2009), while for conversation analysts it is restricted to the linguistic environment in its sequential development and to the elements of the social world to which participants explicitly orient (Schegloff 1987). This very difficulty of delimiting the borders of the contexts within which texts and communicative acts can be understood explains many attempts at producing taxonomies of elements that may be constitutive of them in order to guide the researcher in the interpretation of meaning-making. Perhaps the most famous of these taxonomies is the SPEAKING grid produced by Hymes (1974), which described the environments within which utterances could be placed in order to explain their interpretation. Such environments included both linguistic elements (such as *genre* and *sequence*) and "extralinguistic" elements (such as *participants* and *instrumentalities*). A similar attempt at capturing the various ingredients of context can be found in Ochs' (1979) proposal to look at contexts as defined by settings (social and spatial frameworks), behavioral environments (including bodily behavior), language and background knowledge. These taxonomic efforts reflect, on the one hand, an attempt to make aspects of what we call the context of discourse tangible and, on the other, the need – at the time in which they were produced – to show the relevance of different social and cultural organization patterns to the analysis of language. Without denying the fundamental importance of those models, especially in view of their embedding into an environment of linguistic research that was still dominated by universalistic and essentializing views of language, it must be recognized, as noted by Duranti and Goodwin (1992) in their groundbreaking volume on rethinking context, that providing precise definitions may actually be not only extremely difficult but even, to a certain extent, unproductive. In their words:

> However, it does not seem possible at the present time to give a single, precise, technical definition of context and eventually we might have to accept that such a definition may not be possible ..... From our perspective, lack of a single definition, or even general agreement about what is meant by context, is not a situation that necessarily requires agreement. (1992: 2)

Certainly, as they suggest, in very general terms, defining contexts implies distinguishing focal from non-focal phenomena. Thus, the analyst needs to establish levels of relevance of different aspects of the social that are either evoked or directly brought to bear in the discourse domain and determine how meanings get recognized, what is already shared and what becomes shared through the communication itself. Analysts need to ask: how do people come to understand each other's linguistic and communicative acts while at the same time shaping the social world through them? The work of the contributors to Part I stems from a tradition that has shifted away from static views of context both as a kind of frame within which discourses takes place and as an environment fundamentally determined by well-defined social and cultural organizing structures. The orientation embraced by the contributors to this section reflects approaches to context as highly dynamic, shaped by different structures of knowledge and organization in the social world but also shaping them. Among the most important theoretical methodological points of reference for the reflections presented by the contributors are work of scholars in anthropology and conversation analysis such as Duranti and Goodwin, theorizations on contextualization by Gumperz in interactional sociolinguistics, and ideas proposed by Goffman on interaction and participation. Duranti and Goodwin stress the orientation to emic understandings as a central focus, that is "the importance of, first, approaching context from the perspective of an actor actively operating on the world within which he or she finds him- or herself embedded; and second, tying the analysis of context to study of the indigenous activities that participants use to constitute the culturally and historically organized worlds they inhabit" (1992: 4). As a consequence of this focus on participants, for all contributors, the study of discourse in context can happen only through ethnographic enquiry. From Gumperz (1992), they derive an emphasis on contextualization as a dynamic process in which social actors create connections between discursive elements, social categories, ideologies and common-sense understandings about identities, relations and actions. Finally, following Goffman (1974), they all take as central to the analysis of communicative practices the domain of interaction as the site where structures of action, rules of behavior, social values and identity categories get defined and negotiated. As we will see, authors bring to bear many other influences in their chapters, but the work mentioned above defines their approaches to context as nuanced, participant- and process-centered, and interactionally and ethnographically oriented.

Let us now highlight some of the major themes discussed by the contributors. The chapters present and reflect on some of the fundamental constructs that allow for an analysis of contextualization processes (with the notion of chronotope being particularly salient given its presence in different contributions), ways in which different levels or elements of context are interrelated in communication, and the role of language in relation to other repertoires of semiotic resources. Central to their reflections is also a discussion of how the relationships between simultaneity and historical embedding within contexts have been theorized.

In the Chapter 1, **Moore** focuses on three fundamental constructs that have allowed scholars in sociolinguistics and discourse studies to shift from contexts as rather static sets of spatiotemporal categories surrounding and determining the shape and interpretation of utterances to contextualization as a live, ongoing process. Through the latter, linguistic elements at different levels are related to social meanings which then become recognizable to participants in interaction but also get recycled, recontextualized and transformed. Moore centers his discussion on indexicality and the two interrelated concepts of style and register.

He reconstructs the history of this concept through Peirce's ideas about the sign, Jakobson's work on shifters as linguistic signs with indexical properties and Silverstein's proposals about indexicality as a context-presupposing and context-creating process in which users relate utterances to social categories and, building recursively on these relations, create "orders" that reflect higher levels of ideological saturation. Such orders are revealing of widely shared social norms and expectations. Moore underscores how the shift from the focus on dialects to a focus on registers implies a turn to interaction as a central domain. In his words, "this has immediate 'methodological' implications, because it means that unlike 'dialectal' variants, 'superposed' ones must be observed *in use* in actual contexts of interaction, since they are constituted as reflexive models, as what a (culturally recognizable) type of person would say (i.e., choose from a set of 'permissible alternates') in a recognizable type of situation – or might not – and to what effect" (p. 16). The study of enregisterment has expanded the range of investigation to the ways in which linguistic resources become indexically linked with social meanings but can also be continuously reconfigured. A similar attention to process is shown, in Moore's view, by the growing interest in stylization, rather than style, as a site of linguistic mutability that allows speakers to reconfigure and recombine semiotic and linguistic resources from a variety of repertoires creating ever changing meanings. Moore points to indexicality and the interrelated concepts of style and register as central to current developments in discourse analysis that look at "how participants in discursive interaction orient to the contextualization (and recontextualization) of their own and each other's contributions to semiotically mediated communicative activities, whether these activities unfold online, offline or across these and other modalities of contact" (p. 25).

Central to **Roth-Gordon's** Chapter 2 is the discussion on how discourse analysts can articulate links between texts and different levels of context with a particular focus on the micro–macro dilemma, that is, on the ways in which local interactions can be connected to wide constructs such as ideologies, mainstream discourses and interactional practices. As thoroughly discussed in Chapter 3, this is a notoriously thorny issue within discourse studies since the way analysts approach these levels is revealing of tensions between seeing texts and discourse practices as more or less directly determined and influenced by social structures and by power relations. Roth-Gordon distinguishes among four levels of analysis – linguistic features, interactional context, ethnographic context and sociopolitical context – and argues that showing how all these levels are interconnected is a particular concern for discourse analysts working within an ethnographic tradition. Indeed, such linkages, especially the connections between the first three levels and the sociopolitical context, are revealing of how discourses reflect and at the same time participate in the construction of the social order. In Roth-Gordon's view, it is precisely through ethnographic approaches that such interrelations can be studied and uncovered. Chapter 2 is devoted to the discussion of methodological strategies that facilitate such an approach to discourse in context and the tools that have been developed within different traditions of linguistics. Roth-Gordon focuses on Goffman's notion of participant roles, the concepts of stance and register, and the Bakhtinian notions of genre, intertextuality, voicing and chronotopes as ways of linking "local contexts" to the realms of societal norms, processes and ideologies, but she stresses that it is only through ethnography that these particular concepts can be put to use to articulate how the social informs and is informed by discourse practices.

The issues of levels of context and particularly the micro–macro dilemma are at the center of **Blommaert, Smits and Yacoubi's** Chapter 3 as well, but, as we will see, these authors take a radically different approach from that of Roth-Gordon by effectively denying the relevance of the micro–macro opposition. Like Moore, they explicitly link their approach to a view of contextualization and indexicality as key notions to connect discursive features to "relevant chunks of sociocultural knowledge" (p. 53). In their view, the micro–macro distinction reveals an orientation to discourse in which certain aspects of social life are seen as direct and others as indirect causes of linguistic conduct and in which the micro is related to the anecdotal and the unique, while the macro is taken to represent the generalizable and the stable. The authors argue that such binary opposition is unhelpful since, in fact, the macro can be found only in the observation of the small details of interaction. At the same time, the small details of interaction reveal a high degree of organization and recognizability even when communication processes seem chaotic and complex. Indeed, participants in interaction draw upon available resources that are layered and multiple but also socioculturally marked and therefore recognizable. Recognizability is based on framing, and framing happens in social environments. Blommaert, Smits and Yacoubi propose the notions of chronotopes and scales as capable of capturing some of these regularities. Chronotopes capture the particular spatiotemporal frames that make relevant specific discursive and behavioral scripts, while scales represent "reflections and expressions of how social beings experience dimensions of sociocultural reality as indexical vectors, as informing the general normative patterns that shape formats of action" (p. 59). The authors emphasize how the presence of these different processes and levels of meanings points to the need to recognize simultaneity as central to the construction and interpretation of contexts and argue that it is through recognition of the simultaneous working of different processes of contextualization that discourse analysts can tackle communication in digital environments.

Fabricio and Moita-Lopes offer in Chapter 4 yet another perspective on the micro–macro duality, but they do so from a critical discourse studies standpoint and through the analysis of how different philosophers, social scientists and linguists have reintroduced history as a central concern for language studies. Their focus is on how discourses can be understood as entrenched with different spatiotemporal parameters and the ways in which they show links to both punctual and disperse temporalities. They argue that a great deal of the theorizing around the relationships between discourse and history happened in the past in disciplines other than linguistics, for example through the work of philosophers such as Derrida, Deleuze and Guattari and through that of social theorists such as Foucault who fundamentally contributed to the analysis of how discourses are embedded in power struggles.

The authors focus the second part of the chapter on the constructs of interdiscursivity and intertextuality as key notions to demonstrate the sociohistorical embedding of discourses since they capture both the regularities of discourse meanings and structures (for example types and genres) and change. Indeed, as they argue, "because discourse practices involve the constant repetition-reactualization of prior texts, utterances, and voices, they are inherently destabilizing intertextual phenomena. Therefore, discourses and genres have the potential to materialize in new micro-recontextualizations, which may structure a social field outright" (p. 81).

Fabricio and Moita-Lopes discuss how these understandings of discourse as shaped by and shaping sociohistorical contexts have been enriched by the recent focus on mobility in discourse studies. Such focus has opened the way to the development of the constructs discussed by other authors in Part I – entextualization, scales and chronotopes – which dynamically capture both the processes of circulation and change in discourses and their articulations with diverse spaces and temporalities.

To end this section, Chapter 5 by **De Fina and Georgakopoulou** centers on how orientations to discourse that recognize the multiplicity, fragmentation, context-specificity and performativity of communication practices have revolutionized narrative analysis, particularly in relation to the study of identities. It discusses how the field has shifted from a view of stories as containers of experience to a stress on narratives as practices that are both context-shaped and context-shaping.

The chapter reviews recent work in the area, paying particular attention to ways in which identities are configured within different narrative practices with their own associated resources. Thus, De Fina and Georgakopoulou discuss a variety of constructs and areas of engagement that reflect this shift: First, they turn to small stories as encapsulating an orientation to narrative identities not only as co-constructed, fluid and profoundly contextualized but also as pointing to digital contexts as privileged points of observation of the dynamics between participants' choices and the constraints imposed by technological frames and surveillance mechanisms. Within such research, narrators are seen not as sole producers of identities but as engaged in constant dialogue and negotiation with audiences and affordances provided to them. Second, they note how the centrality of mobility for the study of narratives and narrators has opened the way to investigations of the narrative construction of mobile identities within different media and environments and of ways in which mobile identities are regimented and dealt with in institutional practices. They also discuss how this renewed interest in mobility has brought to light the many imbrications of narratives with space and time (for example through chronotopic constructions) and their embedding within nexi of historical and sociocultural spaces.

References

De Saint Georges, I. (2013). Context in the Analysis of Discourse and Interaction. In A. Chapelle (ed.) *The Encyclopedia of Applied Linguistics*. New York: Wiley-Blackwell. 920–26. DOI: 10.1002/9781405198431.wbeal0194.

Duranti, A. and Goodwin, C. (1992). Rethinking Context: An Introduction. In A. Duranti and C. Goodwin (eds.) *Rethinking Context: Language as an Interactive Phenomenon*. Cambridge: Cambridge University Press. 1–42.

Goffman, E. (1974). *Frame Analysis*. New York: Harper & Row.

Gumperz, J. (1992). Contextualization Revisited. In P. Auer and A. di Luzio (eds.) *The Contextualization of Language*. Amsterdam: John Benjamins. 39–53.

Hymes, D. H. (1974). Ways of Speaking. In R. Bauman and J. Sherzer (eds.) *Explorations in the Ethnography of Speaking*. Cambridge: Cambridge University Press. 433–52.

Ochs, E. (1979). What Child Language Can Contribute to Pragmatics. In E. Ochs and B. Schieffelin (eds.) *Developmental Pragmatics*. New York: Academic Press. 1–17.

Schegloff, E. A. (1987). Between Macro and Micro: Contexts and Other Connections. In J. Alexander, B. Giessen, R. Munch and N. Smelser (eds.) *The Micro-Macro Link*. Berkeley: University of California Press. 207–34.

Van Dijk, T. A. (2009). *Society and Discourse: How Context Controls Text and Talk*. Cambridge: Cambridge University Press.

1

Registers, Styles, Indexicality

Robert Moore

1.1 Introduction/Definitions

Researchers in linguistic anthropology and post-variationist sociolinguistics have over recent decades increasingly converged on a shared focus of attention: the unfolding real-time process of communicative activities that involve language – spoken/heard, written, digitally mediated – in concert with the other semiotic affordances that provide participants with the means to presume upon, and to (re-)create, the very contexts in which these forms of talk take place, with various effects in the here-and-now and beyond (see Silverstein 2017a).

Sociolinguists emerging from the confines of variationism have increasingly abandoned the operationalism and quasi-experimentalism of earlier work in favor of more ethnographically rich accounts that take note of the way that historically situated facts about sociolinguistic variation (e.g. Inoue 2004; Zhang 2017) do not just reflect but also help to constitute identities made manifest in other ways: through modes of dress, bodily practices, consumption patterns, etc.; these patterns – both linguistic and nonlinguistic (e.g. Mendoza-Denton 2008) – are often grouped by sociolinguists under the heading of *style* (see, e.g., Eckert 2003, 2012, 2018).

Linguistic anthropologists, meanwhile, have been increasingly oriented to the way that observed variation in language usage resolves itself into verbal (phonological, lexical, etc.) repertoires keyed to the interactional contours of recurring types of situation with recurring types of participant role – termed *registers*. Linguistic anthropologists have also been alert to the ways in which linguistic and semiotic resources that are by-degrees regularized and presumed upon as "normal" in some contexts are, by that very fact, ripe for creative "recycling" and reuse in other contexts, with different and sometimes surprising effects (see, e.g., Agha 2004, 2005, 2007).

All of these disciplinary and transdisciplinary realignments, I argue, result from the introduction of a single, centrally important analytic concept: *indexicality*. Developed by the American mathematician and logician Charles S. Peirce (1839–1914) and introduced into modern linguistics by Roman Jakobson ([1957]1990) – its implications developed further by Jakobson's student Michael Silverstein (e.g. 1976, 2003) and others – the concept of *indexicality* has drawn scholarly attention to the central importance of sign forms (including expressions of ordinary language such as *I/you, here/there, this/that*, etc.) that function *not* by representing, describing or naming things in the world (including participants in discourse) but by *pointing to* them, which is to say, *indexing* them. The increasing importance of indexicality in studies of language, discourse and interaction has enabled the recent alignment of erstwhile disciplinary forms of inquiry in sociolinguistics and linguistic anthropology (Silverstein 2017a) and seems to be the fulcrum for much of the work now emerging at the intersection of these and other fields, including discourse studies, linguistic ethnography and applied linguistics.

1.2 Overview

As can be seen, the three concepts of *register, style* and *indexicality* are now rather densely interrelated in the work of scholars from several fields. In some work, the (*indexical*) phenomena discussed under the headings of *style* and *register* overlap so much in their conceptualization that the terms become near-synonyms; in other work, processes of *enregisterment* have become central to a more comprehensive theory of the nature of social relations viewed through the lens of communicative practices (e.g. Agha 2007, 2011b).

Clearly, *indexicality* is a term/concept of a more encompassing order than *register* or *style*, since it identifies the semiotic process that makes it possible for participants (and researchers) to link particular forms of speech or conduct to types of social situation and participant in these: all such linkages are by definition *indexical*, hence discussions of *register* and/or *style* are attempts to model the way that participants in interaction engage with linguistic and other semiotic and communicative resources available to them to construe the situations they find themselves in as situations of this or that *type* or category and to project themselves (and their interlocutors) as participants of this or that type or category.

These ideas, and the many projects of empirical and field-based research into communication conduct carried out under their auspices since the 1970s, did not develop in an intellectual vacuum, of course: linguistic anthropology's turn away from a focus on cognition and classification (e.g. Conklin 1962) and toward discourse practices as central to the agentive self-positioning of actors (speakers) negotiating unstable and unequal regimes of power and political economy (e.g. Hill 1985) responded to wider shifts in anthropology (e.g. Ortner 1984), just as sociolinguists answered Goffman's (1964) call for attention to "the neglected situation" of face-to-face interaction with ever more detailed analyses (and transcripts – see Sacks, Schegloff and Jefferson 1974).

Accordingly, then, I will first provide an overview of *indexicality*, the governing concept of this field of study, before passing on to *register(s)* and *style(s)*.

1.2.1 Indexicality

Peirce propounded his semiotic theory as a unified account of logic and cognition, "an attempt to explain the cognitive process of acquiring scientific knowledge as a pattern of communicative activity" (Parmentier 1994: 3). Three elements are crucial: (1) an object, constituted as such not because of its inherent properties but because it enters into a relationship with (2) a sign, which "stands for" it, and finally (3) an interpretant, some form of (human) consciousness that takes account of the standing-for relationship between the sign and its object. Signs are "forms of representation (verbal, graphic, gestural, etc.) which stand for, substitute for, or exhibit the object" to an observing consciousness, this last conceived by Peirce "indifferently, [as] members of a community or [as] sequential states of a single person's mind" (Parmentier 1994: 3).

With respect to the "ground" – the sign–object relationship – Peirce identified three classes of signs, which he called icons, indexes (or indices) and symbols (see Peirce 1955 for details).

Icons are signs that stand for their objects by virtue of resembling them; that is, the sign of itself possesses qualities that are similar to ("iconic" representations of) qualities possessed by the thing it stands for. Icons are "signs whose grounds involve formal resemblance" (Parmentier 1994: 17): think of a Russian *ikon*, a painted image of an Eastern Orthodox saint, with all of his or her ritual paraphernalia; or a painting of cows in the grass (sign) and actual cows in the grass (object); or the highly schematized images of male and female persons that identify gender-specific restrooms.

Indexes are signs that stand for their objects not by virtue of shared qualities (resemblance) but by virtue of the existential fact of a direct physical connection between sign and object: contiguity in space or time. Indexes are signs that in a sense emanate from their objects, are caused to exist by their objects: think of smoke (sign) and fire (object). For Peirce, indexical signs and their objects are in a relationship of "dynamical coexistence" (quoted in Hanks 1999: 124) with each other, which is how they are construed by an interpretant (or observing consciousness). An index, says Peirce, "directs attention to its object by blind compulsion" (Peirce 1931–58, Vol. 2: 306).

One of Peirce's favorite examples of an index is a weathervane "because in the first place it really takes the self-same direction as the wind, so that there is a real connection between them, and in the second place ... when we see a weathercock pointing in a certain direction it draws our attention to that direction" (1931–58, Vol. 2: 286). Smoke (taken as a sign) points to its object (fire); symptoms – say, a skin rash of a certain type, coupled with a fever – point to an underlying disease (measles). A weathervane points out the direction in which the wind is blowing because it was made to do so, by the wind.

In language, so-called deictic expressions such as *I, you; here, there; this, that* are all indexical because they are uninterpretable outside of the context in which they are uttered. More on this in a moment.

Symbols for Peirce are signs that stand for their objects by virtue of a law or convention, there being no necessary linkage based on shared qualities (resemblance; icons) or direct causation (or contiguity; indexes). Symbols, in this sense, are relatively "arbitrary": the color red as used in traffic signals possesses no quality that makes it resemble the activity of stopping a car and certainly is not brought into existence as a sign by cars coming collectively to a stop. In this context, red means "stop" solely by virtue of an agreement, convention or law. Most of the nondeictic expressions in languages(s) – most nouns and verbs – are Peircean symbols.

Jakobson's essay "Shifters, Verbal Categories, and the Russian Verb" (Jakobson [1957]1990) brought Peirce's ideas to the attention of linguists, showing that many core categories of grammar – including tense, mood, evidentiality and person – are irreducibly indexical in character.

Jakobson identified "shifters" as what he called "duplex signs" – signs that contribute to the "conventional" referential content of an utterance (hence, Peircean symbols) but do so only insofar as they have also successfully pointed to (indexed) an aspect of the immediate context in which they are uttered: "The general meaning of a shifter cannot be defined without a reference to the message" (Jakobson [1957]1990: 388).

Jakobson's analysis depended on making a sharp distinction between the speech event or event of speaking (designated as E^s) and the event being spoken about, the narrated event (E^n).[1] The verbal category of tense, then, functions to locate the event(s) being described (E^n) *relative to* the event of describing them (E^s) – for example, as having taken place prior to the event of speaking ("past tense"; *John ate a sandwich*), concurrently with the act of speaking ("present tense"; *John is eating a sandwich*) or as taking place subsequently to the act of speaking ("future tense"; *John will eat a sandwich*). Tense is a shifter.

---

[1] The distinction corresponds to Benveniste's distinction between the *énonciation* or act of speaking (in context), and the *énoncé*, the content of the utterance considered apart from its context of *énonciation* (Benveniste [1956] 1971).

The facts under discussion in Jakobson's essay were indisputable – every language *qua* grammatical system (*langue*) does in fact possess expressions such as *I, here, this,* etc. and major verbal categories such as tense, mood and evidentiality that are uninterpretable apart from their specific context(s) of use (*parole*) – though the implications of this had never been systematically explored.

A second intervention came in 1976 with Michael Silverstein's (1976) essay "Shifters, Linguistic Categories, and Cultural Description." Addressed primarily to anthropologists, it entered a disciplinary "conversation" already underway in which "meaning" was perhaps the central – if ill-defined – concept around which the whole discourse of "symbolic anthropology" ceaselessly revolved, without ever achieving resolution. Clifford Geertz (1926–2006), for example, defined culture as "an historically transmitted pattern of meanings embodied in symbols, a system of inherited conceptions expressed in symbolic forms by means of which men communicate, perpetuate, and develop their knowledge about and attitude toward life" (1966: 3).

In this environment, Silverstein's essay – which presents an explicit theory of semiotics, emphasizing the *pragmatic* (context-dependent and context-creating) and *indexical* functions of language over the more obviously (and technically) "symbolic" *denotational* functions – came as something of a surprise and has had lasting impact. The aim of the essay was to "demonstrate that this 'pragmatic' analysis of speech behavior – in that tradition extending from Peirce to Jakobson – allows us to describe the real linkage of language to culture, and perhaps the most important aspect of the 'meaning' of speech" (1976: 11–12).

Silverstein's essay introduced new and important distinctions into the study of indexicality in language and communication: the distinction, on formal-functional grounds, between *referential* (or denotational) *indexicality* and *non-referential* (or "pure") *indexicality*; and the distinction between two indexical modes, termed *presupposing indexicality* and *entailing* (or "creative") *indexicality*. A third distinction, between different "orders of indexicality" (first and second order or n^{th} and n^{th+1}), emerged in later work (Silverstein 2003). I will develop the implications of these distinctions in sections to follow on "Register(s)" and "Style," but I offer quick preliminary sketches here.

Referential and non-referential indexicality. Jakobson's essay was concerned with shifters (indexical symbols), that is, forms that contribute to the denotational content of the utterances in which they occur, but whose "propositional values ... are linked to the unfolding of the speech event itself" (Silverstein 1976: 29). In addition to these, Silverstein pointed to the importance of what he called "pure" or non-referential indexes: "features of speech which, independent of any referential speech events that may be occurring, signal some particular value of one or more contextual variables" (1976: 29). Such non-referential (or non-denotational) indexes add nothing to the propositional content of what is said but add powerful cues about how an utterance should be interpreted or construed or taken up by interlocutors: think of the way intonation, pitch and prosody can signal sarcasm and other speaker stances. Many languages require speakers to add an element to every sentence that contributes nothing to the referential content of what is said but simply signals that the speaker is (sociologically) female or male (see Agha 2004: 31–2 for Koasati and Lakhota examples).

Presupposing vs. entailing indexicality. "Any indexical sign form, in occurring …, hovers between two contractible relationships to its 'contextual' surround: the signal form as occurring either PRESUPPOSES … something about its context-of-occurrence, or ENTAILS ['CREATES'] … something about its context-of-occurrence" (Silverstein 1993: 36). Presupposing indexicals, in other words, gesture toward aspects of context that interlocutors probably take for granted as relevant; their use presumes upon participants' shared assumptions about the independent existence of whatever is pointed to in/as context (Silverstein 1976: 33). Entailing indexicals, by contrast, are surprising and may force a reassessment by participants of "what is going on" in the interaction, while it is going on. Their use "[brings] into sharp cognitive relief part of the context of speech … seeming to be the very medium through which the relevant aspect of the context is made to 'exist'" (1976: 34).

Orders of indexicality. If *pragmatics* (as here understood) is "the semiotic realm of indexical meaning, including both denotational and nondenotational signs," and if, "in the realtime activity of discursive interaction, an indexical sign points from the ever-moving here-and-now occurrence of some signal (token) to its PRESUPPOSED 'CONTEXT' and/or to its ENTAILED 'CONSEQUENCES'" (Silverstein 1993: 41–2), then *metapragmatics* represents a kind of "second-order" construal of these pragmatic facts: "signs functioning metapragmatically have pragmatic phenomena – indexical sign phenomena – as their semiotic objects; they thus have an inherently 'framing', or 'regimenting' or 'stipulative' character with respect to indexical phenomena" (1993: 33). Second-order indexicality frames, "regiments" and interprets first-order indexicality by assigning (limitlessly varied) pragmatic activities to a (limited) set of "types" or categories – by bringing them into some kind of normative order, in other words. Speakers of French, for example, have the option of addressing their co-conversationalist with *vous* or *tu* (Brown and Gilman 1960). Here is nonreferential indexicality: the two forms can "equally" be used to denote the addressee; the difference between them contributes nothing to denotation but only marks an indexical contrast. Under certain conditions of utterance (a marked asymmetry of status – age, rank, etc. – between the two conversationalists, say), the use of one or the other of these address forms in context – along with accompanying text (and nonlinguistic conduct) containing less obvious indexicals – might be interpreted as rude, polite, presumptuous, contemptuous, graceful or servile. These interpretations "read" first-order usage in terms of second-order (ideologically saturated) values and are always informed by speech-community norms that themselves are unevenly distributed over populations of language users. In some cases, a speaker's skillful deployment of deference indexicals (aka honorific usages) in context(s) can be further interpreted metapragmatically as evidence of their moral probity, good character and the like – and hence as evidence that they themselves deserve to be addressed with the same deference indexicals that they so skillfully use with others. Such inherently metapragmatic models of conduct in speech are culturally and historically specific and are the subject-matter of a now very large literature on language ideologies.[2]

1.2.2 Register(s)

John Gumperz in his 1968 essay on "The Speech Community" presciently identified what might be called the "elementary form of the sociolinguistic life" – the fundamental fact of any sociolinguistic analysis. Note that it is an event:

> An individual's choice from among permissible alternates in a particular speech event may reveal his family background and his social intent, may identify him as a Southerner, a Northerner, an urbanite, a rustic, a member of the educated or uneducated classes, and may even indicate whether he wishes to appear friendly or distant, familiar or deferential, superior or inferior. (Gumperz [1968]1997: 66–7)

Here, Gumperz captures many of the key dimensions of the *register* phenomenon as it has been developed in more recent work (e.g. Agha 2007): our intuition that registers offer different (but denotationally equivalent) ways of "saying the same thing" (here, "permissible alternates"); our sense that speakers, in "choosing" one from among two or more alternates, "reveal" or "indicate" (i.e., index) what Gumperz a few lines later calls "social information" about themselves and about the nature of their participation in the here-and-now of discursive interaction. And notice that more than one kind of "social information" is being (indexically) invoked, in more than one way here: facts about the speaker's identity as a Southerner or a Northerner, perhaps signaled by "accent" ("dialectal" variants in Gumperz's 1968 terminology; first- or n^{th}-order indexicals), are involved, but so too are more complicated diacritics of class ("family background … educated or uneducated"). The key point, which Gumperz implies but does not develop, is that speaking in a way that could be called "rustic" might be a means of performing being "friendly" or "familiar" with one's interlocutors, while talking like an "urbanite" might be a way of performing "distance" and/or "superior[ity]"

---

[2] See, e.g., Silverstein 1979; Kroskrity, Schieffelin and Woolard 1998; Kroskrity 2000; Irvine and Gal 2000; to name only a few.

(or vice versa) – here is second- (or $n^{th}+1^{st}$-) order indexicality, an ideologically saturated construal of 1st-order indexicality. When such configurations of second-order indexicals – in language and in other communicative modes, including dress, posture, vocal quality, etc. – become to some degree publicly known and "naturalized" as emblems of this-or-that type of person participating in this-or-that type of interactional encounter, perhaps acquiring names along the way ("posh," "Cockney," "slang," "street language," etc.), we call them *registers* or, perhaps better, describe a process of *enregisterment*.

Halliday, McIntosh and Strevens ([1964]1968) drew a sharp distinction between "dialect" and "register": "A dialect," they write, "is a variety of a language distinguished according to the user: different groups of people ... use different dialects"; "the name given to a variety of a language distinguished according to its use is a 'register'" (Halliday, McIntosh and Strevens [1964]1968: 149). Halliday's distinction seems to have influenced the distinction that Gumperz drew in the same essay between what he called "dialectal" linguistic variants and "superposed" variants:

> Dialectal relationships are those in which differences set off the vernaculars of local groups ... from those of other groups within the same, broader culture. ... [Dialectal relationships] show characteristics similar to the relationship existing between dialects of the same language. Whereas dialect variation relates to distinctions in geographical origin and social background, superposed variation refers to distinctions between different types of activities carried on within the same group. ... The language of formal speechmaking, religious ritual, or technical discussion, for example, is never the same as that employed in informal talk among friends, because each is a style fulfilling particular communicative needs. ([1968]1997: 69–70)

Note the (non-technical) use of the term "style" here. Most important is to see that the kinds of variations in speech that Gumperz identifies as "dialectal" have a social distribution that in a sense redundantly reflects differences between groups of speakers that can be established on other, nonlinguistic grounds (e.g. of geography).

"Superposed" variants, by a truly orthogonal contrast, are diverse repertoire elements that an (imaginary) single speaker in some sense has under his or her "command" (passively or actively), switching among different registers as appropriate to different activities and situations. "Different types of activities," with different types of participants arrayed with respect to each other in different ways, are "carried on" within a single speech community, and different kinds of communicative resources are required for effective participation in each.

This has immediate "methodological" implications because it means that, unlike "dialectal" variants, "superposed" ones must be observed *in use* in actual contexts of interaction, since they are constituted as reflexive models, as what a (culturally recognizable) type of person would say (i.e., choose from a set of "permissible alternates") in a recognizable type of situation – or might not – and to what effect? The analysis of interaction is fundamental because processes of *enregisterment* provide participants in discourse with the tools to perform an "analysis of interaction" while it is happening, enabling them to use language (and other communicative resources) to "formulate a sketch of the social occasion constituted by the act of speaking" (Agha 2007: 14) while it is underway, and perhaps to "revise" the sketch a millisecond or two later. In any case, "superposed" variability does not match or mirror differences between "groups" that can be arrived at on nonlinguistic grounds; rather, it is intrinsically about the way that people use different forms – and, indeed, different "languages" – in different kinds of situation, and so the study of discourse in context is the *sine qua non* of this whole intellectual project (this point is developed further in Sections 1.2.3 and 1.3; see Chapter 3 in this volume on the concept of "action").

Lexical registers, as mentioned, are always the most salient and obvious types of enregistered phenomena to speakers – think of "legalese," "medicalese" and similar. The best-studied of all lexical registers are honorific registers – often termed "speech levels" in the literature – sets of "permissible alternate" forms arranged in "pragmatic paradigms" (Silverstein 2017b) that enable language users to elaborately express different degrees (and kinds) of respect and deference to an addressee or topic (for overviews, see Agha 1994, 2002).

Over the last decade or so, "register" has become a central organizing concept for many researchers in discourse studies, as fields with roots in linguistics (e.g. pragmatics), interactional sociolinguistics (e.g. linguistic ethnography) and linguistic anthropology have converged on a set of problems that would be impossible to formulate without starting from a concept of indexicality: how do variations in language use – in whatever medium, from face-to-face to Facebook – presume upon or help to create the contexts in which they occur?

Asif Agha defines a register of language as "[a] linguistic repertoire that is associated, culture internally, with particular social practices and with persons who engage in [them]" (2004: 24). For Agha, registers are "cultural models of speech that link speech repertoires to typifications of actor, relationship, and conduct" (2004: 23) – but this, as Agha points out, is a "folk" model ("conceived in intuitive terms"). In analytic terms, the problem is to focus attention on the "*reflexive social processes* whereby such models are formulated and disseminated in social life and become available for use in interaction by individuals" (2004: 23; emphasis in original).

A "register formation," for Agha, is a reflexive model of behavior that evaluates a semiotic repertoire – whether linguistic (as, e.g. lexicon, phonology, prosody, syntax) or nonlinguistic (e.g. gesture, bodily hexis, dress, etc.) – as appropriate to culture-specific types of conduct, types of occasion, types of person (role-fractions) *qua* participants (social relations).

It is the by-degrees "detachability" of enregistered usages from their usual or appropriate contexts that makes possible the creative "recycling" of enregistered utterance-fractions into new and unexpected situations, in "creative" (indexically entailing) usages. John Gumperz presents a classic example:

> The first incident was recorded while I was sitting in an aisle seat on an airplane bound for Miami, Florida. I noticed two middle aged women walking towards the rear of the plane. Suddenly I heard from behind, "Tickets, please! Tickets, please!" At first I was startled and began to wonder why someone would be asking for tickets so long after the start of the flight. Then one of the women smiled toward the other and said, "I told you to leave him at home." I looked up and saw a man passing the two women, saying, "Step to the rear of the bus, please." (1982: 161)

"Americans," notes Gumperz, "will have no difficulty identifying this interchange as a joke" (Gumperz 1982: 161). In lectures during the 1930s, Edward Sapir defined humor as "an unconscious mathematics of changed contexts" ([1930s]2011: 105).

People get socialized into register formations: if the social *domain* of a register is that set of people acquainted with it, then it follows that many more people can recognize the forms (repertoire) and their linkage to reflexive typifications than can fluently use the enregistered forms with the expected indexical effects.

> An individual's *register range* – the variety of registers with which he or she is acquainted – equips a person with portable emblems of identity, sometimes permitting distinctive modes of access to particular zones of social life. In complex society, where no fluent speaker of the language fully commands more than a few of its registers, the register range of a person may influence the range of social activities in which that person is entitled to participate. (Agha 2007: 24)

This asymmetry – the fact that many more people are acquainted with a register than can actively (and convincingly) use the enregistered forms in context – was a key finding of Agha's sociohistorical account of "Received Pronunciation" (RP) in English (latterly, British) English (Agha 2003, 2007) and has informed much recent work. This asymmetry is a fundamental feature of register formations everywhere. It also shows how the study of language use through the lens of register formations presents an opportunity to connect the study of variable use in context to wider concerns about the unequal distribution of power and resources in society.

1.2.3 Style(s)

Of the three terms/concepts under review here, "style" is perhaps the most frequently invoked in the relevant literatures of discourse studies and almost certainly the most elastic in its range of meanings. As we've already seen, some authors use "register" and "style" almost interchangeably, while others insist on drawing a sharp distinction between the two. Accepting for now a very broad definition of style as "the way that individual speakers vary their language in response to different aspects of the social situation" (Cheshire 2007: 432), we can observe how the increasing centrality of "style" in sociolinguistics reflects a broader shift in the field: away from the operationalism and quasi-experimental methodologies of orthodox (Labovian) variationism (e.g. Labov 1966) and toward more ethnographically informed and interpretive approaches that seek to address the indexical function(s) of variable forms of speech and speakers' own (ideologically mediated) understandings of these (see, e.g., Eckert 2003, 2008, 2012).

Discussions of "style," then, reflect a convergence of theoretical and empirical orientations that brings post-variationist work in sociolinguistics into closer alignment with work being done in linguistic anthropology, interactional sociolinguistics and related fields such as linguistic ethnography (e.g. Rampton, Maybin and Roberts 2014). But the continuities between Labov's concept of "contextual styles" and later post-variationist work are as significant as the discontinuities: both focus on the individual speaker's ability to draw upon a repertoire of variant forms (in early work, variant pronunciations) in different situations of use. For the linguistic anthropologist Judith Irvine, "styles in speaking involve the ways speakers, as agents in social (and sociolinguistic) space, negotiate their positions and goals within a system of distinctions and possibilities. Their acts of speaking are ideologically mediated, since those acts necessarily involve the speaker's understandings of salient social groups, activities, and practices, including forms of talk" (2001: 23–4).

Labov defined "style" much more narrowly than this. "Style" in Labov's work is a technical term that enabled him to measure the dimension of "intra-speaker variation in the structured sociolinguistic interview" (Irvine 2001: 25). Labov structured his interviews around a series of standardized "task demands," a method derived from work in experimental psychology, to elicit comparable speech samples from each interviewee (see Chapter 3 in this volume for a methodological critique). Speakers were asked: "Have you ever been in a situation where you thought you were in serious danger of being killed – where you thought to yourself, 'This is it'?" (Labov [1966] 1972c: 93). "If the informant answers yes," Labov explains, "the interviewer pauses for one or two seconds, and then asks, 'What happened?' As the informant begins to reply, ... [o]ften he becomes involved in the narration to the extent that he seems to be reliving the critical moment, and signs of emotional tension appear" ([1966]1972c: 93).

The elicitation of "danger of death" narratives, then, was a technique for eliciting whatever was that particular speaker's most vernacular style – and "styles" are defined by Labov strictly in cognitive psychological terms, as the product of different degrees of the individual speaker's attention to his or her own speech. In "reliving the critical moment," speakers become so "involved in the narration" that their self-monitoring of their own speech is minimized and the speech they produce is accordingly their most "informal" style (Style A). The other tasks included relatively informal back-and-forth between interviewer and interviewee (Style B) and tasks in which interviewees were asked to read a paragraph of written prose aloud (Style C), to read out a list of words containing targeted phonological segments (Style D) and, in some cases, to read out a list of minimal pairs (Style D), the idea being that speakers increase the degree of their attention to their own speech as they move through these different tasks, producing speech in increasingly "formal" styles (Labov [1964] 1972b). If this elicitation of individual speakers' "styles" – "all ranged along a single dimension of attention paid to speech, with casual speech at one end of the continuum and minimal pairs at the other" (Labov [1964] 1972b: 99) – revealed "intra-speaker" variation as one dimension of sociolinguistic variation, the other dimension, termed "social variation," reflected the sorting of speakers into groups based on socioeconomic status (SES) – hence, inter-speaker variation.

At the center of Labov's analysis are phonological variables, elements of pronunciation that are differentially realized in speech across both dimensions – both within the speech of individuals across different "styles" (so defined) and across different speakers grouped according to their place in a macro-social system of class stratification (SES).

Labov's approach has come under critique from within sociolinguistics since the 1970s. Nessa Wolfson questioned the authenticity of Labov's quasi-experimental interview techniques – "there is no single, absolute entity answering to the notion of natural/casual speech. If speech is felt to be appropriate to a situation and the goal, then it is natural in that context" (1976: 124) – and many others have made similar observations (see, e.g., Gregersen et al. 2017). Subsequent work has pointed to the importance of "audience design" and "referee design" (e.g. Bell 1984, 2001) for developing a more sophisticated notion of style that attends to the way that speakers' style choices take account of interlocutors (both real and copresent, and imagined); Coupland's influential studies of a Cardiff radio DJ show how standard and nonstandard features of Cardiff's urban dialect are mixed with features associated with Cockney and US English in projecting a "persona" that is irreducible to stereotypes associated with users of these varieties (2001, 2007).

Much "post-variationist" work interprets "style" much more broadly than as the effect of the individual speaker's attention to his own speech (though Labov's own position has, if anything, become more entrenched since 1966); most of it has likewise rejected Labov's operationalism and his use of quasi-experimental methods in favor of attention to "naturalistic" speech practices as they unfold in their own social contexts – in workplaces, classrooms, call centers, over the radio and in a range of other private or public settings. But two elements have remained at the center of post-variationist work on "style": the individual speaker and the sociolinguistic variable.

Penelope Eckert has given an account of the "three waves of variation study" that have emerged in sociolinguistics since the 1960s. Interestingly, she positions Labov's first significant work – his study of phonological "change in progress" on Martha's Vineyard (Labov [1963]1972a) – as both the historical precursor of the "first wave" (exemplified in Labov 1966) and an exemplar, *avant la lettre*, of the third. In the Martha's Vineyard study, Labov had showed that members and descendants of long-established English-derived fishing families on the island (known locally as "Yankees") were increasingly pronouncing words like *house* and *life* with centralized diphthongs – as [hɜʊs] and [lɜɪf] rather than [haʊs] and [laɪf] – and that this centralized pronunciation was increasingly preferred by "Yankees" who wished to identify themselves as locals, in contrast with the "Summer People," urban professionals from Boston and New York, who were buying up the ancestral houses of the Yankee fisherfolk as vacation homes. Eckert asserts that, with this discovery, Labov "established that the pronunciation of /ay/ had been recruited as an indexical resource in a local ideological struggle" (2012: 88): "This move was a textbook example of the workings of what Silverstein (2003) has termed 'indexical order', by which a feature that had simply marked a speaker as a Vineyarder came to be used stylistically within the island to index a particular kind of Vineyarder, foregrounding a particular aspect of island identity" (2012: 88).

For Eckert, the first wave of variationism is exemplified by Labov's monumental 1966 study of *The Social Stratification of English in New York City* (Labov 1966): "The first wave viewed linguistic change as emerging from pressures within the linguistic system, first affecting the speech of those least subject to the influence of standard language and spreading outward through populations increasingly resistant to change" (Eckert 2012: 90).

The second wave of variation studies is exemplified by studies that moved away from Labov's quasi-experimental interview methods, favoring instead the ethnographic study of language users in their communities: Eckert discusses the well-known work of the Milroys in Belfast (e.g. Milroy 1980) and her own study of a suburban Detroit high school (Eckert 1988, 1989), among others. The analysis still centers on correlations between the frequency of occurrence of certain (usually subphonemic) variables of pronunciation on the one hand, and social facts about speakers on the other, but the social facts now include speakers' "social category membership" (2012: 92) – for example as Jocks or Burnouts in Eckert's Detroit high-school study (Eckert 1988, 1989) – and "patterns of variation" are now seen as "resources in the construction of identity" (2012: 92). Just as important, "[sociolinguistic] variation also emerged as part of a broader stylistic complex including territory and the full range of consumption – such as adornment, food and other substance use, musical tastes – that jocks and burnouts exploit in constructing their mutual opposition" (2012: 92).

If "ethnography brought stylistic practice into view," Eckert writes, "the principal move in the third wave then was from a view of variation as a reflection of social identities and categories to the linguistic practice in which speakers place themselves in the social landscape through stylistic practice" (2012: 93–4). Third wave studies recognize that "variables cannot be consensual markers of fixed meanings; on the contrary, their central property must be indexical mutability. This mutability is achieved in stylistic practice, as speakers make social-semiotic moves, reinterpreting variables and recombining them in a continual process of bricolage" (2012: 94). And, indeed, Eckert asserts that "[i]ndexical order (Silverstein 2003) is central to the mutability of indexical signs" (2012: 94).

It is important to note here that by "mutability" Eckert does not refer to the indexical function(s) of sign forms in the dynamic, processual real-time of discursive interaction – where they "hover" between polar values of presupposition and entailment – but rather to changes in the status of phonological variables over longer scales of temporality: "At some initial stage," she writes, "a distinguishing feature" of pronunciation associated with a group or population "may attract attention"; "once recognized, that feature can be extracted from its linguistic surroundings and come, on its own, to index membership in that population" (2012: 94). This sounds very much like the "register shibboleths" already discussed, functioning at an n+1st order of indexicality: "[I]ndexical order is not linear but can progress simultaneously and over time in multiple directions, laying down a set of related meanings. These meanings at any particular time constitute an indexical field (Eckert 2008) – a constellation of ideologically linked meanings, any region of which can be invoked in context" (Eckert 2012: 94).

A clear example of a variable's (indexical) linkage to "a constellation of linked meanings" is the pronunciation of intervocalic /t/ with full (aspirated) release: such a "hyperarticulated" pronunciation is associated with "nerd girls" in California high schools (Bucholtz 1999), with studiousness in Orthodox Jewish communities (Benor 2001) and with "a playful, diva persona" in US gay men (Podesva 2004): "As a hyperarticulation, /t/ release can index carefulness, precision, and general standardness, attention to detail, or education. As a fortition, it can index emphasis or force, hence focus, power, or even anger" (Eckert 2012: 97).

Note that these elements of a variable's "indexical field" are assembled from summaries of recurring patterns of usage, rather than from "close readings" of their indexical functioning in any actual context(s) of situated (and interested) use, where their uptake by interlocutors in the event, and the interactional effects of such uptake on the subsequent unfolding of a discursive encounter, can be observed and made part of the analysis. Styles, in this literature, begin to take on the qualities of internally cohesive systems – countable and integral, existing somehow separate from their "activation" (or invocation) in contingent and time-bound events.

1.3 Issues and Ongoing Debates

If some post-variationist approaches to "style(s)" seem more oriented to the indexical potentials of phonological variables than to how the activation of these potentials in actual events of use helps to shape people's participation in discursive interaction, a body of work on what is often called "stylization" (e.g. Rampton 2006; Jaspers and Van Hoof 2018) offers a clear alternative. Ben Rampton's study of students' fleeting performances of (often exaggerated) "accents" in a London secondary school (2006) reveals how young people deploy features associated with a continuum of recognizable "accents" and "voices" to evoke an "indexical field" that is labile and not neatly bounded. The continuum is anchored at the metaphorical "top-and-center" by stylizations that Rampton labels as "posh," and at the "bottom" by usages that gesture toward what he calls "Cockney" – marked by features associated with working-class London speech (cf. Møller 2015 for examples from Cophenhagen). Through the use of carefully transcribed extracts from students' everyday interactions (in the classroom and outside of it), Rampton is able to focus precisely on the interactional effects of such "stylizations" and the way that stylization practices enable participants to take up recognizable kinds of stance toward ongoing activities and/or to negotiate transitions from one activity to another – often, from relatively unstructured peer-focused interactions to the official business of classroom tasks. "Stylizations of posh and Cockney," Rampton writes, "can be seen as small pieces of secondary representation inserted into the flow of practical activity – moments of social commentary on some aspect of the activities on hand" (2006: 218). When Hanif, a student of Bangladeshi descent, picks up a booklet in a science class and reads its title aloud to his two classmates with an exaggerated Cockney stylization – *Stars and Galaxies* rendered as a heavily nasalized [stɑːz n gælәksәɪːːz] – "we can plausibly construe his stylized Cockney as a way of managing the transition between chat and study, peer group and school" (2006: 299); and, more than this, we can see how "in rounding the title off with an accent that was often associated with informal sociability, he seems to combine a display of 'being on-task' with signs that he is not a nerd and is still in tune" (2006: 299). A clearer exemplification of "second-order indexicality" could hardly be wished for.

1.4 Implications

The *register* concept – and the way that registers of language (Agha 2004) are situated within a larger framework of the enregisterment of conduct, involving multiple signaling modalities (Agha 2007) – has already proven fertile for researchers addressing a wide range of discourse phenomena. Barbara Johnstone's studies of "Pittsburghese" (Johnstone, Andrus and Danielson 2006; Johnstone 2013), for example, have tracked the enregisterment of an erstwhile dialect as an emblem of locality in a context of socio-economic transformation of this former "rust belt" US city; recent work by Qing Zhang (Zhang 2008, 2017) has explored the emergence of a new register of "Cosmopolitan Mandarin" among white-collar workers in China, while researchers studying the "polylanguaging" practices of diverse populations of young people in urban centers in Europe have shown how complex speech repertoires are organized around registers and register shibboleths as indexical anchors (Jørgensen et al. 2011 and cf. Møller 2015 and refs. therein).

Agha himself has extended the "enregisterment" framework into the realm of commodities (Agha 2011a); other recent work has developed "enregisterment" within a wide frame of reference to include food (e.g. Karrebæk 2012, 2013, 2016), cosmetics (Mendoza-Denton 2008), wine (Silverstein 2003: 222–227, 2009, 2016) and other beverages (Manning 2012), and clothing (Nakassis 2012, 2013), to name only a few.

The concept of "orders of indexicality" has played a central role in the recent work of Jan Blommaert and others on the sociolinguistics of globalization (Blommaert 2010) and has also been used to illuminate how state bureaucracies function in part by managing the circulation of indexical information about documentary artifacts (Hull 2003, 2012) and to show how "leadership" is evidenced in Indonesian politics (Goebel 2014, 2020), to mention only a few examples.

1.5 Future Directions

A new generation of researchers has been developing the concepts and frameworks of *indexicality*, *register* and *style* (and related frameworks of metapragmatics) to analyze and interpret interactions that take place in digital or online environments, including on social media platforms. Hua (Ted) Nie takes full advantage of the affordances that online environments provide to researchers by tracking the invention and "viral spread" of neologisms across Chinese social media platforms: combining data-mining techniques with close readings of the back-and-forth of online interaction, Nie (2017) shows how new items of "internet slang" are disseminated across user networks and become enregistered as emblems of group identity.

In a study of "textually mediated participatory practices on the online platform *reddit.com*," Jack LaViolette focuses on "forms of discourse participation that are unique to online environments, … showing how the online environment facilitates the display and re-entextualization of 'others'' speech" and drawing "parallels with Miyako Inoue's [2004] discussion of the print-mediated metapragmatics of citation that played a central role in the creation of the Japanese schoolgirl stereotype: both are based on overheard utterances" (2017: 2).

Responding to claims in the "new media" literature that online platforms such as Facebook and Twitter, by their very design, precipitate "crises of self-presentation" (Wesch 2008) by automatically "flattening" all audiences into one (Marwick and boyd 2011: 9; the phenomenon known as "context collapse"), researchers in discourse studies have shown that the situation is more complicated (Georgakopoulou 2017; Szabla and Blommaert 2017; Moore 2019). Szabla and Blommaert (2017), for example, bring the tools of discourse analysis to bear on a complex and multiparty conversation on Facebook among Polish immigrants in Belgium, showing that the participants did not in fact experience "context collapse"; rather, they engaged expertly with the "affordances" of the online platform to expand and multiply interactional contexts, using "various mechanisms to solve possible complications in addressee selection," even as they "provided useful correcting information to each other, and completed complex interactional tasks" (2017: 20).

1.6 Summary

In the years since Roman Jakobson ([1957]1990) showed that many core categories of grammar (e.g. person, tense, mood) were irreducibly *indexical* – and his student Michael Silverstein developed the implications of this discovery for the study of language use in context – new research problems and new approaches to analysis have transformed discourse studies as a multidisciplinary field of inquiry. Around the interrelated phenomena of *register(s)* and *style(s)*, remarkably productive bodies of empirical work are continuing to emerge, showing how participants in discursive interaction orient to the contextualization (and recontextualization) of their own and each other's contributions to semiotically mediated communicative activities, whether these activities unfold online, offline or across these and other modalities of contact.

Further Reading

Register
Agha, A. (2007). *Language and Social Relations*. Cambridge: Cambridge University Press.

This develops a social theory of communication centered on the process of enregisterment.

Agha, A. and Frog (eds.) (2015). *Registers of Communication*. Helsinki: Studia Fennica. 18. https://oa.finlit.fi/site/books/10.21435/sflin.18/.

This diverse collection of studies analyzes enregisterment in various linguistic and cultural settings

Style

Coupland, N. (2007). *Style: Language Variation and Identity*. Cambridge: Cambridge University Press.

This is a compilation of important works on language, style and identity.

Eckert, P. and Rickford, J. (eds.) (2001). *Style and Sociolinguistic Variation*. Cambridge: Cambridge University Press.

This influential anthology has contributions from scholars in multiple disciplines.

Indexicality

Hanks, W. (1990). *Referential Practice: Language and Lived Space among the Maya*. Chicago: University of Chicago Press.

This is an exemplary ethnography of indexical practices in a single community.

Lee, B. (1997). *Talking Heads: Language, Metalanguage and the Semiotics of Subjectivity*. Durham, NC: Duke University Press.

This synthesizes the philosophical and anthropological literature on semiotics.

References

Agha, A. (1994). Honorification. *Annual Review of Anthropology* 23: 277–302.
  (2003). The Social Life of Cultural Value. *Language & Communication* 23: 231–73.
  (2004). Registers of Language. In A. Duranti (ed.) *A Companion to Linguistic Anthropology*. Malden, MA/Oxford: Blackwell. 23–45.
  (2005). Voice, Footing, Enregisterment. *Journal of Linguistic Anthropology* 15 (1): 38–59.
  (2007). *Language and Social Relations*. Cambridge: Cambridge University Press.
  (2011a). Commodity Registers. *Journal of Linguistic Anthropology* 21(1): 22–53.
  (2011b). Meet Mediatization. *Language & Communication* 31: 163–70.
  (2002). Honorific Registers. In K. Kataoka and S. Ide (eds.) *Culture, Interaction and Language*. Tokyo: Hituzisyobo. 21–63.
Agha, A. and Frog (eds.) (2015). *Registers of Communication*. Helsinki: Studia Fennica. 18. https://oa.finlit.fi/site/books/10.21435/sflin.18/.
Bell, A. (1984). Language Style as Audience Design. *Language in Society* 13(2): 145–204.
  (2001). Back in Style: Reworking Audience Design. In P. Eckert and J. R. Rickford (eds.) *Style and Sociolinguistic Variation*. Cambridge: Cambridge University Press. 139–69.

Benor, S. (2001). Sounding Learned: The Gendered Use of /t/ in Orthodox Jewish English. In D. E. Johnson and T. Sanchez (eds.) *Penn Working Papers in Linguistics: Selected Papers from NWAV 29*. Philadelphia: University of Pennsylvania Press. 1–16.

Benveniste, É. ([1956]1971). The Nature of Pronouns. In *Problems in General Linguistics*, trans. M. E. Meek. Miami Linguistic Series, No. 8. Coral Gables, FL: University of Miami Press. 217–22.

Blommaert, J. (2010). *The Sociolinguistics of Globalization*. Cambridge: Cambridge University Press.

Brown, R. and Gilman, A. (1960). The Pronouns of Power and Solidarity. In T. Sebeok (ed.) *Style in Language*. Cambridge, MA: MIT Press. 253–76.

Bucholtz, M. (1999). "Why Be Normal?": Language and Identity Practices in a Community of Nerd Girls. *Language in Society* 28(2): 203–23.

Cheshire, J. (2007). Review: Style and Sociolinguistic Variation (ed. by Penelope Eckert and John R. Rickford. Cambridge: Cambridge University Press, 2001. Pp. xvi, 341. ISBN 0521597897. $27.99). *Language* 83(2): 432–5.

Conklin, H. C. (1962). Lexicographical Treatment of Folk Taxonomies. In F. W. Householder and S. Saporta (eds.) *Problems in Lexicography*. Publication 21. Bloomington: Indiana University Research Center in Anthropology, Folklore, and Linguistics. 119–41.

Coupland, N. (2001). Dialect Stylization in Radio Talk. *Language in Society* 30: 345–75.

(2007). *Style: Language Variation and Identity*. Cambridge: Cambridge University Press.

Eckert, P. (1988). Adolescent Social Structure and the Spread of Linguistic Change. *Language in Society* 17(2): 183–207.

(1989). *Jocks and Burnouts: Social Categories and Identity in High School*. New York: Teachers College Press.

(2003). The Meaning of Style. *Texas Linguistic Forum* 47: 41–53.

(2008). Variation and the Indexical Field. *Journal of Sociolinguistics* 3: 428–42.

(2012). Three Waves of Variation Study: The Emergence of Meaning in the Study of Sociolinguistic Variation. *Annual Review of Anthropology* 41: 87–100.

(2018). *Meaning and Linguistic Variation: The Third Wave in Sociolinguistics*. Cambridge: Cambridge University Press.

Geertz, C. (1966). The Impact of the Concept of Culture on the Concept of Man. *Bulletin of the Atomic Scientists* 22(4): 2–8.

Georgakopoulou, A. (2017). "Whose Context Collapse?": Ethical Clashes in the Study of Language and Social Media in Context. *Applied Linguistics Review* 8(2–3): 1–32. https://doi.org/10.1515/applirev-2016-1034.

Goebel, Z. (2014). Doing Leadership through Signswitching in the Indonesian Bureaucracy. *Journal of Linguistic Anthropology* 24 2: 193–215.

(2020). *Global Leadership Talk*. Oxford: Oxford University Press.

Goffman, E. (1964). The Neglected Situation. *American Anthropologist* 66(6 Part 2: The Ethnography of Communication): 133–6.
Gregersen, F., Jørgensen, J. N., Møller, J. S., Pharao, N. and Hansen, G. F. (2017). Sideways: Five Methodological Studies of Sociolinguistic Interviews. *Acta Linguistica Hafniensia*.
Gumperz, J. J. (1982). *Discourse Strategies*. Cambridge: Cambridge University Press.
 ([1968]1997). The Speech Community. In A. Duranti (ed.) *Linguistic Anthropology: A Reader*. Malden, MA/Oxford: Blackwell. 66–73.
Halliday, M. A. K., McIntosh, A. and Strevens, P. ([1964]1968). The Users and Uses of Language. In J. A. Fishman (ed.) *Readings in the Sociology of Language*. The Hague: Mouton. 139–69.
Hanks, W. F. (1990). *Referential Practice: Language and Lived Space among the Maya*. Chicago: University of Chicago Press.
 (1999). Indexicality. *Journal of Linguistic Anthropology* 9(1–2): 124–6.
Hill, J. H. (1985). The Grammar of Consciousness and the Consciousness of Grammar. *American Ethnologist* 12(4): 725–37.
Hull, M. (2003). The File: Agency, Authority, and Autography in an Islamabad Bureaucracy. *Language & Communication* 23: 287–314.
 (2012). *Government of Paper*. Berkeley: University of California Press.
Inoue, M. (2004). *Vicarious Language: Gender and Linguistic Modernity in Japan*. Berkeley: University of California Press.
Irvine, J. (2001). "Style" as Distinctiveness: The Culture and Ideology of Linguistic Differentiation. In P. Eckert and J. R. Rickford (eds.) *Style and Sociolinguistic Variation*. Cambridge: Cambridge University Press. 21–43.
Irvine, J. and Gal, S. (2000). Language Ideology and Linguistic Differentiation. In P. V. Kroskrity (eds.) *Regimes of Language: Ideologies, Polities, and Identities*. Santa Fe, NM: School of American Research Press. 35–84.
Jakobson, R. ([1957]1990). Shifters, Verbal Categories, and the Russian Verb. In L. Waugh and M. Monville-Burston (eds.) *On Language*. Cambridge, MA: Harvard University Press. 386–92.
Jaspers, J. and van Hoof, S. (2018). Style and Stylisation. In K. Tusting (ed.) *The Routledge Handbook of Linguistic Ethnography*. London: Routledge. 109–24.
Johnstone, B. (2013). *Speaking Pittsburghese: The Story of a Dialect*. Oxford: Oxford University Press.
Johnstone, B., Andrus, J. and Danielson, A. E. (2006). Mobility, Indexicality, and the Enregisterment of "Pittsburghese." *Journal of English Linguistics* 34: 77–104.
Jørgensen, J. N., Karrebæk, M. S., Madsen, L. M. and Møller, J. S. (2011). Polylanguaging in Superdiversity. *Diversities* 13(2): 23–37.
Karrebæk, M. (2012). "What's in Your Lunch-Box Today?" Health, Ethnicity and Respectability in the Primary Classroom. *Journal of Linguistic Anthropology* 22(1): 1–22.

(2013). Rye Bread and Halal: Enregisterment of Food Practices in the Primary Classroom. *Language & Communication* 34: 17–34.

(2016). Rye Bead for Lunch, Lasagna for Breakfast: Enregisterment, Classrooms, and National Food Norms in Superdiversity. In K. Arnaut, M. Karrebæk and M. Spotti (eds.) *Engaging Superdiversity: Recombining Spaces, Times and Language Practices*. Bristol: Multilingual Matters. 90–120.

Kroskrity, P. V. (ed.) (2000). *Regimes of Language: Ideologies, Polities, and Identities*. Santa Fe, NM: School of American Research Press.

Kroskrity, P., Schieffelin, B. and Woolard, K. (eds.) (1998). *Language Ideologies: Practice and Theory*. Oxford: Oxford University Press.

Labov, W. (1966). *The Social Stratification of English in New York City*. Washington, DC: Center for Applied Linguistics.

([1963]1972a). The Social Motivation of a Sound Change. In W. Labov, *Sociolinguistic Patterns*. Philadelphia: University of Pennsylvania Press. 273–309.

([1964]1972b). Hypercorrection by the Lower Middle Class as a Factor in Linguistic Change. In W. Labov, *Sociolinguistic Patterns*. Philadelphia: University of Pennsylvania Press. 122–42.

([1966]1972c). The Isolation of Contextual Styles. In W. Labov, *Sociolinguistic Patterns*. Philadelphia: University of Pennsylvania Press. 70–109.

LaViolette, J. (2017). Cyber-metapragmatics and Alterity on *reddit.com*. King's College Working Papers in Urban Language and Literacies, paper 229; also Tilburg Papers in Culture Studies, paper 196.

Manning, P. (2012). *Semiotics of Drink and Drinking*. New York: Continuum.

Marwick, A. E. and boyd, d. (2011). I Tweet Honestly, I Tweet Passionately: Twitter Users, Context Collapse, and the Imagined Audience. *New Media & Society* 13(1): 114–33.

Mendoza-Denton, N. (2008). *Homegirls: Language and Cultural Practice among Latina Youth Gangs*. New York: Wiley-Blackwell.

Milroy, L. (1980). *Language and Social Networks*. Oxford: Basil Blackwell.

Møller, J. (2015). The Enregisterment of Minority Languages in a Danish Classroom. In A. Agha and Frog (eds.) *Registers of Communication*. Helsinki: Studia Fennica. 107–24.

Moore, R. (2019). "Context Collapse" on a Small Island: Using Goffman's Dissertation Fieldwork to Think about Online Communication. *Language, Culture & Society* 1(2).

Nakassis, C. V. (2012). Brand, Citationality, Performativity. *American Anthropologist* 114(4): 624–38.

(2013). Brands and Their Surfeits. *Cultural Anthropology* 28(1): 111–26.

Nie, H. (2017). Memes, Communities, and Continuous Change: Chinese Internet Vernacular Explained. Unpublished PhD thesis, Tilburg University.

Ortner, S. (1984). Theory in Anthropology since the Sixties. *Comparative Studies in Society and History* 26(1): 126–66.

Parmentier, R. J. (1994). Peirce Divested for Non-intimates. In R. Parmentier (ed.) *Signs in Society*. Bloomington: Indiana University Press. 3–22.

Peirce, C. S. (1931–58). *Collected Papers of Charles Sanders Peirce*, 8 vols., ed. by C. Hartshorne, P. Weiss and A. W. Burks. Cambridge, MA: Harvard University Press. Abbreviated as *CP* 2 (*Collected Papers*, Vol. 2).

(1955). Logic as Semiotic: The Theory of Signs. In J. Buchler (ed.) *Philosophical Writings of Peirce*. New York: Dover Publications. 98–119.

Podesva, R. (2004). On Constructing Social Meaning with Stop Release Bursts. Paper presented at Sociolinguistics Symposium 15, Newcastle upon Tyne.

Rampton, B. (2006). *Language in Late Modernity*. Cambridge: Cambridge University Press.

Rampton, B., Maybin, J. and Roberts, C. (2014). Methodological Foundations in Linguistic Ethnography. King's College Working Papers in Urban Language and Literacies, Paper 125.

Sacks, H., Schegloff, E. A. and Jefferson, G. (1974). A Simplest Systematics for the Organization of Turn-Taking for Conversation. *Language* 50(4 Part 1): 696–735.

Sapir, E. ([1930s]2011). *The Psychology of Culture: A Course of Lectures*, reconstituted and ed. by J. Irvine. New York: Mouton de Gruyter.

Silverstein, M. (1976). Shifters, Linguistic Categories and Cultural Description. In K. H. Basso and H. A. Selby (eds.) *Meaning in Anthropology*. Albuquerque: University of New Mexico Press. 11–55.

(1979). Language Structure and Linguistic Ideology. In P. R. Clyde, W. F. Hanks and C. L. Hofbauer (eds.) *The Elements: A Parasession on Linguistic Units and Levels*. Chicago, IL: Chicago Linguistic Society. 193–247.

(1993). Metapragmatic Discourse and Metapragmatic Function. In J. A. Lucy (ed.) *Reflexive Language: Reported Speech and Metapragmatics*. Cambridge: Cambridge University Press. 33–58.

(2003). Indexical Order and the Dialectics of Sociolinguistic Life. *Language and Communication* 23(3–4): 193–229.

(2016). Semiotic Vinification and the Scaling of Taste. In E. S. Carr and M. Lempert (eds.) *Scale: Discourse and Dimensions of Social Life*. Berkeley: University of California Press.

(2017a). Forty Years of Speaking (of) the Same (Object) Language – *sans le savoir*. *Langage et Société* 160–1: 93–110.

(2017b). Standards, Styles, and Signs of the Social Self. *Journal of the Anthropological Society of Oxford* 9(1): 134–64.

Szabla, M. and Blommaert, J. (2017). Does Context Really Collapse in Social Media Interaction? Tilburg Papers in Culture Studies, Paper 201.

Wesch, M. (2008). Context Collapse. http://mediatedcultures.net/youtube/context-collapse/.

Wolfson, N. (1976). Speech Events and Natural Speech: Some Implications for Sociolinguistic Methodology. *Language in Society* 5: 189–209.

Zhang, Q. (2008). Rhotacization and the "Beijing Smooth Operator": The Social Meaning of a Linguistic Variable. *Journal of Sociolinguistics* 12(2): 201–22.

(2017). *Language and Social Change in China: Undoing Commonness through Cosmopolitan Mandarin*. London/New York: Routledge.

2

Situating Discourse Analysis in Ethnographic and Sociopolitical Context

Jennifer Roth-Gordon

2.1 Introduction

For many sociolinguists and linguistic anthropologists, conducting discourse analysis entails paying careful attention to the ways in which texts and speech are simultaneously located in interactional, local, national and global contexts. Speakers themselves make sense of language through a continuous process of contextualization. In this chapter, I examine how scholars working in what we might call a tradition of *ethnographic discourse analysis*[1] seek to address broad anthropological concerns that include the construction of identity and subject formation; power and inequality; and citizenship, rights and belonging, among other topics. This method of conducting discourse analysis bridges the fields of linguistic and cultural anthropology to reveal the linguistic construction of social order. An ethnographic approach allows us to understand that language is both intimately related to culture and central to creating and upholding social structure. Language is given meaning through the cultural, political, economic, and historical aspects of society, which I will describe as the ethnographic and sociopolitical contexts.

In this chapter, I offer examples of ethnographic approaches to discourse, focusing in particular on how linguistic anthropologists have engaged and expanded upon the concepts and theoretical tools offered by Erving Goffman and Mikhail Bakhtin. This includes attention to how

---

[1] My thanks to Jacqueline Messing for first suggesting this term to me. I am also grateful to my graduate students, especially Neşe Kaya, Jessica Ray and Antonio José da Silva, with whom I have explored this topic for many years.

Goffman unpacks interactional *participant roles*, how his concept of footing has been critical to recent interest in *stance*, and also how speakers linguistically shift in and out of *registers*. Drawing on Bakhtin, discourse analysts have turned to explore the productive concepts of *genre*, *intertextuality*, *voicing*, and *chronotopes*. I begin by describing how ethnographic discourse analysis connects levels of discourse and context and relies on specific methodological strategies to capture the dynamic ethnographic and sociopolitical contexts within which language is located and to which it contributes and responds.

2.2 Connecting Levels of Discourse and Context

Discourse is often analyzed on different linguistic, social, and cultural levels ranging from what is commonly called "the micro" to "the macro." An ethnographic approach to discourse analysis makes connections across these levels by joining analysis of strategic linguistic choices made by participants that unfold within an interaction with broader concerns about power and the construction of social order. In order to simultaneously engage in linguistic and cultural analysis, scholars must integrate: (1) linguistic features (2) interactional context (3) ethnographic context and (4) sociopolitical context. On the "micro" end, discourse analysis must attend to the linguistic features of text or speech. More traditional discourse analysis from a linguistic perspective focuses on this level exclusively, analyzing, for example, the process through which discourse markers have undergone grammaticalization into new discursive roles. At the interactional level, participants occupy and negotiate overlapping and competing social roles (teacher, student, expert, novice, parent, child, waiter, customer, etc.). But interlocutors also draw on cultural competence and background knowledge to inform what they must attend to as they interact. These cultural norms and customs constitute a third level that includes the ethnographic context. In order to answer questions about how these interactions are influenced by and help construct larger social structures, analysts must address a fourth level that can be described as the "macro" level of sociopolitical context.

These levels do not come pre-labeled in interactions, of course, and there are no actual lines that separate them. I make these distinctions in order to explain what constitutes an ethnographic approach to discourse analysis. An analysis of the possible grammatical slots that a discourse marker could occupy will remain mostly at the level of discourse features. A study that attends to social roles (between teacher and student, for example) will likely emphasize the interactional level. Research that includes participant observation outside of the classroom and offers background information on appropriate cultural norms associated with these roles will tend to draw on the ethnographic context, while studies that point out inequities (based on, for example, race, class, gender, sexual orientation, religion or other forms of social difference) engage with the sociopolitical context. This type of wide-angle lens allows a researcher to connect the use of specific linguistic features to the construction of power and inequality within a particular society. Though I describe attention to these levels as taking an "ethnographic" approach (as shorthand), the fourth level of sociopolitical context is critical to one's ability to speak to broader anthropological concerns.

In an excellent example of this approach, Rusty Barrett (2006) connects all of these levels in an investigation of the use of Spanish–English codeswitching in a Texas restaurant in which he served as a bartender. His analysis successfully moves from linguistic features to assigned and assumed social roles (such as server/customer), while drawing on ethnographic data gained through participant observation and ending with a larger argument that attends to the consolidation of power and the construction of racial inequality. Barrett begins by diligently documenting the use of Mock Spanish (Hill 1998), including hyperanglicization and the pejoration of Spanish words (as when one Anglo speaker tells another to just say "yellow" when asking a Spanish-speaking coworker for *hielo* or ice). In particular, he notes that a lack of Spanish grammar ("Did you *limpia* the *baño*?") gave the managers the sense that they were making a good faith effort to communicate with their Spanish-speaking employees, without any real concern over the comprehensibility of the utterances they produced. Barrett offers a careful analysis of (1) the linguistic competence that some Anglo speakers did possess in Spanish (as evidenced by their ability to produce fully grammatical sentences in an emergency), but he also attends to (2) the social roles and dynamics of manager–employee or coworker–coworker conversations (at the interactional level), (3) the offhand comments and social interactions that revealed a racial divide between staff (situating the discourse analyzed within ethnographic context) and (4) US language ideologies that locate Spanish speaking and Spanish speakers at the bottom of a linguistic and racial hierarchy (on a sociopolitical level). He skillfully shows how the limited Spanish used by English-speakers contributed not just to maintaining power relations between staff in moment-to-moment interactions but also to constructing racial hierarchy within US culture and society.

2.3 Methodological Strategies

In order to be able to situate discourse within, and shed light on, a larger context, researchers generally seek out deeper knowledge about the speakers, their everyday lives, and the historical background and social structures that influence them. This information can be obtained through a variety of methods, and there is no one magic formula. In the case of

Barrett's (2006) study, his status as an employee allowed him to immerse himself in the various experiences and interactions that take place in a restaurant, affording him opportunities to note patterns through long-term exposure, to gain an "insider" understanding of beliefs, values, and daily practices, and to mine his own personal interactions for data on relevant racial and linguistic dynamics and boundaries. This ethnographic information becomes an important part of his data and discussion. For example, Barrett recounts that he was frequently called a "burrito" (a tortilla and bean dish that is white on the outside and brown on the inside) because of his status as an Anglo who crossed racial boundaries to pursue friendships with Spanish-speaking coworkers. In this case, his personal relationships and his own racial subjectivity allowed him to critically reflect on how the language use he observed is set within local and (trans)national contexts of racial segregation and inequality,

While this type of in-depth and immersive participant observation is a staple of ethnographic fieldwork, it is also possible to gain a deeper understanding of a community through ethnographic interviews (see De Fina 2019), through analysis of written or historical texts set within a context with which one is deeply familiar (Hanks 1987; Inoue 2003; Irvine 2009; Stasch 2010) and within online or virtual settings (Boellstorff et al. 2012). Anthropology's broad understanding of context means that physical copresence is not always required to gain a rich understanding of what speakers are doing. The works summarized below range not only in methodological strategies, but also in the amount of ethnographic information that researchers bring into their analysis. What unites these studies is a desire to set discourse within ethnographic and sociopolitical context in order to think through connections between language, culture and power.

2.4 Participant Roles

Erving Goffman's (1981) contributions to the study of face-to-face interactions have been picked up in various fields, and it is nearly impossible to engage in an ethnographic approach to discourse analysis without embracing his ideas and terminology. His exploration of participant roles is of particular interest to scholars seeking to situate language use in context. Goffman began by deconstructing (and then complicating) the speaker/hearer dyad conceptualized by Saussure. Using the concept of the production format to unpack the speaker role, Goffman included *animators* (who voice or relay a message), *authors* (who create the message), and *principals* (who stand behind the message itself). Within the participation framework, he elaborated various participant roles for listeners: from ratified to unratified participants, including bystanders, overhearers, and eavesdroppers, among others. In what he called frame analysis, Goffman (1997) took up the study of interactional arrangements or frames that guide participants' understandings of how to speak and act appropriately (in a classroom or a restaurant, at a play or a religious service, for example). These frames can be cued, negotiated, conflicting or embedded, as when a parent may launch into a lecture at the dinner table. In such a scenario, one might imagine a child missing, ignoring or trying to subvert this embedded lecture frame (in which the primary speaker holds the floor and interruptions are dispreferred), by asking that parent to pass the ketchup. These interactional struggles of competing frames rely on each participant's knowledge of the larger cultural and sociopolitical contexts that they are situated within, in order to determine what is allowed or unexpected, preferred or a "breaking" of the frame.

Of equal importance to an ethnographic approach to discourse analysis is Goffman's exploration of footing shifts, through which participants work to linguistically align with particular roles and identities. These shifts in alignment can range from "gross changes in stance to the most subtle shifts in tone" (Goffman 1981: 128). Goffman focuses on the significance of the shift itself, as speakers and hearers move in and out of interactional and social roles (from speaker to listener, from expert to novice, etc.). Goffman uses the terms *byplay* to denote communication between ratified participants, *crossplay* to describe interaction between ratified and unratified participants and *sideplay* to label communication between bystanders (or unratified participants). As one example, byplay could include a comment from one "extra" on stage to another; crossplay might entail a cast member turning and addressing the audience; and sideplay would entail audience members whispering to each other. Discourse analyst Gregory Matoesian helpfully notes that footing shifts constitute "the contextualization cues through which speakers and recipients signal who they are and what they are doing at any given interactional moment" (1999: 493).

While analysis of frames, production formats and participant frameworks may seem to draw attention to the interactional level, ethnographers attuned to the study of discourse patterns recognize that it is through these intricate interactional shifts and negotiations that a larger sense of social order is enacted. Linguistic anthropologist Judith Irvine turns to ethnographic context to highlight the process through which different participant roles are created and transformed, particularly through the construction of interdiscursive chains that connect verbal performances (see also the Bakhtinian concept of intertextuality, discussed in Section 2.8). In her classic study of Wolof insult poems, Irvine (1996) explores how speakers reduce their own personal responsibility for utterances through a dispersed interdiscursive chain where those who help craft the potentially damaging insults (the authors) are often not the ones who publicly distribute the message (the animators) – nor are all of the intended recipients necessarily present amongst the audience for whom the poems are recited. Various speech events are linked as the poem is created, edited, presented, repeated and commented upon, and different participant roles (and social relationships) are formed through each related speech event. These "shadow conversations" constitute the discursive histories that surround Wolof insult poems and the social order that these poems uphold. Additional ethnographic studies that attend to participant roles have explored how the projection of imagined audiences (Vigouroux 2010) and imagined discursive figures (Taha 2017) influence language use and help construct identity and belonging for participants.

In a study of the South Indian Tamil popular stage, anthropologist Susan Seizer (1997) examines how male comedians engage in strategic footing shifts away from the audience and toward male "coplayers" with whom they share the stage. The new interactional arrangement (or participant framework) they create through these stage asides successfully creates distance between the comedian and his mixed-gender audience, embedding new relationships and new standards of linguistic appropriateness into the performance. This fancy footwork allows dirty jokes to be told seemingly amongst men, despite an audience of ratified overhearers that includes their mothers, wives, sisters and other female listeners. As Seizer explains, it is not just Tamil morality and cultural identity that are at stake in these risky stage asides in which they talk to fellow stagemates and let audience members just "overhear"; these culturally appropriate and face-saving linguistic strategies serve to naturalize gender separation and hierarchy and work through anxiety-provoking situations of social change that include modernization and globalization. As male comedians "joke" amongst themselves about women out of place in public spaces (from within the safer embedded frames that they have themselves constructed), they linguistically and socially keep women in fixed participant and gender roles. Thus, a careful analysis of participant roles within this specific staged performance affords Seizer the opportunity to offer broader commentary on contemporary gender relations within Tamil society.

2.5 Stance

New research into stancetaking offers an especially fruitful direction for scholars working on discourse analysis from an ethnographic perspective. The concept of stance can be used to directly link specific linguistic choices to the construction of self and other within a broader sociopolitical context. Stance refers to how one positions oneself in relation to utterances, ideas, other interactional participants or broader social groups. Much like Goffman's notion of footing, on which the concept depends, stance is constantly expressed, even as it might be ambiguous, shifting or contradictory. Stance can be expressed through cues that are metalinguistic, linguistic or nonlinguistic. A metalinguistic stance would react to language itself, as in the utterance "Did you really just say that?". Stances can be taken up through linguistically overt responses ("I don't *think* so!"), just as they can be marked nonlinguistically, through a roll of the eyes, a noncommittal shrug or a thumbs-up sign. Stance can also be expressed through the absence of a reaction where one is expected. Irvine (2009) helpfully details three common types of stance: Epistemic stances bring together truth-value and degree of commitment ("I wholeheartedly agree"); affective stances offer a speaker's emotional reaction toward an utterance ("It's so disturbing to hear you say that!"); and a third (unnamed) type of stance positions a speaker in relation to fellow interlocutors and social roles. Irvine (2009: 54) offers the example "And call me 'sir' when you speak to me!" – an utterance we might call a relational stance.

Stance offers participants the opportunity to display identities, evaluate what has been said or is happening within an interaction, align with (or distance themselves from) copresent, nonpresent or imagined interlocutors and react to broader social ideas. Through stancetaking, speakers pick up linguistic features to accomplish both local interactional and broader sociopolitical goals. Irvine usefully reminds us that stances are not speaker or agent-centered and can be "given or accorded, rather than taken" (2009: 70). This is productively discussed through Goffman's (1981) concept of "faultables" – when a listener attributes fault to a previous utterance and attempts to modify or correct it, as in the reaction "I think that is a ridiculous thing to say!". Here the listener not only takes up their own stance (of disagreement) but also shapes the position of the first speaker (as potentially "ridiculous") for present (or future) audiences.

The skilled discourse analyst can also attribute stances that speakers would not necessarily articulate or even agree with. Researching white Kenyans who are experiencing anxious and uncomfortable postcolonial challenges to white settler power, anthropologist Janet McIntosh (2009) found that any mention of the African occult seemed to serve as a "stance prompt" for her interviewees. The descendants of white settler families simultaneously sought to prove their African connections and rightful belonging in Kenya while also needing to justify their positions of relative privilege due to their European heritage. They navigated these competing goals in part through racial appeals to (white) rationality that contrasted strongly with what they portrayed as pagan and primitive African religious practices. In her analysis of some of the contradictory responses she received, such as "I believe … in it [the African occult] … for THEM [black Kenyans]," McIntosh observes: "Stancetaking may not always clarify for white Kenyans where they stand, but it nevertheless expresses some of the realities and contradictions of what it means to be a white African today" (2009: 89).

As in McIntosh's study, stancetaking is most often situationally negotiated and not infrequently ambivalent or shifting; it can also be metalinguistically modeled and rehearsed. Taha (2017) examines the centrality of human rights-oriented stancetaking within a new multicultural curriculum mandated by the Spanish state and designed to promote intercultural tolerance. She analyzes repeated role-playing classroom activities meant to display *convivencia* (conviviality or "getting along") and finds that this socialization into normative "progressive" stances often positions Moroccan immigrant students outside the boundaries of forward-thinking Spain. Stance thus helps reveal the various positioning acts that participants cannot avoid in speech events. As Irvine notes of stance as an analytic concept: "It gives us a chance to situate linguistic detail in a long train of consequences and in a global context" (2009: 55).

2.6 Register

Through the concept of register, discourse analysts can more specifically describe the resources that speakers draw on to connect themselves to others and that listeners use to recognize or contextualize their speech. Registers have been defined as linguistic repertoires that become stereotypically linked to "a system of contrastive social personae" (Agha 2003: 241). Registers describe a particular form of voicing that draws on more established discursive figures that have wide social recognizability and go beyond the voicing of a specific friend or family member or even a well-known individual. For example, registers create personae that call to mind for listeners social attributes (associated with age, gender, sexual orientation, race, class or religion), professions (from doctors and lawyers to criminals), geographic or regional connections (such as "southerner") or other social characteristics (including a worldly cosmopolitanness). Registers create imagined figures by drawing on a range of linguistic features that do not rely solely on linguistic content. As an example of this distinction between linguistic form (ways of speaking) and linguistic content (what is talked about), academics are known for long, wordy utterances, full of jargon and nominalizations, a speech style that can be readily recognized by others as "academese." However, members of other professions such as plumbers or construction workers can be linguistically indexed only through drawing on particular lexical domains (the mention of specific tools, for example) because these trade professions are not associated with a specific way of speaking. Thus, not every identifiable social group or identity is indexed through a linguistic register. Registers also continuously shift and change in terms of the linguistic and paralinguistic features they include, the figures they are associated with and the audiences that are familiar with their meaning.

The use of a register allows speakers to either performatively display aspects of their identity or temporarily "sound like" a particular type of person. Robert Moore (see Chapter 1 in this volume) helpfully describes connections between the concepts of register and style and the way both rely on the process of indexicality. Like any linguistic and therefore social practice, registers are acquired and associated with different amounts of social or cultural capital. Speakers may also be overtly socialized into them (by going to law school or medical school, for example). Asif Agha, who has written extensively on the process of enregisterment (2003, 2005), explains that all registers have a social range (of figures performable through the register) as well as a social domain (in which the people who can recognize and imitate the register outnumber those who actually speak it). Speakers who are not lawyers or doctors can attempt to speak legalese or medicalese to lend an air of authority, respectability and expertise to their speech, just as grandparents can pepper their utterances with slang to sound current and youthful. The invoking of linguistic repertoires associated with registers necessarily upholds metapragmatic stereotypes (not all young people use slang, for example) as well as differential indexical values (offering prestige to those who speak with jargon but not to those who use slang). Most importantly, it is the *contrastive* pattern of language use that marks a register – and makes it linguistically productive. Of critical interest to those who study language in context, registers bind together social and linguistic contrast. As Susan Gal notes: "It takes an active ideological, hence semiotic, process to create a similarity, and the necessary concomitant of similarity: differentiation. . . . Registers are the products of contrast" (2013: 34).

In multilingual contexts, different languages can come to be associated with contrasting figures, as Janet McIntosh (2010) finds in Kenya. The local vernacular of Kigiriama associates speakers with tradition, close kin relations and face-to-face contact, while the lingua franca of Kiswahili evokes the seriousness of everyday affairs surrounding work and commerce. To create a contrast both to the personae of loyal/local kin and to adults dealing with business, Giriama youth have developed an abbreviated international text-messaging "medialect" (based on English) to identify themselves with more modern, mobile and global actors. Youth do not text exclusively in this "succinct and snappy fashion" (McIntosh 2010: 338) but instead codeswitch based on shifting communicative goals. The relatively recent development of this text language reminds us that enregisterment is not always a process of linguistic socialization imposed "from above," as new registers can be created and dispersed by speakers working through their sense of self and other in mundane interactions. And yet the social distinctions that emerge from these small linguistic maneuvers can have big sociopolitical consequences. In my own work in the democratically unstable and highly unequal context of Rio de Janeiro, Brazil, I have found that the enregisterment of slang helps maintain and justify different levels of citizenship. Those who speak *gíria* (slang) and draw on nonstandard lexical items and discourse conventions, including the frequent use of pragmatic markers, are readily associated with blackness, poverty, social and geographic marginality, and crime. They are labeled *bandidos* (criminals) and denied many of the rights and resources offered to members of the whiter middle class, who diligently avoid slang in favor of more "standard" Portuguese. In this context, differentiated speech repertoires are made to index (or point to) opposing citizenship categories and embraced to legitimize a context of extreme racial and social inequality (on the association between language varieties and race, see also Chapter 24 in this volume).

As with stance, what a register socially indexes or "means" must be interactionally produced between speakers and listeners. Even as the linguistic repertoires associated with register offer speakers opportunities to define themselves and accomplish social goals, the meaning of these linguistic choices remains up for grabs, as Jillian Cavanaugh (2012) illustrates through her work on Bergamasco. The use of this Italian vernacular can be associated with regional pride and strong emotion that are valuable to local activists who seek to challenge the nationalist and homogenizing efforts of the Italian state. However, the register has long been associated with "backwards, provincial, and old-fashioned ways of living" (2012: 77) and, more recently, has been picked up by a vocal anti-immigrant political faction called the Northern League. Cavanaugh suggests that the League's public embrace of Bergamasco creates an "interdiscursive trap" for some speakers, who support the local register but not the political ideas and stances now conveyed by the use of Bergamasco. Registers, as "reflexive models of language use" (Agha 2005: 38), have much to tell us about the construction of identity, difference and hierarchy in different cultural and sociopolitical contexts.

2.7 Genre

Genres are most commonly described as orienting frameworks toward discourse or open-ended discursive templates that apply to both spoken and written texts (on this point, see also Chapter 27 in this volume). Writing extensively on the topic, literary theorist Mikhail Bakhtin (1986) foregrounds the connections between speech genres and social life. Participants draw on genres to inform their choice of specific linguistic features which then help set expectations for others about participant roles and relationships. "Once upon a time" will cue listeners that they are about to hear a story, just as a sudden lowering of the voice to speak in hushed tones might indicate that one is about to exchange gossip. The genre of a political speech prefers a certain kind of linguistic content (discussing public matters rather than private ones), a particular tone (exuding confidence and enthusiasm, for example), particular speech acts (such as promises) and acceptable audience responses (applauding). Genres are related to Goffman's notion of frames, but they differ in important ways. Within the linguistic frame of a restaurant, the utterance "Two please" will likely be successfully interpreted as a request for a table, but "Two please" does not fit within a specific and recognizable linguistic genre. Frames can have multiple linguistic genres associated with them: A religious space might be associated with sermons, prayers and confessions, among other linguistic genres. But genres do not live within a specific frame either, and we might find a religious sermon or a confession printed in a newspaper. Genres have a sense of predictability or stability to them, and they work to orient participants as to what is expected of them. But a genre's linguistic conventions can be intentionally violated (often to produce humor) or unintentionally violated, leading a speaker to be judged unsuccessful. For example, a speaker offering up a wedding toast could present overly negative or embarrassing information or talk more about themselves than the people being married, which might cause wedding guests to shift uncomfortably in their seats and offer only scattered applause. Even as that toast might be judged poorly, audience members are likely to stick to the conventions of the genre: Booing the speaker would be highly dispreferred. But these "rules" and reactions will necessarily vary depending on the ethnographic context of a given wedding ceremony. Genres cannot be understood outside of specific local, cultural and historical contexts (Briggs and Bauman 1992).

New genres can be created through the shifting and blending of more established genres. As one example, Rodney Jones (2015) describes the "It Gets Better" YouTube videos (empowering messages sent to LGBTQ teens) as drawing from the genres of narrative, testimony and confession to establish a new blended genre. Genres relate to other genres within a particular linguistic and ethnographic context, a relationship that Robin Shoaps describes as an "ecology of communicative practices within a community" (2009: 465). Genres are also inherently intertextual, forging links between independent speech events, as when unrelated speakers post their own "It Gets Better" videos on YouTube. While the speaker and content and even some of the form may differ, these videos are linked through their adherence to certain linguistic conventions (using the positive refrain "It Gets Better") and through their identification (by the author or by others) as part of a larger, broader but recognizable linguistic genre. Linguistic anthropologist William Hanks describes genres as an "integral part of the linguistic habitus" as they "familiarize and naturalize reality" for speakers and listeners alike (1987: 671, 676). In a study of the shifting classification of Kabyle Berber oral texts within colonial, nationalist and more contemporary global projects, Jane Goodman similarly argues that genres are not neutral classificatory devices but instead operate "as fluid and mutable components of a society's metadiscursive landscape, providing an array of conceptual frames and narrative possibilities through which perceptions of self, other, and world are mediated" (2002: 109).

Brigittine French (2001) uses the lens of genre to study the shifting relationship between Mayan vendors and Ladino customers (who claim

European descent) in Guatemala's highland open-air markets. Examining daily tokens of bargaining speech, she finds that Mayan vendors draw on the stability and predictability of the genre to position themselves as equal to their clients despite a historical context of deep ethnic violence and genocide. By conforming to discursive conventions that include agreement, cooperation, formality and politeness, the female vendors acquire Spanish and take up a greater share of the communicative burden with their clients, but they attempt to force mutual respect (in part through the *Ud./tú* formal/informal pronoun distinctions that Spanish speakers must attend to). She argues that close attention to daily language use helps explain why the market constitutes "a site where social change in the relations between Mayas and Ladinos is discernible ... [as] the subtle and delicate echoes of social change in Guatemala reverberate in the discursive body of bargaining speech" (French 2001: 181).

2.8 Intertextuality

Bakhtin's contributions to the study of language in context were brought to the attention of linguistic anthropologists most clearly by Jane Hill in the late 1980s (Hill 1985, 1986). His concepts of heteroglossia and dialogism recognize the deep connections all language has to other language, or "the inescapably interactive history of every utterance, resonating with multiple pasts and futures" (Haviland 2005: 81). Just as Erving Goffman offered discourse analysts a new framework with which to understand and connect the complicated roles taken up by participants in any speech event (moving beyond the oversimplified speaker and hearer dyad), Bakhtin's work reminds us that all utterances exist in a complicated web of relationships to other utterances. All language depends on and relates itself to prior speech events at the same time that it anticipates future ones (Bakhtin 1986). The text you are currently reading, for example, is connected to a whole range of previous texts, from published books and journal articles, to academic conference presentations and graduate seminar discussions. Along similar lines, I write not just in dialogue with these prior texts and utterances but also in anticipation of how my words might be quoted or referenced in a future text or classroom discussion. Intertextuality describes the many different ways in which written and spoken texts can be connected: Translations rely on – and shape – prior texts; commentaries (religious, political, artistic, etc.) necessarily link separate speech events together; and quotations, citations and narratives all exemplify the strong intertextual relationships between seemingly autonomous speech events or texts.

While Bakhtin denies speakers' claims to originality, autonomy and uniqueness, interlocutors are still afforded room for creativity and intentionality. It is important to recognize, just as was discussed with the concepts of register and stance, that rights of interpretation do not lie solely with the speaker. Listeners can make their own intertextual connections that speakers may or may not agree with ("Isn't that a line from a song?") and intertextual connections do not have to be recognized, acknowledged or even understood by a listener to "count" as examples of heteroglossia. According to Bakhtin, all language is intertextual, but discourse analysts have tended to focus on examples where specific linguistic features make visible and audible the (un)intentional connections between texts. Bauman and Briggs have described some language as characterized by a "prepared-for detachability" (1990: 74) which allows for easy decontextualization (from one text) and recontextualization (into another). Here, their notion of an "intertextual gap" (Briggs and Bauman 1992) allows analysts to describe the ways that speakers strategically seek to either increase the closeness between two texts (using, for example, a direct quote) or maximize the distance between texts to foreground innovation. Parodies call for careful attention to this potential gap: Do you mimic someone by reciting exactly what they have said or by taking up other (sometimes paralinguistic/nonlinguistic) cues while changing the language significantly? Even direct quotes allow for significant transformations of speech as the repetition is given new meaning. Think here of a congressperson choosing to read into the congressional record, verbatim, a letter written by a constituent. As Charles Briggs and Richard Bauman remind us, "the roots of intertextual practices run just as deeply into social, cultural, ideological, and political-economic facets of social life as they do into the minutiae of linguistic structure and use" (1992: 160).

In a classic study of the role of intertextuality and the media, Debra Spitulnik (1997) suggests that the recycling of media discourse offers speakers important opportunities for connection and community building, especially in large-scale societies. Specifically, she looks at how Zambian radio promotes the social circulation of lexical items and catchphrases that can become "common linguistic reference points" (1997: 163). In one well-known example – "Hello, Kitwe?" – a speaker creatively picks up a refrain commonly heard on the radio when transferring between stations to get the attention of a friend who has not noticed her in a store. Through this example, Spitulnik analyzes the heteroglossia that abounds in everyday life, illustrating how "public words" (such as those heard on the radio) are embraced by speakers to establish and reinforce shared experiences and social relationships. The significance of the social circulation of media discourse and its intertextual connections has become ever more evident with the rise of social media in recent decades. In a world now filled with catchy pop culture slogans and the rapid generation and circulation of memes (which often depend on linguistic intertextuality), where even official government business is conducted through tweets that can be easily quoted and commented on, intertextuality proves an especially useful tool for understanding the role of language in the construction of identity, community and power.

2.9 Voicing

According to Bakhtin, a speaker's words are never fully one's own, not only because a speaker relies on intertextual connections but also because speakers spend so much time repeating and quoting the words of others (see also Vološinov 1973). Bakhtin refutes the possibility of unconnected utterances; all messages reference prior speech and contain within them multiple messages. As a modern-day visual, one might picture receiving an email chain that has already been forwarded, responded to and commented upon – one that references outside/unseen conversations and has no clear beginning or end. Bakhtin's notion of voicing pushes us to understand that all utterances – even a single word – bear the marks of prior language use and social struggle. A word like "queer" can be used as a homophobic slur or as a term of empowerment, among other uses, becoming "a translinguistic battlefield, upon which ... ways of speaking struggle for dominance" (Hill 1985: 731). While not all words have as complicated a linguistic history or carry the same political burden, the overall point remains that words are never neutral and come to us already filled with connections to other situations of use that are separate from the speaker using them.

Discourse analysts have most often explored the concept of voicing through careful attention paid to the use of direct and indirect reported speech. Both forms of reported speech allow a speaker to create connection to – and distance from – the words they have spoken. With the use of direct reported speech, an embedded participant framework is created and the listener is brought into the moment of the narrated event: "He said to me, 'Don't go!'" Note how the narrator occupies two participant roles here, as the narrator in the current moment of the reporting context but also as the listener in the embedded frame of the prior reported speech. Indirect speech similarly distances the speaker from an utterance but does not create the same vivid embedded frame: "He told me not to go." The use of reported speech creates an intertextual gap for the speaker, which facilitates various social goals. A speaker can benefit from the construction of alignment or shift the burden of responsibility or establish distance, in particular through mockery. Quoting necessarily includes the words reported to have been spoken along with an evaluation or reaction to those words. Vološinov describes this as a situation of "words reacting on words" (1973: 116) and Bakhtin (1986) details various ways in which utterances can be "double voiced." In her discussion of the multilayered nature of what she calls constructed dialogue, discourse analyst Deborah Tannen reminds us that words are never just accurately, neutrally or innocently "reported." As a provocative example, she cites an Arab proverb: "The one who repeats an insult is the one who is insulting you" (1989: 106).

Speakers are constantly inserting other people's words into their speech and, as in the game of pool, bouncing off of voices they themselves have created in order to construct an interactive sense of self (Haviland 1991). This includes using the metalinguistic device of "self-lamination" (Hill 1995) where speakers voice previous or hypothetical versions of themselves to provide a point of contrast ("I used to say ..." or "Right then I should have said ..."). The other who is voiced need not be an actual "other" and it may be more imagined than "real." Inoue (2003) and Wirtz (2013) bring to our attention contexts in which an "enregistered voice" (Agha 2005) is created and becomes real for people, even when there may be no actual linguistic source for the speakers invoked through the voicing. In each case, the social, political and historical context is critical to understanding how language works "as a nontransparent medium through which social orders are not simply reflected, but actively constructed" (Wirtz 2013: 804).

In one of the most influential studies of voicing, Jane Hill (1995) describes at least twenty voices that appear in a seventeen-minute recorded interview with Don Gabriel, a Mexicano-speaking man who narrates the murder of his son. Hill's analysis of this polyphonic narrative shows how Don Gabriel conveys an understanding of himself and his moral position (what Bakhtin describes as his consciousness) through a dispersed system of voices. The "moral geography" Don Gabriel constructs through his narrative relies heavily on the metalinguistic strategies of reported speech and self-lamination, in addition to codeswitching between Spanish and Mexicano. Through the study of voice, linguistic anthropologists continue to draw on Bakhtin's influential work to show how selves and social order do not preexist social interactions but are instead constituted through them.

2.10 Chronotopes

The concepts of intertextuality and voicing describe how language in context is infused with references to prior texts and other people's words; the Bakhtinian concept of chronotope draws on space and time as closely related social constructs that similarly shape how people speak and situate themselves in the world. Asif Agha glosses chronotopes as "depictions of place-time-and-personhood" (2007: 320), while Jan Blommaert describes them as "invokable chunks of history that organize the indexical order of discourse" (2015: 105). As with registers, the importance and usefulness of the concept of chronotopes lie in their ability to create linguistic and social contrast (Agha 2007: 321). Through chronotopes, speakers bring the past or the future into the here and now, mobilizing participants to align with or distance themselves from the personae associated with these "temporal and spatial imaginaries" (Wirtz 2016: 343). In her own work, Kristina Wirtz (2011, 2013, 2016) analyzes a range of religious and folkloric performances for a repertoire of linguistic features associated with Cuba's colonial past and the imagined speech of African slaves. She finds that this "Bozal" speech register is used along with stereotypical features of dress and dance to create a "chronotopic gap" between "the timeless African past still among us" and modern day audiences (Wirtz 2011: E29), bridging temporal and racializing processes.

As with Wirtz's discussion of the role of a specific speech register in the construction of a chronotope, scholars often rely on multiple and overlapping discursive concepts in their analyses. In his study of Korowai travel accounts, Rupert Stasch (2010) finds that travel writers draw on both chronotopes and intertextuality to help shore up an imagined opposition between modern, civilized travelers and primitive, dark-skinned natives. They narrate their travel to West Papua, New Guinea in terms of visiting "the Stone Age" and going "back in time," linking the physical place they have visited with an "archaic" time which contrasts strongly with the modern "outside world" in which they live. He notes that civilized and primitive constitute salient distinctions within a "mythic" chronotope, "in the specific sense of being temporal epochs and qualities mapped into geography, and geographic locations mapped into time" (Stasch 2010: 7). To strengthen the image of a primitive timespace for their readers, travel writers intertextually connect their experience to movies they have seen (such as *Jurassic Park*) or novels they have read. In addition to these more overt intertextual references, Stasch also notes the strong linguistic overlap between very similar and highly repetitive travelogues. This form of generic intertextuality (Briggs and Bauman 1992) was never acknowledged by authors, however, as it would detract from the perceived originality and uniqueness of their travel experiences and writing. Linking these intertextual and chronotopic discourse features to the level of sociopolitical context, Stasch shows how, in these travel narratives, "white superiority to cultural and racial others is steadily measured, questioned, and affirmed" (2010: 14).

2.11 Conclusion

An ethnographic approach to discourse analysis brings the study of linguistic features and discourse patterns to bear on broader questions about the role of language in the construction of social order. In particular, analysts seek to explain: (1) how interlocutors use language to negotiate interactional roles and social relationships between themselves and others; (2) how they discursively create a sense of self and their place in society; (3) what they accomplish when they (un)intentionally connect the current speech event to the words of others and to other speech events (both in the past and in the imagined future); and (4) how the work they do within specific interactions is influenced by and reconfigures the larger social context. As Gregory Matoesian notes, "our social identities are not static or structurally determined, but contextually situated and interactionally emergent" (1999: 494). In order to be able to show how participants strategically attend to both discourse-internal and discourse-external factors, the researcher must develop a deep understanding not only of what specific linguistic features do but also of what the larger ethnographic and sociopolitical contexts look like. Ultimately, the goal is to demonstrate the incredibly sophisticated understanding of language that all speakers possess and the wide range of social goals they juggle (and accomplish) as they communicate. As anthropologist William Hanks reminds us, "[u]tterances are part of social projects, not merely vehicles for expressing thoughts" (1996: 168). Goffman's concept of participant roles, recent scholarly interest in stance and register that draw on his attention to footing shifts, and Bakhtin's heteroglossic notions of genre, intertextuality, voicing and chronotopes have been particularly useful to linguistic anthropologists who seek to explain how discourse builds the world around us. This connection between the linguistic, the social, the cultural and the political is at the heart of an ethnographic approach to discourse analysis.

Further Reading

Dick, H. P. (2010). Imagined Lives and Modernist Chronotopes in Mexican Nonmigrant Discourse. *American Ethnologist* 37(2): 275–90.

Hilary Parsons Dick shows how speakers evoke chronotopic distinctions between tradition ("here") and progress ("there") to situate themselves in relation to the ever-present reality of transnational migration.

Jacobs-Huey, L. (2006). *From the Kitchen to the Parlor: Language and Becoming in African American Women's Hair Care*. New York: Oxford University Press.

This is a multi-sited exploration of face-to-face and online discourse surrounding African American women's hair care that attends to how women negotiate identity, professional expertise and US race relations.

Roth-Gordon, J. and da Silva, A. J. (2013). Double-Voicing in the Everyday Language of Brazilian Black Activism. In S. T. Bischoff, D. Cole, A. V. Fountain and M. Miyashita (eds.) *The Persistence of Language: Constructing and Confronting the Past and Present in the Voices of Jane H. Hill*. Philadelphia, PA: John Benjamins. 365–88.

The authors illustrate how speakers invoke and then contrast "racist" and "anti-racist" voices in their daily speech in order to display their own racial consciousness.

References

Agha, A. (2003). The Social Life of Cultural Value. *Language & Communication* 23: 231–73.

(2005). Voice, Footing, Enregisterment. *Journal of Linguistic Anthropology* 15 (1): 38–59.

(2007). Recombinant Selves in Mass Mediated Spacetime. *Language & Communication* 27: 320–35.

Bakhtin, M. (1986). *Speech Genres and Other Late Essays*, ed. by C. Emerson and M. Holquist. Austin: University of Texas Press.

Bauman, R. and Briggs, C. L. (1990). Poetics and Performance as Critical Perspectives on Language and Social Life. *Annual Review of Anthropology* 19: 59–88.

Barrett, R. (2006). Language Ideology and Racial Inequality: Competing Functions of Spanish in an Anglo-owned Mexican Restaurant. *Language in Society* 35: 163–204.

Blommaert, J. (2015). Chronotopes, Scales, and Complexity in the Study of Language in Society. *Annual Review of Anthropology* 44: 105–16.

Boellstorff, T., Nardi, B., Pearce, C. and Taylor., T. L. (2012). *Ethnography and Virtual Worlds: A Handbook of Method*. Princeton, NJ: Princeton University Press.

Briggs, C. L. and Bauman, R. (1992). Genre, Intertextuality, and Social Power. *Journal of Linguistic Anthropology* 2(2): 131–72.

Cavanaugh, J. R. (2012). Entering into Politics: Interdiscursivity, Register, Stance, and Vernacular in Northern Italy. *Language in Society* 41(1): 73–95.

De Fina, A. (2019). The Ethnographic Interview. In K. Tusting (ed.) *The Routledge Handbook of Linguistic Ethnography*. Abingdon/New York: Routledge. 154–167.

French, B. M. (2001). The Symbolic Capital of Social Identities: The Genre of Bargaining in an Urban Guatemalan Market. *Journal of Linguistic Anthropology* 10(2): 155–89.

Gal, S. (2013). Tastes of Talk: Qualia and the Moral Flavor of Signs. *Anthropological Theory* 13(1/2): 31–48.

Goffman, E. (1981). *Forms of Talk*. Philadelphia: University of Pennsylvania Press.

(1997). Frame Analysis of Talk. In C. Lemert and A. Branaman (eds.) *The Goffman Reader*. Malden, MA: Blackwell. 167–200.

Goodman, J. E. (2002). Writing Empire, Underwriting Nation: Discursive Histories of Kabyle Berber Oral Texts. *American Ethnologist* 29(1): 86–122.

Hanks, W. F. (1987). Discourse Genres in a Theory of Practice. *American Ethnologist* 14(4): 668–92.

(1996). Exorcism and the Description of Participant Roles. In M. Silverstein and G. Urban (eds.) *Natural Histories of Discourse*. Chicago, IL: University of Chicago Press. 160–220.

Haviland, J. B. (1991). "That Was the Last Time I Seen Them, and No More": Voices through Time in Australian Aboriginal Autobiography. *American Ethnologist* 18(2): 331–61.

(2005). "Whorish Old Man" and "One (Animal) Gentleman": The Intertextual Construction of Enemies and Selves. *Journal of Linguistic Anthropology* 15(1): 81–94.

Hill, J. H. (1985). The Grammar of Consciousness and the Consciousness of Grammar. *American Ethnologist* 12(4): 725–37.

(1986). The Refiguration of the Anthropology of Language. *Cultural Anthropology* 1(1): 89–102.

(1995). The Voices of Don Gabriel: Responsibility and Self in a Modern Mexicano Narrative. In D. Tedlock and B. Mannheim (eds.) *The Dialogic Emergence of Culture*. Urbana: University of Illinois Press. 97–147.

(1998). Language, Race, and White Public Space. *American Anthropologist* 100(3): 680–9.

Inoue, M. (2003). Speech Without a Speaking Body: "Japanese Women's Language" in Translation. *Language & Communication* 23: 315–30.

Irvine, J. T. (1996). Shadow Conversations: The Indeterminacy of Participant Roles. In M. Silverstein and G. Urban (eds.) *Natural Histories of Discourse*. Chicago, IL: University of Chicago Press. 131–59.

(2009). Stance in a Colonial Encounter: How Mr. Taylor Lost His Footing. In A. Jaffe (ed.) *Stance: Sociolinguistic Perspectives*. New York: Oxford University Press. 53–71.

Jones, R. H. (2015). Generic Intertextuality in Online Social Activism: The Case of the It Gets Better Project. *Language in Society* 44: 317–39.

McIntosh, J. (2009). Stance and Distance: Social Boundaries, Self-Lamination, and Metalinguistic Anxiety in White Kenyan Narratives about the African Occult. In A. Jaffe (ed.) *Stance: Sociolinguistic Perspectives*. New York: Oxford University Press. 72–91.

(2010). Mobile Phones and Mipoho's Prophecy: The Powers and Dangers of Flying Language. *American Ethnologist* 37(2): 337–53.

Matoesian, G. M. (1999). The Grammaticalization of Participant Roles in the Constitution of Expert Identity. *Language in Society* 28(4): 491–521.

Morson, G. S. and Emerson, C. (1990). *Mikhail Bakhtin: Creation of a Prosaics*. Stanford, CA: Stanford University Press.

Seizer, S. (1997). Jokes, Gender, and Discursive Distance on the Tamil Popular Stage. *American Ethnologist* 24(1): 62–90.

Shoaps, R. A. (2009). Ritual and (Im)Moral Voices: Locating the Testament of Judas in Sakapultek Communicative Ecology. *American Ethnologist* 36(3): 459–77.

Spitulnik, D. (1997). The Social Circulation of Media Discourse and the Mediation of Communities. *Journal of Linguistic Anthropology* 6(2): 161–87.

Stasch, R. (2010). Textual Iconicity and the Primitivist Cosmos: Chronotopes of Desire in Travel Writing about Korowai of West Papua. *Journal of Linguistic Anthropology* 21(1): 1–21.

Taha, M. (2017). Shadow Subjects: A Category of Analysis for Empathic Stancetaking. *Journal of Linguistic Anthropology* 27(2): 190–209.

Tannen, D. (1989). *Talking Voices: Repetition, Dialogue, and Imagery in Conversational Discourse*. New York: Cambridge University Press.

Vigouroux, C. B. (2010). Double-Mouthed Discourse: Interpreting, Framing, and Participant Roles. *Journal of Sociolinguistics* 14(3): 341–69.

Vološinov, V. N. (1973). *Marxism and the Philosophy of Language*. Cambridge, MA: Harvard University Press.

Wirtz, K. (2011). Cuban Performances of Blackness as the Timeless Past Still Among Us. *Journal of Linguistic Anthropology* 21(S1): E11–E34.

(2013). A "Brutology" of Bozal: Tracing a Discourse Genealogy from Nineteenth-Century Blackface Theater to Twenty-First-Century Spirit Possession in Cuba. *Comparative Studies in Society and History* 55(4): 800–33.

(2016). The Living, The Dead, and the Immanent: Dialogue across Chronotopes. *HAU: Journal of Ethnographic Theory* 6(1): 343–69.

3

Context and Its Complications

Jan Blommaert (with Laura Smits and Noura Yacoubi)

3.1 Introduction: Online–Offline Action

In his classic *Cognitive Sociology*, Aaron Cicourel made this general observation: "The problem of meaning for the anthropologist-sociologist can be stated as how members of a society or culture acquire a sense of social structure to enable them to negotiate everyday activities" (Cicourel 1973: 46). This statement can serve as an extraordinarily accurate description of what was later called and methodologically developed as "contextualization" (Gumperz 1982, 1992; also Auer and di Luzio 1992; Duranti and Goodwin 1992). Yet two components of the statement – "social structure" and "everyday activities" – demand closer attention for, since the beginning of the twenty-first century, the realities of social structure and the range and modes of everyday activities have been profoundly affected by the generalized introduction of a layer of online social life, complicating the offline social world on which these earlier formulations of contextualization were based. In this chapter, we intend to sketch the complications emerging from discourse produced interactionally in such an online-offline environment now serving as the backdrop for what Ron Scollon (2001) called "the nexus of practice": the actual situations in which momentary actions and historical conditions coproduce meanings.

We must pay closer attention to the aspects of contextualization that have changed, but that does not mean that we must do so from within a methodological *tabula rasa*. We believe that the effort can be profitably made by means of some central insights and principles from within the interactionalist tradition of discourse studies. In fact, the scholars mentioned at the start of this chapter belong to the stream of ethnographically grounded studies of actual, situated discursive practice, which has been the richest source of fundamental reflections on the notion of context and its role in social interaction. Observe that this tradition is not mainstream; it is, in fact, rather marginal in its influence on disciplines such as discourse analysis, which makes our discussion slightly idiosyncratic. We shall return to this in our concluding section (3.6).

It is from this tradition then that we can draw the general principles that will guide the discussion in this chapter:

1. Context should not be seen as an abstract, stable or latent presence; it is a resource that is deployed in concrete socially situated meaning-making action: context is always contextualization (Gumperz 1982; Auer and di Luzio 1992). In that sense, it is highly unpredictable, evolving, dynamic and unstable. Also, while contexts operate at various scale-levels and structure a multitude of concrete interactions, the analytical point of departure is their situated effects on making sense. To quote Herbert Blumer in this respect: "People ... do not act toward culture, social structure or the like, they act toward situations" (Blumer 1969: 88).
2. Contextualization is the key to making sense because it consists of interactionally constructed *indexical* connections, that is, connections between actual discursive features and relevant chunks of sociocultural knowledge (Silverstein 1992; Hymes 1996; Gumperz 2003; Agha 2007).
3. Such indexically deployed and invoked knowledge is never neutral but always *evaluative* (and in that sense *moral*, connected to a value system) and, by extension, *identity* related (e.g. Goodwin 2007). Making sense is a moral judgment grounded in socioculturally available normative-behavioral scripts situationally projected onto persons. Goffman (1974) called such moralized scripts "frames"; the ways we implement them have been variously called (with distinctions not overly relevant here) "indexical order" (Silverstein 2003) and "orders of indexicality" (Blommaert 2005). The concepts are joined by their emphasis on (Bakhtinian) evaluative uptake and on the dimension of social order as part of meaning-making practices – recall Cicourel's statement quoted at the start of the chapter.
4. The contextual resources that people draw upon in interaction (i.e. the ordered indexicals mentioned in point 3) have to be *recognizable* but not necessarily *shared* (Garfinkel 2002; also Blommaert and Rampton 2016: 28–31). Sharedness is evolving as the interaction proceeds, but it can also evolve as a shared sense of misunderstanding, that is, a shared sense that very little of substance is shared in the interaction. What needs to be recognizable is the broad outline of a *format* of interaction, a general script for social action.

We can see that these principles, derived from a broad interactionalist tradition of scholarship, favor action over content and participants, and situated and evolving effects over a priori categories (such as speech acts, conversational maxims, "meaning" and "understanding"). The reason for these preferences is that, due to the shift toward an online-offline communicative economy, very little can be taken for granted with respect to what is "ordinary" and "normal" in communication. To name just a few of the widely used assumptions that need to be qualified: The assumption that communication is self-evidently a human-to-human activity has been challenged by human-machine interactions and has thus become a variable rather than a stable feature. This, of course, has numerous knock-on effects on widely used criteria in theories of meaning: intentionality, agency and (human) rationality. Even more widespread is the assumption that the most "normal" or primitive form of communication – in the sense of being the kind of communication on which most discourse-analytic traditions still base their fundamental theoretical imagination – is unmediated, spoken, dyadic, face-to-face interaction in shared physical timespace and between persons sharing massive amounts of knowledge, experience and sociocultural norms within a sedentary community (an offline conversation between similar people, in short). The online world has critically destabilized that assumption by inserting scripted, multimodal, nonsimultaneous, translocally mobile, multiparty and technologically heavily mediated forms of everyday communication into the communicative economies of very large numbers of people, not as peripheral modes of interaction but as important, inevitable ones (cf. Baron 2008). We now communicate intensely with interlocutors with whom we do not share much (not even acquaintance as a natural person and a human subject), across space and time, and through complex modes of nonacoustic (visual-designed) semiotic work.

The core vocabulary and assumptions of many branches of the study of language derive from an implicit sociological imagination that one assumes reflects the true state of things. Changes in the state of things often take some time before they translate into an alternative sociological imagination (cf. Mills 1959; also Blommaert 2018a). In the meantime, however, they render some of our core vocabulary for talking about language, interaction and meaning-making less salient and applicable, and invite a focus on the phenomena we can identify as constants. The constant feature, we would argue, is social *action* – a synonym, as Anselm Strauss (1993), amongst others, emphasized, for *interaction*. Even if we now communicate with machines, with unknown mass audiences (as in mass online gaming), by means of delayed, asynchronous messages scripted in new forms of graphic visualization and design – we are still performing interactions in an attempt to make sense of our world. Taking social action, defined in this sense, as our ontological point of departure enables us to start describing and understanding old and new patterns of interaction, how they intersect and how they structure our social lives.

With these principles established, we shall now engage with four different sets of issues, all of them inspired by the transition from an offline world of communication to an online-offline one. Some of these issues are not new – they have been constant features of debates on context and contextualization – but they demand renewed engagement in view of changes in the world of communication. In reviewing them, we will make proposals for reimagining aspects of them and for adopting another vocabulary in our descriptions of them.

3.2 Beyond the Macro and the Micro: Recognizability and Formatting

A persistent feature of discussions of context and its uses in scholarship is the use of the "micro–macro" dichotomy (occasionally turned into a triad by inserting "meso" in between). "Micro" contexts are the factors affecting and informing local, situated events: the timespace frame, the participants, the immediately and *directly* relevant social roles, the topic and so forth. "Macro," in turn, stands for the nonlocal, broader factors in which the event can be situated and by which it is *indirectly* affected: the wider historical, sociocultural and political parts of the picture making (at least part of) the event understandable (see the discussion in e.g. Goffman 1964; Silverstein 1992; Cicourel 1992; Duranti 1997; Blommaert 2015a).

While such distinctions might be discursively and heuristically helpful, they are methodologically unhelpful from the perspective we have formulated so far. They do point to a fundamental fact – the nonunified and complex nature of context – *any* context – but they do so in an inaccurate way. This is certainly the case when we become aware of the ways in which they rest on a particular sociological imagination and of the ways in which they structure an epistemological field. The sociological imagination on which the dichotomy between "micro" and "macro" rests is one in which we can separate and isolate specific aspects of social life as being the *direct* conditions for conduct – the local, sedentary, individual, variable and mundane aspects – while other aspects appear to only *indirectly* inflect such conditions for conduct, due to their remoteness and their stable, collective character. The first set of facts we could call "processual" factors that would always be unique, while the others would be "procedural" and always general. The first set would index "community" – a specific small-scale group involved in shared practices, but diverse and changeable – while the latter would index "society" – the organized, stable, enduring, systemic large-scale group characterized by common institutional characteristics. Obviously, this imagination of the social world is far removed from what Castells (1996), in a visionary text, called the online-offline "network society" (cf. also Blommaert 2018a).

The dichotomy between "micro" and "macro" also structures an epistemological field in which "micro" would stand for the anecdotal, the concrete, the singular, the possible exception, the empirical and the "token", while "macro" would point to the systemic, the abstract, the generalizable, the norm, the theoretical and the "type." Thus, so-called "micro-sociologists" and ethnographers would be dismissed (for instance, by survey-based researchers) as scholars whose attention to the uniquely situated features of cases precludes any attempt toward valid generalization, because generalization can be made only at a "macro" level of analysis where analytical detail has to be surrendered to abstraction (see the discussions in e.g. Mills 1959; Blumer 1969; Giddens 1984).

From a viewpoint privileging social action, all of this is highly unproductive; the pressing nature of the problem was repeatedly emphasized by Pierre Bourdieu and others. Bourdieu – often seen as a "macro"-sociologist whose work speaks to society at large – considered that concepts such as "habitus" (a *general* concept) could emerge only through ethnographic attention to actual situated practice, not by statistical surveys. It was by observing the struggles of Algerian farmers in coming to terms with a new market economy that Bourdieu saw the actual working of capitalism as propelled into socioculturally inhabited modes of practice (Bourdieu 2000; cf. Blommaert 2015b). The big things reside in the small things, and the most inconspicuous and uniquely situated social action is, in that sense, "systemic" and "typical," as well as the source for theoretical generalization. Evidently, the same insight animated Goffman's work on interactional ritual and frames (1967, 1974): Even if all instances of human interaction are unique, they display general characteristics and patterns sufficient to lift them from "micro" to "macro" relevance (cf. also Rampton 2016).

This is the point where we can start formulating an alternative position in line with the principles already outlined. And we can draw for inspiration on the authors just mentioned, as well as on Garfinkel's (2002) uncompromising formulations of the issue (see Blommaert 2018c for a discussion). Garfinkel saw *recognizability* as the key to understanding the social nature of interaction, although he considered that it should not be equated with sharedness of norms, assumptions and worldviews. It is recognition of the joint potential of specific modes of action that gives such action modes the character of "congregational work" (2002: 190), he argued; work is performed collectively *because* we are jointly involved in it. We enter jointly into an action of which we know very little outside of its possible general features and we jointly construct such actions as forms of *social order*. This order can be entirely ad hoc, temporary and ephemeral. But, while it lasts, it is a firm order that generates roles and identities along with a range of moral codes controlling (mis)behavior.

It is this aspect of recognizability, generating congregational work and its social outcomes, that renders distinctions between the "micro" and "macro" aspects of the act meaningless. Since acts are *social*, they draw on available and accessible social resources – from the different social positions from which we enter the action, the kinds of language and discourse we use, over the topic, to the actual things we say, hear, write or read (cf. also Briggs 2005). And even if we see that such resources are unevenly distributed, a degree of order will emerge from the action itself. The latter was exemplified in a magnificent study by Charles Goodwin (2004), in which a man who, following a stroke, had lost almost all of his linguistic capabilities was shown to engage in lengthy and complex interactions with his friends and relatives. Evidently, the absence of shared linguistic resources imposes constraints on what can happen in such forms of interaction – resources are crucial contexts for interaction (Blommaert 2005: 58–62) – but when we intend to understand what *is* happening, recognizability is the key.

Recognizability, however, is not an empty and random container. We recognize particular social situations and their features *as* something specific – a quarrel, a lecture or a Facebook update – on the basis of perceived properties of the situation (what Garfinkel called "autochthonous order properties" (2002: 245)) associated with, as already mentioned, Goffman's "frames": the ways in which we organize our experience. Recognizing a situation means *framing* it along what we could call a general *indexical vector*, that is, entering that situation as one that imposes and enables specific forms of interaction, one or different orders of indexicality. When we recognize something as a Facebook update, we recognize that it enables (among other actions) different forms of *response* and that it privileges keyboard writing and a specific set of symbols (e.g. emoticons) as techniques for responding to it. When we recognize the particular update as an instance of trolling, we recognize it as enabling an unfriendly response and so forth. This, following Garfinkel, we can call *formatting*: shaping the particular situated interaction in "typical" (i.e. generic, nonunique) ways and bringing the "sense of social structure" mentioned by Cicourel into the particular action we are engaged in with others.

A lot of what we do in the work of contextualization is moving from recognition through framing to formatting. We do so dialogically in congregational work with others and we do so by drawing upon socioculturally marked – indexicalized – resources that acquire a general direction in such activities. This, we propose, is the cornerstone of the argument here. We can now proceed to elaborate it further.

3.3 Chronotopes, Scales and Synchronization

In every moment of interaction, contextualization draws upon *specific* and *nonunified* resources (cf. Cicourel 1967, 1974; Silverstein 1992). Both dimensions are crucial if we wish to avoid undue simplifications such as "*The context* for this utterance is X." The contextual resources drawn upon in contextualizing concrete interactions are inevitably multiple and layered (cf. Blommaert 2005), but they are not infinite and not without structure and pattern. If we draw upon Goffman's frames, we see that social experience is organized into such structures and patterns in which particular forms of interaction – with attributes to be discussed in a moment – are attached to specific social situations in forms comparable to what Bakhtin (1981) called "chronotopes."

Bakhtin developed the notion of chronotope (literally "timespace") as a way to describe the sociohistorical layering in novels, more precisely the ways in which invocations of particular sociohistorical frames structured "voices" in specific situations, infusing them with identity scripts, moral orientations, participation frameworks (Goodwin and Goodwin 1992), expected and unexpected normative modes of conduct and roles within the situation – in short, the full sociocultural value of otherwise random forms of action (see the discussion in Blommaert 2015a and Blommaert and De Fina 2016). Thus, in a fairy tale, the Big Bad Wolf is exactly that: male, big and bad, a threat to the others and someone to be defeated by the others. Chronotopes, seen from this rather orthodox Bakhtinian perspective, provide moralized behavioral scripts in specific social situations (we called them *formats*) and the recognition of social situations as *specific* (e.g. a formal meeting) prompts such scripts: as soon as the chair announces the beginning of the meeting, we are likely to reorganize our conduct, assume a different set of body poses, discursive patterns and relations with the other participants (e.g. respecting the chair's formal leadership and the differential allocation of speaking rights) and align with the congregational work performed by the others. As soon as the meeting is over, we can shift back into another register of conduct, and the opponent during the meeting can turn into an ally in the pub during the post-meeting drink. Chronotopes impose formats on those inhabiting them, meaning that, from the potentially infinite aspects of context animating events, a specific subset will be invoked and deployed as the normative script for conduct within that chronotopic situation, as the *specific* bit of social order to be followed by all those involved. Violating or disrupting that order – Goffman called it frame breaking – comes with moral judgments: Everyday notions such as inappropriateness, rudeness, insolence, being off topic and trolling come to mind (cf. Blommaert and De Fina 2016; see Tagg, Seargeant and Brown 2017 for social media examples).

Chronotopes are, we believe, a useful gloss with which to address the specific nature of context and contextualization, one that forces us to examine with utmost precision what is elsewhere simply called "the context" of actual interactions. The notion also offers us a view of context as *active*, something that structures action and makes it socially recognizable and, thence, socially valued. The demand for precision will almost inevitably lead to outcomes in which particular chronotopes are

(a) composed of several different actions and types of action, as when someone checks their email or takes orders for sandwiches during a formal meeting – where each of these will have to proceed along the specific formats for such actions, as Goffman (1974: 561) clearly

pointed to (using the term "realm statuses" for what we call formats here) and as, for example, Goodwin (2013) excellently discusses; and
(b) connected to other chronotopes, as when the relations between participants in a formal meeting are affected by already existing interpersonal relationships specific to other areas of social life or when the history of a particular issue is invoked as a frame for discussing its present status or even when quoted or indirect speech is introduced into interaction embedding one chronotope and its actual voices into another one (e.g. Voloshinov 1973; Goodwin 2003).

Both outcomes are particularly interesting because they take us to the issue of the nonunified nature of context and bring issues of scale into view (cf. Blommaert 2015a). Scale can best be understood as reflections and expressions of how social beings experience dimensions of sociocultural reality as indexical vectors, as informing the general normative patterns that shape formats of action (cf. Das 2016; Carr and Lempert 2016). Scales, thus, are interpretive and normative-evaluative, suggesting distinctions between what is general and what is specific, what is important and what is not, what is widely known and what is not, what is valid and what is not, what can be widely communicated and what cannot, what can be widely recognized and understood and what cannot. There is nothing stable, absolute or a priori about scales – we can obliquely recall our discussion of the "micro–macro" distinction here – for what we see in actual discursive work are scalar *effects*. To give a simple example: When the history of a particular issue is invoked as a decisive argument in discussing its present status, then that history is presented as a way of upscaling the current issue to normative levels immune to contemporary petty or personal concerns ("We already discussed and decided this point in January, there is no point in returning to it now!"). Conversely, when someone raises a point that is not seen by others as belonging to the most general normative layer of what goes on, it can be downscaled ("This is a detail." or "This is just your personal opinion."). In their actual deployment, scalar effects are indexically ordered degrees of moralization in social actions. Their power lies in the capacity to draw into the moment-by-moment interaction a variety of nonmomentary evaluative dimensions attached to a topic, a kind of interlocutor, an interpersonal history of interaction or imagined aspects of society-at-large. (The last carried Goffman's favor, e.g. Goffman 1971.)

The presence of such nonunified (plural and scaled) contexts in concrete situations brings us to a third notion: synchronization (cf. Blommaert 2005: 131–7, 2018b). The scalar effects we just mentioned occur in real-time and on-the-spot moments of interaction, in a sort of evolving "synchrony" that hides layers of nonsynchronous resources and folds them together into momentary and situated instances of making sense. We call this process synchronization because the highly diverse resources that are deployed as context are focused, so to speak, onto one single point in social action. In other branches of scholarship, this process would be called "decision-making," with strong undertones of individual rational calibration. From an action-centered perspective, synchronization is a collaborative social act in which the format, not the rational calculation of its actors, is predominant (cf. Goodwin 2013; Chapter 13 in this volume).

Within such formats, synchronization ensures the degree of coherence that we expect to find in interactions as an essential component in making sense of situations.

3.4 Formatting and Nonlinear Outcomes

Coherence, however, must not be imagined as a straight line from premises to conclusion. Neither can formats be imagined as closed boxes with extraordinarily transparent orders of indexicality, generally known to all participants. As suggested in Section 3.2, order is evolving and contingent upon the congregational work performed by participants. Recognizing a situation, we explained, proceeds through perceived order properties of such situations that can be framed into formats, then guiding the actions of participants. But outcomes cannot be linearly predicted from the starting conditions because multiple forms of action can emerge within the same format *and be coherent* to the participants. In other words, different kinds of action can be ratified as properly within the format; formats allow *nonlinear* actions, and when it comes to normativity in connection to formats, we see a relatively open and relaxed form of normativity there.

This violates several older assumptions about communication. In speech act theory, J. L. Austin (1962) famously distinguished clear "felicity" conditions for smooth and "correct" interaction, while deviations of them (even a violation of one of them) would make the interaction "unhappy" or "infelicitous." Equally famous are Grice's (1975) "maxims" for conversation – conditions for maintaining a well-ordered mode of interaction with any other interlocutor. Both (and many others) grounded their theories into widely shared folk views of the strong normative order required for interaction. Another set of assumptions that is violated by nonlinearity within the format is that underlying the kind of naïve survey methodology devastatingly criticized by Cicourel (1964) and others. In such survey enterprises, the stability of the format is used as an argument for the stability of its outcomes. Concretely, it is assumed that as long as we ask the same questions in the same format to large numbers of respondents, the answers will be commensurable because each respondent was addressed *identically*. Converted into the terms we are using here, stable formats will generate linear actions, since every action will be an identical response to an identical prompt. Cicourel's penetrating critique targeted the impressive amount of ignorance about actual forms of communication buried inside this methodological assumption, leading to the incredible suggestion that hundreds of different people would all have identical understandings of a question (and its meanings for the analyst) and that the actual (and highly diverse) conditions of the question-and-answer events would not have any effects on the respondents.

The fallacies of such assumptions can be shown through the following example, involving the present authors. In late 2017, as part of his program teaching, Jan Blommaert set up a small practice-based workshop on research interviewing for MA students including Laura Smits and Noura Yacoubi. The instructions were clear: pairs needed to be formed and the roles of interviewer and interviewee needed to be assigned; the interview was to proceed in English and (unbeknownst to the interviewees) had to contain some potentially frame-disturbing elements. One of these elements was the opening question "Who are you *really*?". The format, we can see, was entirely scripted and uniform for all the teams.

Laura and Noura were both interviewees and were interviewed by classmates with whom both had a history of friendly personal encounters and lengthy conversations – in Dutch. All of them – interviewers and interviewees – were also students in the same year of the same program track at Tilburg University. Thus, we can suppose other elements of potential stability to be there: shared membership of a clearly defined community, a shared history of interaction making all participants familiar with each other's speech habits and idiosyncrasies, and also enabling all to know quite well who the other "really" was. Laura and Noura, however, responded to the question in radically different ways. Let us look at the sequences following the question; in the transcript "I" stands for "interviewer" and "R" for "respondent."

Laura's answer
I: SO Laura*, who are you REALLY?
R: Who are I (am) really. Eu::hm. What do you want to know of me. What is–what is really?
I: TELL me something about yourself
R: Okay. I'm Laura . Laura Smits . I a::m twenty-three years old . eu::hm. I study Global Communication here at Tilburg University I play volleyba::ll I have a little sister, I have a boyfriend, and I live in Tilburg eu::hm furthermore<1> I think<1> I am very happy at the mome::nt in the situation I live in . eu::hm ja* enjoying life/ . . .
I: Okay.

Noura's answer
I: Uhm . who are you really?
R: Who I am?
I: Yes
R: Well. what do you mean? What do you want to know?//
I: Yeahh who are you?//
R: That is a. difficult question [Laughing]/

I: Why is it difficult?//
R: Because you are asking *a lot* at the same time. Do you want to know my characteristics, my name, my birth, my hobbies, do you want to know my study?
I: Tell me what *you think* who you really are//
R: *Dude* [Laughing] well I am a … Dutch, well Moroccan-Dutch girl, born here, I'm uuhh twenty-two years old. Uuhm who I am? <2> Well I am a student that is part of my identity, I *feel* as a student, I am. living the life of a student. Uhmm. I am studying global communication/
I: Ohh
R: What a coincidence [Laughing]
I: Me too [Laughing]
R: Can you ask. can you ask the question more specific?//
I: Is this really who you really are?
R: Well it's uhm. it is quite a lot who I am I mean. also history comes into pla::y, also family comes into pla::y uuh who I am yeah I am a human being//
I: Okay but/
R: Punt

We see that Laura and Noura are both initially looking for the right frame, as both ask for clarification of their interviewer's actions ("What do you want to know"?). Both, consequently, receive a reiteration of the question (part of the instructions given by Jan to the interviewers). But what follows are two entirely different courses of action. Laura instantly aligns with the perceived frame and gives what we could call a "profile answer" – the kind of clearly organized factual and affective information offered on social media profiles and in short introductory "pitches" to unknown people. She "neutralizes," so to speak, the interviewer whom she considered to be a close friend, and addresses her in her role as an interviewer performing an unusual kind of interaction, which in the same move is "normalized": this is an interview, it's strange, but we'll do it the way it should be done. The synchronization toward the format is complete in Laura's case. Noura, by contrast, does not exit the interpersonal and intertextual frame, but engages in several turns of metapragmatic negotiation with the interviewer (also someone with whom she maintained a very friendly personal relationship), expressing discomfort and resistance to aligning with the format in utterances such as "Dude" and "Punt" (a Dutch categorical utterance meaning "period," "full stop," "that's it"). And while she does offer a kind of "profile answer" at some point, the answer is followed by a repeated request for clarification of what goes on. The chronotope of interpersonal friendship sits uncomfortably with that of the training interview, and synchronization is a process that demands quite a bit of construction work here. Note, however, that, later in the interview, Noura offers long and detailed autobiographical-narrative answers; the synchronization demands more work but happens eventually.

If Austin's felicity conditions were rigorously applied here, Noura's initial response would perhaps be called "unhappy," a "misfire." Laura's response would, from a similar perspective, be "correct" and "happy," as it articulates the linear uptake of the interviewer's action. From the viewpoint of making sense of the particular situation, however, Noura's actions and those of Laura are equivalent and fit the format in spite of their substantial differences. What we can take from this is that uniformity in format does not guarantee uniformity in actions – a confirmation of Cicourel's critique of assumptions to the contrary – and that diverse lines of action can occur within the same format, even if some actions are not linear responses to what preceded. Formats are not one-size-fits-all and linear-normative units.

3.5 Context Collapse versus Expansion

At this point, our action-centered proposal is complete: we see contextualization as the recognition of a situation through its perceived-order properties that can be framed into formats then used to guide the actions of participants (see Chapter 6 in this volume). We submit that our action-centered proposal is applicable to interaction online and offline, since it avoids many of the core assumptions (and vocabulary) that are challenged by features of online interaction.

In studies of online interaction, "there are great analytical gains to be made by looking very closely at how particular activities are organized" (Goodwin and Goodwin 1992: 96). The advantages of that tactic can be illustrated by looking at an issue widely debated in the world of social media research: "context collapse," that is, "the flattening out of multiple distinct audiences in one's social network, such that people from different contexts become part of a singular group of message recipients" (Vitak 2012: 541).

The theoretical and empirical validity of the concept of context collapse has been criticized by several discourse analysts (Georgakopoulou 2017a, 2017b; Tagg, Seargeant and Brown 2017; Szabla and Blommaert 2018). Indeed, online technology "complicates our metaphors of space and place, including the belief that audiences are separate from each other" (Marwick and boyd 2010: 115; see also Chapter 32 in this volume), and has taken us from a world of relatively transparent audiences to that of far less transparent "networked publics" (boyd 2011). But such complications cannot be solved by drawing on the sociological imagination we sketched earlier: that of "normal" dyadic face-to-face communication with well-known similar people in a tight community – which is what happens in the literature on context collapse. Such an anachronistic imagination spawns an abstract conceptualization of context as something that is transparent only when we situate humans in transparent situations in transparent communities, where "audiences" are known and trusted and people have full control over what they do in social action. When we move into the online world of online audiences and inconspicuous overhearers, of lurkers, aliases and bots, and of algorithms regulating the traffic and distribution of messages, such theoretical and analytic instruments obviously cease to be useful and have to be replaced by more flexible and precise ones.

In a case study of a long and highly complex discussion within a large Facebook group for Polish people living in The Netherlands, we used the action-centered perspective described here (Szabla and Blommaert 2018). At first glance, the case would qualify eminently for context collapse: we had an enormous community of effective and potential participants, large enough to speak of a "networked audience" consisting of people who did not know each other. The lengthy nature of the online discussion may have disturbed our "metaphors of space and place" and the particular rudimentary platform affordances of Facebook may have complicated our expectations of coherence and sequentiality in dialogue, as responses to a prompt may not appear in adjacency but be separated by several intervening responses from others – a practical problem of synchronization, in fact (see Frobenius and Harper 2015). Facebook formats interactions in a curious way, and people may lose their bearings in such formats.

Our first empirical observation obviously complicated things further: the general activity of a "discussion" was, in actual fact, a mosaic of different actions, some linear and connected to the initial action (a request from a Polish-origin journalist for assistance in the making of a documentary on the labor conditions of Polish workers in The Netherlands) and many nonlinear, embedded and parallel to the initial action. People would indeed respond to the journalist's request (and be redirected to the private messaging section of Facebook), but they would also attack the orthographic errors in the Polish writing, discussing linguistic correctness in relation to Polish identity; they would accuse and scold each other relative to specific statements they had made, venture conspiracy theories about journalists and Polish émigrés, offer general observations about the work ethos of Polish and Dutch workers, and so forth. Each of these different lines of action was normatively recognizable as a different chronotopic unit of participants, topics, orders of indexicality and moral codes, and was formatted accordingly.

The second observation, however, was that people found their way around this terrifically complex web of actions. The nonsequentiality of scripted Facebook interaction, the meandering of topics and participants and the generally confusing character of what went on (often emphasized in literature on context collapse) did not appear as an obstacle for participants to participate *in the specific parts of the event in which they got involved*. We saw participation frameworks shift along with topic shifts, in such a way that just handfuls of people would be involved in an action and know quite well who their actual addressees were and how they should proceed, and how they could migrate to another participation framework or exit the discussion when lines actions were closed. In other words: we saw plenty of congregational work shaping formats and subformats and connecting or disconnecting parts of the discussion from other parts. Participants made sense of the *specific actions* in which they were involved – they performed adequate contextualization work throughout, even if that included self- and other-correction and rectification, necessitated by the awkward Facebook discussion affordances. They recognized the specific situations then framed and formatted them into indexically ordered discursive actions. No contexts appeared to collapse; instead, we saw an amazing density and intensity of contextualization work – context *expansion*, if you wish.

3.6 Conclusion

The example of context collapse versus context expansion brings us back to our point of departure: the need to rethink our commonly used notions of context and contextualization so as to make them useful and accurate for addressing a world of communication in which ordinary dyadic face-to-face conversation is no longer the default point of departure and foundation for theory. Contemporary discourse analysts must be aware that the sociological imagination constructed on this foundation is anachronistic, and that we cannot accurately address the phenomenology of contemporary communication without sacrificing that imagination.

Doing that does not mean that we are left empty-handed for the task of analysis. We can fall back on reasonably robust tools and approaches that do not carry that bias of anachronism or that can be refashioned so as to be free of it. The tools we used here were drawn from an old interactionist approach often called ethnomethodology (and never to be confused with mainstream conversation analysis; cf. Garfinkel 1967; Cicourel 1974). In a broader sense, they are part of the ethnographic tradition in the study of language (e.g. Gumperz and Hymes 1972). Within that tradition, it was *language as a feature of social action* that was central, not language per se, and that focus on language-as-action enabled this tradition to ground itself in a sociology of *emerging* order, not just of reproduction. Facing a terrain of new and rapidly changing objects – the online forms of interaction that are deeply transforming communicative economies worldwide – such an open and unfinished sociological footing is a requirement, lest we attempt to squeeze what is thoroughly new into models and frameworks unfit for it.

The proposals we made in this chapter, thus, have a specific direction and talk from a specific viewpoint. Let them be prompts for others to think along, exploring other viewpoints in the process.

Further Reading

Blommaert, J. (2015). Chronotopes, Scales and Complexity in the Study of Language in Society. *Annual Review of Anthropology* 44: 105–16.

Cicourel, A. (1992). The Interpenetration of Communicative Contexts: Examples from Medical Encounters. In A. Duranti and C. Goodwin (eds.) *Rethinking Context*. Cambridge: Cambridge University Press. 291–310.

Goodwin, C. (2013). The Co-operative, Transformative Organization of Human Action and Knowledge. *Journal of Pragmatics* 46(1): 8–23.

Gumperz, J. (2003). Response Essay. In S. Eerdmans, C. Previgniano and P. Thibault (eds.) *Language and Interaction: Discussions with John J. Gumperz*. Amsterdam: John Benjamins. 105–26.

Silverstein, M. (1992). The Indeterminacy of Contextualization: When Is Enough Enough? In P. Auer and A. di Luzio (eds.) *The Contextualization of Language*. Amsterdam: John Benjamins. 55–76.

Szabla, M. and Blommaert, M. (2018). Does Context Really Collapse in Social Media Interaction? *Applied Linguistics Review* 9(2). https://doi.org/10.1515/applirev-2017-0119.

References

Agha, A. (2007). *Language and Social Relations*. Cambridge: Cambridge University Press.

Auer, P. and di Luzio, A. (eds.) (1992). *The Contextualization of Language*. Amsterdam: John Benjamins.

Austin, J. L. (1962). *How to Do Things with Words*. Oxford: Clarendon Press.

Bakhtin, M. (1981). *The Dialogic Imagination*. Austin: University of Texas Press.

Baron, N. (2008). *Always On: Language in an Online and Mobile World*. Oxford: Oxford University Press.

Blommaert, J. (2005). *Discourse: A Critical Introduction*. Cambridge: Cambridge University Press.

(2015a). Chronotopes, Scales and Complexity in the Study of Language in Society. *Annual Review of Anthropology* 44: 105–16.

(2015b). Pierre Bourdieu: Perspectives on Language in Society. In J.-O. Östman and J. Verschueren (eds.) *Handbook of Pragmatics*. Amsterdam: John Benjamins. 1–16.

(2018a). *Durkheim and the Internet: Sociolinguistics and the Sociological Imagination*. London: Bloomsbury.

(2018b). Chronotopes, Synchronization and Formats. *Tilburg Papers in Culture Studies*. Paper 207. www.tilburguniversity.edu/research/institutes-and-research-groups/babylon/tpcs.

(2018c). Online with Garfinkel. https://alternative-democracy-research.org/2018/01/17/online-with-garfinkel/.

Blommaert, J. and De Fina, A. (2016). Chronotopic Identities: On the Spacetime Organization of Who We Are. In A. De Fina, D. Ikizoglu and J. Wegner (eds.) *Diversity and Superdiversity: Sociocultural Linguistic Perspectives* (GURT Series). Washington, DC: Georgetown University Press. 1–15.

Blommaert, J. and Rampton, B. (2016). Language and Superdiversity. In K. Arnaut, J. Blommaert, B. Rampton and M. Spotti (eds.) *Language and Superdiversity*. New York: Routledge. 21–48.

Blumer, H. (1969). *Symbolic Interactionism: Program and Method*. Berkeley: University of California Press.

Bourdieu, P. (2000). Making the Economic Habitus: Algerian Workers Revisited. *Ethnography* 1(1): 17–41.

boyd, d. (2011). White Flight in Networked Publics? How Race and Class Shaped American Teen Engagement with MySpace and Facebook. In L. Nakamura and P. Chow-White (eds.) *Race after the Internet*. New York: Routledge. 203–22.

Briggs, C. (2005). Communicability, Racial Discourse and Disease. *Annual Review of Anthropology* 34: 269–91.

Carr, E. S. and Lempert, M. (2016). Introduction: The Pragmatics of Scale. In E. S. Carr and M. Lempert (eds.) *Scale: Discourse and Dimensions of Social Life*. Oakland: University of California Press. 1–23.

Castells, M. (1996). *The Rise of the Network Society*. London: Blackwell.

Cicourel, A. (1964). *Method and Measurement in Sociology*. New York: The Free Press.

(1967). *The Social Organization of Juvenile Justice*. New York: Wiley.

(1973). *Cognitive Sociology: Language and Meaning in Social Interaction*. Harmondsworth: Penguin Education.

(1974). *Cognitive Sociology: Language and Meaning in Social Interaction*. New York: Free Press.

(1992). The Interpenetration of Communicative Contexts: Examples from Medical Encounters. In A. Duranti and C. Goodwin (eds.) *Rethinking Context*. Cambridge: Cambridge University Press. 291–310.

Das, S. (2016). *Linguistic Rivalries: Tamil Migrants and Anglo-Franco Conflicts*. New York: Oxford University Press.

Duranti, A. (1997). *Linguistic Anthropology*. Cambridge: Cambridge University Press.

Duranti, A. and Goodwin, C. (eds.) (1992). *Rethinking Context*. Cambridge: Cambridge University Press.

Frobenius, M. and Harper, R. (2015). Tying in Comment Sections: The Production of Meaning and Sense on Facebook. *Semiotica* 204: 121–43.

Garfinkel, H. (1967). *Studies in Ethnomethodology*. New York: Prentice Hall.

(2002). *Ethnomethodology's Program: Working Out Durkheim's Aphorism.* Lanham, MD: Rowman & Littlefield.

Georgakopoulou, A. (2017a). "Whose Context Collapse?" Ethical Clashes in the Study of Language and Social Media in Context. *Applied Linguistics Review* 8(2–3): 1–32.

(2017b). Small Stories Research: A Narrative Paradigm for the Analysis of Social Media. In A. Quan-Haase and L. Sloan (eds.) *The Sage Handbook of Social Media Research Methods.* London: Sage. 266–81.

Giddens, A. (1984). *The Constitution of Society.* Berkeley: University of California Press.

Goffman, E. (1964). The Neglected Situation. *American Anthropologist* 66(6 Part 2): 133–6.

(1967). *Interactional Ritual: Essays on Face-to-Face Behavior.* New York: Pantheon Books.

(1971). *Relations in Public: Microstudies of the Public Order.* New York: Basic Books.

(1974). *Frame Analysis: An Essay on the Organization of Experience.* Harmondsworth: Penguin.

Goodwin, C. (2003). Embedded Context. *Research on Language and Social Interaction* 36(4): 323–50.

(2004). A Competent Speaker Who Can't Speak: The Social Life of Aphasia. *Journal of Linguistic Anthropology* 14(2): 151–70.

(2007). Participation, Stance and Affect in the Organization of Practice. *Discourse & Society* 18(1): 53–73.

(2013). The Co-operative, Transformative Organization of Human Action and Knowledge. *Journal of Pragmatics* 46(1): 8–23.

Goodwin, C. and Goodwin, M. H. (1992). Context, Activity and Participation. In P. Auer and A. di Luzio (eds.) *The Contextualization of Language.* Amsterdam: John Benjamins. 77–99.

Grice, H. P. (1975). Logic and Conversation. In P. Cole and J. Morgan (eds.) *Syntax and Semantics, Vol. 3: Speech Acts.* New York: Academic Press. 41–58.

Gumperz, J. (1982). *Discourse Strategies.* Cambridge: Cambridge University Press.

(1992). Contextualization Revisited. In P. Auer and A. di Luzio (eds.) *The Contextualization of Language.* Amsterdam: John Benjamins. 39–53.

(2003). Response Essay. In S. Eerdmans, C. Prevignano and P. Thibault (eds.) *Language and Interaction: Discussions with John J. Gumperz.* Amsterdam: John Benjamins. 105–26.

Gumperz, J. and Hymes, D. H. (eds.) (1972). *Directions in Sociolinguistics: The Ethnography of Communication.* New York: Holt, Rinehart and Winston.

Hymes, D. (1996). *Ethnography, Linguistics, Narrative Inequality: Toward an Understanding of Voice.* London: Taylor & Francis.

Marwick, A. and boyd, d. (2010). I Tweet Honestly, I Tweet Passionately: Twitter Users, Context Collapse, and the Imagined Audience. *New Media and Society* 13(1): 114–33.

Mills, C. W. (1959). *The Sociological Imagination*. New York: Oxford University Press.

Rampton, B. (2016). Foucault, Gumperz and Governmentality: Interaction, Power and Subjectivity in the 21st Century. In N. Coupland (ed.) *Sociolinguistics: Theoretical Debates*. Cambridge: Cambridge University Press. 303–328.

Scollon, R. (2001). *Mediated Discourse: The Nexus of Practice*. London: Routledge.

Silverstein, M. (1992). The Indeterminacy of Contextualization: When Is Enough Enough? In P. Auer and A. di Luzio (eds.) *The Contextualization of Language*. Amsterdam: John Benjamins. 55–76.

(2003). Indexical Order and the Dialectics of Sociolinguistic Life. *Language & Communication* 23: 193–229.

Strauss, A. (1993). *Continual Permutations of Action*. New York: Aldine de Gruyter.

Szabla, M. and Blommaert, M. (2018). Does Context Really Collapse in Social Media Interaction? *Applied Linguistics Review* 9(2). https://doi.org/10.1515/applirev-2017-0119.

Tagg, C., Seargeant, P. and Brown, A. (2017). *Taking Offence on Social Media: Conviviality and Communication on Facebook*. London: Palgrave Pivot.

Vitak, J. (2012). The Impact of Context Collapse and Privacy on Social Network Site Disclosures. *Journal of Broadcasting and Electronic Media* 56(4): 451–70.

Voloshinov, V. (1973). *Marxism and the Philosophy of Language*. Cambridge, MA: Harvard University Press.

4

Historicity, Interdiscursivity and Intertextuality in Discourse Studies

Branca Falabella Fabricio and Luiz Paulo Moita-Lopes

4.1 History as the Outlawed Wanderer of Linguistics

Linguistics as a modern science has never granted a substantial place to history. On the contrary, it has invested its attention in describing structural rules and "trustworthy" parameters. Objectivity, stability and invariance were among its underlying assumptions. By approaching language as a mental system, mainstream linguistics has placed syntactic-morphological-phonological features at its core, isolating them from contextual "contamination." Very much to the scientific taste of modernity, linguistics has focused on specific items in relation to other specific items, deriving foundational categories and universal patterns from idealized structural linguistic patterns or from the so-called researcher's introspective sense of grammaticality. These procedures conceived of language as an autonomous structured entity that created a kind of fixed ontology, relegating historical phenomena to a subaltern position. However, although linguistics ignored historical forces, areas such as social sciences and philosophy have frequently made historicity a central concern. Derrida ([1967]2008: 53) goes so far as to say that history has always been "the outlawed wanderer of linguistics" because, despite having been banished, history "never stopped from following language as its first and most close possibility." Nevertheless, in the field of mainstream language studies, linguistics and history were traditionally kept apart for a long time.

Considering the self-enclosure of linguistics, in this chapter, we begin by discussing how historicity and language are associated by different twentieth-century philosophers. We make a selective recourse to philosophy, by highlighting its insights into historicity since they speak well to contemporary views of language as discourse. We then move into exploring how history is brought into textuality in present-day discourse studies by focusing on the macro–micro theoretical constructs of interdiscursivity and intertextuality. We conclude by drawing upon the relevance of such a theoretical apparatus to account for discourse circulation in fluid and superdiverse contexts.

We are particularly interested in the role of historicity within our increasingly fast-paced and fleeting digital lives. Therefore, a specific question orients our line of reasoning and the pathway we construct as we perambulate: How can we, as discourse analysts, deal with the temporal-spatial horizon of history in view of the accelerated and ephemeral time-space references we experience nowadays? Put differently, we are concerned with the challenges that contemporary chronotopes pose to discourse analysis.

4.2 Historicity: The History of Necessity versus the History of Contingencies

Historicity is a crucial concept in philosophy. It frequently integrates philosophers' approaches when they explore language or discourse. Thinkers as diverse as Volochinov ([1929]1981), Bakhtin ([1975]2002), Derrida ([1967]2008), Deleuze and Guattari ([1980]1995a and 1995b) and Foucault (1994) directly address history in their musings on discourse. Specifically, they draw attention to how, at the outset of structuralism, the field of linguistics left historicity out of its horizon in constructing the "science" of language. With the exception of Foucault, all these thinkers widely built their arguments on the criticism of two pivotal linguists, Saussure and Chomsky. Although the two linguists were separated by almost forty years, they converged on their understanding of the language system as the core of linguistic science. The influential constructs they designed – *langue* (Saussure [1916]1959) and competence (Chomsky 1957, 1965) – attest to the research approach they favored. Their methods were criticized on basically three accounts: firstly, because they orient toward positivist and objectivist theories; secondly, because they overlook historical conjunctures; and, finally, because they sidestep pragmatics, the domain of concrete language practices in meaning-making.

While they disregarded the importance of history, in the 1920s and 1930s, Bakhtin ([1934]1981) and his circle of collaborators (Volochinov being one of them) were following a very different perspective, away from the dogmas concerning knowledge production. They emphatically accentuated the critical relevance of time and space to the comprehension of human life. In fact, Bakhtin drew attention to the inseparability of time and space (termed "chronotopes") in his study of discourse in literary novels. Human beings and the texts we produce were as such fathomed as chronotopical "entities," whose actions orient to particular temporalities and spatialities.

In his *Aesthetics of Verbal Creation*, Bakhtin ([1979]1992: 282) discussed how historicity can be avoided in language studies only if enunciation and alterity are ignored. When we abandon the existing link between language and social life, we bypass historical significance. If this is so, erasing such bonds is what allows for "formalism and abstraction" as orienting perspectives. By the same token, it is the formulation of invariant facts that establishes the contours of the so-called language system, worthy of becoming "the focus of a well-defined science" (Volochinov [1929]1981: 77). Therefore, understanding the materiality of verbal interaction requires comprehension of how social life penetrates language and vice versa (Bakhtin [1979]1992). One's engagement in meaning construction can be considered only if history is conceived as a pervasive phenomenon. That is also the reason why language thrives on concrete enunciations (Volochinov [1929]1981) – understood as acts of producing utterances in specific situations.

The difference between system and enunciation is a crucial point in Bakhtin's work. When he conceptualizes verbal life ([1975]2002), he draws a distinction between centripetal and centrifugal forces operating in all languages. On the one hand, centripetal forces are in action in the production of a "standard language." They are unifying and regulatory forces that pull language elements together. On the other hand, centrifugal forces are at work in drifting language elements away from the center and in keeping them apart and differentiated. Centrifugal forces produce difference and multiplicity (of voices, "languages," semiotic resources, etc.). They are also "compelled by movement, randomness, continual flows and history" (Clark and Holquist [1984]1998: 35). This is an important distinction because it clearly points to the forces that need to be taken into consideration when historicity comes into play in the concrete enactment of verbal interaction. Moreover, it points to a conceptualization of history as fluid and "unstable"[1] (Bakhtin [1934]1981: 129).

In twentieth-century Russia, Bakhtin and his interdisciplinary circle anticipated such a comprehension of history that ties in with contemporary philosophers' interpretations. As discussing their different perspectives in detail is beyond the scope of this chapter, we proceed by concentrating on commonalities among them and by selectively highlighting how historicity comes into their works.

Derrida ([1967]2008), for example, in *Of Gramatology*, questions Saussure's focus on language systems, especially on their phonetic structure. He brings into discussion how Saussure operates from a logocentric

---

[1] "[T]races of historical time (however unstable) turn up in the social heterogeneity of this private life world" (Bakhtin [1934]1981: 129).

logic, committed to truth values, in which meaning is always present or represented. Such a perspective, termed the metaphysics of presence, makes it impossible for Saussure to understand the deferral activity that is constitutive of discourse engagement. According to Derrida, in order to make sense of what meanings are at play during an interaction, we resort to other meanings, which in turn make recourse to other meanings ... ad infinitum. In other words, meanings are constantly deferred, that is, postponed. In his view, that which we experience as communication and understanding would be an illusion created by imprecise actions. This is so because meaning is but an effect produced within indetermination. It is in this vein that Derrida de-essentializes representational meaning that comes out of the *logos*, "the meaning of truth" ([1967]2008: 13).

In criticizing the myths of precision and transmission of meanings, Derrida ([1967]2008: 11) employs the concept of *écriture* to refer to meaning production of any kind;

> not only the physical gestures of the literal, pictographic or ideographic inscription, but also the totality of what makes it possible; and from then on, everything that may open the ground for an inscription in general, literal or not, and even if what it distributes does not belong to the order of voice: cinematography, choreography, without doubt, but also pictural, musical, sculptural, etc. *écriture*.

In *écriture*, the deferral activity or practice is constitutive of discourse engagement, such that signs need to be thought of under erasure, that is, they exist only as traces of meaning. As a consequence of continuous postponement, there is always a residue to be grasped. Therefore, meaning cannot be approached "on the basis of *logos*, genesis, origin or metaphysics" (Wolfreys [2007]2012: 93).

By the same token, subjectivity and history cannot be traced back to an original or founding moment. They are always assumed as in-between space differences and postponing temporalities. Their meanings are always indecisive. They provide us with the delusion that we are in control. Historicity is thus a flowing process in Derrida's vision: "before being the object of history – of scientific history – *écriture* opens the field of History as a constant becoming process" (Derrida [1967]2008: 34). The operations that institutionally stabilize historic discourses are the very ones that flout the deferral "nature" of meaning-making. In light of this discussion, Derrida criticizes Saussure's view of language as obliterating "space differences and temporal deferrals" (Wolfreys [2007]2012: 92). There is always another meaning possible in an infinite number of unfolding historical performativities in language pragmatics. This position is made explicit when Derrida ponders how words and concepts gain meaning only "in the chains of differences" produced throughout history (Derrida [1967]2008: 86).

Sharing a similar position, Deleuze and Guattari ([1980]1995b) build their theorization on language by criticizing Chomsky. The crucial issue for these philosophers in relation to language is the centrality of pragmatics – or the regimes of signs in use that do not depend on the general invariants or universals of grammar or syntax. This is so "because pragmatics is not the complement of a logic, of a syntax or of a semantics, but, on the contrary, it is the basic element on which all the rest depends" (Deleuze and Guattari [1980]1995b: 113). In their very words, "linguistics is nothing outside pragmatics (semiotic or political) which define the effectuation of the language conditions and the use of linguistic elements" (Deleuze and Guattari [1980] 1995b: 27). That is why Deleuze and Guattari also wish to focus on what was put aside by linguistics: pragmatics, or Chomsky's idea of performance. Their argument is based on the impossibility of separating competence from performance. By insinuating itself everywhere, pragmatics underscores all other language dimensions, as syntax and semantics. In this sense, pragmatics is no longer the "garbage bin" ([1980]1995b: 15). This kind of criticism is related to the fact that Chomsky's search for language invariants and language universals puts aside human agency by closing language on itself, isolating it from use.

The production of universals concerning the structure of language is a discursive practice situated in a multiplicity of "happenings" (évenements, in Deleuze 1969) that are not reduced to a specific timespace instance. Universals are ever-becoming affirmatives that remain "as the *happening* which persists in history" (Cardoso 2005: 111). Their effectuation is ephemeral, lingering here and there. This fluidity of history operates within a plurality of encounters that constitute its singularity as a happening. Hence, the nature of the historical forces at play in the production of knowledge is dealt with not in terms of origin but in terms of an assemblage of meanings, contingencies and events (Read 2003). As Deleuze and Guattari themselves affirm ([1972]1983: 140), "universal history is the history of contingencies, and not the history of necessity." This does not imply that everything is contingent nor that necessity is erased. It means that "necessity is the becoming-necessary of contingent encounters" (Althusser 1994: 566). Such events are experienced as natural, rational and objective only when we forget about the unstable historicity pertaining to any mode of production (Read 2003).

Deleuze (1986: 90) pointed out that the convergence of "happening" and history was already present in Foucault's original contribution to the theorizing of practices. However, contrary to the ideas we have explored so far, Foucault did not build his argument by referring to linguistics. As an anti-structuralist, Foucault (1979: 5) was critical of how structuralism did away with the concept of "happening" in the human sciences. In his view, it was necessary to understand that there are "happenings" of different kinds, operating within different scales and within a diverse chronological range. What is of concern, he argued, is to unravel the threads that weave such "happenings" together. In this sense, he adds that "what one should have as reference is not the model of language and of signs, but the war and the battle" (1979: 5), where historicity reigns. "Historicity is belligerent and not linguistic" (1979: 5). It should be analyzed in terms "of strategies and of tactics" (1979: 5). As the philosopher of power-resistance, Foucault was also drawing attention to where action is and to how we are acting. By operating on the capillarity of power, he contended that we act through discourse in the world (Foucault [1972]1984). In discursive practices, the nanoscale, or microphysics of power, is where we can resist solidified meanings. It is where history is transformed.

His involvement with history was related to his concern with the present. In investing a great effort to understand how modern subjects came to be what they are (Foucault 1982), he inquired into ways of reading and combining texts in different historical times. In his methodology, this was done by analyzing how texts and discourses were inserted in large systems or discursive formations (Foucault [1969]1972). A discursive formation comprehends discourses that are linked to a multiplicity of events. These events occur in both punctual moments and disperse temporalities, which makes it possible for them to be "repeated, known, forgotten, transformed" (Foucault [1969]1972: 25). In such circumstances, it is necessary to relinquish the idea of an original discourse, referring it back to the whole discursive formation in which it emerged. This grasp helped him to project a nexus between texts and the wider social order. Specific structural arrangements, displaying internal regularities, are not natural occurrences in history. They are maintained through textual practices such as laws, document and scientific treatises, which are part and parcel of control and policing apparatuses. Foucault did not deny that these surveillance mechanisms operate coercively. Nevertheless, he argued that they do not make social actors completely subjected. In his view, social agents may employ different strategies to violate regulation games. Far from being static, discursive formations and the social practices they articulate are prone to change over time. Transformations are not, however, the actions of sovereign subjects. They are the rearrangement of a whole enunciative field (Foucault [1969]1972).

By drawing attention to historicity, power, resistance and discursive formations, Foucault is emphasizing the relevance of the discourse practices within which we act. In this sense, he broke away from a view of history that moves from an original point to a well-defined end. On disturbing the perception that history is linear and progressive, he drew attention to the plural meanings and discourses that construct the histories within which social subjects operate. Therefore, Foucault's perspective on history is a nontotalizing and incidental one, accounting for the many continuities and discontinuities that "historically constituted western subjectivity" (Castro [2004]2009: 204).

This brief review of how some twentieth-century philosophers have addressed historicity is relevant because they efface the commonsense perception of history as a chronological thread of happenings. Moreover, it foregrounds the discursive practices in which social subjects are contingently situated in space and time. In our view, such perception of historical processes may account for contemporary intensely mobile times. At this junction, we move into how historicity is brought into text through interdiscursivity and intertextuality.

4.3 Historicity, Interdiscursivity and Intertextuality in Discourse Studies

Around the 1980s, linguists from different traditions started establishing a contact zone between linguistics and social sciences. Inspired by a Marxist tradition and intellectuals such as Louis Althusser, Pierre Bourdieu and Michel Foucault, they turned to a conception of language as ongoing social action. The idea of activity came along with a view of language as a situated sociohistorical practice interlaced with signs and texts. In this context, linguistic research was regarded as being profoundly political (Lemke 1995). The aim of such scholars was to develop a critical analytical approach that could combine linguistics, history and politics. The ones following such an orientation came to be grouped together under the umbrella of a discipline named discourse analysis, an area that shelters diverse theoretical-methodological-analytical positions (Maingueneau 1993). As drawing parallels between the myriad works in this area is not our purpose in this section, we turn our attention to how historicity profoundly influenced some discourse analysis theoreticians. Despite their differences, they share a common goal in their attempt to join situated and historical practices through the notions of interdiscursivity and intertextuality.

In the French context, Michel Pêcheux lies among the first to propose a dialogue between linguistics and social sciences. His work was extremely influential. Encouraged by the Marxist project of enhancing social transformations, he focused on political discourse and its ideological dimensions. In fact, he equated discourse and ideology, approaching the latter as the material manifestation of language. Drawing on Althusser's (1971) Marxist theory of ideology, he argued that ideological state apparatuses manipulated reality in the service of economic interests, thus reproducing or mutating systems of oppression. According to such a regime, what one can say or must say is conditioned by ideology (Pêcheux 1982). This guidance occurs within a "discursive formation." Much in the sense employed by Foucault ([1969]1986), a discursive formation emerges and forms within certain economic, political and historical conditions.

Despite the malleability of the Foucauldian concept we highlighted in Section 4.2, its appropriation by Pêcheux was rather deterministic (Baronas 2004). Deeply influenced by Marxism and Althusserianism, he pushed the idea of discursive formations toward an understanding that ideological complexes are fundamentally conditioned by a sociohistorical confluence. This conjuncture, linked to superstructures such as the State, determines social life. It places social subjects in specific positions, directs their conduct, rules their talk, forges specific perceptions and produces ways of thinking and feeling (Pêcheux 1982). Linguistic elements and their combination (the linguistic system) are thus entangled in a structural matrix that is a producer of meaning-effects. They interpellate individuals as discourse subjects who orient thoughtlessly to ideological processes within discursive formations. As they frequently forget about the cause of their discourse, they develop the false consciousness that they freely create their own discourse (Pêcheux 1975). Hence, unknowingly, they reproduce meanings and practices.

Discursive formations consist of a package of relations to other discursive formations, a relationship Pêcheux (1982) referred to as interdiscursivity. His analytical struggles concentrated on text analysis, observing how linguistic elements, as words, expressions or sentences, circulated among different discursive formations. One could think, for the sake of exemplification, that the expression "health industry" is an interdiscourse crossing diverse discursive formations related to economic, commercial and medical practices. In this crossing, the discourses of health and industry interpellate social subjects' discursive production. They incorporate these ideas into their own discourse while presuming its authorship. This is to say that they read off autonomy from what is in fact ideological subjection. According to such an apprehension, interdiscourse is the effect of ideological interpellation. As a consequence, the task of the discourse analyst is to explore key words, expressions and clauses that would be indicative of the ideological apparatus operating surreptitiously, in imperceptible ways. If interdiscourse imposes/dissimulates itself upon social subjects, it curbs possibilities of agency and reconfigurations. Subjects succumb, so to speak, under the weight of external forces: history, discursive formations and interdiscourse. It can thus be argued that Pêcheux, by constructing such deterministic relations, ended up hindering the very project of social innovation he sought.

Followers of Pêcheux, nevertheless, have reviewed this stagnant approach, characterizing discursive formations and interdiscursivity as heterogeneous, ambiguous and changeable. Such features made these concepts susceptible to restructuring (Courtine 1981). Dominique Maingueneau, for example, suggests their reinterpretation, reading them through the lens of the Bakhtinian tradition. Drawing on the notions of "genres" (Bakhtin 1986) and "intertextuality" (Kristeva 1986),[2] he considered that textual production was inseparable from sociohistorical frameworks (Maingueneau 1984). In his view, discourse analysis does not

---

[2] Although the term intertextuality was coined by Kristeva (1986), she builds on the Bakhtinian view of how texts speak to other texts.

approach texts in themselves nor as sociological or psychological objects. Its purpose is the association of texts, through their enunciation apparatus (discourse participants in situated practices), with the social worlds that produce them and that are, in turn, produced by them (Maingueneau 1996). In other words, analysis starts at the textual level, aiming to reach the levels of discourse and discursive formations. This stance enhances the observation of the linguistic and extralinguistic materials (texts and the conditions of enunciation) that contribute to the texturing process of interdiscourse (Maingueneau 2009).

Therefore, Maingueneau's first explorations of interdiscursivity led him not only to study discourse in relation to other discourses but also to explore how this relationship composed the interdiscourse. The latter is taken to be a space of regularity and historical repetition. In interdiscursivity, the same discourse can be employed in different contexts, invoking the memory of what has already been said. This historical inscription in new circumstances may operate transformations in discursive formations. Therefore, discourse analysis has a twofold purpose. While giving primacy to interdiscursivity, it invests in the demarcation of clear boundaries between different discursive formations (Baronas 2004). In this sense, texts simultaneously reactualize what has already been said (in a previous discursive formation) and validate that which it recycles (in a new discursive formation). This relationship of reciprocality is constitutive of interdiscourse.

In the development of his work, however, Maingueneau (1995) re-elaborated the notion of interdiscourse, by establishing a dialogue with other related notions as genre and intertextuality. This movement marked a shift from the focus on discourse and its historical inscription to a concern with the production/interpretation of texts and the conditions of their enunciation. He suggests that attention should be paid to the entanglement of modes of enunciation and specific social places. Such a change resulted in the reconsideration of the idea of discursive formation toward the relationship between texts and discourse genres. Texts form a network of genres that are situated hierarchically, according to different levels of prestige. In processes of socialization, people learn how to shape and apprehend discourse as an activity reporting to a genre, as a discursive institution (Maingueneau 1995). For instance, a single expression like "let's say grace," stated by a parent before a meal, may create the presupposition of several chained actions. Its enunciator and the audience he/she addresses constitute these very actions and the context of enunciation – family dinner in the case at hand. Therefore, discourse analysis should be concerned with texts, the place they occupy in enunciation apparatuses and the different social values attributed to their position. This means observing the association of multiple texts, genres and ranking systems within a discursive formation (Maingueneau 1993, 1999).

4 Historicity, Interdiscursivity, Intertextuality

Such plurality contributes to defining the identity of a discursive formation according to two kinds of relationship. One connection is interdiscursive, having to do with the range of genres and discourse types that regulate interactions in the interior of a specific conjuncture. Enunciations make sense only if they follow typical rhetorical and interactional patterns arbitrated before a momentary statement is made. For example, the communicational routines and discursive practices still enacted in many classrooms worldwide[3] encompass "a body of anonymous historical rules" determined in time and space (Foucault [1969]1972: 117). The other liaison is intertextual and designates the relationship that texts or groups of texts maintain with each other.

The conception of intertextuality has been expanded by Maingueneau, who distinguishes internal from external relationships (Charaudeau and Maingueneau 2004: 288–9). Internal intertextuality is articulated between a specific discourse and another from the same discursive field. Let us consider American President Barack Obama's victory speech as a prototypical case. When the president elect chose "A new birth of freedom" as the theme of his victory speech in 2008, he resonated with Abraham Lincoln's 1863 *Gettysburg Address* in Pennsylvania. The intertextual dialogue established by the enunciations of two political leaders separated in time and space occurs within the same discursive field, orienting to similar genre conventions. External intertextuality, on the other hand, associates discourses from distinct discursive fields (as in Zen psychology, blending Buddhism, a religious discourse, and psychotherapy, a scientific one[4]).

Taken in conjunction, interdiscursivity and intertextuality may account for texts' historical embedding and historical transformation. While they function as the memory of "textual treasure," they are manipulated each time they emerge in new enunciations, troubling taken-for-granted genre boundaries. Hence, despite their historical anchorage (Maingueneau 1993), they may produce new modes of existence. Ignoring such movement would reduce discourse analysis to a simplistic pragmatics of discourse genres. Discourses can be resignified under new conditions of production, which can make room for the materialization of new discursive practices and genres.

In the Anglo-Saxon context, the reflections of many discourse practitioners have also been animated by the 1980s European zeitgeist we have alluded to already. Among such practitioners, British linguist Norman Fairclough stands out as an intellectual captivated by the social and historical signatures of language. He has published intensely in the area of discourse studies, inquiring about the narrow links between situated

---

[3] In this respect, check Cazden (2001).
[4] An example, among many others, is P.-Y. Eisendrath and S. Muramoto (eds.) (2002) *Awakening and Insight: Zen Buddhism and Psychotherapy* (London/New York: Routledge).

discourse events and wider processes. In doing so, he has put forward insightful resources for interrogating these relationships. For the purposes of this chapter, we concentrate on how he deals with the interaction of both ephemeral and durable features of meaning-making.

Norman Fairclough is the major articulator of the field of discourse studies known as critical discourse analysis (CDA) (Sarangi and Coulthard 2000). By making recourse to the work of Michael Halliday – another British linguist who conceived language use and social function as inseparable – he has argued against the isolation of language studies from other social sciences. The road he has trailed is in many ways comparable to that traced by Maingeneau. Arguing for the interdependence of sociocultural life and textual life, he delved into the connections between textual analysis and social analysis, with an eye on how this dialogue can bring about change (Fairclough 1992). He has also argued that textual-social-historical analysis demands transdisciplinary knowledge, a gesture that explains his diverse theoretical affinities as with Mikhail Bakhtin, Michel Foucault, Pierre Bourdieu, Basil Berstein, Ernest Laclau, Chantal Mouffe and Roy Bhaskar, to name but a few.

In Fairclough's view, CDA is a method of historical analysis. As he defined later, it takes a theoretical-methodological-analytical approach to sociohistorical conjunctures (Chouliaraki and Fairclough 1999; Fairclough 2003). Conjunctures are relatively durable assemblies of people, materials, technologies and practices involved in large-scale social projects. Such macro configurations are partly ordered by discourse actions – genres, discourses and all sorts of semiotic activity. That is to say, social life is constituted of practices seen as "habitualized ways, tied to particular times and places in which people apply resources (material or symbolic) to act together in the world" (Chouliaraki and Fairclough 1999: 21).

In spite of such an iterative facet, social life is open to change. This possibility is the very matter of Fairclough's research, which scrutinizes how discursive change is linked to wider sociocultural transformations. Mutations are seen as involving the crossing of boundaries and the innovative combination of conventions and resources. It is in this light that Fairclough recycles the conceptions of discourse, genre, intertextuality and interdiscursivity, viewing them as fluid phenomena. He approaches interdiscursivity as part of intertextuality, making a distinction between "manifest intertextuality" and "constitutive intertextuality" (Fairclough 1992: 85). The former is related to the explicit reference of texts within a text. The latter, also termed interdiscursivity, extends intertextuality to the blurring of boundaries between genres within different orders of discourse. So, instead of putting efforts into demarcating discursive perimeters, as Maingueneau did, he is spellbound by the transgression of borders, or interdiscursivity, that is, "the shifting articulations of different discourses, genres and voices in interactions and texts" (Chouliaraki and Fairclough 1999: 45). For example, he was particularly alert to the way in which discourse practices in the contemporary world have been softening and redrawing boundaries between social spaces, as public/private or advertising/education spheres. These reorganizations have spread globally and have become hegemonic – a perception that has drawn his attention to both dissemination and possibilities of recontextualization. By regarding texts, discourses and genres as unfinished products able to blend, Fairclough suggests that they may metamorphose into new intertextual and interdiscursive conjugations.

The operationalization of such perspective relies heavily on a dialectical view of discourse and social life seen as a cluster of practices that keep constant dialogue with one another. Discourse is one of such practices, linked to all the others. As something that social actors do, discourse practices get articulated within institutional and societal orders of discourse. The latter is a Foucauldian notion that Fairclough favors over discursive formation, to emphasize the idea of rearticulation potential. An order of discourse is the "socially ordered set of genres and discourses associated with a particular social field, characterized by shifting boundaries and flows between them" (Chouliaraki and Fairclough 1999: 58). The instability and openness of orders of discourse can be explained by their constitutive intertextuality.

Texts circulate in intertextual chains, congregating discourse types regulated by conventions of genre. Going back to our previous example, Obama's victory speech entered a complex chain. It was transformed into a diversity of media texts worldwide (as news pieces, editorials and internet posts). It integrated everyday and official conversations. It was replicated in reports, books, academic articles and so on. The variety of discourse types is immense. The circuit they pursue is unpredictable and so are the identities they produce. This trajectory makes all these elements susceptible to transformations, hybridity and heterogeneity. Because discourse practices involve the constant repetition-reactualization of prior texts, utterances and voices, they are inherently destabilizing intertextual phenomena. Therefore, discourses and genres have the potential to materialize in new micro-recontextualizations, which may structure a social field outright.

Nevertheless, Fairclough admonishes that such flexibility does not happen limitlessly since it is embedded in ideological formations, which need to be considered in any critical enterprise. Such a position justifies CDA's theoretical practice toward two concomitant perspectives: "the analysis of communicative events … and the analysis of their structural conditions of possibility and structural effects" (Chouliaraki and Fairclough 1999: 30). Norman Fairclough's endeavors to link micro and macro levels of analysis have contributed to the widening of research interests in the field of discourse studies, highlighting the importance of historical contexts to signify past experiences, to understand present forms of globalization and to construct alternative futures.

In the remainder of this section, we turn our attention to some scholars in the neighboring discipline of linguistic anthropology who have reworked notions of intertextuality, historical processes and text circulation. Such reworkings have, in turn, influenced numerous applied linguistic and sociolinguistic studies. Linguistic anthropologists Richard Bauman, Charles Briggs, Michael Silverstein and Asif Agha engage in heightened reflexivity regarding language and humans' general semiotic activity. Their approach tackles historicity and intertextuality through the notion of entextualization proposed by Bauman and Briggs (1990). Entextualization alludes to the trajectories that texts follow when they leave a particular contextual anchorage and get recited in other semiotic environments. In the authors' own words, "it is the process of rendering discourse extractable, of making a stretch of linguistic production into a unit – a *text* – that can be lifted out of its interactional setting" (Bauman and Briggs 1990: 73).

While keeping the dialogical character of Kristevian intertextuality, entextualization sheds light on the incessant movimentation of texts and the transformations they suffer throughout chains of entextualization-decontextualization-recontextualization. The concept helps us think about intertextuality-in-interaction. As we write this chapter, for instance, the many signs and discourses we entextualize interact with one another, interweave in new ways and produce an aggregate meaning-effect. This is interpreted by different readers who, in turn, mention it in other semiotic encounters. The chain is potentially infinite and, in each phase of the entextualization process, something new is going on: new co-texts, new interlocutors and new communicative surroundings. This processual dynamism captures what Michael Silverstein and Greg Urban have termed the "natural histories of discourse" (Silverstein and Urban 1996).

Textuality is not an inert phenomenon. Texts are always in motion and, in their circulation, they land just provisionally in specific environments. This situatedness, however, is not only local because texts contain the traces of their previous entextualizations-in-context (Silverstein 1996). The entextualization trail can be captured by ethnographic accounts attentive to interdiscursivity (i.e., precedential text occasions). So, entextualization implies that texts' history of earlier uses – or their "secret life" (Silverstein 1996: 81) – is to be considered part of their social existence. Therefore, in any instantaneous interaction, a sociohistorical repertoire is condensed in the routine and typified actions we perform (Agha 2007). According to this angle, "every macro-phenomenon is a micro-phenomenon with respect to a phenomenon at a large scale" (Agha 2007: 11). Such relationality calls the traditional macro–micro divide into question.

Macro and micro are seen as scales invoked in the apprehension and perspectivization of social phenomena, their qualities and their relations (Latour 2005; Carr and Lempert 2016). In this sense, they are projected perspectives that demand complex semiotic labor. The assumption is that what we take to be a social reality is totally enmeshed with semiosis (see Chapter 13 in this volume). What we call reality is in fact semiotized perception. For this reason, macro and micro are not absolute terms and work only when comparisons are defined contextually in the organization of demographic, spatiotemporal, numeric or hierarchical connections. For example, if a famous public figure posts a comment on the Internet, this small-scale activity may have semiotic consequences that affect many subsequent encounters, as it is entextualized in different social spaces, during extended time, becoming known to larger audiences in diverse parts of the world. This digital travel accommodates evaluation practices that may end up taking a human rights committee to make a pronouncement on the topic. It is in this regard that "a single encounter is an element of a larger process" (Agha 2007: 11). In other words, small narratives and grand narratives intersect as far as timespace parameters are concerned.

In the contemporary world, exchanges between distinct human groups, semiotic actions and discourses are much sharper than at any point in history. Our age is marked by the extreme mobility brought about by economic changes, technological advancements and migratory movements. People, languages, texts and signs circulate so fervently that conceptual borders between nations, named idioms and communities are constantly unsettled. And so are spatial and temporal references, as movement increases geographically in space and discursively in time. Multiple transits enhance diversity at the expense of stability. This kind of disturbance has complicated more and more the construction of linear and chronological narratives and, for this reason, has deeply impacted scholarly theorizations on historicity. The dislodgement of some modern tropes is the last trail we follow in our narrative.

4.4 Contemporary Chronotopes: Accelerated Timespace

Superdiversity is taken to be a distinguishing feature of twenty-first-century immigration processes, in reference to the unprecedented level of variability in migratory movements all around the world (Vertovec 2007). Migrants and their sign systems likewise have started turning up in unexpected spaces. More and more, the coexistence of different ethnicities, different languages and different habitus is part of social reality in many contemporary scenarios. In their position paper on superdiversity, Blommaert and Rampton (2011) expanded the concept by associating intensified geographical transit with the frantic digital navigation afforded by the development of internet technology. The central point they make is that translocal people and their resources have been operating a paradigm shift in the way we practice communication.

Superdiversity offers discourse analysts the opportunity to rethink their conceptual framework and epistemological stances in the light of unceasing transportability. In fact, a growing challenge that superdiverse environments pose to the area of discourse analysis nowadays is in creating instability within its objects of study: language, discourse and sign phenomena at large. Moving texts are entextualized in unimaginable corners of the world and blend in unpredictable ways (Pennycook 2012; Chapter 18 in this volume). Furthermore, the signs they aggregate hook up temporarily in particular semiotic spaces and then keep on moving, often uncontrollably, as in the case of textual virality on the web (Blommaert and Varis 2015). And each time they "disembark," however fleetingly, they affect neighboring signs, interpellate surrounding elements and contribute to the local contextualization of meaning (see Chapter 14 in this volume). Evolutionist views of history cannot account for these multidirectional transitions.

In coping with such complex timespace "moorings," different academics have been reactualizing the Bakhtinian chronotope idea, associating it with a scalar perspective. A chronotope refers to the inseparability of timespace domains operating in any social encounter. As such, it pushes linguists to view meaning as "locally enacted historically loaded semiotic effects" (Blommaert 2015: 108) that can be taken along to other semiotic events. Accordingly, signs in use always reconstruct sociohistorical repertoires in the flow of ongoing interactions (Rampton 2006). The dialogue kept between contingent and historical meanings is indexical (Silverstein 2003), in the sense that it points to whole chunks of history framing interaction and meaning activity. Consequently, besides allowing discourse analysts to produce a nexus between historical and momentary agency, indexicality enables the investigation of how social subjects embody historical schemes and patterns in their daily local performances (Blommaert 2015; Blommaert and De Fina 2017).

Ron Scollon and Suzie Scollon (2004) have insightfully penetrated into the pragmatics of the macro-microscopic nexus. In their well-known ethnographic study at the University of Alaska, they have shown how historical discourses, historical bodies and historical spaces are inextricably tied to one another in the interactional order. Their analytical focus is on social actions, their orientation to historically organized experiences, and modes of conduct. This sociohistorical repertoire is in place in every interaction, but its organizations can be reassembled along the way. In their research, the authors follow the displacement of bodies in place when university subjects transition between a panopticon form of life – learned very early in life – and a technology-mediated one.

In a traditional university, class teachers and students have normalized expectations concerning institutional space, institutional bodily conduct and institutional communication. Pupils are generally confined to the same physical space and focus their attention on an individual of greater authority who manages classroom topic and interaction. In a computer-mediated class, on the other hand, participants are dispersed on campus, develop multiple interactions and share interactional control. These different social actions bring about cycles of historical practices that are actualized in several university encounters. Establishing the connection of varied timespace frames and their friction, so to speak, is the task of nexus analysis. It seeks a more complex understanding of how historical itineraries of discourses, bodies and timespace references crisscross in unique moments of social action. This reminds us that interactional environments, bodies and actions are always tied to historical flows, messing past, present and future chronotopes.

Approaching the multilayered historical dimensions entangled in any discourse moment is a challenge that many scholars have been facing lately (Silva 2018; Moita-Lopes and Baynham 2017; Pérez-Milans 2016; Rampton and Charalambous 2010). Most of them converge on the idea that the complexity of contemporary communicational processes requires ethnographic grounded studies. Moreover, they rely on the correlation of entextualizations, chronotopes and indexical meanings to enlighten the intersection of slow historicity, developed along a diachronic line, and emergent historicity in social action (Fabricio 2015; Rymes 2012). By reworking the notions of intertextuality and interdiscursivity, they produce intelligibility about historicity-in-motion, as anticipated by the twentieth-century philosophers we have accompanied throughout this chapter.

4.5 Decentering Modern Boundaries

De Certeau (1988) contends that modernity has unceasingly defined all kinds of border, postulating homogeneous and compartmentalized unities of knowledge, science, language, nation, class, gender and sexuality. These boundary practices have set in motion the production of classifications and dychotomies that have "organized" modern life as many people know it. They have put discourses, bodies and institutions in place. They have divided time. They have narrated history according to chronologically ordered events. Together, they have woven a network of essentialisms, full of Gordian knots whose logical threads are so tight that they have endured over time, ingraining in daily social activities.

Nevertheless, solid roots may be loosened from hardened soils. The multidirectional itineraries we have pursued here, and the travel companions onboard, have helped us to envision such likelihood. Historicity, interdiscursivity and intertextuality were taken as compasses. The paths they indicated foregrounded interdisciplinarity, textual heterogeneity, power relations, hybridity and mobility. It is our view that this salience may potentially bring about multiple decenterings of the modern tenets we have mentioned previously. In a moment when we are experiencing accelerated timespace, it is reasonable to presume that many other displacements are already en route. As Pennycook (2016) ponders, mobile times demand mobile concerns. One of them is that extreme mobility, like a propeller, presses forth the rethinking of habitualized perceptions of history and rememoration processes.

The ideas of *chronos* and *kairos* (the right or opportune moment for action in Ancient Greek) are both disturbed. How will chance figure into our theories? What kind of stability will our investigations be able to invoke? What new combinations involving synchronicity and diachronicity will we put forward? How are we to deal with the ongoing implosion of timespace temporalities that digital communication engenders? What sort of links will we draw among conceptions of archives, files and cloud storage? What kind of dialogue will practices of remembering and forgetting establish? How will the increasingly fast pace of text circulation affect our social imagination? What new interdiscursive and intertextual mixtures will we fathom? What kind of chronotropic memories will social subjects articulate? Rather than a crystal-balling exercise, these questions wander about some of the tracks available to contemporary enquiries.

Further Reading

Bennett, S. (2016). New "Crises," Old Habits: Online Interdiscursivity and Intertextuality in UK Migration Policy Discourses. *Journal of Immigrant & Refugee Studies* 16(1–2): 140–60.

Focusing on Twitter communication in the context of contemporary migration crisis, this study updates the concepts of interdiscursivity and intertextuality.

Fairclough, N. (1992). Intertextuality in Critical Discourse Analysis. *Linguistics and Education* 4(3): 269–93.

This article is one of Fairclough's earliest explorations of intertextuality and interdiscursivity.

Slembrouk, S. (2011). Intertextuality. In J. Zienkowski, J.-O. Östman and J. Verschueren (eds.) *Discursive Pragmatics*, Handbook of Pragmatics Highlights, Vol. 8. Amsterdam: John Benjamins. 156–75.

This chapter is a comprehensive source of information on the development of Kristeva's concept, considering both theoretical and empirical perspectives.

Valverde, M. (2015). *Chronotopes of Law: Jurisdiction, Scale, and Governance*, London: Glasshouse/Routledge.

The purpose of this book is to explore the notions of intertextuality, dialogism and "chronotope" as tools to generate dynamic analyses in the legal context.

Wodak, R. (2001). A Discourse-Historical Approach. In R. Wodak and M. Meyer (eds.) *Methods of Critical Discourse Analysis*. London: Sage.63–94.

This article presents a discourse-historical approach and its operationalization in the context of discriminatory discourse in Austria. It singles out interdiscursivity and intertextuality as important analytical tools.

References

Agha, A. (2007). *Language and Social Relations*. Cambridge: Cambridge University Press.
Althusser, L. (ed.) (1971). *Lenin and Philosophy and Other Essays*. London: New Left Books.
  (1994). Le courant souterrain du matérialisme de la reencontre [The Current Underground of the Materialism of the Encounter], *Écrits philosophiques et politiques*, Vol. 1. Paris: Stock/IMEC. 539–79.
Bakhtin, M. ([1934]1981). *The Dialogical Imagination*, ed. by M. Holquist, trans. by C. Emerson and M. Holquist. Austin: University of Texas Press.
  (1986). *Speech Genres and Other Late Essays*, ed. by C. Emerson and M. Holquist, trans. by V. W. McGee. Austin: University of Texas Press.
  ([1975]2002). Questões de literatura e estética. A teoria do romance. [Questions of Literature and Aesthetics. The Theory of Romance], trans. by A. F. Bernardini et al. São Paulo: Hucitec / Annablume.
  ([1979]1992). Estética da criação verbal [Aesthetics of Verbal Creation], trans. by M. E. Galvão. São Paulo: Martins Fontes.
Baronas, R. L. (2004). Formação discursiva em Pêcheux e Foucault: uma estranha paternidade [Discursive Formation in Pêcheux and Foucault: A Strange Paternity]. In V. Sargentini and P. Navarro-Barbosa (eds.) *M. Foucault e os domínios da linguagem: discurso, poder e subjetividade* [M. Foucault and the Domains of Language: Discourse, Power and Subjectivity]. São Carlos: Claraluz. 45–62.
Bauman, R. and Briggs, C. (1990). Poetics and Performance as Critical Perspectives on Language and Social Life. *Annual Review of Anthropology*, 19: 59–88.
Blommaert, J. (2005). *Discourse: A Critical Introduction*. Cambridge: Cambridge University Press.
Blommaert, J. and De Fina, A. (2017). Chronotopic Identities: On the Spacetime Organization of Who We Are. *Diversity and Superdiversity: Sociocultural Linguistic Perspectives*. GURT. 1–15.
Blommaert, J. and Rampton, B. (2011). Language and Superdiversity. *Diversities* 13(2): 1–21.

Blommaert, J. and Varis, P. (2015). Conviviality and Collectives on Social Media: Virality, Memes, and New Social Structures. www.epubs.ac.za/index.php/multiling/article/view/50.

Cardoso, H. R. (2005). Acontecimento e história: pensamento de Deleuze e problemas epistemológicos das ciências humanas [Happening and History: Deleuzian Thought and Epistemological Problems in Human Sciences]. *TransForm/Ação* 28(2): 105–16.

Carr, E. S. and Lempert, M. (eds.) (2016). *Scale: Discourse and Dimensions of Social Life*. Oakland: University of California Press.

Castro, E. ([2004]2009). *Vocabulário de Foucault. Um percurso pelos seus temas, conceitos e autores* [The Vocabulary of Foucault. A Trajectory through His Themes, Concepts and Authors], trans. by I. Müller Xavier. Belo Horizonte: Autêntica.

Cazden, C. B. (2001). *Classroom Discourse: The Language of Teaching and Learning*, 2nd ed. Portsmouth: Heinemann.

Charaudeau, P. and Maingueneau, D. (2004). *Dicionário de análise do discurso* [A Dictionary of Discourse Analysis]. São Paulo: Contexto.

Chomsky, N. (1957). *Syntactic Structures*. The Hague: Mouton & Co.

(1965). *Aspects of the Theory of Syntax*. Cambridge, MA: MIT Press.

Chouliaraki, L. and Fairclough, N. (1999). *Discourse in Late Modernity: Rethinking Critical Discourse Analysis*. Edinburgh: Edinburgh University Press.

Clark, K. and Holquist, M. ([1984]1998). *Mikhail Bakhtin*. trans. by J. Guinsburg. São Paulo: Perspectiva.

Courtine, J.-J. (1981). Analyse du discours politique: le discours communiste adressé aux chrétiens [Political Discourse Analysis: The Communist Discourse Addressed to Christians]. *Langages*, 62: 9–128.

De Certeau, M. (1988). *The Writing of History*, trans. by T. Conley. New York: Columbia University Press.

Deleuze, G. (1969). *Logique du Sens*. Paris: Minuit.

(1986). *Foucault*. Paris: Minuit.

Deleuze, G. and Guattari, F. ([1972]1983). *Anti-Oedipus: Capitalism and Schizophrenia*, trans. by R. Hurley et al. Minneapolis: University of Minnesota Press.

([1980]1995a). *Mil Platôs* [A Thousand Plateaux], Vol. 1, trans. by A. L. de Oliveira and L. C. Leão. São Paulo: Editora 34.

([1980]1995b). *Mil Platôs* [A Thousand Plateaux], Vol. 2, trans. by A. L. de Oliveira and L. C. Leão São Paulo: Editora 34.

Derrida, J. ([1967]2008). *Gramatologia* [Of Grammatology], trans. by M. Chnaiderman and R. J. Ribeiro. São Paulo: Perspectiva.

Eisendrath, P.-Y. and Muramoto, S. (eds.) (2002). *Awakening and Insight: Zen Buddhism and Psychotherapy*. London/New York: Routledge.

Fabricio, B. F. (2015). Policing the Borderland in a Digital Lusophone Territory: The Pragmatics of Entextualization. In L. P. Moita-Lopes (ed.) *Global Portuguese: Linguistic Ideologies in Late Modernity*. London: Routledge. 66–86.

Fairclough, N. (1992). *Discourse and Social Change*. Cambridge: Polity Press.
  (2003). *Analysing Discourse: Textual Analysis for Social Research*. London: Routledge.
Foucault, M. ([1969]1972). *The Archeology of Knowledge*. New York: Pantheon Books.
  ([1969]1986). *Les mots et les choses*. Paris: Gallimard.
  ([1972]1984). The Order of Discourse. In M. Shapiro (ed.) *Language and Politics*. Oxford: Basil Blackwell. 108–38.
  (1979). Verdade e poder [Truth and Power] (interview with Alexandre Fontana). In *Microfísica do Poder* [Microphysics of Power], trans. by R. Machado. Rio de Janeiro: Edições Graal. 1–14.
  (1982). The Subject & Power. In H. Dreyfus and P. Rabinow (eds.) *Michel Foucault: Beyond Structuralism & Hermeneutics*. New York: Harvester Wheatsheaf. 208–26.
  (1994). *Dits et ècrits IV*. Paris: Gallimard.
Kristeva, J. (1986). Word, Dialogue and Novel. In T. Moi (ed.) *The Kristeva Reader*. Oxford: Basil Blackwell. 24–33.
Lemke, J. L. (1995). *Textual Politics: Discourse and Social Dynamics*. London: Taylor & Francis.
Latour, B. (2005). *Reassembling the Social: An Introduction to Actor-Network Theory*. Oxford: Oxford University Press.
Maingueneau, D. (1984). *Genèses du discours*. Bruxelles: Mardaga.
  (1993). Analyse du discours et archive [Discourse Analysis and Archive]. *Semen*. http://journals.openedition.org/semen/4069.
  (1995). Présentation. *Langages* 29ᵉ année, n°117. Les analyses du discours en France [Discourse Analysis in France]: 5–11. www.persee.fr/doc/lgge_0458-726x_1995_num_29_117_1702.
  (1996). Les livres d'école de la République, Paris. *Linguistik* 26: 114–33. https://doi.org/10.1007/BF03396107.
  (1999). Analysing Self-Constituting Discourses. *Discourse Studies* 1(2): 175–200.
  (2009). Entrevista com Maingueneau [Interview with Maingueneau], *Revista Linguagem*. Universidade Federal de São Carlos. www.letras.ufscar.br/linguasagem/edicao10/entrevista_maingueneau.php.
Moita-Lopes, L. P. and Baynham, M. (eds.) (2017). Meaning Making in the Periphery. *AILA Review* 30.
Pêcheux, M. (1975). *Les vérités de La Palice. Linguistique, sémantique, philosophie (Théorie)*. [The Truths of La Palice. Linguistics, Semantics and Philosophy (Theory)]. Paris: Maspero.
  (1982). *Language, Semantics and Ideology*. London: Macmillan.
Pennycook, A. (2012). *Language and Mobility: Unexpected Places*. Bristol: Multilingual Matters.
  (2016). Mobile Times, Mobile Terms: The Trans-super-poly-metro Movement. In N. Coupland (ed.) *Sociolinguistic Theoretical Debates*. Cambridge: Cambridge University Press. 201–16.

Pérez-Milans, M. (ed.) (2016). Reflexivity in Late Modernity. Accounts from Linguistic Ethnographies of Youth. *AILA Review* 29.

Rampton, B. (2006). *Language in Late Modernity: Interaction in an Urban School*, Cambridge: Cambridge University Press.

Rampton, B. and Charalambous, C. (2010). Crossing: A Review of Research. *Working Papers in Urban Language &; Literacies*. Paper 59. King's College London.

Read, J. (2003). A Universal History of Contingency: Deleuze and Guattari on the History of Capitalism. *Borderlands e-journal* 2(3). www.borderlands.net.au/vol2no3_2003/read_contingency.htm.

Rymes, B. (2012). Recontextualizing YouTube: From Macro-micro to Mass-Mediated Communicative Repertoires. *Anthropology & Education Quarterly* 43(2): 214–27.

Saussure, F. de ([1916]1959). *Course in General Linguistics*, trans. by W. Baskin. New York: McGraw-Hill Book Company.

Sarangi, S. and Coulthard, M. (2000). *Discourse and Social Life*. London: Longman.

Scollon, R. and Scollon, S. W. (2004). *Nexus Analysis: Discourse and the Emerging Internet*. London: Routledge.

Silva, D. N. (ed.) (2018). *Language and Violence: Pragmatic Perspectives*. Amsterdam: John Benjamins.

Silverstein, M. (1996). The Secret Life of Texts. In M. Silverstein and G. Urban (eds.) *Natural Histories of Discourse*. Chicago, IL: University of Chicago Press. 81–105.

Silverstein, M. and Urban, G. (eds.) (1996). *Natural Histories of Discourse*. Chicago, IL: University of Chicago Press.

Vertovec, S. (2007). Super-diversity and Its Implications. *Ethnic and Racial Studies* 30(6): 1024–54.

Volochinov, V. N. ([1929]1981). Marxismo e filosofia da linguagem [Marxism and Philosophy of Language], trans. by M. Lahud and Y. F. Vieira. São Paulo: Hucitec.

Wolfreys, J. ([2007] 2012). Compreender Derrida [Derrida: A Guide for the Perplexed], trans. by C. Souza. Petrópois: Editora Vozes.

Acknowledgments

We are both grateful to the Brazilian National Research Council (CNPq) for the research grants (311578/2016–0 and 302935/2017–7) which make the research reported on in this chapter possible.

5

Rethinking Narrative: Tellers, Tales and Identities in Contemporary Worlds

Anna De Fina and Alexandra Georgakopoulou

5.1 Introduction

The landscape of narrative analysis within discourse analysis and sociolinguistics has changed radically since the turn of the millennium. This has involved rethinking the mainstay ways of defining, exploring and studying stories and in turn their main ingredients: in particular, the role of the teller, story-ownership and of the personal story, a highly valued genre in conventional narrative analysis; the role of time and space/place; and, finally, the role and place of stories themselves in the contemporary world. The focus on the teller as a sole entity, in control and possession of their story, has given way to contextual approaches that view stories as co-constructed and negotiable accounts. In similar vein, the tellers' identities have been increasingly viewed as intricately connected with local purposes and practices of which a storytelling event becomes an integral part, and with participation roles pertinent to them.

This rethinking of narrative has been partly the result of the increasing resonance of contextual, practice-based approaches to language and discourse and partly the result of the rapprochement between text-centered and identity-centered perspectives on narrative. The former originate in narratology, textlinguistics and structuralist methods (e.g. Labov's 1972 model of narrative structure), while the latter have been employed in social scientific research on narrative through research interviews. At the same time, the rethinking of narrative has been necessitated and precipitated by major sociocultural changes, for example the advent of social media communication.

In the light of this, instead of providing an overview of the study of narrative within discourse studies that traces its foundations, our focus in this chapter is on teasing out the key-aspects of rethinking narrative in ways which allow the analyst to address the prime challenges of studying (any) discourse and communication in the twenty-first century. In Section 5.2, we focus on rethinking the teller by discussing the shift to interactional approaches to identities, including small stories research. In Section 5.3, we focus on rethinking the personal story with a focus on political identities. Section 5.4 is devoted to rethinking the role of time and space in relation to identities, while Section 5.5 centers on mobility (5.5.1) and digital environments (5.5.2) as part of rethinking the role of stories and identities in a globalized world.

5.2 Rethinking the Teller

5.2.1 The Shift to Stories and Identities-in-Interaction

The shift to interactional approaches to identities or, as often called, *identities-in-interaction* within discourse studies, sociolinguistics and interactional pragmatics has had a big influence on discourse approaches to narrative. Interactional approaches stress the multiplicity, fragmentation, context-specificity and performativity of communication practices (see De Fina and Georgakopoulou 2012: ch. 6). At the level of analysis, a key commonality in identities-in-interaction research in different strands of discourse analysis is that they draw upon conversation analysis for insights, tools and modes of investigation (see also Chapter 6 in this volume). One of the premises of this type of analysis is that "the events of conversation have a sense and import to participants which are at least partially displayed in each successive contribution, and which are thereby put to some degree under interactional control" (Schegloff 1997: 165). Speakers' actions are therefore contextual and need to be investigated as such. The notion of context is closely associated with that of co-text. Interactions and, in turn, stories are viewed as context/co-text-shaped. Any contribution to an ongoing sequence of events cannot be understood but by reference to the co-text, the immediate configuration of actions, in which it participates. At the same time, stories are also context-shaping: "every contribution shapes a new context for the action that will follow" (Heritage 1984: 242).

The implications of an interactional approach to the study of identities are summarized aptly by Antaki and Widdicombe (1998: 3). For a person to "have an identity" is to be cast into a category with *associated characteristics or features*. Such casting is *indexical and occasioned*: it makes sense only in its local setting and it may point more or less indirectly to an aspect of it. The casting thus *makes relevant* the identity to the interactional business going on and is consequential for it. All the above is visible in people's exploitation of the *structures of conversation* (Antaki and Widdicombe 1998: 3).

Locating identities-in-interaction requires of the analyst to attend to participant perspectives, to the "characterizations that are privileged in the constitution of socio-interactional reality ..., to the endogenous orientations of the participants . . ., what constitutes the relevant context" (Schegloff 1997: 167). From this point of view, identities are an outcome and a result of the analysis rather than a presupposition of it (Schegloff 1997: 170). Identities-in-interaction approaches thus caution the analyst against coding forms and strategies a priori of concrete analyses and according to preconceived theoretical categories.

The analytical priorities of an interactional approach to identities involve finding where, how and why an identity categorization occurs and how it relates to its co-text; similarly, what systematicity (i.e., location, design, responses) it presents and what (other) categorizations, attributions and/or activities it is linked to. Identities are viewed and analyzed as emergent and jointly drafted by participants (e.g. accepted, upheld, contested, negotiated, etc.) in actual interactions. This problematizes the conventional association of identities in much autobiographical research with individual properties of self.

In the light of this, what stories reveal about their tellers' identities is examined with a close eye to their connections with the local environments in which they occur and the social actions that they perform in them. Emphasis on the local context implicates a focus on identities as partly temporary and contingent, situation-bound participation roles (cf. discourse identities, Zimmerman 1998). It is in the interconnections of such roles with the situation in which they occur that the participants' larger, *transportable identities* are brought about. In her study of the conversational stories of a group of female adolescent best-friends, Georgakopoulou (2006) showed how the participants' discourse identities varied systematically in relation to different story components, particularly the plotline and evaluation. This had implications for how they constructed ownership and expertise in the story's reported experiences and for how they presented their feminine identities.

Recognizing and identifying the importance of discourse identities in stories safeguards against treating them as categorical and demographically attestable identities (e.g. gender, age, ethnicity) which can be postulated in advance of the analysis and their significance for the analysis can be presupposed. This has been commonly the case in research interviews aimed at eliciting narratives as well as in earlier discourse analytic studies of storytelling (for details, see De Fina and Georgakopoulou 2012: 151–3). In contrast, within identities-in-interaction, the tellers' identities are sought in their display of, or ascription to, membership of some social category, in the course of the storytelling, with consequences for the interaction in which the display or ascription takes place.

The interest in stories as a significant communication genre for how tellers present themselves as people with a biographically irreducible history and memory has been at the heart of narrative studies. From this point of view, the singular focus of much of identities-in-interaction research in local interactions has been viewed as too restrictive for the project of exploring any durability and stability of identities beyond the here-and-now of interactions and beyond the single speech event. A first point of critique of conversation-analytic approaches to identities involves the difficulty they have in capturing identities that are not "oriented to" by the participants, actively influencing the way that people try to shape both their own actions and the subsequent actions of others. As Zimmerman (1998) shows, the importance of "apprehended" identities, tacitly noticed but not treated as immediately relevant to the interaction on hand, should not be underestimated. To tap into such apprehended identities, many analysts have claimed that it is necessary to go beyond the single event, so as to explore the ways in which multiple and potentially inconsistent subject positions remain available and are carried forward from one context to another (Georgakopoulou 2013; Wortham and Reyes 2015). A related position is that identities are not created from scratch in interactions but are partly predetermined by discourses and can be predicted and inferred by participants from knowledge of the relevant discourse. In Potter and Wetherell's terms, it is important in this respect for the analyst to uncover the participants' interpretative repertoires (1988), which comprise a back-cloth for the realization of locally managed positions in actual interaction. Intepretative repertoires consist of culturally familiar and habitual lines of argument made up of recognizable themes and commonsensical ways of interpreting reality.

Narrative and identities-in-interaction approaches increasingly synthesize insights from conversation analysis, interactional sociolinguistics and linguistic anthropology with a view to producing multilayered approaches (for details, see De Fina and Georgakopoulou 2012: ch. 6). A concept that has been deployed by numerous studies for providing links between linguistic and sequential choices in local context and larger, extra-situational identities as well as nuanced descriptions of context is that of *positioning*. Indexicality, timescales (Wortham and Reyes 2015), stance (Jaffe 2009) and chronotopes, amongst others, are affiliated concepts for investigating discourse-in-context. These concepts, often deployed within ethnographic work on discourse, are useful for exploring the creation of links between semiotic choices and social meanings that may be implicit, indirect and associative (cf. Ochs 1992). Although broadly affiliated with them, positioning affords analysts specific tools for investigating the interanimation of the here-and-now telling worlds with the narrated taleworlds uniquely involved in stories (Schiffrin 1996; Deppermann 2013; Georgakopoulou 2007). In this way, positioning captures representation, action and performance, as well as a biographical, at times temporally structured, individual dimension to identities. The stories' plots, the types of evens and experience that they narrate and the ways in which they are interactionally managed during the telling are all important in this respect. So are the intertextual links of the current story with other, previous and anticipated, stories. Positioning has a long history in discourse studies (see

Deppermann 2013), originating in Foucault's work, but in narrative and identities-in-interaction analysis, it has been specifically associated with the study of three levels (see Section 5.2.2), as postulated by Bamberg (1997) and, later, operationalized by small stories research.

5.2.2 Small Stories Research and Positioning-in-Interaction

The rationale for developing small stories research was that, unless narrative studies rethink and even dispense with some of their traditional tenets, they cannot engage productively with interactional approaches to identities (Georgakopoulou 2006, 2007; Bamberg 2006). A key limitation in that respect was that a range of narrative activities, commonly occurring in everyday conversational contexts, had not been sufficiently studied nor had their importance for the interlocutors' identity-work been recognized. These involved stories with fragmentation and open-endedness of tellings, exceeding the confines of a single speech event and resisting a neat categorization of beginning-middle-end. They were heavily co-constructed, rendering the sole teller's story-ownership problematic. Small stories served as an umbrella term for "tellings of ongoing events, future or hypothetical events, shared (known) events, but also allusions to tellings, deferrals of tellings, and refusals to tell" (Georgakopoulou 2006: 130).

In this way, small stories research was put forth as a countermove to dominant models of narrative studies that defined narrative restrictively and on the basis of textual criteria and that privileged long, relatively uninterrupted, teller-led accounts of past events or of one's life-story, typically elicited in research interviews and often described as "big" stories. It also placed emphasis on the communicative how of stories and its links with tellers' identities as opposed to a focus on the "biographical content" and the "whats" of stories (Phoenix and Sparkes 2009: 222–3). In this sense, the term small stories served as a metaphor for neglected, disenfranchised communication activities in the minutiae of ordinary life. Many of the small stories in face-to-face conversations are indeed small in length, but length is not the key factor in the descriptor of "small." Instead, smallness encapsulates the fleetingness of stories in interactional moments, their embeddedness into local contexts and the analyst's attentiveness to the emergence of plots in the microcosm of everyday life experience.

For its methods of analysis, small stories research has drawn on a synthesis of frameworks from diverse disciplinary traditions, including discourse analysis, (interactional) sociolinguistics, linguistic anthropology and biographical studies. Since its inception, empirical work has added nuance to the general descriptor of small stories, bringing to the fore specific genres of small stories that occur in specific contexts and that ought to be included in the narrative analytic lens. This work has uncovered different types of social organization and relation that warrant or prohibit small stories, from friendship groups to social media platforms, deliberation focus-groups and professional organizations (Juzwik and Ives 2010; Sprain and Hughes 2015; Watson 2007). It has also shown conventional associations between specific types of small stories (ways of telling), social worlds in the tales and tellings (sites) and tellers' discourse, situated (situational) identities as well as larger, extra-situational identities (Georgakopoulou 2007). For example, Georgakopoulou has shown that small stories of *breaking news* on social media, in particular on Facebook statuses, position the teller as somebody who has a story to tell, if there is sufficient interest. Such statuses raise for their Friends the task of showing interest, so that a fuller telling and an update can follow in a subsequent posting (2017).

The identification and the analysis of small stories have been combined with interactional approaches to positioning. Since small stories are "embedded in conversational interaction and occasioned by situated discursive concerns, such as justifying actions, blaming, advice-seeking and -giving, etc., interactional positioning becomes a prime motivation for storytelling and, consequently, for storytellers' self- and other-positioning by the story" (Deppermann 2013: 6). Such research has shown that interactional negotiation, emergence and action-oriented design are pervasive features of positioning in narrative interaction (Bamberg and Georgakopoulou 2008; Georgakopoulou 2013). The three levels put forward by Bamberg and operationalized as a five-step work-up of stories in Bamberg and Georgakopoulou (2008) frequently serve as heuristics for positioning analysis. *Level 1* focuses on how characters are presented in the taleworld, their relations, evaluative attributions, activities and overall placement in time and place. *Level 2* attends to how positioning in small stories can reveal how identity is constructed within interaction. The focus here is on how a story is locally occasioned and distributed; who participates by co-authoring, ratifying, legitimating or contesting which part of the story and how? Finally, *Level 3* emerges from the interaction of Levels 1 and 2 and concerns "how the speaker/narrator positions a sense of self/identity with regards to dominant discourses or master narratives," by which the teller "establishes himself as a particular kind of person" (Bamberg and Georgakopoulou 2008: 391). It involves the aspects of the character(s), events and narrated experience that are presented as generalizable and holding above and beyond the specific story.

There has been a productive debate in the literature on how these three levels of positioning can be extended or further systematized so as to advance our understanding of how "transportable" identities can be attested to in stories. Ethnographic understandings and tracking of iterative choices have been proposed as ways for tapping into operative discourses in stories and into how participants both invoke and are prepositioned by them (De Fina 2013; Georgakopoulou 2013).

Small stories and positioning analysis has been employed in a variety of perspectives on narrative: for example narrative psychology relating to sports, organizational sociology, wellbeing and aging studies, narrative inquiry perspectives on (second) language education (e.g. Norton and Early 2011; Phoenix and Sparkes 2009; Vasquez 2011). Despite differences in the analytical modes employed in these applications, one common thread is the aim to challenge dominant idioms about the self and the lifestory that are supported by (interview) narrative research. In this respect, small stories research has been taken up as a critical framework for identities analysis. This involves interrogating essentialist links between stories and identities, thus bringing to the fore silenced, untold and devalued stories in numerous institutional or research-regulated contexts (e.g. interviews). Small stories then frequently emerge as the *counterstories* that are not encouraged or allowed in specific environments, that do not fit expectations of who the tellers should be or of dominant discourses (e.g. Bock 2018), and through which tellers introduce contradictions, dilemmas and tensions (Ostendorp and Jones 2015). Similarly, small stories have been associated with cases of tellers presenting emergent and hybrid identities for themselves, often as part of life transitions: for example gendered identities in adolescents (Spreckels 2008), ethnicity identities in mobile populations and intercultural encounters (e.g. Lee 2013), etc. Small stories have also offered tools for facilitating projections onto the future (Sools 2012) and for biographical research on neurodivergent individuals who may find it difficult to produce a coherent account of their selves over time (e.g. Lenchuk and Swain 2010).

5.3 Rethinking the Personal Story: Political Identities through Narratives

The notion that narratives are not simply tools for the unmediated expression of identities has been one of the central tenets of the critique leveled by discourse analysts and sociolinguists against biographical approaches to narratives by narrative turn analysts such as Bruner (1990), McAdams (1988) and McIntyre (1984) (see De Fina and Georgakopoulou 2012: ch. 6 and De Fina 2015 on this point). As demonstrated in this chapter, much research has been devoted to showing how identities, far from simply reflecting people's inner selves, are constructed, negotiated and contested within specific semiotic practices. However, it is in the area of the political and public sphere that the complexity of the relations between narrative and identities becomes more evident. We use the elusive term "political" (see Freeden 2008) here to designate the realm of public struggles and discourses about social issues (for details, see De Fina 2018a: 235–6). Narratives are used by politicians and members of diverse social and political movements to construct and contest identities that are crafted for public consumption and that may, or may not, be related to the narrators' personal experiences. At the same time, discourses about social issues may build on personal biographies to enhance their argumentative power, since stories are widely seen as a much more effective persuasion and communication tool than arguments or explanations (Polletta et al. 2011: 110). Much discourse analytic work on the intersections between narrative, identity and politics has focused on the use of master narratives or grand stories about the past, tradition and history in the construction of public, national identities (see, for example, Wodak et al. 2009) or on the use, by politicians, of the personal story or the anecdote in order to convey different types of persona (see Souto Manning 2014; Schubert 2010). The informalization of the public sphere (Goetsch 1991) and the explosion of the public discussion and performance through the use of social media as a political platform have thrown new light on the complexities of the relationships between (master) stories and identities. An aspect of this complexity is related to story-ownership. Recent work on narratives told on social media by members of minority groups, be they undocumented youth (De Fina 2018b) or members of LGBTQ communities (Jones 2015), reflects on the strategies and mechanisms through which personal stories told in different formats (e.g. video posts) and in different social media platforms contribute to the building up of collective images aimed at eliciting empathy and recruiting supporters. These analyses focus on the public storytelling practices that these groups enact, thus showing how personal narratives are collectivized through the use of shared scripts, common themes, signaled, for example, by hashtags or slogans, multimodal resources (e.g. type of visuals), displays of emotions and so forth. These storytelling practices highlight the ambiguous relation between telling a story about the self and owning the experience: tellers appear to be clearly invested in their tellings and show a great deal of involvement with their stories while, at the same time, their narratives are appropriated and embedded into storytelling practices controlled by others and constrained by the affordances of the media in which they are published. Such complexity has been captured in the work of Amy Shuman (2005) on the use of personal stories by entities such as charities and organizations supporting social justice causes. As Shuman notes: "Storytelling is pushed to its limits both by the use of a particular story beyond the context of the experience it represents and by the use of a personal story to represent a collective experience .... We ask, who has the right to tell a story, who is entitled to it?" (2005: 3).

The dilemmas that story-ownership and storytelling rights pose in regard to identity raise questions about how identities are related to personal stories in many domains involving different agents, including, for example, fragile groups such as refugees and asylum seekers whose self-presentations are affected by the politics of suspicion (see Spotti 2018: 69) and whose narratives in both institutional and research contexts are profoundly influenced by the contexts in which they are told (see Chapter 25 in this volume).

5.4 Rethinking the Role of Time and Space

5.4.1 Narrative, Identities and Space

The last two decades have seen a growing interest in the relationships between narratives, identities and space. Some important antecedents to this shift come from work conducted in the early 2000s on the role of place as constitutive of narrative identities rather than simply as informational, backgrounded resources, as proposed by Labov (1972). This work has also contested the almost exclusive attention devoted by narrative scholars to time, as the main structuring element for narrative. This critique (e.g. Baynham 2003; De Fina 2003; Georgakopoulou 2003; Baynham and De Fina 2005) has pointed to, among others, Harvey's (1989) and de Certeau's (1988) ideas about space as defined by and defining of human action, history, experience and interaction, to argue that tellers' identities negotiated in interaction emerge within and through the use of particular types of space and movement in the construction of storyworlds. Focusing on narratives told by migrants, they have shown, for example, that different forms of agency are connected by narrators to different spaces and that certain spaces index particular identities.

Recent investigation of migrants and diasporic populations has also brought to bear the need to shed preconceived categories about their communities' identities, thus recognizing the complexities of people's (dis)affiliations with particular places and the multiplicity of connections that they establish through transnational ties. Work on mobility has also highlighted the role of liminality as a notion that captures ways in which people position themselves within an ambiguous place that does not belong to the center or to the periphery (Scully 2019). In an analysis of narratives told by Zanzibaris who live in different countries, Piazza (2019) notes, for example, how simplistic notions of diaspora as people who are uprooted from their place of origin and who always feel a sense of nostalgic ethnic affiliation to their country are. The analysis shows instead complex positionings through which narrators often place themselves in a liminal space in between different countries and experiences. Work on narrative, space and identity has also focused on the ways in which stories are built around particular physical spaces in order to project certain kinds of identities (Jensen 2007). Research on linguistic landscapes has been particularly important in this connection, since it has shown how narrators recruit a host of semiotic resources to build certain identities through stories. It has also pointed to the complexity of production formats in narratives that are exposed in public places such as museums and neighborhoods (see also Lou 2010 and Chapter 14 in this volume).

5.4.2 Stories in Time and Space: Chronotopes

The growing interest in the role of space in narrative has gone hand in hand with the recent turn in discourse studies toward a refined and improved understanding of the role and constitution of contexts by going beyond the classical opposition between micro and macro and exploring not only different scales but also different ways in which contexts are conformed and interconnected. In narrative studies, this trend has translated into a renewed engagement with the notion of chronotope, which has been productive for the study of identities as well. The concept of chronotope was introduced by Bakhtin ([1981] 1990) who employed it in the study of the novel. According to Bakhtin's definition: "In the literary artistic chronotope, spatial and temporal indicators are fused into one carefully thought-out, concrete whole" ([1981] 1990: 84).

Bakhtin thought of chronotopes as specific timespace configurations in the novel, such as the road, the castle, the salon, the public square, which constituted recognizable units where people met and things happened in a certain way within certain time frames. The notion has, however, been extended to include identities in the nexus of time and space. Agha, for example, argued that "entextualized projections of time cannot be isolated from those of locale and personhood" and therefore that chronotopes are "sketches of personhood in time and space" (2007: 320) that emerge within participation frameworks. In similar vein, Blommaert and De Fina (2017) proposed that "it is possible to see and describe much of what is observed as contemporary identity work as being chronotopically organized" (2017: 1). Indeed, considerations of the suitability of actions and identity displays are closely related to the recognizability of these time/place/person connections within specific frames through habitus and repetition. According to Blommaert (2018), these frames act as scripts that include not only participation frameworks but also participant roles. In terms of narratives and identities, chronotopes have been investigated in the following two areas: (1) research on ways in which people use timespace configurations to negotiate stances and identities in the here-and-now at an interactional level when telling stories and (2) studies on the evoking and recontextualizion of particular chronotopes, including traditional literary ones, as encompassing frames for the identity construction of groups.

Work in the first area has investigated cross-chronotope effects, that is, how the blurring of timespace configurations related to different chronotopes serves the objective of negotiating and redefining identities. In an early application of the Bakhtinian notion to everyday storytelling, Perrino (2007) studied "cross chronotopic" discursive work in a Senegalese man's oral narrative about medical practice in his country. She noted how the narrator used the historical present to blur the distinction between the chronotope of the storyworld and the chronotope of the storytelling world. By eliminating the historical distance between the events depicted and the ones unfolding, the narrator drew the addressee into his narrated world by transforming her into a character.

A second area of study has focused on the analysis of how larger-scale chronotopes are used as spatiotemporal frames in which identities are inscribed and evaluated. This work has examined, for example, the opposition between chronotopes of modernity and tradition and ways in which storytellers and audiences depict and interpret these chronotopes. Merino and De Fina (2019) showed that when Mapuche Indians use brief narrative references to their life as children and other kinds of stories, they do it to reclaim their belonging to a "chronotope of the south" and to reject their attachment to a chronotope of modern life embodied in their city neighborhood. Oppositions between chronotopes of modernity and those of backwardness can be more complex and polycentric, as demonstrated by Koven and Simões Marquez (2015) in their analysis of online reactions to a video narrative depicting a comedic character of Portuguese descent. The authors illustrate how performers and commenters of the video orient to and construct different subsets of oppositions characterizing the modernity and nonmodernity chronotopes based on a stereotypical embodiment of nonmodernity through a variety of semiotic means including accent, use of colloquialisms, clothing and bodily demeanor.

Discourse analysts have also looked at the recontextualization of well-known literary chronotopes into the present as a process generating new identity-related meanings. This is the case of the chronotope of Ulysses (De Fina, Paternostro and Amoruso 2020), the heroic protagonist of *The Odyssey*, which is appropriated by minor asylum seekers in Italy and recontextualized into their present reality in the recounting of their experiences. The historical figure of Ulysses is used to symbolize these youths' new identities as adventurous travelers rather than as poor migrants, through storytelling practices that include oral narratives, the use of drawings and the writing of brief recollections on strips of paper.

To summarize, work on chronotopes in narratives has investigated both the ways in which identities are inscribed and negotiated into time/space frames and the kinds of contrasts that the latter may index. This work can be placed within the shift to narratives as practices in the study of identity, characterized by attention to the local emergence of meanings, participation frameworks and the multimodal resources that are deployed to convey chronotopic identities. At the same time, research in this area also demonstrates a growing interest in the role of history in the constitution and interpretation of contexts, particularly through applications of the notion of scale to the analysis of how chronotopes are circulated and interpreted.

5.5 Rethinking Stories and Identities in a Globalized World

5.5.1 Mobility

Mobility has been at the center of much sociolinguistic inquiry in recent years due to the growing realization that globalization and the technological revolution brought about by it have disrupted and problematized the stability of the links that connect communities and individuals to specific places. Scholars of globalization and modernity such as Appadurai (1996), Castells (2000) and Hannerz (1996) have pointed to mobility as one of the central features of life in late-modern societies. Mobility is associated with the unprecedented flows of people, goods, cultural products and technologies that are typical of our age. Indeed, although most scholars agree that commercial exchanges and migrations are not new phenomena, the intensity and scale of mobilities in the twenty-first century have not been experienced before. Human displacement is much easier than in the past for many categories of people such as businessmen and -women, tourists and members of international organizations. For others, such as refugees and migrants, growing dislocation and uprooting are the consequence of social economic conflicts generated by the increasing centralization of wealth and economic power, the redrawing of borders and the insurgence of wars in different parts of the globe. But there is a new kind of mobility, too, the "virtual" one afforded by the media and new technologies.

The burgeoning interest in issues of mobility within the social sciences, according to Salazar, allows us to talk about a "mobility turn" (2018: 155). Salazar also argues that the meanings and implications of mobility are not uncontested, since there are many who warn against a neoliberal view that uncritically associates mobility with freedom and socially upward movement. In this section, we assess to what extent this shift in focus has happened in narrative studies and how it has influenced approaches and theorizations about identity.

A definite consequence of the surge in interest in mobility has been the greater focus on the interplay among identity, time and space in narrative, as discussed in Sections 5.2–5.4. The areas in which these interconnections have been highlighted are:

1. the study of identities among mobile populations, particularly migrants and asylum seekers but also travelers and displaced people in both institutional and noninstitutional contexts and in virtual and transnational networks;
2. work on relationships between place and identities or on place identities themselves as expressed in narratives; and
3. investigation into the construction of identities within chronotopes and chronotopic relations (see Section 5.4.2).

Much research in the above strands has started to look at mobile individuals' and groups' narratives with an eye to the ways in which narrators tie different places with a variety of identities in their narratives as well as how their identity constructions are entangled within transnational ties of all kinds. The remit has thus expanded from the more traditional investigation of narratives told by migrants that characterized work between the 1990s and the first decade of the 2000s toward a consideration of new groups. Narrative analysts have looked, for example, at the construction of identities amongst different mobile individuals such as travelers (Convery and O'Brien 2012, Piazza 2015), lifestyle migrants (Lawson 2017), peoples displaced within the borders of the same country (Gómez-Estern 2013) and tourists (Avni 2013). These studies have concentrated on the use by narrators of linguistic strategies and components such as pronominal forms, codeswitching, agentive and nonagentive constructions, constructed dialogue and so forth, as projecting and indexing different levels of positioning, and on emotions as structuring elements that indicate affiliation or disaffiliation with in-groups, mostly in interview or focus-group situations.

Another line of inquiry has contributed to diversifying the contexts in which storytelling takes place. Thus, recent research has focused on identity construction and negotiation among digital communities, both diasporic and transnational. Scholars have pointed to the role of digital media in providing new spaces for the negotiation and contestation of identities through narrative genres in different online environments, for example blogs (Kresova and Mouravi 2016), forum discussions (Galasinska and Horolets 2012), instant messaging (Yi 2009) and Facebook groups (Baran 2018).

The stress on mobility which has impacted methodological choices in many areas of discourse analysis has also had its effect on methods in narrative studies. In this respect, the research conducted by Sabaté Dalmau with Ghanaian migrants in Spain is illustrative. Sabaté Dalmau (2018) employed a moving ethnography by soliciting her informants to talk to her through "walk alongs" in which she literally moved with her informants. This technique produced a novel understanding of how migrants relate to particular places, build categories of belonging in relation to those places and make sense of the social order.

Recent years have also seen an increasing interest in the role of storytelling for mobile people within institutional contexts. Work on asylum seekers and asylum-seeking narratives has a particularly central role in this area. Scholars have been interested in the relationship between narratives and identities in this context for some time because narratives elicited in asylum-seeking interviews are centrally about establishing the "true" identity of the narrators while, at the same time, they are conducted in an environment in which migrants and refugees have very few options in terms of the identities that they can claim (see Blommaert 2001; Maryns 2006; Jacquemet 2005; Chapter 25 in this volume). Recently, scholars have also considered the impact of mobility on asylum-seeking procedures by examining the role of what the anthropologist Marco Jacquemet has called "transidiomatic practices": these are "communicative practices of groups of people, no longer territorially defined, that communicate using an array of both face-to-face and long-distance media and in so doing produce and reproduce the social hierarchies and power asymmetries we came to associate with postcolonial, late industrial class relations" (2009: 527). Such work closely examines the effect of transidiomatic practices and environments on the ways in which stories told by asylum seekers are entextualized by immigration authorities into official records focusing on the distortions that derive from cultural frames that are applied to depositions obtained from migrants and the elimination of ambiguities and polyvocality from the narrative record written by migration officers. This research exemplifies the role that new language practices play in the way narratives are produced and received in institutional environments and the effects of this process on some groups of mobile people in terms of receiving or not a just treatment and access to their rights.

5.5.2 Social Media Environments

Research on interactional approaches to stories and identities (see Section 5.2.1) has undoubtedly paid more attention to (para)linguistic and sequential choices in the telling of stories as cues of identities. Less emphasis has been placed on embodied and multisemiotic resources. This bias has begun to be redressed with studies that have shown how the body can function both as a constitutive topic in stories and as an interactional resource that structures the telling of stories (for an overview see Heavey 2015; see also Chapter 15 in this volume). But what has mainly challenged the logocentric idiom of narrative and identities studies is the proliferation of multisemiotic stories on social media. Georgakopoulou (2013) has, to this effect, argued that small stories research prefigured the current situation, when social media affordances have made small stories, as described in Section 5.2.2 above, much more widely available and visible in public arenas of communication. A focus on how small stories on social media remediate other forms and practices of storytelling is combined with a focus on the implications of their pervasiveness for the ways in which we present ourselves and our lives. Identities to this effect are explored on the intersection among media affordances, algorithms and stories. The role of platforms as ideologically laden, designed, sociotechnical spaces (e.g. Beer 2009; Kitchin and Dodge 2011) in the stories we share online and how we share them is increasingly becoming an integral part of the analysis.

A starting point in this exploration, in Georgakopoulou's work, has been the built-in logic and economy of breaking news in many social networking sites. This is linked with the algorithmically shaped preference for recency and timeliness of posts. Georgakopoulou's contention has been that this logic encourages the sharing of everyday life as stories, *sharing-life-in-the moment* (www.ego-media.org). Her analysis of Facebook statuses and selfies posted by female adolescents as well as the circulation of political events on YouTube having to do with the Eurozone (2015, 2016a, 2016b, 2017; Georgakopoulou and Giaxoglou 2018) has attested to the need to define a story's emplotment flexibly and on the basis of the following features:

- **emblematic events**, that is, key shared moments that emerge as central in the mediatization of specific individuals and current affairs on account of their distribution and iterative invocation in (re)tellings;
- **key actors** who, through distribution of specific emblematic events, become "characters" in circulating stories, often with different roles and identities than those in "real life";
- **portable and iterative assessments**, that is, evaluations of key actors' speech, action, values and style that are picked out for circulation and, helped by replicability and distribution, often lead to recyclable quotes; and
- **multi-authorship**, meaning participation roles, rights and affordances in the sharing of a story, including co-narration possibilities.

Georgakopoulou has also shown (2014, 2015) that the sharing of the above plot ingredients relies on two systematic media-afforded practices:

1. **Rescripting**: This involves the deployment of media affordances (e.g. video editing, remixing) for visually and/or verbally manipulating and reworking specific incidents.
2. **Narrative stancetaking**: The brevity and live-sharing affordances are conducive to announcements of stories (*breaking news*) as opposed to full tellings. Conventionalized story-framing devices (e.g. reference to time, place, characters) are used to tell a condensed story or to suggest that there is a story in the making (Georgakopoulou 2017). Narrativity is therefore an emergent property, a process of becoming a story through engagement. This has implications for how tellers are presented and for how their posts are engaged with. For example, the performative display of self in "me selfies" calls for a scrutiny of the self and a positive assessment of it, a "ritual appreciation" (Georgakopoulou 2016a, 2016b), expressed in conventionalized language coupled with emojis (mainly hearts). These semiotic choices tend to be found in sequences of contributions from commenters, which, despite not directly engaging with one another, are strikingly similar, visually and linguistically. At the same time, the identities of friendship and close relationships proposed by "significant other" and "group selfies" were found to be systematically associated with knowing participation from commenters. This involved comments that display knowledge from offline,

preposting activities or any other knowledge specific to the selfie or selfied person(s), as a means of showing alignment and affiliation with the activity of the post and/or the characters (Georgakopoulou 2016a, 2016b). The fact that different types of selfie are associated with different positioning configurations in terms of the characters portrayed, the visual arrangements and placement (e.g. statuses, profile pictures, cover pictures, etc.) and the audience engagement suggests the benefits of a contextualized, interactional approach to stories and identities online. Such an approach has allowed the analyst to add nuance to oversimplifying accounts of selfies as narcissistic expressions of ideal selves (Georgakopoulou 2016a, 2016b).

This approach also pays dividends with regard to how networked audiences engage with others' stories, be they their friends' and followers' or current affairs. For example, Georgakopoulou and Giaxoglou's (2018) study of Yanis Varoufakis, economist and former Minister of Finance in Greece (from January to June 2015), who became a celebrity-economist and the face of the Greek crisis, through his negotiations with the EU about the restructuring of the Greek debt, showed how incidents involving him in his negotiations with members of the Eurogroup were rescripted, at times parodically, mainly on YouTube and Twitter. Such rescriptings placed him and the Greek economy in popular culture-scenarios of one-to-one clashes with the powerful of Europe. In these clashes, Varoufakis was emplotted as a character of "thug life," a "gangsta," an "action superhero," "kicking ass," "the Killah." These characterizations, through wide distribution as iterative quotes (e.g. "Wow you just killed the troika," whispered to Varoufakis by the head of Eurogroup Disselbloem after a tense press conference in January 2015), became part of small stories of contests between him as the "hero" and Eurogroup politicians and bureaucrats as the "villains," David vs. Goliath. Their transmedia distribution (e.g. on T-shirts and other artifacts), enhanced by portable quotes and assessments (e.g. "the Minister of Awesome"), sedimented the iconography and biographing of a maverick, embattled Minister of Finance. This was facilitated by what we call polystorying, that is, media-afforded possibilities for bringing together different plots and for affording multiple modes of audience participation in them: for example, as economy and politics commentators, as fans of the Thug Life videos, as drawn to specific personality aspects or to the lifestyle and physical appearance (e.g. his fashion choices) of Varoufakis, etc.

Studies such as that by Georgakopoulou and Giaxoglou (2018) show the performative, agentive and multi-authoring possibilities involved in producing stories and self- and other-identities online. That said, in the interplay between algorithms, affordances and stories, how algorithms may infer and predict users' identities, what assumptions they make about them and how those shape users' communication choices and self-perceptions should not be underestimated. As Cheney-Lippold puts it: "[O]nline a category like gender is not determined by one's genitalia or even physical appearance. Nor is it entirely self-selected. Rather, categories of identity are being inferred upon individuals based on their web use. Code and algorithm are the engines behind such inference" (2011: 165).

This somewhat deterministic view has been moderated by studies that show that users can be highly reflexive and aware online, developing discursive strategies to tweak and manipulate algorithms (see Chapter 32 in this volume; Beer 2009: 998). There is, however, much scope for exploring the different types of connection involved between algorithmically produced and configured identities in stories and users' compliances, resistances or ways of counteracting them.

One important avenue for further study is how the apps themselves design stories and what kinds of identity those "curate." What definitions and views of stories and storytellers underpin such story-features? What facilities are on offer for posting stories, how are they being branded and why? Georgakopoulou has begun to address these issues with a focus on the design of Instagram and Snapchat stories as a distinct feature (Georgakopoulou 2019). Her corpus-assisted analysis of how stories are launched and subsequently discussed in online media has made apparent certain paradoxes and mismatches between the rhetoric of the design and the affordances on offer. Stories were found to be built on the basis of the algorithmic logic of instant live-sharing, despite setting out to go beyond the moment and to offer facilities for continuity of self. They also promoted visual representations and snapshots of sharing the moment as well as viewing audience engagement practices, despite evoking familiar tropes of textual and telling accounts of one's life. The promise of user control and creativity was found to clash with the abundance of preselections, prior categorizations of experience, templates and menus with specific editing features. Georgakopoulou argued that these mismatches are revealing of a redesignation of key ingredients of stories (time, memories, audience engagement) on the one hand and, on the other hand, of a collapse of the stories' social and relational aspects with the quantification (cf. metricization) of users' activities. Stories are being "curated" in ways that allow them to serve as consumables, as vehicles for advertising and monetization. Taking into account the affordances of distribution and amplification as well as the huge uptake of stories by influencers, this curation has the potential to create normative ways of storying oneself. Similarly, the convergence and replication of story-facilities across apps suggest that drawing on templates to post stories has the potential to become further consolidated as a widely available mode of sharing everyday life, particularly for the main targeted groups of teenagers and young adults (2019).

5.6 Conclusion and Suggestions for Further Research

In this chapter, we have discussed latest developments in discourse studies in how stories and identities have been connected, through reviewing certain basic premises of interactionally oriented studies, key areas in which recent research has been conducted (such as social media, political discourse, translocal and mobile environments) and key concepts and methods (such as small stories research, positioning, chronotopes).

The social interactional approach that we advocated in earlier work (De Fina and Georgakopoulou 2008), that is, the study of how identities are configured within different narrative practices with their own associated resources, has by now led to a sizeable critical mass. We anticipate that this will be further enriched with new directions and domains of study, including digital communication practices. In that respect, as Georgakopoulou has argued (2017), further interrogation of intensified story curation on social media and of its implications for subjectivity should be high on the agenda of small stories research and of narrative investigation in general. This plea can be extended to any research with a posthumanist focus (see Chapter 16 in this volume) on the entanglements of a variety of human (e.g. ordinary users, programmers, influencers, app CEOs, product managers, etc.) and nonhuman (e.g. bots, algorithms) agents with the production and distribution of stories.

Further Reading

Bamberg, M. and McCabe, A. (2000). Special Issue: Narrative and Identities. *Narrative Inquiry* 10(1).

This special issue brings together work on narrative and identities by scholars from a variety of areas, including social psychology, anthropology, sociolinguistics and narratology.

De Fina, A. and Georgakopoulou, A. (eds.) (2015). *Handbook of Narrative Analysis*. Malden, MA: Wiley.

This is a comprehensive volume on main issues and trends in narrative studies, with several chapters following a discourse analytical approach.

De Fina, A. and Perrino, S. (eds.) (2019). *Storytelling in the Digital World*. Amsterdam: John Benjamins.

This volume brings together sociolinguistic and discourse analytic work on stories and identities in digital environments.

Ochs, E. and Capps, L. (2001). *Living Narrative*. Cambridge, MA: Harvard University Press.

This volume presents a flexible, context-sensitive definition of storytelling premised on a dimensional approach to it, which is widely applied in research on narratives and identities.

References

Agha, A., (2007). Recombinant Selves in Mass Mediated Spacetime. *Language & Communication* 27: 320–35.

Antaki, C. and Widdicombe, S. (1998). Identity as an Achievement and as a Tool. In C. Antaki and S. Widdicombe (eds.) *Identities in Talk*. London: Sage. 1–15.

Appadurai, A. (1996). *Modernity at Large: Cultural Dimensions of Globalization*. Minneapolis: University of Minnesota Press.

Avni, S. (2013). Homeland Tour Guide Narratives and the Discursive Construction of the Diasporic. *Narrative Inquiry* 23(2): 227–44.

Bakhtin, M. ([1981]1990). Forms of Time and of the Chronotope in the Novel: Notes toward a Historical Poetics. In M. Holquist (ed.), *The Dialogic Imagination: Four Essays*, trans. by C. Emerson and M. Holquist. Austin: University of Texas Press. 84–258.

Bamberg, M. (2006). Stories: Big or Small? Why Do We Care? *Narrative Inquiry* 16: 147–55.

Bamberg, M. and Georgakopoulou, A. (2008). Small Stories as a New Perspective in Narrative and Identity Analysis. *Text & Talk* 28: 377–96.

Baran, D. M. (2018). Narratives of Migration on Facebook: Belonging and Identity among Former Fellow Refugees. *Language in Society* 47(2): 245–68.

Baynham, M. (2003). Narratives in Space and Time: Beyond "Backdrop" Accounts of Narrative Orientation. *Narrative Inquiry* 13(2): 347–66.

Baynham, M. and De Fina, A. (eds.) (2005). *Dislocations, Relocations, Narratives of Displacement*. Manchester: St. Jerome.

Beer, D. (2009). Power through the Algorithm? Participatory Web Cultures and the Technological Unconscious. *New Media & Society* 11: 985–1002.

Blommaert, J. (2001). Investigating Narrative Inequality: African Asylum Seekers' Stories in Belgium. *Discourse & Society* 12(4): 413–49.

  (2018). "Are Chronotopes Helpful?" https://alternative-democracy-research.org/2018/06/22/are-chronotopes-helpful/.

Blommaert J. and De Fina, A. (2017). Chronotopic Identities: On the Timespace Organization of Who We Are. In A. De Fina, D. Ikizoglu and J. Wegner (eds.) *Diversity and Super-Diversity: Sociocultural Linguistic Perspectives*. Washington, DC: Georgetown University Press.

Bock, Z. (2018). Negotiating Race in Post-Apartheid South Africa: Bernadette's Stories. *Text & Talk* 38: 115–36.

Bruner, J. (1990). *Acts of Meaning*. Cambridge, MA: Harvard University Press.

Castells, M. (2000). *The Rise of the Network Society*. Oxford: Blackwell.

Cheney-Lippold, J. (2011). A New Algorithmic Identity. *Theory, Culture and Society* 2(8): 164–81.

Convery, I. and O'Brien, V. (2012). Gypsy-Traveller Narratives: Making Sense of Place. *Narrative Inquiry* 22(2): 332–47.

De Certeau, M. (1988). *The Practice of Everyday Life*. Berkeley: University of California Press.

De Fina, A. (2003). Crossing Borders: Time, Space and Disorientation in Narrative. *Narrative Inquiry* 13(2): 1–25.

(2013). Positioning Level 3: Connecting Local Identity Displays to Macro Social Processes. *Narrative Inquiry* 23(1): 40–61.

(2015). Narrative and Identities. In A. De Fina and A. Georgakopoulou (eds.) *Handbook of Narrative Analysis*. Malden, MA: Wiley.

(2018a). What Is Your Dream? Fashioning the Migrant Self. *Language & Communication* 59: 42–52.

(2018b). Narrative Analysis. In R. Wodak and B. Forchtner (eds.) *Handbook of Language and Politics*. London/New York: Routledge. 233–46.

De Fina, A. and Georgakopoulou, A. (2008). *Analysing Narratives as Practices*. Qualitative Research 8(3): 379–87.

(2012). *Analyzing Narrative: Discourse and Sociolinguistic Perspectives*. Cambridge: Cambridge University Press.

De Fina, A., Paternostro, G. and Amoruso, M. (2020). Odysseus the Traveler: Appropriation of a Chronotope in a Community of Practice. *Language & Communication*, 70: 71–81.

Deppermann, A. (2013). Editorial: Positioning in Narrative Interaction. *Narrative Inquiry* 23: 1–15.

Freeden, M. (2008). Editorial: Thinking Politically and Thinking Ideologically. *Journal of Political Ideologies* 13(1): 1–10.

Galasinska, A. and Horolet, A. (2012). The (Pro)long(ed) Life of a Grand Narrative: The Case of Internet Forum Discussions on Post-2004 Polish Migration to the United Kingdom. *Text & Talk* 32(2): 125–43.

Georgakopoulou, A. (2003). Plotting "the Right Place" and "the Right Time": Place and Time as Interactional Resources in Narrative. *Narrative Inquiry* 13(2): 413–32.

(2006). Small and Large Identities in Narrative (Inter)action. In A. De Fina, D. Schiffrin and M. Bamberg (eds.) *Discourse and Identity*. Cambridge: Cambridge University Press. 83–102.

(2007). *Small Stories, Interaction and Identities*. Amsterdam/Philadelphia, PA: John Benjamins.

(2013). Special Issue on Positioning: Building Iterativity into Positioning Analysis: A Practice-Based Approach to Small Stories and Self. *Narrative Inquiry* 23: 89–110.

(2015). Sharing as Rescripting: Place Manipulations on YouTube between Narrative and Social Media Affordances. *Discourse, Context & Media* 9: 64–72.

(2016a). From Writing the Self to Posting Self(ies): A Small Stories Approach to Selfies. *Open Linguistics* 2: 300–17.

(2016b). Friendly Comments: Interactional Displays of Alignment on Facebook and YouTube. In S. Leppänen, S. Kytölä and E. Westinen (eds.) *Discourse and Identification: Diversity and Heterogeneity in Social Media Practices*. London: Routledge. 178–207.

(2017). Special Issue [Storytelling in the Digital Age]: Sharing the Moment as Small Stories: The Interplay between Practices and Affordances in the Social Media-Curation of Lives. *Narrative Inquiry* 27: 311–33.

(2019). Designing Stories on Social Media: A Corpus-Assisted Critical Perspective on the Mismatches of Story-Curation. *Linguistics & Education*. Published online: www.sciencedirect.com/science/article/pii/S0898589818304212.

Georgakopoulou, A. and Giaxoglou, K. (2018). Employment in the Social Mediatization of the Economy: The Poly-storying of Economist Yanis Varoufakis. *Language@Internet* 16: article 6. www.languageatinternet.org/articles/2018si/georgakopoulou.giaxaglou.

Goetsch, P. (1991). Presidential Rhetoric: An Introduction. In P. Goetsch and G. Hurm (eds.) *Important Speeches by American Presidents after 1945*. Heidelberg: Winter. 7–31.

Gómez-Estern, M. (2013). Narratives of Migration: Emotions and the Interweaving of Personal and Cultural Identity through Narrative. *Culture & Psychology* 19(3): 348–68.

Hannerz, U. (1996). *Transnational Connections: Culture, People, Places*. London/New York: Routledge.

Harvey, D. (1989). *The Condition of Postmodernity: An Inquiry into the Origins of Cultural Change*. Oxford: Blackwell.

Heavey, E. (2015). Narrative Bodies, Embodied Narratives. In A. De Fina and A. Georgakopoulou (eds.) *The Handbook of Narrative Analysis*. Hoboken, NJ: Wiley-Blackwell. 429–46.

Heritage, J. (1984). *Garfinkel and Ethnomethodology*. Cambridge: Polity Press.

Jacquemet, M. (2005). The Registration Interview: Restricting Refugees' Narrative Performances. In M. Baynham and A. De Fina (eds.) *Dislocations/Relocations: Narratives of Displacement*. Manchester: St. Jerome. 194–216.

(2009). Transcribing Refugees: The Entextualization of Asylum Seekers' Hearings in a Transidiomatic Environment. *Text & Talk* 29 (5): 525–46.

Jaffe, A. (ed.) (2009). *Sociolinguistic Perspectives on Stance*. Oxford: Oxford University Press.

Jensen, O. (2007). Cultural Stories: Understanding Urban Cultural Branding. *Planning Theory* 6(3): 211–36.

Jones, R. (2015). Generic Intertextuality in Online Social Activism: The Case of the It Gets Better Project. *Language in Society* 44(3): 317–39.

Juswik, M. and Ives, D. (2010). Small Stories as a Resource for Positioning Teller Identity: Identity-in-Interaction in an Urban Language Classroom. *Narrative Inquiry* 20: 37–61.

Kitchin, R. and Dodge, M. (2011). *Code/Space: Software and Everyday Life*. Cambridge, MA: MIT Press.

Koven, M. and Simões Marques, I. (2015). Performing and Evaluating (Non)modernities of Portuguese Migrant Figures on YouTube: The Case of Antonio de Carglouch. *Language in Society* 44(2): 213–42.

Kresova, N. and Mouravi, T. (2016). Lifestories as a Lifelogging-Project: Russian Émigré Bloggers and Their Life Stories. In S. Selke (ed.) *Lifelogging: Digital Self-Tracking and Lifelogging – Between Disruptive Technology and Cultural Transformation*. Wiesbaden: Springer. 151–79.

Labov, W. (1972). The Transformation of Experience in Narrative Syntax. In W. Labov (ed.) *Language in the Inner City: Studies in the Black English Vernacular*. Philadelphia: University of Pennsylvania Press. 354–96.

Lawson, M. (2017). Negotiating an Agentive Identity in a British Lifestyle Migration Context: A Narrative Positioning Analysis. *Journal of Sociolinguistics* 21(5): 650–71.

Lee, H. (2013). Telling Stories and Making Social Relations: Transnational Women's Ways of Belonging in Intercultural Contexts. *Applied Linguistics* 36: 151–73.

Lenchuk, I. and Swain, M. (2010). Alice's Small Stories: Indices of Identity Construction and of Resistance to the Discourse of Cognitive Impairment. *Language Policy* 9(1): 9–28.

Lou, J. (2010). Chinatown Transformed: Ideology, Power, and Resources in Narrative Place-Making. *Discourse Studies* 12(5): 625–47.

Maryns, K. (2006). *The Asylum Speaker: Language in the Belgian Asylum Procedure*. Manchester: St. Jerome.

McAdams, D. P. (1988). *Power, Intimacy and the Life Story: Personological Inquiries into Identity*. New York: Guilford.

McIntyre, A. (1984). *After Virtue: A Study in Moral Theory*, 2nd ed. Notre Dame, IN: University of Notre Dame Press.

Merino. M. E. and De Fina, A. (2019). Chronotopic Identities: The South in the Narratives Told by Members of Mapuche Communities in Chile. In R. Piazza (ed.) *Discourses of Identity in Liminal Places and Spaces*. New York/London: Routledge. 15–41.

Norton, B. and Early, M. (2011). Researcher Identity, Narrative Inquiry and Language Teaching Research. *TESOL Quarterly* 45: 415–39.

Ochs, E. (1992). Indexing Gender. In A. Duranti and C. Goodwin (eds.) *Rethinking Context: Language as an Interactive Phenomenon*. Cambridge: Cambridge University Press. 335–58.

Oostendorp, M. and Jones, T. (2015). Tensions, Ambivalence and Contradiction: A Small Story Analysis of Discursive Identity Construction in the South African Workplace. *Text & Talk* 35(1): 25–47.

Perrino, S. (2007). Cross-Chronotope Alignment in Senegalese Oral Narrative. *Language & Communication* 27: 227–42.

Phoenix, C. and Sparkes, A. (2009). Being Fred: Big Stories, Small Stories and the Accomplishment of a Positive Ageing Identity. *Qualitative Research* 9: 209–36.

Piazza, R. (2015). "Since Big Fat Gypsy Weddings [...] Now [People] ... Understand More 'cos of that Programme": Irish Travellers' Identity between Stigmatisation and Self-Image. In R. Piazza and A. Fasulo (eds.) *Marked Identities: Narrating Lives between Social Labels and Individual Biographies*. Basingstoke: Palgrave Macmillan. 16–42.

(2019). With and Without Zanzibar Liminal Diaspora Voices and the Memory of the Revolution. *Narrative Inquiry* 29(1): 99–136.

Polletta, F. et al. (2011). The Sociology of Storytelling. *Annual Review of Sociology* 37: 109–30.

Potter, J. and Wetherell, M. (1988). Discourse Analysis and the Identification of Interpretative Repertoires. In C. Antaki (ed.) *Analysing Everyday Explanation: A Casebook of Methods*. London: Sage. 168–83.

Sabaté Dalmau, M. (2018) Exploring the Interplay of Narrative and Ethnography: A Critical Sociolinguistic Approach to Migrant Stories of Dis/emplacement. *International Journal of the Sociology of Language* 250: 35–58.

Salazar, N. (2018). Theorizing Mobility through Concepts and Figure. *Tempo Social* 30(2): 153–68.

Schegloff, E. A. (1997). Whose Text? Whose Context? *Discourse & Society* 8: 65–87.

Schiffrin, D. (1996). Narrative as Self-Portrait: Sociolinguistic Constructions of Identity. *Language in Society* 25(2) (June): 167–203.

Schubert, C. (2010). Narrative Sequences in Political Discourse: Forms and Functions in Speech and Hypertext Frameworks. In C. Hoffman (ed.) *Narrative Revisited: Telling a Story in the Age of New Media*. Amsterdam: John Benjamins. 143–62.

Scully, M. (2019). Cornish Identity at the Margins and the Pan-Celtic Context. In R. Piazza (ed.) *Discourses of Identity in Liminal Places and Spaces*. New York/London: Routledge. 147–65.

Shuman, A. (2005). *Other People's Stories: Entitlement Claims and the Critique of Empathy*. Urbana: University of Illinois Press.

Sools, A. (2012). Narrative Health Research: Exploring Big and Small Stories as Analytical Tools. *Health* 17: 93–110.

Souto Manning, M. (2014). Critical Narrative Analysis: The Interplay of Critical Discourse Analysis and Narrative Analyses. *International Journal of Qualitative Studies in Education* 27(2): 159–80.

Spotti, M. (2018). "It's All about Naming Things Right": The Paradox of Web Truths in the Belgian Asylum-Seeking Procedure. In N. Gill and A. Good (eds.) *Asylum Determination in Europe*. Palgrave Socio-Legal Studies. Basingstoke: Palgrave Macmillan. 68–89.

Sprain, L. and Hughes, J. M. F. (2015). A New Perspective on Stories in Public Deliberation: Analyzing Small Stories in Discussions about Immigration. *Text & Talk* 35: 531–51.

Spreckels, J. (2008). Identity Negotiation in Small Stories among German Adolescent Girls. *Narrative Inquiry* 18: 393–413.

Vasquez, C. (2011). TESOL, Teacher Identities and the Need for Small Story Research. *TESOL Quarterly* 45: 535–45.

Yi, Y. (2009). Adolescent Literacy and Identity Construction among 1.5 Generation Students from a Transnational Perspective. *Journal of Asian Pacific Communication* 19(1): 100–29.

Watson, C. (2007). "Small Stories" and the Doing of Professional Identities in Learning to Teach. *Narrative Inquiry* 17(2): 371–89.

Wodak, R., de Cillia, R., Reisigl, M. and Liebhart, K. (2009). *The Discursive Construction of National Identity*, 2nd ed. Edinburgh: Edinburgh University Press.

Wortham, S. and Reyes, A. (2015). *Discourse Analysis beyond the Speech Event*. New York: Routledge.

Zimmerman, D. (1998). Identity, Context and Interaction. In C. Antaki and S. Widdicombe (eds.) *Identities in Talk*. London: Sage. 87–106.

Part II

Perspectives and Modes of Analysis

Introduction

As the chapters of this part demonstrate, delimiting the boundaries of an approach within discourse studies or clearly defining it as a method, theory, analytical toolkit or simply a set of procedures is by no means straightforward or unproblematic. Much of the historical labeling in discourse analysis has thus had to rely on taking specific dichotomies at face value, for instance between text and context, language and paralanguage, referential and connotational meaning, speakers and addressees, etc. These received dichotomies in turn led to longstanding methodological debates in the field. For instance, the benefits and limitations of micro-analysis vs. quantitative discourse analysis have been amply discussed. This also applies to social interactional vs. cognitive approaches and to approaches focused on structure vs. those focused on speakers' agency, often discussed in terms of macro vs. micro. The chapters in this part critically assess these longstanding debates in the context of well-established traditions in doing discourse analysis (e.g., conversation analysis, critical discourse analysis), while at the same time demonstrating the field's gradual but decisive move away from binaries in favor of porous boundaries and intersections amongst different perspectives and modes of analysis. For instance, Ancarno's Chapter 8 discusses how corpus-assisted discourse analyses synergize big data mining and compilation of corpora with qualitative micro-analysis of texts. The synergy, she argues, allows for some of the criticisms leveled against both discourse analysis and corpus linguistics to be addressed. Chapter 10 by Demjén and Semino includes proposals to combine different levels in the analysis of metaphors, so as to combine cognitive with situated discourse-analytic approaches to them. Hart's Chapter 9 also showcases the benefits of a synergy of cognitive linguistics assumptions and concepts with critical discourse analytic concerns in relation to the study of metaphors. Heinrichsmeier's Chapter 7 provides a template for drawing on both discourse analysis (conversation-analytic informed micro-analysis of audio recordings) and ethnographic data (recorded interviews and field observations).

These examples of emerging or by now consolidated synergies should not lead us to underestimate the challenges of radically departing from well-established modes of analysis or from their assumptions. Angermuller, for instance, in Chapter 11, discusses the lingering structuralist biases in much of critical discourse analysis and the difficulties that the field has faced in terms of achieving a full rapprochement with poststructuralist views of discourse. Similarly, any necessary synergies of different approaches around topics of current relevance do not automatically mean that they shift away from their conventional perspective, priorities and sets of questions. For instance, the ways in which multimodality and the body are increasingly integrated into conversation analysis, as Hofstetter's Chapter 6 outlines them, are very different to the ways this is done within poststructuralist studies, as Køhler Mortensen and Milani's Chapter 19 documents (see Part IV). In Chapter 9, Hart makes a case for integrating insights from visual and multimodal analysis into cognitive linguistic-critical discourse studies, with the aim of exploring the role of concrete images present in the co-text of particular linguistic constructions that frame metaphors.

Regardless of the extent to which and the ways in which intersections amongst different perspectives are forged, what brings them together is the broadening of the definitions and analyses of discourse beyond language and text. This paradigm shift away from logocentrism and text-based approaches to contextualized, materialist, multisemiotic orientations to discourse is a theme running throughout this handbook and illustrated in different ways by different chapters. The shift to a materialist discourse analysis has implicated a revisioning and rethinking of basic methodological and analytical tenets in well-established approaches. For instance, in Chapter 6, Hofstetter discusses how, in order to analyze the practices of participants involved in multiple activities, verbal, nonverbal, embodied, object-oriented, etc., conversation analysis has had to rethink the concept of activity as a basic unit of organization of sequences. Mondada's work (e.g. 2014), to which Hofstetter refers, demonstrates the benefits and ways in which the concept of multiactivity can be deployed to provide an account of sequences where multiple activities are being conducted.

Despite certain key-differences in terms of how context is conceptualized and operationalized in discourse analysis, as illustrated in Part I, the benefits and value of contextualized discourse analysis are by now well recognized. It is largely in its sensitivity to context and the fine-grained analysis of discourse that linguistically informed discourse analysis normally locates its impact and contribution both to other social science disciplines and to policy and practice. Heinrichsmeier's Chapter 7 shows us how the micro-discourse analysis of older participants' subjective sense of wellbeing can offer insights into public policy and circulating, often stereotypical, discourses about what makes for quality in a particular interaction for the participants themselves. This in turn can help change public discourses on ageing and foster self-esteem and positive identities. In Demjén and Semino's Chapter 10, research on metaphor and framing in actual interactions has been instrumental in investigating how and why different metaphorical framings may help or hinder public understanding of and engagement with public-interest issues, often with a view to shaping public discussions and policy on a wide range of issues from climate change to mental and physical illness. Ancarno's discussion of corpus-assisted discourse analysis, in Chapter 8, argues for the potential of the approach for cross-fertilization with anthropology and other disciplines.

In this part, Chapter 6 by **Hofstetter** provides an overview of how everyday talk can be analyzed as organized into self-regulating sequences. One key principle in this organization is the "next turn proof procedure" by which participants and analysts validate their understanding of prior talk. The benefit of understanding sequence organization is not only to grasp the structures that we use to coordinate interaction but also to have an emic, empirical basis for demonstrating how participants understand and organize their own interactions. The chapter discusses the adjacency pair as the most minimal sequence, and expansion sequences on the base adjacency pair. The discussion shows how sequencing rules provide a basis for understanding interaction as it happens, allowing speakers, for example, to validate whether they have maintained intersubjectivity or to negotiate nuances. Since these behaviors are thus encoded in the interaction itself, and are available to the participants, the organization and its outcomes are available for analysts as well. Conversation analysis is currently moving away from its traditional emphasis on the verbal elements of sequential components to examining how sequence can be accomplished by bodily movement and expression.

Heinrichsmeier's Chapter 7 examines the ways in which a micro-discourse analytic perspective enables us to see how the sense of an individual's wellbeing may be co-constructed in everyday interactions, specifically, in quality interactions. The starting point of the chapter is that much research into interaction with older people has taken place in institutional settings, for example in care homes, often presenting older people as a homogeneous group. Studies that co-examine ageing and wellbeing in everyday settings remain scarce. The discussion showcases the benefits of combining micro-discourse analysis with ethnographic material, with special reference to the author's study of older women's interactions in a hair salon. Bringing in ethnography is seen as a way of addressing much of the criticism leveled against conversation analysis because of how it views and works with wider sociocultural contexts (see Chapter 6 and the chapters in Part I). By infusing ethnographic sensibilities into the micro-analysis of recorded conversations, the discussion shows the negotiation work involved by participants in achieving and maintaining positive identities, the way in which quality in interaction is achieved and how older people are active actors in these interactions rather than the passive recipients they are so often portrayed as being. Overall, the chapter highlights the importance of researching wellbeing in situated interaction and the potential for discourse analysis of this kind to inform public discourses and policy on the matter.

Chapter 8 by **Ancarno** offers practical and theoretical insights into corpus-assisted discourse studies (CADS), an increasingly popular framework for studying language-in-use. By drawing upon both discourse analysis and corpus linguistics, CADS combines methods of text analysis commonly perceived as qualitative and quantitative, respectively. The discussion provides an overview of the main corpus methods for exploring lexical and thematic associations in a body of collected texts, including the identification of keyword lists, collocation lists and multiword expression lists. The chapter makes a case for the strength of CADS as a mixed methods research approach in linguistics. Despite challenges (e.g., the desirability for discourse analysts to familiarize themselves with corpus linguistics and its tools), the author suggests that the main appeal lies in CADS' ability to reconcile close qualitative analyses with the more broad-ranging quantitative analyses made possible by using corpus linguistic methods to analyze language. The chapter provides examples of ways in which qualitative and quantitative approaches to discourse analysis are synergized and triangulated, and how this research can stretch disciplinary boundaries, thus showcasing the value of discourse analysis beyond linguistics.

In Chapter 9, **Hart** discusses the principles and modes of analysis around which cognitive linguistics and critical discourse studies can converge with special reference to the framing of metaphors. Cognitive linguistics seeks to model the conceptualizations invoked by specific language usages and to consider the potential ideological/(de)legitimating functions of competing conceptualizations. The chapter brings into the discussion concepts that are frequently employed in discourse analysis, even if in different ways. Examples are the concept of framing (e.g. see Chapter 10), defined as a portion of background knowledge that creates expectations in communication, and the concept of positioning (see also Chapter 5 in Part I), defined here as the position of the conceptualizer with respect to the conceptual content currently evoked as well as the position of construed elements relative to this egocentric reference point. In line with cognitive approaches to metaphor (discussed in Chapter 10), the discussion shows how metaphor involves the activation of mental imagery which in turn gives rise to framing effects. At the same time, it argues for including multimodal analysis in the analysis of metaphor, as its meaning and framing effect can be shaped by any visual semiotic material with which it may be or have been conventionally associated. Finally, the chapter suggests the need for the use of experimental methods in CL-CDS which currently remain underrepresented.

Demjén and Semino's Chapter 10 co-examines two affiliated phenomena, namely metaphors and metonymy, in terms of their framing potential, that is, of how they can reflect and facilitate different ways of viewing topics, experiences and phenomena as well as being associated with conventionalized linguistic expression. Three main approaches to the framing potential of metaphor are introduced – namely, conceptual metaphor theory, contextualized discourse analysis and experimental research – and their relative strengths and limitations are discussed. On their basis, two main tendencies within work on metaphor and framing are identified: a strand of research that emphasizes the conceptual dimension of metaphor and a strand of research that emphasizes the discoursal dimension of metaphor. The authors present the benefits of the collection and systematic analysis of naturally occurring language data in the analysis of metaphor and on combined approaches to the framing power of metaphors that investigate both the involvement of preexisting conceptual structures and their emergence in everyday interactions. Finally, they present examples of how the investigation of framing effects of metaphor and metonymy in a wide variety of discourse data and contexts can inform practice in relation to issues of societal concern.

Angermuller's Chapter 11 provides an introduction to key assumptions and disciplinary affiliations of an important set of orientations to discourse that can be usefully grouped as poststructuralist discourse studies (PDS). Situated at the interdisciplinary intersection of language and society, PDS aim to bridge structure- and practice-oriented strands of discourse research and to overcome the divisions between linguistics and other disciplines in the social sciences and humanities. While perceiving language as a practice that is constitutive of social order, PDS place emphasis on the critical and reflexive dimensions of discourse research. As proponents of a linguistic turn in social, cultural and political theory, PDS theorists also make the case for posthumanist and antiessentialist epistemologies. The chapter presents the uneasy relationship and the challenges that CDS have faced in their intersections with critical discourse analysis and the French School of discourse studies. Poststructuralism critically interrogates the structuralist heritage in these traditions and the author suggests that there is much scope within much linguistically informed discourse analysis of language and power for departing from the binary opposition between top and bottom, the oppressors and the oppressed. A more explicit engagement with the poststructuralist challenge could be beneficial to these traditions, in the same vein as the emergent poststructuralist synergies within pragmatics, ethnomethodology and positioning analysis as combined with small stories research (see also Chapter 5 in Part 1).

Reference

Mondada, L. (2014). The Local Constitution of Multimodal Resources for Social Interaction. *Journal of Pragmatics* 65: 137–56.

6

Sequence Organization: Understanding What Drives Talk

Emily Hofstetter

6.1 Introduction

Everyday talk is highly organized. This is one of the original findings of conversation analysis (Schegloff 1968) and it has been repeatedly confirmed over decades of work. There is also evidence that this system is present across human languages (Stivers et al. 2009). Earlier conceptions of language claimed that performance, the everyday instances of talk, was disorganized and chaotic, whereas "competence," the rules that theoretically form the basis of our ability to talk, was the only linguistic subject worthy of study (Chomsky 1957). Schegloff and Sacks, in various papers (e.g. Schegloff and Sacks 1973), as well as Jefferson (Sacks, Schegloff and Jefferson 1974), demonstrated this view to be patently false by showing how everyday talk ("performance") is organized, namely, into sequences. This chapter will explain how these sequences work. I will also show how these sequences are self-regulating and provide a "next turn proof procedure" by which participants and analysts validate their understanding of prior talk. The benefit of understanding sequence organization is not only to grasp the structures that we use to coordinate interaction but also to have an emic, empirical basis for demonstrating how participants understand and organize their own interactions. Note that I will refer generally to "participants" and "interaction" as being inclusive, as these structures are applicable to more than verbal components of communication (i.e., not just "speakers" or "talk").

In this chapter, I will outline the basics of sequence organization, starting with the adjacency pair and discussing the "next turn proof procedure." I will then explain how sequences are expanded beyond the adjacency pair sequence and briefly discuss variations on this form of sequence, such as storytelling and some institutional variations. Finally, I will discuss longer sequences and overall sequence organization, before turning to the applications of sequences.

6.2 Overview: The Adjacency Pair and Response Relevance

In this section, I will focus on the base adjacency pair, its "pair parts" and the rule of response relevance. These principles form the basic structure for all interaction, as well as forming the basis for conversation analytic arguments (Schegloff 2007). The data extracts used are examples from real interactions.

The most minimal sequence, and the type of sequence upon which others are structured, is the adjacency pair. An adjacency pair is a set of, at minimum, two turns, where the first turn creates relevance for the second turn and the second turn responds to, and is treated as a sufficient response to, the first turn. Schegloff and Sacks (1973: 295–6) give a more precise definition, wherein:

- an adjacency pair is composed of two turns,
- spoken by different speakers;
- the turns are adjacently placed (one after the other);
- the turns are relatively ordered (there are two parts to the pair – a first pair part (FPP) and a second pair part (SPP) – and the second must follow the first); and
- the turns are pair-type related (the SPP must be of a correct "type" to fit the FPP, such as an SPP denial in response to an FPP accusation, or a greeting with a greeting and a goodbye with a goodbye).

Turns do not "merely" happen one after the other; speakers *make* them happen in this way. Each component of the above definition provides a "rule" – an expectation of how the interaction *should* proceed – and any deviation from that expectation can and *will* be

> heard as qualifying the progressivity of the talk, and will be examined for its import, for what understanding should be accorded it. Each next element of such a progression [sequence] can be inspected to find how it reaffirms the understanding-so-far of what has preceded, or favours one or more of the several such understandings that are being entertained, or how it requires reconfiguration of that understanding. (Schegloff 2007: 15)

In other words, these rules provide a basis for understanding interaction as it happens, allowing speakers, for example, to validate whether they have maintained intersubjectivity or to negotiate nuances. Since these behaviors are thus encoded in the interaction itself, and are available to the participants, the organization and its outcomes are available for analysts as well.

The adjacency pair itself is the most condensed form in which this relationship between turns can occur. An adjacency pair can constitute an entire sequence in itself, and indeed an entire interaction (e.g. waving and reciprocal waving when passing in the street, before moving past an

6 Sequence Organization: Understanding What Drives Talk

acquaintance). Series of "simple" adjacency pairs are especially common in routine interactions, such as greetings:

Extract 6.1: HG

0		FPP1	((ring))
1	Nan:	SPP1	H'llo:?
2	Hyl:	FPP2	Hi:,
3	Nan:	SPP2	HI::.
4	Hyl:	FPP3	How are yuhh.=
5	Nan:	SPP3	=Fi:ne how're you.

In this sequence (see Transcription Conventions at end of chapter), we see three adjacency pairs that open the encounter. Nancy is summoned to the phone by the ring and answers (pair 1, L0–1), they greet and recognize each other (pair 2, L2–3) and they begin opening "how are you?"s (pair 3, L4–5). These pairs occur in quick succession, with no silence between them. Each pair is matched with its type (summons with answer, greeting with greeting, how are you with response and reciprocal how are you). Note that, here, the greeting and mutual recognition of speakers is accomplished via one pair. Schegloff (1979: 34, emphasis original) says Hyla is completing the identification "*en passant*"; through intonation, Hyla both greets and recognizes Nancy's voice (L2), and Nancy does likewise (L3). In this way, multiple pairs can sometimes be condensed. However, these actions can be expanded into more distinct pairs:

Extract 6.2: 01golf

0		FPP1	((Johnny is called to the phone by his partner))
1	Joh:	SPP1	Hello:?
2	Guy:	FPP2	Johnny,
3	Joh:	SPP2	Ye:h.
4	Guy:	FPP3	Guy Detweiler.
5	Joh:	SPP3	Hi Guy

The pairs are similar to above, in that Johnny is called to the phone and responds to the summons (pair 1, L0–1), Guy requests confirmation that it is Johnny speaking now and this is confirmed (pair 2, L2–3), then Guy identifies himself and is recognized (pair 3, L4–5). Regardless of whether Johnny recognized Guy in L2–3 of Extract 1, his failure to *indicate* recognition in his SPP (L3 "Ye:h") makes it relevant for Guy to identify himself. A possible relevant response to Guy's turn in Extract 6.1 L2 would have been to include recognition, but its absence leads to a more explicit version of accomplishing that action.

The question of whether something can be "absent" is important in conversation analysis (CA). As Schegloff writes (2007: 19–20): "There is an indefinitely large and extendable number of things that have not been said. ... For the noting of an absence to be non-trivial, we need a 'relevance rule' that makes it relevant for something to happen or be done or be mentioned. ... We can then speak of it as a 'noticeable absence.'" Sequences provide for what is *relevant* to come next, and thus the lack of that relevant something is an absence. There are many ways in which something can be absent or relevantly present that this chapter does not have room to cover. I refer the reader to some related research on providing the relevant responses (Clayman 2001; Fox and Thompson 2010; Raymond 2003).

The most overtly noticeable absence is silence or a complete lack of response. These absences are treated as accountable and may result in pursuit of the response via further efforts from the FPP speaker. The following extract involves two players at a board game, where one has just chosen to "take" the other's piece.

Extract 6.3: BG 160712 – Tash Kalar

1	Joh:	F	Ooh:::↓ ↑That one,
2			(0.4)
3	Joh:	F$_{Purs}$	↑Really?
4	Kat:	S	That one.

John asks whether Kat will indeed take his piece (L1), but Kat does not respond (L2). John pursues an answer (L3): in "↑Really?", he reissues his request for confirmation. The new form ("↑Really" instead of "↑That one") specifically pursues certainty (whether Kat will indeed do the move), rather than the specificity issue (whether Kat will take that specific piece). Pursuits often alter the format of the action, targeting some additional or different component of the original question, which can make it structurally easier to respond, as well as increasing response relevance with the reissue of the action. Kat now responds with a confirmation (L4). Note that she confirms the original question from L1, indicating that she treats John's pursuit *as* pursuit and that the original question is still relevant.

There *are* situations where a lack of response is not held accountable, in that speakers do not pursue a response, do not complain about inattention, etc. These instances still challenge Sacks, Schegloff and Jefferson's (1974) sequence organization theory. Stivers and Rossano (2010) have begun to address this question by formulating a theory of response relevance. They suggest that a variety of interactional features can be used by participants to encourage an SPP, including where in the sequence a turn lands, the action being accomplished and the design of the turn. These features can be used in combination (both within a single turn, as well as over a sequence) to elicit a response more and more strongly. Their theory accounts for the lack of SPPs in certain extracts and for many design features, especially those used in pursuit of response (as in Extract 6.3; see also Romaniuk 2013). Recent research has also shown how *early* and anticipatory turns can be, particularly when offering assistance to minimal displays of need (Kendrick and Drew 2016), which provides more evidence that participants project what response is relevant.

Finally, what is remarkable about this system of talk is that it provides its own means for establishing intersubjectivity. Each response (each SPP) demonstrates what the current speaker understands and chooses to address in the prior turn (prototypically, the FPP). If there is a problem with that understanding for in the second speaker not responding sufficiently for the first speaker's turn, the first speaker will, in the subsequent turn (e.g. post-expansions or the next FPP), have the opportunity to initiate repair. Analysts can take advantage of this organization. Since participants must inevitably display their understandings of the prior turn when making their next turn in the sequence, analysts can see what any given turn accomplished as an action. The participants display what they took the prior action to be, through giving the relevant next action. This is the "next turn proof procedure," wherein analysts can use participants' own turns in the sequence to understand what speakers are doing, what they take to be relevant and what they project to be happening. For example, when something that is expected is absent from the "next" turn, it can be analyzed for import, just as the speakers are (demonstrably) doing.

In this section, I have discussed the base adjacency pair, its first and second pair parts and the requirement of giving a relevant response in the second pair part. I have given emphasis to understanding these basics because they are the foundation of the sequential organization of interaction, as well as the foundation for providing proof in any conversation analysis via the next turn proof procedure. Next, I will briefly touch on how sequence can be accomplished through nonverbal means, before moving to the expansions in a sequence.

6.2.1 Embodied Response

The above examples have focused on verbal means of accomplishing sequence. Before moving to expansions, it is worth noting that sequential components can be accomplished by bodily movement and expression (see Chapter 15 in this volume). The lack of multimodal analysis in this chapter is for the sake of simplicity (easier transcripts for novices) and space, but segregating modalities in analysis has been rightly criticized (Goodwin 2000). Nonverbal behaviors are integral to interaction, not only in copresent interaction but also where participants are on the phone with each other (Mondada 2008). Nonverbal behaviors have even been shown to be integral to syntactic structures (Keevallik 2018), previously thought to be solely verbal. Conversation analysis has experienced a "multimodal turn" (Neville 2015), enabled in part by widely available and inexpensive video recorders, much as the original work by Sacks, Schegloff and Jefferson (1974) was enabled by newly affordable audio recorders (see Chapter 12 in this volume).

A common example of an embodied sequence is that "Can you pass the salt?", as a first pair part, requires as its second pair part not only agreement but for someone to actually pass the salt. Embodied responses can be useful for their very lack of speech, as in a video in which Adam and Kat are playing a board game. Adam has played a card that lets him move one of Kat's pieces. This is bad for Kat, as the locations of the pieces on the board are critical to effective strategy, and any movement of her piece will almost certainly be a detriment to her getting points. However, Adam does not know which spaces on the board are most effective for Kat – he may inadvertently move her piece to a good spot. Despite the odds, Kat thanks Adam for moving her piece.

Extract 6.4: BG 160712 – Tash Kalar

1	Ka:		↑Thank you,
2	Ad:	F	You like that,
3		S	(1.4) ((Ka smiles))
4	Ad:	F_{Post}	n'Ah: cra:p.

Adam asks for confirmation of the move (L2), and instead of responding with insistence of genuine gratitude (remember gratitude is bad for Adam) or perhaps saying "Just kidding," Kat "merely" smiles, while gazing directly at Adam. This constitutes a sufficient SPP; the fact that Adam takes it as sufficient is seen in his subsequent assessment. It later turns out that Kat is bluffing. Her smile here is highly effective, though, in that it convinces Adam of her sincerity and thus allows her to manipulate him. A verbal SPP may have been less effective and also more morally accountable, as it would have involved repeating or making a new lie. The smile does not reiterate the lie, but coyly allows Adam to make of it what he will.

Adam's assessment turn (L4) brings us to a new type of sequence component, however, as it does not fit in the adjacency pair structure. It is a type of sequence expansion, which will be covered in Section 6.2.2.

6.2.2 Expansions

While talk *can* be done in minimal adjacency pairs, it is very frequently more complex. Speakers expand on the base adjacency pair: before (pre-expansion), between the pair parts (insert expansion) and after (post-expansion). These expansions can and often do include their own first and second pair parts, and expansion sequences can even contain internal expansions within the expansions (leading to occurrences such as "pre-pre-expansions"; Schegloff 1980).

We will see that participants use expansions in systematic ways (Schegloff 2007): pre-sequences are used in dealing with matters that are preliminary to the base pair, such as testing whether someone is available to go out; insert expansions are used to deal with difficulties in giving a base SPP response, including repair; and post-expansions are used to repair misunderstandings displayed in the base SPP or to display a stance to the SPP. The systematic distribution of uses shows that the complexities of sequence expansion are not only analysts' concerns but also participants' concerns.

6.2.2.1 Pre-expansion

Pre-expansions deal with matter that is in some way "preliminary" to the base sequence – that participants treat as necessarily coming before the issue of a base FPP.

Lisa has recommended a book to Rose, and is describing it further. In order to assess the book in a way that is relevant (and that will promote her recommendation), Lisa first checks whether Rose likes the singer with whom she is comparing the book.

Extract 6.5: Callfriend eng-n4984

```
1    Li:    F_pre    you like Tom Waits,
2                    (0.5)
3    Ro:    S_pre    yeah I love [Tom Waits.]
4    Li:    F_b                  [It's like a] <lo:ng Tom Waits song.>
5                    (0.7)
6    Ro:             hh(h)ah (h)ah(h)ah
7    Li:    F_b      Be p[atient,
8    Ro:    S_b          [.hhh Well: I don' know if I like (h)him
                         that
9                    much(h)m(h)m(h)eh(h)m
```

The check (L1) of Rose's enjoyment of Tom Waits is a pre-sequence. If Rose does not like Tom Waits (or has not heard of him), Lisa would be able to abandon that descriptor or alter her recommendation. As it turns out, Rose's professed enthusiasm for Tom Waits may have been misleading, as it provided a structural "go-ahead" for Lisa to use that form of assessment for the book (L4–7), despite Rose not liking Tom Waits "that much(h) m(h)m ..." (L8–9). However, given that Lisa could only work with the pre-expansion supplied, she acted accordingly.

6.2.2.2 Insert Expansion

Insert expansions are initiated by the recipient of the FPP (note that this means that continuations or reversals of the FPP by the FPP speaker are *not* insert expansions) and occur between the FPP and the SPP. They are used to deal with difficulties in giving an SPP, typically either in repairing the FPP (a "post-first insert expansion") or in establishing necessary information to give the SPP (a "pre-second insert expansion"). Here is an example of an insert expansion from the same book-recommending conversation as Extract 6.6.

Extract 6.6: Callfriend eng-n4984

1	LI:		[So I don't know: :,]
2	RO:	F$_b$	[.hhh my friend reads cl]o:ckers right now
3			did you ever read tha:t,
4			(0.5)
5	LI:	F$_{ins}$	Clockers?
6	RO:	S$_{ins}$	Yea:h,
7	LI:	S$_b$	No:.

Here, Rose asks if Lisa has read the book "Clockers" (L3). Lisa initiates repair (L5), most likely checking hearing on the title of the book. Once the book title is confirmed (L6), Lisa provides the SPP (L7). The prototypical insert expansions given are short, as above, but they can be very extensive (see Schegloff 1990 for one that is approximately ninety lines long).

6.2.2.3 Post-expansion

Once the SPP is delivered, the next speaker may comment on it, such as showing they are informed or assessing it. Schegloff (2007) divides these into minimal and nonminimal post-expansions. The former involves a turn that does not make a further response relevant; the latter does make a further response relevant. Both types can proceed in a subsequence of their own, as multiple minimal post-expansions can occur before moving to a new sequence. A minimal example is as follows:

Extract 6.7: NB 06fungus

1	Lot:	F$_b$	When d'ya go:- ther- (.) [yesti-
2	Emm:	S$_b$	[Uh <u>Fri</u>day.
3	Lot:	Post$_m$	<u>O</u>h:.

Here, Lottie asks Emma when she was away (L1), is told (L2) and then reacts to that telling (L3). In this particular case, "Oh" acts as a display of having been informed (Heritage 1984). Indeed, we can see Lottie's transition from an incorrect date ("yesti-", L1) to Emma's informing.

6.2.2.4 Multiple Sequences

Now that the expansions have been briefly explained, we can put these structures together to examine longer extracts and demonstrate how the base pair and expansions may occur in a sequence. For instance, the following is a telephone call between two friends, Deb and Issy, where Issy is in hospital, having just had her first baby. There are multiple sequences here that overlap, so I have numbered the sequences to help. Note that this was recorded before digital photography existed.

Extract 6.8: Callfriend eng-n4889

1	Is:	1F	They took pictures of the baby and brought
2			it up to me which is really good
3			ca[use no one can see her.]
4	De:	1S	[Are you ↑serious, alrea]dy,
5			(0.5)
6	De:	2F	.hhh [Did you name her (>t'day<)]
7	Is:	1Post$_{nm}$	[No they're just like] Polaroids.
8			(0.3)
9	Is:	2F$_{in}$	What?=
10	De:	1Post$_{nm}$,2 F	=That's cute.=Did you name her,
11			(0.3)
12	Is:	S2	Yeah.=Dora Winifred,
13			(0.3)
14	De:	2Post$_m$	That's nice,

Overlap can cause participants to respond out of order, as not all elements may be heard. Furthermore, Deb's assessment of the immediacy of baby pictures (L4) has an ambiguous component: "already" could be part of the assessment, but its tag-position and upward intonation suggest that a further response may be relevant (Stivers and Rossano 2010). The surprise at the time frame in her turn may also suggest that Deb has misunderstood Issy's description – perhaps that they are developed pictures. Issy thus treats Line 4 as requiring a repairing response (L7). As this occurs after some delay (L5), Deb has already moved on to initiating a new sequence, and the turns occur in overlap. Issy repairs (L9), having again not heard due to overlap. Deb repairs the misunderstanding from both sequences by redoing an assessment of the Polaroids situation ("That's cute," L10) and in the same turn redoing her FPP (also L10). The second sequence now continues without difficulty with an SPP (L12) and post-expansion for assessing the SPP (L14).

Everyday talk, as seen in these sequences between friends, can seem far messier than strings of adjacency pairs, but it contains an internal organization that is visible through sequential analysis. In this section, I have shown the basic expansions known to CA (for more detail and subtypes of expansions, see Schegloff 2007) and applied them in two longer stretches of talk to demonstrate their function in a slightly larger context. In Section 6.3, I will examine variations on sequence organization, as found in much institutional talk.

6.3 Other Sequence Organizations

In this section, I will discuss variations seen in sequential organization. This topic has received the most attention in institutional interaction (Drew and Heritage 1992), as these contexts provide for specific rights and responsibilities in talk, but alternate organization is seen in everyday talk as well.

The main alternative to adjacency pair sequences is a storytelling or "telling" sequence, where the teller takes far longer turns and the listener withholds substantial responding turns until the story is concluded (see Georgakopoulou 2010; Goodwin 1984; Goodwin 2015; Chapter 5 in this volume). Such sequences are common in service encounters where a client is telling some kind of trouble or complaint for which they hope to receive service. For example, in the following extract, a citizen is visiting their local Member of Parliament because his benefits have been canceled. He is trying to appeal this decision, but the appeal court refuses to fix a date for appeal. It is worth noting that this particular constituent speaks slowly due to illness, which helps explain the unusually long gaps between turns.

Extract 6.9: MP01.Surgery-1KO_01
```
1     MP:    So. (0.2) How can we:: °how can we help.°
2                   (0.9)
3     C1:    Well, (0.9) I had ay: (0.4) assessment'hh. (0.9) Eighteen
4            months ago,
5     MP:    Right,
6                   (0.9)
7     C1:    Which stated that I was (0.3) fit an' capable, (0.6) For
8            work.=
9     MP:    =Right,
10                  (1.5)
11    C1:    An:d_ (0.4) my dactor: ↓when I phoned him up to tell
12           'im he just (0.3) °laughed his head off.°
13    MP:    °Mm,°
```

Both the constituent (C1) and the MP set up the sequence to allow C1 to do an extended telling. The MP asks "How can we help?" (L1), opening a slot wherein C1 can explain his answer fully. C1 begins his turn with "Well," (L3), which has been shown to indicate that the response will not be straightforward or immediate (Schegloff and Lerner 2009). C1 continues by referencing a past event ("Eighteen months ago"), begging the question of why that event is relevant now and suggesting that C1 will explain the relevance of this event. The MP supports C1's continued telling (L7 onwards) with continuers such as "Right" (L5, L9) and "Mm" (L13), which indicate receipt, but withholds stance until the telling has been completed (Goodwin 1986). CA prefers to use the term "continuer" as opposed to "back-channel" vocalization as it is more specific to the action being accomplished. The opening turns, followed by the use of continuers, set up the interaction to be one of a telling (see Hofstetter and Stokoe 2018). The MP's turns promote the continuation of the story, rather than a transition between speakers. Many institutional contexts have means for accomplishing specific sequences, often with extended turns for one party or another (e.g. interviews, speeches, formal debates, lecturing, etc.). However, although the above extract is institutional data, similar mechanisms support tellings in noninstitutional contexts (Jefferson 1978).

One additional source of sequence variation is in three-part base sequences (rather than two-part base pairs), where the third part is typically a stance toward or receipt of the SPP (Jefferson and Schenkein 1978). From Schegloff's (2007: 13) perspective, these are post-expansions. The alternative argument is that, if participants orient to a third turn as *missing* when absent (i.e., the third turn was not an "optional" component but a normatively, accountably relevant one), then the third turn is a necessary part to the sequence. There is evidence that the third turn is required in some institutional contexts. For example, Kevoe-Feldman and Robinson (2012) have shown how customers must necessarily produce a third-turn acceptance when calling to a computer repair shop and hearing the status of their repair. Repair center staff allow lengthy silences and do not initiate closing of the call until callers have indicated some acceptance of the status update. The most convincing evidence that this is not "merely" a post-expansion is that these third parts are treated as incomplete if they contain only news receipts that respond to the SPP – the independent *acceptance* is required. Similarly, necessary third turns have also been documented in noninstitutional data (Seuren 2018), suggesting this is not a trivial, one-context finding. Thus, it appears that certain actions or activities require more sequential space.

Finally, there are instances where sequential organization is temporarily suspended, specifically when there is a lapse in the sequence and significant silence occurs. Hoey (2015) has explored these moments, finding three types of lapse. First, silence can become the necessary thing to do (reading a document during a meeting, letting the driver manage a busy stretch of road, etc.). Second, silence can be "allowable" – occurring without participants making each other accountable (e.g. while some or all participants are engaging in tasks like studying or cooking and lapse into doing only those tasks instead of simultaneously talking). Third, silence can be accountable when participants act as though talk *ought* to be occurring but is not. Speakers all successively pass on opportunities to initiate a sequence, in what Hoey calls "turn taking hot potato," which is itself a form of sequential organization.

In this section, I have discussed some of the variations on sequential organization, where there is debate on how best to incorporate these alternatives. Although the adjacency pair may not be functioning in the same fashion, the response relevance concept still does. In Section 6.4, I will discuss one further area of debate, though one that does not have as much research: is there an organization to how sequences are put together?

6.4 Beyond One Sequence: Debates in Sequential Analysis

The adjacency pair and expansions can constitute long stretches of talk, even entire interactions. However, most interactions contain multiple sequences, and multiple "activities" as well. This chapter follows Robinson (2013) in using the word "activity" or "unit" to refer to a grouping of sequences that address a task or topic, and in that these units can have an internal organization and may themselves be organized with respect to each other in the overall interaction. For example, within an evening meal there is setting the table, settling down, passing food, eating and talking, closing the meal, washing up and perhaps dessert. Internal to the "washing up" activity may be sequences assigning drying and washing roles. In discussing these instances of complete interaction and sequences, the analysis should still demonstrate that such an organization is consequential to the participants, that the "activities" are not only the analyst's perception (e.g. participants orienting to not eating dessert before the meal). The merits of avoiding an analyst's label have been debated at length (see, e.g., Billig 1999; Schegloff 1999). The ethnomethodological perspective has been particularly criticized for being unable to label an activity as sexist given that sexism often receives no orientation from participants (Kitzinger 2000). However Kitzinger has also argued that this is precisely the advantage of an ethnomethodological/conversation analytic (EMCA) perspective, as it recognizes that sexism is designedly ambiguous.

Robinson in particular has shown (e.g. 2003) how patients and doctors orient to the activities of an acute care doctor's appointment, such as greeting, problem presentation, diagnosis, treatment, etc. Within each activity there is evidence that participants orient to progressing that *activity*, and additionally there is evidence that participants orient to progressing the full interaction. Importantly, Robinson (2013) points out that we cannot delineate how all activities or units are structured, nor full instances of interaction, as the structures vary to serve the tasks and context. The coherence of an activity is found within the structure. They are mutually constituted, both the "project and product" (Drew and Heritage 1992: 19) of participants' actions, and so they can only be locally demonstrated as well as locally created. This is not an analytic shrug of the shoulders but a commitment to analysis grounded in participant behavior.

Activities are culturally recognized and thus culturally grounded (Levinson 2013) and we must be cautious in assigning labels to them, as they can be easily multiply described (a doctor's appointment is as much an "activity" as is the history-taking phase within it (Robinson 2013: 278; see also Sidnell 2017). As the multiple activities or "levels" that can be described are reflexively linked within participant behavior, participants can be orienting to or progressing multiple components of the interaction at the same time, and may even designedly fail (Sidnell 2012; Stokoe 2012) to provide evidence of which component is at issue at any given point.

Early forays into this are seen in Schegloff's (1990) work on the maintenance of coherence across a sequence and Jefferson's (1988) breakdown of how a troubles-telling progresses. Each of these, however, stays within a single sequence, albeit a very large one; the authors themselves argue that their analyses demonstrate coherence over highly expanded, single actions. In addressing activities, there have been multiple approaches in the literature, as follows. One is to examine practices for joining multiple sequences into a coherent framework, such as Heritage and Sorjonen (1994), who showed how "and"-prefaced turns can mark a turn as united to a prior item, thus generating coherence across an activity. Relatedly, Bolden (2009: 996) finds that "so" can be used to indicate that the upcoming turn "has been occasioned by something other than the immediately preceding talk." In other words, a discourse marker is necessary to allow speakers to mention something that has not been made relevant by the prior adjacency pairs. Such behavior is literally marked. Both of these studies show that one reason activities can be difficult to describe is that interactional work occurs to ensure a seamless connection between activities.

A slightly different perspective is to consider moments when the sequence "lapses" (e.g. Hoey 2015), such as at moments of changing topic or in silences. Drew and Holt (1998) have found that figurative expressions can be used both as means to close a sequence relatively sharply but also as means to create a "pivot" point on which to transition topics in a stepwise, gradual manner (Holt and Drew 2005). The difference between these uses, however, is sequential: the former is accomplished by the same speaker as the teller doing the figurative expression, as a close to the story, while the latter is accomplished by the recipient of the telling through an assessment of the story.

One further approach is seen in Evans (2013), who links the practice-generated concept of activity (the "project and product" of the actions seen earlier) to Sacks's (1992) discussion of "membership categorization devices" (MCDs). MCDs are concepts activated through use by speakers in the interaction to invoke category-relevant features. Sacks's famous example is that in the sentences "The baby cried. The mommy picked it up," the mommy is instantly recognizable as *that baby's* mommy, not some other random mommy. The category terms are linked to each other and to specific activities. Evans argues that by invoking an activity, various things can be made relevant through the activity – for example, diagnosis is relevant to a doctor's appointment. This can be more fine-grained as well, working at a single sequence level or at multiple levels. A pain cry during a doctor's examination is relevant to cessation of the movement that causes the pain (as such, it can be an FPP with the SPP being assessment or stopping the movement), as well as to the diagnosis that is ongoing (the activity) and to the overall interaction (the doctor providing service to that patient).

A particularly promising route of investigation has looked at how participants do *multiple* activities at once and how they demonstrate orientations to balancing those activities. Mondada's (2014) discussion provides the most detailed account of the basics of multiactivity. She shows how a surgeon puts various behaviors on hold as contingencies arise in one or another of the activities being done: lecturing and pointing to demonstrative components, coordinating manual movements with the surgery team and manipulating the surgical tools. The benefit of analyzing participants engaged in multiple activities is that they show a range of practices, from implicit to highly explicit comments such as "hold on," that demonstrate their orientation to what constitutes an ongoing activity. This research tends to focus less on activity-as-the-subunit of a whole interaction and more on individual sequences where multiple activities are being done, but it still sheds light on how participants make sense of and create "activity" in real time.

In this section, I have discussed various approaches to researching how sequences are combined into recognizable activities. There is a wide variety of means to tackle this issue, but all are grounded in showing how participants generate "activity." There is still much work to be done in this area, as it pushes the boundaries of sequential analysis. In Section 6.5, I will discuss how sequences and activities can be informative in other research projects and in applied work.

6.5 Implications

As I have emphasized throughout this chapter, sequential organization is present in all interactions – with evidence that the same basic organization runs across languages (Stivers et al. 2009). While it is useful to describe this system in its own right, and to have a method for analyzing talk that demonstrates its findings in a way that is grounded in the participants' own orientations, there are also useful considerations for noninteractional researchers. In particular, it is worth applying the notion of "sequential context" to linguistic and social analyses of *any* kind of talk because this framework explains the occurrence of many features and phenomena found in talk. CA has largely recommended this practice to interview-based studies (Drew, Raymond and Weinberg 2006), but the recommendation applies elsewhere.

When determining what a turn design does, for example, sequential position is critical. Past research has shown that sequential position can change the outcome of utterance (Kent and Kendrick 2016). In other subdisciplines, "outcome" might be called the utterance's meaning or illocutionary force, such as with speech act theory (Searle 1979). Words do not occur in a vacuum but inevitably in sequential position, so their sequential position influences their design and action. Responses in interviews are given in a specific sequential context in the interview, and this sequential context influences what people say because they must design their talk in accordance with the sequence. By demonstrating this sequential context in publication, researchers can both ensure an analysis grounded in the concerns of the participants (which will always include management of the sequence and interaction) and give readers better means to evaluate the analysis of the data collected, which additionally provides for more robust and comparable findings.

Finally, showing the sequence in which utterances occur has also been shown to be effective in applied work such as communication training. Invented examples rely too heavily on assumed situations, and these assumptions have been proven, bluntly, to be inaccurate (Stokoe 2013b). Presenting real sequences to trainees allows them to better understand the context in which their utterances will come about in the work day. This is done with the Conversation Analytic Role-play Method (CARM, Stokoe 2013a) and has also been useful in generating feedback for professionals elsewhere (e.g. Antaki 2011). The key component to CARM and similar work is showing practitioners the sequences of actual talk. In demonstrating to them the sequence in which practical, professional difficulties can occur, and examples of how past practitioners in recordings had avoided, exited or altered that sequence, practitioners see feasible options for communicating differently.

6.6 Future Directions

CA has generated a solid understanding of the internal mechanisms of the sequence, although there is still work to be done – particularly with respect to why SPPs may sometimes not be relevant (Stivers and Rossano

2010; Hoey 2015). It would be helpful now to devote more attention to social action beyond single sequences, such as activities. Despite calls for more research in overall sequence organization (Robinson 2013), there are few studies of activities, and several current explanations of organization that may be further tested or condensed. Earlier, I described how contextually situated and culturally grounded studies of activities have shown that they can be very flexible for participants but difficult to analyze. Furthermore, participants employ resources for maintaining coherence over sequences and multiple sequences, further obscuring potential sites of activity "change." The difficulty in understanding long stretches of multiple sequences is best phrased by Sacks (1992: 190):

> Then there's this other thing about greetings, having to do with their placing, i.e. that greetings go at the beginning of the beginning section, which is altogether independent of adjacency pair organization and has to do with a different type of organization for conversation, i.e., the overall structural organization. And in those terms, there is no information in adjacency pair organization about where the first part of the pair should go in a conversation.

The robust organization found in adjacency pairs and other sequences is internally illuminating, but to discover how these units are linked requires a view beyond the sequences themselves – to zoom back and determine what organization may be found among the larger units. What "next turn proof procedure" can we find outside the sequence, if any?

The need for this information is seen in a pervasive term: "project." The verb form ("to project") is used to refer to the ability of interlocutors to anticipate likely upcoming responses. In its noun form, however, a "project" has been used to describe the activity at hand, with the implication of a goal or agenda. It is a widely used term (e.g. Rossi 2012; Sacks 1992: 56; Walker, Drew and Local 2011) but rarely the topic of research. Levinson (2013: 122) writes:, "A project is not a sequence, for it may or may not be instantiated in a sequence," and indeed analysts will see evidence of projects that run across multiple sequences or appear as extensive sequences that *could* be pre-sequences but then get abandoned before any clear base pair or action. Authors use this term to discuss the goals or agenda of speakers that is seen to be pursued in the talk, but without breaking the CA rule not to assume the mental states of the participants. "Projects" are most clearly visible in institutional interactions where the two parties (the institutional representative and the service seeker) have "projects" that are slightly different or juxtaposed (Hepburn and Potter 2011). Raymond and Zimmerman (2007) show examples of how different callers to emergency services during a large-scale fire demonstrated different projects – some informed about the emergency, some *requested* information or advice. As such, we can see the impact of multiple activities at once (calling emergency lines, informing vs. asking advice) on the sequence.

Furthermore, critiques of the sequential perspective desire that sequences grapple with the context of an interaction (e.g. Billig 1999). An understanding of activities, sequences of sequences and such "mid-level" organization may help address these concerns. Further research into activities may be able to unite the highly "micro"-analytic scale that characterizes EMCA with larger, "macro"-scale (or "meso"-scale, with activities) events that are more recognizable to the layman and to other researchers of discourse. The key will be, as ever, to show how speakers manage to *create* the structures that support these levels of organization (and how they make said structures accountable).

6.7 Summary

In this chapter, I have given a detailed overview of sequential organization, the central mechanism that structures all human interaction, and a means by which to analyze talk. I have described the adjacency pair and its expansions, as well as some variations in sequence organization. I have also discussed how sequences can be linked together into activities, a mid-level unit that can themselves be linked into larger interactions. More research into the concept of "activity" seems necessary, but activities are challenging to define and prove relevant due to their inherent flexibility and context-generated nature. Finally, I have discussed some considerations for other fields and that including the sequential context in analysis provides multiple benefits.

Further Reading

Haddington, P., Keisanen, T., Mondada, L. and Nevile, M. (eds.) (2014). *Multiactivity in Social Interaction: Beyond Multitasking*. Amsterdam: John Benjamins.

This volume has an excellent collection of different ways in which multiactivity can appear in various contexts and with various practices.

Heritage, J. and Maynard, D. W. (eds.) (2006). *Communication in Medical Care: Interaction between Primary Care Physicians and Patients*. Cambridge: Cambridge University Press.

This book covers many of the "stages" found in medical consultations (diagnosis, treatment, etc.) and, as such, provides examples of how full interactions may be broken down into activity units.

Schegloff, E. A. (2007). *Sequence Organization in Interaction: A Primer in Conversation Analysis*. Cambridge: Cambridge University Press.

This is the primary resource for the details of sequential organization.

Abridged Jefferson Transcription Key

t[alk	Square brackets mark the start and end of overlapping speech.
[Yeah,	They are aligned to mark the precise position of overlap.
↑↓	Vertical arrows precede marked pitch movement, over and above normal rhythms of speech. They are used for notable changes in pitch beyond those represented by stops, commas and question marks.
Under<u>lin</u>ing	Indicates emphasis; the extent of underlining within individual words locates emphasis and also indicates how heavy it is.
CAPITALS	Mark speech that is hearably louder than surrounding speech. This is beyond the increase in volume indicated by <u>under</u>lines.
°<u>I</u> know it,°	"Degree" signs enclose hearably quieter speech.
(0.4)	Numbers in round brackets measure pauses in seconds (in this case, four-tenths of a second).
(.)	A micropause, hearable but too short to measure.
((stoccato))	Additional comments from the transcriber, e.g. about features of context or delivery.
((lines omitted))	Also to indicate material omitted for brevity.
(I know)	Text in single round brackets to indicate best guess at hard-to-hear utterance. Can also be blank to indicate something spoken but unhearable.
she wa::nted	Colons show degrees of elongation of the prior sound; the more colons, the more elongation.
hhh	Aspiration (out-breaths); proportionally as for colons.
.hhh	Inspiration (in-breaths); proportionally as for colons.
Yeh,	Comma: "Continuation" marker, speaker has not finished; marked by weak rising intonation, as when delivering a verbal list.
y'know?	Question mark: strong rise in intonation, *irrespective of grammar*.
okay¿	Inverse question mark indicates tone between a comma and a question mark in rise.
Yeh.	Full stop: marks falling, stopping intonation ("final contour"), *irrespective of grammar*, not necessarily followed by a pause.

bu- u-	Hyphens mark a cut-off of the preceding sound.
>he said<	"Greater than" and "lesser than" signs enclose utterances that are faster than surrounding talk.
<he said>	Reverse indicates utterances that are slower than surrounding talk.
solid.=	"Equals" signs mark the immediate "latching" of successive talk,
=We had	whether of one or more speakers, with no interval.
sto(h)p i(h)t	Laughter within speech is signaled by h's in round brackets.

References

Antaki, C. (ed.) (2011). *Applied Conversation Analysis: Intervention and Change in Institutional Talk*. London: Palgrave.

Billig, M. (1999). Whose Terms? Whose Ordinariness? Rhetoric and Ideology in Conversation Analysis. *Discourse & Society* 10(4): 543–82.

Bolden, G. B. (2009). Implementing Incipient Actions: The Discourse Marker "So" in English Conversation. *Journal of Pragmatics* 41(5): 974–98.

Chomsky, N. (1957). *Syntactic Structures*. The Hague: Mouton.

Clayman, S. E. (2001). Answers and Evasions. *Language in Society* 30(3): 403–42.

Drew, P. and Heritage, J. (eds.) (1992). *Talk at Work: Interaction in Institutional Settings*. New York: Cambridge University Press.

Drew, P. and Holt, E. (1998). Figures of Speech: Figurative Expressions and the Management of Topic Transition in Conversation. *Language in Society* 27: 495–522.

Drew, P., Raymond, G. and Weinberg, D. (eds.) (2006). *Talk and Interaction in Social Research Methods*. London: Sage.

Evans, B. (2013). Order on the Court: The Interactional Organization of Basketball Practice Activities. Doctoral thesis, University of Western Sydney.

Fox, B. A. and Thompson, S. A. (2010). Responses to Wh-Questions in English Conversation. *Research on Language and Social Interaction* 43(2): 133–56.

Georgakopoulou, A. (2010). Closing in on Story Openings and Closings: Evidence from Conversational Stories in Greek. *Journal of Greek Linguistics* 10(2): 345–61.

Goodwin, C. (1984). Notes on Story Structure and the Organization of Participation. In J. M. Atkison and J. Heritage (eds.) *Structures of Social Action: Studies in Conversation Analysis*. Cambridge: Cambridge University Press. 225–46.

  (1986). Between and Within: Alternative Sequential Treatments of Continuers and Assessments. *Human Studies* 9(2–3): 205–17.

(2000). Action and Embodiment within Situated Human Interaction. *Journal of Pragmatics* 32: 1489–522.

(2015). Narrative As Talk-in-Interaction. In A. De Fina and A. Georgakopoulou (eds.) *The Handbook of Narrative Analysis*. London: Wiley. 195–218.

Hepburn, A. and Potter, J. (2011). Designing the Recipient: Some Practices that Manage Advice Resistance in Institutional Settings. *Social Psychology Quarterly* 74: 216–41.

Heritage, J. (1984). A Change-of-State Token and Aspects of Its Sequential Placement. In J. M. Atkinson and J. Heritage (eds.) *Structures of Social Action: Studies in Conversation Analysis*. Cambridge: Cambridge University Press. 299–345.

Heritage, J. and Sorjonen, M.-L. (1994). Constituting and Maintaining Activities across Sequences: And-Prefacing as a Feature of Question Design. *Language in Society* 23: 1–29.

Hoey, E. M. (2015). Lapses: How People Arrive at, and Deal with, Discontinuities in Talk. *Research on Language and Social Interaction* 48 (4): 430–53.

Hofstetter, E. and Stokoe, E. (2018). Getting Service at the Constituency Office: Analyzing Citizens' Encounters with Their Member of Parliament. *Text & Talk* 38(5): 551–73.

Holt, E. and Drew, P. (2005). Figurative Pivots: The Use of Figurative Expressions in Pivotal Topic Transitions. *Research on Language and Social Interaction* 38(1): 35–61.

Jefferson, G. (1978). Sequential Aspects of Storytelling in Conversation. In J. Schenkein (ed.) *Studies in the Organization of Conversational Interaction*. New York: Academic Press. 219–48.

(1988). On the Sequential Organization of Troubles-Talk in Ordinary Conversation. *Social Problems* 35(4): 418–41.

Jefferson, G. and Schenkein, J. (1978). Some Sequential Negotiations in Conversation: Unexpanded and Expanded Versions of Projected Action Sequences. In J. Schenkein (ed.) *Studies in the Organization of Conversational Interaction*. New York: Academic Press. 155–72.

Keevallik, L. (2018). What Does Embodied Interaction Tell Us about Grammar? *Research on Language and Social Interaction* 51(1): 1–21.

Kendrick, K. H. and Drew, P. (2016). Recruitment: Offers, Requests, and the Organization of Assistance in Interaction. *Research on Language and Social Interaction* 49(1): 1–19.

Kent, A. and Kendrick, K. H. (2016). Imperative Directives: Orientations to Accountability. *Research on Language and Social Interaction* 49(3): 272–88.

Kevoe-Feldman, H. and Robinson, J. D. (2012). Exploring Essentially Three-Turn Courses of Action: An Institutional Case Study with Implications for Ordinary Talk. *Discourse Studies* 14(2): 217–41.

Kitzinger, C. (2000). Doing Feminist Conversation Analysis. *Feminism & Psychology* 10(2): 163–93.

Levinson, S. (2013). Action Formation and Ascription. In J. Sidnell and T. Stivers (eds.) *The Handbook of Conversation Analysis*. London: Wiley-Blackwell. 103–30.

Mondada, L. (2008). Using Video for a Sequential and Multimodal Analysis of Social Interaction: Videotaping Institutional Telephone Calls. *Forum Qualitative Sozialforschung* 9(3): Art. 39.

(2014). The Temporal Orders of Multiactivity: Operating and Demonstrating in the Surgical Theatre. In P. Haddington, T. Keisanen, L. Mondada and M. Nevile (eds.) *Multiactivity in Social Interaction: Beyond Multitasking*. Amsterdam: John Benjamins. 31–75.

Nevile, M. (2015). The Embodied Turn in Research on Language and Social Interaction. *Research on Language and Social Interaction* 48(2): 121–51.

Raymond, G. (2003). Grammar and Social Organization: Yes/No Interrogatives and the Structure of Responding. *American Sociological Review* 68(6): 939–67.

Raymond, G. and Zimmerman, D. H. (2007). Rights and Responsibilities in Calls for Help: The Case of the Mountain Glade Fire. *Research on Language and Social Interaction* 40(1): 33–61.

Robinson, J. (2003). An Interactional Structure of Medical Activities during Acute Visits and Its Implications for Patients' Participation. *Health Communication* 15(1): 27–59.

(2013). Overall Structural Organization. In J. Sidnell and T. Stivers (eds.) *The Handbook of Conversation Analysis*. London: Wiley-Blackwell. 257–80.

Romaniuk, T. (2013). Pursuing Answers to Questions in Broadcast Journalism. *Research on Language and Social Interaction* 46(2): 144–64.

Rossi, G. (2012). Bilateral and Unilateral Requests in Italian: The Use of Imperatives and Mi X? Interrogatives in Italian. *Discourse Processes* 49(5): 426–58.

Sacks, H. (1992). *Lectures on Conversation*. Oxford: Blackwell.

Sacks, H., Schegloff, E. and Jefferson, G. (1974). A Simplest Systematics for the Organization of Turn-Taking in Conversation. *Language* 50: 696–735. doi: 10.1353/lan.1974.0010.

Schegloff, E. A. (1968). Sequencing in Conversational Openings. *American Anthropologist* 70: 1075–95.

(1979). Identification and Recognition in Telephone Conversation Openings. In G. Psathas (ed.) *Everyday Language: Studies in Ethnomethodology*. New York: Irvington Publishers. 23–78.

(1980). Preliminaries to Preliminaries: "Can I Ask You a Question?" *Sociological Inquiry* 50(3–4): 104–52.

(1990). On the Organization of Sequences as a Source of "Coherence" in Talk-in-Interaction. In B. Dorval (ed.) *Conversational Organization and Its Development*. Norwood: Ablex. 51–77.

(1999). Schegloff's Texts as Billig's Data: A Critical Reply. *Discourse & Society* 10(4): 558–72.

(2007). *Sequence Organization in Interaction: A Primer in Conversation Analysis*, Vol. 1. Cambridge: Cambridge University Press.

Schegloff, E. A. and Lerner, G. H. (2009). Beginning to Respond: Well-Prefaced Responses to Wh-Questions. *Research on Language and Social Interaction* 42(2): 91–115.

Schegloff, E. A. and Sacks, H. (1973). Opening Up Closings. *Semiotica* 8(4): 289–327.

Searle, J. (1979). *Expression and Meaning: Studies in the Theory of Speech Acts*. Cambridge: Cambridge University Press.

Seuren, L. (2018). Assessing Answers: Action Ascription in Third Position. *Research on Language and Social Interaction* 51(1): 33–51.

Sidnell, J. (2012). Declaratives, Questioning, Defeasibility. *Research on Language & Social Interaction* 45(1): 53–60.

(2017). Action in Interaction Is Conduct under a Description. *Language in Society* 46(3): 313–37.

Stivers, T., Enfield, N. J., Brown, P., Englert, C., Hayashi, M., Heinemann, T., ... Levinson, S. C. (2009). Universals and Cultural Variation in Turn-Taking in Conversation. *Proceedings of the National Academy of Sciences of the United States of America*, 106(26): 10587–92.

Stivers, T. and Rossano, F. (2010). Mobilizing Response. *Research on Language and Social Interaction* 43(1): 3–31.

Stokoe, E. (2012). Categorial Systematics. *Discourse Studies* 14(3): 345–54.

(2013a). Overcoming Barriers to Mediation in Intake Calls to Services: Research-Based Strategies for Mediators. *Negotiation Journal* 29(3): 289–314.

(2013b). The (In)Authenticity of Simulated Talk: Comparing Role-Played and Actual Interaction and the Implications for Communication Training. *Research on Language and Social Interaction* 46(2): 165–85.

Walker, T., Drew, P. and Local, J. (2011). Responding Indirectly. *Journal of Pragmatics* 43: 2434–51.

7

Doing Micro-Analysis of Discourse: The Case of Ageing and Wellbeing

Rachel Heinrichsmeier

7.1 Introduction

In this chapter we use ageing and wellbeing as a case study for examining what micro-analysis of interaction can offer. Wellbeing is extensively researched. Scholars the world over research levels, causes and interventions with respect to national populations, in comparative studies, for particular groups considered "at risk" of low wellbeing, and so on. One group often stereotypically perceived as likely to suffer from low wellbeing is older people, and it is on this broad category that we focus in this chapter. Wellbeing has been conceptualized in various ways and can encompass a number of domains of life including economic, health and environment (Andrews and Robinson 1991; Custers et al. 2011). Here we focus on what is variously referred to as subjective wellbeing (SWB), psychological wellbeing or personal wellbeing (Keyes, Shmotkin and Ryff 2002), which – implicitly or otherwise – tends to be taken as encompassing one or more of quality of life, life satisfaction, personal happiness and self-worth (Andrews and Robinson 1991; Steptoe, Deaton and Stone 2015). Unsurprisingly given that this is *subjective* wellbeing we are talking about, these ideas conceptualize wellbeing as essentially inner to an individual. However, as we see in this chapter, a discourse analytic perspective helps us see how wellbeing may be at least partly co-constructed in everyday interactions, specifically in quality interactions.

What, though, constitutes quality interaction? Summarizing from research into older people's interactions and friendships (e.g. Grainger 2004; Rawlins 2004), we may infer that quality interactions are those that are enjoyable or in some way fulfilling for participants, interactions that display attentiveness to the other, alignment to their interactional project (e.g. a complaint, a story, a gossip) and displays of affiliation that show the speakers share the same or similar stances toward the topic of talk. Such interaction might encompass a range of kinds of talk, including laughter and humor, displays of intimacy and interest in each other's lives and the possibility for troubles-telling (e.g. Matsumoto 2009; Moremen 2008; Pomerantz and Mandelbaum 2005). But, ultimately, what constitutes quality in any particular interaction is a *participant's concern*, and this brings us to a brief discussion of the discursive approach adopted in this chapter, which is informed by the ideas of conversation analysis (CA) (see Chapter 6 in this volume).

CA focuses on understanding people's ordinary, everyday sense-making methods in interaction and tries to capture the details of talk – both the words and how they are produced – in transcripts. CA also emphasizes the importance of privileging participants' orientations over those of the analyst. So, although we shall examine what other studies have to say about quality interaction, we shall also scrutinize examples of older people's actual talk in an everyday setting (a hair salon) to see what these tell us about participants' own orientations to the quality or otherwise of particular interactions. In drawing on CA, the analyses in this chapter can be considered to be "applied CA," in that the concepts and analytic frameworks of CA are being used to understand the psychological notion of subjective wellbeing, "respecifying it as [at least in part] a communicative act"' rather than a pre-existing independent state (Antaki 2011: 3). This is similar to the way CA has been used in discursive psychology, such that "[r]ather than seeing the study of discourse as a pathway to individuals' inner life, whether it be cognitive processes, motivations or some other mental stuff, we see psychological issues as constructed and deployed in the discourse itself" (Edwards and Potter 1992: 127).

In Section 7.2, and as an entry-point to the topic, we shall start by considering some actual discourse, in the sense of language use and practice, between participants in a hair salon. We shall then consider why we might want to focus on ageing and what this kind of discourse analysis offers when it comes to examining ageing and wellbeing. In Section 7.3, we shall discuss what other studies say about interaction with older people. As part of this, we shall examine more examples of actual talk to scrutinize participants' own orientations to the quality (or otherwise) of their talk. Finally, we will briefly examine the implications of adopting this CA-informed discourse analytic approach to exploring wellbeing in later life, before closing the chapter with a discussion of possible avenues of future research.

7.2 Wellbeing in Action: Laughter and Positive Identities

The following extract, which derives from my research into older women's identity constructions in a hair salon (Heinrichsmeier 2016,

7 Doing Micro-Analysis of Discourse

2020), helps us start to see what might make for a quality encounter in everyday conversation; importantly, picking up on the discussion in Section 7.1, it helps us see what *participants themselves* might orientate to as quality interaction. As I shall argue, the quality, here, lies both in the immediate enjoyment afforded by the interaction and in the positive sense of self or identity that the encounter also affords for the older participant; and wellbeing accrues from both these elements. The extract comes from audio recordings of talk between a ninety-year-old woman, Mrs. Farming, and her stylist, Joellen, in the hair salon.[1] Rachel is inexpertly (ll.8–10) passing perm rods to Joellen. She, Joellen and another salon-worker have been increasingly consumed by giggles. After one of these laughing fits, Mrs. Farming, who has herself been laughing, and who is smiling as she speaks (indicated by the "£" sign), makes her comment in l.1 (see Appendix for transcription notation).

Extract 7.1 Carrying On[2]
20:43
1.	Mrs. Farming	£I think I'm going home
2.		if you're [(gon)£ he he he he he he
3.	Joellen	[he he he he he he he he ((*sighs*))
4.	Joellen	you love it really=
5.	Mrs. Farming	=yeah [I do
6.	Joellen	[he he he
7.		(9)((*no talk as Joellen focuses on hair*))
8.	Rachel	°°oh which color (.) oh this color°°
9.	Joellen	no >I don't want that color at all now<
10.		[((*clatter as something falls on the ground*))
11.	Mrs. Farming	[I don't know what-
12.	Joellen	oh gaw::d he he
13.	Mrs. Farming	our new girl thinks of Lucy and I
14.		because we ca(h)rry on like we do
15.		in here [you know
16.	Joellen	[ye(h)ah [he he he he he
17.	Mrs. Farming	[sh(h)e £looked a bit stunned£
18.		.he [ha ha ha ha
19.	Joellen	[he he he he

21:11

There is a lot to be said about this extract, but we will focus on the way in which both Mrs. Farming and Joellen orientate to laughter as a good thing: Joellen asserts that Mrs. Farming "loves it really" (l.4), to which Mrs. Farming produces an agreement so swiftly that it comes without

---
[1] Ethical approval was granted by King's College London. All participants' names are pseudonyms except for that of Rachel, the researcher.
[2] Extract taken from pp.191–192 in R.Heinrichsmeier (2020) Ageing Identities and Women's Everyday Talk in a Hair Salon, New York and London: Routledge

pause (l.5). She then makes a claim to act similarly at home (ll.11–17). Laying claim to "loving it" in this way and producing this claim with laughter constructs this kind of "carrying on" as something positive and fun, and Joellen's responsive laughter (ll.16, 19) affiliates with that construction. So, this interaction affords us a glimpse of *participants' orientations to quality interaction*. Such interaction, I suggest, contributes at least fleetingly to participants' wellbeing. Indeed, prior studies involving older people's talk, of both those living in the community and institutionalized older people, have noted the benefit that can accrue from talk involving humor and laughing together, in terms of enjoyment, warmer relationships and positive emotional benefit (e.g. Marsden and Holmes 2014; Matsumoto 2009: 948; see, too, Section 7.4). But there is another aspect of quality here, namely, the way that the interaction affords Mrs. Farming (and indeed Joellen too) a positive identity. Here, identities – including *older* identities – are understood as emergent interactional achievements (re)constructed *through* or the *product of* a range of situated practices (Bucholtz and Hall 2005: 588). Such practices include spoken interaction and written texts; that is, discourse that itself emerges in a particular sociocultural-historical environment.

In this extract, although Mrs. Farming in ll.1–2 is laughing, her words imply a degree of impatience with the giggling; any further evaluation by her could go either way. But then Joellen declares "you love it really" (l.4). The design of this utterance positions Joellen as knowing what Mrs. Farming is "really" like; and it casts Mrs. Farming as (really) the kind of person who enjoys this unconventional behavior in the hair salon. As we've seen, Mrs. Farming not only immediately accepts this positioning but also extends the scope of the claim: it is not just here that she "carries on"; it is how she is more broadly. That is, she makes a claim about her identity: rather than being a stereotypically complaining, depressed and grumpy (older) person (Matsumoto 2009: 933), she is "really" a fun, lively and rather wacky person.

Coupland (2004: 85) argues that "identity in ageing ultimately connects to morale and wellbeing." He continues: "There is an intensity of personal consequence when old people perceive their identities to be spoiled or their narratives … to be 'incoherent.'" Here, by contrast, the interaction has afforded Mrs. Farming the opportunity to co-construct for herself, with Joellen, a positive – an "*un*spoiled" – identity; one that is counterstereotypical enough to "stun" her young cleaner (the "new girl," l.13). This extract thus gives insights into *wellbeing in action* – that is, instead of seeing wellbeing as a purely internal psychological process, we see the way it might actually be achieved in interaction (see, for example, Edwards and Potter 1992); and it is achieved both through the immediate enjoyment of the exchange and through the "unspoiled" identities thereby afforded, for example, through identities that run counter to dominant decremental images of later life. So, we start to get an understanding of both what might constitute quality in an interaction and how this can contribute to people's wellbeing, including that of older people. Why, though, might we be particularly interested in *ageing* and wellbeing? This is what we turn to next.

7.3 Overview: Why Ageing? Why Discourse?

Wellbeing research crosses disciplinary boundaries, with investigations emanating, for example, from economics, health and social studies, and psychology. However, a considerable body of research into wellbeing also stems from social gerontology (Andrews and Robinson 1991; Keyes, Shmotkin and Ryff 2002). Indeed, many studies focusing on other aspects of older age, such as, for example, friendships in later life, claim that the particular factors scrutinized in their research also have an impact on wellbeing (Rawlins 2004). And in terms of discourse, Coupland, Coupland and Giles (1991: 73) proposed that discourse analysis could enhance training for many in the caring professions, thereby contributing to the psychological wellbeing of older people.

But low wellbeing is not an issue confined to older populations. Indeed, there is evidence to suggest that older people – by some measures at least – enjoy higher levels of wellbeing than adults in their middle years (Blanchflower and Oswald 2008). To what extent does a focus on *older people's* wellbeing implicitly construct later life as problematic? This is indeed a risk, but let us for now note that there are several reasons why we might want to focus on wellbeing in later life. For example, not only is there a well-documented rise in the proportion of people over sixty-five, but some research finds that levels of wellbeing in older age differ in different countries (Steptoe, Deaton and Stone 2015) and also are lower for some groups of older people; indeed, there are gaps in our knowledge of particular sections of society. Furthermore, though, one of the circulating ideas or Discourses of later life in much of Western society is of *ageing as decline* – physical, cognitive and social – with low wellbeing often seen as part of this decline.

It is useful at this point to borrow from Gee (2008: 2) and distinguish broadly between two kinds of "discourse." So, on the one hand are discourses (with lower-case "d") in the sense of language use and practices – talk and writing in specific settings and contexts. On the other hand are wider social processes such as ideologies and wider social norms or value systems – Discourses with an upper-case "D." In terms of ageing, later life is often nowadays depicted as a time of renewal and invigoration, particularly in much advertising and in publications aimed at older people (e.g. Calasanti, Sorensen and King 2012; Lumme-Sandt 2011). However, one still-dominant Discourse in much of the Western world is the conceptualization of ageing as inevitable decline. So, in many mainstream media and advertisements, older people are portrayed as increasingly physically and cognitively impaired, weak and complaining, as dependent, vulnerable, passive, and so on (e.g. Coupland 2004; Fealy et al. 2012). In line with this conceptualization, low wellbeing is stereotypically associated with *older* people, inasmuch as they are often conceptualized as lonely, vulnerable, isolated and depressed (Agren 2017; Uotila, Lumme-Sandt and Saarenheimo 2010). Such negative depictions of ageing are powerful and pervasive. They can infuse the talk and shape perceptions of later life of both younger and older people (Ylänne 2015), with consequential impacts on the way in which relationships unfold, on health, and on self-esteem and identities. So focusing on ageing and wellbeing gives us, inter alia, a lens through which to scrutinize the way these broader ideologies play out in local interactions (Coupland 2004). A growing volume of research adopts discourse analysis to examine issues affecting older people, encompassing both wider societal representations and the way such circulating ideas about ageing are orientated to in interaction (e.g. Coupland and Coupland 1999; Fealy et al. 2012; Grainger 2004; Jolanki 2004; Näslund 2017; Ylänne 2015). Nevertheless, studies adopting a micro-discourse analytic approach of the kind used in the example above to focus explicitly on what might support wellbeing for older people are rare.

Wellbeing is of course more than just discourse: a wide range of material factors have been linked to people's wellbeing, particularly good health (Andrews and Robinson 1991; Steptoe, Deaton and Stone 2015). So why adopt a micro-discourse analytic approach? One answer is that it is through discourse – local interaction that draws on, shapes and is shaped by a wider Discursive environment – that older adults construct and are ascribed "spoiled" or "unspoiled" identities. Discourse, too, is central to research about ageing and wellbeing (e.g. via interviews and surveys). We shall illustrate the centrality of discourse and the importance of discourse analysis by picking up on the discussion in Section 7.2 and focusing on the insights that discourse analysis offers about quality interaction and the kinds of identities afforded.

7.4 Quality in Interaction: Issues and Ongoing Debates

Many studies of wellbeing highlight the centrality of meaningful relationships and social roles for the wellbeing of older people (e.g. Ashida et al. 2018; Steptoe, Deaton and Stone 2015), including particularly those in institutional contexts (e.g., Custers et al. 2011). And many social gerontologists researching a range of aspects of older adults' lives likewise argue that friendships and other relationships have a significant impact on older people's lives (Ashida et al. 2018: 15; Moremen 2008). Rawlins (2004: 293), for example, states: "Friends are uniquely valued to talk, reminisce, and judge with, and to keep confidences. They relieve loneliness, help with incidental needs, connect individuals to larger communities, and foster their ongoing enjoyment of life." He goes on to argue that what is critical for older people's psychological wellbeing is not the "quantity of their social encounters" so much as "the quality of interaction characterizing their stable confidant relationships" (Rawlins 2004: 289). Examining what constitutes this quality in interaction is a task for which discourse analysis is well fitted. We shall start by reviewing the research into ageing and interaction in institutional settings and then turn to everyday community-based settings.

7.4.1 Research in Institutional Settings

Much research into interaction with older people has taken place in institutional settings, including many ethnographic studies of relationships in care homes (e.g. chapters in Henderson and Vesperi 1995). As Grainger (2004: 482) shows, where these examine talk in any degree of detail, much of the focus is on *quantity* of talk, with a scrutiny of the number or length of interactions with patients or residents. Summarizing these findings, Grainger (2004: 482) concluded that "institutionalized older adults tend to leave [sic] a communicatively impoverished life" as overall there is little talk with residents, and such talk as there is tends to be focused on completion of the institutional caring task. Later studies have confirmed this finding (e.g. Ward et al. 2008).

Many ethnographic studies do move beyond this kind of quantification and seek to shed light on the quality of interaction and communication in care homes. One focus of such research has been the use of "elderspeak" or "secondary baby talk." A substantial psychological literature claims that stereotypical "decline" views of older people as vulnerable and cognitively incompetent, particularly though not solely those in institutions, shape the use of this kind of talk (e.g. Ryan, Hummert and Boich 1995). This is talk characterized by higher pitch and a particular kind of intonation, involving also features such as use of "we" instead of "I," "softeners" and modal verbs, use of first names as well as talking about the older person in the third person in the presence of another (see discussions in Grainger (2004) and Williams (2011)). This has been claimed to have negative effects on individuals' wellbeing in long-term care (Williams 2011: loc.19); and, indeed, older people themselves claim that such talk affects their wellbeing. Yet other research reports that older people find it nurturing (Williams 2011: loc.333). This last observation highlights the challenges in examining a single kind of talk in isolation: not only does it assume that older people in a particular setting are a homogenous group; it also fails to look at how older people themselves receive and co-construct particular kinds of talk.

Other ethnographic studies highlight a range of positive interactions occurring in care settings "including personal talk, jokes, and non-verbal affective behaviour like smiling" (Custers et al. 2011: 1427). These studies show the interaction that goes beyond task-talk, whether between residents and carers or among residents, and provide invaluable pointers to the kinds of behavior that seem to support wellbeing. However, as Grainger (2004: 484) points out, what is characterized as "personal talk," for example, might turn out, upon closer inspection of the actual interaction, to be in the service of task completion. More broadly, when it comes to verbal interactions, it can be difficult to identify the key factors underpinning problems and successes without minute examination of the detail of talk.

Until recently, there have been relatively few interactionally focused studies of communication in care settings. One such study, though, is Grainger's (2004) detailed examination of interactions with patients in long-stay geriatric wards undertaken in the early 1990s. She argues powerfully that talk orientated toward building a relationship in this institutional setting is subordinated to the demands of caring for the residents, and shows how nurses repeatedly deflect or ignore patients' troubles. The issue for the nurses, argues Grainger, is twofold. Firstly, they have to attend to institutional goals of physical care, which might be put at risk if too much time is spent talking about patients' troubles. Secondly, though, and perhaps more fundamentally, "[n]urses lack the specialized training and expertise to respond effectively to deeply felt emotional or physical stresses" (Grainger 2004: 488); and a failure to respond effectively impacts their own "caring identity."

In the last decade, an increasing number of studies have adopted a discourse analytic perspective on interaction in care settings (e.g. chapters in Backhaus 2011b; Chatwin 2014; Marsden and Holmes 2014), that is, have undertaken close analysis of the detail of people's talk in situated interactions. These studies offer more insights into the detail of interaction in care and nursing institutions and how quality interaction for residents is afforded or constrained. For example, Matsumoto (2019) draws on analysis of a documentary to highlight not only the extent of interaction but also "the significance of affective communication" for Alzheimer's patients. Marsden and Holmes (2014), examining talk in a care home in New Zealand, challenge the universality of the finding that patronizing "elderspeak" dominates in care homes; and Backhaus's (2011a) analysis of talk between carers and residents in a care home in Japan found that parties were able temporarily to suspend or even reverse their institutional roles of carer/caree, highlighting the interactive co-construction of such roles. He suggests that such role shifts are likely to be positive for both carer and resident.

Some studies draw on the tools of conversation analysis to examine the unfolding detail of turns at talk. This can be even more revealing in terms of quality in interaction. For example, Chatwin (2014) presents a case study of an interaction between a care-home resident with dementia and two care-workers. He shows that whereas the resident consistently orientates to the logic of his understanding of the setting, with this observable in his successive turns at talk, the staff members orientate to his talk as if his interactional competence was much more limited. Such misalignments result in repeated daily tensions for both residents and care-workers, with consequent impacts on their well-being. Other CA-informed research on people with dementia has pointed to the identity work that can be facilitated through supported storytelling. For example, Hydén and Örulv (2009) show how staff support enables a woman with Alzheimer's disease (AD) to produce a more temporally coherent story than was possible for her without scaffolding. However, they also argue that attention to the performative aspects of small fragments of stories rather than a focus on overall structural aspects may offer insights into those aspects of their identity that tellers with AD consider most central. Affirmation of those aspects can then help relatives and carers to enhance the AD teller's wellbeing.

7.4.2 Research in Everyday Settings

Whilst there is now an increasing volume of studies examining older people's interaction in institutional settings, studies of such interaction in everyday settings remain rare. Yet, for the majority of older people, such everyday settings will be where the bulk of their relationships play out (Coupland 2011). My research in a hair salon (Heinrichsmeier 2016, 2020) is an example of one such study and it helps us see the way quality in interaction may be done – or not – in quotidian talk. This study drew on both discourse analysis (CA-informed analysis of audio recordings of hair-appointment talk) and ethnographic data (recorded interviews and field observations), in line with much research that falls under the broad linguistic ethnographic umbrella (see Chapter 2 in this volume).

One feature of the site was the opportunities it offered for joking and laughter with clients, of which Extract 7.1 in Section 7.2 is an example. Often, this laughter revolved around improprieties or scatologically orientated anecdotes, as in the following extract from an appointment of a sixty-eight-year-old client, Mrs. France. She and Joellen have been complaining about the smell of slurry from the nearby farm and both agree that it is "horrible." This sparks off Mrs. France's illustrative story about just how "horrible" the smell is. A turn-by-turn analysis shows the way in which participants construct affiliation and positive identities for them both.

Extract 7.2 Scatological Talk³

15:51

1.	Mrs. France	cos I picked somebody up and took them (.)
2.		to Bonnybrook (.)
3.		.h er the other day and (.)
4.		I got the windows o(h)p(h)en i(h)n th(h)e car
5.		and she said
6.		.hh <that's not me:>
7.	Joellen	he he [he he he
8.	Mrs. France	[I said (.)
9.	Joellen	[he he he he he he he he he he he h he he he
10.	Mrs. France	[↑well I didn't think it ↑wa:s he he he he he
11.		he he
12.		.h £I said
13.		if that was [you I think
14.	Joellen	[.h h …
15.	Mrs. France	I ought£ to pu(h)ll o:ver he he [he he
16.	Joellen	[ye(h)ah he
17.		£better chuck you ↑out£ he [he he he
18.	Mrs. France	[ye(h)h he
19.	Joellen	chu(h)ck you in a field he he [he
20.	Mrs. France	[.h £ye:s£

16:13

Unlike in Extract 7.1, here it is the client's talk that generates the laughter. Through a concisely sketched narrative including the use of reported speech (l.6, 10, 13), she depicts her friend and herself treating the smell of slurry as being as bad as a fart to illustrate how awful it was. The laughter Mrs. France embeds in her narrative displays her orientation to the vulgarity of this treatment; and this laughter is mirrored by Joellen (ll.7, 9, etc.). This laughing and the collaborative storytelling (ll.17, 19) are both displays of, and construct, affiliation. Pomerantz and Mandelbaum (2005: loc.8494) suggest: "Engaging in, or resisting, shared laughter in response to an impropriety may also be a way for interactants to enact intimacy or distance with the person who produced the impropriety." The implicit reference to farting here is one kind of impropriety. Arguably, the laughter in which both women engage in relation to that implicit reference *in itself* contributes to both women's wellbeing at this point in (at least temporarily) constructing intimacy. Further, though, earthy jokes "indirectly subvert negative social images of older women" (Kotthoff 2006: 21). So, the scatological humor displayed here and the ribald laughter from both women enable them to construct identities that run counter to stereotypical depictions of

---

[3] Extract adapted from p. 1373 in Heinrichsmeier R. (2018) 'So long as there's hair there still': displaying lack of interest as a practice for negotiating social norms of appearance for older women. *Ageing and Society* 39(7) 1360–1386 (reproduced with permission of The Licensor through PLSclear) © Cambridge University Press 2018

humorless, boring older women. Indeed, like Mrs. Farming, so Mrs. France here also constructs a wider identity through this story: engaging in such ribaldry is constructed as part of who she is, something she does also outside the salon.

Studies of groups of older female friends by Charalambidou (2011) and Matsumoto (2009) have similarly shown the way that collaboratively telling a dirty joke (counterstereotypical behavior for older women) or reframing as humorous serious and painful events such as a husband's death help construct positive older identities. These findings support other, non-discourse-analytic research into older people's relationships that argues that fun and laughter are among the key ingredients in close relationships (Moremen 2008: 158). Furthermore, in recounting the amusing tale or telling the joke, the teller assumes momentary control of the conversation (Kotthoff 2006: 8). She is thus not only positioned through the telling as funny (or wacky or otherwise counterstereotypical) but also interactionally displaying herself as quite other than weak and passive (and so stereotypically "decrementally old").

Unlike the peer group setting of Charalambidou's and Matsumoto's studies, the hair salon, for all its fun and laughter, was not always an environment in which troubles-telling and humorous reframing was afforded. In fact, detailed analysis of the interactions showed that a similar phenomenon in this setting as in Grainger's (2004) data was occasionally observed, namely trouble talk being deflected, particularly that relating to ill-health. I illustrate this with another exchange between Mrs. Farming and the stylist, Joellen.

Extract 7.3 Troubles
09:47

1.	Mrs Farming	I tell you what (.)
2.		I wish (you had) some energy pills
3.		cos I could certainly do with some
4.	Joellen	ah::
5.		(1)
6.	Joellen	I don't think this weather's
7.		helping very much
8.	Mrs Farming	[no
9.	Joellen	[everybody you talk to says that
10.		they're [tired
11.	Mrs Farming	[↑yes
12.		it's ↑terrible
13.		(11)((*audible talk from another client/stylist dyad*))
14.	Mrs Farming	you know I thought yesterday (1)
15.		something I want to do
16.		and thought oh I'll just sit down first
17.		and I thought this is ridiculous
18.		(.)

19.	Joellen	[mm
20.	Mrs Farming	[so (???) I must get down to the doctors
21.		because they haven't got the results
22.		from (.)
23.		what they did (.)
24.		I have from the surgeon
25.		but not from the surgery he's al-
26.		our doctor's already sent two letters
27.		(.)
28.	Joellen	[↓oh
29.	Mrs Farming	[I've igno:red them
30.		(.)
31.	Mrs Farming	ha h[e
32.	Joellen	[ts
33.	Mrs Farming	£I said to Lucy yesterday£
34.		the next thing on the agenda when we get
35.		all this s::ettled (.)
36.		is er the doctors
37.		(.)
38.	Joellen	°you're getting it all sorted now°
39.		(1.5)
40.	Mrs Farming	well we're still not hearing
41.		a bloody word from the:[:
42.	Joellen	[↑reall[y
43.	Mrs Farming	[no
44.		from the er (1) bloke in Blenheim
10:50		

Here, Mrs. Farming makes several oblique references to some health problem: she wishes she had energy pills (l.2); she starts a "small story" (Georgakopoulou 2007) about having to take a rest the previous day (ll.14–17); she launches a further medically orientated "small story" (ll.20–6); and then produces a "projection" (Georgakopoulou 2007: 47ff) about getting to the doctor (ll.33–6). Like the nurses in Grainger's data, Joellen does not ignore Mrs. Farming's attempts to talk of her health. In fact, she displays sympathy (for example ll.4, 28, 32). What she does *not* do, though, despite pauses that would allow her to do so (ll.5, 18, 23, 30), is elicit a story from Mrs. Farming about her lack of energy or medical issues. When at length she *does* elicit a troubles story (l.38), it relates to "all this" (l.35), a reference to ongoing problems with a solicitor, rather than Mrs. Farming's health issues; and even this elicitation is designed to expect the answer yes, and thus no further elaboration. So Mrs. Farming's health trouble remains untold.

As in Grainger's medical setting so in this hair salon, this was not an isolated case of a troubles-telling being deflected. Of course, even more than the nurses in Grainger's study, stylists lack the expertise to address

7 Doing Micro-Analysis of Discourse 155

the sometimes worrying issues of older age. But this deflection of troubles-talk, this lack of alignment with the prospective teller's project, matters, in terms of wellbeing. As Grainger concludes with respect to the patients in her research: "Interactions with staff members constitute the majority of their daily interactional experiences, and yet their communicative agendas repeatedly go unaddressed: Their troubles are consistently avoided, made light of, or dismissed. This, it seems to me, cannot fail to have damaging effects on the physical and mental health of the older recipients of long-term care" (2004: 488). One benefit of troubles-telling, argued Coupland, Coupland and Giles (1991), is that it can be therapeutic and offer the opportunity to display oneself heroically. As Matsumoto (2009: 949) observes, the opportunity to talk about such issues and perhaps represent them more humorously gives older people "the power to be in charge of their self-presentation as their circumstances change." Some older people retain a circle of friends with whom to laugh and share problems. However, bereavement and increasing immobility tend to deprive people of their regular contacts as they age (Charalambidou 2011: 125; Rawlins 2004). So, we might ask, what other opportunities are there for older people to talk about their concerns and win reassurance as well as the opportunity to construct identities for themselves as heroic, troubles resistant and amusing?

The above discussion, adopting a micro-discourse analytic approach, offers insights into what constitutes quality in interaction and points to the way in which such interaction may foster wellbeing. As I have argued, wellbeing is achieved in part through the immediacy of the talk – the opportunity to talk of worries, for example, to a receptive listener or to share laughter. Discourse analysis allows us to see in detail how this is – or is not – achieved in particular encounters. Furthermore, as noted throughout this discussion, wellbeing is promoted – or undermined – through the kinds of identity that are recurrently constructed, as a rather wacky person, as heroic in the face of the odds, for example. The identities achieved in any particular interaction are fleeting; nevertheless, over time, certain self-constructions become routines for participants, giving them the sense that this is how they are (Wetherell 2007). So, it is plausible to suggest that recurrent opportunities to construct oneself as, for example, "fun," during interactions in which one is also "having fun," promote people's longer-term wellbeing in supporting their positive self-constructions as people who *are* "fun," and so on. That is, we see wellbeing being interactionally achieved in both the fulfilling exchange and the positive self it affords over time. This contrasts with the potentially negative impact on older people's wellbeing of being recurrently cast into unremittingly decremental identities, recurrently struggling to reposition themselves in line with more positive, "ageing well" identities; or recurrently having troubles deflected, as in Grainger's (2004) study or with Mrs. Farming above, and thus not being afforded the opportunity to construct themselves as "heroic" or "troubles resistant." Such repeated struggles contribute to the perceived spoiled identities of which Coupland (2004: 85) writes, with a consequent negative impact on wellbeing.

7.5 Implications

In Section 7.4, we focused on quality in interaction as a way of highlighting what micro-discourse analysis can offer research into ageing and wellbeing. Discourse analysis enables us to see both the way wider Discourses emerge and how these infuse interactions. Micro-discourse analysis of talk reveals, inter alia, the negotiation work involved in achieving and maintaining positive identities, the way quality in interaction is done (or not), how older people are active actors in these interactions rather than the passive recipients they are so often portrayed as being, and the way wellbeing may be at least partly co-constructed in interaction. These points have a number of implications. Let us consider just a couple.

First, wider stereotypes and circulating ideas of ageing can have subtle effects on interaction at a local level, including the kinds of identity work afforded or constrained. The kind of discourse analysis advocated here, that is, detailed analysis of spoken interaction, helps us identify the way in which those wider ideas of ageing may be orientated to in interaction. For example, a body of existing research shows how older people orientate to both decline and "ageing well" conceptualizations of ageing in different settings (e.g. Jolanki 2004; Näslund 2017). Research into people's subjective wellbeing draws primarily on instruments like surveys and interviews (Andrews and Robinson 1991; Steptoe, Deaton and Stone 2015). It is thus not only inevitably discursively framed, and uses discourse in its design and execution, but employs what need to be seen as socially situated interactions that take place in a wider Discursive environment. As such, the data emerging, generally decontextualized from people's everyday lives, cannot be unproblematically treated as offering unmediated access to people's "true" beliefs. Rather, these data are co-constructed in interaction (see, e.g., De Fina 2011; Edwards and Potter 1992: esp.77ff; Wooffitt and Widdicombe 2006). The kind of discourse analysis used here has something to offer such research, in helping, for example, to identify how particular claims made in interview are shaped and the work they are doing, which in turn can reveal, for example, participants' orientations to circulating norms about states related to wellbeing, e.g. loneliness.

Secondly, and more briefly, the discussion has implications for how we think of wellbeing. If, as argued here, wellbeing is at least partly constructed in interaction – through the satisfaction of the encounter and the positive identities recurrently afforded – this highlights the importance of researching and enhancing quality in interaction at all points.

7.6 Future Directions

The foregoing discussion points to several areas for future development. We again focus on just a few of these.

First, in the European and North American contexts on which this chapter largely draws, an area of focus relates to possible changing images of ageing: as Generation X follows the Baby Boomer generation into older age, and the latter group themselves increasingly count among the "old old," research is needed into the kinds of images of ageing prevalent among these groups: to what extent, for example, will notions of inevitable decline still be a factor? There is scope for charting the changing Discourses of older age and representations of older people in public discourse, and examining the extent to which such changes shape or are reflected in the micro-detail of local interactions.

Second, the rapid growth of internet technologies and the widespread use of social media cannot be ignored. Given the importance of relationships and social interaction for wellbeing in older age, there are, unsurprisingly, a number of studies examining the potential these technologies may offer to reach older people who are perhaps harder to reach through face-to-face or telephone interventions. Conclusions as to the benefit of internet technologies are, though, as yet inconclusive. For example, Wright and Query (2004) suggested that the Internet might offer older people a way of extending their networks and, having reviewed the evidence at the time, concluded that online relationships could be positive for older people's wellbeing. More recent research suggests that the case for computer and internet technologies to enhance wellbeing has still to be made (Dickinson and Gregor 2006), with some studies arguing that balance is needed if the increased online social networks are not, paradoxically, to reduce older people's feelings of belonging (Wilson 2018). In particular, though, how can micro-discourse analysis help us identify the *kind of online interactions* that might favor wellbeing, for example through fostering positive identities in technologically-mediated encounters, and in which of the ever-newly-emerging platforms?

Finally, there is still plenty of scope to enhance our understanding of the sites and contexts in which older people are able to construct positive – or constrained to accept negative – older identities. Interactional research among older people has to date been largely confined either to research interviews or to different kinds of medical and institutional encounter. But what other kinds of interaction do older people have in their everyday lives? And to what extent are these sites of quality interactions that can contribute to their wellbeing? Similarly, there is also scope for further interactionally-orientated research with older people and their carers at home in the manner exemplified by Heinemann (2011) and Engfer (2011). So, a large growth area – particularly given the increasing older population – is studying interactions with older people in a range of settings and examining the extent to which these can help foster self-esteem and positive identities and thereby contribute to wellbeing. This work needs to take account of the multiple factors shaping older age. Many older people are considerably advantaged compared to younger age groups. But different kinds of disadvantage – e.g. economic, educative – can work together to negate or intensify factors that contribute to wellbeing. So micro-discursive approaches need to extend their reach to different groups of older people, including very old people who are not living in institutions, particular ethnic groups, and so on. As Coupland (2004: 86) reminds us: "Disadvantaged older people will find it far harder to resist living out the stereotyped attributes of an ageist and gerontophobic society," with corresponding impacts on their identity and thereby wellbeing.

Part of this work must include a greater focus on embodiment in communication and identity (see chapters in Coupland and Gwyn (2003) and Chapter 15 in this volume). Goodwin's pioneering work has shown how a tendency to logocentrism leads us to ignore other aspects of communication such as posture, gaze and gesture (see, e.g., Goodwin 2007). Ward et al. (2008) similarly found that careful analysis of video recording in a care home indicated that some residents, unable to communicate verbally, were nevertheless using their body as a means of self-expression. These studies, along with, for example, Hydén and Örulv's (2009) research already discussed, are helpful reminders of the role played by nonverbal means in communication with those with a range of communicative issues, including aphasia, dementia or AD. But more research is needed to understand not only the way the ageing body is pathologized or celebrated in different texts but also how the body itself functions as an entire interactive and expressive resource.

In short, there is considerable scope for more targeted and comparative research into the minute detail of interactions in later life. This includes moving beyond a pathologizing narrative of ageing, for, as Coupland (2004: 87) reminds us, "there is far more to social ageing than disadvantage." There is scope, too, to ensure that older people are themselves involved in designing programs to help foster wellbeing. Finally, there is a role for discourse analysis in framing the object of inquiry. How this is done, as Coupland (2004: 87) likewise states, "tends to determine the questions addressed and therefore what we learn from research." As discourse analysts, we should be interrogating more critically the way that object of inquiry is framed, and thereby bringing new perspectives and insights to discursive research into states like wellbeing in later life.

7.7 Summary

In this chapter we have focused on just one aspect of ageing and wellbeing, namely, quality in interaction, as a case study of doing micro-discourse analysis of spoken interaction informed by CA. Drawing on prior micro-linguistic analytic literature into communications with older people together with worked examples from interactions in an everyday site, I have argued that this kind of micro-discourse analysis, by scrutinizing participants' orientations, offers insights into what makes for quality in a particular interaction for those participants. I have proposed that such quality interaction contributes to participants' wellbeing both through the immediate enjoyment or fulfillment of the talk and through the kinds of identity that that talk affords. I have also argued that we should be wary of treating responses to interviews or surveys as providing unmediated access to what participants "really" believe or think, rather than treating such responses as the products of situated encounters.

Further Reading

Backhaus, P. (ed.) (2011). *Communication in Elderly Care: Cross-Cultural Perspectives*. London/New York: Continuum.

This collection encompasses studies of communication with older people in different care settings. The range of approaches allows readers to appreciate the insights afforded by different methods.

Coupland, N., Coupland, J. and Giles, H. (1991). *Language, Society and the Elderly*. Oxford, UK/Cambridge, MA: Basil Blackwell.

This is a very influential study in the field of discursive approaches to later life. The data are experimental, but the authors show clearly how detailed analysis of participants' actual talk reveals more nuance about what is going on in particular exchanges than simple quantitative measures.

Kenyon, G.M., Bohlmeijer, E. and Randall, W.L. (eds.) (2011). *Storying Later Life: Issues, Investigations, and Interventions in Narrative Gerontology*. Oxford/New York: Oxford University Press.

This collection offers multiple perspectives on narrative and older age, encompassing not only narrative as therapy but also the way different groups construct themselves through narrative.

Nussbaum, J. F. and Coupland, J. (eds.) (2004). *Handbook of Communication and Aging Research*. Mahwah, NJ: Lawrence Erlbaum Associates.

This is an excellent collection of essays encompassing a wide range of aspects of communication and ageing. Although the chapters do not explicitly focus on wellbeing, many argue that wellbeing is at issue (for example those by Coupland and Grainger).

Ylänne, V. (2012). *Representing Ageing: Images and Identities*. Basingstoke: Palgrave Macmillan.

This volume explores representations of ageing from several different disciplinary perspectives. Although not all the authors adopt a strictly language-based discourse-analytic approach, the chapters, as a whole, offer insights into the way everyday discourses connect with wider societal discourses.

References

Agren, A. (2017). What Are We Talking About? Constructions of Loneliness among Older People in the Swedish News-Press. *Journal of Aging Studies* 41: 18–27.

Andrews, F. M. and Robinson, J. P. (1991). Measures of Subjective Wellbeing. In J. P. Robinson, P. R. Shaver and L. S. Wrightsman (eds.) *Measures of Personality and Social Psychological Attitudes*. San Diego, CA: Academic Press. 61–114.

Antaki, C. (2011). Six Kinds of Applied Conversation Analysis. In C. Antaki (ed.) *Applied Conversation Analysis: Intervention and Change in Institutional Talk*. Basingstoke: Palgrave Macmillan. 1–14.

Ashida, S., Sewell, D., Schafer, E. and Schroer, A. and Friberg, J. (2018). Social Network Members Who Engage in Activities with Older Adults: Do They Bring More Social Benefits than Other Members? *Ageing and Society* 39(5): 1050–69.

Backhaus, P. (2011a). "Me Nurse, You Resident": Institutional Role-Play in a Japanese Caring Facility. In P. Backhaus (ed.) *Communication in Elderly Care: Cross-Cultural Perspectives*, Kindle ed. London/New York: Continuum.

—— (ed.) (2011b). *Communication in Elderly Care: Cross-Cultural Perspectives*, Kindle ed. London/New York: Continuum.

Blanchflower, D. G. and Oswald, A. J. (2008). Is Well-Being U-Shaped over the Life Cycle? *Social Science & Medicine* 66(8): 1733–49.

Bucholtz, M. and Hall, K. (2005). Identity and Interaction: A Sociolinguistic Linguistic Approach. *Discourse Studies* 7 (4–5): 585–614.

Calasanti, T., Sorensen, A. and King, N. (2012). Anti-ageing Advertisements and Perceptions of Ageing. In V. Ylänne (ed.) *Representing Ageing: Images and Identities*. Basingstoke: Palgrave Macmillan. 19–35.

Charalambidou, A. (2011). *Language and the Ageing Self: A Social Interactional Approach to Identity Constructions of Greek Cypriot Older Women*. Unpublished PhD thesis, King's College London.

Chatwin, J. (2014). Conversation Analysis as a Method for Investigating Interaction in Care Home Environment. *Dementia* 13(6): 737–46.

Coupland, J. and Gwyn, R. (eds.) (2003). *Discourse, the Body, and Identity*. Basingstoke: Palgrave Macmillan.

Coupland, N. (2004). Age in Social and Sociolinguistic Theory. In J. F. Nussbaum and J. Coupland (eds.) *Handbook of Communication and Aging Research*. Mahwah, NJ: Lawrence Erlbaum Associates. 69–90.

(2011). Preface. In P. Backhaus (ed.) *Communication in Elderly Care: Cross-Cultural Perspectives*, Kindle ed. London/New York: Continuum.

Coupland, N. and Coupland, J. (1999). Ageing, Ageism and Anti-ageism: Moral Stance in Geriatric Medical Discourse. In H. E. Hamilton (ed.) *Language and Communication in Old Age: Multidisciplinary Perspectives*. New York/London: Garland. 177–208.

Coupland, N., Coupland, J. and Giles, H. (1991). *Language, Society and the Elderly*. Oxford, UK/Cambridge, MA: Basil Blackwell.

Custers, A. F. J., Kuin, Y., Riksen-Walraven, M. and Westerhof, G. J. (2011). Need Support and Wellbeing during Morning Care Activities: An Observational Study on Resident–Staff Interaction in Nursing Homes. *Ageing and Society* 31(8): 1425–42.

De Fina, A. (2011). Special Issue: Researcher and Informant Roles in Narrative Interactions: Constructions of Belonging and Foreign-ness. *Language in Society* 40(1): 27–38.

Dickinson, A. and Gregor, P. (2006). Computer Use Has No Demonstrated Impact on the Well-Being of Older Adults. *International Journal of Human-Computer Studies* 64(8): 744–53.

Edwards, D. and Potter, J. (1992). *Discursive Psychology*. London: Sage.

Engfer, H. (2011). Cake or Meat? A Case Study on Dinner Conversations in a Migrant-in-the-Family Household in Germany. In P. Backhaus (ed.) *Communication in Elderly Care: Cross-Cultural Perspectives*, Kindle ed. London/New York: Continuum.

Fealy, G. et al. (2012). Constructing Ageing and Age Identities: A Case Study of Newspaper Discourses. *Ageing and Society* 32(1): 85–102.

Gee, J. P. (2008). *Social Linguistics and Literacies: Ideology in Discourses*, 3rd (Kindle) ed. Abingdon/New York: Routledge.

Georgakopoulou, A. (2007). *Small Stories, Interaction and Identities*. Amsterdam/Philadelphia: John Benjamins.

Goodwin, C. (2007). Interactive Footing. In E. Holt and R. Clift (eds.) *Reporting Talk: Reported Speech in Interaction*. Cambridge: Cambridge University Press. 16–46.

Grainger, K. (2004). Communication and the Institutionalized Elderly. In J. F. Nussbaum and J. Coupland (eds.) *Handbook of Communication and*

Aging Research, Kindle ed. Mahwah, NJ/London: Lawrence Erlbaum Associates. 479–97.

Heinemann, T. (2011). From Home to Institution: Roles, Relations, and the Loss of Autonomy in the Care of Old People in Denmark. In P. Backhaus (ed.) *Communication in Elderly Care: Cross-Cultural Perspectives*, Kindle ed. London /New York: Continuum.

Heinrichsmeier, R. (2016). *The Interactional Construction of Ageing Identities: A Linguistic Ethnography of Older Women's Narratives, Talk and Other Practices in a Hair Salon*. Unpublished PhD thesis, King's College London.

(2020). *Ageing Identities and Women's Everyday Talk in a Hair Salon*. London/ New York: Routledge.

Henderson, J. N. and Vesperi, M. D. (1995). *The Culture of Long Term Care: Nursing Home Ethnography*, Kindle ed. Westport, CT: Praeger.

Hydén, L. C. and Örulv, L. (2009). Narrative and Identity in Alzheimer's Disease: A Case Study. *Journal of Aging Studies* 23(4): 205–14.

Jefferson, G. (2004). Glossary of Transcript Symbols with an Introduction. In G. H. Lerner (ed.) *Conversation Analysis: Studies from the First Generation*. Amsterdam/Philadelphia: John Benjamins. 13–31.

Jolanki, O. H. (2004). Moral Argumentation in Talk about Health and Old Age. *Health* 8(4): 483–503.

Keyes, C. L. M., Shmotkin, D. and Ryff, C. D. (2002). Optimizing Well-Being: The Empirical Encounter of Two Traditions. *Journal of Personality and Social Psychology* 82(6): 1007–22.

Kotthoff, H. (2006). Gender and Humor: The State of the Art. *Journal of Pragmatics* 38(1): 4–25.

Lumme-Sandt (2011). Images of Ageing in a 50+ Magazine. *Journal of Aging Studies* 25(1): 45–51.

Marsden, S. and Holmes, J. (2014). Talking to the Elderly in New Zealand Residential Care Settings. *Journal of Pragmatics* 64: 17–34.

Matsumoto, Y. (2009). Special Issue: Dealing with Life Changes: Humour in Painful Self-Disclosures by Elderly Japanese Women. *Ageing & Society* 29(6): 929–52.

(2019). Looking through the Glasses of Lee, a Woman with Alzheimer's. *Corpora in Language and Aging Research (CLARe4)* (Helsinki, February 27– March 1).

Moremen, R. D. (2008). Best Friends: The Role of Confidantes in Older Women's Health. *Journal of Women & Aging* 20(1–2): 149–67.

Näslund, S. (2017). Age Ascription as a Resource and a Source of Resistance: An Interactional Study of Health Professionals' Castings of Patients into the Category "Old." *Journal of Aging Studies* 41(Supplement C): 28–35.

Pomerantz, A. and Mandelbaum, J. (2005). Conversation Analytic Approaches to the Relevance and Uses of Relationship Categories in Interaction. In K. L. Fitch and R. E. Sanders (eds.) *Handbook of Language and Social Interaction (e-book)*. Mahwah, NJ/London: Lawrence Erlbaum Associates.

Rawlins, W. K. (2004). Friendships in Later Life. In J. F. Nussbaum and J. Coupland (eds.) *Handbook of Communication and Aging Research*. Mahwah, NJ/London: Lawrence Erlbaum Associates. 273–99.

Ryan, E. B., Hummert, M. L. and Boich, L. H. (1995). Communication Predicaments of Aging: Patronizing Behavior toward Older Adults. *Journal of Language and Social Psychology* 14(1–2): 144–66.

Steptoe, A., Deaton, A. and Stone, A. A. (2015). Subjective Wellbeing, Health, and Ageing. *The Lancet* 385(9968): 640–8.

Uotila, H., Lumme-Sandt, K. and Saarenheimo, M. (2010). Lonely Older People as a Problem in Society: Construction in Finnish Media. *International Journal of Ageing and Later Life* 5(2): 103–30.

Ward, R., Vass, A., Aggarwal, N., Garfield, C. and Cybyk, B. (2008). A Different Story: Exploring Patterns of Communication in Residential Dementia Care. *Ageing and Society* 28(5): 629–51.

Wetherell, M. (2007). A Step Too Far: Discursive Psychology, Linguistic Ethnography and Questions of Identity. *Journal of Sociolinguistics* 11(5): 661–81.

Williams, K. N. (2011). Elderspeak in Institutional Care for Older Adults. In P. Backhaus (ed.) *Communication in Elderly Care: Cross-Cultural Perspectives*, Kindle ed. London/New York: Continuum.

Wilson, C. (2018). Is It Love or Loneliness? Exploring the Impact of Everyday Digital Technology Use on the Wellbeing of Older Adults. *Ageing and Society* 38(7): 1307–31.

Wooffitt, R. and Widdicombe, S. (2006). Interaction in Interviews. In P. Drew, G. Raymond and D. Weinberg (eds.) *Talk and Interaction in Social Research Methods*. Thousand Oaks, CA: Sage. 28–49.

Wright, K. B. and Query, J. L. (2004). Online Support and Older Adults: A Theoretical Examination of Benefits and Limitations of Computer-Mediated Support Networks for Older Adults and Possible Health Outcomes. In J. F. Nussbaum and J. Coupland (eds.) *Handbook of Communication and Aging Research*. Mahwah, NJ/London: Lawrence Erlbaum Associates. 499–519.

Ylänne, V. (2015). Representations of Ageing in the Media. In J. Twigg and W. Martin (eds.) *Routledge Handbook of Cultural Gerontology*. London: Routledge. 369–70.

Acknowledgments

The author gratefully acknowledges the support of an Arts and Humanities Research Council doctoral studentship for the research underpinning this chapter. This chapter has also benefited from the helpful comments on an earlier draft by the editors, Anna De Fina and Alexandra Georgakopoulou, and an anonymous reviewer.

Appendix: Transcription Notation (see Jefferson 2004)

(.)	micro-pause
really	emphasis on underlined part of word
>hair bit<	spoken faster or
<only ti:me>	slower than surrounding talk
ti:me	vowel stretched out
en↑joy	pitch shift up in following syllable
£I think£	'smile voice'
ri(h)ght	laughter in word
he he he	laughter particles
=	latching of utterance with the next
[it's	overlapping talk starts

8

Corpus-Assisted Discourse Studies

Clyde Ancarno

8.1 Introduction

8.1.1 Preamble

This chapter provides practical and theoretical insights into corpus-assisted discourse studies (CADS), an increasingly popular framework for studying language-in-use. By drawing upon both discourse analysis and corpus linguistics, CADS combines methods of analysis commonly perceived as qualitative and quantitative respectively (Marchi and Taylor 2018: 2 rightly suggest that this is a misconception). Despite challenges (e.g. the desirability for discourse analysts to familiarize themselves with corpus linguistics and its tools), the main appeal lies in CADS' ability to reconcile close linguistic analyses with the more broad-ranging analyses made possible by using corpus linguistic methods of analysis to analyze language. This allows for insights into micro- and macro-level phenomena to be explored simultaneously. In addition to providing theoretical insights into CADS, this chapter examines what CADS involves from a practical point of view, examples of ways in which qualitative and quantitative approaches to discourse analysis are synergized and triangulated, and the extent to which CADS differs from other kinds of discourse analysis (e.g. discourse analysis using tools from systemic function linguistics, genre and schema theories, CDA, pragmatics or multimodal analysis). Interdisciplinary applications in CADS are also considered.

8.1.2 Chapter Structure

Section 8.2 provides an overview of the field of CADS research. Section 8.3 explores issues and ongoing debates in CADS. Questions related to the breadth of CADS research and its position within the quantitative–qualitative debate in corpus linguistics, for example, are considered. Section 8.4

focuses on the implications of CADS research for linguistics and other disciplines, while Section 8.5 discusses the scope and direction of future CADS research. As its name suggests, CADS involves combining corpus linguistics and discourse analysis. As I will explain, in this chapter they are considered to be two methodological approaches in linguistics. Before moving into Section 8.2, a brief overview of corpus linguistics is provided.

8.1.3 Corpus Linguistics

Modern corpus linguistic research using digital technology can be traced back to the 1950s when computer technology started becoming more widely available (for a full account of the history of corpus linguistics, see McEnery and Hardie 2013). Corpus linguistics can therefore be defined as "the study of language via computer-assisted analysis of very large bodies of naturally occurring text" commonly called *corpora*[1] (McEnery and Hardie 2013: 727).

A key feature of debates concerning corpus linguistics is its framing as a theory and methodology. Although it is sometimes referred to as an *approach, discipline, paradigm, toolbox of techniques*, these labels have not received as much attention as those of *theory* and *methodology*. These last two labels have been widely discussed as part of one of the most well-known debates in corpus linguistics. On the one hand, some argue that corpus linguistics is a discipline/theory:[2] for example Halliday 2005: 130; Sinclair 2004; Tognini-Bonelli 2001; Stubbs 1993: 2. On the other hand, others suggest it is best understood as a methodology: the stance of most corpus linguists in the Centre for Corpus Approaches to Social Sciences CASS),[3] for example.[4] In this chapter, I espouse McEnery and Hardie's view that corpus linguistics is "a set of procedures or methods, for studying language" (2012: 2). In other words, I posit that corpus linguistics is a set of methods used to explore large amounts of digitally available texts with corpus tools – primarily by linguists, although increasingly frequently by scholars outside linguistics, too. Like Thompson and Hunston (2006: 8), I consider that, rather than being regarded as a theory, corpus linguistics is best understood in reference to how it can be aligned with any theory. This position assumes that the tools used to conduct an analysis (methods of

---

[1] The tools used to explore corpora are varied. They can be found online (e.g. Brigham Young University's suite of corpora available at https://corpus.byu.edu/) or consist of downloadable software. Some corpus tools are also free and/or open source (for a comprehensive list of tools see https://corpus-analysis.com/). One of the most widely used commercial corpus tools is *Sketch Engine*.

[2] This can also be understood as the *corpus-driven corpus linguistics as theory orientation*. This is often opposed to the *corpus-based corpus linguistics as method(ology) orientation* (for further information concerning this distinction see Tognini-Bonelli 2001).

[3] "CASS is a Centre designed to bring a cutting-edge method in the study of language – the corpus approach – to a range of social sciences. In doing so it provides an insight into the use and manipulation of language in society in a host of areas of pressing concern, including education, hate crime and communication about health and illness" (http://cass.lancs.ac.uk/).

[4] Literature useful in understanding this debate includes Gries (2010) and Taylor (2008).

analysis) and specific approaches to doing research (methodologies) are distinct. Kothari (2004) establishes a similar distinction. Following this position, methods of linguistic analysis include, for example, the analysis of corpus outputs (e.g. keyword lists, collocate lists, concordance lists[5]) and of turn-taking in a conversation, whereas examples of linguistic methodologies comprise conversation analysis and discourse analysis. There is no denying, however, that boundaries between methods and methodologies, in linguistics as well as other disciplines, can fluctuate, be challenged or reified, and that such a distinction may at times be untenable.

Texts are not randomly combined to create a corpus. Corpora are compiled to represent a specific segment of a language. Corpus compilation therefore follows a range of careful considerations, such as how big should the corpus be? Which texts should be included? Where can these texts be found? Corpora are compiled for a range of reasons, for example generic corpora for dictionary makers, parallel corpora for translators or translation studies, small specialized thematic corpora for discourse studies (e.g. legal discourse, academic discourse, social media interactions). Once texts have been compiled into a corpus, the latter can be annotated in a range of ways. Tagging, for example, is an important form of corpus annotation and concerns the assignment of linguistic information to individual or groups of words. The kind of information added to corpora can concern grammatical, morphological, lexical, phonological and semantic aspects of language use. For example, for us to know that *be*, *were* and *been* are different instances (i.e. lemmas – see Section 8.1.3.1) of the verb *to be* involves lexical tagging of the corpus. The most common kind of tagging is *part-of-speech* (also known as *POS/PoS tagging* or *word category disambiguation*). This consists in indicating which lexical class (e.g. noun, verb, adjective) words in a corpus belong to. Tagging can be done manually or (semi)automatically. For POS tagging of corpora of English, *CLAWS*[6] is commonly used to assign this lexical class information automatically to words in these corpora. An annotated corpus is therefore a lot richer than one that is not. It allows, for example, differentiation between different grammatical uses of a word, for example *attack* as a noun or a verb.

I will now introduce four key corpus outputs in corpus linguistic and CADS research. Word lists (lists of words appearing in a text/group of texts organized in order of frequency) are the first point of entry into any corpus. As this corpus output is self-explanatory, I will focus in Sections 8.1.3.1, 8.1.3.2, 8.1.3.3 and 8.1.3.4 on concordance, keyword, collocation and multiword expression lists. As will become apparent, statistics are central to many corpus outputs (see Brezina 2018) and are widely held to help corpus linguists generalize with greater certainty, for example by helping to evaluate hypotheses better.

---

[5] It must be noted that here is now a number of corpus tool-specific outputs. *Word sketches* in *Sketch Engine*, for example, combine insights into the collocational and grammatical behavior of a word, i.e. they rely both on statistics to identify collocates and on the tagging of the corpus under scrutiny to know which grammatical role a word fulfills.
[6] CLAWS part-of-speech tagger for English official website: http://ucrel.lancs.ac.uk/claws/.

8.1.3.1 Concordance Lists

These are lists of all occurrences of a given word/phrase in a corpus. A concordance line, unless expanded, consists of a single line of text with the given word/phrase in the center and a few words before and after. Concordance lines can be ordered alphabetically so that frequently occurring phrases can easily be identified – for example based on the word immediately preceding or succeeding the word/phrase under scrutiny. Figure 8.1 shows concordances for the lemma *cat* in a corpus of answers from the general public following a directive issued in 2009 by the *Mass Observation Project*[7] (MOP) on the topic of animals and humans (Figure 8.1 is a key words in context list, but in *Sketch Engine* concordance lines could also have been presented as whole sentences).

```
              age . 1 rabbit : when I was about 12 or 13 . 2   cats   : late secondary school age to when I
          was very upset when the gerbils rabbit and           cats   died . I do n't have any pets at the moment
                 's house . I really miss the company that     cats   ( ! ) and dogs provide . When I first moved
              ) flat I was adopted by a couple of female       cats   ( one was black and the other was a brown and
           last one died in 2006 . I was very fond of the      cats   . I was probably more attached to the
                    more attached to the tortoiseshell         cat    as she was the one that demanded the most
          do n't know . I do n't think I considered the        cats   or the rabbit as anything other than pets .
                   about animals though I do love my two       cats   ! I really struggle with the concept of
             pens or cages . I currently am ruled by two       cats   . They allow me to stay in the house feed
                  pet or stroke them . They are true           cats   barely looking up when I come in from
         and I had a budgie and when that died I had a         cat    which later died from eating rat poison
                   mere creatures to be exploited . I have a   cat    living with me Molly . Until a few weeks ago
               last thirty years or so I have had several      cats   - dogs were not an option as I was out at work
                   be cruel ; they had other priorities so the cat    camped on my doorstep until I took her in .
                  she became mine and started a trend ! The    cats   have been wonderful companions as
                  in the house to greet me when I come in .    cats   are not subservient as dogs can be . They
                     to think of getting another . The         cat    who was with me the longest time was Henry .
          you are sad and be there when you get home .         cats   do not enable you to meet people but I have
            walking them . Over the years I have had six       cats   . Five times I have had to make the decision
                    anything else . To us the idea of eating   cats   or dogs is appalling but this is largely
```

Figure 8.1 Concordances for the word *cat* (*MOP animals corpus*): keyword in context (KWIC) view

---

[7] The MOP, based at the University of Sussex, UK, sends out two or three directives a year to about 500 correspondents. The animals and humans directive (Nickie Charles's initiative) includes a range of open-ended questions and prompts concerning our relationship with and experience of animals; for example: "What do animals mean to you?". The MOP animals corpus comprises 103 responses to this directive (174,938 tokens) and was compiled as part of the Leverhulme-funded project *'People', 'Products', 'Pests', and 'Pets': the discursive representation of animals*. I worked on this project as a researcher (see Sealey and Pak 2018, Sealey and Charles 2013 for further information about this corpus).

Searching for lemmas means that all forms of a word are searched for simultaneously. The word forms of the verb *to be*, for example, include *was*, *were*, *been*. Deciding whether to search for a specific word form or a lemma will depend on what the analyst is interested in. For example, searching for the lemma *cat* presupposes that the analyst is interested in finding out about the noun *cat*, not only *cat* (singular form) or *cats* (plural form).

This small random sample of concordance lines goes some way to providing opening insights into how the lemma *cat* is used in everyday discourse. It notably seems to suggest that (1) emotions are an important feature of how we talk about cats (see the verbs *be fond of*, *love* and *miss*); (2) cats are an integral part of some humans' lives; and (3) they have a particular status in the lives of humans (see references to companionship).

8.1.3.2 Keyword Lists

Keywords are often used to explore texts' "aboutness" (e.g. Scott 2001: 48). A keyword is a word that is statistically more frequent in one set of texts ("focus corpus") in comparison to another ("reference corpus"). In other words, a reference corpus[8] is the corpus a focus corpus is compared with to identify unusually frequent/infrequent words. Keyword lists are therefore a comparative corpus output and allow analysts to establish how distinctive a focus corpus is in terms of the frequency of occurrence of its words, its collocations, etc. When talking about a keyword in corpus linguistic terms, we are therefore referring to the quality a word or phrase has of being "key" (unusually salient) in its context, and keyness analysis consists in exploring keyword lists. Table 8.1 is a list of the top twenty keywords for the corpus of newspaper articles about animals also gathered as part of the *'People'*, *'Products'*, *Pests'*, *and 'Pets'* project. The reference corpus was a corpus of English broadsheet newspaper articles entitled *SiBol/Port corpus* and available via *Sketch Engine*:

The top three keywords correspond to: (1) the contracted negation as in *won't*; (2) the possessive particle or contracted form of *is* as in *Josie's/it's*; and (3) the negation in the contracted negation as in *doesn't*. Also, *ve* and *re* indicate grammatical contractions as in *they've* and *they're*. All other words in the list demonstrate the aboutness of the focus corpus, a thematic corpus about animals. Some refer to animals in generic terms, for example *species*, *wildlife*, while others point to specific animals. The specific animals featuring in this keyword list – *fish*, *dog*, *horse*, *salmon* – underscore the kinds of animal who are most salient in the focus corpus. Understanding why this is in further detail would require looking at concordances.

Corpus tools use specific statistical calculations to compile keyword lists (see Kilgariff 2009 for further information), that is, to determine how

---

[8] The choice of a reference corpus should be given careful consideration since the composition of the reference corpus will determine what will get included and excluded from a keyword list, hence reflecting genre differences between the focus and the reference corpus (see Baker 2004; Scott 2009; Culpepper 2009). The term *comparator corpus* is also sometimes used.

Table 8.1 *Top twenty keywords for a corpus of newspaper articles about animals (reference corpus: SiBol/Port corpus)*

	Freq	Freq/mill	Freq_ref	Freq_ref/mill
T	1074	2144.8	2807	7.2
S	3746	7480.8	101782	262.6
N	1097	2190.7	9292	24
animal	572	1142.3	12099	31.2
animals	572	1142.3	14016	36.2
fish	579	1156.3	20622	53.2
dog	506	1010.5	17513	45.2
dogs	433	864.7	11196	28.9
horse	406	810.8	19709	50.9
birds	342	683	12447	32.1
species	332	663	11492	29.7
ve	214	427.4	151	0.4
replaced-dns	197	393.4	0	0
bird	228	455.3	8556	22.1
horses	241	481.3	14124	36.4
wild	253	505.2	16524	42.6
re	160	319.5	1184	3.1
meat	212	423.4	11410	29.4
salmon	173	345.5	4616	11.9
wildlife	164	327.5	5970	15.4

unusually frequently/infrequently particular words are used in a focus corpus, in comparison with a reference corpus. Keyword lists will therefore differ depending on which statistical calculation is used to compile the lists. For example, log-likelihood (LL) focuses on statistical significance but not on how large/small a difference is. Kilgariff (2009) devised the "simple maths calculation" which is used in *Sketch Engine* to identify more or less common/rare words. This calculation involves choosing a parameter to determine whether the focus in the keyword list should be on common/rare words (Kilgariff 2012: 6).[9]

8.1.3.3 Collocation Lists

These are lists of words/phrases within a given span of another node word/phrase, that is, they capture the reality that certain words appear together more often than would be expected by chance. These can be listed in order of raw frequency or specific statistical measures can be used to devise these lists, for example LL score (mentioned already in relation to keyword lists), t-score. Table 8.2 shows the top twenty collocates from the collocation list for the word *cat* in the *MOP animals corpus* (a total of 1,040 occurrences of the word *cat* were considered to devise this list). Two statistical tests often

---

[9] For the keyword list in Table 8.1, I used a parameter of 100. Note that "generally, the higher value (100, 1000, ...) of Simple maths focuses on higher-frequency words (more common words), whereas the lower value (1, 0.1, ...) of Simple maths will rather prefer the words with lower frequency (more rare words)" (www.sketchengine.eu/documentation/simple-maths/).

Table 8.2 *Top twenty collocates for the word cat in the MOP animals corpus*

Concordance size	1040 Co-occurrence count	Candidate count	MI	LL
My	131	5366	7.97306	1207.297
Called	40	1221	8.39735	388.752
My	23	672	8.46051	225.1936
Cat	39	1949	7.68615	340.1795
House	28	1132	7.99197	255.8858
Rescue	17	332	9.04169	180.3109
Child	18	557	8.37766	174.0546
Flap	12	53	11.18631	165.1861
Lived	16	447	8.52514	158.0031
Died	20	918	7.80885	177.5044
Had	144	13825	6.7442	1083.044
Love	17	744	7.87757	152.4606
Pets	18	850	7.76787	158.6902
Always	32	2414	7.09206	252.4834
husband	12	257	8.90861	124.9547
Garden	16	730	7.81752	142.1354
Siamese	10	88	10.19177	122.5814
another	33	2718	6.96533	254.6139
Our	86	8792	6.65356	630.9579
Having	25	1891	7.08819	196.9497

combined for the identification of collocates (LL and MI score) were used, and all collocates in the table are statistically significant in both tests.

This collocate list gives us a sense of what respondents to the survey usually associated with cats. By clicking on any of the words when the output is viewed online, the analyst can see the concordances of the word when it is used with *cat*. In *Sketch Engine*, it is also possible to review all the concordances for that word, regardless of whether they are used with the focus term *cat*. It is also possible to compile lists of lemmatized collocates.

Using cut-off points, as I have done here by selecting only the top twenty words from a collocation list, is common in corpus linguistic research. Researchers should duly explain these and I contend that cut-off points should also always be used with an acknowledgment that there might be interesting insights to be gained into the data beyond the cut-off points. In other words, to avoid the pitfalls of subjectivity and cherry-picking, whole lists should ideally be explored before deciding to use a cut-off point.

8.1.3.4 Multiword Expression Lists

These are also sometimes termed *n-gram*, *word cluster*, *lexical bundle*, *lexical phrase*, *chunk* and *multiword (lexical) unit*[10] and are lists of contiguous sequences of words. The number of words may be specified, for example,

---

[10] Note that there are some differences and that not all multiword expressions consist of a series of contiguous words (e.g. phrasal verbs).

Table 8.3 *Top twenty fourgrams for the* MOP *animals corpus*

WORD	FREQ
part of the family	54
but I do n	33
when I was about	30
had to be put	30
to be put down	27
a member of the	24
and I do n	23
not involved in any	22
when I was a	21
never worked with animals	21
I am not involved	21
have never worked with	20
I was a child	20
part of our family	19
I have never worked	19
am not involved in	18
I would like to	17
when I was very	16
to an animal charity	16
of the family and	16

in the case of n-grams, focus may be on *bigrams* (these effectively capture collocates), *trigrams*, *fourgrams*, etc. Multiword expressions occur frequently and indicate a pattern of use. They provide insights into a well-recognized phenomenon in linguistics: phraseology, namely fixed and variable word combinations (Hunston 2002). Often cited phraseological units, albeit very rigid, include well-known sayings such as proverbs and idioms. Table 8.3 is a list of the top twenty fourgrams for the MOP *animals corpus*:

For the researchers involved in the 'People', 'Products', Pests', and 'Pets' project who were interested in human–animal interaction, these fourgrams are valuable points of entry into everyday discourse about animals and the ways in which animals feature in our lives. What is most noticeable about this list, for example, is the particular way in which cats seem to feature in humans' lives, namely as family members and hence evoking the topics of anthropomorphism, personification, etc. The recurrent references to *family* are relevant to this point. *Put down* also evokes animals' death, which may seem surprising considering debates in the human–animal studies literature concerning the widespread occultation of animals' death. As with the keyword list, the analysis of multiword expressions is often supplemented by concordance analyses. For example, concordances for the multiword expressions containing *put down* reveal that it is the lives of a specific kind of animal – *pets*, animals usually perceived as family members – which are discussed. This therefore evokes the hierarchization of animals which largely goes unnoticed (e.g. animals being ranked on the basis of how useful or similar they are to us). I feel confident that further investigation into this topic would indicate that the death of pets is discussed far more frequently than that of animals bred for human consumption in everyday discourse.

8.2 Overview of CADS

In this section, I first attempt to define CADS. I then review two key topics: the relevance to CADS of the qualitative–quantitative debate in linguistics and CADS research design.

8.2.1 CADS

CADS is used here as a superordinate term to designate research combining corpus linguistics and discourse analysis. It therefore de facto includes a broad spectrum of research, for example corpus-based CDA, corpora and discourse studies, discourse-oriented corpus studies. The reason I chose the term CADS (instead of *corpus-assisted discourse analysis*, for example) to refer to all research combining corpus linguistic and discourse analytic methods of analysis is comparable to arguments suggesting that *discourse studies* accounts better for the interdisciplinary nature of much discourse analytic research than the term *discourse analysis* (deemed to apply mostly to linguistic research). Besides, using a single term to refer to such research might help unify its variegated landscape and therefore increase its visibility. I contend that CADS is flexible enough to encapsulate all research combining corpus linguistics and discourse analysis.

CADS research first emerged in the mid-1990s (e.g. Hardt-Mautner 1995). It has been defined in a range of ways with some definitions, such as Partington's (2010: 88), stressing its methodological roots: "The investigation and comparison of features of particular discourse types, integrating into the analysis, where appropriate, techniques and tools developed within corpus linguistics." Taylor and Marchi's (2018) definition focuses on its role in uncovering truths about the social world. They therefore contrast CADS with conventional corpus linguistic research which is primarily concerned with uncovering facts about the workings of language:

> CADS in particular seeks to capture the recurring traces left by social routines … by discursively producing and reproducing habitual patterns of understanding and acting. From this point of view, the starting point of the analysis is not linguistic but social (Biber 1993: 244): what CADS seeks to characterise is not a particular language or linguistic variety but rather a particular situation, purpose or function repeatedly enacted within a speech community.   (Taylor and Marchi 2018: 61)

CADS's usefulness, as a linguistic methodological synergy, is now widely recognized. For some, this synergy was apparent early on. This applies to Flowerdew (1998) and Sinclair (2004: 11), for example, who describes discourse analysis and corpus linguistics as "twin pillars of language research" and suggests that they have a "long-standing and natural synergy." The arguments put forward by Sinclair at the time notably included the ability of both linguistic fields to encourage the formulation of new kinds of hypothesis and to engage with patterns larger than those commonly handled in linguistic research. Judging by the burgeoning of publications and events dedicated to the combination of these two fields,[11] Sinclair's prediction seems to have been proven true (this natural synergy is recognized elsewhere, e.g. Baker et al. 2008). However, the strength of CADS as a mixed methods research approach in linguistics has largely been overlooked. The following definition of mixed methods research shows the extent to which this is unfortunate: "Mixed methods research, with its focus on the meaningful integration of both quantitative and qualitative data, can provide a depth and breadth that a single approach may lack by itself" (Ivankova and Creswell 2009: 135).

8.2.2 CADS and the Quantitative–Qualitative Debate in Linguistics

As mentioned, CADS is often considered to combine quantitative and qualitative approaches to language study. CADS therefore reopens long-standing debates concerning the strengths and weaknesses of both approaches in linguistics.

CADS research is often presented as discourse analysis whose validity is boosted by the use of corpus methods of analysis perceived as more "scientific" or "empirical." This chimes with discussions around the scientific validity and adequacy of linguistic research in which corpora are seen to reduce subjectivity (or increase objectivity – see Marchi and Taylor 2018: 2). This bodes well in an era where much research, as evidenced for example by research funders' agendas, seems to be driven by an obsession with truth, objectivity and accuracy. This view of CADS as enhanced discourse analysis is centered on a variety of claims concerning, for example, the inductive underpinnings of CADS (Stubbs 2006: 17 cited in Partington 2010: 281), the decreased partiality and increased representativeness of CADS findings because it utilizes corpus evidence, the possibility to generalize from CADS findings and the serendipitous effect of CADS research (Partington 2010: 279). What these claims have in common is an

---

[11] In recent years, an increasing number of publications and events dedicated to CADS has emerged, e.g. *Critical Approaches to Discourse Analysis across Disciplines/CADAAD* conference since 2006, *Corpora & Discourse International* conference since 2012, *CADAAD Journal* since 2007, *Journal of Corpora and Discourse Studies* since 2017. Corpus linguistic publications also contain an increasing number of CADS articles, e.g. *Corpora* and *International Journal of Corpus Linguistics*.

assumption that CADS evidences a concern for observation, whereas discourse analysis is seen to rely more on introspection.

Alternatives to these discourse-analysis-as-deficient views of CADS exist. Some argue that the qualitative methods of analysis such as those used in discourse analysis (e.g. introspection, intuition, manual coding) can benefit corpus linguistic insights. In other words, discourse analysis in CADS research is perceived to be helping the soundness of corpus analyses because it can notably provide richer insights into the context in which language is used. Focus on context in such discussions of CADS can be attributed to the fact that it is a key feature of discourse analysis – the latter is often defined as the analysis of language "in context" – but also to the fact that quantitative results yielded by corpus analyses were traditionally perceived to be unable to provide insights into context.

A third, non-dualistic, view of the quantitative–qualitative debate in linguistics emphasizes the value of synergizing the methods of analysis from discourse analysis and corpus linguistics, namely methods based on introspection and data observation, respectively. This echoes the view of Marchi and Taylor (2018: 6) who argue against a polarized outlook on the quantitative–qualitative debate and suggest a more fluid and flexible view of methodology as a more fruitful approach. Such a view, which I also endorse, embraces the complexity and fuzzy nature of much CADS research and therefore stands a better chance of accounting for CADS research.

8.2.3 CADS Research Design

To comprehend the design of CADS research, it can be useful to ask whether it is primarily driven by (1) corpus linguistics – corpus linguists doing discourse analysis, which will tend to be corpus-driven – or (2) discourse analysis incorporating corpus linguistic methods, which will tend to be labeled as corpus-assisted/based – or (3) whether the two areas of linguistics are fully synergized. As will become apparent in this chapter, there are many ways in which corpus linguistic and discourse analytic methods of analysis can be combined and understanding/reporting the design of CADS research can therefore be challenging, especially given the breadth of corpus linguistic and discourse analysis.

Corpus linguists have sometimes been accused of being "vague about the methods they use" (Stubbs 2006: 17 cited in Partington 2009: 278) and there is evidence of CADS researchers being so too. As rightly suggested by Partington (2009: 278), not being vague means not only accounting for the techniques used to conduct the analyses but also reflecting on "the scientific validity and adequacy of what corpus linguists do." Being clear about the exact nature of research questions asked is clearly a critical step in this process. Identifying whether a research question is hypothesis-driven – this tends to be corpus-assisted/based research – or data-driven can be really useful. For example, it can help understand the relevance of philosophy of science concepts such as induction, deductive falsification, and so on and therefore provide better descriptions of methods used in CADS research. Indeed, depending on whether the approach adopted is purely inductive or whether induction is interspersed with hypothesis[12] testing will notably have an impact on how a research project is designed. In some cases, the analysis itself, for example keyword analysis, might lead to the formulation of a hypothesis or intuitions which the researcher(s) then attempts to answer by means of other analyses. In other words, it is not uncommon to have an overall data-driven CADS project riddled with hypothesis/intuition-driven questions. It is also worth noting that CADS research, like much linguistic research, does not tend to deal with universal statements but instead relies on statements highlighting the probability of something happening and the various aspects of social life phenomena analyses are linked to/rely on. This is illustrated in the following example (taken from Partington (2009): 285): "[I]n media discussions of war reporting, if the item *armchair* is used as a modifier, then it has a very high probability of displaying an unfavourable evaluative prosody and a high probability of being employed as an over-the-fence term."

A review of key journals and books in CADS evidences the variety of ways in which corpus linguistic methods and discourse analytic methods are "put in conversation" in research. As far as the input of corpus linguistic methods is concerned, it is notable that different corpus outputs are used to different extent, for example some CADS utilize a single corpus output while others draw on several kinds of output. Some studies use a range of corpus tools or are centered on a particular analytical approach, comparative keyword analysis, semantic categorization. Similarly, the contribution of discourse analysis to CADS also varies tremendously, with some CADS research drawing on the tools offered by a single kind of discourse analysis, for example conversation analysis, while other CADS research may take a more flexible approach to doing discourse analysis, for example close linguistic analysis of a range of texts with the view of identifying themes. I contend that this makes it imperative for CADS researchers to explicitly account for the extent to which they draw on corpus linguistics and discourse analysis, and to explain which specific methods from these two areas of linguistics they utilize. Admittedly, in some such research, corpus and discourse analyses are kept separate. However, and as the remainder of this section suggests, there are instances when corpus linguistic and discourse analytic methods of analysis interact with each other.

The question underpinning the rest of this section is therefore as follows: How do CADS researchers exploit and alternate between corpus

---

[12] Partington (2009: 282) suggests that it might at times be difficult to differentiate between a "hypothesis" and an "explicitly formulated intuition."

linguistics and discourse analysis in their work, that is, between inductive and deductive methods of analysis? I use Marchi's funneling down approach (2010) to start this discussion, a currently widely used approach in CADS. Marchi argues that we should move from a macro- to a micro-level analysis. The protocol she outlines is as follows:

1. word lists/keyword lists to identify key semantic domains, that is, to establish central themes;
2. collocation lists to explore the textual behavior of key terms, that is, to identify patterns or start classifying terms from the corpus outputs (keyword and collocate lists);
3. concordance lists to explore further dominant patterns in context.

The funneling down approach is by no means the sole approach to designing CADS research, but it is useful in recalling that strong CADS research accounts for how it has been designed and for the input of corpus linguistics and discourse analysis. The funneling down approach is an exclusively corpus-driven approach, that is, the discourse context is explored by means of corpus outputs only. It is noteworthy, however, that it is now often possible to expand concordance lines, for example by clicking on the search term, and therefore to gain insight into the context of language use. In the light of our discussion so far, a fourth step could be added to Marchi's funneling down approach, namely:

4. close linguistic analysis informed by discourse analytic methodologies, for example thematically coded texts, conversation analyses of samples of interaction.

With this fourth step, CADS research is no longer corpus-driven in that the researchers gain insights into their data by looking beyond corpus outputs – and possibly beyond the corpus itself. This four-step funneling down approach corresponds to much research carried out in CADS to date. Researchers, however, rarely follow this sequentially and instead allow their research design to be shaped by their research questions. In other words, their CADS research tends to be exploratory. This means that certain steps will be decided only as the research unfolds. For example, they might take an iterative approach where initial explorations into word lists and keyword lists (1–2) might be followed by explorations into concordance lists for specific terms (3). This would then inform the analysis of a downsample[13] of texts from the original corpus or even a single text (4), which could then be followed by further explorations into concordances (3) and so on. Rather than seeming daunting, this should be seen as a strength of CADS.

---

[13] Downsampling is an important consideration in CADS. Baker (2018b) makes a timely contribution to this debate by comparing insights gained from four different downsampling techniques with the insights obtained from corpus-driven analyses, concluding that combining corpus analyses with the analysis of a downsample allows for the richest insights.

As CADS research is still establishing itself as a field, there are currently few established protocols, hence undertaking CADS research will feel like a leap in the dark for many. The design of CADS research testing hypotheses, namely less data-driven/inductive approaches, tends to be more straightforward.

Subcategories of CADS research not only show that it is growing in recognition but also evidence the nuanced insights into discourse that it permits. The nature of the linguistic data under scrutiny accounts largely for such nuances. For example, corpora from different but recent times are studied in *modern diachronic* CADS (MD-CADS, see special edition of *Corpora* 5(2) 2010). CADS involving the comparison of languages has come to be labeled as *cross-linguistic* CADS (C-CADS) and concerns CADS research studying comparable, non-parallel corpora of different languages (e.g. Drasovean 2017). Other CADS research attaches itself to specific schools of thought, for example CDA for corpus-assisted critical discourse studies (e.g. Samaie and Malmir 2017; Wright and Brookes 2019).

8.3 Issues and Ongoing Debates

Despite its relative recency, CADS has raised important questions concerning the nature of investigations into discourse. In doing so, it has reopened existing debates, for example debates concerning the qualitative–quantitative debate in linguistics (see Section 8.2), while also causing new debates to emerge, for example those concerning the challenge of multimodal corpora.

To a large extent, the chapter has already hinted at two of the issues inherent to CADS. First there is the need to have a unified approach, the position adopted here being that using a single term to refer to CADS research might be useful in supporting this process of unification (Mautner (2016) speaks of reducing "academic tribalism"). Second, I have also alluded to the challenge of designing robust CADS research projects.

What has perhaps not been articulated as explicitly is the challenge of having expertise in both discourse analysis and corpus linguistics. Although in many instances researchers take on this challenge alone – this often involves additional training for researchers to acquaint themselves with the methods used in one or both fields – at times, it requires a collaboration of researchers, for example one or more researcher(s) with expertise in discourse analysis and one or more researcher(s) with expertise in corpus linguistics become involved in a project. As rightly evoked by Baker (2018a: 288), the expectation is not for CADS scholars to become "academic polymaths."

On a practical note, there is also the challenge of familiarity with corpus tools but also digital tools used by discourse analysts, for example qualitative data analysis software such as *Nvivo* and *Atlas.ti* which may be used to assist with the close linguistic analysis of texts. While the latter are optional, CADS research cannot be conducted without recourse to corpus tools. Besides – and this is a challenge for corpus linguists too – understanding certain corpus outputs/analyses requires statistical knowledge. The need for corpus linguists to develop skills in statistics and computer programming has recently received attention, see Anthony (2016).

An additional issue concerns the "consumers" of such research, for whom issues of level of proficiency in discourse analysis and/or corpus linguistics also apply. To a certain extent, CADS shares some of the challenges faced by interdisciplinary research more generally: namely, it can sometimes be difficult to choose the right publication platform. For those whose background was previously either in corpus linguistics or in discourse analysis, getting their peers to read their mixed methods research might be difficult.

Besides the qualitative–quantitative debate, new debates have also emerged as the field is establishing itself. The current undertheorization of CADS, for example, has come under intense scrutiny. This is hardly surprising considering its short history as a field of linguistic study. However, it might also be linked to the relative undertheorization of corpus linguistics itself: O'Halloran (2017), for example, suggests that corpus linguistic work's focus on techniques, methods and analysis has been at the expense of adequate theorization of the field.

Judging by current work in CADS such as Taylor and Marchi's 2018 edited book which is framed as an attempt to provide theoretical insights into CADS, it appears that CADS researchers may have learned from the mistakes of corpus linguists and are showing a willingness to reflect on the relevance of their research to discussions posed in philosophy of science (e.g. Partington 2009). I would argue that it is also critical for CADS researchers to engage with the specificities of mixed methods research, to be able to determine, for example, whether their CADS research (following Ivankova and Creswell 2009) adopts an *explanatory, exploratory, triangulation* or *embedded* design.

Another recent debate in CADS concerns its interdisciplinary applications. Taylor and Marchi (2018) underscore that such applications, for example, raise important epistemological questions – for example, how do we know what we know, and what do we accept as suitable forms of evidence? – as well as more practical questions – for example, how do we relate corpus/textual data to social reality? In my collaborative work with two anthropologists – Insa Nolte and Rebecca Jones (see, e.g., Nolte, Ancarno and Jones 2018) – we have had to think very carefully about the ways in which the introspective methods of analysis used in anthropology can be used in research where corpus tools are often seen to reduce subjectivity. This has led the three of us to embrace the fact that, for example, some of the corpus outputs are best analyzed using introspection primarily. Corpus-assisted anthropological research methodology enhances the quality of our research because Nolte, Jones and I are able to confirm or cast a new light on known patterns, as well as reveal new patterns in the anthropological survey data we analyze. Contrary to much CADS research, achieving greater impartiality is not the driving force of such research.

8.4 Implications

This chapter has illustrated that CADS projects vary in their design and the extent to which researchers draw on corpus and discourse analyses, for example corpus methods of analysis might be used to merely supplement discourse analyses or, on the contrary, corpus methods may be their driving force. The implications of combining corpus and discourse methods are therefore multifarious. On the one hand, it might be considered to broaden the scope of discourse analysis and corpus linguistics. On the other hand, CADS constitutes a potentially useful methodological apparatus for a range of social scientists whose source of data is language. Considering the increasing number of interdisciplinary applications in CADS (see Ancarno 2018 for insights into such applications), it is apparent that CADS research stretches disciplinary boundaries in unprecedented ways, thus showcasing the value of linguistics-informed analyses of language outside of linguistics.

CADS is therefore changing the landscape of linguistics quite significantly, while also starting to impact on other disciplines too. The fact that corpus technology is used in some courtrooms and that the British National Health Service approached CASS to analyze some of its patient feedback with corpus tools (see Brookes and Baker 2017), as well as other recent developments, seems to suggest that recognition of CADS is likely to resonate beyond academia. Recent developments notably include Lorenzo-Dus's collaborations with various law enforcement units such as the United Nations Interregional Crime and Justice Research Centre, the Global Drugs Policy Observatory on the topic of cryptodrug markets and violent extremism, and the NSPCC, specifically to develop online child sexual grooming prevention material (Lorenzo-Dus and di Cristofaro 2018; Lorenzo-Dus, Izura and Pérez-Tattam 2016).

8.5 Future Directions

Judging by the current developments in CADS – for example the increasing number of specialist publications such as Marchi and Taylor's 2018 textbook dedicated to CADS – it is likely that CADS will continue to establish itself as a linguistic field in its own right.

We can also safely predict that interdisciplinary applications will become increasingly frequent, as the range of disciplines using CADS methods of analysis is growing. Work in geography, for example, combines corpus linguistic methods with geographic information systems (GIS) technology (Gregory and Hardie 2011). While raising a range of timely questions concerning differences between disciplines in the way they conceive of, compile, analyze and discuss knowledge, these interdisciplinary applications underscore the contributions that corpus linguists can make beyond linguistics. In our interdisciplinary collaborative work, what Nolte, Jones and I found to be of paramount importance was being clear about our epistemological beliefs, including beliefs about our sources of data. For example, we came to realize that our understanding of our unit of analysis – the text – was different and that therefore our expectations of what it could tell us about the world varied.

CADS research is also symptomatic of broader changes in corpus linguistics. Where the definition of corpora as, for example, large sets of electronically available naturalistic language use would have seemed unproblematic until fairly recently, current debates in corpus linguistics suggest otherwise. Corpora seem to be undergoing a mutation process with some corpora now capturing elicited data (e.g. interview data) or being relatively small (e.g. thematic or specialized corpora of a few thousand words). Technological advances mean that existing corpus tools keep being improved, with new ones also being developed to address the new demands of corpus linguistic research. The reverse is also true, that is, the affordances of tools allow for new insights into language to be gained. The possibility of using tools such as *BootCaT* to develop trillion-word corpora – "mega" corpora – of language from online sources almost effortlessly illustrates this. Thanks to technology, corpus tools have changed tremendously. Their functionalities have broadened in scope – for example, *GraphColl* allows the compilation of collocation networks. There is also an increasing number of online corpus tools – for example *CQPWeb*, *Sketch Engine*, and corpora with their own search interface such as the *BYU corpora*.[14]

In addition, corpora have diversified. For example, a wider range of languages is now represented, languages with a short history of being written are also tackled and corpora of social media offer an opportunity to explore internet language. A lot of corpus linguistic research now also examines spoken and multilingual corpora, which raises unprecedented questions. This is particularly significant since corpus tools were originally developed with monolingual and almost exclusively English corpora in mind.

---

[14] The private sector also funds the development of corpus tools and/or develops or has recourse to tools sharing similarities with corpus tools (e.g. *Google Search and Ngram Viewer*, sentiment analysis tools used to track social marketing success).

8.6 Summary

This chapter defined CADS research in reference to two linguistic methodological approaches – corpus linguistics and discourse analysis. To help fully appreciate the scope of CADS research, including the relevance of statistics to it, four key corpus outputs were defined: concordance, keyword, collocation and multiword expression lists. Prior to exploring CADS per se, it was argued that to ensure the visibility of the wide range of researchers combining the abovementioned linguistic methodologies, it was necessary to use a single term. CADS was deemed to be an appropriate term which speaks to the growing interdisciplinary nature of research in this field. Three broad types of CADS research were singled out, namely those that (1) draw mostly on the methods of analysis in corpus linguistics, (2) rely mostly on the methods of analysis in discourse analysis and (3) constitute a full synergy between the linguistic methodologies. These three broad approaches draw attention to the limitless possibilities in CADS research design. It was therefore argued that it is primordial to be clear about the extent to which CADS research draws on corpus linguistic and/or discourse analytic methods of analysis, and about the specific steps of CADS analyses (e.g. adapting Marchis's funneling down approach). In terms of its being a mixed methods approach to the study of language-in-use, I also considered the relevance of CADS to the quantitative–qualitative debate, in linguistics in particular, emphasizing that the "corpus linguistics as quantitative" and "discourse as qualitative" view is misled. To conclude, I suggested that CADS research will continue to make timely contributions to the scarcity of mixed methods research in linguistics, while highlighting that some of its most innovative work currently lies at its interdisciplinary boundaries.

Further Reading

Baker, P. (2008). *Using Corpora in Discourse Analysis*. London: Continuum.

    This textbook assumes no prior knowledge of corpus linguistics. It is a useful introduction to how corpus tools can be used in discourse analysis.

Baker, P. and McEnery, T. (eds.) (2015). *Corpora and Discourse Studies: Integrating Discourse and Corpora*. Palgrave Advances in Language and Linguistics. Basingstoke: Palgrave Macmillan.

    This is a substantial edited book comprising thirteen independent studies where corpus linguistics and discourse analytic methodologies are practically combined.

Taylor, C. and Marchi, A. (eds.) (2018). *Corpus Approaches to Discourse: A Critical Review*. London/New York: Routledge.

This complements the previous two books in that it encourages students and researchers to critically reflect on CADS research.

References

Ancarno, C. (2018). Interdisciplinary Approaches in Corpus Linguistics and CADS. In C. Taylor and A. Marchi (eds.) *Corpus Approaches to Discourse: A Critical Review*. London/New York: Routledge. 130–56.

Anthony, L. (2016, February). Arguments For and Against DIY Corpus Tools Creation: A Debate about Programming. Keynote lecture given at the Corpus Statistics Group Launch Event, Department of English Language and Applied Linguistics, University of Birmingham, UK.

Baker, P. (2004). Querying Keywords: Questions of Difference, Frequency, and Sense in Keywords Analysis. *Journal of English Linguistics* 3: 346–59.

(2018a). Conclusion: Reflecting on Reflective Research. In C. Taylor and A. Marchi (eds.) *Corpus Approaches to Discourse: A Critical Review*. 281–92.

(2018b). Which Techniques of Down-Sampling Best Complement a Corpus-Assisted Discourse Analysis? A Case Study on Press Representations of Obesity.

Baker, P., Gabrielatos, C., Khosravinik, M., Krzyzanowski, M., McEnery, T. and Wodak, R. (2008). A Useful Methodological Synergy? Combining Critical Discourse Analysis and Corpus Linguistics to Examine Discourses of Refugees and Asylum Seekers in the UK Press. *Discourse & Society* 19: 273–306.

Brezina, V. (2018). *Statistics in Corpus Linguistics: A Practical Guide*. Cambridge: Cambridge University Press.

Brookes, G. and Baker, P. (2017). What Does Patient Feedback Reveal about the NHS? A Mixed Methods Study of Comments Posted to the NHS Choices Online Service. *British Medical Journal Open* 7.

Culpeper, J. (2009). Keyness: Words, Parts-of-Speech and Semantic Categories in the Character-Talk of Shakespeare's Romeo and Juliet. *International Journal of Corpus Linguistics* 14: 29–59.

Drasovean, A. (2017). A Cross Linguistic Corpus-Assisted Study of the Representation of Animals in Romanian and British Online Newspapers. Unpublished PhD dissertation.

Flowerdew, L. (1998). Corpus Linguistic Techniques Applied to Textlinguistics. *System* 26: 541–52.

Gregory, I. N. and Hardie, A. (2011). Visual GISting: Bringing Together Corpus Linguistics and Geographical Information Systems. *Lit Linguist Computing* 26: 297–314.

Gries, S. T. (2010). Corpus Linguistics and Theoretical Linguistics: A Love–Hate Relationship? Not Necessarily . . .. *International Journal of Corpus Linguistics* 15: 327–43.

Halliday, M. A. K. (2005). *Computational and Quantitative Studies*, ed. by J. J. Webster. Collected Works of M. A. K. Halliday, Vol. 6. London: Continuum.

Hardt-Mautner, G. (1995). "Only Connect": Critical Discourse Analysis and Corpus Linguistics. UCREL Technical Paper 6. Lancaster: University of Lancaster. 1–31.

Hunston, S. (2002). *Corpora in Applied Linguistics*. Cambridge: Cambridge University Press.

Ivankova, N. V. and Creswell, J. W. (2009). Mixed Methods. In *Qualitative Research in Applied Linguistics: A Practical Introduction*. Basingstoke: Palgrave Macmillan.135–61.

Kilgariff, A. (2009). Simple Maths for Keywords. In M. Mahlberg, V. González Díaz and C. Smith (eds.) Proceedings of the Corpus Linguistics Conference (CL2009). University of Liverpool.

(2012). Getting to Know Your Corpus. In P. Sojka, A. Horak, I. Kopecek and K. Pala (eds.) Proceedings of Text, Speech, Dialogue (TSD2012). SpringerLink. https://link.springer.com/book/10.1007/978-3-642-32790-2.

Kothari, C. R. (2004). *Research Methodology: Methods and Techniques*. New Delhi: New Age International.

Lorenzo-Dus, N. and di Cristofaro, M. (2018). "I Know This Whole Market Is Based on the Trust You Put in Me and I Don't Take That Lightly": Trust, Community and Discourse in Crypto-drug Markets. *Discourse & Communication* 12: 608–26.

Lorenzo-Dus, N., Izura, C. and Pérez-Tattam, R. (2016). Understanding Grooming Discourse in Computer-Mediated Environments. *Discourse, Context & Media* 12: 40–50.

Marchi, A. (2010). "The Moral in the Story": A Diachronic Investigation of Lexicalised Morality in the UK Press. *Corpora* 5: 161–89.

Marchi, A. and Taylor, C. (2018). Introduction: Partiality and Reflexivity. In C. Taylor and A. Marchi (eds.) *Corpus Approaches to Discourse: A Critical Review*. London/New York: Routledge. 1–15.

Mautner, G. (2016). Checks and Balances: How Corpus Linguistics Can Contribute to CDA. In R. Wodak and M. Meyer (eds.) *Methods of Critical Discourse Studies*. London: Sage Publications. 154–79.

McEnery, T. and Hardie, A. (2012). *Corpus Linguistics: Method, Theory and Practice*. Cambridge Textbooks in Linguistics. Cambridge: Cambridge University Press.

(2013). The History of Corpus Linguistics. In K. Allan (ed.) *The Oxford Handbook of the History of Linguistics*. Oxford: Oxford University Press. 725–45.

Nolte, I., Ancarno, C. and Jones, R. (2018). Inter-religious Relations in Yorubaland, Nigeria: Corpus Methods and Anthropological Survey Data. *Corpora* 13: 27–64.

O'Halloran, K. (2017). *Posthumanism and Deconstructing Arguments: Corpora and Digitally-Driven Critical Analysis*. London/New York: Routledge.

Partington, A. (2009). Evaluating Evaluation and Some Concluding Thoughts on CADS. In J. Morley and P. Bayley (eds.) *Corpus-Assisted Discourse Studies on the Iraq Conflict: Wording the War*. London/New York: Routledge. 261–304.

(2010). Modern Diachronic Corpus-Assisted Discourse Studies (MD-CADS) on UK Newspapers: An Overview of the Project. *Corpora* 5: 83–108.

Samaie, M. and Malmir, B. (2017). US News Media Portrayal of Islam and Muslims: A Corpus-Assisted Critical Discourse Analysis. *Educational Philosophy and Theory* 49: 1351–66.

Scott, M. (2001). Comparing Corpora and Identifying Key Words, Collocations, and Frequency Distributions through the WordSmith Tools Suite of Computer Programs. In M. Ghadessy, A. Henry and R. L. Roseberry (eds.) *Small Corpus Studies and ELT: Theory and Practice*. Amsterdam: John Benjamins. 47–67.

(2009). In Search of a Bad Reference Corpus. In D. Archer (ed.) *What's in A Word-List? Investigating Word Frequency and Keyword Extraction*. London/New York: Routledge. 99–112.

Sealey, A. and Charles, N. (2013). "What Do Animals Mean to You?": Naming and Relating to Nonhuman Animals. *Anthrozoös* 26: 485–503.

Sealey, A. and Pak, C. (2018). First Catch Your Corpus: Methodological Challenges in Constructing a Thematic Corpus. *Corpora* 13: 229–54.

Sinclair, J. M. (2004). *Trust the Text: Language, Corpus and Discourse*. London/New York: Routledge.

Stubbs, M. (1993). British Traditions in Text Analysis: From Firth to Sinclair. In M. Baker, G. Francis and E. Tognini-Bonelli (eds.) *Text and Technology: In Honour of John Sinclair*. Amsterdam: John Benjamins. 1–36.

Taylor, C. (2008). What Is Corpus Linguistics? What the Data Says. *ICAME Journal* 32: 179–200.

Taylor, C. and Marchi, A. (eds.) (2018). *Corpus Approaches to Discourse: A Critical Review*. London/New York: Routledge.

Thompson, G. and Hunston, S. (2006). *System and Corpus: Exploring Connections*. London: Equinox.

Tognini-Bonelli, E. (2001). *Corpus Linguistics at Work*. Studies in Corpus Linguistics, Vol. 6. Amsterdam: John Benjamins.

Wright, D. and Brookes, G. (2019). "This Is England, Speak English!": A Corpus-Assisted Critical Study of Language Ideologies in the Right-Leaning British Press. *Critical Discourse Studies* 16: 56–83.

9

Cognitive Linguistic and Experimental Methods in Critical Discourse Studies

Christopher Hart

9.1 Introduction

Critical discourse studies (CDS) is an approach to language study which theorizes the instrumentality of language in creating and sustaining power and inequality in social actions, identities and relations. Through detailed semiotic analysis, it also seeks to highlight (and resist) which lead to social inequalities and injustices (van Dijk 1993; Wodak 2016). Several "schools" of CDS can be identified, characterized primarily by the theoretical and methodological frameworks that underpin their analyses (Hart and Cap 2014; Wodak and Meyer 2016). CDS is multifaceted in this sense, exploiting a range of frameworks suitable for analyzing different types of data (relating, for example, to topic, feature, mode or genre of communication) and answering different research questions. In relation to the last, for example, different schools or approaches are concerned, to lesser or greater extents, with processes of text-production versus text-reception. One recent approach to CDS explicitly concerned with issues of text-reception is cognitive linguistic CDS (CL-CDS) (e.g. Chilton 2004; Hart 2014). CL-CDS places an emphasis on cognition as a necessary mediator in the constitutive relationship between texts and social action. In cognitive linguistics, meaning is viewed as a dynamic process of *conceptualization* in which language connects with background knowledge and domain-general cognitive processes to yield a rich, modal rather than amodal, mental representation of the target scene (Croft and Cruse 2004). Drawing on frameworks in cognitive linguistics, then, CL-CDS seeks to model the conceptualizations invoked by specific language usages and consider the potential ideological/(de)legitimating functions of competing conceptualizations.

Cognitive linguistics is not a specific theory but comprises a number of frameworks united by a common set of assumptions about, and perspectives on, the nature of language (Croft and Cruse 2004). Frameworks include Conceptual Metaphor Theory (Lakoff and Johnson 1980, 1999), cognitive grammar (Langacker 1991, 2008), frame semantics (Fillmore 1982, 1985) and conceptual semantics (Talmy 2000). These frameworks are all available to CL-CDS which, unsurprisingly, also inherits the core epistemological commitments that unite them. In this chapter, I begin by introducing key principles of CL-CDS. I then go on to highlight some of the linguistic/conceptual phenomena that it has investigated. Finally, I consider some of the issues facing CL-CDS and the future directions it may take. One especially pertinent issue for CL-CDS is that the analyses offered of particular language usages and the conceptualizations they invoke remain only as hypotheses. Although cognitively plausible claims are made about text-reception, these are not actually empirically verified. Cognitive linguistics itself now makes more and more use of empirical methods to evidence its claims, exploiting a range of paradigms, including both "offline" paradigms like native speaker acceptability judgments and norming tasks and "online" paradigms like cross-modal priming, eye-tracking and neuro-imaging (see Gonzalez-Marquez et al. 2007). A more recent development in CL-CDS, then, in line with cognitive linguistics more generally, is hypothesis-testing using experimental methods. Since most hypotheses in CL-CDS concern the ideological effects that different language usages and the conceptualizations they evoke have on audience attitudes, emotions, judgements, decisions, etc., most of this research relies on offline methods such as rating-scale questions in a post-stimulus-text questionnaire. At the end of this chapter, I briefly point to a small number of CL-CDS studies adopting experimental methods.

9.2 Overview of the Topic

A key claim of cognitive linguistics, and thus CL-CDS, is that meaning construction – semiosis – is a conceptual process. The language system is made up of a set of **symbolic assemblies** in which both words and grammatical constructions are paired with abstract conceptual structures that are imagistic in nature. This is known as the **symbolic thesis**. A further key claim is that the conceptual structures associated with linguistic units are not specific to the language system but are based in real-world experiences, including physical, social and semiotic experience. This is known as the **experientialist thesis**. Although words and grammatical constructions are immediately paired with particular conceptual structures, meaning is not "closed." Words and constructions evoke their conceptual counterparts which, in turn, provide access to large networks of interconnected conceptual structure. This is known as the **encyclopedic thesis**. In discourse, then, meaning construction takes place as words and grammatical constructions act as prompts for an array of conceptual processes and the recruitment of background knowledge to produce an intersubjectively shared mental representation of the referential situation.

From these epistemological commitments, a number of significant corollaries arise. For example, it follows from the symbolic thesis that grammar and the lexicon are not distinct components of the language system. Lexical and grammatical units both have conventionalized semantic content, which is distinguished only by its degree of abstractness, and are stored in the same way in the "constructicon." The distinction between literal and figurative language similarly breaks down. The processes involved in understanding metaphorical expressions are principally no different from those involved in understanding literal expressions in so far as both forms involve the invocation of abstract imagery. From the experientialist thesis, it follows that language is not an autonomous cognitive faculty. The cognitive processes that support language are not unique to language but are, rather, manifestations of more general cognitive processes found to function in other nonlinguistic domains like memory, perception and action. The conceptual processes which provide meaning in discourse therefore have analogues in other areas of experience and can be described accordingly. It also follows from the experientialist thesis that much of the conceptual system on which language depends is derived from experiences we have with our bodies in interacting with or observing our physical environment. In this sense, cognitive linguistics and CL-CDS subscribe to an **embodied cognition** view of language. Crucially, for a critical perspective, it follows from all three theses that alternate language usages, that is, those involving different linguistic formulations, are functional in effecting competing **construals** of the same situation which may be indexical of wider ideological worldviews or discourses and which may contribute to the (de)legitimation of social actions, identities and relations.

It is the aim of CL-CDS to model the conceptualizations invoked by specific language usages and to disclose the ideological qualities and (de)legitimating potentials of those conceptualizations. To this end, drawing from across frameworks in cognitive linguistics, CL-CDS has focused on a number of conceptual parameters or **construal operations** that make possible the discursive enactment of ideology and (de)legitimation.

In the CL-CDS framework, construal operations are set out against the more general cognitive systems on which they rely, on the one hand, and

Table 9.1 *Construal operations, cognitive systems and discursive strategies*

System Strategy	Gestalt	Comparison	Attention	Perspective
Structural configuration	Schematization			
Framing		Categorization Metaphor		
Identification			Figure/ground Granularity Viewing frame	
Positioning				Point of view Deixis Modality

the discursive strategies which they potentially realize, on the other (see Table 9.1).[1]

9.2.1 Structural Configuration Strategies

Structural configuration is the most basic-level strategy and concerns the internal event-structure imposed on the scene described. Conceptually, this strategy is realized as alternative **image schemas** are invoked to provide raw models of the referential situation or event. Schematization relies on a more general cognitive ability to analyze complex scenes in terms of gestalt structures. Image schemas are abstract, holistic knowledge structures distilled from repeated patterns of prelinguistic embodied experience (Johnson 1987; Mandler 2004). They arise in basic domains like ACTION, FORCE, SPACE and MOTION to provide folk theories of the way the world works, encoding information relating to such matters as topology, sequence and causation. In discourse, competing linguistic constructions cue alternative image schemas to define an event's domain and internal structure in ideologically invested ways. For example, in a study of media discourse on immigration, Hart (2011) showed that right-wing media especially construe the demographic process of migration as

---

[1] Three things should be noted here. (1) Table 9.1 is an attempt to synthesize several lines of research applying cognitive linguistics in CDS. This takes in, for example, research conducted under the rubrics of Critical Metaphor Analysis and Proximization Theory. Not all scholars working in these programs would necessarily locate their work with respect to the broader framework outlined here. (2) Many of the notions featured in Table 9.1, such as framing and positioning, overlap with similar notions in other approaches to discourse analysis like interactional sociolinguistics. Subjecting these notions to a specifically cognitive linguistic treatment, the emphasis in CL-CDS is on how such discursive strategies and effects are enabled linguistically and enacted conceptually. (3) The classification in Table 9.1 should be seen as relatively fluid and malleable. The discursive strategies do not operate independently of one another but, rather, function interdependently, conspiring together to construct overall patterns of representation. They should therefore be viewed as contributing different layers or dimensions of meaning. Likewise, the same construal operation is not tightly bound to any one strategy and may realize more than one strategy simultaneously. And, of course, further construal operations may be incorporated into the framework.

a force-dynamic event rather than a force-neutral motion event. The contrast can be seen in Examples (1) and (2).

(1) It is estimated that between 1,000 and 1,200 asylum seekers are coming into the country every month. (*The Mirror*, May 10, 2002)
(2) Downing Street acknowledges that illegal immigration is an issue because of the growing frustrations over the stream of people getting into Britain from France through the Channel Tunnel. (*Daily Telegraph*, May 21, 2000)

In (1), the process, designated by the verb "coming," is construed as one of unimpeded motion. The image schema invoked represents a canonical motion event in which an agent (A) moves freely into an open region (R). By contrast, in (2), the verb "getting" suggests a closed barrier that is being breached in the realization of the process.[2] In force-dynamic terms (Talmy 2000), a stronger (+) agonist (AGO) is able to overcome a weaker antagonist (ANT) and realize its intrinsic force-tendency (>). The respective image schemas evoked by (1) and (2) to constitute our most basic understandings of the target situation are modeled in Figures 9.1a and 9.1b.[3] While neither example is celebratory of migration, the force-dynamic construal encoded in (2) arguably articulates a more negative discourse by denying the right to free movement and presenting migrants as devious and pernicious in finding a way through the barriers in place.

In a study of media representations of violence at political protests, Hart (2013a, 2013b) showed that the media, when describing interactions in which protesters are agents, construe the interaction as an ACTION event

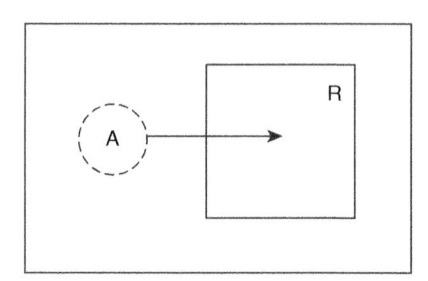

Figure 9.1a Free motion schema

---

[2] Force-dynamic indicators are not restricted to verbs, but closed-class elements like prepositions and conjunctions can similarly encode force-dynamic construals.

[3] Analyses in CL-CDS are replete with diagrams such as these. It is important to recognize that linguistic knowledge is not claimed to be encoded in precisely this format. Rather, the diagrams are a notational device – heuristics – used to capture a range of intuitively meaningful distinctions missed by other characterizations of grammar and semantics. At the same time, they are not arbitrary or ad hoc. Their spatialized format reflects a view of language as embodied, having a grounding in visual perception, and their iconicity is intended to capture semantic properties such as distance, direction and orientation, in at least a systematic fashion (see Langacker 2008: 9–12 for further discussion).

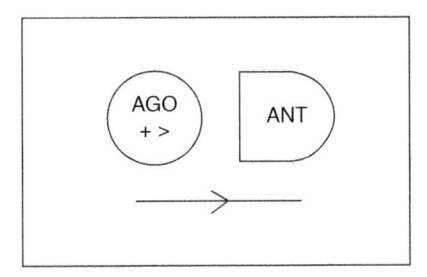

Figure 9.1b Force-dynamic schema

but, by contrast, when describing interactions in which the police are agentive, construe the interaction as a FORCE or MOTION event. Consider Examples (3) to (5).

(3) A number of police officers were injured as they came under attack from the protesters. (*The Times*, November 10, 2010)
(4) Pockets of demonstrators pushed forward and were held back by police. (*The Independent*, November 24, 2010)
(5) About 50 riot police moved in just after 5pm. (*The Independent*, November 10, 2010)

In (3), the event is schematized as an ACTION event in which there is a transfer of energy from an agent (protestors) to a patient (police officers) resulting in a change in state (injuries) in the patient. The construal encoded is modeled in Figure 9.2a. As the sole agent in the interaction, protesters are delegitimated as instigators of violence. By contrast, in (4) the interaction is conceived as a FORCE event. There is no transfer of energy from an agent to a patient; rather, what is at issue are the location and freedom to move of one participant as determined by the other. The police in (4) are not agents of a violent action, only an attempt to block the advances of protesters. The police are therefore legitimated as engaging only in efforts to maintain the status quo. The schema evoked is modeled in Figure 9.2b where the police are the stronger entity able to prevent the protesters from realizing their intrinsic force tendency.

In (5), the police are agents in a nontransactive MOTION event. That is, there is no interaction with a second participant. The construal encoded entirely glosses over any form of resistance met by the police and their response to that resistance. Example (5) may therefore be described as euphemistic and close to metaphorical. The schema invoked is the same as that modeled in Figure 9.1a. Examples like (3) to (5), then, articulate a discourse of deviance in respect to civil disorder in which protesters are seen as perpetrators of violence while the police are seen as peaceful protectors.

Events construed as belonging to the same domain are subject to further levels of construal as they may still be configured in subtly different ways or conceived from different perspectives (for discussion of perspective see

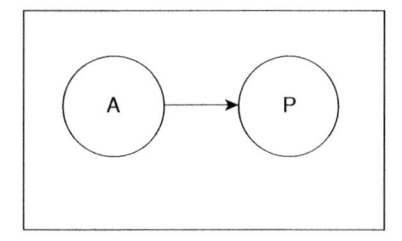

Figure 9.2a One-tailed action schema

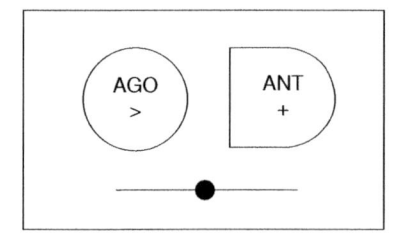

Figure 9.2b Force-dynamic schema

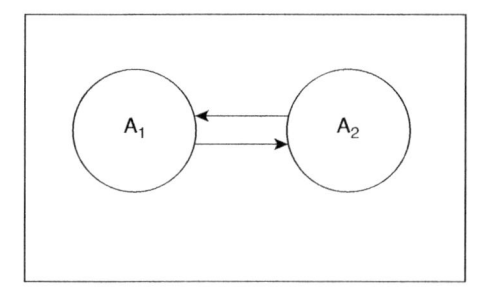

Figure 9.3 Two-tailed action schema

Section 9.2.4). For example, Hart (2013a, 2013b) further found that when construing violent interactions between police and protesters as ACTION events, the right-wing press construed the events in terms of a one-sided action schema with protesters as the sole agent, while liberal newspapers more often construed the same events in terms of a two-sided action schema in which both participants are agentive. Consider the contrast between (6) and (7).

(6) A number of police officers were injured as they <u>came under attack from</u> the protesters. (*The Times*, November 10, 2010)

(7) Police wielding batons <u>clashed with</u> a crowd hurling placard sticks, eggs and bottles. (*The Guardian*, November 10, 2010)

The schema invoked by (6) is the one modeled in Figure 9.2a. The schema invoked by (7) is modeled in Figure 9.3. Ideologically, reciprocal constructions like (7) and the two-sided action schema they invoke to make sense of the situation serve to apportion blame and responsibility for the violent encounter more equally and thus at least recognize a discourse of state violence.

The examples discussed in this section serve to highlight the blurred boundaries between literal and figurative language as well as between structural configuration and framing strategies. I turn to framing strategies in the following section.

9.2.2 Framing

If structural configuration strategies determine the most elementary properties of an event, imposing image schemas derived from embodied experience to define its domain and internal "logic," framing strategies "flesh out" the conceptualization by drawing on rich, encyclopedic knowledge structures in the form of **frames**. Framing strategies rely on a basic cognitive ability to compare real-world phenomena with idealized models. Frames are stereotyped structures representing areas of sociocultural experience (Fillmore 1982, 1985). In discourse, frames are activated all at once by lexical units that refer either to the frame itself or to its elements. When activated, frames serve to attribute more affective qualities to the actors and actions involved in the target situation or event. Conceptually, framing strategies are realized through processes of categorization and metaphor. Every act of categorization involves the apprehension of a particular frame. For example, when an individual is categorized as a "refugee" versus an "economic migrant" or as a "rioter" versus a "demonstrator," competing frames are conjured that carry different ideological and evaluative baggage. Consider the contrast between headlines in Examples (8) and (9). The RIOT frame accessed by (8) contains entries to do with violence and vandalism and thus connotes opportunistic criminality rather than an organized display of political discontent. The categorization in (8) is thus likely to invite a more negative appraisal of the actors involved.

(8) Rioters loot RBS as demonstrations turn violent. (*The Telegraph*, April 1, 2009)
(9) G20 Protests: Riot police clash with demonstrators. (*The Guardian*, April 1, 2009)

The competing frames in (8) and (9) both offer literal interpretations of the situation. Very often, however, frames are applied figuratively, cued by metaphorical expressions in discourse. The framing functions of metaphor have been investigated in a wide variety of discourse contexts and genres and from a range of different perspectives (see Chapter 10 in this volume for an overview).

In CL-CDS, **metaphor** is investigated under the banner of critical metaphor analysis (Charteris-Black 2004; Chilton 1996; Koller 2004; Musolff

2004, 2016; Santa Ana 2002) where it is identified as a key index of ideology and an important device in the discursive (de)legitimation of social action. From this perspective, metaphor is understood to be a cognitive process of frame projection whereby a source frame is mobilized to provide a template for sense-making inside an otherwise underspecified target frame. Metaphors in discourse are therefore not just convenient tropes but invitations to particular modes of understanding. In accessing particular stores of knowledge, metaphors construe the target situation in particular ways, profiling certain aspects of reality while backgrounding others and making certain inferences available at the expense of others. In so doing, metaphors define how social situations are to be understood, reasoned about, reacted to emotionally and ultimately responded to materially.

While target frames are typically underspecified, representing subjective, unfamiliar or contested areas of experience, source frames tend to be richly populated, representing concrete and familiar areas of experience. In social, economic and political discourses, certain frames are identified as playing a recurrent structuring role. These include: JOURNEY, BUILDING, WEATHER, WATER, ILLNESS, WAR, GAMES and GAMBLING.[4] For example, the BUILDING frame, instantiated specifically in a HOUSE frame, has been found to function in discourses of migration (Hart 2010), discourses of the European Union (Chilton and Ilyin 1993) and Cold War discourses of national security (Chilton 1996). The JOURNEY frame is frequently invoked to conceptualize political policies, such as the 2010–2019 austerity program, and various forms of social and political "progress" (Charteris-Black 2004; Hart 2014). WAR frames are found to feature in media discourses of migration (El Refaie 2001; Hart 2010), business mergers and acquisitions (Koller 2004), political protests (Fridolfsson 2008) and industrial disputes (Hart 2017). Naturalized themes are also frequently drawn upon so that, for example, the financial market is routinely conceptualized as WEATHER (Charteris-Black 2004), immigration is conceptualized as WATER (Charteris-Black 2006; El Refaie 2001; Hart 2010; Santa Ana 2002), civil disorder is conceptualized as FIRE (Charteris-Black 2017; Hart 2018a; Hawkins 2014) and various (perceived) social problems are conceptualized in terms of a DISEASE affecting the national BODY-POLITIC (Musolff 2003, 2007).

Metaphors in discourse are ideologically so significant because, when mobilized in metaphorical construals, frames impose their own "logic," cultural associations and emotional valence on the target situation, giving rise to potential **framing effects** in our judgments, decisions and

---

[4] In metaphor, structural configuration and framing strategies can most clearly be seen to overlap as many frames have as inherent properties particular image schemas. For example, the BUILDING frame possesses as a structural component the CONTAINER schema. Likewise, the JOURNEY frame may be said to instantiate or elaborate the SOURCE-PATH-GOAL schema. Metaphor therefore often involves schematization and thus simultaneously performs a structural configuration and framing function.

ultimately our actions. For example, conceptualizing migration as war, as in (10) and (11) where immigrants are construed as an invading army, not only problematizes migration by presenting immigrants as an aggressive Other to be feared but also creates the space for a military solution to the "problem." As El Refaie (2001: 368) states, the use of war metaphors in discourses of migration "makes it conceivable to treat defenceless human beings as dangerous enemies and seems to justify a war-like reaction to them."

(10) <u>The invasion of Britain</u> by illegal immigrants continues unabated. (*The Sun*, May 17, 2002)
(11) <u>The army of asylum seekers</u> flooding into Britain every year would populate the city of Cambridge, it was admitted yesterday. (*Daily Mail*, March 4, 2003)

Naturalized themes such as found in Examples (12)–(14) serve a dehumanizing function. In discourses of economics, exemplified in (12), construing the financial market as a natural phenomenon that fluctuates of its own accord rather than due to human influence neglects the role that particular financial institutions and political systems play in bringing about financial crises. In discourses of migration, exemplified in (13), construing immigration as a catastrophic natural event, such as a flood, tidal wave or tsunami, not only problematizes migration by construing it as a natural disaster but, in so doing, ignores the individual human stories behind migration and thereby makes it easier to condone inhumane treatments of people. In discourses of civil disorder, exemplified in (14), construing social unrest as a fire breaking out or a volcano erupting detaches the events from any human causes or concerns, thus depoliticizing the events and ignoring the structural conditions that may have given rise to them.

(12) As our biggest trading partner, the problems in the Eurozone are affecting Britain too. As we prepare for the potential <u>storms</u> we should be both resolute and confident. (David Cameron, May 17, 2012)
(13) Tony Blair failed to win virtually any help from the French last night in the battle to stem <u>the flood of illegal immigrants</u> pouring into Britain. (*Daily Mail*, February 10, 2001)
(14) Violence has <u>erupted</u> across London and in other major UK cities following the fatal shooting of a man by police in Tottenham last week. (*BBC News*, August 9, 2011)

Metaphor analysis in CL-CDS, it should be noted, is not restricted to the linguistic modality. Many of the same metaphorical frame projections identified above are invoked by realizations in the visual modality too or via specific combinations of the two semiotic modes. For example, El Refaie (2003) shows how Europe is construed as a building and immigration is construed as moving water in Austrian political cartoons. In a study of media coverage of two political protests in Sweden, Fridolfsson (2008: 137) notes that the news photography was "charged with visual references to war aesthetics like people hunching down in the streets or frightened faces taking protection in a smoky environment." Hart (2017, 2018a) studied media coverage of the 1984–85 British Miners' Strike and found that news photographs and political cartoons appealed, often via intertextual references, to culturally specific frames for World War I and World War II in order to make sense of the strike.

9.2.3 Identification

Identification strategies concern the presence and relative salience of social actors, actions and events within the conceptualization invoked. Identification strategies rely on a general cognitive capacity for distributing attention. They are realized in various construal operations which Langacker (2002) groups together under the banner of **focal adjustments**. If schematization is responsible for conceptual content, determining the structure and domain of a given scene, then focal adjustments add a further level of construal in directing how that conceptual content is viewed. As Langacker (2008: 55) states, "every symbolic structure construes its content in a certain fashion" whereby "what we actually see depends on how closely we examine it, what we choose to look at, which elements we pay most attention to, and where we view it from." Here, I take just one focal adjustment in **viewing frame** (see Hart 2016 for discussion of others).

In apprehending any scene, we can distribute our attention over a greater or lesser portion of that scene. That is, our **viewing frame** can be broader or narrower in scope. One area where this shows up in language is in the expression of causation. In discourses of migration, for example, reasons for movement can be acknowledged or not. This may be indexed explicitly by means of causative conjunctions (*because*) or implicitly by means of temporal conjunctions (*before, after*), among other linguistic means. Expanding the viewing frame can serve different ideological functions depending on the discursive context. In migration discourses, the viewing frame may be expanded to include "push" factors (war, poverty, natural disasters) likely to invite a more sympathetic attitude toward migrants or "pull" factors, as in (15), more likely to invite hostility.[5]

(15)   There have been claims that the Romanians had travelled to Britain again <u>because</u> of the lure of free housing and benefits given to their relatives in Britain. (*Mail on Sunday*, March 25, 2001)

---

[5] The viewing frame can also be moved around to focus attention on different facets of a scene or event. This can be seen in verbs describing migration. Verbs *leave* and *flea (from)* focus attention on the initial stage of the process while verbs *arrive* and *head (to)* focus attention on the final stage.

In discourses of disorder, the viewing frame is often expanded to include some previous mitigating event or circumstance that explains the actions in which police are agentive. In expanding the viewing frame, as in (16), police actions are construed as provoked, retaliatory or restorative rather than gratuitous. The viewing frame is rarely expanded in conceptualizing the actions of protesters.

(16) Hundreds of protesters cheered as office equipment including a printer was carried out of the building before riot police wielding batons managed to force the crowds back. (*The Telegraph*, April 1, 2009)

The viewing frame can also be contracted to conceal causation. In discourses of disorder, this often occurs in relation to injuries sustained by protesters and is realized by means of nominalization among other linguistic phenomena. In (17), for example, there is no reference to how the injuries were acquired. The viewing frame focuses only on the result of an interaction and thus ignores the potential role of the police in causing the injuries. This is in contrast to reporting injuries sustained by police officers as in (6). Restricted versus expanded viewing frames are modeled in Figures 9.4a and 9.4b where E represents some previous event that would, of course, have its own internal structure.

(17) At least 14 people were treated for their injuries in hospital and 32 arrested. (*The Times*, November 10, 2010)

I have argued elsewhere that the scope of the viewing frame, as well as other distinctions in attentional distribution, is a function of positioning

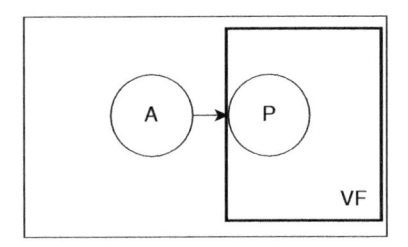

Figure 9.4a Restricted viewing frame

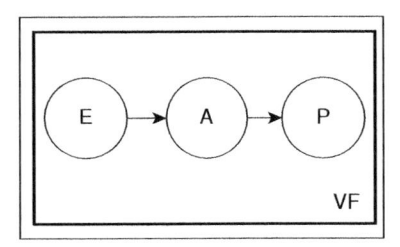

Figure 9.4b Expanded viewing frame

strategies as realized in shifts in spatial point of view (Hart 2016). In the case of viewing frame, an expanded viewing frame may be said to represent a distal point of view while a restricted viewing frame may be said to represent a close-up point of view (Hart 2016). I turn to positioning in Section 9.2.4.

9.2.4 Positioning

Positioning strategies concern the position of the conceptualizer with respect to the conceptual content currently evoked as well as the position of construed elements relative to this egocentric reference point. Positioning strategies rely on a general cognitive capacity for perspective-taking and are realized in construal operations of **point of view** and **deixis**. Positioning is not restricted to spatial positioning; it also includes positioning in temporal, epistemic and deontic dimensions. Construal operations indexed by stancetaking acts in discourse may therefore also be considered to realize positioning strategies (Marín Arrese 2011).

Various forms of positioning strategy are described across the CL-CDS literature (Cap 2006; Chilton 2004; Hart 2016). Hart (2016) proposes an embodied grammar of spatial **point of view** modeled in three aspects: anchor, angle and distance. The claim is that grammatical constructions include as part of their meaning a point of view specification with coordinates in all three dimensions. Meaningful distinctions between grammatical alternates are analyzed as point of view shifts in one or other of these aspects. For example, transitive versus reciprocal verb constructions found in competing discourses of civil disorder are said to encode not only alternative schematizations in one-sided versus two-sided action schemas but also alternative anchorage points from which that conceptual content is further construed. One-sided action schemas evoked by transitive verbs are construed along the sagittal axis with voice determining whether the action is construed from the perspective of the agent or the patient. Two-sided action schemas evoked by reciprocal verbs are construed transversally with information sequence determining the relative left–right arrangement of actors. This gives rise to four alternative construals as modeled in Figure 9.5.

The ideological significance of point of view as a semiotic feature has been most widely studied in relation to images in multimodal discourse analysis (Kress and van Leeuwen 1996; Machin 2007). Here, as Kress and van Leeuwen (1996: 146) state, "the addition of perspective adds nothing to the representational meaning but it does add attitudinal meaning." Specifically, on the horizontal plane, the difference between oblique and frontal angles is the difference between "detachment" and "involvement" (Kress and van Leeuwen 1996: 136). The claim made in Hart (2016) is that point of view should not be expected to function any differently in mental imagery invoked by language. Thus, the conceptualizations invoked by transitive verb constructions, which involve a frontal angle, may be said to

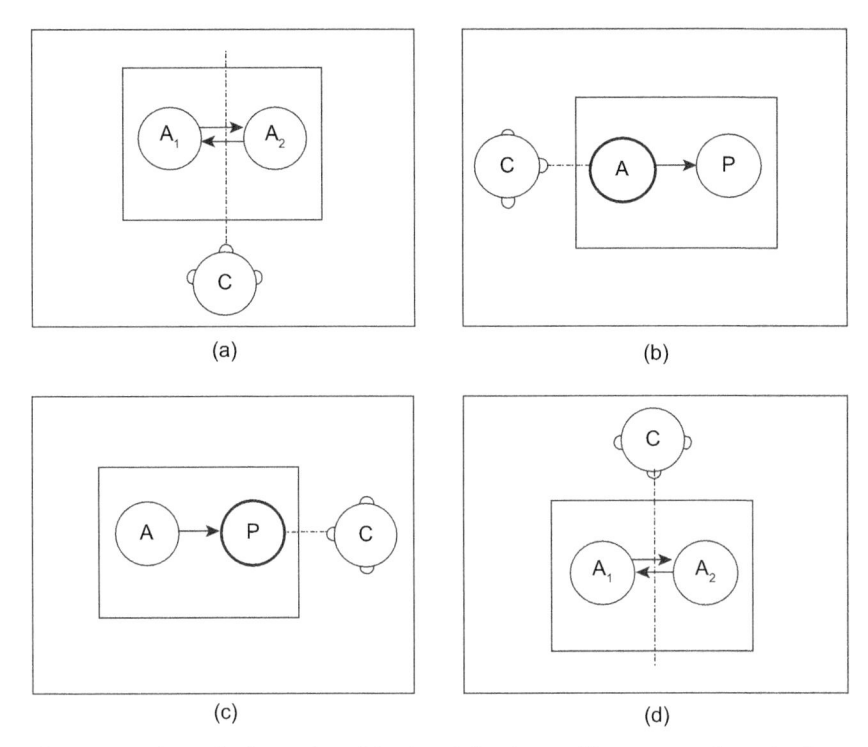

Figure 9.5 Schematization and spatial point of view in transitive versus reciprocal verb constructions

offer a more involved perspective with the conceptualizer invited to "take a side." By contrast, the conceptualizations invoked by reciprocal verb constructions, which involve an oblique angle, offer a more detached and therefore more neutral perspective with respect to the actors designated. The oblique angle encoded by reciprocal verbs is not entirely ideologically neutral, however. This is because spatial values right and left are, from an embodied perspective, associated with positive and negative valence, respectively (Casasanto 2009). Thus, the alternative left–right arrangements invoked by (7) and (9) compared to (18), modeled in Figures 9.5a compared to 9.5d, invite slightly different evaluations of and attitudes toward the social actors represented.

(18) Twenty-three people were arrested as protesters clashed with police around the Bank of England. (*The Telegraph*, April 1, 2009)

Further forms of positioning described across the CL-CDS literature are based on **deixis** or **modality** and involve a point of view which is not encoded in the semantics of grammatical constructions but determined with reference to the communicative situation or in relation to the communicated proposition. One positioning strategy that involves a deictic construal operation is **proximization** (Cap 2006, 2008). Proximization involves a dynamic simulation in which an entity, event, scenario, state of affairs or worldview, constructed as negative and positioned as remote from the conceptualizer, is reconstrued as moving toward or already having arrived at a deictic point of reference in an abstract, three-dimensional mental space. The deictic point of reference represents what the conceptualizer takes as their spatial, temporal and axiological **ground.** Proximization has been shown to be a salient feature of "interventionist" discourses including anti-immigration discourses and discourses justifying military action (Cap 2006; Hart 2010, 2014). Three basic types of proximization are identified (see Hart 2014 for full typology). In **spatial proximization**, a physical threat is presented as moving toward and potentially entering the conceptualizer's spatial ground, leading to corporeal harm. Spatial proximization can be seen in Example (19). Proximization construals are prompted not by single lexical or grammatical units but by combinations of units that together work to fulfill the proximization script.

(19) This new world faces a new threat of disorder and chaos born either of brutal states like Iraq armed with weapons of mass destruction or of extreme terrorist groups . . . . My fear, deeply held, based in part on the intelligence that I see, is that these threats come together and deliver catastrophe to our country and our world. (Tony Blair, March 20, 2003)

In axiological proximization, some ideological threat is established and presented as entering and transforming the conceptualizer's axiological ground (i.e., their presumed system of shared values). This can be seen in Example (20).

(20) In order to ensure the continuity of our culture and its institutions, the English Defence League stands opposed to the creeping Islamisation of our country, because intimately related to the spread of Islamic religion is the political desire to implement an undemocratic alternative to our cherished way of life: the sharia. (English Defence League *Mission Statement*)

Different discourses tend to rely on different proximization strategies. The same discourse, however, can shift between strategies depending on changes in context. For example, Cap (2006) showed that US official discourse justifying military action in Iraq moved from relying on spatial proximization strategies to relying on axiological proximization strategies when it was discovered and accepted that Saddam Hussein did not, in fact, have access to weapons of mass destruction.

The third type of proximization strategy is **temporal proximization**, which presents the events defined in spatial and axiological strategies as being close in time to realization. Temporal proximization is indexed by a range of linguistic features, including markers of present tense and progressive aspect, temporal deictics and temporal adverbial phrases. This strategy is exemplified in (21).

(21) Some of these countries are <u>now a short time away from</u> having a serviceable nuclear weapon. (Tony Blair, March 18, 2003)

Proximization is a powerful rhetorical strategy in interventionist discourses because it construes once remote "problems" as directly affecting the addressee "in the here and now" and thus requiring immediate redressive action.

One form of positioning strategy based in modality concerns the stance that the conceptualizer assumes with respect to the realization of events. Marín Arrese (2011) distinguishes between **effective** and **epistemic stance**. Effective stance is expressed through deontic and volitional modality to construe events as necessary, desirable, etc. Epistemic stance is expressed through epistemic modality and evidentiality to construe the likelihood of an event or the validity of an assertion designating an event. Thus, while epistemic stance acts represent an assessment of reality, effective stance acts represent an attempt to alter the course of reality itself. Both are exploited in the discursive legitimation of social action:

(22) <u>I am in no doubt that</u> the threat is serious and current, that he <u>has</u> made progress on WMD, and that he <u>has to</u> be stopped. (Tony Blair, September Dossier 2002)

A further positioning strategy related to stance is realized though the construal operation of **subjectification/objectification**. This construal operation concerns the extent to which the role of the speaker or other source, as appraiser, is acknowledged as part of the conceptualization evoked. In Langacker's terms, the predication source is **objectified** if they are placed "onstage," by explicit mention, as on object of conception. They are **subjectified** if they remain "offstage" as only an implicit source of predication.[6] In (22) and (23), Tony Blair is objectified by "I am in no doubt that" and "in my judgement," respectively. In such cases of objectification, the speaker explicitly appeals to their own authority as a reason to believe the claims being made.

(23) The possibility of … terrorist groups in possession of weapons of mass destruction, even of a so-called dirty radiological bomb, is now, <u>in my judgement</u>, a real and present danger to Britain and its national security. (Tony Blair, March 20, 2003)

9.3 Issues, Implications and Future Directions

A major claim of CL-CDS, which follows from the symbolic thesis in cognitive linguistics, is that the conceptualizations invoked by linguistic

---

[6] Somewhat confusingly, the way Langacker applies these terms means that utterances usually described as subjectifications, i.e those which explicitly mark the speaker's attitude toward the proposition (e.g. Traugott 1995), are in Langacker's framework treated as objectifications. Consequently, elsewhere I have described examples (22) and (23) from a different analytical perspective as instances of subjectification (e.g. Hart and Fuoli 2020).

expressions in discourse are modal rather than amodal in nature, possessing properties usually associated with visual, including visual semiotic, experience. Such properties have been extensively analyzed in multimodal discourse analysis (MDA; see also Chapter 12 in this volume). Since there is no principled reason to think that these semiotic features should function differently across communicative modalities, it follows not only that the conceptual processes involved in understanding language can be characterized in the same terms as used in MDA but also that studies in MDA can shed crucial light on the most subtle ideological aspects of linguistic meaning. In this chapter, this argument has surfaced most apparently in relation to spatial point of view and suggests the need for researchers in linguistics and CL-CDS to work more closely with researchers in MDA. Although research in MDA has been strongly influenced by linguistics, it has yet to feed back and have the same kind of impact on research in linguistics, including applied linguistics in the form of CDS.

A further, related claim of CL-CDS, which follows from the experientialist thesis in cognitive linguistics, is that the meaning of any linguistic construction is, to a large extent, a function of the visual semiotic material with which it has been associated in the past (see Hart 2016 for discussion). The question thus arises: what patterns of visual representation conventionally occur in the co-text images of particular linguistic constructions? This is an empirical question which to answer would require quantitative methods such as are found in corpus linguistics. One potentially fruitful avenue for future research, then, would be to use corpus linguistic methods to investigate the visual collocates of key linguistic units.

A third major claim of CL-CDS, which follows from all three theses in cognitive linguistics, is that different language usages encode different construals, which gives rise to ideological/(de)legitimating effects in the way in which the target situation is understood and responded to. However, as with all forms of CDS, claiming ideological/(de)legitimating effects for specific language usages, without any empirical evidence, is problematic and the researcher is in danger of intruding their own subjectivity into the analysis and overinterpreting the impact of language choices on other, ordinary readers (O'Halloran 2003; Stubbs 1997; Widdowson 2004). Moreover, any long-term ideological effects of texts are likely to be cumulative, based on repeated exposure to conventionalized practices. CL-CDS, then, like other approaches to CDS, faces two significant challenges: How can analyses be "upscaled" to enable generalizations over larger, more representative sets of data? And how can hypothesized ideological/(de)legitimating effects of particular language usages be empirically verified?

To meet these challenges means an empirical turn exploiting quantitative methodologies. In relation to the first, researchers in CDS increasingly make use of corpus linguistic methods to check that patterns of representation remain significant within larger data sets (e.g. Baker 2006). A major advantage of corpus linguistics for CDS is that computer software can be used to identify patterns of representation in large data sets quickly and reliably (see Chapter 8 in this volume on this point). The starting point here is often an automatic semantic annotation or "tagging" of the data (some manual check and override procedure is still usually required to ensure reliability). In CL-CDS, corpus linguistic methods have been used to identify patterns of metaphoric conceptualization in various social, political and economic discourses (Charteris-Black 2004; Koller 2005). This involves tagging lexical items for their semantic frames or domains, based on an underlying category system, and then seeing which frames or domains feature most frequently as metaphorical vehicles construing a given target. However, while corpus software can automatically parse linguistic data and fairly reliably assign tags for frames and domains (Koller et al. 2008; Semino et al. 2005), current programs do not take into account the other kind of semantic distinctions made in cognitive linguistics. Any corpus linguistic analysis of semantic features beyond frames and domains would therefore be reliant on manual annotation procedures that are very labor intensive.

In relation to the second challenge identified, there is now a small but growing body of work in CDS using experimental methods to investigate the cognitive and ideological import of textual choices (Fuoli and Hart 2018; Hart 2018b, 2018c; Hart and Fuoli 2020 Subtirelu and Gopavaram 2016). An experimental turn is particularly apposite for CL-CDS because CL-CDS makes explicit hypotheses concerning reader response.

Experiments in CL-CDS may target one or both of two levels of analysis: the conceptualizations invoked by particular language usages and/or the ideological/(de)legitimating effects of those conceptualizations.

For example, Hart (2019) investigated the conceptualizations associated with transitive versus reciprocal action verbs. Specifically, Hart used a sentence-image matching task to test hypotheses concerning point of view in transitive versus reciprocal action verb constructions. The primary hypothesis was that transitive verbs construe the designated action along the sagittal axis while reciprocal verbs construe the action along the transversal axis. Secondary hypotheses were that differences in voice and information sequence within transitive and reciprocal verb constructions construe the action in 180° rotations on the primary axes. Using a within subjects design, participants in the experiment were given thirty-two "action" sentences (eight items per type) in four conditions: (i) transitive, active voice; (ii) transitive, passive voice; (iii) reciprocal, sequence AB; (iv) reciprocal, sequence BA. Verbs included *attack, hit, strike* (transitive) and *clash with, fight with, collide with* (reciprocal). To avoid interference from personal politics and target specifically the semantics of the verbs and constructions presented, agents and patients were given as "the circle" and "the square." In transitive constructions, the agent was always "the circle." At the same time, participants saw an image schema made up of a circle and a square connected by a line in four orientations: (i) sagittal, circle front/square back; (ii) sagittal, square front/circle back; (iii) transversal,

```
┌─────────────┬─────────────┐
│ A           │ B           │
│    ▫        │             │
│   ○         │   ○──▫      │
├─────────────┼─────────────┤
│ C           │ D           │
│    ○        │             │
│   ▫         │   ▫──○      │
└─────────────┴─────────────┘
```

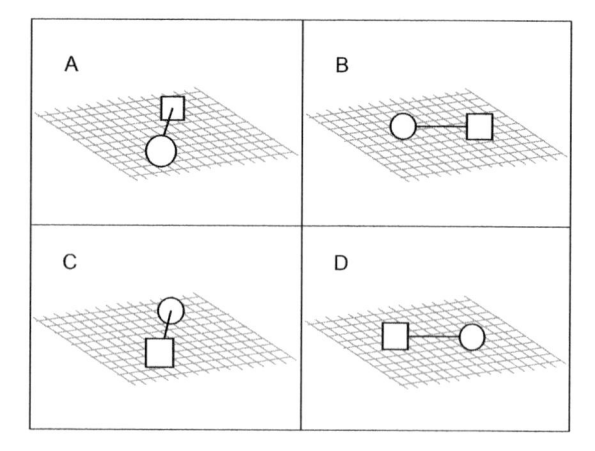

1. The circle attacked the square   [ ]
2. The circle clashed with the square   [ ]

Figure 9.6 Sentence-image matching task (Hart 2019)

circle left/square right; (iv) transversal, square left/circle right. For each sentence, participants had to indicate which schema best represents the event described (see Figure 9.6). The dependent variable was then consistency among subjects in their selection of image schema orientations. The results revealed a significant relationship between verb type and primary axis. For transitive verbs, a sagittal schema was selected the majority of the time, while for reciprocal verbs, a transversal schema was selected the majority of the time. Moreover, within reciprocal verbs, the specific transversal schema selected reflected the left–right linearity of the clause in nearly all cases. Interestingly, however, no equivalent pattern was found for voice alternates within transitive verbs where the majority of sagittal selections in both conditions were from the perspective of the agent.

The high degree of convergence among subjects in this experiment suggests that there are common underlying representations associated with transitive and reciprocal action verbs which include point of view as a meaningful component. The experiment thus helps establish the schematic-level construals evoked by language usages like (6), (7) and (18). But what of the ideological functions of such construals? In another experiment, Hart (2018b) tested the effects of transitive vs reciprocal verbs on blame assignment and perceptions of aggression in news reports of violence at a political protest. Participants were given a short news story, made up of a headline and a lead paragraph, reporting violence at a recent political protest in a fictitious city. Crucially, in a between subjects design, participants were presented with the text in one of four conditions using the different transitive and reciprocal verb constructions to describe the violent interactions. Participants were then asked to indicate where they would place the blame for the violence that occurred and how aggressive they perceived the police and protesters to be. Results were consistent with analyses of event-structure and point of view. Participants given reciprocal verb constructions, which encode a two-sided action schema, distributed blame more equally than participants given transitive verb constructions, which encode a one-sided action schema. Protesters were also judged as more aggressive when they were sole agents in a one-sided action schema encoded by transitive verbs than when they were an agent in a two-sided action schema encoded by reciprocal verbs. Point of view also seemed to be a significant factor. For example, within reciprocal verb constructions, participants judged agents as more aggressive when they occurred first in the clause and thus on the left in the conceptualization invoked, a position associated with negative valence and character traits.[7]

Of course, primary axis is concomitant with differences in event-structure and the effects of information sequence within reciprocal verbs may have to do with sentential position independent of spatial position. To be more confident that point of view is a functional semantic feature of the sentence types under consideration, Hart (2019) conducted a similar experiment using equivalent visual stimuli. If point of view in actual images shows effects in the same direction as language usages that are, by the hypothesis, congruent, then this is further evidence that point of view is a significant semiotic feature of these linguistic forms. In this study, then, participants were shown illustrations of a violent encounter between a police officer and a protester in which point of view was the only relevant variable (see Figure 9.7). They were then asked to make judgments about blame and aggression. The results were indeed consistent with those for hypothesized linguistic counterparts. Participants given transversal images (B and D) were more likely to assign equal blame than participants given sagittal images (A and C). And within transversal images, participants judged actors as more aggressive when they occurred in the left region of the image than when they occurred in the right.

The effects of other construal operations have also been tested experimentally. For example, evidence for a metaphor framing effect has been found across a range of discursive contexts (Landau, Sullivan and Greenberg 2009; Robins and Mayer 2000; Thibodeau and Boroditsky 2011; see Chapter 10 in this volume for an overview). Metaphors in discourse establish frame-structure correspondences and invite inferences about the target situation that are structurally consistent with the source frame. In the context of discourses of disorder, Hart (2018c) investigated

---

[7] Perception of aggression did not change within transitive verb constructions. However, this is to be expected in light of results from the image schema orientation experiment, which suggested that voice alternates are not associated with shifts in point of view.

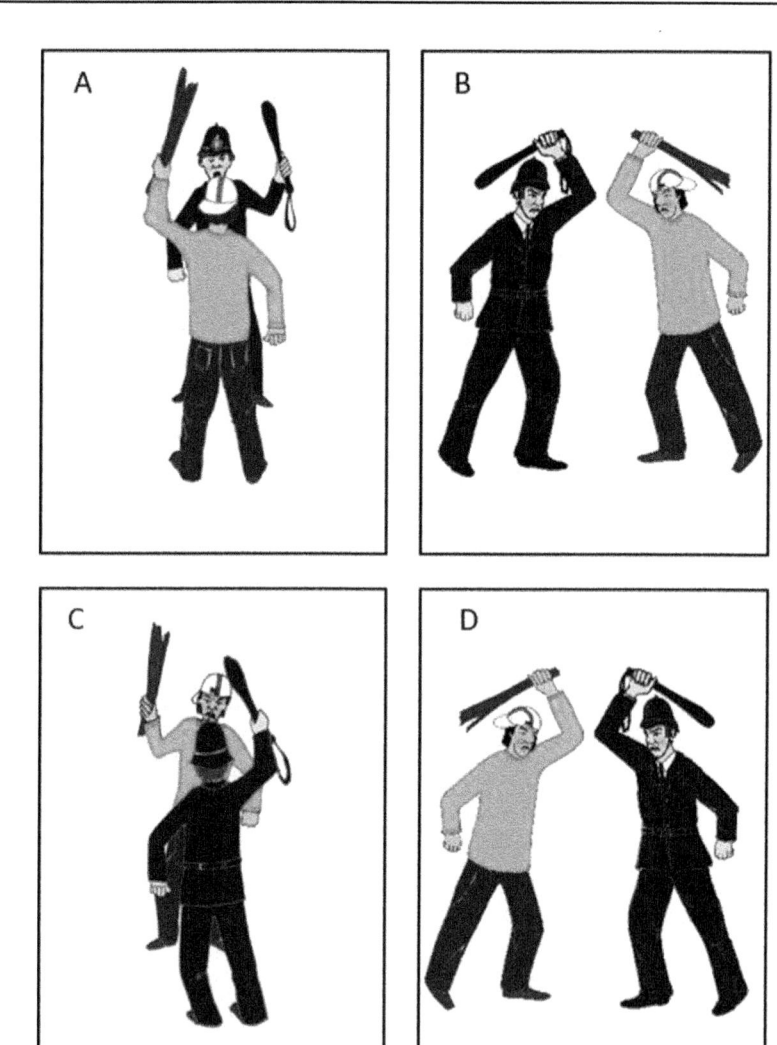

Figure 9.7 Image stimuli (Hart 2019)

the framing effects of a conventional metaphor CIVIL UNREST IS FIRE. Hart tested the hypothesis that, because the conventional means of controlling fire is with water, then the conceptual metaphor CIVIL UNREST IS FIRE, articulated in expressions like "riots engulfed the city," would facilitate support for police use of water cannon as a means of controlling civil disorder.

The design of the study targeted both the presence of fire imagery in the conceptualizations invoked by fire metaphors (source frame activation) and the import of such imagery in this context (framing effects). It was reasoned that if fire metaphors involved the activation of fire imagery, then the presence of fire in images and in metaphorical language usages should have convergent effects. Participants in the study read a newspaper front page reporting a recent instance of civil unrest in a fictitious city that resulted in police deployment of water cannon. Crucially, the text used either fire metaphors (*riots engulfed the city, spread to other cities, and continued to rage all day*) or literal equivalents (*riots overwhelmed the city, extended to other cities, and continued to occur all day*) to describe the events. Images were also taken into account so that the text included photographs containing fire (such as a man setting light to a car), photographs not containing fire (such as a man vandalizing a car) or no photographs at all. Participants were then asked to judge the legitimacy of the police response. Results were as follows. Participants presented with fire-related images but the literal version of the written text were more likely to see the use of water cannon as legitimate compared to participants presented with non-fire-related images. Participants presented with fire metaphors were similarly more likely to see the use of water cannon as legitimate compared to participants presented with literal descriptions but only in the absence of competing, non-fire-related images. Participants presented with non-fire-related images were unaffected by the presence of fire metaphors. The results were interpreted as evidence not only for the framing power of metaphor but also for image-simulation accounts of metaphor processing (e.g. Walsh 1990). Metaphor involves the activation of mental imagery, which in turn gives rise to framing effects. However, the formation of mental imagery in response to metaphor and thus the potential for a metaphor framing effect is inhibited by concrete, incongruent images present in co-text. Both sets of experiments described here point to the modal nature of meaning construction and the significance of multimodality for CDS.

9.4 Summary

In this chapter, I have introduced a particular approach to critical discourse studies grounded in cognitive linguistics (CL-CDS). The focus of CL-CDS is on the conceptualizations invoked by specific language usages and the potential ideological functions that those conceptualizations may have. A number of conceptual parameters along which ideology may be encoded/enacted have been identified and discussed. These different construal operations are described in relation to the ideological discursive strategies they potentially realize and the domain-general cognitive systems on which they rely. A recurrent theme in CL-CDS, inherited from principles in cognitive linguistics, is that meaning construction is an imagistic process resulting in modal rather than amodal mental representations. I have therefore suggested that CL-CDS can benefit from incorporating into its analyses insights from visual semiotics. The link between language and image also has consequences for the way in which language is processed when accompanied by images. The multimodal contexts in which language usages are embedded must therefore be taken into account in one's analyses. Finally, as part of an empirical turn in CDS, I have shown how experimental methods may be exploited in CL-CDS to help verify hypotheses concerning reader response. So far, however, only a very small number of experimental studies have been conducted. Hopefully, a substantial body of experimental evidence for the influence of textual choices can be amassed as part of future research programs.

Further Reading

Charteris-Black, J. (2004). *Corpus Approaches to Critical Metaphor Analysis*. Basingstoke: Palgrave.

This book provides an introduction to corpus-assisted critical metaphor analysis with applications to a range of discursive contexts including politics, economics and religion.

Chilton, P. (2004). *Analysing Political Discourse: Theory and Practice*. London: Routledge.

This book discusses a range of discursive strategies and linguistic features from a critical cognitive linguistic perspective with example analyses of discourses of national security, war and immigration.

Hart, C. (2014). *Discourse, Grammar and Ideology: Functional and Cognitive Perspectives*. London: Bloomsbury.

This book provides an introduction to cognitive linguistic critical discourse studies with chapters on structural configuration, identification, framing and positioning. A range of contemporary discourses are analyzed including discourses of riots, strikes and protest, discourses of austerity, discourses of military intervention and discourses of immigration.

Kress, G. and van Leeuwen, T. (2006). *Reading Images: The Grammar of Visual Design*. 2nd ed. London: Routledge.

This book provides an introduction to multimodality and considers, from a social semiotic perspective, the functions of different parameters, including point of view, in visual and multimodal texts.

References

Baker, P. (2006). *Using Corpora in Discourse Analysis*. London: Continuum.

Cap, P. (2006). *Legitimisation in Political Discourse*. Newcastle: Cambridge Scholars Publishing.
  (2008). Towards a Proximisation Model of the Analysis of Legitimisation in Political Discourse. *Journal of Pragmatics* 40(1): 17–41.
Casasanto, D. (2009). Embodiment of Abstract Concepts: Good and Bad in Right- and Left-Handers. *Journal of Experimental Psychology* 138(3): 351–67.
Charteris-Black, J. (2004). *Corpus Approaches to Critical Metaphor Analysis*. Basingstoke: Palgrave.
  (2006). Britain as a Container: Immigration Metaphors in the 2005 Election Campaign. *Discourse & Society* 17(6): 563–82.
  (2017). *Fire Metaphors: Discourses of Awe and Authority*. London: Bloomsbury.
Chilton, P. (1996). *Security Metaphors: Cold War Discourse from Containment to Common House*. New York, Peter Lang.
  (2004). *Analysing Political Discourse: Theory and Practice*. London: Routledge.
Chilton, P. and Ilyin, M. (1993). Metaphor in Political Discourse: The Case of the "Common European House." *Discourse & Society* 4(1): 7–31.
Croft, W. and Cruse, A. (2004). *Cognitive Linguistics*. Cambridge: Cambridge University Press.
El Refaie, E. (2001). Metaphors We Discriminate By: Naturalised Themes in Austrian Newspaper Articles about Asylum Seekers. *Journal of Sociolinguistics* 5(3): 352–71.
  (2003). Understanding Visual Metaphor: The Example of Newspaper Cartoons. *Visual Communication* 2(1): 75–96.
Fillmore, C. (1982). Frame Semantics. In Linguistics Society of Korea (ed.) *Linguistics in the Morning Calm*. Seoul: Hanshin Publishing Co. 111–37.
  (1985). Frames and the Semantics of Understanding. *Quaderni di Semantica* 6: 222–54.
Fridolfsson, C. (2008). Political Protest and Metaphor. In T. Carve and J. Pikalo (eds.) *Political Language and Metaphor: Interpreting and Changing the World*. London: Routledge. 132–48.
Fuoli, M. and Hart, C. (2018). Trust-Building Strategies in Corporate Discourse: An Experimental Study. *Discourse & Society*. doi.org/10.1177/0957926518770264.
Gonzalez-Marquez, M., Mittleberg, I., Coulson, S. and Spivey, M. (eds.) (2007). *Methods in Cognitive Linguistics*. Amsterdam: John Benjamins.
Hart, C. (2010). *Critical Discourse Analysis and Cognitive Science: New Perspectives on Immigration Discourse*. Basingstoke: Palgrave.
  (2011). *Critical Discourse Studies in Context and Cognition*. Amsterdam: John Benjamins.
  (2013a). Event-Construal in Press Reports of Violence in Political Protests: A Cognitive Linguistic Approach to CDA. *Journal of Language and Politics* 12(3): 400–23. Pre-proof version. Manuscript accepted for publication in *Applied Linguistics*.

(2013b). Constructing Contexts through Grammar: Cognitive Models and Conceptualisation in British Newspaper Reports of Political Protests. In J. Flowerdew (ed.) *Discourse and Contexts*. London: Continuum. 159–84.

(2014). *Discourse, Grammar and Ideology: Functional and Cognitive Perspectives*. London: Bloomsbury.

(2016). Viewpoint in Linguistic Discourse: Space and Evaluation in News Reports of Political Protests. *Critical Discourse Studies* 12(3): 238–60.

(2017). Metaphor and Intertextuality in Media Framings of the (1984–85) British Miners' Strike: A Multimodal Analysis. *Discourse & Communication* 11(1): 3–30.

(2018a). Metaphor and the (1984–5) British Miners' Strike: A Multimodal Analysis. In C. Hart and D. Kelsey (eds.) *Discourses of Disorder: Representations of Riots, Strikes and Protests in the Media*. Edinburgh: Edinburgh University Press. 133–53.

(2018b). Event-Frames Affect Blame Assignment and Perception of Aggression in Discourse on Political Protests: An Experimental Case Study in Critical Discourse Analysis. *Applied Linguistics* 39(3): 400–21.

(2018c). "Riots Engulfed the City": An Experimental Study Investigating the Legitimating Effects of Fire Metaphors in Discourses of Disorder. *Discourse & Society* 29(3): 279–98.

(2019). Spatial Properties of ACTION Verb Semantics: Experimental Evidence for Image Schema Orientation in Transitive vs. Reciprocal Verbs and Its Implications for Ideology. In C. Hart (ed.) *Cognitive Linguistic Approaches to Text and Discourse: From Poetics to Politics*. Edinburgh: Edinburgh University Press.

Hart, C. and Cap, P. (eds.) (2014). *Contemporary Critical Discourse Studies*. London: Bloomsbury.

Hart, C. and Fuoli, M. (2020). Objectification strategies outperform subjectification strategies in military interventionist discourses. *Journal of Pragmatics* 162: 17–28.

Hawkins, S. (2014). Teargas, Flags and Harlem Shake: Images of and for Revolution in Tunisia and the Dialectics of the Local in the Global. In P. Werbner, M. Webb and K. Spellman-Poots (eds.) *Global Protest: The Arab Spring and Beyond*. Edinburgh: Edinburgh University Press. 31–52.

Johnson, M. (1987). *The Body in the Mind: The Bodily Basis of Meaning, Imagination and Reason*. Chicago, IL: University of Chicago Press.

Koller, V. (2004). *Metaphor and Gender in Business Media Discourse: A Critical Cognitive Study*. Basingstoke: Palgrave.

(2005). Critical Discourse Analysis and Social Cognition: Evidence from Business Media Discourse. *Discourse & Society* 16(2): 199–224.

Koller, V., Hardie, A., Rayson, P. and Semino, E. (2008). Using a Semantic Annotation Tool for the Analysis of Metaphor in Discourse. *metaphorik.de* 15: 141–60.

Kress, G. and van Leeuwen, T. (1996). *Reading Images: The Grammar of Visual Design*. London: Routledge.

Lakoff, G. and Johnson, M. (1980). *Metaphors We Live By*. Chicago, IL: University of Chicago Press.

(1999). *Philosophy in the Flesh: The Embodied Mind and Its Challenge to Western Thought*. New York: Basic Books.

Landau, M. J., Sullivan, D. and Greenberg, J. (2009). Evidence that Self-Relevant Motives and Metaphoric Framing Interact to Influence Political and Social Attitudes. *Psychological Science* 20(11): 1421–6.

Langacker, R. W. (1991). *Foundations of Cognitive Grammar, Vol. II: Descriptive Application*. Stanford, CA: Stanford University Press.

(2002). *Concept, Image, and Symbol: The Cognitive Basis of Grammar*, 2nd ed. Berlin: Mouton de Gruyter.

(2008). *Cognitive Grammar: A Basic Introduction*. Oxford: Oxford University Press.

Machin, D. (2007). *An Introduction to Multimodal Analysis*. London: Bloomsbury.

Mandler, J. M. (2004). *The Foundations of Mind: Origins of Conceptual Thought*. Oxford: Oxford University Press.

Marín Arrese, J. (2011). Effective vs. Epistemic Stance and Subjectivity in Political Discourse: Legitimising Strategies and Mystification of Responsibility. In C. Hart (ed.) *Critical Discourse Studies in Context and Cognition*. Amsterdam: John Benjamins. 193–224.

Musolff, A. (2003). Ideological Functions of Metaphor: The Conceptual Metaphors of Health and Illness in Public Discourse. In R. Dirven, R. M. Frank and M. Pütz (eds.) *Cognitive Models in Language and Thought: Ideology, Metaphors and Meanings*. Berlin: Mouton de Gruyter. 327–52.

(2004). *Metaphor and Political Discourse: Analogical Reasoning in Debates about Europe*. Basingstoke: Palgrave.

(2007). What Role Do Metaphors Play in Racial Prejudice? The Function of Antisemitic Imagery in Hitler's Mein Kampf. *Patterns of Prejudice* 41 (1): 21–43.

(2016). *Political Metaphor Analysis: Discourse and Scenarios*. London: Bloomsbury.

O'Halloran, K. (2003). *Critical Discourse Analysis and Language Cognition*. Edinburgh: Edinburgh University Press.

Robins, S. and Mayer, R. E. (2000). The Metaphor Framing Effect: Metaphorical Reasoning about Text-Based Dilemmas. *Discourse Processes* 30(1): 57–86.

Santa Ana, O. (2002). *Brown Tide Rising: Metaphors of Latinos in Contemporary American Public Discourse*. Austin: University of Texas Press.

Semino, E., Hardie, A., Koller, V. and Rayson, P. (2005). A Computer-Assisted Approach to the Analysis of Metaphor Variation across Genres. In J. Barnden, M. Lee, J. Littlemore, R. Moon, G. Philip and A. Wallington (eds.) *Corpus-Based Approaches to Figurative Language*. Birmingham: University of Birmingham School of Computer Science. 145–53.

Stubbs, M. (1997). Whorf's Children: Critical Comments on Critical Discourse Analysis (CDA). In A. Ryan and A. Wray (eds.) *Evolving Models of Language*. Clevedon: British Association for Applied Linguistics. 100–16.

Subtirelu, N. C. and Gopavaram, S. R. (2016). Crowdsourcing Critical Discourse Analysis: Using Amazon's Mechanical Turk to Explore Readers' Uptake of Comments about Language on RateMyProfessors.com. *CADAAD* 8(1): 38–57.

Talmy, L. (2000). *Toward a Cognitive Semantics*. Cambridge, MA: MIT Press.

Thibodeau P. H and Boroditsky, L. (2011). Metaphors We Think With: The Role of Metaphor in Reasoning. *PLoS ONE* 6(2): e16782. https://doi.org/10.1371/journal.pone.0016782.

Traugott, E. (1995). Subjectification in grammaticalisation. In D. Stein and S. Wright (eds.), *Subjectivity and Subjectivisation: Linguistic Perspectives*. Cambridge: Cambridge University Press. 31–54.

Van Dijk, T. (1993). Principles of Critical Discourse Analysis. *Discourse & Society* 4(2): 249–83.

Walsh, P. (1990). *Imagery as a Heuristic in the Comprehension of Metaphorical Analogies: Representation, Reasoning, Analogy and Decision-Making*. New York: John Wiley.

Widdowson, H. G. (2004). *Text, Context, Pretext: Critical Issues in Discourse Analysis*. Oxford: Blackwell.

Wodak, R. (2016). Critical Discourse Studies: History, Agenda, Theory and Methodology. In R. Wodak and M. Meyer (eds.) *Methods in Critical Discourse Studies*. London: Sage. 1–22.

Wodak, R. and Meyer, M. (eds.) (2016). *Methods in Critical Discourse Studies*. London: Sage.

10

Metaphor, Metonymy and Framing in Discourse

Zsófia Demjén and Elena Semino

10.1 Introduction

Metaphor matters in discourse analysis because different metaphors can reflect and facilitate different ways of viewing topics, experiences and phenomena. This potential effect of metaphor is itself metaphorically captured by the notion of "framing." In this chapter, we review research on the framing function of metaphor and also consider the related phenomenon of metonymy as a potential framing device. We begin by providing definitions of metaphor, metonymy and framing (Section 10.2), then briefly overview the relationships between them (Section 10.3). Section 10.4 focuses on metaphor specifically and discusses three main approaches to its framing potential, drawing from Conceptual Metaphor Theory (Lakoff and Johnson, 1980), discourse analysis and experimental research. In Section 10.5, we consider some areas of debate and show how the different strands of research discussed in Section 10.4 can be brought together. In Section 10.6, we consider the practical implications of the different approaches to metaphor, metonymy and framing, both for research and for practice in different areas. We finish by encouraging further research into the topic of this chapter in Section 10.7.

10.2 Definitions

Metaphor – from the Greek "meta" meaning "over, across" and "pherein" meaning "to carry, bear" – involves talking and, potentially, thinking about one thing in terms of another, where the two things are different but some form of similarity can be perceived between them (Semino 2008).

As this definition suggests, metaphor relies on the perception of similarities or correspondences between unlike entities and processes, so that one can experience, think and communicate about one thing in terms of another – difficulties as battles, relationships as journeys, emotions as external forces, and so on. These similarities or correspondences, however, are only ever partial; they foreground certain aspects of the entity or process in question, while backgrounding others. For example, in "I have kind of prepared myself for a battle with cancer" (from an online forum for people with cancer), "battle" foregrounds those aspects of the cancer experience that are related to danger, determination, intense effort and uncertain but clear-cut outcomes. On the other hand, this metaphor backgrounds other potential aspects of the experience, such as acceptance of living with the disease long term, a renewed appreciation for life and empathy with others sharing the same experience. More importantly, this metaphor may suggest that not getting better is a personal failure, as it corresponds to "losing the battle." This, in a nutshell, is how metaphors frame topics in different ways.

In the analysis of verbal data, the best-established method for identifying metaphorically used words (or metaphorical expressions[1]) is known as the Metaphor Identification Procedure (MIP) (Pragglejaz Group 2007). This procedure requires the researcher to consider the meaning that each word (or multi-word expression) has in a given discourse context and decide whether that "contextual meaning" contrasts with a more "basic" meaning of that word/expression in other contexts. "Basic meaning" for this purpose is defined as a meaning that is more concrete; related to bodily action; more precise as opposed to vague; and, usually, historically older. If such a basic meaning is identified, the researcher then needs to establish whether the contextual meaning can be understood in comparison with the basic meaning. If this is the case, the word/expression is considered to be metaphorically used (Pragglejaz Group 2007; see also Steen et al. 2010 for an extension on the original MIP procedure known as MIPVU and Charteris-Black (2004) for an approach to metaphor identification based on the notion of incongruity). In the example above, "battle" is not used in its basic meaning of "a fight between two armies in a war" (macmillandictionaryonline.com) but to refer to attempting to recover from cancer. The latter meaning can be understood in comparison with the former on the basis of the perception of several possible similarities, such as that they both denote difficult, effortful enterprises that are potentially painful and life-threatening. Within this approach, verbal metaphors include not just striking and creative uses of language but also metaphorical expressions that are so conventional as to be barely noticeable (e.g. "going through" to refer to coping with difficult experiences, rather than to physical movement). Metaphoricity in language can also be realized through "similes" and other explicit statements of comparison between unlike things, such as "cancer is just like a long and winding country road" (Semino et al. 2018:

---

[1] The term "metaphorical expression" allows for the fact that metaphors can consist of more than one word.

135). When we talk generally about "metaphor" in discourse in this chapter, we include similes alongside metaphorical expressions.

From a cognitive perspective, metaphor has been influentially defined as a cross-domain mapping, i.e. as a set of correspondences between a "source" conceptual domain (e.g. BATTLE) and a "target" conceptual domain (e.g. ILLNESS) (Lakoff and Johnson 1980; see also Chapter 9 in this volume). From this theoretical perspective (known as Conceptual Metaphor Theory), metaphorical expressions such as "battle" in our example are linguistic realizations of conceptual metaphors, that is, patterns of metaphorical thought that can become conventionalized and entrenched in language.[2] This approach to metaphor provides an account of the framing power of metaphor, to which we will return in Section 10.3.

Metonymy – from the Greek "meta" meaning, in this case, "change" and "onoma," that is, "name" – is often discussed alongside and in contrast with metaphor. From a linguistic perspective, it also involves talking about one thing in terms of another but on the basis of a "stand for" relationship of association or contiguity (rather than similarity), such as when the phrase "the White House" (which literally refers to a building) is used to refer to the President of the United States of America and the team of advisors usually based in that building. From a conceptual perspective, metonymy involves a mapping within (rather than across) conceptual domains, such as between different entities within the conceptual domain for US GOVERNMENT (Kövecses 2010; Littlemore 2015). In the terms of Dancygier and Sweetser (2014: 104), "metaphorical mappings project structure from frame to frame, while metonymic patterns focus on parts of frames but give access to the frames as wholes." Metonymies are particularly reliant on relevant background knowledge: one needs to know that the US President is based in a building known as "the White House" in order to make sense of metonymic uses of that phrase. This is particularly obvious with more context-specific metonymies. Deignan, Littlemore and Semino (2013) discuss, for example, the use of "veg bowls" and "meat bowls" by staff in a UK nursery to refer to children who eat, respectively, vegetarian and meat-based lunches.

The term "framing" has been used in a range of different fields, including in classic studies in sociology (Goffmann 1967), artificial intelligence (Minsky 1975) and semantics (Fillmore 1985). While there are various, sometimes conflicting uses of the term, in general, a "frame" tends to be defined as a portion of background knowledge that (i) relates to a particular aspect of the world, (ii) generates inferences and expectations in communication and action and (iii) tends to be associated with particular verbal expressions (see also explanation in Chapter 9 in this volume). Entman (1993) provides an overarching definition of "framing" that aims

---

[2] For a classic discussion of "universality" and cultural specificity in relation to conceptual metaphors, see Kövecses (2005).

to reconcile the different uses of the term in different disciplines in relation to communication, including any kind of verbal data: "Framing essentially involves *selection* and *salience*. To frame is to *select some aspects of a perceived reality and make them more salient in a communicating text, in such a way as to promote a particular problem definition, causal interpretation, moral evaluation, and/or treatment recommendation* for the item described" (Entman 1993: 52; italics in original). Having defined our key terms, we now go on to consider their relationships in more detail.

10.3 Overview of Metaphor, Metonymy and Framing

10.3.1 Metaphor and Framing

At least as far back as classical antiquity, there has been a steady interest in metaphor, particularly within the rhetorical tradition that developed at the interface between philosophy, literature and politics. In *The Art of Rhetoric*, Aristotle already pointed out that metaphors are frequently used in communication and that they "bring things vividly 'before the eyes' of listeners or readers" (Mahon 1999: 76). This, he argued, makes metaphor particularly helpful as a tool of learning and persuasion. An awareness of the persuasive potential of metaphor has in fact regularly resulted in metaphors being viewed with suspicion, and led to warnings against it for fear that it could be used to mislead (e.g. Locke [1690]1979). In the late 1970s, for example, sociologist Susan Sontag (1979) denounced the negative implications of military metaphors for illnesses such as cancer, especially for patients' morale and self-esteem, and proposed as a solution the removal of all metaphors from communication about illness.

The development of Conceptual Metaphor Theory, since the 1980s, into the dominant theoretical approach to metaphor across disciplines has had a number of relevant implications. It has placed metaphor center-stage in the study of language, communication and cognition. It has argued that metaphor is a crucial tool for thinking and communicating. It has provided a theoretical account for how different metaphors frame topics in different ways, and potentially without the conscious awareness of those who produce or interpret instances of those metaphors.

On the other hand, Conceptual Metaphor Theory has tended to neglect the linguistic and discoursal aspects of metaphor, and created an unnecessary and counterproductive opposition between its own conceptual view of metaphor and the view of metaphor as a rhetorical tool that dates back at least to Aristotle (e.g. Mahon 1999).

As a result, it is possible to identify two main tendencies within work on metaphor and framing over the last few decades: a strand of research that emphasizes the conceptual dimension of metaphor and a strand of research that emphasizes the discoursal dimension of metaphor, even when being influenced by Conceptual Metaphor Theory. In Section 10.4, we consider each of these strands in turn. We then briefly review some empirical work on the effects of metaphors in comprehension and reasoning, which provides evidence for the framing power of metaphor and is relevant to both strands. Indeed, in Section 10.5, we show how the conceptual and discourse-based approaches to metaphor and framing can and ought to be combined to do justice to the richness and complexity of the uses and functions of metaphors in discourse (see also Hampe 2017).

10.3.2 Metonymy and Framing

While the connection between metaphor and framing is a theme that emerges again and again in discussions of metaphor, the same cannot be said about metonymy and framing. This may be due to several reasons. Although the literature on metonymy is substantial (e.g. Littlemore 2015 for an overview), it does not even closely approximate the amount of work that has been carried out on metaphor. In addition, research on metonymy has traditionally employed artificial examples to explain different kinds of metonymy as cognitive mechanisms (e.g. Barcelona 2000). As a result, it has tended to focus on metonymies that do not have strong evaluative, emotional or ideological implications, such as "White House," or even the practice of referring to children via the food they are meant to eat while organizing lunch in a nursery. Nonetheless, the choice of a particular association as the basis for a metonymic reference is often based on relevance in context from a particular perspective (e.g. that of nursery staff trying to serve lunch in their workplace). Depending on the context and perspective, there may therefore be important implications for framing. For example, the expression "having a blonde moment" is sometimes used to describe situations in which someone (usually a woman, whether with blonde hair or not) behaves in a way that is perceived as stupid or naïve. The use of "blonde" here is metonymic: it both relies on and reinforces a sexist association between blonde women and stupidity, and reflects the prejudiced belief that women cannot be both attractive and intelligent. When applied to a particular incident (even if humorously), this metonymy frames it as being the result of that particular kind of lack of intelligence, rather than as the result of something else.

Recent work on metonymy from the perspective of discourse analysis and applied linguistics has begun to highlight the framing biases of at least some uses of metonymy, especially in interaction with metaphor. Metonymic references to people always have the potential to dehumanize the individual or groups involved. This may not have major consequences in cases like the meat/veg bowls, as these metonymic references to the children are limited to lunchtimes, and partly aimed at making sure that everyone is given the correct lunch. In contexts such as hospitals, in contrast, the practice of referring to patients via their disease, or their bed number, could undermine the person-centered, empathetic approach that should be the aim of healthcare systems. In the words of a doctor writing on an online forum analyzed in Semino et al. (2018: 166): "Alas, few of us 'see' our patients. We see only a duodenal ulcer, or hypertension, or major depression."

In the context of media reporting, Pinelli (2016) considers the metaphors and metonymies used in two Russian newspapers to report on a terrorist attack against a school in the town of Beslan in September 2014. The two newspapers differ in how they use the country's name "Russia" ("Rossija") metonymically. One newspaper uses it to stand for the Russian people and the government, while the other uses it to stand for the Russian people only, excluding the government. This results in different framings of the broader situation in which the terrorist incident occurred, namely as part of an external attack against Russia as a whole or in the context of internal conflict within Russia.

Littlemore (2015) is the first book-length account of metonymy that brings together research on metonymy based on a wide range of discourse data. While the book's subtitle aptly describes metonymies as "hidden shortcuts in language, thoughts and communication," Littlemore also shows that metonymies can perform a variety of functions in discourse. These include persuasive, evaluative and ideological functions, which, Littlemore argues, may be conveyed even more subtly than with metaphor, as metonymies may be even harder to notice and therefore to question or challenge.

Persuasive functions can also be performed by expressions that combine metaphor and metonymy. For example, Semino and Koller (2009) mention Silvio Berlusconi's tendency to refer to taxation as "putting the hands in the Italians' pockets" ("mettere le mani nelle tasche degli italiani"), while he was Prime Minister of Italy. The scenario evoked by this expression involves metonymic associations between pockets and money, and between putting one's hands in someone else's pockets and depriving them of money. This whole scenario then functions as a metaphor for taxation. Crucially, however, this scenario is reminiscent of pickpocketing, and it is this allusion to theft that Berlusconi relied upon, to justify not just his low-taxation policies but also his condoning of tax evasion, including in relation to his own affairs.

As there are still relatively few studies on metonymy and framing in discourse, the rest of this chapter will focus on metaphor, where the relevant literature is large.

10.4 Different Approaches to Metaphor and Framing

10.4.1 Framing and Metaphor in Conceptual Metaphor Theory

As we have already outlined, within Conceptual Metaphor Theory, in line with its cognitive linguistic orientation, Lakoff and Johnson (1980) see metaphors first and foremost as mappings across different domains, or areas of background knowledge, in conceptual structure, for example

BATTLE and BEING ILL WITH CANCER. From this perspective, much of our thinking relies on conventional conceptual metaphors – systematic sets of correspondences between, typically, more concrete, image-rich and intersubjectively accessible "source" domains such as BATTLE and more abstract, subjective and poorly delineated "target" domains such as BEING ILL WITH CANCER (Lakoff and Johnson 1980; see also Gibbs 2008). Conventional patterns of metaphors in language, such as the tendency to talk about having cancer as a "battle," are seen as linguistic realizations of, and one type of evidence for, the conceptual metaphors we think by.

Lakoff and Johnson's notion of conceptual domain has its roots in the tradition of frame semantics associated with Fillmore (1985). As we mentioned earlier, "frame" denotes a "prefab" chunk of knowledge structure, which can be evoked by any expression referring to any aspect of the chunk (Dancygier and Sweetser 2014: 17–18). As an example, Dancygier and Sweetser (2014) provide the terms "husband," "wife," "divorce" and "in-laws," which all relate to, and therefore potentially activate, the MARRIAGE frame.

Consistently with this link between conceptual domains and frames, Lakoff and Johnson (1980: 10–13 et passim), albeit without using the term "framing," emphasize that the choice of source domain highlights some aspects of the target domain and hides others. For example, the conventional conceptual metaphor ARGUMENT IS WAR highlights the competitive, antagonistic aspect of arguments and hides their potential collaborative aspects. This highlighting and backgrounding happens because the choice of source domain makes available a particular set of entities, processes and relationships to be mapped onto the target domain, resulting in particular "entailments" (i.e. inferences and patterns of reasoning). Amongst others, the ARGUMENT IS WAR metaphor gives rise to the entailment that if one destroys the other participant's views, one wins the argument (see also Croft and Cruse, 2004: 197–8). Metaphors, especially the choice of source domains, are therefore important, Lakoff and Johnson (1980) argue, because they reflect and influence how we think about different kinds of experiences and potentially also how we act. This line of argument is broadly consistent with Entman's (1993) definition of framing introduced earlier.

In subsequent work, Lakoff uses the terms "frames" and "framing" explicitly, in a series of studies on US politics. In a paper on the US administration's reaction to the 9/11 attacks (Lakoff 2001), for example, he discusses the different ways in which the attacks were framed by conservatives (in its political sense) using metaphors like IMMORAL PEOPLE ARE ANIMALS to describe the terrorists and SECURITY IS CONTAINMENT to suggest ways of minimizing the threat. He shows how these different framings link with preferences for overarching conservative vs. liberal frames for the role of government in public life (what he calls the STRICT FATHER VS. NURTURANT PARENT frames). Lakoff's (2004) discussion of US political discourse begins with a chapter entitled "Framing 101: How to Take Back Public Discourse," which makes the central claim that "every word, like 'elephant', evokes a frame" (Lakoff, 2004: 3). He argues that metaphorical political language, such as the term "tax relief," can be particularly effective at convincing the public, and can make it particularly hard for anyone to uphold opposing views: "When the word 'tax' is added to 'relief', the result is a metaphor: Taxation is an affliction. And the person who takes it away is a hero, and anyone who tries to stop him [sic] is a bad guy. This is a frame. It is made up of ideas, like 'affliction' and 'hero'" (Lakoff, 2004: 4). More recently, Lakoff (2010) has also applied this approach to other issues, such as discussions of the environment. Here, Lakoff makes the case for working toward coherent and consistent framings of environmental issues, without which environmentalism, he argues, cannot be successful.

Research on metaphor and framing in this tradition has been used to investigate how and why different metaphorical framings may help or hinder public understanding of and engagement with public-interest issues, sometimes with a view to shaping public discussions (e.g. Schön 1993; Grady 2017). While linguistic realizations of metaphors are of course discussed, these studies focus on the relationship between different linguistic (or visual) metaphors and different ways of thinking about particular topics, but do not involve the collection and systematic analysis of naturally occurring language data. This contrasts with the strand of research on metaphor that we turn to in Section 10.4.2.

10.4.2 Framing and Metaphor in Discourse

A rich and growing tradition of research has taken a (critical) discourse analytic approach to the use of metaphor and its framing implications. This kind of work involves the collection of authentic linguistic data (spoken, written and/or multimodal, and of different sizes) and detailed and systematic qualitative and/or quantitative analyses of metaphor choices and patterns in that data. The findings are then used as the basis for discussions of the framing implications of those choices and patterns, whether or not the term "framing" is explicitly used. These implications may concern, for example, prejudice against immigrants via flooding metaphors (El Refaie 2001), gender biases via sports and war metaphors in business media discourse (Koller 2004), the delegitimization of striking miners via war metaphors (Hart 2017), the sensationalization of problems to do with bacterial infections via apocalyptic metaphors (Nerlich 2009) and the success of processes of reconciliation in conflict situations through the reuse of others' metaphors (e.g. Cameron 2011). These studies tend to make use of explicit methods for the identification of metaphor-related expressions, such as MIP or MIPVU (Pragglejaz Group 2007; Steen et al.

2010) and often employ corpus linguistic methods (e.g. Charteris-Black 2004; L'Hôte 2014).

Although Conceptual Metaphor Theory provides the theoretical foundation for much of this work, these studies tend to problematize the claims made by Lakoff and colleagues (e.g. Deignan 2005) and to reveal patterns of regularity and variation within and across texts and genres that require different explanations (e.g. Zinken 2007; Deignan, Littlemore and Semino 2013). For example, Deignan (2005) points out that some metaphors drawing from the ANIMAL source domain seem to occur only as nouns (e.g. *cow* as an offensive term for a woman), while others occur only as verbs (e.g. *horsing around*) and yet others occur as both nouns and verbs but not necessarily with the same meaning (e.g. *racist pigs* and *pigging out on food*) (Deignan 2005: 153). Cameron (2011) shows how the collaborative development of metaphors in the course of several lengthy conversations between two people is influenced by the interaction of several different co-textual and contextual factors, such as previous conversations and turns, emotional distancing and alignment, and so on. In other words, while conceptual metaphors may explain why certain (groups of) words develop particular conventional metaphorical meanings over time in a specific language, they cannot adequately account for how metaphorical expressions are used in actual discourse situations.

In addition, some studies have found that the notion of "conceptual domain" adopted within Conceptual Metaphor Theory is too broad to account for the complexity and variety of manifestations of metaphor in discourse. In an influential paper on metaphors in British and German press reports on the single European currency, for example, Musolff (2006) suggests that the metaphorical patterns in his data require explanations at a more specific level than general conceptual domains. He therefore adopts the notion of "scenario" as a "specific sub-domain category" akin to "mini-narratives" (2006: 24) and defines it as "a set of assumptions made by competent members of a discourse community about 'typical' aspects of a source-situation, for example, its participants and their roles, the 'dramatic' storylines and outcomes, and conventional evaluations of whether they count as successful or unsuccessful, normal or abnormal, permissible or illegitimate, etc." (Musolff 2006: 28; see also Semino 2008; Musolff 2016). Musolff shows how some specific uses of metaphor in his press data exploit different specific scenarios from the broad conceptual domain of MARRIAGE, such as END-OF-HONEYMOON and ADULTERY. These specific scenarios each frame the debate in different ways; they enable people not just to "apply source to target concepts but to draw on them to build narrative frames for the conceptualization and assessment of socio-political issues and to 'spin out' these narratives" (Musolff 2006: 36). This definition of metaphor scenarios is compatible with the notion of "frame" that is adopted in some cognitive approaches to metaphor (e.g. Sullivan 2013; Dancygier and Sweetser 2014). It also has echoes of the sociological definition of "frame" (e.g. Goffman 1967) in its foregrounding of expectations and background knowledge with regard to events and potential storylines.

In a series of studies on metaphor patterns in different kinds of discourse data, Cameron, Low and Maslen have similarly suggested that analyses of metaphorical framing in actual language use require a level more specific than conceptual metaphors (2010: 138). They put forward the notion of "systematic metaphor" to capture the use of semantically related linguistic metaphors in relation to the same topic within a particular discourse event. For example, they formulate the systematic metaphor A RESPONSE TO TERRORISM IS NEGATIVE LABELING OF MUSLIMS to capture one of the ways in which a group of Muslim participants in a focus group discussion talked about the response to terrorism on the part of the UK authorities (e.g. "they'll just label all of us"). According to Cameron, Low and Maslen (2010: 137), systematic metaphors "emerge from the metaphor analysis as ways of 'framing' the ideas, attitudes and values of discourse participants."

This attention to specific linguistic metaphor use in context has led to insights and advances in relation to what is included within framing effects. For example, several studies have highlighted the importance of evaluations, emotions, perceptual simulations, as well as surrounding non-metaphorical language, for the framing implications of different metaphors (e.g. Ritchie 2013; Ritchie and Cameron 2014; see also Lakoff 2010). Ritchie and Cameron (2014), for example, explicitly consider the evaluative implications of particular framings. They show how contrasting framings of a public discussion of a fatal shooting of an African American woman on the part of police officers, including via different metaphors, can account for why no common ground was achieved among the groups involved. While public officials attempted to frame the discussion as an "open conversation among equals," members of the public referred to it as "smoke and mirrors" and "dancing around the issues."

Another direction of discourse-based metaphor research, mostly by Cameron, Deignan and Gibbs, incorporates further macro- and micro-level aspects of the communicative situation into an explanation of specific framing effects. The claim here is similar to those already discussed: the framing power of metaphors does not just depend on the involvement of preexisting conceptual structures; it emerges in the dynamic interaction of people "talking and thinking" in specific discourse contexts. This approach explicitly adopts a dynamic systems view of communication and argues that the meanings and functions of metaphorical expressions can be adequately explained only by showing "how various cognitive, linguistic, social and cultural forces simultaneously shape" the understanding and use of metaphor (Gibbs and Cameron 2008: 74). Cameron and Deignan (2006) more specifically state that the meaning of any metaphor in discourse "evolves and changes in the dynamics of language use between individuals, and that this local adaptation leads to the emergence of certain stabilities of form, content, affect, and pragmatics" (Cameron and Deignan 2006: 675). This emergent specificity of meaning, including the values, attitudes and emotions of participants in communication, will influence the specific framing effects of any metaphor as much as any conceptual structures involved. Cameron and Deignan (2006) propose the term "metaphoreme" to capture this phenomenon, which Gibbs and Cameron later define as "a bundle of stabilized but flexible word-meaning links that incorporate particular affective and pragmatic values with particular lexico-grammatical forms and cultural preferences" (2008: 73). Among other examples, Cameron and Deignan (2006) discuss the metaphorical uses of the noun "baggage" in English as an example of a metaphoreme. When used metaphorically, "baggage" tends to refer to experiences or relationships that are always negatively evaluated (e.g. "emotional baggage," "psychological baggage"). This specific meaning (and therefore the specific framing of the experience) derives partly from conventional conceptual metaphors such as DIFFICULTIES ARE BURDENS and LIFE IS A JOURNEY but also has emergent linguistic forms in usage: it occurs as a noun with an adjectival premodifier (e.g. "emotional") and/or as the direct object of verbs such as "carry" and "dump" (Cameron and Deignan 2006). Although "baggage" is an example of a fairly widely used metaphoreme (at least among users of British English), and, indeed, Cameron and Deignan (2006) use "metaphoreme" to refer to very conventionalized meanings, Semino and Demjén (2017) have argued that the same principles apply at more local levels where specific discourse communities are involved. They describe "cancer card" as a context-specific metaphoreme on an online support forum for people with cancer, because of the way it was humorously and creatively developed by a small number of contributors to one specific thread on the forum.

Both strands of work on metaphor and framing we have discussed so far beg the question of whether and how metaphor choices in discourse affect and/or reflect the views of those who hear or use them. This is what we turn to in Section 10.4.3.

10.4.3 Evidence for the Framing Power of Metaphors from Experimental Research

The framing power of metaphor is not easy to provide evidence for in laboratory conditions. Our views take shape over time, through multiple influences, and are often resistant to change. However, several recent empirical studies have shown that metaphor can have a powerful influence over people's reasoning, particularly about problems and possible solutions (see Thibodeau, Hendricks and Boroditsky 2017 for an overview of relevant research). Thibodeau and Boroditsky (2011) presented two groups of university students with different versions of a media crime report. In one case, crime was described in terms of a virus and, in the other, in terms of a beast. They found that, when an increase in crime was described as the effect of a "virus," participants tended to reason within the same biological framing and to propose exploring the causes of the problem. When increased crime was described in terms of a "beast," however, they preferred capturing and jailing criminals. This echoes Schön's (1993) earlier study which suggested that describing slums metaphorically as a "blight" versus an "ecosystem" called for rather different policy actions.

In the context of healthcare, Hauser and Schwarz (2015) found that metaphorical descriptions of cancer as an enemy to be fought reduced the extent to which people said they intended to engage in prevention that involved limiting or restricting behaviors (e.g. not smoking), but did not increase people's intentions to engage in proactive behaviors that would be preventative (e.g. taking regular exercise). Similar results have emerged for nonverbal metaphors as well. In a study involving multimodal data, Hart (2017) investigated the "legitimating framing effects" of fire metaphors in news reports about social unrest. The results suggested that the presence of images of fire (in the absence of competing images) alongside verbal fire metaphors increased support for the use of water cannon on the part of the police to disperse crowds.

At a general level, all these findings can be related back to metaphor's selectivity in foregrounding certain aspects of topics, as opposed to others (cf. Entman 1993).

10.5 Issues and Ongoing Debates

While the different strands of work on metaphor and framing share some key assumptions and concerns, there are differences in emphasis and focus. These relate particularly to the precise definition of framing; the relative amounts of attention that are given to conceptual structures vs. authentic data, that is, whether investigations focus on the specifics of linguistic (or indeed multimodal) manifestations or on generalizing to broader patterns of cognition; what kinds of conceptual structure are invoked; what kinds of claim and generalization are made; and what kinds of evidence are provided for these claims and generalizations.

In the original version of Conceptual Metaphor Theory, Lakoff and Johnson (1980) use the term "domain" rather broadly, resulting in a wide variety of concepts and types of knowledge being labeled domains, for example WAR, ARGUMENT, LIFE, DEATH, TIME, MONEY, LOVE, etc. Subsequent developments of the theory have explicitly raised this as an issue (e.g. Croft and Cruse 2004: 7–39; Sullivan 2013; Dancygier and Sweetser 2014: 13–21) and used a variety of terms to capture more specific conceptual structures involving representations of particular situations, such as "scenes" (Grady

1997) and "frames" (e.g. Sullivan 2013). Sullivan (2013) suggests that a domain can subsume multiple frames: for example, the BODY domain includes frames such as EXERCISE, INGESTION and many others. Despite such attempts at classification and clarification, there is still variation and sometimes disagreement on the level at which framing analysis is most appropriate and useful as far as metaphor is concerned. Cameron, Low and Maslen (2010: 138), for example, describe conceptual metaphors as "overarching frames which inform and influence discourse," and caution that "[c]laims about metaphor framing need to avoid the danger of overgeneralization, beyond what is warranted by empirical data."

In this context, there are increasing attempts to reconcile and, in some cases, combine different approaches. Musolff's (2006) analysis at the level of metaphor scenarios (as we discussed in Section 10.4.2) is one attempt at bringing together cognitive and discourse-based approaches to metaphor and framing. He argued that scenarios extracted from discourse data provide "a platform to link the conceptual side of metaphor to its usage patterns in socially situated discourse" (Musolff 2006: 36). Cameron, Low and Maslen (2010) see the role of systematic metaphors in much the same way (see Section 10.4.2). Both of these approaches, as well as others drawing on Dynamic Systems Theory (e.g. Cameron and Deignan 2006; Semino and Demjén 2017), allow framing effects to be analyzed at the more specific level of linguistic metaphors, taking into consideration conceptual metaphors but not ignoring the implications of particular contexts and uses.

Proposals to combine different "levels" in metaphor analysis have been made by Dancygier and Sweetser (2014) from a cognitively-oriented perspective and by Semino, Demjén and Demmen (2018). The latter paper is an attempt to combine cognitive and discourse-analytic approaches to metaphor and framing in ways that also take into account potential practical applications.

More specifically, Semino, Demjén and Demmen (2018) propose that metaphors can be analyzed for their framing effects at three levels of generality or abstraction. At the highest level of generality, the conceptual metaphors of Lakoff and colleagues can be seen as overarching frames that allow broad generalizations at the level of a whole language or for contrasting different languages and cultures (cf. Cameron, Low and Maslen 2010). At a lower level of generality, Musolff's (2006) "scenarios" capture more specific framing effects that apply in local discourse contexts. At the most specific level, systematic metaphors and metaphoremes involve specific (groups of) linguistic expressions and potentially discourse community-specific meanings, including particular evaluations and emotional associations. This approach is exemplified by Semino, Demjén and Demmen (2018) in relation to a corpus-based study of metaphors for cancer. This is an area where metaphors have been shown to have an important and potentially beneficial role (e.g. Appleton and Flynn 2014) but where considerable controversy exists. In particular, this concerns the framing implications of military metaphors, as we mentioned in Section 10.3 (e.g. McCartney 2014; Sontag 1979), and their potential to imply that patients who do not recover are weak or did not try hard enough.

Semino, Demjén and Demmen (2018) introduce the following six excerpts from their data, all produced by people with cancer posting in an online forum dedicated to the disease:

1. It's sad that anyone, but especially younger people like yourself, find themself with this <u>battle</u> to <u>fight</u>.
2. I feel such a failure that I am not <u>winning</u> this <u>battle</u>.
3. But the emotional side of cancer and of BC [breast cancer] in particular is the real <u>killer</u> – it <u>strangles</u> and <u>shocks</u> your soul.
4. I'm new to the forum and wanted to know if there are any other younger bowel cancer <u>fighters</u> amongst us.
5. Also it [the online forum] allows me to leave a record for my family, showing them how much I love them and how much I am <u>fighting</u> to stay with them for as long as possible.
6. Your words though have given me a bit more of my <u>fighting spirit</u> back. I am ready to <u>kick</u> some cancer <u>butt</u>!

At the level of conceptual domains, these can all be seen as manifestations of a conceptual metaphor along the lines of BEING ILL WITH CANCER IS A VIOLENT CONFRONTATION WITH DISEASE, which is a specific version of a general BEING ILL IS A VIOLENT CONFRONTATION WITH DISEASE. At an even higher level, these metaphors can be explained in terms of a more general conceptual metaphor DIFFICULTIES ARE OPPONENTS, which, in Grady's (1997) terms, can be described as a "primary" metaphor arising from an experiential correlation between difficulties and aggressors. At this level of generality, the examples suggest a consistent framing of the experience of illness. When mentioned, the patient is explicitly placed in the role of fighter and the disease is implicitly placed in the role of opponent, aggressor or enemy (more explicitly in example 3); being cured or living longer is construed as winning the fight; and not recovering or dying corresponds to losing on the part of the patient.

Such generalizations can be useful in that they can account for a wide variety of linguistic expressions and can be used to make comparisons within and across languages and cultures. Nonetheless, there are also differences among the examples, particularly in terms of the relationship between the person and the disease, which arguably result in different framings. This is where the second, more specific level of analysis becomes necessary.

At the level of metaphor scenarios, the different kinds of metaphorical expressions previously captured in terms of the broad source domain VIOLENT CONFRONTATION and the target domain BEING ILL WITH CANCER can be grouped and labeled according to the more specific type of violent scenario they suggest. For example:

- A PATIENT'S ATTEMPT TO GET BETTER IS ENGAGING IN A FIGHT or PHYSICAL ATTACK ON AN EXTERNAL AGENT, e.g. "fighting to stay with them for as long as possible" and "ready to kick some cancer butt."
- THE EFFECT OF THE DISEASE ON THE PATIENT IS PHYSICAL ATTACK FROM AN EXTERNAL AGENT, e.g. "But the emotional side of cancer and of BC in particular is the real killer – it strangles and shocks your soul."
- A PATIENT GETTING OR NOT GETTING BETTER IS THE OUTCOME OF A CONFRONTATION, e.g. "I'm not winning this battle."

These scenarios vary in terms of the position of the patient as attacker or attacked and the degree to which they express negative emotions and place the patient in a disempowered position. They therefore vary in how they frame the cancer experience. This is particularly obvious in example 2: the fact that treatment has not worked is described as the patient "not winning this battle," which makes her feel "a failure." In contrast, in examples 4–6, the expressions "fighters," "fighting" and "kick butt" are used to emphasize patients' own agency and determination in difficult circumstances, and suggest a sense of pride in one's own efforts.

However, Semino, Demjén and Demmen (2018) caution that the precise framing implications of particular scenarios can vary further still depending on who uses them, how and in what specific co-text and context. At this third level of specificity, the authors show that individual linguistic realizations of metaphors can also display distinctive tendencies in terms of how they frame the patient's experience. They present the noun "fighter" as an example that is always used by patients to present themselves and others as active, determined and optimistic, in spite of finding themselves in adverse circumstances. This particular use of "fighter" is consistent with the metaphorical use of this noun in English generally, which is captured by the Macmillan Dictionary as follows: "someone who refuses to be defeated even in the most difficult situations" (macmillandictionaryonline.com). The use of this noun in Semino, Demjén and Demmen's (2018) data set is a specific application to cancer patients and is consistently used for (self or mutual) praise and encouragement. In Cameron and Deignan's (2006) terms, "fighter" can therefore be seen as an example of a discourse community-specific metaphoreme, as it has very specific semantic, affective and pragmatic qualities.

This multilevel framework shows that the framing implications or potential consequences for individual patients of violence-related metaphors can be fully accounted for only at a level of analysis that is firmly grounded in the specific context of communication from which the pattern emerges. More generally, the different conclusions about framing effects that can be drawn at each level of generality should prevent hasty decisions about whether certain metaphors are "good" or "bad" for patients. Blanket rejections of particular metaphors and the uncritical promotion of others are at best unrealistic and at worst harmful, as they may deprive some patients of helpful resources for meaning-making and coping.

10.6 Implications for Research and Practice

There is overwhelming theoretical and empirical evidence that metaphors and, to a lesser extent, metonymies have framing implications that need to be taken into account in research and practice in a wide variety of areas. From the point of view of research, metaphors need to be investigated systematically and interrogated for their implications at different levels, especially in areas that involve vulnerable individuals, be they immigrants or people with serious illnesses, as the stakes are particularly high with regard to how such individuals are viewed or view themselves. From the point of view of practice, dominant metaphors may be usefully challenged, while both new and conventional metaphors can be more actively harnessed to foster, for example, a better understanding of issues such as climate change (e.g. Grady 2017), more effective interactions between therapists and people with mental health problems (Tay 2017) and greater empathy for others in conflict situations (Cameron 2017).

As suggested in Section 10.5, metaphor and framing researchers need to be aware of and explicit about which tradition they are operating within and how they are using key terms such as "frame" and "framing." They also need to be aware of what conclusions can and cannot be safely drawn within their adopted approach. As studies by Musolff (2006) and Cameron, Low and Maslen (2010) show, framing effects can differ substantially within specific scenarios or systematic metaphors, even if they appear to belong to broadly the "same" conceptual metaphors. The same is true at the even more specific level of discourse community-specific metaphoremes (e.g. Semino and Demjén 2017) and particular lexicalizations of broader metaphor patterns (e.g. Semino et al. 2018; Grady 2017). Metaphor framings are also influenced by the metaphorical and nonmetaphorical co-text of specific usages as well as who uses them (e.g. Ritchie and Cameron 2014). For example, a specific group of cancer patients choosing to refer to each other as "fighters" can be motivating, empowering and community-building. However, the same metaphor used by charities or the media to refer to patients in general may be perceived as glorifying an antagonistic approach to the disease that some people may find unacceptable or inappropriate. The nonmetaphorical co-text is also important: "I feel such a failure" intensifies the disempowerment and specifies the affective connotation implied in "I'm not winning this battle."

With regard to practitioners, whether in education, healthcare, policy-making, the media, etc., we reiterate Semino, Demjén and Demmen's

(2018) point that decisions about which metaphors to adopt and which to avoid need to be based on appropriate evidence and to take into account both general patterns and variation according to context, genre and individuals. It is, for example, too simplistic, as we have shown, to treat violence metaphors for cancer as imposing a single and necessarily negative framing. On the one hand, there is indeed evidence that could support the decision to avoid violence metaphors in mass communication with patients or the public, and to beware of imposing them in communication with individual patients. On the other hand, it also needs to be recognized that they can be helpful for some patients, especially when there is still the prospect of a cure. It is also possible to make a distinction between using violence metaphors for the individual's experience of cancer vs. the societal and scientific enterprise of finding a cure for cancer, as used in slogans such as President Nixon's "War on cancer." While the latter use of military metaphors is also controversial, it frames the disease as a collective rather than an individual opponent and may work effectively to galvanize people to donate to cancer research charities, depending on how it is used (see Flusberg, Matlock and Thibodeau 2018).

The results of these studies suggest that, because of the alternative framings they facilitate, different metaphors are best seen as potentially useful but inevitably imperfect resources to be assessed and exploited depending on one's purposes and contexts.

10.7 Future Directions

As we have suggested, the potential framing effects of *metonymy* need greater attention, from all the different perspectives we have discussed in relation to metaphor. Future work on *metaphor* and framing would in turn benefit from greater interaction and mutual influences among the different strands of research we have discussed. We have already indicated how it is possible to profitably combine cognitive and discourse-analytic approaches to metaphor. An additional interaction that has been proposed as important for the future of research on metaphor is between the findings of discourse-analytic studies of metaphorical framings and those of laboratory-based experimental studies (Boeynaems et al. 2017): on the one hand, scholars that operate in the discourse analysis tradition could attempt to generate and, potentially, test the claims they make on the basis of their textual analyses (e.g. Hart 2017 and Chapter 9 in this volume); on the other hand, the stimuli used in experimental research, including laboratory-based studies, could be formulated to be as similar as possible to naturally occurring examples (Thibodeau, Hendricks and Boroditsky 2017: 9). This can lead to ever better understandings of the circumstances and ways in which metaphor and metonymy can have framing effects.

For both metaphor and metonymy, the investigation of framing effects in a wide variety of discourse data can inform practice in relation to issues of societal concern, from understanding climate change to combating the stigma associated with mental and physical illness. Future work in this area can therefore both advance research and contribute to individual and collective wellbeing.

10.8 Summary

This chapter has provided an overview of how metaphor and, to a lesser extent, metonymy can have framing effects, that is, both reflect and influence how we reason and feel about topics, concepts and experiences. We have discussed different strands of research on metaphor and framing in particular (conceptual, discourse-based and experimental) and shown how these different strands could be usefully brought into greater mutual interaction. Among other things, we have argued that this can benefit the practical application of metaphors (and potentially metonymies) to the tackling of important issues in many different societal domains.

Further Reading

Pinelli, E. (2016). The Role of Metaphor and Metonymy in Framing Terrorism: The Case of the Beslan School Siege in the Russian Media. *Metaphor and the Social World* 6(1): 134–55.

This shows how metaphor and metonymy are used to promote particular interpretations of a conflict event in Russia. It is argued that, in this way, the structure of the event itself is modified.

Semino, E., Demjén, Z. and Demmen, J. (2018). An Integrated Approach to Metaphor and Framing in Cognition, Discourse and Practice, with an Application to Metaphors for Cancer. *Applied Linguistics* 39(5): 625–45.

This outlines cognitive, discourse-analytic and practice-based perspectives to metaphor and framing, arguing that each is best suited for particular types of research goals. It sets out a blueprint for how different approaches to metaphor and framing can be integrated into a coherent model.

Thibodeau, P. H., Hendricks, R. K. and Boroditsky L. (2017). How Linguistic Metaphor Scaffolds Reasoning. *Trends in Cognitive Science* 21(11): 852–63.

This is a review of the state of knowledge on how and under what conditions metaphors have been found to shape thinking. Theoretical and practical implications, as well as key challenges and opportunities for future research, are highlighted throughout.

References

Appleton, L. and Flynn, M. (2014). Searching for the New Normal: Exploring the Role of Language and Metaphors in Becoming a Cancer Survivor. *European Journal of Oncology Nursing* 18(4): 378–84.

Barcelona, A. (ed.) (2000). *Metaphor and Metonymy at the Crossroads*. Berlin: Mouton de Gruyter.

Boeynaems, A., Burgers, C., Konijn, E. A. and Steen, G. J. (2017). The Effects of Metaphorical Framing on Political Persuasion: A Systematic Literature Review. *Metaphor and Symbol* 32(2): 118–34.

Cameron, L. (2011). *Metaphor and Reconciliation: The Discourse Dynamics of Empathy in Post-Conflict Conversations*. New York: Routledge.

  (2017). Using Metaphor for Peace-Building, Empathy and Reconciliation. In E. Semino and Z. Demjén (eds.) *The Routledge Handbook of Metaphor and Language*. New York: Routledge. 426–42.

Cameron, L. and Deignan, A. (2006). The Emergence of Metaphor in Discourse. *Applied Linguistics* 27(4): 671–90.

Cameron, L., Low, G. and Maslen, R. (2010). Finding Systematicity in Metaphor Use. In L. Cameron and R. Maslen (eds.) *Metaphor Analysis: Research Practice in Applied Linguistics, Social Sciences and the Humanities*. London: Equinox. 116–46.

Charteris-Black, J. (2004). *Corpus Approaches to Critical Metaphor Analysis*. Basingstoke: Palgrave Macmillan.

Croft, W. and Cruse, D. (2004). *Cognitive Linguistics*. Cambridge: Cambridge University Press.

Dancygier, B. and Sweetser, E. (2014). *Figurative Language*. Cambridge: Cambridge University Press.

Deignan, A. (2005). *Metaphor and Corpus Linguistics*. Amsterdam: John Benjamins.

Deignan, A., Littlemore, J. and Semino, E. (2013). *Figurative Language, Genre and Register*. Cambridge: Cambridge University Press.

El Refaie, E. (2001). Metaphors We Discriminate By: Naturalized Themes in Austrian Newspaper Articles about Asylum Seekers. *Journal of Sociolinguistics* 5(3): 352–71.

Entman, R. (1993). Framing: Toward Clarification of a Fractured Paradigm. *Journal of Communication* 43(4): 51–8.

Fillmore, C. (1985). Frames and the Semantics of Understanding. *Quaderni di Semantica* 6(2): 222–53.

Flusberg, S. J., Matlock, T. and Thibodeau, P. H. (2018). War Metaphors in Public Discourse. *Metaphor and Symbol* 33(1): 1–18.

Gibbs, R. W., Jr. (ed.) (2008). *The Cambridge Handbook of Metaphor and Thought*. Cambridge: Cambridge University Press.

Gibbs, R. W., Jr. and Cameron, L. (2008). The Social-Cognitive Dynamics of Metaphor Performance. *Journal of Cognitive Systems Research* 9(1–2): 64–75.

Goffman, E. (1967). *Interaction Ritual: Essays in Face-to-Face Behaviour*. Chicago, IL: Aldine Publishing Company.

Grady, J. (1997). *Foundations of Meaning: Primary Metaphors and Primary Scenes*. Unpublished PhD thesis, University of California.

(2017). Using Metaphor to Influence Public Perceptions and Policy: How Metaphors Can Save the World. In E. Semino and Z. Demjén (eds.) *The Routledge Handbook of Metaphor and Language*. New York: Routledge. 443–54.

Hampe, B. (ed.) (2017). *Metaphor: Embodied Cognition and Discourse*. Cambridge: Cambridge University Press.

Hart, C. J. (2017). Metaphor and Intertextuality in Media Framings of the (1984–85) British Miners' Strike: A Multimodal Analysis. *Discourse and Communication* 11(1): 3–30.

Hauser, D. and Schwarz, N. (2015). The War on Prevention: Bellicose Cancer Metaphors Hurt (Some) Prevention Intentions. *Personality and Social Psychology Bulletin* 41(1): 66–77.

Koller, V. (2004). *Metaphor and Gender in Business Media Discourse: A Critical Cognitive Study*. Basingstoke: Palgrave Macmillan.

Kövecses, Z. (2005). *Metaphor in Culture: Universality and Variation*. Cambridge: Cambridge University Press.

(2010). *Metaphor: A Practical Introduction*, 2nd ed. New York: Oxford University Press.

L'Hôte, E. (2014). *Identity, Narrative and Metaphor: A Corpus-Based Cognitive Analysis of New Labour Discourse*. Basingstoke: Palgrave Macmillan.

Lakoff, G. (2001). September 11. *Metaphorik.de*. www.metaphorik.de/auf saetze/lakoff-september11.htm.

(2004). *Don't Think of an Elephant: Know Your Values and Frame the Debate*. White River Junction, VT: Chelsea Green Publishing Company.

(2010). Why It Matters How We Frame the Environment. *Environmental Communication* 4(1): 70–81.

Lakoff, G. and Johnson, M. (1980). *Metaphors We Live By*. Chicago, IL: University of Chicago Press.

Littlemore, J. (2015). *Metonymy: Hidden Shortcuts in Language, Thought and Communication*. Cambridge: Cambridge University Press.

Locke, J. [1690](1979). *An Essay Concerning Human Understanding*, ed. by P. H. Nidditch. Oxford: Oxford University Press.

Mahon, J. E. (1999). Getting Your Sources Right: What Aristotle Didn't Say. In L. Cameron and G. Low (eds.) *Researching and Applying Metaphor*. Cambridge: Cambridge University Press. 69–80.

McCartney, M. (2014). The Fight Is On: Military Metaphors for Cancer May Harm Patients. *British Medical Journal* 349: g5155.

Minsky, M. (1975). A Framework for Representing Knowledge. In P. Winston (ed.) *Knowledge and Cognition*. New York: Lawrence Erlbaum. 201–310.

Musolff, A. (2006). Metaphor Scenarios in Public Discourse. *Metaphor and Symbol* 21(1): 23–38.

(2016). *Political Metaphor Analysis: Discourse and Scenarios*. London: Bloomsbury.

Nerlich, B. (2009). "The Post-Antibiotic Apocalypse" and the "War on Superbugs": Catastrophe Discourse in Microbiology, Its Rhetorical Form and Political Function. *Public Understandings of Science* 18(5): 574–88.

Pinelli, E. (2016). The Role of Metaphor and Metonymy in Framing Terrorism: The Case of the Beslan School Siege in the Russian Media. *Metaphor and the Social World* 6(1): 134–55.

Pragglejaz Group. (2007). MIP: A Method for Identifying Metaphorically Used Words in Discourse. *Metaphor and Symbol* 22(1): 1–39.

Ritchie, L. D. (2013). *Metaphor*. Cambridge: Cambridge University Press.

Ritchie, L. D. and Cameron, L. (2014). Open Hearts or Smoke and Mirrors: Metaphorical Framing and Frame Conflicts in a Public Meeting. *Metaphor and Symbol* 29(3): 204–23.

Schön, D. (1993). Generative Metaphor: A Perspective on Problem-Setting in Social Policy. In A. Ortony (ed.) *Metaphor and Thought Cambridge*, 2nd ed. Cambridge: Cambridge University Press. 137–63.

Semino, E. (2008). *Metaphor in Discourse*. Cambridge: Cambridge University Press.

Semino, E. and Demjén, Z. (2017). The Cancer Card: Metaphor and Humour in Online Interactions about the Experience of Cancer. In B. Hampe (ed.) *Metaphor: Embodied Cognition and Discourse*. Cambridge: Cambridge University Press. 181–99.

Semino, E. and Koller, V. (2009). Metaphor, Politics and Gender: A Case Study from Italy. In K. Ahrens (ed.) *Politics, Gender and Conceptual Metaphors*. Basingstoke: Palgrave Macmillan. 36–61.

Semino, E., Demjén, Z. and Demmen, J. (2018). An Integrated Approach to Metaphor and Framing in Cognition, Discourse and Practice, with an Application to Metaphors for Cancer. *Applied Linguistics* 39(5): 625–45.

Semino, E., Demjén, Z., Hardie, A., Payne, S. and Rayson, P. (2018). *Metaphor, Cancer, and the End of Life: A Corpus-Based Study*. New York: Routledge.

Sontag, S. (1979). *Illness as Metaphor*. London: Allen Lane.

Steen, G. J., Dorst, A. G., Herrmann, J. B., Kaal, A. A., Krennmayr, T. and Pasma, T. (2010). *A Method for Linguistic Metaphor Identification: From MIP to MIPVU*. Amsterdam: John Benjamins.

Sullivan, K. (2013). *Frames and Constructions in Metaphoric Language*. Amsterdam: John Benjamins.

Tay, D. (2017). Using Metaphor in Healthcare: Mental Health. In E. Semino and Z. Demjén (eds.) *The Routledge Handbook of Metaphor and Language*. New York: Routledge. 371–84.

Thibodeau, P.H. and Boroditsky, L. (2011). Metaphors We Think With: The Role of Metaphor in Reasoning. *PLoS ONE* 6(2): e16782.

Thibodeau, P. H., Hendricks, R. K. and Boroditsky, L. (2017). How Linguistic Metaphor Scaffolds Reasoning. *Trends in Cognitive Science* 21(11): 852–63.

Zinken, Jörg. (2007). Discourse Metaphors: The Link between Figurative Language and Habitual Analogies. *Cognitive Linguistics* 18(3): 445–66.

Acknowledgments

Sections 10.5 and 10.6 of this chapter draw in part from Semino et al. (2018).

11

Poststructuralist Discourse Studies: From Structure to Practice

Johannes Angermuller

11.1 Introduction

"Poststructuralism" designates theoretical and political debates in the social sciences and humanities that have crucially contributed to the growing interdisciplinary interest in the problem of discourse since the 1970s. Poststructuralism is typically associated with intellectuals from France and theorists from the Anglo-American world who are in dialogue with "Continental" traditions. As proponents of a linguistic turn in social, cultural and political theory, these theorists defend post-humanist and antiessentialist epistemologies against the background of a crisis of political and aesthetic representation. Poststructuralism has put "discourse" center-stage in the interdisciplinary theoretical discourse of the social sciences and humanities. Yet in discourse studies, where there is a division between linguistics and other disciplines in the social sciences and humanities, the label "poststructuralism" is still a controversial one. Earlier "critical" and "French School" discourse researchers are indebted to structuralist conceptions of language and society, which are challenged by poststructuralism.

11.2 Overview

In this contribution, I will give an account of poststructuralist discourse studies (PDS), which is an umbrella term for various interdisciplinary strands studying the social production of meaning. PDS turns around the nexus of power, language and subjectivity while reflexively accounting for the critical effects of discourse research on society. In Section 11.3.1, I will discuss the term "poststructuralism," map the controversies around it and spell out its consequences for discourse studies. In Section 11.3.2, I will discuss earlier tendencies in "French School" as well as Critical Discourse Studies. With its critique of closed container structures and of the centered subject, PDS questions lingering structuralist conceptions of language and/or society in discourse studies (Section 11.3.3). In the future (Section 11.4), one may expect a more systematic exchange over key problems in PDS across disciplinary fields, notably between linguistics and the other social sciences as well as between Anglophone and Francophone traditions. Key problems turn around a perceived "methodological deficit" as well as the stance that PDS takes toward the critique of power.

11.3 Issues and Ongoing Debates

11.3.1 A Brief Account of "Poststructuralism"

Poststructuralism is a theoretical debate that crosses the disciplines in the social sciences and humanities. It exists at the intersection of three disciplinary clusters: a) the humanities, where poststructuralism deals with the dilemmas of political and aesthetic representation (Spivak 1988); b) the social sciences, where the question is how social order is constituted in discursive practices; and c) the interdisciplinary space of language and society, which revolves around the uses of language in context.

One can distinguish between a narrow understanding, which equates "poststructuralism" with a short-lived fashion in literary theory around 1980 (especially deconstructivism), and a wider understanding of the interdisciplinary theoretical debate about subjectivity, language and power since the late 1960s that has involved theorists and activists in the intellectual arena that was once founded by Marxism and psychoanalysis. It is in the latter sense that I will discuss the contributions of poststructuralism to discourse studies (cf. Benoît 2017).

Even though "poststructuralism" is associated with canonical theorists from France (and some other "Continental" thinkers), it has never had currency in France (Angermuller 2015). Poststructuralism has resulted from the way these theorists have been received internationally, notably in the Anglophone world. The prefix "post" does not necessarily mean that poststructuralism is "antistructuralist." In fact, many poststructuralists share the relational methodology and the antiessentialist thrust of structuralism. Nor is poststructuralism necessarily related to postmodernity (i.e. post-Enlightenment political theory) and postmodernism (i.e. new aesthetic tendencies since the late 1960s). If Marxist cultural theorists such as Jameson (1991) have theorized poststructuralism as the theoretical equivalent to postmodernist developments in aesthetics and postfordist developments in the economy, the supposed "founding fathers" of poststructuralism, notably Foucault ([1983]1994: 447) and Derrida (1999: 241f), never accepted the labels "poststructuralism" and "postmodernism" (Angermuller 2015). These terminological problems notwithstanding, since the 1980s, "poststructuralism" has become an established point of reference in the interdisciplinary debate, where it designates a body of reflexive, antiessentialist and posthumanist theory.

Broadly speaking, poststructuralism has resulted from three conjunctures. A first conjuncture took place in the 1960s and 1970s in Paris, where some theorists and intellectuals engaged in the controversy over structuralism, understood as the application of Saussure's differentialist theory of language to cultural and social life more generally (Ducrot et al. 1968). If structuralism proper remained a fairly short-lived fashion around 1966/7, those who have become the canonical figures of poststructuralism reacted in various ways: Foucault's early work (1966) clearly builds on structuralist insights, which he later renounces, whereas Derrida's deconstructive philosophy (1967) radicalizes Saussure's relational method in order to reveal its inherent aporias. Some theorists of poststructuralism never adhered to structuralism (Deleuze 2002: 238ff.; Lyotard 1983) whereas others remained faithful (Althusser [1966]2003).

The label "poststructuralism" was established during the second conjuncture around 1980 (Angermuller 2015: 69–82), when French (and other "Continental") theorists were received in the North American humanities (Ehrmann 1970). Initially, the second generation of poststructuralist intellectuals can be divided into an "East Coast" (Yale) branch promoting Derridian deconstruction as a text-centered method in literary criticism (e.g. Bloom et al. 1979) and a Californian branch where Foucault's more historical and sociological work on knowledge/power met with resonance (e.g. Dreyfus and Rabinow 1983). During the 1980s, poststructuralism helped spawn a number of "studies," most paradigmatically cultural studies (e.g. Grossberg, Nelson and Treichler 1992).

These literary and cultural fields testify to a number of "turns" in the social sciences and humanities (Bachmann-Medick 2006) that have constituted a third conjuncture of poststructuralism since the 1990s. The paradigmatic one is the "linguistic turn," which is inspired by both analytical philosophers of language (Rorty 1967) and semiotic-structuralist traditions (Fraser 1995; Guilhaumou 1993) and challenges the idea of language mirroring a reality before and outside language. More recently, one can register a practice turn that focuses on practices as performative and creative rather than as reflecting an intention or following a given script (Schatzki, Knorr-Cetina and von Savigny 2001), a visual turn that refers to the uses of images in contemporary life (Kress and van Leeuwen 2006), a material turn that insists on the materiality of social and cultural practices (or New Materialism, Beetz and Schwab 2017) and a political turn that argues for the primacy of the political over the social (Butler, Laclau and Žižek 2000).

Table 11.1 *Three conjunctures of poststructuralism (Angermuller 2015: 19)*

Discussion highlights	Around 1970 in France	Around 1980 in the USA	Since the mid-1990s in Europe
Common labels	*structuralisme Marxisme psychanalyse*	(high) theory, (cultural) studies, especially Yale: poststructuralism	In Germany: *Poststrukturalismus, Dekonstruktivismus*
Key representatives	Lacan, Jacques Althusser, Louis Foucault, Michel Lévi-Strauss, Claude Deleuze, Gilles Derrida, Jacques Lyotard, Jean-François Barthes, Roland De Certeau, Michel Kristeva, Julia Baudrillard, Jean	de Man, Paul Butler, Judith Spivak, Gayatri Jameson, Fredric Said, Edward Bhabha, Homi	Žižek, Slavoj Laclau, Ernesto Mouffe, Chantal Agamben, Giorgio Negri, Antonio Rancière, Jacques Badiou, Alain perhaps Luhmann, Niklas
(Imaginary) opponent	humanism	(European) modernity, essentialism, binary opposition	"Old European theory," autonomous subject, container society
Leading discipline	linguistics	Literary criticism (mostly English)	Political philosophy and theory, especially in Germany: radical and cognitive constructivism
Disciplines concerned	*sciences humaines* (with linguistics, against philosophy)	humanities (without social sciences, linguistics, philosophy)	In Germany: *Sozial- undGeisteswissenschaften*
"Paradigm"			Poststructuralism

With its insistence on the nexus of language and power, poststructuralism has been a crucial source of inspiration to social scientists and humanists interested in discourse. It is no wonder, therefore, that many observers equate poststructuralism with discourse theory and discourse analysis. Poststructuralist discourse theories can be found in political science (think of Laclau and Mouffe's hegemony and discourse analysis approach (1985); also known as postfoundational discourse analysis (Marttila 2016), in cultural and political sociology (Hall et al. 1980; Dean 1994), in history (cf. White 1987), in psychology (e.g. earlier work in discursive psychology of Potter and Wetherell 1987 and later work in critical psychology of Parker and Pavón-Cuéllar 2014) and in cultural studies (Said 1978). In these fields, "discourse analysis" and "poststructuralism" are used interchangeably, often drawing on Foucault's work on knowledge/power and governmentality, Derrida's deconstructive critique of Western "logocentrism" or on Lacan's interrogations of the split subject.

In these interdisciplinary debates, poststructuralism touches on a number of questions that more specialized disciplinary knowledge easily loses sight of, such as:

a) the question of constitutive representation: If language does not simply represent social reality, how do linguistic representations contribute to constituting what is considered as real in society?
b) the question of constructed subjectivity and agency: If actors do not use language to express their intentions, how are they enacted as "free," "autonomous," intentional beings through discourse practices?
c) the question of reflexive critique: If knowledge is constructed under conditions of power and inequality, how can discourse scholars account for the critical effects that their own discursive practice has on their objects?

11.3.2 Challenging the Structuralist Heritage of Discourse Studies

While "poststructuralism" has promoted the linguistic turn in the social sciences and humanities, it has stimulated the intellectual imagination of other linguists interested in "social and cultural stuff." If concepts such as "translanguaging," "crossing" and "superdiversity" resonate with poststructuralist tropes and themes, it is within the area of applied linguistics, where poststructuralist ideas have been cited most explicitly. Some linguists explicitly refer to poststructuralism in order to reexamine the epistemological bases of the field and cite it as a model for a reflexive critique of power (McNamara 2012; Busch 2012; Norton and Morgan 2013; Schmitz 2017). In language teaching, poststructuralism has helped revalue subjective experience (Pavlenko 2002; Bernstein 2016; Kramsch 1998), whereas, in sociolinguistics, it has helped articulate antiessentialist perspectives on identity and agency (Baxter 2016; Carter 2013; Kiesling 2006; Motschenbacher 2009).

However, if poststructuralism has been so successful in establishing discourse as an interdisciplinary problematic, why have many linguistic discourse analysts been reticent to claiming the label? Many strands in linguistic discourse analysis, whose name goes back to Harris's distributionalism (1952), started to develop long before the poststructuralist engagements with social, cultural and political theory. And more than poststructuralist discourse theories, linguistic discourse analysis places emphasis on the wide range of tools and methods for analyzing linguistic material.

Linguistic discourse analysis typically aims at opening linguistic analysis to levels beyond words and sentences. It comprises a number of perspectives, for instance quantitative approaches such as corpus linguistics, that use quantifying tools to reveal patterns in large collections of text, as well as qualitative tools from interactional analysis that insist on the sequential place of utterances within a dialogue. Early discourse analysts were often influenced by textlinguistics, which flags up the co-text of an utterance, that is, the way utterances are woven together as a text. And it is difficult to underestimate the influence of functional and pragmatic views on language that reflect on the context in which utterances are used (cf. the "French" tradition of enunciative pragmatics, Benveniste 1974; "Anglosaxon" systemic functionalism, Halliday 1978; and "German" functional pragmatics, Ehlich 1986).

In the late 1960s, the first (linguistic) discourse analysts began to dialogue with social theory, especially with macrosociological, Marxist concepts of power and inequality. As a result, two schools of discourse studies were born, namely "French School" or "French" discourse studies (FDS, cf. Williams 1999; Maingueneau 1994) and "critical discourse analysis" or "critical discourse studies" (CDS, Flowerdew and Richardson 2017), which are the internationally most recognized ones. While FDS was influenced by structuralist Marxism and Lacanian psychoanalysis (Pêcheux 1975), the theoretical references of CDS are more eclectic and include critical realism as well as dialectical Marxism (Fairclough 2017). FDS and CDS do not normally claim the label "poststructuralism" even though both like to cite (French) discourse theorists, especially Michel Foucault and Michel Pêcheux. FDS shows a strong affinity to poststructuralist ideas such as the opaque materiality of language and the heterogeneity of discourse. Yet FDS researchers usually see the term "poststructuralism" as an invention of Anglophone colleagues (Žižek 1991: 142; Angermüller 2007). And while CDS theorists such as Fairclough and Jäger are strongly influenced by Foucault and Pêcheux (Fairclough 2013: 185; Jäger [1993]2007), they normally don't share the constructivist, antihumanist and reflexive orientations of poststructuralist discourse theorists whose emphasis tends to be on conceptual work.

One may cite many more strands in discourse research, notably those who have engaged explicitly with poststructuralism, for example in textlinguistics in Germany (a perspective from Germany, Warnke 2007) or in critical research on language commodification (a perspective from Spain, Rojo 1997). In the following, I will focus on the internationally more recognized strands of FDS and CDS, which have overcome structuralism only partially. Nobody in CDS is in favor of structuralist conceptions (Wodak 2007) and even FDS has largely turned toward pragmatics (Angermuller 2014; Maingueneau 1990). Yet power and inequality ("the social") are still conceived of in structuralist terms, namely as a structural opposition between top and bottom, between the oppressors and the oppressed. Against this background, both FDS and CDS cannot but benefit from a more explicit engagement with poststructuralist ideas.

FDS goes back to a group of Paris-based linguists and philosophers who applied linguistic methods, including corpus analysis and distributionalism, to account for communication in the political arena as early as in the 1960s (e.g. Robin 1973). With their pioneering discourse theoretical works, Michel Foucault (1969) and Michel Pêcheux (1969) put "discourse" on the agenda of a broader intellectual debate that was under the impression of Marxism, psychoanalysis and structuralism. Unlike Foucault, who was always a solitary intellectual and soon turned back to more historical questions, Pêcheux became the head of what is sometimes called the French School of Discourse Analysis (Pêcheux 1990). For Pêcheux, discourse operates with utterances under the conditions of class struggle. Utterances form networks of utterances (i.e. discursive formations) through which discourse participants relate to their place in the class structure. In the wake of these highly recognized theorists, a "French" debate about discourse has emerged that has been highly productive conceptually speaking (Charaudeau and Maingueneau 2002; Détrie, Siblot and Verine 2001) and is characterized by its analytical focus on written texts taken in their "opaque materiality" (Conein et al. 1981). Since the 1980s, FDS has since seen a turn toward pragmatics and "enunciation," that is, the activity of using texts in context, which undermines the division into two separate domains of language and of society (Charaudeau 1983; Maingueneau 1991). If today in France there is an increasing interest in investigating discourse as empirical objects (rather than in theorizing it in terms of "poststructuralism"), the more intellectual and theoretical, the political and critical orientations of earlier generations in FDS are especially alive in Brazil (Orlandi 1990; Possenti 2009), where they sometimes merge with the interdisciplinary debates about poststructuralism. FDS has also been taken up in countries with Francophone or Francophile research cultures including Switzerland (Pêcheux 1975), Belgium (Rosier 1999), Israel (Amossy 2005) and Portugal (Pinto 1997).

The other internationally branded strand is critical discourse studies (CDS), which has currency in the countries of the Commonwealth, including the United Kingdom, Australia, Hong Kong, as well as in the German-speaking and Spanish-speaking world. Just like FDS, CDS has fired the imagination of linguists who consider language a social phenomenon and like to dialogue with the social sciences. CDS goes back to the late 1970s, when critical linguists started to explore the relationship of language use and its social conditions. By the 1990s, the label of critical discourse analysis had become an umbrella term of theoretically eclectic strands of discourse research that are oriented toward social problems. To distinguish between "French" and "Critical" strands of discourse studies is not without problems since some of their references are the same. And while discourse researchers with the "French" label are not necessarily French, many "French" discourse researchers have seen themselves in the critical tradition of Marxism (Angermuller 2017).

Just like FDS today, the major protagonists of CDS concur in the rejection of language as an abstract system, which has been summed up by Norman Fairclough's dictum of discourse as "simultaneously a piece of text, an instance of discursive practice, and an instance of social practice" (Fairclough 1992: 4). Based on pragmatic and interactional models of discourse, Reisigl and Wodak (2009) insist on the social and historical context of language use. Thus, both FDS and CDS conceptualize discourse as a meaning-making activity that shapes and is shaped by the social structures in which language is used. And just like FDS, CDS questions structural linguistics. Yet neither one has challenged structuralist conceptions of society. CDS tends to rely on Marxist class models, perhaps through British sociology during the 1970s, when Bernstein (1971) collaborated with M. A. K. Halliday (whose systemic-functional linguistics is the basis for a great deal of CDA work, Fairclough 1995; Kress and van Leeuwen 2006).

11.3.3 Poststructuralism in Discourse Studies

From a poststructuralist viewpoint, FDS and CDS have come only halfway in freeing themselves from their structuralist heritage. While they have turned to pragmatic conceptions of language in use, they tend to view society as a power structure where all social positions are clearly defined top down. Such a view is problematical since it risks reifying "society" as a reality to which discourse researchers claim privileged access. While structuralist explanations have come under attack from many corners of the social sciences since the late 1970s (as well as within linguistics if one thinks of the turn toward the actor in sociolinguistics), CDS and FDS would do well to discuss the shortcomings of sociological structuralisms more explicitly.

If poststructuralist orientations insist on the nexus of language, power and subjectivity, they have initiated a turn toward the praxis dimension of linguistic and social order. In particular, poststructuralism invites us to theorize the way in which structures are made and unmade in discursive practices without giving up a critical reflexive take on the question of power and inequality. Occupying the critical intellectual space that was instituted by Karl Marx's and Sigmund Freud's work on the hidden forces of inequality and the unconscious during the twentieth century, PDS follows the linguistic turn, which invites social, cultural and political theorists to apply linguistic models – notably those of Saussure and of the later Wittgenstein – to nonlinguistic problems and objects and the practice turn, which builds on a broad alliance from the pragmatists, Wittgenstein to Foucault and Bourdieu. The question, then, is how social and linguistic structures are constituted by discursive practices (which intentional, strategic actors are never entirely in control of).

In order to reveal the constructed foundations of the social, poststructuralism is sympathetic with views on doing the social and sometimes resonates with interactionist and pragmatist work if one thinks of such developments as early discursive psychology (Potter and Wetherell 1987), positioning theory (van Langenhove and Harré 1999), the small story approach (Bamberg and Georgakopoulo 2008), feminist (e.g. Smith 1999) and "new materialist" ethnographies (Latour 1987), more theoretically minded ethnomethodology (Widmer 1986), the sociology of scientific knowledge (Ashmore, Myers and Potter 1995) and the "new pragmatism" in sociology (Boltanski and Thévenot 1991). If, in linguistics, the structuralist hegemony ended long ago, the social sciences, too, have seen a crisis of structuralist logics of explanation. Just like structuralism in linguistics, social scientists have suspected structuralism for its

- proclivity for abstraction. Can there be structural rules that are applied independently of the specific situation and circumstances of action?
- implied normativity. Do practices always need to conform to a structural code or system in order to be socially meaningful?
- epistemological God's-eye view. Does the analyst occupy a privileged epistemological position vis-à-vis the practical knowhow of language users?

While FDS and CDS see discourse as a practice within more or less constituted social structures, poststructuralist discourse theories consider discursive practices as constitutive of the social. More than FDS and CDS, poststructuralism places emphasis on the way in which representations are made "real," knowledge "true" and relationships "natural." While, for Pêcheux, language is functional for class struggle (Pêcheux 1975), poststructuralist discourse theorists ask how discourse articulates the social as an antagonistic space. And more than representatives of CDS who believe that there are true or false representations of the social, poststructuralists see discourse as a practice that not only represents the social but, through representation, also brings it forth. Poststructuralist discourse theorists, in other words, problematize the social as a given, stable and naturalized order before and outside language. It is against this background that a number of poststructuralist discourse theorists have examined the ways in which practices and structures are articulated in discourse, for instance:

- In the *Archaeology*, Michel Foucault (1969) formulated the contours of a pragmatic discourse theory that perceives the utterance (*énoncé*, sometimes translated as "statement") as the smallest unit of discourse and ask how utterances are organized in organized ensembles (i.e. discursive formations). In the 1970s, Foucault proposes a number of historical case studies to undermine the view of power as the property of one centralizing source ("the government"). In some interviews of the 1970s (Foucault 1980), he stresses the "productive" dimensions of power that does not repress but makes possible certain practices. And in his lectures on governmentality (Foucault 2004; Mills 1997), Foucault testifies to his more sociological interests in power as a set of discursive practices that produce and reproduce social order. As governance from a distance, neoliberalism has subjects act in the mode of "freedom" and subjects a large population to a framework of control and supervision (Rose 1989; Bröckling, Krasmann and Lemke 2000; Dean 1994).

- In *Hegemony and Socialist Strategy*, Ernesto Laclau and Chantal Mouffe (1985) outlined a political theory of hegemony that turns against the determinism of Marxist social theory. For Laclau and Mouffe, political practice is never entirely determined by underlying social structures or lawlike rules. The political is perceived as an articulatory practice that combines elements (such as "demands") to form a hegemonic bloc. This practice is contingent in as much as it does more than merely reproducing a given social order. In their view, discourse refers to the way political acts create chains of equivalence between different elements. Promising to fill a constitutive lack in the social, political subjectivities needs to be seen as a result of discursive practices rather than as their source (Torfing 1999; Howarth and Glynos 2007; de Cleen and Stavrakakis 2017).

- In *Gender Trouble*, Judith Butler (1990) takes on the heterosexual matrix as an institutionally established regime of male–female gender difference. For Butler, gender identities are not naturally given; they are enacted and constructed in discursive practices. And, through performative repetition, such identities can be reinforced or undermined. In *Bodies That Matter*, Butler (1993) responds to critics who warn against seeing all, notably biological, realities as discursively constructed. Butler does not object to some distinctions such as between male and female or between (biological) sex and (cultural) gender being considered more material than others (Cameron and Kulick 2003). Her question is how such oppositions turn into material and objective facts through performative repetition (cf. the performative turn in discourse studies, Licoppe 2010).

Against this background, PDS asks how order emerges from linguistic practices that are neither intentionally controlled nor structurally determined, at least not entirely. To perceive discourse as a social practice of using language does not deny the existence of structures. Rather, while PDS rejects the causalist idea of the social as an objective ground of discursive practice, it considers discursive practices as shaping, and being shaped by, the social.

The major questions, themes and interests of PDS can be summed up in the following four points (cf. Angermuller 2014: 83–102):

- First, while PDS is critical of the intentional strategic actor and the author as authority, it is interested to analyze the discursive construction of subjectivity. It is important to understand how recognition and visibility are allocated in discourse through discursive subject positions. PDS reveals the intricate entwinements of subjectivation with the dynamics of power. It asks how individuals turn into subjects in performative acts of naming and how they are established in symbolically mediated processes. It perceives agency as an effect of discursive practices rather than as their source. It insists on the divisions of a subject that can never be one with itself. The subject engages in discursive practices in order to create an illusion of inner unity.

- Second, PDS emphasizes the practices constituting the social. Rather than expressing a strategy, these practices need to be understood in their opaque materiality, that is, in terms of their institutional function rather than as an intentional project of actors. Practices are grounded in the material world. They mobilize human as well as nonhuman resources, cognitive and material stuff. And language is a medium through which practices can be performed and orchestrated. While discursive practices rely on language used in a context, discourse participants enter discourse by performing speech acts through which the social is articulated.
- Third, the social is seen as an open and fluid terrain of subjectivities rather than a closed container of fixed positions. It is a heterogeneous space where elements are tied together in discursive formations. Through discourse, the social is subject to "policing" practices that flatten and smooth out the social, making it governable. By entering discourse, the participants occupy subject positions all of which are not equal. A few discourse participants occupy highly valuable positions while many none at all (Angermuller 2018a).
- Fourth, as a space that shapes and is shaped by discursive practices, the social is subject to reflexive critique (Angermuller 2018b). Critique, in other words, is immanent to the social: it is based on criteria that are the very product of the society it subjects to critique (Herzog 2016). It recognizes the critical awareness of the discourse participants. As critical experts, discourse analysts are never neutral; they, too, take part in the struggles over what counts as truth and what is valuable (Zienkowski 2017; Nonhoff 2017).

11.4 Three Challenges for Poststructuralist Discourse Studies

Poststructuralist orientations have struggled to become established within discourse studies, not least because of considerable disciplinary cleavages between linguistics, where discourse analysis designates a well-established subfield, and other fields in the social sciences and humanities, where "discourse" is more likely to be used to designate certain theoretical schools and intellectual fashions. With its focus on posthumanist, anti-essentialist and constructivist epistemologies, poststructuralism has resonated with the theoretical and interpretive social sciences and humanities. And while one typically associates poststructuralism with the linguistic turn in social theory, it is important to point out a certain mismatch between the ways in which language and society are conceptualized across the disciplines. This situation leads me to point out three challenges of PDS: (a) the challenge of interdisciplinary communication, (b) a methodological deficit and (c) the normative challenge.

a) Interdisciplinary communication is riddled by divergences between disciplinary debates. To give an example, while almost no linguist nowadays would self-identify as a structuralist – and even in FDS, which originated under the influence of structuralism, pragmatics and other currents have taken over – some commentators outside linguistics refer to Saussurean structural linguistics as if it reflected the current state of the art in linguistics. Conversely, there are probably few professional sociologists or political scientists today who would make the case for society as a top-down power structure, which FDS and CDS sometimes assume.

If one wants to make the case for poststructuralist orientations within discourse studies, it is important to deal with such asymmetries (or misunderstandings?) in cross-disciplinary communication. Moreover, more than PDS, CDS and FDS are heavily indebted to debates among linguists with little interest in constructivist, antihumanist and practice-oriented developments in other social sciences. A first challenge for the future, therefore, is to reflect on those hidden (or not so hidden) cleavages that make discourse researchers choose this rather than that label. And one may also point out the important role of language as a medium of scientific communication. If poststructuralism sometimes draws on a "French" philosophical culture, it has been crucially stimulated by transatlantic encounters between North America and France. Yet one needs to recognize important contributions from outside the Western world, from Latin America and elsewhere, where one can also find French-speaking discourse analysts. Yet how does PDS relate to an unequal global space where certain intellectual styles and cognitive orientations are hegemonic?

b) A second challenge for PDS is what has been called the methodological deficit in poststructuralist discourse theory (Zienkowski 2012; Marttila 2016). While some have also been motivated by activist considerations, many practitioners of PDS came to discourse analysis through theoretical works, especially from such theorists as Foucault, Laclau and Mouffe, and Butler. It is clear that poststructuralism has appealed to those academics with conceptual obsessions, which is reflected in the elaborate body of theoretical work that comments on various aspects of discourse theory. However, since it is easy to fall into the traps of repetition and intellectual routine, PDS should have the courage not only to leave trodden theoretical paths but also to apply its insights and intuitions to new social problems and to empirical objects. While some of the canonical figureheads of PDS have enjoyed enormous publicity (which has entailed misrecognition of so many other figures, which should be an object of a reflexive critique in the field in its own right), the creative work that has been done to come up with viable research designs, methodological solutions and new conceptual models has perhaps not always been given the recognition that it should have been. Is this the reason why more theoretically minded discourse researchers in the poststructuralist vein do not easily see the impressive number of tools and devices for the analysis of linguistic material that more linguistic-oriented discourse research has been working with? The list of methodological tools and approaches seems almost endless. It has required and will require more integration and synthesis to make the many methodological tools of discourse analysis available to discourse researchers (Angermuller et al. 2014; Angermuller, Maingueneau and Wodak 2014).

c) More than CDS, PDS has perhaps particular self-reflexive ambitions concerning the claims it makes and the critical projects it pursues. Some of the more activist colleagues in discourse studies have therefore reproached PDS for being overly self-reflexive and sometimes even for indulging in academic navel-gazing. For PDS, it is crucial to ask how it can make a positive, critical contribution to the social world. PDS is always part and parcel of the struggles it wants to investigate. Yet this does not mean that all scientific and nonscientific claims are equal. Rather, discourse researchers would do well to reflect on the social conditions of their own discursive practice. They should ask who becomes visible and recognized in discourse studies? They should reflect on what makes discourse researchers aware of critical, political questions and on how they become relevant in nonacademic struggles. And while PDS should have no illusions over the difference that some academics can make in view of great societal challenges such as environmental disasters and capitalist exploitation, racism and post-democracy, it should insist on the value of discourse research both within the academic world as well as without (cf. Angermuller 2018b).

11.5 Summary

"Poststructuralism" designates ongoing theoretical and political debates since the 1970s that have placed "discourse" center-stage in the theoretical discourse of the social sciences and humanities. Occupying the intellectual space of Marxism and psychoanalysis until the 1960s, poststructuralism comprises intellectuals such as Michel Foucault, Jacques Derrida and Louis Althusser in France and Judith Butler, Gayatri Spivak, and Ernesto Laclau and Chantal Mouffe in the Anglo-American world. These poststructuralist theorists are known for their theoretical accounts of the entanglements of language, subjectivity and power as well as for their critical role in contemporary struggles (e.g. over gender, postcolonialism, populism). While discourse is a central notion in their interrogations, discourse studies as a field has shown ambivalence toward poststructuralism. Among the more established strands in linguistics, the "French School," that is, the post-Pêcheux developments in French-speaking discourse studies, commonly does not accept the term, which is widely seen as an invention by international colleagues, and does not share the strong epistemological, intellectual and political impetus of first-generation discourse theorists. Furthermore, CDS, which has dominated in the Commonwealth countries, prefers (critical) realism over the more radical constructivism in poststructuralism (Fairclough 2013: 181ff.). However, many discourse researchers, especially outside linguistics, are crucially inspired by poststructuralism, which is why poststructuralism is a major reference point for the interdisciplinary debate and for linguistics as well.

PDS goes beyond structuralist conceptions of language and society. While it has opened up structuralist accounts of power and inequality to the practical dimensions of discourse, the productive encounters between poststructuralism and practice theories have led to posthumanist conceptions of subjectivity. PDS draws on poststructuralist topoi (such as the critique of the sovereign subject and language as a socially constitutive practice) and formulates a critique of the structuralist, top-down logic of explanation that characterized earlier tendencies. At the same time, it insists on reflexivity as a method of accounting for the critical effects that discourse analysts have on their objects of investigation. Therefore, PDS fills an important gap as it bridges structure and practice perspectives on discourse in order to account for the discursive construction of social reality.

Further Reading

Angermuller, J., Nonhoff, M., Herschinger, E., Macgilchrist, F., Reisigl, M., Wedl, J., ... Ziem, A. (eds.) (2014). *Diskursforschung. Ein interdisziplinäres Handbuch. Zwei Bände. Band 1: Theorien, Methodologien und Kontroversen. Band 2: Methoden und Analysepraxis Perspektiven auf Hochschulreformdiskurse.* Bielefeld: transcript.

Angermuller, J., Maingueneau, D. and Wodak, R. (eds.) (2014). *The Discourse Studies Reader: Main Currents in Theory and Analysis.* Amsterdam: John Benjamins.

Baxter, J. (2016). *Positioning Language and Identity: Poststructuralist Perspectives*. In S. Preece (ed.) *The Routledge Handbook of Language and Identity*. Oxford/New York: Routledge. 34–49.

Mills, S. (1997). *Discourse*. New York: Routledge.

Torfing, J. (1999). *New Theories of Discourse: Laclau, Mouffe and Žižek*. Oxford: Blackwell.

References

Althusser, L. ([1966]2003). *The Humanist Controversy and Other Writings (1966–67)*. London/New York: Verso.

Amossy, R. (2005). *L'argumentation dans le discours*. Paris: Armand Colin.

Angermuller, J. (2007). Qu'est-ce que le "poststructuralisme français"? A propos de la réception des tendances françaises de l'analyse du discours en Allemagne. *Langage et société* 120: 17–34.

(2014). *Poststructuralist Discourse Analysis: Subjectivity in Enunciative Pragmatics*. Basingstoke: Palgrave Macmillan.

(2015). *Why There Is No Poststructuralism in France: The Making of an Intellectual Generation*. London: Bloomsbury.

(2017). Renouons avec les enjeux critiques de l'Analyse du Discours. Vers les Études du discours. *Langage & société* 160–61:145–61.

(2018a). Accumulating Discursive Capital, Valuating Subject Positions: From Marx to Foucault. *Critical Discourse Studies* 15(4): 415–25. https://doi.org/10.1080/17405904.2018.1457551.

(2018b). Truth after Post-Truth: For a Strong Programme in Discourse Studies. *Palgrave Communications* 4(30): 1–8. www.nature.com/articles/s41599-018-0080-1.

Angermuller, J., Maingueneau, D. and Wodak, R. (eds.) (2014). *The Discourse Studies Reader: Main Currents in Theory and Analysis*. Amsterdam: John Benjamins.

Angermuller, J., Nonhoff, M., Herschinger, E., Macgilchrist, F., Reisigl, M., Wedl, J., Wrana, D. and Ziem, A. (eds.) (2014). *Diskursforschung. Ein interdisziplinäres Handbuch. Zwei Bände. Band 1: Theorien, Methodologien und Kontroversen. Band 2: Methoden und Analysepraxis Perspektiven auf Hochschulreformdiskurse*. Bielefeld: transcript.

Ashmore, M., Myers, G. and Potter, J. (1995). Discourse, Rhetoric, Reflexivity: Seven Days in a Library. In S. Jasanoff, G. Markle, T. Pinch and J. Petersen (eds.) *Handbook of Science and Technology Studies*. London: Sage. 321–42.

Bachmann-Medick, D. (2006). *Cultural Turns: Neuorientierung in den Kulturwissenschaften*. Hamburg: Rowohlt [transl. *Cultural Turns: New Orientations in the Study of Culture*, Berlin/New York: de Gruyter, 2016].

Bamberg, M. and Georgakopoulo, A. (2008). Small Stories as a New Perspective in Narrative and Identity Analysis. *Text & Talk* 28(3): 377–96.

Baxter, J. (2016). Positioning Language and Identity: Poststructuralist Perspectives. In S. Preece (ed.) *The Routledge Handbook of Language and Identity*. Oxford/New York: Routledge. 34–49.

Beetz, J. and Schwab, V. (eds.) (2017). *Material Discourse – Materialist Analysis: Approaches in Discourse Studies*. London: Palgrave.

Benoît, D. (2017). What Is Poststructuralism? *Political Studies Review* 15(4): 516–27.

Benveniste, É. (1974). *Problèmes de linguistique générale, Vol. 2*. Paris: Gallimard.

Bernstein, B. (1971). *Class, Codes, and Control*, 4 vols. London: Routledge & Kegan Paul.

Bernstein, K. A. (2016). Post-Structuralist Potentialities for Studies of Subjectivity and Second Language Learning in Early Childhood. *Contemporary Issues in Early Childhood* 17(2): 174–91.

Bloom, H., de Man, P., Derrida, J., Hartman, G. H. and Hillis Miller, J. (eds.) (1979). *Deconstruction and Criticism*. London: Routledge & Kegan Paul.

Boltanski, L. and Thévenot, L. (1991). *De la justification. Les économies de la grandeur*. Paris: Gallimard [transl. *On Justification: Economies of Worth*. Princeton, NJ: Princeton University Press, 2006].

Bröckling, U., Krasmann, S. and Lemke, T. (eds.) (2000). *Gouvernementalität der Gegenwart*. Frankfurt am Main: Suhrkamp.

Busch, B. (2012). The Linguistic Repertoire Revisited. *Applied Linguistics* 33 (5): 503–23.

Butler, J. (1990). *Gender Trouble: Feminism and the Subversion of Identity*. London/New York: Routledge.

(1993). *Bodies That Matter: On the Discursive Limits of "Sex."* London: Routledge.

Butler, J., Laclau, E. and Žižek, S. (2000). *Contingency, Hegemony, Universality*. Paris: Verso.

Cameron, D. and Kulick, D. (2003). *Language and Sexuality*. Cambridge: Cambridge University Press.

Carter, P. M. (2013). Poststructuralist Theory and Sociolinguistics: Mapping the Linguistic Turn in Social Theory. *Language and Linguistics Compass* 7 (11): 580–96.

Charaudeau, P. (1983). *Langage et discours. Eléments de sémiolinguistique*. Paris: Hachette.

Charaudeau, P. and Maingueneau, D. (2002). *Dictionnaire d'analyse du discours*. Paris: Seuil.

Conein, B., Courtine, J.-J., Gadet, F., Marandin, J.-M. and Pêcheux, M. (1981). *Matérialités discursives, Actes du Colloque des 24–26 avril 1980, Paris X-Nanterre*. Lille: Presses Universitaires de Lille.

Dean, M. (1994). *Foucault's Methods and Historical Sociology*. London/New York: Routledge.

De Cleen, B. and Stavrakakis, Y. (2017). Distinctions and Articulations: A Discourse Theoretical Framework for the Study of Populism and

Nationalism. *Javnost – The Public: Journal of the European Institute for Communication and Culture* 24(4): 301–19.

Deleuze, G. (2002). *L'Île déserte et autres textes*. Paris: Minuit [transl. *Desert Islands and Other Texts (1953–1974)*. New York: Semiotexte, 2004].

Derrida, J. (1967). *De la grammatologie*. Paris: Minuit [transl. *Of Grammatology*. Baltimore, MD: Johns Hopkins University Press, 1976].

  (1999). Marx & Sons. In M. Sprinker (ed.) *Ghostly Demarcations: A Symposium on Jacques Derrida's Specters of Marx*. London/New York: Routledge. 213–69.

Détrie, C., Siblot, P. and Verine, B. (2001). *Termes et concepts pour l'analyse du discours. Une approche praxématique*. Paris: Honoré Champion.

Dreyfus, H. L. and Rabinow, P. (1983). *Michel Foucault: Beyond Structuralism and Hermeneutics* 2nd ed. with afterword by/interview with Michel Foucault. Chicago: University of Chicago Press.

Ducrot, O., Todorov, T., Sperber, D., Safouan, M. and Wahl, F. (1968). *Qu'est-ce que le structuralisme?* Paris: Le Seuil.

Ehlich, K. (1986). Funktional-Pragmatische Kommunikationsanalyse – Ziele und Verfahren. In W. Hartung (ed.) *Untersuchungen zur Kommunikation – Ergebnisse und Perspektiven (Internationale Arbeitstagung in Bad Stuer, Dezember 1985)*. Berlin: Akademie. 15–40.

Ehrmann, J. (ed.) (1970). *Structuralism*. Garden City, NY: Anchor-Doubleday.

Fairclough, N. (1992). *Discourse and Social Change*. Cambridge/Oxford: Polity Press.

  (1995). *Critical Discourse Analysis: The Critical Study of Language*. London/New York: Longman.

  (2013). Critical Discourse Analysis and Critical Policy Studies. *Critical Policy Studies* 7(2): 177–97.

  (2017). CDA as Dialectical Reasoning. In J. Flowerdew and J. E. Richardson (eds.) *The Routledge Handbook of Critical Discourse Studies*. Abingdon: Routledge.

Flowerdew, J. and Richardson, J. (eds.) (2017). *The Routledge Handbook of Critical Discourse Studies*. London: Routledge.

Foucault, M. (1966). *Les Mots et les choses. Une archéologie des sciences humaines*. Paris: Gallimard [transl. *The Order of Things. An Archeology of the Human Sciences*. London: Routledge, 2002].

  (1969). *L'Archéologie du savoir*. Paris: Gallimard [transl. *The Archeology of Knowledge and the Discourse on Language*. London: Routledge, 1989].

  (1980). *Power/Knowledge: Selected Interviews and Other Writings 1972–1977*. New York: Pantheon Books.

  ([1983]1994). Structuralisme et poststructuralisme. In *Dits et écrits, tome 4. 1980–1988*. Paris: Gallimard. 431–457 [transl. Structuralism and Post-Structuralism. In J. D. Faubion (ed.) *Aesthetics, Method, and Epistemology: Essential Works of Foucault, 1954–1984*. New York: The New Press, 1998, 433–58].

(2004). *Territoire, population, sécurité*. Paris: Gallimard, Seuil [transl. *Security, Territory, Population: Lectures at the College de France*. Basingstoke: Palgrave Macmillan, 2007].

Fraser, N. (1995). Pragmatism, Feminism, and the Linguistic Turn. In S. Benhabib, J. Butler, D. Cornell and N. Fraser (eds.) *Feminist Contentions: A Philosophical Exchange*. New York: Routledge. 157–72.

Grossberg, L., Nelson, C. and Treichler, P. (eds.) (1992). *Cultural Studies*. New York/London: Routledge.

Guilhaumou, J. (1993). A propos de l'analyse de discours: les historiens et le "tournant linguistique." *Langage & société* 65: 5–38.

Hall, S., Hobson, D., Lowe, A. and Willis, P. (eds.) (1980). *Culture, Media, Language*. London: Hutchinson.

Halliday, M. A. K. (1978). *Language As Social Semiotic*. London: Edward Arnold.

Harris, Z. S. (1952). Discourse Analysis. *Language* 28: 1–30.

Herzog, B. (2016). *Discourse Analysis as Social Critique: Discursive and Non-discursive Realities in Critical Social Research*. London: Palgrave Macmillan.

Howarth, D. and Glynos, J. (2007). *Logics of Critical Explanation in Social and Political Theory*. London: Routledge.

Jäger, S. ([1993]2007). *Kritische Diskursanalyse. Eine Einführung*. Münster: Unrast.

Jameson, F. (1991). *Postmodernism, or The Cultural Logic of Late Capitalism*. Durham, NC: Duke University Press.

Kiesling, S. (2006). Hegemonic Identity-Making in Narrative. In A. De Fina, D. Schiffrin and M. Bamberg (eds.) *Discourse and Identity*. Cambridge: Cambridge University Press. 261–87.

Kramsch, C. (1998). *Language and Culture*. Oxford: Oxford University Press.

Kress, G. and van Leeuwen, T. (2006). *Reading Images: The Grammar of Visual Design*, 2nd ed. London: Routledge.

Laclau, E. and Mouffe, C. (1985). *Hegemony and Socialist Strategy: Towards a Radical Democratic Politics*. London/New York: Verso.

Latour, B. (1987). *Science in Action*. Milton Keynes: Open University Press.

Licoppe, C. (2010). The "Performative Turn" in Science and Technology Studies: Towards a Linguistic Anthropology of "Technology in Action." *Journal of Cultural Economy* 3: 181–8.

Lyotard, J.-F. (1983). *Le Différend*. Paris: Minuit.

Maingueneau, D. (1990). *Pragmatique pour le discours littéraire*. Paris: Dunod.

(1991). *L'Analyse du discours. Introduction aux lectures de l'archive*. Paris: Hachette.

(1994). Die ‚französische Schule' der Diskursanalyse. In K. Ehlich (ed.) *Diskursanalyse in Europa*. Frankfurt am Main: Peter Lang. 187–95.

Marttila, T. (2016). *Post-Foundational Discourse Analysis: From Political Difference to Empirical Research*. London: Palgrave.

McNamara, T. (2012). Poststructuralism and Its Challenges for Applied Linguistics. *Applied Linguistics* 33(5): 473–82.

Mills, S. (1997). *Discourse*. New York: Routledge.

Motschenbacher, H. (2009). Speaking the Gendered Body: The Performative Construction of Commercial Femininities and Masculinities via Body-Part Vocabulary. *Language in Society* 38: 1–22.

Nonhoff, M. (2017). Discourse Analysis As Critique. *Palgrave Communications* 3(17074).

Norton, B. and Morgan, B. (2013). Poststructuralism. In C. A. Chapelle (ed.) *The Encyclopedia of Applied Linguistics*. London: Wiley.

Orlandi, E. (1990). *Análise de discurso: princípios e procedimentos*. Campinas: Pontes.

Parker, I. and Pavón-Cuéllar, D. (eds.) (2014). *Lacan, Discourse, Event: New Psychoanalytic Approaches to Textual Indeterminacy*. London/New York: Routledge.

Pavlenko, A. (2002). Poststructuralist Approaches to the Study of Social Factors in Second Language Learning and Use. In V. Cook (ed.) *Portraits of the L2 User*. Bristol: Multilingual Matters. 275–302.

Pêcheux, M. (1969). *Analyse automatique du discours*. Paris: Dunod [transl. *Automatic Discourse Analysis*. Amsterdam/Atlanta, GA: Rodopi, 1995].

(1975). *Les Vérités de La Palice*. Paris: Maspero [transl. *Language, Semantics and Ideology: Stating the Obvious*. London: Macmillan, 1982].

(1990). *L'inquiétude du discours*. Paris: Edition des Cendres.

Pinto, A. G. (1997). *Publicidade: um discurso de sedução*. Porto: Porto Editora.

Possenti, S. (2009). *Questões para analistas do discurso*. São Paulo: Parábola Editorial.

Potter, J. and Wetherell, M. (1987). *Discourse and Social Psychology*. London: Sage.

Reisigl, M. and Wodak, R. (2009). The Discourse-Historical Approach (DHA). In R. Wodak and M. Meyer (eds.) *Methods of Critical Discourse Analysis*. London: Sage. 87–121.

Robin, R. (1973). *Histoire et linguistique*. Paris: Colin.

Rojo, L. M. (1997). El orden social de los discursos. *Discurso* 21(22): 1–37.

Rorty, R. (ed.) (1967). *The Linguistic Turn: Essays in Philosophical Method*. Chicago: Chicago University Press.

Rose, N. (1989). *Governing the Soul: The Shaping of the Private Self*. London: Free Association.

Rosier, L. (1999). *Le discours rapporté: histoire, théories, pratiques*. Bruxelles: Duculot.

Said, E. W. (1978). *Orientalism*. London: Penguin.

Schatzki, T. R., Knorr Cetina, K. and von Savigny, E. (eds.) (2001). *The Practice Turn in Contemporary Theory*. London/New York: Routledge.

Schmitz, J. R. (2017). English as a Lingua Franca: Applied Linguistics, Marxism, and Post-Marxist Theory. *Revista Brasileira de Linguística Aplicada* 17(2): 335–54. Epub March 23, 2017. https://doi.org/10.1590/1984-6398201710866.

Smith, D. E. (1999). *Writing the Social: Critique, Theory, and Investigations*. Toronto: University of Toronto Press.

Spivak, G. C. (1988). Can the Subaltern Speak? In C. Nelson and L. Grossberg (eds.) *Marxism and the Interpretation of Culture*. Urbana: University of Illinois Press. 271–313.

Torfing, J. (1999). *New Theories of Discourse: Laclau, Mouffe and Žižek*. Oxford: Blackwell.

Van Langenhove, L. and Harré, R. (1999). Introducing Positioning Theory. In R. Harré and L. van Langenhove (eds.) *Positioning Theory: Moral Contexts of Intentional Action*. Oxford: Blackwell. 14–31.

Warnke, I. (ed.) (2007). *Diskurslinguistik nach Foucault: Theorie und Gegenstände*. Berlin: Walter de Gruyter.

White, H. (1987). *The Content of the Form: Narrative Discourse and Historical Representation*. Baltimore: The Johns Hopkins Press.

Widmer, J. (1986). *Langage et action sociale. Aspects philosophiques et sémiotiques du langage dans la perspective de l'ethnométhodologie*. Fribourg: Editions Universitaires Fribourg Suisse.

Williams, G. (1999). *French Discourse Analysis*. London: Routledge.

Wodak, R. (2007). Pragmatics and Critical Discourse Analysis: A Cross-Disciplinary Analysis. *Pragmatics and Cognition* 15(1): 203–25.

Zienkowski, J. (2012). Overcoming the Post-Structuralist Methodological Deficit: Metapragmatic Markers and Interpretive Logics in a Critique of the Bologna Process. *International Pragmatics Association* 22(3): 501–34.

(2017). Reflexivity in the Transdisciplinary Field of Critical Discourse Studies. *Palgrave Communications* 3(17007).

Žižek, S. (1991). *Looking Awry: An Introduction to Jacques Lacan through Popular Culture*. Cambridge, MA/London: MIT Press.

Part III

Discourse Materialities and Embodiment

Introduction

In this part, we have included chapters that present, assess and take stock of the recent momentum within discourse studies in terms of expanding the field's focus beyond language and text to a wide range of communicational modalities and multisemiotic resources, objects, artifacts, nonhuman agents, as well as the participants' bodies in communication acts. Crossing the boundaries between language, bodies and the material world is arguably the biggest transformative paradigm shift within discourse studies, notably absent from earlier handbooks of discourse analysis. At the time of its publication, this handbook is thus uniquely placed to register this shift and help consolidate its hard-fought-and-earned place within discourse studies. Material, multisemiotic and multisensorial modalities have traditionally been underrepresented in discourse studies, viewed as peripheral or, in Busch's terms, treated as "epiphenomena in the analysis of communicative acts" (Chapter 15 in this volume, p. 328). It is widely recognized, as we can see in the discussion of Chapters 13, 15 and 16, that the history of discourse analysis as a primarily logocentric field with a dematerialized view of language has been shaped by structuralist and Saussurean views of language as sets of binaries (e.g. signifier–signified) and as a system isolated from the social world of its users. At the same time, the influence of approaches that could be seen as precursors to the current decisive shift toward a materialist view of language and discourse should not be underestimated. Busch reminds us that Garfinkel's ethnomethodological approach influenced later works, mainly within conversation analysis, that recognized the importance of para- and nonverbal features (such as body posture and gesture). The place of Scollon and Scollon's influential nexus analysis, also referred to as geosemiotics and mediated discourse analysis (e.g. Scollon and Scollon 2003, 2004), as a precursor to multimodal frameworks of analysis, is also well-recognized and acknowledged across the chapters.

Turning attention to the multisemioticity, materiality and corporeality of communication implicates working with new material and different foci of analysis. It is no accident that the chapters in this part include reflections on "data" decidedly outside of the areas of concern of conventional discourse analysis, such as the role of monuments and public spaces as sites of contestation, human–sea turtle relationships, the semiotic implications of a hopscotch grid (in the work of Goodwin 2017; referred to in Chapter 13 in this volume), etc. Language in these cases becomes part of social actions and practices produced through the interactions and meaning-making of diverse semiotic and corporeal elements.

The chapters' discussion shares a concern with how different, established approaches (e.g. critical discourse analysis, social semiotics, conversation analysis) have addressed the complex problems arising from studying the integration of language with other resources, such as images, gesture, movement, space and so forth. As Tan, O'Halloran and Wignell remark in Chapter 12, the designations of terms that refer to traditions originally developed for the analysis of spoken and written communication, such as "conversation analysis" and "systemic functional linguistics," have broadened in meaning and application beyond the confines of the study of language, and thus no longer match the scope of the disciplines they used to described in the past. This renders certain terms as misnomers, for instance linguistic landscaping, which, as Seargeant and Giaxoglou observe in Chapter 14, has had its meaning broadened to include all forms of (public) semiotic landscaping. From this point of view, traditionally distinct areas of inquiry can nowadays be brought together and viewed as affiliated through the lens of a posthumanist, materialist orientation that cuts across their sets of tools, modes of analysis and choice of material.

This decisive disruption of longstanding boundaries and the remit of different areas is not without challenges. A particular challenge that the chapters collectively point to is the development of adequate systems for the transcription, visual representation and analysis of gestures, embodied actions, interaction with material objects, movement in space and so on. As Tan, O'Halloran and Wignell discuss in Chapter 12, various digital approaches have been developed to handle the multidimensional complexity of multimodal analysis, in particular for the analysis of dynamic media such as videos. Such approaches include, amongst others, the development of mixed methods, purpose-built software tools and automated techniques.

The opening up of discourse to materialist, posthumanist, multisemiotic approaches is essentially questioning the definition and primacy of human agency. Partly influenced by Actor-Network Theory (see Chapter 16), a prevalent position in this respect is that agency is distributed across an ontologically heterogeneous field and emerges as a relational achievement of heterogeneous entities. A related issue concerns the nature and type of relationships amongst language, artifacts, objects, and multimodal and multisensorial semiotic resources. The structuralist accounts of the relations between text and context that pose cause–effect, one-to-one relationships have clearly been problematized. But what the nature of relationships in a materialist view of discourse is and what the unit of discourse analysis is or becomes are far from settled, agreed upon issues. There seems to be convergence on the fact that relationships are multiple and dynamic, that the elements involved are heterogeneous and that this needs to be recognized in the analysis. Terms such as entanglement, assemblage and nexus are often used to describe the sorts of relationships involved, as even a cursory look at the chapters suggests. "Action" is often referred to as a unit of analysis, but there is much scope for specifying what exactly it covers and how it concurs with or can be brought into dialogue with existing modes of analysis and concepts in different traditions of doing discourse analysis. Action often encompasses "emergent, open-ended, intertwined affective-discursive patterns evident in social life," as Busch suggests in Chapter 15, following Wetherell (2013: 351). The comparable unit of momentary, fragmented, ephemeral moments of engagement-in-place is invoked in Chapter 14 in its connections with key events, past or present, and a narrative orientation to the world, following Georgakopoulou's work on small stories. The importance of the analytic orientation to the "moment" is also discussed in Chapter 18 in this volume. How such an orientation can be brought together with concepts such as positioning and stance (see Chapter 13) should be an issue of interest in the area.

As Lamb and Higgins caution us, to see the assemblages or entanglements of language, discourse, multisemioticity, embodiment and affect within moments of social action as a flat ontology that distributes agency indiscriminately across people and objects raises a number of methodological concerns. First, it skews unequal communicative encounters that require critical perspectives on power relations. Another related challenge is to "recognize how researchers themselves become entangled in this messy relational ontology of research practice that posthumanist theory encourages" (Chapter 16, p. 362). Finally, the affordances that come with specific modalities (visual, verbal, embodied), what they enable and constrain, need to be scrutinized for different communication acts in different contexts, as opposed to viewing multisemioticity as a level playing field. In the case of research on social media, it is important to identify and analyze the types of discourse and communication they afford and in turn the kinds of agentive potentials, empowering or disempowering, that these shape (e.g. see Chapters 5 and 32).

A view of the material and embodied aspects of discourse within a framework of power relations inevitably brings into focus the extent to which a distinction between resources as situated and as shaped by and bringing about capital D- or macro-discourses is relevant or useful for the analysis. Although the distinction between micro- and macro- as a way of conceptualizing the contextualization of language has by now been problematized (see chapters in Part I), we see the continuing relevance of the distinction between macro- and micro-interactional approaches to discourse in some of the work on discourse, embodiment and affect, as Busch shows us in Chapter 15. This is partly explicable by the areas of influence in this kind of work, which consist in feminist studies, queer studies, critical race theory, studies on colonialism, all of which are invested in the role of power relations, dominant discourses and subjective experiences in "answering back." A macro-view of discourse is invoked in much of the work here in terms of capturing how emotions, etc. are conceived of in specific historical, spatial contexts. The question of how site-specific semiotic events are pulled into broader discourses is also examined in Chapter 14, where Seargeant and Giaxoglou talk about how meaning is generated through the complex layering of contexts, the interplay between multiple signs, and the dialogic possibilities presented by social media which allow local meanings to be upscaled and reconfigured.

Materialist approaches to discourse are still a new area with many, exciting directions of research and a rich agenda, as identified in the chapters. These include both forging (further) links with methodological and analytical approaches (e.g. ethnography as suggested by Sidnell (Chapter 13) and by Lamb and Higgins (Chapter 16); narrative analysis as suggested by Busch (Chapter 15); and small stories research as suggested by Seargeant and Giaxoglou (Chapter 14)) and developing (further) research foci, for example examining the role of objects in interaction. Finally, the concept of affect emerges throughout the chapters as "an energetic force that triggers relational exchanges beyond the threshold of language or representations and which connects us to the material and ecological world through more visceral emotional and corporeal channels of meaning-making" (Chapter 16, p. 357, citing Thrift, 2008).

In Chapter 12 by **Tan, O'Halloran and Wignell**, the study of multimodality is undoubtedly more consolidated in discourse studies than that of embodiment; the chapter provides an overview of the terminological issues (e.g. the use of the term multimodal as opposed to that of multisemiotic) and analytical concerns within the constantly evolving framework of multimodal discourse analysis (MDA), also referred to as systemic functional multimodal discourse analysis (SF-MDA). MDA is not alone in multisemiotic approaches to discourse in having been informed by and pulling together insights by a number of fields, from social semiotics and critical discourse analysis, to photography, film theory and visual design. In turn, the participating discourse analytic areas have expanded their brief and modes of analysis to include a wide range of embodied multimodal resources. As other chapters, too, suggest, this opening up has also been the case in conversation analysis, under the umbrella of what is now often called multimodal interaction analysis. Increasingly, as the chapter shows, MDA has had to develop ways of modeling, analyzing and interpreting multimodal texts, especially videos and nowadays digital material. This is an ongoing operation with much potential for exploiting big data techniques. The authors present the examples of purpose-built software applications for text, image and video analysis, developed by Kay O'Halloran and her team. The use of these tools for what could be labeled "critical discourse analysis," for example for the investigation of the meanings arising from text and images in violent extremist discourse (e.g. O'Halloran et al. 2017; Wignell et al. 2017; Tan et al. 2018), is indicative of the directions that multimodality can take with the further development of mixed methods and sophisticated data modeling.

Chapter 13 by **Sidnell** begins by tracing the dematerialization of language in the sign theory underlying the Saussurean approach to language. Saussure saw the linguistic system (langue) and its internally constituted elements as cordoned off from social life, thus excluding any consideration of the material or physical properties of the sign. After considering the materialist critique of Voloshinov, who essentially suggests that language and social life are inextricably linked via ideology, the chapter moves to a discussion of Peirce's influential theory of signs, which can be viewed as providing a foundation for the materiality of discourse. As is explained, the materiality of discourse includes the physical character of the signs as well as the ways in which they are used to make reference to the world of an interaction and to construct consequential action. The participants' embodiment also becomes an integral part of this material configuration of interactions. Accepting the materiality of discourse essentially involves attending to the rich social, cultural and linguistic contexts in which discourse occurs and, from this point of view, strong connections of discourse analytic work with an ethnographic and anthropological approach are both desirable and necessary. The author suggests that such research should include further exploration of deixis and the indexical character of reference in discourse. In addition, it should include a focus on the discursive practices by which material features of the world are semiotically articulated, a plea that cuts across the chapters in this part.

Seargeant and Giaxoglou's point of departure in Chapter 14 is that research into the way that linguistic and other semiotic signs are displayed in public space has opened up a productive field for social language analysis over the last few years, referred to as linguistic landscaping. With a focus on the policy implications of public signage, linguistic landscape research has since its inception engaged with issues of politics and ideology and thus, indirectly, discourse. In recent years, it has also begun to theorize the ways in which semiotic artifacts and practices interact in explicitly dialogic ways, thus generating meaning. To date, however, theorizing that is directed specifically at the relationships between linguistic landscape studies and discourse studies has been scarce, at least in the way it has addressed the subject in explicit terms. This chapter explores the nature of this relationship by focusing on select case studies that exemplify the way in which acts of linguistic and semiotic display in the public arena operate as key sites for social organization and for political regulation and contestation. The chapter's focus on how public spaces and semiotic artifacts can be used to demarcate places of affect, whereby specific narratives, along with participant positions of (dis)alignment to discourses in, often transmedial, circulation about key events, are created as beacons for how this area can intersect with research on discourse and affect, narrative analysis and, last but not least, social media communication. In similar vein as in Chapter 13, semiotic signs are approached here as emplaced discourse complexes, which are part of broader communication and (social) media ecologies.

Busch's Chapter 15 provides an overview of the main ways in which discourse analysis has slowly but decisively been turning its attention to bodies and emotions, both inextricably involved in all forms of subjective experience and social practice. The author identifies feminist approaches, gender and queer studies, studies on colonialism and racism as major influences in the recent reorientation of discourse analysis toward conceptions of embodiment, that is, the thinking about and through bodies. Three main perspectives on embodiment and emotions are teased out from an ongoing, growing body of work and discussed: a focus on how bodies and emotions are involved and deployed in situated interactions; a focus on how bodies and emotions are conceived and formed through historically and spatially situated social practices and discourses, that is, how everyday practices and discourses are inscribed into the body; and finally, a focus on how they are lived, experienced and narrated by subjects. The first perspective is closely associated with interactional approaches, the second with critical discourse analysis and the third with cognitive, phenomenological and narrative approaches. As the author suggests, depending on which of these perspectives one chooses, the meaning of the term "embodiment" changes, from standing for enactment (in interaction) through incarnation (of discursively established positions) to incorporation (of lived experience). In the debate on interconnections amongst discourse, emotion and embodiment, how the three perspectives outlined and discussed in the chapter can combine insights and be brought together remains one of the most topical questions.

Another productive area for further research involves cases in which the bodily and emotionally lived experience does not match discursively established norms and categorizations, a gap that is crucial in areas that research discourse, inclusion and diversity (see chapters in Part V).

Finally, Chapter 16 by **Lamb and Higgins** maps the emerging conceptual terrain of posthumanism and its relevance for discourse studies, with a particular focus on sociolinguistics and applied linguistics work. Posthumanism is a label applied to a range of theoretical and methodological approaches across the humanities and social sciences that are calling into question dominant assumptions generated by Western Enlightenment thinking about "the human" by giving greater consideration to the role of material objects, animals and the environment in understanding the social world. Posthumanism thus considers the implications of the central role of materialism in our understandings of human agency, language, cognition and society. For discourse studies, a turn to posthumanism requires us to examine the role of discourse in how humans become entangled with the material world through their everyday embodied interactions with objects, artifacts, technologies, plants, animals, and the built and natural environment. Discourse is thus located at the nexus of semiotic and material affordances, but the analysis of it is also important for posthumanism, not least in the form of circulating ideological stances about human–material relations. Through embracing an activity-oriented perspective toward human–nonhuman entanglements, the authors argue that the implications are that we must rethink modernist categorical boundaries between subject/object, human/nonhuman and society/nature, both within meta-discourses about these dichotomies and through a more micro-analytic lens in the analysis of text and talk. In similar vein as in Chapter 15, the former set of concerns falls within critical discourse analysis while the latter within conversation and more generally interactional analysis. In general, posthumanist discourse studies are well placed to offer insights into multi-species studies by investigating how plants, animals and ecosystems become agentive and integral partners in social practices. Posthumanist discourse studies, the authors argue, push us to consider how discourse analysts might show the multisensorial knowing of the world through research. Taking risks with alternative forms of knowledge production in the field will be especially important when seeking to share this expertise beyond the boundaries of academic debate.

References

Goodwin, C. (2017). *Co-operative Action*. Cambridge: Cambridge University Press.
O'Halloran, K. L., Tan, S., Wignell, P. and Lange, R. (2017). Multimodal Recontextualisations of Images in Violent Extremist Discourse. In

S. Zhao, E. Djonov, A. Björkvall and M. Boeriis (eds.) *Advancing Multimodal and Critical Discourse Studies: Interdisciplinary Research Inspired by Theo Van Leeuwen's Social Semiotics*. London/New York: Routledge. 181–202.

Scollon, R. and Scollon, S. W. (2003). *Discourses in Place: Language in the Material World*. London: Routledge.

(2004). *Nexus Analysis*. London: Routledge.

Tan, S., O'Halloran, K. L., Wignell, P., Chai, K. and Lange, R. (2018). A Multimodal Mixed Methods Approach for Examining Recontextualisation Patterns of Violent Extremist Images in Online Media *Discourse, Context & Media* 21: 18–35.

Thrift, N. (2008). *Non-representational Theory: Space, Politics, Affect*. London: Routledge.

Wetherell, M. (2013). Affect and Discourse – What's the Problem? From Affect as Excess to Affective/Discursive Practice. *Subjectivity* 6(4): 349–68.

Wignell, P., Tan, S., O'Halloran, K. L. and Lange, R. (2017). A Mixed Methods Empirical Examination of Changes in Emphasis and Style in the Extremist Magazines *Dabiq* and Rumiyah. *Perspectives on Terrorism* 11 (2): 2–20.

12

Multimodality

Sabine Tan, Kay O'Halloran and Peter Wignell

12.1 Introduction: Definitions and Background

Multimodality has become a buzzword for scholars working in different disciplinary areas and domains, including linguistics, film and media studies, journalism studies, cultural studies, anthropology and psychology. Over the past two decades, interest in multimodal approaches has expanded exponentially, with a corresponding cornucopia of monographs, handbooks and textbooks being published on the subject (e.g. Bateman, Wildfeuer and Hiippala 2017; Jewitt 2014; Jewitt, Bezemer and O'Halloran 2016; Kress 2010; Machin 2007; O'Halloran 2004; O'Halloran and Smith 2011).

This chapter provides an overview of recent theoretical, methodological and analytical trends in multimodal research. More specifically, it focuses on how different approaches such as critical discourse analysis, social semiotics, systemic functional linguistics, conversation analysis and interaction analysis have addressed the complex problems arising from studying the integration of language with other resources such as images, gesture, movement, space and so forth. In doing so, the chapter discusses how traditional divisions in discourse studies (e.g. Jewitt 2014; Jewitt, Bezemer and O'Halloran 2016) have become somewhat blurred, given the evident need to account for resources other than language and the meanings that arise as choices combine in texts, interactions and events.

The chapter also explores how various digital approaches have been developed to handle the multidimensional complexity of multimodal analysis, in particular for the analysis of dynamic media such as videos (e.g. Bateman and Schmidt 2012; Tan, Wignell and O'Halloran 2016; Wildfeuer 2014; Wildfeuer and Bateman 2016). This discussion includes the development of mixed methods approaches, purpose-built software, automated techniques and the latest trends in big data approaches to multimodal analysis (e.g. Bateman et al. 2016; Bateman et al. 2019; O'Halloran, Tan and Wignell 2016).

In what follows, the chapter first introduces some definitions of the term "multimodality" and its background. This is followed by an overview of approaches to multimodal research from different discourse analytical perspectives in Section 12.2. The subsequent sections look at some of the issues related to the complexity of research in multimodal phenomena in the digital age (Section 12.3) and the implications of this for research and practice (Section 12.4) and future directions (Section 12.5). The chapter concludes with a brief summary in Section 12.6. Suggestions for further reading are presented in Section 12.7.

For Jewitt (2014: 1), multimodality means approaching "representation, communication and interaction as something more than language." Multimodality, she explains, extends the social interpretation of meaning in a culture to the whole repertoire of representational and communicational modes or semiotic resources available for meaning-making, including image, text, symbolism, gaze, gesture, posture and sounds (Jewitt, 2014: 1).

According to Jewitt, Bezemer and O'Halloran (2016: 2), the term multimodality first appeared in the mid "to late 1990s in different parts of the world," where it was used by scholars working independently of each other across different disciplines. In the literature (e.g. Machin 2013, 2016), the introduction of multimodality is frequently attributed to Gunther Kress and Theo van Leeuwen, who first used the term in their books *Reading Images: The Grammar of Visual Design* ([1996]2006) and *Multimodal Discourse: The Modes and Media of Contemporary Communication* (2001). Around the same time, the term was also being used by Charles Goodwin (2000) to model the construction of social action as accomplished through combinations of different kinds of semiotic resource in talk-in-interaction.

The notion that human beings in a culture use a whole range of different semiotic resources available to them for meaning-making and communication, however, has a much longer history and can be traced to the works of scholars working in different linguistic and philosophic traditions in the late nineteenth and early twentieth centuries. For instance, it laid the foundations for the pioneering work in semiotics by Charles S. Peirce ([1867–71]1984) and Ferdinand de Saussure ([1916]1983), and formed the basis of French philosopher Roland Barthes' ([1957]1987, 1977) groundbreaking work in semiotics, literary criticism and social theory, providing a bridge between structuralism (e.g. Saussure and Levi-Strauss) and post-structuralism, as exemplified by Foucault (1926–1984), Derrida (1930–2004) and others.

Likewise, the study of semiotic resources such as sound, gesture, gaze, body posture and proxemics, as used together with language in social interaction contexts, has been the subject of interest in a host of other research traditions, such as anthropology and sociology, for instance (e.g. Goffman 1981; Hall 1968; Kendon 2004).

While some scholars argue that the field of multimodality is and remains fragmented, even today, with "insufficient consistency or agreement" in how the term is used or defined (Machin 2016: 323), others contend that the concept we now refer to as multimodality has long transcended traditional research boundaries (e.g. Bateman et al. 2017). As Jewitt, Bezemer and O'Halloran (2016: 2) explain, it was precisely

> that recognition of the need for studying how different kinds of meaning making are combined into an integrated, multimodal whole that scholars attempted to highlight when they started using the term "multimodality." It was a recognition of the need to move beyond the empirical boundaries of existing disciplines and develop theories and methods that can account for the ways in which we use gesture, inscription, speech and other means together in order to produce meanings ….

According to Jewitt (2014), multimodality as a research tradition evolved in close "conversation with different historical influences and research interests to realize *interconnected* but distinctive approaches to multimodal research" (Jewitt 2014: 12; emphasis added), each with its own concepts, tools, processes, methods and terminology (see also Machin 2016). In the widest sense, multimodality can thus be regarded "as a theory, a perspective or a field of enquiry or a methodological application" (Jewitt 2014: 12).

In Section 12.2, we provide an overview of some of the multimodal approaches that have been developed from different analytical, theoretical and methodological perspectives, such as social semiotics, systemic functional linguistics, critical discourse analysis, conversation and interaction analysis, and others.

12.2 Overview of the Topic

A common trend in the literature on multimodality is to delineate what appear to be distinctive approaches in terms of select sets of conventionally agreed research traditions or disciplines (e.g. Jewitt 2014; Jewitt, Bezemer and O'Halloran 2016). There are also numerous books and edited volumes that offer valuable insights into the distinctive ways in which multimodality is approached and applied within a particular field or discourse domain (e.g. Bateman and Schmidt 2012; Djonov and Zhao 2014; O'Halloran and Smith 2011; Sindoni, Wildfeuer and O'Halloran 2017). According to Deppermann (2013: 2), "multimodality" is a label that "has become most fuzzy by its use in various strands of semiotics, discourse and media analysis." Jewitt, Bezemer and O'Halloran (2016: 7) argue that the "same can be said about the names of the originating disciplines. The terms 'conversation analysis' or 'systemic functional linguistics' no longer match the scope of the disciplines they describe."

In what follows, we provide a summary of multimodal approaches developed from different analytical, theoretical and methodological perspectives. In this context, it must be noted that multimodality is fundamentally a *transdisciplinary* field of research and application. Although "the different sub-fields that lie under the umbrella of multimodality have concepts, tools and processes of analysis designed to do very different things, and which are generated from very different starting points" (Machin, 2016: 323), there are many overlaps and intersections between individual approaches. As Jewitt, Bezemer and O'Halloran (2016: 13) point out, "[i]n many studies, selected elements of one of the [other] approaches have been adopted and brought into connection with concepts and methods from other disciplines."

The most influential works that can be credited with establishing multimodality as a transdisciplinary field of research are perhaps Kress and van Leeuwen's *Reading Images: The Grammar of Visual Design* ([1996]2006) and *Multimodal Discourse: The Modes and Media of Communication* (2001), and Michael O'Toole's *The Language of Displayed Art* ([1994]2011) (see also Bateman, Wildfeuer and Hippala 2017; Djonov and Zhao 2017; Machin 2016). These works all built upon by the combined principles of semiotics and social theory (e.g. Hodge and Kress 1988) and Michael Halliday's (1978) systemic functional theory (SFT).

Developed most fully as systemic functional linguistics (SFL) (e.g. for a collection of Halliday's extensive work in theoretical and applied linguistics, see Halliday 2009, 2018), SFT is "a theory of meaning as choice, by which language, or any other any other semiotic system, is interpreted as networks of interlocking options," whereby the particular choices that are made are not to be viewed as the result of conscious decisions but rather as unconscious choices from "a set of possible alternatives" (Halliday, 1994: xiv–xxvi), and where semiotic resources are conceptualized in terms of the functions they have come to serve in society. One of the key tenets in SFT is Halliday's metafunctional principle (e.g. Halliday 1978; Halliday and Matthiessen 2014), which proposes that language and other semiotic resources used for meaning-making in a culture are structured to make three kinds of meaning simultaneously: (a) *ideational* meaning for construing our experience and knowledge of the world (i.e. experiential meaning) and for making logical connections in that world (i.e. logical meaning); (b) *interpersonal* meaning for enacting social relations; and (c) *textual* meaning for organizing meanings and for forming connections with other signs to produce coherent texts.

Robert Hodge and Gunther Kress expanded upon these principles in *Social Semiotics* (1988) to explore different sets of semiotic resources, including nonverbal modes, which people use in everyday life, such as writing and images (Bezemer and Jewitt 2009). Kress and van Leeuwen further extended the social semiotic approach to the analysis of visual images in *Reading Images: The Grammar of Visual Design* ([1996]2006). Drawing on the key principles of Halliday's systemic functional theory, "along with a broader agenda of concern with 'multimodality'" (Kress and van Leeuwen [1996]2006: vii), they developed a comprehensive, metafunctionally-based, social semiotic framework for the analysis of a wide variety of visual texts and artifacts, ranging from line drawings, maps, photographs, paintings and advertisements to material objects such as sculpture, children's toys and architectural designs. Highly interdisciplinary in outlook and design, *Reading Images* combines social semiotic theory with insights from art history, film, iconography, structural semiotics and cognitive psychology. Kress and van Leeuwen's multisemiotic approach, which aims "to provide inventories of the major compositional structures which have become established as conventions in the course of the history of visual semiotics, and to analyse how they are used to produce meaning by contemporary image-makers" (Kress and van Leeuwen [1996]2006: 1), has proved enduringly influential and continues to inform and underpin the work of multimodal scholars to this day (see also Bateman, Wildfeuer and Hippala 2017).

In *Multimodal Discourse: The Modes and Media of Communication* (2001), Kress and van Leeuwen took a different approach, moving away from close detailed analysis of multimodal texts and artifacts "to explore the common principles behind multimodal communication" (Kress and van Leeuwen 2001: 2). Aimed at identifying the broader semiotic principles that apply across communicative design processes and practices, the book focused more on "discourse" rather than "semiotics" and established a close connection between social semiotics and discourse (Bezemer and Jewitt 2009: 2).

The social semiotic inspired approaches to multimodal discourse analysis proposed by Kress and van Leeuwen have left an "enduring legacy in two strands of discourse studies – multimodal and critical discourse studies, and ultimately served as a catalyst for their merger" (Djonov and Zhao 2017: 3). The approaches have since been adapted and extended, by Kress and van Leeuwen themselves, and colleagues, to the analysis of color (Kress and van Leeuwen 2002), music and sound (van Leeuwen 1999, 2012), typography (van Leeuwen 2006; van Leeuwen and Djonov 2015), children's toys (Machin and van Leeuwen 2009), lighting in film (van Leeuwen and Boeriis 2017) and many other discourse domains.

A complementary application of Halliday's SFT for the analysis of visual and material semiotic artifacts can be found in Michael O'Toole's *The Language of Displayed Art* ([1994]2011). Drawing on insights from film studies, iconography and art history, O'Toole proposes detailed metafunctionally-orientated frameworks for understanding the meaning-making propensity of paintings, sculpture and works of architecture. While, according to Machin (2016: 324–5), perhaps "less influential outside of linguistics than *Reading Images* yet providing the inspiration for much multimodal scholarship from within linguistics … the book is more systemic as is the body of work it has inspired." O'Toole's contributions to multimodality and the process of interpretation in literature and the visual arts are documented in the collection of his works *The Hermeneutic Spiral and Interpretation in Literature and the Visual Arts* (2018).

Kress and van Leeuwen's and O'Toole's approaches to multimodality provided the theoretical foundations for what is now often called multimodal discourse analysis (MDA) (e.g. Jewitt 2014; O'Halloran 2011), also referred to as systemic functional multimodal discourse analysis (SF-MDA) (e.g. O'Halloran 2008; O'Halloran, Tan and Wignell 2019). As O'Halloran (2011: 120) explicates:

> The terminology in MDA is used somewhat loosely at present as concepts and approaches evolve in this relatively new field of study. For example, language and other resources which integrate to create meaning in "multimodal" (or "multisemiotic") phenomena (e.g. print materials, videos, websites, three-dimensional objects and day-to-day events) are variously called "semiotic resources," "modes" and "modalities." MDA itself is referred to as "multimodality," "multimodal analysis," "multimodal semiotics" and "multimodal studies."

SF-MDA extends beyond the simple adaptation of established systemic functional approaches "which were largely developed for modeling discourse and grammatical systems in language" (O'Halloran 2008: 446). SF-MDA is concerned with the theory and analysis of semiotic resources and the semantic expansions that occur as semiotic choices combine in multimodal phenomena. That is, it is concerned with the development – and integration – of different, yet complementary, models and approaches for the study of multimodal semiosis (O'Halloran 2011).

In the approach, key conceptual ideas in SFT, such as Halliday's metafunctional principle, as well as notions of register and genre, realization, stratification and constituency (e.g. Martin 1992, 2002; Martin and White 2005), are combined and extended to other semiotic resources to provide a detailed account of how meaning arises through *combinations of semiotic choices* – that is, from semiotic interactions within and across different resources rather than from individual system choices – and how these meanings can be modeled, analyzed and interpreted (O'Halloran et al. 2019). Complemented and informed by insights from social semiotics, critical discourse analysis, photography, film theory and visual design, this has resulted in the formulation of visual systems that function to structure our experience of the world in terms of participants, processes and circumstances. SF-MDA thus provides an unrivaled platform for modeling, analyzing and interpreting multimodal texts, interactions and events involving language and other resources such as images, scientific symbolism, sound, embodied action and so forth (e.g. O'Halloran 2011;

O'Halloran et al. 2019). Early works in this tradition include O'Halloran's (1999, 2000) multisemiotic (i.e. multimodal) approach to mathematics, which explores the functions and integration of language, images and mathematical symbolism in mathematics texts and mathematics classroom discourse (see O'Halloran 2015).

As Jewitt, Bezemer and O'Halloran (2016) point out, approaches inspired by social semiotics and SFT have gained in popularity over the past decade, giving evidence of the appliability of the theory, its concepts, tools and methods, which have been variously adapted to the study of phenomena such as 3D spaces, museum exhibitions, buildings, websites, online news, body language, children's picture books and disciplinary knowledge (e.g. mathematics, science and history) (e.g. Dreyfus, Hood and Stenglin 2011; Jones and Ventola 2008; Kress et al. 2014; O'Halloran 2008; Unsworth 2008).

As a domain of enquiry, such an approach also encourages "engagement and cross-fertilisation with other disciplines" (O'Halloran 2011: 123). Because of its extensive coverage and amenability, the approach then also becomes accessible to the kinds of ideological arguments and critiques commonly pursued within the field of critical discourse analysis (CDA) (e.g. Machin and Mayr 2012). The influence of the multimodal approach on CDA, which "seeks to reveal buried ideologies in texts, to show how the powerful seek to re-contextualise social practice in their own interests and maintain control over ideology" (Machin 2016: 322), is perhaps most evident in van Leeuwen's *Discourse and Practice: New Tools for Critical Discourse Analysis* (2008). Drawing on a range of ideas from anthropology, sociology and psychology, and bringing together Halliday's concept of "register" and Basil Bernstein's (1990) "recontextualisation principle," van Leeuwen proposes extensive social semiotic frameworks for the critical analysis of discourse practices. Built upon the assumption that all discourses recontextualize social practices (van Leeuwen 2008: vii), developed in earlier work on representations of social actors and social actions (van Leeuwen 1995, 1996), the aim was to show how changes in social practices involving representations of social actors, activities and circumstantial elements take place recursively across sequences of multimodal activities, and thus "reveal how discourses help perpetuate or expose and challenge social boundaries, oppression in inequality" (Djonov and Zhao 2017: 8). The contribution of van Leeuwen's approach to CDA is significant in the sense that it also accounts for the role of nonverbal and multimodal representations in the reinforcement or reconstitution of dominant ideologies in discourse (Djonov and Zhao 2017: 9). Multimodal approaches to CDA inspired by the work of van Leeuwen and others have been found to offer more robust sets of tools than those available for the analysis of language alone and have been adapted and applied to the critical analysis of a range of multimodal discourses, including discourses of globalization in lifestyle and women's magazines (e.g. Machin and Mayr 2012; Machin and van Leeuwen 2007) and discourses of unity and purpose in fascist music (Machin and Richardson 2012). As Bateman, Wildfeuer and Hippala (2017: 68–9) note, multimodal approaches to the study of human communication and social interaction also overlap with and complement other, more linguistically and/or socially orientated approaches to CDA (e.g. Flowerdew and Richardson 2017; Wodak and Meyer 2015), as well as approaches to discourse that employ ethnographic methods, such as conversation analysis, multimodal interaction analysis and multimodal pragmatics.

Conversation analysis (CA), probably the most established of these approaches, was developed in the United States in the mid-1960s and early 1970s by Sacks, Schegloff and Jefferson (see Chapter 6 in this volume). In their groundbreaking publication "A Simplest Systematics for the Organization of Turn-Taking for Conversation" (1974), Sacks et al. provided a detailed account of turn-taking in conversation, with a focus on the role played by both verbal and nonverbal elements used by human beings in social situations. As Bateman, Wildfeuer and Hippala (2017) explicate, CA "began its life addressing the fundamental question of how social order emerges from the moment-by-moment acts of participants in everyday social interactions" (Bateman, Wildfeuer and Hippala 2017: 240).

Although the term "multimodality" was for a long time not endemic in most CA-based work, CA procedures and methodologies have since been appropriated and extended to include a wide range of embodied multimodal resources used in human communication, such as body posture and movement, gaze, gesture, proxemics and so forth, under the umbrella of what is now often called multimodal interaction analysis (e.g. Goodwin 2000; Mondada 2014, 2016; Streek 2009). As Deppermann (2013: 2) notes, "the turn to multimodal interaction is a consequential move for a discipline which aims at a comprehensive understanding of human interaction and which sets as its goal to uncover the practices by which social interaction is produced."

Another body of research that is concerned with the study of human interaction in social situations within the umbrella term multimodal interaction analysis is the work pioneered by Ron Scollon and Suzie Wong Scollon at the beginning of the millennium. Combining interactional sociolinguistics, intercultural communication and multimodal semiotics, their ethnographic-orientated work resulted in a variety of eclectic research strands in intercultural communication, in which microscopic observation and analysis of communication events are placed against macroscopic sociohistorical and cultural changes. Their work, advanced variably as "nexus analysis," "geo-semiotics" and "mediated discourse analysis" (e.g. Scollon 2001; Scollon and Scollon 2003, 2004), provided the foundations for Sigrid Norris's (2004) multimodal framework for understanding and investigating the multiple modes and resources used in human interaction. Deliberately crossing the "boundaries between linguistics, non-verbal behavior and the material world," Norris aimed to show how the different research strands can be combined purposefully to study human communication practices in all their complexity (Norris 2004: 10).

Additional transdisciplinary approaches to the analysis of multimodal communication have been developed from within the perspective of pragmatics, as proposed by Pennock-Speck and Del Saz-Rubio (2013), for example, who combine Brown and Levinson's (1987) verbal politeness strategies together with a detailed analysis of facework (e.g. Goffman 1967) as realized through multimodal modes of communication in their analysis of British television advertisements; and O'Halloran, Tan and E (2014), who demonstrate the usefulness of a multimodal pragmatics approach by combining pragmatics concepts with social semiotic theory to explore how informal, casual online conversation, visual resources and action are integrated to accomplish formal learning tasks in collaborative computer-mediated communication.

Perspectives on multimodality also emerged from within cognitive linguistics and cognitive linguistic critical discourse studies (CL-CDS). Hart (2016), for example, argues that, in these disciplines, meaning-making is traditionally understood as involving the construction of what he calls "fully modal" mental representations (Hart 2016: 336), and shows how insights from multimodal discourse analysis could be usefully integrated within CL-CDS to illuminate the connections between language, image and ideology in the creation of meaning (also see Chapter 9 this volume).

In the same manner, scholars with an interest in Cognitive Metaphor Theory have long incorporated insights from the field of multimodal studies, as demonstrated, for example, in Forceville's (1996) and Forceville and Urios-Aparisi's (2009) work on creative and conceptual metaphors in advertisements, cartoons, films and comics, as well as other discourse genres (e.g. see also Machin 2016).

In this section, we have provided an overview of existing multimodal approaches developed from different analytical, theoretical and methodological perspectives. At the same time, we have tried to show that multimodality can also act as a uniting force for scholars working within different disciplines. Many of the multimodal approaches we cited have gained new insights from blending and absorbing analytical and methodological perspectives from other fields within their own research traditions, actively paving the way for further theorizing and testing applications of multimodality in this rapidly expanding field.

12.3 Issues and Ongoing Debates

Added to the challenge of the emergence of multimodality as a field of research in its own right, multimodal representations and practices are themselves undergoing rapid change (Jewitt 2014: 2). One of the most pressing issues faced by multimodal researchers today is the fact that multimodality as a field of enquiry is becoming increasingly data-driven. While only a decade ago it may have been possible to employ traditional, largely text-based analytical methods, for example, by transcribing and presenting findings and observations sorted according to certain criteria in the form of simple lists or tables (e.g. see also Bateman, Wildfeuer and Hippala 2017), multimodal analysis and transcription in the digital age has become a complex and challenging task. In this and the following sections, we discuss some of the digital approaches and methods that have been developed for the analysis of multimodal discourse, specifically dynamic media such as film and videos, and the challenges in dealing with large collections of multimodal data.

Multimodal data, as represented by webpages, film and video, for example, is dynamic, multifaceted and multidimensional. In order to capture such rich multimodal phenomena in all their complexity, new digital tools and methods are required which can "accompany data analysis at all stages: organising data according to coding categories, exploring the data by annotating it and searching for content, integrating data from various sources, as well as helping interpretations by performing searches for patterns of varying sophistication" (Bateman, Wildfeuer and Hippala 2017: 162).

One example of such a tool are the purpose-built software applications for text, image and video analysis *Multimodal Analysis Image* (2012)[1] and *Multimodal Analysis Video* (2013),[2] developed by Kay O'Halloran and her team in the Multimodal Analysis Lab at the Interactive and Digital Media Institute, National University of Singapore. The software applications are specifically designed for exploring semiotic interactions in static (e.g. written texts and images) and dynamic media (e.g. videos), and include facilities for importing and organizing video files; creating and editing catalogues of system frameworks and system choices for video annotation; storing and consolidating projects of analyses; annotating and analyzing videos by creating time-stamped annotations; visualizing combinations of multimodal choices; and exporting data from the analyses to Excel spreadsheets for further data processing and visualization. Rather than surmising how multimodal semiosis takes place through the limited, labor-intensive, manual analysis of a small sample of multimodal texts, O'Halloran and colleagues have demonstrated variously (e.g. O'Halloran, Tan and Wignell 2016; Tan, O'Halloran and Wignell 2016; Tan, Wignell and O'Halloran 2016) that using purpose-built software for the analysis of rich multimodal data sets not only allows analysts to observe the complex interplay between different semiotic resources as they unfold over time and space

---

[1] http://multimodal-analysis.com/products/multimodal-analysis-image/index.html
[2] http://multimodal-analysis.com/products/multimodal-analysis-video/index.html

but also enables them to base their theories, analyses and interpretations on empirical evidence.

Other scholars have similarly noted the growing body of research in recent years that is concerned with investigating how multimodal phenomena, particularly dynamic audiovisual media such as film, can be explored empirically by utilizing automated or semi-automated analytical techniques (e.g. Bateman 2014; Wildfeuer and Bateman 2016; Wildfeuer 2014), which can provide a wealth of information that traditional manual analysis could not have been able to reveal.

12.4 Implications

The proliferation of new digital tools and techniques marks an important shift "away from one-off, single studies to larger-scale research" (Bateman, Wildfeuer and Hippala 2017: 154). However, it also presents new challenges, in particular when dealing with large sets of data. Large-scale analyses of language, images and videos still consider the potential meanings of these modalities separately, whereas in reality meaning arises from a complex integration of the contributions made by linguistic, visual and aural choices. As O'Halloran and colleagues have shown, the use of such existing tools and techniques remains insufficient for capturing this complexity in large data sets, and for mapping discourse patterns and trends over time. Dealing with large amounts of multimodal data in a principled way that is supportive of empirical research also carries methodological implications (e.g. see also Bateman, Wildfeuer and Hippala 2017: 154), especially since current computational approaches and tools available for the analysis of large data sets continue to be grounded in content- and/or platform-focused analyses, such as social network analysis. While such analyses can offer important insights, they are predominantly language-based and lack theoretically well-founded methods for addressing the meanings that emerge from juxtapositions of visual messages, such as images and videos. As a consequence, they remain insufficient for understanding the impact of multimodal messages and their impact on society effects within a variety of contexts. To address these issues, studies have begun to integrate multimodal analysis with computational techniques. O'Halloran, Chua and Podlasov (2014) demonstrate, for example, how interactive visualizations can be used as a valuable resource for mapping socio-cultural trends in their investigation into variations of language and image use in urban Singapore, while another study (Podlasov and O'Halloran 2014) illustrates how the integrated automated analysis of photographs, data visualization techniques using self-organizing maps and topology learning algorithms can be feasibly combined with multimodal analysis to map patterns and trends in Japanese street fashion. These studies and others, for example Cao and O'Halloran's (2014) large-scale investigation of photo shooting patterns across diverse locations and cultures, demonstrate how different levels of analysis (i.e. multimodal discourse, context and culture) can be integrated using mixed methods digital approaches.

Building upon this work, O'Halloran and colleagues (2017, 2019) propose a mixed methods approach that integrates qualitative methods of multimodal discourse analysis, informed by Halliday's systemic functional linguistic theory and social semiotics, with quantitative methods of data mining and information visualization. This approach has already been applied successfully in their investigations of the meanings arising from text and images in violent extremist discourse (e.g. O'Halloran et al. 2017; Wignell et al. 2017; Tan et al. 2018).

12.5 Future Directions

New computational methods to multimodal discourse analysis, as used and proposed by O'Halloran and colleagues, and others (e.g. Bateman et al. 2016, Bateman, Wildfeuer and Hillapa 2017, Bateman et al. 2019), not only demand a rather different mindset to that commonly found in more traditional fields of study but also require interdisciplinary collaboration with the wider scientific community. Researchers from the humanities, arts and social sciences have rich theories and conceptual frameworks for investigating human behavior and associated sociocultural influences, but not necessarily the capabilities to move beyond traditional research methods that involve typically manual analysis and qualitative interpretation of a small number of texts, interactions and events. These methods are insufficient, given the ways in which individuals, groups and societies function in the digital world and the available data today. At the same time, while science-based disciplines have methods for big data analytics, they do not possess the necessary conceptual frameworks and approaches for understanding the human aspects of the phenomena being studied: for example, approaches employing big data-based methodologies to human interactions are grounded in content and/or platform-focused analyses that are inadequate for understanding the impact of human communications and their effects within a variety of contexts critical for shaping public opinion and actions.

Going forward, O'Halloran and colleagues propose to further advance the mixed methods in order to demonstrate how automated techniques for language, image and video processing can be enhanced through a context-based multimodal approach to human communication. Supported by theories and methodologies from cultural sociology, political science, visual communication theory and critical discourse analysis, and computational techniques, the methodology to be developed involves using MDA for investigating the meaning arising from the integration of language, images and other resources in texts, interactions and events, coupled with state-of-the-art methods in computer vision, natural language understanding and machine learning. As O'Halloran, Tan and Wignell (2016) explain, the proposed approach endeavors to resolve the gap that exists between decontextualized big data approaches on the one hand and highly-detailed, contextualized, close analyses of small samples of multimodal texts on the other hand, by incorporating and building upon recently developed and emerging multidisciplinary theories and techniques of multimodal analysis, and enhanced further by theoretical and methodological models from the fields of social sciences, visual communication and CDA perspectives.

12.6 Summary

This chapter has been concerned with the issue of multimodality. In Section 12.1, we introduced some definitions of the term and its background. This was followed, in Section 12.2, by an overview of different multimodal approaches that have been developed from different discourse analytical perspectives, including social semiotics, systemic functional linguistics, CDA, conversation analysis, interaction analysis and others. In Section 12.3, we looked at some of the issues related to the complexity of multimodal research in the digital age, and the digital approaches that have been developed to handle complex multimodal data, such as encountered in the analysis of film and video. In Section 12.4, we discussed the challenges and implications for multimodal analysis in dealing with "big data," including the development of mixed methods approaches and computational techniques. The emerging trends in "big data" approaches to multimodal analysis with an outlook toward the future were discussed in Section 12.5.

Further Reading

Bateman, J., Wildfeuer, J. and Hiippala, T. (2017). *Multimodality Foundations, Research and Analysis: A Problem-Oriented Introduction*. Berlin: Mouton de Gruyter.

This offers an introduction to multimodality from a practice-based perspective and approaches multimodal phenomena from different theoretical perspectives and disciplinary angles.

Jewitt, C. (2014). *The Routledge Handbook of Multimodal Analysis*, 2nd ed. London: Routledge.

This provides a comprehensive introduction to various theoretical approaches to multimodality from different disciplines (e.g. visual studies, anthropology, conversation analysis, sociocultural theory, etc.).

Jewitt, C., Bezemer, J. and O'Halloran, K. L. (2016). *Introducing Multimodality*. London/New York: Routledge.

This presents an accessible introduction to multimodality that illuminates the potential of multimodal research for understanding the ways in which people communicate. Offering a wide range of examples, clear practical support and a glossary of terms, the book is an ideal reference guide for beginners in multimodal analysis.

Kress, G. and van Leeuwen, T. ([1996]2006). *Reading Images: The Grammar of Visual Design*, 2nd ed. London: Routledge.

This is an essential resource for researchers interested in multimodal communication. Drawing on an enormous range of examples including children's drawings, textbook illustrations, photojournalism, advertising images, fine art, websites, as well as three-dimensional material artefacts such as sculpture, the book presents a comprehensive account of the ways in which images communicate meaning.

Machin, D. and Mayr, A. (2012). *How to Do Critical Discourse Analysis: A Multimodal Introduction*. London: Sage.

This presents a systematic toolkit of theories, concepts and techniques for carrying out critical discourse analysis of language and images. Based on a variety of case studies and examples drawn from a range of traditional and new media genres, the book is an essential resource for beginners in critical discourse analysis.

References

Barthes, R. ([1957]1987). *Mythologies*. New York: Hill & Wang.
　(1977). *Image, Music, Text*. London: Fontana Press.
Bateman, J. (2014). Looking for What Counts in Film Analysis: A Program of Empirical Research. In D. Machin (ed.) *Visual Communication*. Berlin: Mouton de Gruyter. 301–30.
Bateman, J. and Schmidt, K.-H. (2012). *Multimodal Film Analysis: How Films Mean*. London/New York: Routledge.
Bateman, J., McDonald, D., Hiippala, T., Couto-Vale, D. and Costetchi, E. (2019). Systemic Functional Linguistics and Computation: New Directions, New Challenges. In G. Thompson, W. L. Bowcher, L. Fontaine and D. Schönthal (eds.) *The Cambridge Handbook of Systemic Functional Linguistics*. Cambridge: Cambridge University Press. 561–86.
Bateman, J., Tseng, C. I., Seizov, O., Jacobs, A., Lüdtke, A., Müller, M. G. and Herzog, O. (2016). Towards Next-Generation Visual Archives: Image, Film and Discourse. *Visual Studies* 31(2): 131–54.

Bateman, J., Wildfeuer, J. and Hiippala, T. (2017). *Multimodality Foundations, Research and Analysis: A Problem-Oriented Introduction*. Berlin: De Gruyter Mouton.

Bernstein, B. (1990). *Class, Codes and Control, Vol. IV: The Structuring of Pedagogic Discourse*. London: Routledge.

Bezemer, J. and Jewitt, C. (2009). Social Semiotics. In J.-O. Östman, J. Verschueren and E. Versluys (eds.) *Handbook of Pragmatics: 2009 Installment*. Amsterdam: John Benjamins.

Brown, P. and Levinson, S. D. (1987). *Politeness: Some Universals in Language Usage*. Cambridge: Cambridge University Press.

Cao, Y. and O'Halloran, K. L. (2014). Learning Human Photo Shooting Patterns from Large-Scale Community Photo Collections. *Multimedia Tools and Applications* 24: 11499–516.

Deppermann, A. (2013). Multimodal Interaction from a Conversation Analytic Perspective. *Journal of Pragmatics* 46(1): 1–7.

Djonov, E. and Zhao, S. (2014). *Critical Multimodal Studies of Popular Discourse*. New York: Routledge.

  (2017). Social Semiotics: A Theorist and a Theory in Retrospect and Prospect. In S. Zhao, E. Djonov, A. Björkvall and M. Boeriis (eds.) *Advancing Multimodal and Critical Discourse Studies: Interdisciplinary Research Inspired by Theo Van Leeuwen's Social Semiotics*. London/New York: Routledge. 1–18.

Dreyfus, S., Hood, S. and Stenglin, M. (2011). *Semiotic Margins: Meaning in Multimodalities*. London/New York: Continuum.

Flowerdew, J. and Richardson, J. (2017). *Routledge Handbook of Critical Discourse Studies*. London: Routledge.

Forceville, C. (1996). *Pictorial Metaphor in Advertising*. London: Routledge.

Forceville, C. and Urios-Aparisi, E. (2009). *Multimodal Metaphor*, Vol. 11. Walter de Gruyter.

Goffman, E. (1967). *Interactional Ritual: Essays on Face to Face Behaviour*. New York: Garden City.

  (1981). *Forms of Talk*. Oxford: Blackwell.

Goodwin, C. (2000). Action and Embodiment within Situated Human Interaction. *Journal of Pragmatics* 32(10): 1489–522.

Hall, E. T. (1968). Proxemics. *Current Anthropology* 9(2/3): 83–108.

Halliday, M. A. K. (1978). *Language as Social Semiotic*. London: Edward Arnold.

  (1994). *An Introduction to Functional Grammar*, 2nd ed. London: Edward Arnold.

Halliday, M. A. K. and Matthiessen, C. M. I. M. (2014). *Halliday's Introduction to Functional Grammar*. London/New York: Routledge.

Halliday, M. A. K. (2009). *Collected Works of M. A. K. Halliday*, ed. by J. J. Webster. Vol. 10. London: Bloomsbury Academic.

  (2018). *Halliday in the 21st Century: Collected Works of M. A. K. Halliday*, ed. by J. J. Webster. Vol. 11. London: Bloomsbury Academic.

Hart, C. (2016). The Visual Basis of Linguistic Meaning and Its Implications for Critical Discourse Studies: Integrating Cognitive Linguiic and Multimodal Methods. *Discourse & Society* 27(3): 335–50.

Hodge, R. I. V. and Kress, G. (1988). *Social Semiotics*. Cambridge: Polity Press.

Jewitt, C. (2014). *The Routledge Handbook of Multimodal Analysis*, 2nd ed. London: Routledge.

Jewitt, C., Bezemer, J. and O'Halloran, K. L. (2016). *Introducing Multimodality*. London/New York: Routledge.

Jones, C. and Ventola, E. (2008). *From Language to Multimodality: New Developments in the Study of Ideational Meaning*. London: Equinox.

Kendon, A. (2004). *Gesture: Visible Action as Utterance*. Cambridge: Cambridge University Press.

Kress, G. (2010) *Multimodality: A Social Semiotic Approach to Contemporary Communication*. London: Routledge.

Kress, G. and van Leeuwen, T. ([1996]2006). *Reading Images: The Grammar of Visual Design*. London: Routledge.

—— (2001). *Multimodal Discourse: The Modes and Media of Contemporary Communication*. London: Arnold.

—— (2002). Colour as a Semiotic Mode: Notes for a Grammar of Colour. *Visual Communication* 1(3): 343–68.

Kress, G., Jewitt, C. L., Ogborn, J. and Tsatsarelis, C. (2014). *Multimodal Teaching and Learning: The Rhetorics of the Science Classroom*, 2nd ed. New York: Bloomsbury Academic.

Machin, D. (2007). *Introduction to Multimodal Analysis*. London: Hodder Arnold.

—— (2013). What Is Multimodal Critical Discourse Studies? *Critical Discourse Studies* 10(4): 347–55.

—— (2016). The Need for a Social and Affordance-Driven Multimodal Critical Discourse Studies. *Discourse & Society* 27(3): 322–34.

Machin, D. and Mayr, A. (2012). *How to Do Critical Discourse Analysis: A Multimodal Introduction*. London: Sage.

Machin, D. and Richardson, J. E. (2012). Discourses of Unity and Purpose in the Sounds of Fascist Music: A Multimodal Approach. *Critical Discourse Studies* 9(4): 329–45.

Machin, D. and van Leeuwen, T. (2007). *Global Media Discourse: A Critical Introduction*. New York: Taylor & Francis.

—— (2009). Toy As Discourse: Children's War Toys and the War on Terror. *Critical Discourse Studies* 6(1): 51–64.

Martin, J. R. (1992). *English Text: System and Structure*. Amsterdam: Benjamins.

—— (2002). Meaning beyond the Clause: SFL Perspectives. *Annual Review of Applied Linguistics* 22: 52–74.

Martin, J. R. and White, P. R. R. (2005). *The Language of Evaluation: Appraisal in English*. London: Palgrave Macmillan.

Mondada, L. (2014). The Local Constitution of Multimodal Resources for Social Interaction. *Journal of Pragmatics* 65: 137–56.

(2016). Challenges of Multimodality: Language and the Body in Social Interaction. *Journal of Sociolinguistics* 20(3): 336–66.

Norris, S. (2004). *Analyzing Multimodal Interaction: A Methodological Framework*. London/New York: Routledge.

O'Halloran, K. L. (1999). Towards a Systemic Functional Analysis of Multisemiotic Mathematics Texts. *Semiotica* 124(1/2): 1–29.

(2000). Classroom Discourse in Mathematics: A Multisemiotic Analysis. *Linguistics and Education* 10(3): 359–88.

(2004). *Multimodal Discourse Analysis*. London/New York: Continuum.

(2008). Systemic Functional-Multimodal Discourse Analysis (SF-MDA): Constructing Ideational Meaning Using Language and Visual Imagery. *Visual Communication* 7: 443–75.

(2011). Multimodal Discourse Analysis. In K. Hyland and B. Paltridge (eds.) *Bloomsbury Companion to Discourse Analysis*. London: Bloomsbury. 120–37.

(2015). The Language of Learning Mathematics: A Multimodal Perspective. *Journal of Mathematical Behaviour* 40(Part A): 63–74.

O'Halloran, K. L. and Smith, B. A. (2011). *Multimodal Studies: Exploring Issues and Domains*. New York/London: Routledge.

O'Halloran, K. L., Chua, A. and Podlasov, A. (2014). The Role of Images in Social Media Analytics: A Multimodal Digital Humanities Approach. In D. Machin (ed.), *Visual Communication*. Berlin: Gruyter. 565–88.

O'Halloran, Kay L., Tan, Sabine, and E, Marissa K. L. (2014). Multimodal Pragmatics. In K. Schneider and A. Barron (eds.) *Pragmatics of Discourse*. Berlin: De Gruyter Mouton. 239–68.

O'Halloran, K. L., Tan, S., Pham, D.-S., Bateman, J. and Vande Moere, A. (2018). A Digital Mixed Methods Research Design: Integrating Multimodal Analysis with Data Mining and Information Visualization for Big Data Analytics. *Journal of Mixed Methods Research* 12(1): 11–30. DOI: 10.1177/1558689816651015.

O'Halloran, K. L., Tan, S. and Wignell, P. (2016). Inter-Semiotic Translation as Resemiotization: A Multimodal Perspective. *Signata* [Special Issue on Translating: Signs, Texts, Practices] 7(1): 199–229.

(2019). SFL and Multimodal Discourse Analysis. In G. Thompson, W. L. Bowcher, L. Fontaine and D. Schönthal (eds.) *The Cambridge Handbook of Systemic Functional Linguistics*. Cambridge: Cambridge University Press. 433–61.

O'Halloran, K. L., Tan, S., Wignell, P. and Lange, R. (2017). Multimodal Recontextualisations of Images in Violent Extremist Discourse. In S. Zhao, E. Djonov, A. Björkvall and M. Boeriis (eds.) *Advancing Multimodal and Critical Discourse Studies: Interdisciplinary Research Inspired by Theo Van Leeuwen's Social Semiotics*. London/New York: Routledge. 181–202.

O'Toole, M. ([1994] 2011). *The Language of Displayed Art*, 2nd ed. London/New York: Routledge.

Peirce, C. S. (1984). *Writings of Charles S. Peirce: A Chronological Edition, Vol. 2: 1867–1871*. Bloomington: Indiana University Press.

Pennock-Speck, B. and Del Saz-Rubio, M. M. (2013). A Multimodal Analysis of Facework Strategies in a Corpus of Charity Ads on British Television. *Journal of Pragmatics* 49(1): 38–56.

Podlasov, A. and O'Halloran, K. L. (2014). Japanese Street Fashion for Young People: A Multimodal Digital Humanities Approach for Identifying Socio-Cultural Patterns and Trends. In E. Djonov and S. Zhao (eds.) *Critical Multimodal Studies of Popular Culture*. New York: Routledge. 71–90.

Saussure, F. de ([1916]/1983). *Course in General Linguistics*, trans. by R. Harris. London: Duckworth.

Sacks, H., Schegloff, E. A. and Jefferson, G. (1974). A Simplest Systematics for the Organization of Turn-Taking for Conversation. *Language* 50(4): 696–735.

Scollon, R. (2001). *Mediated Discourse: The Nexus of Practice*. London: Routledge.

Scollon, R. and Scollon, S. W. (2003). *Discourses in Place: Language in the Material World*. London: Routledge.

―― (2004). *Nexus Analysis*. London: Routledge.

Sindoni, M. G., Wildfeuer, J. and O'Halloran, K. L. (2017). *Mapping Multimodal Performance Studies*. London/New York: Routledge.

Streeck, J. (2009). *Gesturecraft*. Amsterdam: Benjamins.

Tan, S., O'Halloran, K. L. and Wignell, P. (2016). Multimodal Research: Addressing the Complexity of Multimodal Environments and the Challenges for CALL. *ReCALL* [Special Issue on Multimodal Environments in CALL] 28(3): 253–73.

Tan, S., O'Halloran, K. L., Wignell, P., Chai, K. and Lange, R. (2018). A Multimodal Mixed Methods Approach for Examining Recontextualisation Patterns of Violent Extremist Images in Online Media *Discourse, Context & Media* 21: 18–35.

Tan, S., Wignell, P. and O'Halloran, K. L. (2016). From Book to Stage to Screen: Semiotic Transformations of Gothic Horror Genre Conventions. *Social Semiotics* [Special Issue: The Languages of Performing Arts: Semiosis, Communication and Meaning-Making] 26 (4): 404–23.

Unsworth, L. (2008). *Multimodal Semiotics: Functional Analysis in Contexts of Education*. New York: Continuum.

van Leeuwen, T. (1995). Representing Social Action. *Discourse and Society* 6 (1): 81–106.

―― (1996). The Representation of Social Actors. In C. R. Caldas-Coulthard and M. Coulthard (eds.) *Texts and Practices: Readings in Critical Discourse Analysis*. London: Routledge. 32–70.

―― (1999). *Speech, Music, Sound*. London: MacMillan.

(2006). Towards a Semiotics of Typography. *Information Design Journal* 14 (20): 139–55.

(2008). *Discourse and Practice: New Tools for Critical Discourse Analysis*. London: Oxford University Press.

(2012). The Critical Analysis of Musical Discourse. *Critical Discourse Studies* 9(4): 319–28.

van Leeuwen, T. and Boeriis, M. (2017). Towards a Semiotics of Film Lighting. In J. Wildfeuer and J. A. Bateman (eds.) *Film Text Analysis: New Perspectives on the Analysis of Filmic Meaning*. New York/Abingdon: Routledge. 24–45.

van Leeuwen, T. and Djonov, E. (2015). Notes towards a Semiotics of Kinetic Typography. *Social Semiotics* 25(2): 244–53.

Wignell, P., Tan, S., O'Halloran, K. L. and Lange, R. (2017). A Mixed Methods Empirical Examination of Changes in Emphasis and Style in the Extremist Magazines *Dabiq* and *Rumiyah*. *Perspectives on Terrorism* 11 (2): 2–20.

Wildfeuer, J. (2014). *Film Discourse Interpretation: Towards a New Paradigm for Multimodal Film Analysis*, Vol. 9. London/New York: Routledge.

Wildfeuer, J. and Bateman, J. A. (2016). *Film Text Analysis: New Perspectives on the Analysis of Filmic Meaning*, Vol. 50. New York: Taylor & Francis.

Wodak, R. and Meyer, M. (2015). *Methods of Critical Discourse Analysis*, 3rd ed. London: Sage.

13

Sign Theory and the Materiality of Discourse

Jack Sidnell

13.1 Overview of the Topic

To understand both the actual materiality of discourse and the historical circumstances within which it was dematerialized, we must go to the very foundations of linguistic thinking, as this developed in theories of the sign. It was in his conception of the sign, after all, that Ferdinand de Saussure effected a radical break between language on the one hand and the (material) world on the other. In broad outline, at least, Saussure's argument was not particularly novel. Locke, for instance, had proposed that words were the signs of ideas or conceptions (see Hacking 1975; Short 2007). What Saussure contributed was a systematic theory built upon the premise that the physical and material properties of language are accidental, contingent and of little or no theoretical interest. Saussure's Cartesian dichotomies between *langue* and *parole* and between signifier and signified provided a basis not only for a synchronic theory of language but also for a structuralist semiology that identified such binary oppositions at the very heart not just of culture but of the human mind itself. But Saussure's *Cours* also attracted critique. Perhaps the most important of these, at least for present purposes, is that elaborated by Valentin Vološinov ([1929] 1986). As we will see, while Vološinov challenged many of Saussure's central ideas including, to some extent, the latter's conception of the sign, he ultimately accepted the most basic underlying assumptions that served to dematerialize language.

By the time Saussure gave his famous course, Charles Sanders Peirce had been thinking about signs along radically different lines for more than thirty years. Peirce, who died in 1914, continuously revised his ideas about signs throughout his life and over hundreds of manuscripts, only a small number of which were published during his lifetime. Unlike Saussure, Peirce developed his theory of signs as a contribution to logic (i.e. the systematic study of valid forms of inference), and it thus does not assume a reductive, immaterial conception of language. Indeed, Peirce was more or less forced, in the course of his investigations, to reckon with the ways in which signs, including those of language, are both a part of, and capable of articulating with, the world. Whereas Saussure was a nominalist, Peirce was a realist and a pragmatist, and this led him to argue for a radically alternate conception of signification.

Peirce's conception of the sign and of semiosis provides the basis for a novel sense of the materiality of discourse, argument I attempt to make in what follows, first through a schematic sketch of semiotic theory and second by applying the results of this survey to a small number of empirical case studies.

13.1.1 Ferdinand de Saussure

Saussure's *Course in General Linguistics* begins with a short history of the discipline before turning to the problem of how to delimit the object of study. Here, in a preview of the larger argument that he is to make, he notes that "[e]verything in language is basically psychological, including its material and mechanical manifestations" ([1916]1959: 6) and that, for this reason, linguistics might be seen as a branch of social psychology. He defers discussion of this possibility, suggesting that the line between linguistics and the study of the "physiology of sounds" is much easier to draw. Then, in a striking example of what Latour (1993; see also Keane 2007: 23) calls "purification," Saussure (1959: 7) pronounces: "The thing that constitutes language is ... unrelated to the phonic character of the linguistic sign." The course of lectures that follows can be read as a single, sustained argument for this claim, an argument that begins with the famous dichotomies between signifier and signified, between individual and society, and between synchrony ("established system," "existing institution") and diachrony ("evolution," "product of the past"). The presence of these dualities and the multiple perspectives they seem to offer lead Saussure to propose (1959: 8) that whereas "other sciences work with objects that are given in advance," linguistics must begin by delimiting the object of study. This he does by isolating language (*langue*) from speech:

> But what is language [*langue*]? It is not to be confused with human speech [*langage*], of which it is only a definite part, though certainly an essential one .... Language ... is a self-contained whole and a principle of classification. As soon as we give language first place among the facts of speech, we introduce a natural order into a mass that lends itself to no other classification. (Saussure 1959: 9)

It is this cordoning off of the linguistic system (*langue*) and its internally constituted elements and values that allows Saussure to excise any consideration of the material or physical properties of the sign itself. As he

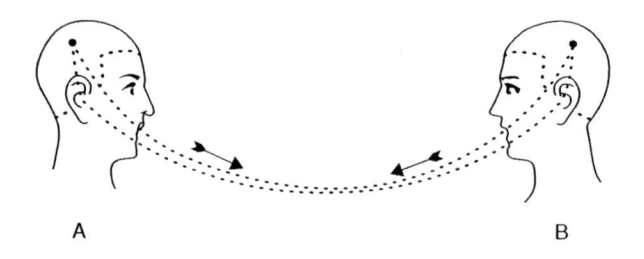

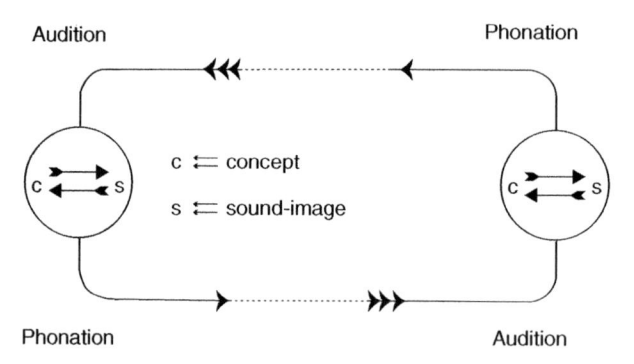

Figure 13.1 Two representations of "the speech circuit" (Saussure 1959: 11, 12)

says (1959: 10): "language is a convention, and the nature of the sign that is agreed upon does not matter."

Saussure then sets himself the task of separating "from the whole of speech the part that belongs to language" (1959: 11), which he attempts to do by imagining the components of "the speech circuit." Here we get the famous diagram of two talking heads connected by a looping, dotted line (figure 13.1). By means of this analysis, Saussure proposes to have isolated the "physical (sound waves)" and the "physiological (phonation and audition)" from the psychological parts which he describes as "word-images and concepts" (1959: 12). Language, Saussure concludes, is a "well-defined object" that can be "localized in the limited segment of the speaking-circuit where an auditory image becomes associated with a concept" (1959: 14). Indeed, language, he goes on to say, "is a system of signs in which the only essential thing is the union of meanings and sound-images, and in which both parts of the sign are psychological" (1959: 15). These signs, the only truly *linguistic* realities, have their "seat in the brain" (1959: 15).

Having in this way defined language, Saussure continues the work of purification focusing specifically on the sign itself. The sign is composed of two parts, Saussure tells us, the signifier and the signified, and the relation between them is arbitrary. Saussure proceeds with a series of examples, one of which is that the idea of "sister" is linked to "the succession of sounds s-ö-r" (in the case of French *sœur*) solely by convention and that the fact that "it could be represented equally by just any other sequence is proved by differences among languages" (1959: 68). As Benveniste (1971) pointed out, Saussure is playing a shell-game here. According to his own arguments about value and the system-internal set of relations by which it is conferred on any given lexical item, other languages don't (and couldn't possibly) have an exactly parallel sign, one in which some other set of sounds is linked to the same concept as that tied to the French *sœur*. As such, the arbitrariness, to the extent that it is real, is between the signifier and the thing in the world to which the word may be used to make reference (what Saussure calls the word's *signification* and what we today describe as the referential extension, denotation or denotatum). Be that as it may, Saussure treats arbitrariness as the *sine qua non* of the linguistic sign and spends some time dealing with those phenomena he sees as possible exceptions to the rule such as onomatopoeia and interjections.[1] These he characterizes as "limited in number" (1959: 69), "of secondary importance" (1959: 69) and tending, over time, toward arbitrariness. He also briefly considers "natural signs" such as pantomime but suggests that even if these are to be included within the future science of semiology, "its main concern will still be the whole group of systems grounded on the arbitrariness of the sign" (1959: 68). In fact, according to Saussure (1959: 68), "every means of expression used in society" is based on convention. Orientalizing, he proposes that even in the Chinese custom of "bowing down to the ground nine times" to greet the emperor, it is the "rule and not the intrinsic value of the gestures that obliges one to use them" (1959: 68). The example is instructive as it shows the way Saussure confounds the thirdness exhibited by the sign – the bowing custom is a legisign, that being the sense in which it is a "rule" – with the thirdness exhibited by the relation of sign to object – it's not a symbol but rather an index (on thirdness, legisign, symbol, index and other Peircean notions, see Section 13.1.3).

Having established the arbitrary, wholly psychological sign as the elemental fact of language, Saussure's final, and decisive, theoretical move is to show how such signs are linked together to form a "system of pure values" (1959: 111). Here Saussure begins by claiming that thought, without connection to words, is a "shapeless and indistinct mass" (1959: 111), "a vague, uncharted nebula" (1959: 112). Words, then, do not represent already preexisting ideas; rather word-images and the concepts they are associated with are mutually delimiting. Saussure's well-known analogy here is to a sheet of paper – "thought is the front and the sound the back" (1959: 113) – but the key idea is that the value of any given item is determined by its relations with the others. As he puts it, "language is a system of interdependent terms in which the value of each term results solely from the simultaneous presence of the others" (1959: 114). In this

---

[1] Saussure (1959: 69) writes: "[F]or most interjections we can show that there is no fixed bond between their signified and their signifier. We need only compare two languages on this point to see how much such expressions differ from one language to the next." Some sense of just how wrong Saussure was about this can be had from Dingemanse, Torreira and Enfield (2013).

way, Saussure doubles down on the arbitrariness argument suggesting that "[w]ithin the same language, all words used to express related ideas limit each other reciprocally" (1959: 116) and that "synonyms like French *redouter* 'dread,' *craindre* 'fear,' and *avoir peur* 'be afraid' have value only through their opposition" (1959: 114). If words name preexisting concepts, Saussure asserts, we should find exact equivalents across different languages. But instead of "pre-existing ideas," language consists entirely of "values emanating from the system" (1959: 117) and "concepts are purely differential ... defined not by their positive content but negatively by their relations with the other terms of the system. Their most precise characteristic is in being what the others are not" (1959: 117).

As Jakobson (1978) noted, Saussure in this way extended an argument from phonology, in which values *are* purely differential, to the whole of language. The result is a picture of a perfect system in which, as Meillet (1925: 12) put it, "tout se tient." Moreover, this wholly psychological system, which exists in the brains of individuals and yet is nevertheless somehow fundamentally social, stands apart from and in a fundamentally arbitrary relation with a world which it is used, as its sole purpose, to represent.[2] The effect is a total dematerialization of language – language is cut off from the world at every pass and emerges as a purely psychological, conceptual and, although Saussure (1959: 15, 102) denied it, abstract entity.

13.1.2 Valentin Vološinov

Saussure's critics are many, but it was Vološinov who perhaps most directly challenged the notion of language as a system isolated from the social world of its users. Vološinov takes Saussure as the prime representative of the approach he labels "abstract objectivism," the exclusive focus of which is the "self-identical forms comprising the immutable system of language" (1986: 56). But, Vološinov (1986: 65) asks, can such a system "be considered a real entity?". In his answer to this question, Vološinov begins by noting that "if we were to look at language in a truly objective way ... we would discover no inert system of self-identical norms. Instead we would find ourselves witnessing the ceaseless generation of language norms" (1986: 66). And yet, even if from an objective point of view there is no system of self-identical norms, perhaps such a system exists "with respect to the subjective consciousness of members of some particular community" (1986: 66). But even this, according to Vološinov, is untenable. Rather,

> the speaker's focus of attention is brought about in line with the particular, concrete utterance he is making. What matters to him is applying

---

[2] Irvine (1989: 248) writes: "Perhaps one of the most durable legacies of Saussure's *Course in General Linguistics* is its radical separation of the denotational sign (qua sign) from the material world."

a normatively identical form in some particular concrete context..... [W]hat is important for the speaker is not that it is a stable and always self-equivalent signal, but that it is an always changeable and adaptable sign.
(1986: 67)

In sum, abstract objectivism, in positing a system of self-identical norms, reifies language to a level divorced from its use in actual, ideological contexts.

Against the view of abstract objectivism, Vološinov suggests that language and social life are inextricably linked via ideology: "Everything ideological possesses meaning: it represents, depicts, or stands for something lying outside itself. In other words, it is a sign. Without signs, there is no ideology" (1986: 9). Here, Vološinov suggests that all ideology is semiotic. Later, he asserts: "The domain of ideology coincides with the domain of signs. They equate with one another" (1986: 10). This implies that language, consisting as it does of signs, does not exist as a system of self-identical norms but rather as a dynamic medium of social intercourse that not only reflects but also, as Vološinov insists, refracts reality (1986: 10). Although language "has the capacity to register all the transitory, delicate, momentary phases of social change" (1986: 19), Vološinov's focus is on the intersection of "differently oriented social interests within one and the same sign community" (1986: 23), which he glosses as "the class struggle." He goes on: "The ruling class strives to impart a supraclass, eternal character to the ideological sign, to extinguish or drive inward the struggle between social value judgments which occurs in it, to make the sign uniaccentual" (1986: 23). This conceptualization of language and ideology allows Vološinov to resituate language in social (and political) life. The materiality of language is seen in its link to ideology and to the struggle of social accents. Moreover, Vološinov asserts that every "ideological sign is not only a reflection, a shadow, of reality, but is also itself a material segment of that very reality. Every phenomenon functioning as an ideological sign has some kind of material embodiment, whether in sound, physical mass, colour, movements of the body, or the like" (1986: 11).

At the same time, Vološinov's fundamental assumptions about the sign also create a theoretical and imaginative roadblock through which he is unable to pass. Specifically, he's not able to articulate an account of signs that goes beyond a rather vague sense of symbolism. These limitations are most obvious in the opening pages of the book. Here Vološinov suggests that "side by side with the natural phenomena, with the equipment of technology, and with articles for consumption, there exists a special world – the world of signs" (1986: 10). Semiosis is thus conceptualized as something radically separate from the rest of social life. Take, for instance, his discussion of a tool which he claims is, by itself, "devoid of any special meaning" (1986: 10) and simply fulfills its "designated function" (1986: 10). The tool, he suggests, serves its purpose "as the particular, given thing that it is, without reflecting or standing for anything else" (1986: 10). Such a tool can, however, be "converted" into an ideological sign. Vološinov gives the example of the hammer and sickle insignia of the Soviet Union, which has come to "possesses a purely ideological meaning" (1986: 10). And, though a tool may be aesthetically enhanced, it does not, Vološinov asserts, "itself become a sign" (1986: 10). There is, he claims, a "distinct conceptual dividing line" (1986: 10) – "the tool, as such, does not become a sign; the sign, as such, does not become an instrument of production" (1986: 10).

These arguments are repeated for consumer goods which may, like tools, be combined with ideological signs but nevertheless remain fundamentally separate according to Vološinov. Bread and wine become the body and blood of Christ in the course of the Eucharist, but even such a transubstantiation does not alter the fundamentally nonsemiotic character of the material elements. Thus, for Vološinov, although the sign itself must be embodied in some material form and although things in the world can be made into signs, the line between the two is absolute. As Vološinov puts it, these are two worlds that exist "side by side." Signs are material and ideology consists of signs, but, ultimately, signs are conceptualized as "symbols" that reflect and refract reality.

This, of course, won't do. If a tool were not itself a sign, we would not know how to use it. A hammer presents its handle and, as Mead proposed, a chair invites us to sit on it.[3] These uses do not exhaust the affordances of a tool, broadly conceived, but, to the extent that they are available to us, they appear as signs inherent in the design. And the semiotic meaning of consumer goods (commodities) is not a simple overlay on top of their functional significance; it is essential to what they are (see e.g. Kockelman 2006; Agha 2011; Gal 2017). In sum, signs do not exist "side by side" with the world of tools and commodities – it's one and the same world, and semiotic mediation is our means of access to it.

13.1.3 Charles Sanders Peirce

Peirce took his first steps toward what was to become his theory of signs, what he called "semeiotic," in May of 1867. In his presentation to the American Academy of Arts and Sciences that month, Peirce sought to reveal the fundamental structures of thought through an examination of its organizing categories. Peirce, in other words, attempted to develop a new set of categories which could be justified as necessary elements in any account of human experience. Whereas Kant had proposed four triads under the headings Quantity, Quality, Relation and Modality, Peirce concluded that all experience could be reduced to just three fundamental

---

[3] Mead (1962: 280) writes: "The chair is something we sit down in, the window is something that we can open, that gives us light or air."

categories which in 1867 he referred to as Quality, Relation and Representation but which would eventually become firstness, secondness and thirdness, respectively (Peirce 1992: 6). These categories provided the underlying conceptual framework for Peirce's thinking throughout the rest of his long career and are central to his theory of signs in particular. Already in 1867, he uses them to generate one of his three most famous trichotomies: icon (*Likenesses*), index (*Indices*) and symbol (1992: 7).[4]

Whereas the "new list" was meant to revise Kant, the important works Peirce published the following year in the *Journal of Speculative Philosophy* challenged fundamental assumptions in Descartes. Specifically, in "Some Questions Concerning Certain Faculties Claimed for Man," Peirce argued against the possibility of intuition and introspection, suggesting that our knowledge of both the external and the internal world is mediated by signs. In "Some Consequences of the Four Incapacities," he summarizes his conclusions thus (1992: 30):

1. We have no power of Introspection, but all knowledge of the internal world is derived by hypothetical reasoning from our knowledge of external facts.
2. We have no power of Intuition, but every cognition is determined logically by previous cognitions.
3. We have no power of thinking without signs.
4. We have no conception of the absolutely incognizable.[5]

Peirce reasons that all thought "must necessarily be in signs" (1992: 24) and since it "is the essence of a sign" to "address itself to some other" (1992: 24), it follows that cognition involves a seemingly infinite series of signs running in two directions, one toward whatever is thought about (what Peirce calls the object) and the other toward what is thought about it (what Peirce calls the interpretant).

Thus, at this early stage, Peirce, like Saussure and following in the tradition of Locke, had developed a largely mentalist theory of signs and one that faced many of the same deep theoretical problems, as did those which preceded it (see Short 2007). Moreover, in his early explorations, Peirce was concerned primarily with symbols, which are "general" signs (e.g. "dog," not "that dog"), as these seemed to be the signs most obviously constitutive of thought and the most relevant to the study of logic. In the following years he wrestled with these familiar problems and eventually came to rethink the importance of secondness within his overall theory of signs and his distinctive approach to logic (see, e.g., Short 2007; Lee 1997: 108ff). Secondness, which includes not only "relation" but also "existence,"

---

[4] He also mentions another trichotomy in the new list, that of term (later rheme), proposition (later dicent) and argument (Peirce 1992: 8–9), but these distinctions are not yet integrated with the former. In fact, Peirce (1868) discussed this trichotomy at the April meeting of the American Academy of Arts and Sciences just a month before he presented the "new list."

[5] This last point is Peirce's challenge to Kant's *ding an sich*, "thing in itself."

"effort and resistance," introduces a decisive break with much previous mentalist thinking about signs.

Signs themselves involve a relation of thirdness, which is to say they mediate relations. This is a crucial point for properly appreciating Peirce's theory. Whereas Saussure (and many others) conceptualized the sign as a duality, a combination of two distinct forms of reality, namely a sound image and a concept, a signifier and a signified, for Peirce, the sign is an element in a relation; it is a relatum. More specifically, a sign (or what Peirce sometimes calls a representation and later a representamen) mediates the relation between an object and an interpretant. It is a common mistake, even among some specialists, to suppose that for Peirce the sign consists of three things whereas for Saussure it consists of two.[6] For Peirce, the sign is one element in a triadic relation. This is what Peirce means when he says sign. Thus, it is also not appropriate to talk of a "sign vehicle" in Peirce's theory since the sign just *is* the vehicle and the object and interpretant are part of the semiotic relation but not part of the sign itself. Another way to put this: the representamen is the sign, not a part of the sign. Many confusions can be avoided by resisting the temptation to think of the sign as anything other than one node in a triadic relation. For starters, it should dissuade us from identifying things as "signs." Anything may function or serve as a sign, but there is no special class of things in the world (even the words in a human language) that are signs in and of themselves, that is, outside of that special triadic relation in which they mediate between an object and an interpretant (see Ransdell 1976, 1977; Parmentier 1994).

Although different aspects of semiosis are highlighted, this conceptualization of a triadic relation which the sign activates is constant throughout Peirce's writings. Thus, in 1897, Peirce (1998: 228) writes that a sign "is something which stands to somebody for something in some respect or capacity. It addresses somebody, that is, creates in the mind of that person an equivalent sign, or perhaps a more developed sign." Ten years later, in a letter to his friend and fellow philosopher Lady Welby, Peirce (1958: 404) wrote that a sign is "anything which is so determined by something else, called its Object, and so determines an effect upon a person, which effect I call its interpretant, that the latter is thereby mediately determined by the former." After 1903, we find Peirce insisting that the sign determines an interpretant which stands in the same relation to the object as the sign itself does. For instance, in 1904 Peirce (1958: 390) proposed that a sign "is an object which is in relation to its object on the one hand and to an interpretant on the other, in such a way as to bring the interpretant into a relation to the object, corresponding to its own relation to the object." Kockelman (2005: 234) usefully glosses this in terms of a correspondence-preserving projection:

---

[6] See, for instance, Atkin (2016: 128): "[S]igns are composed of three interrelated parts: a sign, an object and an interpretant." See also his misleading use of the term "sign-vehicle" to mean the representamen.

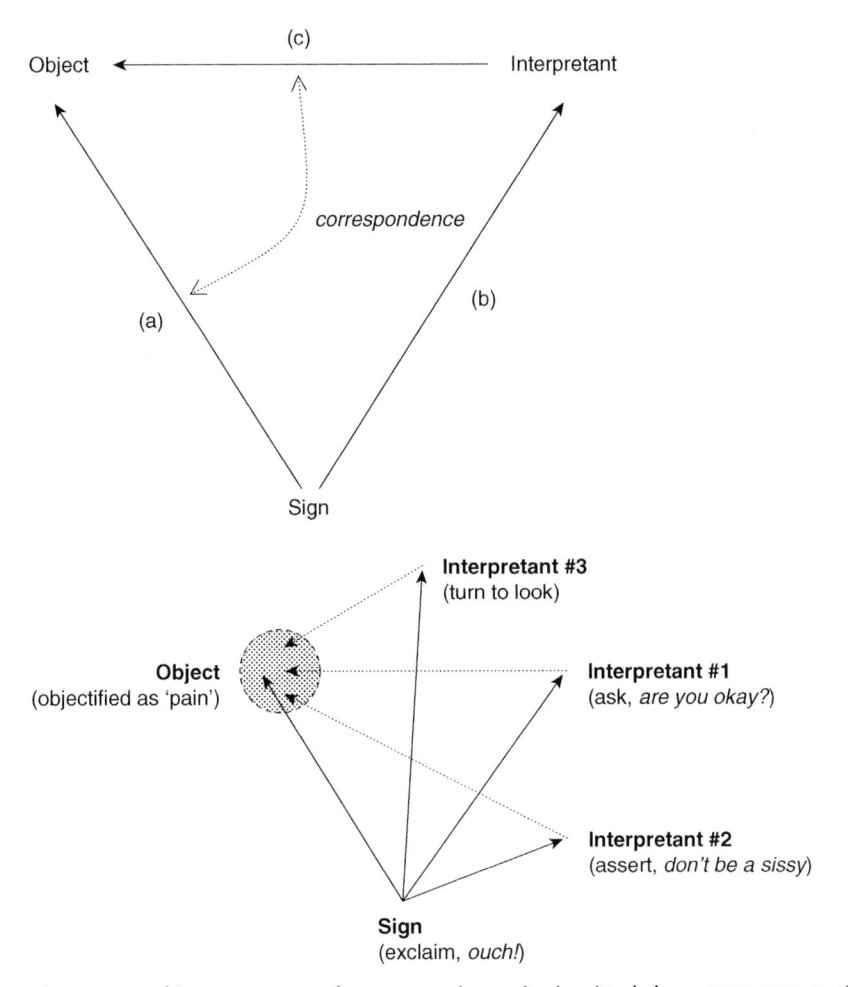

Figure 13.2 Object as correspondence-preserving projection (Kockelman 2005: 236, 242)

"a sign stands for its object on the one hand, and its interpretant on the other, in such a way as to make the interpretant stand in relation to the object corresponding to its own relation to the object."

In the present context, we should take note of a qualification that Peirce (1958: 404) appends to his definition in the letter to Welby, namely that his "insertion of 'upon a person' is a sop to Cerberus," included in an effort to make his "broader conception understood." In fact, as Kockelman (2005: 236) points out, a Peircean conception of the sign does not commit us to the view that signs must be addressed, interpreters must be human and interpretants must be mental.[7]

---

[7] There's some disagreement as to how far Peirce's semeiotic should be extended. On the one hand, Short (2007: 177) suggests: "Outside of purposeful action, which appears to be limited to animals, no mistakes are possible, and where no mistakes are possible, there can be no intentionality, hence, no interpretation; but all significance is relative to potential interpretation." On the other hand, Kohn (2013), as I understand him, suggests that semiotic relations are a characteristic of all biological systems (in a word, of all life) and not just animal ones. Although Peirce admittedly did

Peirce developed several different typologies, the most famous being that of 1903 in which he employed three trichotomies to arrive at ten classes of signs.[8] Peirce (1998: 291) writes:

> Signs are divisible by three trichotomies: first, according as the sign in itself is a mere quality, is an actual existent, or is a general law; secondly, according as the relation of the sign to its Object consists in the sign's having some character in itself, or in some existential relation to that Object, or in its relation to an Interpretant; thirdly, according as its Interpretant represents it as a sign of possibility, or as a sign of fact, or a sign of reason.

So, the first trichotomy distinguishes qualities that are signs, from actual existents that are signs, from general laws that are signs. Consider a well-known example adapted from Savan (1988), that of a red paint chip. Obviously, the chip itself is an existent, and if I arrive home to find it on the kitchen table, or taped to the wall, I will assume that someone has been to the paint store and perhaps that they intend to paint the room. In this case, it is a sinsign. At the same time, I will recognize it as an instance of a type: it is after all a paint chip and not just a red piece of cardboard. In that sense, it is (the replica of) a legisign. Finally, if I now use the chip to decide whether I should paint the room red, I will abstract from the actual existent sinsign and the general type or legisign that it exemplifies to consider the particular quality of red that is embodied; I will treat it as a qualisign.

The second trichotomy is the most familiar. This distinguishes signs according to the nature of the "ground," which is to say the relation between representamen and object. Thus, there are those that involve formal resemblance or likeness (icons), those that involve contiguity or dynamical coexistence (indexes or indices) and those that involve convention (symbols).

Finally, the third trichotomy is premised on recognition of the fact that the interpretant can represent a sign–object relation in a way other than it actually is (see Ball 2014). Another way to think about this is in terms of the kind of information that a sign provides. Thus, if someone suddenly says "Ouch!" the sign is rhematic, only suggesting a possibility (the utterer is in pain). If, on the other hand, the same person says "That hurts!" the sign is dicent in so far as, while again suggesting a qualitative possibility, it also

---

conceive of "mind" in a remarkably broad sense, he nevertheless seems committed to the view that semiosis requires some kind of intelligence. Thus, he writes that if a scientist is uncertain whether some "motion of an animalcule is guided by intelligence, of however low an order, the test . . . is to ascertain whether event, A, produces a second event, B, *as a means* to the production of a third event, C, or not." In other words, for Peirce, semiosis requires purposeful action. This is what distinguishes it from dyadic, brute relations.

[8] Several important, indeed crucial, distinctions came later, including that between the dynamic and immediate object as well as that between immediate, dynamic and final interpretants. Also important in, for example, the work of Paul Kockelman and N. J. Enfield is the distinction between affective, energetic and representational interpretants which is part of a later typology (see Jappy 2017; Short 2007).

indicates the source of the pain and thus provides some information about what is ailing the speaker. Or to take a similar example from Peirce, when someone says "Hello!" the sign is rhematic (conveying no information but merely a feeling, a qualitative possibility), whereas if a vendor says "Tickets, tickets, we got tickets here!" the sign is dicent.[9] An argument, the most developed sign in Peirce's 1903 typology, is a sign of law which not only provides information but also gives reasons by conveying something about the relation between component propositions.

According to Peirce, any given sign can be classified according to each of the three trichotomies.[10] Mathematically, that should result in twenty-seven possible signs, but, as Jappy (2013: 164) puts it, "in no case is it possible to attribute to the sign a higher phenomenological status in the hierarchy than it had in preceding criterion." Thus, qualisigns are necessarily rhematic icons and arguments are necessarily symbolic legisigns. The result is a set of ten possible sign classes.

Our concern here is specifically with the materiality of language and discourse and for that reason we will focus on secondness: sinsigns, indexes and dicents.[11]

13.2 Implications: Secondness and the Material Quality of Signs

Anything that is to function as a sign must take some sensible, which is to say perceivable, form (though see Kockelman 2005: 240). A sign is something that can be sensed – felt, smelt, seen, heard, tasted, etc. – and thus understood (in the broadest sense) as standing for something other than itself (see also Kockelman 2017). It is for this reason that a qualisign must be embodied in some sinsign and any legisign can only function as a sign through its replicas. Semiosis, then, must run through the bottleneck of existence in the form of sinsigns. As early as 1868, Peirce called attention to this, noting: "Since a sign is not identical with the thing signified, but differs from the latter in some respects, it must plainly have some characters which belong to it in itself, and have nothing to do with its representative function. These I call the material qualities of the sign" (1992: 40).

---

[9] See Peirce's extensive consideration of the dicent or dicisign from 1903 (1998: 275–85).

[10] It is commonplace among linguistic anthropologists, following Roman Jakobson (1965, 1970), to describe certain linguistic items (demonstrative pronouns, for instance,) as "indexical symbols" and other signs as "indexical icons." For discussion of this issue see Short (1998: 100–9).

[11] Although materiality, being itself a quality, might lead us to a focus on firstness (rather than secondness), as Chumley and Harkness (2013: 9) write: "Materiality can be regarded as an attribution of qualities to objects in an external world, which can then be experienced and acted upon through qualia." See also Gal (2017: 129): "The goal now is to grasp the conventional cultural meanings of, say, a porcelain plate taken as a sign in a specific social order, while simultaneously analyzing how the plate's undeniable material qualities – say, its hardness and nonporousness – are themselves semiotically achieved through an institutionally and ideologically guided formulation that provides categories for objects and materializes particular qualities in them that shape how the plate is known, used, and actually produced."

And in a manuscript from 1873, he writes that a sign, "like any other thing ... must have qualities which belong to it whether it be regarded as a sign or not. Thus, a printed word is black, has a certain number of letters and those letters have certain shapes. Such characters of a sign I call its material quality" (Peirce 1992: 141). We can compare what Peirce says here with Saussure's claim that "the nature of the sign that is agreed upon does not matter." There's some irony in the choice of words here, but beyond that we can see that the Peircean and Saussurean approaches will lead us down very different paths.

A first manifestation of the materiality of discourse then lies in the material character of the signs themselves. Many linguistic anthropologists have elaborated this point through the semiotic analysis of "material things" (see, e.g., Keane 1997, 2003, 2007, 2018; Manning 2012). One particularly important work that illustrates well the methods and key assumptions associated with this line of inquiry is Matthew Hull's (2003, 2012) study of bureaucracy in Islamabad. Hull (2003: 288) suggests that "successful bureaucratic processes result in action that is not dissolvable into the agency of distinct individuals" and shows how this is accomplished through the circulation and continuous modification of documents within the setting he studied. Hull's focus is on the "file" – an organized collection of documents that is created when a government office receives a "written communication on a subject for which no file in the directorate already exists" (2003: 296–7). The file consists of several documents gathered together in a single folder and travels throughout the bureaucracy accumulating annotations, signatures, stamps, instructions and so on as it moves from one government agent to the next. Importantly, although portions of the file may be copied for inclusion in another file, the file itself is unique; there's only one copy. It's obvious then that the materiality of the file (its composition and the record of its own production which it embodies) is key to its significance, to its life as a sign. Its use and reuse effect new materializations, new modifications to the nature of the sign itself (see Nakassis 2013 for a subtle discussion of this and many other issues). Hull's analysis of the file, the graphic-artifacts that it includes, as well as the various forms of writing and other practices by which it is constituted thus illustrates vividly the material nature of the sign. At the same time, Hull shows the way in which signs are subject to nondiscursive happenings, what Keane describes as "the vicissitudes to which material signs are prone" (1997: 31). A file, or one of its documents, may be lost, damaged, hidden, stolen, destroyed, forgotten, defaced, redacted and so on.

As it travels within the government office, the file accumulates signatures and stamps, two forms of inscription that, as Hull (2003: 294) notes, have an autographic component; these signs "anchor discourse in the world because they are the causal result of physical events involving the file." Signatures and stamps are treated as "officially sanctioned indexes ...

of person, place, or time" (Hull 2003: 294). The signature, because it involves "an ostensibly inimitable biomechanical act of signing," indexes an individual through a relation of physical causality. In contrast, the stamps with which a file is also annotated are understood as portable (and possibly forged) and thus vulnerable to counterfeit or otherwise unauthorized use. Hull's study illustrates, then, the way the material qualities of a sign (and the worldly contingencies of a sign's production, circulation and so on) necessarily shape its interpretation.

Cody's study of a group of neoliterate women who brought a petition to the Pudukkottai district collector's office in Tamil Nadu provides a useful counterpoint – here we see the making of a "written communication" which might lead to the eventual production of a government file. The Dalit women Cody describes were, at the time of his study, newly literate and the activist who encouraged them to submit the grievance suggested that one of them should, if possible, write the petition text that would precede the listing of their signatures. Cody argues that, certain complexities notwithstanding, through the written medium the Dalit women were able to self-represent as citizen petitioners. Specifically, he suggests (2009: 356) that writing fits with a conception of enlightenment as transparency, "insofar as it can be detached from interest-laden contexts of enunciation and weighed in terms of its own rational, denotational content, ridding communication of that which might be thought to stand between the writing subject and her addressee." And he shows the ways in which these ideas shaped the writing of the petition text itself, encouraging the inclusion of some elements and the exclusion of others that might index "an intercaste pleading register" (2009: 364). Still, the women petitioners were disappointed when they were unable to deliver the petition to the collector in person.

Of particular interest is Cody's discussion of the signature. The neoliterate signatures that accompanied the petition contrast with the sure-handed writing of the petition text (which, in the end, was produced by the literacy activist). But the very material qualities of the signatures do more than index the individuals who produced them (via biomechanical causation). They also embody the newness of their ability and thus serve as traces of their path toward enlightenment. And whereas the signatures in the Islamabad bureaucracy stand in relation to the official stamps of office, among the newly literate Dalit villagers, the signature takes its significance, in part, from the fact that it is alternative to a thumbprint.

> The thumbprint that many nonliterates still use to identify themselves on government documents has always carried connotations of ignorance, marginality, and even criminality, and it is increasingly stigmatized as an anachronism by the literacy movement and by the district administration ... A petition signed by the very villagers who are acting as petitioners ... allows the petitioner to be fully present as a citizen,

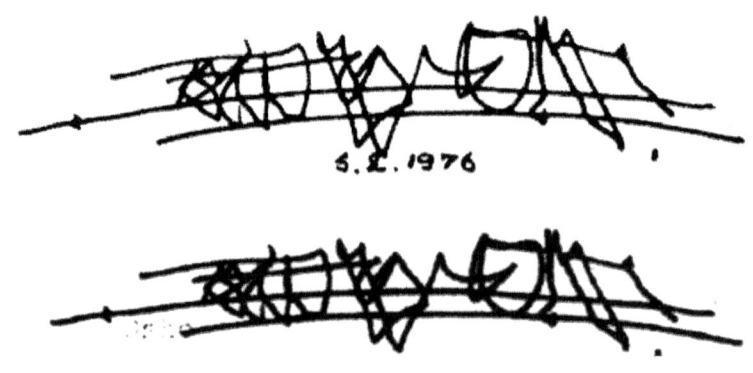

Figure 13.3 Osho's signature, 1976 version (top), from the will (bottom)

rather than a simple body, in their very absence. Signature is perhaps the most important cultural form signaling one's ability to operate in modern spheres of activity associated with the state. (2009: 358–9)

Thus, the material qualities of a signature are precisely what makes it the kind of sign it is. To abstract away from these qualities, as Saussure suggests we must, would be to erase the very significance of the sign itself. This can be seen, for instance, in cases of purported forgery. In 2013, twenty-three years after his death, the apparently certified will of famed guru Osho (formerly Bhagwan Shree Rajneesh) was submitted to the court in Pune by one of his caretakers. Other disciples subsequently challenged the authenticity of the will and suggested that the signature had been forged. Those challenging the will claimed that the signature was similar, indeed identical, to one that had been included in a published book. Thus, the signature, as a sign, is inimitable not because it is impossible to produce an exact copy but because one cannot produce a *nonexact copy*, which is to say a unique replica of the legisign rather than a duplicate of another replica.

We needn't, however, turn to written language and documents to see the materiality of discourse. Consider a case discussed by Charles Goodwin (2017) in which three girls are playing hopscotch. After Diana throws her beanbag into a square and begins hopping back through the grid, Carla objects, describes her as a cheater and subsequently blocks Diana's passage through the game space with her own body.

As Goodwin notes in his analysis of this episode, the action is produced by bringing together various diverse semiotic modalities (or fields). In the first place, the action of the game itself is produced within the framework provided by the grid of squares painted on the cement. The grid here defines a set of spaces within which the game-relevant actions become visible. Like the files of an Islamabad bureaucracy and the petition of Dalit villagers, the hopscotch grid has an obvious material existence. At the same time, the grid imposes semiotic structure on material reality, the

13 Sign Theory and the Materiality of Discourse   297

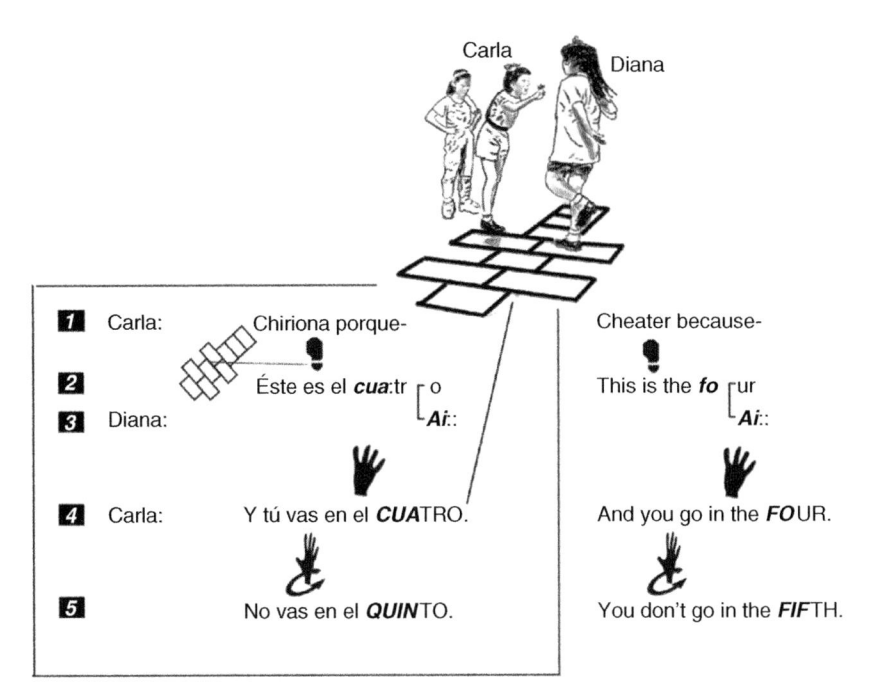

1	Carla:	Chiriona porque-	Cheater because-
2		Éste es el *cua*:tr ⌈o	This is the *fo* ⌈ur
3	Diana:	⌊Aï::	⌊Aï::
4	Carla:	Y tú vas en el *CUA*TRO.	And you go in the *FO*UR.
5		No vas en el *QUIN*TO.	You don't go in the *FIF*TH.

Figure 13.4 Diana and Carla, 1

world within which the game of hopscotch takes places. The grid itself is the replica of a legisign and at the same time a constitutive component in the more encompassing legisign of the game of hopscotch.

Diana's movements though the space of the grid are themselves embodied signs and they follow a sequence that is projectable. When Carla blocks Diana's movement through the grid, she uses her whole body as a sign, and it is difficult to imagine a better illustration of secondness, which Peirce characterized as "effort" and "resistance" (e.g. 1998: 268) and as the "outward clash" (1992: 233), than the way Carla purposefully interrupts Diana's movement, first by walking into the grid and then by occupying the square to which Diana must jump next. The two girls momentarily meet, Diana still attempting to stand on one foot, and then they push off from one another. Carla, standing directly in front of Diana and within the space of the game-grid, now gives reasons for her claim that Diana has violated the rules.

Carla does this using both linguistic and gestural signs. With, *Este es el cuatro*, "This is the four," she uses the indexical expression (what Peirce classified as a rhematic indexical legisign) *este*, "this," to refer to something within the immediate surround, something that she treats Diana as having perceptual access to. Such signs serve to anchor talk to the context in which it is used. If we are to avoid the temptations of Saussurean dematerialization, we must carefully attend to these signs, indexes that, as Peirce (1992: 226) puts it, assert "nothing" and instead take "hold of our eyes ... forcibly" directing "them to a particular object."

Carla links this *este* (the object of which is a particular space defined by the grid) to another indexical expression, *el cuatro*, "the four," using the copular verb *es*. Such an expression treats that which is referred to as something already known about; the definite determiner is an index that ties the expression to what Peirce described as "collateral experience." The utterance as a whole is a dicent which, by joining together an indexical referring expression (*este*) with a predicate (which, while including another indexical expression, can be thought of as an icon, something that presents a kind of picture or image), conveys information (whether correct or not) about the world. This, then, is another aspect of secondness and of the materiality of discourse. Not only are signs themselves unavoidably and consequentially material but they also ubiquitously butt up against the world in which they are used. Any adequate account of discourse must thus avoid the ideologically motivated temptation of imagining a gap between language on the one hand and world on the other, an account of language which is used solely to refer to the world "out there" (see Irvine 1989).

As Peirce realized through a consideration of quantifiers in the 1880s, reference to particulars (individuals) is possible only through the use of indexical signs. A symbol (or an arbitrary linguistic sign à la Saussure), on its own, refers only to a general class, such as "dog" or "pet" etc., not to the particular one that lives in my home and barks at the neighbor. Peirce (1998: 7) summarizes: "No combination of words (excluding proper nouns, and in the absence of gestures or other indicative concomitants of speech) can ever convey the slightest information." He illustrates the point with an example in which one man, Ben, tells another, Abe, "The owner of that house is the richest man in these parts." Thus, Abe, Peirce notes, has "acquired information." But if Abe now walks to a distant village and pronounces, "The owner of a house is the richest man in those parts," he will not have conveyed any information since "the remark will refer to nothing, unless he explains to his interlocutor how to proceed from where he is in order to find that district and that house."

To return to the example of Carla and Diana, as she says, *Y tu vas en el CUATRO*, "and you go in the four," Carla holds her right hand in front of Diana's face, palm forward and thumb folded in so as to present four fingers. As she continues with the subsequent, *No vas en el QUINTO*, "not in the fifth," she flips her hand around, still suspended in front of Diana's face, and shows four fingers in addition to the thumb thus displaying "five." As Goodwin notes, in terms of propositional content it seems as if this merely duplicates part of what has been said, but in terms of semiotic action the hand shapes play a distinct role in the unfolding interaction. Not only does Carla's hand stand in for her now withdrawn body to block Diana's further progress through the grid, it presents to Diana a target for gaze, a place to look. In this way, it requests that Diana's attention be directed to the challenge Carla is producing and away from the grid and the turn in the game that Diana was in the course of producing. The spontaneous choreography of what follows is remarkable – Diana, still standing on one foot, is looking at Carla's hand but then, apparently starting to lose her balance, tries to catch herself and turns to look at the ground. Just as she does this, Carla releases the hand gesture and produces a deictic gesture with her foot, stomping in the square on the grid that she claims is the five just as Diana's gaze moves to that very spot.

Reference to a particular square within the grid is accomplished by several quite different kinds of sign – first, the nominal expression, *el quinto*, which combines an ordinal number with the definite determiner; second, the iconic manual sign of five outstretched digits; third, the indexical gesture accomplished by stomping the right foot in the square referred to. Clearly these signs differ in terms of the material qualities of the signs themselves. This material difference has consequences for what may be termed the collateral effects of the sign (see Sidnell and Enfield 2012) – in the case of the verbal expression, *el quinto*, the square is formulated as one in a series; in the case of the manual gesture, the hand provides an alternate focus of attention and also works to interrupt the course of action with which Diana is otherwise engaged; and in the case of the foot-point, the gesture draws attention toward the physical spaces within the grid the identities of which (as fourth or fifth) are being contested.

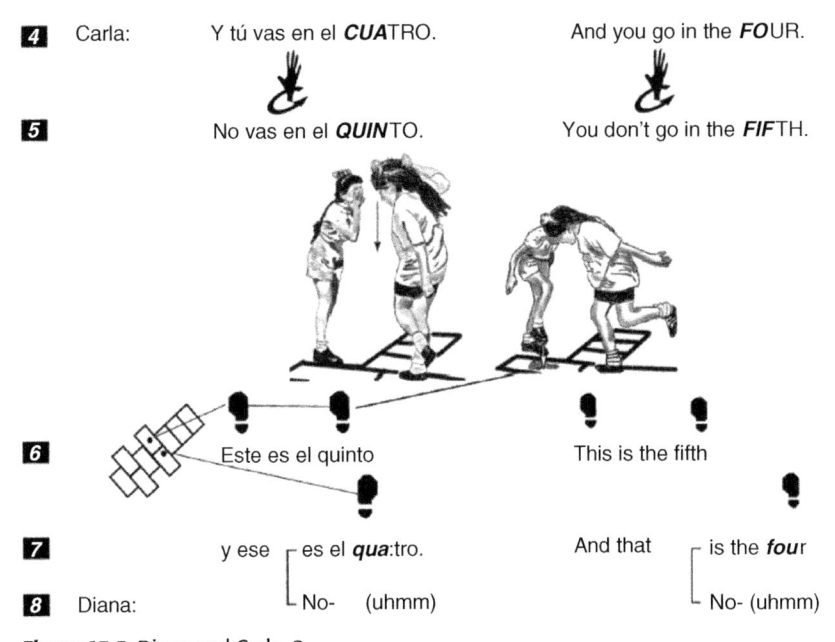

4	Carla:	Y tú vas en el **CUA**TRO.	And you go in the **FO**UR.
5		No vas en el **QUIN**TO.	You don't go in the **FIF**TH.
6		Este es el quinto	This is the fifth
7		y ese ⌈ es el **qua**:tro.	And that ⌈ is the **fou**r
8	Diana:	⌊ No- (uhmm)	⌊ No- (uhmm)

Figure 13.5 Diana and Carla, 2

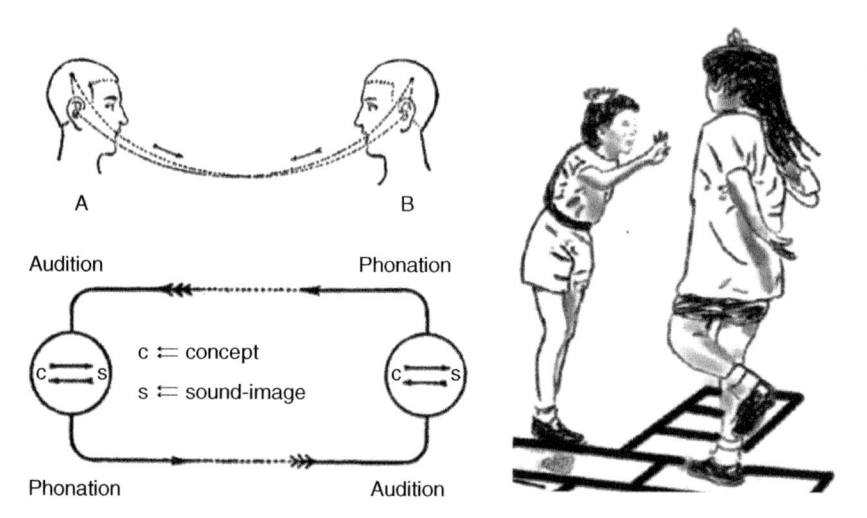

Figure 13.6 Language and interaction as disembodied heads à la Saussure (left) and as fully embodied participation à la Goodwin (right)

The materiality of discourse, in other words, includes not just the physical character of the signs themselves but also the particular ways in which they are used (1) to make reference to the world in which interaction takes place and (2) to construct consequential action. Crucially, reference involves a form of semiotic mediation that is all but excluded from Saussurean theory – this is one in which there is some existential, causal relation between the sign and that to which reference is made (object). According to Peirce, this is a "degenerate" sign form since one of the constitutive three relations (sign-object, sign-interpretant, interpretant-object) holds independently of the others.

We can see then that the very bodies of the interactants, their hands, eyes, feet and the configuration of the whole relative to one another, provide a material basis within which language and interaction are embedded. At this point, we might note how far we are from the disembodied heads of Saussure's *Cours* (see figure 13.6).

13.3 Future Directions

The foregoing discussion suggests three possible directions for future research. First, and most obviously, a focus on the materiality of discourse should encourage the continuing development of our understanding of embodied interaction including the various ways in which language and world articulate through referential practices. Such research should include further exploration of deixis and the indexical character of reference in discourse. It should also include consideration of gesture and other aspects of embodied interaction (see Enfield 2009; Goodwin 2017; also Latour 1999).

Second, the preceding discussion has touched upon some aspects of a specifically ethnographic approach to the materiality of discourse. Research in this area has considered the ways in which material qualities are semiotically articulated and subject to various forms of evaluation, assessment and so on (see especially Gal 2017; Keane 2003). Some research in this area has focused on the material qualities of language itself as an object of semiotic elaboration (see Harkness 2013; Keane 2007). Included also here is work that considers the ways in which language and other sociomaterial forms (e.g. beards and brands) are combined and configured within registers that allow for the formation of recognizable social persona (see especially Agha 2011; Nakassis 2016).

A third possible direction would focus on what might be thought of as discursive materializations – the various discursive practices by which material features of the world are semiotically articulated. International borders involve walls, gates and security checks, and passing through them involves providing documentation that is inspected, recorded, marked and so on. An international border is, at one level, an institutional reality (Searle 2010) – epistemically subjective, ontologically objective fact – but, treated semiotically, it involves a complex combination and coordination of signs, some built out of language, some involving complex activities of looking, checking, recording, some architectural and so on.

13.4 Summary

This chapter began by tracing the dematerialization of language in the sign theory underlying the Saussurean approach to language. After briefly considering the materialist critique of Volosinov, we sketched, in broad outline, a Peircean approach based on the assumptions of semiotic realism. Peircean semiotic realism refuses any *a priori* opposition of representation and world and the associated assumption of an incognizable reality as is implied by Saussurean sign theory. Instead, within a Peircean approach, it is suggested that all thinking involves signs and that, as such, internal and external reality are fundamentally continuous. This does not deny the existence of an external world – quite the opposite. But that external world is continuous with the internal one; both are mediated by signs. Still, if all thinking is in signs, we must ask how it is possible to refer to particular things in the world, how it is possible for the series of signs to ever terminate, to connect with objective reality. Peirce's answer to this question rests on his ideas of secondness. Sinsigns are existent signs that take some kind of material form. Indexes are signs in which sign and object are related by some form of determinate coexistence, contiguity or causal relation. Dicent signs are those that convey some information about the world by combining determinate reference with predication. With these distinctions in place, it is possible to build an ethnographic and anthropological approach to the materiality of discourse. As seen in the work reviewed here, this involves attending to the rich social, cultural and linguistic contexts in which discourse occurs and to which it is inevitably linked.

Further Reading

Chumley, L. (2017). Qualia and Ontology: Language, Semiotics, and Materiality: An Introduction. *Signs and Society*, 5(S1): S1–S20.

This very useful introductory essay is partly concerned with the semiotic mediation of material qualities.

Goodwin, C. (2017). *Co-operative Action*. Cambridge: Cambridge University Press.

Goodwin's magnum opus brings together his lifelong concern with gesture, materiality, language and embodiment in an argument about the cooperative character of human action.

Hull, M. (2012). *Government of Paper: The Materiality of Bureaucracy in Urban Pakistan*. Berkeley: University of California Press.

This is an important attempt to apply the linguistic anthropological approach to the study of documents in their contexts of use.

Irvine, J. (1989). When Talk Isn't Cheap: Language and Political Economy. *American Ethnologist* 16(2): 248–67.

In this classic, pioneering essay, the author explores ways of thinking about language across a range of contexts and challenges a simplistic application of Saussurean sign theory to the ethnographic study of language in context.

Keane, W. (2003). Semiotics and the Social Analysis of Material Things. *Language and Communication* 23(2/3): 409–25.

This is an important and influential intervention in which the author shows the utility of Peircean sign theory in a semiotic consideration of material objects.

Nakassis, C. (2013). Materiality, Materialization. *Hau: Journal of Ethnographic Theory* 3(3): 399–406.

In this short but brilliant comment on Hull's ethnography, the author draws upon Derrida and some of the ethnographic details Hull reports on to articulate larger questions about the relationships among language, discourse and materiality.

Short, T. L. (2007). *Peirce's Theory of Signs*. Cambridge: Cambridge University Press.

This is a useful, recent and quite comprehensive survey of Peirce's writings on signs.

References

Agha, A. (2011). Commodity Registers. *Journal of Linguistic Anthropology* 21(1): 22–53.
Atkin, A. (2016). *Peirce*. New York: Routledge.
Ball, C. (2014). On Dicentization. *Journal of Linguistic Anthropology* 24(2): 151–73.
Benveniste, E. ([1939]1971). The Nature of the Linguistic Sign. In *Problems in General Linguistics*, trans. by M. E. Meek. Oxford, OH: University of Miami Press.
Chumley, L. (2017). Qualia and Ontology: Language, Semiotics, and Materiality: An Introduction. *Signs and Society* 5(S1): S1–S20.
Chumley, L. and Harkness, N. (2013). Introduction: Qualia. *Anthropological Theory* 13(1/2): 3–11.
Cody, F. (2009). Inscribing Subjects to Citizenship: Petitions, Literacy Activism, and the Performativity of Signature. *Cultural Anthropology* 24(3): 347–80.
Dingemanse, M., Torreira, F. and Enfield, N. J. (2013). Is "Huh?" a Universal Word? Conversational Infrastructure and the Convergent Evolution of Linguistic Items. *PLoS ONE* 8(11): e78273.
Enfield, N. J. (2009). *The Anatomy of Meaning: Speech, Gesture, and Composite Utterances*. Cambridge: Cambridge University Press.
Gal, S. (2017). Qualia as Value and Knowledge: Histories of European Porcelain. *Signs and Society* 5(S1): S128–53.
Goodwin, C. (2017). *Co-operative Action*. Cambridge: Cambridge University Press.
Hacking, I. (1975). *Why Does Language Matter to Philosophy?* Cambridge: Cambridge University Press.
Harkness, N. (2013). *Songs of Seoul: An Ethnography of Voice and Voicing in Christian South Korea*. Berkeley: University of California Press.
Hull, M. (2003). The File: Agency, Authority, and Autography in an Islamabad Bureaucracy. *Language and Communication* 23: 287–314.
  (2012). *Government of Paper: The Materiality of Bureaucracy in Urban Pakistan*. Berkeley: University of California Press.
Irvine, J. (1989). When Talk Isn't Cheap: Language and Political Economy. *American Ethnologist* 16(2): 248–67.
Jakobson, R. (1965). Quest for the Essence of Language. *Diogenes* 13(51): 21–37.
  (1970). Shifters, Verbal Categories, and the Russian Verb. In *Selected Writings, Vol. 2: Word and Language*. The Hague: Mouton. 130–47.

(1978). *Six Lectures on Sound and Meaning*. Cambridge, MA: MIT Press.
Jappy, T. (2013). *Introduction to Peircean Visual Semiotics*. New York: Continuum.
(2017). *Peirce's Twenty-Eight Classes of Signs and the Philosophy of Representation*. New York: Continuum.
Keane, W. (1997). *Signs of Recognition: Powers and Hazards of Representation in an Indonesian Society*. Berkeley: University of California Press.
(2003). Semiotics and the Social Analysis of Material Things. *Language and Communication* 23(2/3): 409–25.
(2007). *Christian Moderns: Freedom and Fetish in the Mission Encounter*. Berkeley: University of California Press.
(2018). On Semiotic Ideology. *Signs and Society* 6(1): 64–87.
Kockelman, P. (2005). The Semiotic Stance. *Semiotica* 157(1–4): 233–304.
(2006). A Semiotic Ontology of the Commodity. *Journal of Linguistic Anthropology* 16: 76–102.
(2017). Semiotic agency. In N. J. Enfield and P. Kockelman (eds.) *Distributed Agency*. New York: Oxford University Press.
Kohn, E. (2013). *How Forests Think: Toward an Anthropology beyond the Human*. Berkeley/Los Angeles: University of California Press.
Latour, B. (1993). *We Have Never Been Modern*, trans. by C. Porter. Cambridge, MA: Harvard University Press.
(1999). *Pandora's Hope*. Cambridge, MA: Harvard University Press.
Lee, B. (1997). *Talking Heads: Language, Metalanguage, and the Semiotics of Subjectivity*. Durham, NC: Duke University Press.
Manning, P. (2012). *Semiotics of Drink and Drinking*. New York: Continuum.
Mead, G. H. (1962). *Mind, Self and Society*. Chicago: University of Chicago Press.
Meillet, A. (1925). *La Méthode Comparative En Linguistique Historique*. Paris: Champion.
Nakassis, C. (2013). Materiality, Materialization. *Hau: Journal of Ethnographic Theory* 3(3): 399–406.
(2016). *Doing Style: Youth and Mass Mediation in South India*. Chicago: University of Chicago Press.
Parmentier, R. (1994). *Signs in Society: Studies in Semiotic Anthropology*. Bloomington: Indiana University Press.
Peirce, C. S. (1868). On the Natural Classification of Arguments. In *Proceedings of the American Academy of Arts and Sciences* (581st meeting, April 9, 1867) 7: 261–87.
(1958). *Values in a Universe of Chance: Selected Writings of Charles S. Peirce*, ed. by P. P. Weiner. New York: Doubleday.
(1992). *The Essential Peirce, Vol. 1: Selected Philosophical Writings, 1867–1893*. Bloomington: Indiana University Press.
(1998). *The Essential Peirce, Vol. 2: Selected Philosophical Writings, 1893–1913*. Bloomington: Indiana University Press.
Ransdell, J. (1976). Another Interpretation of Peirce's Semiotic. *Transactions of the Charles S. Peirce Society* 12(2): 97–110.

(1977). Some Leading Ideas in Peirce's Semiotic. *Semiotica* 19: 157–78.

Saussure, F. de ([1916]1959). *Course in General Linguistics*, trans. by W. Baskin. New York: Philosophical Library.

Savan, D. (1988). *An Introduction to C.S. Peirce's Full System of Semeiotic*. Toronto: Toronto Semiotic Circle.

Searle, J. (2010). *Making the Social World: The Structure of Human Civilization*. New York: Oxford University Press.

Short, T. L. (1998). Jakobson's Problematic Appropriation of Peirce. In M. Shapiro (ed.) *The Peirce Seminar Papers, Vol. 3: Essays in Semiotic Analysis*. New York: Peter Lang. 89–123.

(2007). *Peirce's Theory of Signs*. Cambridge: Cambridge University Press.

Sidnell, J. and Enfield, N. J. (2012). Language Diversity and Social Action: A Third Locus of Linguistic Relativity. *Current Anthropology* 53: 302–33.

Volosinov, V.N. ([1929]1986). *Marxism and the Philosophy of Language*, trans. by L. Matejka and I. R. Titunik. New York: Seminar Press.

14

Discourse and the Linguistic Landscape

Philip Seargeant and Korina Giaxoglou

14.1 Introduction: Defining the Linguistic Landscape

14.1.1 Discursive Roundabouts

Over a three-day period in March 2018, traffic signs in the small town of Didcot in the south of England became the focus for a developing news story that mixed together themes of vandalism, creative expression and the regulative responsibilities of the local authority. An unknown party had altered the road signs at some of the town's major roundabouts so that, alongside signs to places such as Wallingford, Sutton Courtenay and the local power station, there were suddenly directions to Narnia, Gotham City and Neverland (BBC News, 2018a). When the news media managed to track down the mysterious prankster, he explained that his motivation was to change perceptions of the place, which had recently been branded "the most normal town" in England (BBC News, 2018b). For the local council, however, although they admitted it was vaguely amusing, this was nevertheless a case of vandalism and a potential risk to drivers, as it could easily distract them when approaching the affected roundabouts. By the third day of the media saga, the signs were removed and a sense of normality restored (BBC News, 2018c).

This small incident combines together a number of elements illustrating key facets of the relationship between discourse and the linguistic landscape. Road signs of various types have been one of the chief focal points of linguistic landscape research since its emergence as a field of study within sociolinguistics. In the case outlined above, road signs are operating, albeit for a very condensed period of time, as a site for the expression of competing discourses about the cultural identity of the town. They function primarily as an artifact that is part of a particular regulatory discourse about behavioral expectations in the public space – that is to say, they direct the way road-users are required to conduct themselves when driving. In this way, they map a social representation of the town onto the geography of the physical space. The intervention by the unknown prankster (who turned out to be a local artist) uses the grounded "reality" of this everyday regulatory discourse as a context in which to offer an alternative imagining of the town. This was linked, by means of a few place names from well-known fantasy literature, with an imaginary universe far removed from the mundanity of local urban planning regulations.

Public signs have both a spatial and a semiotic scope. They are used to demarcate and map out areas of human geography, and in so doing address a range of different-sized audiences. As Blommaert notes (2018: 85), "the semiotic scope of the road sign is wider than that of the 'apartment for rent' sign, and is in this sense more *public* – it addresses more potential interlocutors and excludes fewer." As the above example shows, it is the wide semiotic scope of the road sign that makes it possible to turn it into a public forum where a local artist can inscribe an alternative imagining of the town's cultural identity. This intervention addresses not only passing-by drivers but also the media and a wider public who may never come near these roundabouts. Without overwriting the existing place names, the intervention rewrites Didcot on the map and claims a different relationship to the place.

Research into the way that linguistic and other semiotic signs are displayed in public space and the meaning-making work they do in terms both of identity and regulation has opened up a productive field for sociolinguistic analysis (see Section 14.1.2 for an overview). This has often centered on the policy implications of public signage and as such this research has, from the very beginning, engaged with issues of politics, ideology and thus discourse. Yet, despite this focus, theorizing that is directed specifically at the relationship between linguistic landscape research and discourse studies has been slight, at least in terms of addressing the subject in explicit terms.

In this chapter we explore the relevance of discourse studies to linguistic landscape research by examining the various ways in which acts of linguistic and semiotic display in the public arena operate as key sites for the creation and negotiation of meaning. We look, more specifically, at how meaning is generated through the complex layering of contexts, the interplay between multiple signs, the dialogic possibilities presented by social media which allow local meanings to be upscaled and reconfigured, and the narrative-affective potential of linguistic landscapes, all of which, we suggest, pull site-specific semiotic events into much broader discourses and materialities.

Our aim is to make explicit the different levels of intersection between linguistic landscape research and discourse studies. In the remainder of this introduction, we review the development of linguistic landscape research and outline the issues it seeks to address. In Section 14.1.2, we draw up a system of categorization for the various types of relationship between discourse studies and linguistic landscape research, before going on to discuss and illustrate these in Section 14.2.

14.1.2 Linguistic Landscape Research: A Brief Overview

In their study of the attitudes of French-speaking Canadian high school students toward the multilingual signs in Quebec, Landry and Bourhis (1997) explicitly defined the concept of *linguistic landscapes* for the first time, and showed how signs in public space act as either a symbol or an index for the different language community identities in the city. The research area that grew from their study has typically examined patterns of signage in urban environments as a way of mapping the concrete manifestation of the linguistic diversity of an area in terms of the way that different languages are publicly inscribed in various artifacts (see, for example, the collection edited by Shohamy and Gorter (2009) for an early conceptualization of the range and aims of the field).

Given that the linguistic landscape has a higher degree of permanence than spoken language, it has also been possible to discern historical patterns in the language use of the communities that have successively inhabited particular parts of town, and in this way examine the influence of dynamic migration patterns on the linguistic profile of an area. Researchers have investigated a variety of ways in which the organization of visually displayed language in public places indicates and relates to social patterns of language use, showing how this is predominantly the result either of top-down language planning initiatives – regulations laid out by city councils, for example (Shohamy 2006) – or of more ad hoc bottom-up practices carried out by local communities who lack regulative authority over the public space. Examples of the latter include handwritten signs placed in shop windows (Blommaert 2013) and graffiti (Pennycook 2009). In many instances they can, of course, be a dialogue between top-down and bottom-up practices, as in the example of Didcot's roundabout signs. In context of this sort, the material nature of the sign often acts as a key index of the difference in status, with top-down signs having a more permanent and crafted physical nature (being "professionally" produced) and bottom-up signs tending more to the ephemeral or "home-made."

Even though linguistic landscape research has traditionally focused on "the use of language in its written form in the public sphere" (Gorter 2006: 2), it also includes all types of semiotic display in the public arena. Jaworski and Thurlow (2010) introduced the alternative term *semiotic landscapes* in order to acknowledge this, while Blommaert (2013: 14) has drawn attention to processes of semiotization that turn physical space into social, cultural and political space. It appears, however, that due to the fact that *linguistic landscape* is the more established term, its meaning has been broadened to include all forms of public text irrespective of their discursive modality and type of semiotic display (see Pütz and Mundt 2018). This is therefore how we will be using it in this chapter.

Blackwood (2017: 221) notes that what he calls "ante-lettram linguistic landscape research," that is, research conducted before linguistic landscape research, emerged as a distinct field, focused primarily on multilingualism. While this continues as an important focus, the research scope has broadened considerably since then, reflecting theoretical developments in sociolinguistics such as the recognition of the importance of the body and embodiment in the production and interpretation of meaning (Bucholtz and Hall 2008; Chapter 15 in this volume) and the paradigmatic shift in multilingualism from stability to mobility which has brought to the fore a concern with the relevance of superdiversity and translanguaging for the analysis of people's actual communicative practices. These developments have led to the emergence of new areas of study, new questions and new methods for investigating them.

A major impetus to the opening up of the field was Shohamy and Waksman (2009) who led the drive to expand the field's focus beyond signage to a range of semiotic artifacts, such as monuments and moving vehicles. Over the last decade, this expansion of scope is attested in analyses both of *core* texts, that is, place-names, road signs and public notices, and *peripheral* texts, including T-shirts (Coupland 2010), product labels, tickets, banknotes and flyers (Sebba 2010), as well as non-stationary signs, for example mobile train graffiti (Karlander 2018). In addition to the visible and material manifestations of languages, linguistic landscape research now also covers the study of various forms of *-scapes* including, for example, the study of "soundscapes" (Scarvaglieri et al. 2013), body tattoos making up "skinscapes" (Peck and Stroud 2015) and ethnographies of urban "smellscapes" (Pennycook and Otsuji 2015) (for an overview see Gorter 2018). This expansion of the field has been accompanied by a concern with how the linguistic landscape is produced, consumed and commodified and how it is invested with meaning by those who experience it (see, for example, Lou's sociolinguistic ethnography of Chinatown in Washington (2016)).

In terms of methods, the unit of analysis in linguistic landscape research is indeterminate and based on procedural decisions that depend on the scope and breadth of the study (Androutsopoulos 2014: 85). The tendency of early studies for contrastive counting and categorizing of linguistic tokens in a designated survey area that were then used to quantify the extent to which different languages are used in the environment, gauging examples of dominance and marginalization of minority languages, has given way to qualitative accounts of *signs in context*. Irrespective of the type of data collection and sample size, linguistic landscape studies involve some form of fieldwork, including photographs, (walking) interviews and observations. More recently, the blending of collaborative ethnographies with creative arts activities has also been used as a method, aimed at encouraging young people to become ethnographers of their own communities (Bradley et al. 2018).

In terms of the concerns of the current chapter, developments in the field have also entailed a shift from the examination of how public signs reflect language hierarchies to how signs work as communicative acts within their context, and what this indicates about the complex and changing sociolinguistic profile of a particular area (Blommaert and Maly 2014). This shift to the consideration of context in the interpretation of signs is most notably articulated in Scollon and Scollon's (2013) approach to the study of linguistic landscapes, known as *geosemiotics*, at the interface between semiotics and the physical world.

This concern with "signs-in-place" and their contextualization is one area where discourse studies becomes particularly relevant. Another such area is work around how physical space is constructed as social, cultural and political space, or as "a space that offers, enables, triggers, invites, prescribes, proscribes, polices or enforces certain patterns of social behaviour; a space that is never no-man's-land, but always *somebody*'s space; a *historical* space, therefore, full of codes, expectations, norms and traditions; and a space of *power* controlled by, as well as controlling, people" (Blommaert 2013: 3).

Interestingly, it is rare to find extensive discussions of the different ways in which linguistic landscapes research relates to discourse studies; in most cases, discourse is taken for granted, whether as a heuristic, as an analytic concept or as a method. In Section 14.2, we will provide some working definitions of discourse before moving on to map out the different elements of the relationship between discourse and linguistic landscape research, thus providing a list of theoretical assumptions for study within the area.

14.2 Discourse and Linguistic Landscapes

While at the most basic level discourse is often defined as "language in use" (Jaworksi and Coupland 1999: 7), it can also have a more specific meaning, referring to the way that text works within (or, indeed, as) context (Georgakopoulou and Goutsos 2004) or, more broadly, as a general mode of semiosis (i.e. meaningful symbolic behavior) that reflects, shapes and maintains the ideologies that constitute a culture (Blommaert 2005: 2). In this chapter we understand discourse as a social practice of meaning-making in linguistic and other modes, which is at the center of human activity and experience, as well as an analytical heuristic that can be used to address a range of questions (Johnstone 2018: 8). While discourse is a mode of semiosis, the linguistic landscape then constitutes a modality for articulating, regimenting, prescribing and proscribing, reinforcing or contesting sociosymbolic behavior. In this respect, the relationship between the two is double-edged: discourse(s) shapes and is shaped by the linguistic landscape(s). We can therefore explore this relationship in the way that it is manifest in the nature, display and interactions of specific semiotic artifacts in context.

Signs can exist in different modes or combinations thereof. As Blommaert (2018) notes, the different modalities in which signs are created need to be seen as affordances which have a cultural, social, political and historical (normative) dimension. Signs, thus, have a semiotic scope but also a spatial one: they operate in specific, identified spaces, and demarcate such spaces. They can divide a space into micro-spaces where particular rules and codes operate in relation to specific audiences (for example, a "no-smoking" sign being placed near entrances to or exits from a public building). This demarcating effect also defines identities by selecting possible addressees and making them potentially legitimate – or illegitimate – users of the demarcated space. Such categorizations are also social and political categories in the sense that they set the dynamics of power in public space through claims of entitlement to its use. Instances where such claims are contested can reveal wider social and political conflicts, as in the example Blommaert gives of police being instructed by shopping mall management to remove groups of young immigrants, homeless people and skaters who gather in shopping malls after closing time, that is, after the time when displays of "shopping behaviour" are sanctioned (2018: 85).

Signs draw their social meaning from their material placement and discourse(s), as Scollon and Scollon note (2003: 2), foregrounding the centrality of *context* in the study of semiotic artifacts in public space (see Chapters 1, 2 and 3 in this volume). Indeed, a primary purpose of linguistic landscape artifacts – by which we mean any socially and culturally meaningful signage in the public arena – is that they contribute to, while taking their meaning from, the notion of "public" space – that is, space that is structured around ideas of communal identity and shared values and codes. In this way the very context of the public space is itself a discourse. Artifacts within the linguistic landscape are thus instruments that manifest the regulatory, historical and normative discourses creating the ideological structures for the creation and maintenance of social order. This is only one type of dynamic in the relationship between linguistic landscapes and discourse; in the discussion that follows, we categorize the range of different relationships that link the two.

14.2.1 Linguistic Landscape Artifacts Enact Discourses

As noted, the very idea of the linguistic landscape is, in fact, founded on a specific discourse: the complex of beliefs and regulations about what constitutes public space in society. Signs can regulate communal behavior in ways that would be neither expected nor appropriate in private space.

Specific signs within the linguistic landscape are, then, artifacts of, and ways of articulating and maintaining, particular ideologies that structure behavior within society. In directing behavior, they are a means of managing aspects of social organization which, from issues such as traffic regulation to the display of official languages, create the social matrices and indexical orders in which we live. Linguistic landscape artifacts can also enact hierarchies about social identity, for example, marking the dominance of certain languages – and thus language communities – above others, and contributing to the way this dominance is discursively constructed through practice.

14.2.2 Discourses Assign Meaning to Linguistic Landscape Artifacts

The obverse of the relationship mentioned in Section 14.2.1 is that, just as linguistic landscape artifacts enact discourses, they also rely on these discourses for their meaning. In other words, signs are indices of particular discourses; in order to be able to interpret them, a familiarity with related discourses is needed, and this emerges in and through routine practices. A road sign, for example, is meaningful within the wider context of the social and legal contract that regulates driver behavior on public roads. Borrowing the example again from Scollon and Scollon (2003), a "STOP" sign being transported on the back of a lorry does not have the same legal or social meaning as one positioned by the side of a junction. We know this because any speech act is reliant on both text and context. Context here is not merely a physical location; it is also a regulatory discourse.

14.2.3 Linguistic Landscape Artifacts Become Symbolic Sites around Which Conflicting Discourses Are Played Out

As we saw with the Didcot roundabout example, bottom-up interventions around top-down signs can be a means of challenging a mainstream discourse by altering the message of the sign. In instances such as this, two or more discourses come into direct conflict, with the modified sign becoming a symbolic touchstone for social debate.

14.2.4 Linguistic Landscape Artifacts Mobilize Further Discursive Articulation or Contestation

In the case of inventions of the sort described in the Didcot example, the modified artefict often then triggers further debate or discussion in public forums and the media. Such discussions can be in the form of a moral panic or public outcry (at least in the way these are framed in the media), in which two conflicting discourses are pitted against each other. As we shall see in Section 14.2.5, this generation of discussion and debate can be either purposeful or the result of evolving ideologies in society. In recent years, social media has played a major role in mediating the local and supralocal, pulling site-specific meanings into broader discourses.

14.2.5 Linguistic Landscape Artifacts that Are in Conversation with Each Other Can Create Meaning that Extends beyond the Level of the Individual Sign

As Blommaert notes, the "meanings and effects of signs ... are specific to the space in which they are emplaced and to the addressees they select" (2018: 86). Most surveys of the embedded ideologies in the linguistic landscape focus on the semiotic work being done by individual signs (or a collection of such signs). There are, however, also instances where meaning is created not just by the context in which an artifact is placed but also by its juxtaposition with other artifacts, and the discourse that this then creates as these "converse" with one another.

14.2.6 Linguistic Landscapes Have Narrative Potential

Linguistic landscape research has paid little attention so far to the narrative potential of landscapes, despite the recognition that place narratives in particular are intricately connected with others' lives and others' stories in what Massey calls *spatial times*, that is, the contemporaneous existence of others in space as "a simultaneity of stories so far" (2005: 9).

In addition to landscapes in the broad sense, public signs also have important narrative potential. As Blommaert (2013: 16) notes, "signs in public space document complexity – they are visual items that tell the story of the space in which they can be found, and clarify its structure." There is, therefore, much scope for further clarifying how signs and other artifacts create spaces invested with affective meanings through narrative. There are particularly fruitful connections between linguistic landscape and *small story* research (Georgakopoulou 2015a), whereby explorations of narrative landscapes encompass not only the life-stories associated with place-making but also those fragmented ephemeral moments of engagement-in-place with key events, past or present, which show a narrative orientation to the world (De Fina and Georgakopoulou 2012: 116; Chapter 4 in this volume). As the examples in Section 14.3.6 show, it is important to look at how public spaces and semiotic artifacts can be used to demarcate *places of affect*, whereby specific narratives along with participant positions of alignment or disalignment to discourses in circulation about key events come to be created and shared in the context of specific critical incidents.

There is, inevitably, some overlap or slippage between the various categories described so far that sometimes coexist in the same landscape or artifact. In Section 14.3, we discuss each in turn in further detail, illustrating them through select examples.

14.3 Discussion of Case Studies

14.3.1 Linguistic Landscape Artifacts Enact Social Discourses

The ways in which the linguistic landscape enacts discourses is, perhaps, the most salient form of relationship between the two. We noted already how signs help create the notion of public space – how road signs, for instance, operate as specific tokens relating to a legally mandated set of rules for behavior within the public space. Much work in the area has also explored how the uses of different languages on public signage, especially in environments with politically contested histories, are manifestations of official policies that relate particular languages to community identity. For example, Tufi (2013) has looked at the ways in which the Slovenian-speaking community in Trieste, despite having achieved equality in terms of the legal status of its language, is still marginalized in that Slovenian is not accorded the same status in relation to Italian signage around the city. In this way, she argues, "public use of the Slovenian language [becomes] central to the performance of a material border" (2013: 391). To put it another way, the distribution of signs becomes a material enactment of a discourse of unequal power relations between the majority and the minority language communities.

Another example of the way that signs enact social discourses can be seen in the design of pedestrian signs on traffic lights. Not only do these form part of the general regulatory discourse of public space but they also encode particular cultural stereotypes about gender in their iconography in the way that the default figure is seemingly male. In recent years, traffic lights have been targeted for their role in the maintenance and reinforcement of dominant ideologies about cultural gender identity, with campaigns aimed at altering the type of imagery used (ITV News, 2017). In 2017 in Melbourne, Australia, for instance, male figures on some traffic lights were replaced with female ones by campaigners as a way of promoting gender equality and mobilizing the public through the routine act of crossing the street.

14.3.2 and 14.3.3 Discourses Assign Meaning to Linguistic Landscape Artifacts; and Linguistic Landscape Artifacts Become Symbolic Sites around Which Conflicting Discourses Are Played Out

When violent protests by white supremacist groups broke out in the city of Charlottesville, Virginia, in August 2017, they were initially sparked by a dispute over the fate of a public monument. A statue of the Confederate general Robert E. Lee was due to be removed from its place in the center of Emancipation Park. For many people this, along with other Confederate statues, was a symbol of the United States' racist past. In other words, the meaning of these statues as semiotic artifacts in the public space is inextricably tied up with the history related to their subjects, and the discourse of the cultural and political identity of modern-day America. The controversies over these statues was pointedly political – even if some commentators at the time attempted to argue that their meaning should first and foremost be an aesthetic one. Donald Trump (2017) himself, for example, tweeted against the calls for having them removed by lamenting "the beauty that is being taken out of our cities, towns and parks [which] will be greatly missed and never able to be comparably replaced!" But the fact that disputes over a statue led to violent street clashes and an extended public conversation about how to deal with historical injustice indicates the ways that semiotic artifacts draw their meaning from broader cultural discourses and can become sites for the production and contestation of these discourses.

14.3.4 Linguistic Landscape Artifacts Mobilize Further Discursive Articulation or Contestation

An example of the way that linguistic landscape artifacts can act as a prompt for the contestation of discourses can be seen in the controversy that broke out following a decision by Manchester Art Gallery to temporarily remove from display the painting *Hylas and the Nymphs* by John William Waterhouse. This was the result of an intervention by the artist Sonia Boyce, who was working with the art gallery on a project exploring the intersection between cultural identity and curating practices. As Boyce is quoted in *The Guardian* as saying, "Taking the picture down had been about starting a discussion, not provoking a media storm" (Higgins 2018).

The media storm it did provoke was structured around a conflict between two notable contemporary discourses – or what are referred to in the popular media as culture wars: those of freedom of expression and of gender identity politics. Boyce's project was a means of exploring the practices involved in decisions about how the work in the galleries is selected, displayed and presented, who gets to decide what gets to be seen and what does not, and the ideas of cultural value that this creates in society. In her conversations with those working at the gallery, the topic of the representation of gender frequently came up: "There seemed to be two roles played by women: femmes fatales, driving men to their deaths, or figures of beauty in quiet contemplation, but without being active agents" (Higgins 2018). The painting in question depicts a scene from the story of Hylas, a servant of Heracles, who was abducted by female water nymphs; in the composition, he is partially clothed while they are naked. The topic has been used repeatedly as a subject in Western art and is often seen as a metaphor for predatory female sexuality. As an editorial in The Guardian (2018) wrote, removing the painting from view "may have been a clumsy gesture – but it stimulated an important debate," that is, an intervention within the linguistic landscape became a prompt for a wide-ranging discussion about discourses of cultural representation, as well as regulation of social behavior.

As this example illustrates, linguistic landscapes and the media (both old and new) are interconstituted, and discourse circulation is thus a transmedia process. A case aptly illustrating interconnections between traditional media, social media and linguistic landscapes is the reactions to the terrorist attacks at the offices of the satirical magazine Charlie Hebdo in Paris in 2015. The attacks took place around 11:30 a.m. (local time) on January 7, and journalists immediately started covering the events in live reports appearing on television, radio, news blogs, and Twitter. At 12:52 p.m. (local time) French designer Joachim Roncin posted via his Twitter account a logo using the masthead of the magazine featuring the words *Je Suis Charlie*. Seven minutes later, the logo was retweeted by Twitter user Thierry Puget, who further added the hashtag *#JeSuisCharlie*. This has since been used more than five million times on Twitter alone (Morrison 2015). The hashtag was recontextualized in media reports as a way of encoding public sentiment around the event, and it also became the topic of many media articles. During the day of the attack, both the logo and the hashtag migrated from Twitter onto the streets of cities in France via personalized placards held up by demonstrators. Images of people holding these placards were then shared on social media, accompanied by messages reusing the hashtag as a metadiscursive marker used to tag the message as part of a developing backchannel to people's rallies on the ground and remediate the experience of "being-there." The hashtag inscribed a stance of solidarity and defiance into retellings of the shared story about the attack, which circulated around the (Western) world (see Giaxoglou 2018), serving as a resource for what Georgakopoulou (2015b) has termed *narrative stancetaking*, that is, taking up the position of a teller in the here and now. This transmedia circulation of the hashtag attests to what Seargeant and Monaghan (2017) describe as a "close choreography between traditional and new forms of communications technology." The slogan also became part of the physical landscape, featuring as a sticker and graffiti on the monument of the Place de la République, as well as on street walls all over cities across Europe.

The articulation of the slogan in these different modalities afforded a wide-ranging and extensive semiotic scope for the slogan, so that it very rapidly turned into a cultural meme, that is, a shared cultural reference as well as a public sign of solidarity and alignment bonding affective publics at a global scale (Papacharissi 2014). The scope of the expression *jesuis* widened to the extent that, over subsequent months, it acquired a more general meaning associated with mourning, solidarity or (dis)alignment. It was then used in the wake of other terror attacks as in the case of *Je Suis Ankara* referring to the bomb attacks in Ankara in October 2015 or the case of *Je suis Orlando* in 2016 expressing solidarity with the victims of the terrorist attack in the gay nightclub "Pulse" in Orlando, Florida. The expression *jesuis* has, thus, turned into an emblem of social identity (De Cock and Pizarro Pedraza 2018: 209) also used to reject particular social identities, as in the case of the slogan *Je ne suis pas Charlie*.

This pragmatic and semiotic extension of the expression attests to moments of heightened interconnectivity amongst traditional media, social media and landscapes through which local events are upscaled to global events, creating superspectacles that unfold across modalities, platforms and contexts. Despite their seemingly ephemeral nature, transmedial discourse assemblages are organized around particular narratives, which invite audiences to participate as more or less distant witnesses to key events, and align or disalign themselves to circulating stances to these. Importantly, these also contribute to shaping the direction of discourses about particular events and issues by sedimenting specific narrative positions, hence increasing the visibility of certain voices in physical and (social) media landscapes. This example therefore points to the need to look at social media as part of a wider media and communication ecology in which social media overlap and interconnect with traditional broadcast and print media, as well as physical spaces of gathering (Kavada 2018).

14.3.5 Linguistic Landscape Artifacts that Are in Conversation with Each Other Can Create Meaning that Extends beyond the Level of the Individual Sign

The way that slogans such as *Je suis Charlie* get reworked for different events, resulting in examples such as *Je ne suis pas Charlie* or *Je suis Ankara* and *Je suis Orlando*, illustrates how certain texts within the linguistic landscape are dialogically motivated by others. There are also ways in which semiotic artifacts can be in direct "conversation" with each other, however, creating discursive meaning that is generated by the juxtaposition of, rather than the individual placement of, these artifacts. A good example of this sort of "conversation" is that between the multiple statues that have appeared in the Wall Street area of New York. In May 2017 an artist named Alex Gardega added a small statue of a urinating dog to a site in the Bowling Green area of the neighborhood which already boasted two different examples of public art. In doing so, he was adding to a conversation about gender that had been played out in the public sphere by means of the placement and juxtaposition of statues, and the media discourse that was prompted by this. Gardega's statue of a dog was urinating up against the statue known as the *Fearless Girl*, which depicts a young girl adopting a defiant pose with her hands on her hips. This in turn had been installed in juxtaposition to another statue, that of the *Charging Bull*.

Each of these statues has fueled a debate about cultural identity – a debate that is primarily based on the interpretation of the symbolism of the different statues, as well as their provenance and placement, which generates a contested discourse of gender politics as these relate to the social context of twenty-first century Western feminism. The meaning of the statues is, thus, being generated not simply by what they depict (and what this might symbolize) but also by their emplacement in relation to the surrounding statues.

To recap the history that forms part of the discursive context for this, the statue of the *Charging Bull* was initially installed without official permission outside the New York Stock Exchange at the end of 1989. The intention, according to its artist Arturo Di Modica, was to symbolize "the strength and power of the American people" following the stock market crash in 1987. Almost thirty years later, in March 2017, the *Fearless Girl* was erected directly opposite the *Charging Bull*. It was created for International Women's Day by Kristen Visbal and sponsored by the investment firm State Street Global Advisors. Their stated aim was to draw attention to the gender gap on the boards of large US corporations, as well as to promote their Gender Diversity Index fund, which offers investment to companies who are committed to gender diversity. From an advertising perspective, it appears to have been extremely effective and has apparently helped produce a 347 percent increase in the size of the Gender Diversity Index fund (Thakker 2017).

The final statue in the conversation is the small dog urinating up against the leg of the *Fearless Girl*. According to the artist responsible, it is meant to draw attention to the fact that the *Fearless Girl* should in fact be seen predominantly as a publicity stunt rather than an act of feminism, and that it also belittles Di Modica's *Charging Bull* (Fugallo and Jaeger 2017). Both these issues had been voiced prior to the appearance of the urinating dog: when the *Fearless Girl* was first erected, the sculptor of the *Charging Bull* complained that it violated his artistic copyright because it fundamentally changed the dynamic of his work (*The Guardian* 2017). For many, including New York Mayor Bill de Blasio, this response was seen as evidence of a deep-rooted sexism in society, rather than being an issue about artistic integrity.

Debates about these various interpretations have played out predominantly in the media. An article in the *New York Times*, for example, noted that the firm behind the *Fearless Girl* itself had a very poor record in terms of promoting women to senior management positions (Bellafante 2017). In *Rolling Stone*, the journalist Helena Fitzgerald was concerned that, despite the surface message of empowerment that the statue gave, underpinning this was the idea that the goal for women, as for men, is simply to make more money, which in fact addresses none of the numerous systemic inequalities in society (Fitzgerald 2017).

Yet, at the same time, the symbolism of the urination in Gardega's statue creates a very transparent message. Writing in *Harper's Bazaar*, Jennifer Wright argues that Gardega has inadvertently created a perfect metaphor for the sort of experiences that ambitious women endure on a day-to-day basis. Whatever success they achieve in their careers, nevertheless "some remarkably mediocre man is going to come along and insure you get pissed on" (Wright 2017).

As we have seen, one of the contentious issues about the *Fearless Girl* has been that it takes its meaning from its position in front of the *Charging Bull* – and in doing this alters the meaning of the *Charging Bull* itself. This is an interesting case of recontextualization as contextualization that does not involve decontextualiation. Typically, recontextualization is a transformational process in the circulation of texts which involves the decontextualization of a stretch of discourse (or an image) from one social context and recentering in another, resulting in a change in meaning (Bauman and Briggs 1990). In this case, the emplacement of additional statues in a public space resignifies the context as well as the artifacts without them having otherwise been moved or transformed in any other way. But in resignifying the context in this way, a new context of interpretation of each artifact is created, extending and contesting the semiotic scope of the artifacts that populate it and opening up a debate about issues ranging from capitalism and patriarchy, to the influence that commercial companies versus civic bodies should have over public space.

14.3.6 Linguistic Landscapes as Narrative Landscapes

The semiotic scope of linguistic landscapes – and the artifacts within them – can also be extended and subject to resignification through different narratives and stances made available to publics. The final set of examples discussed in this section attests to this narrative potential of the linguistic landscape. The examples illustrate the negotiation and sedimentation of narrative stances and positions, the creation of identities and the regulation of affective behavior and reactions as manifest in memorial-*scapes* and the discourses related to them.

In the last few years, memorial practices in the linguistic landscape have started to attract a fair amount of scholarly attention, focusing on the physical and cultural materialities of *gravescapes* (Morris 2006), their examination as sites of queer rhetorical action (Dunn 2016) or as manifestations of broader cultural shifts, indexing, for instance, shifts from collective Muslimhood to personalized memoryscapes in the case of Danish-Muslim cemeteries (Nielsen 2018). Other work is looking at memorial-scapes as sites of and for *acts of unforgetting* tied up with discursive tensions around memory-making, as in the case of Hillsborough memorials in Liverpool (Monaghan 2018).

Acts of unforgetting seem to have become an integral part of everyday landscapes as the public reacts to terror attacks, local tragedies or even the death of celebrities. These acts involve narrative practices embedded in other social practices and discourses relating to the politics of memory and often issues of justice.

An example of this is the way that, following the attack on London Bridge on June 16, 2017, a vigil was organized and an impromptu memorial set up on the site. This accumulated flowers and handwritten tributes, many of which took the form of Post-it Notes of different colors placed one on top of another (BBC News, 2017). This wall of tributes read as a single message of solidarity and love, with key phrases such as "Together We Stand," "Prayers for London," "Stay Strong" or "Love" attracting the attention of passers-by. The use of Post-it Notes here is different from their everyday use; for example, a Post-it Note left on a door saying "John, I'll be back in five minutes" acting as a small-scale "private" interaction carried out in a public space (Blommaert 2018: 85). Post-it Notes in public memorials are used with a much wider semiotic scope, while still drawing on the association with "private" moments of connection. Memorial Post-it messages select intimate publics, blending the private and the public, the individual and the collective, and the local and the global. The accumulation of these messages on a wall in the corner of London Bridge, for instance, transformed an everyday busy street into a micro-space for passers-by to participate in an event of public mourning, prompting them to add their own tribute, stop to read the messages in silence, take pictures and remediate the act of unforgetting via social media or comment further in other contexts on the emerging story about the attack. This can be seen as an example of how signs can act as instruments for moving from one scale to another, including a move from the identity of mourner to the identity of "Londoner," legitimizing a much wider group of people to participate in the memorial event.

In this case, memorialization involves the demarcation of public space and its reconfiguration as a semi-ritual space for unforgetting, whereby narratives about the event and its main participants are interwoven through tributes contributed by family members, friends and members of the public. These acts of unforgetting, thus, create affective spaces that demand public attention and invite members of the public to take up participant positions as spectators or witnesses to what becomes a shared narrative about the event.

Impromptu memorials such as this are increasingly gaining official recognition, as evident in the announcement in March 2018 of the creation of an official memorial for the victims of the four recent attacks in London. In this memorial, offline and online modes of remembrance were combined in a digital book of hope at City Hall, the use of the hashtag #LondonUnited on social media and messages projected onto a map of the capital on the Houses of Parliament, London Bridge, Finsbury Park Mosque and Parsons Green Tube Station on the anniversaries of the attacks.

Such sites should not be seen as neutral spaces for individual and collective narrativization of mourning, however, but as sites of discursive tension about grievable lives (Butler, 2006) and issues of social inequality (starkly illustrated by the tragic Grenfell Tower fire; see Snow 2017).

Memorial-scapes raise important questions about the politics of mourning and also about story entitlement: whose stories make it into the sphere of public mourning in the form of physical, media and social media memorials, what (or who) are they about and who has the right to tell them? They offer a key example of narrative landscapes as "a place of affect" (Jaworksi and Thurlow 2010) and furnish opportunities for extending linguistic landscape research into the examination of how media and public discourses interconnect, affording and distributing particular stances on events and upscaling them from local to global levels. This line of research calls for transmedia methods for data collection and analysis as a supplement to existing ethnographic approaches.

14.4 Conclusion

Scholars are still in some disagreement about the scope that linguistic landscape research should take and the methods appropriate to its study. Among the discussions around this, Blommaert has called for a social or materialist semiotic approach to the study of the meanings and effects of signs in actual social life, adopting an ethnographic perspective (2018: 86). As a contribution to discussions of this nature, the present chapter has sought to clarify some of the interconnections between linguistic landscapes and discourse as a step toward opening up the scope of this type of research and analyzing the ways in which the linguistic landscape is semiotized.

More specifically, we have called attention to the many ways in which linguistic landscapes and the artifacts that constitute them enact and mobilize discourses (and vice versa), noting how linguistic landscapes can become symbolic sites around which discourses are pitted against each other and negotiated. Such negotiations make available different participant positions of alignment or disalignment to particular stances. We have foregrounded linguistic landscapes as sites for creative practices of meaning-making where regulatory (normative) discourses can be contested, extended or subverted. We have approached semiotic signs as emplaced discourse complexes which are part of broader communication and (social) media ecologies. And finally, we have called attention to linguistic landscapes as "places of affect" (Jaworski and Thurlow 2010) by pointing to the narrative potential of landscapes for demarcating affective micro-spaces, which attract public attention and create opportunities for participation in specific kinds of event and their storying.

Our suggested categories of the interface between discourse and linguistic landscape research have important methodological implications. They call for the inclusion of data collection decisions that allow a more systematic consideration of (re)contextualization and narrativization processes, moving beyond the individual sign or groups of signs in a delimited survey area, to tracking the emergence and change of signs' meanings in place, by analyzing incidents and discourses around critical moments or events (see Georgakopoulou 2014). Applying this method for data collection and analysis can bring together aspects of signs' emplacement and uptake across physical, media and social media environment.

Given the issues outlined here, there is great scope for linguistic landscape research to revisit its connections to the disciplines of geography and sociology, where the landscape is studied in relation to sociopolitical formations (Sassen 2016), as well as its connections to developments in discourse studies, including, for example, critical discourse analysis, small story research and social media communication studies. In systematically merging theories and analytical frameworks from discourse studies with the aims and approaches that constitute linguistic landscape research, this area of study will continue to flourish as an important window on the complex relationships between language, culture and society.

Further Reading

Blommaert, J. (2013). *Ethnography, Superdiversity and Linguistic Landscapes: Chronicles of Complexity*. Bristol: Multilingual Matters.

This case study of the linguistic landscape of Antwerp, Belgium explores the way in which multilingual signs chronicle the complex histories of a place.

Jaworski, A. and Thurlow, C. (eds.) (2010). *Semiotic Landscapes*. London: Continuum.

This is an important collection about linguistic landscapes, with a focus on language and visual discourse and on spatial practices.

Scollon, R. and Scollon, S. B. K. (2003). *Discourses in Place: Language in the Material World*. London: Routledge.

This classic text explores the ways in which the meaning of public texts is dependent on a rich understanding of the social and physical context in which they exist.

Shohamy, E. and Gorter, D. (eds.) (2009). *Linguistic Landscape: Expanding the Scenery*. London: Routledge.

This is one of the earliest collections of linguistic landscape research; it gives a good overview of the scope of the field.

References

Androutsopoulos, J. (2014). Computer-Mediated Communication and Linguistic Landscapes. In J. Holmes and K. Hazen (eds.) *Research*

Methods in Sociolinguistics: A Practical Guide. Malden, MA: Wiley-Blackwell. 74–90.

Bauman, R. and Briggs, C. L. (1990). Poetics and Performance as Critical Perspectives on Language and Social Life. *Annual Review of Anthropology* 19: 59–88.

BBC News. (2017). London Attack: Crowds Gather for Vigil to Honour Victims. June 5. www.bbc.co.uk/news/in-pictures-40159030.

(2018a). Didcot Signs Point to Narnia, Gotham City and Middle Earth. March 19. www.bbc.co.uk/news/uk-england-oxfordshire-43459598.

(2018b). Didcot's Narnia and Middle Earth Sign-Changer Found. March 20. www.bbc.co.uk/news/uk-england-oxfordshire-43470241.

(2018c). Didcot's Narnia and Middle Earth Signs Removed. March 21. www.bbc.co.uk/news/uk-england-oxfordshire-43486855.

Bellafante, G. (2017). The False Feminism of "Fearless Girl." *New York Times*, March 16. www.nytimes.com/2017/03/16/nyregion/fearless-girl-statue-manhattan.html.

Blackwood, R. (2017). Introduction: Methodology in Linguistic Landscape Research. *Linguistic Landscape* 3(3): 221–5.

Blommaert, J. (2005). *Discourse: A Critical Introduction*. Cambridge: Cambridge University Press.

(2013). *Ethnography, Superdiversity and Linguistic Landscapes: Chronicles of Complexity*. Bristol: Multilingual Matters.

(2018). *Dialogues with Ethnography: Notes on Classics, and How I Read Them*. Bristol: Multilingual Matters.

Blommaert, J. and Maly, I. (2014). Ethnographic Linguistic Landscape Analysis and Social Change: A Case Study. *Working Papers in Urban Language & Literacies*. Paper 133: 1–20.

Bradley, J., Moore, E., Simpson, J. and Atkinson, L. (2018). Translanguaging Space and Creative Activity: Theorising Collaborative Arts-Based Learning. *Language and Intercultural Communication* 18(1): 54–73.

Bucholtz, M. and Hall, K. (2008). All of the Above: New Coalitions in Sociocultural Linguistics. *Journal of Sociolinguistics* 12(4): 401–31.

Butler, J. (2006). *Precarious Life: The Power of Mourning and Violence*. London/New York: Verso.

Coupland, N. (2010). *Welsh Linguistic Landscapes "from Above" and "from Below."* In A. Jaworski and C. Thurlow (eds.) *Semiotic Landscapes: Language, Image, Space*, London: Continuum. 77–101.

De Cock, B. and Pizarro Pedraza, A. (2018). From Expressing Solidarity to Mocking on Twitter: Pragmatic Functions of Hashtags Starting with #jesuis across languages. *Language in Society* 47(2): 197–217.

De Fina, A. and Georgakopoulou, A. (2012). *Analyzing Narrative: Discourse and Sociolinguistic Perspectives*. Cambridge: Cambridge University Press.

Dunn, T. (2016). *Queerly Remembered: Rhetorics for Representing the GLBTQ Past*. Columbia: University of South Carolina Press.

Fitzgerald, H. (2017). Why "Pissing Dog" Statue beside "Fearless Girl" Statue Is Misogynistic. *Rolling Stone*, May 31. www.rollingstone.com/culture/why-nyc-pissing-dog-statue-is-misogynistic-w484932.

Fugallo, N. and Jaeger, M. (2017). Pissed-Off Artist Adds Statue of Urinating Dog next to "Fearless Girl." *New York Post*, May 29. http://nypost.com/2017/05/29/pissed-off-artist-adds-statue-of-urinating-dog-next-to-fearless-girl/.

Georgakopoulou, A. (2014). Small Stories Transposition and Social Media: A Micro-perspective on the Greek Crisis. *Discourse & Society* (Special Issue: From Grexit to Grecovery: Euro/Crisis Discourses, ed. by R. Wodak and J. Angouri) 25 (4): 519–39.

(2015a). Small Stories Research: Methods – Analysis – Outreach. In A. De Fina and A. Georgakopoulou (eds.) *Handbook of Narrative Analysis*. Malden, MA: John Wiley & Sons 256–71.

(2015b). Life/Narrative of the Moment: From Telling a Story to Taking a Narrative Stance. In B. Schiff, A. E. McKim and S. Patron (eds.) *Life and Narrative: The Risks and Responsibilities of Storying Experience*. Oxford: Oxford University Press.

Georgakopoulou, A. and Goutsos, D. (2004). *Discourse Analysis: An Introduction*. Edinburgh: Edinburgh University Press.

Giaxoglou, K. (2018). #JeSuisCharlie? Hashtags as Narrative Resources in Contexts of Ecstatic Sharing. *Discourse, Context, and Media* (Special Issue on: Discourse of Social Tagging, ed. by C. Lee) 22: 13–20.

Gorter, D. (ed.) (2006). *Linguistic Landscape: A New Approach to Multilingualism* Clevedon: Multilingual Matters. 67–80.

(2018). Methods and Techniques for Linguistic Landscape Research: About Definitions, Core Issues and Technological Innovations. In M. Pütz and N. Mundt (eds.) *Expanding the Linguistic Landscape: Multilingualism, Language Policy and the Use of Space as a Semiotic Resource*. Bristol: Multilingual Matters.

Higgins, C. (2018). "The Vitriol Was Really Unhealthy": Artist Sonia Boyce on the Row over Taking Down Hylas and the Nymphs. *The Guardian*, March 19. www.theguardian.com/artanddesign/2018/mar/19/hylas-nymphs-manchester-art-gallery-sonia-boyce-interview.

ITV News. (2017). Female Traffic Light Signals a Step Forward for Equality. March 7. www.itv.com/news/2017-03-07/female-traffic-light-signals-a-step-forward-for-equality/.

Jaworksi, A. and Coupland, N. (eds.) (1999). *The Discourse Reader*. London/New York: Routledge.

Jaworski, A. and Thurlow, C. (eds.) (2010). *Semiotic Landscapes: Language, Image, Space*. London: Bloomsbury.

Johnstone, B. (2018). *Discourse Analysis*, 3rd ed. Hoboken, NJ: Wiley Blackwell.

Karlander, D. (2018). Mobile Semiosis and Mutable Metro Spaces: Train Graffiti in Stockholm's Public Transport System. In A. Peck, C. Stroud and Q. Williams (eds.) *Making Sense of People and Place in Linguistic Landscapes*. London: Bloomsbury.

Kavada, A. (2018). Editorial: Media and the "Populist Moment." *Media, Culture & Society* 40(5): 742–4.

Landry, R. and Bourhis, R. (1997). Linguistic Landscape and Ethnolinguistic Vitality. *Journal of Language and Social Psychology* 16(1): 23–49.

Lou, J. (2016). *The Linguistic Landscape of Chinatown: A Sociolinguistic Ethnography*. Bristol: Multilingual Matters.

Massey, D. (2005). *On Space*. London: Sage.

Monaghan, F. (2018). Unforgetting Hillsborough: Researching Memorialisation. Poster presentation at X-Scapes Linguistic Landscape Workshop, May 2–4, Bern, Switzerland.

Morris, R. (2006). Death on Display. In L. J. Prelli (ed.) *Rhetorics of Display*. Columbia: University of South Carolina Press. 2014–29.

Morrison, K. (2015). #JeSuisCharlie Used More than 5 Million Times on Twitter. Adweek, January 12. www.adweek.com/digital/jesuischarlie-used-5-million-times-twitter/.

Nielsen, H. L. (2018). Branding Muslimhood or Mourning the Dead? What Muslim Gravescapes Can Tell Us about the Living. Paper presented at X-Scapes Linguistic Landscape Workshop, May 2–4, Bern, Switzerland.

Papacharissi, Z. (2014). *Affective Publics: Sentiment, Technology and Politics*. Oxford: Oxford University Press.

Peck, A. and Stroud, C. (2015). Skinscapes. *Linguistic Landscape* 1(1): 133–51.

Pennycook, A. (2009). Linguistic Landscapes and the Transgressive Semiotics of Graffiti. In E. Shohamy and D. Gorter (eds.) *Linguistic Landscape: Expanding the Scenery*. London: Routledge. 302–12.

Pennycook, A. and Otsuji, E. (2015). Making Scents of the Landscape. *Linguistic Landscape* 1(3): 191–212.

Pütz, M. and Mundt, N. (eds.) (2018). *Expanding the Linguistic Landscape: Multilingualism, Language Policy and the Use of Space as a Semiotic Resource*. Bristol: Multilingual Matters.

Sassen, S. (2016). Land as Infrastructure for Living. In C. Girot and D. Imhof (eds.) *Thinking the Contemporary Landscape*. New York: Princeton Architectural Press. 30–8.

Scarvaglieri, C., Redder, A., Pappenhagen, R. and Brehmer, B. (2013). Capturing Diversity: Linguistic Land- and Soundscaping. In J. Duarte and I. Gogolin (eds.) *Linguistic Superdiversity in Urban Areas: Research Approaches*. Amsterdam: John Benjamins. 45–74.

Scollon, R. and Scollon, S. B. K. (2003). *Discourses in Place: Language in the Material World*. London: Routledge.

Seargeant, P. and Monaghan, F. (2017). Street Protests and the Creative Spectacle. *Diggit Magazine*, March 20. www.diggitmagazine.com/articles/street-protests-and-creative-spectacle.

Sebba, M. (2010). Discourses in Transit. In A. Jaworksi and C. Thurlow (eds.) *Semiotic Landscapes: Language, Image, Space*. London: Continuum.

Shohamy, E. (2006). *Language Policy: Hidden Agendas and New Approaches*. New York: Routledge.

Shohamy, E. and Gorter, D. (eds.) (2009). *Linguistic Landscape: Expanding the Scenery*. London: Routledge.

Shohamy, E. and Waksman, S. (2009). Linguistic Landscape as an Ecological Arena: Modalities, Meanings, Negotiations, Education. In E. Shohamy and D. Gorter (eds.) *Linguistic Landscape: Expanding the Scenery*. New York: Routledge. 313–31.

Snow, J. (2017). Grenfell Proved It: The British Media Are Part of a Disconnected Elite. *The Guardian*, August 23. www.theguardian.com/commentisfree/2017/aug/23/grenfell-british-media-divide.

Thakker, K. (2017). Fearless Girl Takes Home 3 Top Awards at the Cannes Ad Festival. *Fortune*, June 20. http://fortune.com/2017/06/20/fearless-girl-cannes-awards/.

The Guardian. (2017). "Charging Bull" Sculptor Says New York's "Fearless Girl" Statue Violates His Rights April 12. www.theguardian.com/us-news/2017/apr/12/charging-bull-new-york-fearless-girl-statue-copyright-claim.

(2018). The Guardian View on Hylas and the Nymphs: Not Censorship. February 7. www.theguardian.com/commentisfree/2018/feb/07/the-guardian-view-on-hylas-and-the-nymphs-not-censorship.

Trump, J. D. (@realDonaldTrump) "... the beauty that is being taken out of our cities, towns and parks [which] will be greatly missed and never able to be comparably replaced!" https://twitter.com/realDonaldTrump/status/898172999945392131. 17 Aug. 2017. 06:21am. Tweet.

Tufi, S. (2013). Shared Places, Unshared Identities: Vernacular Discourses and Spatialised Constructions of Identity in the Linguistic Landscape of Trieste. *Modern Italy* 18(4): 391–408.

Wright, J. (2017). How to Be Fearless in the Face of a Pissing Pug. *Harper's Bazaar*, June 1. www.harpersbazaar.com/culture/features/a9960542/fearless-girl-pissing-pug-statue-nyc/.

15

Discourse, Emotions and Embodiment

Brigitta Busch

15.1 Introduction

Over a long period, social sciences and humanities were heavily influenced by the so-called "linguistic turn," an umbrella term that designated orientations based on constructionist thinking and following the assumption that language rather constitutes and structures than merely describes "reality." Since the 1970s, a plethora of other turns were proclaimed pointing to aspects that seemed neglected within predominantly logocentric perspectives. This is the case for approaches which are sometimes summarized as body or corporeal turn respectively, as emotional or affective turn and which, as disparate as they may be, in one way or another challenge the classical Western division between mind and body, between rationality and emotionality.

In the works of the "founding fathers" of sociology in the twentieth century, bodies played a role of "absent presence" (Shilling 1993: 19); corporeal and affective phenomena were primarily perceived as disturbing factors interfering with the research process and the rational explication of the world. However, early exceptions from the rule could be mentioned: Bergson ([1896]2012) developed in the late nineteenth century a concept of embodied memory, Husserl ([1929]1960), not much later, emphasized the body dimension of the subject's being-in-the world. To a certain extent, both anticipated elements of what characterizes current approaches in social research and humanities: bodies and emotions are considered not only as objects of social research but also as being inextricably involved in all forms of subjective experience and social practice.

Feminist approaches, gender and queer studies, studies on colonialism and racism, all of which are interested both in the "making" of bodies by dominant Discourses[1] and in the role of subjective experiences in

---

[1] Following a frequently applied practice, we differentiate throughout this chapter between *Discourse* with a capital D when referring to Discourses on a societal macro-level and *discourse* when referring to speech in situated interaction.

"answering back," have played a decisive role for this reorientation toward conceptions of embodiment, that is, the thinking about and through bodies. The persisting interest in approaches focusing on body and/or emotion is reflected by a growing number of handbooks and specialized academic journals in a range of disciplines. Many of these works draw on theoretical conceptions developed in the course of the twentieth century. To mention only a few which will be discussed in more detail later in the chapter: Merleau-Ponty's (1962) distinction between the body as an observable object and the perceiving body subject; Vygotsky's ([1934]1994) thoughts on the role of emotional experience in the process of adaption to social environments; Goffman's (1959) interest in bodies involved in situated social interactions; Garfinkel's (1967) ethnomethodological considerations on para- and nonverbal features in interaction; Lakoff and Johnson's (1980) work on basic metaphors derived from bodily experience; Douglas's (1970) understanding of the body as a symbolic system reflecting social structures; Bourdieu's (1991) concept of hexis and habitus as embodied social positions; Foucault's (1973) studies on the history of medicine, sexuality and biopolitics; and Butler's (1997) concept of subjectivation developed in her work on the production of gendered bodies. Increasingly also, neurosciences, often employing imaging techniques, begin to recognize the role of emotion and body for cognition and memory.

In applied linguistics, the so-called corporal and affective turns arrived rather late, roughly around the millennium turn. However, bodily and emotional phenomena have played a certain role in linguistics from the early days, for example in phonetics (interested in the physiological production and auditory perception of speech sound), in ethnographic approaches (interested in non- and paraverbal semiotic practices in the process of meaning-making) or in semantic-lexical studies (interested in how emotions are expressed and conceptualized in different languages). In this context, the groundbreaking works of Bühler ([1934]1990) and Jakobson (1960) on language and communication who point out that an expressive or emotive component is present in every act of communication and constitutes one of the basic functions of language should not go unmentioned. In fact, emotion can come into play with regard to all three variables of Bühler's organon model of language: the emotive function which is associated with the sender, the representational which is associated with the object of the utterance and the appellative which is associated with its receiver.

Generally speaking, however, physical and/or emotional aspects were for a long time considered mainly as epiphenomena in the analysis of communicative acts. Only more recently have a number of approaches appeared in sociolinguistics or applied linguistics that, though committed to different theoretical and methodological orientations, concur in moving the idea of subjects that are bodily and emotionally involved in interactions with other subjects to the center of their interest. Taking into account the bodily and emotional dimensions of discourse is, as I will argue, more than an "add-on" to the understanding of verbal interaction. Also, focusing on bodily and emotional aspects can shed new light on other phenomena. This, of course, has implications for theory and methodology too.

The recent focus on the role of bodies and affects in sociolinguistic, conversation analytical and discourse analytical research correlates with an understanding of meaning-making as a cooperative, dialogical process across different modes or sign systems (including making use of objects and spatial arrangements). This entails a growing interest in the "material" quality and the spatial embeddedness of the linguistic/communicative sign as emphasized in "post-human" and process-based approaches that embrace a "concept of affective practice" (Wetherell 2012: 3). In Mondada's (2016: 336) words, the challenge is to overcome "a logo-centric vision of communication, as well as a visuo-centric vision of embodiment." However, this reorientation is still in early stages and, as Bucholtz and Hall (2016: 173) note, a broad discussion within sociocultural linguistics concerning the theoretical relationship between language and embodiment is still largely lacking.

From the angle of discourse studies, rather than being interested in bodies and emotions as such, we try to understand bodily and affective phenomena as intentional moves in interaction. The term "intentional" thereby is not to be equated with "deliberate"; it solely indicates that affect and body moves are, in a quite similar way as discourse, directed or oriented toward someone or something. In this, I follow Ahmed (2004: 6) who understands emotion as a phenomenon of contact that resides neither in the subject nor in the object but involves "the subject, as well as histories that come before the subjects" and presupposes a (socially and historically informed) "process of reading." Ahmed uses the term "impression" to elucidate her understanding of emotion as a contact phenomenon, an understanding that "allows us to associate the experience of having an emotion with the very affect of one surface upon another, an affect that leaves its mark or trace" (2004: 6). The idea of "impression" includes affective, corporal and cognitive dimensions and, according to Ahmed (2004: 6), allows "to avoid making analytical distinction between bodily sensation, emotion, and thought as if they could be 'experienced' as distinct realms of human 'experience.'" Although some of the literature discussed in this chapter focuses either on affects or on bodies in interaction, I suggest that emotions and bodies should be thought of as intimately intertwined and as representing dimensions always present in discourse in interaction. In a similar direction, Wetherell (2013: 351) argues that social research requires methods that deal with entanglements of embodiment and discourse and that a privileged unit for the analysis in this domain are the "emergent, open-ended, intertwined affective-discursive patterns evident in social life."

According to different disciplines and theoretical approaches, authors define emotion or affect in various ways, sometimes seeking to subdivide the realm of emotions into different categories and subcategories and to establish semantic distinctions between terms such as feeling, emotion, affect, arousal, desire, etc. In contrast to psychological approaches that understand emotions primarily as "inner states," the focus when exploring the nexus discourse–embodiment–emotion is on social and intersubjective parameters, on how affects are conceived by Discourse in specific historical and spatial contexts and how they are deployed and interpreted in situated interactions. From such a perspective, Ahmed (2004) suggests that "emotions" are prefigured by cultural scripts, while "affect" focuses on the specific performance and its effects. For the purpose of this chapter, I will use the two terms in most cases synonymously or according to the use by the authors referred to.

The notion of embodiment, roughly speaking, refers to the capacity of the senso-motoric body to internalize information from the material and social world, making the body an informed body that incorporates or embodies the relation with the "world" (historical and material conditions, power relations, social/discursive practices, etc.). The current concept of embodiment is inspired by earlier thinking that conceives of the body as a mediating instance between the inner and the outer world (e.g. Vygotsky [1934]1994). In this context, it is also important to remind of the distinction made in phenomenological thinking (e.g. Husserl [1929]1960; Merleau-Ponty 1962) between the observable object body that one "has" and the perceiving and acting subject body that one "is."

In Section 15.2, I will first give an overview on literature dealing with the nexus discourse–embodiment–emotion. Within this section, the survey is structured according to different strands of research: approaches committed to interaction research (Section 15.2.1), to Discourse theory (Section 15.2.2) and to cognitive science or phenomenology (Section 15.2.3). These approaches not only differ in their theoretical and methodological implications but also correspond to different ways of "looking" at bodies and emotions: the focus can be on how they are deployed in (observable) interactions; on how they are constructed in and made object of Discourse; or on how they are lived and experienced by subjects. Focusing on the concepts of positioning (Section 15.3.1) and of lived experience of language (Section 15.3.2), Section 15.3 addresses ongoing debates on how these different takes can be thought of as complementary with regard to affect and embodiment.

15.2 Overview of the Topic

15.2.1 Emotions and Bodies in Interaction

In this first subsection, I will discuss literature that focuses on the observation of situated communicative events on a micro-level and conceives of bodies and emotions as resources on which actors rely in dialogical processes of meaning-making. This perspective is mainly represented in research oriented toward linguistic anthropology, ethnography of communication, interactional sociolinguistics, ethnomethodology or conversation analysis. I will first go back to some founding concepts within this strand of social and cultural theory and then explore how these concepts were made productive in different fields of linguistics.

Many of the works focusing on embodiment and affect in interaction refer to Goffman, who already in his seminal book *The Presentation of Self in Everyday Life* (1959) drew attention to the importance of bodily and emotional aspects in face-to-face encounters. In his view, an individual will try to control the impression others receive of the situation. Goffman is mainly concerned with the participant's staging problems and the techniques they employ to sustain the intended impressions. Emotions come into play, for instance, when events occur within an interaction that contradict the participants' expectations linked to the definition of the situation: "At such moments the individual whose presentation has been discredited may feel ashamed while the others present may feel hostile, and all the participants may come to feel ill at ease, nonplussed, out of countenance, embarrassed, experiencing the kind of anomy that is generated when the minute social system of face-to-face interaction breaks down" (Goffman 1959: 12). Elsewhere Goffman insists: "Indeed it is impossible to utter a sentence without coloring the utterance with some kind of perceivable affect – even if (in special cases) only with the emotionally distinctive aura of affectlessness" (Goffman 1978: 813). He devotes special attention to forms of blurted vocalization: namely, response cries (interjections), self-talk and imprecations, which present an element of public display of affect. He considers them to be highly conventionalized as to form, occasion of occurrence and social function. Goffman addresses the bodily dimension of social interaction under the term "social portraiture" (1979: 6). This refers to "individuals' use of 'faces and bodies' in social situations" so as to present themselves in the way they want to be seen whereby they draw on models provided, for example, by commercial advertisements.

Garfinkel's ethnomethodological approach has heavily influenced later works mainly within conversation analysis that recognize the importance of para- and nonverbal features (such as body posture and gesture, facial expression, prosody, eye gaze, spatial orientation, etc.) in situated interaction. These bodily components also contribute to evoke what is assumed in specific settings as "normal" and thereby also to produce "normality." Garfinkel's (1967) famous case study of "Passing and the managed achievement of sex status in an 'intersexed' person" was the first to discuss a topic that, in our days, takes an important place when it comes to interrelations between language and body.

With reference to both Goffman and Garfinkel, Gumperz (1992), in his notion of contextualization cues, that is, signs by which interactants indicate which presuppositions they must rely on to maintain conversational involvement and assess what is intended, relates verbal and nonverbal forms of interaction such as prosody, gesture, mimics and posture to each other.

Conversation analysis – initially rather inclined toward a certain logocentrism – received new impetus from using audiovisual data. Thanks to his professional training in film production, Goodwin played a pioneering role already in the beginning of the 1980s. One example for the interest in the use of bodies in situated communication events is Goodwin's (2000) very detailed analysis of the video recording of a conflictual interaction between three young girls playing hopscotch. He shows how the participants deploy a range of different kinds of semiotic resource, whereby gestures are not necessarily "simply a visual mirror of the lexical content of the talk, but a semiotic modality in their own right" (2000: 1498), and he pleads for an analysis of human action that "takes into account simultaneously the details of language use, the semiotic structure provided by the historically built material world, the body as an unfolding locus for the display of meaning and action, and the temporally unfolding organization of talk-in-interaction" (2000: 1517). Goodwin (2007) also shows that taking an affective stance plays a significant role in expressing willingness or refusal to participate in a cooperative interaction. Goodwin's work has been especially influential in workplace studies.

A particular challenge for the analysis of audiovisual data is the development of adequate systems for the transcription and visual representation of gestures, embodied actions, interaction with material objects, movement in space, etc. (cf. Norris 2004). Mondada (2016) gives an overview of the growing interest in embodiment in conversation analysis and draws attention to specific challenges for transcription. In particular, she shows that sequentiality in interactions is a less linear phenomenon than it appears just on the basis of talk. A precise transcription of timing reveals that sequentiality "relies on subtle ways of arranging and adjusting prior and next actions in real time" (Mondada 2016: 346). As she explains, "an action can be initiated before the turn is actually uttered; an action can be responded to very early, and even responded to while the previous action is being produced, either in the form of a turn or an embodied movement" (2016: 346).

The question of affect and embodiment has also frequently been raised in linguistic anthropology, especially in the context of work on rituals understood as firmly established ideologically founded orders of practice. Under the telling title "Language has a heart," Ochs and Schieffelin (1989), in an oft cited paper, set out to sketch a general framework for the understanding of language and affect. They are interested in how speakers display features in language to key affect to others as well as in how "interactants seek out affective information from significant others in their social environment to better understand and respond to uncertain information" (Ochs and Schieffelin 1989: 21). They specify that linguistic resources for expressing affect include not only lexicon (interjections, response cries, respect and disrespect vocabulary, etc.) and phonology (intonation, voice quality, sound symbolism, etc.) but also grammatical features (use of pronouns, determiners, mood, etc.) and discourse structure (code-switching, affective speech, etc.), whereby these affect markers can serve a range of different pragmatic functions. Social referencing, the ability to read and to express affect, is considered to be central for cooperation and communication in all spheres of life.

With regard to the importance of body dimensions of communication, a study by the anthropologist Duranti is seen as pioneering. Based on audiovisual recordings of sequential acts of ceremonial greetings in Western Samoa, Duranti (1992: 657) investigates "the interpenetration of words, body movements, and living space in the constitution of a particular kind of interactional practice." He pays special attention to "sighting" as an interactive step by which interactants engage in a negotiated process at the end of which they find themselves physically located in the relevant social hierarchies. With his empirical findings, he contests the idea of supremacy of the verbal mode: "The body (e.g. body postures, gestures, eye gaze) not only provides the context for interpretation of linguistic units (words, morphemes, etc.), as argued by linguists working on deixis, but helps fashion alternative, sometimes complementary, sometimes contradictory messages" (Duranti 1992: 663).

From the broader perspective of interaction or communication analysis, early works treated phenomena of body motion primarily as phenomena accompanying talk often using the term of kinesics. The concept of multimodality which is linked to the work of Kress and van Leuwen (2001), however, assumes that meaning-making is spread across all modes involving a plurality of semiotic resources. Detailed patterns of body postures that come together with specific linguistic constructions in given sequential environments constitute, as Mondada (2016: 344) argues, "complex multimodal Gestalts," whereby the term *Gestalt*, borrowed from psychology, suggests that the whole has qualities that are more than the sum of its parts. Some authors (Pennycook 2017; Canagarajah 2018) prefer the term *assemblage*, coined by Deleuze and Gutattari (1987), thereby emphasizing that semiotic assemblages emerge from the interplay between bodies, actions, artifacts and spaces that concur in momentary, constantly changing constellations. According to Pennycook (2017), the notion of assemblages allows for an understanding of how different trajectories of people, semiotic resources and objects meet at particular moments and places, and thus emphasizes the significance of things, bodies and places alongside the meanings of linguistic resources.

In sum, within the interactional paradigm, the bodily-affective dimension in and of communication has received attention mainly as *display* of affect or as body *enactment*, of course with regard to the functions that bodily and affective phenomena accomplish in a specific moment of situated interaction. As Pépin (2008) summarizes, from an interactional perspective, emotions cannot be understood as isolated, decontextualized, individual phenomena but rather as situated in particular sociocultural environments and interactional settings. They are understood as closely intertwined with the sequential organization of talk-in-interaction and as jointly constructed, deconstructed and reconstructed by the participants. They are linked to the fluidity of talk-in-interaction allowing participants to turn, within short lapses of time, toward very different emotional displays. The body is seen as an essential vehicle for the deployment of emotions in interaction. Emotions are distributed amongst different modes of verbal and nonverbal communication (intonation, gesture, body posture, etc.), the interacting participants, and different resources exploited in interaction, e.g. space and surrounding objects.

15.2.2 Body and Emotion Shaped by Discourse and Practice

Whereas from an interactional perspective researchers are primarily interested in how bodies and affects are deployed in accomplishing communicative tasks, works based on theories of Discourse (Foucault) or Practice (Bourdieu) are more interested in how bodies and emotions are conceived and formed through historically and spatially situated social practices and Discourses, that is, in how everyday practices and discourses are inscribed into the body. Whereas the focus in the former is on the micro-level of situated interactions, in the latter it is rather on power relations and inequalities on the macro-level of societies.

Foucault, one of the founding figures in Discourse theory, attaches particular attention to the body. In his work on the clinic (Foucault 1973), he offers a cultural and historical account of how, in the eighteenth century, the clinical gaze constructed the body in a new way. The body became something that could be mapped; disease became subject to new rules of classification. The construction of the body in a specific way is understood as part of the process of becoming a subject. This process operates not only through disciplinary power, interdictions and restrictions but also by "technologies of the self" that human beings use to address and understand themselves, to effect operations "on their own bodies and souls, thoughts, conduct, and way of being" (Foucault 1988: 17).

In Bourdieu's works, the focus is less on historical discourse formations than on everyday practices of social production and reproduction. His concept of habitus and hexis is often referred to when dealing with interrelations between language dispositions and society. According to Bourdieu, a particular position in society or within a particular social field is characterized and reinforced by sets of specific everyday practices that are in turn condensed in personal, bodily dispositions, in what he calls habitus and hexis and by which he understands "a certain durable way of standing, speaking, walking and thereby of feeling and thinking" (Bourdieu 1991: 13). Bourdieu uses the two terms to some extent interchangeably whereby hexis rather foregrounds observable bodily aspects while habitus foregrounds the process of how social power relations become internalized, incorporated or incarnated mainly beyond the grasp of consciousness and will.

Bourdieu (1991) exemplifies the habitus concept by analyzing class- and gender-specific ways of speaking. According to him, speaking is always oriented toward a specific linguistic market, on which specific ways of speaking are evaluated according to their symbolic value and judged as acceptable or not: "The sense of acceptability which orients linguistic practices is inscribed in the most deep-rooted of bodily dispositions: it is the whole body that responds by its posture, but also by its inner reactions or, more specifically, by the articulatory one's, to the tension of the market" (Bourdieu 1991: 86).

In this sense, the habitus anticipates the demands of the field, which can, as Bourdieu shows, result, for example, in falling silent or in self-censorship when one's own linguistic practices seem inappropriate. Through socialization and habitualized practice, language becomes a "body technique," "a life style 'made flesh'" (Bourdieu 1991: 86).

Judith Butler's work on performativity, subjectivation and gender, which draws on both Foucault and Bourdieu, is frequently referred to when it comes to questions of body and gender in discourse. In line with Foucault, Butler (1997) emphasizes the double character of discourse in constituting and in subjugating the subject. One becomes a subject by being repeatedly allocated to previously established identity categories. Every such recognition is at the same time a misrecognition because it reduces heterogeneous and ambiguous elements to either-or categories. The social and performative constitution of the body is a cornerstone in Butler's concept of subjectivation. She develops Bourdieu's concept of the habitus, which she understands as produced and structured by repeated performative acts. Referring to Althusser's (1971) idea that the subject is constituted in being "interpellated" (addressed) by ideologies, Butler notes: "The social life of the body is produced through an interpellation that is at once linguistic and productive" (Butler 1997: 153). And later: "[T]he habitus constitutes a tacit form of performativity, a citational chain lived and believed at the level of the body" (1997: 155).

Butler (1993: xvii) illustrates the way in which interpellation and performativity operate with the famous example of the medical discourse that "shifts an infant from an 'it' to a 'she' or a 'he', and in that naming, the girl is 'girled', brought into the domain of language and kinship through the interpellation of gender." This founding interpellation is then reiterated by various authorities and throughout various intervals of time. "The naming is at once the setting of a boundary, and also the repeated inculcation of a norm" (Butler 1993: xvii). In her analysis of hate speech, Butler (1997) also discusses the somatic dimension of linguistic injury and linguistic pain. If the subject is constituted by language, language can also threaten its existence. Linguistic injury not only represents a metaphorical violence but is also inscribed onto the body; with every new injuring utterance, previous ones are reinvoked.

The discourse theoretical perspective on corporeity and emotionality has proven to be particularly productive in gender and queer studies (e.g. Motschenbacher 2010; Milani 2017) as well as in critical race theory (e.g. Alim 2016), both of which challenge essentialist or naturalizing conceptualizations and categorizations. Ahmed (2004) suggests a methodology for reading the emotionality of texts and discusses the role of emotions in political debates on topics such as terrorism, asylum or reparation. Also, recent works have increasingly explored how discourses on emotionality and corporeality contribute to translating neoliberal notions of self-responsibility, self-optimization, emotional competence or creativity into everyday practices and techniques of the self, thereby facilitating the adaption of the involved subjects to the requirements of post-industrial capitalism (e.g. Reckwitz 2006; Illouz 2007; Lordon 2014). Other studies (e.g. Wellgraf 2018) deal with the reverse side of these processes, namely the emotional experience of ascribed inferiority and of exclusion.

15.2.3 Bodily-Emotional Experience in Cognitive and Phenomenological Approaches

While the approaches discussed so far foreground either situated interaction or Discourse on the macro-level of society, cognitive and phenomenological approaches start from the (individual) speaking subject. According to cognitive sciences, both language and emotions are located (mainly) in the brain, while according to phenomenological approaches, language and emotions are part of our bodily being-in-the-world.

In the heterogeneous field of cognitive linguistics, informed by neuroscience and brain research, emotion and language are seen as complex mental systems consisting of different knowledge subsystems that interact in manifold ways and mediate between the "inner" and the "outer" world. In a meta-analysis of approximately 500 scientific publications on the interconnection between language and emotion, Lüdtke and Polzin (2015) show that a continuously intensifying interest can be identified from the 1980s onwards. In cognitive linguistics, there has been growing attention to emotive aspects of language and language processing, for example analyzing the emotion vocabulary, emotive metaphors, morphological items, connotative meanings, etc. A large segment of research is dedicated to comparisons between different languages in the expression of emotions (for an overview see Pavlenko 2005; Dewaele 2013) or else to exploring emotions "from a language-independent perspective" searching for (decontextualized) semantic universals, for a universal understanding of emotions Wierzbicka (1995: 236).

In cognitive science, different schools of thought can be identified that developed over time and are also currently pursued (Schwarz-Friesel 2015). The for-a-long-time dominant paradigm followed the linear model of perceiving–evaluating/processing–acting. Current embodied-mind theories claim that the mind is inherently embodied and that even abstract thinking is firmly grounded in senso-motoric experience. Another current of thought, sometimes labeled the "emotional revolution" in cognitive science (e.g. Damásio 1999), challenges the traditional view of an autonomous cognition and sees emotions as mental states that help to classify and evaluate the world we live in: "Emotions ... help us to position and define ourselves to other people, objects, states, and events, to evaluate our own behavior and mental states (e.g., shame, regret, pride), to react to specific situational circumstances (e.g., fear, happiness, anger, mourning)" (Schwarz-Friesel 2015: 158).

The increasing emphasis on intersubjectivity (Trevarthen 2015) and the role of emotions and the body for cognitive processes of conceptualization and evaluation mark a shift away from a strictly mentalist understanding of the mind to perspectives that recognize the relevance of prereflexive cognitive operations and of the social realm.

With regard to the concept of embodied cognition, the works of Lakoff and Johnson in the 1980s and 1990s had big impact, in particular the book with the speaking title *Philosophy in the Flesh: The Embodied Mind and Its Challenge to Western Thought* (Lakoff and Johnson 1999). In their view, which brings elements of phenomenological thinking, in particular from the French philosopher Merleau-Ponty, into cognitive linguistics, the human concept system follows, to a considerable extent, processes of metaphor-formation where the meaning of bodily lived experiences is transferred to other levels of thinking.

The current interest in Merlau-Ponty's work in social sciences and linguistics can be understood by the emphasis he puts on the experiencing subject, on the emotionally and bodily lived subjective experience – thus challenging biological as well as social-discursive determinism (which sees the body exclusively as effect of discursive practices). Inspired by Husserl's phenomenology, Merleau-Ponty (1962) developed in the 1940s a theory bringing together body, perception, language and emotion. He makes a terminological distinction between the physical body [*corps physique*] as an object that is observable and measurable and the living body [*corps vivant*] as the subject of perception, feeling, experience, action and interaction. He illustrates the ambiguity of the body as simultaneously observing and observed, as affecting and affected, with the example of the left subject hand that touches and feels the right object hand.

Merleau-Ponty sees the bodily being as the foundation of the subject. The body positions the subject in the world and the movement of the body is the basis of the faculty that allows to relate to the world and engage with it. Language as well as emotion are seen primarily as bodily phenomena. Like gesture and emotion, language is, first and foremost, about positioning oneself in relationship to the world, about projecting oneself toward the other – and only then is it also a mental act of representation and symbolization. "The spoken word is a genuine gesture, and it contains its meaning in the same way as the gesture contains its. This is what makes communication possible" (Merleau-Ponty 1962: 212). Through repeated interaction with other subjects and the world, the subject acquires what Merleau-Ponty (1962: 164) calls a "senso-motoric style," understood as "the power to respond with a certain type of solution to situations of a certain general form."

The "rediscovery" of phenomenological thinking in social and cultural sciences can be related to a growing interest in how subjects experience and interpret their interactions with their social and material environment. This is particularly relevant when the bodily and emotionally lived experience does not match discursively established norms and categorizations, a gap that is crucial in research areas such as dis/ability studies (e.g. Heavey 2015), gender and queer studies (e.g. Ahmed 2006; Milani 2017), narrative medicine (e.g. Charon 2006), deaf studies (e.g. Kusters et al. 2017) or research on linguistic diversity (e.g. Busch 2017). One characteristic of phenomenologically inspired approaches is that, through the collection of first-person accounts, the research participants are more actively involved in the research process and given a voice. In autoethnographic studies, researchers make their own experiences, which include corporeality and emotionality, the object of their research.

15.3 Issues and Ongoing Debates: How to Connect Interaction, Discourse and Experience?

In Section 15.2, we discerned three epistemological stances toward bodies and emotions in discourse: the first focusing on how bodies and affects are deployed and made meaning of on the micro-level of locally situated interactions (Section 15.2.1); the second interested in how bodies and emotions are conceived of and constructed on the macro-level of historical formations, societies or groups (Section 15.2.2); and the third asking how subjects experience and interpret their social and material environments (Section 15.2.3). In doing so we have consecutively shifted from a *third-person perspective* represented by interaction research (what people are doing with their bodies and emotions), to a *second-person perspective* represented by the analysis of Discourse (that tells you who you are and how you should look and feel), and from there to a *first-person perspective* grounded in phenomenology (how my body and my emotions are involved in making sense of the world).

An original contribution to thinking these different takes as complementary was developed by Scollon and Scollon in what they call nexus analysis. They claim that social action should be understood as situated at the intersection of "discourse in place" (spatial aggregates of discourses), "interaction order" (social arrangements in which people come together) and the "historical body" (the embodied history of personal experience) (Scollon and Scollon 2004: 19). In the debate on interconnections between discourse, emotion and embodiment, one of the most topical questions remains that of how to combine insights from the analysis of interaction, Discourse and lived experience. In the following subsections we will therefore take a look at how emotion and/or embodiment are seen in concepts such as positioning, stance, voice (Section 15.3.1) and lived experience of language (Section 15.3.2).

15.3.1 Emotions or Bodies in Conceptualizations of Positioning, Stance and Voice

In narrative analysis, the concept of positioning builds, as Deppermann (2013) shows, on Foucault's (1972) notion of subject positions which are simultaneously made available and constrained by Discourses that assign subjects to "allowed" positions with regard to status, power, knowledge and practices. In De Fina's (2013: 45) view, concepts of positioning are situated in "a middle ground between CA based approaches ... and orientations that view identities from a macro perspective as already given in the social world and merely manifested in discourse."

It is interesting to recall that concepts of positioning originally developed from the preoccupation with emotions in discourse. In their early concept of positioning in narratives, Davies and Harré (1990) consider positioning activities such as the display of emotion as the primary site of the discursive production of selves. Also, Bamberg (1997) develops his three-level model of positioning from empirical inquiry into what he calls emotion talk. His study is based on how narrators position themselves and others in elicited first-person accounts of so-called "emotion experiences" as well as on how narrators ascribe emotions to characters of narrated (third-person) stories in order to position the characters in relation to each other. In both cases, emotions are referred to or ascribed with the purpose of presenting an evaluative stance. Rather than how emotions are expressed in communication, Bamberg is thus interested in how they are discursively constructed in narratives.

Current works in narrative analysis taking into account affective or body dimensions demonstrate how beneficial it can be to pay attention equally to interactions on the micro-level, societal Discourses on the macro-level and lived experiences related by narrators. Referring to Ochs and Capps's (2001) model of narrative analysis that considers psychological/physiological response to unexpected events or complicated actions as an important component of storytelling, Relaño Pastor (2014) analyzes, from an interactional perspective, narratives of language experiences at the US–Mexican border related by Mexican women. She shows that emotions occur on all three levels of positioning introduced by Bamberg (1997): on the level of the emotionally lived language experience in the past, which the women tell about; on the level of the interaction with the interviewer, in which these emotions are revived, reenacted and reevaluated; and on the level of the social construction of self. In the case of the Mexican women, this involves feelings of shame linked to situations of powerlessness giving rise to developing agency and pride. Relaño Pastor emphasizes that the interactional dimension of emotions is a central linguistic device not only found in constructed dialogues (reported speech) but also emergent in the whole narrative structure. In the narrative analysis of stories about bodies affected by illness or other bodily crisis, Heavey (2015) regards the body from two angles: as producing narratives and as constructed by narratives.

She elaborates on how, in individual narratives, by constructing, performing and making meaningful their own body, participants draw simultaneously on lived embodied experiences (for which she refers to Merleau-Ponty) and to master narratives or shared discourses about, for instance, masculinity or disability.

Emotion/affect in connection with positioning is discussed not only in narrative analysis in the stricter sense but also in sociolinguistic approaches to stancetaking. Jaffe (2009) distinguishes between epistemic and affective stances, whereby the former refer to speakers' knowledge about the propositions being made, the latter to their emotional states. Du Bois and Kärkkäinen (2012) develop a model of stancetaking in which they include emotion as a salient factor. In their view, every utterance contributes to the enactment of stance; affect is, even if not overtly marked, always present and interactionally relevant. Based on the stance triangle developed earlier by Du Bois (2007), the authors suggest the following model: (1) A stance object (a person, a situation, etc.) is evaluated through an affective reaction, thus affect requires a stance object; (2) the subject positions herself by the act of affective stancetaking as the kind of person who would make that kind of evaluation about that kind of thing; (3) she thereby aligns with others comparing and contrasting with the stances of copresent others. Stancetaking in the here and now of an interaction serves to link affect to aspects of ideological systems and their expressions.

In their book chapter on "Embodied Sociolinguistics," Bucholtz and Hall (2016) call for a recognition of the central role of bodies and embodiment in sociolinguistics. In their understanding of the body as "a dialogic product, co-constructed in the back and forth of speakers and hearers" (2016: 183), they point to voice as the "embodied heart of language: It emerges from the body, and through indexicality it auditorily locates the body in social space as being of a particular kind" (2016: 178). Voice is employed by speakers and interpreted by listeners especially in relation to categories of gender, sexuality and race. But rather than directly indexing such categories, voice phenomena perform specific cultural and interactional functions and, in doing so, these phenomena come to be ideologically associated with specific social categories and iconically linked to particular types of people who are believed to use their bodies and voices in particular ways.

15.3.2 Bodily and Emotionally Lived Experience of Language

In a similar move, the concept of lived experience of language (*Spracherleben*) developed in my own work (e.g. Busch 2017) aims at merging interactional, poststructuralist and phenomenological perspectives. The focus is on the subject's emotionally and bodily lived experience of verbal or nonverbal interactions with others, that is, on how we perceive ourselves in relation to and interacting with others. This being said, we have to add two caveats or clarifications. First: the experiencing subject cannot be thought of as pregiven but should be considered as being brought into life by discourses (or "interpellations") that assign to an individual certain defined social positions that it can inhabit. Thus, as Vološinov ([1929] 1973: 36) underlines, experience is already ideologically filled: "We do not feel or see an experience – we understand it ...[. W]e engage our experience into a context made up of other signs we understand." Second: not only is experience made in and related to specific situated interactions or scenes but it is also accessible only by being reconstituted – be it by introspection or by narration – in another specific context with its specific prerequisites.

If we imagine the three perspectives on body and emotions discussed in Section 15.2 – i.e. the interaction, the Discourse and the subject perspective – as forming the vertices of a triangle, we can gain a better understanding of the ways in which these perspectives have to be thought of as being reciprocally interrelated in multiple manners:

(1) Discourses about bodies and emotions, bundles of ideological representations, scientific knowledge and power relations that, although subjected to permanent transformation, claim validity when established for a certain time within a certain space. These can be thought of as structured and structuring only in so far as they are, on the one hand, constantly reiterated and reinforced in ritualized forms of local interaction and, on the other hand, firmly anchored in real subjects' routines of perceiving the world, of desiring, feeling, thinking.

(2) Observable situated interactions in which bodies and emotions are involved and deployed then are the site where, on the one hand, discourses (that become Discourse by reiteration) are produced, reproduced and enforced, and where, on the other hand, subjects make or recall the situated experiences that shape their perception of the world.
(3) Consequently, emotionally and bodily experiencing subjects can be thought of as an instance where Discourse and interaction intersect. They "incarnate" social positions assigned to them by at times contradictory Discourses. They store or incorporate lived interactions with others in what can be termed communicative repertoire (Gumperz), habitus (Bourdieu) or senso-motoric style (Merleau-Ponty).

However termed, this kind of disposition should be conceived of not as belonging to the individual but, in the same manner as Bakhtin (1981: 294) characterizes language, as lying "on the borderline between oneself and the other," as inherently dialogic and intersubjective. Drawing on Merleau-Ponty, Fuchs (2011) uses the term "intercorporeality" to emphasize both the intersubjective and the embodied quality of language dispositions. In what he calls "body memory," situations and interactions experienced in the past fuse together and, through repetition and superimposition, form a structure, a style that sticks to the subject.

The messy archive of bodily stored experience allows subjects to imagine themselves in terms of biographical continuity and coherence, at least as long as the way in which the subject perceives her- or himself is not seriously called into question by being suddenly exposed, in situated interaction, to an altered Discourse telling her or him who she or he is or ought to be. Such disrupting experiences raised in autobiographical narratives are typically linked to various forms of displacement (Busch 2012) and discrimination (Busch 2016), or when radical sociopolitical changes force subjects to reposition themselves with regard to dominant ideologies (Busch 2010).

While processes of adapting oneself (i.e. one's communicative repertoire) to altering social environments take place mostly unconsciously, they become salient when linked to situations, events or scenes that are experienced as being irritating, disturbing, stressing or traumatizing, thus when linked to strong emotional and bodily feelings. Not the situation as such but the way it is lived through and the (intersubjectively acquired) capacity to relate it to previous experiences and memories are decisive for whether it can or cannot easily be assimilated. This is an idea that Vygotsky ([1934]1994) sketched out in his notes on the emotional experience (*perezhivanie*).

Emotional and bodily experience thus often becomes palpable *ex negativo*, from perceiving oneself in relation to others as disregarded, powerless or excluded, from the feeling that one's communicative, linguistic, emotional etc. repertoire is not situationally appropriate and does not fit the requirements and expectations one is confronted with, that the way of being categorized by others does not correspond to one's self-perception.

To illustrate this, I will refer to extracts from autoethnographic texts written by students in the course of a seminar at Vienna University. The texts have in common that their authors left Bosnia as children during wartime (1992–5), spent some years in exile and were forced to remigrate to Bosnia after the end of the war. All of them tell about experiencing linguistic ostracism by classmates and teachers when returning to their country of birth and early childhood. These emotionally unsettling experiences were based on perceived, or rather assumed, differences in the pronunciation of particular affricates, considered to be a shibboleth allowing to identify those who had left their country "for a better life" abroad (Busch and Spitzmüller forthcoming). The following extracts are translated from German by me:

> I am in my country, but because of my pronunciation, I am seen as Austrian or rather as "bauštelac."[2] (Aida)

> Finally it was my turn, and when I started to read, the murmuring started. My class mates giggled all the time. First I thought that there was a funny word in the story as I did not understand everything. Then I realized that they were laughing about me and my pronunciation. (Lejla)

> When I was called for an oral question, I got so scared that I hardly managed to get a word out. (Sanela)

> I felt so humiliated that I refused to speak with my class mates altogether. ... The feeling of shame made me seclude myself so that my self-esteem and my marks suffered. (Lejla)

Here, experiences linked to depreciating evaluations by others of one's own language repertoire are described as being heavily loaded with emotion (being "scared," "humiliated," "ashamed") but also as having a bodily dimension (could not "get a word out," made me "seclude myself").

Such moments in which the perceiving subject-body suddenly turns into a self-perceived object-body, moments of apprehended discrepancy between personal experience and normative Discourse, can become occasions to "read" such norms, to question and, potentially, to subvert them – in other words, to reconsider situated interactions as sites where Discourse is not just reiterated but can also be modified. In any case, it is such moments or scenes that leave strong traces, both in retrievable memory and in bodily memory which is not immediately accessible to consciousness.

The interplay between the three angles of the imagined triangle (see figure 15.1), that is, subject (1), Discourse (2) and interaction (3), can be exemplified

---

[2] Derogatory term for migrants working abroad as blue-color workers on construction sites.

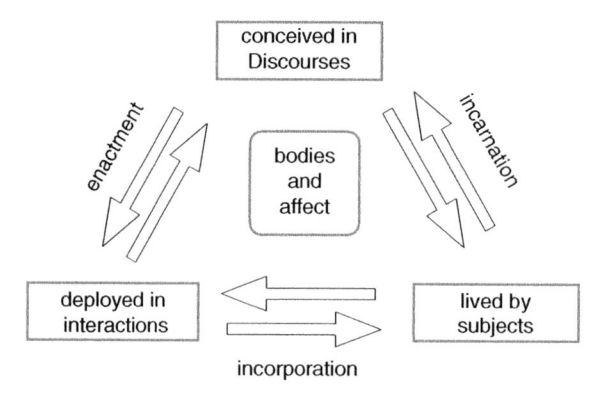

Figure 15.1 Bodies and affects as conceived in Discourse, deployed in interaction and lived by subjects; "embodiment" standing for enactment (in interaction), incarnation (of discursively established positions) or incorporation (of lived experience).

by taking feelings of shame as an example, an affect that is a recurrent topic in language biographical narrations (e.g. Relaño Pastor 2014; Busch 2017). Feelings of shame are most often related to particular scenes or situations of interaction in which we believe to have acted in an inappropriate way; the subject perceives her- or himself through the eye of a real or imagined other as an inappropriate "object-body" (1). Shame in this case is the response to a "call to order" by Discourses that establish norms of appropriateness. The exposure to shame enforces the power of moral norms but also, in some cases, can lead to questioning them (2). Shame is situationally lived as a bodily arousal that can be displayed toward others; but obviously one can also hide feelings of shame or perform such feelings without being affected (3).

15.4 Summary

Taking body and affect seriously has far-reaching implications for almost all domains of linguistic research as persistent language ideologies are widely spread in everyday life, in public Discourse and, of course, also in academic work. In particular, ideas of language as a transparent, neutral vehicle are being questioned. Important contributions to this agenda came from feminist, gender and queer studies, postcolonial studies, dis/ability studies and critical race theory. The use of audiovisual recordings in the analysis of communicative events awakened broader interest in considering the role of the body in interactions and a certain revival of biographical methods drew attention to representations of emotionally lived experience.

This chapter provided an overview of interactional, Discourse theoretical and phenomenological approaches to affect and embodiment. It argued that concepts of positioning or of lived experience of language suggest that the correlation between language, body and emotion can best be conceptualized when considering them from different angles: from how bodies and emotions are involved and deployed in interaction, from how they are conceived in Discourse and from how they are lived by subjects. Depending on which take one chooses, the term "embodiment" will noticeably change in the coloration of its meaning, from standing for *enactment* (in interaction) through *incarnation* (of discursively established positions) to *incorporation* (of lived experience).

Further Reading

Bucholtz, M. and Hall, K. (2016). Embodied Sociolinguistics. In N. Coupland (ed.) *Sociolinguistics: Theoretical Debates*. Cambridge: Cambridge University Press. 173–97.

This chapter offers a well-founded overview of key questions in sociolinguistics from the angle of body and embodiment. It deals with topics such as embodied indexicality, style as embodied self-presentation, embodied discourse and embodied agency.

Busch, B. (2017). Expanding the Notion of the Linguistic Repertoire: On the Concept of Spracherleben – The Lived Experience of Language. *Applied Linguistics* 38(3): 340–58.

The concept of bodily and emotionally lived experience of language is developed in detail and grounded in post-structuralist and phenomenological thinking.

Goodwin, C. (2007). Participation, Stance and Affect in the Organization of Activities. *Discourse & Society* 18(1): 53–73.

This is one of Goodwin's famous studies on how interactants make use of their bodies and display affects to achieve collaborative action. It is based on a sequence in which a father is helping his daughter do homework.

Relaño Pastor, A. M. (2014). *Shame and Pride in Narrative: Mexican Women's Language Experiences at the U.S.–Mexico Border*. Basingstoke/New York: Palgrave Macmillan.

The book analyzes personal experiences of language through the voices of Mexican immigrant women in the United States, in relation to racialization discourses. The author emphasizes that the interactional dimension of emotions is a central linguistic device not only found in constructed dialogues (reported speech) but also emergent in the whole narrative structure.

Wetherell, M. (2012). *Affect and Emotion: A New Social Science Understanding*. London/Thousand Oaks, CA: Sage.

This book presents a new social science understanding of affect and emotion and offers insights into approaches from psycho, neuro, bio and social sciences.

References

Ahmed, S. (2004). *The Cultural Politics of Emotion.* Edinburgh: Edinburgh University Press.

(2006). *Queer Phenomenology: Orientations, Objects, Others.* Durham, NC: Duke University Press.

Alim, H. S. (2016). Who's Afraid of the Transracial Subject? Raciolinguistics and the Political Project of Transracialization. In H. S. Alim, J. R. Rickford and A. F. Ball (eds.) *Raciolinguistics: How Language Shapes Our Ideas about Race.* New York: Oxford University Press. 33–50.

Althusser, L. (1971). Ideology and Ideological State Apparatuses (Notes towards an Investigation). In *Lenin and Philosophy, and Other Essays.* London: New Left Books. 127–88.

Bakhtin, M. (1981). Discourse in the Novel (1934–35). In M. Holquist (ed.) *The Dialogic Imagination.* Austin: University of Texas Press. 259–422.

Bamberg, M. (1997). Emotion Talk(s): The Role of Perspective in the Construction of Emotion. In R. Dirven and S. Niemeier (eds.) *The Language of Emotions: Conceptualization, Expression, and Theoretical Foundation.* Amsterdam: John Benjamins. 209–29.

Bergson, H. (1896/2012). *Matière et mémoire. Essai sur la relation du corps à l'esprit.* Paris: Editions Flammarion.

Bourdieu, P. (1991). *Language and Symbolic Power*, trans. by G. Raymond and M. Adamson. Oxford: Polity Press.

Bucholtz, M. and Hall, K. (2016). Embodied Sociolinguistics. In N. Coupland (ed.) *Sociolinguistics: Theoretical Debates.* Cambridge: Cambridge University Press. 173–97.

Bühler, K. (1934/1990). *The Theory of Language: The Representational Function of Language.* Amsterdam: John Benjamin.

Busch, B. (2010). New National Languages in Eastern Europe. In N. Coupland (ed.) *Language and Globalization.* Malden, MA: Blackwell. 182–200.

(2012). The Linguistic Repertoire Revisited. *Applied Linguistics* 33(5): 503–23.

(2016). Regaining a Place from which to Speak and to Be Heard: In Search of a Response to the "Violence of Voicelessness." *Stellenbosch Papers in Linguistics PLUS* 49: 317–30.

(2017). Expanding the Notion of the Linguistic Repertoire: On the Concept of Spracherleben – The Lived Experience of Language. *Applied Linguistics* 38(3): 340–58.

Busch B. and Spitzmüller J. (forthcoming) Indexical borders: The sociolinguistic scales of the shibboleth. *International Journal of Sociolinguistics*.

Butler, J. (1993). *Bodies that Matter: On the Discursive Limits of "Sex."* London/New York: Routledge.

(1997). *Excitable Speech: A Politics of the Performative*. New York: Routledge.

Canagarajah, S. (2018). Translingual Practice as Spatial Repertoires: Expanding the Paradigm beyond Structuralist Orientations. *Applied Linguistics* 39(1): 31–54.

Charon, R. (2006). *Narrative Medicine: Honoring the Stories of Illness*. New York: Oxford University Press.

Damásio, A. (1999). *The Feeling of What Happens: Body and Emotion in the Making of Consciousness*. New York: Harcourt Brace.

Davies, B. and Harré, R. (1990). Positioning: The Discursive Production of Selves. *Journal for the Theory of Social Behaviour* 20(1): 43–63.

De Fina, A. (2013). Positioning Level 3: Connecting Local Identity Displays to Macro Social Processes. *Narrative Inquiry* 23(1): 40–61.

Deleuze, G. and Guattari, F. (1987). *A Thousand Plateaus: Capitalism and Schizophrenia*. Minneapolis: University of Minnesota Press.

Deppermann, A. (2013). Editorial: Positioning in Narrative Interaction. *Narrative Inquiry* 23(1): 1–15.

Dewaele, J.-M. (2013). *Emotions in Multiple Languages*, 2nd rev. ed. Basingstoke: Palgrave Macmillan.

Douglas, M. (1970). *Natural Symbols: Explorations in Cosmology*. London: Barrie & Rocklif.

Du Bois, J. W. (2007). The Stance Triangle. In R. Englebretson (ed.) *Stancetaking in Discourse: Subjectivity, Evaluation, Interaction*. Amsterdam: John Benjamins. 139–82.

Du Bois, J. W. and Kärkkäinen, E. (2012). Taking a Stance on Emotion: Affect, Sequence, and Intersubjectivity in Dialogic Interaction. *Text & Talk* 32(4): 433–51.

Duranti, A. (1992). Language and Bodies in Social Space: Samoan Ceremonial Greetings. *American Anthropologist* 94(3): 657–91.

Foucault, M. (1972). *The Archeology of Knowledge and the Discourse on Language*. New York: Pantheon Books.

(1973). *The Birth of the Clinic: An Archeology of Medical Perception*. London: Tavistock.

(1988). Technologies of the Self: Lectures at Vermont University in October 1982. In *Technologies of the Self*, ed. by L. H. Martin et al. Amherst: University of Massachusetts Press. 16–49.

Fuchs, T. (2011). Body Memory and the Unconscious. In D. Lohmar and D. J. Brudzinska (eds.) *Founding Psychoanalysis: Phenomenological Theory of Subjectivity and the Psychoanalytical Experience*. Berlin: Springer. 86–103.

Garfinkel, H. (1967). *Studies in Ethnomethodology*. Englewood Cliffs, NJ: Prentice Hall.

Goffman, E. (1959). *The Presentation of Self in Everyday Life*. New York: Doubleday.
  (1978). Response Cries. *Language* 54(4): 787–815.
  (1979). *Gender Advertisements*. New York: Harper & Row.
Goodwin, C. (2000). Action and Embodiment within Situated Human Interaction. *Journal of Pragmatics* 32: 1489–522.
  (2007). Participation, Stance and Affect in the Organization of Activities. *Discourse & Society* 18(1): 53–73.
Gumperz, J. J. (1992). Contextualization and Understanding. In A. Duranti and C. Goodwin (eds.) *Rethinking Context: Language as an Interactive Phenomenon*. Cambridge: Cambridge University Press. 229–52.
Heavey, E. (2015). Narrative Bodies, Embodied Narratives. In A. De Fina and A. Georgakopoulou (eds.) *Handbook of Narrative Analysis*. Oxford: Wiley-Blackwell. 429–46.
Husserl, E. ([1929]1960). *Cartesian Meditations: An Introduction to Phenomenology*. The Hague: Nijhoff.
Illouz, E. (2007). *Cold Intimacies: The Making of Emotional Capitalism*. Malden, MA: Polity Press.
Jaffe, A. (2009). Introduction: The Sociolinguistics of Stance. In A. Jaffe (ed.) *Stance. Sociolinguistic Perspectives*. Oxford: Oxford University Press. 3–28.
Jakobson, R. (1960). Linguistics and Poetics. In T. A. Sebeok (ed.) *Style in Language*. New York: Wiley. 350–77.
Kress, G. and van Leeuwen, T. (2001). *Multimodal Discourse: The Modes and Media of Contemporary Communication*. London: Arnold.
Kusters, A., Spotti, M., Swanwick, R. and Tapio, E. (2017). Beyond Languages, Beyond Modalities: Transforming the Study of Semiotic Repertoires. *International Journal of Multilingualism* 14(3): 219–32.
Lakoff, G. and Johnson, M. (1980). *Metaphors We Live By*. Chicago: University of Chicago Press.
  (1999). *Philosophy in the Flesh: The Embodied Mind and Its Challenge to Western Thought*. New York: Basic Books.
Lordon, F. (2014). *Willing Slaves of Capital*. London/New York: Verso.
Lüdtke, U. and Polzin, C. (2015). Research on the Relationship between Language and Emotion. In U. Lüdtke (ed.) *Emotion in Language: Theory – Research – Application*. Amsterdam: John Benjamins. 211–40.
Merleau-Ponty, M. (1962). *Phenomenology of Perception*, trans. by C. Smith. London: Routledge & Kegan Paul.
Milani, T. M. (2017). Queering Critique: Discourse, Body, Affect. In P. Handler, K. Kaindl and H. Wochele (eds.) *Ceci n'est pas une festschrift. Texte zur Angewandten und Romanistischen Sprachwissenschaft für Martin Stegu*. Berlin: Logos. 245–58.
Mondada, L. (2016). Challenges of Multimodality: Language and the Body in Social Interaction. *Journal of Sociolinguistics* 20(3): 336–66.
Motschenbacher, H. (2010). *Language, Gender and Sexual Identity: Poststructuralist Perspectives*. Amsterdam: John Benjamins.

Norris, S. (2004). *Analyzing Multimodal Interaction: A Methodological Framework*. London/New York: Routledge.

Ochs, E. and Capps, L. (2001). *Living Narrative: Creating Lives in Everyday Storytelling*. Cambridge: Harvard University Press.

Ochs, E. and Schieffelin, B. (1989). Language Has a Heart. *Text* 9(1): 7–25.

Pavlenko, A. (2005). *Emotions and Multilingualism*. Cambridge: Cambridge University Press.

Pennycook, A. (2017). Translanguaging and Semiotic Assemblages. *International Journal of Multilingualism* 14(3): 269–82.

Pépin, N. (2008). Introduction to the Special Issue: Studies on Emotions in Social Interaction. *Bulletin suisse de linguistique appliquée* 88: 1–18.

Reckwitz, A. (2006). *Das hybride Subjekt. Eine Theorie der Subjektkulturen von der bürgerlichen Moderne zur Postmoderne*. Weilerswist: Velbrück Wissenschaft.

Relaño Pastor, A. M. (2014). *Shame and Pride in Narrative: Mexican Women's Language Experiences at the U.S.–Mexico Border*. Basingstoke/New York: Palgrave Macmillan.

Scollon, R. and Scollon, W. S. (2004). *Nexus Analysis: Discourse and the Emerging Internet*. London/New York: Routledge.

Shilling, C. (1993). *The Body and Social Theory*. London: Sage.

Schwarz-Friesel, M. (2015). Language and Emotion. The Cognitive Linguistic Perspective. In U. Lüdtke (ed.) *Emotion in Language: Theory – Research – Application*. Amsterdam: John Benjamins. 157–73.

Trevarthen, C. (2015). The Developmental Psychology and Neuropsychology of Emotion in Language. In U. Lüdtke (ed.) *Emotion in Language: Theory – Research – Application*. Amsterdam: John Benjamins. 3–26.

Vološinov, V. N. (1929/1973). *Marxism and the Philosophy of Language*. New York: Seminar Press.

Vygotsky, L. S. ([1934]1994). §14. The Problem of the Environment (1934). In R. van der Veer and J. Valsiner (eds.) *The Vygotsky Reader*. Hoboken, NJ: Wiley-Blackwell. 338–54.

Wellgraf, S. (2018). *Schule der Gefühle. Zur emotionalen Erfahrung von Minderwertigkeit in neoliberalen Zeiten*. Bielefeld: transcript.

Wetherell, M. (2012). *Affect and Emotion: A New Social Science Understanding*. London/Thousand Oaks, CA: Sage.

(2013). Affect and Discourse – What's the Problem? From Affect as Excess to Affective/Discursive Practice. *Subjectivity* 6(4): 349–68.

Wierzbicka, A. (1995). Emotion and Facial Expression: A Semantic Perspective. *Culture and Psychology* 1: 227–58.

16

Posthumanism and Its Implications for Discourse Studies

Gavin Lamb and Christina Higgins

16.1 Introduction

Hundreds of people are walking along a beach, maneuvering around its rocky shore, wading into the water and even swimming and snorkeling further offshore. The majority of people are here to see green sea turtles, that emerge from the ocean at unpredictable intervals to crawl up on the warm sand to sleep for several hours at a time. When a sea turtle emerges from the ocean, it moves slowly, pulling itself up inch by inch, stopping occasionally to look around then pressing on further up the sand, seemingly unfazed by the hordes of people who dash over with cameras. "Give the honu space," someone yells from behind, using the Hawaiian word for green sea turtle. She then unfurls a red rope to create a barrier between the people and the creature. "Do not touch" signs are promptly staked into the ground to create a perimeter around the sea turtle, and on the signs, the sea turtle's name, Brutus, is provided for the visitors. The person marking off the turtle's space is wearing a badge, blue shirt and blue hat, all adorned with the logo of a sea turtle and embroidered with the name of the community-activist organization of which this volunteer is a member: "Mālama na Honu," or "Care for the sea turtles," in Hawaiian.

This is an illustration of what Pennycook (2018: 445) describes as the posthumanist question: "how and why we have come to think about humans in particular ways, with particular boundaries between humans and other animals, humans and artefacts, humans and nature." In posthumanist thinking, discourse plays an important role in meaning-making, though its power to account for our understanding of our social worlds is limited by the material world in which discourse circulates. While discourse studies are usually anchored in social constructionist and postmodern ontologies that privilege meaning-making at the level of language and semiotics, posthumanism emphasizes the importance of materiality in making sense of our worlds. Rather than viewing discourse as emanating only from human cognition and human-made relationships, posthumanism locates discourse at the nexus of semiotic and material affordances. Discourse is important for posthumanism in the form of circulating ideological stances about human–material relations. For example, "Big-D" (Gee 2015) discourses about human agency and nature are the result of people enacting socially and historically significant identities through their actions and values. On the one hand, the scene above illustrates a Discourse of sea turtle tourism, mobilized in part by a tourism industry that uses wildlife to stage tourists' thrilling anticipations and encounters with sea turtles frolicking in their natural habitat. On the other hand, we see a rather different Discourse of sea turtle conservation and protection that designates green sea turtles as a protected species and that admonishes tourists' behavior accordingly, framing such conservation via the Hawaiian language. This Discourse of sea turtle protection mobilizes an institutional infrastructure of laws protecting sea turtles, educational outreach and the recruitment of volunteers to carry out the communicative goals of sea turtle protection and education (Lamb 2019). Human–sea turtle interactions have only recently come into being in the past few decades as Hawaiian green sea turtle populations have recovered from near extinction in the 1960s. Here, at Laniākea Beach, on the island of O'ahu, Hawai'i, posthumanism helps to understand how new arrangements of discourse, culture and nature are taking shape as different actors, human as much as nonhuman, converge and conflict. In terms of Gee's (1986) "little-d" discourses of conversational interactions and texts, we can monitor how these arrangements are dynamically produced and altered in dialogue with the material aspects of transportation routes, sea turtles, the ocean and the beach.

Discourse plays an important role in mediating the boundaries between the human and the nonhuman, for it is through discourse that we signify events and relations among people, things, history and actions. Discourses constrain knowledge about how to behave around endangered sea life and also enable new knowledge formations to be produced in relations of power, as expressed through language and actions (Foucault [1966]1970). Discourses are also embedded in the material world through histories of actional and discursive resemiotization, as meaning is transformed into more durable objects and built infrastructure (Iedema 2001; Scollon and Scollon 2003). Laniākea Beach offers a rich illustration of how discourse operates as humans come to understand their role in the material world, and how discourses in turn are "concretized" into material effects that shape both human and nonhuman action (Latour 1990). In the case of green sea turtles in Hawai'i, discourses of tourism, which naturalize the human entitlement to nature as spectacle, come into contact with discourses that assert conservation and that question that entitlement.

Moving away from human–animal encounters, consider human–airplane relations for a moment. As Thurlow (2016) points out, airplane travel, as a microcosm of social class relations, provides insight into global consumption practices, class ideologies and material and structural inequalities dividing identities, communities, nation-states and hemispheres (Thurlow 2016). His critical discourse analysis of elite travel discourse tells us as much. But he also takes us onboard and beyond or behind the first-class curtain of logocentric and visiocentric dimensions of discourse analysis, to experience the materiality of classed plane travel. Here, we are also made to hear and touch how class divisions are realized in the sounds of clinking cutlery echoing from first class, the soft touch of first-class pajamas provided to elite travelers (and denied to others) or the "snap-snap-snap" of a flight attendant buttoning up a blue curtain separating coach from elite class, with a sign reading "world class business (only) – lavatories in rear." Plane spaces, with their tight juxtaposition of eliteness and the rest, do not just turn on the material and embodied semiotics of inclusion and exclusion; they are also shot through with, and economically dependent on, seemingly more immaterial affective effects that strategically circulate euphoria, excitement, disappointment, disgust, jealousy and desire among target consumers. In this way, the semiotic landscapes of aerospace elite mobility "do not just get into one's head; they also get under one's skin" (Thurlow 2016: 496). The physicality of class division and the affect felt through being given "superior" service (or the desire for it) come together with language as a means of knowing and being in the world. Posthumanist discourse studies push us to consider how discourse analysts might show this multisensorial knowing of the world through our research.

Of course, those elite few who travel on planes – as all plane travel is essentially elite considering that the vast majority of human beings will never step foot on a plane – are increasing their carbon footprint on the planet exponentially beyond what they might if they were to stay on the ground. Climate change discourse implores us to fly less, as every flight we take adds to the global-warming gases wreaking havoc on the planet. Rising sea-levels, desertification, coral reef die-offs, industrial animal agriculture, species extinction, deforestation; the list of human-induced ecological devastation goes on, a global socioecological catastrophe captured by the idea of the Anthropocene, the scientific diagnosis of our current era. The Anthropocene indicates that humans are influencing every micro and macro aspect of earthly existence, from genetics to the global climate, leaving traces of our signature in the fossil record for millennia to come: "we" have become a geological force of nature. But in lumping all humanity together in this global we – Anthropos – the Anthropocene blurs human responsibility for the ecological crises proliferating around the world. These current ecological crises underscore the point that "mainstream linguistics has forgotten, or overlooked, the embedding of humans in the larger systems that support life" (Alexander and Stibbe 2014: 585). More fundamentally, attending to the embedding of humans in the living and material world involves a recognition of the foolishness of human exceptionalism. This is an idea that has fueled the violent and exploitative treatment of animals and the natural world. But it also shows how human exceptionalism insidiously worked its way through centuries of colonialism and capitalism to position some humans as more human than others along lines of racial, gender, class and sexual discrimination.

Posthumanism is an umbrella term for a range of approaches across the social sciences and humanities that, at their core, challenge this liberal Enlightenment notion of human exceptionalism. Posthumanism raises questions about human entanglements with material objects, technologies and living beings. In attending to these entanglements, posthumanism asks what it means to be human when we recognize the empirical flimsiness of modernist divides between society and nature that have erected ideological boundaries between the human and what is deemed to be nonhuman. In one sense, posthumanism suggests that we have never been modern (Latour 2012); phrased another way, we have always been posthuman. In this chapter, we present posthumanism as a challenge to notions of human exceptionalism and human hubris undergirded by a Western philosophical tradition privileging the liberal Enlightenment human subject. Rather than a new academic turn, we recognize that "scholars working across varied fields in sociocultural linguistics have contributed to a general posthumanist perspective for some time now, even if they rarely identify [...] as such and may not entirely align with these theoretical frameworks" (Bucholtz and Hall 2016: 187). Important contributions include discourse research on embodied interaction with objects, technologies and the built landscape (Goodwin 2000; Jones 2009; Norris 2004; Pennycook 2018; Scollon and Scollon 2003). This work examines the semiotic-material alliances forged between bodies, objects, discourse and place through embodied interaction. Materiality is not mere, passive "stuff"; through semiosis, it becomes a vibrant, dynamic and active partner in human action. In this chapter, then, we suggest that posthumanism offers an important re-turn for discourse studies to questions of what it means to be human when we recognize our embeddedness in the material world and the larger systems that support life, or what posthumanist geographer Sarah Whatmore (2006: 602) calls a "return to the livingness of the world."

16.2 Overview of the Topic

In this section, we briefly map out five key areas contributing to posthumanist thinking in the social sciences and humanities. These broad academic engagements with posthumanism include critiques of humanism,

Actor-Network Theory, assemblage theory, new materialisms, and critical plant/animal studies. In briefly discussing these approaches, our aim is not to provide a comprehensive overview of what posthumanism is but rather to highlight some of the threads in this wide-ranging body of work that we see as offering fruitful theoretical and methodological avenues for discourse analysts to pursue.

16.2.1 Provincializing Western Knowledge about the Human

One important point of departure for posthumanist approaches is an argument for "provincializing" (Chakrabarty 2000) the classic narrative of modernity inherited from European Enlightenment thinking about the human. This modernist narrative has sought to standardize and universalize a rational, culture-neutral and value-free science of human reason and progress across the globe. The kind of knowledge produced by this modernist project is justified as universal because it is claimed to be context-independent and therefore can (and should) be applied everywhere and to anyone. One profound outcome of this narrative is the notion of a universal human subject undergirded by a shared human nature. While this perspective helps to advocate for inclusivity in the realm of universal human rights, Western humanism has just as often been used as a powerful political technology of exclusion. Universal humanism has largely served mainly white, Western male elites who police the boundaries around the category of the human to determine who qualifies as fully human and who does not: historically people of color, women and people with disabilities. Furthermore, the universal capacity for language is an important scaffold for the modernist notion of humanism. But in another exclusionary move, people whose language is deemed as divergent from its particular model of humanity, such as creole speakers and the Deaf community, have been historically stigmatized and denigrated by those with authority.

In light of these concerns, one way to understand posthumanism is as an umbrella term for projects trying to critically rethink these representationalist-realist debates about (human) society and (nonhuman) nature by more directly engaging with the concept of ontology. The intellectual impasse between social constructionism and scientific realism is due to the fact that both perspectives "subscribe to a form of representationalism that the new materialism can help us avoid" (Pennycook 2018: 458). Traditional notions of representationalism are grounded in a Cartesian mind–body dualism and Saussurean structuralism that theorizes an insurmountable divide between linguistic representation and the material world. In resisting these dualisms, posthumanist approaches are asking how discourse, language and representation are emergent from and continuous with the embodied and material world. In this sense, they are seeking not just to bridge this language–materiality divide but to potentially dissolve it altogether. From this perspective, discourse is grounded in and made possible through its *entanglements* with materiality, a view that emphasizes how matter is active and continuous with discourse rather than passive and set apart from it (Barad 2003). The aim here is to open up ways for discourse analysts to bring the material and living world more forcefully into our analyses.

Broadly speaking, a posthumanist call to "provincialize" Western divides between human/nonhuman, society/nature and representation/materiality aims not to get rid of these divides but to situate them within a particular knowledge-making lineage emanating from Europe. In doing so, a posthumanist stance aims to dethrone this lineage of ontological dualisms and situate it among other knowledge traditions, including non-Western and Indigenous sources of knowledge production about human–nonhuman relations. Next, we summarize how key approaches in the realm of posthumanism engage in this epistemological reterritorialization.

16.2.2 Actor-Network Theory

Actor-Network Theory (ANT) has been a major stream of inspiration for posthumanist arguments critiquing human exceptionalism and giving greater appreciation for the role of nonhuman agency in explanations of "the social." Bruno Latour's (2005) work is a major touchstone among posthumanist approaches, and particularly in ANT's diasporic set of research concerns across a wide range of interdisciplinary research interests. In his book, *We Have Never Been Modern*, Latour ([1993]2012) challenges modernist divisions between nature and society, arguing that these categories work to purify the indeterminate "hybrid" natureculture entities and beings that proliferate in the world. Building on this, ANT proposes a flat or symmetrical ontology that rejects a priori distinctions between subjects and objects or society and nature. Instead, ANT develops an analytic set of concepts to aid researchers in maintaining a sensitivity to the indeterminacy and open-ended emergence of what comes to count as social or natural in practice.

Classic ANT is largely concerned with the network-building and network-consolidating practices of social actors, whether an individual, a group or some human–nonhuman collective. *Translation* is one of the key notions in classic versions of ANT to describe these network-building processes (Callon 1984). Here, translation involves a dialogic process of semiotic-material transformation. The concept aims to describe how social actors come into being and extend their influence by reshaping the discursive grounds for relation-making in order to recruit other entities and beings into their strategic projects of network-building. ANT is perhaps most well-known for its claims about nonhuman agency or the capacity for material objects to act. In making this argument, ANT begins with two basic theoretical moves: first, agency is destabilized as a manifestation or emanation of individual human intention. Thus, researchers investigate how agency emerges as a relational achievement spun among heterogeneous entities and beings all coming together in a network of relations to make some course of action possible. A second move, building from the first, is to decouple binaries such as subject–object, society–nature, mind–body and time–space, where human qualities of intention and agency are primarily placed on the first element in these binaries. Instead, rather than assume these binaries in advance, emphasis is placed on investigating how agency emerges in these relations in situated practice. That nonhuman entities and beings can be actors – a turtle, a plane, a door or a rock – has been one of ANT's more controversial claims. However, ANT's approach is not to attribute human-like agency to nonhuman objects but to disentangle intentionality from agentive potential and focus instead on effects: any entity that has an effect in a network – that makes a difference – is agentive (Law and Mol 2008).

16.2.3 Assemblages

Assemblage is an English translation derived from the French word *agencement* ("arrangement, fitting, fixing") in the spatial philosophy of Deleuze and Guattari, (1987) and it shares many concerns with the human–nonhuman practices of relation building in ANT. Whereas early versions of ANT were vague about what lies beyond networks and what forces destabilize them, assemblages help give greater focus to the fluidity, nonlinearity and unpredictability of association-making in actor-networks. There are two insights in particular that have been especially influential in this work. The first involves how assemblages theorize not just the provisional assembly of heterogeneous entities but also how relations among bodies, objects, practices and places are transformed along trajectories of discursive movement. These trajectories are described with the metaphors of rhizomes, on the one hand, and trees on the other. Rhizomes (such as ginger roots) grow horizontally under the surface of the earth and are mobilized as a metaphor to describe nonhierarchical and nonlinear network-building trajectories, where associations can be made at any node along the rhizome. In contrast, arboreal structures, like trees, are hierarchical, static and rooted in the ground. Their dendritic logic seeks to impose structure, controlling the trajectory of networks for strategic purposes. As Deleuze and Guattari (1987: 25) describe it: "The tree imposes the verb 'to be,' but the fabric of the rhizome is the conjunction, 'and … and … and.'" This point about assemblages is not that they emphasize change over stasis but that they seek to explore how stasis and change, or fixity and fluidity (Pennycook and Otsuji 2015), always operate together, along dynamic pathways of discursive transformation.

In seeking to better understand the complex kinds of semiotic association that link discourse with human bodies acting in the material world, the concept of assemblage also draws attention to the alternative forces of human–nonhuman connection that lie beyond or exceed humanist discursive representation. Affect, in particular, has emerged as an energetic force that triggers relational exchanges beyond the threshold of language or representations and that connects us to the material and ecological world through more visceral emotional and corporeal channels of meaning-making (Thrift 2008).

16.2.4 New Materialisms

Another central body of work informing posthumanist perspectives on human relations with the material and living world are a variety of "new materialisms." These approaches draw on a different line of thinking from the historical materialism of Marxism, which focused on the economic relations in societies as the explanation for their development. New materialisms extend insights from feminist and phenomenological theories of the body's situated entanglement with the material world, drawing attention to the material inequities related to gender, race, class and sexuality. Emerging understandings in physics describing the vitalism and agentive qualities of matter also play an important role here as well. Nature is no longer conceived of as a reliable script that humans can simply read off; it is a vibrant and unpredictable participant in human meaning-making processes. As Bennett (2010: 47) argues, new materialism aims to experiment with "narrating events (a power blackout, a crisis of obesity) in a way that presents non-human materialities (electricity, fats) as themselves bona fide agents rather than as instrumentalities, techniques of power, recalcitrant objects, or social constructs." The major impetus behind this approach is to challenge the human hubris that assumes nature to be a passive and instrumentalized resource for human use and control. The ontological division between human subjects and nonhuman objects inherited from Enlightenment thinking fuels human hubris as the sole conductor of the world, "preventing us from detecting (seeing, hearing, smelling, tasting, feeling) a fuller range of the nonhuman powers circulating around and within human bodies" (Bennett 2009: ix).

Barad's (2003) notion of posthumanist performativity has also been influential in theorizing new materialisms. It "calls into question the givenness of the differential categories of human and nonhuman, examining the practices through which these differential boundaries are stabilized and destabilized" (Barad 2003: 66). Notably, this approach challenges Western notions of representationalism inherited from a Cartesian legacy that presupposes an ontological chasm between words and things, mind and matter, and culture and nature. This is also a challenge to Saussurean structuralist representationalism which posits language as arbitrary and untethered from its relations to the material world. In this regard, new materialist approaches draw attention to the silencing effects that representationalism has had on our recognition of the agentive participation of materiality in discursive practices (Coole and Frost 2010: 6–7). To emphasize the active role of matter in constituting human activity, this approach brings focus to discursive practices as materializing practices that continually compose and (re)configure human–nonhuman relations in the world (Barad 2003: 809).

To a new materialist, then, a sea turtle tourism destination is not simply about the discursive practices, social relationships or even the discursive representations embedded in objects and signs that can be found there; it is better understood as a multifaceted, vibrant assemblage of sand, emotions, transportation infrastructure, seawater, social media, adventure travel lifestyles, ecotourism, sunglasses, credit cards, the excitement of anticipation, and sea turtles. The point is not to make an exhaustive list of all possible entities and beings that make an appearance but to be attuned to how nonhuman entities and beings interpellate human discursive practices. In other words, it pushes discourse analysts to consider how objects, through their material presence and semiotic intervention in our lives, have consequences for human action and "make people happen" (Kell 2015). In addressing this admittedly difficult terrain of ideas on how to address the agency of nonhuman materiality in relation to human discourse and practice, posthumanist plant and animal studies have provided important insights here, an area of research we turn to next.

16.2.5 Posthumanist Plant and Animal Studies

While many posthumanist approaches examine the semiotic-material interactions between humans and objects, technologies and built infrastructure, there is a growing body of work across the social sciences taking up posthumanist concerns to explore more lively and organic human engagements such as with viruses, insects, pets, wild animals and forests. Ethnography emerges as a key method in this disparate body of work spread across anthropology, geography and the environmental humanities, to attune researchers to the situated practices humans engage in within the nonhuman living world. As Kirksey and Helmreich (2010: 545) argue in their introduction to multispecies ethnography, "[c]reatures previously appearing on the margins of anthropology – as part of the landscape, as food for humans, as symbols – have been pressed into the foreground." These studies examine the kinds of relationship people construct with a diverse range of creatures, and what kinds of alliance, conflict and entanglement emerge in these encounters. Exploring these human–nonhuman entanglements raises important questions about how the agency of plants and animals intervenes in human social practices, as well as what kinds of boundary between nature and culture are being made or unmade in these "more-than-human" assemblages (Whatmore 2006).

Posthumanist ethnographic approaches to human discursive and interactional practices with animals and natural places serve as a key point of departure for these studies. This work argues that language and discourse have been given too dominant a role, obscuring our understanding of other nondiscursive connections being forged in these encounters. For example, in exploring the interactions of the Quichua-speaking Runa in Ecuador's Upper Amazon with their dog companions, Kohn (2007) examines how people and dogs become entangled in one another's lives through their co-constitutive semiotic practices. Arguing that human language is not radically separate from (or exceptional to) animal forms of communication, he seeks to show how meaning is built on more fundamental embodied semiotic processes used by all living organisms to sense and instigate actions in the world around them. Perhaps most fundamentally, multispecies studies are asking symmetrical questions about how plants, animals and ecosystems become agentive and integral partners in the emergence of human social practices.

16.3 Implications for Discourse Studies

These posthumanist frameworks deeply challenge most of the current treatment of language as a key component of discourse in sociolinguistics and applied linguistics, which are two fields that have claimed a major stake in discourse studies. These are also the perspectives that we are most familiar with ourselves as scholars who study multilingual practices from a social and semiotic perspective. Much of this research presupposes that language is the primary focus of analysis, and hence largely brackets nonlinguistic elements off, regarding them as "context" for the analysis of language. In fact, most academic journal articles that examine discourse data contain a section for the context wherein authors describe the linguistic, demographic, and sometimes historical context of the situation and then move on to the analysis with no further attention to the context. Several longstanding discourse approaches have taken a deeply contextual view to the analysis of language, including Fairclough's (1989) three dimensional approach known as Critical Discourse Analysis (CDA) and interactional sociolinguistics (e.g. Gumperz 1982), an approach to studying conversational interactions with attention to not only what is "brought about" in language but also what is "brought along" (Giddens 1976) from the material world, including structures of inequality. Still, these approaches have largely treated language as indexical to their sociopolitical contexts, rather than as enmeshed within and resulting from networks or assemblages involving material and human actors. The result is that most discourse research in these areas has privileged language as the starting point for analysis.

In our view, *nexus analysis* was the first approach to point to a posthumanist orientation that included language as part of an interconnected set of semiotic dynamics. Scollon and Scollon (2003) and Scollon (2008) use "nexus" to refer to the intersection of historical trajectories of people, discourses, objects and places to illustrate sites of engagement. While human action takes a central role, the Scollons' examination of how technology and history mediate human action embraced the posthumanist interest in the material world's role in human experiences. Their study on the effort to improve Native Alaskans' access to higher education in the 1980s tied the practices in the classroom and the community to the economic boom brought by the discovery of oil. They analyzed these changes ethnographically, examining how human action was equivalent to a set of cycles of discourse that were mediated by technology for teaching and learning and, particularly, the early days of the Internet. Their framework privileged human activity as a series of "itineraries of relationships among text, action, and the material world through what [they] call a nexus analysis" (Scollon 2008: 233). Scholars working in this tradition have since used nexus analysis to analyze discourse from a holistic, integrated and materially informed perspective. For example, Norris and Jones (2005) offer illustrations of how texts such as AIDS education pamphlets and computer instructions are used as tools for human action and resources for constructing identities. More recently, Lou (2016) analyzed how the linguistic landscape in Washington DC's Chinatown intersected with the material processes of gentrification and city planning measures which tended to exclude the Chinese community.

Discourse research has also more recently drawn on the metaphor of the rhizome to examine the trajectories of interdiscursive assemblages that interweave together in complex ways to shape people's discursive practices. In early work in this area, Ramanathan (2006) discussed how the selection and translation of texts and their embedding into other academic texts exemplifies how studying the assemblage of texts invites us to see their constructed nature and encourages us to realize that they are one of many possible assemblages, thereby drawing our attention to the politics of knowledge construction. In more recent work, Pietikäinen (2015) explores the potentialities that Sámi language speakers are experiencing at the current historical juncture where Indigenous languages and multilingual resources are increasingly valued but also commodified and contested. In analyzing how Sámi in the village of Inari is represented and used, she illustrates how historical, material and discursive elements rhizomatically produce and constrain opportunities to use the Sámi language. In tracing these interdiscursive networks, this work raises critical questions about the location of agency, subjectivity and linguistic competence. Rather than attributing language maintenance to individual efforts and capacities, the analysis shows that the capacity for minority languages is a relational achievement spun from shifting networks of objects, bodies, people and places, all human as much as nonhuman, and that come together at different moments to make our day-to-day discursive practices possible. Canagarajah (2018), for example, references the rhizome to describe how a Korean STEM scholar reworked a series of several drafts of an article for publication. In producing this text, the scholar engaged with a multifaceted and shifting trajectory of discursive and material networks that worked to transform his polysemiotic interactions into an academic English product along the way. Here, the communicative competence is not an individual capacity but a capacity to "align" a shifting network of embodied practices, objects, technologies, texts, images and interactions with his communicative objective: publishing an article.

Very recently, posthumanist work in applied linguistics has foregrounded the primacy of semiotics other than language. Pennycook and Otsuji (2015), for example, begin one study of *metrolingual practices* in Sydney by researching a cucumber whose origins in Japan (and consequent reputation for crunchiness) are what cause people to travel to particular markets, thereby producing new spatial repertoires involving not only the languages that they encounter and use but also the cucumbers themselves. Similarly, Zhu Hua, Wei and Lyons (2017) analyze Polish cornershops in London, noting how the spatial layout of the shop, the display of goods for sale, body movements, gaze and language work together to form communicative zones in which customers and the employee engage in sense-making activities. In our own different studies on language in the tourism landscape in Hawai'i, nonhuman elements play a pivotal role in the expansion of Japanese as an important language for communication with tourists, including transportation routes, sought-after food items such as pancakes with macadamia nut sauce, and Hawaiian turtles (Higgins and Ikeda 2019; Lamb 2019). All of this research has highlighted the need to shift focus from language as the starting point and to pay greater attention to the ways that humans are enmeshed in dynamic relationships with the material world.

16.4 Issues and Debates

There are several issues and challenges that arise for discourse researchers drawing on posthumanist theory. The issue of nonhuman agency, and the flat ontology it implies, challenges researchers in fields such as anthropology and human geography to reattune their theories and methods so as to give equal weight to the role of materiality and the agency of animals as participants in human activity. Adopting a flat ontology rejects the a priori dualism dividing subjects and objects to foreground instead how nonhuman entities and beings come to provoke, instigate, inspire, resist, block, interpellate and otherwise demand attention of human experiences and practices. As already mentioned, discourse researchers have pointed to a flatter posthumanist view of human agency in their work, in treating agency not as an individual capacity but as a relational achievement spun between mediational means and the mediated actions these resources make possible. However, a flat ontology also raises a number of methodological concerns. Canagarajah (2018), for example, has suggested that, while illuminating in a number of ways, a flat ontology that distributes agency indiscriminately across people and objects may also risk diluting a critical lens on power relations in unequal communicative encounters. Another challenge related to this is to recognize how researchers themselves become entangled in this messy relational ontology of research practice that posthumanist theory encourages (Law 2004; Jones 2018).

Moreover, a posthumanist symmetrical stance on research phenomena encourages researchers not to assume in advance what discursive and material resources will ultimately mediate the focal event under study but instead to trace what resources become relevant for the participants themselves in moments of action, and across longer chains of events. A concern here arises if language itself emerges as more or less irrelevant to the participants' activity(ies) under focus. For discourse researchers who ostensibly study "language and discourse," this raises questions about what the object of study actually becomes from a posthumanist approach to discourse analysis, when language ends up being of not so great importance. To give one example, in wildlife tourism settings such as the sea turtle tourism site in the introduction to this chapter, much of the human interaction with these creatures may involve little verbal engagement, relying much more or entirely on modalities such as gaze, pointing, body positioning and other modal aggregates of sense-making such as "touch-response" feel (Norris 2012).

This also raises the challenging issue of how posthumanist discourse research that is more ecologically grounded in the global systems that support life might account for the participatory "actions" of other living beings and ecosystems, such as sea turtles and their habitats. For example, how might discourse researchers better include a much wider terrain of nonhuman agency and meaning-making in their theoretical and methodological frameworks? This question raises more fundamental concerns about what constitutes "discourse" in the field, and thus what the boundaries and reach of discursive inquiry ought to include.

One fruitful entry point into these questions is to turn to research on semiotic landscapes in sociolinguistics (Jaworski and Thurlow 2010) foregrounding the body, and the multisensorial rapport of forces it imbricates us in as a central locus of discourse analysis (Pennycook and Otsuji 2015). Building on mediated discourse analysis (Norris and Jones 2005; Scollon 2002), Thurlow and Jaworski (2014) analyze tourists' embodied *kinesic displays* (e.g. postures, pointing, poses, gestures, gaze, camera-holding, walking) in their movements through the site of the Leaning Tower of Pisa in Italy. The mostly silent embodied movements of tourists are seen not as individual, isolated acts but as interdiscursive upwellings of activity produced from an irreducible assemblage of bodies, discourse and place. From another perspective, in analyzing the interactional organization of tactility and tasting of gourmet cheese, Mondada (2018) shows how conversation analytic methods can demonstrate the materiality and multisensorial nature of objects constituting intersubjectivity. Perhaps more controversially, a posthumanist approach would also direct discourse or conversation analysts to acknowledge objects like cheese not just as object-like resources for interaction but also as actors in their own right (Ren 2011).

16.5 Implications

The ontology of posthumanism has many implications for how we go about doing research in the fields of applied linguistics, sociolinguistics and related fields such as linguistic anthropology and literacy studies. At present, much of the writing about posthumanism remains at a conceptual level, with illustrations of the key concepts provided via real-world examples. However, the more practical methodologies remain underdescribed, in our view. Currently, researchers who embrace posthumanism in these fields engage in ethnography as the key framework for understanding particular actor-networks, nexuses and assemblages. While ethnography is essential to developing a holistic understanding of a place, community or context, more attention is needed on how researchers' experience in doing ethnography can be documented and reported on with reference to the concept of a flat ontology. An example of such work is Pennycook and Otsuji (2015) who characterize their team-based ethnographic work as steady engagement with the unexpected in markets, restaurants and city streets in Sydney and Tokyo. Their transcripts of recordings were particularly difficult to accomplish, as the mixtures of languages challenged the multilingual transcribers to identify what language and what meanings were being conveyed, and showed many disagreements over the details. The mobile quality of their data led them to follow individuals as they navigated through spaces while using a range of semiotic resources. They also chose to analyze spaces from a more static perspective, identifying how resources emerged and were used in those spaces. For particular contexts, they realized the importance of objects in producing multilingual networks of mobility, so they focused on tracing the connections between items like Japanese cucumbers, and the actions of distributing, buying and consuming these cucumbers, all of which occurred while people engaged in multilingual multitasking.

Posthumanism calls for researchers to focus on all semiotic affordances from a posthumanist/assemblage perspective, rather than beginning with language or discourse. This holistic view makes issues like the idea of transcription difficult, particularly since many nodes of the rhizome or actants in the network are not synchronous. This leads to the problem of what semiotic modes to transcribe and what to include and exclude. Mediated and multimodal discourse analysis (Norris 2004; Norris and Jones 2005) offer models for transcription that include nonhuman aspects such as furniture and "frozen actions" such as a plate of warm food, indicating the actions taken prior. Nonetheless, this leaves out many macro-level considerations, including historically dominant ideologies that shape interaction. An illustration of this is found in Pietikäinen (2015), which shows how the legacy of political oppression toward the Sámi is part of the confluence of forces acting on speakers today. Though the language has become endangered, it is also a cultural commodity that draws tourism around new developments such as reindeer farms, where visitors are apprenticed in how to lasso a reindeer by a Sámi-speaking expert whose use of the language authenticates him or her as a member of an "exotic" and "traditional" culture that has been long displaced.

Noting the challenges, Canagarajah (2018) analyzes STEM scholars' work, where he adopts a narrative, case-study approach that allows him to draw on affordances from different spatiotemporal scales. An example is the analysis of a scientific diagram produced by a STEM scholar, Gunter, whose sedimented experience of reading many academic articles intersected with the human resources in his lab, including a fellow scholar who worked with him to transform his ideas into an effective diagram to show how the honeybee population declines in winter. After they had produced the diagram, Gunter questioned his original logic, and the result was that his own thinking about the relationship linking bee pheromones, foraging and maturation changed. Canagarajah writes (2018: 278): "The visual model did not simply convey preconstructed ideas or supplement words, but was itself agentive in shaping human thinking and communication." We suggest that future posthumanist scholars do more to show others how the research process unfolds through the "methodology of following" the networks, as Latour (1987) advocates. In addition to the rich description of fieldwork, researchers might consider sharing the process of following networks through open science platforms that allow others to engage in the process.

Beyond implications for research methodology, posthumanism itself creates new discourses around the issue of origins, cause and effect, and chronology. In recent work on tourism on O'ahu Hawai'i for example, it has become clear that Japanese celebrities play a key role in the ways in which restaurants and shops become must-visit destinations for Japanese visitors in the residential town of Kailua (Higgins and Ikeda 2019). A discourse that has emerged there is a protectionist one, as many residents voice their concern over their hometown becoming overrun with tourists, thus losing its appeal. However, this discourse is in constant dialogue with other discourses from other nodes on the rhizome, including discourses that are both critical of and supportive of gentrification, a process that has taken place in Kailua due to land ownership changes over the past twenty years and ensuing retail and condo development. Japanese celebrities visit Kailua because it is charming, but it is charming because of the gentrification. At the same time, as economic opportunities for tourism have arisen in Kailua, the state's tourism agency has created its own commodification discourses for Kailua, which have in turn been challenged by residents who have called for the agency to stop recommending Kailua as a destination for Japanese tourists. The result is that Kailua has become a place where NIMBY ("not in my backyard") discourses about development and gentrification coalesce with material changes that push these forces forward, resulting in discourses of resistance and critique in the process. It is important to examine other contexts in which competing discourses about social change and social problems arise in the nexus of material, discursive and embodied engagements, and to explore the role of discourse in these entanglements.

16.6 Future Directions

We have argued that discourse researchers are already contributing to posthumanist concerns by retheorizing the relation between discourse and key concepts in the field such as (non)human agency, materiality, embodiment and representation. This work is raising fundamental questions about the embedding of human discursive activity in the more-than-human material and living world. Here, we raise some issues we see as especially important for continued dialogue between discourse studies and posthumanist theory.

How does embracing a flat ontology lead to more dynamic understandings of discursive practices, not as emanating from a purely human source but rather as an emergent effect of human imbrications with objects, tools, technologies, across both physical and virtual places? One challenge presented by a posthumanist perspective will be to examine how the current era of "the digital" is imbricating embodied and material worlds with virtual worlds in dynamic and unpredictable ways. A focus on the digital raises questions about how embodied-virtual interactivity across online and offline spaces empowers people to disperse and reassemble their discursive repertoire, agentive reach and sense of subjectivity in new ways. This is evident in how social media platforms such as YouTube and Twitter have become increasingly powerful as technologies for amplifying political activism such as during the Arab Spring and #BlackLivesMatter movements (Bonilla and Rosa 2015; Shiri 2015). At the same time, humans are also becoming caught up in the digital landscapes of state surveillance regimes (Jones 2017). As these digital tools become powerful technologies in the hands of corporations and nation-states, it will be important to understand how these global online–offline assemblages produce diverse forms of agentivity, carrying both empowering and disempowering agentive potentials for those – human and nonhuman alike – entangled with them (cf. Jones 2009).

While a flat ontology sensitizes researchers to the agentive participation of material and digital worlds in human semiotic practices, a further area of concern for discourse researchers to address will be how these practices are shaped through human interactions with the nonhuman living world. For instance, what agency potentials do plants, animals and natural places bring to the formation of social processes and discursive formations? Here, anthropogenic ecological crises from climate change to species extinction are spurring a new urgency for interdisciplinary scholarship in this area. In particular, posthumanist theory is increasingly invoking the idea of the Anthropocene to call attention to the ethically problematic and damaging kinds of relationship being forged between human and nonhuman beings in their relational cobecomings within assemblages. By this token, an important task will be to remain vigilant of where power, inequality and responsibility lie in these assemblages. This will require researchers to be precise in explaining how agency comes to be distributed across human–nonhuman assemblages through discursive practices, and develop a sensitivity to more partial vehicles of human and nonhuman agency such as "actants" and "mediants" (Appadurai 2015).

Addressing how these and many other questions might be taken up through the ongoing dialogue between discourse studies and posthumanist theory is beyond the scope of this chapter, but much of this work is already underway in the field of discourse studies, as we have argued. In examining the interconnectivity among humans, discursive processes and the nonhuman material and living world, this dialogue will continue to open up interdisciplinary conversations on a range of important empirical topics, theoretical concerns and methodological innovations. Notably, in pointing to the material, embodied and more-than-discursive ways of knowing and being in the world, future work should continue to embrace supplementing more traditional text-based genres of academic knowledge production with multisensorial representations of knowing, being and doing in the world. Taking risks with alternative forms of knowledge production in the field will be especially important when seeking to share this expertise beyond the boundaries of academic debate.

16.7 Summary

This chapter maps the emerging conceptual terrain of posthumanism and its relevance for discourse studies, with attention to sociolinguistics and applied linguistics work. As a label applied to a broad range of theoretical and methodological approaches, a fundamental aspect of posthumanism is its aim to call into question dominant assumptions generated by

Western Enlightenment thinking about "the human." This critical stance toward the category of the human runs in parallel with efforts to recognize the importance of material objects, animals and the environment in constituting social processes. For discourse studies engaging in dialogue with posthumanist theory, these interdisciplinary conversations will continue to offer insight into the role of discourse in how humans become entangled with the material world through their everyday embodied interactions with objects, artifacts, technologies, plants, animals and the built and natural environment.

Further Reading

Canagarajah, S. (2018). Materializing "Competence": Perspectives from International STEM Scholars. *Modern Language Journal* 102(2): 268–91.

This article offers a reframing of "competence" by examining how multilingual STEM scholars engage in their work through linguistic, embodied and material resources. Building on conceptual insights from new materialism and Actor-Network theory, it explores some of the methodological implications of posthumanist thinking for discourse analysts.

Kohn, E. (2013). *How Forests Think: Toward an Anthropology beyond the Human.* Berkeley: University of California Press.

In dialogue with emerging posthumanist multispecies studies, this ethnography investigates the semiotic entanglements of Ecuadorian Quichua-speaking Runa with the plants, animals and ecosystems they interact with in the Amazon. In challenging anthropocentric thinking about language, discourse and representation, the book offers an innovative understanding of semiosis as not only human but an emergent property of all living beings or "selves."

Latour, B. (2005). *Reassembling the Social: An Introduction to Actor-Network-Theory.* Oxford: Oxford University Press.

This book offers an in-depth introduction to Actor-Network theory from one of the key figures in its development. Divided into two parts, it first provides an overview of the theoretical influences motivating ANT's call for a shift from a "sociology of the social" to a "sociology of associations." The second part guides readers through the methodological principles underpinning ANT.

Pennycook, A. (2017). *Posthumanist Applied Linguistics.* New York: Routledge.

This book introduces posthumanism to the field of applied linguistics by arguing against the popular conception that language is the key to human exceptionalism. Pennycook dismantles this logic by drawing attention to the embodied, material and distributed nature of language.

Scollon, S. W. (2004). *Nexus Analysis: Discourse and the Emerging Internet.* New York: Routledge.

This book offers an introduction to nexus analysis and remains a cutting-edge example of a posthumanist orientation to ethnographic discourse analysis. The method is illustrated through an investigation of how early internet communication mediated Alaska Natives' access to various institutional assemblages in the 1980s. The appendix of the book further summarizes the key principles of nexus analysis in a highly useful "field guide" for examining posthumanist actor-networks and assemblages.

References

Alexander, R. and Stibbe, A. (2014). From the Analysis of Ecological Discourse to the Ecological Analysis of Discourse. *Language Sciences* 41: 104–10.

Appadurai, A. (2015). Mediants, Materiality, Normativity. *Public Culture* 27 (276): 221–37.

Barad, K. (2003). Posthumanist Performativity: Toward an Understanding of How Matter Comes to Matter. *Signs* 28(3): 801–31.

Bennett, J. (2009). *Vibrant Matter: A Political Ecology of Things.* Durham, NC: Duke University Press.

(2010). A Vitalist Stopover on the Way to a New Materialism. In D. Coole and S. Frost (eds.) *New Materialisms: Ontology, Agency, and Politics.* Durham, NC: Duke University Press.

Bonilla, Y. and Rosa, J. (2015). #Ferguson: Digital Protest, Hashtag Ethnography, and the Racial Politics of Social Media in the United States. *American Ethnologist* 42(1): 4–17.

Bucholtz, M. and Hall, K. (2016). Embodied Sociolinguistics. In N. Coupland (ed.) *Sociolinguistics: Theoretical Debates.* Cambridge: Cambridge University Press. 173–97.

Callon, M. (1984). Some Elements of a Sociology of Translation: Domestication of the Scallops and the Fishermen of St Brieuc Bay. *Sociological Review* 32: 196–233.

Canagarajah, A. S. (2018). Materializing "Competence": Perspectives from International STEM Scholars. *Modern Language Journal* 102(2): 1–24.

Chakrabarty, D. (2000). *Provincializing Europe: Postcolonial Thought and Historical Difference.* Princeton, NJ: Princeton University Press.

Coole, D. and Frost, S. (2010). *New Materialisms: Ontology, Agency, and Politics.* Durham, NC: Duke University Press.

Deleuze, G. and Guattari, F. (1987). *A Thousand Plateaus: Capitalism and Schizophrenia.* Minneapolis/St Paul: University of Minnesota Press.

Fairclough, N. (1989). *Language and Power.* London/New York: Longman.

Foucault, M. ([1966] 1970). *The Order of Things: An Archaeology of the Human Sciences*, trans. by A. M. S. Smith. New York: Vintage Books.
Gee, J. P. (2015). Discourse, Small d, Big D. In K. Tracy, C. Ilie and T. L. Sandel (eds.) *The International Encyclopedia of Language and Social Interaction*. Boston, MA: Wiley-Blackwell. 418–22.
Giddens, A. (1976). *New Rules of Sociological Method*. London: Hutchinson.
Goodwin, C. (2000). Action and Embodiment within Situated Human Interaction. *Journal of Pragmatics* 32: 1489–522.
Gumperz, J. J. (1982). *Discourse Strategies*. Cambridge: Cambridge University Press.
Higgins, C. and Ikeda, M. (2019). The Materialization of Language in Tourism Networks. *Applied Linguistics Review*. https://doi.org/10.1515/applirev-2019-0100
Iedema, R. (2001). Resemiotization. *Semiotica* 137(1/4): 23–39.
Jaworski, A. and Thurlow, C. (eds.) (2010). *Semiotic Landscapes: Language, Image, Space*. London: Continuum.
Jones, R. H. (2009). Dancing, Skating, and Sex: Action and Text in the Digital Age. *Journal of Applied Linguistics* 6(3): 283–302.
  (2017). Surveillant Landscapes. *Linguistic Landscape* 3(2): 149–86.
  (2018). Messy Creativity. *Language Sciences* 65: 82–6.
Kell, C. (2015). "Making People Happen": Materiality and Movement in Meaning-Making Trajectories. *Social Semiotics* 25(4): 423–45.
Kirksey, S. E. and Helmreich, S. (2010). The Emergence of Multispecies Ethnography. *Cultural Anthropology* 25(4): 545–76.
Kohn, E. (2007). How Dogs Dream: Amazonian Natures and the Politics of Transspecies Engagement. *American Ethnologist* 34(1): 3–24.
Lamb, G. (2019). Towards a Green Applied Linguistics in the Anthropocene: Human–Sea Turtle Semiotic Assemblages in Hawai'i. *Applied Linguistics*. https://doi.org/10.1093/applin/amz046
Latour, B. (1987). *Science in Action: How to Follow Scientists and Engineers through Society*. Cambridge, MA: Harvard University Press.
  (1990). Technology Is Society Made Durable. *Sociological Review* 38 (supplement): 103–31.
  (1993/2012). *We Have Never Been Modern*. Cambridge, MA: Harvard University Press.
  (2005). *Reassembling the Social: An Introduction to Actor-Network Theory*. Oxford/New York: Oxford University Press.
Law, J. (2004). *After Method: Mess in Social Science Research*. New York: Psychology Press.
Law, J. and Mol, A. (2008). The Actor-Enacted: Cumbrian Sheep in 2001. In C. Knappett and L. Malafouris (eds.) *Material Agency*. Dusseldorf: Springer. 57–77.
Lou, J. (2016). *The Linguistic Landscape of Chinatown: A Sociolinguistic Ethnography*. Bristol: Multilingual Matters.

Mondada, L. (2018). The Multimodal Interactional Organization of Tasting: Practices of Tasting Cheese in Gourmet Shops. *Discourse Studies* 20(6): 743–69.

Norris, S. (2004). *Analyzing Multimodal Interaction: A Methodological Framework*. New York: Routledge.

(2012). Teaching Touch/Response-Feel: A First Step to an Analysis of Touch from an (Inter)active Perspective. In S. Norris (ed.) *Multimodality in Practice: Investigating Theory-in-Practice-through-Methodology*. New York: Routledge. 7–19.

Norris, S. and Jones, R. (2005). *Discourse in Action: Introducing Mediated Discourse Analysis*. New York: Routledge.

Pennycook, A. (2018). Posthumanist Applied Linguistics. *Applied Linguistics* 39(4): 445–61.

Pennycook, A. and Otsuji, E. (2015). *Metrolingualism: Language in the City*. London: Routledge.

Pietikäinen, S. (2015). Multilingual Dynamics in Sámiland: Rhizomatic Discourses on Changing Language. *International Journal of Bilingualism* 19(2): 206–25.

Ramanathan, V. (2006). Of Texts AND Translations AND Rhizomes: Postcolonial Anxieties AND Deracinations AND Knowledge Constructions. *Critical Inquiry in Language Studies* 3(4): 223–44.

Ren, C. (2011). Non-human Agency, Radical Ontology and Tourism Realities. *Annals of Tourism Research* 38(3): 858–81.

Scollon, R. (2002). *Mediated Discourse: The Nexus of Practice*. New York: Routledge.

(2008). Discourse Itineraries: Nine Processes of Resemiotization. In V. Bhatia, J. Flowerdew and R. Jones (eds.) *Advances in Discourse Studies*. London: Routledge. 233–44.

Scollon, R. and Scollon, S. W. (2003). *Discourses in Place: Language in the Material World*. New York: Routledge.

Shiri S. (2015). Co-constructing Dissent in the Transient Linguistic Landscape: Multilingual Protest Signs of the Tunisian Revolution. In R. Rubdy and S. B. Said (eds.) *Conflict, Exclusion and Dissent in the Linguistic Landscape: Language and Globalization*. London: Palgrave Macmillan. 239–59.

Thrift, N. (2008). *Non-representational Theory: Space, Politics, Affect*. London: Routledge.

Thurlow, C. (2016). Queering Critical Discourse Studies or/and Performing "Post-Class" Ideologies. *Critical Discourse Studies* 13(5): 485–514.

Thurlow, C. and Jaworski, A. (2014). "Two Hundred Ninety-Four": Remediation and Multimodal Performance in Tourist Placemaking. *Journal of Sociolinguistics* 18(4): 459–94.

Whatmore, S. (2006). Materialist Returns: Practising Cultural Geography in and for a More-than-Human World. *Cultural Geographies* 13(4): 600–9.

Zhu Hua, Li Wei, and Lyons, A. (2017). Polish Shop(ping) as Translanguaging Space. *Social Semiotics* 27(4): 411–33.

Part IV

(Trans)Locations and Intersections

Introduction

There are a number of threads that bind together the chapters in this section. Authors focus their work on concepts that have to do with the transgression of boundaries, both in the sense of crossing borders between disciplinaries and deconstructing received categories and tools for analysis, and in the sense of pointing our attention to phenomena related to fluidity and change rather than stability and permanence. Contributors also analyze intersections, that is, the reciprocal influence of identity categories and the joining together of different methods for analyzing linguistic phenomena. In addition, they discuss the many ways in which communication happens through the nexus of a variety of resources working together with language and through networks of connections among people, discourse occasions, texts and so forth. Another theme that runs through the chapters is the importance of hybridity and processes of assemblage against a received focus on homogeneity and continuity in the study of discursive phenomena at different levels: from the individuation of speech communities and participants' identity categories, to the definition of languages and languages varieties, to the description of genres.

These foci of attention reflect shifts in discourse studies that have emerged in great part as a response to the sweeping social changes brought about by globalization. Together with the technological revolution, possibly the most important of these changes has been the unprecedented increase in mobility of people, goods and resources, which has been at the center of theorizations by scholars of globalization and modernity such as Appadurai (1996), Castells (2000) and Bauman (1998) and of linguistic anthropologists such as Agha (2006). The realization of the role of mobility in society has brought about a deep rethinking in discourse studies, particularly of the relationships among identities, languages and places. Such rethinking has first been evident in the critique of the construct of the *speech community*, conceptualized as an aggregate of people having regular interactions and sharing sets of resources (Gumperz 1968). Rampton (2010: 274) noted how scholars are no longer interested in "'big' communities that pre-exist us" but are increasingly focused on the processes though which communities emerge, while at the same time shifting their attention toward new communities and interactions at the margins of established ones. It can be argued that this critique of the speech community is one of the clearest symptoms of twenty-first-century discourse analysts' discomfort with notions of stability in the connections among communities, languages and places. Reflections on mobility have also led to a new centrality of space in discourse and sociolinguistics research. But geographical location is not seen as a determining factor in language variation and use. Indeed, attention has been shifted toward the way in which speakers position themselves in relation to linguistic elements and repertoires connected to certain spaces, particularly in digital environments.

With the recognition of the permeability and fluidity of space, the idea of crossing borders has also taken center-stage. This is particularly evident in work on transnational identities with its recognition of the multiplicity of ties that migrants and mobile subjects establish with different communities, as illustrated in Chapter 17 by Goebel. It also underlies theoretical reflections that invite us to transcend and problematize barriers existing not only between disciplines but also between language varieties usually regarded as separate. The latter is exemplified in Chapter 20, in which Schreiber, Shahri and Canagarajah's characterize academic English both as an area that encompasses a variety of disciplinary approaches and as a construct combining diverse language varieties, and in Chapter 18, in which Tong King Lee and Li Wei view translanguaging as going beyond named languages boundaries.

The theme of intersections underlies Køhler Mortensen and Milani's analysis of how different categories combine and contribute in unique ways to people's identities, in Chapter 19, and in the arguments in this chapter and in Chapter 17 about connections created by discursive activity between phenomena at different scales. The idea of the centrality of the connections between different resources as a basis for understanding actual communication is present in all the chapters: in particular in the conception of languages in use as being repertoires of resources that underlie the construct of translanguaging (see Lee and Li, Chapter 18), in the argument that effective communication involves a performative ability to bring together semiotic elements of different nature (Chapters 17 and 20, respectively by Goebel and Milani and Køler Mortensen and Milani) and in the analysis of emotions as an arena of encounter between the bodily, the discursive and the social (Chapter 19 by Køler Mortensen and Milani).

Finally, hybridity and assemblage are constructs that underlie not only research and theorization on translanguaging and translingual practices, as based on the mixing and combination of very diverse elements (Chapter 18 by Lee and Li) coming from a variety of semiotic systems, but also the argument, made by different authors, that discourse analysts need to "bring into sharp relief the interactions among bodies, artifacts, spatial resources and other material conditions" (Chapter 20, p. 442). Next we highlight some of the contribution made by each individual chapter in this section.

Goebel's Chapter 17 analyzes how the development of the concepts of transnationalism, globalization and superdiversity represents both a reflection of the impact on discourse studies of global flows with their associated changes in the social and economic sphere and a symptom of where much of the research in the area is going. He sketches some of the common roots and methodological choices that underlie the use of those concepts and presents reflections on how they have also been problematized and debated within the field, with particular reference to superdiversity. Among the elements of common ground that he underscores are the rejection of fixed associations between places, social identities and language varieties, the stress on both discourse circulation and the investigation of connections between communicative resources and events, and the interest in analyzing how power issues play out in the global sphere. The latter has led to recognition of the polycentricity and scalar nature of resources. In terms of methodological common ground, Goebel underscores the use of ethnography and the appropriation of many of the tools offered by conversation analysis and the talk-in-interaction orientation that allow for close attention to the local management of communication. The focus of the chapter is, however, on exploring ways in which analysts have studied connections among speakers, discourses and communicative events at different scales, and therefore on bringing to light the implications of doing discourse analysis with an emphasis on mobility and diversity.

Like Goebel, **Lee and Li**, in Chapter 18, start from a reflection on how theorizations on liquid modernity (Bauman 2000) have affected the way we think about languages. They concentrate on translanguaging and associated concepts as an alternative to multilingualism as a simple juxtaposition of languages. Indeed, in their view, translanguaging captures the "spontaneous convergence of different languages (or language varieties and registers), semiotic modalities, or technology-driven media" and underscores "a sense of immediacy, transiency and momentarity" (p. 395). The chapter traces the origins and development of the concept and sketches the authors' conceptualization of it. Lee and Li put stress on the fact that translanguaging captures linguistic behavior happening in between systems, that it reflects a variety of functions and objectives beyond the representational, and that it is deeply transformative. The authors note that the objective of translanguaging studies is not to deny the existence and reality of named languages but rather to show how participants in discourse events constantly transgress those boundaries, thus revealing their permeability. Much of the emphasis here is on the creativity that underlies language users' communicative practices and on the embracing of a critical stance toward language studies. Indeed, according to the authors, it is through changing the way in which we orient to multilingual discourse that different tools for studying it can emerge. Hence, generalization is much less important to translingual studies than punctual observation of specific patterns of interaction among multilingual speakers.

In Chapter 19, **Køhler Mortensen and Milani** take up the theme of intersectionality and its application to the study of identities and affect. Intersectionality has represented a response to views of identities based on isolated or juxtaposed categories, by shifting the emphasis on the ways in which categories interconnect and influence each other in unique ways. For the authors, intersectionality should not be regarded as a theory – a point of animated debate within the field – but rather as a stance favoring instead an orientation to this construct as a heuristics that allows for more nuanced analyses about identities and power relations. At the same time, it is the authors' view that scholars should take a critical attitude with regard to applications of this orientation that focus exclusively on macro categories, favoring instead "thicker intersectionalities" (Yep 2016), that is, "a context-based sensitivity to how apparently similar constellations of identity nexus points may be experienced very differently by individuals, depending on context and person" (p. 420). It is precisely an orientation to this kind of finer and more nuanced analysis that, according to Køhler Mortensen and Milani, leads to a renewed appreciation of the importance of emotions in discourse, as emotions represent a point of intersection among social practices, social structures and agency. Emotions are also seen here as mediating between the individual and the collective, the mind and society. Studying emotions crucially involves the analysis of "visible discourse practices," that is, of how emotions like hate or shame are socially produced, but without losing sight of the individual investment and agency in such processes of discursive production.

Finally, in Chapter 20, **Schreiber, Shahri and Canagarajah** discuss how understandings of academic English have changed in the last thirty years from a focus on a single variety to one that accepts the plural and multifaceted nature of academic Englishes and from a stress on structure to an orientation to practice. These shifts have implied abandoning a text-centered view and recognizing the need to analyze and study the diverse discursive practices that constitute such object of study. The authors highlight, for example, the contributions of genre and corpus-based discourse analysis in showing both the plurality of genres that are used by academics in their writings and the many ways in which patterns and thematic associations occur within large databases. However, the reliance of these approaches on written English has been criticized and Schreiber, Shahri and Canagarajah highlight how a focus on "literate activity" rather than on texts allows for widening the focus of analysis to physical setting and actual interactions. The centrality of activity has opened the way to a conception of academic discourses as hybrid – that is, as incorporating different discursive forms and genres – and multimodal. Another significant trend in the area has been the investigation of pragmatic strategies in the use of English as a lingua franca with particular emphasis on their translingual nature. The authors discuss some implications of these theoretical changes: first, that the recognition that academic discourse is produced within a nexus of agents, material resources and social networks implies a consequent focus on the connections of these elements; second, that the need to rethink communicative competence has to do with the performative ability to use different resources rather than the ability to function in one language variety; and finally, that the realization of the centrality of the individual and the human in research needs to be tempered by recognition of materialities and concrete environments as a fundamental factor in the production of knowledge.

References

Agha, A. (2006). *Language and Social Relations*. New York: Cambridge University Press.

Appadurai, A. (1996). *Modernity at Large: Cultural Dimensions of Globalization*. Minneapolis: University of Minnesota Press.

Bauman, Z. (1998). *Globalization: The Human Consequences*. New York: Columbia University Press.

 (2000). *Liquid Modernity*. Cambridge: Polity.

Castells, M. (2000). *The Rise of the Network Society*. Oxford: Blackwell.

Gumperz, J. (1968). The Speech Community. In D. L. Sills and R. K. Merton (eds.) *International Encyclopedia of the Social Sciences*: London: Macmillan. 381–6.

Rampton, B. (2010) Speech Community. In J., Östman and J. Verschueren (eds.) *Society and Language Usage*. Amsterdam: John Benjamins. 274–303.

Yep, G. (2016). Toward Thick(er) Intersectionalities: Theorizing, Researching, and Activating the Complexities of Communication and Identities. In K. Sorrells and S. Sekimoto (eds.) *Globalizing Intercultural Communication*. Thousand Oaks, CA: Sage. 85–94.

17

Transnationalism, Globalization and Superdiversity

Zane Goebel

17.1 Introduction

This chapter focuses on transnationalism, globalization and superdiversity. It starts by examining how these concepts have been developed in the broader field of humanities and social sciences and then analyzes how they have developed within sociolinguistics. I identify some of the common concerns, especially the need to focus on understanding complex connections between multiple communicative events, as well as some of the conceptual developments that have been part of work in the field. In doing so, I sketch some of the common intellectual roots, and the common theoretical and methodological approaches associated with the concepts of transnationalism, globalization and superdiversity.

17.2 Overview of the Topic

The terms *transnationalism* and *globalization* both refer to the movement or flow of people, goods, services and ideas between nation-states or countries, the complex connections among all of these and the effects of these processes on individuals and on populations (Appadurai 1996; Portes, Guarnizo and Landolt 1999; Stiglitz 2006). Work on superdiversity has focused on these aspects too, while exploring how these flows relate to identity, inequality and social cohesion (Vertovec 2007). In what follows, I examine each of these constructs in turn, starting with transnationalism.

In 1992, Nina Glick Schiller and colleagues put together a collection of papers entitled "Towards a Transnational Perspective on Migration: Race, Class, Ethnicity, and Nationalism Reconsidered." In their introduction to this collection, they pointed out that this volume recognized the increasing use in scholarly writing of the term "transnationalism" (Glick Schiller,

Basch and Blanc-Szanton 1992). As a move toward conceptualizing what they saw as a new phenomenon, they defined transnationalism as follows:

> When comparing our observations of the social relations of immigrants to the United States from three different areas – the eastern Caribbean, Haiti, and the Philippines – we found that migrants from each population were forging and sustaining multi-stranded social relations that linked their societies of origin and settlement. We called this immigrant experience "transnationalism" to emphasize the emergence of a social process in which migrants establish social fields that cross geographic, cultural, and political borders.   (Glick Schiller, Basch and Blanc-Szanton 1992: ix)

A later special edition devoted to this topic, by Portes et al. (1999), continued to emphasize the newness of this phenomenon, especially in regard to what was seen as a critical mass of migrants who constituted an emergent "social field." The latter was defined as being "composed of a growing number of persons who live dual lives: speaking two languages, having homes in two countries, and making a living through continuous regular contact across national borders" (Portes et al. 1999: 217). As with Glick Schiller, Basch and Blanc-Szanton (1992), scholarly focus was on the economic, political and social initiatives of the people who were seen as constituting transnational social fields. However, the authors also pointed out that many different methodological approaches existed in the area – for example, the empirical focus could be on individuals, groups, organizations or states – and that this methodological diversity worked against producing a coherent field that could be referred to as the study of transnationalism (Portes et al. 1999: 218).

In making the case for defining transnationalism as a new concept, Portes et al. (1999: 218–19) suggested that the phenomena in question needed to involve large numbers of people over a sustained period of time; high intensity of exchanges between those who migrate in both the host and the home contexts; new forms of interaction; and increases in the types of activity that require sustained cross-border travel and contact. In addition, they suggested delimiting the unit of analysis to enable a focus on one of the following elements: individual activity; networks of social relations; and institutional structures (e.g. local and national governments). While they suggested delimiting these units of analysis, they also proposed a methodological route of initial interviews of individuals and their support networks (Portes et al. 1999: 220). These interviews could then be followed by forays into examining the connections between interviewees and more complex issues, such as community formation. They went on to note that seeking to understand the relationship of community formation to economic and political situations could come at later stages of inquiry. In short, they were mirroring anthropological approaches to understanding community formation through the analysis of interactions that occur among small groups of people. In the same special issue, Vertovec (1999: 456–7) placed more emphasis on the need to link these different social domains, which he referred to as "scales," via the use of "multi-sited ethnography" (see Marcus 1995 on this term); which essentially traces people, things and ideas across multiple offline and online research sites.

In this early definitional work, and in subsequent research that focused on the experience of transnationalism, migrants' identities were conceptualized as classed, gendered, ethnic and national, and often collective, hyphenated or hybrid; such as in the case of Japanese-Brazilian's living in Japan and Chinese-Dutch-Indonesians living in Australia (Ang 2003; Tsuda 2003; Vertovec 1999). For example, Glick Schiller, Basch and Blanc-Szanton (1992: x) suggested that migrants constructed "collective identities" as a response to political and economic conditions in their country of origin and settlement. These processes are highlighted in Tsuda's (2003) account of mobility between Brazil and Japan and how Brazilians of Japanese heritage who went to Japan for work organized Mardi Gras and other activities in Japan that socially identified them as Brazilian, rather than Brazilians of Japanese heritage.

This early work on transnationalism interpreted transnationalism as an effect of economic conditions, arguing that when populations found it difficult to seek a better life in their own country, they moved to another country (Glick Schiller, Basch and Blanc-Szanton 1992: x; Portes et al. 1999: 220). This economic "push" explanation of migration was complemented with a "pull" explanation. The pull explanation was accounted for with reference to developments in transportation infrastructures – such as air travel – and communication technology infrastructures that enabled instantaneous communication, such as long-distance telephone, facsimile communication and email (Castells 1996; Portes et al. 1999: 223–7; Vertovec 1999: 447). These infrastructures not only compressed space and time (Harvey 1989) but they also enabled relatively easy and cheap contact between migrants and those in their country of origin, while also enabling people to imagine new lives (Appadurai 1996). For example, in his book entitled *Modernity at Large: Cultural Dimensions of Globalization*, Appadurai (1996) suggested that video technology was a facilitator of migration. This was so because communication between migrants and those from their country of origin fueled people's imagination about other places and the opportunities that they presented. This work also started to seek to understand connections between flows of people and other flows (e.g. ideas, capital, goods and services, technology, communication), although Appadurai discursively linked these flows and the connections between them with a phenomenon he referred to as "globalization."

In the following decade, time-space compression, expansion, connection, flows of people, flows of ideas, flows of technology, flows of capital and communicative flows were common topics covered in discussions of both transnationalism (Ferguson and Gupta 2002; Vertovec 2007) and globalization (Poynting et al. 2004; Stiglitz 2006; Tsing 2005). Definitions of globalization often overlapped across disciplines. For example, the Nobel prize winning economist Joseph Stiglitz's (2006) definition of globalization has much in common with Appadurai's (1996) ideas about globalization, in terms both of flows and of the aspirations driving some of them:

> Globalization encompasses many things: the international flow of ideas and knowledge, the sharing of cultures, global civil society, and the global environmental movement... the closer economic integration of the countries of the world through the increased flow of goods and services, capital, and even labor. The great hope of globalization is that it will raise living standards throughout the world: give poor countries access to overseas markets so that they can sell their goods, allow in foreign investment that will make new products at cheaper prices, and open borders so that people can travel abroad to be educated, work, and send home earnings to help their families and fund new businesses. (Stiglitz 2006: 4)

Stiglitz (2006: 8) and others (Poynting et al. 2004; Tsing 2005; Wallerstein 2004) have also identified other, less palatable characteristics of globalization, such as unemployment, environmental degradation, inequality and xenophobia. Flows create more flows, as in Appadurai's (1996) thesis, and are thus also an effect of globalization, as are inequality and xenophobia.

Diversity, as an effect of globalization, has also received increased attention, especially after the publication of a paper by Steven Vertovec (2007) entitled "Super-Diversity and Its Implications." In this paper, which primarily focused on the effects of mobility in the United Kingdom, he defined superdiversity as follows:

> In the last decade the proliferation and mutually conditioning effects of additional variables shows that it is not enough to see diversity only in terms of ethnicity, as is regularly the case both in social science and the wider public sphere. Such additional variables include differential immigration statuses and their concomitant entitlements and restrictions of rights, divergent labour market experiences, discrete gender and age profiles, patterns of spatial distribution, and mixed local area responses by service providers and residents. Rarely are these factors described side by side. The interplay of these factors is what is meant here, in summary fashion, by the notion of "super-diversity." (Vertovec 2007: 1025)

This diversification, including linguistic diversification, was perceived as a problem for those responsible for providing public services, such as schooling, transportation and health (Vertovec 2007: 1034–48). Vertovec also pointed to a need to better understand how social relationships were formed, maintained and broken in everyday encounters between migrants and hosts, and between migrants themselves (Vertovec 2007: 1045). Even so, and this is a critique of all the studies noted so far, the sociological and anthropological disciplinary backgrounds of the scholars cited here meant that while language and communication issues came up regularly, they were never engaged with: enter discourse analysis.

17.3 Issues and Ongoing Debates

The ideas of transnationalism and globalization have been developed in diverse ways within the broad field of sociolinguistics. Discourse analysts of all stripes commonly referred to as sociolinguists have a long history of engaging with issues of human contact, social cohesion, identity and inequality (Gumperz 1982; Rampton 1995). They have also developed theories and methodologies for understanding connections between different communicative events across different settings (Agha 2007; Wortham 2006). This section examines how sociolinguists have engaged with ideas of transnationalism and globalization.

Much of the research on transnationalism and globalization has many common intellectual roots. For example, ideas about social value and its relationship to inequality owe much to Bourdieu's (1991) work on language and symbolic power, while ideas about how profit seeking and markets impact on human mobility owe much to the work of Wallerstein (2004). For example, Heller et al. (2015) draw on general insights about how the movement of capital relates to resource exploitation, market saturation, mobility and the valuation of different languages. Similarly, Blommaert's (2010) ideas on value, polycentric norms (defined shortly) and how they relate to the policing of social conduct are inspired by these same scholars, as well as by Foucault (1978).

Common across recent sociolinguistic scholarship on transnationalism (De Fina and Perrino 2013; Lorente 2018; Park 2017), globalization (Blommaert 2010; Dovchin 2018; Heller et al. 2015) and superdiversity (Arnaut, Blommaert, Rampton and Spotti, 2015; Arnaut et al. 2016) is an increased focus on complex connections between the communicative resources used in one communicative event occurring in one time and place (i.e. scale) and another, and their relationship to social value. Blommaert (2010), for example, argues for a focus on connection, as an appropriate concern for a sociolinguistics of globalization: "Sociolinguistics in the age of globalization needs to look way beyond the speech community, to sociolinguistic systems and how they connect and relate to one another" (Blommaert 2010: 41). Concrete examples of studies seeking to understand connection include Wortham and Rhodes' (2013) paper, published as part of a special issue on transnational identities (De Fina and Perrino, 2013), and work by Lorente (2018). Both invite us to explore relationships between different bundles of data from different scales. For example, Lorente's (2018) study of transnational domestic workers examines the connections between social value and communicative practices emanating from the Philippine government, those emanating from labor recruiting firms and their effects on women from the Philippines who go to Singapore to become foreign domestic workers. I will return to these studies in Section 17.4 where I will look more closely at research methods.

Scholars of transnationalism and globalization, such as Wortham and Rhodes (2013), Blommaert (2010) and Heller et al. (2015), also highlight the importance of historicizing research participants' life trajectories, while viewing different data sets as providing insights into the creation of different centers of value. Their work emphasizes how mismatches and inequalities emerge when mobile people use language resources associated with one center of value in a new setting that evaluates these language resources differently. For example, Heller et al. (2015) show how one variety of French brought to a frontier mining town in Canada had less social value than another, resulting in different employment opportunities and ultimately life trajectories for some of her research participants.

Blommaert (2010: 38–9) refers to these types of difference in social value via two concepts: "orders of indexicality" and "polycentricity" (see also Chapter 3 in this volume). Orders of indexicality refers to the ability to evaluate different social domains (e.g. some might place more value on the social domain of high finance than on the social domain of a restaurant). This concept also incorporates the idea that, within these social domains, there is also a hierarchy of persons and communicative resources (e.g. highly paid managers and the lower-paid workers within a company). The concept "polycentricity" refers to the multitude of social domains that exists and to ideas about the appropriate use of communicative resources held by those who inhabit particular roles within these social domains. For example, in earlier work on asylum interviews, Blommaert (2006) shows how one set of norms for how to tell a story (i.e. those of the asylum seeker) was inappropriate in another setting where a different set of norms for how to tell stories applied (in this case, the migration officer's). This difference led not just to mismatches in meaning but also to negative outcomes for asylum seekers.

Centers and peripheries and their relationship to value have become another area of sociolinguistic work on globalization. Some of this research examines how ideas and language practice associated with a center are reused (or receive uptake) in another setting, sometimes referred to as a periphery (Dovchin 2018; Kroon and Swanenberg 2018). In this sense, centers can be cities, "the West" or middle-income groups, while peripheries can be rural areas, the global South or low-income groups. Other streams of scholarship explore the effects of the movement of capital on specific groups, including how they appropriate ideas about the links between nation and language to revitalize their communities (Heller et al. 2015; Pietikäinen and Kelly-Holmes 2013; Pietikäinen et al. 2016). For example, they explore how language and discourses that link language to tradition and/or tourism have been used to address rural–urban shift, as in the case of dying towns. Another stream of work seeks to understand the discursive processes that construct territories (and those that inhabit them) as centers and peripheries (Goebel 2018; Goebel et al. 2020). For example, Goebel (2018) examines how newspaper reports and blogs construct different areas in Indonesia as a center or a periphery.

Being nourished by many of the ideas described so far, the concept of superdiversity has received sustained uptake within sociolinguistics. Even so, and as is common in scholarly discourse, the idea of superdiversity has been used in different ways by different authors. Some use superdiversity as a descriptor for what are seen as new forms of human contact in contemporary urban spaces across the globe (Jacquemet 2011; Jørgensen 2012). In other cases, superdiversity has been interpreted as an ascalar perspective (Reyes 2014), a construct that overemphasizes the role of migration in creating the types of complexity covered by it (Goebel 2015), a way of talking about diversity (Faudree and Schulthies 2015) and an exemplar of academic faddism and branding (Pavlenko 2017). Just as importantly, the idea of superdiversity has contributed to a solidification of a whole new set of concepts for thinking about language, community, contact and context (Arnaut et al. 2016). In what follows, I expand on some of these perspectives.

In examining the mismatches between the language use of asylum seekers and the expectations of language use by the bureaucrats responsible for granting asylum, Jacquement (2011) used the idea of superdiversity as a descriptor to refer to what he perceived as new effects of globalization:

> Late-modern communication as experienced in these [asylum] proceedings is no longer embedded in a single dominant language relating to a strong minority language, but in the multilingual practices that arise with global cultural flows and their power relations. We are witnessing a more complex kind of diversity than the one encountered by Gumperz, where the origin of people, their presumed motives for migration, their "career" as migrants (sedentary versus short-term and transitory), or their sociocultural and linguistic features cannot be presupposed – we have entered, in the words of sociologist Steve Vertovec (2007), a "super-diverse" world.
> (Jacquemet 2011: 493–4)

While Jacquemet's claims of newness are qualified through his contrast with the institutional contact settings examined by Gumperz (1982) and those Jacquement currently researches, others have questioned many aspects of the superdiversity turn. For example, Reyes (2014) wondered about the extent of this newness, how "super" as against "regular" diversity could be distinguished, whether this was a Eurocentric view of contemporary language and social relations, and whether what we were seeing was merely the result of people commenting upon differences that they encountered. The last point became a focus of a special issue on diversity talk (Faudree and Schulthies 2015), while Pavlenko (2017) used scholarship on superdiversity to illustrate some of the processes involved in academic branding. In short, academic branding is discussed as a process whereby new terminology gets a foothold in scholarly circles through scholarly practices, such as the organization of workshops, panels and conferences, and the writing of programmatic papers and books. Ultimately, the imitation (not replication as precise copy) of some of the ideas in these academic forums enables the term to become widely recognized and often associated with a particular scholar or group of scholars (Pavlenko 2017).

However, superdiversity scholarship has also produced sustained and ongoing conceptual development. For example, drawing on a critique of work in the area of codeswitching (Alvarez-Cáccamo 1998; Meeuwis and Blommaert 1994; Rampton 1998), new concepts have been developed as part of efforts to reconceptualize everyday multilingual language practices. Some of the terms that reflect these new ways of looking at multilingual processes include *truncated competence* (Blommaert 2010), *polylanguaging* (Jørgensen et al. 2011), *translanguaging* (Garcia and Wei 2014; see also Chapter 18 in this volume), *transglossia* (Sultana 2015), *linguascapes* (Dovchin 2018), *metrolingualism* (Pennycook and Otsuji 2015), *diversity talk* (Faudree and Schulthies 2015) and *knowledging* (Goebel 2015). While there are some subtle differences among these terms, what is common to all is the idea that we can't assume that the semiotic resources used in interaction can be associated in any straightforward way with a set of speakers often referred to as a community belonging to a geographically defined territory (see Chapter 18 in this volume). What is equally common is the idea that, in interaction people use sign fragments that have different semiotic potential and that it is only through attention to streams of interaction that we can get a sense of which signs are recognized and how they affect a communicative moment and/or chains of communicative moments.

Other scholars have focused on instances of human contact, asking how rules for social conduct are constructed in settings characterized by transience (Goebel 2010a, 2019; Lønsmann et al. 2017). In line with the broad arguments in the special issue edited by Faudree and Schulthies (2015), Goebel (2019) suggests a need to focus on different forms of discourse that comment upon, model and police different types of human contact. Related to this are ideas of conviviality, especially how sign fragments, such as kin terms, are used to build and perform both positive and negative social relationships among strangers (Blommaert and Varis 2015; Goebel 2010b; Williams and Stroud 2013).

17.4 Implications

In addition to having many common intellectual roots in the area of theory, work on transnationalism, globalization and superdiversity also shares a number of methodological roots. This section identifies some of these, which include ethnography, analysis of talk-in-interaction, analysis of communicative modalities other than talk, and the relationships among all of these. I point to the implications of these methodologies for our understanding of some of the areas that have become the focus of discourse analytic studies of transnationalism, globalization and superdiversity.

Taking inspiration from Hymes (1974, 1996), Gumperz (1982), Goffman ([1959]1969, 1981), Scollon and Scollon (1981), Sacks et al. (1974), Silverstein (1976, 1992) and other pioneers of the study of language in social life, sociolinguists working in the areas of transnationalism, globalization and superdiversity have used multiple methods to gather and interpret data. One method can be roughly summarized as ethnographic. In brief, conducting research ethnographically includes the observations of and participation in research subjects' lives over a year or more (Agar 1996; O'Reilly 2012). This participation includes regular informal conversations with research participants as well as timetabled recorded interviews. Such work requires the ethnographer to establish and maintain productive working relationships with participants (Marcus 1998), while keeping in mind how representations of such relationships privilege and hide inequalities between researchers and participants (Clifford and Marcus 1986).

Within sociolinguistics, ethnographic methods also include the audio or audiovisual recording of interactions among a number of participants, as well as the recording of interviews (De Fina and Perrino 2011; Duranti 1997; Rampton et al. 2004). These recordings are then transcribed and interpreted using insights from work in conversation analysis, as well as insights from the analysis of ethnographic data (see Chapter 6 in this volume). What is common to ethnographic approaches and those that use ethnographic methods to examine talk-in-interaction is that both approaches share similar epistemological stances about the need to examine communicative practice from participants' perspectives (Bucholtz and Hall 2008). It is also common to see these methods used in conjunction with semiotic approaches to language, which include analysis of written documents, television and radio programs, and social media, as well as explorations into the relationships among these different texts (Dovchin 2018; Goebel 2010b, 2015; Lorente 2018).

While there are many excellent accounts of methods and theories (Blommaert 2013; Dovchin 2018; Heller et al. 2015), here I will draw on two recent studies to illustrate some of the ways in which work in sociolinguistics in the areas examined has dealt with methodological choices. This work provides a view of the wide range of historicized data that can be used to understand complex connectivity. In their account of their research on and with Mexican migrants who settled in the United States, Wortham and Rhodes (2013: 542) thus describe their methodology:

> We have been conducting ethnographic and sociolinguistic research with multiple families, across multiple institutions, for >7 years in one Mid-Atlantic suburb that we call Marshall. Data include almost 1,000 fieldnotes, interviews, and videotaped interactions in schools, churches, community institutions, businesses, and individuals' homes. Researchers have spent the past 3 years collecting data with Allie and her family in Marshall. We have spent time with Allie and her family on >50 occasions – at home, in church, on family trips, and at academic events in and out of school. We have over a dozen hours of video footage with Allie and her family, and they are central characters in a documentary we have completed. Our ethnographic analyses follow Emerson et al. (1995) and Maxwell (1996), iteratively drawing patterns out of fieldnotes, documents, transcribed interviews, and videotaped classes. (Wortham and Rhodes 2013: 542)

Very much in line with how Glick Schiller, Basch and Blanc-Szanton (1992) imagined the future of scholarship on transnationalism, the study by Wortham and Rhodes (2013) documents the impacts of events in both Mexico and the United States on the life trajectories of their migrant subjects. More specifically, and building on earlier work by Wortham (2006), this collaborative study provides us with insights into the complex processes surrounding social identification. By examining how someone becomes socially identified across communicative events, in this case as a "good reader," this work shows how the multiple data sets noted here can be used to interpret specific instances of interaction. In particular, this work points to the importance of analyzing how different signs and different semiotic processes across a person's lifespan come together in one communicative event. In doing so, this study also speaks to the limitations of using any one method, while increasing what I refer to in Goebel (2020) as the "believability" of our interpretations of language in social life.

In more recent work, Lorente (2018) provides a long list of different methods used to help answer her question of how different communicative events contributed to the continued marginalization of Filipino women working as domestic servants in Singapore.

> In this ethnographically informed study, I draw from different types of data, including newspaper articles and opinion pieces about the language situation in the Philippines and foreign DWs [domestic workers] in Singapore; websites and advertisements of Singapore-based maid agencies; official documents circulated by Philippine government agencies; interviews with FDWs [foreign domestic workers]; sociolinguistic questionnaires; class cards and language journals collected from the students

I taught under the Filipino Overseas Workers in Singapore (FOWS) skills training program from 2001 to 2006; ethnographic information recorded and gleaned from Sundays at the Bayanihan Center; visits to Lucky Plaza, a shopping mall along Orchard Road (the main shopping road of Singapore) where Filipinos and FDWs congregate to buy Philippine-made products, eat Philippine food, send remittances back to the Philippines, etc.; and conversations with FDWs from my English classes, from other classes at the center and in my own neighborhood. (Lorente 2018: 21–2)

While "transnational" is part of the title of her book, this important work is, in fact, very much about the sociolinguistics of globalization. It traces how discourses about the value of a competitive labor market within the Philippines have been impacted upon and are connected with flows of discourses and ideologies about "the market" from elsewhere, and how all of this affects the lives of women who are employed as domestic workers.

As Lorente (2018) notes, these discourses and ideologies about one component of a specific market, that of domestic service, are scripted by the Philippine state and by labor brokers. This scripting mimics specific social conventions and emotions in order to socially value and to sell domestic workers' labor to the world and to employers in places such as Singapore, Hong Kong, the Middle East and Canada. Such practices are scripted via state-generated discourses about domestic work and via the provision of training by the state. Similar discourses and similar scripts are imitated in the advertisements and training sponsored by labor hire companies. For example, the one hundred or so hours of free language training offered by the state to aspiring domestic workers in the Philippines includes the scripting of deferential politeness formulas of address, such as "maam" and "sir." These same formulas are also taught in the courses offered to the domestic workers who register with labor hire companies (Lorente 2018).

In addition to pointing out how such discourses and scripting practices contribute to continued inequities in the global labor market, another strength of Lorente's (2018) study is how she details some of the unintended consequences of discourses about domestic workers and scripting practices. For example, the author shows how the state and labor hire companies discursively produce hierarchies of nation-states, employers and domestic workers by evaluating languages and their speakers: that is, "orders of indexicality" (Blommaert 2010: 38). She also documents how those who become domestic workers draw upon and reuse elements of these hierarchies in their own narrative accounts of their working lives to create their own linguistic hierarchies; some of which reproduce those fashioned by the state and labor companies, and some which reconfigure these hierarchies. For example, she shows how these domestic workers value their own Philippine English resources as more authentic than many of their Singaporean bosses' English resources. In short, one contribution of this book for the sociolinguistics of transnationalism, globalization and superdiversity is how it offers a detailed empirical account of the fact that linguistic resources often do not travel well or are totally reconfigured when reused by those who are poor and mobile (see Blommaert 2010). In doing so, it highlights the import of studying transnationalism and globalization from a sociolinguistic perspective.

Another strength of this study is its illustration of how ideologies about language condition present and imagined lifeways, while providing a basis for commentaries about such expectations. Lorente (2018) shows how ideologies about different varieties of English and the territories and persons authorized to use them are a constant point of talk in her participants' narratives about their lives: something that I have referred to as "contact discourse" (Goebel 2019). Just as importantly, her work also shows how the ability to be communicatively flexible, through what has been referred to as "adequation" (Bucholtz and Hall 2004), is an important aspect of performing and inhabiting a convivial self with unfamiliar interlocutors in unfamiliar spaces and times, or chronotopes (see Chapter 3 in this volume). In highlighting flexibility and conviviality, this work also offers one answer to Vertovec's (2007: 1045) question about how social relationships are formed, maintained and broken in everyday encounters between migrants and hosts.

17.5 Summary

Transnationalism, globalization and superdiversity are emergent ideas used for thinking about and understanding flows of people, information, capital, texts and ideas, as well as how they are connected. While there are many differences in these terms and the processes that they refer to, this entry has highlighted both commonalities of focus and common intellectual roots in terms of theory and methods. Much of the early work in these areas was carried out by sociologists, anthropologists and those working in cultural studies with the result that a key aspect of these processes, communication, continued to be understudied in these fields. In contrast, I have pointed out that, within sociolinguistics, the use of these ideas and the study of the phenomena described by them have been characterized by a constant drive to understand connections between communicative events that are part of these flows, how and why different communicative events are valued, and how and why such differences can create inequality.

In doing so, I have pointed out that much of the work in the sociolinguistics of transnationalism, globalization and superdiversity has also led to the creation of new concepts and invitations to reconceptualize language in social life. Such concepts include: ways of discussing language practices (e.g. truncated competence, polylanguaging, metrolingualism, translanguaging); ways of discussing how languages are valued in social life (orders of indexicality, polycentricity, knowledging, contact discourse); and ways in which social relations are managed in unfamiliar contexts (e.g. conviviality and adequation).

Further Reading

Agha, A. (2007). *Language and Social Relations*. Cambridge: Cambridge University Press.

This provides a comprehensive discussion of contemporary semiotics.

Arnaut, K., Blommaert, J., Rampton, B. and Spotti, M. (eds.) (2015). *Language and Superdiversity*. New York: Routledge.

This explores the sociolinguistics of superdiversity, as do the two works that follow (Arnaut et al. 2016; Blommaert and Varis 2015).

Arnaut, K., Karrebæk, M., Spotti, M. and Blommaert, J. (eds.) (2016). *Engaging Superdiversity: Recombining Spaces, Times and Language Practices*. Bristol: Multilingual Matters.

Blommaert, J. and Varis, P. (2015). The Importance of Unimportant Language. *Multilingual Margins* 2(1): 4–9.

De Fina, A. and Perrino, S. (2013). Transnational Identities. *Applied Linguistics* [Special Issue: Transnational Identities] 34(5): 509–15.

For a survey of recent directions and conceptual work being undertaken in the area of language and transnationalism, see this special edition, in particular the article on transnational identity.

Faudree, P. and Schulthies, B. (2015). Introduction: "Diversity Talk" and Its Others. *Language & Communication* 44: 1–6.

This discusses the sociolinguistics of superdiversity.

Kroon, S. and Swanenberg, J. (eds.) (2018). *Language and Culture on the Margins: Global/Local Interactions*. New York: Routledge.

This deals with the area of language and globalization as it relates to centers and peripheries.

Lønsmann, D., Hazel, S. and Haberland, H. (2017). Introduction to Special Issue on Transience: Emerging Norms of Language Use. *Journal of Linguistic Anthropology* 27(3): 264–70.

This also explores the sociolinguistics of superdiversity.

Pietikäinen, S., Kelly-Holmes, H., Jaffe, A. and Coupland, N. (2016). *Sociolinguistics from the Periphery: Small Languages in New Circumstances*. New York: Cambridge University Press.

This looks at language and globalization relative to centers and peripheries.

References

Agar, M. (1996). *The Professional Stranger: An Informal Introduction to Ethnography*. San Diego, CA: Academic Press.

Agha, A. (2007). *Language and Social Relations*. Cambridge: Cambridge University Press.

Alvarez-Cáccamo, C. (1998). From "Switching Code" to Code-Switching. In P. Auer (ed.) *Code-Switching in Conversation: Language, Interaction and Identity*. New York: Routledge. 29–48.

Ang, I. (2003). Together-in-Difference: Beyond Diaspora into Hybridity. *Asian Studies Review* 27: 141–54.

Appadurai, A. (1996). *Modernity at Large: Cultural Dimensions of Globalization*. Minneapolis: University of Minnesota Press.

Arnaut, K., Blommaert, J., Rampton, B. and Spotti, M. (eds.) (2015). *Language and Superdiversity*. New York: Routledge.

Arnaut, K., Karrebæk, M., Spotti, M. and Blommaert, J. (eds.) (2016). *Engaging Superdiversity: Recombining Spaces, Times and Language Practices*. Bristol: Multilingual Matters.

Blommaert, J. (2006). Applied Ethnopoetics. *Narrative Inquiry* 16(1): 181–90.

(2010). *The Sociolinguistics of Globalization*. Cambridge: Cambridge University Press.

(2013). *Ethnography, Superdiversity and Linguistic Landscapes: Chronicles of Complexity*. Bristol: Multilingual Matters.

Blommaert, J. and Varis, P. (2015). The Importance of Unimportant Language. *Multilingual Margins* 2(1): 4–9.

Bourdieu, P. (1991). *Language and Symbolic Power*. Cambridge: Polity Press in association with Basil Blackwell.

Bucholtz, M. and Hall, K. (2004). Theorizing Identity in Language and Sexuality Research. *Language in Society* 33(4): 469–515.

(2008). All of the Above: New Coalitions in Sociocultural Linguistics. *Journal of Sociolinguistics* 12(4): 401–31. doi.org/10.1111/j.1467-9841.2008.00382.x.

Castells, M. (1996). *The Rise of the Network Society*. Cambridge, MA: Blackwell.

Clifford, J. and Marcus, G. (eds.) (1986). *Writing Culture: The Poetics and Politics of Ethnography*. Berkeley: University of California Press.

De Fina, A. and Perrino, S. (2011). Introduction: Interviews vs. "Natural" Contexts: A False Dilemma. *Language in Society* 40(Special Issue 1): 1–11.

(2013). Transnational Identities. *Applied Linguistics* 34(5): 509–515.

Dovchin, S. (2018). *Language, Media and Globalization in the Periphery: The Linguascapes of Popular Music in Mongolia*. London: Taylor & Francis.

Duranti, A. (1997). *Linguistic Anthropology*. New York: Cambridge University Press.

Faudree, P. and Schulthies, B. (2015). Introduction: "Diversity Talk" and Its Others. *Language & Communication* 44: 1–6.

Ferguson, J. and Gupta, A. (2002). Spatializing States: Toward an Ethnography of Neoliberal Governmentality. *American Ethnologist* 29 (4): 981–1002.

Foucault, M. (1978). *The History of Sexuality, Vol. 1: An Introduction*, trans. by R. Hurley. New York: Pantheon Books.

Garcia, O. and Wei, L. (2014). *Translanguaging: Language, Bilingualism and Education*. Basingstoke: Palgrave Macmillan.

Glick Schiller, N., Basch, L. and Blanc-Szanton, C. (1992). Towards a Definition of Transnationalism: Introductory Remarks and Research Questions. *Annals of the New York Academy of Sciences* 645: ix–xiv.

Goebel, Z. (2010a). Identity and Social Conduct in a Transient Multilingual Setting. *Language in Society* 39(2): 203–40.

(2010b). *Language, Migration and Identity: Neighborhood Talk in Indonesia*. Cambridge: Cambridge University Press.

(2015). *Language and Superdiversity: Indonesians Knowledging at Home and Abroad*. New York: Oxford University Press.

(2018). Reconfiguring the Nation: Re-territorialisation and the Changing Social Value of Ethnic Languages in Indonesia. In S. Kroon and J. Swanenberg (eds.) *Language and Culture on the Margins: Global/Local Interactions*. New York: Routledge. 27–52.

(2019). Contact Discourse. *Language in Society* 48(3): 331–51.

(2020). *Global Leadership Talk: Constructing Good Governance in Indonesia*. New York: Oxford University Press.

Goebel, Z., Cole, D. and Manns, H. (eds.) (2020). *Contact Talk: The Discursive Organization of Contact and Boundaries in Indonesia*. New York: Routledge.

Goffman, E. ([1959]1969). *The Presentation of Self in Everyday Life*. London: Allen Lane/Penguin Press.

(1981). *Forms of Talk*. Philadelphia: University of Pennsylvania Press.

Gumperz, J. (1982). *Discourse Strategies*. Cambridge: Cambridge University Press.

Harvey, D. (1989). *The Condition of Postmodernity: An Enquiry into the Origins of Cultural Change*. Oxford: Blackwell.

Heller, M., Bell, L., Daveluy, M., McLaughlin, M. and Noel, H. (2015). *Sustaining the Nation: The Making and Moving of Language and Nation*. New York: Oxford University Press.

Hymes, D. (1974). *Foundations in Sociolinguistics: An Ethnographic Approach*. Philadelphia: University of Pennsylvania Press.

(1996). *Ethnography, Linguistics, Narrative Inequality: Toward an Understanding of Voice*. Washington, DC: Taylor & Francis.

Jacquemet, M. (2011). Crosstalk 2.0: Asylum and Communicative Breakdowns. *Text & Talk* 31(4): 475–97.

Jørgensen, J. N. (2012). Ideologies and Norms in Language and Education Policies in Europe and Their Relationship with Everyday Language Behaviours. *Language, Culture and Curriculum* 25(1): 57–71.

Jørgensen, J. N., Karrebæk, M. S., Madsen, L. M. and Møller, J. S. (2011). Polylanguaging in Superdiversity. *Diversities* 13(2): 22–37.

Kroon, S. and Swanenberg, J. (eds.) (2018). *Language and Culture on the Margins: Global/Local Interactions*. New York: Routledge.

Lønsmann, D., Hazel, S. and Haberland, H. (2017). Introduction to Special Issue on Transience: Emerging Norms of Language Use. *Journal of Linguistic Anthropology* 27(3): 264–70.

Lorente, B. (2018). *Scripts of Servitude: Language, Labour Migration and Transnational Domestic Work*. Bristol: Multilingual Matters.

Marcus, G. (1995). Ethnography in/of the World System: The Emergence of Multi-sited Ethnography. *Annual Review of Anthropology* 24: 95–117.

 (1998). *Ethnography through Thick and Thin*. Princeton, NJ: Princeton University Press.

Meeuwis, M. and Blommaert, J. (1994). The "Markedness Model" and the Absence of Society: Remarks on Codeswitching. *Multilingua* 13(4): 387–423.

O'Reilly, K. (2012). *Ethnographic Methods*, 2nd ed. London: Routledge.

Park, J. (2017). Transnationalism as Interdiscursivity: Korean Managers of Multinational Corporations Talking about Mobility. *Language in Society* 46(Special Issue 1): 23–38.

Pavlenko, A. (2017). Superdiversity and Why It Isn't: Reflections on Terminological Innovation and Academic Branding. In S. Breidbach, L. Küster and B. Schmenk (eds.) *Sloganizations in Language Education Discourse*. Bristol: Multilingual Matters.

Pennycook, A. and Otsuji, E. (2015). *Metrolingualism: Language in the City*. New York: Routledge.

Pietikäinen, S. and Kelly-Holmes, H. (eds.) (2013). *Multilingualism and the Periphery*. New York: Oxford University Press.

Pietikäinen, S., Kelly-Holmes, H., Jaffe, A. and Coupland, N. (2016). *Sociolinguistics from the Periphery: Small Languages in New Circumstances*. New York: Cambridge University Press.

Portes, A., Guarnizo, L. and Landolt, P. (1999). The Study of Transnationalism: Pitfalls and Promise of an Emergent Research Field. *Ethnic and Racial Studies* 22(2): 217–37.

Poynting, S., Noble, G., Tabar, P. and Collins, J. (2004). *Bin Laden in the Suburbs: Criminalising the Arab Other*. Sydney: Institute of Criminology.

Rampton, B. (1995). *Crossing: Language and Ethnicity among Adolescents*. London: Longman.

 (1998). Language Crossing and the Redefinition of Reality. In P. Auer (ed.) *Code-Switching in Conversation: Language, Interaction and Identity*. London: Routledge. 290–317.

Rampton, B., Tusting, K., Maybin, J., Barwell, R., Creese, A. and Lytr, V. (2004). *UK Linguistic Ethnography: A Discussion Paper*. Coordinating Committee of the UK Linguistic Ethnography Forum. London.

Reyes, A. (2014). Linguistic Anthropology in 2013: Super-New-Big. *American Anthropologist* 116(2): 366–78.
Sacks, H., Schegloff, E. A. and Jefferson, G. (1974). A Simplest Systematics for the Organization of Turn-Taking for Conversation. *Language* 50: 696–735.
Scollon, R. and Scollon, S. (1981). *Narrative, Literacy, and Face in Interethnic Communication*. Norwood, NJ: Ablex.
Silverstein, M. (1976). Shifters, Linguistics Categories, and Cultural Description. In K. Basso and H. Selby (eds.) *Meaning in Anthropology*. Albuquerque: University of New Mexico Press. 11–56.
 (1992). The Indeterminacy of Contextualization: When Is Enough Enough? In P. Auer and A. di Luzio (eds.) *The Contextualization of Language*. Amsterdam: John Benjamins. 55–76.
Stiglitz, J. (2006). *Making Globalization Work*. New York: W. W. Norton & Company.
Sultana, S. (2015). Transglossic Language Practices: Young Adults Transgressing Language and Identity in Bangladesh. *Translation and Translanguaging in Multilingual Contexts* 1(2): 202–32.
Tsing, A. (2005). *Friction: An Ethnography of Global Connection*. Princeton, NJ: Princeton University Press.
Tsuda, T. (2003). *Strangers in the Ethnic Homeland: Japanese Brazilian Return Migration in Transnational Perspective*. New York: Columbia University Press.
Vertovec, S. (1999). Conceiving and Researching Transnationalism. *Ethnic and Racial Studies* 22(2): 447–62.
 (2007). Super-Diversity and Its Implications. *Ethnic and Racial Studies* 30(6): 1024–53.
Wallerstein, I. (2004). *World-Systems Analysis: An Introduction*. Durham, NC: Duke University Press.
Williams, Q. and Stroud, C. (2013). Multilingualism in Transformative Spaces: Contact and Conviviality. *Language Policy* 12(4): 289–311.
Wortham, S. (2006). *Learning Identity: The Joint Emergence of Social Identification and Academic Learning*. Cambridge: Cambridge University Press.
Wortham, S. and Rhodes, C. (2013). Life as a Chord: Heterogeneous Resources in the Social Identification of One Migrant Girl. *Applied Linguistics*, 34(5): 536–53.

18

Translanguaging and Momentarity in Social Interaction

Tong King Lee and Li Wei

18.1 Introduction

The twenty-first century has witnessed the emergence of an alternative version of modernity in contemporary society. Described by Bauman (2000) as "liquid modernity," this new epistemology operates beyond the modernity–postmodernity dyad; it foregrounds the fluidity rather than fixity of location, the itinerancy rather than rootedness of identity, and the instantaneity rather than premeditation of action. In this milieu of flux, where change is the default mode of lived experience, how can we begin to rethink language, discourse and communication?

The condition of liquid modernity has given rise to two phenomena of interest to us. The first is the enhancement of mobility – not just of people, as in the spatial dispersal and displacement of populations in global migrations, but also of information and technology, as in the vast proliferation of data across intensely networked media. A corollary of these different mobilities is the increased mobility of language that is manifested in the heteroglossic tendencies of communication, particularly in superdiverse urban settings. Here, social interaction is *intersection*, where borders of different kinds are nuanced, negotiated or simply negated; new subterranean formations, varieties or registers of language may rise and fall depending on the sociolinguistic contingencies in question. What ensues is a Babelian realm where a plethora of tongues disrupt traditional categorical spaces in relation to language.

As a term and concept, multilingualism in our view no longer adequately captures the dynamics of human communication in late modernity. Discourses generated by the spontaneous convergence of different languages (or language varieties and registers), semiotic modalities and technology-driven media, and marked by a sense of immediacy, transiency and momentarity, exceed multilingualism. Indeed, we are entering the phase of *postmultilingualism* (Li 2016a), the second phenomenon of liquid modernity that interests us. Unlike multilingualism, postmultilingualism is not satisfied with the simple coexistence of different languages within a given timespace. Rather, it causes turbulences through identity politicking within the strategic deployment of hybrid repertoires in postmodern contexts, where postmultilingual individuals do not merely *use* several named languages separately; they also *manipulate* the space between them to advance particular causes, such as the critique of top-down ideologies. Postmultilingualism additionally points to discursive experiences that are organized not exclusively by human language but through the mobilization of linguistic and what have traditionally been termed non-linguistic resources.

This chapter introduces translanguaging as an analytical lens through which we can understand the linguistic behaviors of people with multiple named languages. Broadly, translanguaging refers to speakers' dynamic and creative use of resources across the borders of named languages. It is premised on the view that multilingual individuals have an innate ability to draw flexibly upon a repertoire of linguistic features (phonetic, morphological, semantic, orthographic and so forth) that originate in more than one named language, as well as what has been termed extralinguistic or nonlinguistic meaning-making resources, including bodily and sensory resources. Translanguaging is performative, and this includes everyday performances in mundane situations; it exudes creativity and criticality, generating *positive disturbance* to social interaction.

In the following sections, we first trace the origin of translanguaging and highlight the salient issues and debates surrounding the concept. We then use three examples from the Sinosphere – East and Southeast Asian countries, cultures and languages that have historically come under influence from the politics, culture, religion and languages of China (Matisoff 1990) – to explain how translanguaging works. This is followed by a discussion of the theoretical implications of deploying the concept of translanguaging for multilingual discourse studies. We end the chapter with some hypotheses on what we call the Translanguaging Moment.

18.2 Overview of Translanguaging

The origin of the term translanguaging is often attributed to Colin Baker and his student Cen Williams. Williams (1994) observed a pedagogical practice in Welsh revitalization programs where the teacher was trying to teach in Welsh while the pupils responded largely in English. He used the Welsh word *trawsieithu* to describe the practice and argued that, rather than seen in a negative light in the Welsh policy context, this allowed learners, and also teachers, to maximize their bilingual capacity in the process of knowledge construction. In introducing Williams' work to the wider world, Baker (2001) initially translated *trawsieithu* as "translinguifying," and later termed it translanguaging. Along with Williams, Baker emphasized the positive contributions of this pedagogical approach to learning. Subsequently, García (2009), when studying the education of minoritized learners labeled as "bilingual" in the United States, extended the notion of translanguaging to refer to "multiple discursive practices in which bilinguals engage in order to make sense of their bilingual worlds" (2009: 45). She highlighted the empowering and transformative potential of translanguaging for minoritized language users and their communities in enabling them to utilize their full linguistic repertoire and construct their subjectivities through flexible and dynamic language practices.

Our use of the term follows a separate development, with Li (2011) deriving the term translanguaging by adding the *trans-* prefix to the psycholinguistic notion of "languaging." Languaging refers to the process of using language to gain knowledge, to make sense of one's world, to articulate one's thoughts and to communicate about using language (Swain 2006). Work on "languaging" has a long tradition. In a short commentary on Newmeyer's (1991) essay on the origins of language, Becker (1991) borrowed the term languaging from the Chilean biologist and neuroscientist Humberto Maturana and his coauthor Francesco Varela (1980), and invited us to think that "there is no such thing as Language, only continual languaging, an activity of human beings in the world" (Becker 1991: 34). This reiterates Ortega y Gasset's (1957: 242) argument that language should not be regarded "as an accomplished fact, as a thing made and finished, but as in the process of being made."

This argument has been further pursued from the perspectives of distributed cognition and distributed language, where languaging refers to "an assemblage of diverse material, biological, semiotic and cognitive properties and capacities which languaging agents orchestrate in real-time and across a diversity of timescales" (Thibault 2017:82). Following Love (e.g. 1990, 2004), scholars such as Cowley, Thibault, and Steffensen set out to challenge what they call the "code view" of language. The "code view" sought to identify abstract verbal patterns, morphosyntax or lexicogrammar divorced from cognitive, affective and bodily dynamics in real-time and to specify rules for mapping forms to meanings and meanings to forms. Scholars working on distributed cognition and distributed language now regard language thus identified and specified as a *second-order construct*, the product of *first order activity*, that is: languaging (Cowley 2017; Thibault 2011, 2017; Steffensen 2009, 2011). They argue that "human languaging activity is radically heterogeneous and involves the interaction of processes on many different time-scales, including neural, bodily, situational, social, and cultural processes and events" (Thibault 2017: 3) and urge linguists, psychologists and others working on human communication to "grant languaging a primacy over what is languaged" (Cowley 2017: 48).

With its use of the *trans-* prefix, translanguaging captures multilingual language users' dynamic practices that transcend the boundaries of named languages and the boundaries between language and other cognitive as well as semiotic resources that human beings use in sense- and meaning-making. In the meantime, the *–ing* in translanguaging urges us to focus on the instantaneity and the transient nature of human communication.

Following Li, our current position on translanguaging is premised on how it transcends and transforms our experience of the languaged world. This may be summarized as follows (Li 2011: 1223):

1. Translanguaging involves going *between* different linguistic structures and systems; it is also about going *beyond* language as conventionally understood, in recognition of the intersections among different modalities of communication, such as speaking, writing, signing, listening, reading and remembering.
2. Translanguaging includes the full range of linguistic performances of multilingual language users, for purposes that transcend the combination of structures, the alternation between systems, the transmission of information, and the representation of values, identities and relationships.
3. Translanguaging is transformative; it creates a social space for the multilingual language user by bringing together different dimensions of their personal history, experience and environment, their attitude, belief and ideology as well as their cognitive and physical capacity, into one coordinated and meaningful performance, and making it into a lived experience.

18.3 Issues and Debates

Today, translanguaging is very much in vogue in sociolinguistics and applied linguistics, including discourse studies, as well as in semiotics and human communication studies. With that come various uses and abuses of the term. This section clarifies some of the arising issues in discussions and debates on translanguaging.

18.3.1 Translanguaging vs. Codeswitching

One of the most controversial issues about translanguaging is whether it is sufficiently differentiated from codeswitching to justify its existence; in other words, do we really need the term/concept translanguaging or is it just another neologism for vanity rather than substance?

It should be pointed out that the concept of translanguaging was never invented with the intention of its replacing codeswitching. Codeswitching is a term used primarily by descriptive linguists to investigate grammatical constraints on bilingual interaction. Premised on the model of Separate Bilingualism and the principle of Complementary Distribution, it describes the movement between two or more neatly delineated languages (or "codes"), each having its own set of structural features. Translanguaging is conceptually and epistemologically distinct from codeswitching. It builds on an idea of language that runs opposite to the "code-view" of language and operates on the model of Dynamic Bilingualism. In this model, multilingual speakers do not access features from discrete named languages but rather from within a unified heterogeneous *repertoire* (García and Li 2014: 12–16; see also Otheguy, García and Reid 2015, 2018).

The idea of repertoire is central to translanguaging. It highlights the dynamic permutation and combination of integrated semiotic resources at the disposal of multilingual persons, as opposed to a mechanical *switching* from one language to another.

Li, who studied codeswitching as an interactional resource (e.g. Li and Milroy 1995), maintains that it has its place in multilingual communication (e.g. Green and Li 2014) – and translanguaging does not dispute that. Indeed, there is a substantial body of literature that sees codeswitching as an interactional resource for accomplishing local organization of conversation, as well as for self-presentation, stylizations and so on (see contributions in Auer 2013). Nevertheless, conventional, grammatical approaches to codeswitching cannot account for creative and critical practices that strategically manipulate the space between languages or language varieties for various purposes: for example, to produce a tentative idiolect to resist certain structures of power, to express sociopolitical views in a sardonic manner, to create specific social groupings that cannot be defined by named languages or to inject a dose of linguistic entertainment into discourse. Whatever the motivation, translanguaging is not about the habitual to-and-fro, back-and-forth shift between codified languages – these are some of the features of codeswitching; rather, it is about the spontaneous activation of elements from a continuum of signifying resources to positively disturb monolingual discourse.

18.3.2 On Named Languages

A corollary issue is the status of named languages. Because codeswitching is about oscillating between languages, and translanguaging establishes itself as a different practice from codeswitching, translanguaging is sometimes said to reject the existence of languages as conventionally understood. That is not the case. Translanguaging is not at all in denial that we live in a world populated by named languages that do not by necessity overlap with standard or official languages, which are by default "named."

It recognizes the empirical reality of distinct boundaries between languages, but highlights the ideological constructedness of those boundaries, which are instituted through historical and political circumstances and sedimented through education and socialization.

By exposing the contingency and artificiality of language borders, translanguaging opens up the way to attenuating those borders – without repudiating their objective existence – and developing a vibrant and fluid view of communication that gives us a more accurate picture of how multilinguals think and maneuver their social worlds. On this view, multilinguals do not so much "switch" between Language A and Language B as they *transcend* the binary to create new semiotic spaces (called translanguaging spaces; see Section 18.6) through social interaction. Hence, it is not that named languages are no longer relevant; rather, it is that translanguaging equips us with the lens to be ever more vigilant so as to interrogate the boundaries between our acquired languages and to destabilize our discourse to creative and/or critical ends.

18.3.3 Beyond a Code-View of Language: Multimodality

Translanguaging exceeds the narrow definition of language, including in its purview nonlinguistic modalities of communication. It is therefore not just a multilingual but also a multimodal, multisensory practice, involving embodied participation on the part of language users (Baynham and Lee 2019; Chapter 15 in this volume). In this connection, translanguaging echoes Halliday's view of language as a semiotic system, "not in the sense of a system of signs, but a systemic resource for meaning" (Halliday 1985: 192). Halliday described language as a "meaning potential" and defined linguistics as the study of "how people exchange meanings by 'languaging'" (1985: 193). Translanguaging affiliates itself with this social semiotic approach to discourse, taking into account *mode* (meaning-making resources such as speech, writing, image, layout and so on that are socially and culturally determined) and *medium* (the material platform on which meaning is expressed) to derive an understanding of communication that goes beyond language or languages as such (Kress 2010; Chapters 12 and 16 in this volume). Through a translanguaging lens, communication takes place by way of *orchestrating* languages, modes and media available in the repertoire of language users, where the orchestra metaphor points to the seamless, performative combination of features from an ensemble of resources.

With this in mind, we now turn to an interesting example of multimodal communication as reported by Li (2018a), focusing on two signs in a fruit shop. Li spotted the first sign (Figure 18.1) during a morning stroll in Chungyuan, Taiwan. It caught his attention because it explicitly violates the standard grammatical rules of codeswitching, which state that function words such as *be* and possessive markers such as the English *'s* are not to be switched (e.g. Myers-Scotton 1997). The sign reads: "Today's fruit is watermelon," and even though this is an extremely simple message that can easily be written in unmarked Chinese, it is here communicated by marshaling a host of semiotic resources, including words from three languages (Chinese, Japanese, English) and a hand-drawn picture of two slices of watermelon.

A codeswitching analysis would not go much further than the following observations: (a) the two Chinese characters at the top mean "today"; (b) the Japanese character の (*no*) is the equivalent of the English possessive marker *'s*; (c) the two Chinese characters in the middle mean "fruit"; and (d) English is introduced into the text by way of the BE verb "is." Such an analysis may leave out parts of the sign represented by visual cues, that is, the drawing and the color scheme.

Yet, beyond the surface manifestation of the sign, there is so much more to be read. The single Japanese character brings in the colonial history of Taiwan, which was occupied by Japan between 1895 and 1945, and the cultural identification with Japan among the younger generation in Taiwan today. The Japanese word for watermelon is pronounced *suika*, which sounds very similar to the Chinese term *shuikuo* (in Wade-Giles) for "fruit." The two "foreign" elements, the Japanese possessive marker and the English verb, are in the same color, whereas the Chinese characters are in a different one.

Figure 18.1 Translanguaging sign (1): Watermelons (For a full colour version, see https://blog.oup.com/2018/05/translanguaging-code-switching-difference/)

Figure 18.2 Translanguaging sign (2): Pineapples

The second picture (Figure 18.2) was taken a few days later, in the same shop, by a former student of Li. The sign reads "Pineapples on discount today" but, like the watermelon example, this apparently straightforward piece of marketing communication is semiotically complex. Compared to the first sign, the space for the characters for fruit is now occupied by a cut-out picture of skinned pineapples. Instead of the word "is," the English word "cut" is handwritten. At the bottom left, we see an image of pineapple slices; to its right, a hand sign is placed alongside the Chinese word for discount (literally "special price") and the English word "cut" is repeated. The hand sign itself has multiple indexes – it can be understood as the victory sign, a popular photography pose expressing happiness or cuteness, or a gesture meaning "to cut," or any combination thereof depending on the cultural context. A codeswitching reading of this poster can, of course, reveal certain aspects of the juxtaposition of the different linguistic codes. But a translanguaging reading has the capacity to reveal much more of the social semiotics of these multimodal signs, which transcend the boundaries between named languages as well as between linguistic and nonlinguistic cues.

In this regard, the composite sign at the bottom-right corner in Figure 18.2 is exemplary: it deploys two languages (the English word "cut" and the Chinese word for "special price") and a visual sign that may give rise to multiple interpretations simultaneously to express the meaning of "discount." It is overdetermined in that its meaning is expressed through multiple cues or resources that corroborate each other to create a *semiotic gestalt* – a semiotic entity made up of separate components but consumed in a holistic manner. The convergence of these various cues also opens up ambiguous spaces for ludic readings. Here the word "cut" not only expresses the meaning of the Chinese characters for "special price" (as in cutting prices); it also evokes the corporeal act of cutting pineapples when coupled with the image of sliced pineapples, where the hand sign both intersemiotically translates the word "cut" and indexically expresses a sense of victory or delight.

18.4 Illustrations from Kongish and Singlish

To illustrate how translanguaging works as an analytical concept, we now explore two further examples from Kongish (Hong Kong English) and Singlish (Singapore English) discourse, respectively.

On August 3, 2015, an important discourse event took place – the creation of a Facebook page called *Kongish Daily*. The creators were a group of young applied linguists in Hong Kong, who wanted to collect data on everyday language practices by ordinary citizens of Hong Kong through social media. The page received more than 10,000 "likes" overnight, and now has a population of steady followers of over 66,000. It is essentially a news sharing site where the owners of the Facebook page choose to translate news items into a hybrid form of Cantonese, Hong Kong English, standard English, alphabetic spelling, Chinese characters, emoji, and other signs and languages, and repost items for entertainment purposes but also to critique controversial social issues. The owners normally add their own commentaries on repostings, and the followers contribute their comments in response.

Throughout the pages of *Kongish Daily*, there is a huge amount of language play. Here is an example from the "Our Story" page (Figure 18.3).

Let us unpack this discourse to see how it exemplifies the features of translanguaging:

- Kongish ng hai exac7ly Chinglish
  This reads: "Kongish is not exactly Chinglish," where *ng hai* is the negative form of the Cantonese verb to be, and *exac7ly* uses the coda of the Cantonese word for the number 7 (romanized as "cat" but sounding more like "chat") to stand in for the "t" sound. Importantly, the number 7 connotes silliness or stupidity in Cantonese, such that *exac7ly* embeds an ironic tone within its transcriptual construction.
- The site is founded bcoz we want to collect relly research how people say Kongish by looking at everyone ge replies ... and share this finding to all people who think Chinglish=Kongish.

18 Translanguaging and Momentarity in Social Interaction

Our Story

KONGISH DAILY《未語日報》 MONDAY, 8 APRIL 2019

Kongish Daily is a local site sharing news in "Kongish".

Kongish =/= Chinglish; Kongish also =/= romanised Cantonese only; Kongish dou ng exactly hai Hong Kong English. If you ask little editers Kongish hai mud? Little editer can light light dick tell you: Kongish is a collective creation used and understood by Hongkongers 💚

Only knowing English or Cantonese ng wui give you the full picture, you have to be a Hongkonger sin can fully understand our page, Kongish Daily 😉

The site is founded to collect Kongish examples and research how people say Kongish by looking at everyone ge replies, including you and me, and share this finding to all people who think Chinglish = Kongish. But actcholly, Kongish hai more creative, more flexible, and more functional ge language practice.

PS for secondary school chicken:
If you want to learn English, Sor(9)ly, this site ng wui help you learn more English, but to share news with you in Kongish, finish.

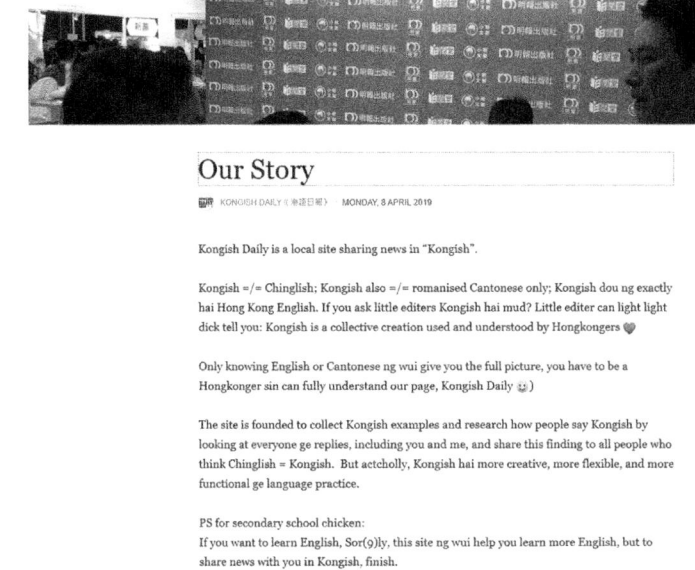

Figure 18.3 "Our Story" page, *Kongish Daily*

This explains the motivation for founding the website, which is to look into how people use Kongish in practice by examining their replies to posts. The form *bcoz* is contracted from "because," *relly* is a corruption of "really" and *ge* 嘅 is a possessive marker in Cantonese. Here the phrase "everyone ge replies" is not a case of codeswitching; rather, *ge* stands in functionally for *'s*, so this is the result of an English phrase *worked through* Cantonese grammar.

- actcholly, Kongish hai more creative, more flexible, and more functional ge variety.

  Actcholly mimics the way "actually" is sometimes pronounced by HongKongers. Unlike the *ge* above, the *ge* here functions as a suffix to the adjective "functional," yet we see the same translingual operation of writing/reading *English-through-Cantonese*: "[a] more functional variety" would work in English, but "functional *ge* variety" transgresses ordinary English discourse by calquing a Cantonese syntactical structure (and eliding the indefinite pronoun). This kind of translingual inflection eludes the term codeswitching: it makes little sense to say we are "switching" from an English adjective into a Cantonese particle and then into an English noun. The phrase is essentially a Cantonese phrase calqued in English, leaving the Cantonese particle protruding as a distinctive marker of Kongish.

- PS for secondary school chicken: If you want to learn English, Sor(9)ly, this site ng wui help you learn more English, but to share news with you in Kongish, finish.

  Secondary school chicken is a calque of a Cantonese slang expression *zung hok gai* 中學雞 meaning "immature secondary school students," where "chicken" has a mildly pejorative sense here, in addition to a possible play with its visual similarity with "children." Like exac7ly versus "exactly," sor(9)ly gives an ironic twist to "sorry." The transcriptual form, pronounced sor-gau-ly (where gau is read swiftly), plays with the Cantonese sound for the number 9 (gau); it invokes the homophone 鳩, which in classical Chinese refers to a species of bird but is appropriated in Cantonese to refer to the male sexual organ. At the same time, this vulgar meaning is masqueraded with the visuality of the number 9 and meshed into the sound sequence of the English "sorry." The phrase ng wui means "will not." The closing word "finish" stands in for the Cantonese zau gam 就噉 ("that's all"); and although it renders the English syntax broken, the sentence reads perfectly well when processed translingually in Cantonese.

It would be erroneous to understand these examples as instances of "bad" English. On the contrary, English is here being strategically manipulated to make a metalinguistic statement on the mission of *Kongish Daily*, which is to promote a vernacular variety of English in Hong Kong, where Cantonese is the dominant medium. What is apparently a piece of English discourse is in fact heavily infiltrated with a strain of Cantonese. Yet, to say that these exemplars of Kongish discourse demonstrate codeswitching is to miss the point entirely: there is no switching as such from one language to another; rather Cantonese grammar and syntax operate beneath the façade of English to create a kind of palimpsest, giving rise to an uncanny breed of English that both is and is not English. The creativity of Kongish lies precisely in the way it hijacks the orthographic form of English to subvert English *from within*.

As Li and Zhu (2019) argue, this kind of playful language is an example of what Raessens (2006) described as the "ludification of culture" – the mocking of authorities, the creation of alternative meanings and realities, the subversion and deception of roles, and the breaking of boundaries through play. As a Facebook page, the postings, repostings and followers' reactions (including "likes" and "comments") should all be read as signs holistically for their meaning potential. They are translanguaging signs that transcend a number of boundaries, between named languages, writing systems, semiotic systems and media (many of the postings contain videos).

Our next example is a Singlish poster created on Facebook (Figure 18.4).

The design and color scheme of this poster parody multilingual warning posters. The titles feature the four official languages of Singapore: English, Chinese, Malay and Tamil. But simply placing four languages alongside one another does not result in translanguaging. The way the four titles are emplaced gives rise to the visual impression that they translate one another, when in fact they are dialogic. While the English title carries the neutral-official tone of instructional discourse, its Chinese counterpart is a vulgar imperative in a local Chinese dialect (literally, "don't cry-father-

HOW TO HAVE A CIVIL DISCOURSE

不　要　哭　爸　哭　妈

JANGAN　　　　　TENSION

ரிலேக்　　　லா　　　மச்சி

A Singaporean way of confronting opposing viewpoints without womiting blood.

ZHUN BO?
Always fact-check. Because when your information can *confirm plus guarantee*, you can engage differing views with evidence, not emotion.

GOT PAY ATTENTION OR NOT?
Listen actively. It may seem *lecheh*, but it helps you to better reflect, question, and clarify conflicting views.

WHY SO NGEOW?
Avoid binary thinking. Robust discussions can be achieved when we recognise *cheem* issues aren't always black and white.

DON'T ANYHOW CHUT PATTERN
Focus on what you are for, not on *abuden* rhetorics or what you are against.

YAYA FOR WHAT?
Be humble. If you're right, you'd seem welcoming to other views; if you're wrong, then won't so *paiseh lor*.

SORRY GOT CURE
Admit when you're wrong. Apologising isn't *malu* at all; it simply re-establishes common ground.

© 2017 Andrea Lau

Figure 18.4 A Singlish poster (image courtesy of Andrea Lau) (For a full color version, see https://www.reddit.com/r/singapore/comments/6ll9pm/how_to_have_a_civil_discourse_singapore_style/)

cry-mother") used to deride people for complaining about things too dramatically. The Malay *Jangan tension* means "take it easy," resonating with the Chinese title in sense though not in register. The Tamil version is a phoneticization of the vernacular expression *relac lah machi* ("relax, my friend"), where *relac* is a Singlish variant on "relax," *lah* is a ubiquitous sentence-final particle in Singlish and *machi* is a slang address term in Tamil used with friends. Taken together, the Chinese, Malay and Tamil titles are not translations of but ludic responses to the English "How to have a civil discourse." This dialogic play between languages and unlikely juxtaposition of registers, all occurring within a discursive frame that evokes a translation relationship, is translanguaging.

The lead (the line below the titles), "A Singaporean way of confronting opposing viewpoints without womiting blood," sounds like a moderately formal piece of language. Yet a nonword has been surreptitiously sneaked in: *womiting*, a deliberate corruption of "vomiting" playing on how the word is sometimes pronounced by Singaporeans. The rest of the piece is divided into six blocks of text, each headed by a Singlish expression that describes an issue. Below each heading is a text largely in standard English and shaped along the lines of informative writing – except that, in each case, one Singlish word or phrase is introduced: *confirm plus guarantee* (the words mean as they do in standard English but the V-plus-V structure is distinctively Singlish), *abuden* (a conflation and phonetic corruption of "or, but then," meaning "if not, then what?"), *lecheh* (cumbersome), *paiseh lor* (to feel embarrassed), *cheem* (too profound to understand), *malu* (to make a fool of oneself). The body text, written largely in standard English, can be read as a response to or resolution of the issue described by the Singlish heading. For example, *zhun bo?* literally means "Is [the information] accurate?", and the body text responds to this with "Always fact-check"; *Yaya for what* means "Why be cocky?", and this is resolved by the exhortation to "be humble."

The result of this twisting together of registers is a hybrid and ironic discourse that is stylistically marked – even to native speakers of Singlish. For, although all the vernacular words and expressions featured in the poster are unmarked in Singlish, the way they are deployed to intersect and interact with a more formal English register is unusual, producing a humorous effect. Therein resides the linguistic creativity that is key to translanguaging.

Yet this image was not designed purely for linguistic entertainment. According to the creator Andrea Lau (personal communication, 2018), the poster was conceived in July 2017 amidst "a growing number of sociopolitical issues that were getting Singaporeans hot under the collar." This prompted Lau to create the graphic "to share practical ways on how we can navigate differing views and cultivate fruitful conversations out of them." The work, therefore, is motivated by a critical stance toward social issues, speaking to our second ingredient of translanguaging: criticality. The exuberant multilingualism and heteroglossia are meant to heighten the sensational value of the language, in the creator's words, to "elevate the sentiment of the content and solicit an emotional response" from readers, thereby producing an interface between creativity and criticality. And, as demonstrated in this and the previous example, the affordances of new communication media clearly provide new opportunities for creative and critical translanguaging.

18.5 Implications

Translanguaging as a theoretical concept has fundamental implications for our understanding of the nature of language (Li 2018b). As pointed out earlier, languages have hitherto been considered as differentiated systems of codes, and the use of various languages has accordingly been theorized as the interaction of different self-sufficient structures. Without denying the value of structural approaches to language, our translanguaging approach breaks decisively with the assumption that languages are discretely managed in multilingual discourse. The idea of repertoire already discussed suggests instead a distributed view of language, that is, the view that language is not a concentrated essence locked into some structural template but spatially disseminated as diverse linguistic, semiotic and material resources. In any given interactional situation, these resources assemble and interact in certain constellations as mediated through the actions, beliefs, experiences and capacities of language users. Meaning, as it were, is the accrued *effect* of that constellation or assemblage; it does not emanate exclusively from the structural forms of the languages involved in social interaction (see Pennycook 2018: 40–55).

This new conception of language compels us to rethink multilingual communication as a more complex kind of discourse, one that is intensively worked through by languages, language varieties and registers, but also by multiple modalities and medialities, all of which are engaged in tandem by language users in making sense of their social world. In this light, multilingual capacity needs to be construed not as proficiency in separate languages but rather as *linguistic multicompetence* (see Cook and Li 2017), going beyond the language dimension to factor sensory-embodied and perceptual-cognitive skills into the equation. In the final analysis, translanguaging gives us an angle from which to revisit the notion of "text," which connotes a stable signifying frame. Dynamic multilingual and multimodal interactions destabilize the idea of "text," for they take us not just between textual frames but also beyond them. Hence the significance of the *trans-* prefix in translanguaging, which puts a multilingual and multimodal spin on the concept of languaging.

Translanguaging has implications for how we understand the cognitive aspects of language use. These may be framed as two arguments, pertaining respectively to two theoretical issues in linguistics, namely Language and Thought, and Modularity of Mind (Li 2018b: 18):

1. *Language and Thought*: Multilinguals do not think unilingually in a politically-named linguistic entity, even when they are in a so-called "monolingual mode" and producing one namable language only for a specific stretch of speech or text.
2. *Modularity of Mind*: Human beings think beyond language, and thinking requires the use of a variety of cognitive, semiotic, and modal resources

of which language in its conventional sense of speech and writing is only one.

By changing the way in which we think about the nature of multilingual discourse and the cognition of multilingual speakers, translanguaging also changes the way we study it. As compared with prevailing approaches to the study of language-in-use, translanguaging is much less interested in generalizing broad patterns about how multilingual speakers interact. Indeed, the idea of generalizing patterns, with its implications of reiterability and predictability, can be seen as contradictory to the two primary attributes of translanguaging, namely creativity and criticality.

Translanguaging is rather invested in the moment-by-moment unfolding of interaction, not purporting to make systemic predictions about linguistic behavior, but instead to appreciate the epiphanies of creativity and criticality in multilingual settings. In highlighting the dynamism and instantaneity of communication, translanguaging brings our attention to the moment (more on this in Section 18.6) as a new unit of analysis in language study. It attempts to capture the fleetingness, the minuteness, the contingencies of language use, which are largely ignored or suppressed in linguistics where structural thinking has long held sway.

18.6 Future Directions

Moving forward, one question that deserves attention is how translanguaging actually happens. What are the circumstances that make translanguaging possible in discourse or interactional situations? And if translanguaging is not a "thing" that we can simply put a finger on, then how do we go about studying it? In the following, we outline our approach to these questions by proposing the notion of the Trialectics of Translanguaging, with a further focus on the Translanguaging Moment.

18.6.1 The Trialectics of Translanguaging

We hypothesize that translanguaging occurs at the confluence of three ingredients, namely Translanguaging Space, Translanguaging Instinct and Translanguaging Potential. Together, these constitute what we call the Trialectics of Translanguaging.

A Translanguaging Space is a space produced by and for translanguaging practice. It can be thought of as a kind of clearing house in discourse, converging, exchanging and trading various social practices and linguistic codes that are otherwise constructed as distinct entities outside this space. A Translanguaging Space pulls together language users and their linguistic repertoires, dovetailing different dimensions of their histories, experiences, environments; their attitudes, beliefs and ideologies; and their cognitive and physical capacities into a single coordinated performance (Li 2011: 1223; Li 2018b: 23). It not only transcends institutionalized language systems and structures but also transforms these systems and structures as well as the cognitive realm of participants. A Translanguaging Space is therefore more than an intermediate or hybridized space *between* two or more languages; it is also a space *beyond* institutionalized categories that organize our social and linguistic sensibilities. It is a *rhizomatic* space, to borrow Deleuze and Guattari's (1987: 27) term – "always in the middle, between things, interbeing, intermezzo," where connections are made laterally across nodes instead of being structured top-down. The idea of "nodes" links with Latour's (1996) Actor-Network Theory, which helps us think of a Translanguaging Space as a relational, productive and heterogenous space built on weak ties rather than stable points of reference. Translanguaging Spaces are therefore also assemblages. At once deterritorializsing and reterritorializing, they "establish territories as they emerge and hold together but also constantly mutate, transform, and break up" (Žižek, Ruda and Hamza 2018: 19).

The idea of Translanguaging Instinct derives from the notion of "interactional instinct," the biological drive for infants and children to affiliate with people around them (in turn inspired by Steven Pinker's "language instinct") (Li 2016b). Translanguaging Instinct refers to the innate motivation in multilinguals "to go beyond narrowly defined linguistic cues and transcend culturally defined language boundaries to achieve effective communication" (Li 2018b: 24–5). It speaks to the idea of multicompetence, the ability to handle communication across named languages and sensory modalities. This innate cognitive capacity in multilinguals for complex semiotic management is premised on a Principle of Abundance (Li 2018b: 25). On this view, the process of sense-making in social interaction is, again, overdetermined: from a translanguaging perspective, speakers simultaneously draw on and exploit a multitude of cues and resources in a coordinated manner, while making real-time evaluations on weighing and balancing these various cues and resources (recall the pineapple poster in Figure 18.2). Importantly, Translanguaging Instinct highlights the fact that language users do not just bring their language faculties to bear on social interactions; their sensory modalities, emotions and cognitive skills as well as their embodied experience with and conceptual knowledge of human sociality are all roped into a holistic execution of communication.

Whereas Translanguaging Instinct lies within the language user, Translanguaging Potential lies in the exterior realm, within the sign or utterance that triggers the Translanguaging Moment. Translanguaging cannot happen on the basis of a blank slate. Although translanguaging itself is not rarefied, there must nonetheless be some entity in the material world to introduce a ripple into the discourse in the first instance. Without this entity, translanguaging runs the risk of becoming a purely imaginative event with no objective reference, which means that one can then read any sign into a translanguaging event at his or her whim and fancy. The entity in question must minimally contain within its semiotic constitution the potentiality for intersection or fusion – a potentiality because translanguaging does not actually unfold in the sign or utterance itself but through dynamic interaction between the language user (who has Translanguaging Instinct) and the sign or utterance. Translanguaging Potential can assume a variety of forms, such as calquing, onomatopoeia, transliteration, literal translation, tranßripting (different scripts transfusing into a single visual sign; see Li and Zhu 2019) as well as other ways in which the discourse maneuvers the gap between languages (language varieties, registers), between sensory modes (visual-verbal, oral-aural, tactile-kinetic, olfactory-gustatory), between media, or any combination thereof. In other words, translingual, intersemiotic and multimedia texts are exemplary of, though not exhaustive of, texts with Translanguaging Potential.

In the Trialectics of Translanguaging, a Translanguaging Moment represents a dynamic instant arising at the intersection of Space, Instinct and Potential. When multilinguals come into interaction with one another – or into contact with artifacts – they co-create a social semiotic space (Translanguaging Space). Here, the various participants instinctively (Translanguaging Instinct) deploy their linguistic repertoires and sensory modalities within the material and medial environment of the interaction. They bring along their personal histories, ideologies, emotions, perhaps biases and idiosyncrasies, together with an entire spectrum of physical-cognitive capacities, into a spontaneous performance of language and identity. This interaction may serendipitously produce translingual, intersemiotic or multimedia signs or utterances, giving rise to a possible window for transgression or transformation (Translanguaging Potential). At this point of convergence of Space, Instinct and Potential, a creative disturbance, even turbulence, is introduced into the subjective consciousness of the language user, and a Translanguaging Moment is born.

18.6.2 On the Translanguaging Moment

Translanguaging is a timespace phenomenon. The notion of Translanguaging Space enables us to think of dynamic communicative practices in spatial terms, leaving us with the issue of temporality: what is the nature of time in respect of translanguaging? This question remains to be fully explored, but preliminary work has highlighted the concept of momentarity and its ancillary methodology: Moment Analysis (Li 2011).

Here, a "moment" is a point in time, or a period of time, that captures the "spontaneous, impromptu, and momentary actions and performances of the individual" and is marked by a "distinctiveness and impact on subsequent events or developments" (Li 2011: 1224). A Translanguaging Moment is thus in part objective, constituted by recordable interactional sequences played out in an empirically observable way and whose duration is measurable in terms of clock time. This includes perceptible linguistic behavior and the feedback triggered by such behavior, as in the responses and reactions of interlocutors.

Yet, there is also a subjective dimension to the Translanguaging Moment, aptly expressed by the phrase "spur-of-the-moment." Its duration is not determined by clock time (it makes little sense to speak of minutes or hours here); it must be *experienced* into being through and within all the circumstances of the interactional situation. Methodologically, this experiential dimension can be elicited only post-event by metalanguaging data through post hoc interviews, focus-group discussions or participants' reflective journals. The purpose of gathering such data is to gain insight into language users' personal understanding of their linguistic behavior, the motivations behind such behavior as well as how they articulate or position themselves vis-à-vis others within the interactional discourse (Li 2011: 1224). Moment Analysis is therefore a "double hermeneutic": it consists of the process of the analyst methodically tracking spontaneous actions in social interactions *and* of unveiling the subtle flux within the subjective consciousness of language users.

Future research would further elaborate on this last point, with all its implications for the methodological apparatus of Moment Analysis. We advance two views here that are purposefully radical so as to push the envelope on how dynamic language practices may be conceptualized.

18.6.2.1 There Is No Translanguaging without the Subjective Language User

Where does the Translanguaging Moment subsist? An obvious answer would be: between multilinguals engaged in social interaction or, as the case may be, between multilinguals and artifacts with Translanguaging Potential. Translanguaging occurs within the space-between where creative-critical linguistic practices unfold. Yet this view assumes that the parties on each side of the interaction are consciously bouncing off each other on some point of linguistic interest, say a new lexical pun. It precludes the possibility that translanguaging may come into being as an experience within the subjective consciousness of language users, even if that is not intended by them or anticipated by their interlocutors.

Imagine, for example, that you hear an utterance while walking on the street. Because of some phonetic coincidence, you accidentally misconstrue one word in that utterance as a word belonging to another named language you happen to know. Almost instantly you realize the slippage and arrest it, and although you have technically misheard something (it was a "mistake," as we would normally say), you nonetheless find this interesting. In this serendipitous event, you have in a fleeting moment produced a conflation of two languages. Notwithstanding that the speaker has completely no idea that his or her utterance was processed by you in such an anomalous way, you have virtually meshed the border of two languages by way of confounding one sound with another. Translanguaging has occurred – not within the signifying patterns of the utterance but as a flux within your cognition.

A better view is thus that the Translanguaging Moment takes place within the subjective consciousness of an individual who is co-creating a Translanguaging Space, either with other individuals or with artifactual signs. Translanguaging, therefore, is not wholly "owned" by individuals; it is an emergent effect arising from the triangulation of the Translanguaging Instinct innate to the language user; the Translanguaging Potential immanent in the semiotic constitution of an utterance or artifact; and the Translanguaging Space (both material and cognitive) co-created by all participants, including inanimate ones.

18.6.2.2 Translanguaging Moments, as a Complementary Construct to Translanguaging Spaces, Manifest as Transitory Movements of Creativity

Translanguaging is impermanent. As a dynamic practice, it destabilizes Language (with a capital "L"), punctuating its continuity, iterability and hence predictability. Accordingly, then, translanguaging manifests not as an ontologically definable entity: it makes absolutely no sense to speak of "one translanguage" or "several translanguages" (whereas by contrast "translation" can act as a countable noun when referring to the product, not the process; see Baynham and Lee 2019: 35). Any creative act comes about through interplay between adherence to and experimentation with norms, and translanguaging exemplifies such interplay. It represents a perennial state of drift, always in the progressive (*–ing*) rather than in the perfective (*–ed*), refusing to settle into lexical or grammatical formations. Once such stable formations occur, translanguaging becomes normativized into Language, in which case it loses its flux and fossilizes. In this sense, translanguaging does not operate outside the box, as it were. Rather, it continually engages with and creatively responds to normative Language, where instances of creativity become conventionalized with the currents of time and usage, at the same time as new instances of creativity are generated within the Trialectics of Translanguaging.

Take, for example, the coinage of a new term or slang expression in a vernacular setting, say, a local market. Prior to the uptake of this term or expression, it goes through a formative discursive process that negotiates, selects and recombines different features from what we may call the "market repertoire." Initially it would be highly marked, and this is a symptom of translanguaging. As it continues to circulate among participants (such as vendors, shoppers, deliverers and so on), its markedness gradually fades. At some point it crosses the invisible threshold and enters the "market register" of the language, and this is where translanguaging ceases.

Translanguaging can thus be conceived as a field of creative energy moving along a continuum from markedness on the one pole to unmarkedness on the other. It sets in when different features of a repertoire are spontaneously activated and converged to create temporary forms; sustains itself through the period of the *perceived* creativity of such forms (within the perceptual-cognition of the "persons in the culture"); and terminates when those forms are fully embedded into everyday parlance. There is therefore a momentarity to translanguaging: as all creative and dynamic linguistic practices must eventually lapse into Language and become static and mundane (to be succeeded by other creative and dynamic practices), any particular instance of translanguaging is temporally finite. Translanguaging happens in the here and now.

18.7 Conclusions

The motif of *trans-* is now trending. The humanities and social sciences are now witnessing ongoing developments on how *trans-* as a conceptual method can help us think across and beyond modalities and disciplines. Translanguaging can be seen as an instantiation in linguistics of the broader idea of "performing the trans" or *trans-ing* (Mylona 2016: 65), as articulated in performance research (e.g. Jones 2016; cf. Brubaker 2016 on the use of *trans-* as method in cultural studies). If the *trans-* prefix suggests "exceeding, moving towards, changing" as well as "going across, over or beyond," then the *–ing* suffix in trans-ing links all of these qualities toward the performative – "saying as doing, or that which performs something while articulating it" (Jones 2016: 1). In this light, translanguaging is a discursive and semiotic performance, one that is dynamic and processual, and in which the language-user as performer constructs social experiences and identities by weaving across the complex fabric of multilingual and multimodal discourse.

References

Auer, P. (ed.) (2013). *Code-Switching in Conversation: Language, Interaction and Identity*. London: Routledge.

Baker, C. (2001). *Foundations of Bilingual Education and Bilingualism*, 3rd ed. Clevedon: Multilingual Matters.

Bauman, Z. (2000). *Liquid Modernity*. Cambridge: Polity.

Baynham, M. and Lee, T. K. (2019). *Translation and Translanguaging*. Abingdon: Routledge.
Becker, A. L. (1991). Language and Languaging. *Language & Communication* 11 (1–2): 33–5.
Brubaker, R. (2016). *Trans: Gender and Race in an Age of Unsettled Identities*. Princeton, NJ: Princeton University Press.
Cook, V. and Li, W. (eds.) (2017). *The Cambridge Handbook of Linguistic Multi-Competence*. Cambridge: Cambridge University Press.
Cowley, S. J. (2017). Changing the *Idea* of Language: Nigel Love's Perspective. *Language Sciences* 61: 43–55.
Deleuze, G. and Guattari, F. (1987). *A Thousand Plateaus: Capitalism and Schizophrenia*, trans. by B. Massumi. Minnesota: University of Minnesota Press.
García, O. (2009). *Bilingual Education in the 21st Century: A Global Perspective*. Oxford: Wiley-Blackwell.
García, O. and Li, W. (2014). *Translanguaging: Language, Bilingualism and Education*. London: Palgrave Macmillan.
Green, D. W. and Li, W. (2014). A Control Process Model of Code-Switching. *Language, Cognition and Neuroscience* 29(4): 499–511.
Halliday, M. A. K. (1985). Systemic Background. In J. D. Benson and W. S. Greaves (eds.) *Systemic Perspectives on Discourse*, Vol. 1. Norwood, NJ: Ablex. 1–15.
Jones, A. (2016). Introduction: *Trans-ing* Performance. *Performance Research* 21(5): 1–11.
Kress, G. (2010). *Multimodality: A Social Semiotic Approach to Contemporary Communication*. Abingdon: Routledge.
Latour, B. (1996). On Actor-Network Theory: A Few Clarifications Plus More than a Few Complications. *Soziale Welt* 47: 369–81.
Love, N. (1990). The locus of languages in a redefined linguistics'. In H. G. Davis and T. J. Taylor (eds.) *On Redefining Linguistics*. London: Routledge, pp. 53–117.
Love, N. (2004). Cognition and the language myth. *Language Sciences*, 26, 525–44.
Li, W. (2011). Moment Analysis and Translanguaging Space: Discursive Construction of Identities by Multilingual Chinese Youth in Britain. *Journal of Pragmatics* 43: 1222–35.
  (2016a). New Chinglish and the Post-Multilingualism Challenge: Translanguaging ELF in China. JELF 5(1): 1–25.
  (2016b). Multi-competence and the Translanguaging Instinct. In V. Cook and W. Li (eds.) *The Cambridge Handbook of Multi-Competence*. Cambridge: Cambridge University Press. 533–43.
  (2018a). Translanguaging and Code-Switching: What's the Difference? OUP blog. https://blog.oup.com/2018/05/translanguaging-code-switching-difference.

(2018b). Translanguaging as a Practical Theory of Language. *Applied Linguistics* 39(1): 9–30.
Li, W. and Milroy, L. (1995). Conversational Code-Switching in a Chinese Community in Britain: A Sequential Analysis. *Journal of Pragmatics* 23 (3): 281–99.
Li, W. and Zhu, H. (2019). Tranßcripting: Playful Subversion with Chinese Characters. *International Journal of Multilingualism* 16(2): 145–61.
Matisoff, J. A. (1990). On Megalocomparison. *Language* 66(1): 106–20.
Maturana, H. and Varela, F. (1980). *Autopoiesis and Cognition: The Realization of the Living*. Boston Studies in the Philosophy of Science, 42. Dordrecht: Reidel.
Myers-Scotton, C. (1997). *Duelling Languages: Grammatical Structure in Codeswitching*. Oxford: Oxford University Press.
Mylona, S. (2016). Trans-ing. *Performance Research* 21(5): 65–7.
Newmeyer, F. J. (1991). Functional Explanation in Linguistics and the Origins of Language. *Language and Communication* 11(1–2): 3–28.
Ortega y Gasset, J. (1957). What People Say: Language. Toward a New Linguistics. In *Man and People*, trans. by W. Trask. New York: Norton. Ch. II.
Otheguy, R., García, O. and Reid, W. (2015). Clarifying Translanguaging and Deconstructing Named Languages: A Perspective from Linguistics. *Applied Linguistics Review* 6(3): 281–307.
(2018). A Translanguaging View of the Linguistic System of Bilinguals. *Applied Linguistics Review*. https://doi.org/10.1515/applirev-2018-0020.
Pennycook, A. (2018). *Posthumanist Applied Linguistics*. Abingdon: Routledge.
Raessens, J. (2006). Playful Identities or the Ludification of Culture. *Games and Culture*. 1: 52–7.
Steffensen, S. V. (2009). Language, Languaging and the Extended Mind Hypothesis. *Pragmatics and Cognition* 17(3): 677–97.
(2011). Beyond Mind: An Extended Ecology of Languaging. In S. J. Cowley (ed.) *Distributed Language*. Amsterdam, John Benjamins. 185–210.
Swain, M. (2006). Languaging, Agency and Collaboration in Advanced Second Language Learning. In H. Byrnes (ed.) *Advanced Language Learning: The Contributions of Halliday and Vygotsky*. London: Continuum, pp. 95–108.
Thibault, P. J. (2011). First-Order Languaging Dynamics and Second-Order Language: The Distributed Language View. *Ecological Psychology* 23: 210–45.
(2017). The Reflexivity of Human Languaging and Nigel Love's Two Orders of Language. *Language Sciences* 61: 74–85.

Williams, C. (1994). *Arfarniad o ddulliau dysgu ac addysgu yng nghyd-destun addysg uwchradd ddwyieithog* [An evaluation of teaching and learning methods in the context of bilingual secondary education]. Unpublished doctoral thesis, Bangor: University of Wales.

Žižek, S, Ruda, F. and Hamza, A. (2018). *Reading Marx.* Cambridge: Polity Press.

19

Intersectionality, Affect and Discourse

Kristine Køhler Mortensen and Tommaso M. Milani

19.1 Introduction: Intersecting Identity Categories and Affective Outbursts

As Doctor Christine Blasey Ford stood up to testify against US Supreme Court nominee Brett Kavanaugh in 2018, the event brought back memories of a similar occasion in 1991 when Anita Hill witnessed against her supervisor and then nominated Supreme Court Judge Clarence Thomas. In both cases, women gave testimony of experiences of male sexual harassment and assault, and the hearings led to the same result: the accused man was eventually exonerated and went on to occupy one of the most powerful positions in US society, that of Supreme Court judge. The similar gendered constellation in the two events illustrates a recognizable power asymmetry in which women are victims of male sexual aggression and face difficulties in being perceived as credible when testifying their experiences (cf. Ehrlich 2014).

The distinguishing factor lies in the sociological makeup of the people involved: a white female plaintiff against a white male defendant, both middle-aged; a young Black female complainant against a middle-aged Black male offender. As for the latter, the intersection of age and race meant that Anita Hill fell between chairs. Feminist activists recognizing her experience of male harassment supported her. However, a large part of the Black community saw Anita Hill's testimony as a threat against a long-fought battle for Black governmental influence (Crenshaw 1993) – at least this is how it was rhetorically framed and interpreted by many. In fact, Clarence Thomas defended himself by presenting the accusations against him as a "high-tech lynching" (Bhabha 1993: 235). In this way, he emphasized race by locating Anita Hill's accusations in a long history of violence against Black people. At the same time, such foregrounding downplayed the gendered nature of the offense on trial. As a result, Thomas turned from perpetrator to victim. Put differently, age and race turned against

Anita Hill: as a young victim of an older Black man's sexual harassment, she was in a structural position in which she could not mobilize full credibility and sympathy for her case.

In the hearing against Kavanaugh, gender asymmetry was indeed the primary vector of power and oppression. However, another element emerged, one that had not been as evident twenty-seven years earlier, that is, affect. Although Clarence Thomas had expressed his indignation by connecting the accusations to the violent history of Black oppression, his words were delivered in a controlled tone of voice. Similarly, Anita Hill's testimony was conveyed in a measured and precise wording without affective outbursts. In contrast, Kavanaugh's defense has been described by a YouTube commentator as "all capital letters" and was compounded by tears. In Western contexts, such an affective response is not expected of men in public and is typically frowned upon, as is testified by the well-known admonishment "men don't cry." What we want to highlight for the purpose of this chapter is the performative power of Kavanaugh's affect in relation to his subject position of white heterosexual man, which enabled him to go against the grain and engage in non-normative public display of emotions while not losing credibility. How was it possible? As Eve Kosofsky Sedgwick has explained, heterosexual male tears have a quasimagical property:

> The sacred tears of the heterosexual man: rare and precious liquor whose properties, we are led to believe, are rivaled only by the lacrimae Christi whose secretion is such a specialty of religious kitsch. What charm, compared to this chrism of the gratuitous, can reside in the all too predictable tears of women, of gay men, of people with something to cry about?
> ([1990]2008: 145–6)

Would Judge Thomas have been as convincing if he had lost his temper or cried? Would his racial affiliation have blocked the unique sacred connection between maleness, heterosexuality and suffering from which Kavanaugh benefited? (See Crenshaw 2018 about blackness and rage.)

We believe that these examples vividly encapsulate the nexus between intersecting identities and affect (or lack thereof), and how these are conveyed through discursive means. It is such an *intersectional perspective* that we want to present in this chapter, focusing in particular on existing scholarship that brings together a nuanced attention to discourse with sensitivity to emotions and an awareness of the double binds of identity categories (see also Chapter 15 in this volume). In what follows, we begin by defining the three main concepts underpinning this chapter: intersectionality, affect and discourse. We then move on to offer an overview of existing discourse analytical work that has engaged with affect and intersectionality. We conclude with a few reflections about potential future avenues for further investigation.

19.2 Definitions: Intersectionality, Affect, Discourse

Intersectionality highlights that subject formations are more than the sum of separate identity categories (i.e. gender, race, class, sexuality) since "each aspect of identity redefines and modifies all others" (Pavlenko and Blackledge 2004: 16). A person can belong to the category "woman," but she may have very different lived experiences about how she is perceived by, say, professional employers or sexual partners depending on her racial and/or class affiliations.

Historically, intersectionality originated within Black feminist activism and scholarship. Law scholar Kimberlé Crenshaw is often attributed the first authorship of the concept in her 1989 article "Demarginalizing the Intersection of Race and Sex: A Black Feminist Critique of Antidiscrimination Doctrine, Feminist Theory and Antiracist Politics." Whereas this publication played a key role in theorizing intersectionality and disseminating it widely to academic audiences, the intersecting workings of identity categories had been raised before by Black feminist activists who drew upon their own experiences of oppression as Black *and* women (Collins and Bilge 2016) in order to argue against the idea of a universal womanhood within the feminist movement. The genealogy of intersectionality has been presented and discussed at length elsewhere (e.g. Carbin and Edenheim 2013) and some scholars (e.g. Tomlinson 2013) have bemoaned the fact that a concept originally formulated by Black activists and scholars has been appropriated by white academics who have mutated it into a trendy and all-encompassing term lacking critical and deconstructive scope (Crenshaw 2011; Salem 2018).

Whether intersectionality is a *theory* is an issue of debate (Nash 2008). Intersectionality research has taken many different forms over the past decades, deploying a plethora of methods in different disciplines within the humanities and social sciences (for a recent overview see Gray and Cooke 2018: 404). Rather than an all-encompassing theory with a matching toolkit, intersectionality can be viewed as a heuristic stance – a position from which to critically understand the social world. More specifically, an intersectional perspective seeks to "reveal how power works in diffuse and differentiated ways through the creation and deployment of overlapping identity categories" (Cho, Crenshaw and McCall 2013: 797). Analytically, then, intersectionality can be operationalized by "asking the other question," as Mari Matsuda (1997) pithily puts it. Such an exercise can be summarized as follows: "When I see something that looks racist, I ask 'Where is the patriarchy in this?' When I see something that looks sexist, I ask 'Where is the heterosexism in this?'" (Matsuda 1997: 66). By doing so, it is possible to unravel the interconnectedness and mutual constitution of different processes of discrimination in which, say, hatred against non-normative sexualities is tightly interwoven with racism and sexism (see also Levon and Mendes 2016).

Because of its emphasis on power and identity, intersectionality has been employed in a variety of studies that critically investigate the role played by language/discourse in identity production and power negotiations. While David Block and Victor Corona (2014) illustrate how social class intersects discursively with other identities such as age, gender, race and ethnicity in the lives of a group of Latino adolescents in Barcelona, the contributions to Erez Levon and Ronald Mendes's (2016) edited collection offer a breadth of analytical techniques – from sociophonetic analysis to multimodal critical discourse analysis – through which to investigate the ways in which sexuality is imbricated with other axes of social categorization across geopolitical contexts.

Though increasing in popularity in both academic and activist circles, intersectionality has been criticized (e.g. Puar 2007) for its overreliance on the possibility of dividing up the social world according to social categories. As a result, intersectionality may paradoxically end up homogenizing people falling within a specific intersectional nexus (e.g. Black women) and erasing the particularity of individual experiences *within* the intersectional bundle under investigation. This is because intersectional scholarship privileges a focus on macro-structural inequalities; consequently, the lived experiences of such inequalities at micro-level become blurred.

As an alternative, John Gray and Melanie Cooke (2018) suggest combining intersectionality with a queer theoretical thrust to "articulate the problems and leakages of identity categories" (Yep 2003: 39). This is with a view to achieving what Gust Yep calls "thicker intersectionalities" (2016), that is, a context-based sensitivity to how apparently similar constellations of identity nexus points may be experienced very differently by individuals, depending on context and person (e.g. Cashman 2017). We would argue that the realm of the affective could also be a fruitful avenue in the pursuit of such "thicker" intersectional analysis, for emotions lead us to pay attention to the *visceral workings* of oppression and resistance to it (see also Chapter 15 in this volume).

We want to state upfront that a focus on affect does not necessarily entail abandoning the discursive study of identity. Rather, we believe that we should investigate the discursive production of identities *at the same time as* we cast a critical gaze at what lies *beside*, and give affective valences to them both. In this respect, Sedgwick suggested that the English preposition *beside* "seems to offer some useful resistance to the ease with which *beneath* and *beyond* turn from spatial descriptors into implicit narratives of, respectively, origin and telos" (Sedgwick 2003: 8; see also Thurlow and Pennycook 2018). As the examples that follow illustrate, a bifocal perspective on identities and affect allows us to achieve a more nuanced understanding of social structures and social practices and to gain deeper insights into the ways in which *politics* and *agency* work (see also Peck and

Stroud 2015; Milani 2015; Cashman 2017; Ferrada, Bucholtz and Corella 2020). Before delving into the overview of the field, however, we first want to define the concept of affect.

Drawing upon the work of cultural theorist Sarah Ahmed, we believe that emotions should be taken into consideration less for their ontological status than for their performative ability to "do things, ... align individuals with communities – or bodily space with social space – [and] mediate the relationship between the psychic and the social, and between the individual and the collective" (Ahmed 2004: 119). According to such a performative understanding, emotions are not states lodged somewhere in people's minds or bodies, and are therefore invisible, but they are *social forces* that are produced, circulated and materialize semiotically through discourse. Here, by discourse, we do not just include spoken and written codes but also other meaning-making systems such as images, music and the body – what is often referred to as multimodality (e.g. Kress and van Leeuwen 1996; Peck and Stroud 2015; Bucholtz and Hall 2016). Analytically, focusing on affect does not require discourse analysts to embark on an esoteric quest of what is *prior* or *external* to the realm of the semiotic. As Margaret Wetherell puts it,

> feelings are not *expressed* in discourse so much as *completed* in discourse. That is, the emotion terms and narratives available in a culture, the conventional elements so thoroughly studied by social constructionist researchers, realise the affect and turn it for the moment into a particular kind of thing. What may start out as inchoate can sometimes be turned into an articulation, mentally organized and publicly communicated, in ways that engage with and reproduce regimes and power relations.　　　　　　　　　　　　　　　　　　　(Wetherell 2012: 24)

Investigating affect then entails focusing on the visible *discursive practices* through which emotions are produced and that are taken up within specific constraints. This does not mean losing sight of power. Rather, it implies reorienting our attention to the often subtle ways in which discipline and control operate, not so much through the mobilization of individuals' "rational capacities to evaluate truth claims but through affects" (Isin 2004: 225). In what follows, we showcase a selection of studies that, through detailed analysis of discourse, offer nuanced analyses of the affective and intersectional workings of power.

It goes without saying that this chapter cannot do justice to the richness of theoretical frameworks, methodological techniques and empirical insights of the growing body of scholarship on intersectionality, affect and discourse. The texture of our narrative has been woven following our own historical bodies (Scollon and Scollon 2004), which include, inter alia, an academic formation as discourse analysts, an epistemological allegiance to poststructuralism and a multitude of other structures of feelings and beliefs, which, as the Scollons (2004) remind us, might not be immediately accessible to our consciousness but nonetheless permeate our research production.

19.3 Current Research

19.3.1 Hate

Research on discourses of loathing against non-normative sexualities – what is called heterosexism and/or homophobia – has occupied a key place in research on language and sexuality (see also Leap 2010). By the same token, both overt and more covert forms of contempt against women – sexism and/or misogyny – have been the targets of feminist linguistic analysis since the inception of gender and language as a field of inquiry (e.g. Cameron 1985). It is only more recently, though, that transfeminist scholars (e.g. Gomes de Jesus 2015; Vergueiro 2015) have pointed to the failure of the concepts of homophobia and sexism to describe the specificities of discourses and practices directed against trans people, which fall under the labels of transphobia, transmisandry and/or cissexism.

What these investigations share is the difficulty to theorize the *social production* of hate without losing sight of the deeply affective layering involved in such processes. In this regard, it has been argued that the suffix -*phobia* is misleading because, whether directed against sexual or gender non-normativities, linguistic and bodily aggression "is not due to an 'irrational' fear, nor can it be understood from a purely psychological framework, that is, as a fear or hatred that resides in an individual's psyche …[; rather,] it is a socially produced form of discrimination located within relations of inequality" (Murray 2009: 3). It is with a view to moving away from a mentalist view that the labels heterosexism and cissexism have been proposed as alternatives. Analogous to other -isms, these terms seek to capture the *structural* dimensions of hatred against sexual and gender variance. However, as Don Kulick (2009: 25) points out, "[a] problem with terms like *sexism* and *racism* (or the alternative often proposed for *homophobia*, *heterosexism*) is that while they do indeed lead us to pay attention to social structure, they background an exploration of the emotional investment that people come to have in those structures."

With this caveat in mind, it is also worth interrogating whether disdain against women as well as against gender and sexual non-normative individuals is a form of discrimination that revolves around sexuality and gender alone. A cogent example of intersectional approach to homophobia is offered in a study of anti-gay speech against two mayors in France. Hatred against same-sex practices is, in this specific case, deeply imbricated with anti-Semitic and racist sentiments (Provencher 2010). Also investigating the intersections of race, gender and sexuality, Zethu Matebeni (2013) demonstrates how court processes on the increasing violence and sexual assault against Black lesbians in South Africa tend to erase the sexual identity of the victims. In numerous cases, violent acts are described and explained with reference to class issues (poverty) and to some extent gender relations, whereas the offenders' knowledge of the sexual identity of the victim is left out of the picture.

Moreover, the labels employed to describe the disciplining of non cis-gendered behavior in South Africa are themselves problematic. The terms punitive, corrective and curative rape are unfortunate because they rest upon the perpetrator's understanding rather than the victim's experience (Matebeni 2013). This means that homosexuality is viewed as something that needs to be punished, cured and corrected (see also Swarr 2012) rather than a legitimate subject position against which oppression and violence are directed. A noticeable circumstance connected to the violence against Black lesbians in South Africa is that all the attacks listed in Matebeni's study have been committed in public places, not in the private sphere of the home. Hence, the public domain works as a stark spectacle that circulates hatred beyond the borders of the concrete crime itself, and in turn instills fear among potential victims in the entire community (Matebeni 2013: 176–7).

South Africa, however, is not an exception, and homosexuality is certainly not the only reason underpinning hate against women, as is testified by the innumerable cases of sexual harassment and violence as well as the violent killings driven by misogynist worldviews such as those in Utøya 2011, Isla Vista 2014, Oregon 2015, Texas 2018 and Toronto 2018. Such hate against women was publicly announced by the perpetrators through elaborate "manifestos" and videos published online. In particular, the texts related to the mass killings in Isla Vista, a student neighborhood adjacent to the campus of University of California, Santa Barbara have been subject to discourse analytical investigations (Bucholtz 2016; Blommaert 2017). What is particularly interesting is that the perpetrator left considerable textual evidences, having engaged in online activities in the so-called "Manosphere" (Nagle 2017; Schmitz and Kazyak 2016; Ging 2017). This is a network of online platforms for men claiming to have been betrayed by women who reject engaging in erotic interaction with them and thus put them into "involuntary celibacy" (abbreviated *incel*) (Bucholtz 2016: 2). The arguments advanced on the Manosphere and through other men's rights movements are based on the following logic: as women gain more equal rights, men are in turn oppressed and subordinated; they are victims of female power, which works by prohibiting men's fulfillment of erotic pleasure.

Yet, whereas reverse gender hierarchy was singled out in the Isla Vista shootings as a reason underpinning the perpetrator's act, the intersections of race and class also played an important role in relation to his misogynistic affective stances. For example, he explicitly referred to his Malaysian origin as one of the main reasons underlying his experienced social exclusion and lacking erotic success with women (Bucholtz 2016). His Asian identification notwithstanding, the offender was highly invested in promoting traditional racial hierarchies of white superiority, even though these worked to his own detriment. This is not particularly surprising because, as Ameeriar points out, "minorities can still be invested in whiteness. Socially, there are unearned benefits and advantages to those invested in whiteness, which often but does not always mean exclusively white people. This possessive investment in whiteness crosses racial lines" (2014). The perpetrator, for example, desired and fetishized white blonde girls while despising them for their lack of sexual interest in him. Moreover, he expressed hatred against Black, Latino and Asian men romantically engaged with white women (Bucholtz 2016; Ameeriar 2014).

Issues of social class were also significant for this affective stance of hatred, anger and revenge. The offender subscribed to the belief that wealth inherently leads to erotic success. Hence, the inability to impress women with expensive presents compounded his gendered, sexual and racial experiences of exclusion and oppression. The massacre in Isla Vista thus demonstrates how affective stances are steeped into intersecting axes of domination and oppression such as misogyny, racism and classism.

Whereas it is easy to describe the killings at Isla Vista as an exceptional deed performed by a radicalized individual belonging to what Blommaert calls a "light community" (2017: 17), "an online zone of social activity ... relatively isolated and enclosed" with no "offline equivalent to it" (2017: 2), Cameron (2018) cautions against the exceptionalization of extreme violence. She proposes that these acts should be seen not as isolated aberrances but as extensions of other less extreme but nonetheless violent acts of misogyny, such as the sexual assault and harassment of Anita Hill and Kristine Blasey Ford, which we discussed at the beginning of this chapter.

The Isla Vista massacre also raises an important methodological and analytical quandary for discourse analysis, that of the researcher's affective involvement. As academics who were themselves part of the community under attack, Bucholtz and Ameeriar disclose that their scholarly background had not prepared them adequately to deal with the emotions they experienced. However, rather than dismissing such emotional involvement, Bucholtz reveals that her "own and other's affective experiences were and continue to be vital to ... [her] ongoing sense-making process" (Bucholtz 2016: 1), and, as a result, she turned to the essay genre as a way of incorporating her feelings into the analysis of this terrible event. Blommaert (2017) also expresses repulsion of the deed. However, he does not engage personally or analytically with the affective impact that misogynistic acts and ideologies have on his researcher's positionality. Whereas, in his paper, Blommaert (2017) reproduces *verbatim* what the offender said and wrote in order to critically analyze the argumentative logic of the texts, Bucholtz (2016) insists that we should resist quoting the perpetrator in order to avoid reproducing his problematic discourses and to puncture the affective circulation of his hateful sexual desire.

19.3.2 Desire

In the same way as research summarized in Section 19.3.1 has highlighted the social production of hate, so discourse analytical work has developed an approach "that focuses on the social mediation of desire: to construct a view of desire that is simultaneously internal and individual, and external and shared" (Eckert 2002: 100). Analytically, such a social perspective entails "showing how particular desires seek to attach to a varieties of bodies, objects, statuses and relationships" in such a way that, for example, "differences of race, age or class may be extremely important in some people's erotic lives" (Cameron and Kulick 2003: 144). Most crucially, such preferences are not idiosyncratic or ahistorical, as Milani illustrates in an investigation of *meetmarket* – a South African online community for men who are looking for other men.

While studies of language and desire typically employ qualitative methodologies in order to analyze spoken data (e.g. Pichler 2017; Mortensen 2015, 2017; Kiesling 2013), Milani (2013) uses corpus techniques for analyzing written texts. This quantitative approach allows him to interrogate a large corpus of personal profiles (N: 4738), with a view to mapping *meetmarket*'s "libidinal economy" (Lyotard 2004) and thereby teasing out which identities are valorized by the members of this online community (see also Bogetić 2013). Similar to the point made with regard to Provencher's (2010) study of homophobia in Section 19.3.1, the analysis of *meetmarket* points to the *intersectional* nature of desire, showing how specific nexus points of race and masculinity are consistently imbued with higher value than other identity configurations. The "libidinal economy" (Lyotard 2004) of *meetmarket* seems to follow a well-known hegemonic system of gender normality in which masculinity is the most valuable currency and femininity is rejected as worthless and undesirable.

That being said, the men on this online community make male same-sex desire visible and heard in a context like South Africa where, despite the official recognition of LGBT rights, attitudes toward same-sex desire remain largely negative among the majority of the population. Through the valorization of masculinity, they are also countering problematic indexicalities that tie male homosexuality with femininity. However, through their nearly misogynist attitudes, these men ultimately end up reinforcing dominant societal discourses that valorize masculinity at the expense of femininity. Hence, their complicity in reproduction of hegemonic masculinity is not innocuous insofar as it allows them to reap the "patriarchal dividend" (Connell 1995) of passing as a man's man. Moreover, the content of the online *meetmarket* profiles also indicates that the tapestry of same-sex desire is woven in racially monochromatic patterns, most likely a vestige of the past regime's enforced sexual normality. Thus, members of *meetmarket* do not seem to be rebelling against the "normal" but are, instead, happily reproducing different "normalities" in which the past intersects with the present.

Shifting attention from race to social class and geographical locale, Barrett (2017) demonstrates how American gay bears desire a very different male ideal from the middle-class slim and slender archetype in US mainstream gay culture. Here the label bear metaphorically refers to heavyweight body structure and hair growth. Moreover, such a hairy, stocky model is linked to cultural symbols and practices typically associated with blue-collar workers and rurality such as heavy work, camping, watching sports and listening to country and bluegrass music (Barrett 2017: 84). Whereas the privileging of working-class masculinity might be interpreted as problematically reproducing conservative patriarchal masculine ideals, the valorization of a body type that is typically disdained on the mainstream gay scene is not dissimilar from the body positivism proposed by radical feminists (e.g. Daly 1978). That being said, US Southern rurality and redneck symbols valued by gay bears carry with them a long history of racism. These ambivalences point once again to the importance of an intersectional analysis of desire. While, on the one hand, gay bears' fetishizing of stocky and hairy Southerner blue-collar workers can, on one axis, be seen as emancipatory of certain body types, on a different axis, it may be (unintentionally) (re)inscribing oppressing structures such as that of racism. All in all, the case of gay bears in the United States illustrates how identities and desires may carry with them conflicting cultural belief systems that lead to contradictory dynamics.

The connection between sexuality and class affiliation has also been highlighted in understanding processes of migration and second-language acquisition. In her investigation of Japanese women's projects of learning English and migrating to Western English-speaking countries, Kimie Takahashi (2013) demonstrates how the desire to learn English is linked to an aspiration to move up the social ladder as well as to a romantic and erotic idealization of white Western men. Through consumption of Hollywood culture, many Japanese women are socialized into desiring the white Western man, a desire that is subsequently exploited by English teaching companies in their advertising material. Through visuals of attractive white male teachers, learning English is marketed as the most successful way to romantically engage with white men and, as a result, improve one's own social standing (see also Piller and Takahashi 2006). This study cogently demonstrates how the desire to learn a language is not only imbricated with sexual desire but also compounded by specific intersections of race, class, gender and sexuality.

Despite methodological and analytical differences, the scholarship presented in this section shares a commitment to demystifying the "naturalness" of desire (Eckert 2002), unpicking the sociocultural and historical situatedness of its production and circulation. Moreover, this body of literature seems to agree that identity and desire are not a zero-sum game; the one does not exclude the other; rather, they influence and constitute the other.

19.3.3 Shame

At the risk of falling into undue oversimplification, desire and love operate by "sticking figures together," as Ahmed would say, a sticking that also has evaluative aspects – "love is a way of valuing something" (Ahmed 2004: 127). Quite the contrary, the dyad shame/guilt typically works through a process of devaluing. As Ahmed puts it, "[i]f we feel shame, we feel shame because we have failed to approximate an ideal that has been given us through the practices of love. What is exposed in shame is the failure of love" (2004: 106). This failure, in turn, is not necessarily momentary or idiosyncratic but can be structurally inscribed in nation-state policies. A forceful case in point is provided by Don Kulick and Jens Rydström (2015) in an ethnographic study of people with disabilities in Sweden and Denmark, and how different national affiliations translate into very different opportunities for being sexual.

Sweden is characterized by an idea of "statist individualism": a particular type of contract between the individual and the state in which the state is assumed to regulate and provide the best possible means for the individual to flourish (Kulick and Rydström 2015: 227–32). However, people with disabilities are considered helpless and thus grouped within the same category as innocent children, that is, without sexual drives and desires (2015: 6). In light of this view, the Swedish social security system rejects supporting and assisting sexual activities for people with disabilities. As a result, claiming to have sexual desire as a person with disability becomes imbued with shame. For example, a Swedish participant in Kulick and Rydström's study reports on how her attempt to facilitate an open discussion with careworkers about the sexual lives of people with disabilities was eventually silenced by accusations of perversion and utterances of disgust (2015: 88–9). In Denmark, on the contrary, the state has developed specific regulations in an attempt to enable people with disabilities to have a sexually active life. As Kulick and Rydström suggest (2015: 224–7), such support may be rooted in a Danish tradition of *frisind* (free-spirit or broadmindedness): an idea of an open and tolerant mindset and individual autonomy. Dating as far back as to the 1850s, *frisind* has become particularly influential since the 1930s and has been connected to Danish deregulation of pornography in the 1970s. Since Kulick and Rydström's study, *frisind* has been even more outspokenly connected to Danishness by the Danish government's incorporation of the notion into the "Denmark Canon"; a collection of ten core national values.[1] In sum, different "nation-state mindsets" thus set up differing frames in which citizens/bodies can be legitimately sexual or shamed to silence and invisibility.

Besides people with disability in relation to the nation-state, there are many examples in which gender and sexual non-normative individuals are shamed for not fitting into existing normative structures. These are not only the standards of heteronormative masculinity and femininity but also normative ideas about what it means to be gay, lesbian or bisexual. A particularly telling example of the affective backlash of homonormativity is given in Lisa Thorne's (2013) insightful analysis of feeling shameful in the context of an LGBT student union for not being convincingly bisexual.

While shame can indeed be employed as a normalizing tool, queer scholars have highlighted that shame does not necessarily need to be viewed as a negative affective process of devaluation but "has political potential as it can provoke a separation between the social convention demarcated within hegemonic ideals, enabling a re-inscription of social intelligibility" (Munt 2007: 4). A case in point of the potentials of turning shame into power is offered by a multimodal discourse analysis of a protest against the annual Johannesburg Pride parade in 2012 (Milani 2015). For contextual purposes, it is important to mention that, since the enactment of the democratic dispensation in 1994, which indeed sanctioned sexuality-based rights, Johannesburg Pride has changed its character from an openly political march in the city's socially mixed center to a street parade in the wealthy suburb of Rosebank, followed by a profit-driven Mardi Gras on the grass of the nearby Zoo Lake. It is also notable in this respect that, whereas Black activists had been the main leaders in the original Pride marches, white middle-class entrepreneurs increasingly took over the management of the subsequent parades. It is in this context that the members of the feminist activist group One in Nine performed a so-called die-in as a form of protest against Johannesburg Pride: A group of Black women carrying human-sized figures ran before the incoming parade and lay down on the street tarmac, as if dead. A few other women went to stand behind this carpet of bodies, carrying the signs "No cause for celebration" and "Dying for justice." Their aim was to make the participants in Johannesburg Pride stop and hold a minute of silence in memory of all the Black lesbians and gender non-normative individuals that had been killed in South Africa because of their noncompliance with gender and sexuality normativities. The sudden interruption set off viciously angry responses from the jubilant walkers. As can be seen on many YouTube videos of the event, a Pride participant aggressively urged the demonstrators to "go back to the *lokshinis* [townships]"; a parade marshal

---

[1] www.danmarkskanon.dk/.

Figure 19.1 *One in Nine*, Joburg Pride 2012

headbutted a protesting woman; Jenni Green – the Joburg Pride board member responsible for the logistics of the event – yelled from her golden Mercedes: "This is my route"; and the chairperson of Joburg Pride, Tanya Hartford, ended up in a bodily confrontation with the protesters.

The bodily and linguistic assemblage represented in Figure 19.1 is less an attempt to seek recognition from their immediate interlocutor – the incoming parade – than a powerful strategy of defiance geared to unsettle the affective structure of the parade itself. It is not sexual identities as such that are the target of the One in Nine intervention but the very affective glue that binds the parade together: Pride. As Sarah Ahmed (2004: 119) notes, emotions "work by sticking figures together (adherence), a sticking that creates the very effect of a collective (coherence)." The dead bodies and the slogan "No cause for celebration" worked like a Bakhtinian "crooked mirror" (Bakhtin 1984: 127) put in front of the parade. The beautiful *Pride* looks at the One in Nine protest and sees itself reflected back as ugly *Shame*. Since affect is always performative – it does things, it has an effect (Ahmed 2004) – it is unsurprising, albeit unjustifiable, that the production of shame set off an affective counterresponse of anger from the participants in the Pride parade, who experienced that as a dissolution of their collective coherence. Through the production of shame, One in Nine could puncture the very idea of a unified South African lesbian and gay "community," revealing its emptiness. As a result, the NGO that organized Johannesburg Pride was disbanded, and a plethora of new, promising political initiatives burgeoned in the wake of the One in Nine's protest, such as the highly politicized Johannesburg People's Pride.

To conclude, shame can be either a way through which non-normative individuals are silenced or, conversely, one of the most powerful affective strategies through which sexual non-normativity can speak back to power affectively. It is an exercise of "cruising utopia" (Muñoz 2009), a loud cry of disidentification from, and resistance against, normalizing forces. And, like all utopias, it carries the hope for a better and perhaps unattainable future; like sexual cruising, it gives a head-rush but always comes with risks attached.

19.4 Where Could We Be Heading?

We began this chapter by highlighting how a focus on affect does not entail ignoring power although it does entail considering the often subtle ways in which discipline and control operate. In this respect, a potentially fruitful avenue of research is to understand the ways in which allegedly liberal nation-states currently police migration, sifting "good" from "bad" migrants on the basis of specific "structures of feelings" (Williams 1977). These are not just the practices that require asylum seekers on the basis of sexual orientation to "come out" for the state as gay, lesbian or transgender in order to be granted the right to stay (Murray 2014); they are also more subtle *affective checkpoints* about what it means to be a "good husband," a "good wife" or simply what it means to be a "man" or a "woman" according to Western democratic ideas. To give an example, the intersectional connections among gender, sexuality and nationality have become increasingly debated across Europe after an incident in Cologne on New Year's Eve 2016 when the German police received 1054 reports of sexual assaults against women perpetrated by drunken men of "foreign heritage." In Denmark, reports of the event quickly led to a discussion about the need to "educate" newly arrived asylum seekers, "schooling" them into sober (legal) romantic and sexual behavior. As a result, compulsory education in "Danish sexual morals" was introduced as part of a general introductory culture course for asylum seekers in Denmark in the summer of 2016. In the Danish context, this process is particularly interesting since, as we have noted, sexual *freedom* has historically been highlighted as an important trait of Danish history and culture, and has led to state support of the sexual desires and practices of people with disabilities. However, in the debate initiated by the multiple sexual assaults on women in Cologne, the general public in Denmark as well as Danish politicians started drawing strict moral boundaries along ethnic and racial lines. We still know too little about these "affective checkpoints" in which intersectional nexus points of gender, sexuality and "national mores" are strategically deployed in the service of the "dirty work of boundary maintenance" (Crowley

1999), reinforcing strict lines between the "good" national Self and the "evil" immigrant Other.

Exclusion and the creation of the "evil" Other, however, never remains uncontested – not only through shame, as we saw, but also through "hope" (see Silva 2017; Peck, Williams and Stroud 2019). An example of semiotic practices of hope is given in a study of public responses against increasing manifestations of misogynist and homophobic discourses in the wake of the impeachment of Brazilian president Dilma Rousseff (Borba 2019). Taking as a case in point the reaction to injurious homophobic words spray-painted on the shutters of a bookshop in Rio de Janeiro, Borba illustrates how hateful words were repainted with two hands joined in solidarity in the rainbow colors. Such a semiotic practice leads him to conclude that "if, in the broader political scenario, hate appears to have won, in local contexts and grassroots activism hope for a better future thrives. ... In fact, it is an openness to the future that local semiotic acts of hope materialize and, thus, help intervene in the broader ideological scenario of this political (and representational) crisis" (Borba 2019: 178). While we began this chapter in dark tones, we want to conclude it in lighter colors. In a time of Donald Trump, Boris Johnson, far-right parties and Nazi revival, what's most pressing as both an academic pursuit and an activist practice is engaging more strongly with the politics of *hope*. An intersectional perspective on hope is perhaps where we should be heading.

Further Reading

Cashman, H. (2017). *Queer, Latinx and Bilingual: Narrative Resources in the Negotiation of Identities*. London: Routledge.

This monograph offers an illuminating analysis of the relationships among bilingualism, gender, sexuality, ethnicity and race among Latinx in the United States.

Gray, J. and Cooke, M. (2018). Special Issue: Intersectionality, Language, and Queer Lives. *Gender and Language* 12(4).

This insightful special issue illustrates how intersectionality can be analytically useful in the study of queer lives in a variety of contexts.

Levon, E. and Mendes, R. (2016). *Language, Sexuality, and Power*. Oxford: Oxford University Press.

This important edited collection showcases sociolinguistic studies that operationalize the notion of intersectionality with the help of different analytical and methodological techniques.

Wetherell, M. (2012). *Affect and Emotion: A New Social Science Understanding*. Thousand Oaks, CA: Sage.

This useful book summarizes debates about emotions and affect in the social sciences and offers clear examples of the ways in which discourse analysts can go about analyzing emotions in discourse.

References

Ahmed, S. (2004). Affective Economies. *Social Text* 22(2): 117–39.

Ameeriar, L. (2014). *Investing in Whiteness: The UCSB Tragedy and Asian America*. Social Text Online. https://socialtextjournal.org/investing-in-whiteness-the-ucsb-tragedy-and-asian-america/.

Bakhtin, M. M. (1984). *Problems of Dostoevsky's Poetics*. Minneapolis/St Paul: University of Minnesota Press.

Barrett, R. (2017). *From Drag Queens to Leathermen: Language, Gender, and Gay Male Subcultures*. Oxford/New York: Oxford University Press.

Bhabha, H. K. (1993). A Good Judge of Character: Men, Metaphors, and the Common Culture. In T. Morrison (ed.) *Racing Justice, Engendering Power: Essays on Anita Hill, Clarence Thomas, and the Construction of Social Reality*. New York: Pantheon. 232–49.

Block, D. and Corona, V. (2014). Exploring Class-Based Intersectionality. *Language, Culture and Curriculum* 27(1): 28–42.

Blommaert. J. (2017). Online-Offline Modes of Identity and Community: Elliot Rodger's Twisted World of Masculine Victimhood. *Tilburg Papers in Culture Studies*, Paper 200. www.tilburguniversity.edu/upload/5a9ff4f6-4c84-4b93-8724-500f32578cd0_TPCS_200_Blommaert.pdf.

Bogetić, K. (2013). Normal Straight Gays: Lexical Collocations and Ideologies of Masculinity in Personal Ads of Serbian Gay Teenagers. *Gender and Language* 7(3): 333–67.

Borba, R. (2019). Injurious Signs: The Geopolitics of Hate and Hope in the Linguistic Landscape of a Political Crisis. In A. Peck, Q. E. Williams and C. Stroud (eds.) *People in Place: Making Sense of Linguistic Landscapes*. London: Bloomsbury. 161–81.

Bucholtz, M. (2016). Why Bodies Matter: Discourse and Materiality after Mass Murder. Unpublished essay. www.linguistics.ucsb.edu/faculty/bucholtz/research.

Bucholtz, M. and Hall, K. (2016). Embodied Sociolinguistics. In N. Coupland (ed.) *Sociolinguistics: Theoretical Debates*. Cambridge: Cambridge University Press. 173–98.

Cameron, D. (1985). *Feminism and Linguistic Theory*. Basingstoke: Palgrave Macmillan.

  (2018). Is "Terrorism" the Right Word? Language: A Feminist Guide https://debuk.wordpress.com/2018/05/01/is-terrorism-the-right-word/.

Cameron, D. and Kulick, D. (2003). *Language and Sexuality*. Cambridge: Cambridge University Press.

Carbin, M. and Edenheim, S. (2013). The Intersectional Turn in Feminist Theory: A Dream of a Common Language? *European Journal of Women's Studies* 20(3): 233–48.

Cashman, H. (2017). *Queer, Latinx and Bilingual: Narrative Resources in the Negotiation of Identities*. London: Routledge.

Cho, S., Crenshaw, K. and McCall, L. (2013). Toward a Field of Intersectionality Studies: Theory, Applications, and Praxis. *Signs* 38 (4): 785–810.

Collins, P. H. and Bilge, S. (2016). *Intersectionality*. Cambridge: Polity Press.

Connell, R. W. (1995). *Masculinities*. Cambridge: Polity Press.

Crenshaw, K. (1989). Demarginalizing the Intersection of Race and Sex: A Black Feminist Critique of Antidiscrimination Doctrine, Feminist Theory and Antiracist Politics. *University of Chicago Legal Forum* 1989(1): 139–67.

(1993). Whose Story Is It Anyway? Feminist and Antiracist Appropriations of Anita Hill. In T. Morrison (ed.) *Racing Justice, Engendering Power: Essays on Anita Hill, Clarence Thomas, and the Construction of Social Reality*. New York: Pantheon. 402–40.

(2011). Postscript. In H. Lutz, M. T. Herrera Vivar and L. Supik (eds.) *Framing Intersectionality: Debated on a Multi-faceted Concept in Gender Studies*. Farnham: Ashgate. 221–33.

(2018). *We Still Haven't Learned from Anita Hill's Testimony*. www.nytimes.com/2018/09/27/opinion/anita-hill-clarence-thomas-brett-kavanaugh-christine-ford.html.

Crowley, J. (1999). The Politics of Belonging: Some Theoretical Considerations. In A. Geddes and A. Favell (eds.) *The Politics of Belonging: Migrants and Minorities in Contemporary Europe*. Aldershot: Ashgate. 15–41.

Daly, M. (1978). *Gyn/ecology: The Metaethics of Radical Feminism*. Boston, MA: Beacon Press.

Eckert, P. (2002). Demystifying Sexuality and Desire. In K. Campbell-Kibler, R. J. Podesva, S. J. Roberts and A. Wong (eds.) *Language and Sexuality: Contesting Meaning, Theory and Practice*. Stanford, CA: CSLI Publications. 99–110.

Ehrlich, S. (2014). Language, Gender and Sexual Violence: Legal Perspective. In S. Ehrlich, M. Meyerhoff and J. Holmes (eds.) *The Handbook of Language, Gender, and Sexuality*, 2nd ed. Oxford: Wiley Blackwell. 452–70.

Ferrada, J. S., Bucholtz, M. and Corella, M. (2020). "Respecta mi idioma": Latinx Youth Enacting Affective Agency. *Journal of Language, Identity, and Education*, 19(20): 79–94.

Ging, D. (2017). Alphas, Betas, and Incels: Theorizing the Masculinities of the Manosphere. *Men and Masculinities* OnlineFirst. www.researchgate.net/publication/316845210_Alphas_Betas_and_Incels_Theorizing_the_Masculinities_of_the_Manosphere.

Gomes de Jesus, J. (2015). *Homofobia: identificar e prevenir*. Rio de Janeiro: Metanóia.

Gray, J. and Cooke, M. (2018). Intersectionality, Language, and Queer Lives, *Gender and Language* 12(4): 401–15.

Isin, E. (2004). The Neurotic Citizen. *Citizenship Studies* 8(3): 217–35.

Kiesling, S. F. (2013). Flirting and "Normative" Sexualities. *Journal of Language and Sexuality* 2(1): 101–21.

Kress, G. and van Leeuwen, T. (1996). *Reading Images: The Grammar of Visual Design*. London: Routledge.

Kulick, D. (2009). Can There Be an Anthropology of Homophobia? In D. A. B. Murray (ed.) *Homophobias: Lust and Loathing across Time and Space*. Durham, NC: Duke University Press. 19–33.

Kulick, D. and Rydström, J. (2015). *Loneliness and Its Opposite: Sex, Disability, and the Ethics of Engagement*. Durham, NC: Duke University Press.

Leap, W. L. (2010). Introducing the Special Issue. *Gender and Language* 4(2), 179–185.

Levon, E. and Mendes, R. (eds.) (2016). *Language, Sexuality, and Power*. Oxford: Oxford University Press.

Lyotard, J. P. (2004). *Libidinal Economy*. London: Continuum.

Matebeni, Z. (2013). *Exploring Black Lesbian Sexualities and Identities in Johannesburg*. PhD thesis, Faculty of Humanities, University of Witswatersrand. http://wiredspace.wits.ac.za/bitstream/handle/10539/10274/Matebeni%20PhD%20thesis%202011.pdf?sequence=2&isAllowed=y.

Matsuda, M. (1997). *Where Is Your Body?* Boston, MA: Beacon Press.

Milani, T. M. (2013). Are "Queers" Really "Queer"? Language, Identity and Same-Sex Desire in a South African Online Community. *Discourse & Society* 24(5): 615–33.

(2015). Sexual Citizenship: Discourses, Spaces and Bodies at Joburg Pride 2012. *Journal of Language and Politics* 14(3): 431–54.

Mortensen, K. K. (2015). A Bit Too Skinny for Me: Women's Homosocial Constructions of Heterosexual Desire in Online Dating. *Gender and Language* 9(3): 461–88.

(2017). Flirting in Online Dating: Giving Empirical Grounds to Flirtatious Implicitness. *Discourse Studies* 19(5): 581–97.

Muñoz, J. E. (2009). *Cruising Utopia: The Then and There of Queer Futurity*. New York: NYU Press.

Munt, S. (2007). *Queer Attachments: The Cultural Politics of Shame*. Aldershot: Ashgate.

Murray, D. A. B. (2009). Introduction. In D. A. B. Murray (ed.) *Homophobias: Lust and Loathing across Time and Space*. Durham, NC: Duke University Press. 1–15.

(ed.) (2014). Special Issue: Queering Borders. *Journal of Language and Sexuality* 3(1).

Nagle, A. (2017). *Kill All Normies: Online Culture Wars from 4chan and Tumblr to Trump and the Alt-Right*. London: Zero Books.

Nash, J. C. (2008). Re-thinking Intersectionality. *Feminist Review* 89: 1–15.

Pavlenko, A. and Blackledge, A. (2004). Introduction: New Theoretical Approaches to the Study of Negotiation of Identities in Multilingual Contexts. In A. Pavlenko and A. Blackledge (eds.) *Negotiation of Identities in Multilingual Contexts*. Clevedon: Multilingual Matters. 1–33.

Peck, A. and Stroud, C. (2015). Skinscapes. *Linguistic Landscape* 1(1–2): 133–51.

Peck, A., Williams, Q. E. and Stroud, C. (eds.) (2019). *People in Place: Making Sense of Linguistic Landscapes*. London: Bloomsbury.

Pichler, P. (2017). "You Are Stupid, You Are Cupid": Playful Polyphony as a Resource for Affectionate Expression in the Talk of a Young London Couple. *Gender and Language* 11(2): 153–75.

Piller, I. and Takahashi, K. (2006). A Passion for English: Desire and the Language Market. In A. Pavlenko (ed.) *Bilingual Minds: Emotional Experience, Expression, and Representation*. Clevedon: Multilingual Matters. 59–83.

Provencher, D. M. (2010). "I Dislike Politicians and Homosexuals": Language and Homophobia in France. *Gender and Language* 4(2): 287–321.

Puar, J. (2007). *Terrorist Assemblages: Homonationalism in Queer Times*. Durham, NC: Duke University Press.

Salem, S. (2018). Intersectionality and Its Discontents: Intersectionality as Traveling Theory. *European Journal of Women's Studies* 25(4): 403–18.

Schmith, R. M. and Kazyak, E. (2016). Masculinities in Cyberspace: An Analysis of Portrayals of Manhood in Men's Rights Activist Websites. *Social Sciences* 5(2): 1–16.

Scollon, R. and Scollon, S. W. (2004). *Nexus Analysis: Discourse and the Emerging Internet*. London: Routledge.

Sedgwick, E. K. ([1990]2008). *The Epistemology of the Closet*. Berkeley: University of California Press.

   (2003). *Touching Feeling: Affect, Pedagogy, Performativity*. Durham, NC: Duke University Press.

Silva, D. (2017). The Pragmatics of Hope, or How to Emancipate Yourself from Violent (Speech) Acts. Paper presented at AILA 2017, Rio de Janeiro, July 23–28.

Swarr, A. L. (2012). Paradoxes of Butchness: Lesbian Masculinities and Sexual Violence in Contemporary South Africa. *Signs* 37(4): 961–86.

Takahashi, K. (2013). *Language Learning, Gender and Desire: Japanese Women on the Move*. Clevedon: Multilingual Matters.

Thorne, L. (2013). "But I'm Attracted to Women": Sexuality and Sexual Identity Performance in Interactional Discourse among Bisexual Students. *Journal of Language and Sexuality* 2(1): 70–100.

Thurlow, T. and Pennycook, A. (2018). *Affecting Sociolinguistics*. Panel presented at Sociolinguistics Symposium 22, Auckland, New Zealand, June, 27–30.

Tomlinson, B. (2013). Colonizing Intersectionality: Replicating Racial Hierarchy in Feminist Academic Arguments. *Social Identities* 19(2): 254–72.

Vergueiro, V. (2015). *Por inflexões decoloniais de corpos e identidades de gênero inconformes: uma análise autoetnográfica da cisgeneridade como normatividade*. Dissertação de Mestrado. Bahia: Universidade Federal da Bahia.

Wetherell, M. (2012). *Affect and Emotion: A New Social Science Understanding*. Thousand Oaks, CA: Sage.

Williams, R. (1977). *Marxism and Literature*: Oxford: Oxford University Press.

Yep, G. (2003). The Violence of Heteronormativity in Communication Studies. *Journal of Homosexuality* 45(2–4): 11–59.

   (2016). Toward Thick(er) Intersectionalities: Theorizing, Researching, and Activating the Complexities of Communication and Identities. In K. Sorrells and S. Sekimoto (eds.) *Globalizing Intercultural Communication*. Thousand Oaks, CA: Sage. 85–94.

20

Expanding Academic Discourses: Diverse Englishes, Modalities and Spatial Repertoires

Brooke R. Schreiber, Mohammad Naseh Nasrollahi Shahri and Suresh Canagarajah

20.1 Introduction

In this chapter we will discuss how scholarly understandings of academic discourse have shifted over the past thirty years in response to increasing globalization and changes in theorizations of language. We will look at how the definition of and boundaries around academic discourse have widened, shifting from a singular academic discourse to plural discourses, and from a focus on language to a focus on practices, in the process of accommodating more diverse Englishes. In particular, we will consider how the study of academic discourse has exposed the increasingly blurry boundaries not only between languages but also between modes, and how discourse includes not only text but also other resources for making meaning, such as images, sound, gesture and material artifacts. We will consider how English's role as the academic lingua franca has influenced these shifting definitions and concepts. Finally, we will consider the implications of this diversification for pedagogy and for frameworks for future discourse studies.

First, what do we mean by "academic discourse"? Academic discourse is defined as "ways of using language and thinking which exist in the academy" (Hyland 2009: 1). Academic discourse, as we understand it, is neither fixed nor singular; there are many forms of academic discourse, and these forms change over time (Bizzell 2002). In this chapter, the term academic discourse encompasses an intentionally broad territory. It includes writing, reading, listening and speaking across institutes of education, embracing not only actual texts that are used in academic settings (e.g. journal articles, books, grant proposals, course papers and emails) but also talk that surrounds and supports these texts (e.g. conference presentations, classroom lectures, group discussions, peer reviews and co-writing talk). Some scholars wish to take into consideration all acts of communication that occur in the academic setting, such as application letters for jobs, resume writing and creative writing for student magazines and university newspapers (see Ivanic 2009). Though these activities might influence the shaping of academic texts, we restrict our focus to discourses that relate to "academic" content and objectives.

Second, what do we mean by "diverse Englishes"? In this term, we include what would traditionally be called World Englishes (e.g. Kachru 1986): varieties of English spoken in English-dominant settings like the United States and Great Britain; in places where English is one of the official languages, such as India, Singapore and the Philippines; and in places where English is learned as a foreign language, such as China, Germany and Brazil. In the World Englishes model, these locations are often classified as Inner Circle, Outer Circle and Expanding Circle. We must note that multiple dialects of English are spoken within these national contexts. In the United States, this includes varieties such as Southern English, Brooklynese, and African-American Vernacular English (AAVE). We include also supranational dialects of English, such as English spoken in lingua franca settings, defined as "any use of English among speakers of different first languages for whom English is the medium of choice, and often the only option" (Seidlhofer 2011: 7), as well as varieties of English that have emerged in digital spaces (e.g. Crystal 2012).

Along with these more traditional definitions, we also recognize recent translingual orientations that emphasize that what we call "English" is not a clearly separate entity with sharp boundaries. In communication, speakers do not simply turn off one language when using another; rather, they use all the languages at their disposal to make meaning: they mesh together verbal resources from what is labeled the "English" language with resources from other languages and semiotic systems (images, gestures, etc.) to generate hybrid (or "code meshed") texts (see Canagarajah 2017; Horner et al. 2011; Young 2004).

20.2 Overview of the Topic

20.2.1 Evolving Understandings of Academic Discourse

Academic discourse has been studied mainly in the context of the university, although in recent years there have been notable attempts to challenge this dominance (e.g. Johns and Snow 2006; Schleppegrell 2004). Early studies of academic discourse were "text-oriented" (Hyland, 2009), meaning that they used written academic documents such as research articles and peer reviews as the primary source of data. These early studies took as their principal organizing construct the concept of genre, defined as "a distinctive category of discourse of any type, spoken or written" (Swales 1990: 33). Significant in this tradition of research was the analysis of moves in discourse. A move is a "bounded communicative act that is designed to achieve one main communicative objective" (Swales and Feak 2000: 35). The analysis carefully attended to the relation between moves and the linguistic features that realized them. It also brought out the role of the rhetorical and disciplinary contexts behind the moves. Such research was also concerned with the concept of discourse communities, which are defined as categories of people driven by particular communicative purposes that determine what kinds of tasks speakers engage in (Swales 1990).

A key insight from these genre studies was the discovery of "occluded genres," genres that are "out of sight," concealed from public scrutiny (Swales 1996: 46). Within academic discourse, these include such genres as book reviews, cover letters to journals, research grant proposals and application letters. The identification of these genres was important as they are pervasive throughout the academy, serving necessary functions, and their discovery paved the way for pedagogical initiatives centered on these less-known genres.

Pedagogically, genre studies proved to be a useful approach to the teaching of academic discourse. The analysis of genres and the concomitant identification of their linguistic patterns provide students with examples of a particular genre and its typical features as they learn how to produce it (Tardy 2011; also see Chapters 1 and 27 in this volume). In other words, genres can become heuristics for learning socially significant forms of discourse. Although this approach has been critiqued for portraying academic genres as static and rigid, and therefore turning academic writing into mere templates or rules for students to follow, recent genre scholarship draws attention to the creativity and diversity possible within genres (Tardy 2016).

Closely related to genre is a corpus-based approach (see Chapter 8 in this volume) to academic discourse (Hyland 2004; Biber 2006; Coxhead 2000). This strand of research grounds the analysis of academic discourse in large databases of texts, identifying patterns of word frequency and lexical and thematic association. As a result, corpus studies supply robust descriptions of genres (Hyland 2009). A significant finding of these studies involves the identification of lexical bundles, recurring word sequences in texts (Biber et al. 1999). These lexical bundles, alternatively referred to as chunks or clusters, allow for fluency in the use of academic discourse (Coxhead and Byrd 2007). Significantly, this line of research has explored both written and spoken genres. The description of these bundles has also been used to inform pedagogy particularly in the form of lessons explicitly aimed at familiarizing students with the notions of bundles and illustrations of their use (e.g. Cortes 2006; Meunier and Granger 2008; Weber 2001). However, genre and corpus-based approaches to academic discourse tend to focus narrowly on textual data to the exclusion of interactional data showing how texts are used or produced.

Such interactional data are the object of analysis in context-oriented approaches, advanced by Prior (1998), who advocated a shift from written texts as the unit of analysis to *literate activity*, which recognized that the physical setting and interactions are usually concealed when we focus only on the final written product. Adopting a sociocultural framework, Prior deconstructed the myth of individual authorship, emphasizing the deeply intertextual nature of writing and how human activity around texts infuses them with various voices. Similarly, Myers (1990) underscores the social construction of texts, carefully demonstrating the profound effect of negotiations with readers, reviewers and journals on the written product. These more contextually oriented studies appeal for more recognition of the social nature of the process of writing, the features of the context around writing, and how these factors are incorporated into the final product. These studies can be seen as attempts to place written texts as academic discourse within the contexts of their production and reception. The effect has been to broaden what is taken as academic discourse, from only written texts to the social activity around those texts. Such an orientation has paved the way for considering discourse as a practice that involves speakers/writing engaging with diverse social networks and material ecologies, and accommodating various semiotic resources beyond language, as we will discuss in the following paragraphs.

A move toward diversification of academic discourses is also discernible in more text-based studies. Hyland (2002), for instance, debunks the idea of an easily defined general academic English that shares broad features across disciplines. Taking this line of reasoning further, Hyland (2004) notes that academic discourses within disciplines are the products of various negotiations within academic fields marked by divergent views of what constitutes knowledge.

Using corpus approaches, complemented by interviews, he examines these negotiations by looking at issues such as citations and intertextuality. In this view, language choices result from the typical social negotiations informing academic discourses. Negotiations are particularly important in the global periphery where academic texts are mediated by "literacy brokers" and "literacy sponsors," which can include formal editors and translators but also informal networks of colleagues, friends and family members who read and suggest changes to texts during the writing process (Lillis and Curry 2010).

Another significant step toward the diversification of academic discourses was taken by New Literacy Studies (Gee 2015; Heath 1983; Street 1984). This line of research originally arose in opposition to a psychological approach to literacy, which limited literacy to the individual's mind. New Literacy Studies instead highlighted the multiplicity of linguistic practices that students should be able to command as they switch from one educational context to another (Street 1998). Together with recognizing the multiple literacies involved in academic life, New Literacy Studies made a compelling argument that a skill-dominated view of literacy was inadequate since literacy is not merely a set of neutral skills that can easily be transferred between contexts but rather a range of socially constructed practices, varying from one cultural context to the next. As such, academic literacies are always anchored in particular worldviews and are, thus ideological (Gee 2015; Street and Besnier 1994). In this view, then, academic literacies are seen as representing a diverse range of ideologically shaped practices based on "socially constructed epistemological principles" (Street 2014: 4). For the purposes of the discussion here, it is significant that New Literacy Studies drew attention to the existence of plural literacies rather than a singular literacy, underpinned by a variety of practices.

This shift toward activity, practices and diversity set the scene for the emergence of the conception of academic discourses as hybrid and multimodal. Kress (2010) makes a case that it is no longer valid to privilege writing and speaking as central means of meaning-making, in a digital age in which other modes of communication dominate. This attention to other modes such as the visual and the gestural has also percolated to scholarship on academic discourse (also see Chapter 12 on multimodality, in this volume). Molle and Prior (2008), for instance, showed that academic discourse is essentially multimodal with images accompanying texts. Similarly, Shipka (2016) emphasizes that texts are both multimodal and translingual. In a similar vein, Haneda (2014), drawing on Vygotsky (1999), Tomasello (1999) and Lave and Wenger (1991) within sociocultural theory, makes an argument for expanding the study of academic language to a broader notion of academic communication in which a variety of semiotic resources beyond writing are merged to achieve student goals. So, too, Heller and Morek (2015) caution that the dominant tendency in studies of academic discourse to focus on generalizable features of academic discourse results in insufficient attention to actual language use. In propounding a "situated practice" view of academic discourse, Heller and Morek (2015) underscore the necessity of taking account of oral instantiations of academic discourse such as classroom discourse, which is "bound to the particular conditions of orality" while being about academic content (Heller and Morek 2015: 180).

Alongside heightened attention to the multimodal dimensions of academic discourses, scholars such as Molle and Prior (2008) and Duff (2003) brought to the surface the intertextuality of academic discourses. Duff's study, for instance, challenges the picture of academic discourse as isolated from other discourses, revealing how the intrusion of references to popular culture into tenth grade class discourse results in hybrid discourses, posing challenges for immigrant students. This line of research also contributes to the disruption of the assumed homogeneity of academic discourses. These studies further widen what counts as academic discourse by bringing to the fore the hybridity generated by traditionally-considered nonacademic discourses involved in the production and reception of academic discourses.

More recently, language use and discourse are treated as an "assemblage" (Deleuze and Guattari 1987; Latour 2005), to bring into sharp relief the interactions among bodies, artifacts, spatial resources and other material conditions (see Chapter 16 in this volume). In this perspective, influenced by poststructuralist theories, discourse is understood as emerging from more expansive material, social and semiotic resources and networks (see Toohey and Dagenais 2015). These recent approaches have significant implications pertaining to academic discourse (Canagarajah 2018). In accord with the new sensitivity in academic discourse studies toward multimodality, language is seen as only one among a varied array of semiotic resources, not the center of communication. By way of illustration, research suggests that international STEM scholars who have limited proficiency in English perform successfully in academic work as they are adept at orchestrating diverse semiotic resources (i.e. visuals, technology, artifacts, texts) and expansive social networks to their advantage (see Canagarajah 2018). Languages, such as English, play only a partial role in accounting for academic discourse and success. In addition, the divide between text and context is lessened to the point where context is seen as being part of the text, not just the background to it (see Kunitz and Markee 2017 for a discussion of context in conversation analysis and ethnography). This is because what has traditionally been seen as contextual is recast as being an integral part of the spectrum of multimodal resources deployed in the production of the text.

The general thrust of the recent developments sketched so far is to bring to the fore a more diverse notion of academic discourse: cutting across multiple modalities and deeply embedded in material conditions and social interactions. It is thus more appropriate to speak of academic discourses in the plural.

20.2.2 Evolving Understandings of English

As the theoretical understanding of academic discourses has broadened, so has the understanding of the role of English in academia globally. English has been widely recognized as the academic lingua franca, not only the language of international conferences and publications but also increasingly the medium of instruction even in non-English-dominant academic settings – a process that is both driven by and drives increased international student mobility (e.g. Fraiberg, Wang and You 2017). However, the rising dominance of English has not been without controversy: there have been critiques of how that dominance works with other forces of globalization to exclude local discourses, knowledge and practices (see Canagarajah 2005). Scholars are also increasingly critical of the dominance of center-based scholars in academic publications and, thereby, intellectual life. Beyond just the differences in the way English is used by scholars outside "native speaker" communities, scholars are also critical of genre conventions, voice and rhetorical preferences biased in favor of Western communities, leading to a near monopoly of academic publishing and communication by English-dominant scholars (Canagarajah 2002).

Yet it is important to understand that the English that is employed as an academic lingua franca is not, in practice, tied to native-speaker norms and standards. Drawing on a general English as a Lingua Franca (ELF) framework, scholars have begun to study the features of English as a Lingua Franca in Academia (ELFA), such as the elimination of grammatical redundancy, innovative use of tenses and the invention of new words and collocations (Jenkins 2011; Mauranen et al. 2010). Crucially, these differences from the academic English of monolingual English speakers are "neither random nor idiosyncratic, but rather, are indicative of the emergence of new ELF patterns" (Jenkins 2011: 929). This line of research has shed light on a deep gap between the everyday language practices in academic settings – in classrooms, research labs and academic conferences – and the narrow native-speaker language standards that are used in teaching, testing and publication (Tardy 2015).

The emphasis in ELFA studies has shifted from efforts to collect and catalogue differences in production to efforts to understand the pragmatic strategies that make lingua franca communication successful: namely, codeswitching and accommodation (Jenkins 2011). ELFA is viewed not as a static variety but rather as a set of skills, an ability to use knowledge of English as one resource among many in making meaning. This means that the conception of a skilled user of English has also shifted, from "someone who has 'mastered' the forms of a particular native variety of English" to "someone who has acquired the pragmatic skills needed to adapt their English use in line with the demands of the current lingua franca situation" (Jenkins 2011: 931–2). In other words, a person who is successful in academic discourse will be able not to replicate one privileged dialect but to use their knowledge of English together with other semiotic resources in a flexible way, adapting to the context.

The ELFA perspective on the fluidity of academic discourse coincides with a movement within US composition scholarship to question how "standard" Standard Written English (SWE) truly is. As Elbow (1999: 359) points out, SWE, "what is called correct by prestige readers," is hardly codified: it varies between contexts and even between individual readers. Even published academic writing has vastly different requirements across contexts; a skillful user of academic English must shift their rhetorical and linguistic strategies to fit their local or global audiences (Canagarajah 2006b) and some scholars already skillfully insert nonstandard features into their writing for voice and rhetorical effect (Canagarajah 2006a). There are also differences in practice among disciplines; while the natural sciences tend to expect normative (SWE) writing, the humanities accommodate greater diversity, although discourse within all academic disciplines is shaped by interaction between genre conventions and writers' individual topics, purposes and personalities (Paltridge, Starfield and Tardy 2016; Thaiss and Zawacki 2002).

However, across these differences, the most widely accepted forms of academic discourse generally reflect "the cultural preferences of the most powerful people in the community" (Bizzell 2002: 1; see also Royster 2002) and therefore tend to reflect white, middle-class, monolingual ways of speaking and writing. Composition scholars are exploring how academic discourses might accommodate different dialects and varieties that are historically devalued, including those of indigenous people (Lyons 2000), women, people of color (Young et al. 2014) and those who speak English as an additional language (J. W. Lee 2017). At the heart of this movement are two crucial recognitions: first, that academic English is no one's first language and monolingual English speakers still need to acquire it; and second, that forcing all students to conform to (white, male, middle-class) standards is problematic at best and racist at worst, and yet students do still need to master – or at least access – this "code of power" in order to become successful in a world that views nonstandard dialects and accents as inferior (Delpit 1995; Elbow 1999; Young 2004).

Building on this line of inquiry, scholars have argued for a "translingual" approach to academic discourse. The translingual approach is connected to the practice of translanguaging, in which speakers use all of their linguistic resources "to make meaning, transmit information, and perform identities" (Creese and Blackledge 2010: 109). A translingual approach to academic discourse emphasizes that multilingualism is the norm rather than the exception; that language boundaries are fluid, that both language norms and genres are constantly changing, and that language differences are not "a barrier to overcome or a problem to manage, but … a resource for producing meaning" (Horner et al. 2011: 303). The translingual approach, like ELF studies, reflects the ways in which academic discourse in English is often preceded by texts and interactions in diverse languages and informed by their influences. It emphasizes that asking academics to conform to a "standard" English is a goal that is not only impossible but also counterproductive to effective communication, framing all deviations from an imagined standard as errors (Horner et al. 2011).

20.3 Issues and Ongoing Debates

The developments in research and scholarship relating to the understanding of academic discourses described in this chapter are not universally accepted. The ongoing debates arising from these changing understandings center both on how learners can best acquire academic discourses and on how professional academics' discourse practices have developed.

The first major debate is whether these new understandings about the true diversity of academic discourse have permeated the world of academic publishing. It has long been clear that academic publishing in English favors those in the global center, who not only have easier access to resources like recent publications, conferences and laboratories but are also trained in the dominant genres and discourses, to which scholars from the periphery and semiperiphery are expected to conform, devaluing their local ways of knowing (Bennet 2014; Canagarajah 2002). Some scholars have argued that despite the rise of the new approaches to academic discourse outlined in this chapter – from World Englishes and ELF to translingual – those in gatekeeping positions such as journal editors and reviewers still adopt narrow standards that continue to privilege center-based scholars (Lillis and Curry 2010). In particular, Heng Hartse and Kubota (2014) argue that, even among scholars who are deeply committed to pluralizing academic discourse, the dominant norms for publishing are still based on native varieties of English. They point out that the guidelines applied by journal editors are often vague and idiosyncratic, inconsistent across journals and commonly tied to "native speaker standards of acceptability" (2014: 76). Heng Hartse and Kubota describe their own process of putting together an edited collection and note that, despite their strong intentions "to respect NNES writers' voices" by copyediting lightly, "almost all decisions about what to change, delete, or insert were made based on native-speaker intuition" (2014: 80) even though the native speaker in question was a graduate student with far less experience than the authors. Thus, they argue, while creativity is encouraged in writing classrooms, there remains a large gap between that creativity and publication practices.

Secondly, the translingual approach itself is the subject of no small amount of controversy. Some critics have argued that by emphasizing the visible incorporation of other codes into academic discourse, studies on creativity in academic discourse are exoticizing diversity, creating a sort of "linguistic tourism" that is ultimately harmful (Matsuda 2014).

In the teaching of academic discourse, there is a debate around whether translingual approaches address second language writers' needs and expectations of mastering standard academic English for their own purposes (Atkinson et al. 2015; Gevers, 2018).

These recent criticisms echo longstanding disagreements within the teaching of academic discourse. As Fox (2002: 59) describes, to join academic conversations, many students (particularly students of color) must discard and distance themselves from their home discourses, which can be both "confusing and disheartening." Scholars have noted that well-meaning teachers experience a great deal of anxiety around their desires to validate their students' home dialects, but at the same time enable students "to produce the language they need in order to avoid stigmatization by other teachers and readers" (Elbow 1999: 366; see also Schreiber and Worden 2019). The new pluralistic models of academic discourse described in this chapter offer multiple frameworks for teachers grappling with this dilemma, which Matsuda and Matsuda (2010: 371) call "the complex push–pull relationship between standardization and diversification" in academic discourse. Teachers might provide students opportunities to use their own dialects for drafting and other low-stakes writing (Elbow 1999), teach students strategies of code-meshing (Canaragrajah 2006a) or teach standard academic discourse while also emphasizing the socially constructed and fluid nature of that discourse (Matsuda and Matsuda 2010). Debate continues between those who support translingual approaches and those who do not (Gevers 2018; Schreiber and Watson 2018), though there is one point of agreement: they caution teachers to be aware of the potentially negative consequences for students, who are often in marginalized positions, of deviating from the status quo, and encourage teachers "to play a greater role in challenging the undue privileging of the dominant discourses" (Matsuda and Matsuda 2010: 373; also see Chapter 23 in this volume).

Finally, there are ideological debates on the diversification of academic discourses: are the evolving diverse conventions truly democratizing academic communication, empowering a greater range of users of English to participate in the reception and production of academic discourses, or are they instead a new, equally restrictive set of requirements established by neoliberal economics? Scholars like Flores (2013) and Kubota (2014) have argued that translingualism and hybridity are privileged by neoliberal agencies for purposes of profit and marketization. In other words, the new global capitalism demands a type of language fluidity closely aligned with discourses of hybridity. Such fluid language practices are valued by global businesses looking to expand their consumers. They also argue that the new conventions become popular for the sake of spawning new publications and scholarship, maintaining the status quo without broad-based changes that democratize knowledge-making activity and represent the values and interests of marginalized communities.

20.4 A New Definition of Competence

The developments sketched out in this chapter, particularly the recognition of academic discourses as diverse and multimodal, carry important implications for notions of competence in applied linguistics and discourse studies more generally. Specifically, it is no longer theoretically viable to view competence as being located or contained within an individual person. When we understand academic discourses as socially constructed, resulting not from an individual's solo actions but from the alignment of various resources strategically mobilized for meaning-making purposes in social networks (Canagarajah 2018), competence in academic discourses must lie in the networks responsible for producing texts and not the individual mind. Without social networks that include material resources, other individuals and connections among them, academic texts would not take the form that they do. An emphasis on individual competence downplays the role of material resources and networks of authors in enabling the authorship of academic texts (Lillis and Curry 2010; Prior 1998).

A second implication is that competence in academic discourses is not about mastery of a single language. Even though the finished text may resemble a standard variety of a language depending on the situation, competence is the result of the use of a variety of resources (Canagarajah 2018). In fact, many of the new theoretical understandings of language (translingualism, plurilingualism and others) suggest that communicative competence is "a transformative ability to merge language resources" (Donahue 2018: 27) as well as an attitude of flexibility that comes from "openness to uncertainty" (Donahue 2018: 33). In other words, competence in academic discourse is about being able to use what you know of multiple languages as an integrated whole, in a way that adapts to the communicative situation. In this definition of competence, it's also important to understand that meaning is not simply transmitted from the speaker or writer to the listener or reader; it is co-constructed by all participants (Donahue 2018). And just as competence is not restricted to one language, it is not restricted to one mode (namely, writing). Rather, it cuts across various modalities, and competent users of academic discourse must construct texts that build on several modes. Given these two implications, competence in using academic discourses becomes the strategic deployment of available resources, both linguistic and nonlinguistic, in the advancement of social action, centered on semiotic repertoires (Kusters et al. 2017).

The term "emplacement," used in studies of rhetoric (Pigg 2014; Rickert 2013), is well suited to take account of these two implications for our understanding of competence. Defined as "the strategic and ongoing attunement to an assemblage of agents and resources in expansive spatiotemporal scales for the emergence of thinking and meaning in activity" (Canagarajah 2018: 18), emplacement indexes the importance of the physical activity of locating oneself within the ecology of practice to be able to align various resources. It highlights the equal importance of all resources and participants within networks. The notion implies human agency tempered by the significance of spatial resources, which allows for the possibility of creative and strategic human activity in pursuit of meaning-making (Cangarajah 2017).

Finally, undertaking research on academic discourses in relation to the ways in which it is being diversified will also raise new methodological implications. When diverse social and material networks contribute to shaping language and texts, what should be the unit of analysis? To understand how academic texts are shaped, scholars like Paul Prior (1998) favor adopting longitudinal ethnographies that take into account the social interactions and life histories of scholars, extending far beyond the academy. Similarly, Lillis and Curry (2010) adopt the method of "talk around the text" to reconstruct the social and material networks shaping the text by interviewing the authors. Canagarajah (2018) discusses the new challenges in studying academic discourse from such expansive contexts and semiotic resources, suggesting that analysis encompasses the range of scales and resources that become relevant in the study. Digital environments have made academic interactions virtual and distributed across social and material networks, requiring scholars to go beyond bounded texts and interactions. Scholarship has to engage seriously with the question of what data to include in ways that are responsive to diverse notions of academic discourses.

20.5 Future Directions

We see several future directions for the study of academic discourse under the new pluralistic understandings. First, we expect further explorations into translingual writing pedagogy, looking for more concrete strategies for implementing these new understandings of discourse in classroom practices and reporting on how these strategies have worked (see Horner and Tetreault 2017). We anticipate more research on translingual practice, to clarify how translingual writing is more than visible code-mixing. A promising direction is suggested by the term "spatial repertoires." The notion draws attention to the role of resources attached to places where communication takes place (Pennycook and Otsuji 2015). Spatial repertoires refer to the multiplicity of semiotic resources, including environmental affordances and artifacts alongside verbal and nonverbal resources from various spatiotemporal scales, assembled in communicative contexts in cooperation with other participating individuals (Canagarajah 2018). This perspective allows for more nuanced approaches attuned to the complexity of contemporary communication in academic settings. The studies cited throughout this chapter adopt methods such as multi-sited ethnography, multimodal conversation analysis and critical discourse analysis.

We also expect to see research moving toward a clearer description of the dispositions and strategies that teachers and students use to support the negotiation of academic discourses in situationally effective ways. Traditionally, the research focus has been on language and text construction, rather than on the attitudes and techniques that facilitate the successful construction and reception of hybrid or alternative texts. Notions such as "rhetorical attunement" (E. Lee 2017; Leonard 2014), which describes an approach to communication that expects, appreciates and negotiates with linguistic multiplicity, may provide an important framework, as scholars study how readers and writers work together to generate meanings in academic communication marked by diverse norms and resources.

Next, we expect that scholars interested in contesting the narrow definitions of academic writing will begin to look more closely into the reception of hybrid or translingual discourses beyond the university. Donahue (2018: 34) calls for research that identifies the features of successful discourse in a variety of contexts, both formal and informal, what she calls "the new linguistic norms in everyday practice." This line of inquiry will help composition teachers to close the gap between outdated teaching standards and the real-world practices beyond the university, and may ultimately "lead to wider acceptance of non-standard lexis and grammar in published texts" (Heng Hartse and Kubota 2014: 75).

It is also important to observe how technology and communication changes might provide new affordances for diversifying writing. Online platforms for academic publications provide spaces to publish in diverse styles and in languages other than English: publishing the abstracts in multiple languages, for example, or inviting authors to include multimodal data as supplements to articles. There are fewer restrictions of length in online publications, allowing for more experimentation and creativity. Most importantly, as many journal submissions adopt online platforms, scholars from diverse communities around the world are enjoying more access to publishing networks as both readers and writers. It remains to be seen how these developments will influence the increasing diversification of academic discourse.

Finally, our new understanding of "competence" in English and in academic discourses, as something beyond separate languages and the individual, will require teachers to explore how to harness this new concept to develop better teaching resources. Specifically, we will need to investigate how to reconcile these new notions with more traditional orders of academic spaces. While discourses of education around the world are constructed around individual competence in dominant languages, how can educational endeavors be designed in ways that, while theoretically attuned to newer concepts of competence, actually help learners? Donahue (2018: 35), for example, suggests that we must adopt "a new understanding of what it might mean to be 'competent,' one that redirects our attention away from specific language features to strategies, tools, and meta-awarenesses." As teachers move past the dichotomy between "correct" and "incorrect" language, recognizing the hybrid, fluid and socially constructed nature of academic discourse, they may find they need to focus not on grammar but on dispositions. That is, they might focus on developing capabilities in their students such as language awareness, rhetorical sensitivity and negotiation strategies (Canagarajah 2018). Since scholars and students have to negotiate academic discourses in situated contexts, in response to the specific audience, purpose, venue and disciplines addressed, they have to develop the capacity to negotiate the established norms in relation to these factors. Based on such negotiations, the grammatical and genre norms they adopt for the context will vary. Therefore, working more on developing the sociolinguistic awareness and strategies to negotiate changing communicative contexts might be helpful for students and scholars in the long run.

20.6 Summary

In this chapter, we have traced how the expansion in the understanding of academic discourse as a form of multimodal, translingual practice has allowed for greater creativity and diversity in the use of language. The traditional notion of academic discourse – as a single, homogeneous form with a normative use of English – limited writers' voices, reproduced dominant forms of knowledge and restricted access in publishing and educational institutions. As we move toward treating academic discourses as a negotiated practice, one that takes different forms in relation to diverse audiences, genres and purposes, we also see how students and scholars are finding spaces for diverse varieties of English and even other languages in academic communication. Though publishing policies and pedagogical practices have not always kept up with the expanding research and theoretical orientations, we have outlined some ways in which teachers can support students' negotiation of discourses in relation to established conventions.

Further Reading

Canagarajah, S. (2002). *Critical Academic Writing and Multilingual Students*. Ann Arbor: University of Michigan Press.

This foundational text lays out a critical approach to the teaching of academic discourse, in which academic discourse is understood as a situated, historical, social and ideological practice, rather than a neutral product. Canagarajah examines many aspects of writing pedagogy (e.g. error correction, voice and plagiarism), looking at how teachers can accommodate the linguistic and cultural knowledge of multilingual writers.

Schroeder, C., Fox, H. and Bizzell, P. (eds.) (2002). *ALT DIS: Alternative Discourses and the Academy*. Portsmouth, NH: Boynton/Cook.

This edited volume presents insightful discussions around various alternative forms of discourse that are now present in the academy. The chapters take up related issues including the role of traditionally non-standard discourses, dialects, hybridity and the new conditions engendered by multilingual students in composition courses and in writing across the curriculum.

Tardy, C. M. (2016). *Beyond Convention: Genre Innovation in Academic Writing*. Ann Arbor: University of Michigan Press.

This book discusses how the conventions of academic genres are formed and how they are creatively flouted. Tardy, an expert on academic genre, here offers insights from her own research on genre innovation, as well as guidance for teachers on incorporating innovation and playfulness into the teaching of academic genres.

Young, V. A., Barrett, R., Young-Rivera, Y. and Lovejoy, K.B. (2014). *Other People's English: Code-Meshing, Code-Switching, and African American Literacy*. New York: Teachers College Press.

This book argues for the value of code-meshing, the blending of African-American language styles with Standard English in academic discourse, as a way of empowering young people of color. The authors address the history of code-meshing, how this technique pushes back against racial segregation and negative stereotypes, and how it can be implemented in education.

References

Atkinson, D., Crusan, D., Matsuda, P. K., Ortmeier-Hooper, C., Ruecker, T., Simpson, S. and Tardy, C. (2015). Clarifying the Relationship between L2 Writing and Translingual Writing: An Open Letter to Writing Studies Editors and Organization Leaders. *College English* 77(4): 383–6.

Bennett, K. (ed.) (2014). *The Semiperiphery of Academic Writing: Discourses, Communities and Practices*. Basingstoke: Palgrave Macmillan.

Biber, D. (2006). *University Language: A Corpus-Based Study of Spoken and Written Registers*. Amsterdam: John Benjamins.

Biber, D., Johansson, S., Leech, G., Conrad, S. and Finegan, E. (1999). *Longman Grammar of Spoken and Written English*. Harlow: Longman.

Bizzell, P. (2002). The Intellectual Work of "Mixed" Forms of Academic Discourses. In C. Schroeder, H. Fox and P. Bizzell (eds.) *ALT DIS: Alternative Discourses and the Academy*. Portsmouth, NH: Boynton/Cook. 1–10.

Canagarajah, A. S. (2002). *A Geopolitics of Academic Writing*. Pittsburgh, PA: University of Pittsburgh Press.

(ed.) (2005). *Reclaiming the Local in Language Policy and Practice*. London/New York: Routledge.

(2006a). The Place of World Englishes in Composition: Pluralization Continued. *College Composition and Communication* 57: 586–619.

(2006b). Toward a Writing Pedagogy of Shuttling between Languages: Learning from Multilingual Writers. *College English* 68(6): 589–604.

(2017). Translingual Practice as Spatial Repertoires: Expanding the Paradigm beyond Structuralist Orientations. *Applied Linguistics* 39(1): 31–54.

(2018). Materializing Competence: Perspectives from International STEM Scholars. *Modern Language Journal* 102(2): 1–24.

Cortes, V. (2006). Teaching Lexical Bundles in the Disciplines: An Example from a Writing Intensive History Class. *Linguistics and Education* 17: 391–406.

Coxhead, A. (2000). A New Academic Word List. *TESOL Quarterly* 34(2): 213–38.

Coxhead, A. and Byrd, P. (2007). Preparing Writing Teachers to Teach the Vocabulary and Grammar of Academic Prose. *Journal of Second Language Writing* 16(3): 129–47.

Creese, A. and Blackledge, A. (2010). Translanguaging in the Bilingual Classroom: A Pedagogy for Learning and Teaching? *Modern Language Journal* 94(1): 103–15.

Crystal, D. (2012). *English as a Global Language*. Cambridge: Cambridge University Press.

Deleuze, G. and Guattari, F. (1987). *A Thousand Plateaus*. Minneapolis: University of Minnesota Press.

Delpit, L. (1995). *Other People's Children: Cultural Conflict in the Classroom*. New York: The Press.

Donahue, C. (2018). Rhetorical and Linguistic Flexibility: Valuing Heterogeneity in Academic Writing Education. In X. You (ed.) *Transnational Writing Education: Theory, History, and Practice*. London: Routledge. 21–40.

Duff, P. A. (2003). Intertextuality and Hybrid Discourses: The Infusion of Pop Culture in Educational Discourse. *Linguistics and Education* 14(3): 231–76.

Elbow, P. (1999). Inviting the Mother Tongue: Beyond "Mistakes," "Bad English," and "Wrong English." *Journal of Advanced Composition* 19(2): 359–88.

Flores, N. (2013). The Unexamined Relationship between Neoliberalism and Plurilingualism: A Cautionary Tale. *TESOL Quarterly* 47(3): 500–20.
Fraiberg, S., Wang, X. and You, X. (2017). *Inventing the World Grant University: Chinese International Students' Mobilities, Literacies, and Identities*. Logan: Utah State University Press.
Fox, H. (2002). Being an Ally. In C. Schroeder, H. Fox and P. Bizzell (eds.) *ALT DIS: Alternative Discourses and the Academy*. Portsmouth, NH: Boynton. 57–67.
Gee, J. P. (2015). *Social Linguistics and Literacies: Ideology in Discourses*, 5th ed. New York: Routledge.
Gevers, J. (2018). Translingualism Revisited: Language Difference and Hybridity in L2 Writing. *Journal of Second Language Writing* 40: 73–83.
Haneda, M. (2014). From Academic Language to Academic Communication. *Linguistics and Education* 26: 126–35.
Heath, S. B. (1983). *Ways with Words: Language, Life, and Work in Communities and Classrooms*. Cambridge: Cambridge University Press.
Heller, V. and Morek, M. (2015). Academic Discourse as Situated Practice: An Introduction. *Linguistics and Education* 31: 174–86.
Heng Hartse, J. and Kubota, R. (2014). Pluralizing English? Variation in High-Stakes Academic Writing. *Journal of Second Language Writing* 24: 71–82.
Horner, B., Lu, M., Royster, J. J. and Trimbur, J. (2011). Language Difference in Writing: Toward a Translingual Approach. *College English* 73(3): 303–21.
Horner, B. and Tetreault, L. (eds.) (2017). *Crossing Divides: Exploring Translingual Writing Pedagogies and Programs*. Boulder: University Press of Colorado.
Hyland, K. (2002). Specificity Revisited: How Far Should We Go Now? *English for Specific Purposes* 21(4): 385–95.
  (2004). *Disciplinary Discourses*. Ann Arbor: University of Michigan Press.
  (2009). *Academic Discourse: English in a Global Context*. London: Continuum.
Ivanic, R. (2009). Bringing Literacy Studies into Research on Learning across the Curriculum. In M. Baynham and M. Prinsloo (eds.) *The Future of Literacy Studies*. Basingstoke: Palgrave Macmillan. 100–22.
Jenkins, J. (2011). Accommodating (to) ELF in the International University. *Journal of Pragmatics* 43(4): 926–36.
Johns, A. and Snow, M. A. (eds.) (2006). Special Issue: Academic English in Secondary Schools. *Journal of English for Academic Purposes* 5(4).
Kachru, B. B. (1986). *The Alchemy of English: The Spread, Functions and Models of Non-native Englishes*. Oxford: Pergamon.
Kress, G. R. (2010). *Multimodality: A Social Semiotic Approach to Contemporary Communication*. London: Routledge.
Kubota, R. (2014). The Multi/Plural Turn, Postcolonial Theory, and Neoliberal Multiculturalism. *Applied Linguistics* 33: 1–22.
Kunitz, S. and Markee, N. (2017). Understanding the Fuzzy Borders of Context in Conversation Analysis and Ethnography. In S. Wortham,

D. Kim and S. May (eds.) *Discourse and Education*, 3rd ed. Heidelberg: Springer. 15–27.

Kusters, A., Spotti, M., Swanwick, R. and Tapio, E. (2017). Beyond Languages, Beyond Modalities: Transforming the Study of Semiotic Repertoires. *International Journal of Multilingualism* 14(3): 219–32.

Latour, B. (2005). *Reassembling the Social: An Introduction to Actor-Network-Theory*. Oxford: Oxford University Press.

Lave, J. and Wenger, E. (1991). *Situated Learning: Legitimate Peripheral Participation*. New York: Cambridge University Press.

Lee, E. (2017). *Translingual Disposition, Negotiation Practices, and Rhetorical Attunement: Multilingual Writers Learning of Academic Writing*. Unpublished PhD dissertation, Pennsylvania State University.

Lee, J. W. (2017). *The Politics of Translingualism: After Englishes*. New York: Routledge.

Leonard, R. L. (2014). Multilingual Writing as Rhetorical Attunement. *College English* 76(3): 227–47.

Lillis, T. M. and Curry, M. J. (2010). *Academic Writing in a Global Context: The Politics and Practices of Publishing in English*. Abingdon: Routledge.

Lyons, S. R. (2000). Rhetorical Sovereignty: What Do American Indians Want from Writing? *College Composition and Communication* 51(3): 447–68.

Lu, M.-Z. (1994). Professing Multiculturalism: The Politics of Style in the Contact Zone. *College Composition and Communication* 45(4): 442–58.

Matsuda, P. K. (2014). The Lure of Translingual Writing. *PMLA* 129(3): 478–83.

Matsuda, A. and Matsuda, P. K. (2010). World Englishes and the Teaching of Writing. *TESOL Quarterly* 44(2): 369–74.

Meunier, F. and Granger, S. (eds.) (2008). *Phraseology in Foreign Language Learning and Teaching*. Amsterdam/Philadelphia: John Benjamins.

Molle, D. and Prior, P. (2008). Multimodal Genre Systems in EAP Writing Pedagogy: Reflecting on a Needs Analysis. *TESOL Quarterly* 42(4): 541–66.

Myers, G. (1990). *Writing Biology: Texts in the Social Construction of Scientific Knowledge*. Madison: University of Wisconsin Press.

Paltridge, B., Starfield, S. and Tardy, C. (2016). *Ethnographic Perspective on Academic Writing*. Oxford: Oxford University Press.

Pigg, S. (2014). Emplacing Mobile Composing Habits: A Study of Academic Writing in Networked Social Spaces. *College English* 66(2): 250–75.

Prior, P. (1998). *Writing/Disciplinarity: A Sociohistoric Account of Literate Activity in the Academy*. Mahwah, NJ: Lawrence Erlbaum Associates.

Rickert, T. (2013). *Ambient Rhetoric*. Pittsburgh, PA: University of Pittsburgh Press.

Royster, J. J. (2002). Academic Discourse or Small Boats on a Big Sea. In C. Schroeder, H. Fox and P. Bizzell (eds.) *ALT DIS: Alternative Discourses and the Academy*. Portsmouth, NH: Boynton/Cook. 23–30.

Schleppegrell, M. J. (2004). *The Language of Schooling: A Functional Linguistics Approach*. Mahwah, NJ: Lawrence Erlbaum Associates.

Schreiber, B. R. and Watson, M. (2018). Translingualism≠Code-Meshing: A Response to Gevers' "Translingualism Revisited." *Journal of Second Language Writing* 42: 94–7.

Schreiber, B. R. and Worden, D. (2019). "Nameless, Faceless People": How Other Teachers' Expectations Influence Our Pedagogy. *Composition Studies* 47(1): 57–72.

Schroeder, C., Fox, H. and Bizzell, P. (eds.) (2002). *ALT DIS: Alternative Discourses and the Academy*. Portsmouth, NH: Boynton/Cook.

Seidlhofer, B. (2011). *Understanding English as a Lingua Franca*. Oxford: Oxford University Press.

Shipka, J. (2016). Transmodality in/and Processes of Making: Changing Dispositions and Practice. *College English* 78(3): 250–7.

Street, B. (1984). *Literacy in Theory and Practice*. Cambridge: Cambridge University Press.

(1998). New Literacies in Theory and Practice: What Are the Implications for Language in Education? *Linguistics and Education* 10(1): 1–24.

(2014). New Literacies, New Times: Developments in Literacy Studies. In N. H. Hornberger (ed.) *Encyclopedia of Language and Education*. New York: Springer.

Street, G. and Besnier, N. (1994). Aspects of Literacy. In T. Ingold (ed.) *Companion Encyclopedia of Anthropology: Humanity, Culture, and Social Life*. London: Routledge. 527–62.

Swales, J. (1990). *Genre Analysis: English in Academic and Research Settings*. Cambridge: Cambridge University Press.

(1996). Occluded Genres in the Academy: The Case of the Submission Letter. In E. Ventola and A. Mauranen (eds.) *Academic Writing: Intercultural and Textual Issues*. Philadelphia, PA: John Benjamin. 45–58.

Swales, J. M. and Feak, C. (2000). *English in Today's Research World: A Writer's Guide*. Ann Arbor: Michigan University Press.

Tardy, C. M. (2011). The History and Future of Genre in Second Language Writing. *Journal of Second Language Writing* 20(1): 1–5.

(2015). Discourses of Internationalization and Diversity in US Universities and Writing Programs. In D. Martins (ed.) *Transnational Writing Program Administration*. Logan: Utah State University Press. 243–64.

(2016). *Beyond Convention: Genre Innovation in Academic Writing*. Ann Arbor: University of Michigan Press.

Thaiss, C. and Zawacki, T. M. (2002). Questioning Alternative Discourses: Reports from across the Disciplines. In C. Schroeder, H. Fox and P. Bizzell (eds.) *ALT DIS: Alternative Discourses and the Academy*. Portsmouth, NH: Boynton/Cook. 80–96.

Tomasello, M. (1999). *The Cultural Origin of Human Cognition*. Cambridge, MA/London: Harvard University Press.

Toohey, K. and Dagenais, D. (2015). "That Sounds So Cool": Entanglements of Children, Digital Tools and Literacy Practices. *TESOL Quarterly* 49(3): 461–85.

Vygotsky, L. S. (1999). Tool and Sign in the Development of the Child. In R. W. Rieber (ed.) *The Collected Works of L. S. Vygotsky, Volume 6: Scientific Legacy*. New York: Kluwer Academic/Plenum. 3–68.

Weber, J.-J. (2001). A Concordance- and Genre-Informed Approach to ESP Essay Writing. *ELT Journal* 55(1): 14–20.

Young, V. (2004). Your Average Nigga. *College Composition and Communication* 55: 693–715.

Young, V. A., Barrett, R., Young-Rivera, Y. and Lovejoy, K. B. (2014). *Other People's English: Code-Meshing, Code-Switching, and African American Literacy*. New York: Teachers College Press.

Part V

Ethics, Inequality and Inclusion

Introduction

The chapters in this section are generally focused on ways in which discourse studies deal with social and moral problems both in society and in research. Questions regarding the relationship between discourse and social issues have always been at the core of many areas of discourse studies. The pursuit of the right to recognition of the discursive practices and cultural traditions of minority groups such as indigenous communities has been central to the work of anthropologists such as Dell Hymes (1981) and Jane Hill (1995) who painstakingly described the styles of speaking and linguistic resources of different indigenous groups. In sociolinguistics, Labov (1972) devoted much research to studying and highlighting the discursive and linguistic skills of African Americans. The negative impact of differences in the use of communicative resources on reciprocal understandings between members of different ethnic communities in interaction was a main preoccupation for John Gumperz (1982) and the thrust for the development of his theory about contextualization. The tradition of critical discourse analysis (Fairclough 1989; Wodak and Meyer 2009) was founded on the premise that discourse studies need to reveal the mechanisms through which discourses contribute to the dominance and maintenance of mainstream ideologies, unequal power relations and processes. These are just a few examples of the many ways in which prominent discourse analysts and traditions have engaged with inequality and social justice. What has changed in our time, a change that is reflected in the chapters collected in this section, is the fact that awareness of the relevance of ethics questions in discourse studies has been steadily growing. In addition, there has been a decisive shift away from studying the characteristics of the discourses used in perpetrating social injustice with a focus on dominant classes and outlets; more recently, studies have been moving toward analyses of how discursive processes and practices concretely participate in the reproduction of ideologies and conditions that sustain inequalities, both in institutional encounters and in everyday communication, and on how these meanings are negotiated. The chapters also reflect the further problematization of research and analytical issues connected to ethics and social justice in a world characterized by mobility and instability.

Authors deal with two main questions. One relates to how to approach the analysis of ways in which discourse and discursive practices foster or contest world inequalities; the second to how research practice can deal with inequalities and injustices and how it may contribute to expose or redress them. The first question points to discourse practices in the world outside academia, while the second interrogates the impact of academic discourses and practices on participants in research and/or social agents and processes.

The issue of the contributions of discourses to inequalities is investigated respectively in the domain of education in Chapters 23 by Lai and King and 26 by Lytra, in asylum seeking procedures in Chapter 25 by Shuman and Bohmer and in mundane talk in Chapter 24 by Zavala and Back. A perspective generally shared by the authors is that the relationships among discourse, social exclusion and inequalities need to be investigated through a close study of the interactive dimensions of the discursive practices that contribute to establishing and perpetrating social injustice.

In relation to the second problem, the potential contribution of researchers and research to inequality, issues that come to the forefront are the relationships between researchers and participants, the choice of methods for investigating situations where inequalities are produced, circulated and negotiated, and the neglect of potentially important research domains. Lai and King in Chapter 23 and Zavala and Back in 24 both pose the question of the relationship between structure and agency, by highlighting how structures such as ideologies cannot be understood independently of the social subjects who negotiate them in interaction. Talking about racial ideologies, Zavala and Back note in that respect: "If we define discourse as racist in terms of what it *does* and not what it *says*, racism is no longer defined by the content or the tropes alluded to during an interaction. Therefore, it is crucial to ask *who* hears certain linguistic forms and structures as racial: after all, racialization processes have to do more with the exercise of power than with what the speaker does or does not do" (p. 539).

All papers also deal with the issue, so prevalent in this handbook, of how the changing societal landscape of the twenty-first century has affected ways in which we look at social issues and moral dilemmas. For example, in Chapter 21 Hammersley notes the new challenges that working with virtual communities poses for ethics in research, and Wee in Chapter 22 discusses how mobility has affected our views of language rights and citizenship, while both Li and King in Chapter 23 and Lytra in Chapter 26 point to the importance of multimodal resources in research within educational environments when dealing with contemporary phenomena.

Chapter 21 is devoted to the role of ethics in research. **Hammersley** introduces a useful distinction between *epistemic and nonepistemic values*, that is, values related to the pursuit of knowledge (epistemic) and more general moral values that may be seen as affecting the relationships with participants (nonepistemic). Both influence the ways in which ethics considerations are applied to research. However, such sets of values are linked to very different principles of action: in the case of epistemic values, what takes priority is consideration of possible negative consequences for the research process, while in the second case (nonepistemic values) what is important are potential and actual effects of the research on other people. Hammersley discusses the clashes between these two sets of principles and some of the dilemmas that present themselves to the researcher, many of which have received and continue to receive much attention in discourse studies. In particular, the degree to which anonymity should be respected even in the face of opposition by participants, and the balance between respecting participants' feelings about how their speech is represented and following the research imperative of representing data in the most accurate way possible. Another amply debated issue to which Hammersley devotes attention is the problem of informed consent, which is becoming more and more salient, given the tightening of regulations of research in the humanities and social sciences by ethics boards. Hammersley discusses how, in some situations, seeking consent can hamper and even prevent the research taking place, and highlights practical difficulties in securing informed consent in certain environments such as online chat rooms and multi-player real-time virtual worlds. Finally, questions related to reciprocity include whether and how to compensate communities and individuals who participate in research. The approach that Hammersley proposes is grounded in common sense, and in the careful appraisal of specific situations, rather than being an all-or-nothing attitude based on abstract principles.

Central to **Wee**'s Chapter 22 is the relationship between three concepts: *migrants, citizenship* and *language rights*, and the implications of the way these relationships are defined for discourse studies. Wee argues that language rights for migrants cannot be understood as separate from the other two concepts because societies generally link the idea of specific individual rights (excluding the so-called universal human rights) to the nation-state. The existence of this connection explains why states continuously threaten the right of migrants since the latter are basically regarded as stateless. Wee discusses, however, how complex and contradictory definitions of the construct of migrant are, since mobile individuals leave their countries for a variety of reasons and the different statuses, situations and motivations that characterize them can hardly be captured by one general concept. Citizenship itself is not without contradictions as the right to be a citizen seems to be accorded depending on the interests of the states and as boundaries continuously shift in our contemporary world. Linguists and discourse analysts have tried to redress this situation of inequality in which migrants are stuck by recurring to the idea of defining what the linguistic rights of groups are. Wee's chapter is largely devoted to arguing against this approach since, in his words, there are serious issues involved in trying to identify those rights "by delimiting the contours of both the bearer of a language right and the object of the right" (p. 490). Indeed, from Wee's perspective, a discourse based on language rights presupposes that communities can be clearly identified by ethnic or territorial criteria and that their sets of linguistic resources can also be enumerated. Both premises are often unworkable (particularly in the case of migrants) and may lead to undesirable effects such as selectivity in defining one language variety as worthy of protection vis-à-vis others or essentialization of the characteristics of communities. The alternative proposed by Wee is the idea of "linguistic citizenship," defined by Heugh (2018: 75) as "the individual claim and exercise of the right of citizens to voice, to be heard, and to act upon whichever dimension of a person's linguistic repertoire as may be useful in circumstance or purpose."

Lai and King's Chapter 23 looks at how discourse studies have dealt with inequalities in education. The authors highlight the role of work in discourse in documenting how everyday classroom routines and cross-cultural differences contribute to marginalizing or alternatively legitimizing certain communicative styles and interactional participation structures and in demonstrating the power of both agency and structure in the construction of inclusion and exclusions. Research in discourse has also documented the impact of language policies on minorities and marginalized groups' access to education. Lai and King present some of the current dilemmas and debates within the field and trace emerging trends. As mentioned, they discuss the tension between stress on structure and that on agency in discourse studies. On one end of this continuum, there is the tendency of qualitative, interactive studies to emphasize the role of local practices, neglecting their links with higher processes of power and domination. On the other end, critical discourse studies have been accused of privileging deterministic social forces, thus failing to explain how social processes are negotiated at a local level.

In reviewing recent trends in the field, the authors highlight a shift from a focus on expected styles of speaking and ideologies deployed by teachers and students in relation to language and social categories, toward the divide between official policies regarding diversity and school practices. They also emphasize the increasing interest in the analysis of transmodal resources (for example in studies of the use of stylization to marginalize members of outer groups) and the more general tendency toward the use of multiple approaches and interdisciplinarity, together with close attention, to tackle the complexity of school-based research.

Zavala and Back, in Chapter 24, focus their contribution on discourses of racialization. Their approach to the issue is based on a view of linguistic racialization as a set of sociocultural processes "through which race – as an ideological dimension of human differentiation – comes to be imagined, produced and reified through language practices" (p. 529). The authors look both at how discourse constructs racialized views of the world (not necessarily by using racist categories but also by using indirect strategies) and at how linguistic categories are used to index race. The chapter constructs racism as something that is done through discourse practices in many different ways and is negotiated by different groups, including racialized minorities. Focus is then not on identity categories or fixed power relationships, as race is not seen as an inherent feature of the body but as a process of social differentiation that is embedded in specific spatiotemporal dimensions. The authors highlight the importance of research that works with indexical processes rather than with open racist discourses or the discriminatory use of racial categories. Such research includes work on "race talk," that is, talk that racializes individuals or communities without openly referring to race, or research that deals with the negotiation of ethnic and racial categories in different contexts. These analyses show that racial terms do not have stable meanings but are used by participants in the context of different positioning processes that can vary even at the individual level. However, the authors also point to the importance of the study of processes of enregisterment and their role in the fixation of the socially shared views about race and racial categories that form the basis of such interactional negotiations. At the same time, Zavala and Back note how recent research (particularly in raciolinguistics) highlights intersubjectivity, agency and emotions as central to racialization processes, thus further inviting the investigation of concrete social practices rather than ideological formations.

In Chapter 25, **Shuman and Bohmer** see discourse in action in the sense that narrative is examined in relation to how it participates in the fostering of social inequalities. The authors analyze the "conditions of production" of asylum seekers' narratives and the criteria that underlie their assessment. They bring to light the fact that such conditions already create a situation that is fraught with obstacles for asylum seekers, by looking, for example, at the roles that genre, mode of interaction, tellability, moral stance and coherence play in the evaluation of asylum seekers' narratives. Indeed, asylum seekers are required to produce cohesive and detailed stories even though the experiences they went through do not lend themselves to coherence and organization. Their recountings are judged based on expectations about what is possible and what is normal that are modeled from the lived experiences of people in receiving countries, not in countries of origin. Shuman and Bohmer underscore the different levels involved in the analysis of how asylum seekers' narratives enter into processes of inequality. At one level, they look at the concrete obstacles and hurdles that are posed to asylum seekers in narrating their experience; at another level, they underscore how the "internal logics" through which such narratives are assessed respond to a set of institutional discursive practices that shape the ways in which migrant voices are heard. Yet at another level, asylum seekers' narratives are part of a circulation of discourses that include the stories that are told by refugees and others before and during the asylum process, reports on and discussions of political asylum in the media, and legal and other policy discourses. Central to institutional and media discourses is what the authors call the "production of the suspicious subject," that is, a process through which asylum seekers are presumed guilty even before they produce their stories.

Finally, Chapter 26 by **Lytra** examines the relationships between discourse and religion in educational settings. Lytra notes how religion has played a marginal role in dominant discourses about education but, until recently, also in discursive studies of educational settings. An exception to this trend is represented by anthropologically oriented studies of religious literacy and socialization practices in everyday lives that have shown the central role played by religion in everyday settings.

In her contribution, Lytra argues for the need to redress this neglect, stating that discourse studies can gain a great deal of insight on both learning strategies and processes and the formation and negotiation of identities. Religion is seen in the chapter as a contested category and as a cultural practice embedded within sociohistorical and political contexts. For the discourse analyst, it constitutes a vast interdisciplinary field. One central area of investigation and debate in discourse studies has been the intersection of religion with the teaching of English as a global language. Indeed, while some scholars have pointed to the use of the teaching of English as a proselitizing enterprise by religious teachers, others have emphasized the complexity of teachers' investment in religious beliefs and their different ways of relating to their credo in their educational practice. Lytra critiques the almost exclusive focus of these studies on secular settings and points to religious schools as an important research setting given their number and influence in many parts of the world. Another area that has produced important insights is the investigation of ways in which identity, socialization, pedagogy and language policy are intertwined within local and global contexts and social processes such as gender differentiation, the fostering of ethnic identification and the strengthening of literacy in minority languages. New trends in the investigation of the nexus between religion and discourse point to the growing impact of religious practices for migrant populations and the significance of digital contexts for the study of how religion is negotiated and incorporated into both educational contexts and everyday life.

References

Fairclough, N. (1989). *Language and Power*. London: Longman.

Gumperz, J. (1982). *Discourse Strategies*. Cambridge: Cambridge University Press.

Heugh, K. (2018). Commentary: Linguistic Citizenship: Who Decides Whose Languages, Ideologies and Vocabulary Matter? In L. Lim, C. Stroud and L. Wee (eds.) *The Multilingual Citizen*. Bristol: Multilingual Matters. 174–89.

Hill. J. (1995). The Voices of Don Gabriel: Responsibility and Self in a Modern Mexicano Narrative. In D. Tedlock and B. Mannheim (eds.) *The Dialogic Emergence of Culture*. Urbana: University of Illinois Press. 97–147.

Hymes, D. (1981). *"In Vain I Tried to Tell You": Essays in Native American Ethnopoetics*. Philadelphia: University of Pennsylvania Press.

Labov, W. (1972). *Language in the Inner City: Studies in the Black English Vernacular*. Philadelphia: University of Pennsylvania Press. 354–96.

Wodak, R. and Meyer, M. (eds.) (2009). *Methods of Critical Discourse Analysis*, 2nd rev. ed. London: Sage.

21

Ethics and the Study of Discourse

Martyn Hammersley

21.1 Introduction

Attention to ethical issues is always important in carrying out research involving human beings, in the field of discourse studies as elsewhere. There is a longstanding literature on these issues, but discussion of them has been strongly shaped in recent decades by the spread of ethical regulation: "institutional review boards" or "research ethics committees" controlling what research can be pursued in order to reduce the risk of unethical practices. Equally important have been growing debates among researchers about the politics and ethics of their work.

21.2 Overview

Since discourse research can take a variety of forms, and is carried out across diverse types of geographical and social context, there will be some variation in the ethical considerations that need to be taken into account. Nevertheless, there are key values that apply to all research in this field, though they are by no means uncontentious.

I will begin by drawing a distinction between epistemic and nonepistemic values. Epistemic values relate to the pursuit of knowledge. In the past, it was widely assumed that the production of factual knowledge should serve as the only goal of academic research; indeed, the meaning of the term "research" is frequently *defined* in this way. However, there have been challenges to the priority given to epistemic values, and these challenges have been especially strong in recent times.

Nonepistemic values concern what is good or bad, right or wrong. One set of values of this kind has been central to much discussion of research ethics, relating primarily to the relationship between researcher and researched. This set includes minimizing harm, showing respect for autonomy and protecting privacy. I will discuss these values, and the types of ethical reasoning that underpin them, before going on to consider reciprocity, another nonepistemic value that informs some discussions of research ethics in the field of discourse studies. This last value connects with the relationships among research, advocacy and empowerment, topics that are central for some discourse researchers.

Nevertheless, my assumption will be that only epistemic values define the *goal* of research, even though nonepistemic ethical values are an essential constraint on its pursuit. Furthermore, I will argue that there is a *range* of other considerations that need to be taken into account in making research decisions, of a prudential kind; that values often conflict; and that good judgment is required, rather than the following of procedures (Kubanyiova 2008). At the same time, I will consider some influential views that challenge these assumptions. I will conclude by noting the problems that a more proceduralist approach, characteristic of much ethical regulation, can cause.

21.3 Epistemic Values

My starting point, then, is a distinction between *epistemic* values, which relate directly to the task of producing knowledge, and *nonepistemic* values, especially those that concern the relationship between researcher and researched. This distinction is important because it relates to significant disagreements about sociocultural research and ethical issues.

The main epistemic value is truth. If the goal of all forms of research is to produce knowledge, this requires commitment to the value of truth since, in general usage, for something to count as knowledge it must be taken to be true. There are complex philosophical issues surrounding the concept of truth, of course, and some researchers have adopted skeptical epistemological positions – for example under the headings of constructionism or poststructuralism.[1] Nevertheless, it is usually recognized that, in practice, researchers have an obligation to try to ensure that the knowledge claims they produce are true. For instance, while some discourse analysts deny that what people say should be taken as referring to phenomena that exist independently of their utterances, so that the validity of their accounts cannot be assessed, they nevertheless present their own analyses of discursive practices as true representations.

A second, closely related, epistemic value is justifiability. This demands that sufficient evidence be supplied in support of research conclusions. We can believe the truth without being justified in doing so; and we can be justified in believing something even though it is false. For instance, my

---

[1] For an excellent clarification of some of these issues, aimed at the field of education but applicable more generally, see Bridges 1999.

suspicion that academic publishing is now wholly motivated by calculations of profit or loss could be correct even though I do not have sufficient evidence to warrant it; and, while President Trump's mode of talk may be strong evidence for diagnosing a cognitive deficit, his claim to be a genius could still be true – after all, the relationship between linguistic and cognitive capacities is highly mediated.

A third epistemic value, of a rather different kind, concerns the degree of importance of the research questions being addressed. Commitment to this value arises from the fact that not *all* knowledge is worthwhile. It is of worth only if it refers to matters that are of interest to human beings. The most obvious case of such worth is where the issues addressed are key cultural, social or political problems. However, there are *degrees* of importance and there is likely to be disagreement about the relative priority of different issues at any particular time. Furthermore, there can be nonpragmatic relevance, arising from intellectual interest in puzzling features of sociocultural events and practices. Indeed, it has been argued that research motivated solely by intellectual concerns can nevertheless turn out to have great practical relevance. However value is to be judged, though, researchers have an obligation to pursue *worthwhile* knowledge.

The final epistemic value I will mention is feasibility: researchers are under an obligation to tackle questions to which they have a reasonable chance of finding true answers. Of course, what is feasible may change over time, partly as a result of technological developments (for instance, these have made making audio and even video recordings much easier, as well as creating online sites where novel forms of language use can be studied). What can be investigated effectively will also change as knowledge in a field increases. At the same time, commitment to this value must be sustained against a desire on the part of researchers themselves, and pressure from elsewhere, to address big issues whose investigation is not currently feasible.

Closely associated with these four epistemic values are what we can refer to as epistemic *virtues*. A virtue is a personal disposition that is desirable, in contrast to ones whose possession is undesirable (vices). Since Aristotle, it has been recognized that many virtues stand midway between extremes. So, we could say that it is an epistemic virtue for researchers to be neither overconfident nor underconfident in the truth of their conclusions. Similarly, researchers should be neither perfectionist nor cavalier in going about their work: the first is likely to result in the inquiry never being completed, while the second increases the chances that false conclusions will be reached.[2]

However, there are other epistemic virtues that do not seem to have the character of golden means. One of these would be honesty in reporting how the research was done. This is crucial if fraud and/or plagiarism are to

---

[2] For elaboration of the role of virtues in the context of research ethics, see Macfarlane 2008 and Emmerich 2018.

be avoided or minimized. Another could be a willingness to follow an argument wherever it leads, even if the conclusions are uncomfortable (though it is also a virtue to recognize that improbable conclusions may indicate that a false route has been taken). As a final example of an epistemic virtue, there is the willingness to engage with criticism of one's work by colleagues and to give it due weight. It is perhaps worth saying that these virtues are not always on full display amongst researchers.

As I noted earlier, it has been traditionally assumed that epistemic values define the character of academic research as a distinctive type of activity: in these terms, the sole operational goal of this activity should be the production of knowledge. However, this view has never gone entirely uncontested, and challenges to it have become particularly common in recent times. There have been several lines of criticism.

The first relates to the very possibility of knowledge. The fact that we can never be *absolutely* certain of the truth or falsity of factual claims is sometimes taken to imply that no knowledge is possible. It is seen as leading to a "crisis of representation" (see Clifford and Marcus 1986; Nöth 2003). Thus, it is not uncommon for researchers to avoid use of the words "truth," "true" and "fact," preferring euphemisms like "valid," "cogent," "sound" and "reliable." And where "truth" and "fact" *are* used, they are generally clothed in scare quotes, to distance the author from any commitment to what they imply. Yet some knowledge claims would be regarded by most of us as beyond all *reasonable* doubt (for example that English is the most commonly spoken language in North America, or that the rise of email, text messaging and social media has involved significantly changed patterns of written English). Furthermore, the fact that we can never know with absolute certainty whether a factual statement is true or false does not render these words unusable in their standard senses. Indeed, we would be very hard pressed in our everyday lives, as well as in doing research, to avoid using them or substitutes for them. This reflects the fact that a thoroughgoing epistemological skepticism is unsustainable. In short, while it is true that all factual claims are fallible, this does not mean that we cannot claim to be justified in believing that some are true and others false (Hammersley 2009a).

The other main line of criticism questions whether the production of knowledge (even that relevant to human concerns) has sufficient value to serve as the sole aim of inquiry (Cameron et al. 1992). In light of this, as Lewis (2018: 325) argues in the case of sociolinguistics, research is often conducted "with social change goals in mind, aiming to improve social conditions for participants in their research or for other members of a society." It may be argued that the production of knowledge, in itself, does not lead to any improvement in people's lives and that research must be pursued in a different way to ensure that it does. Thus, Lewis (2018) criticizes sociolinguists for failing to identify and adopt effective strategies for bringing about social change.[3] His argument, like that of many others, is that research must serve the interests of groups that are oppressed, exploited or marginalized, so as to reduce social inequality. Along the same lines, in the case of critical discourse analysis the task is to identify how particular discursive practices reproduce social divisions, *with a view to disrupting that process* (see Kress 1996: 15).

However, combining academic inquiry with practical or political goals creates serious dilemmas: if either type of goal is to be pursued in the most effective way possible, it must be treated as the priority, and this often opens up divergent courses of action – it cannot be assumed that the requirements of the two goals are in alignment (see Hammersley 1995, 2000, 2017). These tensions are evident in the history of "action research," where (in practice) the emphasis tends to fall on one or another component of that phrase (see Hammersley 2004). A likely result of seeking to serve a practical or political goal is an increased risk that the findings produced will be false: the true does not necessarily serve the good.

It is important, though, to distinguish the goal of research from the motives that researchers have for engaging in it or for researching particular topics. It is, of course, quite legitimate to do research because one believes that the knowledge produced can contribute to social improvement; it is only if the latter is taken to be the *goal* of inquiry that the threat of bias is likely to be increased, for the reason already outlined. For example, I may engage in research on discrimination against minority languages because I want to help reduce this, but if I collect and analyze data specifically to serve this goal I may be tempted to exaggerate the scale of discrimination, and to oversimplify its causes, because this will serve my political goal more effectively than a more cautious academic investigation. In summary, while potential bias is ever-present in social research, it is likely to be increased where the researcher is serving practical goals as well as seeking to produce knowledge.

21.4 Nonepistemic Values

There is a wide range of nonepistemic values, concerning what is the good life for human beings, or the good society, and what actions are right or wrong. However, discussions of research ethics have focused on a relatively small number of values, relating especially to researchers' treatment of the people they study. The most commonly discussed are: minimizing harm, respecting autonomy, protecting privacy, and

---

[3] For an assessment of this argument, see Hammersley 2018.

ensuring reciprocity. These values are normally employed in the evaluation of *actions*; retrospectively or prospectively. For example, in considering the adoption of a particular research method or strategy, we will often need to take account of ethical arguments. An extreme example is the case of covert research, which is widely judged unethical but has its justifications (see Roulet et al. 2017). It is important to emphasize, though, that none of these values, in itself, can tell us what should or should not be done in particular situations. This is because decisions must take account of *all* relevant values, epistemic and ethical, as well as of what is (or was) possible and prudent in the circumstances.

The values usually treated as central to research ethics mostly depend upon two influential modes of argument. One is to do with the consequences a decision or course of action is likely to have, or has had; these being evaluated as good or bad for the people directly affected and/or for others. This is often labeled *consequentialism*. An example would be the importance of maintaining confidentiality – of researchers not revealing who has said what – which stems largely from a concern about negative consequences for participants if they are revealed to be the source.

The other mode of argument, often given the label "deontological," concerns ideas about what forms of action are right *in themselves*, irrespective of whatever consequences they have had or are likely to have. For example, it may be argued that promises should not be broken, including those involved in initial contracts (implicit or explicit) between researcher and researched. Or it may be insisted that researchers should be completely honest, for instance in the information they provide to participants at the start of their research and subsequently. There is sometimes a tendency for researchers to be "economical with the truth"; and occasionally the information offered is misleading in significant respects, albeit perhaps for good consequentialist reasons. However, from a "deontological" point of view, this is likely to be judged illicit.

There has been much philosophical debate about these two approaches and about whether there is some superior alternative. However, most people in their everyday ethical evaluations probably employ both, and this includes researchers. In fact, it seems to me that a single consequentialist value (minimizing harm) and a single deontological value (respecting autonomy) cover between them a very large proportion of the ethical issues that researchers face in doing their work, in discourse studies and elsewhere. The third ethical value I mentioned, respecting privacy, seems reducible to the first two: we seek to protect people's privacy because not doing this may result in harm and/or because we believe that, as persons, they have a *right* to privacy, which relates to the value of autonomy. A fourth value – reciprocity – does *not* seem to be covered by these two values, and I will discuss this separately.

21.4.1 Minimizing Harm

There are different ways in which the issue of harm can arise in research. A study may involve an intervention that promises benefits but could also entail the risk of harm of particular kinds; as, for example, with some kinds of experimental or action research. While most discourse studies do not involve such interventions, the actions of researchers can still have unintended consequences that could be beneficial or harmful to participants: normal patterns of activity may be disrupted; attention could be focused on people who normally do not receive much, and this may be good or bad; information can be communicated that has a negative effect on people's reputations; and so on. A third way in which the issue of harm arises is when a researcher becomes aware of serious harm done to, or by, one or more of the people being studied, or by someone else. Here the researcher is, directly or indirectly, a witness to, rather than a cause of, harm. But questions nevertheless arise about whether and when a researcher should intervene, and if so how – the consequences for the people involved, including the victim(s), and also for the research (such as a threat to continued access) need to be taken into account here (unless we adopt an entirely deontological position).

I have formulated the value principle involved here as "*minimizing* harm" because avoiding *all* risk of *any* kind of harm is unrealistic. There are three component judgments involved in assessing harm: what the consequences of the action being evaluated have been or are likely to be, given that other factors are always involved; whether these consequences constitute benefit or harm, in what sense *and to what degree*; and, where the evaluation is prospective, what the *likelihood* of harmful consequences occurring is, and what is and is not an acceptable level of risk for different types and levels of harm. So, for example, in considering whether it would be ethical to study discourses in online "pro-ana" websites covertly (see Brotsky and Giles 2007; Hammersley and Treseder 2007), it is necessary to anticipate what consequences this might have, how likely these are, and how serious they would be.

The first of these judgments is factual in character, but it operates within a value-relevance framework relating to for what a researcher could and could not reasonably be deemed responsible. For example, what if the presentation of interim research findings on an organization to its members, in which examples of sexual innuendo that could amount to harassment were mentioned, is followed immediately by the sacking of those involved, even though they had not been named in the presentation? Assuming, for the moment, that their sacking constituted harm, could the researcher reasonably be held responsible for this? After all, precautions were taken to disguise their identities, and perhaps they were very likely to be dismissed anyway, so that the research presentation was simply a trigger or even an excuse to sack them. Judgments of this kind rely on necessarily rather speculative counterfactual assessments about what would have happened if the researcher had acted differently. It is also important to underline that, frequently, our judgments about these matters will be highly sensitive to what information we have available about the situation in which the action took place, or in which it will take place. Lack of such information, or inaccurate assumptions, is one reason why judgments made by research ethics committees about what would and would not be ethical, or standard protocols that purport to determine this, may often be mistaken.

The second type of judgment is also open to dispute. In the example just used, we could acknowledge that people losing their jobs has negative consequences for them without accepting that they have been harmed either by the researcher or even by the person who sacked them. For example, it may be argued that they caused harm to others and harmed themselves by doing what was reported by the researcher.

Finally, in relation to prospective evaluations, there is the issue of the *likelihood* that particular harms will occur. Once again, there can be differences in view about this, and about what is an acceptable level of risk.

So, there is often room for disagreement about what is and is not (would and would not be) harmful, as well as about who is (or could be) responsible for it, about what is minor and serious harm, and about what sorts of risk are acceptable. Such disagreement underpins many of the disputes about ethics amongst researchers and also their differences in attitude toward ethical regulation. Some commentators, of whom I am one, believe that the level of harm likely to result directly from most social research, especially that in discourse studies, is low, by comparison both with that involved, say, in medical trials and with the kinds of harm that people risk in many routine aspects of their everyday lives. Of course, this can easily lead to complacency, and this must be countered by judicious assessment of all the relevant considerations. This points to the fact that there are virtues associated with ethical as well as with epistemic values – above all, what Aristotle calls "phronesis," which can be translated here as "wise judgment." This is required in assessing the likelihood of different outcomes, as well as the benefits and costs they entail, and the implications of the values involved in their assessment.

The issue of harm can arise in relation to various aspects of the research process. For instance, research may deal with sensitive topics which can be distressing for participants and/or carry dangers for them (see Hydén 2008). At the same time, it may be important for them to have the opportunity to speak about these matters, and in ways that do not position them simply as victims. It should be added that what is sensitive, and why, is by no means always immediately obvious. So, there is a need for researchers both to anticipate sensitivities and to deal with them wisely when they arise. And this is particularly true where research deals with those, such as young children or elderly people, who may be regarded as especially vulnerable.[4]

In discourse studies, much research involves reliance on transcriptions of speech, and there are ethical as well as methodological questions surrounding how this is done – particularly how people's speech is represented in extracts included in research publications (see Kingston 2020). Particular ways of transcribing people's speech may be viewed as carrying implications about their social status or personal characteristics; and these can cause embarrassment or possibly even more serious consequences if the person can be identified. There are several aspects to this: decisions about whether to represent the words spoken in standard orthography or to change them to capture the distinctiveness of pronunciation; whether to present the order of words *as spoken* or to modify this to satisfy the demands of standard syntax; whether to represent hesitations, false starts and repetitions. In much discourse research, there would be a strong commitment to avoid "tidying up" the orality of the text, for methodological but perhaps also for ethical reasons – for instance, because this would falsely imply the superiority of standard forms. However, research participants will not always share the same views as researchers about these matters. Participants may object to having their speech represented "with all its warts," especially when the surrounding text is in formal academic language.

A third issue concerns whether the data obtained, or analysis of it, should be "fed back" to participants. It is sometimes argued that they have a right to this. However, this is open to question and it must be remembered that feeding back information can sometimes have undesirable effects. Nor can the researcher control what use is made of information provided (as in the example used earlier where people were sacked). This is a particular problem where data or analyses are about *multiple* participants, since here participants are given access to information about one another.

Another issue is whether to anonymize participants in research reports. This is often done routinely by researchers, largely to reduce the risk of harm. However, some participants may wish to speak through the research in their own names (Thomas-Hughes 2018) and people sometimes find it distressing to see their own words pseudonymized (Grinyer 2002). Furthermore, in studying some types of people – for instance, politicians – it may be impossible to disguise them.

Of course, benefits as well as harms can result from research: people may enjoy their contacts with researchers or they may value the research itself: speakers of a minority language could welcome the fact that it is treated as worthy of study, for example. This means that it may be

---

[4] Though care is needed in handling this concept of vulnerability: see van den Hoonaard 2018.

necessary to "weigh" costs against benefits; though this cannot be done mechanically or with precision. Furthermore, this process of "weighing" may be necessary not only as regards the consequences for the people being studied but also for what would be in the general interest. In this, there will need to be an assessment of the value of the research results that are likely to be produced. Of course, any such judgment will itself be uncertain. Moreover, if too much is expected of research in terms of the impact of its findings, it may be that no research will be judged warranted, given its limits and that some costs are always involved.

All that can reasonably be expected of researchers is that they try to make the best judgments they can about actual or likely harm and benefit, and that they are able to justify or excuse their actions in these terms with reasonable cogency.

21.4.2 Respecting Autonomy

An implication often derived from the principle that people's autonomy ought to be respected is that they should be able to choose whether or not they supply data and/or are included within the focus of a study; and perhaps also that they ought to be able to withdraw from a study at any time, and in doing so withdraw all of the data about themselves. However, interpretations of this value are sometimes extended beyond this to suggest that people have a right to participate in the decision-making associated with any research project that includes them: that research should be carried out *with* them rather than *on* them; on the grounds that the latter amounts to an infringement of their right to control their own lives.

As regards the issue of informed consent, a first question is whether consent is always necessary. It may *not* be needed when collecting data that are publicly available, whether in physical contexts – in bars or train carriages, for example – or in online sites that are openly accessible. Indeed, some have argued that covert research can be legitimate even when studying *private* settings, especially where access is likely to be refused or seeking it will distort the data, *so long as what can be discovered promises to be of sufficient value* (see Calvey 2017).[5] However, there are often prudential reasons for seeking consent even when observing and recording people in public settings. For example, if one tries to video-record social interaction in a café, staff or security personnel may intervene and there could be a hostile reaction from those being observed. So, it may often be prudent to obtain permission (from at least some of those involved), irrespective of any ethical considerations. On the other hand, in some contexts (for example online chat rooms or multi-player real-time virtual worlds) gaining informed consent may be difficult or impossible,

---

[5] The distinction between what is private and what is public is not a straightforward one, perhaps especially online: see Whiteman 2012: ch 3; Giaxoglou 2017.

even if it is felt to be ethically appropriate, because there is a shifting population of participants, because seeking consent would seriously disrupt group activity, and/or because it turns out to be impossible to contact the people concerned (see Giaxoglou 2017: 237–8).

Even where initial access has been negotiated, questions may arise about whether consent should be sought for collecting particular kinds of data. An example is Harvey's (1992) clandestine recording of the conversations of Peruvian peasants during social rounds of drinking. This could be regarded as a breach of the principle of respecting autonomy; though, even if this is true, it does not necessarily follow that it was unethical or the wrong decision. Despite misgivings, she decided that verbatim recording was essential for her research. More generally, researchers do not usually indicate to participants, in detail, what data are being collected and what is to be done with it. And there can be good reasons for this.

In the case of interviews, gaining consent is generally unavoidable; whether to seek consent is not therefore, first and foremost, an ethical matter. But ethical questions *do* arise regarding what would count as *informed* and *free* consent. In providing information about the research, judgment has to be made about what is important for people to know, and this is not always easy to decide. Furthermore, initially, there will often be much that the researcher her- or himself does not yet know about what the investigation will involve, so there is a limit to the information that can be provided. Furthermore, people may not tolerate lengthy descriptions of the research or bother to read the description on a consent form. Alcadipani's experience is by no means unusual:

> I was very concerned to secure informed consent from individuals as the research progressed. In practice, this proved very difficult to achieve in any meaningful way; securing informed consent from ... 10 busy managers at the outset of each meeting, posed a range of difficulties. After a few weeks in the field, a customary response to requests for consent was "F*ck off mate, you always ask this sh*t. Of course I agree, pal."
> (Alcadipani and Hodgson 2009:135–6)

There is also the problem that participants may fail to understand the information provided, or they may consent (or refuse to consent) for reasons that are not well founded. For example, in doing research on tribunals hearing refugees' claims for asylum, Tomkinson (2015: 33) discovered that, despite having fluent English, a participant had not understood the account provided: he had assumed that she was an intern working for his lawyer rather than a researcher. The issue that then arose was: could she use evidence from his hearing in her research?

There may also be aspects of the research that it is undesirable to disclose, for instance because doing so could affect participants' behavior in ways that would threaten the validity of the findings. For instance, to tell teachers that one is interested in whether they normally ask girls as many questions as boys in the classroom could produce false results, since they may make an effort (consciously or unconsciously) to equalize their interactions in this respect when being observed (but see Spender 1982: 56). A slightly different issue arises where the focus of analysis will not be on the substantive matters about which people are being questioned in interviews but rather on *the language they use*, for instance the discourses they deploy. Here, again, explaining the focus to participants prior to interviews could significantly affect the data. Eckert (2013: 15) comments: "Sociolinguists prefer to downplay their interest in language in order to elicit as unselfconscious speech as possible." Moreover, this problem takes on a particularly sharp form in relation to studies of discourse adopting a constructionist perspective, since participants are unlikely to share that perspective: while the analyst may treat the phenomena participants talk about as constituted in and through their talk, *they* are unlikely to regard those phenomena this way (see Hammersley 2014).

Ethical considerations also arise about whether participants' consent decisions have been subject to illegitimate constraint. While in interview situations where the researcher has recruited the participants this can usually be avoided, the situation is very different where participants are encountered in an organizational context to which the researcher has negotiated access. Here it is often hard to know what pressures operate on members of the organization, and attempts to secure their informed consent may even be regarded as disrespecting or challenging the authority of the gatekeeper. Similar problems can arise in studying small, highly integrated communities.

It is also important to recognize that seeking informed consent, and particularly allowing subsequent withdrawal, can cause serious methodological difficulties in carrying out research. For example, in group contexts, if one person refuses to be observed this may mean that even those who *have* consented cannot be observed. Similarly, if consent is withdrawn by one person during observation, or after it has taken place, the data of all participants involved on that occasion may have to be discarded. Much the same is true with group interviews and focus groups.

Given all this, there are sometimes grounds for *not* seeking informed consent. It should not be assumed that obtaining this is essential: whether it is required is a matter of judgment *in context*. Autonomy is not an all-or-nothing matter, and this principle must be weighed against others. Of course, this is a controversial conclusion to reach. It is at odds with some views of ethics, usually deontological in character, that would treat gaining informed consent as an absolute requirement, not one that can legitimately be compromised.

There is also the question of what people are consenting *to* when they agree to be involved in a research project. One issue here concerns ownership of the data. Does giving consent for data to be collected mean assigning to the researcher the right to use it in any way he or she sees fit? If not, must the researcher renegotiate new uses of the data each time? Indeed, it is sometimes argued that people have a right to control *any* uses to which what they say or write is put, as regards both face-to-face interview data and online material. There are sharply contrasting views here. Many years ago, Lincoln and Guba (1989: 236) argued that "when participants do not 'own' the data they have furnished about themselves, they have been robbed of some essential element of dignity, in addition to having been abandoned in harm's way." However, others do not take this view. Eckert (2013: 12) indicates a reason for this in one particular kind of study:

> Linguists, particularly those working on endangered languages, generally feel a responsibility to the language itself, as a living, and all too often a dying, practice. This sense of responsibility is often shared with the communities who speak (or spoke) the language, opening possibilities for fruitful collaborations. But linguists' dependence on, and commitment to, linguistic diversity also leads us to a view of language and languages as the property not just of their speakers, but of humankind more generally. The analogy between linguistic and biological diversity intensifies this view, putting the linguist in the position of righteous activist.

It is also worth noting that sometimes researchers will need to resist efforts by powerful groups, such as governments or commercial companies, to control the use of information about them, blocking inquiry or seeking to steer it for their own purposes – and, in such contexts, the principle of informed consent may be manipulated by them for this purpose.

There are some other reasons for questioning the idea that people have a right to control the data they produce. One is that data are coproduced (the researcher also plays a role). Furthermore, "ownership" of what is said is not usually respected in people's ordinary social interactions, where there is much reporting of others' comments, sharing of personal emails and text messages, etc. Also relevant are the severe practical difficulties that treating participants as owning data would cause for many kinds of research.

As I noted earlier, some commentators regard respect for autonomy as requiring that people be invited to participate in the decision-making process of any research project studying them – so that research is carried out "with" rather than "on" them. This is hard to justify *as a general principle*, which would require it to be applied not just in studying marginalized groups with whom we sympathize but also when investigating powerful organizations, people committed to racist ideology, etc. Moreover, there are genuine questions to be asked about whether the researcher can legitimately delegate responsibility for the proper pursuit of research to others. Such "inclusion" can make it more difficult, sometimes perhaps even impossible, for researchers to exercise their epistemic, and for that matter their ethical, responsibilities. Furthermore, usually, people's participation or nonparticipation in a research project is *insignificant* for any assessment of the extent to which they are in control of their own lives; and, indeed, many participants will not want to spend time engaging in research decision-making. All this is not to deny that there may be circumstances where involving participants in this way would be ethical or prudent.

21.4.3 Reciprocity

Central to the value of reciprocity is the requirement that participants are not exploited or oppressed by the researcher. The key idea here, often, is that, since researchers benefit from doing research (being paid to do it, gaining an educational qualification as a result, and/or furthering their careers through publications based on it), so too should the participants. An example is Labov's (1982: 173) "principle of the debt incurred," which he formulates thus: "An investigator who has obtained linguistic data from members of a speech community has an obligation to make knowledge of that data available to the community, when it has need of it." However, often researchers seek to maintain reciprocity by a variety of other means, including disclosing information about themselves in a way that partially mirrors what they have asked of informants, providing minor services, and paying for participation.

Some discussions of the value of reciprocity adopt a relatively narrow focus, concerned with what participants are being requested to do (that they would not otherwise do); what entitlements they are granting to the researcher; whether they are significantly deprived (in some respect) in absolute terms or compared to other people; and what benefits they gain from participation in the research (for example an enhanced sense that they and their activities are important, or an opportunity to talk about themselves and what they do). There can, of course, be variation in each of these matters across research projects and indeed across participants within the same project.

A frequently discussed issue is whether participants should be paid for their participation. Sometimes there are strong prudential reasons for doing this: people may not participate otherwise. But there can also be ethical reasons, for instance where what the research requires of them is especially demanding or because they are impoverished. However, there are some important issues to be resolved here: whether the level of pay that can be offered (or *any* offer of payment) would be considered insulting; whether payments can be equitable, respecting the different levels of contribution by participants; and whether paying people will shape their behavior in ways that could threaten the validity of the research findings (for instance, leading them to change their normal behavior significantly or even to invent data).

Sometimes arguments about reciprocity take a more radical turn, claiming that the research relationship involves an illegitimate power imbalance, since it is researchers who make the decisions about what is to be studied, how, where and when; as well as how the findings will be produced and disseminated. As a result, it is argued, researchers produce conclusions that necessarily reflect not only their own personal and social characteristics but also the assumptions characteristic of social research as an institution, viewed as part of a wider power system. This underpins both Cameron et al.'s (1992) influential argument that research should empower the people studied and the widespread advocacy of "participatory" or "inclusive" forms of research (see Nind 2014).

A third issue is whether researchers should serve as advocates on behalf of the people whose discourse is being studied. This is sometimes requested by these people themselves, but researchers may also be inclined to take on this role because they believe that the issue of reciprocity must be viewed in a broader context. For example, where a researcher from the global North is carrying out research in the global South, or a researcher from an ethnic majority is doing research involving people from ethnic minorities, or where a man is doing research involving women, it is sometimes argued that the research must work to counter the social inequalities these people suffer. Here the task becomes to expose and criticize existing power relations and perhaps to work with others to destabilize them. At the same time, questions have been raised about whether it is legitimate to speak "on behalf" of those who are subordinated or marginalized (Gray 1990; Alcoff 1991–2). One response to this has been to suggest that the task of the researcher is to enable members of such groups to speak on their own behalf.

Even in relation to what I have referred to as the narrow view of reciprocity, there are many difficult issues involved, and it would be unwise to suggest that any single conclusion is the only justifiable one. That research should not involve gross exploitation would probably be generally agreed, but there is more variation in views about what is and is not fair as regards research relations, including about whether participants should be paid. Furthermore, the notions of social justice involved in arguments about the exploitative character of research are often vague and problematic. As I noted, one of these is the idea that there is an imbalance of power that must be equalized. But the problem is that the word "power," used in abstract, is close to meaningless: what is at issue is always the power to do particular things. So, while it is true that researchers have power in relation to participants and informants in some respects – including in how the latter are represented in the research – they by no means always have greater power than the people they study in other respects. In particular, they are often dependent upon the granting of access and agreement for the research to take place, and usually do not control what goes on in the situations they study. Moreover, even when the people studied do not have much control over economic and political resources in society, neither (usually) do researchers. And research is sometimes carried out on groups that *are* powerful in this sense.

There are also problems with arguments for equalizing power relations, as advocated in "participatory" or "inclusive" inquiry of various kinds. There is a sense in which to equalize power is to eliminate it; and without power of some kind nothing will get done. As this suggests, power is not intrinsically bad: it can be enabling, not just constraining (and some constraints are, in any case, justifiable). Whether the exercise of power is bad depends upon whether or not it is legitimate, what it is used to do, etc. – so we are forced to address the question of what types of power, exercised in what ways and by whom, are and are not desirable (and from what perspective)? My point is that equalizing power within the research relationship is by no means obviously desirable.

As regards advocacy, while there are circumstances where providing this, or facilitating people in representing themselves, would be appropriate, in my view it is essential to maintain a clear distinction between doing this and carrying out research – because the goals of these activities are different. Advocacy may be an important political task, but it is not the same as research. While there seems to be a temptation for some to redefine the goal of research to include it (see, for instance, Lewis 2018), this amounts to abandoning the distinctive mission of research or at least introducing competing priorities. Furthermore, the complexities of advocacy must not be overlooked: groups are rarely entirely homogeneous in their interests and attitudes, and the question of what is in whose interests, or in the common interest, is always difficult to resolve and frequently controversial (Hastrup and Elsass 1990). Nor will particular participants, aided by the researcher, necessarily represent even their own interests effectively.

As I noted, commitment to engaging in advocacy often stems from viewing the research relationship in a broad context concerned with social divisions in the wider society or globally, and researchers must certainly take account of relevant aspects of this context when they are carrying out their work. However, context is always open to multiple, and frequently contested, descriptions – and care must be taken not to adopt too crude an interpretation of it. Even where participants view research as implicated in general patterns of social injustice, domination, or oppression, their interpretation of this will not necessarily correspond to that of the researcher. For instance, opposition to "Western imperialism" can be grounded in a variety of ideologies, religious as well as secular, populist as well as democratic, not all of which should be judged desirable or progressive. Similarly, there are different versions of feminism and different attitudes toward it on the part of women. Furthermore, most research does not have any significant effect on wider social structures, in either reinforcing or undermining them, despite many researchers' belief that this is the case.

My purpose in underlining these complexities is not to deny that researchers ought to be aware of issues of social justice relating to the research relationship and of how their research connects with wider power structures, such as unjust social divisions and oppressive institutional arrangements. But here, as with the other values I have discussed, there is a danger of what can be referred to as moralism (Hammersley and Traianou 2011, 2012): of distorting the practice of research in order to make it serve other purposes, or requiring it to satisfy excessive requirements framed in terms of nonepistemic values.

21.5 Ethical Regulation

As I noted at the beginning of this chapter, in the past few decades, across many countries, social research, including that concerned with studying discourse, has come under processes of ethical regulation. It is important to note that these usually take a mandatory and preemptive form: researchers are required to submit research proposals to institutional review boards (IRBs) or research ethics committees (RECs) who then decide whether or not the research can go ahead; or, at least, what changes in plan are necessary for this to be allowed. There has been a great deal of debate about the warrant for this type of regulation and about its effects on research (see, for instance, van den Hoonard and Hamilton 2016). Here I can do no more than summarize some of the arguments that have been presented.

One question concerns whether, prior to the introduction of regulation, social research, including that in the field of discourse studies, was seriously defective in ethical terms. As should be clear from the discussion in this chapter, this is a question that could receive very different answers depending upon the particular approach to ethical issues taken. However, it is a striking fact that the regime of preemptive ethical regulation was not extended to social research because the latter had been shown to be ethically deficient, but largely to allow organizations, such as funding bodies or universities, to deflect potential legal liability for any problems caused by research they had sponsored (Dingwall 2008).

A second issue is whether a *preemptive* regulatory regime is warranted, as against, say, a system in which complaints about unethical behavior on the part of researchers would be referred to a body that could adjudicate on them and administer penalties for ethical offenses (as is the case with doctors). It has been argued that a preemptive regime infringes academic freedom, conceived not just in terms of the proper autonomy of researchers but also as a requirement if academic research is to be done well (Hammersley 2009b). Equally important is that much research in the discourse field adopts an emergent, flexible process of research design, so that research proposals supplied to an IRB/REC are unlikely to be accurate, at least in their details. One implication of this is that it may be necessary to gain agreement from the relevant ethics committee every time there is deviation from the initial plan, as Bruce et al. (2016: 4–5) found in their longitudinal narrative study of people with life-threatening illnesses. At the same time, this may seriously disrupt the research process.

One of the most common complaints is that the type of regulatory regime now in operation foreshortens the time available for actually carrying out projects, thereby potentially damaging their quality. Equally, it can lead to researchers becoming preoccupied with whether or not what they propose will meet the requirements of the relevant IRB or REC, rather than considering ethical issues in their own terms.

A final point is that, by its very nature, a preemptive regulatory regime tends to operate on the basis of a proceduralist notion of ethics; in other words, ethical behavior is interpreted as compliance with rules.[6] An example would be the widespread treatment of informed consent as a *requirement*, one that is to be waived only under very special circumstances, if at all. The problem with this is not just that, as noted earlier, it may not be feasible or desirable to seek informed consent but also that the gaining of such consent tends to be reduced to getting participants to sign a consent form. Not only are there problems in some contexts with requiring *written* consent, but the fact that a person has signed a form, or orally given consent, does not in itself tell us whether this consent was well-informed or free. Nor does it absolve researchers of their responsibility to protect participants from serious harm.

21.6 Summary

This chapter has outlined some of the key values that ought to govern research in discourse studies and in other fields, distinguishing between epistemic and specifically ethical values. I argued that epistemic values define the goal of research and supply its essential virtues, whereas ethical values are necessary external constraints on its pursuit. It was also emphasized that value principles need to be *interpreted* and judgments made about their relative priority, *in particular situations*. This was illustrated in discussions of the importance of minimizing harm, respecting autonomy and ensuring reciprocity. Finally, the consequences of the current mode of ethical regulation were examined. While these may not be entirely negative, some almost certainly are.

---

[6] This reflects the character of ethical regulation as concerned with "accountability." See O'Reilly et al's (2009) discourse analysis of letters from ethics committees to researchers who had submitted research proposals to them.

Further Reading

British Association for Applied Linguistics. (2006). Recommendations on Good Practice in Applied Linguistics. www.bbk.ac.uk/linguistics/research/baal%20ethics%20and%20good%20practice%20in%20research%20guidelines%202006.pdf.

This is perhaps the most useful set of ethical guidelines for the field of discourse studies; it provides comprehensive and helpful coverage of the issues.

Cameron, D., Frazer, E., Harvey, P., Rampton, M. B. H. and Richardson, K. (1992). *Researching Language: Issues of Power and Method.* New York: Routledge.

This is a seminal work which takes a very different stance from that adopted in this chapter. Several chapters provide illuminating insights into concrete ethical problems.

Cassell, J. and Jacobs, S.-E. (1987). *Handbook on Ethical Issues in Anthropology.* Special Publication No. 23. Washington DC: American Anthropological Association. www.psi.uba.ar/academica/carrerasdegrado/psicologia/sitios_catedras/obligatorias/723_etica2/material/normativas/handbook_on_ethical_issues_in_anthropology.pdf.

This handbook examines ethical dilemmas via discussion of a wide variety of actual cases; it is designed for teaching anthropology students but is of wider value.

Eckert, P. (2013). Research Ethics in Linguistics. In R. Podesva and D. Sharma (eds.) *Cambridge Handbook in Research Methods in Linguistics.* Cambridge: Cambridge University Press. 11–26.

This is a thoughtful and helpful discussion of ethical issues specifically relating to linguistic fieldwork.

Hammersley, M. and Traianou, A. (2012). *Ethics in Qualitative Research.* London: Sage.

This general account of research ethics, in the context of qualitative research, elaborates on the arguments presented in this chapter.

Iphofen, R. and Tolich, M. (eds.) (2018). *The Sage Handbook of Qualitative Research Ethics.* London: Sage.

This recent handbook contains thirty-five chapters discussing a wide range of ethical issues that can arise in carrying out qualitative research.

Kubanyiova, M. (2012). Ethical Debates in Research on Language and Interaction. In C. Chapelle (ed.) *Encyclopedia of Applied Linguistics.* New York: Wiley.

A useful discussion of a range of ethical debates relating to applied linguistics.

Lazaraton, A. (2012). Ethics in Qualitative Research. In C. Chapelle (ed.) *Encyclopedia of Applied Linguistics*. New York: Wiley.

This is a review of issues arising in qualitative research in the field of applied linguistics and of some of the contrasting views taken about them.

References

Alcadipani, R. and Hodgson, D. (2009). By Any Means Necessary? Ethnographic Access, Ethics and the Critical Researcher. *Tamara Journal* 7(4): 127–46.

Alcoff, L. (1991–2). The Problem of Speaking for Others. *Cultural Critique* 20: 5–32.

Bridges, D. (1999). Educational Research: Pursuit of Truth or Flight into Fancy? *British Educational Research Journal* 25: 597–616.

Brotsky, S. and Giles. D. (2007). Inside the "Pro-ana" Community: A Covert Online Participant Observation. *Journal of Eating Disorders* 15(2): 93–109.

Bruce, A., Beuthin, R., Sheilds, L., Molzahn, A. and Schick-Makaroff, K. (2016). Narrative Research Evolving: Evolving through Narrative Research. *International Journal of Qualitative Methods* 15(1): 1–6.

Calvey, D. (2017). *Covert Research*. London: Sage.

Cameron, D., Frazer, E., Harvey, P., Rampton, M. and Richardson, K. (1992). *Researching Language: Issues of Power and Method*. London/New York: Routledge.

Clifford, J. and Marcus, G. (eds). (1986). *Writing Culture: The Poetics and Politics of Ethnography*. Berkeley, CA: University of California Press.

Dingwall, R. (2008). The Ethical Case against Ethical Regulation in Humanities and Social Science Research. *Twenty-First Century Society* 3 (1): 1–12.

Eckert, P. (2013). Research Ethics in Linguistics. In R. Podesva and D. Sharma (eds.) *Cambridge Handbook in Research Methods in Linguistics*. Cambridge: Cambridge University Press. 11–26.

Emmerich, N. (ed.) (2018). *Virtue Ethics in the Conduct and Governance of Social Science Research*. Bingley: Emerald.

Giaxoglou, K. (2017). Ethics Revisited: Rights, Responsibilities and Relationships in Online Research. *Applied Linguistics Review* 8(2–3): 229–50.

Gray, A. (1990). On Anthropological Advocacy. *Current Anthropology* 31(4): 387–90.

Grinyer, A. (2002). The Anonymity of Research Participants: Assumptions, Ethics and Practicalities. *Social Research Update* 36: 1–5.

Hastrup, K. and Elsass, P. (1990). Anthropological Advocacy: A Contradiction in Terms? *Current Anthropology* 31(3): 301–11.

Hammersley, M. (1995). *The Politics of Social Research* London: Sage.

  (2000). *Taking Sides in Social Research*. London: Routledge.

  (2004). Action Research: A Contradiction in Terms? *Oxford Review of Education* 30(2): 165–81.

  (2009a). Challenging Relativism: The Problem of Assessment Criteria. *Qualitative Inquiry* 15(1): 3–29.

  (2009b). Against the Ethicists: On the Evils of Ethical Regulation. *International Journal of Social Research Methodology* 12(3): 211–25.

  (2014). On the Ethics of Interviewing for Discourse Analysis. *Qualitative Research* 14(5): 529–41.

  (2017). On the Role of Values in Social Research: Weber Vindicated? *Sociological Research Online* 22(1): 1–12.

  (2018). Revisiting Objectivity and Commitment in Sociolinguistics: From Labov to Lewis. Unpublished paper. https://martynhammersley.wordpress.com/documents/.

Hammersley, M. and Traianou, A. (2011). Moralism and Research Ethics: A Machiavellian Perspective. *International Journal of Social Research Methodology* 14(5): 379–90.

Hammersley, M. and Treseder, P. (2007). Identity as an Analytic Problem: Who's Who in "Pro-ana" Websites? *Qualitative Research* 7(3): 283–300.

Harvey, P. (1992). Bilingualism in the Peruvian Andes. In D. Cameron, E. Frazer, P. Harvey, M. Rampton and K. Richardson (eds.) *Researching Language: Issues of Power and Method*. London/New York: Routledge.

Hydén, M. (2008). Narrating Sensitive Topics. In M. Andrews, C. Squire and M. Tamboukou (eds.) *Doing Narrative Research*. London: Sage. 121–36.

Kingston, A. (2020). Feminist Research Ethics. In R. Iphofen (ed.) *Handbook of Research Ethics and Scientific Integrity*. Basingstoke: Palgrave-Macmillan. 531–549.

Kress, G. (1996). Representational Resources and the Production of Subjectivity: Questions for the Theoretical Development of Critical Discourse Analysis in a Multicultural Society. In C. Caldas-Coulthard and M. Coulthard (eds.) *Text and Practice: Readings in Critical Discourse Analysis*. London: Routledge.

Kubanyiova, M. (2008). Rethinking Research Ethics in Contemporary Applied Linguistics: The Tension between Macroethical and Microethical Perspectives in Situated Research. *Modern Language Journal* 92(4): 503–18.

Labov, W. (1982). Objectivity and Commitment in Linguistic Science: The Case of the Black English Trial in Ann Arbor. *Language in Society* 11(2): 165–201.

Lewis, M. (2018). A Critique of the Principle of Error Correction as a Theory of Social Change. *Language in Society* 47: 325–84.

Lincoln, Y. S. and Guba, E. G. (1989). Ethics: The Failure of Positivist Science. *Review of Higher Education* 12(3): 221–40.

Macfarlane, B. (2008). *Researching with Integrity*. London: Routledge.

Nind, M. (2014). *What Is Inclusive Research?* London: Bloomsbury.

Nöth, W. (2003). Crisis of Representation? *Semiotica* 143(1/4): 9–15.

O'Reilly, M., Dixon-Woods, M., Angell, E., Ashcroft, R. and Bryman, A. (2009). Doing Accountability: A Discourse Analysis of Research Ethics Committee Letters. *Sociology of Health & Illness* 31(2): 246–61.

Roulet, T., Gill, M., Stengers, S. and Gill, D. (2017). Reconsidering the Value of Covert Research: The Role of Ambiguous Consent in Participant Observation. *Organizational Research Methods* 20(3): 487–517.

Spender, D. (1982). *Invisible Women: The Schooling Scandal*. London: Writers and Readers Publishing Co-operative Society with Chameleon Editorial Group.

Thomas-Hughes, H. (2018). Ethical "Mess" in Co-produced Research: Reflections from a U.K.-Based Case Study. *International Journal of Social Research Methodology* 21(2): 231–42.

Tomkinson, S. (2015). Doing Fieldwork on State Organizations in Democratic Settings: Ethical Issues of Research in Refugee Decision Making [46 paragraphs]. *Forum Qualitative Sozialforschung/Forum: Qualitative Social Research* 16(1): Art. 6. http://nbn-resolving.de/urn:nbn:de:0114-fqs150168.

Van den Hoonaard, W. (2018). The Vulnerability of Vulnerability: Why Social Science Researchers Should Abandon the Doctrine of Vulnerability. In R. Iphofen and M. Tolich (eds.) *The Sage Handbook of Qualitative Research Ethics*. London: Sage.

Van den Hoonard, W. and Hamilton, A. (eds.) (2016). *The Ethics Rupture*. Toronto: University of Toronto Press.

Whiteman, S. (2012). *Undoing Ethics: Rethinking Practice in Online Research*. New York: Springer.

22

Migrants, Citizenship and Language Rights

Lionel Wee

22.1 Introduction

This chapter is concerned with the relationships between a tripartite of concepts: migrants, citizenship and language rights, and the implications of these relationships for discourse studies. I will begin by looking at how the concept of citizenship is defined since, as we will see shortly, it is this concept that undergirds the ways in which the other two tend to be understood. It needs to be emphasized, however, that the definitions of all three concepts are by no means unproblematic. The differences and contestations regarding how these terms are to be understood – as well as how they can be said to connect to one another – should be taken as indicative of the need for further scholarly investigations into the discourses that surround the migrant-citizen-language nexus.

22.2 Definitions

Citizenship has been described as "a bundle of rights and obligations that define a person's societal role" (Ciprut 2008: 17). Moreover, this societal role is typically understood as being in the context of the state so that an individual who is formally recognized as a citizen *by* the state might then claim rights *from* the state while also having obligations *toward* the state.

It has to also be noted that citizenship, far from being a one size fits all concept, is in fact being increasingly defined by "gradations of esteem" (Carver and Mottier 1998: 14), where different kinds of rights and responsibilities accrue to different subcategories of citizens. Ong (2006: 500) describes this as the notion of citizenship "mutating": "[I]nstead of all citizens enjoying a unified bundle of citizenship rights, we have a shifting political landscape in which heterogeneous populations claim diverse rights and benefits associated with citizenship, as well as universalizing criteria of neoliberal norms or human rights." Thus, there are different conceptions of what it means to be a citizen even when this is a formal status accorded by the state. This includes issues such as what kinds of rights or obligations come along with being a citizen, what subcategories of citizen can be considered acceptable (e.g. whether classifications involving religion, gender, ethnicity or birthplace should be recognized) and the extent to which neoliberal values that emphasize productivity should be factored into the valuing of citizens.

Having noted some of the problematics involved in defining citizenship, we can move on to the concept of migrants. Individuals who are considered migrants are often interpreted as constituting a residual group that cannot be absorbed into other categories such as citizen or permanent resident (Maher 2002: 22; Somers 2008: 21). This way of conceptualizing the migrant – that is, as a residual category vis-à-vis that of the citizen or permanent resident – has tended to construe the migrant as someone who is stateless and, moreover, is oftentimes stigmatized precisely because of this statelessness. Ong (2006: 499) refers to this as the "citizenship-versus-statelessness" model, and the relevance of this model becomes questionable when, as Faist (2000: 37) points out, the factors that might impact on a person's decision to migrate are actually highly varied and may involve, among other things, a quest for better income, status, adventure, personal freedom or to join up with friends or family: "In this view the potential migrant could not only be a worker, a member of a household or a kinship group, but also a voter, a member of ethnic, linguistic, religious, and political groups, a member of a persecuted minority, or a devotee of arts or sports." Such a differentiated and more nuanced understanding of migrants makes clear that some migrants are likely to be more valued or welcome than others. This in turn complicates the understanding of citizenship because migrants who may be considered more attractive to the host society (e.g. those who are skilled in particular art forms or specific sports, those who are economically well-off or those who have professional qualifications) may be courted by the state to consider taking up citizenship while their less desired counterparts may be barred from doing the same. Consequently, migrants who are more attractive to their host societies may in fact end up having more in common with some of their more "esteemed" citizen counterparts.

Let us now consider the third concept that this chapter is concerned with, that of language rights. The general motivation behind the concept of language rights "is to ensure that an identifiable group – usually an ethnic minority – is granted specific forms of protection and consideration on the basis of their associated language" (Wee 2011: 5). But there are serious conceptual problems with the notion of language rights (Wee 2011: 4):

Exactly what is meant by the concept of language rights, however, is not always clear, since it has been variously asserted that the holders of such rights need not be speakers of languages, but can include the languages themselves, usually on the grounds that languages are intrinsically valuable. If speakers have rights, then we need to further clarify whether such rights accrue to speakers as individuals or by virtue of their status as members of particular groups. And if languages also have rights, then we need to ask whether we are in danger of reifying a social practice that is inherently changeable and variable by dissociating it from the interests of speakers.

Since we are concerned with language rights as these pertain to migrants and citizens, I leave aside the problematic matter of whether languages themselves can be considered to have rights (see Wee 2011: 62). Instead, I focus on the issue of what it means to suggest that speakers – in particular, speakers categorized as citizens or migrants – have language rights. I will also discuss the issue of language obligations, which seems to be ignored or certainly at least underdiscussed in comparison with the prominence that has been accorded to language rights.

22.3 Overview of the Topic

The migrant-citizen-language nexus, at bottom, revolves around the issue of boundaries, how boundaries might be established, legitimized and sustained. There are, for example, boundaries that separate citizens from noncitizens, such as migrants. These boundaries are sociopolitical boundaries and, as such, can and have been redrawn in different ways at different times by different polities and communities. Thus, the earlier Westphalian interpretation of citizenship – "based on sovereign claims over territory and on the exclusive loyalty of those recognized by the sovereign as belonging to his estate" – has since proven to be deeply problematic because globalization "has created a mosaic of social, economic, and political spaces that transcend and weaken the political boundaries of physical space" (Ciprut 2008: 17).

In this regard, there is a need to come to grips with a contemporary milieu where neoliberalism is an increasingly influential force in how the workings of citizenship are understood (Ong 2006; Somers 2008). Neoliberalism takes the position that "human well-being could best be advanced by liberating individual, entrepreneurial freedoms within an institutional framework of private property rights, free markets and free trade" (Harvey 2005: 2). Consequently, as we have just noted, how the state decides to accord "sovereignty" to the citizenry may be increasingly informed by considerations of relative productivity, with the consequence that different kinds of privilege then accrue to different subcategories of citizens. Productive and skilled foreigners may even share in some of the same kinds of sovereignty as highly valued citizens, giving them greater commonality with their skilled citizen counterparts. But neoliberalism's emphasis on free markets also means an increase in the mobility of individuals so that the language rights (and obligations) of both citizens and migrants have to be considered in a transnational context rather than just within the confines of a (nation-)state. As Ho (2018, citations omitted) observes:

> Where once the label "diaspora" was reserved for forced exile, it is invoked by migrant-sending states today to lay claim to citizens or former citizens abroad. Recognising the transnational ties that migrants maintain with their countries of origin, migrant-sending states extend symbolic membership and selective rights to emigrant populations by flexibly extending components of citizenship beyond the national territory. Such changes happening to citizenship have been described as extraterritorial, emigrant or external citizenship.
> Even as migrant-sending states flexibly decouple components of citizenship to proactively engage emigrants, there are implications for immigration societies when migrants move across national contexts during different junctures of their life-course. For example, migrants are conscious that their social reproduction concerns, such as familyhood and retirement planning, extend across different national contexts or transnational social fields across the life-course … How might we approach analyses of citizenship differently if we consider competing accounts of membership, rights and duties invoked by different social groups inhabiting the same space at the same time or traversing different national territories across the life-course?

It should be clear that shifting community boundaries are likely to lead to concomitant changes in the kinds of rights and obligations that go along with being a citizen or being a migrant. However, while it is generally agreed that these boundaries do shift (even if they do not always shift in ways that are unanimously accepted), there is greater reluctance to accept that the boundaries of languages, too, can shift, as can the relationships between languages and their speakers (be they citizens or migrants). This reluctance becomes compounded when there is talk of language rights. This is because a key problem with the notion of language rights is that it cannot comfortably address the question of who the bearer of the rights ought to be. Wee (2011: 21) discusses this as the problem of boundary marking, and shows that there are serious issues involved in trying to identify by delimiting the contours of both the bearer of a language right and the object of the right. This is an important concern because if there is no clarity as to who the bearer is or what the object of the right is, then how can we tell if language rights have indeed been violated, that is, what merits do we give petitions that someone's (individual's or group's) language rights are in need of protection?

The bearer is usually presumed to be a (minority) group or community of speakers rather than an individual speaker. But this presumption is itself problematized by the fact that we cannot necessarily assume that there will be any consensus among the members of the relevant group/community as to which linguistic variety is sufficiently prestigious or culturally significant so as to warrant being treated as the object of the right. As Blackledge and Creese (2008) show, there can be significant disputes over whether a particular variety is too informal or too elitist to be treated as emblematic of a group's identity and heritage. For example, in their study of Bangladeshi immigrants in Britain, Bengali (the literate variety) is proposed by school administrators as the heritage language as distinct from Sylheti (a regional vernacular which also indexed lower status). But this way of positioning the two varieties tended to be rejected by Sylheti speakers, who viewed the two as being largely the same language (2008: 543–5).

However, there are even more serious conceptual issues involved, since the preceding statement already relies on the assumption that the group/community as well as the candidate language can themselves all be easily identified (i.e. bounded and thus distinguished from other groups/communities and languages). But the outlines of a group or community are fluid as are the individuals who make up the group, given the fact of migration. And likewise, the outlines of a variety are also not easily defined or stabilized given that language change, borrowing, contact and innovation are all inevitable concomitants of regular language use. In other words, there is a problematic assumption that the issues involved "merely" have to do with trying to forge consensus among the community members (i.e. this is a matter *internal* to the community) and the issue on which consensus is needed concerns *which* linguistic variety to select from among a set of distinct and distinguishable contenders. That is, language rights are typically invoked in order to ensure speakers have access to or support for the continued use of their heritage (ethnic) languages. But such an invocation of language rights does not address the intralinguistic variability found within the community of speakers (Wee 2005). Neither does it address the thorny question of how language rights can or ought to be protected in the case of mobile individuals such as migrants, a question that is increasingly in need of urgent discussion (Wee 2011: 126–7).

22.4 Issues and Ongoing Debates

The foregoing indicates that questions such as the following need to be considered: Is it the state that bears the responsibility of protecting a citizen's language rights? If not, then who? What about the language obligations of a citizen to his or her community since a citizen is defined in terms of not only rights but also obligations? What might these language obligations be? And similar questions can and should be asked regarding migrants: What language rights and obligations do migrants have, and how might these be protected or discharged?

These questions remain pertinent despite attempts at constructing relatively sweeping accounts of citizenship and rights, such as that offered by Somers (2008). In trying to address the complexities surrounding studies of citizenship, Somers (2008: 5–6, italics in original) offers a view of citizenship as "the *right to have rights*":

> I stipulate that the first right to political membership must equally include the *de facto* right to *social* inclusion in civil society. By social inclusion I mean the right to *recognition* by others as a moral equal treated by the same standards and values and due the same level of respect and dignity as all other members. The second bundle of rights contains the civil-juridical ones, often summed up in Marshallian terms as civil, political, and social rights, and recently expanded to include such rights as cultural, economic, indigenous and same-sex rights. In addition, I insist that both kinds of rights must include human rights, since they too require the recognition that only membership and social inclusion can ensure.

Somers aims to draw together disparate strands concerning rights and citizenship into an integrated vision of what it means to be a member of a political community. Somers claims that individuals have a right to political membership and, furthermore, that this right, while in principle distinct from the right to social inclusion, cannot be meaningfully exercised if the two are separated. She emphasizes that political communities can be of various sizes and, consequently, the notion of citizenship should not only be viewed in relation to the nation-state. She also stresses that social inclusion must involve recognition as a "moral equal" of cultural, economic, indigenous and same-sex rights, thus bringing her understanding of citizenship into the domain of identity politics. Finally, she claims that both the right to political membership and the right to social inclusion must encompass human rights.

Given that Somers wants her interpretation of citizenship to encompass what might be broadly described as "identity politics" (since it embraces as relevant to the notion of citizenship cultural, ethnic and sexual identity issues, among other possibilities) as well as human rights, her conceptualization of citizenship brings into its ambit the notion of language rights for two reasons. One, a prominent argument for recognizing language rights – the Linguistic Human Rights Movement (LHRM) (Phillipson and Skutnabb-Kangas 1995; Skutnabb-Kangas 2000) – does indeed claim that language rights have to be treated as a form of human rights. For example, Skutnabb-Kangas (2000: 498, bold in original) asserts that:

> Necessary rights are rights which, in human rights language, fulfill basic needs and are a prerequisite for living a dignified life .... Only the necessary rights should be seen as linguistic human rights. Enrichment-oriented rights, for instance the right to learn foreign languages, can be

seen as **language** rights but I do not see them as inalienable human rights, i.e., they are not linguistic **human** rights.

Two, both the LHRM and the Minority Language Rights Movement (MLRM) (May 2001, 2005), where the latter does not necessarily subscribe to the claim that language rights are a form of human rights, emphasize the importance of language rights as a way of respecting the ethnic and cultural identities of minority communities. Thus, Phillipson and Skutnabb-Kangas (1995: 485) claim that "[r]ights pertaining to the use of a given language are an eminent example of the way in which the rights of the individual presuppose their social and collective exercise" and May (2005: 322–3) criticizes what he sees as an attitude of "unquestioned legitimacy" of "majority languages" in which there is a failure to recognize the historical processes by which these languages and speakers became dominant, often at the expense of speakers of minority languages.

To accommodate the admittedly broad sweep of issues that she wants to capture under her conceptualization of citizenship, Somers (2008: 20) acknowledges that citizenship has to be ultimately understood as involving "shifting" and "discursive" relationships where the state, market and civil society are engaged in a power struggle. But there are problems with Somers' proposal. While she recognizes that what counts as citizenship (and, by implication, what counts as a migrant and what might count as language rights) can and does shift, by situating her proposal within the notion of rights, she is in a very real sense already placing significant constraints on the kinds of shifts that can occur. This is because, as we already noted, in the case of language rights, there are indeed serious problems with trying to identify the bearer of the right as well as the object of the right. In addition, rights discourse, despite its "emancipatory aura," is neither ethically unambiguous nor neutral (Cowan, Dembour and Wilson 2001: 11). A rights discourse in fact imposes the following three effects (Wee 2011: 26):

1. Selectivity: Since not all the practices associated with a social group are appropriate candidates as the objects of rights, a rights discourse exerts pressure such that only a few selected practices are privileged over others (Ford 2005: 71).
2. Reinvention: In some cases, the pressure to come up with appropriate practices can lead a group to engage in reinvention, such as modifying the practices in ways that fit the demands of a rights discourse. This may include providing the practices with the necessary authentication demanded by rights-conferring authorities, and asserting that these practices unanimously reflect the collective history of the group (Tamir 1993: 47).
3. Neutralization: A rights discourse neutralizes the distinction between strategic and non-strategic essentialism. This means that an essentialist claim (strategic or otherwise), once locked into the rights discourse, has

no clear "exit strategy," making it difficult for such a claim to work as a temporary tactic. (Ford 2005: 68)

The result is that "rights may be *constitutive* of cultures and their associated identities" (Cowan, Dembour and Wilson 2001: 11, italics in original; see also Ford 2005: 73), rather than simply protecting them. For example, consider Ford's (2005) discussion of *Renee Rogers, et al. v. American Airlines, Inc.* (1981), where the plaintiff was a black woman seeking damages against the airline for prohibiting employees from wearing an all-braided hairstyle. Rogers' assertion was that "the 'corn row' style has been, historically, a fashion and style adopted by Black American women, reflective of cultural, historical essence of the Black women in American society" (quoted in Ford 2005: 23). Ford (2005: 25, italics in original), however, points out:

> Even if we take it on faith that cornrows represent black nationalist pride as against the integrationist and assimilationist coiffure of chemically straightened hair, it's clear that a right to cornrows would be an intervention in a long-standing debate *among* African-Americans about empowerment strategies and norms of identity and identification .... A right to group difference may be experienced as meddlesome at best and oppressive at worst even by some members of the groups that the rights regime ostensibly benefits. For the black woman who dislikes cornrows and wishes that no one – most of all black women – would wear them, the right not only hinders her and deprives her of allies, but it also adds insult to injury by proclaiming that cornrows are *her* cultural essence as a black woman.

The observations by Ford are relevant to Somers' attempt to absorb both human rights and what might be termed "cultural rights" under the ambit of citizenship, and it extends to the arguments made for language rights by the LHRM as well as the MLRM. Notice, for example, that the autonomy of the rights-claiming group vis-à-vis other groups or society at large is secured on the basis that the cultural practice in question is supposed to represent the group's collective identity. Thus, the autonomy of the group is privileged over the possibility that individual members within the group may in fact have a different view of said practice or may even reject its putative role as a representative practice. The group's autonomy is being achieved at the expense of that of its individual members. Given that we are interested in language rights, there is no reason to assume that all members of the group will share the same views toward "their" language. These problems apply regardless of whether the group in question happens to be a group of citizens or a group of migrants.

These considerations mean that Somers' conception of citizenship is vulnerable to two uncomfortable but related scenarios. The first is where certain linguistic and cultural practices are recognized only by the state because the claimants involved happen to be citizens and not migrants. That is, the substantive nature of the practices themselves is thus less relevant than the identities of the claimants when considering whether or not to award rights. This is particularly problematic in the case of human rights (which Somers absorbs under her notion of citizenship and to which the LHRM also appeals), since these should be awarded on the basis of the claimant being an *individual human* rather than happening to occupy a formal status such as that of citizen.

The second, related to the first, is that the question of which actor (if any) has an obligation to ensure that the rights of migrants are protected is left unaddressed. If citizens can appeal to the state, who can migrants appeal to for protection of their rights? If language rights are supposed to be treated as a type of human rights (as claimed by the LHRM), then there are major problems since human rights are uncontroversial only when understood as individual rights (i.e. rights that we each have as human beings). Human rights are typically individual rights rooted in a conception of "universal personhood" (Maher 2002: 21) and, as such, cannot be territorially bounded. This is what happens with the basic human right to freedom from torture, for example. But language rights are intended by their proponents to be collective or group rights since they are intended as reflections of a group's identity. And group rights are not easily transferable across state boundaries. This is because the reasons why groups can lay claim to language rights tend to be territorially specific. For example, under Malaysia's bumiputra policy, the Malays were awarded special rights on the basis that they are the "original people" of the land. But when a group of Malays migrates to another state, say, the basis for such historical ties no longer holds. The issue of establishing some original tie to the land is specific to groups who claim to be national minorities (Kymlicka 1995). But even ethnic minorities face territorially specific problems since the notion of a minority is a relative one and is identifiable only within the context of a particular state. It thus becomes highly problematic to assume that the language rights of a particular group are transferable across state boundaries since what counts as a minority in the context of one state may count as a majority in the context of another and vice versa. However, if language rights are not treated as belonging to the category of human rights, then any claims that migrants might have toward the host society are just as problematic. This is because the host society has no historical or cultural obligation to help a group of migrants preserve their ethnic or heritage language. It is therefore unclear exactly what kinds of obligation migrants can expect from the state in which they happen to be resident.

Broadly speaking, the fact is that the boundaries demarcating what counts as a language, and what it means to be a citizen or a migrant, can and do shift. Moreover, these shifts are likely to be harder to avoid and may well even be accelerated as societies become increasingly complex and diverse due to individuals becoming ever more mobile and developments in communicative technologies that make it easier for mobile individuals to stay in contact with a variety of communities around the globe. Thus, Blommaert and Rampton (2016: 22), in their discussion of "superdiversity" (Vertovec 2007), suggest:

> Superdiversity is characterized by a tremendous increase in the categories of migrants, not only in terms of nationality, ethnicity, language, and religion, but also in terms of motives, patterns and itineraries of migration, processes of insertion into the labor and housing markets of the host societies, and so on (cf. Vertovec 2010). The predictability of the category of "migrant" and of his/her sociocultural features has disappeared.

And Jacquemet (2005: 269) describes the communicative practices at a family reunion where "the Albanian language blended with English, Italian, and occasionally German …. The TV was on, broadcasting in Spanish, while from another room you could hear the beat of Nuyorican hip hop …" and because some of the family members were keen to learn Italian, these individuals "in their peer group … displayed these newly acquired linguistic skills in a mixed idiom of Albanian, Italian, English, and personal slang" (2005: 270).

Such shifts are highly problematic for the notion of language rights, which tend to insist on a fixed relationship between a particular language and its speakers (the latter two themselves being understood as fixed and clearly identifiable entities). Neither does the notion of language rights address the question of what languages might be needed for a group of speakers to realize any aspirations they might have for upward socioeconomic mobility – which might actually involve them shifting away from their putative heritage language. And finally, an appeal to language rights says nothing about those language practices that might serve as quotidian lingua franca but have no status as recognizable varieties of any sort (cf. Maryns and Blommaert 2001), much less whether these quotidian practices deserve to be treated as the objects of language rights. Consequently, as Wee (2011: 45–6) points out:

> And this brings us to what is perhaps the most serious problem with the notion of language rights: the ontological assumption that there is an identifiable linguistic variety that can be coherently treated as the object of a rights discourse …. An approach that advocates language rights, however, is likely to find it extremely difficult to deal with such a situation, where sociolinguistic categories and practices are not only unstable, but so incipient that no clear named varieties can yet be said to exist ….
>
> The kind of hybridity that is characteristic of contact situations and the problems it raises for language rights should in fact *not* be considered exceptional; rather it should be treated as a characteristic of languages in general.

There is, however, an alternative way of thinking about language responsibilities, one that avoids the problems involved when the notion of rights is invoked. This is the concept of linguistic citizenship (Stroud 2001, 2018a, 2018b). Linguistic citizenship refers to "the individual claim and exercise of the right of citizens to voice, to be heard, and to act upon whichever dimension of a person's linguistic repertoire as may be useful in circumstance or purpose" (Heugh 2018: 175–6). It therefore does not begin with the presumption that named varieties are always necessarily relevant to the needs and experiences of individuals. It may be a mix of resources that have no established linguistic name. It instead emphasizes "language-as-a-mode-of-action" and the roles that linguistic resources play in giving voice to speakers (Deumert 2018: 289, 295). Unlike the concept of language rights, which starts by privileging named varieties and, in so doing, loses sight of the fact that speakers require the ability to voice their concerns and this may not involve such recognized varieties, linguistic citizenship is "fundamentally an invitation to rethink our understanding of language through the lens of citizenship and participatory democracy" and it does this by interrogating "the historical, sociopolitical and economic determinants of how languages are constructed, at the same time as it pinpoints the linguistic, structural and institutional conditions necessary for change" (Stroud 2018b: 20).

The notion of citizenship here is not restricted to the formal status of being a citizen that is accorded by the state. While the notion of linguistic citizenship may involve speakers exercising agency through a rights framework as well as through institutionalized means of recognizing political participation, it also acknowledges and indeed gives equal if not more emphasis to

> the use of language (registers, etc.) or other multimodal means in circumstances that may be orthogonal, alongside, embedded in, or outside of, institutionalized democratic frameworks for transformative purposes .... It refers to what people do with and around language(s) in order to position themselves agentively, and to craft new, emergent subjectivities of political speakerhood, often outside of those prescribed or legitimated in institutional frameworks of the state. (Stroud 2018a: 4)

Here is an example (Stroud 2018a: 5):

> Somali refugees in Ugandan camps are also exercising linguistic citizenship when they use the resources – teaching spaces under trees, chalk and boards, etc. – provided by a foreign NGO to teach English literacy for their own purposes of learning to read the Quran (Kathleen Heugh, Personal communication, August 2015). They are exercising their agency, and pursuing a goal that is important to *them*, but likely not to the "keepers" of the programme. They are doing so on the sidelines and margins of the formally structured literacy programme, taking part in "informal" networks of learning at the same time as they create the conditions for participating in new roles in alternative communities of practice.

In this way, the notion of linguistic citizenship is compatible with Somers' argument that citizenship can be relevant to communities of various sorts and not just the state, and it can and should be open to multiple identity dimensions. But what linguistic citizenship manages to do is to avoid the entrapments and encumbrances that come with the adoption of a rights discourse, and it emphasizes instead the importance of noninstitutional acts of citizenship alongside institutional ones. This means that not just officially recognized citizens but migrants as well can all engage in acts of linguistic citizenship. Finally, in giving equal attention to acts of citizenship across institutional as well as everyday or noninstitutional contexts, it stresses the importance of attending to discourses emanating from a multitude of actors, thus bringing us to the focus of Section 22.5.

22.5 Implications for Discourse Studies

We have seen that concepts such as migrant, citizen and language are by no means unproblematic or unchanging, and this has significant implications for any attempt to appeal to the notion of language rights. An important role that discourse studies can play is, of course, to clarify the different and changing meanings of these concepts. Obviously, the point here is not for discourse studies to identify the "correct" or "true" meanings of these concepts, but rather to highlight the ways in which they are differently understood (sometimes by the same individual or group and perhaps even within the same stretch of discourse). The contribution that this can make is to emphasize the extent to which the meanings of these concepts tend to shift to reflect changing priorities or goals, even when the speakers themselves may not be aware of the shifts.

Consider the persistent belief that languages are autonomously existing bounded entities (Heller 2008), a belief that is at odds with sociolinguistic reality (on this point also see Chapters 3 and 18 in this volume). In fact, the linguistic knowledge that all individuals carry with them is always knowledge of some social language. A social language (Gee 2001: 652) is a set of "lexical and grammatical resources (whether in speech or writing) that a recognizable group of people uses to carry out its characteristic social practices." It is never knowledge of this nonexistent fully developed delimitable system. As individuals move into new environments, form new relationships and social networks, they either acquire new social languages or modify (perhaps imperceptibly) the ones they already possess, or both. As should be clear by now, a world of mobile humans cannot therefore be multilingual in the sense of individuals possessing multiple sets of sharply delimitable systems; rather, it must be multilingual in a much more fluid, porous and perhaps even ephemeral manner, where individuals' linguistic repertoires consist of multiple social languages that are demarcatable only gradiently from each other. Many of the activities undertaken by mobile humans are also likely to be much more transitory in nature, and this will be reflected in the associated social languages (Wee 2007). For example, a Chinese academic who spends three weeks in Paris, first attending a conference and then staying on for a holiday, may acquire bits of French as part of ordering food or commuting between her hotel and the conference site. Crucially, her social language for ordering food, which will become more "fluent" toward the end of her stay, will probably involve a mixture of French and English. But knowledge of this particular social language may begin to fade once she returns to China.

In this regard, a rights-based discourse is useful if the particular right under consideration is one that is assumed to have universal validity and is unlikely to change over time. The idea of human rights therefore works best when it concerns properties that are universally accepted as part of what it means to be a person in the sense that these are properties that individuals invariably carry with them regardless of where they may happen to be. The corollary is that such properties need to be isolable from a person's changing circumstances. But this also means that social languages are not good candidates for human rights, as any given social language is not a property of an individual (or group even) but emerges from the relationship the individual/group has to their environment. To treat specific social languages as the rights of particular groups, as the LHRM paradigm would presumably attempt to do, is to enshrine language as essential/stable/isolable, whereas the entire point of a social language is to capture the flux, changeability and potentially transitory nature of various communicative practices. There is therefore an urgent need to critique highly persistent and problematic assumptions regarding the nature of language, especially when these assumptions feed into politically charged arguments regarding migrants and citizens.

At the bottom of these considerations is the issue of personhood. What kinds of person are migrants, citizens or speakers of languages? Whilst this has been less of an issue in the case of citizens (notwithstanding our earlier observation that some subtypes of citizen may be more valued than others), migrants have tended to be denied the status of full personhood when compared with citizens, especially when they are considered to have entered the country illegally. And this has implications for the kinds of responsibility a state might have toward ensuring their wellbeing. As Maher (2002: 28, italics in original) points out in her discussion of the United States: "What this means in practice is that it has been possible to imagine undocumented immigrants as *outside civil society*, outside the bounds of civil law, since the polity has never approved their presence." And given the liberal assumption of rational, autonomous action by all individuals, migrants who have "chosen" to cross state borders without authorization are imagined to have consented to the conditions of "rightslessness." Their border crossing involves a "knowing defiance" of American law, a "calculated risk" (Schuck and Smith 1985) in which migrants exchange their right to rights for economic opportunity. Thus, in clarifying the different understandings of what it means to be a citizen or migrant or what a language is, it is important for discourse studies to link these various articulations of the concepts to broader discourses concerning volition, autonomy and personhood. It should be noted at this point that discourse is inevitably implicated in all of these issues. How, why and when the boundaries that demarcate specific communities or specific categories of individuals are drawn, what the concomitant implications are for those inhabitants within those communities (such as citizens or migrants) and, in particular, what kinds of language right (if any) should accrue to these inhabitants – these are all ultimately matters of discourse (see Chapter 23 in this volume on this point). They are matters that are debated, argued and (where possible) agreed upon, even if only temporarily. In this sense, it is discourse in the relatively common understanding as spoken or written communication that occurs in some social setting that is relevant.

In recent times, perhaps the most well-known of such cases revolves around the "Dreamers" in the United States. The Deferred Action for Childhood Arrivals is part of American immigration policy, one that allows those individuals who came to the country as minors (and, therefore, not necessarily of their own volition) to defer deportation, assuming various conditions such as not having a criminal conviction are met. These individuals are sometimes known as "Dreamers" after the passing of the Dream Act Bill in 2001, a bill intended to provide them with pathways to citizenship, especially if during their stay in the country they completed a college degree or served in the military. Here, then, we have a category of individuals who are technically not citizens but who are not migrants, much less illegal migrants, as the term is usually understood. And debates over how to handle the issues raised by these Dreamers are less about accessing or preserving a specific language than about voice.

Hence, the concept of language rights is of little relevance; it is that of linguistic citizenship that has the potential to give discourse studies greater purchase. This is because linguistic citizenship emphasizes "acts of citizenship" as those "practices whereby new actors, seeking recognition in the public space in order to determine a new course of events, shift *the location of agency and voice*" (Stroud 2018b: 21; see also Isin 2009). In the case of the Dreamers, it is about tracking and analyzing changes in personhood since the Dreamer is not a typical migrant. And there are important repercussions for voice. As individual Dreamers grow up, their passage from young children to adults offers them different opportunities and platforms from which to directly voice their concerns as opposed to having others speak for or against them, with consequent implications for the kinds of uptake or response that they might then have to face (e.g. Lind 2018).

Thus, Bass (2018) describes a series of writing workshops aimed at countering the rising antiimmigrant sentiment that the Dreamers debate has become swept up in. As she observes, the goal of the workshops is

> to elevate the voices of young aspiring writers who struggle with the realities of their undocumented status and with other obstacles. For these young poets, essayists, and storytellers, the political debate over DACA and the DREAM Act is not an abstract political conversation; it is a debate over whether their voices – and existence – are welcome in the United States.
>
> ...
>
> The uncertainty surrounding their status has driven many DREAMers into the shadows, like many of this country's other undocumented residents. As a result, the current debate about their future is taking place largely without their own stories being heard: without the voices of the vast majority of the approximately 800,000 people in the DACA program and without the voices of other undocumented people, many of whom have lived here in the United States – working, raising families, and contributing to this country's welfare – for years. PEN America's DREAMing Out Loud program is one small effort to bring more of those voices into the conversation.

The point of such writings is for Dreamers to be seen, heard and understood as actual individuals with specific goals and feelings rather than as members of the category "undocumented immigrant." Such a phenomenon finds no theoretical purchase from a language rights perspective; it is linguistic citizenship that provides us with a framework for understanding what these young writers are trying to do.

22.6 Future Directions

While there are, of course, many different directions that the study of migrants, citizenship and language rights could take, I want to highlight two in this closing section.

The first is to probe more carefully and critically into whether it is at all even useful to be invoking the notion of language rights. Linguistic citizenship has been presented here as an important concept that allows for much more nuanced explorations of the complex interrelationships between citizens, migrants and language. It is not held hostage to the strictures of a rights discourse and, concomitantly, neither to the ontological presumptions that come along with being the bearer of right or the object of a right.

The second is to chart newer and changing notions of what it means to be a citizen and migrant. For example, virtual migration – where workers remain in their home countries whilst their skills and labor migrate abroad, as in the case of call center-workers based in India working for American companies – complicates the all too common arguments that migrants physically present in the host societies are responsible for taking away jobs from citizens. Relatedly, even as migrants are often scapegoated for taking away the jobs that citizens "deserve," the rise of the gig economy also has to be taken into account for potentially creating a labor market with low-paying precarious work (a precarity to which migrants and citizens are vulnerable). This, of course, means that a discourse approach has to contextualize language, migration and citizenship in relation to the larger political economy.

22.7 Summary

As public understandings of what it means to be a migrant and a citizen continue to shift and change, it is necessary to also be appreciative that understandings of what a language is, too, cannot be taken for granted or presumed to be self-evident. In this regard, a rights-based approach is probably not the best way forward if we are to give proper cognisance to the complex issues raised by migration and citizenship. This is because it goes against the basic point that languages derive their values relationally, depending on their environments. This is why it makes more sense to think in terms of social languages and to contextualize social languages in relation to linguistic citizenship.

Further Reading

Bohman, J. (1996). *Public Deliberation*. Cambridge, MA: MIT Press.

This book addresses the complex question of how inclusivity and diversity can be fostered in a democracy. It proposes a model of public deliberation based on the public reasoning and discussions of citizens so as to encourage cooperation amidst increased social complexity.

Lim, L., Stroud, C. and Wee, L. (eds.) (2018). *The Multilingual Citizen*. Bristol: Multilingual Matters.

This volume elaborates on the notion of linguistic citizenship, presenting studies from the global South. It shows how addressing speakers' vulnerability and need to exercise agency requires first deconstructing ideas of what language is.

Milani, T. (ed.) (2017). *Language and Citizenship*. Amsterdam: John Benjamins.

This volume highlights the importance of approaching the language–citizenship nexus from a multivocal, multimodal and semiotic perspective.

Drawn from a variety of case studies, it shows how conflicting notions of citizenship can be understood only if institutional discourses are combined with more ethnographic data.

References

Bass, K. G. (2018). Amplifying Dreamer Voices: The DACA Debate and Free Expression. Pen America, April 11. https://pen.org/amplifying-dreamer-voices-the-daca-debate-and-free-expression/.

Blackledge, A. and Creese, A. (2008). Contesting "Language" as "Heritage": Negotiation of Identities in Late Modernity. *Applied Linguistics* 29(4): 533–54.

Blommaert, J. and Rampton, B. (2016). Language and Superdiversity. In K. Arnaut, J. Blommaert, B. Rampton and M. Spotti (eds.) *Language and Superdiversity*. New York: Routledge. 21–48.

Carver, T. and Mottier, V. (1998). Introduction. In T. Carver and V. Mottier (eds.) *Politics of Sexuality: Identity, Gender, Citizenship*. London: Routledge. 1–12.

Ciprut, J. V. (2008). Citizenship: Mere Contract, or Construct for Conduct? In J. V. Ciprut (ed.) *The Future of Citizenship*. Cambridge, MA: MIT Press. 1–29.

Cowan, J. K., Dembour, M. and Wilson, R. A. (2001) Introduction. In J. K. Cowan, M. Dembour and R. A. Wilson (eds.) *Culture and Rights: An Anthropological Perspective*. Cambridge: Cambridge University Press. 1–26.

Deumert, A. (2018). Commentary: On Participation and Resistance. In L. Lim, C. Stroud and L. Wee (eds.) *The Multilingual Citizen*. Bristol: Multilingual Matters. 289–99.

Faist, T. (2000). *The Volume and Dynamics of International Migration and Transnational Social Spaces*. Oxford: Oxford University Press.

Ford, R. T. (2005). *Racial Culture: A Critique*. Princeton, NJ: Princeton University Press.

Harvey, D. (2005). *A Brief History of Neoliberalism*. Oxford: Oxford University Press.

Heller, M. (2008). Language and the Nation-State: Challenges to Sociolinguistic Theory. *Journal of Sociolinguistics* 12(4): 504–24.

Heugh, K. (2018). Commentary: Linguistic Citizenship: Who Decides Whose Languages, Ideologies and Vocabulary Matter? In L. Lim, C. Stroud and L. Wee (eds.) *The Multilingual Citizen*. Bristol: Multilingual Matters. 174–89.

Ho, E. (2018). *Citizens in Motion: Emigration, Immigration, and Re-migration Across China's Borders*. Stanford, CA: Stanford University Press.

Isin, E. (2009). Citizenship in Flux: The Figure of the Activist Citizen. *Subjectivity* 29: 367–88.

Lind, D. (2018). "I Want More than Anything to Just Live My Life": DREAMers Wrestle with Being Used as "Hostages" in Immigration

Debate. Vox, January 30. www.vox.com/policy-and-politics/2018/1/30/16945222/daca-dream-act-trump-support.

Maher, K. H. (2002). Who Has a Right to Rights? Citizenship's Exclusions in an Age of Migration. In A. Brysk (ed.) *Globalization and Human Rights*. Berkeley: University of California Press: 19–43.

Maryns, K. and Blommaert, J. (2001). Stylistic and Thematic Shifting as a Narrative Resource: Assessing Asylum Seekers' Repertoires. *Multilingua* 20(1): 61–84.

May, S. (2001). *Language and Minority Rights*. London: Longman.

(2005). Language Rights: Moving the Debate Forward. *Journal of Sociolinguistics* 9: 319–47.

Ong, A. (2006). *Neoliberalism as Exception*. Durham, NC: Duke University Press.

Phillipson, R. and Skutnabb-Kangas, T. (1995). Linguistic Rights and Wrongs. *Applied Linguistics* 16: 483–504.

Schuck, P. and Smith, R. (1985). *Citizenship without Consent: Illegal Aliens in the American Polity*. New Haven, CT: Yale University Press.

Skutnabb-Kangas, T. (2000). *Linguistic Genocide in Education: Or Worldwide Diversity and Human Rights*. Mahwah, NJ: Lawrence Erlbaum Associates.

Somers, M. R. (2008). *Genealogies of Citizenship: Markets, Statelessness and the Right to Have Rights*. Cambridge: Cambridge University Press.

Stroud, C. (2001). African Mother-Tongue Programmes and the Politics of Language: Linguistic Citizenship versus Linguistic Human Rights. *Journal of Multilingual and Multicultural Development* 22: 339–55.

(2018a). Introduction. In L. Lim, C. Stroud and L. Wee (eds.) *The Multilingual Citizen*. Bristol: Multilingual Matters. 1–14.

(2018b). Linguistic Citizenship. In L. Lim, C. Stroud and L. Wee (eds.) *The Multilingual Citizen*. Bristol: Multilingual Matters. 17–39.

Tamir, Y. (1993). *Liberal Nationalism*. Princeton, NJ: Princeton University Press.

Vertovec, S. (2007). Super-Diversity and Its Implications. *Ethnic and Racial Studies* 30(6): 1024–54.

(2010). Towards Post-Multiculturalism? Changing Communities, Contexts and Conditions of Diversity. *International Social Science Journal* 199: 83–95.

Wee, L. (2005). Intra-language Discrimination and Linguistic Human Rights. *Applied Linguistics* 26: 48–69.

(2007). Linguistic Human Rights and Mobility. *Journal of Multilingual and Multicultural Development* 28(4): 325–38.

(2011). *Language without Rights*. Oxford: Oxford University Press.

Legal Case

Renee Rogers, et al. v. *American Airlines, Inc.* (1981) 527 F. Supp. 229, 232, United States District Court for the Southern District of New York.

23

Diversity and Inclusion in Education

Yi-Ju Lai and Kendall A. King

23.1 Introduction

The discourse study of diversity and inclusion in educational contexts encompasses a broad range of disciplinary, theoretical and methodological approaches and purposes. This work has expanded rapidly over these past decades, and this theoretically informed close analysis of discourse-in-interaction has advanced our understanding of the practices of inclusion and exclusion in education in myriad, specific ways. This chapter reviews some of the seminal, classic studies of discourse in education, together with current, cutting-edge research examining diversity and inclusion in and outside of formal classrooms. Concomitantly, we argue that the study of discourse in education has advanced the field's understanding of discourse processes more broadly.

As highlighted in the overview in Section 23.2, discourse studies have documented how ordinary classroom routines and cross-cultural differences work to marginalize and legitimize certain communicative styles and interactional participation structures. Simultaneously, discourse studies have illustrated the role of both institutional power and individual agency in constructing inclusion and exclusion. An additional line of work has taken up discourse analysis tools to evaluate the impact of language and education policies and revealed the unintended consequences of those policies within classrooms. While there is general agreement on these points across the field, debates at both theoretical and methodological levels remain unsettled, including differences in the relative analytical weight of agency and structural constraint; disagreements in what constitutes legitimate discourse data, how it should be analyzed and the claims that might be made; and active discussion around the productivity of translanguaging as a construct in language education policy. We overview these ongoing issues in the second half of the chapter. We end the chapter by considering the implications of this work for practice and policy moving ahead.

23.2 Overview

23.2.1 Cross-Cultural Differences in Everyday Classroom Discourse

An early line of discourse research examined how diversity, inclusion and exclusion were patterned within daily, routine practices of talk in classrooms. These scholars identified how linguistic and interactional practices were legitimized through classroom instructional interactions, as well as the differences across home and school language socialization practices (e.g. Michaels 1981). Early examples include the now classic studies of Philips (1983) and Heath (1983), both of which provided field-shaping insights into how routine classroom interactions marginalized the home and community-based discourse and literacy practices favored in minoritized communities, and impacted students' participation and achievement in school activities. Philips's microethnographic study analyzed the classroom participant structures of Indigenous students at a Native American school on the Warm Springs Indian Reservation in the US state of Oregon. She documented the verbal and nonverbal patterns of classroom instructional communication between Indigenous students and their teachers, and then compared those patterns with European-American classroom patterns she observed in a non-Indigenous school (off the reservation). Philips argued that different primary language socialization practices made it challenging for Indigenous students to fully participate in the mainstream or dominant classroom interaction structures (e.g. initiation-response-evaluation exchanges). This so-called cultural mismatch across home and school led to miscommunication and often positioned the Indigenous students as less capable.

Heath's (1983) ethnography of communication, in turn, directed our attention to how language was acquired and used at home and in school in communities in the southeastern United States. Compared to the children from the white working-class community of Roadville, children in the African American working-class community of Trackton experienced greater challenges in school literacy activities. Those challenges were rooted, according to Heath, in the different storytelling and everyday conversation patterns at home and in school. However, both Trackton and Roadville children faced increasing difficulties when the school tasks required creativity and critical reflection as such activities were relatively unfamiliar to students and not common in the primary language socialization patterns at home. Heath's study powerfully demonstrated that communities' different "ways with words" and varied ways of engaging in family literacy activities had consequences for children's educational experiences and outcomes.

This early work inspired a second generation of scholars to continue to explore differences across students' primary language socialization experiences and mainstream institutional language practices, and how particular discourse practices contribute to the marginalized educational trajectories of some minoritized students (e.g. Delpit 1995/2006; Gutiérrez, Morales and Martinez 2009; Moore 2006). This research has challenged deficit ideologies that blame students and families for the so-called "achievement gap" between dominant and minoritized students. This line of work more explicitly takes inclusion and exclusion as social interactional achievements and analyzes the role of language in everyday educational discourses as an instrument of power and control that perpetuates social inequalities (Anyon 1980).

From this vantage point, education serves as a key site for the reproduction and legitimization of dominant power structures and ideologies. For example, Razfar (2006) used conversation analysis to explore the repair practices situated within instructional interactions in a US urban secondary school with a predominant bilingual Latina/o population. Razfar (2006: 410) reported that teachers often engaged their English learners in "other repair" in classroom interactions as the "normative assistance strategy employed by instructors to facilitate oral literacy skills" of English language learners. Taking up broader work on language ideologies, Razfar showed how these "other repair" practices were deployed to correct learners' pronunciation in ways that align with speaking and sounding white. In response to studies such as this, critical scholars have noted that rather than engaging in "other repair," institutions should allow space for language learners to access school routines to more fully participate in classroom interactions using their existing repertoires (Baquedano-López, Solís and Kattan 2005).

23.2.2 Diversity and Homogeneity in Classroom Instruction

Global trends in migration, and in particular the increasing transnational flows of immigrants and refugees (UNHCR 2018), have resulted in a robust body of work examining transnational students' experiences within their new schools. This work has documented how institutional and societal discourses concerning diversity and inclusion can play out in everyday classroom interactions where immigrant students' agency is constrained by their ethnolinguistic backgrounds and by school practices (e.g. Archakis 2014; Mökkönen 2013). Although multilingual and multicultural pedagogies of diversity and inclusion are frequently normalized in institutional discourses (e.g. school slogans and "international celebration" days), close analysis of classroom discourse and everyday interactions has uncovered how taken-for-granted ideologies of homogeneity (e.g. hierarchization, traditional ethnolinguistic categories) are embedded in educational practices. For instance, García-Sánchez (2013) used classroom discourse analysis in conjunction with linguistic anthropology to explore the politics of citizenship and belonging among Moroccan immigrant preadolescent students in southern Spain. Her analysis revealed that central to the production of inclusionary and exclusionary institutional discourses were classroom participation and homework assignments, including tokenization and formulations of membership categories based on students' ethnocultural, linguistic and national backgrounds. For instance, immigrant students were often selected by teachers as a representative (diversity token) of their ethnicity. Those students were also assigned to give an ethnically-based example to meet a class objective, which was discursively naturalized as the "marked." Despite the overt discourses of inclusion in the school, these processes had unintended paradoxical consequences of further marginalizing the immigrant students as non-Spanish "Others."

In recent years, scholars have paid increasing attention to the role of educational institutions in producing and distributing knowledge and other forms of symbolic capital (Bourdieu 1991). This work considers how classroom instructional interactions across teachers–students or peers (re)produce legitimized and marginalized identities and memberships within diverse populations and perpetuate existing ideologies and patterns of privilege. For instance, Pérez's (2013) critical discourse analysis illustrated how the performance strategy of humor served as a mechanism for expressing ethnic and racial stereotypes in schools, and how students in a southern US California comedy school were socialized differently to engage in racial discourses that ostensibly claimed to reject explicit racial stereotypes in public. White students were taught distance and denial strategies that allowed them to participate in overt racial discourses and deny racist intent. In contrast, students of color often were encouraged to engage in racial stereotypes uncritically. Pérez argued that this legitimation of learning to make racism funny exemplified the symbolic capital and power (Bourdieu 1989) of the instructors to impose their racial ideologies on students.

23.2.3 Linguistic Varieties and Diversity

Another important line of related research examines how diversity, inclusion and exclusion are constructed in educational contexts through particular varieties of language. In this work, language use is of central interest in identifying (and critiquing) both covert and overt forms of privilege that normalize and reproduce oppressive hierarchies and educational inequalities, and for connecting such critiques to pedagogical practice. Here scholars have asked how different language varieties function to negotiate social status, identities and relationships within peer groups, classrooms and school cultures. This work has documented how these processes are established, often through the creation and maintenance of boundaries of inclusion and exclusion, to allow participants in interaction to simultaneously position themselves as a certain type of person and marginalize others within local social orders (e.g. Cook-Gumperz and Szymanski 2001; Shankar 2008).

This research has been taken up from a range of different disciplinary stances, including critical sociocultural, sociolinguistic and anthropological perspectives. For example, using linguistic anthropological and conversation analysis approaches to frame her ethnographic study in a southern US California elementary school, Goodwin (2006) examined how preadolescent girls participated in the embodied and discursive construction of their own social identities and forms of social organization. In this mixed ethnicity and mixed social-class school, the so-called "popular" girls touted democratic values of diversity and equity while undermining those values to situationally define memberships. Other interactions devolved into aggressive rituals of degradation. For instance, a marginalized African-American girl was stigmatized by words such as a "tagalong," ensuring that she was an excluded "nobody" who could not be mistaken as an included "somebody" in the popular girl group. Goodwin's analysis of co-constructed turns-in-conversation shows how social class distinction and stigma were indexed through the use of language that reflected the hierarchical structures of the school.

More recently, Goodwin and Alim (2010) used interactional sociolinguistic approaches to examine transmodal stylizations – that is, how popular girls mocked a "tagalong" African-American girl by using particular linguistic features associated with legitimized wealthy white "Valley Girls," while simultaneously producing gestures related to marginalized working-class black "Ghetto Girls." These forms of transmodal stylization were indexed "through the use of different yet mutually elaborating communicative modalities" (Goodwin and Alim 2010: 179). As noted by many scholars, such mocking transmodal stylizations and stancetaking in interaction are embedded within larger discourses and histories of class, gender, race and oppression (e.g. Bucholtz 2010; Chun 2009; Jaspers 2011; Lamb 2015). In its connecting of both the co-construction of moment-by-moment interactional identities and the coproduction of broader social identity categories, the study of diversity and inclusion in interaction requires understanding of the ecology of sign systems, including not only language but also other semiotic resources (e.g. Delfino 2016; Johnson 2017; see Chapter 15 in volume). This line of work has highlighted how language functions as a means of symbolic dominance that (re)produces hegemonic ideologies toward marginalized populations. Scholarship in this vein has shown how these everyday encounters have important implications for students' identity, membership construction and, ultimately, educational achievement.

While studies of diversity, inclusion and exclusion in education have shown how interactions in school settings can be a source of marginalization, closely related research has analyzed how marginalized and mainstream identities and memberships are constructed as part of everyday socialization practices in educational contexts (e.g. Abdi 2011; Chrisomalis 2015). An important example is Talmy's (2008, 2010) critical ethnographic study examining the dynamic competing cultural reproductions of assigned marginalized identities toward English as a second language (ESL) students in a Hawaiian high school: "oldtimer Local" and "newcomer FOB (fresh off the boat)." Situating his language socialization study within a critical ethnographic and discourse analysis approach, Talmy analyzed how routine classroom interactions socialized students into these "oldtimer Local" and "newcomer FOB" identities. Students exercised their agency to resist school-based ideological practices toward ESL 1.5 generation students and new immigrants by demonstrating oppositional linguistic behaviors and alternative identities in interactions. These conflicting perspectives about what it means to be "ESL" were reflected in a hegemonic, institutionally sanctioned ESL identity that positioned and labeled students in particular ways in everyday educational interactions.

A related line of research examines the growing number of English as an additional language (EAL) international students in higher education institutions around the world. This work has revealed how activities and interactions in academic contexts can index international students' identities and memberships as relative newcomers or linguistic and cultural *Others* (e.g. Morita 2009; see Chapter 20 in this volume). Othering works to "reify idealized, stereotypical imaginings of students' past over their present circumstances, denying students the possibilities of more complex, hybrid, and shifting affiliations and identities in favor of an enduring, exoticized nostalgia" (Talmy 2004: 150). For instance, Vicker's (2007) ethnographic study documented the interactional construction and negotiation of memberships between EAL international and US undergraduate students in science and engineering. Taking up both language socialization and conversation analysis approaches, Vicker demonstrated how international and domestic students positioned themselves in interactions as recognized experienced engineers or silent Others, respectively. They did so within conversational moves in regular team meetings, including the organization of the conversational floor, that revealed their research experiences, disciplinary epistemologies and access to educational opportunities.

Fotovatian (2012), as another example, drew on sociocultural theories of second language use and learner agency in interaction to investigate institutional identity construction among some EAL international graduate students in an Australian university. Her analysis of students' narratives demonstrated how the construction of identity and membership was discursively mediated in and through participation and engagement in institutional interactions. The term "international students" functioned as marked identity that underestimated student agency and positioned international students as excluded *Others*.

These close examinations of the social (re)production (Giddens 1979) of the marginality and stigma of students from diverse backgrounds suggest that linguistic and cultural learning, as well as identity construction and membership negotiation, are best understood as fundamentally contextualized and interactionally mediated processes. The close analysis of linguistic and semiotic resources is critical to gaining in-depth understandings of complex situated learning and communicative practices over time and across individual development in educational settings (Garrett and Baquedano-López 2002). Analysis of school discourse practices from a range of methodological perspectives has yielded powerful insights into how inclusion and exclusion are constructed through the local-level movements of verbal and nonverbal (e.g. gestures) acts in conjunction with larger-level sociocultural and political processes (Wortham 2012).

23.2.4 Language and Education Policies

An additional line of work has focused more explicitly on educational policies and practices and the ways in which these constructs allow for student inclusion or exclusion. This body of research has looked closely at classroom discourse in light of national, state or local language and education policy. A classic and influential example in this vein is Hornberger's (1987) analysis of bilingual education in Puno, Peru, which evaluated the impact of a language education policy intended to include a marginalized population in the state educational system. Hornberger compared two schools in the region, one of which had adopted a Quechua-Spanish bilingual education policy and program to serve its Quechua-speaking students, and one that continued to use Spanish only to instruct its Quechua-dominant Indigenous students. Her close analysis of everyday classroom discourse revealed how students in the bilingual education program participated more in classroom discussions and activities, with turns that were both longer and more linguistically complex. More broadly, bilingual education classrooms were characterized by fluid teacher–student interaction (rather than solely teacher-fronted) and by activities that were pedagogically meaningful (e.g. summarizing and discussing readings rather than copying letters from the board). Findings revealed ways in which educational policies around medium of instruction (MOI) profoundly shaped classroom discourse and learning opportunities and had the power to include even the most disenfranchised, in this case, rural Quechua-speakers, in formal education.

A powerful counterpoint to this work is Chick's (1996) analysis of what he characterized as "safe-talk" by teachers and students in Zulu-English classrooms. So-called safe-talk, defined by rhythmic, chorusing sequences, serves social rather than academic functions in classrooms where policy mandates that the MOI is a language in which students (and sometimes teachers) are not proficient. Safe-talk allows for teachers and students to avoid the loss of face associated with (in this case) English language incompetence and to maintain a sense of purpose and accomplishment. Through ritualistic safe-talk discourse patterns, Zulu-speaking students could participate in English-medium instruction that was mandated by South African educational policy at the time. Chick's micro-ethnographic discourse analysis points to the ways in which these patterns simultaneously allowed for inclusion, as all students had access to these repetitious choral structures, and exclusion, as these structures limited academic engagement and content learning (Hornberger and Chick 2001).

More contemporary work has taken up discourse analysis methods to analyze how particular language and education policies, such as those promoting translanguaging, potentially construct more inclusive classroom contexts and productive learning environments. As suggested by Baker (2001), translanguaging has the potential to promote deeper and fuller understanding of the subject matter; to develop students' weaker language(s); to facilitate home-school links and cooperation; and to promote the integration of fluent speakers with early learners (see Chapter 18 in this volume). While translanguaging approaches remain controversial (see "debates" in Section 23.3), a growing body of work has examined the impact of these (typically local) translanguaging educational policies on students' engagement and participation in classroom instructional interactions. For instance, Velasco and García (2014) took up Fairclough's (2007) notion of "intertextuality" to critically examine written texts produced by five bilingual learners in which translanguaging was used in the planning, drafting and production stages of writing. In turn, Martin-Beltrán (2014) used interactional ethnography and microgenetic analysis to investigate how students who were learning English alongside students learning Spanish activated their multilingual repertoires as they participated in a school program that promoted reciprocal learning. Her findings revealed fluid and reciprocal affordances for language learning during interactions among linguistically diverse peers as they drew upon translanguaging practices.

Lastly, a final line of research meriting mention has engaged in close, discursive analysis of language and education policies themselves. For instance, Haque and Patrick (2015) took up critical historical and discursive analysis to analyze language policy in Canada. They showed how racial hierarchies and language ideologies favored French and English dominance, and, furthermore, that the text of the language and education policies reinforced the marginalization of Indigenous groups, who were defined in terms of a socially constructed and assigned category of race. King and Bigelow (2017, 2019) likewise took up discourse analysis tools to analyze a recently passed US state law promoting multilingualism. Drawing on interviews with key policy officials and close analysis of the text of law, they examined the development and implementation of the law. Through their close analysis of the positioning within narrative accounts, King and Bigelow demonstrated how local culture, in particular what has been termed "Minnesota Nice," shaped both the law's development and its implementation path. They argued that, despite the inclusive rhetoric of the law, the implementation trajectory to date seems unlikely to alter the well-established exclusionary practices in place.

23.3 Debates

Most of the discursive processes of inclusion and exclusion overviewed so far are widely documented and neither controversial nor contested. However, within the study of discourse in education, there are other areas of ongoing debates concerning the conceptual/theoretical, methodological and implicational dimensions of this work; we highlight three of these in Sections 23.3.1, 23.3.2 and 23.3.3.

23.3.1 Agency versus Structural Constraints

At the conceptual and theoretical level, there is ongoing debate about the relative importance of agency (co)construction in language-in-interaction, on the one hand, and constraint in relation to institutional and sociocultural structures, on the other. Micro-analysts often approach the contingent emergence of linguistic patterns with reference to the demonstration of agency as free will or resistance in interaction. By contrast, macro-analysts often emphasize their insights into constraint with reference to the structure and ideology at the institutional and societal levels. Differences concerning the relative analytical weight to be given to agency versus structural constraint have deep roots.

Micro-analysts' focus on the contingent emergence of linguistic patterns in educational discourses, especially those used to include and exclude participation and memberships, attempts to move beyond the earlier deterministic accounts evident in initial home-school mismatch literature, for instance. In current work, linguistic patterns or practices are analyzed to more fully describe individuals' particular lived experiences; those practices can either reproduce or transform the structures that shape them. To that end, micro-analysts often conceptualize and theorize unexpected language behaviors and their referential meanings at multiple sociolinguistic scales (Blommaert 2007) with an emphasis on agency. Here, agency is usually equated with free will or the resistance of individuals in interaction.

A central concern in taking agency as a synonym for free will is that this approach "ignores or merely gives lip service to the social nature of agency and the pervasive influence of culture on human intentions, beliefs, and actions" (Ahearn 2001: 114). Moreover, treating agency as a synonym for resistance has the potential to lead to a "romance of resistance" (Abu-Lughod 1990), minimizing the constraining power of structures and norms (e.g. linguistic, economic, sociopolitical in nature) and resulting in a more deductive view of agency and language practices. For most scholars, pure free will or resistance does not exist because the exercise of agency is complicated and contradictory, reflecting and simultaneously being shaped by multiple sociolinguistic scales (Ahearn 2001).

In contrast, macro-analysts tend to emphasize the role that structural constraint plays in understanding the emergence of unexpected language practices in inclusion and exclusion in educational discourses. They critique the missing links between the close analyses of linguistic patterns and spatial and temporal scales in micro-analytic studies exploring enduring questions on social power domination and inequality (Silverstein 1992). However, macro-analysts' focus on the structural constraint often leads to an (over)emphasis on deterministic social forces that fails to more fully explain individuals' ethnographic experiences at local level and how those experiences reflect longer and broader temporal and spatial scales (Wortham 2012).

Agency is not merely an individual's demonstration of free will. Agency is also not resistance in interaction. This is because, as Fairclough (2007) notes, social agents are not free agents. Social agents are socially constrained, but their actions are not totally socially determined given that "agents have their own 'casual power,' which is not reducible to the causal powers of social structures and practices" (Fairclough 2007: 22). In this way, agency is mediated through not only larger social structures and political ideologies but also linguistic forms and meanings co-constructed in conversation (Agha 2007). One approach to this tension outlined here is to take agency as multiple agentive acts that involve accommodation to, or reinforcement of, one's positions in relation to others in discourse (Al Zidjaly 2009). Individuals actively construct and constrain, rather than passively engaging in meaning formation and identity and membership construction that are socially mediated and intertextually situated within a bound of larger discourses (Ahearn 2001). Approaches such as this, including scalar analysis (e.g. Blommaert 2007: Wortham 2012), allow analysts to make connections among phenomena at different levels of analysis (Warriner 2012) and to examine the interplay of the shared moments that "add up to social life" (Lemke 2000: 273).

23.3.2 Boundaries of Analysis

At the methodological level, perhaps the most longstanding and salient debate concerns the boundaries of analysis. As suggested, micro-analytic research (e.g. discourse or conversation analysis) into educational diversity and inclusion have been critiqued for failing to fully engage with critical social theories and longer and broader sociological scales. Conversely, macro-analytic studies that approach inclusion and exclusion from a critical theoretical stance (e.g. critical race theory) have been critiqued for their lack of close linguistic analysis of discourse and conversation structure, and sometimes sweeping claims (Rogers 2011). Bringing together a critical theoretical perspective (e.g. poststructuralism) and aspects of discourse analysis, critical discourse analysis (CDA) attempts to describe, interpret and explain the ways in which talk constructs, is constructed by, demonstrates and is demonstrated by cultural practices across diverse populations and speech communities (Wodak and Meyer 2015).

Many scholars agree that discourse practices in education are never neutral; rather, they reflect and reproduce broader inequalities. An explicitly critical approach has been taken by some to consider how the production of knowledge is mediated by the values of individuals and discourse communities (van Dijk 2011; Wodak 2011). These CDA scholars take up a postdiscourse view of knowledge construction that emphasizes experiences, subjectivity, reflexivity and more holistic understanding shaped by the social and power relations of capitalist production (Rogers 2011). They engage with critical social-theoretical frameworks to analyze how power structures (privilege, hegemony) and social inequities are demonstrated, legitimized and resisted by and through the use of language in educational and sociopolitical contexts (van Dijk 2015).

Yet there are longstanding debates between scholars of CDA and conversation analysis (CA), particularly on their fundamentally different views of text and talk (Hammersley 2003; Schegloff 1997; van Dijk 1999, 2015; Wetherell 1998; see Chapter 3 in this volume). Both CDA and CA recognize that text and talk are structured under the constraints of the social situation where they occur. However, the ways in which CDA and CA contextualize text and talk are quite different. In principle, CDA adopts a critical social-theoretical framework to examine the interrelatedness between human agency and social structures within larger institutional or societal systems (Wodak and Meyer 2015). Put differently, CDA considers the hierarchical structure of power as well as communicative norms and habitus as a function of the structure that guides and regulates cultures and conduct. In contrast, CA does not usually share this broad research goal of theorizing and analyzing relationships across human agency, language use and society. Therefore, for some scholars of CA, contextual and interpersonal categories (e.g. power, gender, race) are not often prior considerations for the analysis of talk, and become relevant only if they emerged through the participants' talk-in-interaction.

This debate has broader methodological implications for the study of discourse, including, perhaps most importantly, the role of the researcher in the research context and their relationships to participants and data. On one (extreme) side of this debate is the position held by some conversation analysts that demands minimal involvement of the researcher in the context, seeking to audio/video record data as if the researcher is not present. From this perspective, the researcher is a neutral data collector and the objective is to transcribe closely to uncover the organization of everyday talk. Other approaches to discourse studies, including those grounded in more anthropological or ethnographic perspectives, view neutrality as impossible and acknowledge (and seek to understand how) the researcher's positionality in shaping the theorizing and designing of studies as well as the collection and analysis of data (van Dijk 2015). These lines of work tend to see that a fundamental component of critical research is developing "a nexus of shared practice and discourse that productively mediates differences between researchers' and [participants'] respective Discourses or habituses" (Jaffe 2012: 350). From this vantage point, the goal is not to neutralize or invisibilize the role of researcher in a study but to make apparent and to take into account the ways in which research data are shaped by researcher positionalities in relation to others (Martin-Jones 2015).

A relevant debate concerns the authority of the researcher relative to study participants, including questions of who counts as an insider or outsider and who has the authority and legitimacy to make claims about whom. In discourse and educational research, these tensions are not surprisingly most evident in contexts where power differences are highly salient. For instance, Native American language scholars and non-Indigenous scholars working to support Native American languages note myriad tensions in navigating this work (Thorne, Siekmann and Charles 2015). These include questions of who the research is intended to benefit (e.g. the scholarly community or the language community) and who has the authority to record, analyze and make claims about the language of others or even of one's own group.

This researcher–researched tension is also apparent in the ongoing discussion of the role of interviews in applied linguistics. Talmy (2011), for instance, contrasted what he called the *research interview as social practice* approach with the *interview as research instrument* approach. While some scholars reject interviews outright as overly dependent on the researcher and thus non-naturalistic, many scholars have attempted to treat (and conduct) interviews as neutral research instruments for collecting language and education data. Increasingly, scholars (e.g. Talmy and others) have taken a more reflexive approach to interviews, analyzing interview talk itself as an interactional and self-presentation work (De Fina and King 2011).

23.3.3 Translanguaging as an Educational Policy

A final area of ongoing debate concerns the efficacy and appropriateness of language-in-education policies. Perhaps the most current and vociferous of these is the disagreement surrounding the pedagogies and policies of translanguaging. In broad terms, translanguaging is a conceptual innovation that embraces positive, holistic and fluid notions of bilingualism and multilingualism, and takes seriously the productive potential of using students' languages as resources for communication and full engagement in educational contexts (Caldas and Faltis 2017; Flores and García 2013; García, Johnson and Seltzer 2017). Over the last decade, as the notion of translanguaging has been taken up by a growing number of scholars, there has been debate over how the term is defined and, in particular, its implications for research, policy and practice. Some have taken translanguaging as a psycholinguistic construct, suggesting that translanguaging, by definition, demands repudiation of the notion that multilinguals hold competencies in different, discrete so-called "named" languages. From this vantage point, multilingual individuals have internally undifferentiated, unitary language systems (Otheguy, García and Reid 2015) or at least an integrated multilingual knowledge base (Herdina and Jessner 2002).

Others have adopted what MacSwan (2017) has termed a multilingual take on translanguaging. This perspective emphasizes that multilingualism is psychologically "real" (acknowledging that speakers do move between different and often recognizable languages) but also points to the ways that translanguaging is productive for learning and engagement in classrooms. This perspective makes clear the longstanding language ideologies that have privileged monolingual language use (and, correspondingly, diminished and problematized use of additional languages), and points to the ways in which codeswitching in the classroom can productively enhance both language and content learning while also contributing to culturally sustaining pedagogies (García, Johnson and Seltzer 2017; Paris 2012).

There is some empirical evidence pointing to the productivity of translanguaging practices for facilitating learning in school. This is sometimes referred to as pedagogical or intentional translanguaging (to contrast with the fluid, everyday use of languages outside of school). Productive, intentional pedagogical approaches might entail reading a text in one language and discussing it in another or alternating the languages used for input and output systematically. For instance, researchers in New Zealand found that Māori language literacy increased when students were permitted to use their first language (in this case, English) to discuss Māori medium texts (Lowman et al. 2007). Similarly, recent work with Deaf adults in the United States suggests that translanguaging served as a bridge from American Sign Language to English literacy (Hoffman et al. 2017). Vaish (2018) reported that for Malay and Chinese-dominant children who were struggling English readers, translanguaging pedagogical approaches seemed to stimulate metalinguistic awareness, which helped learners with nuances of orthography, grammar and meaning-making.

Other scholars, in particular those concerned with nondominant, endangered or Indigenous languages, argue that translanguaging approaches are less applicable or perhaps wholly inappropriate for minority language contexts. As Cenoz and Gorter (2017) noted, in situations where the balance of power of the languages is uneven, school is often a prime (and perhaps the only) site where minority languages can be protected and practiced. There is concern that translanguaging pedagogies might impact both the language status (crowding out limited "space" for use of the language) and the language corpus (leading to loss of particular forms and a simplified language), as by researchers of the Basque case (Cenoz and Gorter 2017; Zarraga 2014). Other scholars have emphasized the longstanding lines of research supporting separation of languages in the classroom and maximizing target language use, and have argued for the need for more classroom research prior to adopting translanguaging approaches (Fortune and Tedick 2018).

23.4 Implications

Taken together, the discourse study of diversity and inclusion has demonstrated, in close detail and with solid empirical evidence, multiple ways that everyday discourse in educational contexts reflects, enacts and reproduces social structures, including the exclusion and segregation of minoritized groups. Using a variety of theoretical and methodological approaches, scholars have uncovered how discourse in educational practices and policy work, covertly and overtly, (re)produces inclusion and/or marginalization simultaneously in interaction.

In some cases, this work has directly informed school practice and policy. For instance, King and Bigelow (2018) used discourse analysis tools to examine the administration of a common placement test for English language learning newcomers to US schools. They found that test takers and test administrators locally negotiated this test in ways that allowed them to save face while still meeting local and federal policy requirements and expectations. Moreover, they found that the nationally used test failed to differentiate adequately across students with widely different literacy skills and formal schooling experiences. As a result of this work, the state now encourages additional testing in students' native languages and supports the development and dissemination of these assessments.

A second contribution of this work is at the theoretical and methodological levels. Many researchers studying discourse of diversity and inclusion in education have taken up multiple methodological tools to understand the dynamics of diversity and inclusion in classroom interactions. This tendency toward multidisciplinary, layered approaches is driven both by the complexity of school-based research (e.g. any particular classroom is porous, shaped by myriad school, district, state and federal policies and practices) and by the limited and variable access that forces researchers to do the most and best with what they have. In part of this reason, scholars of discourse in education in many instances have been pioneers in combining or layering (King and Mackey 2016) research approaches to discourse.

23.5 Future Directions

One important future direction for the study of discourse in education will be closer analysis of informal contexts of learning, and in particular learning, relationship building and organizing through social media and online platforms. While there is a growing body of work on digital, online interaction, the field needs to advance theoretically and to keep pace with the development of technology. As data suggest that youth spend nine hours per day online, and that significant differences exists in technology use across youth with multilingual and multicultural backgrounds (Watkins 2012). understanding more about discourse and including and exclusion processes in this domain is of paramount importance.

An additional future direction concerns the need for our work to engage more deeply with the analysis of gender (including LGBTQR+ populations), race and raciolinguistic inequalities (Flores and Rosa, 2015; see Chapter 24 in this volume). While discourse analysts have long been interested in how gender, race and ethnicity influence and are influenced by talk, continued research in this direction is important in future years as we debate and continue to work through differences, race and social inequality. This work is particularly urgent and concomitantly more accessible as increasing numbers of individuals have access to social media, political organizing and advocacy work.

In addition, an area of continuing and ongoing work concerns agency and structural constraint, as we discussed in Section 23.3.1. Specifically, researchers need to reconsider and develop approaches to bridge what has sometimes been termed the "micro" versus "macro" divide. Scholars from diverse disciplines are interested in making links across everyday talk, on the one hand, and broader discourses and ideologies, on the other. While numerous approaches (e.g. scalar analysis, nexus analysis) have been introduced to build these links analytically, more theoretical and methodological work is needed here.

Another gap is the need for deeper theoretical understanding of organizational structures of classroom discourses. Classroom-oriented, critical discourse studies of instructional interactions have been theorized by "a continued privileging of mono-cultural epistemology" (Rogers 2011: 9). These studies are also analyzed methodologically by a Western-based view of organizational structures of classroom discourse that stands in opposition to Eastern perspectives of classroom interactions, in which the speaker's intention is often oriented toward their listeners, the intersubjective nature of conversation and focus on the collective culture with the individuals as part of the group (Shi-xu 2009). A more nuanced theoretical and methodological approach should be locally grounded and globally mediated, considering a postdiscourse view (e.g. postcolonization) of meaning construction that emphasizes experience, subjective, reflexivity and more holistic understanding shaped by local and global, social and power relations of capitalist production (Flowerdew 2002).

23.6 Conclusion

The discursive study of diversity and inclusion in education has enriched our collective understanding of how social power and inequality are enacted, (re)produced and resisted through discourse-in-interaction in educational contexts. In this chapter, we reviewed a number of influential and current works, highlighting what the study of discourse has contributed to field's understanding of diversity, inclusion and exclusion in education, locally and broadly. While some theoretical and methodological debates remain unresolved, we have no doubt that the field will continue to grow and to make productive contributions to our understanding of language in the organization of social life, both in and out of schools.

Further Reading

To further learn about how different discourse approaches applied to critically examine diversity and inclusion in educational contexts, how locally situated practices and identity shape and are shaped by broader institutional or sociopolitical ideologies, and the relationships between researcher and the researched, we recommend the following three books:

Bucholtz, M. (2010). *White Kids: Language, Race, and Styles of Youth Identity*. New York: Cambridge University Press.

Bucholtz examines how white teenage students use their linguistic resources (e.g., Valley Girl speech, African American English) to demonstrate identities based on race and youth cultures, and to position themselves and others in accordance with the school's racialized social order.

Gardner, S. and Martin-Jones, M. (eds.) (2012). *Multilingualism, Discourse, and Ethnography*. New York: Routledge.

This edited book discusses multilingualism and discourse from different sociolinguistic and/or ethnographic perspectives, reviews conceptual and methodological concerns and challenges that researchers face, and suggests future directions in the relevant fields.

Wodak, R. and Meyer, M. (eds.) (2015). *Methods of Critical Discourse Analysis*, 3rd ed. Thousand Oaks, CA: Sage.

This edited book provides an introduction to critical discourse analysis, reviewing various theories and methods associated within the fields of applied linguistics and linguistic anthropology. It also examines how critical discourse analysis, as a theory and method, is applied to the research of diversity, exclusion and inclusion in educational and societal contexts.

References

Abdi, K. (2011). "She Really Only Speaks English": Positioning, Language Ideology, and Heritage Language Learners. *Canadian Modern Language Review* 67(2): 161–90.

Abu-Lughod L. (1990). The Romance of Resistance: Tracing Transformations of Power through Bedouin Women. *American Ethnologist* 17(1): 41–55.

Agha, A. (2007). *Language and Social Relations*. Cambridge: Cambridge University Press.

Ahearn, L. M. (2001). Language and Agency. *Annual Review of Anthropology* 30: 109–37.

Al Zidjaly, N. (2009). Agency as an Interactive Achievement. *Language in Society* 38(2): 177–200.

Anyon, J. (1980). Social Class and the Hidden Curriculum of Work. *Journal of Education* 162(1): 67–92.

Archakis, A. (2014). Immigrant Voices in Students' Essay Texts: Between Assimilation and Pride. *Discourse & Society* 25(3): 297–314.

Baker, C. (2001). *Foundations of Bilingual Education and Bilingualism*. Clevedon: Multilingual Matters.

Baquedano-López, P., Solís, J. L. and Kattan, S. (2005). Adaptation: The Language of Classroom Learning. *Linguistics and Education* 16(1): 1–26.

Blommaert, J. (2007). Sociolinguistic Scales. *Intercultural Pragmatics* 4 (1): 1–19.

Bucholtz, M. (2010). *White Kids: Language, Race, and Styles of Youth Identity*. New York: Cambridge University Press.

Bourdieu, P. (1989). Social Space and Symbolic Power. *Sociological Theory* 7 (1): 14–25.

(1991). *Language and Symbolic Power*. Cambridge, MA: Harvard University Press.

Caldas, B. and Faltis, C. (2017). Más allá de poly, multi, trans, pluri, bi: ¿De qué hablamos cuando hablamos de translinguismo? *NABE Journal of Research and Practice* 8(1): 155–6.

Cenoz, J. and Gorter, D. (2017). Minority Languages and Sustainable Translanguaging: Threat or Opportunity? *Journal of Multilingual and Multicultural Development* 38(10): 901–12.

Chick, J. K. (1996). Safe-Talk: Collusion in Apartheid Education. In H. Coleman (ed.) *Society and the Language Classroom*. Cambridge: Cambridge University Press. 21–39.

Chrisomalis, S. (2015). What's So Improper about Fractions? Prescriptivism and Language Socialization at Math Corps. *Language in Society* 44(1): 63–85.

Chun, E. (2009). Speaking like Asian Immigrants: Intersections of Accommodation and Mocking at a US High School. *Journal of Pragmatics* 19(1): 17–38.

Cook-Gumperz, J. and Szymanski, M. (2001). Classroom "Families": Cooperating or Competing – Girls' and Boys' Interactional Styles in a Bilingual Classroom. *Research on Language and Social Interaction* 34(1): 107–30.

De Fina, A. and King, K.A. (2011). Language Problem or Language Conflict? Narratives of Immigrant Women's Experiences in the U.S. *Discourse Studies* 13(2): 163–88.

Delfino, J. B. (2016). Fighting Words? Joining as Conflict Talk and Identity Performance among African American Preadolescents. *Journal of Sociolinguistics* 20(5): 631–53.

Delpit, L. (1995/2006). *Other People's Children: Cultural Conflict in the Classroom*. New York: The New Press.

Fairclough, N. (2007). *Analysing Discourse: Textual Analysis for Social Research*. New York: Routledge.

Flores, N. and García, O. (2013). Linguistic Third Spaces in Education: Teachers' Translanguaging across the Bilingual Continuum. In D. Little, C. Leung and P. van Avermaet (eds.) *Managing Diversity in Education: Languages, Policies, Pedagogies*. Tonawanda, NY: Multilingual Matters. 243–56.

Flores, N. and Rosa, J. (2015). Undoing Appropriateness: Raciolinguistic Ideologies and Language Diversity in Education. *Harvard Educational Review* 85: 149–71.

Flowerdew, J. (2002). Globalization Discourse: A View from the East. *Discourse & Society* 13(2): 209–25.

Fortune, T. W. and Tedick, D. J. 2018, Context Matters: Translanguaging and Language Immersion Education in the US and Canada. In M. Haneda and H. Nassaji (eds.) *Perspectives on Language as Action*, Tonawanda NY. 27–44.

Fotovatian, S. (2012). Three Constructs of Institutional Identity among International Doctoral Students in Australia. *Teaching in Higher Education* 17(5): 577–88.

García, O., Johnson, S. I. and Seltzer, K. (2017). *The Translanguaging Classroom: Leveraging Student Bilingualism for Learning*. Philadelphia, PA: Caslon.

García-Sánchez, I. M. (2013). The Everyday Politics of "Cultural Citizenship" among North African Immigrant School Children in Spain. *Language & Communication* 33(4): 481–99.

Garrett, P. B. and Baquedano-López, P. (2002). Language Socialization: Reproduction and Continuity, Transformation and Change. *Annual Review of Anthropology* 31: 339–61.

Gutiérrez, K. D., Morales, P. Z. and Martinez, D. C. (2009). Re-mediating Literacy: Culture, Difference, and Learning for Students from Nondominant Communities. *Review of Research in Education* 33(1): 212–45.

Giddens, A. (1979). *Central Problems in Social Theory: Action, Structure, and Contradiction in Social Analysis*, Vol. 241. Berkeley and Los Angeles, CA: University of California Press.

Goodwin, M. H. (2006). *The Hidden Life of Girls: Games of Stance, Status, and Exclusion*. Malden, MA: Blackwell.

Goodwin, M. H. and Alim, H. S. (2010). "Whatever (Neck Roll, Eye Roll, Teeth Suck)": The Situated Coproduction of Social Categories and Identities through Stancetaking and Transmodal Stylization. *Journal of Linguistic Anthropology* 20(1): 179–94.

Hammersley, M. (2003). Conversation Analysis and Discourse Analysis/ Methods or Paradigms? *Discourse & Society* 14(6): 751–81.

Haque, E. and Patrick, D. (2015). Indigenous Languages and the Racial Hierarchisation of Language Policy in Canada. *Journal of Multilingual and Multicultural Development* 36(1): 27–41.

Heath, S. B. (1983). *Ways with Words: Language, Life and Work in Communities and Classrooms*. New York: Cambridge University Press.

Herdina, P. and Jessner, U. (2002). *A Dynamic Model of Multilingualism: Perspectives of Change in Psycholinguistics*, Vol. 121. Tonawanda, NY: Multilingual Matters.

Hoffman, D., Wolsey, J.-L., Andrews, J. and Clark, D. (2017). Translanguaging Supports Reading with Deaf Adult Bilinguals: A Qualitative Approach. *Qualitative Report* 22(7): 1925–44.

Hornberger, N. H. (1987). Bilingual Education Success, but Policy Failure. *Language in Society* 16(2): 205–26.

Hornberger, N. H. and Chick, J. K. (2001). Co-constructing School. In M. Heller and M. Martin-Jones (eds.) *Voices of Authority: Education and Linguistic Difference*, Vol. 1. Westport, CT: Ablex. 31–56.

Jaffe, A. (2012). Collaborative Practice, Linguistic Anthropological Enquiry and Mediation between Researcher and Practitioner Discourses. In S. Gardner and M. Martin-Jones (eds.) *Multilingualism, Discourse, and Ethnography*. New York: Routledge. 334–52.

Jaspers, J. (2011). Talking Like a "Zerolingual": Ambiguous Linguistic Caricatures at an Urban Secondary School. *Journal of Pragmatics* 43(5): 1264–78.

Johnson, S. J. (2017). Agency, Accountability and Affect: Kindergarten Children's Orchestration of Reading with a Friend. *Learning, Culture and Social Interaction* 12: 15–31.

King, K. A. and Bigelow, M. (Fall, 2017). Minnesota (Not so) Nice?: LEAPS Policy Development and Implementation. (Invited article.) *MinneTESOL Journal*. http://minnetesoljournal.org/fall-2017-issue/minnesota-not-nice-politics-language-education-policy-development-implementation.

(2018). The Language Policy of Placement Tests for Newcomer English Learners. *Educational Policy* 32(7): 936–68.

(2019). The Politics of Language Education Policy Implementation: Minnesota (Not so) Nice? In T. Ricento (ed.) *Language and Politics in the U.S. and Canada*. Cambridge: Cambridge University Press. 192–211.

King, K. A. and Mackey, A. (2016). Research Methodology in Second Language Studies: Trends, Concerns, and New Directions. *Modern Language Journal* 100: 209–27.

Lamb, G. (2015). "Mista, Are You in a Good Mood?": Stylization to Negotiate Interaction in an Urban Hawai'i Classroom. *Multilingua* 34(2): 159–85.

Lemke, J. (2000). Across the Scales of Time/Artifacts, Activities, and Meanings in Ecosocial Systems. *Mind, Culture, and Activity* 7(4): 273–90.

Lowman, C., Fitzgerald, T., Rapira, P. and Clark, R. (2007). First Language Literacy Skill Transfer in a Second Language Learning Environment. *SET* 2: 24–8.

Otheguy, R., García, O. and Reid, W. (2015). Clarifying Translanguaging and Deconstructing Named Languages: A Perspective from Linguistics. *Applied Linguistics Review* 6(3): 281–307.

MacSwan, J. (2017). A Multilingual Perspective on Translanguaging. *American Educational Research Journal* 54(1): 167–201.

Martin-Beltrán, M. (2014). "What Do You Want to Say?" How Adolescents Use Translanguaging to Expand Learning Opportunities. *International Multilingual Research Journal* 8(3): 208–30.

Martin-Jones, M. (2015). Multilingual Classroom Discourse as a Window on Wider Social, Political and Ideological Processes: Critical Ethnographic Approaches. In N. Markee (ed.) *The Handbook of Classroom Discourse and Interaction*. Malden, MA: Blackwell. 446–60.

Michaels, S. (1981). "Sharing Time": Children's Narrative Styles and Differential Access to Literacy. *Language in Society* 10(3): 423–42.

Mökkönen, A. C. (2013). Newcomers Navigating Language Choice and Seeking Voice: Peer Talk in a Multilingual Primary School Classroom in Finland. *Anthropology & Education Quarterly* 44(2): 124–41.

Moore, L. C. (2006). Learning by Heart in Qur'anic and Public Schools in Northern Cameroon. *Social Analysis* 50(3): 109–26.

Morita, N. (2009). Language, Culture, Gender, and Academic Socialization. *Language and Education* 23(5): 443–60.

Paris, D. (2012). Culturally Sustaining Pedagogy: A Needed Change in Stance, Terminology, and Practice. *Educational Researcher* 41 (3): 93–7.
Pérez, R. (2013). Learning to Make Racism Funny in the "Color-Blind" Era: Stand-Up Comedy Students, Performance Strategies, and the (Re)production of Racist Jokes in Public. *Discourse & Society* 24(4): 478–503.
Philips, S. U. (1983). *The Invisible Culture*. Long Grove, IL: Waveland Press.
Razfar, A. (2006). Language Ideologies in Practice: Repair and Classroom Discourse. *Linguistics and Education* 16(4): 404–24.
Rogers, R. (ed.) (2011). *An Introduction to Critical Discourse Analysis in Education*. New York: Routledge.
Schegloff, E. A. (1997). Whose Text? Whose Context? *Discourse & Society* 8(2): 165–87.
Shankar, S. (2008). Speaking like a Model Minority: "FOB" Styles, Gender, and Racial Meanings among Desi Teens in Silicon Valley. *Journal of Linguistic Anthropology* 18(2): 268–89.
Shi-xu. (2009). Reconstructing Eastern Paradigms of Discourse Studies. *Journal of Multicultural Discourses* 4(1): 29–48.
Silverstein, M. (1992). The Indeterminacy of Contextualization: When Is Enough Enough? In P. Auer and A. Di Luzio (eds.) *The Contextualization of Language*. Amsterdam: John Benjamins. 55–75.
Talmy, S. (2004). Forever FOB: The Cultural Production of ESL in a High School. *Pragmatics* 14(2): 149–72.
 (2008). The Cultural Productions of the ESL Student at Tradewinds High: Contingency, Multidirectionality, and Identity in L2 Socialization. *Applied Linguistics* 29(4): 619–44.
 (2010). Becoming "Local" in ESL: Racism as Resource in a Hawai'i Public High School. *Journal of Language, Identity, and Education* 9(1): 36–57.
 (2011). The Interview as Collaborative Achievement: Interaction, Identity and Ideology in a Speech Event. *Applied Linguistics* 32(1): 25–42.
Thorne, S. L., Siekmann, S. and Charles, W. (2015). Ethical Issues in Indigenous Language Research and Interventions. In P. I. de Costa (ed.) *Ethics in Applied Linguistics Research: Language Researcher Narratives*. New York: Routledge. 142–60.
UNHCR. (2018). Figures at a Glance. www.unhcr.org/en-us/figures-at-a-glance.html.
Vaish, V. (2018). Translanguaging Pedagogy for Simultaneous Biliterates Struggling to Read in English. *International Journal of Multilingualism* 16 (3): 286–301.
Van Dijk, T. A. (1999). Critical Discourse Analysis and Conversation Analysis. *Discourse & Society* 10(4): 459–60.
 (ed.) (2011). *Discourse Studies: A Multidisciplinary Introduction*. Thousand Oaks, CA: Sage.

(2015). Critical Discourse Analysis. In D. Tannen, H. E. Hamilton and D. Schiffrin (eds.) *The Handbook of Discourse Analysis*. Malden, MA: Wiley Blackwell. 466–85.

Velasco, P. and García, O. (2014). Translanguaging and the Writing of Bilingual Learners. *Bilingual Research Journal* 37(1): 6–23.

Vickers, C. H. (2007). Second Language Socialization through Team Interaction among Electrical and Computer Engineering Students. *Modern Language Journal* 91(4): 621–40.

Warriner, D. S. (2012). When the Macro Facilitates the Micro: A Study of Regimentation and Emergence in Spoken Interaction. *Anthropology and Education Quarterly* 43(2): 173–91.

Watkins, C. (2012). Digital Divide: Navigating the Digital Edge. *International Journal of Learning and Media* 3(2): 1–2.

Wetherell, M. (1998). Positioning and Interpretative Repertoires: Conversation Analysis and Post-Structuralism in Dialogue. *Discourse & Society* 9(3): 387–412.

Wodak, R. (2011). Critical Discourse Analysis. In K. Hyland and B. Paltridge (eds.) *The Continuum Companion to Discourse Analysis*. New York: Continuum. 38–53.

Wodak, R. and Meyer, M. (eds.) (2015). *Methods of Critical Discourse Analysis*, 3rd ed. Thousand Oaks, CA: Sage.

Wortham, S. (2012). Beyond Macro and Micro in the Linguistic Anthropology of Education. *Anthropology & Education Quarterly* 43(2): 128–37.

Zarraga, A. (2014). Hizkuntza-ukipenaren ondorioak. www.erabili.eus/zer_berri/muinetik/1410777403/1410864140.

24

Discourse and Racialization

Virginia Zavala and Michele Back

24.1 Introduction

The modern concept of race derives from a European history of colonization and exploitation of non-European Others within the framework of the "discovery" of other continents (De la Cadena 2008; Wade 2017). This construction of race occurred at the service of a hierarchized society whose economic model focused on exclusion and where the division of labor corresponded with skin color (Quijano 2000). As we discuss in this chapter, discourse, in the sense of language as social practice, had a crucial role in creating the powerful idea of "race" and racialized categories and identities, with consequential unequal material conditions and embodied experiences.[1]

Currently, researchers in numerous fields recognize race as a social construction and racial categories as not corresponding to significant biological differences (Delgado and Stefancic 2017; Yudell et al. 2016). For this reason, many believe that race is merely an illusion and/or that we live in a "postracial" society. Yet the idea of race is still very much real, although its reality depends upon certain social ontological schemes and practices (Alcoff 2006). In the framework of contemporary skepticism regarding race as "real," we highlight its social reality and power as a category of social differentiation, both of which have political, sociological and economic consequences. Goldberg's (1992) assessment that race is irrelevant, but that everything is race, rings especially true in this context.

Despite its detractors (Goldberg 1992; Rattansi 2005; Fields 2001), the increasing use of the terms "racialization" and "racialized" (in contrast, for instance, to "racial classification" and "racial formation") helps to analyze the notion of race in terms of ongoing processes rather than as

---

[1] Some of the discussions in this chapter come from Zavala and Back (2017) and Back and Zavala (2019).

a fixed construct (Hochman 2018). As García (2003: 285) states, while "race" is something one supposedly has, "racialization is something that is done to a group, by some social agent, at a certain time, for a given period, in and through various processes, and relative to a particular social context." In fact, the terms "racialization" and "racialized" highlight how current ideas about race and racial categorization are the contingent, changeable result of specific historical, cultural, political and, above all, ideological processes (Chun and Lo 2016). According to Hochman (2018), the process of racialization, as a form of (false) biologization, can be applied to groups, individuals, social structures and a range of other phenomena, such as hairstyle, types of dress or ways of speaking. Hence, racial ideas, as products of racializing processes, do not refer only to phenotypical cues and skin color, and physical features do not solely determine racial meaning (Roth-Gordon 2017).

Racialization as a sociocultural practice entails that race and culture are interrelated and that it is impossible to distinguish biological from cultural racism (De la Cadena 2000; Gotkowitz 2011). Biological understandings are anchored in culture (the culturalization of race) and culture is conceived as a biological force (the naturalization of culture). Race has always been connected to both nature and culture; even nineteenth-century scientific theories contained powerful discourses regarding morality and what we now denominate as culture. For many researchers, the force of race resides precisely in the synthesis of the cultural and the biological (Gotkowitz 2011). This ambiguous connection is precisely what favors the emergence, production and force of racialized thought. By acquiring diverse forms to fit changing historical circumstances, racism can be used to maintain economic and social privileges in different contexts. The combination of rigid and flexible becomes the essence of racism and is fundamental to its adaptability and power.

Due to these complex, situated racializing processes, it is very difficult to depend upon a transcendental, transhistoric definition that includes everything that we intuitively want to include as racial. Perhaps, instead of defining race and racism with a single meaning, we should ask ourselves how race functions according to each historical moment and social particularity (Bailey 2010). This implies moving beyond emphasizing the *ideology* of racism toward emphasizing its *ideological practice* (Wetherell and Potter 1992). Researchers should cease analyzing racist ideology as a fixed system of ideas, instead observing how these ideas function in a particular context. For example, an ideological approach proposes that if a statement makes an allusion to genetic and/or phenotypical characteristics and locates social groups in a hierarchy, then it could be considered racist. In contrast, an ideological practice approach assumes racism as a series of ideological effects with flexible, fluid and varied content. What is important is the effect rather than the content, as the latter will always be changing. In this way, discourse would be defined as racist due to what it *does* and not necessarily what it *says*.

Language, though generally overlooked in research on race, is central to how race is culturally understood, to the form it takes in different contexts and to semiotic processes of racialization. Through racialization as a key semiotic process and sociocultural practice, people read and interpret bodies racially in order to naturalize difference. In this chapter, we will focus on *linguistic racialization*, or "the sociocultural processes through which race – as an ideological dimension of human differentiation – comes to be imagined, produced and reified through language practices" (Chun and Lo 2016: 220). These processes work differently in different contexts, where race usually intersects with other identity components (such as gender, social class and education) in complex ways (see Chapter 19 in this volume for a discussion of intersectionality). We will illustrate how certain cultural practices, but also the use of specific linguistic and orthographic features, are discursively racialized in articulation with ideologies of class and education. In addition, we will show another example where "deracialization" processes occur as a reaction to more classic racist practices.

In this chapter, we discuss in detail the role of discourse in creating race and racialized categories, providing examples from recent research where applicable. Section 24.2 provides a historical overview of the topic, with an emphasis on two main theoretical approaches pertaining to discourse in this area: *racial discourse* and *racialized linguistic practices*. Section 24.3 is devoted to a discussion of issues and ongoing debates in the area of racialization and discourse, and Section 24.4 looks at implications. In Section 24.5 we discuss future directions, and we conclude with suggestions for further reading. Throughout this chapter we highlight the flexible, contextual nature of discourse and racialization and the need to analyze its effects on racialized subjects, as its content is always shifting.

24.2 Overview of the Topic

Although American anthropologists developed ideas about race and language early on, sociolinguists did not establish a connection between language and race until the 1960s. In any case, these scholars viewed language as a closed structural system shared by group members characterized in terms of linguistic features (Labov 1972; Baugh 1983) or discourse strategies (Goodwin 1990; Mitchell-Kernan 1972). This "distinctive ethnoracial language paradigm" (Chun and Lo 2016: 221) attended to linguistic patterns that distinguished ethnoracial groups. Despite the fact that this research revealed the workings of linguistic racism, it favored correlational studies that did not address situated language use and assumed that language reflected a speaker's "real" identity (Chun and Lo 2016).

Assuming language as discourse, we propose that language and race intersect in two main ways. First, both intersect in discourse that takes race as its topic. This is what we call "racial discourse" or, in the words of Alim, Rickford and Ball (2016), "languaging race," in which people's ways of using language construct reality in racialized terms. Second, language and race intersect in the language use associated with specific racialized groups. This is what we call "racialized linguistic practice," in which certain linguistic features or ways of speaking are racialized through indexical processes connecting language forms to certain societal groups. While the first phenomenon involves the creation of referential meaning by the use of categories or talk commonly associated with race, the second involves symbolic associations between linguistic forms and racialized meanings (Bucholtz 2011). The latter relates more to interpersonal meanings and shows how racial identities can be negotiated through specific ways of using language. In Sections 24.2.1 and 24.2.2, we offer further details about both ways in which language and race intersect, with the help of examples.

24.2.1 Racial Discourse

Racial discourse includes all talk or text about race or racialized issues. Analysis of this discourse considers content in the sense of what is said but also how it is said within the social context in which it is produced, consumed and distributed by others (Fairclough 2002). This type of discourse has been studied by different schools of applied and sociocultural linguistics, including critical discourse analysis (CDA), linguistic anthropology, discursive psychology and conversation analysis (CA).

This dimension of the intersection between language and race includes the use of racialized terms. However, racial discourse cannot be reduced to the use of these terms, as identifying racist practices has become more and more difficult. Indeed, today, most people do not express racist sentiments directly; rather, they demonstrate an ambivalent, contradictory discourse that often attempts to hide such sentiments. Scholars have turned to the term "race talk" to refer precisely to this phenomenon, which implies using racial rhetoric without alluding to race (Anderson 2008; Bucholtz 2011). For example, a central characteristic of contemporary racist discourse is the rejection of race through negations such as "I'm not racist, but ...."

Racial discourse has been studied in CDA since the 1980s, particularly in the work of Van Dijk (2003) and Wodak (2002) on how privileged speakers engage in discursive moves to normalize discrimination and deny prejudice. Within this perspective, racism has been defined as a system of social domination controlled by symbolic elites, with discourse posited as an instance where racism is reproduced. The elite spheres analyzed in this scholarship include media, political settings, organizations and schools, with an emphasis on immigration policy and the treatment of asylum seekers. CDA has also focused on how people use discourse to normalize racism in noninstitutional contexts when engaging in explicitly prejudiced talk, mainly through the use of disclaimers for avoiding potential negative judgments. For example, Van Dijk (2012) noted that news reporting on immigration emphasizes "illegal" "foreigners" who ostensibly commit crimes and acts of violence in higher numbers than native-born citizens. This type of reporting serves to position immigrants systematically as threats or problems to a white, majority "Us" while avoiding potential sanctioning of this discourse as racist, even though the individuals portrayed in these reports are overwhelmingly people of color.

From the framework of discursive psychology, Augoustinos and Every (2007) highlighted the existence of five forms in which people present negative visions of others as reasonable and justified: (1) rejecting prejudice; (2) presenting personal points of view as reasonable and rational reflections of the outside world; (3) developing positive self-presentations (through "tolerance") in contrast with negative presentations of others (as "criminals"); (4) discursively deracializing negative representations of others with the use of nonracial terms; and (5) appealing to liberal arguments about liberty, equality and progress through nondemocratic ends. For her part, Bucholtz (2011) further developed the fourth point from a linguistic anthropological approach, introducing discursive strategies such as *erasure, delay* and *displacement*. Hence, the significance of race is *erased* in discourse and not named; in other cases, it is *delayed* through hesitations, mitigations or silences; and in still others, it is *displaced* to categories of education, language or class. However, even though speakers generally do not use explicit racial categories, their rhetoric can be strongly oriented toward race by biologizing and essentializing certain social groups through other categories with the goal of hierarchizing and excluding them.

In the following example, a speaker in his mid-fifties from a high socioeconomic class in Lima justifies the existence of private beaches in Peru, reproducing a postcolonial, segregated society with an unequal distribution of resources (Zavala and Zariquiey 2009). The following excerpt, from a focus group discussion where one of the authors asked about this polemic topic, shows the workings of implicit reference in talk that alludes to race but does not name it:[2]

> This isn't a problem of occupying the same space, the problem is that there is no space. And you don't have to come here if you don't (...) this is not a place, let's say, that is prepared for this type (...) go farther away! But it's not a problem that I don't want them to come, what I don't want is

[2] All translations from the original Spanish are the authors'.

a polluted beach, have you imagined what it could be like with ten thousand people peeing in the sea? Do you have an idea of (...) the level of pollution that could happen in that moment? So, that's what you're discriminating, you're not discriminating the person, you're discriminating the consequence of a saturation that shouldn't happen if the authorities enact (...) enact their duties, right?[3]

In this example, the speaker constructs an argument based on apparent denials, which reveals one strategy of contemporary racism: the rejection of prejudice. "This isn't a problem of occupying the same space"; "you're not discriminating the person." Nevertheless, the speaker tries to justify why some people should not be admitted into private beaches, enacting representations of the Other within a racial rhetoric that erases, delays and displaces race. First, the speaker displays difficulties in naming the Other or using categories that have been historically associated with racial subjects in Peru, such as *"indio," "serrano"* or *"cholo."* This difficulty of naming is also revealed when the speaker delays making reference to the Other during the interaction, as accomplished through silences, hesitations and hedges: "This is not a place, let's say, that is prepared for this type (...) go farther away!". Third, race is displaced to tropes such as space transgression or pollution, which have been studied in other contexts (Van Dijk 2003).

Although these tropes do not refer directly to the Others' cultural practices or ways of being, both the allusion to pollution and the example about urinating in the sea presuppose the ascription of certain characteristics to a discriminated Other. The question "have you imagined what it could be like with ten thousand people peeing in the sea?" works as a strategy with a clear racial rhetoric that presents negative aspects of Others with excessive detail. This rhetoric not only exaggerates and overgeneralizes but also assumes that this practice belongs or is intrinsic to these Others as a social group. These tropes are intertextually linked to the ways in which indigenous people have been historically represented as lacking civility, discipline and "culture" (Roth-Gordon 2017; De la Cadena 2008).

Finally, this argument constructs a fallacy that interpellates social consciousness with environmental tropes. The speaker presents personal points of view as reasonable reflections of the outside world and deracializes negative representations of Others with the use of nonracial terms. Although racial categories are not mentioned, the effect is a clearly ideological racializing practice: the speaker inferiorizes a social group under apparently rational arguments in order to legitimize the privatization of beaches in Peru. He does this by projecting his own interest (that of maintaining his private beach) as the interest of Peruvian society as a whole – even of these Others – under the guise of protecting the environment. This is a clear example of the classic ideological premise in which

---

[3] (...) indicates a pause.

one's own interest is presented as common societal interest and taken as the only possible representation of reality (Marx and Engels 1968).

This aspect of the intersection between language and race includes not only talk or text *about* a third party but also the use of racial or racialized terms to position oneself and the interlocutor during an interaction. We see this positioning in Wong's (2019) analysis of a Peruvian Facebook page, in which the word *cholo*, a denigrating term for Peruvians with indigenous ancestors, is used in its traditional racializing sense by some speakers, then taken up and reflexively reframed as a term of pride by others. Wong analyzes the Facebook page *Vergüenza Democrática* [Democratic Shame] (VD), created during the second round of Peru's 2011 presidential elections to denounce a series of hateful posts against the followers of presidential candidate Ollanta Humala, which were posted by many Peruvians on their personal Facebook pages. The interactants responded to extracts of posts that the VD administrators reentextualized. The original posts expressed unhappiness with the advance of Humala to the second round and sympathy for presidential candidate Pedro Pablo Kuczynski (PPK), who was associated with the White population from higher social classes. On one occasion, the interactants aligned among themselves and with the administrators in relation to the signifier *cholo* as a reaction to one reentextualized post: "That is why the cholos must be happy with Ollanta":[4]

> Hahahahahaha, first of all, cholo refers to people from the *chala* and the coast, my dear ignorant ones, ... why the racism? (Intervention 4)
> ... But I am definitely a happy "chola" who will defend her ideals, position, and the search for democracy in the second round. (Intervention 6)
> I'd rather be a happy cholo than to be like one of them ... (Intervention 7)
> I am a happy chola because I did not vote for PPK, so? (Intervention 15)

The alignment is produced by participants' positioning as *cholos*, in this way constructing an Us opposed to an Other who *cholea* (discriminates against *cholos*). The responses showed an alignment to the identity marker *cholo* through both positive resignification (and deracialization) of the word as a term of pride and critical positioning of the racial category. Hence, the social meaning of *cholo* is reoriented from an apparently fixed racial term to an identity category that is intersubjectively negotiated. It is important to emphasize that the alignment produced among some participants when they position themselves as *cholos* is not motivated by shared racial characteristics but by the necessity of conjointly reacting against the original post in that particular moment and situation. This relational, situated stance is seen, for example, when *cholo* is linked to the search for democracy (Intervention 6), to not being "one of them" (Intervention 7) and to not having voted for Kuczynski (Intervention 15).

---

[4] In the following interaction, there are interventions that have not been included.

Wong's analysis demonstrates that the *cholo* identity, like any other identity, is negotiated in social practice. Interactional-scale analyses reveal the nuanced negotiations of indexical value when multiple ideologies coexist. Terms like "Asian American," "Black" or "*cholo*" do not have stable senses across contexts, since meanings are emergent and negotiated (Reyes 2011). People can fluidly position themselves in relation to figures of personhood (Chun and Lo 2016). They can adopt these figures in acts of alignment, distance themselves from them in situations of mockery, inhabit the figure in a parodic style or comment on them seriously or ironically. In all cases, becoming a member of a racial group is accomplished through some level of performance.

24.2.2 Racialized Linguistic Practice

Language and race also relate to each other through language ideologies, understood as beliefs about language that position subjects in a social order (Kroskrity 2000; Rosa and Burdick 2016). Opinions about languages, varieties of languages or specific ways of using language are racialized in the sense that they evoke racial characteristics in implicit ways (Shuck 2006). In other words, ways of speaking are racialized through indexicality, which connects language forms with certain societal groups (Bucholtz 2011 and Chapter 1 in this volume). Indexicality is the process of creating a link between a semiotic form, such as a linguistic structure, and a contextually specific meaning, such as an identity, via juxtaposition or co-occurrence in a particular context. Language ideologies are central to the construction of identity because they are not primarily about language; they are, rather, more basic ideologies about social groups. Beliefs that certain linguistic forms are the property of specific racialized groups, for example, are used to reinforce social divisions by means of linguistic divisions. It is important to highlight that language ideologies are not limited to personal misconceptions or beliefs but "are always linked to the interests of differently positioned social actors and often embedded within institutionalized practices" (Lewis 2018: 328).

An example of racialized linguistic practice is the Peruvian phenomenon of *motoseo*, in which beliefs about vocalic interference (the supposed blurring of high- and mid-range vowels, such as pronouncing /i/ for /e/ and /u/ for /o/) in the Spanish of Quechua speakers are used to position these speakers as "Indian," with all the pejorative characteristics implied within (Zavala 2011).[5] The following statement was spoken by a student from the University of Cusco during a focus group, where she refers to an Other *motoso*[6] from an affirmative action program under study:

---

[5] Although the Spanish speaker perceives a vowel reversion, what the Quechua speaker does when coming across a Spanish e, i, o, or u is produce a sound located in the [i]–[e] or [u]–[o] continuum, as in his phonological system this continuum constitutes only one functional unit.

[6] *Motoso* and *nonmotoso* constitute adjectives that characterize those people who reproduce the phenomenon of *motoseo* and those who do not, respectively.

> Because usually when they get to the History major, for example, they enter with low grades, not so low, but most are that way, as in they come from the countryside or they haven't been well informed and they start talking to you. Then someone messes up [referring to the *motoseo*] and, "oh my! What type of education have they had?" Most definitely in the countryside. Normally people think that in the countryside the teaching is bad because that is the norm and I, too, have had that type of, "oh my! Poor girl, she is going to be alone, no one is going to help her," because that's usually what happens, they get together in their own group and leave her out. Among the girls who are from the countryside, the only support they have is each other, no one else.

Speaking with *motoseo* – that is, producing an expected phenomenon for a Quechua speaker who learned Spanish as a second language – can index a person as being from a rural community, lacking a good education, possibly being poor and having illiterate parents. Thus, cultural and intellectual inferiority is attributed to a linguistic characteristic. This indexical process produces an apparently inherent link between this characteristic and a social group, when in reality the established connection is historical, contingent and conventional. Representing the phenomenon of *motoseo* in this way validates inequality.

Another dimension is the use or practice of racialized language either unconsciously or consciously. When speakers speak with *motoseo*, they are racialized by others, although this racialization is not entirely based on the speaker's production. Speakers themselves can enact racial identities through linguistic and nonlinguistic resources. Understanding this process requires attention to the social semiotics of language, that is, the particular use of linguistic forms such as pronunciation, vocabulary and grammatical structures as symbols of social meaning. Moreover, linguistic signs work together with nonlinguistic signs, such as clothing, makeup, gesture and body language.

Roth-Gordon (2017) addressed the phenomenon of "situational whiteness" or "behavioral whiteness" in Brazil. This constitutes people's need to look and act White by taking on cultural and linguistic practices associated with intellectual capacity, rationality and cultural refinement, and discarding African and indigenous cultural practices in situations where their phenotype makes them especially vulnerable. Roth-Gordon discussed how dark-skinned youth from a poor and stigmatized area of Rio continually negotiated racial readings of their bodies by speaking calmly and politely, demonstrating their familiarity with standard Portuguese, avoiding the use of slang and, in general, using linguistic strategies of good behavior that could associate them with White spaces and White professions. Roth-Gordon (2017) referred to this as "racial malleability," a process through which racial appearance is constantly negotiated through daily practices, including language.

These symbolic associations between linguistic forms and racialized meanings construct ethnolects, or ways of speaking that align with race-defined speakers. A key contribution of linguistic anthropology is its recognition of ethnolects as ideological and the indexical relationship as indeterminate. Through language ideologies, languages and ways of speaking become enregistered (Agha 2005) as racialized objects, linguistic differences are created and mapped onto social differences, including race, and these webs of social meaning are then mapped onto discursive practice (Chun and Lo 2016).

This idea is exemplified by Brañez's (2019) study about a Facebook page where administrators and users collected images of *amixers* and uploaded them to the page for public ridicule. The signifier *amixer* emerged as a replacement for the classical racial term *cholo* discussed previously and was mostly used online as an epithet for others. In the absence of face-to-face interaction, writing and spelling are racialized and added to other dimensions linked to the speaker, such as phenotype (as seen in uploaded photos), class and education. Through cultural processes of racialization and enregisterment constructed through interactions, certain ways of writing are associated with race-defined speakers, or *amixers*. Some characteristics of this emerging register are specific lexicon, alternation between upper and lower cases (OlItAs for *holitas*), insertion of decorative typographical signs ("#$!eM¶rE*" for *siempre*), reduplication of symbols, ("genteeeee" for *gente*) and numerals that function as letters or syllables ("100pre" for *siempre*, "h0l4" for *hola*), among other features. This *amixer* Spanish, or way of writing associated with this racialized group, is also used by "non-*amixers*" within a double-voiced mode or parodic style that seeks to confer a status of disrepute on the ridiculed subject.

The racialized identities of the *motoso* and the *amixer* show how race is part of the continued rearticulation of colonial distinctions in postcolonial relations. These more ambiguous categories replace classical racial ones in a society where postcolonial subjects try to copy practices associated with colonizers, such as attending university or interacting online, and the latter produce new recursive divisions (see also Reyes 2017). Nevertheless, these divisions are often constructed by people whose skin color is not different from the ones they racialize. In Rosa and Flores's (2017: 629) words: "Whiteness functions as a structural position that can be inhabited by whites and nonwhites alike depending on the circumstances."

Recent scholarship on raciolinguistics (Flores and Rosa 2015; Rosa and Flores 2017) frames the language racialization process as an encounter between a listening subject (Inoue 2006) and a speaking subject, rather than as an objective empirical reality. In this way, raciolinguistic ideologies of listening subjects conflate racialized bodies with linguistic deficiency, apart from any objective linguistic practices of speaking subjects (Flores and Rosa 2015). The link between race and language is so strong that the process of racialization does not only occur when people speak in face-to-face situations, as seen in Brañez's study; it happens when these speakers are imagined and even when interacting with them in writing online. Therefore, it is crucial to ask *who* hears certain linguistic forms and structures as racial: after all, racialization processes have to do more with the exercise of power than with what the speaker does or does not do.

24.3 Issues and Ongoing Debates

In this chapter, we do not align with a sole approach to analyzing discourse but acknowledge that these approaches constantly intersect and enrich each other in the study of language and race. In this section, we discuss how some of these approaches contribute to the study of these topics and what considerations we must take into account in order to assume an integrative view.

First, the perspective of language as social practice can be contrasted with research that situates prejudice in psychologically based attitudes. Instead of discussing racism from a cognitive dimension, we propose a constructivist focus that views race and racism as social practices in which language takes on a central role. This means that the "race talk" we discussed earlier is the product of a racist society rather than a particular individual. Because of this, the focus of analysis is not the racist individual but rather the discursive and rhetorical resources available in any society where inequality is reproduced.

Despite the groundbreaking work of CDA in relation to the study of race and racism, some scholars have criticized how it takes the existence of groups for granted. The following quote from Van Dijk, for example, reifies the existence of ethnic group membership as if it antecedes language use: "Racism is defined as a specific social system of domination in which ethnic groups and their members in various ways abuse their power in their interaction with other ethnic groups and their members" (Van Dijk 2016: 384). This has led some scholars to argue that CDA uses some categories in an unproblematically general way and tends to orient itself to static assumptions about power relations (e.g. oppressors/oppressed or majority/minority; Pennycook 2012; Pietikainen 2017). As we saw in Wong (2019), alignments and boundaries among participants – and groups themselves – emerge in interaction and are more fluid than some trends in CDA suggest.

While critical discourse analysts examine how discourse constructs and distributes power relations, especially those of elite speakers, conversation analysts have focused on how references to race are taken up in ordinary speakers' naturally occurring interactions (Robles 2015; Whitehead 2015). Rather than imposing racial categories on participants, this approach examines how participants orient to talk as racist and how this is negotiated across sequences of situated actions. Conversation analysts discuss race (as with other social categories) only if it emerges from the data and they define participants' discourse as racist only if interlocutors treat it as such. Schegloff (1997) argued that the analyst cannot conclude that macro-discursive resources or participants' social history influence what happens in any interaction unless they are taken up by the participants. Thus, while CDA can run the risk of "imposing" researcher categories, CA can lead to an "especially narrow analytic gaze on that data and its context" (Wetherell 2007: 671).

CA has also been questioned by discursive psychologists, a heteregenous group of scholars who have studied race and racism focusing on discourse as people's investments in particular identity positions. From an anti-cognitivist standpoint, they take discursive practices, rather than the individual, as their unit of analysis and study how people do emotions, memory, gender, identity, attitudes, intergroup relations, prejudice, racism, etc. in talk and text. The emphasis is "on the publicly available social practices which constitute the psychological" (Wetherell 2007: 671). Researchers from this school of thought take a dynamic approach to social categories in general, including racialized discourse. According to Davies and Harré (1990: 59–60), interactive positions shift from moment to moment and at times even appear contradictory, given interlocutors' abilities to construct different "possible selves" both for themselves (reflexive positioning) and for others (interactive positioning). Hence, the structures of power authorized by institutional discourse are less central, and the agency of social actors takes center-stage as speakers negotiate meaning within interaction.

With its emphasis on the semiotic aspects involved in what race *does* in discursive practice (and in situated contexts), the linguistic anthropological approach approximates a more dynamic examination of the social phenomena outlined in CDA. In a special issue of the *Journal of Linguistic Anthropology* (2011: E3–E4), Dick and Wirtz pointed out that race is best studied "not [as] fixed categories of people and things, but [as] processes by which people become marked as exemplars of racial imaginaries." Ostensibly, even when constructed covertly, racialized forms of social difference are traceable in the semiotic characteristics that instantiate race as inherent and natural. Hence, in contrast to CDA, linguistic anthropologists ask: How does racialization happen? How do processes of social indexicality produce racializing codes? How does racialization work when direct invocations of race are left implicit? (Dick and Wirtz 2011). For example, how has talk in the United States about "illegal aliens" become code for "Mexican immigrants"? Or how has talk in Peru about "*amixers*" become code for "*cholos*" or "Indians"? The tensions between imposing researcher categories and limiting interpretations to what emerges in the data could be solved with an ethnographic approach. After all, studying race talk without ethnography runs the risk of treating the phenomenon with preconceived theories, pointing to speakers as "racists" without making sense of their viewpoints and overlooking the ways in which race talk is tied to the local context in which it is produced (Bucholtz 2011).

Another issue under debate is the ontological reality of both race and language. As a social construction, race is always subject to situated interpretation and regimes of power. It is not an object to which we have access in neutral ways. The same happens with language, in the sense that when we hear someone speak, we never have access to his/her production in an objectified way but always through ideological frames. Despite the fact that critical poststructuralist sociolinguistics is gaining more and more visibility, modernist conceptualizations of language (and race) still haunt the field (Lewis 2018; Makoni and Pennycook 2006).

According to Roth-Gordon (2017), this type of flexibility, discussed in gender studies for some time, has not been embraced in reflections about race because scholars have been more concerned with "racial classification" and "racial identity." In certain Latin American contexts, race is malleable and does not define social status as much as class, in contrast to what often occurs in North American contexts (Wade 2017). Yet scholars of linguistic anthropology and other disciplines are currently addressing the instability of race as experienced in social interactions in North America (e.g. Chun 2011; Bucholtz 2011). Through acts such as reading race, speakers assign racialized meaning to linguistic and cultural signs and contribute to the recirculation of these links. On the one hand, people use language and other cultural behavior to change how they racially appear to others; and on the other hand, people "read" other people's bodies for racial cues, both emphasizing and erasing certain features in the service of power.

24.4 Implications

These new debates around the relationship between language and race have important implications for research, policy and pedagogical practice. One consequence for policy is the move beyond an emphasis on racist *ideologies* to an emphasis on its *ideological practice*, as we discussed previously. If we define discourse as racist in terms of what it *does* and not what it *says*, racism is no longer defined by the content or the tropes alluded to during an interaction. This is crucial in our contemporary world, where it is more and more difficult to address and challenge potentially racist assertions and assessments. The same argument, for example that of equal opportunity, can be used to reject racist practices and benefit minoritized groups or to reinforce the interests of the dominant group and justify the exclusion of others (Augoustinos, Tuffin and Every 2005). Therefore, instead of working with a restrictive meaning of racism, we must acknowledge that racism acquires diverse and new forms to fit changing historical circumstances and maintain economic and social privileges (Gotkowitz 2011).

Moreover, as we have argued, instead of thinking of racialized discourse as tied to supposed differences in physical appearance, it must be thought of as related to social inequality and power within histories of colonialism. Race is not an inherent feature of human bodies; rather, it is always part of a dynamic process of social differentiation (and racialization), with distinct configurations and meanings through time and space. Clearly, if racialized identities are negotiated through discursive positioning, and power is not something that is possessed but rather something that is exercised, then it is not surprising that the discriminating and discriminated subject do not coincide with fixed identities. Racism is activated in different moments, circulates through all participants in society, functions in a relational manner and is located not only in people's psychology or cognitive dimensions but also in their actions and interactions. This is why critical language research must be complemented with critical race scholarship (Rosa and Flores 2017).

These approaches to race and discourse have strong implications for education. As Flores and Rosa (2015) argued, certain linguistic practices in educational contexts often hide racialized discourses in their emphasis on "appropriate" and "standard" ways of speaking. The authors discussed the effect of what they termed "raciolinguistic ideologies" on individuals classified as English language learners in the United States. As stated by the authors, "the appropriateness-based model of language education not only marginalizes the linguistic practices of language-minoritized communities but is also premised on the false assumption that modifying the linguistic practices of racialized speaking subjects is key to eliminating racial hierarchies" (Flores and Rosa 2015: 155). This has fundamental implications for pedagogical practice, which should go beyond methodologies based on appropriateness and even critical language awareness if it aims to empower racialized and minoritized students. Students and educators must reflect on the idea that racism does not depend entirely on how people talk or behave, that raciolinguistic ideologies fuse certain racialized bodies with linguistic deficiencies in spite of the existence of "objective" language practices and that racializing representations of language support specific material conditions and social positions (Lewis 2018).

24.5 Future Directions

The study of discourse's role in situating race and racialization has made great strides in recent years. Today, researchers are more conscious of the fluid, context-sensitive nature of race and race talk, as well as the importance of looking at different social actors in these interactions. To continue examining the issues that arise in racial discourse, researchers need to implement interdisciplinary approaches such as sociocultural linguistics, which allows for the examination of discourse content as well as the details of linguistic and interactional structure, in addition to consideration of context at multiple levels: the immediate level of the social interaction, the local level of the ethnographic situation and the broader social, cultural and political levels that inform and are shaped by each instance of race talk and racialized linguistic practice. This also means that the study of language and race should follow a theory of racialized language perception; that is, it should be speaker–hearer-based, rather than solely speaker-based (Bell 2016). While arguably more complex for the researcher, this approach offers a richer analysis of the discourse in question, while building a strong foundation for studies in several different contexts.

The spatiotemporal nature of racialized discourse cannot be ignored, and therefore we argue that an analysis of time and space should be incorporated into every study on race and discourse (Chun and Lo 2016). Taking up frameworks such as Bakhtin's (1981, 1984) notion of chronotopes (see Blommaert 2015; Chapters 3 and 5 in this volume) enables researchers to move away from one-dimensional or even binary micro–macro models of analysis to those that take into account the multiscalar nature of interactions, addressing their "connection to historical and momentary agency" (Blommaert 2015: 109).

Finally, the function of racism in virtual (online) contexts merits special attention, as new practices have developed there that are specific to the dynamic generated in this space. Despite original conceptions of the Internet as a democratizing space, interactions in virtual scenarios continue to reinforce essentialist ideologies of race and ethnicity. Daniels (2013) noted that, although virtual contexts did promote new ways of speaking about these topics, they continued to perpetuate many of the traditional forms of these discourses. The Internet's origins within a predominantly White racial framework, combined with the relative lack of inhibition that many commentators feel when interacting in virtual spaces, contribute to a racism that is at once old and new.

24.6 Summary

In this chapter, we have discussed the idea that discourse is central to how race is culturally understood and the form it takes in different contexts. We have pointed out that race is not subject to a closed definition because it is always reinventing itself to naturalize social difference and exercise power. The terms "racialization" and "racialized" refer to the semiotic and ideological processes through which race comes to be produced and reified through language practices. We have argued that studying ideological processes instead of fixed racial categories entails moving beyond the study of the ideology of racism toward the study of its ideological practice.

We have also discussed how the links between race and language emerge dynamically through discursive practice. We have proposed that language and race intersect in two main ways: in "racial discourse" or discourse that takes race as its topic and in "racialized linguistic practice" or the use of language associated with specific racialized groups. We have suggested integrating the different discursive approaches that address language and race under the wider perspective of language as social practice. This entails researching what race does in specific contexts through the understanding of how power relations emerge in local contexts, how people make sense of their social practices and how wider social structures influence discursive practices.

Further Reading

Alim, H. S., Rickford, J. R. and Ball, A. F. (eds.) (2016). *Raciolinguistics: How Language Shapes Our Ideas about Race*. New York: Oxford University Press.

In this multi-authored work, Alim, Rickford and Ball introduce the concept of raciolinguistics, or how language and ideas about race intersect. In three sections, "Languaging Race," "Racing Language" and "Language, Race, and Education in Changing Communities," researchers from several global contexts offer new perspectives on racialization, racial malleability and marginalization, among other topics addressing race and discourse.

Back, M. and Zavala, V. (eds.) (2019). *Racialization and Language: Interdisciplinary Perspectives from Peru*. New York/London: Routledge.

Back and Zavala situate Peruvian ideas about race and racialization in the overall context of Latin American scholarship on race. Each empirical study in this multi-authored work offers a unique glimpse into the complex construction of racialized identities and "race talk" in both real-world and virtual contexts.

Chun, E. and Lo, A. (2016). Language and Racialization. In N. Bonvillain (ed.) *Routledge Handbook of Linguistic Anthropology*. New York: Taylor and Francis. 220–33.

This excellent chapter proposes three main approaches in the study of language, race and ideology: the distinctive ethnoracial language, the acts of ethnoracial identity and the racialization approach. It discusses critical issues for addressing the key role of language in semiotic processes of racialization.

Rosa, J. and Flores, N. (2017). Unsettling Race and Language: Toward a Raciolinguistic Perspective. *Language in Society* 46: 621–47.

This article establishes the research agenda of a raciolinguistics perspective after the groundbreaking article from Flores and Rosa (2015, see references). It theorizes the historical and contemporary co-naturalization of language and race and discusses five key components of this perspective.

Roth-Gordon, J. (2017). *Race and the Brazilian Body: Blackness, Whiteness, and Everyday Language in Rio de Janeiro*. Oakland: University of California Press.

In this book, the author discusses how racial ideas and structural racism permeate the lives of shantytown youth and people from the middle class in Rio de Janeiro, Brazil. She argues that the amount of whiteness or blackness a body displays is determined not only through observations of phenotypical features but also through attention paid to always malleable cultural and linguistic practices.

References

Agha, A. (2005). Voice, Footing, Enregisterment. *Journal of Linguistic Anthropology* 15(1): 38–59.
Alcoff, L. (2006). *Visible Identities: Race, Gender, and the Self*. Oxford: Oxford University Press.
Alim, H. S., Rickford, J. R. and Ball, A. F. (2016). Introducing Raciolinguistics. In H. S. Alim, J. R. Rickford and A. F. Ball (eds.) *Raciolinguistics: How Language Shapes Our Ideas about Race*. New York: Oxford University Press. 1–30.
Anderson, K. (2008). Justifying Race Talk: Indexicality and the Social Construction of Race and Linguistic Value. *Journal of Linguistic Anthropology* 18(1): 108–29.
Augoustinos, M. and Every, D. (2007). Contemporary Racist Discourse: Taboos against Racism and Racist Accusations. In A. Weatherall, B. M. Watson and C. Gallois (eds.) *Language, Discourse and Social Psychology*. New York: Palgrave. 233–54.
Augoustinos, M., Tuffin, K. and Every, D. (2005). New Racism, Meritocracy and Individualism: Constraining Affirmative Action in Education. *Discourse & Society* 16(3): 315–40.
Back, M. and Zavala, V. (eds.) (2019). *Racialization and Language: Interdisciplinary Perspectives from Peru*. New York/London: Routledge.
Bailey, B. (2010). Language, Power, and the Performance of Race and Class. In K. Korgen (ed.) *Multiracial Americans and Social Class: The Influence of Social Class on Racial Identity*. New York/London: Routledge. 72–87.
Bakhtin, M. (1981). *The Dialogic Imagination*, trans. by C. Emerson and M. Holquist. Austin: University of Texas Press.
  (1984). *Rabelais and His World*, trans. by H. Iswolsky. Cambridge, MA: Harvard University Press.

Baugh, J. (1983). *Black Street Speech: Its History, Structure, and Survival.* Austin: University of Texas Press.

Bell, A. (2016). Succeeding Waves: Seeking Sociolinguistic Theory for the Twenty-First Century. In N. Coupland (ed.) *Sociolinguistics: Theoretical Debates.* Cambridge: Cambridge University Press. 391–416.

Blommaert, J. (2015). Chronotopes, Scales, and Complexity in the Study of Language in Society. *Annual Review of Anthropology* 44: 105–16.

Brañez, R. (2019). "Amixer Detected!": Identities and Racism in Peruvian Cyberspace. In M. Back and V. Zavala (eds.) *Racialization and Language: Interdisciplinary Perspectives from Peru.* London/New York: Routledge. 162–88.

Bucholtz, M. (2011). "Not that I Am Racist": Strategies of Colorblindness in Talk about Race and Friendship. In M. Bucholtz (ed.) *White Kids: Language, Race and Styles of Youth Identity.* Cambridge: Cambridge University Press. 164–86.

Chun, E. W. (2011). Reading Race beyond Black and White. *Discourse & Society* 22(4): 403–21.

Chun, E. and Lo, A. (2016). Language and Racialization. In N. Bonvillain (ed.) *Routledge Handbook of Linguistic Anthropology.* New York: Taylor and Francis. 220–33.

Daniels, J. (2013). Race and Racism in Internet Studies: A Review and Critique. *New Media & Society* 15(5): 695–719.

Davies, B. and Harré, R. (1990). Positioning: The Discursive Production of Selves. *Journal for the Theory of Social Behaviour* 20(1): 43–63.

De la Cadena, M. (2000). *Indigenous Mestizos: The Politics of Race and Culture in Cuzco, Peru, 1919–1991.* Durham, NC: Duke University Press.

 (ed.) (2008). *Formaciones de indianidad. Formaciones raciales, mestizaje y nación en América Latina.* Buenos Aires: Envión.

Delgado, R. and Stefancic, J. (2017). *Critical Race Theory: An Introduction.* New York: New York University Press.

Dick, H. P. and Wirtz, K. (2011). Introduction-Racializing Discourses. *Journal of Linguistic Anthropology* 21(S1): E2–E10.

Fairclough, N. (2002). *Discourse and Social Change.* London: Polity Press.

Fields, B. J. (2001). Whiteness, Racism, and Identity. *International Labor and Working-Class History* 60: 48–56.

Flores, N. and Rosa, J. (2015). Undoing Appropriateness: Raciolinguistic Ideologies and Language Diversity in Education. *Harvard Educational Review* 85(2): 149–71.

García, J. (2003). Three Scalarities: Racialization, Racism, and Race. *Theory and Research in Education* 1(3): 283–302.

Goldberg, D. T. (1992). The Semantics of Race. *Ethnic and Racial Studies* 15(4): 543–69.

Goodwin, M.H. (1990). *He-Said-She-Said: Talk as Social Organization among Black Children.* Bloomington: Indiana University Press.

Gotkowitz, L. (2011). Introduction: Racisms of the Present and the Past in Latin America. In L. Gotkowitz (ed.) *Histories of Race and Racism: The Andes and Mesoamerica from Colonial Times to the Present*. Durham, NC: Duke University Press. 1–53.

Hochman, A. (2018). Racialization: A Defense of the Concept. *Ethnic and Racial Studies* DOI: 10.1080/01419870.2018.1527937.

Inoue, M. (2006). *Vicarious Language: Gender and Linguistic Modernity in Japan*. Berkeley: University of California Press.

Kroskrity, P. (ed.) (2000). *Regimes of Language: Ideologies, Polities and Identities*. New Mexico: School of American Research Press.

Labov, W. (1972). *Language in the Inner City: Studies in the Black English Vernacular*, Vol. 3. Philadelphia: University of Pennsylvania Press.

Lewis, M. (2018). A Critique of the Principle of Error Correction as a Theory of Social Change. *Language in Society* 47(3): 325–46.

Makoni, S. and Pennycook, A. (eds.) (2006). *Disinventing and Reconstituting Languages*. Clevedon: Multilingual Matters.

Marx, K. and Engels, F. (1968). *La ideología alemana*. Montevideo: Pueblos Unidos.

Mitchell-Kernan, C. L. (1972). Signifying and Marking: Two Afro-American Speech Acts. In J. Gumperz and D. Hymes (eds.) *Directions in Sociolinguistics*. New York: Blackwell. 161–79.

Pennycook, A. (2012). *Language and Mobility: Unexpected Places*. Bristol: Multilingual Matters.

Pietikainen, S. (2017). Critical Debates: Discourse, Boundaries and Social Change. In N. Coupland (ed.) *Sociolinguistics: Theoretical Debates*. Cambridge: Cambridge University Press. 263–81.

Quijano, A. (2000). Colonialidad del poder, eurocentrismo y América Latina. In E. Lander (ed.) *La colonialidad del saber: eurocentrismo y ciencias sociales. Perspectivas Latinoamericanas*. Buenos Aires: Clacso. 201–46.

Rattansi, A. (2005). The Uses of Racialization: The Time-Spaces and Subject-Objects of the Raced Body. In K. Murji and J. Solomos (eds.) *Racialization: Studies in Theory and Practice*. New York: Oxford University Press. 271–301.

Reyes, A. (2011). "Racist!": Metapragmatic Regimentation of Racist Discourse by Asian American Youth. *Discourse & Society* 22(4): 458–73.

(2017). Inventing Postcolonial Elites: Race, Language, Mix, Excess. *Journal of Linguistic Anthropology* 27(2): 210–31.

Robles, J. (2015). Extreme Case (Re)formulation as a Practice of Making Hearably Racist Talk Repairable. *Journal of Language and Social Psychology* 34(4): 390–409.

Rosa, J. and Burdick, C. (2016). Language Ideologies. In O. García, N. Flores and M. Spotti (eds.) *The Oxford Handbook of Language and Society*. Oxford: Oxford University Press. 103–23.

Rosa, J. and Flores, N. (2017). Unsettling Race and Language: Toward a Raciolinguistic Perspective. *Language in Society* 46: 621–47.

Roth-Gordon, J. (2017). *Race and the Brazilian Body: Blackness, Whiteness, and Everyday Language in Rio de Janeiro*. Oakland: University of California Press.

Schegloff, E. (1997). Whose Text? Whose Context? *Discourse & Society* 8: 165–87.

Shuck, G. (2006). Racializing the Nonnative English Speaker. *Journal of Language Identity, and Education* 5(4): 259–76.

Van Dijk, T. A. (2003). Critical Discourse Analysis. In D. Schiffrin, D. Tannen and H. E. Hamilton (eds.) *The Handbook of Discourse Analysis*. Hoboken, NJ: Wiley-Blackwell. 352–67.

(2012). The Role of the Press in the Reproduction of Racism. In M. Messer, R. Schroeder and R. Wodak (eds.) *Migrations: Interdisciplinary Perspectives*. New York/Dordrecht/London: Springer. 15–28.

(2016). Racism in the Press. In N. Bonvillain (ed.) *The Routledge Handbook of Linguistic Anthropology*. New York: Routledge. 384–92.

Wade, P. (2017). *Race and Ethnicity in Latin America*, 2nd ed. New York: Pluto.

Wetherell, M. (2007). A Step Too Far: Discursive Psychology, Linguistic Ethnography and Questions of Identity. *Journal of Sociolinguistics* 11(5): 661–81.

Wetherell, M. and Potter, J. (1992). *Mapping the Language of Racism: Discourse and the Legitimation of Exploitation*. New York: Columbia University Press.

Whitehead, K. (2015). Everyday Antiracism in Action: Preference Organization in Responses to Racism. *Journal of Language and Social Psychology* 34(4): 374–89.

Wodak, R. (2002). Discourse and Politics: The Rhetoric of Exclusion. In R. Wodak and A. Pelinka (eds.) *The Haider Phenomenon*. Piscataway, NJ: Transaction. 33–60.

Wong, I. (2019). Racist Practices in Virtual Democracy: Constructing the "Ppkausa" on Facebook. In M. Back and V. Zavala (eds.) *Racialization and Language: Interdisciplinary Perspectives from Peru*. London/New York: Routledge. 214–36.

Yudell, M., Roberts, D., DeSalle, R. and Tishkoff, S. (2016). Taking Race out of Human Genetics. *Science* 351(6273): 564–5.

Zavala, V. (2011). Racialization of the Bilingual Student in Higher Education: A Case from the Peruvian Andes. *Linguistics and Education* 22: 393–405.

Zavala, V. and Back, M. (2017). *Racismo y lenguaje*. Lima: Fondo Editorial PUCP.

Zavala, V. and Zariquiey, R. (2009). "I Segregate You because Your Lack of Education Offends Me": An Approach to Racist Discourse in Contemporary Peru. In T. van Dijk (ed.) *Racism and Discourse in Latin America*. New York: Lexington Books. 259–89.

25

Discourse and Narrative in Legal Settings: The Political Asylum Process

Amy Shuman and Carol Bohmer

25.1 Introduction

A discourse approach to the study of narrative in legal settings examines the production and circulation of stories told as part of cultural conventions for communication. Narratives play many roles in legal exchanges and are told by a variety of participants, including lawyers, judges, litigants and witnesses. John Conley and William O'Barr (1998), Peter Brooks and Paul Gewirtz (1998), Max Travers (2006) and others have surveyed the multiple dimensions of narrative and law, from analyses of courtroom proceedings to representations of narrative and law in literature. Using a rationale of neutrality, legal settings often ignore different cultural conventions for narrating, and many people find themselves in a legal setting without prior knowledge of the particular conventions of a court or without access to opportunities for self-representation and self-determination. The great variation in legal settings further contributes to conflicting expectations.[1] Legal settings often produce what Jan Blommaert has described as "narrative inequalities" in which "the rights to use particular narrative modes are unevenly distributed, and this pattern of distribution disenfranchises those who have to rely on 'disqualified' narrative modes for conducting their business in society" (2001: 13–14).

---

[1] Anthea Vogl (2013: 65) argues: "When the law responds to events and accidents within refugee testimony, narrative expectations are at play – but that the precise terms of these standards and the content of good, orderly narratives are implicit, shifting and inconsistent. Insofar as these standards are often arbitrary or unarticulated, they have the potential to be invisible to both the applicant and the decision-maker."

Paul Gewirtz describes narrative in legal settings as argument (1996: 4). As such, narratives provide possibilities for multiple, sometimes conflicting interpretations, which, in Martha Minnow's (1998: 254) terms, can "shake up some assumptions" about how to assess a legal case. Referring to Robert Cover's work, Jerome Bruner describes the "jurisgenic stories" that govern legal decisions and are "expressions of a culture's deeper, axiomatic nomos" (2010: 47). As we will discuss, larger, cultural narratives inform how individuals' stories are understood and assessed in legal settings.

Although narrative in legal settings is always used as a vehicle of persuasion, not everyone narrates an argument and, in fact, witnesses and individuals can be specifically excluded from arguing. Their warrant to narrate is similarly constrained. A discourse approach to the study of narrative and law examines the cultural and interactive dimensions of legal texts and events by calling attention to questions of tellability (who can tell what to whom, in what contexts), positionality (how narrators position themselves and others in their accounts) and narrative logics (assumptions about what makes sense in an account. The study of narrative as a discourse in legal settings also draws on narrative research more generally, including observations about how texts are produced or entextualized (Bauman and Briggs 1990) and about the role of memory in producing accounts of traumatic events (Eastmond, 2007: 258; Medved and Brockmeier 2008; Brockmeier 2002; Paskey 2016).

Susan Philips (1992) outlines some of the particularities of constituting information as evidence in legal settings, including who can present evidence and what counts as hearsay or as legitimate. The political asylum hearings we discuss here have additional constraints in part because corroboration of facts is difficult (Shuman and Bohmer 2018). In many legal settings, such as those we will analyze, narratives are told as responses to questions (Bohmer and Shuman 2007; Maryns 2014). In these cases, the frame of the question, rather than the cultural frames of, for example, disclosure, testimony or accusation, determine the genre and put the questioner in the position of categorizing the narrative, for example, as hearsay, as credible or as implausible. Narrators are often asked to relate traumatic, stigmatized experiences that would not be tellable in other circumstances; lacking a script for a story that is rarely or ever told and responding to questions rather than telling a story from one's own point of view can compromise the ability to tell a coherent narrative. As we will discuss, narrative inequalities have implications for what counts as evidence and how the credibility of narrators is assessed.

Political asylum narratives, one example of how narratives are used in legal settings, often are told without the aid of legal counsel. In the political asylum process, applicants often rely extensively on their narratives as evidence of the atrocities they have suffered. Narrative evidence alone rarely occupies such a central role in legal processes (Millbank

2009: 2), but political asylum applicants often arrive in the country where they are seeking refuge without passports, birth certificates or other identity documents and without other evidence that they would be in danger if they were to be deported to their home country. As a result, the narratives are central to asylum cases and are carefully scrutinized by hearing officers; even minor inconsistencies become grounds for suspicion. Hearing officers are in the difficult position of attempting to determine the legitimacy of applicants' claims based primarily on those narratives, supplemented by knowledge about the political situation in the applicant's home country.[2] At the same time, immigration officials expect to receive additional supporting documentation, and a narrative alone is rarely sufficient for a successful case (Shuman and Bohmer 2018).

Narratives are complex modes of communication rather than straightforward statements of information (see Chapter 5 in this volume), but the use of narrative in legal deliberations is concerned almost entirely with information. The production of narrative also depends on cultural conventions for what is told, to whom, when and how (Briggs 1996: 13). The immigration legal bureaucracy is designed to use standard measures to assess applications, and officials rarely take into account the cultural conventions for narrating atrocity and for including or omitting particular kinds of detail.[3] Cultural conventions for narration can be especially relevant for how people recount horrific experiences that are difficult to comprehend. Writing about the political asylum process, E. Valentine Daniel (1996: 142) refers to the "unshareability and incommunicability of pain and terror" in the production of political asylum narratives. Michael Baynham and Anna De Fina (2005: 172) observe: "Institutional discursive practices work against the contextualization of a narrative producing, progressively, effects of misunderstanding, communicative entropy, anger and silencing." In the political asylum process, the institutional discursive practices of the legal bureaucracy often work against identifying the complex cultural factors that might make a narrative appear, on the surface, to be inconsistent and/or incoherent and thus less credible.

In this chapter, we focus on how narratives are interrogated and formed in political asylum hearings. We consider not only the obstacles to the adequate, fair and accurate consideration of narratives in political asylum hearings but also the institutional discursive practices that shape how narrative is assessed. In Section 25.2, we present an overview of the political asylum narrative. We then discuss the dimensions that are relevant to understanding how these narratives function within legal settings. In Sections 25.3–25.9, we look at different aspects in the production and

---

[2] Hearings increasingly rely on digitally available information (Jacquemet 2005b).
[3] See Smith-Kahn's discussion of expectations that asylum seekers will provide particular kinds of and sufficient details (2017: 520).

evaluation of asylum seekers' narratives and analyze three specific court cases. We end with some conclusions and future directions.

25.2 Overview

Legal assessments of whether applicants qualify for political asylum in a country of refuge rely primarily on the applicants' narratives and on their answers to questions posed by immigration officials during a face-to-face hearing. It is incumbent upon the applicants to attempt to persuade the officials of their credibility and of the merits of their cases (Jacquemet 1996; Macklin 1998; Millbank 2009). In their assessments, the officials take into account the applicant's demeanor, ability to recount a coherent narrative and other often unarticulated measures of credibility (Macklin 1998). Lacking other evidence, or in the face of disputed identity documents, assessments of discourse are central to political asylum decisions. Mistranslation and the failure to determine an applicant's dialect sometimes result in significant mistakes (Jacquemet 2005b). In some cases, applicants' narratives raise suspicion not because of inconsistencies in the details they report but because the actions they describe seem implausible or logically inconsistent or do not conform to the officials' assumptions and expectations (Millbank 2009: 11).

We describe several dimensions of discourse and narrative in the political asylum process. In a close examination of narrative form and structure, we discuss how narratives are produced, reshaped and circulated in different stages of the process. The circulation of narrative is not a linear trajectory from an individual's personal story to the telling of the story in an immigration hearing but instead is dynamic and dialogic. Each individual story is shaped within a cultural context of norms and expectations for how to talk about or not talk about experiences. Asylum narratives are complex; like any trauma narratives told by people who have suffered atrocities beyond anything that could be imagined or expected, political asylum narratives are not necessarily coherent at first glance (Herlihy et al. 2002; Zagor 2011; Blommaert and Maryns 2000). For example, the orienting details might be missing or elements might be repeated.[4] They can include what the officials regard as extraneous or missing information or they can appear to be too similar to accounts told by other applicants and thus appear to be memorized or contain what are regarded as stock elements (McDougall 2015). Our discussion of narrative attends to the ways in which discourses are evaluated by immigration officials, whether as too familiar or too strange, as insufficiently coherent, as missing details or as contradictory. Building on Blommaert's work (2001), we observe how

---

[4] We provide a more extensive discussion of the role of orientation in political asylum narratives in Bohmer and Shuman 2017. See also Anna De Fina's discussion of orientation in border crossing narratives (2003).

bureaucratic contexts contribute to what become assessed as inadequate narratives. We suggest that closer attention to the narratives and the cultural conventions for narrating is crucial for assessing the validity of the applicants' accounts.

Importantly, we are not arguing that problems in assessing the applicants' narratives can be attributed to the failure of applicants to tell their stories. Nor are we arguing that narratives are inherently faulty in representing accounts of events. By saying that narrative is a form of communication that depends on particular, and often culturally informed, forms and strategies, we are not suggesting that narrative is a false construction of reality. To the contrary, we are arguing for greater understanding of the processes of narration as crucial for the accurate assessment of asylum applications.

25.3 Issues and Ongoing Debates

Our central argument, one with great consequences for assessing political asylum applications, is that assessments of the merits of a narrative as credible and as a form of evidence in legal settings depend on understanding the complexity of narrative production and circulation, including dimensions of form and interaction. An analysis of narratives used in political asylum hearings (and other high-stakes contexts) requires a reassessment of some of the ways in which scholars have considered narrative in the past, especially a hermeneutic approach that regards narrative as shaped by context and open to interpretation (Ricoeur 1981). A "hermeneutics of demystification," the idea that a "narrative does not fully make sense on its own terms ... [and that] the meaning is hidden and in need of deciphering" (Josselson 2004: 18), grants authority to the interpreter, whether a discourse analyst or a political asylum hearing officer, to attribute motives or explain what the interpreter perceives to be gaps in the narrative. In this chapter, drawing on those discussions as well as on the extensive research on unreliable narration in literary studies of narrative (Phelan 2007), we propose a shift in how we conceptualize narrative, from the idea of narrative as constructed and potentially unstable, to the study of the conditions of the production of narrative and the ways in which those conditions are used strategically, both to credit and discredit narrators. Building on Blommaert's discussion of narrative inequality in the political asylum system (2001), we demonstrate how narrators and immigration officials (1) position themselves and others in relation to the events; (2) use narrative logics to make sense out of those events;[5] and (3) use various narrative strategies to categorize asylum seekers as credible or fraudulent.

---

[5] Agnes Woolley (2017: 4) argues: "The process of claiming asylum follows its own rigid plotlines, producing an idealized refugee personhood rooted in the 1951 Convention."

Scholars have offered several ways of thinking about political asylum narrative including discussions of the centrality of credibility assessment in the political asylum process (Barsky 1994; Byrne 2008; Cabot 2013; Daniel and Knudsen 1995; Jacquemet 1996; Macklin 1998). The political asylum process includes several forms of discourse, including interviews, interrogations, reports and narratives, and several channels of communication, including written forms and reports, internet sources, letters, medical documents and reports, among others.

In our first essay on the topic, we proposed the categories of time; relevance; chronology and coherence; emotional presentation; corroboration; dates, details and evidence; and plausibility (Shuman and Bohmer 2004) to describe the primary areas in which immigration officials questioned the validity of the applicants' narratives. In particular, we focused on cultural differences in narrative production that often served as obstacles to successful asylum hearings. For example, applicants often included details that the officials regarded as irrelevant and failed to include the kind of corroborating detail that the officials expected. Marco Jacquemet's framework for considering how narratives are assessed covers the same issues, but he also focuses on the importance of Charles Goodwin's conceptualization of "participation frameworks" as the interactions among participants in a narrative exchange. He observes that, whether understated (minimizing the atrocities they have experienced) or overstated (exaggerating atrocities),

> refugees' stories run the risk of losing a measure of their truth, of their integrity and thus of their credibility. This is partly due to the fact that these stories are not shared casually with friends, but are told to strangers in institutional settings invested with the infinitesimal techniques, tactics and devices through which authority, legitimacy, and dominance operate. (Jacquemet 2005a: 201)

All of these dimensions contribute to assessments of the credibility of political asylum narratives.

25.4 Narrative as Evidence

Particular dimensions of narrative, especially information about places, times and chronologies of events, receive the most scrutiny in political asylum hearings. This information corresponds to what William Labov (1972) described as the orientation part of a narrative, which situates the account. However, as many scholars have observed, narrators do not necessarily provide all of the needed information at the beginning of an account and instead insert orientating details throughout the narrative (Modan and Shuman 2011; De Fina 2003). Further, narrators omit some details and emphasize others depending on many factors, including what they assume their listeners already know and what they deem to be most important. These assumptions about what can or cannot be said (Shuman 2005), what goes without saying (Warhol 2005) and what is difficult or unreportable (Labov 1972) are part of the narrative logics that govern how a story is told (Herman 2002).

Narrative always requires listeners to fill in the gaps, but in the immigration officials' assessments of political asylum narratives, some gaps are regarded as inconsistencies and mark the narrator as not credible. How we fill in gaps also depends on larger assumptions about expected behavior in particular kinds of situation, whether situations of political violence or natural disasters (Horigan 2018). Personal accounts of violence or disruption circulate in larger cultural networks as rumors and legends; the larger discourses, in different media, shape and are shaped by the personal (Goldstein 2015; Erikson 1994). Katryn Maryns (2014) observes how credibility hearings remove narratives from their cultural contexts, resulting in misunderstandings. The bureaucratic context of the hearings requires reference to exact times and places, but the experiences of displacement often make it difficult, if not impossible, for applicants to provide that information (Maryns 2014: 185; De Fina 2003: 383). Lacking precise information and the possibility of corroborating the validity of an account, immigration officials either identify discrepancies as evidence of a lack of credibility or determine that the events described are implausible, based on the official's often erroneous assumptions. If the narrative is considered less than credible, the applicant is sometimes assumed to be an economic migrant rather than a victim of persecution. In other words, the ability to produce a coherent, consistent narrative is often a condition for asylum, even though the circumstances of violence and disruption make such narrative production difficult, if not impossible. Many asylum seekers know (or quickly learn) that a coherent narrative is necessary for a successful application (Daniel and Knudsen 1995: 22; Jacquemet 2005a: 200), so they tailor their narratives to what they believe to be the officials' expectations.

25.5 Narrative Production

On one hand, inconsistencies can be a potentially useful way to identify fraudulent narratives. On the other hand, in many cases, the details seem so insignificant as to make the interrogation look frivolous or perfunctory, a means of dismissing applicants. Attention to narrative production (how the narratives are shaped), both before and during the hearing process, is helpful for understanding the many contributing factors that produce seemingly faulty narratives. First, narrative production includes how narrative gets distilled or translated into legal language (Trinch 2010). Following political asylum policy and law, political asylum narratives describing past events are also mapped onto possible future events. Asylum is granted when applicants have a "well-founded fear of return" to their native countries; even if applicants can substantiate persecution in the past, though, if they are then unable to demonstrate that they would be persecuted in the future, they might not qualify. Second, the hearing process, as we discuss in Sections 25.6–25.9, often includes requests for explanations and for the resolution of what the immigration officials regard as inconsistencies or implausibilities. Thus, the hearing process is an occasion for retelling and reshaping narrative accounts. Narratives are shaped by questions in the interview process (McCormick 2005: 148; Trinch and Berk-Seligson 2002).

25.6 Narrative Interaction and the Larger Discourses of Asylum

The asylum process includes a variety of narrative interactions, including accounts written on legal application forms, narratives produced as part of legal hearings, letters of refusal and explanations rebutting the refusal. These different but intersecting narrative forms are each shaped and constrained by particular contexts of interaction.

Both narrative as evidence and narrative production depend upon particular contexts and the roles of participants in them. What can be said, to whom and how depends on these interactional contexts. Participants in a political asylum hearing include the applicants, witnesses, translators, NGO reports, Country of Information reports and the larger discourses about asylum and immigration. As we discuss in Sections 25.8–25.10, the hearing process can be a devastating encounter for the applicants, not only because it requires them to relive the atrocities they experienced but also because they are disbelieved and placed in the position of having to prove that they are who they claim to be.

In the larger discourses about asylum and immigration, especially in the media (see Chapter 9 in this volume), fraudulent asylum seekers are labeled as economic migrants (Adelson 2004) or as possible terrorists. Other larger discourses include policy discussions, NGO statements and accounts, Country of Origin Information reports and scholarship (such as our own) that influences how asylum seekers are assessed. Powerful metanarratives can provide accurate, helpful background information or can misinform (McDougall 2015: 124). In any case, other forms of discourse about asylum often have more authority than the applicants' accounts of their experiences of persecution and flight.

25.7 The Application Form and the Production of Narrative

The asylum application itself, a legal document, shapes how the narrative is told. The application requires written responses, so some applicants rely on more literate family members or professionals (not always reputable) to fill in the forms. We discovered that some applicants, unfamiliar with such legal documents, believed that they needed to use the space provided in the form, rather than additional pages, to answer the questions (Bohmer and Shuman 2008). The following is excerpted from the US application as an example of the kinds of question used:

> When answering the following questions about your asylum or other protection claim ... you should provide a detailed and specific account of the basis of your claim to asylum or other protection. To the best of your ability, provide specific dates, places, and descriptions about each event or action described. You should attach documents evidencing the general conditions in the country from which you are seeking asylum or other protection and the specific facts on which you are relying to support your claim. If this documentation is unavailable or you are not providing this documentation with your application explain why in your responses to the following questions ...
>
>   1. Why are you applying for asylum or withholding of removal?
>
>   The applicant must check boxes marked race, religion, nationality, political opinion, membership in a particular social group, and/or torture convention.
>   A. Have you, your family, or close friends or colleagues ever experienced harm or mistreatment or threats in the past by anyone?
>   1. What happened;
>   2. When the harm or mistreatment or threats occurred;
>   3. Who caused the harm or mistreatment or threats; and
>   4. Why you believe the harm or mistreatment or threats occurred.
>   B. Do you fear harm or treatment if you return to your home country?
>   1. What harm or mistreatment you fear;
>   2. Who you believe would harm or mistreat you; and
>   3. Why you believe you would or could be harmed or mistreated.
>   2. Have you or your family ever been accused, charged, arrested, detained, interrogated, convicted and sentenced or imprisoned in any country other than the United States.
>   3A. Have you or your family ever belonged to or been associated with any organizations or groups in your home country, such as, but not limited to, a political party, student group, labor union, religious organization, military or paramilitary group, civil patrol, guerrilla organization, ethnic group, human rights group, or the press or media? (Department of Homeland Security n.d. I-589)

Question 1, requesting the reason for the application, requires applicants to choose among the five designated categories that qualify for asylum. (The form adds the additional category of the torture convention.) The narrative must provide evidence of persecution on account of race, religion, nationality, political opinion, membership in a particular social group and, further, as implied by Part B, the account should provide evidence that the applicant's home country has not and will not provide protection against that persecution. The category of membership in a social group is particularly fraught (Shuman and Bohmer 2018), and even if, for example, a country specifically states that it will not protect sexual minorities against prosecution, applicants face obstacles in qualifying for asylum. Applicants whose narratives describe fear of persecution by gangs in Latin America may satisfy the requirement of the fear of return and they may even have proof of prior persecution, including the murder of family members, but refusal to join a gang may not qualify as membership in a social group. In other words, the narrative may be competent and coherent, but the criteria for political asylum may still be insufficient, especially when applicants are suspected of belonging to the categories of economic migrant, terrorist or other, more vague designations of people assumed to be taking advantage of the asylum system.

Part A of the application seems straightforward enough as a request for an account of what happened, but victims of persecution do not always know "Who caused the harm or mistreatment or threats" or "Why you believe the harm or mistreatment or threats occurred." A Sierra Leonean asylum seeker who we worked with had been a boarding school student, far from his home town, when his town was ransacked, his family was killed and he was dismissed, out on the street, without any idea of which side of the conflict had attacked his community. Often, as in this case, an NGO does the research to provide an applicant with the larger context needed to explain a fear of return.

Part B also seems to contain relatively simple questions, but if applicants cannot demonstrate that they, personally, would be in danger were they to be returned to their home countries, their applications will fail. We are aware of several examples. An Algerian woman was raped by police but the rape was anonymous, so she could not prove that she would be targeted again (Bohmer and Shuman 2008: 243). Sexual minorities persecuted in Uganda were told by the authorities where they sought asylum to move to other parts of the country and act more discreetly, to avoid persecution. These discretion directions have been outlawed, but some NGOs representing asylum seekers believe that they are still used (Lewis 2013).

Part 3A is often complicated. An applicant might have belonged to an organization that later became recognized as a terrorist group (Bohmer and Shuman, 2007). We note that the list of organizations includes human rights groups. Membership in a group might or might not be the basis of the persecution; the group might be one that makes the applicant sympathetic or suspicious (Millbank 2009: 4). Responses to this question often become the subject of investigation in an asylum hearing. As we discuss in

Section 25.9, in one of the Burmese cases, applicants' accounts of their political activity are compared with official Country of Origin Information reports that describe unrest, persecution and the activities of political groups. These multiple, intersecting narratives often contain more gaps than confirmations; in some cases, applicants are asked to reconcile the differences in the hearing; in other cases, the officials, finding discrepancies, dismiss the application as not credible. In either case, little attention is paid to the difference between a personal account of persecution and an official report about general conditions as very different sorts of narrative with inevitable discrepancies.

25.8 Assessment: The Letter of Refusal

Written refusals of asylum application provide some understanding of how applications are assessed (Good 2003; Souter 2011) and often demonstrate how immigration hearing officers impute motivations or offer alternative explanations for what they perceive to be implausible or incomplete accounts. One letter denying asylum began: "The events you described do not constitute past persecution." The letter further explained that although the applicant had been questioned by authorities in Burma, this "did not rise to the level of persecution." Further, addressing the applicant's claim to be in fear of returning to Burma, the denial letter continued: "You also claim to have a fear of future persecution. To establish a well-founded fear of future persecution, an asylum applicant must show that her fear is both subjectively genuine and objectionably reasonable. An asylum applicant may establish an objectively reasonable fear by demonstrating that there is a reasonable possibility of suffering persecution." For the rebuttal to this decision, the applicant included two letters from United States NGOs describing the threat she would face upon return to Burma. The president of an NGO wrote:

> I am extremely familiar with the methods of persecution of the SPDC (military government of Burma) and believe that (name of applicant) is in imminent danger not just of an arbitrary arrest on political grounds, but, of being secretly picked up by the SPDC officials and "disappeared." (Name of applicant's) name and face are familiar to those in the SPDC intelligence in sector (X). In fact, when I was with (name of applicant) in Rangoon in 2003, officers forced us out of a University Building. If I had not been with (name of applicant) she would, in all likelihood, have been arrested. (2006)

The NGO's letter includes a specific actual occasion to demonstrate the applicant's "reasonable possibility of suffering persecution." Asylum narratives must satisfy conditions of both specificity (this happened to me and this could happen to me again) and generality (already substantiated facts about the situation in a country). Navigating between these two conditions is a major problem for asylum narratives and, without guidance from a reputable lawyer or NGO, asylum applicants often fail to meet these conditions.

25.9 The Hearing Interrogation and the Production of Suspicious Subjects

In asylum hearings, immigration officials introduce their own narrative logics, based on their own assumptions of what someone might/should do when facing danger. The hearings, which reshape narratives, are described by Blommaert as "remouldings" and "renarrations" (2001: 438). Each of the following Burmese cases, observed by Carol Bohmer, provides an example of how the immigration official imposed an alternative narrative logic on the applicant's account. These alternative logics are informed, in part, by the officials' knowledge of conditions in the applicant's home country; in the final example, we include excerpts from the Country of Origin Information report to better understand how political asylum narratives work intertextually (see Chapter 4 in this volume for a discussion of intertextuality). In addition to the Country of Origin Information report, immigration officials (home officers in the UK) might draw upon their knowledge of other Burmese cases or of other cases generally. The applicants themselves often have knowledge of how other applicants shaped their narratives. Also, of course, other means of corroboration are used in asylum cases; we discuss those in Bohmer and Shuman (2017). Here we focus on the production of suspicious subjects, drawing on multiple, sometimes conflicting narratives, in interrogation hearings. Carol Bohmer was present for the hearings and assisted the lawyers representing one of the applicants.[6] We have deliberately created a composite of cases to blur individual identities and avoid any possibility of causing harm to the applicants or their families. In all of the cases, the applicants faced suspicion about whether they had reason to fear returning to Burma.

In the following hearing in the UK, an immigration official interrogates one of the Burmese applicants about why he "delayed" two months before leaving Burma after learning that he was in danger. The immigration official introduces the idea of delay, and the applicant attempts to explain the sequence as, instead, a necessary course of events. (HO refers to Home Office and AP refers to Applicant.)

HO   When did the military intelligence come to your house?
AP   In May
HO   This year, last year?

---

[6] Translators were present for the hearings. Carol Bohmer took notes in English, and although she noted when particular attention was given to translation problems, we do not have the benefit of an exact transcription including discussion in the applicants' languages.

25 Discourse and Narrative in Legal Settings

AP   2010
HO   I'll come to that in a minute. What I'm asking you is about last July. You say your grandfather paid someone to sign in on your behalf. That's the time I asking about. Did that person go to the police station once, in July, or more than once?
AP   My family arranged for that so I don't know. I was in Rangoon by that time.
HO   Who did you live with in Rangoon?
AP   I stayed in safe places
HO   Who were you staying with?
AP   Alone, but sometimes my grandfather's friends came to see me.
HO   Now, we know that your application for your visa to come to the UK was on 27 September. Why did you wait two months to apply for a visa?
AP   At the time while I was in hiding, his (grandfather's) friends consulted each other and decided to advise me to come to this country.
HO   But the decision was taken in July for you to leave, so why did it take two months for the decision to leave and the application for the visa?
AP   No, that's not true, because it was impossible to stay in M (his town where he lived with his grandparents)
AP   I went to Rangoon to hide there
HO   You're still not answering the question. I understand that you went to Rangoon to stay in a safe house. I also understand that you could not stay in M for fear. What I don't understand is the decision was made by your grandfather in July that you had to leave Burma, but the application for a visa wasn't made until 27 September. What reason, if any, was there for the delay?
AP   It's not easy to leave the country immediately, we had to collect enough funds for the trip.
HO   Where did you get the funds?
AP   My family supported me.
HO   When you say family, who do you mean?
HO   AP My aunts, my mother, my grandfather.

The HO characterizes the period between the time the decision was made to leave (July) and the time the application was made (September) as a delay. The applicant counters this characterization by saying, "No, that's not true, because it was impossible to stay in M," but the HO continues by saying, "You're still not answering the question . . .." The HO reiterates the question, "What reason, if any, was there for the delay?" In legal hearings, the interrogator, not the applicant, maintains control of the narration. He guides the discussion by insisting that his question was not answered. Further, the applicant's response is *about* not having control of the circumstances. He was unable to leave because he had not procured the necessary funds.

The HO's request for a reason, "if any," is the crux of the difference between two narrative logics. The "delay" is easily enough explained by the need to collect funds for travel, and, to the applicant, it makes sense.

One makes a decision to leave, one acquires funds for travel and one applies. For the HO, however, delay indicates that perhaps the situation was not truly dangerous. What looks like an inconsistency to the immigration official, casting doubt on the applicant's credibility, is actually a familiar characteristic of narratives by people fleeing danger. Often, they do not have control over the conditions of their departure. As Anna De Fina explains in her study of border crossing narratives, this experience of lack of control is evident in the narratives, marked by vagueness and disorientation (2003: 380). Legitimate asylum seekers might not be able to produce the kind of detail required by the immigration officials.

In many cases, immigration officials request an explanation but continue to insist on their own, alternative narrative. In a second example of competing narrative logics, an applicant was asked why her sister had not accompanied her to provide a witness for her claim. The official asked:

HO: Given that your sister may be in a position to corroborate your claim, why hasn't she written a witness statement and come to court today to back you?

AP My solicitors never advised me anything with regard to that matter, that's why I did not do that.

In this case, the sister's situation and her absence from the hearing became grounds for denying the claim. In the letter of denial, the official wrote:

> (Her sister) was told that she (the applicant) was in danger and therefore she should leave. Her (the sister's) evidence would have been relevant. The sister left Burma legally using her own passport. It was the opinion of the family she would be in danger; it is not my assessment. As for the case of (name of applicant), the issue is whether she was a genuine activist or a hanger-on.

The applicant's solicitor responded:

> The fact that her sister can return to the UK and is not here to give evidence: her sister a) had no problems and b) had no direct evidence of what had happened. There is no reason for her to give evidence; she would have been dismissed by the Home Office as self-serving. There is no evidence that she would have been at risk because of her sister's activity.

Often, applicants (and even their lawyers) cannot anticipate what will damage the credibility of a narrative. In this case, the sister's absence made the HO suspicious that the applicant was not truly in danger.

In a final Burmese case, the HO was suspicious because the applicant, who claimed to have been in danger because he participated in political protests, had acquired a passport. The HO said, "If he had any political profile he would not have been issued with a passport." Referring to the Country of Origin Information report, the HO said that in Burma, the applicant would have had to have obtained the passport in person and, further, the applicant reported having been in the hospital, related to his political activities, which would have produced official records requiring him to sign in with authorities. Skeptical of the applicant's account, the HO said, "He can't have it both ways; on the one hand, the authorities made him sign-in; on the other hand, he was of so little interest that he could get a passport and an exit visa. He makes reference to an incident at the border with Thailand – that factor in itself did not indicate any interest in him because he left the country under his own name. There was no interest in him in November 2009 when he left, no evidence that there is interest in him now." Further, the HO disputed whether the applicant's protests at the Burmese Embassy in the UK would have brought him to the attention of Burmese authorities because the only photo the applicant produced was taken at a large event, not at the embassy.

The applicant's lawyer countered that during the Saffron revolution it would have been possible for the applicant to make an appointment for a passport and to leave the country legally. Further, the lawyer said, "(The applicant) describes how he was treated during the three-day detention. His grandfather got him released, by having paid a bribe. This is consistent with the objective evidence. The second incident was consistent with the objective evidence. Both incidents are set out in the witness statement. The country guidance case – (the applicant) is someone clearly committed to the cause."

The Country of Origin Information report, issued yearly by the US Department of State, provides additional evidence that might corroborate or contradict an applicant's claims to be afraid of being persecuted upon return. The Country of Origin Information report for Burma at the time of these applications (2010 and earlier) clearly identifies the kind of persecution the applicants describe. The Country of Origin Information report also provides brief narratives about particular acts of persecution.

> The regime continued to abridge the right of citizens to change their government and committed other severe human rights abuses. Government security forces were responsible for extrajudicial killings, custodial deaths, disappearances, rape, and torture. The government detained civic activists indefinitely and without charges. In addition, regime-sponsored mass-member organizations engaged in harassment and abuse of human rights and prodemocracy activists. The government abused prisoners and detainees, held persons in harsh and life-threatening conditions, routinely used incommunicado detention, and imprisoned citizens arbitrarily for political motives. The army continued its attacks on ethnic minority villagers, resulting in deaths, forced relocation, and other serious abuses. The government routinely infringed on citizens' privacy and restricted freedom of speech, press, assembly, association, religion, and movement. The government did not allow domestic human rights nongovernmental organizations (NGOs) to function independently, and international NGOs encountered a difficult environment. Violence and societal discrimination against women continued, as did recruitment of child soldiers, discrimination against ethnic minorities, and trafficking

in persons, particularly of women and girls. Workers' rights remained restricted. Forced labor, including that of children, also persisted. The government took no significant actions to prosecute or punish those responsible for human rights abuses. (www.state.gov/j/drl/rls/hrrpt/2010/eap/154380.htm)

In a legal asylum hearing, elements of a narrative can take on different significance than they have for the people describing their personal experiences. In the Burmese cases, one such element was accounts of leaving Burma, including the perception of imminent danger that prompted their departures, a delay in departing, and difficulties (or lack of difficulties) acquiring a visa and crossing the border. In the three cases in which Carol Bohmer participated, these elements of the narrative became cause for suspicion of the validity of the claim. The immigration officials reasoned that if people are truly in danger, they would leave immediately. The delay, even though explained by the need to get money or make arrangements, signified a lack of urgency to the officials. Similarly, the ease of crossing the border, although explained by the use of bribes, signified a lack of danger for the individual. We have written elsewhere about the ways in which immigration officials impose their own narratives or refuse to recognize the role of bribery in crossing borders (Shuman and Bohmer 2018: 97–112). The Country of Origin Information reports, also referenced in the refusal, provide an additional narrative that might refute an applicant's account of persecution. In the final example, the immigration official refers to political tensions in Burma in 2007 and evidence that someone with a political profile would not have been able to obtain a passport (concerning an applicant who did successfully obtain a passport though he claims to have been identified as participating in political protests).

Beyond disputes about the facts of the case, including whether or not applicants are who they purport to be, have endured persecution as described and have a claim to fear return, competing narrative logics also play a role in determining how applicants are assessed, whether as suspicious or as legitimate. In the final example, the immigration official finds a discrepancy in an account of someone who was wanted by authorities but who was able to obtain a passport. The lawyers explain that the applicant's grandfather provided a bribe such that he was released and then offer, as further evidence, the Country of Origin Information report describing corruption and persecution of political dissidents in Burma. In the three Burmese cases we have described, one official questioned a delay in applying for a visa; a second official questioned the absence of a sister who could have served as a witness; and a third official questioned how someone wanted by authorities was able to obtain a passport and leave under his own name. All of these questions are, of course, legitimate, and all are, for the applicants, somewhat irrelevant to their concerns for safety.

As the Country of Origin Information report indicates, some people in Burma are in danger of persecution. This is not disputed. The question, for immigration officials, is whether the particular applicant is in danger. In a hearing context that begins with suspicion, what are the conditions for producing a credible narrative?

25.10 The Production of Suspicious Subjects

Suspicious political asylum narrators are quite different from unreliable narrators in fiction, but both share the characteristic of being ethically or morally questionable (or both). In fiction, the narrator, differentiated from the author, tells the story and may choose to omit or exaggerate or to lead the reader to false conclusions. In some cases, the narrator can convey a distasteful point of view, leaving readers to decide how to align themselves. For the most part, narrators in fiction are presumed to knowingly mislead their readers. Famous examples include Sherlock Holmes' assistant Dr. Watson, who, as narrator, typically leads readers down an obvious but ultimately erroneous path to solving the mystery. Watson is not, then, accused of subterfuge; instead, the author has successfully persuaded the reader to believe in Watson's reliability, contributing to surprise and satisfaction at the unexpected conclusion. In a legal proceeding, a narrator who produces a less than coherent, credible narrative is suspected of being deliberately misleading or of lying (Coutin 2001; Josselson 2004: 15). Any contradiction in an asylum seeker's narrative is likely to be considered deliberately fraudulent rather than to be attributed to the complexity of the situation described, to lapses in memory or to a failure to understand the immigration official's question. Liisa Malkki (2007: 340–1) writes: "The survivors of rape, torture, and other forms of violence are made to feel like imposters, having to prove and perform their grounds for seeking asylum."

In asylum hearings, asylum applicants do not have authority over their own stories. The immigration officials often already know a great deal about the circumstances of the applicant's country, whether through Country of Origin Information reports or other media, and the applicant's account is measured against that knowledge. As the Burmese cases demonstrate, in narrating their accounts, applicants often face suspicion when they describe complex associations, especially connections across enemy lines, and including their form of participation in political protest.[7]

Positioning oneself as credible is especially difficult when the given, taken for granted assumption is that asylum seekers are likely to be opportunists, economic migrants or terrorists (Bohmer and Shuman 2017; Malkki 2007). For the most part, narrative scholarship begins

---

[7] See Wood (2008) for a discussion of social networking across different affiliations.

with the assumption that people are the narrators of their own stories and that they have the right to control their circulation. Arguing against this position, Shuman points out that stories often circulate beyond their "owners" (Shuman 2005). The problem of story-ownership and authority is exacerbated in legal proceedings in which applicants must prove that they are who they claim to be. Further, many or even most asylum applicants are also economic migrants. They flee their native countries not only because they fear violence but also because earning a livelihood is no longer possible. In today's conflicts, the line between victims, defending themselves, and aggressors, perpetrating violence, is not always clear; neither is the line between friend and enemy. Often, to escape, people rely on associations with characters they do not regard as trustworthy. Thus, the problem of the suspicious asylum seeker is in part a problem of intersecting narratives. The narrative of persecuted people frequently intersects with the narratives of economic migrants, though poverty is insufficient as a claim to political asylum. The narratives of people fleeing violence intersects with narratives of people paying bribes to be released from detention, crossing enemy lines to escape and crossing borders illegally.

The application form asks asylum seekers to categorize themselves according to one or more of the legitimate categories: victims of persecution, fearful of future harm, and, more specifically, members of particular social groups, religions or political organizations. In recent years, fraudulent asylum seekers have been characterized as criminals, guilty of illegal border crossing. Crossing borders to declare asylum is not illegal.

Narratives can be a reputable source for representing experience. We do not argue that the narratives provided in the cases described above represent the truth; instead, we observe problems in the criteria used to assess them as false. The gap in time (between deciding to leave and making the application) did not invalidate the first case. In the officials' assessments of both that case and the second, based on the failure of the sister to appear as a witness, the applicant was suspected of not being sufficiently afraid – the officials reasoned that a truly fearful person would have acted differently. The denial of the third case similarly rests on the official's suspicions about the applicant's account of procuring a passport. All three cases are examples of officials imposing their own, alternative narrative logics on the applicants' accounts. In each case, the applicants or their lawyers were able to explain what looked like a discrepancy or contradiction to the official. The question at stake in each of these cases is whether the applicant has a "well-founded fear." The officials' interrogations about how the person managed to leave and when they left are designed to explore that question. The officials' reference to border crossing is not necessarily relevant to assessments of the credibility of the applicant's claim to a "well-founded fear" of persecution.

25.11 Implications for Policy and Research

Discussions of political asylum practices and policies necessarily integrate research and practice. Such integration is especially important in legal settings where "narrative inequalities," imbalances in who can speak and who can interpret a story, can produce injustices. When immigration activists, lawyers and scholars have convened to identify better practices, they have been able to challenge each other's theories and methodologies, for example in discussions of what counts as expert testimony (Berger et al. 2015). Although we are primarily scholars, from the beginning our work has blurred the boundary between scholarship and policy. Carol Bohmer worked as a pro bono lawyer assisting individuals applying for asylum through an NGO, Community Refugee Immigration Services, in Columbus, Ohio. She continues to provide pro bono legal assistance, primarily to attorneys who request her services. Amy Shuman joined Bohmer as a narrative scholar, and together we wrote an initial book designed to outline the political asylum process, for use by the general public. Our second book, designed for use by scholars, activists and policy makers, attempted to describe the culture of suspicion in political asylum decisions. We were particularly interested in observing some of the inaccurate and misleading measures used to identify asylum fraud. We also discussed cases of known asylum fraud. During the two decades that we have been undertaking this work, we have seen policies changes, primarily in how the category "membership in a particular social group" has been defined. In all of our work, we have used narrative analysis to help asylum seekers and their lawyers to better understand the complexities of producing a coherent, credible narrative.

25.12 Future Directions

We are living in a time when truths are dismissed and easily manipulated (see Chapter 28 in this volume). Narrative analysis has perhaps placed too much attention on the crafting of the text and thus has unwittingly contributed to the idea that truth cannot be ascertained from people's accounts of their experiences. In this essay, we demonstrate how narrative continues to be an effective means for conveying truths about complex situations, and we continue to identify the tools for understanding how narratives are shaped as part of cultural conventions for communication and interaction among participants in different contexts (in this case, legal contexts). By articulating some of the complexities of narrative production, we anticipate future scholarship that will demonstrate how people use narrative in multiple ways, shaping and shaped by both realities and imagination.

25.13 Summary

Narrative plays a significant role in political asylum hearings, but the methods used to assess the credibility of those narratives rarely take into account either the difficulties applicants face in producing a coherent, consistent account of the atrocities they have experienced or the cultural differences in producing narrative. Instead, immigration officials deny applications with what they regard to be discrepancies or discontinuities. We have argued that the applicants' narratives can be more accurately assessed by attending to how the narratives are produced. In particular, we considered how the immigration officials impose their own narrative logics on applicants' accounts. We reviewed three Burmese cases in which immigration officials identified discrepancies that the applicants or their lawyers were able to explain and that involved the imposition of alternative narrative logics.

Further Reading

Berthold, S. M. and Libal, K. R. (eds.) (2019). *Refugees and Asylum Seekers: Interdisciplinary and Comparative Perspectives*. Santa Barbara, CA: Praeger.

This volume provides global perspectives on the laws and policies of political asylum.

Jacquemet, M. (1996). *Credibility in Court: Communicative Practices in the Camorra Trials*. Vol. 14. Cambridge: Cambridge University Press.

This volume remains a foundational study on the ways in which narratives function in legal settings.

McKinnon, S. (2016). *Gendered Asylum: Race and Violence in U.S. Law and Politics*. Urbana: University of Illinois Press.

This is an important study of the gendered dimension of asylum.

References

Adelson, W. (2004). Economic Migrants and Asylum Seekers in the U.K.: Crafting the Difference. *Michigan Journal of Public Affairs* 1: 1–25.

Barsky, R. F. (1994). *Constructing a Productive Other: Discourse Theory and the Convention Refugee Hearing*, Vol. 29. Amsterdam: John Benjamins.

Bauman, R. and Briggs, C. L. (1990). Poetics and Performances as Critical Perspectives on Language and Social Life. *Annual Review of Anthropology* 19(1): 59–88.

Baynham, M. and De Fina, A. (2005). *Dislocations, Relocations, Narratives of Migration*. Manchester: St. Jerome.

Berger, I., Hepner, T. R., Larance, B. N., Tague, J. T. and Terretta, M. (2015). *African Asylum at a Crossroads: Activism, Expert Testimony, and Refugee Rights*. Athens, OH: Ohio University Press.

Blommaert, J. (2001). Investigating Narrative Inequality: African Asylum Seekers' Stories in Belgium. *Discourse & Society* 12(4): 413–49.

Blommaert, J. and Maryns, K. (2000). Stylistic and Thematic Shifting as a Narrative Resource: Assessing Asylum Seekers' Repertoires. Working Papers on Language, Power & Identity 6. Ghent: Belgium Department of Education. http://hdl.handle.net/1854/LU-122620.

Bohmer, C. and Shuman, A. (2007). Producing Epistemologies of Ignorance in the Political Asylum Application Process. *Identities: Global Studies in Culture and Power* 14(5): 603–29.

(2008). *Rejecting Refugees: Political Asylum in the 21st Century*. London: Routledge.

(2017). *Political Asylum Deceptions: The Culture of Suspicion*. New York: Palgrave.

Briggs, C. L. (ed.) (1996). *Disorderly Discourse: Narrative, Conflict, & Inequality*, Vol. 7. Oxford: Oxford University Press.

Brockmeier, J. (2002). Remembering and Forgetting: Narrative as Cultural Memory. *Culture and Psychology* 8(1): 15–43.

Brooks, P. and Gewirtz, P. (eds.) (1998). *Law's Stories: Narrative and Rhetoric in the Law*. New Haven, CT: Yale University Press.

Bruner, J. (2010). Narrative, Culture, and Mind. In D. Schiffrin, A. De Fina and A. Nylund (eds.) *Telling Stories: Language, Narrative, and Social Life*. Washington, DC: Georgetown University Press. 45–9.

Byrne, R. et al. (eds.) (2008). *The Refugee Law Reader*. Budapest: Hungarian Helsinki Committee.

Cabot, H. (2013). The Social Aesthetics of Eligibility: NGO Aid and Indeterminacy in the Greek Asylum Process. *American Ethnologist* 40 (3): 452–66.

Conley, J. M. and O'Barr, W. M. (1998). *Just Words: Law, Language, and Power*. Chicago, IL: University of Chicago Press.

Coutin, S. B. (2001). The Oppressed, the Suspect, and the Citizen: Subjectivity in Competing Accounts of Political Violence. *Law & Social Inquiry* 26(1): 63–94.

Daniel, E. V. (1996). *Charred Lullabies: Chapters in an Anthropology of Violence*. Princeton, NJ: Princeton University Press.

Daniel, E. V. and Knudsen, J. (eds.) (1995). *Mistrusting Refugees*. Berkeley: University of California Press.

De Fina, A. (2003). Crossing Borders: Time, Space, and Disorientation in Narrative. *Narrative Inquiry* 13(2): 367–91.

Department of Homeland Security. (n.d.). U.S. Citizenship and Immigration Services I-589 Application for Asylum and for Withholding of Removal.

Eastmond, M. (2007). Stories as Lived Experience: Narratives in Forced Migration Research. *Journal of Refugee Studies* 20(2): 248–64.

Erikson, K. (1994). *A New Species of Trouble: The Human Experience of Modern Disasters*. New York: W.W. Norton.

Goldstein, D. (2015). Vernacular Turns: Narrative, Local Knowledge, and the Changed Context of Folklore. *Journal of American Folklore* 128(508): 125–45.

Good, A. (2003). Anthropologists as Experts: Asylum Appeals in British Courts. *Anthropology Today* 19(5): 3–7.

Herlihy, J. et al. (2002). Discrepancies in Autobiographical Memories: Implications for the Assessment of Asylum Seekers. *British Medical Journal* 324: 324.

Herman, D. (2002). *Story Logic: Problems and Possibilities of Narrative*. Lincoln, NE: University of Nebraska Press.

Horigan, K. P. (2018). *Consuming Katrina: Public Disaster and Personal Narrative*. Jackson: University Press of Mississippi.

Jacquemet, M. (1996). *Credibility in Court: Communicative Practices in the Camorra Trials*, Vol. 14. Cambridge: Cambridge University Press.

  (2005a). The Registration Interview: Restricting Refugees' Narrative Performances. In M. Baynham and A. De Fina (eds.) *Dislocations, Relocations, Narratives of Migration*. Manchester: St. Jerome. 194–216.

  (2005b). Transidiomatic Practices: Language and Power in an Age of Globalization. *Language & Communication* 25: 257–77.

Josselson, R. (2004). The Hermeneutics of Faith and the Hermeneutics of Suspicion. *Narrative Inquiry* 14(1): 1–28.

Labov, W. (1972). The Transformation of Experience in Narrative Syntax. In W. Labov (ed.) *Language in the Inner City: Studies in the Black English Vernacular*. Philadelphia: University of Pennsylvania Press. 354–96.

Lewis, R. A. (2013). Deportable Subjects: Lesbians and Political Asylum. *Feminist Formations* 25(2): 174–94.

Macklin, A. (1998). Truth and Consequences: Credibility Determinations in the Refugee Context. Conference Paper, International Association of Refugee Law Judges.

Malkki, L. H. (2007). Commentary: The Politics and Trauma of Asylum: Universals and Their Effects. *Ethos* 35(3): 336–43.

Maryns, K. (2014). *The Asylum Speaker: Language in the Belgian Asylum Procedure*. London: Routledge.

McCormick, K. (2005). Working with Webs: Narrative Constructions of Forced Removal and Relocation. In M. Baynham and A. De Fina (eds.) *Dislocations, Relocations, Narratives of Migration*. Manchester: St. Jerome. 143–73.

McDougall, E. A. (2015). The Immigration People Know the Stories: There's One for Each Country. In I. Berger et al. (eds.) *African Asylum at a Crossroads: Activism, Expert Testimony, and Refugee Rights*. Athens, OH: Ohio University Press. 121–40.

Medved, M. I. and Brockmeier, J. (2008). Continuity amid Chaos: Neurotrauma, Loss of Memory, and Sense of Self. *Qualitative Health Research* 18(4): 469–79.

Millbank, J. (2009). "The Ring of Truth": A Case Study of Credibility Assessment in Particular Social Group Refugee Determination. *International Journal of Refugee Law* 21: 1–33.

Modan, G. and Shuman, A. (2011). Positioning the Interviewer: Strategic Uses of Embedded Orientation in Interview Narratives. *Language and Society* 40: 13–25.

Minnow, M. (1998). Stories in Law. In P. Brooks and P. Gewirtz (eds.) *Law's Stories: Narrative and Rhetoric in the Law*. New Haven, CT: Yale University Press. 24–37.

Paskey, S. (2016). Telling Refugee Stories: Trauma, Credibility, and the Adversarial Adjudication of Claims for Asylum. *Santa Clara Law Review* 56(3): 457–530.

Phelan, J. (2007). Estranging Unreliability, Bonding Unreliability, and the Ethics of Lolita. *Narrative* 15(2): 222–38.

Philips, S. U. (1992). Evidentiary Standards for American Trials: Just the Facts. In J. H. Hill and J. T. Irvine (eds.) *Responsibility and Evidence in Oral Discourse*. Cambridge: Cambridge University Press. 248–59.

Ricoeur, P. (1981). *Hermeneutics and the Human Sciences*, ed. and trans. by J. B. Thompson. Cambridge: Cambridge University Press.

Shuman, A. (2005). *Other People's Stories: Entitlement Claims and the Critique of Empathy*. Urbana: University of Illinois Press.

Shuman, A. and Bohmer, C. (2004). Representing Trauma: Political Asylum Narrative. *Journal of American Folklore* 117(466): 394–414.

(2018). Political Asylum Narratives and the Construction of Suspicious Subjects. In B. Haas and A. Shuman (eds.) *Technologies of Suspicion and the Ethics of Obligation in Political Asylum*. Athens, OH: Ohio University Press. 245–64.

Smith-Kahn, L. (2017). Telling Stories: Credibility and the Representation of Social Actors in Australian Asylum Appeals. *Discourse & Society* 28(5): 512–34.

Souter, J. (2011). A Culture of Disbelief or Denial? Critiquing Refugee Status Determination in the United Kingdom. *Oxford Monitor of Forced Migration* 1(1): 48–59.

Travers, M. (2006). Understanding Talk in Legal Settings: What Law and Society Studies Can Learn from a Conversation Analyst. *Law & Social Inquiry* 31(2): 447–65.

Trinch, S. (2010). Disappearing Discourse: Performative Texts and Identity in Legal Contexts. *Critical Inquiry in Language Studies* 7(2–3): 207–29.

Trinch, S. L. and Berk-Seligson, S. (2002). Narrating in Protective Order Interviews: A Source of Interactional Trouble. *Language in Society* 31(3): 383–418.

Vogl, A. (2013). Telling Stories from Start to Finish: Exploring the Demand for Narrative in Refugee Testimony. *Griffith Law Review* 22(1): 63–86.

Warhol, R. (2005). Neonarrative, or, How to Render the Unnarratable in Realist Fiction and Contemporary Film. In J. Phelan and P. Rabinowitz (eds.) *Blackwell Companion to Narrative Theory*. Oxford: Blackwell. 220–31.

Wood, E. J. (2008). The Social Processes of Civil War: The Wartime Transformation of Social Networks. *Annual Review of Political Science* 11: 539–61.

Woolley, A. (2017). Narrating the "Asylum Story": Between Literary and Legal Storytelling. *Interventions* 19(3): 376–94.

Zagor, M. (2011). Recognition and Narrative Identities: The Legal Creation, Alienation and Liberation of the Refugee. ANU College of Law Research Paper No. 11–22. https://ssrn.com/abstract=1906507.

26

Discourse and Religion in Educational Practice

Vally Lytra

26.1 Introduction/Definitions

> It makes me think that anyone can make a difference, no matter what age, race, gender, or nationality. It shows us that there are more important things than ourselves, and that no one should be alone in the world. We were not made to be alone, we were made so that we could comfort, not kill, so that we could heal, not hurt, and so that we could help our earth become the better, cleaner, kinder earth that God created it to be. Juan Mann's story shows us that no one should suffer being alone. We are all humans. We are all equal. We are all His creations, and He blessed each and every one of us differently, but all the same, He blessed each and every one of us. I think that the Free Hugs campaign was a small bit, but it helped the people he hugged, and the people who saw, and cared.
> (student reflection, May 12, 2017, reported in Lytra 2018: 45)

The students in this sixth grade classroom had been talking about how the actions of a single person could affect the lives of many as part of the central idea of the unit of inquiry the students had been exploring at the time: "Through small actions, everyone can make an impact." The student who wrote the reflection above was referring to the Free Hugs movement that sprang up in Australia in 2004. It was initiated by Juan Mann from Sydney who started giving free hugs in his local shopping mall. His actions were spurred by the realization that people were living increasingly disconnected lives and he wanted to do something about it. The idea caught hold of people's imagination and spread across the globe. Earlier that day, I had had an informal conversation with the class teacher about my research interest in the role of religion in children's learning and social identification. He had commented that he hadn't given the topic much thought in his pedagogical practice; later in the day, he sent me the abovementioned student's reflection via email with the following comment: "Interestingly and coincidently, just after you left a classmate wrote this. Funny time, *non*?" [French for "no" in the original].

The student's reflection and the teacher's comments provide several useful insights to the investigation of the nexus of discourse and religion in secular educational settings and wider society more broadly. First, the student employs a religious interpretative frame to make sense of academic learning (understanding and evaluating the actions of Juan Mann in relation to the central idea of the unit of inquiry). Besides invoking a higher power, the student signals a style shift by appropriating textual features, such as syntax, lexis and repetition, which allude to religious registers and genres, such as sermons. Indeed, language in both written and oral form has played a key role in the development of religion; in constructing and clarifying doctrine, in representing religious experiences and beliefs and in participating in religious practices. The relationship between language and religion is encapsulated in Keane's (1997: 47) observation that "the effort to know and interact with an otherworld tends to demand highly marked uses of linguistic resources." Returning to the example above, the efficacy of the religious frame in lending moral authority to the student's response draws on the status of religion as a source of knowledge. Equally importantly, the student's use of a religious frame demonstrates the central role that religion plays in identity development. It illustrates their sense of self and their understanding and interpretation of the world and their place within it as well as how individual self-identity is intertwined with social identity aspects, such as religious and learner identities (Gregory, Lytra et al. 2013). Framing their response in religious terms demonstrates how the student draws upon the full range of their linguistic and cultural resources (including religious sources of knowledge) across home, community and school settings to successfully participate in the school-assigned writing task. In so doing, the student's reflection indicates that "being a learner takes on wider moral and spiritual dimensions" (Kenner et al. 2016: 213), highlighting the centrality of a faith dimension to learner identity. While the student's reflection provides a window into writing as a process of "inscribing ourselves and others in particular ways of doing/thinking/being" (Lillis 2013: 126), it sits uncomfortably with long-held binaries between secular and sacred, private and public spaces, school and religious literacies in many contemporary societies. It points to the existence of more porous and fluid boundaries, what Baquedano-López and Ochs (2002: 175) have referred to as the "entanglement" of secular and sacred worlds. In secular educational practice in particular, the role of religion in students' achievement, socialization and identity development tends to be ignored, disparaged or unfavorably compared to that of school literacies (Genishi and Dyson 2009; Gregory, Long and Volk 2004; Lytra, Volk and Gregory 2016b; Skerrett 2013). The teacher's comment that he hadn't given much thought to the role of religion in students' school learning is indicative of many teachers' stance toward religious literacies (Dávila 2015; Long 2016). The marginal position of religion in secular education in many contemporary societies echoes dominant discourses that consider religion a very private and personal matter. More often than not, students and teachers are expected to keep aspects of their identities, including their religious identities, outside schools and classrooms. At the same time, the significance of religion and its relationship to schooling and society more broadly has become increasingly topical. It has been linked to concerns about pluralism and social cohesion as well as debates about citizenship, nationality and belonging, gender and sexuality, violence and terrorism (Baker, Gabrielatos and McEnery 2013; Hemming 2015; Hoque 2015).

Similar to language, culture or community, religion is understood as a complex and contested category. In this chapter, religion is viewed as an essential part of culture; a cultural practice that is historically situated and embedded in specific local and global contexts (Barton and Hamilton 1998; Gregory and Williams 2000; Heath 1983; Lytra, Volk and Gregory 2016b). A religion as cultural practice perspective examines religion in social activity, in people's histories of participation in religious practice and groups, both offline and increasingly online, as the studies in Rosowsky (2018a) attest to. While recognizing that each person may experience and participate in religious practices in personal and deeply theological ways (Watson 2018), it stresses the social alongside the subjective or experiential dimension of religion. In this sense, it resonates with Geerzt's (1973: 112–3) assertion that it is "out of the context of concrete acts of religious observance that religious conviction emerges on the human plane." In addition, it highlights the importance of examining religious practices in their historical, sociopolitical, economic and ideological contexts (Badenhorst and Makoni 2017; Han 2018). Through socialization in culturally appropriate practices and behaviors and the mobilization of linguistic and other semiotic resources but also affective, social and material resources, people construct and affirm their membership in religious communities. It is important to bear in mind that, similar to religions, religious communities are understood as internally diverse and religious practices as adapting, evolving and transforming across times, spaces, generations and technologies. Moreover, individuals may identify with a particular religious community (and disassociate themselves from others) to varying degrees, enabled by their unique autobiographies, life experiences and choices and limited by larger constraints over which they may have no control. Central to identity construction is how people present themselves and are seen by others both inside and outside of their own religious communities; also central, as we saw in the student's reflection, are how religious identity is woven together with other identity aspects and under what conditions one's religious identity is foregrounded or privileged over other identity aspects. Religious identities are far from homogeneous and static and levels of religiosity are wide-ranging, confirming Badenhorst and Makoni's (2017: 599) observation that "religious subjectivities exist on a continuum that ranges from nominal membership to life-transforming modes of personal devotion."

26.2 Overview of Topic

Historically, religion has been an important driving force worldwide and it remains such in today's globalized world despite changes in the religious landscape. These include, on the one hand, the influence of secularization and, on the other hand, the persistence or resurgence of religion and the increasingly multi-faith nature of many contemporary societies. Religion is considered a resource providing moral and material support, comfort and hope for many individuals and communities as they navigate the challenges and opportunities of a globalized world. This is especially true for individuals and communities new to a country or facing hardship and discrimination. For instance, several scholars have investigated the role of religion as a resource to resist racism, structural discrimination and marginalization (see studies by Baquedano-López and Ochs 2002; Ek 2005; Volk 2016 with Latino families in the United States; Bigelow 2008 with Somali Muslim adolescents also in the United States; Han 2009, 2011 with Evangelical Christian Chinese skilled immigrants in Canada). Others have examined the historical significance of the Black Church in the United States in supporting African American youth to develop resilience and educational achievement (Barrett 2010; Haight 2002; McMillon and Edwards 2000; Peele-Eady 2011, 2016; Jordan and Wilson 2017). At the same time, religion is regarded as a constraint. All religions involve processes of boundary-making with the purpose of including those who belong to the group, thereby enabling group cohesion, and crucially excluding those who break away from cultural conformity and group identity, as Rumsey (2016) has illustrated with regard to religious practices associated with coming of age, adult baptism and shunning among the Amish, in the United States. Moreover, religion is often associated with sowing seeds for social division and prejudice and the ills of colonialism, neocolonialism and proselytism (Edge 2003; Pennycook and Coutand-Marin 2004). Negative representations of religion are compounded by mainstream media reports, which tend to emphasize religious fanaticism and extremism, often stereotyping or misrepresenting particular religions and religious communities (Ahmed 2015; Baker, Gabrielatos and McEnery 2013; Haque 2004; Pihlaja and Thomspon 2017). Rather than ignoring or dismissing religion in social life, its role should be critically investigated through in-depth empirical research. Yet, empirical studies of discourse and religion, particularly in educational practice, which is the focus of this chapter, have received limited scholarly attention.

In this chapter, I set out to explore the intersection of discourse and religion as a growing interdisciplinary field. As discussed elsewhere, "religion does not heed subject boundaries"; rather it "weaves a thread in and across disciplines and fields" (Lytra, Volk and Gregory 2016b: 2). Echoing Han (2018), I argue that the greater inclusion of religion in education research agendas is both an important and a timely task. First, I present research strands that have explored different aspects of discourse and religion in educational practice. The chapter continues with implications for pedagogical practice and concludes with some reflections on future directions in the present context of ever-increasing mobilities and technological innovations worldwide.

26.3 Issues and Ongoing Debates

The investigation of discourse and religion in discourse studies has been overlooked even though, as Pennycook and Makoni (2005: 137) remark, to say "that language and religion are profoundly linked is to state the obvious." In their paper "The Modern Mission: The Language Effects of Christianity," they critically discuss how Christian missionary work influenced the promotion and spread of European languages, especially English, as well as the role of missionary linguists in describing, inventing and constructing languages and producing Bible translations in indigenous languages in the context of the problematic historical relationship among colonization, empire building and language teaching as well as in more recent missionary activities. They point out that the effects of the missionary language and literacy projects were not limited to linguistic structures but also affected social and cultural structures where "languages and literacy practices are brought into existence as Christian languages and literacy practices, molded along Western lines" (Pennycook and Makoni 2005: 151–2).

Their discussion echoes an ongoing debate in educational and professional fora regarding the place and purpose of religion in general and evangelical Christianity in particular in English Language Teaching (ELT) programs. While holding a marginal position within broader debates, it has centered on the impact of religion on the goals of ELT, ethical practice, the moral and political dimensions of teaching and the formation of professional identities among English teachers. Edge (1996, 2003) criticized the use of English teaching for the purpose of mission work and religious conversion, highlighting concerns about teachers concealing their religious goals and calling for the need to make these goals explicit. As Edge (2003: 704) argued, "if, for some, religious conversion is their goal and TESOL is their means, then I believe that these people have a moral duty to make that instrumental goal and means relationship absolutely explicit at all stages of their work." Moreover, the author associated such

Christian Evangelical religious goals in ELT with a broader imperialist agenda, arising historically as an inheritance of the British Empire and culminating in the contemporary hegemony of the United States, especially in the aftermath of 9/11 and the 2003 invasion of Iraq and likening English language teachers to a "second wave of imperial troopers" (Edge 2003: 703). Writing from a critical pedagogical standpoint, Pennycook and Coutand-Marin (2003: 337) raised similar concerns about transparency and the cultural politics involved "in us[ing] the global spread of English to further the spread of Christianity" in the context of what they called "the massive current project of teaching English as a missionary language." Using materials from websites and pamphlets of missionary organizations aimed at recruiting English language teachers, they asserted that teaching English as a missionary language among certain Christian Evangelical circles was exploited as a vehicle to promote a particular set of beliefs: "[A] particular vision of globalisation, neoliberal values and capitalist accumulation [is] celebrated as part of a missionary message" (Pennycook and Coutand-Marin 2003: 345). Instead they maintained that "any good critical approach to ELT must start from a position of respect and engagement with students' cultures and ideas" (2003: 350).

Taking their cue from the growing presence of Christian Evangelicals in the field of TESOL worldwide and the paucity of empirical studies addressing the interplay between Christianity, language learning and ETL, Varghese and Johnston (2007) conducted a series of interviews with preservice English teachers in two evangelical Christian colleges in the United States. The first empirical study on teachers' religious beliefs and how they intersected with their teaching, it sought to avoid essentializing evangelical teachers and treating them as a homogenous group with fixed views and clear denominational demarcations (Varghese and Johnston 2007: 12). Their study reveals that teachers developed a complex and nuanced relationship with teaching as a form of service, which did not necessarily involve conversion or preaching to students. Rather teachers used the metaphor of "planting seeds" as "the process by which learners are made curious and want to know more about the faith that motivates their teacher" inspired by "the teacher acting in a Christlike fashion" (2007: 18). According to Varghese and Johnston (2007: 27), the relationship between teachers' religious beliefs and how they inform their teaching raises a fundamental moral dilemma; on the one hand, the desire to share religious belief through the practice of witnessing and, on the other hand, valuing, respecting and accepting students' beliefs and not wishing to change them. In his recent ethnographic study, Johnstone (2017) examined the cross-cultural encounters between North American Evangelical English language teachers and their Polish Catholic students in an English language school with a Bible-based curriculum in Poland. He probed into the aforementioned dilemma through the use of what he termed "ecumenical discourse" by one of the participant teachers understood as "a way of using language to address religious and spiritual matters that carefully eschews any reference to denomination-specific terms, practices and values, and that restricts itself to words, phrases and concepts that can be readily understood and accepted (even if in different ways) by anyone who thinks of himself or herself as a Christian" (Johnstone 2017: 135). The use of the ecumenical discourse, he argued, created discursive spaces within classroom discourse where religious and theological discussions could be possible across denominational lines. However, attention was drawn to how these discussions fell short of engaging with participants' divergent religious beliefs (2017: 138–9).

Christian Evangelical educators have responded to the critiques leveled against them regarding the lack of transparency about their identities and purposes by claiming to be forthcoming about their religious beliefs and "mak[ing] them attractive and available in a free market" (Stevick 1996: 6) rather than seeking to covertly impose them on their students and their families. This line of argument has been taken up by Purgason (2004: 711) who, in response to Edge (2003), further argued for a commitment to professionalism and high-quality teaching by all English teachers while recognizing that "all teachers convey their values to students, and may have agendas both conscious and unconscious" which, in turn, can influence their students' beliefs and conduct (see Griffith 2004 for a similar argument). Baurain (2007) challenged the perceived incompatibility between the practice of witnessing (akin to what Varghese and Johnston (2007) described through the metaphor of "planting seeds") and respecting students' values and beliefs, claiming that "all teaching is teaching for change" (Baurain 2007: 205). He compared Christian teachers with what teachers more generally do, that is, seek to influence and change their students' ways of thinking, seeing and acting with the purpose of creating better people and a better world (2007: 208). In the case of Christian teachers, he argued, neither their own nor their students' spiritual and moral beliefs can be separated from the educational process. While acknowledging that most Christian teachers believe in some absolute truths, Baurain cautioned that religious belief needs to be approached with humility and that true conversion should be a matter of choice rather than the outcome of imposition or coercion.

In a later publication based on his doctoral research, Baurain (2015) explored the interconnections between Evangelical Christian teachers' personal religious beliefs and their professional knowledge, practices and identities. Mainly through interviews with a group of Evangelical Christian ESOL educators working in secular higher education contexts in Southeast Asia, he identified the multifaceted understandings and interpretations of their professional goals, practices and identities in terms of their religious beliefs as well as the moral and spiritual challenges they engendered. A key finding of the study was that the teachers' narratives challenged the assumption that personal religious beliefs are a private matter that do not belong to the public sphere, thereby questioning the binary between secular and religious, public and private spheres (Baurain 2015: 11). In an edited collection of data-driven studies, Wong, Kristjánsson and Dörnyei (2013) further examined the interplay between Christian faith and English language teaching and learning by bringing an insider perspective and focusing on teachers' identities, different English language learning contexts and the influence of faith on motivation and learning. Attempts to establish a dialogue between scholars with religious and nonreligious perspectives on the role of faith and spirituality in English language teaching led to the publication of an edited volume by Wong and Canagarajah (2009). Nevertheless, debate has been dominated by a focus on teachers (largely Caucasian, English-speaking Evangelical Christians teaching or in the processes of gaining qualifications to teach abroad), their identities and the diversity of their perspectives and less so on those of the learners and processes of language teaching and learning (with the notable exception of Johnstone's (2017) ethnography).

Within the wider educational field, there is an emergent scholarship that has examined the interplay of religion and teaching and learning in religious and increasingly secular settings. The limited research on discourse and religion in educational settings has been compounded by the privileging of secular schools and classrooms as the main sites for teaching and learning. Places of worship, religious and faith-inspired day schools and religious education classes tend to be underexplored. At the same time, day schools with a religious character continue to grow in Britain (Hemming 2015; Sagoo 2016) and in other national contexts (see, for instance, Avni 2012 and Fader 2009 in the United States). While many of these schools tend to give admissions priority to students of the same faith, others may be serving religiously and ethnically diverse student populations (LeBlanc 2017). In a similar vein, limited attention has been given to the intersection of religious literacies and schooling in secular schools and classrooms, which, as I argued in Section 26.1, is consonant with the peripheral position of religion in secular education in many societies. Yet, as the Douglas Fir Group (2016: 23) asserts in "A Transdisciplinary Framework for SLA in a Multilingual World," long-held binaries between the "real world" and the "classroom" setting in second language acquisition (SLA) are being rendered problematic as "affordances for language learning and use arise in multilingual and multimodal encounters with different interlocutors for diverse purposes, across space and time, and in face-to-face and virtual contexts." Moreover, there is recognition of and an attempt to integrate religious beliefs, practices and identities into theories of language learning. For instance, the Douglas Fir Group's transdisciplinary framework for SLA places religious values alongside political, cultural and economic values comprising the macro-level of ideological structures and places of worship as part of the framework's meso-level of sociocultural institutions and communities, which includes families, schools, neighborhoods, places of work and social organizations (Douglas Fir Group 2016: 25) (see also Chapter 23 in this volume on the interaction of school and other social environments in student learning processes).

While the move to recognize and integrate religious beliefs, practices and identities in theories of language learning may be relatively new to SLA research, it is important to stress that investigations of religion as a situated cultural practice have featured more prominently in scholarship in the related fields of social psychology, anthropology and literacy studies, particularly within New Literacy Studies. Seminal studies by Scribner and Cole (1981), Street (1984), Heath (1983), Barton and Hamilton (1998) and Gregory and Williams (2000) urged language and literacy researchers to extend their analytical gaze beyond formal schooling models of literacy to literacies in everyday life of which religious literacies are an integral part for many individuals and communities worldwide. In so doing, they focused on how more experienced group members apprenticed new members into the culturally and socially appropriate languages and literacies of the group. These ethnographically informed studies have demonstrated "the intertwining of language and literacy practices associated with faith with broader repertoires of everyday social and cultural practices and the breadth and scope of faith as a force for learning, socialisation and belonging for individuals and communities" (Lytra 2020). Moreover, they have documented that religious literacies bridge home, school and community in fluid and dynamic ways, and that language and literacy resources, spiritual and moral beliefs and values travel across time, space, generations and technologies (see also the collection of studies in Lytra, Volk and Gregory 2016a).

In Section 26.3, I discuss selected studies at the intersection of religion and discourse across teaching and learning contexts. Studies have explored issues of identity, socialization, pedagogy and language policy and how they are intertwined with local and global contexts and processes in present day societies. In this context, it is worth highlighting that faith learning has an additional moral and spiritual dimension, which makes its purpose unique compared to learning in other contexts. The knowledge, competences and performances practiced, performed and perfected over time are the means not only to gain membership in the religious community but also, more importantly, to build a relationship with a higher and eternal being (Gregory, Lytra, Ilankuberan et al. 2012; Lytra, Volk and Gregory 2016b).

A common theme in these studies has been the way in which language learning is inextricably linked with the construction of a shared religious identity treasured and transmitted to the next generation. Studies have explored not merely how religious identities are negotiated and produced but also the complexities and struggles involved in achieving membership in a faith community (Rumsey 2016). They have taken a broad constructionist approach to identities that stress their multiplicity, fluidity, fragmentation and changeability across time and place (Pavlenko and Blackledge 2004; also see Chapter 5 in this volume). At the same time, they have alerted us to an apparent contradiction between the researchers' theoretical orientations toward identities as negotiated and discursively constructed and how members of religious communities themselves may often reify, essentialize or romanticize religious identities (Baquedano-López and Ochs 2002; Souza 2016; Lytra, Volk and Gregory 2016b). Han (2009) examined the central role that Evangelical churches (also referred to as minority, immigrant or ethnic churches) played in supporting the linguistic, socioeconomic and spiritual needs of many skilled adult immigrants from Mainland China faced with language, employment and other systemic barriers and in facilitating their settlement and integration in Canadian society. She illustrated how practicing, rehearsing and performing a variety of roles for a wide range of religious and social activities and events in church served as a vehicle for using and learning English and building leadership skills with the purpose of evangelizing others. In this respect, the author argued, minority Evangelical Christian communities have been fostering "an alternative space where Chinese immigrants and their children can support each other and assert their legitimacy as being simultaneously Chinese, Christian, and Canadian" (Han 2009: 665). In subsequent publications, Han (e.g. 2011) explored how the construction of religious identities intersected with racial and national identities, linking immigrants to larger networks and communities of Chinese Evangelicals in Mainland China and around the world (for a discussion of intersectionality in identities see Chapter 19 in this volume).

Most studies investigating the interplay between language learning and religious identity development have focused on children's and adolescents' religious socialization in minority and immigrant contexts. In one such study, Avni (2012) examined Hebrew learning in religious socialization and cultural identification in a non-Orthodox Jewish elementary day school in New York. Students were exposed to and interacted with different varieties of Hebrew associated with reading, reciting and studying the Bible and sacred texts as well as learning Modern Hebrew. The school promoted a Hebrew-only language policy for prayer and religious study, which explicitly devalued English translation and was rooted in claims of authenticity and legitimacy of Hebrew as the liturgical language of Judaism and the centrality of religious literacy in Hebrew in sustaining Jewish religious practices in the diaspora. Her study illustrated how students challenged the uniqueness of Hebrew and sought to authenticate English and other languages as a means of experiencing and expressing religious belief. At the same time, it showed the multiplicity and complexity of Jewish American subjectivities. In a study of Hasidic (nonliberal)

Jewish girls' language socialization, anthropologist Ayala Fader (2009) demonstrated how language learning and language use of different forms of Biblical Hebrew, Yiddish, English and Hasidic English was linked to the girls' socialization to gendered roles and identities and a Hasidic form of femininity, "a religious way of life" that Fader explained as "the ability to be 'with it' enough to selectively use and even enjoy the secular and the Gentile world, while never becoming Jews who are modern or secular" (Fader 2009: 3). Also employing a language socialization lens, Baquedano-López (2000) examined how Spanish-based Catholic religious education classes served to reinforce the link between language, religion and ethnicity among school-age Mexican immigrant children in Southern California through the ideological orientation regarding the importance of sustaining Spanish in a diasporic context. Through tellings of the religious narrative of "Nuestra Señora de Guadalupe" (Our Lady of Guadalupe, the patron saint of Mexico) almost exclusively in Spanish, children learned "to narrate being Mexican, locating themselves across a distal colonial past in Mexico and their immediate postcolonial present as immigrants in Los Angeles" (Baquedano-López 2000: 450). These studies point to how far and in what ways language learning and language use are shaped by language ideologies, language hierarchies and language policies circulating locally in the religious institutional settings and beyond. They also show how the negotiation and construction of religious belonging intersect with other identity categories linked to gender, ethnicity, race, nationality or that of becoming a successful language learner, as adults and children learn to navigate different social worlds.

Moreover, studies on religion and language teaching and learning have explored the language interrelationship between liturgical, minority and majority languages, written and oral forms. Religious literacies are based on learning to read, recite and study sacred texts (such as the Bible, the Quran, the Vedas) and devotional texts (songs, chants, hymns and other forms of verse and prose used to mediate religious experience) in one or more languages or language varieties, thereby cutting across language barriers. In a comparative study of British-born children learning to read sacred texts in a Jewish Cheder, a Sikh Gurdwara and a Muslim Mosque, Rosowsky (2013) recorded the enduring significance and resilience of liturgical languages (Biblical Hebrew, Classical Punjabi and Qu'ranic Arabic, respectively) and the symbolic and aesthetic values attributed to learning to read in a liturgical language intimately connected to the children's developing religious subjectivities. In another study, Gregory, Lytra et al. (2013) explored how children learned important sacred and devotional texts in four faith communities (Ghanaian Pentecostal, Polish Catholic, Tamil Hindu and Bangladeshi Muslim) in London, utilizing a range of languages (Qu'ranic Arabic, different forms of Tamil, Twi, Polish and English) and textual practices (translation and transliteration) with the expert mediation of faith teachers, parents, siblings and other faith community members. The authors remarked that "although the texts presented and the faiths they belong to are very different, they share much in common in terms of their symbolic meanings, how and in what ways they are learned and their special syncretic nature as they are negotiated in the new host country" (Gregory, Lytra et al. 2013: 345).

Reciting sacred texts and performing certain rituals are inherently multimodal and multisensory activities. Investigating religious literacies goes beyond an exclusive focus on language as a meaning-making resource to examine the broader relationships between language and other communicative modalities, including gesture, body posture, image, song, dance, chant and artifacts as well as the materiality and technological dimensions of these practices (Gregory, Choudhury et al. 2013; Lytra, Gregory and Ilakuberan 2016). In examining Quranic learning among the Fulbe in Northern Cameroon, Moore (2008) observed how the faith teacher relied on the interweaving of Qur'anic Arabic and Fulfulbe alongside the use of other semiotic resources (posture, pointing, gaze) to impart religious knowledge as well as spiritual and moral beliefs and values. Souza, Barradas and Woodham (2016) discussed how one Polish Catholic child, Adam, developed a wealth of symbolic knowledge through language and other modes (position, gaze, movement, food, cloths) as he participated in his family's Easter celebrations in their London home. Gregory, Choudhury et al. (2013: 323) have proposed to examine religious literacies and the learning potential they offer through the analytical lens of "syncretism" understood as "representing a diverse treasure trove, an array of linguistic, artistic, social and cultural resources from which children can draw," with the purpose of "creat[ing] something that is greater than just the sum of the constituent parts." Seen together, these studies suggest that faith learning entails syncretizing different languages, modalities, cultures and (re)interpreting texts across time and space as children learn to live in multiple or "simultaneous" worlds (Kenner 2004: 43).

For scholars of discourse in educational settings, the selected studies at the intersection of religion and language teaching and learning in religious settings reviewed in this section reveal a holistic approach to learning and achievement where novices are guided by more expert members to develop a wealth of linguistic, cultural, social, scriptural and embodied practices and competences, values and dispositions and to achieve a sense of self-worth, community and belonging. Moreover, the exploration of religious language and literacy practices in different settings (places of worship, religious education classes, religious and faith-inspired day schools, homes) highlights issues of permeability, boundaries and movement across settings. In this respect, the studies raise important questions about the transferability of religious language and literacy practices, identities, values and dispositions to secular school contexts to which I turn in Section 26.4.

26.4 Implications for Pedagogical Practice

As I argued in Section 26.3, the role of religious language and literacy practices in secular schools and classrooms has not been adequately explored, despite the growing diversity of the student population and the ever-growing role of religion in the lives of many young people in many contemporary societies. Therefore, how might religious language and literacy mediate meaning in secular schools? What are the opportunities and challenges? In one such ethnographic study, Sarroub (2005) examined how Yemeni-American adolescent girls sought to negotiate home and school worlds and competing expectations for success and academic achievement and how, in turn, these expectations influenced their use of secular and religious texts for the negotiation of personal and collective identities inside and outside school. Reyes (2009) described how Zulmy, a high-school Latina, used her science scrapbook to document the activities of the school's biology club in which she participated with photographs, maxims, friends' letters and Bible verses and to explore her Christian religious identity alongside the development of her group membership and friendships. The author argued that the biology club afforded a "safe space where she could give voice to her church girl identity," while her engagement with this literacy activity allowed her to feel "confident that her beliefs would not be questioned or attacked" (Reyes 2009: 264). Both studies drew on the concept of "in-betweeness" to explore the creation of spaces in schools and classrooms that can afford students with possibilities "to explore, negotiate, interact, counteract, and inscribe multiple selves" (Reyes 2009: 269).

Skerrett (2013) discussed a rare case study where students and teachers actively incorporated religious literacies in the secular classroom. The teacher leveraged the students' religious literacies to arrive at more complex literary understandings and interpretations in analyzing and understanding secular texts and producing academic writing. The author remarked on how the teacher's knowledge of her students' religious beliefs as well as her own religious knowledge and understanding supported instructional practices that "involved a critical reframing of the literacy curriculum as teacher and students made official students' religious literacies in school" (Skerrett 2013: 243). This reframing, she continued, "enabled students to engage in transformed practice, employing their religious literacies for academic literacy learning in school" (2013: 243). Seen through the theoretical lens of a pedagogy of multiliteracies (New London Group 1996), the study illustrated the opportunities for building critical literacy through engaging with religious literacies in the classroom. These findings echo calls by other scholars to recruit religious literacies in academic learning, arguing that it can serve as a vehicle for literacy development and a creative and cognitive endeavor. LeBlanc (2017: 77) has argued for "greater attention to the potential for students' religious practices and identities to contribute to a robustly relevant pedagogy that honors a variety of cultures and values" (see also Long 2016; Papen 2018).

At the same time, Skerrett (2013) has alerted us to some of the tensions and conflicts involved in navigating different religious and nonreligious perspectives and interpretations that may accompany the use of religious literacies in the classroom. In her study, she documented how the teacher and the students sought to address these challenges by foregrounding "their shared commitment to classroom community, pursuing understanding of one another's perspectives, and seeking underlying commonalities of different, or differently articulated, religious beliefs" (Skerrett 2013: 245). Scholars have identified other limitations in engaging with faith literacies in the classroom. Spector (2007) examined how middle-school students and teachers responded to the Holocaust memoir "Night" by Elie Wiesel in two US public schools. While students drew upon Christian religious narratives, knowledge and beliefs to understand and interpret the Jewish experience of the Holocaust, this engagement did not further the curriculum objectives of increasing tolerance and civic pluralism. Moreover, teachers avoided responding to students' religious framings and, in subsequent debriefings with the author, explained their reactions, thus: "I kind of tread lightly with the religious things" and "[religion] is a place I don't want to go" (Spector 2007: 45). Their reactions suggested that they viewed religion as a controversial topic, which resonated with findings from Dávila's (2015) study of pre-service teachers' responses to the religious content and significance of a children's book.

These studies have highlighted the importance of a critical analysis where students and teachers can work together to explore, confront and transform existing religious identities, knowledge and beliefs. They support Damico and Hall's (2014: 196) argument for teachers to "capitalize on teachable moments in the curriculum when religious knowledge or experience might be crucial to more deeply engaging academic content. This includes not only helping students understand and value the ways that their religious frames are important and powerful; it must also involve helping them understand the potential constraints and limitations of these frames."

26.5 Future Directions

Research on discourse and religion has indicated that in many religious settings there remains an enduring link between language, ethnicity and religion (Souza 2016). At the same time, schools both secular and faith-based are serving increasingly religiously and ethnically diverse student populations. This is compounded by the diversification of the state school sectors, for instance with the proliferation of charter schools in the United States and academies in the UK usually situated in multi-faith urban areas where religion may play a central role in the school's ethos and curriculum. A case in point is Avni's (2018) investigation of Jewish dual language charter schools in the United States where Modern Hebrew and Jewish history are taught as part of the curriculum to students beyond the religious community, thereby rendering the link between language, ethnicity and religion problematic. As schools strive toward pluralistic, democratic and equitable approaches to education, it is important for educators to inquire further into: (a) teaching and learning practices in out-of-school contexts that are meaningful to students' lives, religious settings being some of the most salient ones; (b) the opportunities and challenges for both students and teachers of engaging with religious language and literacy practices in schools and classrooms and the potential academic, social and political learning that students can accrue; and (c) the development of critical knowledge and pedagogies as well as professional preparation and support necessary for such engagement.

Moreover, the intensification of population flows, the confluence of old and new mobilities and the advent of new communication technologies have seen the emergence of new religious practices, such as the virtual attendance of religious services and rituals (Rosowsky 2018b; Sawin 2018; Padharipande 2018) as well as the sharing of religious experiences through social networking sites such as Facebook (Souza 2018) and online video sharing platforms (Peuronen 2017). These studies have raised questions regarding the authenticity of online religious practices and the fragmentation of religious authority alongside the development of more individualized forms of religious expression as opposed to more communal ones through offline religious practices (Rosowsky 2018a). They have also demonstrated the potential for linguistic innovation and transformation (Rosowsky 2018a). New communication technologies have also transformed religious expression and interaction online between people of other religions or no religious beliefs. Pihlaja (2018) explored language use and identity positionings in a series of videos in the social media pages of three public religious figures (an Evangelical Christian, a Muslim and an atheist) and the commentaries they elicited. One of the themes that emerged in his study was how social media users dealt with difference in religious belief, how they framed disagreement vis-à-vis those with whom they shared and those with whom they did not share religious belief. Pihlaja's work seeks to contribute to the ongoing debate regarding to what extent and in what ways social media might facilitate or hinder interreligious dialogue and understanding between people of same, different or no religious beliefs, that is, whether they provide spaces for interaction that reinforce the polarization of positions, fanning the flames of conflict, and/or promote engagement and respectful coexistence among users. This debate is particularly pertinent as acts of religiously-motivated bias and violence have become commonplace, and dehumanizing representations or misrepresentations of religious communities have proliferated in both new and traditional media. To this end, recent work by Baker, Gabrielatos and McEnery (2013) combining critical discourse analysis and corpus linguistics (see Chapter 9 in this volume for a discussion of this mixed methodology) has investigated the discursive representations of Muslims and Islam in the British national press between 1998 and 2009 and whether mainly negative categories of representation might have changed over time and across newspapers. The aforementioned studies on discourse and religion in new and traditional media compel us to engage in further work to dismantle binaries between "us" and "them," especially when we consider the impact that the perpetuation of binaries can have on educational practice and wider society more broadly.

26.6 Summary

This chapter has explored the intersection of discourse and religion as a growing interdisciplinary field, arguing that the greater inclusion of religion in discourse studies research agendas is both an important and a timely task. It has presented research strands within applied linguistics and then moved on to discuss empirical studies from related fields that can provide useful insights and directions for discourse studies too. The chapter has also drawn implications for pedagogical practice and concluded with some reflections on future directions in the present context of ever increasing mobilities and technological innovations worldwide.

Further Reading

Han, H. (2018). Studying Religion and Language Teaching and Learning: Building a Subfield. *Modern Language Journal* 102: 432–45.

This is the Position Paper for the Perspectives followed by five commentaries.

Johnston, B. (2017). *English Teaching and Evangelical Mission: The Case of the Lighthouse School*. Bristol: Multilingual Matters.

This is an ethnographic exploration of the intersection of ELT and evangelical Christianity in the context of an English language school with a Bible-based curriculum in Poland.

Lytra, V., Volk, D. and Gregory, E. (eds.) (2016). *Navigating Languages, Literacies and Identities: Religion in Young Lives*. New York: Routledge.

This edited collection investigates how children and adolescents leverage rich and complex multilingual, multiscriptal and multimodal resources associated with religion for meaning-making and the performance of religious subjectivities in homes, religious education classes, faith-inspired schools and places of worship across a range of religious communities.

References

Ahmed, S. (2015). The Voices of Young British Muslims: Identity, Belonging and Citizenship. In M. K. Smith, N. Stanton and T. Wylie (eds.) *Youth Work and Faith: Debates, Delights and Dilemmas*. Lyme Regis: Russell House. 37–51.

Avni, S. (2012). Translation as a Site of Language Policy Negotiation in Jewish Day School Education. *Current Issues in Language Planning* 13: 76–104.

(2018). What Can the Study of Hebrew Learning Contribute to Applied Linguistics? *Modern Language Journal* 102: 446–8.

Badenhorst, P. and Makoni, S. (2017). Migrations, Religions, and Social Flux. In S. Canagarajah (ed.) *The Routledge Handbook of Migration and Language*. New York: Routledge. 595–637.

Baker, P., Gabrielatos, C. and McEnery, T. (2013). *Discourse Analysis and Media Coverage: The Representation of Islam in the British Press*. Cambridge: Cambridge University Press.

Baquedano-López, P. (2000). Narrating Community in Doctrina Classes. *Narrative Inquiry* 10(2): 429–52.

Baquedano-López, P. and Ochs, E. (2002). The Politics of Language and Parish Storytelling: Nuestra Senora de Guadalupe Takes on "English Only." In P. Linell and K. Aronsson (eds.) *Selves and Voices: Goffman, Viveka and Dialogue*. Linköping, Sweden: Linköping University. 173–91.

Barrett, B. (2002). Religion and Habitus: Exploring the Relationship between Religious Involvement and Educational Outcomes and Orientations among Urban African American Students. *Urban Education* 45(4): 448–97.

Barton, D. and Hamilton, M. (1998). *Local Literacies: Reading and Writing in One Community*. London: Routledge.

Baurain, B. (2007). Christian Witness and Respect for Persons. *Journal of Language, Identity and Education* 6(3): 201–19.

(2015). *Religious Faith and Teacher Knowledge in English Language Teaching*. Newcastle-Upon-Tyne: Cambridge Scholars.

Bigelow, M. (2008). Somali Adolescents' Negotiation of Religious and Racial Bias in and out of School. *Theory into Practice* 47: 27–34.

Damico, J. S. and Hall, T. (2014). The Cross and the Lynching Tree: Exploring Religion and Race in the Elementary Classroom. *Language Arts* 92(3): 187–98.

Dávila, D. (2015). #WhoNeedsDiverseBooks? Preservice Teachers and Religious Neutrality with Children's Literature. *Research in the Teaching of English* 50(1): 60–83.

Douglas Fir Group. (2016). A Transdisciplinary Framework for SLA in a Multilingual World. *Modern Language Journal* 100: 19–47.

Edge, J. (1996). Cross-Cultural Paradoxes in a Profession of Values. *TESOL Quarterly* 30: 9–30.

(2003). Imperial Troopers and Servants of the Lord: A Vision of TESOL for the 21st Century. *TESOL Quarterly* 37(4): 701–8.

Ek, L. (2005). Staying on God's Path: Socialising Latino Immigrant Youth to a Christian Pentecostal Identity in Southern California. In A. C. Zantella (ed.) *Building on Strength: Language and Literacy in Latino Families and Communities*. New York: Teachers College Press. 77–92.

Fader, A. (2009). *Mitzvah Girls: Bringing Up the Next Generation of Hasidic Jews in Brooklyn*. Princeton, NJ: Princeton University Press.

Geertz, C. (1973). *The Interpretation of Cultures*. New York: Basic Books.

Genishi, C. and Dyson, A. H. (2009). *Children, Language, and Literacy: Diverse Learners in Diverse Times*. New York: Teachers College Press.

Gregory, E. and Williams, A. (2000). *City Literacies: Learning to Read across Generations and Cultures*. London: Routledge.

Gregory, E., Choudhury, H., Ilankuberan, A., Kwapong, A. and Woodham, M. (2013). Practice, Performance and Perfection: Learning Sacred Texts in Four Faith Communities in London. *International Journal of the Sociology of Language* 200: 27–48.

Gregory, E., Long, S. and Volk, D. (eds.) (2004). *Many Pathways to Literacy: Young Children Learning with Siblings, Grandparents, Peers and Communities*. New York: Routledge Falmer.

Gregory, E., Lytra, V., Choudhury, H., Ilankuberan, A., Kwapong, A. and Woodham, M. (2013). Syncretism as a Creative Act of Mind: The Narratives of Children from Four Faith Communities in London. *Journal of Early Childhood Literacy* 13(3): 322–47.

Gregory, E., Lytra, V., Ilankuberan, A., Choudhury, H. and Woodham, M. (2012). Translating Faith: Field Narratives as a Means of Dialogue in Collaborative Ethnographic Research. *International Journal of Qualitative Methods* 11(3): 196–213.

Griffith, T. (2004). Readers Respond to Julian Edge's "Imperial Troopers and Servants of the Lord": Unless a Grain of Wheat ... *TESOL Quarterly* 38(4): 714–16.

Haight, W. L. (2002). *African-American Children at Church: A Sociocultural Perspective*. Cambridge: Cambridge University Press.

Han, H. (2009). Institutionalised Inclusion: A Case Study on Support for Immigrants in English Learning. *TESOL Quarterly* 43(4): 643–68.

(2011). "Love Your China" and Evangelise: Religion, Nationalism, Racism and Immigrant Settlement in Canada. *Ethnography and Education* 6(1): 61–79.

(2018). Studying Religion and Language Teaching and Learning: Building a Subfield. *Modern Language Journal* 102: 432–45.
Haque, A. (2004). Islamophobia in North America: Confronting the Menace. In B. van Driel (ed.) *Confronting Islamophobia in Educational Practice*. Sterling, VA: Trentham. 1–18.
Heath, S. B. (1983). *Ways with Words: Language, Life and Work in Communities and Classrooms*. Cambridge: Cambridge University Press.
Hemming, P. (2015). *Religion in the Primary School: Ethos, Diversity, Citizenship*. New York: Routledge.
Hoque, A. (2015). *British-Islamic Identity: Third-Generation Bangladeshis from East London*. London: Trentham Books at IOE Press.
Johnston, B. (2017). *English Teaching and Evangelical Mission: The Case of the Lighthouse School*. Bristol: Multilingual Matters.
Jordan, D. H. and Wilson, C. M. (2017). Supporting African American Student Success through Prophetic Activism: New Possibilities for Public School–Church Partnerships. *Urban Education* 52(1): 91–119.
Keane, W. (1997). Religious Language. *Annual Review of Anthropology* 26: 47–71.
Kenner, C. (2004). Living in Simultaneous Worlds: Difference and Integration in Bilingual Script-Learning. *International Journal of Bilingual Education and Bilingualism* 7(1): 43–61.
Kenner, C., Kwapong, A., Choudhury, H. and Ruby, M. (2016). Supporting Children's Learner Identities through Faith: Ghanaian Pentecostal and Bangladeshi Muslim Communities in London. In V. Lytra, D. Volk and E. Gregory (eds.) *Navigating Languages, Literacies and Identities: Religion in Young Lives*. New York: Routledge. 213–26.
LeBlanc, R. J. (2017). Literacy Rituals in the Community and the Classroom. *Language Arts* 95(2): 77–86.
Lillis, T. M. (2013). *The Sociolinguistics of Writing*. Edinburgh: Edinburgh University Press.
Long, S. (2016). Conclusion. In V. Lytra, D. Volk and E. Gregory (eds.) *Navigating Languages, Literacies and Identities: Religion in Young Lives*. New York: Routledge. 227–33.
Lytra, V. (2018). Faith Literacies Matter: Reflecting on the Role of Faith as a Force for Learning, Socialisation and Personal and Collective Identification in Young People's Lives in a Global City. In A. Fuentes Calle (ed.) *Languages and Spiritual Traditions: Linguistic Diversity and Religious Diversity in the City of Barcelona*. Papers on the LinguaPax-30 Years Conference, Barcelona, November 24, 2017. Barcelona: LinguaPax. 45–56.
(2020). Faith Communities. In K. Tusting (ed.) *The Routledge Handbook of Linguistic Ethnography*. Abingdon: Routledge. 312–25.
Lytra, V., Gregory, E. and Ilankuberan, A. (2016). Children's Representations of the Temple in Text and Talk in a Tamil Hindu/Saiva Faith Community in London. In V. Lytra, D. Volk and E. Gregory

(eds.) *Navigating Languages, Literacies and Identities: Religion in Young Lives*. New York: Routledge. 141–58.

Lytra, V., Volk, D. and Gregory, E. (eds.) (2016a). *Navigating Languages, Literacies and Identities: Religion in Young Lives*. New York: Routledge.

(2016b). Introduction. In V. Lytra, D. Volk and E. Gregory (eds.) *Navigating Languages, Literacies and Identities: Religion in Young Lives*. New York: Routledge. 1–17.

McMillon, G. T. and Edwards, P. A. (2000). Why Does Joshua "Hate" School ... but Love Sunday School? *Language Arts* 78(2): 111–20.

Moore, L. C. (2008). Body, Text, and Talk in Maroua Fulbe Qur'anic Schooling. *Text & Talk* 28(5): 643–65.

New London Group. (1996). A Pedagogy of Multiliteracies: Designing Social Futures. *Harvard Educational Review* 66(1): 60–92.

Padharipande, R. V. (2018). Online Satsang and Online Puja: Faith and Language in the Era of Globalisation. In A. Rosowsky (ed.) *Faith and Language in Digital Spaces*. Bristol: Multilingual Matters. 185–208.

Papen, U. (2018). Hymns, Prayers and Bible Stories: The Role of Religious Literacy Practices in Children's Literacy Learning. *Ethnography and Education* 13(1): 119–34.

Pavlenko, A. and Blackledge, A. (eds.) (2004). *Negotiation of Identities in Multilingual Contexts*. Clevedon: Multilingual Matters.

Peele-Eady, T. (2011). Constructing Membership Identity through Language and Social Interaction: The Case of African American Children at Faith Missionary Baptist Church. *Anthropology & Education Quarterly* 42(1): 54–75.

(2016). "The Responsive Reading" and Reading Responsively: Language, Literacy and African American Student Learning in the Black Church. In V. Lytra, D. Volk and E. Gregory (eds.) *Navigating Languages, Literacies and Identities: Religion in Young Lives*. New York: Routledge. 85–109.

Pennycook, A. and Coutand-Marin, S. (2004). Teaching English as a Missionary Language (TEML). *Discourse: Studies in the Cultural Politics of Education* 24(30): 338–53.

Pennycook, A. and Makoni, S. (2005). The Language Effects of Christianity. *Journal of Language, Identity, and Education* 4(2): 137–55.

Peuronen, S. (2017). *Language, Participation and Spaces of Identification: The Construction of Socio-Ideological Meanings in a Christian Life Style Sports Community*. Unpublished PhD dissertation, University of Jyväskylä.

Pihlaja, S. (2018). *Religious Talk Online. The Evangelical Discourse of Muslims, Christians and Atheists*. Cambridge: Cambridge University Press.

Pihlaja, S. and Thomspon, N. (2017). "I Love the Queen": Positioning in Young Muslim Discourse. *Discourse, Context & Media* 20: 52–8.

Purgason, K. B. (2004). Readers Respond to Julian Edge's "Imperial Troopers and Servants of the Lord": A Clearer Picture of the "Servants of the Lord." *TESOL Quarterly* 38: 711–13.

Reyes, C. (2009). "El Libro de Recuerdos" (Book of Memories): A Latina Student's Exploration of the Self and Religion in Public School. *Research in the Teaching of English* 43(3): 263–85.

Rosowsky, A. (2013). Faith, Phonics and Identity: Reading in Faith Complementary Schools. *Literacy* 47(2): 67–78.

(ed.) (2018a). *Faith and Language Practices in Digital Spaces*. Bristol: Multilingual Matters.

(2018b). Virtual Allegiance: Online "Baya'a" Practices within a Worldwide Sufi Order. In A. Rosowsky (ed.) *Faith and Language in Digital Spaces*. Bristol: Multilingual Matters. 209–33.

Rumsey, S. (2016). Coming of Age: Amish Heritage Literacy Practices of *Rumspringa*, Adult Baptism, and Shunning. In V. Lytra, D. Volk and E. Gregory (eds.) *Navigating Languages, Literacies and Identities: Religion in Young Lives*. New York: Routledge. 56–68.

Sagoo, G. K. (2016). *Making and Shaping the First Nishkam Nursery: A Linguistic Ethnographic Study of a British Sikh Project for Childhood*. Unpublished PhD thesis, University of Birmingham.

Sarroub, L. (2005). *All American Yemeni Girls: Being Muslim in a Public School*. Philadelphia: University of Pennsylvania Press.

Sawin, T. (2018). Re-parishing in Social Media: Identity-Based Virtual Faith Communities and Physical Parishes. In A. Rosowsky (ed.) *Faith and Language in Digital Spaces*. Bristol: Multilingual Matters. 19–44.

Scribner, S. and Cole, M. (1981). Unpackaging Literacy. In M. Farr Whiteman (ed.) *Writing: The Nature, Development and Teaching of Written Communication*. Hillsdale, NJ: Lawrence Erlbaum Associates. 57–70.

Skerrett, A. (2013). Religious Literacies in a Secular Literacy Classroom. *Reading Research Quarterly* 49(2): 233–50.

Souza, A. (2016). Language and Faith Encounters: Bridging Language-Ethnicity and Language-Religion Studies. *International Journal of Multilingualism* 13(1): 134–48.

(2018). Facebook: A Medium for the Language Planning of Migrant Churches. In A. Rosowsky (ed.) *Faith and Language in Digital Spaces*. Bristol: Multilingual Matters. 45–67.

Souza, A., Barradas, O. and Woodham, M. (2016). Easter Celebrations at Home: Acquiring Symbolic Knowledge and Constructing Identities. In V. Lytra, D. Volk, and E. Gregory (eds.) *Navigating Languages, Literacies and Identities: Religion in Young Lives*. New York: Routledge. 39–55.

Spector, K. (2007). God on the Gallows: Reading the Holocaust through Narratives of Redemption. *Research in the Teaching of English* 42(1): 7–55.

Stevick, E. (1996). Response to Julian Edge's "Keeping the Faith." *TESOL Matters* 6(6): 6.

Street, B. V. (1984). *Literacy in Theory and Practice*. New York: Cambridge University Press.

Varghese, M. and Johnston, B. (2007). Evangelical Christians and English Language Teaching. *TESOL Quarterly* 41: 9–31.

Volk, D. (2016). Home Worship Service/Bible Reading/Reading Lesson: Syncretic Teaching and Learning in a Puerto Rican Family. In V. Lytra, D. Volk and E. Gregory (eds.) *Navigating Languages, Literacies and Identities: Religion in Young Lives*. New York: Routledge. 21–38.

Watson, J. A. (2018). *Religere* like You Mean It: A Meditation on Han's "Studying Religion and Language Teaching and Learning: Building a Subfield." *Modern Language Journal* 102: 458–62.

Wong, M. S. and Canagarajah, S. (eds.) (2009). *Christian and Critical English Language Educators in Dialogue: Pedagogical and Ethical Dilemmas*. New York: Routledge.

Wong, M. S., Kristjánsson, C. and Dörneyi, Z. (eds.) (2013). *Christian Faith and English Language Teaching and Learning*. New York: Routledge.

Part VI

Discourses, Publics and Mediatization

Introduction

How can discourse analysis inform policy and practice and how can discourse analysts engage with participants and publics around issues of interest to them? What are the opportunities or, equally, the limits and limitations of such an endeavor? This is a longstanding question in the field with a renewed momentum and relevance in the era of social media and the amplification that accompanies them, and in a climate of post-truth, destabilization and mistrust of expertise. Traditionally, a concern for critical discourse analysts only, the role of discourse analysis beyond (just the) analysis has increasingly become an integral part of the discussions and rationale in every single discourse analytic study, as the chapters of this handbook attest. So, although we recognize the involvement of discourse analysis in "real-world" issues as a cross-cutting theme of this collection, we have chosen to bring together in this part a set of chapters with a dedicated and explicit focus on domains of public engagement that foreground the role of discourse analysts: (corporate) organizations, finance, politics, media. In their discussion of how to identify, analyze and interpret changing values and practices in these domains, all the chapters address the issue of the role and involvement of discourse analysts in uncovering discourse practices that are grounded in unequal power relations and that set out to be persuasive or manipulative. Discourse in these cases becomes a powerful weapon: part of rhetorical tactics, legitimation strategies, branding, constructing, positioning, and policing subjects and publics.

One issue of contention are the very definitions and remits of critical and critique in discourse analysis in these cases. The subfield of critical discourse analysis (CDA) has been traditionally associated with an interest in ideologies and how these regulate textual choices and genres; what links specific, core characteristics of ideological phenomena such as populism, as discussed in by Rheindorf Chapter 28, with specific discursive strategies? By revealing what is ideological, hegemonic and taken for granted, in organizations and elsewhere, which can then form the foundation for a critique with the potential of raising critical awareness, CDA has been associated with an emancipatory knowledge interest, as Björkvall reminds us in Chapter 27. In his discussion of critical discourse approaches to genres, he distinguishes CDA from critical genre analysis (CGA) that is focused on professional practices and actions. More ethnographic in method and outlook, this approach to criticality is not aimed at bringing about social change but at "enhance our understanding of and motivation for the construction of professional genres and actions" (Bhatia 2017: 27 cited in Chapter 27, p. 694).

A different form of critique involves taking an extra step beyond critiquing hegemonic norms to suggesting and promoting alternatives, as Mooney discusses in Chapter 29 on discourses of and about money. To take this step, the discourse analyst needs to dispense with "objectivity" and instead formulate value judgments that would allow them to make concrete suggestions for policy reform as well as linguistic and ideological innovation. This is an example of a participatory research approach that goes beyond empowering and giving voice to any disenfranchised participants by means of generating alternative discourses, frames and explanations for ongoing problems. This kind of activism, based on the production of alternative discourses, is generally absent from work in the field of language and money, Mooney claims. She also aptly discusses the issues of ethics raised when discourse analysts effectively make value judgments about the phenomena they study, and then translate this analysis into action. Another danger of discourse analysts' interventionist approaches involves offering tools that are ultimately co-opted and used for the further legitimation of specific ideologies by organizations, as Jaworska warns us in Chapter 30.

The question of *where* the analysis should primarily be located in cases of CDA of this sort – that is, at the level of text and textual choices; at the level of discursive or social practice; or at the level of organizational and societal ideologies – and of how links amongst these levels should be established remains an ongoing discussion, as we have seen in other chapters too (especially in Part I). The question of methodologies is also unresolved; there seems to be a historical divide between approaches focused on ideologies that are more text-centered and approaches focused on actions and practices that tend to be based on ethnography. One concept that seems to cut across these methodological differences is that of recontextualization: developed both within CDA and in linguistic anthropological and ethnography of communication approaches. It has been deployed to capture changes that textual and generic configurations undergo in different contexts of discourse production, dissemination and engagement as well as the different potentials for meaning-making that these bring about: what kinds of social relation and subject position they naturalize and normalize in the process, what they legitimate and make acceptable, visible and widely available and what they silence.

Another ongoing point of discussion within critical approaches to discourse is what is or should be considered as relevant context and interpretative framework for a study, what the level of generality in posing questions is or should be. For many studies, the role of neoliberal discourses and late capitalism, at least in Western societies and at times of (social, financial and cultural) crisis, should be identified from the outset as part of the contextualization of organizational and institutional discourses (e.g. Chapters by Mooney and Jaworska). The role of (social) media and mediatization both in changing social actions and practices of participation and in the construction of individuals and publics is acknowledged and addressed in all chapters, especially Chapters 31 and 32, respectively by Deschriver and Jones.

The first chapter in this part, Chapter 27 by **Björkvall**, tackles genre, a key concept in discourse studies, amply researched in terms of text-internal structures, functions and social actions, as discussed in Chapter 1 too. Björkvall's chapter zooms into how genre has been theorized and analyzed in two major critical approaches to it, namely, CDA and CGA. While the former relates the textual aspects of genres to broader ideologies in society at large, the latter connects them to specific, mainly professional practices and social actions. The critical endeavor in each of these two approaches has different aims and purposes: CDA is aimed at bringing hidden ideologies to the fore and critiquing them, while CGA is aimed at demystifying how professionals within an organization produce and use texts as part of social actions. This knowledge interest is ethnographically attestable and oriented toward the views and practices of managers as well as other employees in an organization. Connected with these differences are differences in focus and questions asked. Within CDA, there is interest in the hybridization and interdiscursivity of genres. These refer to how prototypical features of a number of genres (and discourses) are mixed within texts, a routine practice in modern organizations. Inspired by Fairclough, studies of interdiscursivity within CDA have pointed to the marketization of public discourse as well as to a tendency of genres of governance and control to be presented as if they were something else. CGA, on the other hand, has been more interested in explaining why "professional practices and actions behind texts set up *interdiscursive* connections to well-established genres in public administration and in the judicial and legal sectors" (p. 605). The opening up of discourse to multimodality and materiality, as seen in Part IV, still has some way to go in these studies. Björkvall also recommends a further shift toward ethnographic studies of genre.

The notion of populism which Chapter 28 by **Rheindorf** focuses on has attracted debates around its status as ideology or style, as a danger to democracy or not, and so on. The chapter shows how linguistic methods and concepts applied to study populist rhetoric have been largely qualitative and include a range of devices at different levels: for example nomination and predication strategies, polarization strategies (e.g. us vs. them dichotomies), topoi, argumentation and fallacy, cognitive schemata, multimodality, discursive shifts, normalization. A wide variety of discourse-analytic approaches have been adopted to study populism, all of which share a commitment to critique, but it is mainly within CDA and the discourse-historical approach that populism has been studied as a discursive phenomenon. The main foci of this research include: "the reasons for populist successes in a particular context; commonalities and differences between populist phenomena across time or space; populism's effects on democracy, institutions or policy, and the workings of populism, conceptualized as discourse, rhetorics, strategies or performances" (p. 629). Populism has been widely found to be premised on mobilization of discourse strategies especially at the level of a personalist leadership, political party and social movement. "In addition, scandalization and calculated ambivalence are often used by populists to capture and maintain media attention" (Engel and Wodak 2012). Social media have been instrumental for populist politicians on account of their amplification and reach affordances as well as their interactivity, which allows networked audiences to distribute and generate populist content. The chapter overall shows how taking a critical perspective on populist discourse requires recognizing textual and contextual choices in populist discourse as strategic.

The starting point for Chapter 29 by **Mooney** is that any studies of money talk or discourses about money need to recognize the polysemy of the term, as a store of value, a medium of exchange, a unit of account, etc., coupled with the fact that it is used in particular contexts, by specific people to do specific things. Much of the research on "money" in this respect has deployed Lakoff and Johnson's Cognitive Metaphor Theory, which is also discussed in Chapters 9 and 10. Such analysis has not just identified metaphors but has also shown their rhetorical and ideological effects, especially in terms of erasing humans and human agency, personifying nonhuman entities and naturalizing economic processes. The range of metaphors that researchers have found to this effect is considerable and it includes organic metaphors, including growth and health, war, body, and water metaphors. The chapter also considers work that focuses on texts and ideology, including research in the CDA tradition, to show the contribution that this work has made in terms of understanding the post-2008 global financial crisis (GFC) and its causes and in showing the utility of taking a multimodal approach to analysis. In similar vein, work that deals with austerity, poverty and poverty porn is explored. While this strand of work is not entirely new, with rising inequality it has become even more relevant. Paying attention to the ways in which economic and financial events are represented is important in understanding political structures, ideology and the experiences of real people. The potential of this type of work is demonstrated with reference to the Framing the Economy project (FTE) undertaken in the UK. Given the analysis involved and the alternatives generated, this is presented as a kind of constructive critique in the domain of language, economics and money.

Jaworska focuses in Chapter 30 on corporate discourse defined as a set of social practices that "supposes acceptance of a common ideological position, a process of socialisation of members, a set of preferred discourse forms … that act as symbols of membership and a structured system of relationships, both inside the domain and with outsiders" (Breeze 2013: 23, cited on p. 667). The chapter stresses the importance of looking at practices and how discourses and practices feed each other as part of a study of corporate discourse.

Studies concerned with internal corporate talk have found that, contrary to the common perception that corporate talk is dry and purely transactional, there is prominence of interpersonal discourse features (e.g. hedges, humor, politeness, impoliteness), highlighting that, in corporate life, relational goals are as important as transactional ones. Research on corporate communication with the outside world has focused specifically on discursive strategies that corporations employ to legitimize their actions and to persuade or dissuade stakeholders. A major focus of inquiry here concerns the study of employee branding, that is, the ways in which corporate organizations employ diverse and increasingly sophisticated symbolic, semiotic and discursive means to create a sense of corporate community and persuade the employees of the merits of the company. Studies of corporate discourse are increasingly addressing the role of social media as an important site for creating and maintaining public relations. The chapter concludes with a discussion of some of the practical and ethical issues that arise when "doing" a critical analysis of corporate discourses, before it outlines some of the opportunities and benefits that criticality and language awareness can bring to corporate life.

Chapter 31 by **Deschrijver** proposes and discusses mediatization as a concept and perspective well-suited to the discourse analytic investigation of globally occurring changes and innovations in communication, but one that is at the same time amenable to local contexts and attentive to emanations of shifting linguistic features. Despite the concept's elusiveness and multiple uses and applications, it can be illuminated through the fruitful dichotomy of institutional vs. social-constructionist perspectives on it (Hepp 2014 cited on p. 689). The former conceptualizes media as "more or less independent social institutions with [their] own sets of rules," exerting (material and discursive) influence on society or on various social domains (Hepp 2014: 51). The latter, in contrast, embeds media in sociocultural reality, investigating how media partake in their communicative construction. The chapter provides an overview, on the one hand, of research within CDA that has tended to follow the institutional conceptualizations of mediatization and, on the other hand, of research within sociolinguistics and linguistic anthropology that could be construed as more social constructionist in focus. The discussion argues for a (further) integration of discourse analytic methodologies to the study of mediatization to strengthen its empirical basis. It also puts forward the importance of investigating linguistic reflexivity as part of a study of mediatization in the spirit of Agha's work and his definition of mediatization as "[reflexive linking] ... of communication to processes of commoditization" (Agha 2011, cited on p. 691). The focus on how ordinary people are able to orient to language (e.g. definitions and uses of specific words) in mediatized communicative encounters is seen as a productive route into the investigation of "'mediatized moments' as providing opportunities and 'massively parallel inputs to recontextualization'" (Agha 2011: 167). Such metapragmatically-oriented discourse analysis can be conducive to the investigation of historically contrastive research and of differences between media types and contexts. Finally, the chapter suggests three main avenues for research: (1) multimodal mediatization research, (2) global mediatization research and (3) social mediatization research.

Chapter 32 by **Jones**, the last in both this part and this volume, turns its attention to a phenomenon of major significance that is interwoven with the rise of social media: surveillance. Surveillance is viewed as being tied up with everyday life practices, for example searching the Internet, engaging with our friends on social media, shopping, showing off. Shying away from exoticizing digital surveillance or treating it as necessarily nefarious and untoward, the discussion stresses that what makes it possible has to do with how more traditional semiotic modes such as text and images are deployed to lure users into making compromising decisions. It is the interaction among social relationships, discourse practices and technological tools in contemporary digital and physical spaces that has created an ecology where interactions can be generative of data that can then be of (monetary) value for internet companies, advertisers and governments. The chapter provides a systematic overview of the main discursive processes involved in digital surveillance, including *participation, pretexting, entextualization, recontextualization* and *inferencing*, showing how they are altered when mediated through digital technologies. At the heart of these processes are ways in which people alter and report altering the way they communicate online based on their algorithmic imaginary, that is, on how they believe algorithms might process and act upon their words. This has to be explored in parallel with the ways in which certain interfaces are designed so as to prompt and inspire honesty and a willing disclosure of personal data. With its conceptual apparatus, the chapter provides a roadmap for future discourse studies of surveillance showcasing both continuity in conceptualization and analysis of the intimate links between discourse and the production of social relations and social life as well as innovation, especially in methodology for exploring digital communication.

References

Agha, A. (2011). Meet Mediatization. *Language & Communication* 31: 163–70.

Bhatia, V. K. (2017). *Critical Genre Analysis: Investigating Interdiscursive Performance in Professional Practice*. New York: Routledge.

Breeze, R. (2013). *Corporate Discourse*. London: Bloomsbury.

Engel, J. and Wodak, R. (2012). "Calculated Ambivalence" and Holocaust Denial in Austria. In R. Wodak and J. E. Richardson (eds.) *Analysing Fascist Discourse: European Fascism in Talk and Text*. New York: Routledge. 73–96.

Hepp, A. (2014). Mediatization: A Panorama of Media and Communication Research. In J. Androutsopoulos (ed.) *Mediatization and Sociolinguistic Change*. Berlin: Mouton de Gruyter. 49–66.

27

The Critical Analysis of Genre and Social Action

Anders Björkvall

27.1 Introduction

Whereas the concept of *discourse* has always been at the core of critical analysis in the field of critical discourse analysis (CDA) and the renamed critical discourse studies (CDS), it can be argued that this has not really been the case for *genre*. To some extent this can be explained considering the focus of CDA on the connection between discourses, in a Foucauldian sense, and representations of, for instance, power relations, gender and social injustices. Following that approach, texts systematically present certain groups in society as being without agency and more or less under the control of other groups and therefore they *draw on* or *realize* normative discourses. Such discourses call for deconstruction, critique and potential transformation, which is an ongoing endeavor in CDA.[1] It cannot be argued that genre has been rendered irrelevant in relation to the critical analysis of texts, contexts and social practice in CDA – as it has been used by key researchers such as Fairclough (2003, 2010), van Leeuwen (1993, 2005a, 2005b) and Wodak (2003, 2013). But the notion is usually applied as part of analytical frameworks with goals other than the critique of genres per se, or as a means for identifying texts for further (critical) analysis.

How, then, can genre analysis be relevant to discourse analysts? Van Leeuwen (1993) distinguishes between, on the one hand, the aforementioned Foucauldian perception of discourses as *representations* of knowledges and social practices and, on the other, discourse as *social action*. He argues that CDA must be concerned with both of these aspects, that is, both with discourse as representation – as "the instrument of the social construction of reality" – and as "the instrument of power and control"

---

[1] Since most of the research referred to in this chapter still makes reference to CDA rather than CDS, CDA will be used henceforward.

through which people do something to or with other people (Van Leeuwen 1993: 193). The latter aspect of discourse is closely connected to how Miller (1984: 151) – a key researcher in genre studies – defines genre: "[A] rhetorically sound definition of genre must be centered not on the substance or the form of discourse but on the action it is used to accomplish."[2] The present chapter deals with this *genre aspect of discourse*, so to speak. Paying particular attention to organizational change, the chapter argues that it can be useful for discourse analysts to focus on the critical analysis of genre in cases where the critique is primarily directed at changing social actions rather than at various representations of knowledge.

A short introductory example can further frame the theme of the chapter. Figure 27.1 shows the first two pages of the Code of Ethics of the Department of Correction in the State of Connecticut in the United States and Figure 27.2 presents a page from the Strategy of the Food Safety Authority of Ireland.

Weber ([1922]1978: 7) broadly defines social actions as meaningful actions in social contexts. The text in both Figure 27.1 and Figure 27.2 can be interpreted as, among other things, realizing the social action of controlling the behavior of the civil servants in the respective institutions. However, the overall design of the document in Figure 27.1, explicitly labeled "ADMINISTRATIVE DIRECTIVE," relates it to a vast number of other directives in the United States and elsewhere with the explicit purpose of directing employees in the public sector. For instance, the heading of the document contains formal information such as "Directive Number"; there are references (under the heading of "2. Authority and Reference") to legal documents and decrees legitimizing the Code of Ethics; and modal auxiliaries ("shall"), other verbs ("comply") and nouns (e.g. "obligations," "conduct") of obligation are used to make clear that this document regulates behavior: "Department employees shall comply with all the provisions of this directive regarding their ethical conduct and obligations as employees." The design of text in Figure 27.2 is very different. It is multimodal and presents boxes in full color containing salient and value-laden lexical items ("innovation," "passion," etc.) as well as a number of illustrations. It also lacks the linguistic markers of obligation that are so prominent in the text in Figure 27.1.

How can we think about the differences between these texts? One option would be to relate the textual observations to broader *discursive* and *sociocultural* practices as well as to ideologies in society at large (e.g. Fairclough 1993; Ledin and Machin 2016a, 2016b; see also Chapter 14 in this volume). In this perspective, the texts in Figures 27.1 and 27.2 could, for instance, be analyzed in terms of how closely they connect to

---

[2] The role of discourse in action is also the main interest of mediated discourse analysis (MDA) (e.g. Norris and Jones 2005). Genre, however, is not.

State of Connecticut Department of Correction	Directive Number 1.13	Effective Date 4/15/2005	Page 1 of 6
ADMINISTRATIVE DIRECTIVE	Supersedes	New Directive	
Approved By	Title Code of Ethics		

1. **Policy**. Employees of the Department of Correction, as representatives of the State of Connecticut, are assigned to positions of trust and responsibility that require them to observe the highest ethical standards. Strict compliance with the provisions of this directive is an essential aspect of employment with the Department.

2. **Authority and Reference**.

    A. United States Code, 5 USC Sections 1501 through 1508.
    B. Connecticut General Statutes, Sections 1-79 through 1-86, 1-86e through 1-89a, 5-266a and 18-81.
    C. Executive Order No. 1, Governor Rell.
    D. Regulations of Connecticut State Agencies, Sections 1-81-1, 1-81-14 through 1-81-38 (inclusive) and 5-266a-1.
    E. DAS General Letter No. 214-D, revised 1995.
    F. American Correctional Association, Standards for the Administration of Correctional Agencies, Second Edition, April 1993, Standards 2-CO-1A-05, 2-CO-1A-29, 2-CO-1C-04 and 2-CO-1C-24.
    G. American Correctional Association, Standards for Adult Correctional Institutions, Fourth Edition, January 2003, Standards 4-4012, 4-4024, 4-4048 and 4-4069.
    H. American Correctional Association, Performance-Based Standards for Adult Local Detention Facilities, Fourth Edition, June 2004, Standards 4-ALDF-7B-05, 4-ALDF-7C-02, 4-ALDF-7C-03, 4-ALDF-7D-06 and 4-ALDF-7E-01.
    I. American Correctional Association, Standards for Adult Probation and Parole Field Services, Third Edition, August 1998, Standards 3-3019, 3-3032, 3-3047, 3-3068 and 3-3069.
    J. American Correctional Association, Standards for Correctional Training Academies, First Edition, May 1993, Standards 1-CTA-1A-11, 1-CTA-1C-01 and 1-CTA-1C-12.
    K. Administrative Directives 2.1, Equal Employment Opportunity and Affirmative Action; 2.2, Sexual Harassment, 2.17, Employee Conduct and 2.22, Workplace Violence Prevention Policy.

3. **Definitions**. For the purposes stated herein, the following definitions apply:

    A. **Gift**. A gift shall mean anything of value, which is directly and personally received, unless consideration of equal or greater value is given in return.

    B. **Substantial and Potential Conflicts**. In reference to section 4(B)(1) of this directive, financial interests that "substantially conflict" include those from which the employee, the employee's spouse, dependent child or associated business would derive a direct monetary gain or suffer a direct monetary loss by reason of the employee's official activity.

Figure 27.1 *Code of Ethics*, Connecticut Department of Correction

neoliberal ideologies of performance management and the soft government (Mulderrig 2011) of postbureaucratic organizations. This is characteristic of CDA's take on a number of issues regarding texts and ideology in society. Key questions here could be: What are the relations between dominating ideological and social conditions in society which have led to social actions realized in texts like the ones in Figure 27.1 and Figure 27.2? And can it be the case that *ideology-driven* performance management has pushed the Strategy of the Food Safety Authority of Ireland further away from the more traditional, rule-based genres of public administration which the Code of Ethics in Figure 27.1 represents?

Directive Number 1.13	Effective Date 4/15/2005	Page 2 of 6
Title	Code of Ethics	

If the employee is faced with taking official action that will directly affect the employee's financial interest, or that of a family member or associated business, distinct from others in the employee's occupation or group (e.g., taking official action on the awarding of a contract to a private business the employee owns), the employee has a "substantial conflict" of interest under Section 1-85 of the Connecticut General Statutes and may not act under any circumstances. The employee shall not be considered to have a substantial conflict if the employee's financial interest is shared by the other members of the employee's profession, occupation or group. If, in the discharge of the employee's official duties, the employee is required to take action that would directly affect the employee's financial interest, or that of a family member (i.e., the employee's spouse, parent, brother, sister, child or child's spouse) or a business with which the employee is associated, the employee may have a "potential conflict" of interest. In that case, unless the interest is insignificant (i.e., less than $100 in a calendar year), or no different than that of a substantial segment of the general public (e.g., a regulatory official approving an increase in residential electric rates), the employee must follow the rules outlined in Section 1-86 of the Connecticut General Statutes. Specifically, the employee must prepare a written report that describes the potential conflict and submit the report to the appropriate supervisor who shall reassign the matter.

4. Ethical Conduct. All Department employees shall comply with the requirements set forth in the Connecticut State Ethics Commission Code of Ethics for Public Officials. Furthermore, all Department employees shall comply with all the provisions of this directive regarding their ethical conduct and obligations as employees.

   A. Employees of the Department of Correction shall:
   1. Strive in their professional and personal life to exemplify the Department's motto of P.R.I.D.E., Professionalism, Respect, Integrity, Dignity, and Excellence.
   2. Uphold the Department's fundamental duty to protect and serve the public, protect staff, and to safeguard the lives and property of offenders under the Department's supervision.
   3. Treat, with respect and dignity, the public, staff, and offenders in accordance with Administrative Directive 2.17, Employee Conduct.
   4. Ensure a workplace free of sexual harassment, discrimination, and workplace violence in accordance with Administrative Directives 2.1, Equal Employment Opportunity and Affirmative Action; 2.2, Sexual Harassment, 2.17, Employee Conduct and 2.22, Workplace Violence Prevention Policy.
   5. Be firm, fair, and consistent in the performance of all their assigned duties.

Figure 27.1 (cont.)

Another take on the texts in Figures 27.1 and 27.2 would be that of critical genre analysis (CGA) (Bhatia 2010, 2015, 2017). Here, *professional* practices and specific social actions connected to them would be brought to the forefront. The critical endeavor would not so much be to relate the texts to ideologies in society at large but to *demystify* how professionals within an organization produce and use texts as part of social actions. The knowledge interest would be oriented toward the views and practices of

Figure 27.2

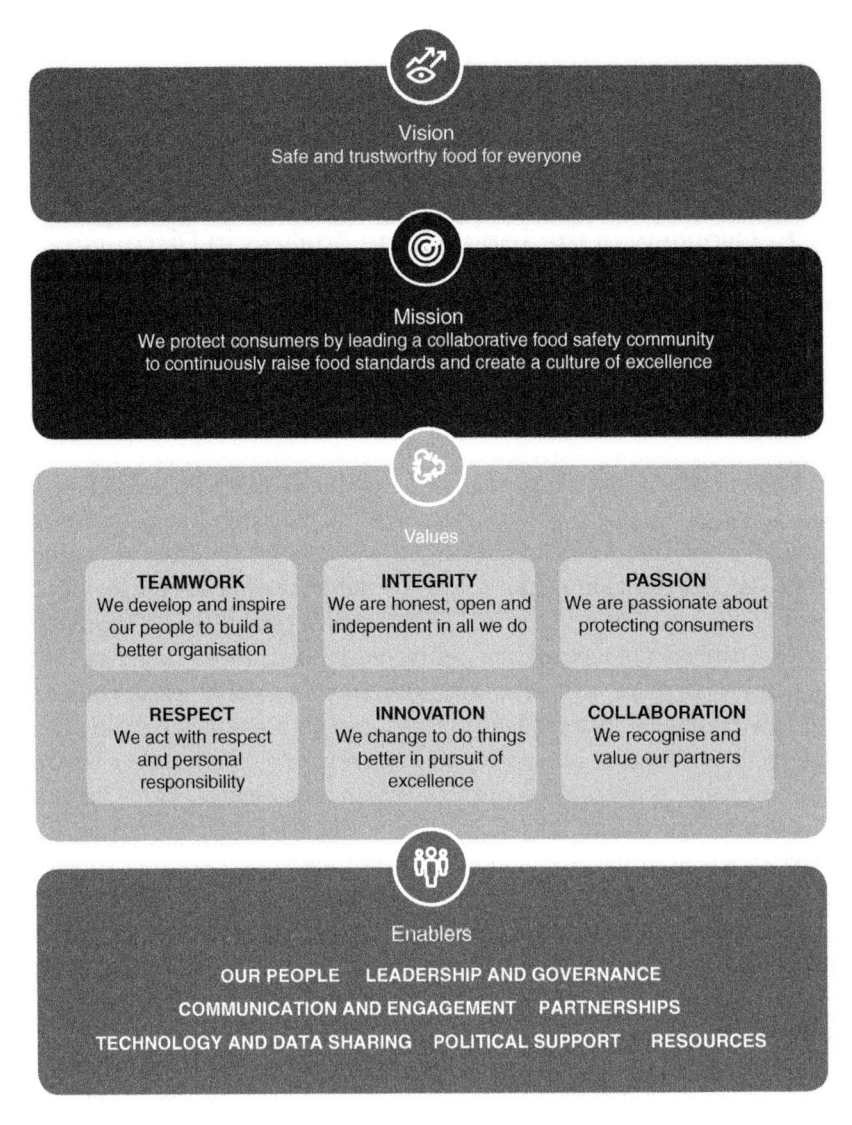

Vision
Safe and trustworthy food for everyone

Mission
We protect consumers by leading a collaborative food safety community to continuously raise food standards and create a culture of excellence

Values

TEAMWORK	INTEGRITY	PASSION
We develop and inspire our people to build a better organisation	We are honest, open and independent in all we do	We are passionate about protecting consumers

RESPECT	INNOVATION	COLLABORATION
We act with respect and personal responsibility	We change to do things better in pursuit of excellence	We recognise and value our partners

Enablers
OUR PEOPLE   LEADERSHIP AND GOVERNANCE
COMMUNICATION AND ENGAGEMENT   PARTNERSHIPS
TECHNOLOGY AND DATA SHARING   POLITICAL SUPPORT   RESOURCES

Figure 27.2 Strategy 2016–2018 of the Food Safety Authority of Ireland (FSAI)

managers as well as other employees in an organization. A typical question would be: Why do the professional practices and actions behind the text in Figure 27.1 set up *interdiscursive* connections (on this concept see Chapter 4 in this volume) to well-established genres in public administration and in the judicial and legal sectors, whereas the text in Figure 27.2 connects to genres in the private sector and, perhaps, to advertising through illustrations and "buzzwords" (Mautner 2005)?

With this short example as a backdrop, the overarching aim of this chapter is to give an introduction to the critical analysis of genre and social action with a particular focus on organizations. The chapter presents, above all, two theoretical approaches to the critical analysis of genre: CDA and CGA. It also gives an overview of how genre has been theorized and analyzed in the broader field of discourse studies.[3]

27.2 Overview of the Topic: Genre Analysis in Discourse Studies, Critical Discourse Analysis and Critical Genre Analysis

The concept of genre has a long history in both classic rhetoric and literature studies. However, it was not until what has sometimes been referred to as a *social* or *pragmatic* turn (Berge and Ledin 2001) in linguistics in the early 1980s that genre analysis started to develop into a field in its own right in discourse studies. The work of Bakhtin has been highly influential for the development of genre theory in linguistics. Bakhtin (1986: 64) defines genres as "relatively stable thematic, compositional and stylistic types of utterances." This "relative" stability is a key factor in genre analysis. Much of the genre research in linguistics has been focused on language and communication in professional, organizational and educational contexts. Such contexts are often characterized by typified, recurring ways of interacting through text and talk, but they have at the same time proven to be open to continuous change. From Bakhtin (1986) come also the notions of *addressivity* and *dialogicity*: utterances (and texts) are always directed at someone and they always set up dialogical relations to other (previous, future and contemporary) utterances, texts and genres. This line of thought forms the foundation for descriptions of the *hybrid* and *interdiscursive* (Bhatia 2017; Fairclough 2003) nature of genres (see also Chapter 20 in this volume). Indeed, "clean" and uniform genres are rarely found.

Three dominating approaches to genre can be identified in linguistics or language studies (cf. Solin 2009; Berge and Ledin 2001): the New Rhetoric (which is sometimes also labeled Rhetorical Genre Studies), the Sydney School of genre analysis and the English for Special Purposes (ESP) approach. These will be presented before we move on to a more detailed description of genre analysis in CDA and CGA.

Perhaps more than any of the other approaches, the New Rhetoric can be seen as a continuation of the thoughts presented by Miller (1984) in a paper that has come to play a key role in genre research. Miller (1984: 159) states that genres are "typified rhetorical actions based in recurrent situations." One implication of this view of genre is that the observations of the design

---

[3] The chapter is based on research conducted within the project *The archaeology of a new genre: Vision and values texts of public authorities in Sweden* financed by Riksbankens Jubileumsfond (The Swedish foundation for humanities and social sciences), 2016–2018 [grant number P15-0119].

and lexicogrammar of the texts in Figures 27.1 and 27.2 are only genre-relevant insofar as they can be related to the recurring social actions in the specific contexts in which they are found. And an understanding of such contextual, "recurrent situations" requires more than analysis of texts; it calls for ethnographic or at least practice-oriented methodologies.

Even though the focus on genre as social action would seem to point out an array of critical questions regarding, for instance, the politics and ideologies behind such actions, much of the research in this tradition has been descriptive rather than critical. For instance, Freedman and Medway (1994: 11) write that "the main reservation to be entered about North American students of genre … is that they have tended to be descriptive, with the accompanying tendency to an uncritical acceptance of status quo." Further, with reference to the edited volume that they introduce, Freedman and Medway (1994: 11) write that "in the essays collected here, for example, researchers have set themselves the task of describing such genres as those of government and social work, without yet extending their inquiry to encompass the political issues entailed."

In the Sydney School of genre analysis, the critical question of *access* to genres is foregrounded. With one foot in Hallidayan systemic functional linguistics (SFL) and the other in Bernstein's code theory, researchers such as Rothery, and Christie and Martin (cf. Rothery 1996; Christie and Martin 1997) developed rather text- and language-oriented genre descriptions with the purpose of empowering underprivileged students through access to, above all, school genres. The critical dimension of the Sydney School is described by Martin and Rose (2008: 18): "Inequalities in access to the privileged genres of modern institutional fields is a concern for developing democratic pedagogies, but also more generally for understanding how symbolic control is maintained, distributed and challenged in contemporary societies." More generally speaking, Martin and Rose claim that "in this kind of social complex, the scope of our control over genres of power in turn conditions our status ranking in social hierarchies, our claim to authority in institutional fields, and our prominence in public life" (Martin and Rose 2008: 19). Thus, for individuals and social groups, control over genres of power equals emancipation and the possibility of making one's voice heard in public life. Creating equal access to this type of control – or command of such genres – is the main critical mission of the Sydney School.

The roots in SFL, with its focus on socially constructed meaning and practical function, have led to genre definitions like that of Martin (1997: 13) who defines genres as "staged goal-oriented social processes." While it shares the view of genres as social action with the New Rhetoric, the Sydney School tends to focus on the detailed analysis of generic structures and meanings of texts rather than on ethnographic or other situated analyses. In other words, the Sydney School argues that the "socialness" of genres to a large extent can be found in the structure and semantics of the texts themselves; the New Rhetoric argues that it is primarily found in social practice. As Martin and Rose (2008: 20) put it: Sydney School genre analysis is "social semiotic rather than ethnographic."

Genre analysis in ESP shares with the Sydney School its focus on genres in education (although usually higher education in the case of ESP) and with the New Rhetoric its focus on genre in professional practice and the necessity of ethnographic and practice-oriented methods and tools. Genre analysis in the ESP tradition serves as a means for uncovering and identifying *communicative purposes* recognized by experts in *discursive communities* (for instance, researchers in an academic field) in order to help learners of these genres. If matched with the practices and values of discursive communities, communicative purposes can be described through concrete *move analysis* of the genre structures of texts. Such an analysis identifies more or less obligatory moves in texts – each move corresponding to a communicative purpose. A move, in turn, often consists of different *steps* with more specific purposes that together realize the move in question. The typical example is Swale's CARS (Creating A Research Space) analysis of moves and steps in introductions to research articles (Swale 1990: 141).

The critical aspect of genre analysis in ESP is similar to that of the Sydney School in terms of emancipation: one aim is to give non-native speakers of a language – often English – access to its professional and expert genres. Researchers like Bhatia (2004, 2017) have endeavored to move beyond the pedagogical applications of ESP and to develop what he calls a *critical understanding* of genres in professional practices, which will be discussed as CGA.

The three approaches introduced here are exclusively concerned with the concept of genre and genre analysis. In CDA, however, genre has often been used as a component in other frameworks for analysis. For instance, and importantly, genre constitutes a salient part of Fairclough's (e.g. 2003) analysis of *orders of discourse*, that is, the combination of genres, discourses and styles within an organization or a social domain. Van Leeuwen (2005a, 2005b, 2008) has also incorporated genre in his critical analysis. Another key researcher in the field of CDA, Wodak, includes genre in her discourse-historical approach (DHA) (Reisigl and Wodak 2016) applied in, for instance, critical analysis of populist discourses (Wodak 2003), but also when critically examining meetings in organizations as genres (2013). The latter can serve as a concrete example of how Wodak applies the concept of genre in order to increase our critical understanding of meetings in organizations. Following Bax (2011), Wodak (2013: 191) argues that the *prototype genre of meeting* is constructed according to the material and social context of the meeting, the issues and topics being discussed, the actions of the chair, and the level and extent of participation of other persons in the meeting, including how they construe their opinions as legitimate and how they present arguments. Wodak then analyzes how the prototype genre of meeting is enacted in specific meetings. She pays particular attention to meetings with the social function of making consensual decisions in political as well as business organizations. The analysis shows how the success of consensual decision-making meetings depends on, among other things, how participants manage to negotiate the issue at stake as important and urgent to the organization, but also on the extent to which powerful actors refrain from dominating the meeting (2013: 211).

Van Leeuwen (2008) discusses how the rise of, for instance, managerialism and marketization in society at large in the 1970s led to an increased interest in rationalized, proceduralized and purpose-driven strategic social action: "In rationalized social interaction, it is therefore no longer consensual representation which binds the members of society together, but common practice, procedures" (van Leeuwen 2008: 3). This salience of strategic and proceduralized social action can partially explain the aforementioned growing interest in genre analysis in the 1970s and 1980s. In other words, the interest in genre analysis was motivated by changes in society at large but, with a few exceptions such as Kress and Threadgold (1988), it lacked the critical awareness of CDA (van Leeuwen 2008: 4).

Inspired by Mitchell's ([1957]1975), Hasan's (1979) and Ventola's (1987) studies of the generic structure of buying and selling, much of van Leeuwen's critical analysis of genres can be described as text-oriented in the sense that it takes *speech acts* ("the minimum unit that can realize a unit of discursive practice" (van Leeuwen 1993: 195)) and their organization in texts as a starting point. Van Leeuwen also recognizes the multimodal nature of genres, something which becomes important in the critical analysis of global media genres such as the "hot-tips" genre (which provides advice for women) in global magazines such as *Cosmopolitan* (Machin and van Leeuwen 2007; van Leeuwen 2005a).

As mentioned, Fairclough (1993, 2003, 2010) uses genre as one of three cornerstones in his analysis of orders of discourse. Genres are defined as "ways of (inter)acting discoursally" (2003: 26), and the other parts of his model are discourses, defined as "ways of representing" (knowledge or social practices, for instance) and styles: "ways of being" such as presenting identities through bodily behavior or other linguistically realized stylistic choices. The relation between genres – *genre chains* – is defined by Fairclough as how different genres are linked together and in that process enabling social actions to "transcend differences in space and time, linking together social events in different social practices, different countries and different times, facilitating the enhanced capacity for 'action at a distance' ... and therefore facilitating the exercise of power" (Fairclough 2003: 31). An example of a genre chain is how the Code of Ethics of the Department of Correction in Figure 27.1 has probably been negotiated through, for instance, meeting genres as described by Wodak (2013, already mentioned) and will also be connected to interactional genres involving and affecting the communication and relations between prison guards and inmates. In other words, the written Code of Ethics is what Fairclough (2003) refers to as a *genre of governance* – a vehicle of power "within an institution or organization directed at regulating or managing some other (network of) social practice(s)" (2003: 32).

Connected to (but still distinct from) the concept of genre chain are those of *hybridization* and *interdiscursivity* of genres. These refer to how prototypical features of a number of genres (and discourses) are mixed within texts (which is the rule rather than the exception in texts from modern organizations). The strategy of the Food Safety Authority of Ireland in Figure 27.2 is an example of this insofar as it shares some properties with more traditional, rules-oriented genres within public authorities and some with advertising and other promotional genres through, for instance, the use of illustrations and "buzzwords." A Faircloughian analysis of this interdiscursivity could further point to the marketization of public discourse as well as to a tendency of genres of governance and control to be presented as if they were something else. For instance, it could be argued that, despite its potential functions in steering and control, the strategy text in Figure 27.2 is mainly presented as a positive PR text that just describes how the civil servants act and think.

Interdiscursivity of genres is also a key component in CGA as presented by Bhatia (2010, 2015, 2017). Bhatia's genre research has its roots in the ESP tradition, but, through the establishment of CGA, he aims at extending the scope further by developing a more comprehensive model for understanding professional communication in and through organizations. The exclusive focus on *professional* genres and practices partly distinguishes CGA from, for instance, genre research in CDA, which focuses on an array of genres and practices, not the least political and commercial ones. It is significant that in Bhatia's (2017: 5) model of discourse realization, the higher levels above texts are not the more general social practice (cf. van Leeuwen 2008) or sociocultural practice (Fairclough 2010: 133) but *professional practice* and *professional culture*. According to Bhatia, we can achieve fuller understandings of genres in organizations only when they are analyzed as tools for performing *professional actions* as part of professional practices related to professional cultures.

It is also within these professional relations that interdiscursivity plays a key role. Bhatia (2017: 35) says that what he calls "text-external resources," such as "conventions that contain generic constructs as well as professional practices," must be analyzed in order to gain any type of comprehensive understanding of professional communication. For Bhatia, then, interdiscursivity must be analyzed at levels in organizations beyond the genre hybridity directly observable in texts. More precisely, an analysis of interdiscursivity would require identifying not only relationships between texts in organizations but also data such as video recordings of meetings and longitudinal observations of everyday professional activities that allow for deeper understandings of professional conventions. Accordingly, Bhatia's analysis of interdiscursivity, and his CGA in general, calls for ethnographic and highly practice-oriented methodologies (see Section 27.3).

In summary, it can be concluded that the text-internal, purpose-driven structures and functions of genres have been thoroughly explored, analyzed and described in applied linguistics since the early 1980s, especially in the Sydney School and ESP approaches to genre analysis but also, for instance, in the *textually oriented discourse analysis* advocated by Fairclough (2003, 2010). In other words, we know a lot about how genres (particularly in education and professional organizations) are realized and unfold as generic moves and how specific features of texts, such as speech acts, narratives or argumentations, are used as resources in those processes. But genres have also – in the spirit of Miller (1984) – been studied through the use of more practice-oriented and ethnographic methods, most prominently in the New Rhetoric tradition and in genre analysis in the ESP tradition (e.g. Swales 1998). The question of *where* the analysis should primarily be located – in texts, at the level of discursive practice, social practice, at various organizational levels, or at all of the above – remains open for discussion, which will be addressed in Section 27.3. Genre analysis as a critical endeavor (or not) within the different approaches has also been touched upon; this issue will also be further discussed in Section 27.3.

27.3 Issues and Ongoing Debates

There have been a number of debates in genre studies over the years. Solin (2009), for instance, in an overview of genre research, points to the discussions of the extent to which texts (based on either text-internal or -external criteria) really can be classified as "belonging" to specific genres, and to the discussion of the stability of genres with regard to hybridization. These are long-running and still ongoing debates in the field, but this chapter focuses on another issue, primarily with regard to CDA and CGA: how *critical* is used differently in relation to the analysis of social actions and genres in organizations.

Fairclough (2005: 933–4) discusses CDA in relation to organization studies, and he writes that whereas ideological critique is quite familiar to everyone in the field of CDA, *strategic critique* is often more appropriate in the critical analysis of hegemonic struggle within organizations, including organizational change in which discourses, genres and styles are changing. Directly related to strategic critique is *operationalization*: strategies are operationalized in different ways, and the discourses that they draw upon may be transformed into genres:

For instance, the discourse of 'appraisal' entered higher educational organizations in Britain as a discourse, an imaginary for change, which was then enacted as universities negotiated and adopted procedures for appraising staff. And, as this example indicates, enactment includes the dialectical transformation of discourses into genres: these procedures included new genres, including the 'appraisal interview', which was designed to regulate interaction between appraiser and appraisee in particular ways .... (Fairclough 2005: 934)

This view of genres as regulating social relations *ideologically* is quite common within the broader field of CDA. Jaworski and Thurlow (2010: 22) point to how genres do ideological work by positioning people as, for instance, teacher and student, storyteller and listener, or manager and employee.

Briefly put, genre analysis (as any other type of analysis) in CDA always comes with an interest in revealing what is ideological, hegemonic and taken for granted, in organizations and elsewhere, which can then form the foundation for a critique with the potential of raising critical awareness but above all making a significant contribution to change in society at large. To which extent CDA has been successful in that endeavor is an open question, but critical analysis, in this research tradition, undoubtedly connects directly to an emancipatory knowledge interest.

In the later genre-work of Bhatia (2010, 2015, 2017) "critical" is framed quite differently with respect to CDA. Bhatia distances his genre analysis from ideology and issues of empowerment. Instead, his CGA is primarily concerned with explaining genre as part of professional actions and practices in "everyday professional life" (Bhatia 2017: 23). In terms of knowledge interest, Bhatia's approach is practical rather than emancipatory: through rigorous and multileveled analysis, professional genres, actions and practices can be demystified and we can reach a fuller, more diversified understanding of them. That is, "the aspect of criticality drawn on by CGA is similar to its use in the analysis and understanding of literature, in the sense that it is not necessarily oriented toward radical social change, or even toward the analysis of society" but aims "to establish and enhance our understanding of and motivation for the construction of professional genres and actions" (Bhatia 2017: 27).

It should be noted that whereas CDA is interested in genre in relation to social practices, actions and hegemonies in society at large as well as in any domain where power and, say, racism and sexism are present, Bhatia limits his analysis to professional practices, actions and genres in organizations, private companies and public authorities. In fact, he even suggests that "any attempt to consider genre as general social practice will essentially obscure the nature of analysis and hence will not be successfully rigorous and multiperspective for professional genres" (Bhatia 2017: 28). A key aspect of CGA, according to Bhatia, is to move beyond a *textually oriented discourse analysis* (Fairclough 2003, 2010) which relies on text analysis in order to study social actions and practices. Bhatia suggests that ethnographic and practice-oriented methods must always complement the analysis of texts in order to gain an understanding of genre as professional action and practice.

27.4 Implications for Theory and Methodology

The discussions so far have a number of theoretical as well as methodological implications for the critical analysis of genre and social actions in organizations. These include how to frame the critical part of the analysis, toward which level or instance of the social action the analysis should be oriented and, accordingly, which genre analytical tools should be applied (e.g. ethnographic, including interviews, field studies or questionnaires or more text-oriented tools). These aspects of the critical analysis of genres in organizations will be illustrated through a more detailed analysis of the aforementioned strategy text from the Food Safety Authority of Ireland (Figure 27.2).

In the context of texts and actions at public organizations and authorities, the text in Figure 27.2 is to be considered as part of an emerging set of genres such as strategies, vision and values and platform of values. The emergence of new genres actualizes a number of issues for critical inquiry, for instance: Which changing social actions are these genres part of? Such questions also call for a theoretical stance. We need to make clear whether we are framing the analysis epistemologically as looking for a critical and demystifying understanding of the professional actions and practices that the genre is part of or whether we are looking for a genre analysis that can form the basis for a critique of ideologies, for instance, those connected to managerialism and New Public Management (NPM). Such theoretical stances also have methodological implications. A textually oriented genre analysis in the spirit of Faircloughian CDA could, for example, be used to connect certain textual features to other genres, social actions, discourses, social practices and ideologies in society at large. A CGA-inspired analysis, on the other hand, would more specifically focus on the professional practices and actions within organizations, irrespective of their textual realizations.

Starting with a more textually oriented analysis, the strategy text in Figure 27.2 has a multimodal design and contains a number of rather short, catchy sentences and "buzzwords" such as "teamwork," "innovation" and "passion" – all with exclusively positive connotations. Another generic feature of the text in Figure 27.2 is the use of nonmodalized statements simply describing how and what the employees as a collective *are*, *act*, *feel* and *do*; for example, "We change to do things better in pursuit of excellence." Finally, due to its multimodal design, the text in Figure 27.2 (just like many other similar texts from public authorities) does not easily lend itself to an analysis of sequentially unfolding moves and steps with different communicative purposes. In other words, spatiality rather than sequentiality is an important organizing principle for the text (for example, through a number of framing devices, such as contrasting colors of the plates on which the "vision," "mission," "values" and "enablers" are found), even though we can assume that most people read the text somewhat sequentially, from top to bottom.

How can a CDA-inspired genre analysis approach the question of social actions in this case? As touched upon, there is a large body of research in CDA that addresses the marketization of public discourse and genres in general. One aspect of this is an increasing competitiveness between public authorities. Broadly speaking, authorities that previously gained legitimacy primarily from appropriation of directions, rules and regulations now have to compete with other authorities and organizations for securing funding and esteem. From this perspective, the social action partially realized in Figure 27.2 would be that of external promotion of the authority (which, as a contrast, would not be the result of an analysis of the Code of Ethics in Figure 27.1). Interdiscursively, the use of positive "buzzwords" and condensed, slogan-like sentences like "Safe and trustworthy food for everyone" connects to promotional genres such as advertising. So does the elaborate use of colors (ranging from darker to lighter blue and green).

Another CDA-inspired reading could relate the generic construct of the text in Figure 27.2 to changing management ideologies in public administration at large. In organization theory, there have been discussions about transitions from *rule-based organizations* (RBO) – prototypically a traditional public authority – to *post-bureaucratic* (PBO) or *neo-bureaucratic organizations* (NBO), characterized by individualization and flexibility rather than the formal hierarchies of RBO (Reed 2011). Connected to PBO and NBO is a new type of *soft power* (Mulderrig 2011), that is, a softer type of exercise of control in organizations where steering of behavior of employees can no longer be performed exclusively through overt directives and commands; it must now be achieved through the continuous promotion of shared values and attitudes. It is plausible that texts such as the strategy in Figure 27.2 play important roles in providing and negotiating common values in organizations, as part of social actions of control.

An analysis of the organization of speech acts can shed further light on how soft power is exercised in the strategy text of the FSAI (cf. van Leeuwen 1993, 2005a, 2005b). The cluster of sentences found under the headline of "Values" in Figure 27.2 are all statements. Generally, the *indicative mood* tends to be preferred whenever values are presented in vision and values texts, strategies and so on. However, in SFL, a theory that has informed much of – but by no means all of – the text analysis performed in CDA, these statements may very well, in this context, be interpreted as *interpersonal metaphors of mood* (Halliday and Matthiessen 2014: 698–707). Whereas statements do not directly aim at regulating behavior, *commands* do. And from the perspective of any employee at the FSAI, "We act with respect and personal responsibility," despite the indicative mood, is not primarily a simple statement about the situation at the authority; it is a command to align with these values or to be excluded from the value-based community of that organization. But in the spirit of the "soft power" of the post- or neo-bureaucratic public authority, this is systematically done through the less intrusive use of plain statements.

If we move the focus away from the connection between generic features of the texts and issues of power and marketization at other levels in society, and look at the text in Figure 27.2 through the lens of CGA, the following genre questions can be actualized: Which are the changing *professional* practices and actions inside of *actual* public authorities that texts and genres like the one in Figure 27.2 are part of? How do civil servants *themselves* and the human resources (HR) officers that usually direct the processes of producing core values and the platform of values perceive these practices, actions and texts?

Nyström Höög and Björkvall (2018) present the results of a focus group discussion with senior HR officers responsible for value-driven practices at seven public authorities in Sweden along with the results from a quantitative questionnaire about value texts and practices to all employees at three major public authorities in Sweden (492 employees completed the questionnaire, which gave a response rate of 58 percent). Even though these methods and tools are not ethnographic in the sense that they, for instance, include long-term field studies in organizations, they are, in this case, practice-oriented. And even though the results come from the Swedish context, it is likely that they are relevant for value work in other European countries as well, such as Ireland.

First, Nyström Höög and Björkvall's (2018) study shows that the most commonly recognized function of the platform of values text, according to the questionnaire, is that it "helps to think and act when we cooperate as employees" and "helps to think and act when we meet the citizens." In other words, value texts and practices are above all perceived as tools that actually facilitate internal collaboration as well as interactions with citizens. Interestingly, the least frequent answer of all (only 4 percent) is that the value texts and practices are tools that help management to govern public authorities. Further, it was clear from the focus group discussion that none of the participants thought about value texts as something that can be used to promote the authority externally. Instead, they thought of them as exclusively internal texts, as ethical compasses for civil servants to use, again when collaborating and meeting citizens. Finally, one of the most conclusive results of the questionnaire study and the focus group combined is that a main goal of value texts, genres and practices, from the perspective of HR officers, is to promote a continuous ethics- and value-driven discussion among employees. Accordingly, the vast majority of respondents to the questionnaire (79 percent) say that they actually have discussed the content of their authority's platform of values with colleagues during the past six months.

In the spirit of CGA, these results connect to professional practices rather than to further-reaching social practices and power-related ideologies. Do they contradict or complement the CDA-inspired genre analysis of the FSAI text in Figure 27.2? It stands clear that neither senior HR officers nor civil servants perceive the platform of values genre as part of a social action of steering and control of organizations. However, there is a very strong perception of these texts and practices as tools for *goal fulfillment*: they are tools that help the authorities reach their goals, and it is also this aspect of them that is most commonly discussed when employees talk about their platform of values. Goal fulfillment has reached a hegemonic status as the principle through which organizations must function. And it seems not to be perceived as a control device, even though it could be argued that it is intrinsically related to performance management as part of NPM practices.

Second, the status of value texts as external promotion of an authority, reflected in the interdiscursive and to some extent multimodal design of value texts such as the one in Figure 27.2, can be challenged. So, even though a number of features of the text from the FSAI as such invite an analysis pointing to communicative purposes of external communication (related to marketization of public authorities), an analysis that focuses on the professional practices in public authorities may point out other, more internal directions to take if we want to understand the development of value work genres.

Nyström Höög and Björkvall (2018) elaborate further on the finding that one of the main actions of the value genre is to keep the internal discussion of ethics alive among employees at public authorities. This result can be interpreted as related to the type of exercise of soft power already discussed, but it also points to how complex the roles of texts as genres are in contemporary organizations. In the case of platforms of values, the text is to a certain extent a tool for generating everyday talk and discussion about values. As Nyström Höög and Björkvall (2018: 29) put it: "[S]ome of the focus group participants actually suggested that, in practice, PV [platform of values] texts should remain unchanged over time. It does not matter whether they become aged or inaccurate as long as they continue to be fuel for discussions and debate." This is a good example of what a genre analysis directed at a *critical understanding* of genre as professional action in organizations can result in, but also of what may, due to both methodological choices and research interest, end up under the radar of CDA.

27.5 Future Directions

Although the multimodality of genres has been recognized in most of the approaches discussed in this chapter (and thoroughly analyzed by researchers like van Leeuwen (2005a, 2005b)), there is much potential for development in terms of both theory and methods. This has been vehemently pointed out by Bateman (2008) and, for instance, Hiippala (2016, 2017). Bateman chose genre as a key concept in the development of the Genre and Multimodality model (GeM), which is more formal than many of the approaches presented here in the sense that it advocates a quite detailed analysis – in many layers – of the structure of multimodal documents as genre. It also makes explicit use of large text corpora in that analysis.

Another future direction is probably a further shift toward ethnographic studies of genre. Genre-as-text has been thoroughly analyzed and described for many years, but more research is needed on, for instance, social actions in organizations in which the texts have functions that can be fully grasped only through a thorough understanding of organizational cultures. As discussed, that type of genre research requires other methodological tools than those most prevalent in text-oriented genre studies.

27.6 Summary

The chapter has discussed the critical analysis of genre and social action in organizations. The issues have been illustrated through value texts from public authorities. Apart from presenting the most prominent approaches to genre within discourse studies (broadly speaking), it has, more specifically, discussed a CDA approach to genre in relation to that of CGA as described by Bhatia. One conclusion is that the critical analysis of genre in CDA connects texts to broader social practices and actions. This could be referred to as a sociological approach to genre, one advantage being that the analysis of texts as parts of genres in organizations can be productively related to critical theory and a number of other domains in society in which power and ideology are operationalized. CGA, on the other hand, distances itself from critical theory and focuses on professional actions and practices in organizations. This can be described as an ethnographic-organizational approach to genre. The chapter has pointed to how this type of approach can further our understanding of the specific social actions that texts in organizations are part of, although these cannot fully be traced by text-oriented genre analysis.

Further Reading

Bhatia, V. K. (2017). *Critical Genre Analysis: Investigating Interdiscursive Performance in Professional Practice* Abingdon: Routledge.

In this book, Bhatia introduces, discusses and positions CGA (primarily in relation to CDA).

Cap, P. and Okulska, U. (eds.) (2013). *Analyzing Genres in Political Communication: Theory and Practice*. Amsterdam: John Benjamins.

This edited volume contains a number of genre-oriented studies of political communication, including the analysis of meetings by Wodak (2013) and a chapter by Krzyżanowski (2013) on policy genres in the European Union.

Fairclough, N. (2003). *Analysing Discourse: Textual Analysis for Social Research*. London/New York: Routledge.

This is one of the more accessible introductions to Fairclough's uses of genre within his CDA framework.

Freedman, A. and Medway, P. (eds.) (1994). *Genre and the New Rhetoric*. London/New York: Taylor & Francis.

The volume introduces the New Rhetoric and also contains Miller's (1984) classic paper "Genre as Social Action."

Martin, J. R. and Rose, D. (2008). *Genre Relations: Mapping Culture*. London: Equinox.

This book presents the foundations and a number of applications of Sydney school genre analysis.

Reisigl, M. and Wodak, R. (2016). The Discourse-Historical Approach (DHA). In R. Wodak and M. Meyer (eds.) *Methods of Critical Discourse Studies*, 3rd ed. Los Angeles: Sage. 87–121.

The chapter describes how genre is perceived within the discourse-historical approach (DHA).

Solin, A. (2009). Genre. In J. Verschueren and J.-O. Östman (eds.), *Handbook of Pragmatics*. Amsterdam: John Benjamins. 1–18.

This chapter gives a good overview of the New Rhetoric, the Sydney school and genre analysis in ESP.

Swales, J. M. (1990). *Genre Analysis: English in Academic and Research Settings*. Cambridge: Cambridge University Press.

Swales' book is a key reading regarding genre analysis in ESP.

Van Leeuwen, T. (2005b). Multimodality, Genre and Design. In S. Norris and R. H. Jones (eds.) *Discourse in Action: Introducing Mediated Discourse Analysis*. Milton Park/Abingdon/New York: Routledge. 73–94.

This introduces van Leeuwen's multimodal genre analysis.

References

Bakhtin, M. M. (1986). *Speech Genres and Other Late Essays*. Austin: University of Texas Press.

Bateman, J. A. 2008. *Multimodality and Genre: A Foundation for the Systematic Analysis of Multimodal Documents*. New York: Palgrave Macmillan.

Bax, S. (2011). *Discourse and Genre: Analysing Language in Context*. Basingstoke: Palgrave Macmillan.

Berge, K. L. and Ledin, P. (2001). Perspektiv på Genre [Perspectives on Genre]. *Rhetorica Scandinavica* 18: 4–16.

Bhatia, V. K. (2004). *Worlds of Written Discourse: A Genre-Based View*. London: Continuum.

  (2010). Interdiscursivity in Professional Communication. *Discourse & Communication* 4(1): 32–50.

  (2015). Critical Genre Analysis: Theoretical Preliminaries. *Hermes: Journal of Language and Communication in Business*. 54: 9–20.

  (2017). *Critical Genre Analysis: Investigating Interdiscursive Performance in Professional Practice*. Abingdon: Routledge.

Cap, P. and Okulska, U. (eds.) (2013). *Analyzing Genres in Political Communication: Theory and Practice*. Amsterdam: John Benjamins.

Christie, F. and Martin, J. R. (1997). *Genre and Institutions: Social Processes in the Workplace and School*. London: Cassel.

Fairclough, N. (1993). Critical Discourse Analysis and the Marketization of Discourse: The Universities. *Discourse & Society* 4(2): 133–68.

  (2003). *Analysing Discourse: Textual Analysis for Social Research*. London/New York: Routledge.

  (2005). Discourse Analysis in Organization Studies: The Case for Critical Realism. *Organization Studies* 26(6): 915–39.

  (2010). *Critical Discourse Analysis: The Critical Study of Language*. Harlow: Longman.

Freedman, A. and Medway, P. (eds.) (1994). *Genre and the New Rhetoric*. London/New York: Taylor & Francis.

Halliday, M. A. K. and Matthiessen, C. M. I. M. (2014). *Halliday's Introduction to Functional Grammar*. Abingdon: Routledge.

Hasan, R. (1979). On the Notion of Text. In J. S. Petöfi (ed.) *Text vs Sentence: Basic Questions of Text Linguistics*, Vol. II. Hamburg: Helmut Buske. 369–90.

Hiippala, T. (2016). *The Structure of Multimodal Documents: An Empirical Approach*. New York: Routledge.

  (2017). An Overview of Research within the Genre and Multimodality Framework. *Discourse, Context & Media* 20: 276–84.

Jaworski, A. and Thurlow, C. (2010). Introducing Semiotic Landscapes. In A. Jaworski and C. Thurlow (eds.) *Semiotic Landscapes: Language, Image, Space*. London: Continuum. 1–40.

Kress, G. and Threadgold, T. (1988). Towards a Social Theory of Genre. *Southern Review* 21(3): 215–43.

Krzyżanowski, M. (2013). Policy, Policy Communication and Discursive Shifts: Analyzing EU Policy Discourses on Climate Change. In P. Cap and U. Okulska (eds.) *Analyzing Genres in Political Communication: Theory and Practice*. Amsterdam: John Benjamins. 101–33.

Ledin, P. and Machin, D. (2016a). A Discourse-Design Approach to Multimodality: The Visual Communication of Neoliberal Management Discourse. *Social Semiotics* 26(1): 1–18.

(2016b). Performance Management Discourse and the Shift to an Administrative Logic of Operation: A Multimodal Critical Discourse Analytical Approach. *Text & Talk* 36(4): 445–67.

Machin, D. and van Leeuwen, T. (2007). *Global Media Discourse: A Critical Introduction*. London: Routledge.

Martin, J. R. (1997). Analysing Genre: Functional Parameters. In F. Christie and J. R. Martin (eds.) *Genre and Institutions: Social Processes in the Workplace and School*. London: Cassel. 3–39.

Martin, J. R. and Rose, D. (2008). *Genre Relations: Mapping Culture*. London: Equinox.

Mautner, G. (2005). The Entrepreneurial University: A Discursive Profile of a Higher Education Buzzword. *Critical Discourse Studies* 2 (2): 95–120.

Miller, C. R. (1984). Genre as Social Action. *Quarterly Journal of Speech* 70: 151–67.

Mitchell, T. F. ([1957]1975). The Language of Buying and Selling in Cyrenaica: A Situational Statement. In T. F. Mitchell (ed.) *Principles of Firthian Linguistics*. London: Longman. 167–200.

Mulderrig, J. (2011). The Grammar of Governance. *Critical Discourse Studies* 8 (1): 45–68.

Norris, S. and Jones, R. H. (eds.) (2005). *Discourse in Action: Introducing Mediated Discourse Analysis*. Milton Park/Abingdon/New York: Routledge.

Nyström Höög, C. and Björkvall, A. (2018). Keeping the Discussion among Civil Servants Alive: "Platform of Values" as an Emerging Genre within the Public Sector in Sweden. *Scandinavian Journal of Public Administration* 22(3): 17–38.

Reed, M. I. (2011). The Post-Bureaucratic Organization and the Control Revolution. In S. Clegg, M. Harris and H. Höpfl (eds.) *Managing Modernity: Beyond Bureaucracy?* Oxford: Oxford University Press. 230–56.

Reisigl, M. and Wodak, R. (2016). The Discourse-Historical Approach (DHA). In R. Wodak and M. Meyer (eds.) *Methods of Critical Discourse Studies*, 3rd ed. Los Angeles: Sage. 87–121.

Rothery, J. (1996). Making Changes: Developing an Educational Linguistics. In R. Hasan and G. Williams (eds.) *Literacy in Society*. London/New York: Longman. 86–123.

Solin, A. (2009). Genre. In J. Verschueren and J.-O. Östman (eds.) *Handbook of Pragmatics*. Amsterdam: John Benjamins. 1–18.

Swales, J. M. (1990). *Genre Analysis: English in Academic and Research Settings*. Cambridge: Cambridge University Press.

(1998). *Other Floors, Other Voices: A Textography of a Small University Building*. Mahway, NJ: Lawrence Erlbaum Associates.

Van Leeuwen, T. (1993). Genre and Field in Critical Discourse Analysis: A Synopsis. *Discourse and Society* 4(2): 192–223.

(2005a). *Introducing Social Semiotics*. London: Routledge.

(2005b). Multimodality, Genre and Design. In S. Norris and R. H. Jones (eds.) *Discourse in Action: Introducing Mediated Discourse Analysis*. Milton Park/Abingdon/New York: Routledge. 73–94.

(2008). *Discourse and Practice: New Tools for Critical Discourse Analysis*. Oxford: Oxford University Press.

Ventola, E. (1987). *The Structure of Social Interaction: A Systemic Approach to the Semiotics of Service Encounters*. London: Pinter.

Weber, M. ([1922]1978). The Nature of Social Action. In W. G. Runciman (ed.) *Max Weber: Selections in Translation*. Cambridge: Cambridge University Press. 7–32.

Wodak, R. (2003). Populist Discourses: The Rhetoric of Exclusion in Written Genres. *Document Design* 4(2): 132–48.

(2013). Analyzing Meetings in Political and Business Contexts: Different Genres – Similar Strategies? In P. Cap and U. Okulska (eds.) *Analyzing Genres in Political Communication: Theory and Practice*. Amsterdam: John Benjamins.

28

Rhetorics, Discourse and Populist Politics

Markus Rheindorf

28.1 Introduction

Although the notion of "populism" in the sense of politics focused on supposedly unmediated access to the will of the *populus* goes back to antiquity, the twenty-first century has seen a surge in such movements. This trend has been labeled the "populist era" (Krastev 2012), the "populist Zeitgeist" (Mudde 2004: 542) and the "populist revival" (Roberts 2007: 3), and has led to a similar increase of academic interest, especially in terms of rhetoric, discourse and politics. Thus, the subjects of "populist rhetorics," "populist discourse" and "populist politics" have become the focus of numerous academic disciplines, including political science, sociology, communication and media studies, applied linguistics in general and critical discourse studies in particular, reinvigorating existing research traditions and generating new approaches. Indeed, the "spectre" of populism (Ionescu and Gellner 1969) has long haunted both the political sphere and academia. Given the intersection between the political, the social and the linguistic in the case of populism's successes, it is no surprise that studies in any of these fields have tended to adopt or incorporate, more or less rigorously, approaches from the others. In other words, political studies have found it necessary to address the discursive and rhetorical dimensions of populism, just as discourse analysts have engaged with debates on the political nature of populism and its relation to democracy.

Fundamental conceptualizations of populism as a political phenomenon differ in terms not only of definition but also of evaluation. Thus, the popular agency approach views populism as a positive force for the mobilization of the people (Goodwyn 1976); the Laclauan approach sees it as the essence of politics and an emancipatory force (Laclau 2005); and the socioeconomic approach regards it as irresponsible economics (Dornbusch and Edwards 1992). Recent approaches developed by Cas Mudde and Cristóbal Rovira Kaltwasser (2017), Jan-Werner Müller

(2016) and Benjamin Moffitt (2016) focus on the ideological, strategic and performative aspects of populism. The above-listed conceptualizations have been highly influential in the social sciences and are therefore discussed here with respect to their impact on discourse-analytic research on populism. Taken together, they also represent the full range of theoretical positions on the value or danger of populism in the contemporary world.

In studying populist rhetorics and discourse, discourse analysts have drawn on diverse types of data, used various methods and analyzed a plethora of linguistic features pertaining to the core traits of populism: dividing society into "the people" and "the elite" while also moralizing this dichotomy, claiming to exclusively represent the "will of the people," appealing to "crises," breaking taboos, creating charismatic leadership and resorting to mediatization. Data used to study the rhetorical and discursive dimensions of populism have included party programs and manifestos, political speeches, campaign rallies and events, posters and slogans, websites, social media postings and tweets, television and radio interviews as well as debates (on the relationships between politics and social media practices, see also Chapters 5 and 14 in this volume). Linguistic methods and concepts applied to study populist rhetoric have been largely qualitative and include nomination and predication strategies, topoi, argumentation and fallacy, cognitive schemata, multimodality, discursive shifts and normalization (for a good cross-section of linguistic approaches to populism, see Wodak and Krzyżanowski 2017; Wodak, KhisraviNik and Mral 2013).

For instance, populists may use *nomination* strategies to construct a social group in a particular way, for example as a threat ("flood") or to delegitimize their status ("economic refugees"); the same social group might be characterized through *predication* as engaged in aggressive or illegal activities ("rioting"), as ungrateful ("rejecting food") or undeserving ("reckless"). Populists may draw on established *topoi* ("history as a teacher") to *argue* for or *legitimate* specific policies ("we must close our borders or suffer the fate of the Roman Empire") as well as to *delegitimize* their political opponents' positions ("unless you personally take refugees into your home, you have no right to call on the state to do so"). Populist discourse frequently employs well-established *cognitive schema* (on this topic see Chapter 9 in this volume) to simplify complex situations and problems, for example by discussing border policy in terms of privately owned homes and national economics in terms of household budgets. Populists often excel at *multimodal meaning-making*, combining musical, visual and performative elements in their campaigns or rallies. And through all of these, populist movements have attempted, with some success, to shift public discourse in their favor, often by monopolizing media attention through deliberate provocation. In many well-documented cases, this has also led to the normalization of marginal or taboo discourses.

28.2 Overview: Core Features of Populism and Their Discursive Realization

Despite the "elusive and complex nature" of populism (Wodak and Krzyżanowski 2017b: 474), it is widely agreed that populism has several core traits. Thus, most "minimal definitions" of populism, that is, definitions that seek to cover a wide range of empirical phenomena, include the following characteristics: divisiveness and homogenizing dichotomies, in particular "the people" and "the elite"; a moralizing logic that may be ethnicized, racialized or culturalized; the claim that populists and only they know "the will of the people"; the construction, propagation and instrumentalization of "crises"; characteristic modes of mobilization, frequently focused on strong leaders and their performance of charisma, authenticity and disregard for established modes of conduct; a reliance on media and the effects of mediatization; and finally a complex relationship with democracy, although the nature of this relationship is contested. As these traits are not uniquely populist and are not equally present in all instances, the relationship between different forms of populism has been likened to a Wittgensteinian "family resemblance" (Brubaker 2017: 361).

Central among the traits identified in populism is its **divisiveness**: It seeks to divide society into two homogenous and antagonistic camps, "the people" and "the elite" (Mudde and Kaltwasser 2017; Müller 2017; Moffitt, 2016). Populist rhetoric constructs and addresses both groups through moralization, creating the characteristic dichotomy of the "pure people" versus the "corrupt elite," and it aligns populist actors with the former. Constructions of "the elite" vary and may include "the establishment" or "the system", but they can also be distinctly cultural ("the media," "Hollywood"), academic ("the intellectuals") or economic ("Wall Street"). Constructing all other political parties as a homogenous power block allows populists to play the role of victim in political debates, claiming that all other parties are not only the same but colluding against them. Thus, ruling out government coalitions with populist parties plays into their rhetorical strategy of victimhood. Populist rhetorics frequently express this idea by fusing the names of other parties into one word (e.g. "UMPS" by the French Front National, "SPÖVP" by the Austrian Freedom Party).

"The people" figure in populist rhetorics in three forms: as sovereign (the source of political power), as the common people (a particular socioeconomic status) and as the nation (a particular nationality, often ethnicized or culturalized). While "the people" is a malleable construct, its status as an "empty signifier" (Laclau 2005) or "corpus mysticum" (Müller 2017) is contested on a conceptual level: such terms risk obscuring rather than analytically grasping the strategic work of populist appeals to "the people," which always involves the strategic recontextualization of existing discourses (e.g. Wodak 2017). Populist politics can thus be seen as involving or hinging on a form of exclusionary identity politics: Only some of the people are really "the people"; and, crucially, the power to define this belonging rests with the populists themselves. Populist constructions of "the people" and "the elite" are thus *antipluralist* by denying diversity within either group but also by delegitimizing all other views among the populace and political competitors (Müller 2017: 21). Especially right-wing populism alleges an alliance between "the elite" and marginal groups, such as refugees, immigrant workers or particular social and ethnic groups, which are cast not only as *not of* the people but also as *against* the people. Populists tend to scapegoat already stigmatized and disenfranchised groups as "enemies of the people" (Wodak 2015, 2017) and to accuse "the elite" of favoring them over "the people."

The Othering in such stark "Us vs. Them" constructions has been described as "vertical opposition" and, combined with the "horizontal opposition" between "the people" and "the elite," has been theorized as populism's "two-dimensional visions of social space" (Brubaker 2017: 362). Discursive constructions of "enemies within" vary in degree, with McCarthyism and some contemporary forms representing particularly strong cases: Especially when in power, populists may seek to discursively delegitimize NGOs and other elements of civil society that oppose them on policy issues. Indeed, civil society presents a symbolic problem to populism as it potentially undermines its claim to exclusive representation of the people (Müller 2017: 48). For instance, when a liberal contender for the Austrian presidency presented a list of supporters in 2016, emphasizing that they came from different political parties, the arts and respected professions, the Freedom Party's candidate Norbert Hofer reviled all of them as "Hautevolee" (from French *haute volée*, indicating a detached and privileged social elite) and contrasted them to his own supporters, whom he described as "Menschen" ("human beings") (Wodak 2017). This dichotomy may further be linked to larger oppositions between "national" and "international" interests, in which "the elite" is cast as colluding with international actors, for example transnational organizations or businesses, against "their own people" (Richardson 2013).

The **representative claim** of populist actors asserts that they alone represent "the people," demanding that "the will of the people" be raised over all other considerations, while also claiming that this is the one and true imperative of democracy (majoritarianism). This is symbolic rather than empirical representation, based on a *pars pro toto* argument (Reisigl, 2005) through which the populist party or even leader is equated with "the people." Thus, populists may reject the results of elections or plebiscites by way of a "silent majority" argument, although they ostensibly endorse direct democratic forms of government (Müller 2016: 20–9). Thus, Geert Wilders has tried to delegitimize the Dutch parliament by calling the Tweede Kamer a "fake parliament."

Equations between "the people" and populist parties or leaders have been observed in many contexts: For instance, Viktor Orbán after losing the 2002 Hungarian elections claimed that "the nation cannot be in opposition." The Austrian Freedom Party used posters showing their leader, Heinz-Christian Strache, with slogans like "ER will, was WIR wollen" ("HE wants what WE want") or "Er sagt, was Wien denkt" ("He says what Vienna thinks") (Reisigl 2005: 62–3). Even more explicit were Hugo Chávez's slogans "Chávez es Pueblo!" ("Chávez is the people!") and "Chávez somos milliones, tú también eres Chávez!" ("Chávez we are millions, you are also Chávez!"). Such rhetoric elides "the people," leaving only "the presence of the leader by fiat of tacit authorization" (Arditi 2007: 65).

Discursively, populist constructions of the unified will of "the people" are premised, first, on a homogenous and knowable people; second, on populists' claim to authenticity and "common sense"; and third, on disavowing established political norms and expert knowledge. Because the representative claim is not based on actual election results, some have expanded the category of "unelected representatives" (Moffitt 2016) to include "populist media actors" such as television and radio hosts (Keane 2013).

While early discussions of populism assumed that it arose from **crises**, recent work recognizes that populist actors discursively construct, propagate and maintain a sense of acute crisis (Moffitt 2016: 113–32). Sensationalist media play a significant role in these efforts (Mazzoleni 2008; Triandafyllidou, Wodak and Krzyżanowski 2009). Such constructions may "spectacularize" the "failures" of those in power (Moffitt 2016: 8), if the populists are in opposition, or of those previously in power, if the populists are in government and need to deflect blame (Reisigl 2005). Populist scenarios of crisis draw on a general distrust of modern bureaucracy and the complexity of consensus-oriented, slow politics (Moffitt 2016: 120). In any populist crisis scenario, it is "the people" who are most threatened by the crisis, while "the elite" either are safe from or even benefit from the crisis. Such crises are constructed to require urgent action to prevent dire consequences: Populists create a sense of impending doom by presenting society as facing apocalyptic confrontations or a continuous state of siege (Müller 2017: 43; Pappas 2014; Angouri and Wodak 2014). For instance, the Austrian Freedom Party has repeatedly warned that "Europe will burn" if immigration continues (Rheindorf and Wodak 2019). Ultimately, such constructions of constant crisis serve populist aims in several ways: they divide "the people" from "the elite," align the populists with "the people" as their defenders, advertise their own strong leadership as a method for overcoming the crisis and radically simplify the political terrain into a common sense choice of either-or (Müller 2017: 43).

Although three forms of **populist mobilization** can be distinguished – personalist leadership, political party and social movement (Mudde and Kaltwasser 2017: 42–61) – most populist formations include a strong leader whose charismatic appeal and authenticity resonate with their electorate

(Moffitt 2016; Wodak 2015). While *personalist* and *party mobilization* often appear in combination, social movements are prone to falter over time unless they develop into one of the other forms mentioned (Mudde and Kaltwasser 2017). Populist leaders have traditionally been male and of the "strongman" type, ostensibly embodying masculine ideals such as quick and decisive action, bravery, virility or entrepreneurial spirit. Female leaders like Marie Le Pen and Sarah Palin have also risen to prominence, crafting equally gendered personas of "mother" or "housewife of the nation," manifesting in Palin's reference to "kitchen economics," "hockey mums" and "mama grizzlies" (Burns, Eberhardt and Merolla 2013; McCabe 2012).

Populist **leaders** typically flaunt their anti-intellectualism and disregard for scientific expertise (on "post-truth," see Montgomery 2017; Lakoff 2017). Although often referred to, the "charisma" of such leaders remains a contested and undertheorized trait (Mudde and Kaltwasser 2017: 66; Barr 2009). Nonetheless, much work on populism draws on Weber's ([1924] 1997) notion of "charismatic authority" as a personal trait ascribed to the leader (Wodak 2015). Individual studies have described the persona of specific leaders as the "Le Pen effect" (Christofferson 2003) or the "Haider phenomenon" (Wodak and Pelinka 2009). Taking a more general approach, Moffitt (2016: 3) argues that populism must always be performed, embodied and enacted. Charisma has also been linked to the celebrity image that some populists have constructed or built on as a form of political capital, as demonstrated by Donald Trump (Nolan and Brooks 2015).

In today's media-pervaded world, charisma is strongly connected to the media (Moffitt 2015). The relationship between populism and the media is highly complex. On the one hand, populists rely on the reach and mechanisms of mass media and typically enter into a "love–hate relationship" with them (Kavada 2018). Thus, populist politics represent a particular case of **mediatization** in the sense of the political sphere being "submitted to, or ... dependent on, the media and their logic" (Strömbäck 2008: 113). These include many rhetorical means identified as typical of populist rhetoric, such as simplification, polarization, intensification, personalization, stereotypization, emotionalization and sports- or military-based dramatization (Moffitt 2016: 74–81; Reisigl 2005: 61–6). In addition, scandalization and calculated ambivalence are often used by populists to capture and maintain media attention (Engel and Wodak 2015) in what has been termed the "perpetuum mobile" of populism (Wodak 2015).

On the other hand, populist actors have frequently attacked and sought to delegitimize media who do not report favorably on them, alleging that they collude with or are part of "the corrupt elite." Although Donald Trump may be credited with popularizing the term "fake news" for this goal, he was not the first populist to use it (Kellner 2017). In confronting established media, populists frequently draw on **conspiracy theories** (Castanho, Vegetti and Littvay 2017), which appear not as an addition but as rooted in the logic of populism. Due to their reach and interactivity, but also because they cut across traditional patterns of media consumption (e.g. region, class, socio-economic status or educational background), online media and social media have been instrumental for many populists: They bypass established media and construct the kind of immediacy between populist actors and "the people" that enables strong identification (Moffitt 2016: 88–94). With the proliferation of user-generated content, the followers of populist actors have effectively become "prosumers" who amplify populist discourse. Indeed, the "antagonistic sphere" and seeming lack of accountability on the Internet, giving rise to "uncivil society" (Krzyżanowski and Ledin 2017), appear ideally suited for populism's dichotomization of politics and society, specifically the rhetorics of hate speech and conspiracy theories (Postill 2018).

Populist leaders' public image is linked to a **coarsening** of political rhetoric, opposing "political correctness" by breaking taboos and publicly showing offensive behavior. The resultant "mix of scandal, provocation, transgression and passion" (Sauer, Krasteva and Saarinen 2017) has been termed "bad manners" (Moffitt 2016: 44), "tabloid style" (Canovan 1999: 5) or "low rhetoric" opposite formal, rational and technocratic language use (Ostiguy 2009). In male populist leaders, this often takes strikingly sexist forms, such as Silvio Berlusconi's *bunga bunga* sex parties. Such performances help to construct the male populist leader's persona as down-to-earth and virile, while also flaunting his disregard for political correctness (Mudde and Kaltwasser 2017: 64). In the case of the so-called "Access Hollywood Tape" that documented Donald Trump's boasts about sexually harassing women, his remarks, downplayed as "locker room talk," did not significantly undercut his popularity (Kellner 2017).

In the mediated performances of populist actors, their use of **symbolism** typically appropriates "national symbols," e.g. flags, national colors, landscapes, public spaces, buildings, anthems or music (Wodak et al. 2009), to intimate unity, homogeneity and cohesion among "the people." In many contexts, there is thus a strong multimodal component to populist performances (Wodak and Forchtner 2014; Richardson and Colombo 2013; Machin and Richardson 2012). The appropriation of symbols of national identity helps populist actors to construct scenarios of crisis, for example by visualizing the threat of immigration as boots trampling the nation's flag or picturing minarets as missiles piercing the national body (both used by the Austrian Freedom Party; Wodak and Rheindorf 2019).

28.3 Populism: A Global Phenomenon with Local Specifics

Beyond minimal definitions focused on universal features of populism, recent empirical research investigates (a) the reasons for populist successes in a particular context, (b) commonalities and differences between populist phenomena across time or space, (c) populism's effects on democracy, institutions or policy, and (d) the workings of populism, conceptualized as discourse, rhetorics, strategies or performances. Views differ on whether previous work has been too local or too universalist. Mudde and Kaltwasser (2017) as well as Moffitt (2017) argue for approaching populism as a global phenomenon, whereas most discourse-analytic research focuses on case studies or limited comparisons (Wodak and Krzyżanowski 2017b). Nonetheless, broad regional distinctions are widely used in the field.

In North America, the term populism holds largely positive connotations going back to late-nineteenth-century prairie populism in Canada and the United States. These agrarian movements were strongly producerist – that is, they emphasized the greater value of those members of society who produced tangible wealth – depicting farmers as the pure, hardworking people whose spirit and morals would never be corrupted (Kuzminski 2008). The anti-communist movement during the Cold War, especially McCarthyism, opposed patriotic common people to corrupt cultural and political elites, accusing the latter of un-American socialist ideas such as redistributing the wealth of hardworking people to a racialized underclass of non-whites (Taggart, 2002). The rhetorics of Ross Perot and Nixon, in particular his "silent majority" argument, have also been studied as expressions of North American populism (Brown, 1997). Throughout, the key imaginary has been constant: the "American way of life" is under attack from liberal elites in politics, education, arts and business, using the powers of the federal state to oppress the spirit of "the true people" while giving privileges to racial, migrant or social minorities. This imaginary has recently manifested, on the right, in the Tea Party (Savage 2013) and, on the left, the Occupy Wall Street movement (Milner 2013), each engendering its own rhetoric and discourse. In their respective slogans, for example "D.C.=District of Corruption" and "Main Street against Wall Street," both movements recontextualize key characteristics of populism. While the Tea Party strongly relies on producerism, the "heartland" and an implicitly racialized construction of "the people," Occupy Wall Street claims to speak for "the 99%" in rhetoric reminiscent of other "silent majority" populism. Significantly, both movements have positively self-identified as populist.

Populism has a long and pronounced history in Latin America, linked to high levels of socioeconomic inequality (Dornbusch and Edwards 1992; Roberts 2007; de la Torre 2014). This inequality as well as a history of colonization and foreign influence has lent itself to populist rhetoric, most prominently in combination with socialist ideas. In Latin American populism, *el pueblo* is typically pitted against both an internal *oligarquía* and outside powers. This brand of populism is allied with *Americanismo*, the idea that all Latin American peoples share an identity and imperialist enemies – inspiring the view that Latin American populism tends to be inclusive while European populism tends to be exclusive (Filc 2015). The first wave of Latin American populism is exemplified by Juan Domingo Perón, followed by a second wave in the 1990s, including Alberto Fujimori in Peru; the third wave was sparked by Hugo Chávez in Venezuela, followed by Bolivian Evo Morales and others. Latin American populists have had extensive electoral success and periods in government (Mudde and Kaltwasser 2017). Mexico, specifically, has an enduring tradition of agrarian populism spanning from the revolution to the contemporary "La Vía Campesina" (Martinéz-Torres and Rosset 2010).

Although populism was a marginal phenomenon in Europe until recently, much current research focuses on it (Wodak and Krzyżanowski 2017; Aalberg et al. 2017; Wodak, KhosraviNik and Mral 2013). Histories of populism include the agrarian movements in Russia at the end of the nineteenth century and in Eastern Europe in the early twentieth century (Mudde and Kaltwaser 2017). Twentieth-century communism and fascism shared traits with populism, and present-day extremist movements sometimes embrace populist rhetoric (Wodak and Richardson 2013). The resemblance between fascism and some contemporary populism is largely due to the ideological combinations that populism enters into rather than the populist core traits. The French Front National and Austrian Freedom Party were first to mold European far-right parties into successful populist parties, making the latter the first far-right party governing an EU member state (Wodak, KhosraviNik and Mral 2013). Other parties have since followed that route, including Forza Italia, the United Kingdom Independence Party and a plethora of movements in post-communist countries (Colombo 2012; Ruzza and Balbo 2013). Today, the Polish Law and Justice and Hungarian Fidesz parties stand out, not least because they have been able to remain in power (Krzyżanowski 2012; Csigó and Merkovity 2017). Using the "refugee crisis" of 2015 as a potent mobilizer, many European populists have recently achieved significant electoral wins (Rheindorf and Wodak 2017; Vollmer and Karakayali 2017). Left-wing populist parties such as Syriza in Greece and Podemos in Spain have also won elections in the wake of economic recession and the Eurozone crisis. In Italy, the far-right Lega Nord under the populist leadership of Salvini has formed a government with leftist Cinque Stelle, itself a populist movement and strongly anti-establishment. While both right- and left-wing populist parties regard the EU as part of the elite, the latter do so with social rather than nationalist arguments (Aslanidis and Kaltwasser 2016; Boukala and Dimitrakopoulou 2015; Stavrakakis and Katsambekis 2014).

Australasia has seen the rise of populist parties similar to those in Western Europe in the 1990s. Both New Zealand First and the Australian One Nation party can be seen as responses to immigration and economic neoliberalism, and both claimed to speak for "the native people," albeit with different outlooks: The former asserted itself as the voice of the indigenous Maori, while the latter claimed to speak for the descendants of white colonizers (Leach, Stokes and Ward 2000). While One Nation's leader Pauline Hanson relied strongly on the role as political outsider and woman, Thaksin Shinawatra in Thailand and Rodrigo Duterte in the Philippines are prime examples of strongmen flaunting "bad manners" (Curato 2016; Moffitt and Tormey 2013).

Populist parties have recently gained prominence in the Middle East, in the form of ruling parties and political leaders. A prominent case is the Justice and Development party in Turkey, led by Recep Tayyip Erdogan, which has maintained its populist rhetoric while campaigning and governing (Dinçşahin 2012). In Israel, the populist rhetorics of Benjamin Netanyahu of Likud have drawn attention from discourse analysts (Musolff 2018; Boukala 2018) and political scientists (Filc 2010).

28.4 Discourse-Analytic Studies of Populism

A wide variety of discourse-analytic approaches have been adopted to study populism as a discursive phenomenon, sometimes broadly to include all social meaning-making and sometimes more narrowly as rhetorics. In principle, these approaches are equally viable for the study of populism, but especially strong contributions have come from work that identifies as critical discourse analysis and embraces frameworks such the discourse-historical approach (Wodak et al. 2009), the dialectal-relational approach (Fairclough 2015) and social semiotics or multimodal discourse analysis (Kress and van Leeuwen 2001). The commitment to critique and the view of discourse as social practice shared by these approaches are perhaps best seen not as a prerequisite to studying populist discourse but as tenets that make them particularly well-suited to the study of populist phenomena as discussed in political science.

Within these discourse-analytic approaches, the concepts of "recontextualization" and "normalization" have provided ways to describe how elements of populist rhetoric and the fringe ideologies they are combined with are appropriated and sometimes become acceptable in hegemonic discourse (Wodak 2018; Rheindorf 2019). Indeed, it is a key strategy of populist politics to test and gradually extend the limits of the sayable through provocation, scandalization and calculated ambivalence (Engel and Wodak 2015; Hatakka, Niemi and Välimäki 2017). Taking a critical perspective, such studies go beyond a descriptive approach to rhetorics or style, recognizing contextual, linguistic and discursive choices in populist discourse as strategic (Ekström, Patrona and Thornborrow 2018).

Analytically, it is the link between core characteristics of populism, on the one hand, and specific discursive strategies and rhetorical or, more broadly, linguistic means of realization, on the other, that characterizes discourse-analytic studies of populism. Analytical focus has been on a variety of discursive features or levels and their contribution to the overall aims of populist actors, including but not limited to argumentation and topoi, legitimation, nomination and attribution, performance, visual or multimodal design. Empirically, discourse studies have traced populist discourses in genres within the field of politics (particularly in election campaigns), including speeches at rallies (Schoor 2017), parliamentary speeches (Hafez 2017; Ekström, Patrona and Thornborrow 2018), commemorative speeches (Ekström, Patrona and Thornborrow 2018), televised debates (Ekström, Patrona and Thornborrow 2018), party programs and manifestos (Rheindorf and Wodak 2019), pamphlets and posters (Wodak 2015) as well as social media (Ruzza and Pejovic 2019; Krämer 2017; Engesser, Fawzi and Larsson 2017).

Unlike political science, discourse-analytic studies on populism are predominantly contextualist and specific not only in terms of data but also in approaching populist discursive practices as situated in a specific social and cultural context, with the success of particular discursive strategies and rhetorical choices depending on how well they activate contextual and historical specifics. Numerous case studies have thus analyzed populist discourses in national contexts such as Austria (Rheindorf and Wodak 2019), the UK (Zappettini and Krzyżanowski 2019), France (Chilton 2017) or Greece (Boukala and Dimitrakopoulou 2015). Contrastive perspectives, whether through the compilation of individual contributions in edited volumes or special issues (Wodak, KhosraviNik and Mral 2013; Engesser, Fawzi and Larsson 2017) or directly comparative research (Ekström, Patrona and Thornborrow 2018; Stavrakakis et al. 2017), have further enriched discourse-analytic understanding of the variety and specificity of populist discourses in relation to its core characteristics.

28.5 Conceptual Issues and Ongoing Debates

In studying populism, discourse analysts have looked to social sciences for conceptually sound and empirically grounded definitions. Although the field offers many insightful approaches, it is far from homogenous in its conceptualization of populism. Ongoing debates of interest for discourse analysts concern populism's relationship to democracy and the interrelationship between its core traits and (socio)linguistic concepts such as discourse, argumentation, legitimation, recontextualization and normalization. Behind this looms the larger question of the status of populism itself. While some scholars define populism as an *ideology* (Mudde and Kaltwasser 2017), others regard it as a *syndrome* in the nonpathological sense of a variable cluster of non-necessary features (Wiles 1969). While some argue that it *combines* specific forms with specific contents (Pels 2011), others maintain that it is a *style* (Brubaker 2017; Moffitt 2016) or *strategy* (Ware 2002). Some argue that populism today is a danger to democracy (Müller 2016, 2017) or to liberal democracy (Mudde and Kaltwasser 2017), while others see it as an integral part of democracy and positive force (Laclau 2005). Although these controversies need not impact the analysis of discursive features, they have far-ranging consequences for discourse-analytical perspectives on populism.

The controversy over populism partly stems from the geographical and historical scope of different approaches. In their attempt to address this issue, Mudde and Kaltwasser (2017: 2) offer an "ideational approach" that covers populist phenomena not only across the political left-right spectrum but also across the globe and across centuries. Given the diverse historical and social contexts, the resulting definition of populism as a "thin-centered ideology" posits only two core elements: pitting "the pure people" against "the corrupt elite" and arguing that politics should be a direct expression of the *volonté générale*. Note that "ideology" here denotes a "mental map through which individuals analyze and comprehend political reality" (Mudde and Kaltwasser 2017: 6) or "interpretative frameworks that emerge as a result of the practice of putting ideas to work in language as concepts" (Stanley 2008: 98). As a thin-centered ideology, populism necessarily assimilates to other ideologies.

In contrast, Moffitt (2016: 38) focuses on contemporary populism, leading him to conceptualize populism as a "political style" in the sense of "the repertoires of embodied, symbolically mediated performance" (see also Brubaker 2017). While this approach covers much the same core traits as others, it strongly emphasizes populist leaders (rather than parties) and conceptualizes them as *performers*, regards "the people" as both a *construction* and the *audience* of the performance, and sees crisis and media as the *stages* of this performance. Despite its limited scope, Moffitt's theoretical framework can be applied to both left- and right-wing populism and may lend itself particularly well to discourse-analytical studies due to its focus on situated performance, mediatization and multimodality (see Chapter 12 in this volume on the impact of this construct on discourse studies in general).

A further influential approach was elaborated by political scientist Jan-Werner Müller, who defines populism not as ideology or style but as "a set of distinct claims and ... inner logic" (Müller 2017: 10). Content in the sense of ideological claims (rather than policy) is here combined with form: Contemporary populism is understood as politics based on principled, moralized antipluralism and a non-institutionalized notion of "the people," using rhetorical or discursive strategies to claim a direct connection with the essence of "the people." Populism must thus be able to construct the leader's image as being one *of* the people and yet *apart* from them, speaking *as* and *for* the people. The content needed to specify that populist claims beyond this may come from the left or right (Müller 2017: 93).

Controversy also surrounds **populists' ability to govern**. Because their success hinges on the ability to mobilize "the people" against "the elite," it has been argued that populists cannot sustain themselves as populists once they are in power. However, there is evidence that they cannot only stay in power and be re-elected, but even maintain much of their rhetoric by redefining it, turning against institutions outside direct electoral control such as courts, the media and civil society (Reisigl 2005) or against an enemy outside the nation, for example an international economic elite or Jewish conspiracy (Mudde and Kaltwasser 2017: 13–14). This phenomenon was described as the "paranoid style of politics" (Hofstadter [1964]2008) and also characterizes the rhetorics of Hugo Chávez and Viktor Orbán.

The most contentious issue is populism's **relationship to democracy**. Some argue that it is intrinsically democratic (Canovan 1999) or the essence of democratic politics, because the construction of "the people" qua populism is a sine qua non of democratic functioning (Laclau 2005). Taking a less pronounced stance, many argue that populists promote repoliticization of topics insufficiently addressed by the establishment, such as immigration in Europe (Mudde and Kaltwasser 2017: 19). While at odds with liberal democracy, that is, pluralism, minority rights, constitutional safeguards and independent institutions, it may "reveal the dysfunctions of contemporary democratic systems" (Moffitt 2016: 143–4). Independent institutions are easily cast as part of "the elite" and an enemy of the people, since they constrain the direct rule of the popular will. Populists' endorsement of direct democratic mechanisms has been debunked as an "elective affinity" because populists will embrace any mechanism that helps construct an authentic relationship with their constituencies, while the general will is presumed to be already known by virtue of that intimacy (Mudde and Kaltwasser 2017: 17).

The general will thus constructed, Wodak (2017) argues, serves to hide what are in fact authoritarian tendencies in populism. Modern populism thus inherits Carl Schmitt's belief that a strong, authoritarian leader supposedly in tune with "the people" is more democratic than any election-based representative democracy or parliament (Müller 2017). Such a belief necessarily denies diversity among "the people" and their will, legitimizing the exclusion of anyone who threatens this homogeneity. Thus, many European scholars argue strongly against the view of democracy as having two separate pillars – one being majoritarianism, the other liberalism/constitutionalism – which might make populism "the bad conscience of liberal democracy" or an "illiberal democratic response to undemocratic liberalism" (Mudde and Kaltwasser 2017: 116). Instead, they regard populism as "blatantly alleged antidemocratic" in its rejection of the irreducible diversity of citizens (Müller 2017: 3–11). This discussion becomes even more critical with right-wing populism, given such parties' ties to extreme-right groups (Wodak, KhosraviNik and Mral 2013; Reisigl 2012; Wodak 2015;

Rydgren 2017). In short: the more virulent the ideology that populism combines with, the more authoritarian its stance toward all nondirect democratic institutions.

From their global perspective, Mudde and Kaltwasser (2017: 86–96) argue that one must distinguish different forms of democracy in relation to populism. Clearly, the political system within which populist actors must work strongly impacts the effects that populism has on the local democratic regime. International treaties or unions such as the European Union can counter some effects of populists in power, yet populists have found ways to recontextualize international pressure as unwanted "meddling" in internal affairs, bolstering their electoral support. For instance, when the Austrian Freedom Party came into power in 2000, international sanctions taken by other EU members effectively rallied national support (Wodak et al. 2009).

A separate issue with possibly far-reaching consequences for discourse analysis is the interdisciplinary framework within which the successes of populism are explained and empirically tied to populist rhetoric. Often-cited models link populism to political beliefs, socioeconomic positions and/or psychological states of its supporters. This view is strongly opposed by Müller (2017) as derived from 1950s and 1960s modernization theory. Recent work attempts to empirically test for the impact of populist rhetoric and seems to confirm the assumption that less educated and politically cynical voters are more susceptible to populism (Bos, Sheets and Boomgaarden 2018; Hameleers, Bos and de Vreese 2017).

There are, furthermore, conflicting views as to whether populism should be conceptualized as *categorical*, where a political actor, politics or rhetoric is either populist or nonpopulist, or as *gradational*, where a specific instance can be more or less populist (Gidron and Bonikowski 2013: 8). While work that regards populism as ideology or strategy tends to see it as categorical even when combined with other ideologies (Mudde and Kaltwasser 2017), work that emphasizes discursive, rhetorical or performative aspects tends to see populism as gradational (Bos, van der Brug and de Vreese 2013; Reisigl 2005), focusing on how and to which extent that actor *employs* populism (Gidron and Bonikowski 2013: 15). There are also concerns that the term "populist" has been used misleadingly to describe radical right-wing parties who may be using populist strategies but whose determining characteristics are not populist (Rydgren 2017).

28.6 Implications

Given the importance that social sciences attribute to discourse, rhetorics and performance in populist successes, discourse-analytic research is highly pertinent beyond the field of linguistics. To the degree that populism is seen as dangerous to democracy, and to the extent that populist rhetoric is found to be manipulative, such research is also relevant to the political field, education, and civil society beyond that. It relates to ongoing debates about plebiscites and provides evidence on the effects of mainstream politicians adopting populism in the attempt to secure electoral success. Even more critically, populism may undermine current political systems and international treaties or organizations. Research indicates that democratic systems may need to develop new forms of participation to counter the populist claim to exclusive representation of "the people." Other research has shown how media, despite their own political orientation or ethical standards, can become complicit in populist successes.

28.7 Future Directions

Research into populism is likely to proliferate further across the social sciences, and both discourse and rhetorics are sure to attract substantial attention. Future studies will continue to provide local, regional and global analyses of populism, yielding contextualized as well as comparative perspectives. In interdisciplinary dialogue, discourse analysis can contribute nuanced and empirically grounded insights into the rhetorical and discursive dimensions of populism. However, this requires strong visibility and positioning with regard to the often vague and inconsistent use of terminology in the field. Take, as a case in point, the fact that Moffitt's (2016) overview of "the discourse approach" fails to acknowledge any work in applied linguistics. This is evident in his claim that "discursive approaches focus primarily on discursive 'content' and have a tendency to sideline the ways in which this content is presented, framed, performed, enacted or broadcast" (Moffitt 2016: 40). In fact, what Moffitt calls the performative aspects of populism closely resemble an understanding of discourse as social practice; his argument that "the people," "crisis" and other populist notions are discursively constructed equates a fundamental premise of discourse-analytical approaches. At the same time, Moffitt's insights into the multimodal aspects of populist embodiment and into populism's relationship with (social) media might provide a valuable impulse to discourse studies. Whether the future holds success or failure for populism, the interplay among rhetoric, discourse and multimodal media contexts will be crucial.

Further Reading

Mény, Y. and Surel, Y. (eds.) (2002). *Democracies and the Populist Challenge*. London: Palgrave Macmillan.

This edited volume's insightful contributions on the forms and effects of populism across the globe remain relevant to this day.

Moffitt, B. (2016). *The Global Rise of Populism: Performance, Political Style, and Representation*. Stanford, CA: Stanford University Press.

Moffitt's book makes a strong case for taking a close look at the performative dimension of populism, in particular the performances of its leaders in relation to crises and the media.

Mudde, C. and Kaltwasser, C. R. (2017). *Populism: A Very Short Introduction*. Oxford: Oxford University Press.

This aptly named introduction manages to give a comprehensive overview of populism across time and space in all its varied forms, providing a concise framework for comparative studies of populism.

Müller, J. W. (2016). *What Is Populism?* Philadelphia: University of Pennsylvania Press.

This concise work, first published in 2016 and updated a year later, provides an accessible and passionate discussion of contemporary populism, focusing on its inner logic and threat to democracy.

Wodak, R. and Krzyżanowski, M. (eds.) (2017a). Special Issue: Right-Wing Populism in Europe & USA: Contesting Politics and Discourse beyond "Orbanism" and "Trumpism." *Journal of Language and Politics* 16(4).

This special issue covers right-wing populism in Europe and the United States and brings together varied approaches from applied linguistics and social sciences.

References

Aalberg, T., Esser, F., Reinemann, C., Stromback, J. and de Vreese, C. (eds.) (2017). *Populist Political Communication in Europe*. London: Routledge.

Angouri, J. and Wodak, R. (2014). They Became Big in the Shadow of the Crisis: The Greek Success Story and the Rise of the Far Right. *Discourse & Society* 25(4): 540–65.

Arditi, B. (2007). *Politics on the Edges of Liberalism: Difference, Populism, Revolution, Agitation*. Edinburgh: Edinburgh University Press.

Aslanidis, P. and Kaltwasser, C. R. (2016). Dealing with Populists in Government: The SYRIZA-ANEL Coalition in Greece. *Democratization* 23(6): 1077–91.

Barr, R. (2009). Populists, Outsiders and Anti-establishment Politics. *Party Politics* 15(1): 29–48.

Bos, L., Sheets, P. and Boomgaarden, H. G. (2018). The Role of Implicit Attitudes in Populist Radical Right Support. *Political Psychology* 39(1): 69–87.

Bos, L., van der Brug, W. and de Vreese, C. H. (2013). An Experimental Test of the Impact of Style and Rhetoric on the Perception of Right-Wing Populist and Mainstream Party Leaders. *Acta Politica* 48(2): 192–208.

Boukala, S. (2018). False Reasoning and Argumentation in the Twitter Discourse of the Prime Minister of Israel. *Journal of Language Aggression and Conflict* 6(1): 58–78.

Boukala, S. and Dimitrakopoulou, D. (2015). The Politics of Fear vs. the Politics of Hope: Analysing the 2015 Greek Election and Referendum Campaigns. *Critical Discourse Studies* 14(1): 39–55.

Brown, G. (1997). Deliberation and Its Discontents: H. Ross Perot's Antipolitical Populism. In A. Schedler (ed.) *The End of Politics? Explorations into Modern Antipolitics*. 115–48.

Brubaker, R. (2017). Why Populism? *Theory and Society* 46(5): 357–85.

Burns, S., Eberhardt, L. and Merolla, J. L. (2013). What Is the Difference between a Hockey Mom and a Pit Bull? Presentations of Palin and Gender Stereotypes in the 2008 Presidential Election. *Political Research Quarterly* 66(3): 687–701.

Canovan, M. (1999). Trust the People! Populism and the Two Faces of Democracy. *Political Studies* 4(1): 2–16.

Castanho, S. B., Vegetti, F. and Littvay, L. (2017). The Elite Is Up to Something: Exploring the Relation between Populism and Belief in Conspiracy Theories. *Swiss Political Science Review* 23(4): 423–43.

Chilton, P. (2017). "The People" in Populist Discourse: Using Neurocognitive Linguistics to Understand Political Meanings. *Journal of Language and Politics* 16(4): 582–94.

Christofferson, T. (2003). The French Elections of 2002: The Issue of Insecurity and the Le Pen Effect. *Acta Politica* 38(2): 109–23.

Colombo, M. (2012). Discourse and Politics of Migration in Italy: The Production and Reproduction of Ethnic Dominance and Exclusion. *Journal of Language and Politics* 12(2): 157–79.

Csigó, P. and Merkovity, N. (2017). Hungary: Home of Empty Populism. In T. Aalberg, F. Esser, C. Reinemann, J. Stromback and C. de Vreese (eds.) *Populist Political Communication in Europe*. London: Routledge. 299–310.

Curato, N. (2016). Flirting with Authoritarian Fantasies? Rodrigo Duterte and the New Terms of Philippine Populism. *Journal of Contemporary Asia* 47(1): 142–53.

De la Torre, C. (2014). Populism in Latin American Politics. In D. Woods and B. Wejnert (eds.) *The Many Faces of Populism: Current Perspectives*. Bingley: Emerald. 79–100.

Dinçşahin, Ş. (2012). A Symptomatic Analysis of the Justice and Development Party's Populism in Turkey, 2007–2010. *Government and Opposition* 47(4): 618–40.

Dornbusch, R. and Edwards, S. (1992). *The Macroeconomics of Populism in Latin America*. Chicago, IL: University of Chicago Press.

Ekström, M., Patrona, M. and Thornborrow, J. (2018). Right-Wing Populism and the Dynamics of Style: A Discourse-Analytic Perspective on Mediated Political Performances. *Palgrave Communications* 4(83). https://doi.org/10.1057/s41599-018-0132-6.

Engel, J. and Wodak, R. (2013). "Calculated Ambivalence" and Holocaust Denial in Austria. In R. Wodak and J. E. Richardson (eds.) *Analysing Fascist Discourse: European Fascism in Talk and Text*. London: Routledge. 73–96.

Engesser, S., Fawzi, N. and Larsson, A. O. (2017). Populist Online Communication: Introduction to the Special Issue. *Information, Communication & Society* 20(9).

Fairclough, N. (2015). *Language and Power*, 3rd ed. London: Routledge.

Filc, D. (2010). *The Political Right in Israel: Different Faces of Jewish Populism*. London: Routledge.

  (2015). Latin American Inclusive and European Exclusionary Populism: Colonialism as an Explanation. *Journal of Political Ideologies* 20(3): 263–83.

Gidron, N. and Bonikowski, B. (2013). *Varieties of Populism: Literature Review and Research Agenda*. Harvard, MA: Weatherhead Center for International Affairs.

Goodwyn, L. (1976). *Democratic Promise: The Populist Moment in America*. New York: Oxford University Press.

Hafez, F. (2017). Debating the 2015 Islam law in Austrian Parliament: Between Legal Recognition and Islamophobic Populism. *Discourse & Society* 28(4): 392–412.

Hameleers, M., Bos, L. and de Vreese, C. H. (2017). The Appeal of Media Populism: The Media Preferences of Citizens with Populist Attitudes. *Mass Communication & Society* 20(4): 481–504.

Hatakka, N., Niemi, M. K. and Välimäki, M. (2017). Confrontational yet Submissive: Calculated Ambivalence and Populist Parties' Strategies of Responding to Racism Accusations in the Media. *Discourse & Society* 28(3): 262–80.

Hofstadter, R. ([1964]2008). The Paranoid Style in American Politics. In *The Paranoid Style in American Politics, and Other Essays*. New York: Vintage Books.

Ionescu, G. and Gellner, E. (eds.) (1969). *Populism, Its Meaning and National Characteristics*. London: Weidenfeld and Nicolson.

Kavada, A. (2018). Editorial: Media and the "Populist Moment." *Media, Culture & Society*. Published online: doi.org/10.1177/0163443718772144.

Keane, J. (2013). *Democracy and Media Decadence*. New York: Cambridge University Press.

Kellner, D. (2017). *American Horror Show: Election 2016 and the Ascent of Donald J. Trump*. Rotterdam: Sense.

Krämer, B. (2017). Populist Online Practices: The Function of the Internet in Right-Wing Populism. *Information, Communication & Society* 20(9).

Krastev, I. (2012). The Populist Moment. *EUROZINE*, September, 18. www.eurozine.com/the-populist-moment/.

Kress, G. R. and van Leeuwen, T. (2001). *Multimodal Discourse: The Modes and Media of Contemporary Communication*. London/New York: Oxford University Press.

Krzyżanowski, M. (2012). Right-Wing Populism, Opportunism and Political Catholicism: On Recent Rhetorics and Political Communication of Polish PiS (Law and Justice) Party. In A. Pelinka and B. Haller (eds.) *Populismus: Herausforderung oder Gefahr für die Demokratie?* Vienna: New Academic Press. 111–26.

Krzyżanowski, M. and Ledin, P. (2017). Uncivility on the Web: Populism in/and the Borderline Discourses of Exclusion. *Journal of Language and Politics* 16(4): 566–81.

Kuzminski, A. (2008). *Fixing the System: A History of Populism, Ancient and Modern*. New York: Bloomsbury.

Laclau, E. (2005). *On Populist Reason*. London: Verso.

Lakoff, R. T. (2017). The Hollow Man: Donald Trump, Populism, and Post-Truth Politics. *Journal of Language and Politics* 16(4): 595–606.

Leach, M., Stokes, G. and Ward, I. (2000). *The Rise and Fall of One Nation*. Queensland: University of Queensland Press.

Machin, D. and Richardson, J. E. (2012). Discourses of Unity and Purpose in the Sounds of Fascist Music: A Multimodal Approach. *Critical Discourse Studies* 9(4): 329–45.

Martinéz-Torres, M. E. and Rosset, P. M. (2010). La Vía Campesina: The Birth and Evolution of a Transnational Social Movement. *Journal of Peasant Studies* 37(1): 149–75.

Mazzoleni G. (2008). Populism and the Media. In D. Albertazzi and D. McDonnell (eds.) *Twenty-First Century Populism*. London: Palgrave Macmillan. 49–64.

McCabe, J. (2012). States of Confusion: Sarah Palin and the Politics of US Mothering. *Feminist Media Studies* 12(1): 149–53.

Milner, R. M. (2013). Pop Polyvocality: Internet Memes, Public Participation, and the Occupy Wall Street Movement. *International Journal of Communication* 7: 2357–90.

Moffitt, B. (2015). How to Perform Crisis: A Model for Understanding the Key Role of Crisis in Contemporary Populism. *Government and Opposition* 50(2): 189–217.

  (2016). *The Global Rise of Populism: Performance, Political Style, and Representation*. Stanford, CA: Stanford University Press.

Moffitt, B. and Tormey, S. (2013). Rethinking Populism: Politics, Mediatisation and Political Style. *Political Studies* 62(2): 381–97.

Montgomery, M. (2017). Post-Truth Politics? Authenticity, Populism and the Electoral Discourses of Donald Trump. *Journal of Language and Politics* 16(4): 619–39.

Mudde, C. (2004). The Populist Zeitgeist. *Government and Opposition* 39(4): 542–53.

Mudde, C. and Kaltwasser, C. R. (2017). *Populism: A Very Short Introduction.* Oxford: Oxford University Press.

Müller, J. W. (2016). *What Is Populism?* Philadelphia: University of Pennsylvania Press.

Musolff, A. (2018). Nations as Persons: Collective Identities in Conflict. In B. Bös, S. Kleinke, S. Mollin and N. Hernández (eds.) *The Discursive Construction of Identities On- and Offline: Personal, Group and Collective.* Amsterdam: John Benjamins. 249–66.

Nolan, D. and Brooks, S. (2015). The Problems of Populism: Celebrity Politics and Citizenship. *Communication Research and Practice* 1(4): 349–61.

Ostiguy, P. (2009). The High–Low Political Divide: Rethinking Populism and Anti-Populism. *Political Concepts: Committee on Concepts and Methods Working Paper Series* 35.

Pappas, T. (2014). *Populism and Crisis Politics in Greece.* London: Palgrave Macmillan.

Pels, D. (2011). The New National Individualism: Populism Is Here to Stay. In E. Meijers (ed.) *Populism in Europe.* Vienna/Brussels: PlanetVerlag/GEF.

Postill, J. (2018). Populism and Social Media: A Global Perspective. *Media, Culture & Society.* Published online: doi.org/10.1177/0163443718772186.

Reisigl, M. (2005). Oppositioneller und regierender Rechtspopulismus: Rhetorische Strategien und diskursive Dynamiken in der Demokratie. In S. Fröhlich-Steffen and L. Rensmann (eds.) *Populisten an der Macht. Populistische Regierungsparteien in West- und Osteuropa.* Wien: Braumüller. 51–68.

  (2012). Rechtspopulistische und faschistische Rhetorik: ein Vergleich. *Totalitarismus und Demokratie* 9: 303–23.

Rheindorf, M. (2019). Disciplining the Unwilling. Normalisation of (Demands for) Punitive Measures against Immigrants in Austrian Populist Discourse. In M. Kranert and G. Horan (eds.) *Doing Politics: Discursivity, Performativity and Mediation in Political Discourse.* Amsterdam: John Benjamins. 179–208.

Rheindorf, M. and Wodak, R. (2017). Borders, Fences, and Limits: Protecting Austria from Refugees. *Journal of Immigrant and Refugee Studies* 16(1–2): 15–38.

  (2019). "Austria First" Revisited: A Diachronic Cross-Sectional Analysis of the Gender and Body Politics of the Extreme Right. *Patterns of Prejudice* 53(3): 302–20.

Richardson, J. E. (2013). Ploughing the Same Furrow? Continuity and Change on Britain's Extreme-Right Fringe. In R. Wodak, M. KhosraviNik and B. Mral (eds.) *Right-Wing Populism in Europe: Politics and Discourse.* London: Bloomsbury. 105–20.

Richardson, J. E. and Colombo, M. (2013). Continuity and Change in Anti-immigrant Discourse in Italy: An Analysis of the Visual Propaganda of the Lega Nord. *Journal of Language and Politics* 12(2): 180–202.

Roberts, K. M. (2007). Latin America's Populist Revival. *SAIS Review* 28 (1): 3–15.

Ruzza, C. and Balbo, L. (2013). Italian Populism and the Trajectories of Two Leaders: Silvio Berlusconi and Umberto Bossi. In R. Wodak, M. KhosraviNik and B. Mral (eds.) *Right-Wing Populism in Europe: Politics and Discourse*. London: Bloomsbury. 163–76.

Ruzza, C. and Pejovic, M. (2019). Populism at Work: The Language of the Brexiteers and the European Union. *Critical Discourse Studies* 16(4): 432–48.

Rydgren, J. (2017). Radical Right-Wing Parties in Europe: What's Populism Got to Do with It? *Journal of Language and Politics* 16(4): 485–96.

Sauer, B., Krasteva, A. and Saarinen, A. (2017). Post-Democracy, Party Politics and Right-Wing Populist Communication. In M. Pajnik and B. Sauer (eds.) *Populism and the Web*. London: Routledge. 14–35.

Savage, R. (2013). From McCarthyism to the Tea Party: Interpreting Anti-Leftist Forms of US Populism in Comparative Perspective. *New Political Science* 34(4): 564–84.

Schoor, C. (2017). In the Theater of Political Style: Touches of Populism, Pluralism and Elitism in Speeches of Politicians. *Discourse & Society* 28 (6): 657–76.

Stanley, B. (2008). The Thin Ideology of Populism. *Journal of Political Ideologies* 13(1): 95–110.

Stavrakakis, Y. and Katsambekis, G. (2014). Left-Wing Populism in the European Periphery: The Case of SYRIZA. *Journal of Political Ideologies* 19(2): 119–42.

Stavrakakis, Y., Katsambekis, G., Nikisianis, N., Kioupkiolis, A. and Siomos, T. (2017). Extreme Right-Wing Populism in Europe: Revisiting a Reified Association. *Critical Discourse Studies* 14(4): 420–39.

Taggart, P. (2002). Populism and the Pathology of Representative Politics. In Y. Mény and Y. Surel (eds.) *Democracies and the Populist Challenge*. London: Palgrave Macmilla. 62–80.

Triandafyllidou, A., Wodak, R. and Krzyżanowski, M. (eds.) (2009). *The European Public Sphere and the Media: Europe in Crisis*. Basingstoke: Palgrave Macmillan.

Vollmer, B. and Karakayali, S. (2017). The Volatility of the Discourse on Refugees in Germany. *Journal of Immigrant and Refugee Studies* 16(1–2): 118–39.

Ware, A. (2002). The United States: Populism as Political Strategy. In Y. Mény and Y. Surel (eds.) *Democracies and the Populist Challenge*. London: Palgrave Macmillan. 101–19.

Weber, M. ([1924]1997). *The Theory of Social and Economic Organization*. New York: Simon & Schuster.

Wiles, P. (1969). A Syndrome, Not a Doctrine: Some Elementary Theses on Populism. In G. Ionescu and E. Gellner (eds.) *Populism: Its Meaning and National Characteristics*. London: Weinfeld & Nicolson. 197–211.

Wodak, R. (2015). *The Politics of Fear: What Right-Wing Populist Discourses Mean*. London: Sage.

　(2017). The "Establishment", the "Élites", and the "People": Who's Who? *Journal of Language and Politics* 16(4): 551–65.

Wodak, R., de Cillia, R., Reisigl, M., Liebhart, K., Hirsch, A., Mitten, R. and Unger, J. W. (2009). *The Discursive Construction of National Identity*, 2nd ed. Edinburgh: Edinburgh University Press.

Wodak, R. and Forchtner, B. (2014). Embattled Vienna 1683/2010: Right-Wing Populism, Collective Memory and the Fictionalisation of Politics. *Visual Communication* 13(2): 231–55.

Wodak, R., KhosraviNik, M. and Mral, B. (eds.) (2013). *Right-Wing Populism in Europe: Politics and Discourse*. London: Bloomsbury.

Wodak, R. and Krzyżanowski, M. (2017). Right-Wing Populism in Europe & USA: Contesting Politics & Discourse beyond "Orbanism" and "Trumpism." *Journal of Language and Politics* 16(4): 471–84.

Wodak, R. and Pelinka, A. (eds.) (2009). *The Haider Phenomenon in Austria*. New Brunswick/London: Transaction.

Zappettini, F. and Krzyżanowski, M. (eds.) (2019). Special Issue: The Critical Juncture of Brexit in Media & Political Discourses: From National-Populist Imaginary to Cross-National Social and Political Crisis. *Critical Discourse Studies*. https://doi.org/10.1080/17405904.2019.1592767.

29

The Discourses of Money and the Economy

Annabelle Mooney

29.1 Introduction

Long before the most recent financial crisis of 2007–8, linguists were interested in money. This has not always been immediately apparent, however, because "money" is abstract. As Bjerg argues, "money eludes a comprehensive theory" (2014: 84). Nevertheless, because linguists interested in discourse tend to focus on particular domains, practices and texts, they have been able to analyze the language used when people talk about and do things with money. That is, discourse about "money" is not always about money as such. Researchers may appear to focus on news reports, textbooks, conversations during transactions or talk about gambling, but they are in fact examining "money talk." Money is used in particular contexts, by specific people to do specific things. It is by paying attention to texts produced while undertaking or describing these activities that linguists can access money talk.

Because money is so abstract and contested, I discuss it in Section 29.2. In Section 29.3, I provide an overview of the rich body of work that linguists have undertaken on the topic. As much of this research has used Lakoff and Johnson's Cognitive Metaphor Theory (CMT), I deal with that first (Section 29.3.1). While, on the face of it, such analysis may appear to simply identify metaphors, because of the rhetorical and ideological effects that flow from metaphors together with the steep rise in use of metaphors in the financial domain in the wake of the global financial crisis (GFC), it is important to understand the complexity of this work and its findings. Specifically, the metaphors that scholars analyze give us insight into the economic ideological status quo as well as indicating possible lines of resistance. In Section 29.3.2 I consider work that focuses on texts and ideology, including research in the CDA tradition, to show the contribution this work has made to money talk and in understanding the GFC and its causes. I show the utility of taking a multimodal approach to analysis in the financial domain in Section 29.3.3. In Section 29.3.4 I explore work that deals with austerity, poverty and so-called "poverty porn." While this strand of work is not entirely new, with rising inequality it has become even more important. In Section 29.4, I consider the implications and impact of linguistic work in the field while in Section 29.5 I draw on recent work in critical discourse analysis (CDA) to suggest ways in which this impact could be brought to the attention of those outside our discipline.

29.2 Overview: The Problem with "Money"

The problem with "money" is as much a social, cultural and ideological one as a linguistic one. It is therefore important to consider what money is, how the term is used and to pay attention to the semantic field of money more generally. At the outset, it is important to notice that the term "money" is not only polysemic; it is multivalent. "Money" may refer to money objects like notes, coins and credit cards, but it may also refer to the system of rules that underpins the functioning of money itself. This difference is reflected in the distinction made between the *money object* and the *money system*. The difference between the money object (notes and coins) and the money system (the financial and economic system that guarantees the value of these objects) is reasonably straightforward. Indeed, the relationship is not unlike Saussure's distinction between langue and parole (where langue is the money system).[1]

The classic economic account of the functions of money is a good place to begin when determining what money is and what linguists interested in money talk may be working on. This definition sets out money's three functions: money is (1) a store of value, (2) a medium of exchange and (3) a unit of account. While this classic description has been subject to critique (Bjerg 2014; Ingham 1996), knowing how something functions is often a useful departure point for thinking about other uses and meanings. For example, as money is a medium of exchange, we know that people must be involved. This suggests, as Ingham argues (1996), that money is a social relation. Therefore, in order to find appropriate linguistic data, we simply need to find examples of language use, interaction and discourses where each function is relevant.

In relation to money as a store of value, company reports to shareholders (Lischinsky 2011) or the branding of banks (Koller 2007) would be appropriate focal points. A good example of using money as a medium of exchange is found in Haakana and Sorjonen's (2011) work on talk around lottery ticket purchases in Finland. Finally, knowing that money is used to

---

[1] The comparison cannot be taken too far, however, as parole speech acts do not function in the same way as exchanges involving money.

keep accounts may cause us to think of the meanings of "debt" (Davidko 2011), and the myriad ways in which this is sold (Brookes and Harvey 2017a, 2017b) and recovered (Custers 2017). Scholars have also paid attention to the vast array of historical and slang terms for money (Coleman 2006) and analyzed the comprehensibility of instant lottery tickets (Butters 2004) and the semiotics of banknotes (Marten and Kula 2008). Consideration of money also connects to work on class and consumption, poverty and social justice.

As money is always embedded in social relations, it is nearly impossible to elicit or identify money talk (either spoken or written) as such. Certainly, economic texts abound, as do news reports and texts produced by significant actors in the economy (businesses, government institutions). But money talk can also be found in the domains of consumption, advertising, family talk, autobiography and narrative more generally. To hope for an ideal kind of money talk is analogous to looking for a kind of ideal language use. Money, like language, is used to *do* things. Even a simple financial exchange can have different purposes and therefore different meanings (see Mooney and Sifaki 2017: 21–7). To further complicate matters, money, as a thing, a system and a mode of reckoning, has been naturalized at an ideological level. This is clear in the discourses used to talk about money, and specifically in the metaphors used in this domain.

29.3 Areas of Work

29.3.1 Metaphor

In this section, I explore work that examines money and related fields using Lakoff and Johnson's ([1980]2003) Cognitive Metaphor Theory (CMT). This model has been extremely productive in documenting the metaphors that we live by in the economic and financial world and in relation to money more generally. Exactly because money and economics are so abstract, CMT is an ideal tool with which to analyze texts in these domains as it makes sense that people would turn to metaphor in order to comprehend and represent money and associated economic processes.

As is well known, metaphor in Lakoff and Johnson's terms is not a mere ornament or stylistic feature. Rather, metaphors are cognitive structures (hence Cognitive Metaphor Theory) that are realized in language (for an account of metaphor and framing, see Chapter 10 in this volume). Metaphors are conceptual and abstract (e.g. TIME IS MONEY) but evidence for them can be found in language (e.g. I *wasted* all afternoon on this). The metaphor, then, resides at a cognitive level with language being the evidence for the existence of the conceptual metaphor. This can be further explained with an example provided by Lakoff and Johnson: inflation. Showing that inflation is personified and given agency, they suggest that people conceptualize inflation as a person or adversary (e.g. "*Inflation is backing us* into a corner," Lakoff and Johnson 2003: 26): the respective conceptual metaphors are INFLATION IS A PERSON and INFLATION IS AN ADVERSARY. Lakoff and Johnson explain the consequences of thinking (and speaking) in this way:

> Viewing something as abstract as inflation in human terms has an explanatory power of the only sort that makes sense to most people. When we are suffering substantial economic losses due to complex economic and political factors that no one really understands, the INFLATION IS AN ADVERSARY metaphor at least gives us a coherent account of why we're suffering these losses. (Lakoff and Johnson 2003: 34)

As they are sense-making mechanisms, metaphors are also framing devices. Thus, they both suggest causality and encourage appropriate further action. If we see inflation as an *enemy*, then the appropriate response is to *fight* it in some way. The way something is represented changes not only how we understand it but also what we do about it. That is, metaphors both ground and entail arguments. They have persuasive consequences.

The range of metaphors researchers have found in the financial and economic domain is considerable. Tomoni reports that "four domains recur frequently" in economics texts: "organic metaphors" including growth and health; "war metaphors"; "machine metaphors" whereby the economy is a machine; and "water metaphors" especially in relation to "liquidity" and "flows" (2012: 204). These domains are readily found in the same text and can be put to different uses according to the target domain involved. I deal with each in turn. As will become clear, the most significant effects of the metaphors are their erasure of humans and human agency, the personification of nonhuman entities and the naturalization of economic processes.

In the case of organic metaphors, the economy is represented as a natural entity, as either an organism (a person, animal or plant) or as a body (usually human or animal) (Charteris-Black and Ennis 2001: 256; Horner 2011; Gil 2016). This body will have agency (Charteris-Black 2000) and thus be able to make things happen, it may be ill and thus require treatment and, depending on the specific kind of body, it will have particular attributes. Human metaphorical bodies will have emotions (Charteris-Black and Ennis 2001; Ho 2016) and may become ill (Horner 2011) while animal bodies will be more prone to instinctive reactions. Ho also finds that emotions themselves may have agency and at least some corporeality in financial news reports. Focusing specifically on living things and emotion post GFC, she found metaphors in the semantic fields of fear and anxiety with emotion represented as "opponents" (Ho 2016: 306). For example, "worries" were represented as acting to "hobble" companies (2016: 307). Ho observes: "The emotions of fear and anxiety were used as a tool to increase the negative perception of readers" making reports more newsworthy by promoting a "negative perception" of events (2016: 309).

Other entities in the general field of economics are also given bodies. Currencies and companies are both personified in a particularly corporeal way. When such entities are personified, they may be given certain attributes as a consequence. Charteris-Black and Musolff (2003) identify relational features (e.g. "parent company"), while Semino (2002) documents a currency (the euro) being represented as a baby. In the wake of the GFC, whole nations were personified. Early economic casualties like Greece were represented as being victims of the crisis, with "stronger" economies serving as rescuing heroes (Bickes, Otten and Weymann 2014). Ho found that the crisis itself was given agency, represented as "sowing" seeds of fear (2016: 306), bringing together in a single frame both bodies and plants. These metaphors are not just simple personification; they are embedded in networks of human relation, production and procreation. This is clearly a form of naturalization of nonhuman entities and actions.

The market is also represented as an environment (Oberlechner, Slunecko and Kronberger 2004) where natural and environmental forces and processes (e.g. growth) are located (White 1997, 2003). These representations are not always positive and may even be classed as dysphemism. The "toxic assets" that were much discussed post GFC are a good example. This poison metaphor, framed almost as an environmental disaster, spread through the economic system and was applied to all kinds of financial processes, generating expressions such as toxic loans, debts, banks, securities and mortgages (Nerghes, Hellsten and Groenewegen 2015: 116). Exactly because spreading toxins is not desirable, action and interventions were required. Moreover, as Horner (2011) argues, as these metaphors erase human culpability for the GFC, they distract attention from any other possible underlying causes that should be remedied.

As companies, corporations and the conduct of business are closely tied to the economy, texts about and from this domain have been much examined. A common metaphor found in financial and economic texts is BUSINESS IS WAR, with businesses and business people in violent conflict with each other (Charteris-Black and Musolff 2003; Charteris-Black and Ennis 2001). Companies, like people, also undertake journeys (Alejo 2010) and engage in competition, especially in the domain of sport (Oberlechner, Slunecko and Kronberger 2004). In contrast, companies might also be seen as containers and as entities lacking in agency thus subject to the forces and whims of the market. In such cases, "the market" stands in for a human actor.

The erasure of agency is also found in mechanistic metaphors. When THE ECONOMY IS A MACHINE, the clear consequence is that it should be kept running in an orderly way (Oberlechner, Slunecko and Kronberger 2004). Related to this mechanistic view is the construction of economic entities such as currencies, companies and even economic actors as inanimate objects. While this erases agency, it does make the object subject to natural forces: an inanimate object, like a ball, that can rise, fall or bounce (Charteris-Black 2000).

These metaphors, together and singly, may be culturally familiar. Nevertheless, it is important to pay attention to them (and to other more foundational metaphorical constructs) in order to trace their consequences for how society thinks about financial matters and how people behave in response to certain representations. Further, Alejo (2010: 1139) cautions that without close attention to texts we may miss other models used to make sense of economics and money. Alejo's work focuses on economics textbooks and a very common metaphor: the container metaphor. In the economic context, it can be easily identified: "the marketplace" is represented as an actually bounded physical space, while something happening "in the market" is also a clear example of the container metaphor (Alejo 2010: 1144). Within this metaphorical container, other metaphorical processes and presences can be found. For example, in the container of the economy, money is water, a liquid that moves with speed (see Tomoni 2012: 225).[2] As Alejo notes, seeing the economy as a container allows both the mechanistic model (THE ECONOMY IS A MACHINE) and the organic model (THE ECONOMY IS AN ORGANISM) to exist side by side (2010: 1147). Moreover, when the economy is a container, it is quite separate from other domains of life.

Analyzing these representations helps us understand how people think about money and, according to CMT, this should connect to how people behave. Evidencing this connection, however, is very difficult. At least some connection can be found in Boers and Demecheleer's work (1997; see also Ho 2016). Examining ten years of editorials in *The Economist*, they document the prominence of health metaphors such as THE ECONOMY IS A PATIENT (e.g. the economy is sick, ailing, fading; see also Charteris-Black 2000: 156). Boers and Demecheleer found these ill health metaphors to be more common in the winter months, suggesting that the use of metaphor is driven by seasonal salience. That is, as illness is more marked in the winter months, a higher number of illness metaphors are used.

Taking the connection further, De Landtsheer (2015) argues that metaphor choices in news media change the audience's view of the world. In the case of financial news, the representations may even have an effect on the stock market. Analyzing Flemish-Belgian and Dutch news coverage of the financial crash (over eight years of data), De Landtsheer queried whether the frequency and intensity (intensity referring to the "novel and original character" (2015: 220)) of metaphors changed over the pre-

---

[2] A physical realization of the economy as a closed system in which water (money) flows can be seen at the Science Museum in London. It was built by Bill Phillips (https://beta.sciencemuseum.org.uk/stories/2016/11/3/how-does-the-economy-work).

and post-crash periods. She also examined whether there was any correlation between the use of metaphor and the state of the economy (based on figures such as GDP, unemployment and consumer confidence). Both trends were found. Metaphor use increased markedly with the onset of the GFC and the metaphors used were more innovative and emotionally laden. The level of metaphor use also correlated with economic indicators to a greater (e.g. unemployment) or lesser extent (e.g. consumer confidence). She concludes: "The increase in unemployment rates and public debt, and the drop in trust in financial institutions and in consumer trust, seem to translate immediately into stronger media rhetoric and metaphor style" (De Landtsheer 2015: 218).

Certainly, correlation is not causation. But one correlation does seem to be causally motivated: the rise of metaphorical invention in the wake of the GFC. During the financial crisis and subsequent government actions, a number of lexical items were created and others brought to public attention. Nerghes, Hellsten and Groenewegen describe "the financial crisis as the trigger for 'one of the largest metaphor spikes in recent history'" (2015, 109, citing the Metaphor Observatory; see www.metaphorobservatory.com).

To return to specific metaphors, there is one final domain that it is necessary to explore. What should already be clear is that people (real people) are not directly present in any of the metaphors that researchers have identified, despite the presence of bodies, agency, nature and illness. Thus, the final metaphorical figure I want to discuss is that used to represent a real human. The metaphor used for a real person is a consequence of the types of metaphor that, as we have seen so far, are created to explain economic processes and objects. That is, if the economy is a mechanistic and therefore logical system, it follows that the economic actor (the human) *must* behave rationally and logically. This rational, logical figure is revealed when metaphors used to expound economic theory are examined. Pessali's (2009) analysis of transaction cost economics reveals a person in economic theory: the "contractual man." Contractual man is "an economic man based on rationality and motivational features" (Pessali 2009: 325). The only kind of person who fits the rational economic market is an entirely rational one. But as we know, and as behavioral economics shows, people do not in fact behave rationally in the market. The neoclassical model of the market works only with rational people; it functions only if it remains a container apart from the rest of the world. Real people do not belong in the market. Once the metaphorical die is cast, other consequences follow in the manner of a logical necessity.

It is worth recalling the abstract nature of money and the economy. This abstractness is precisely why metaphors about bodies, nature and machines are so common; the existence of economies, businesses and money needs to be represented into being. As Oberlechner, Slunecko and Kronberger argue in their paper on foreign exchange markets, "[m]etaphors thus not only describe and illustrate such a target domain as the foreign exchange market, but they also carry normative assumptions about what is right and what is wrong" (2004: 135). They argue that the market, even a specific market like foreign exchange trading, has no objective existence. Rather, it is constituted by the way in which people think, speak and behave. The same can be said of the economy. It has no objective existence. The economy is the sum total of all economic activity. The economy, then, has been represented into existence. It is thus crucial that we pay attention to the forms that it takes and the consequences these have for the "real" economy and real people.

29.3.2 Discourse and Ideology

Metaphor is not the only way that representations and arguments can be framed. Work in both discourse analysis and CDA has been extremely productive in the field of money, debt and the financial crisis. Key here is the way that ideologies are encoded and communicated. It is therefore worth noting the connection between discourse and practice and how pronounced it is in relation to late neoliberal capitalism. Fairclough observes that "now … neo-liberal capitalism has come into what may be a terminal crisis, the crisis is clearly in part a crisis of its discourse" (2013: 13). This crisis, however, is a complex one. Like all ideologies, neoliberal capitalism depends on a close relationship between discourse and practice, and while the real-world crisis may be obvious (see austerity in Section 29.3.4), the discursive crisis is less obvious. That is, the same discursive repertoires that neoliberal capitalism has always used are now being used in its defense.

A focus on particular crisis moments in late capitalism necessarily involves attention being paid to neoliberalism more generally. There is a wealth of work in this field, which is beyond the scope of this chapter. This work considers not just the financial scene but also the impact of neoliberalism on "commodities" like language, education and the linguistic market more generally (see Mautner 2010; also see Chapter 20 in this volume). Nevertheless, it is important to understand the ideological structure of late capitalism in order to found the analysis and critique of particular events. In particular, understanding prevailing ideological norms is paramount in understanding representations in the wake of the GFC.

It is worth stressing that the GFC did not produce a stark shift in how money and economics were represented. Rather, the crisis resulted in an intensification of these representations and therefore brought them to a wider audience. Discourse analytic work post-crisis, therefore, should be understood as a continuation of the research already undertaken. Nevertheless, because of the "crisis" nature of the GFC, it has been possible to see more clearly the causes and effects of ideology.

In the wake of the GFC, public attention focused on who to blame. And while the responsibility of large financial institutions and government economic policy should have been obvious, these actors were able to represent the GFC in such a way as to preserve their positions and the general contours of the economic system. Campbell (2017), for example, analyzes the public talk of Alan Greenspan (Chairman of the Federal Reserve in the United States at the time) in the wake of the GFC. Campbell shows that rather than the crisis being a threat to neoliberalism, the threat is simply absorbed into neoliberalism's ideological logic. As with the lack of blame and fault entailed by the choice of some of the metaphors illustrated above, in Greenspan's talk, Campbell finds a preponderance of "happening" processes, that is, processes without human agents. As Greenspan "does not attribute agency" to the events that led to the GFC, it follows that no one can be blamed (Campbell 2017: 63). And while there are moments when Greenspan appears to admit at least some responsibility for the GFC, these are short-lived: "[I]n the end it [the crisis] was [presented as] largely inevitable and self-engendered processes that unfolded in time, caused by events mostly out of anyone's control" (Campbell 2017: 71). Greenspan is an ideal choice for analysis as Campbell argues that "he was perceived as a prophet" by politicians and those involved in economic matters (2017: 56). When the oracle of late capitalism can appear to defend it even when it is in deep crisis, the ideological power of the construct is shown to be practically unassailable. Even in moments of acute crisis, hegemonic ideologies can shift and flex in order to maintain current power relations.

Whittle and Mueller (2016) also highlight the importance of structure and agency in their discourse analysis of bankers' testimony provided to a public inquiry on the crisis. While the bankers presented themselves as being *without* full individual agency, the questioners positioned them in exactly this way. That is, politicians sought to blame the individuals in front of them rather than questioning the responsibility of government, specifically, their own role in changing regulatory frameworks. Whittle and Mueller document a range of linguistic techniques for both kinds of positioning, but the contrast can clearly be seen in pronouns. While questions from politicians were phrased using "you" singular, they were answered by bankers with an institutional "we," arguably to resist individual accountability. However, whether someone in fact has agency or not is, as Whittle and Mueller argue, not the right question. The issue is rather that agency is constructed in both discourse and practice. In terms of allocating blame, therefore, it is crucial that the way agency is distributed among individuals and throughout institutions is properly understood. It is also important that representations of events allow a range of people to exert agency in presenting their views.

Walsh (2016) shows how this agency can be exerted. In her analysis of then UK Chancellor of the Exchequer Alistair Darling's post-crash budget speech, she demonstrates how he was able to protect the "normal" functioning of the economic system by using and responding to "popular criticism of the financial system and financial elites" (2016: 44). In appearing to take this criticism at least somewhat seriously, he was able to ensure that "the fundamental base of the financial system – asset capital – was protected" (2016: 44). Walsh also points out that Darling's rhetorical strategies provide a template for other elites to follow. In the "post-Crash epoch," it may be wise for the politically and economically powerful to provide some "concessions" in order to remain in their elite positions and yet provide the appearance of full engagement with their critics (2016: 54). This is how capitalism survives. Greenspan and the bankers promoted the view that the GFC was an act of god, but, as Campbell observes, "it has to be said that while it was 'not an act of God', it was action by men who acted as if they were gods" (2017: 73).

The defense of the core of capitalism is prefigured by a more general appeal to normality that was common during the crisis. As Hartz writes in his examination of media coverage pre- and post-crisis in Germany: "To put it simply, the present market is either in a normal state of affairs or in a period of re-normalization" (Hartz 2012: 151). Indeed, describing the GFC as a "crisis" already signals something abnormal. The logical reaction to a crisis is to resolve it, by putting everything "*back* to normal" as soon as possible. In times of "crisis," there is little representational space for planning new and improved ways of life.

29.3.3 Multimodal Analysis

It seems reasonably clear that neoliberal capitalism is hegemonic. It is an authoritative discourse, producing an array of ideologies and texts and influencing a range of practices that real people engage in. This was clear even before the GFC, but the effects of this hegemonic ideology nevertheless continue to grow, especially in the context of online and mediated communication. Multimodal analysis should not be understood as distinct from work on discourse, ideology and metaphor (see Chapter 12 in this volume). Rather, it builds on the kind of analysis discussed in this section by adding further semiotic dimensions to the analysis.

This is clear in the work of Catalano and Waugh (2013) who pay attention to metonymy and its effect on how the financial crisis is understood (for a discussion of metonymy, see Chapter 10 in this volume). Undertaking a multimodal analysis of news stories about the GFC, they argue that "metonymy in image plays an equally important role in (re)producing ideologies but is often harder to detect and easier to deny as subjective because it is accomplished through suggestion or connotation and by appealing to barely conscious, half-forgotten knowledge" (2013: 35). As they show, when images and text are read in relation to each other, the effects are particularly powerful. While the texts they analyze rehearse familiar metaphors (for example, the NATION IS A FAMILY metaphor), images work along the lines of metonymy (e.g. PLACE FOR PEOPLE, CLOTHES FOR STATUS). The combined result of this is a "focus on peripheral parts or properties of the scenario" that avoids "mentioning specific results or those responsible" (Catalano and Waugh 2013: 55).

While not focusing on the GFC itself, Brookes and Harvey's work, which also uses multimodal analysis, is important in understanding how text and image interact to position and persuade an audience. In their article "Just Plain Wronga?", they analyze the multimodal semiotic techniques used on the website of a well-known pay day loan provider, Wonga (2017a). They argue that by using "subtle semiotic techniques" (Brookes and Harvey 2017a: 169), Wonga represents its customers as empowered and responsible. This is not only an appealing subject position (and not too far distant from "contractual man"); these semiotic choices also work to normalize these high-cost loans. Their analysis covers not only language but also the visual subject positions offered to the customer. "Loans" are transformed into "products," customers are given an illusion of control through the use of interactive tools (Brooks and Harvey 2017a: 173) and naturalistic visual representations offer viewers an appealingly normal subject position. Color is also key to the positioning and persuasion of viewers. For example, Brookes and Harvey describe Wonga's use of blue and white as "cleansing and calming" but also reassuring and authoritative (2017a: 173).

Their work on Cash Convertors is similarly incisive. Analyzing the app that customers are encouraged to use, they show how pawning goods for money is represented as a pleasurable, empowering activity replete with positive interpersonal interaction. Brookes and Harvey show that while the "fringe economy is ruthless, fuelled as it is by financial desperation and indebtedness" (2017b: 233), the business portrays itself in routine frames of pleasure and consumerism. Brookes and Harvey document the "subtle semiotic techniques" which "manipulate discourse and emotions … deemphasising the unforgiving reality of indebtedness and the attendant risks of relying on quick and easy high interest credit" (2017b: 234). This attention to indebted lives and the regimes that we all labor under is crucial in any consideration of late capitalism. When considering debt, it is important to take a broader context into account, including but not limited to class, the labor market and the emotional impact of debt itself (see Custers 2017).

Finally, there is a long line of research on the semiotics of money objects, especially paper money (e.g. Blaazer 1999; Penrose 2011; Penrose and Cumming 2011; Sørensen 2014). While not always rooted in linguistics (though see Marten and Kula 2008; Mooney 2017), this work explores the importance of design elements (including color, typeface, representations of people and places) in legal tender in the construction of trust, authority and nation. Legal tender is a potent communicative form, all the more so perhaps because it is often so taken for granted. Nevertheless, as

Sørensen argues, "[t]he imagery of national money provides states a political tool with which to cultivate collective identity and promote imagined communities" (2014: 4).

It is in relation to money objects that interesting strategies of resistance can be seen. Community currency ("money" used in local areas to support local business; see North 2010), along with various forms of art money, seeks to reconfigure national and global economic systems and to critique the production of money itself (Thunder 2004 on J. S. G. Boggs). A very recent example is the work of the Hoe Street Central Bank in the London area of Walthamstow. Here, "money" bearing the faces of local community figures is being hand-produced and sold. The proceeds are used to support the local area and to buy back local debt. The entire project is one of artistic creativity and resistant, multimodal communicative action (Bank Job 2018).

In terms of linguistic attention to resistance, there is less to say. Given the consuming impetus of neoliberalism in terms of discourse, practice and reality, the scant attention to modes of resistance is explicable. Certainly there has been work that analyzes representations of resistance (see, for example, Gregoriou and Paterson 2017 on the representation of Occupy), but the ability of neoliberal discourses to accommodate critique and absorb attack means that if researchers want to analyze alternate economic discourses, they will have to search for them away from mainstream representations. This move also raises ethical questions in relation to the role of the analyst. I return to this in Section 29.4.

29.3.4 Austerity and Poverty Porn

In the difficult economic climate after the GFC, a number of governments implemented austerity measures. As a reduced role for the state is a key tenet of neoliberalism, austerity can be understood as a neoliberal tactic that takes advantage of the crash itself (Mylonas 2014) even though it is presented as a solution to the crisis. It is, however, a policy with high human costs (e.g. Reeves et al. 2015).

Italy and Spain were early victims of the GFC and therefore of austerity policies. In his work, Borriello (2017) examines the lexical and metaphorical choices made during the post-crash period in order to uncover the often-hidden ideologies on which austerity policies depend. He argues that "austerity discourse should be critically assessed for masking its own political nature and acting as an ideological distortion of the debatable nature of economic policy" (2017: 242). Borriello contends that the dominance of neoliberal economic discourses both "restructures" the relationship between the economic and noneconomic "spheres of social activity" (2017: 244) and treats the economy as something separate from everything else. At the same time, the discourse also "rescales" social practices so that, rather than being seen as local or even national, issues are construed as global and connected to particular political and economic practices outwith the nation-state.

This research shows clearly how ideology and metaphor are closely intertwined. Representing the economic crisis as illness or natural disaster, and seeing the economy as a human body, entails actions and constructs ideological points of view. As well as demonstrating the hegemonic (yet flawed) logic of neoliberal capitalism's economic and political policies, it also clearly demonstrates the link between micro-textual features and more abstract ideological structures. For example, seeing the national economy in the same way as a household budget (Boriello 2017: 248) personifies the national economy and naturalizes the "common sense" idea that people (including nations) cannot spend more than they earn. This ignores the fact that households do take on debt when it is productive to do so (e.g. mortgages) as well as erasing the fact that nations may be able to borrow cheaply to invest in areas that either produce returns (e.g. infrastructure investment) or minimize future costs.[3] Further, when nations are embedded in a global neoliberal context, these "common sense" responsibilities have far-reaching consequences. Nations must be competitive; they must have balanced budgets; and they must take measures to rectify the effects of "unforeseen" and agentless economic crises. This strand of neoliberalism holds that nations, like people, must be ideal entrepreneurial subjects.

As nations see themselves compelled to enact austerity measures, it is perhaps to be expected that citizens will be presented with material that seeks to persuade them of the logic of these policies. In addition to news media, official speeches and the like, "entertainment" in the form of television programs can also be identified as part of (a perhaps unconscious) effort to persuade the public of the logic of austerity. Indeed, the post-crash period roughly coincides with a rise of poverty porn of a particular kind. The most recent form of poverty porn describes a genre largely found on television, where poorer people, most usually those in receipt of state welfare support, are represented in their daily lives. Programs may focus on hardship, alleged illegal activity or lifestyle choices (e.g. alcohol, drug use, number of children). While poverty porn has long been used to evoke sympathy (and charitable donations), newer programs are not so clearly framed. Viewers may choose to approve of or judge those represented. The more recent kind of poverty porn has been defined as "the media portrayal of the feral and feckless poor as the source of social breakdown" (Squires and Lea 2013: 12 cited in Paterson, Coffey-Glover and Peplow 2016: 197). According to Paterson, Peplow and Grainger, "[p]overty porn appears designed to homogenise those on benefits and set them up for mockery, as their ways of life are evaluated

---

[3] For example, investing in disease prevention has the potential to save significant amounts of money in health budgets. These returns might not be immediate, but they can be considerable and they can be quantified.

negatively" (2017: 207). While this demonization of the poor has a long history, during periods of economic scarcity it may take on new power and force, motivated perhaps by a kind of "divide and rule" strategy.

The division between us and them takes a number of forms. In the UK, for example, the distinction is between the hardworking taxpayer and "scroungers"/"skivers" (Fairclough 2016: 73) while in the United States the figure of the "welfare queen" may be more familiar (Albiston and Nielsen 1994). The negative stereotypes that are attached to benefit claimants, commonly represented as "scroungers," are attested in Paterson, Coffey-Glover and Peplow's work (2016), which analyzes data from focus groups talking about a well-known piece of UK poverty porn, *Benefits Street*. But they also demonstrate the separation that viewers of poverty porn may make between themselves and the people depicted (Paterson, Coffey-Glover and Peplow 2016). This separation is not consistent: viewers of these programs see those portrayed as "other" but also as "normal." These distinctions are found across communicative platforms. In Twitter data relating to *Benefits Street*, Baker and McEnery (2015) find evidence of a range of discourses including the "idle poor"; but also representations of the poor as victims together with a negative portrayal of financial inequality recognized in the trope of "the rich getting richer." While this demonstrates the complexity of public opinion, as few people would self-identify as a scrounger, most people accept both the existence of "scroungers" and the austerity policies that follow (Fairclough 2016: 73).

29.4 Real-World Applications and Constructive Critique

The detailed text analysis that linguists undertake has, at least potentially, far-reaching effects. This potential can be demonstrated by examining the Framing the Economy project (FTE) undertaken by NEON, NEF, FrameWorks Institute and PIRC in the UK (2018). The goal was to determine how the British public might be persuaded to see that another economic system was not only possible but desirable. They found that "the British public draws on a number of 'powerful but thin' models to think about what the economy is and how it works" (2018: 27). Like the metaphors described in Section 29.3.1, they are powerful in that they "structure people's understanding of the economy" but thin in that they provide little understanding of "the mechanisms behind economic outcomes" (2018: 27).

After gathering and analyzing data from ordinary people, the FTE developed new ways to frame the economy. These were tested to see how they were understood and what kinds of entailments these new models had. For example, they found that talking about the UK being self-reliant led to xenophobic views, with a distinction made between "us and them" (2018: 33). Two framings, however, were more positively productive and "effective in shifting public thinking" (2018: 42). They can be described in terms of narrative. The first, the "populist story," foregrounds the importance of resisting corporate power, especially its power over government. The second, the "common ground story," focuses on fulfillment: the value of creating an economy that addresses the real needs of real people. The project also developed evidence-based activist tools to help determine which communicative tropes and strategies to use in various contexts. That is, a set of interventions are provided together with advice about which is most suitable for different kinds of people. The goal of all this work is to persuade the British public that another kind of society, a different kind of economy, is both possible and desirable. While this may seem to be manipulative in the sense that it takes advantage of the effect of framing on the ways in which people think and make decisions, it is arguably a necessary tactic given the powerful framing effects of neoliberal ideologies. Given the analysis involved and the alternatives generated, this is a kind of constructive critique in the domain of language, economics and money.

There is some work in linguistics that undertakes similar constructive critique in the field. Knezevic et al.'s (2014) work on food security is a good example. While people going hungry might not immediately seem to be about economics or money, "money" is never just about money. It is always about something else. Knezevic et al. show that the food insecure are marginalized socially, practically and ideologically and "internalize the neoliberal discourse that insists on individual responsibility and self-blame" (2014: 236). Their participatory research approach is positive not only in giving voice to marginalized people but also in terms of generating alternative discourses, frames and explanations for ongoing problems. They write: "[A]lternative discourses do indeed hold the potential to re-construct the hierarchy of perceived power and thus alter the lived reality of those who experience participatory approaches" (2014: 239).

This kind of activism, this kind of production of alternative discourses, is generally absent from work in the field of language and money. While descriptive, analytical and critical work is clearly valuable, given the very real human costs of current economic systems, it does seem reasonable to ask what might be possible in the discipline and in the world. The positive discourse analysis (PDA) approach offers a great deal of scope in the domain of money and economics (Martin 2004). Analyzing progressive discourse and highlighting its strategies is one strand; the other is creating constructive responses to hegemonic power and damaging practices by designing interventions in the manner of language reform. This may involve working with communities and with other disciplines. However, the costs involved (in all kinds of domains) in doing so are considerable, especially in the context of increasing pressure on research budgets. It is therefore also worth considering how we might be able to engage in generating alternative visions of the world by drawing on and extending linguistic understanding of both language and ideology.

For a while, the work of behavioral economics seemed to offer a bridge between close linguistic analysis and changes to public behavior. The popular success of Thaler and Sunstein's Nudge Theory (2008) offered some hope that using language to influence behavior could be turned to the public good. This is still a viable path. A potential stumbling block, however, is the way that Nudge Theory has also been absorbed into neoclassical economics. In their analysis of the World Bank's *World Development Report 2015: Mind Society and Behaviour*, Fine et al. observe that in the report's recommendations, "the insights from psychology that are deployed in the behavioural economics approach are filtered through their compatibility with neoclassical economics' technical apparatus, resulting in a lack of genuine engagement with other behavioural sciences" (2016: 649). They also demonstrate that nudging works only if root causes are properly understood. To take one example, the World Bank recommends educating people about the details of pay day loans (Fine et al. 2016: 655), ignoring the fact that people are driven to these providers out of sheer economic desperation and not because they fail to grasp what an expensive product it is (Brookes and Harvey 2017a, 2017b).

It seems reasonable to claim that linguists can, at the very least, identify discursive root causes. The question that then arises is whether it is possible (or permissible) to objectively critique current hegemonic norms and on that basis suggest and promote alternatives. In order to do the former, a clear value in which constructive critique can be grounded is required. In order to do the latter, the discipline needs to accommodate work that would make suggestions for linguistic innovation, policy reform and ideological renovation.

There is some movement in the development of a value that could ground this kind of approach. Recently in CDA there has been a preoccupation with ethics (see Chapter 21 in this volume). A special issue of *Critical Discourse Studies* (2018) is emblematic of this. While attention to ethics, or to something that grounds the critique of CDA, has not been wholly absent (see Graham 2018 for a history and suggestions for future work), the recent attention to "values" is welcome, especially in relation to work on money, the economy and neoliberalism. Van Leeuwen (2018: 151) argues that CDA "should support and endorse discourses that bring people together, positive discourses" that challenge stereotypes and encourage community. This may be done by careful analysis of existing positive discourses, but the positive values must be made explicit and be open to debate. While procedures and objectivity in relation to analysis are important, as Graham notes: "To make a judgement about something is to evaluate it according to some standard or other" (2018: 187). If a standard can be identified, it can be used to both evaluate existing discourse and practice and generate positive innovations.

Having an ethical framework that is "appropriately contingent and subjective" (in that it is sensitive to interpersonal relationship context, Roderick 2018: 165) is necessary both in order to make a defensible value judgment and in order to translate analysis into the world of action. Especially in the light of the erasure of real people from the representation of the economy, moves to place human beings at the heart of this framework are appropriate. Indeed, Herzog's (2018) argument for seeing "suffering" as key in critical approaches suggests an approach that is both flexible and human. He writes: "Suffering thus combines philosophical approaches with individual, psychological dimensions of affective reactions, sociological analysis and a political perspective. Suffering here is seen as the driving engine for critique and social change" (Herzog 2018: 118). Human suffering should be identified and it should be negatively assessed. Moreover, if there is any potential for linguistic analysis of the language of money to develop new discourses that would help alleviate suffering, such suggestions should be both made and encouraged.

29.5 Summary

The research that has been undertaken in discourse studies and linguistics more generally demonstrates the vitality and longevity of the field as well as the broad reach of money and economics. Money, like language, is a human construct that can be used to do a range of things and is understood in a variety of ways. Paying attention to the ways in which economic and financial events are represented is important in understanding political structures, ideology and the experiences of real people. Work on metaphor demonstrates the connection between language and thought, persuasion and ideology. It also demonstrates the way that textual structure, from the lexical level all the way to the text, is informed and shaped by interests that are both ideological and invested in the consequences of representations.

Because of the close attention that researchers pay to language, its ideological origins and its real-world effects, they are well placed to make a positive contribution not only to the discipline but also to broader society. Recent work on ethics, particularly in the field of CDA, provides a basis for both ethical critique and positive interventions in language, representation and thought. While this may at first glance appear to be manipulative, if grounded in a robust ethical approach it can only serve to contest the harm inflicted by hegemonic ideologies and practices. It seems to me that some values really do trump others and precisely the problem in relation to discourses of money and debt and the GFC more generally is that people have been erased. National economies are rated as more important than the state of someone's pantry. The metaphorical life of a company or a national economy is considered more valuable than the life of a real person. I am not suggesting that economic events don't have consequences for real people; as austerity shows, they most certainly do. The question is whether control over both events and consequences can be wrested back from the agentless processes and metaphorical natural disasters that we have been presented with. It seems to me that they can be and it seems right to me that they should be.

Further Reading

Chun, C. W. (2017). *The Discourses of Capitalism: Everyday Economics and the Production of Common Sense*. London: Routledge.

Working with audience responses to an artwork "Capitalism Works for Me!" (by Steve Lambert), Chun analyzes responses to and critiques of people's understanding of capitalism in their lives.

Holborow, M. (2015). *Language and Neoliberalism*. Abingdon: Routledge.

This book offers an incisive account of neoliberal ideology and its effects on both language and practice in contemporary life. It examines the increasing reach of the "market" and the key figure of the "entrepreneur." It provides a robust treatment of ideology and how this links to language specifically and linguistics more generally.

Mautner, G. (2010). *Language and the Market Society: Critical Reflections on Discourse and Dominance*. London: Routledge.

This landmark book documents and critically analyzes the effect of market thinking in domains like education, government, religion and self-promotion. The context of each domain is clearly provided while detailed analysis of texts ranges from the lexical through the multimodal to the linguistic landscape.

References

Albiston, C. R. and Nielsen, L. B. (1994). Welfare Queens and Other Fairy Tales: Welfare Reform and Unconstitutional Reproductive Controls. *Howard Law Journal* 38: 473–519.

Alejo, R. (2010). Where Does the Money Go? An Analysis of the Container Metaphor in Economics: The Market and the Economy. *Journal of Pragmatics* 42(4): 1137–50.

Baker, P. and McEnery, T. (2015). Who Benefits When Discourse Gets Democratised? Analysing a Twitter Corpus around the British Benefits Street Debate. In P. Baker and T. McEnery (eds.) *Corpora and*

Discourse Studies. Palgrave Advances in Language and Linguistics. London: Palgrave Macmillan. 244–65.

Bank Job. (2018). https://bankjob.pictures/bank/.

Bickes, H., Otten, T. and Weymann, L. C. (2014). The Financial Crisis in the German and English Press: Metaphorical Structures in the Media Coverage on Greece, Spain and Italy. *Discourse and Society* 25(4): 424–45.

Bjerg, O. (2014). *Making Money: The Philosophy of Crisis Capitalism*. London: Verso.

Blaazer, D. (1999). Reading the Notes: Thoughts on the Meanings of British Paper Money. *Humanities Research* 1: 39–53.

Boers, F. and Demecheleer, M. (1997). A Few Metaphorical Models in (Western) Economic Discourse. In W. A. Liebert, G. Redeker and L. R. Waugh (eds.) *Discourse and Perspective in Cognitive Linguistics*. Amsterdam: John Benjamins. 115–30.

Borriello, A. (2017). "There Is No Alternative": How Italian and Spanish Leaders' Discourse Obscured the Political Nature of Austerity. *Discourse and Society* 28(3): 241–61.

Brookes, G. and Harvey, K. (2017a). Just Pain Wronga? A Multimodal Critical Analysis of Online Payday Loan Discourse. *Critical Discourse Studies* 14(2): 167–87.

(2017b). The Discourse of Alternative Credit: A Multimodal Critical Examination of the Cash Converters Mobile App. In A. Mooney and E. Sifaki (eds.) *The Language of Money and Debt: A Multidisciplinary Approach*. Cham: Palgrave. 233–56.

Butters, R. R. (2004). How Not to Strike It Rich: Semantics, Pragmatics, and Semiotics of a Massachusetts Lottery Game Card. *Applied Linguistics* 25 (4): 466–90.

Campbell, C. (2017) Neoliberal Ideology Only "Partially" to Blame in the Global Financial Crisis? A Critical Discourse Analysis of Alan Greenspan's Public Discourses on the 2007/8 GFC. In P. Mickan and E. Lopez (eds.) *Text-Based Research and Teaching*. Cham: Palgrave. 55–74.

Catalano, T. and Waugh, L. R. (2013). The Language of Money: How Verbal and Visual Metonymy Shapes Public Opinion about Financial Events. *International Journal of Language Studies* 7(2): 31–60.

Charteris-Black, J. (2000). Metaphor and Vocabulary Teaching in ESP Economics. *English for Specific Purposes* 19(2): 149–65.

Charteris-Black, J. and Ennis, T. (2001). A Comparative Study of Metaphor in Spanish and English Financial Reporting. *English for Specific Purposes* 20: 249–66.

Charteris-Black, J. and Musolff, A. (2003). "Battered Hero" or "Innocent Victim"? A Comparative Study of Metaphors for Euro Trading in British and German Financial Reporting. *English for Specific Purposes* 22: 153–76.

Coleman, J. (2006). Slang Terms for Money: A Historical Thesaurus. In G. Caie (ed.) *The Power of Words: Essays in Lexicology, Lexicography and Semantics in Honour of Christian Kay*. Amsterdam: Rodopi. 23–34.

Custers, A. (2017). Falling Behind: Debtors' Emotional Relationships to Creditors. In A. Mooney and E. Sifaki (eds.) *The Language of Money and Debt: A Multidisciplinary Approach*. Cham: Palgrave. 163–85.

Davidko, N. (2011). The Concept of DEBT in Collective Consciousness (a Socio-historical Analysis of Institutional Discourse). *Studies about Languages* 19: 78–88.

De Landtsheer, C. (2015). Media Rhetoric Plays the Market: The Logic and Power of Metaphors behind the Financial Crisis since 2006. *Metaphor and the Social World* 5(2): 204–21.

Fairclough, I. (2016). Evaluating Policy as Argument: The Public Debate over the First UK Austerity Budget. *Critical Discourse Studies* 13(1): 57–77.

Fairclough, N. (2013). *Critical Discourse Analysis: The Critical Study of Language*, 2nd ed. Harlow: Longman.

Fine, B., Johnston, D., Santos, A. C. and Waeyenberge, E. (2016). Nudging or Fudging: The World Development Report 2015. *Development and Change* 47(4): 640–63.

Gil, M. M. (2016). A Cross-Linguistic Study of Conceptual Metaphors in Financial Discourse. In J. Romero-Trillo (ed.) *Yearbook of Corpus Linguistics and Pragmatics 2016*. Cham: Springer. 107–26.

Graham, P. (2018). Ethics in Critical Discourse Analysis. *Critical Discourse Studies* 15(2): 186–203.

Gregoriou, C. and Paterson, L. L. (2017). "Reservoir of Rage Swamps Wall St": The Linguistic Construction and Evaluation of Occupy in International Print Media. *Journal of Language Aggression and Conflict* 5(1): 57–80.

Haakana, M. and Sorjonen, M.-L. (2011). Invoking Another Context: Playfulness in Buying Lottery Tickets at Convenience Stores. *Journal of Pragmatics* 43: 1288–302.

Hartz, R. (2012). Reclaiming the Truth of the Market in Times of Crisis: Course, Transformation and Strategies of a Liberal Discourse in Germany. *Culture and Organization* 18(2): 139–54.

Herzog, B. (2018). Suffering as an Anchor of Critique: The Place of Critique in Critical Discourse Studies. *Critical Discourse Studies* 15(2): 111–22.

Ho, J. (2016). When Bank Stocks Are Hobbled by Worries: A Metaphor Study of Emotions in the Financial News Reports. *Text & Talk* 36(3): 295–317.

Horner, J. R. (2011). Clogged Systems and Toxic Assets: News Metaphors, Neoliberal Ideology, and the United States "Wall Street Bailout" of 2008. *Journal of Language and Politics* 10(1): 29–49.

Ingham, G. (1996). Money Is a Social Relation. *Review of Social Economy* LIV(4): 507–29.

Knezevic, I., Hunter, H., Watt, C., Williams, P. and Anderson, B. (2014). Food Insecurity and Participation. *Critical Discourse Studies* 11(2): 230–45.

Koller, V. (2007). "The World's Local Bank": Globalisation as a Strategy in Corporate Branding Discourse. *Social Semiotics* 17(1): 111–30.

Lakoff, G. and Johnson, M. ([1980]2003). *Metaphors We Live By*. Chicago, IL: University of Chicago Press.

Lischinsky, A. (2011). In Times of Crisis: A Corpus Approach to the Construction of the Global Financial Crisis in Annual Reports. *Critical Discourse Studies* 8(3): 153–68.

Marten, L. and Kula, N. C. (2008). Meanings of Money: National Identity and the Semantics of Currency in Zambia and Tanzania. *Journal of African Cultural Studies* 20(2): 183–98.

Martin, J. R. (2004). Positive Discourse Analysis: Solidarity and Change. *Revista Canaria de Estudios Ingleses* 49(1): 179–202.

Mautner, G. (2010). *Language and the Market Society: Critical Reflections on Discourse and Dominance*. London: Routledge.

Mooney, A. (2017). Reading That which Should Not Be Signified: Community Currency in the UK. In S. Zhao, E. Djovnov, A. Björkvall and M. Boeriis (eds.) *Advancing Multimodal and Critical Discourse Studies: Interdisciplinary Research Inspired by Theo van Leeuwen's Social Semiotics*. London/New York: Routledge. 95–114.

Mooney, A and Sifaki, E. (2017). The View from the Ground. In A. Mooney and E. Sifaki (eds.) *The Language of Money and Debt: A Multidisciplinary Approach*. Cham: Palgrave. 1–30.

Mylonas, Y. (2014). Crisis, Austerity and Opposition in Mainstream Media Discourses of Greece. *Critical Discourse Studies* 11(3): 305–21.

Neon, NEF, FrameWorks Institute, and PIRC. (2018). Framing the Economy: How to Win the Case for a Better System. http://publicinterest.org.uk/framing-economy-report/.

Nerghes, A., Hellsten, I. and Groenewegen, P. (2015). A Toxic Crisis: Metaphorizing the Financial Crisis. *International Journal of Communication* 9: 106–32.

North, P. (2010). *Local Money: How to Make It Happen in Your Community*. Totnes: Green Books.

Oberlechner, T., Slunecko, T. and Kronberger, N. (2004). Surfing the Money Tides: Understanding the Foreign Exchange Market through Metaphors. *British Journal of Social Psychology* 43: 133–56.

Paterson, L., Coffey-Glover, L. and Peplow, D. (2016). Negotiating Stance within Discourses of Class: Reactions to Benefits Street. *Discourse & Society* 27(2): 195–214.

Paterson, L., Peplow, D. and Grainger, K. (2017). Does Money Talk Equate to Class Talk? Audience Responses to Poverty Porn in Relation to Money and Debt. In A. Mooney and E. Sifaki (eds.) *The Language of Money and Debt: A Multidisciplinary Approach*. Cham: Palgrave. 205–31.

Penrose, J. (2011). Designing the Nation: Banknotes, Banal Nationalism and Alternative Conceptions of the State. *Political Geography* 30(8): 429–40.

Penrose, J. and Cumming, C. (2011). Money Talks: Banknote Iconography and Symbolic Constructions of Scotland. *Nations and Nationalism* 17(4): 821–42.

Pessali, H. F. (2009). Metaphors of Transaction Cost Economics. *Review of Social Economy* 67(3): 313–28.

Reeves, A. et al. (2015). Economic Shocks, Resilience, and Male Suicides in the Great Recession: Cross-National Analysis of 20 EU Countries. *European Journal of Public Health* 15(3): 404–9.

Roderick, I. (2018). Multimodal Critical Discourse Analysis as Ethical Praxis. *Critical Discourse Studies* 15(2): 154–68.

Semino, E. (2002). A Sturdy Baby or a Derailing Train? Metaphorical Representations of the Euro on British and Italian Newspapers. *Text* 22(1): 107–39.

Sørensen, A. R. (2014). "Too Weird for Banknotes": Legitimacy and Identity in the Production of Danish Banknotes 1947–2007. *Journal of Historical Sociology*. https://doi.org/10.1111/johs.12077.

Squires, P. and Lea, J. (2013). Introduction: Reading Loïc Wacquant – Opening Questions and Overview. In P. Squires and J. Lea (eds.) *Criminalisation and Advanced Marginality: Critically Exploring the Work of Loïc Waquant*. Bristol: Policy Press. 1–18.

Thaler, R. and Sunstein, C. (2008). *Nudge*. London: Penguin Books.

Thunder, A. (2004). Living On … Counterfeit Money: J.S.G Boggs and the Borderlands of Economic Criticism. *Textus* XVII: 417–30.

Tomoni, B. (2012). Using Money Metaphors in Banking Discourse: Three Possible Scenarios. *Metaphor and the Social World* 2(2): 201–32.

Van Leeuwen, T. (2018). Moral Evaluation in Critical Discourse Analysis. *Critical Discourse Studies* 15(2): 140–53.

Walsh, C. (2016). Protesting Too Much: Alastair Darling's Constructions after the Financial Crash. *Critical Discourse Studies* 13(1): 41–56.

White, M. (1997). The Use of Metaphor in Reporting Financial Market Transactions. *Cuadernos de Filología Inglesa* 6(2): 233–45.

  (2003). Metaphor and Economics: The Case of Growth. *English for Specific Purposes* 22(2): 131–51.

Whittle, A. and Mueller, F. (2016). Accounting for the Banking Crisis: Repertoires of Agency and Structure. *Critical Discourse Studies* 13(1): 20–40.

30

Corporate Discourse

Sylvia Jaworska

30.1 Introduction and Definitions

When we think of modern corporations, what comes to mind is probably something like the skyline of Manhattan with monolithic skyscrapers or possibly glass buildings with quirky designs dotting the Silicon Valley. But the buildings would have no corporate purpose if it were not for the people who work in them. Essentially, corporations are groups of people who come together to get work done and achieve organizational and interpersonal goals. The way in which they do it is primarily by communicating, that is, using talk and text with one another. Meetings, emails, negotiations with customers, job interviews, annual reports and so on are all forms of discursive event conducted through language. Decisions, actions and even the shared understanding of corporate goals all grow out of interactions in a multitude of discursive events. It is simply impossible to imagine a corporation without any form of discourse. Discourse is the key tool of performing corporate goals; it is what "talks" and "writes" corporations into being (cf. Boden 1994).

To discourse-analytical ears, this statement sounds like a platitude, but it is only recently that language in general and discourse in particular have started to receive scholarly attention in the field of business communication instigated by the so-called "linguistic turn" in social sciences (Alvesson and Kärreman 2000). Applied linguists and discourse analysts, too, began to explore aspects of corporate communication, and this chapter is primarily dedicated to showcasing this work and outlining its implications for the field of discourse studies and corporate communication.

The notion of corporate discourse underlying this chapter draws on Breeze's (2013) understanding of corporate discourse as a set of social practices that comprise a cohesive discourse system (Scollon, Scollon and Jones 2012) that "supposes acceptance of a common ideological position, a process of socialisation of members, a set of preferred discourse forms ... that act as symbols of membership and a structured system of relationships, both inside the domain and with outsiders" (Breeze 2013: 23). In this sense, corporate discourse goes beyond the notion of discourse as language in use and emphasizes what Gee (2014) calls the big D Discourse, understood as ways of being, that is, thinking, acting, interacting, believing, etc. Corporate discourse can therefore be understood as ways of corporate being. Although these ways of corporate being are voluntary, they are "underpinned by a cohesive though not explicit ideological system" (Breeze 2013: 23), of which empiricism, utilitarianism and individualism are, at least in the Western corporate world, the core principles.

Corporate discourse is closely tied with corporate practices. As such, corporate discourse is never static; it changes as new practices arise. It is important to bear in mind that corporate practices are not always transparent and often hide much more than they reveal. Analyzing discourses through which corporate practices are constituted can be a way into this hidden world of corporations. At the same time, it needs to be emphasized that these discourses are likely to be opaque too. It is therefore imperative to read between the lines and scrutinize what is said, how it is said and also what is not said (Breeze 2013). This is where the tools and methods of (critical) discourse analysis come in handy.

This chapter begins with an overview of the major topics and directions in research on corporate discourse. First, studies concerned with internal corporate talk are discussed. Contrary to the common perception that corporate talk is dry and purely transactional, discourse-analytical and sociolinguistic studies of corporate talk have shown the prominence of interpersonal discourse features such as hedges, humor, politeness and impoliteness, highlighting that, in corporate life, relational goals are as important as transactional ones. The chapter moves on to outline research on corporate communication with the outside world, focusing specifically on discursive strategies that corporations employ to legitimize their actions and to persuade or dissuade stakeholders. Increasingly, social media have become an important site for maintaining public relations. Yet, context collapse poses a challenge to business as usual and opens up ways for a wider public scrutiny of corporate practices. The chapter concludes with a discussion of some of the practical and ethical issues that arise when "doing" a critical analysis of corporate discourses, before outlining some of the opportunities and benefits that criticality and language awareness can bring to corporate life.

30.2 Overview of the Topic

Given the understanding of corporate discourse as corporate practice, this section focuses on research that explores the role of discourse in creating and maintaining corporate identity and performing corporate goals. Studies concerned with specific lexical, grammatical and generic features of business genres, often with a teaching purpose in mind and conducted under the banner of ESP, have been extensively reviewed elsewhere (e.g. Bargiela-Chiappini, Nickerson and Planken 2007) and will not be discussed here. Since corporate discourse as corporate practice is inherently context-bound, only studies that are based on authentic data collected in corporate settings are considered. Research using methods that do not emphasize authentic contexts, for example simulations, is excluded.

30.2.1 Discourse and the Inner World of the Corporation

A corporation is a legal entity which in order to exist needs to be formally "incorporated" into a registrar of companies. For example, in the UK this is the House of Companies. The most important part of this process is the completion of a specific text known as the Memorandum of Association and giving the company a name. In this way, a corporation is entextualized into being; it cannot exist otherwise. From that moment, texts and talk will define much of the structure and inner workings of a corporation.

However, it was only recently that the role of text and talk in the corporate inner life has been recognized. For a long time, research concerned with business communication has been premised on the understanding that communication is just about transferring information; if the information is clear and well defined, then it will be received in the intended way. This was equated with communicative efficiency and much effort was spent on creating business communication manuals based on this one-dimensional, transactional and instrumental model of communication (Baxter 2010).

Seminal work by Lampi (1986) who used discourse analysis to study business negotiations is one of the first contributions challenging this output–input model. Her research has shown that business communication is largely about relationships and that the lexical choices made by participants reflect the degree of mutual involvement and the corporate context in which the negotiation takes place.

This contextual and interpersonal nature of business and corporate communication has been demonstrated in subsequent studies concerned with different types of spoken business discourse (see also Chapter 27 in this volume). Interrogating the Cambridge and Nottingham Corpus of Business English (CANBEC), Handford (2010) demonstrates the saliency of interpersonal dimension in business interactions as evidenced by the frequent use of routinized chunks (*you know, I think*) and the pervasiveness of *we*. In a similar vein and using a corpus-based methodology, Koester (2006) analyzes workplace talk and also finds a prevalence of language features typical for interpersonal language use such as hedges, vague language, idioms and metaphors.

One of the major contributions to our understanding of the role of language in the inner workings of business contexts has been the *Language in the Workplace* (LWP) project based at the University of Wellington in New Zealand and conducted by a team of linguists under the direction of Janet Holmes. Many studies with different foci sprang from this undertaking and it is beyond the scope of this chapter to discuss the breadth and depth of the LWP research.[1] What is relevant to highlight is that, in contrast to other studies concerned with discourse in business environments, the LWP project foregrounded the role of discourse in maintaining and negotiating power relationships in business organizations. It also introduced the theoretical notion of a workplace as a form of community of practice (CfP) (Holmes and Stubbe 2003) drawing on the understanding of CfP developed by Wenger (1998). Accordingly, the workplace has been conceptualized as a place based on three indispensable components that constantly intersect, namely joint enterprises (goals), mutual engagements (ties and activities) and shared repertoires (symbolic and behavioral practices).

The LWP project amassed authentic interactions from various business contexts with diverse participates representing different gender and ethnic backgrounds. One of the contributions of LWP has been to show the importance of small-talk in interactions in business contexts as a means of filling a gap between work activities (Holmes and Stubbe, 2003). Humor, too, has been identified as an important feature of business interactions serving a multitude of functions including maintaining of collegiality and good relationships with coworkers and helping to smooth face-threatening acts. It can be a powerful tool for those having a higher status in the managerial hierarchy to assert authority. Equally, humor is used by subordinates to challenge power relationships and express criticism in a "softer" way (Holmes 2000).

The intersection of power and gender has been of particular interest to the LWP project challenging some of the common assumptions and stereotypes about women's and men's talk. For example, Holmes and Marra (2004) have shown that the way women and men talk in the workplace depends on contextual factors, of which power status seems to be an important indicator of a communicative style rather than gender. For example, although use of directives has been commonly associated with a "masculine communicative style," women in managerial positions also use directives to get things done (Holmes and Stubbe 2003).

Similar findings were obtained by Mullany (2007) in the context of British workplace interactions. In her ethnographic study, she observes

---

[1] The project website can offer further insights into the multitude of LWP research projects and relevant publications: www.victoria.ac.nz/lals/centres-and-institutes/language-in-the-workplace.

that women in higher status positions use discourse patterns normally associated with a stereotypical notion of "masculine communicative style"; for example, they talk in a direct manner without using mitigating devices. Similarly, Baxter (2010) has demonstrated the significance of status and context on the ways in which female and male employees deploy language in business interactions. Challenging the stereotypical notion of women's and men's language, she shows how female leaders combine repertoires of both feminine and masculine speech styles to perform transactional and relational goals. The female style seems distinctive in that it is more proscribed and based on nuanced linguistic strategies, which, in Baxter's (2010: 169) view, is needed "in order to preempt negative evaluation in a business world that continues to be male-dominated."

While spoken interactions are a major part of the internal workings of a corporation, employees also spend a significant proportion of their everyday activities on engaging with written discourse, through either documents or text-based digitally mediated communication formats (Darics 2015). Digital technologies, email in particular, have enabled new levels of interactivity and contributed to changes in norms and discursive practices of business communication, blurring at times the distinction between professional, corporate and lay discourse (Darics 2015). More informal, personalized discourse styles emerged, also influencing face-to-face encounters (e.g. Gimenez 2000).

Given that, increasingly, organizations and corporations are multinational and engage in business across the world, teams are likely to be composed of members of different ethnicities and nationalities with different discursive and communicative styles. This can be as much an enrichment as an obstacle to effective communication at work. English is now the dominant language of business communication, with many large corporations switching to English as the official corporate language (Neeley 2012). For example, Airbus, Daimler-Chrysler, Nokia, Renault, Samsung, Siemens, SAP, Microsoft in Beijing and Mikitani use English only and many more corporations plan to follow suit. This creates a scenario in which most employees communicate in a language that is not their first or native language and this might be perceived as a problem for effective communication. Research by Incelli (2013) shows to the contrary, however; she compared business emails written in English by native speakers of English and speakers of Italian and found that native speakers use a range of accommodation strategies to adapt to the kind of English produced by Italian colleagues. Overall, grammatical and lexical errors seem interactionally irrelevant as long as the purpose and technical aspects are understood. Cultural norms seem to play a role too, and differences in communication strategies were observed in the degree of formality or informality used in the emails, with Italians showing a tendency toward a more casual style, while the English native speakers exhibited a more formal register.

Alongside emails, other digital technologies, most notably instant messaging (IM), are increasingly adopted for the purpose of internal communication in corporations (Darics 2013). Garrett and Danziger (2007) argue that IM can be a useful tool of interaction management allowing users to communicate in more efficient ways. For example, Quan-Haase, Cothrel and Wellman (2005) show that IM can facilitate conversations about sensitive matters, while Dennis, Rennecker and Hansen (2010) conclude that IM can be useful for social and task support. The perceived informality of IM conversations is helpful in creating an atmosphere of trust and collegiality, which is achieved through the use of specific linguistic and discursive resources such as emoticons, capitalization, letter repetition and various politeness strategies (Darics 2013).

Communication in professional and organizational settings is predominantly a type of frontstage communication (Goffman 1971) assumed to be rational and polite. Indeed, forms of impoliteness such as swearing are less expected because they are associated with offensive behavior that would be socially sanctioned. Yet, as studies by Jay (2000) and Chaika (1982) show, swearing occurs in the workplace and can even be quite prevalent in the context of backstage communication. Similar to humor, it can be used to exercise power. It can also be an important tool of resistance to authority contributing to the redefinition of power relationships. Mak and Lee (2015) investigate the use of expletives in IM in the context of white-collar workplaces in Hong Kong and conclude that swearing in IM is much more intentional and strategic than in face-to-face communication. Alongside expressions of frustration, expletives in IM can help employees release work-oriented pressure, preface bad news or help share negative feelings. The authors argue that swearing in the workplace should not always be regarded as "bad" as it can strengthen relationships and mutual engagements.

One aspect of internal corporate workings which is increasingly given prominence is employee branding (Breeze 2013). Nowadays, companies invest a great deal of resources into the creation of a system of values that gives a perception of a cohesive, well-working community, and employee branding is an important part of the socialization of employees into that community. Research has shown that employees who identify with the corporate identity develop loyalty and are more likely to go the extra mile (Ellsworth 2002). The benefits for corporations are obvious and it is perhaps not surprising that, increasingly, human resources (HR) departments join in efforts with public relation specialists to devise ways in which to increase the "match" between employees' attitudes and corporate values (Breeze 2013). They do so by employing diverse and increasingly sophisticated symbolic, semiotic and discursive means to create a sense of corporate community and persuade the employees of the merits of the company. Induction meetings, company newsletters with stories of achievements, requests to wear outfits that display company brand and brand-associated qualities, and team-building exercises are implemented to enhance employees' engagement and win their hearts and minds (Breeze 2013).

Given the general difficulties in obtaining access to internal corporate materials and settings, there is little research exploring the discourse of employee branding. One of the few examples is a study by Lischinsky (2018) who scrutinizes training materials given to new employees in the UK retail corporation John Lewis. This corporation is interesting in that it is owned (but not co-managed) by its employees who are normally referred to as partners. Using corpus tools and methods, Lischinsky (2018) looks specifically at the lexical profiles of the terms *partner* and *partnership* and shows how the corporation overemphasizes its uniqueness and reciprocity in the relations between employees and the organization. Also, affiliative and emotional links are created by reinforcing the message that "we are all in it together" and everyone is responsible for the financial situation of the corporation. In this way, employees are made to believe that they are joining structures based on total equality in which responsibility is shared by all, while existing managerial power structures are conveniently downplayed.

Employee branding is a highly problematic discursive practice; it can be seen as an attempt to "mold" employees' minds by co-opting them to think and behave in the ways desired by the corporation, which essentially turns them into a commodity ready to be used as a competitive advantage for increasing profits. On the other hand, it is worth noting that employees who strongly identify with corporate goals and corporate identity might actually be happier employees, as they might feel a harmony between what they do and what the organization expects them to do.

30.2.2 Corporate Discourses and the Outside World

If we look at public documents, brochures and websites of corporations in any sector across the world, there will be one dominant theme that they all will have in common: a positive self-image. Companies invest a great deal of time and resources into public relations (PR) activities whose main task is to create and communicate a positive self-understanding and reinforce the message that whatever activities a company engages with, the goals are desirable and pertain to "do" some social good. Literature in management and organizational studies describes it as organizational legitimacy (Suchman 1995).

Legitimacy is a key aspect of corporate reputation, which, in turn, can ensure competitive advantage and enhance organizational credibility and trustworthiness. Conversely, weak legitimacy and damaged reputation can weaken a corporation's status, making it vulnerable to scrutiny, which could pose a risk to business operations. It is therefore not surprising that the area of PR is at the heart of corporate workings.

There are two main streams of PR work in corporations: creation of a positive corporate image and dissemination of that image to both internal and external stakeholders. Since we have already touched upon employee branding as an example of internal PR work, this section focuses on communication with external audiences.

Corporate identity is normally understood as a set of values and beliefs that define the self-understanding of a corporation, that is, how the corporation perceives itself and how it wants to be perceived by its stakeholders and the wider world. Corporate identity can create a sense of cohesion and belonging not dissimilar to the ways in which national identity fosters an imagining of a larger community (Anderson 1991). Yet, as Breeze (2013) highlights, corporate identity differs considerably from national identity in that a corporation is purposefully created and managed by a few who are on top of the organizational hierarchy. Bottom-up redefinitions are rare, and those in lower ranks are seldom invited to participate in decision-making processes and to contribute to the formulation of corporate identity or image. Because these processes are, for the most part, created and negotiated through discourse, there is almost no official room for counter or oppositional discourses to emerge, meaning that discontent will be vented, if at all, in a back kitchen or private space. Corporate identity is essentially a top-down discursive process controlled, negotiated and strictly supervised by the top management (Breeze 2013). Its prime textual manifestation is the mission statement.

Many of the notions underlying corporate identity feed into the creation of a corporate image. Corporate image differs from corporate identity in that it is the representation of the company disseminated to its internal and external audiences. It is essentially a creation of perceptions about a company's products, services and strategies that a company desires to impress on its audiences. Company image is part of branding activities and, as such, is embedded in a complex ensemble of semiotic and symbolic practices directed at the creation of a unique and easily recognized brand, as a set of associations to engage consumers, influence their tastes and preferences and increase their loyalty. Whereas, in the industrial economies, branding focused on information about products and services, given the rise in mass production and mass consumerism in the twentieth century and the need for distinctiveness, branding nowadays emphasizes symbolic dimensions of products and services with corporations shifting their branding activities toward the management of emotions, images and ideas (Lischinsky 2018).

Corporations utilize a whole range of avenues to communicate with their audiences and to disseminate their image. From the corporations' perspective, the audiences are normally divided into internal and external stakeholders. Internal stakeholders include stakeholders directly involved in business operations such as investors, employees, customers and suppliers as well as shareholders. External audiences can be communities, governments and the public at large. Different types of document are produced to engage with different groups of stakeholders.

The primary tool of communication with investors and shareholders is the annual report, which is required by law. In its basic form, it includes information about the company's directors and its financial situation so that investors and shareholders know how the company is performing and can make informed decisions about whether to invest further or sell their shares. Although originally annual reports were intended as collections of hard financial data, increasingly they are evolving to become a kind of promotional tool (Breeze 2013). Beattie, Dhanani and Jones (2008) examined the changes in the structure and form of annual reports produced by UK firms over the last forty years and revealed a threefold increase in the number of pages, with voluntary material increasing faster than mandatory content. This increase has been accompanied by a significant rise of visual material, much of which is used to depict nonfinancial data. The authors conclude that, from being compact and "technical" documents, annual reports are evolving into PR materials. The increased multimodality of the annual report is observed in a study by Breeze (2013: 89–91) who investigated forty annual reports published in 2010 by different sectors. She notes the existence of diverse linguistic and semiotic features including linguistic and visual metaphors, prevalent representations of people and human faces, magazine-like designs, highlighting of key information using various fonts and colors, visual displays of financial data and inclusion of photographs of board members.

One of the most prominent parts of the annual report is the CEO letter, also known as the letter to shareholders. Its significance is emphasized by placing it at the beginning of the document. CEO letters have received a great deal of attention from discourse analysis. Using corpus tools and methods, Hyland (1998) examined metadiscourse in CEO letters produced by companies in Hong Kong. The study shows pervasiveness of emphatics, hedges and relational markers all used to project a positive image. Nickerson and De Groot (2005) compare CEOs' and Chairmen's statements in British English and Dutch annual reports and identified a number of similarities and differences. For example, projection of a positive image is common to both the CEO letter and the Chairman's statement. Yet, the authors also note that British CEOs tend to be more factual and informative, whereas Dutch CEOs seem to be more relational.

Combining genre analysis with corpus tools and methods, Rutherford (2005) studies word frequencies in whole annual reports in order to assess the effect of the Pollyanna principle, which presumes that positive, affirmative words are used more frequently than negative words. His analysis shows that, indeed, the Pollyanna principle is prevalent in the studied sample and deployed particularly frequently by poorly performing companies, possibly to disguise bad financial news. Adopting CDA, Merkl-Davies and Koller (2012) examined forms of impersonalization and evaluation in a chairman's statement in an annual report produced by a defense firm. The detailed analysis shows how passivization, nominalization and grammatical metaphors are purposefully deployed to obfuscate the relationship between causes and effects, playing a major role in presenting military violence as an essentially abstract entity.

Alongside mandatory disclosures, companies increasingly produce types of disclosure that are not required by law, including press releases, conference calls and corporate social responsibility (CSR) reports. Voluntary reporting of CSR, specifically, has been identified as the most dynamic practice of current corporate communications and an important means by which corporations attempt to influence public discourse and perceptions (Livesey 2002). The damaging effects of business practices on the environment, ecological sustainability, communities and employees began to feature in the media in the 1970s and have been continuing to grab public attention ever since. Increasingly, internal and external stakeholders demand more transparency and higher ethical standards. In response, companies have institutionalized CSR and begun to produce CSR reports, first in the form of shorter narratives included in annual reports and then, since the mid-1990s, as standalone reports. Originally, the focus of CSR reporting was on environmental matters, but gradually the reports have expanded to include a wider range of issues such as organizational governance, human rights, the environment, fair operating practices and community involvement (Bhatia 2012; Jaworska and Nanda 2018). Critics argue that CSR reporting gives prominence to planned CSR activities while we learn little about their impact (Vigneau, Humphreys and Moon 2014). Thus, the potential of CSR to contribute to the development of a sustainable future should not be overestimated. Nonetheless, research has shown that voluntary disclosures – making corporate plans and intentions public – can be challenged by stakeholders, the wider public and academic researchers, leading potentially to changes in business practices (e.g. Livesey and Kearins 2002).

Discourse analysis with a critical edge offers a useful analytical framework to reveal discursive devices and strategies that companies employ to create positive "spins" in constructing a socially and environmentally responsible image. Alexander's work (1999, 2009) is one of the first important contributions showing how two terms – "sustainable" and "sustainability" – were used in environmental reports produced by Shell in ways that erased the company's agency and responsibility. In this sense, "sustainability" becomes an elusive concept used to demonstrate "commitment" in a noncommittal way. Combining CDA with corpus linguistic tools and methods, Lischinsky (2011) investigated instances of self-reference in a corpus of fifty CSR reports issued by Swedish companies in 2009 and noted a prevalence of affiliative voices evidenced by the frequent use of affiliative pronouns *we* and *our*. In the view of the author, this creates a perception of unity which "fosters a view of the organisation as a cooperative whole, while maintaining a level of generality that hampers criticism and falsification" (Lischinsky 2011: 272).

The area in which discursive spins acquire prominence is in the context of crisis communication. Corporations often find themselves in a situation in which they have to respond to criticism or where there is a belief that a wrongdoing happened. A crisis situation can have a damaging effect on the corporation, especially if it affects the whole organization. Revealing a corporate wrongdoing is in the public interest and could potentially lead to important changes in business practices with positive social and ecological outcomes. Yet, from a corporation's point of view, a crisis is a threat to its organizational goals and its corporate image and reputation (Coombs 1998). Thus, companies invest a great deal of resources in crisis management, of which crisis communication is the key.

Responses to a crisis are a form of discourse (e.g. press release, statement in the annual report, letter to shareholders) and, for restoration of the company's image, much depends on that discourse. Crisis communicators use a range of different discourse strategies to repair the tarnished image, most of which will be defensive in nature and aimed at maintaining corporate legitimacy (Breeze 2013). These include nonexistence, distance, ingratiation, mortification and suffering (Benoit 1997; Coombs 1998). Corporations will normally choose a mix of strategies to respond to criticism depending also on the audiences (Creelman 2015). However, it seems that a true apology is the "hardest"; companies are reluctant to apologize publicly and will revert first to other strategies before they say sorry. This is because an apology essentially means accepting the responsibility which could delegitimize corporate goals and actions. This, in turn, could undermine trust and credibility, leading to a collapse of share prices and inviting lawsuits (Benoit 1997; Breeze 2013).

Breeze (2012) studied the discourse of legitimization in letters to stakeholders published in the annual reports of five leading oil companies following the environmental disaster in the Gulf of Mexico in 2010. Her analysis reveals that companies drew on the "survivor" and "lesson learned" narratives in order to restore a positive image of the industry and evoke solidarity on the part of stakeholders. Discursive strategies involved in the reestablishment of trust following the Deepwater Horizon spill in 2010 are also of interest to Fuoli and Paradis (2014). Analyzing the letter from BP's CEO, published in the 2010 annual report, the researchers demonstrate how the company attempted to rebuild trustworthiness by adopting two strategies: neutralizing the negative and emphasizing the positive.

In the same way in which digital technology has contributed to changes in some practices of business interactions (Darics 2015), it has also had an effect on practices of corporate communication with the wider world. The potential to address diverse audiences, including existing and potential customers, has made social media an incredibly useful platform for disseminating and enhancing a positive corporate self-image and expanding corporations' customer base (Creelman 2015). Social media are nowadays firmly integrated in corporate communications because they offer attractive and multimodal forms of self-presentation. Yet, social media are public tools with a high level of interactivity; the context collapses and ambient publics make it difficult to predict who the viewers and readers are (see Chapters 3 and 5 in this volume). This makes the content published on corporate social media accounts open to public scrutiny. Social media empower ambient publics to air their criticism, which can quickly become viral and grab the attention of offline media (Davis, Glantz and Novak 2016).

Research in business and management studies has dedicated much attention to exploring strategies of crisis management online with a view to devising best practices for social media communication (e.g. Austin and Yin 2018). Yet, this research mostly presumes that criticism expressed by ambient publics is threatening and needs to be managed in a way that poses minimal risks to organizations and their profitability, so that companies can continue "business as usual." Ambient criticism has the potential to disrupt this corporate mechanics and contribute to changes with wider societal and positive impacts. For example, Davis, Glantz and Novak (2016) have shown how a meme campaign *Let's Go*, instigated by Greenpeace against Shell's Arctic drilling, inspired and motivated the participation of the public at large. The campaign was based on creating memes mostly with an image of a polar bear and using Shell's corporate voice to ridicule Shell's justifications for the drilling in Alaska. Within a few days, the campaign went vital, with users contributing some 8800 (user-generated) memes. The campaign was successful in that it put pressure on Shell and made it stop Arctic drilling (at least for a while). This example shows how social media uses engage critically and creatively with problematic corporate policies and create counterdiscourses with the potential to change business-as-usual practice.

At the time of writing this chapter, the social networking giant Facebook was revealed as having violated consent decree by allowing a third party – a political consulting company, Cambridge Analytica – to harvest the personal data of nearly 50 million users. Once the news broke out, it created public outrage, which quickly spread on social media. It led to an online campaign with the hashtag #deletefacebook urging users to deactivate their Facebook accounts. The campaign secured support from high profile celebrities, authors and scientists. It is difficult to estimate how many people deleted their Facebook account because Facebook has refused to provide the data. Some estimates indicate that 10 percent of American users deactivated their Facebook profiles following the privacy breach.[2] The case has also demonstrated the tricks that technology

---

[2] http://uk.businessinsider.com/delete-facebook-statistics-nearly-10-percent-americans-deleted-facebook-account-study-2018-4.

companies such as Facebook and Google deploy to make it difficult for users to tune their settings to more private ones, with free choices being impeded and privacy-friendly settings kept hidden[3] (see Chapter 32 in this volume on surveillance mechanisms).

The ways in which corporations engage with audiences, whether on social media or through user privacy settings, are all discursive. Scrutinizing these discourses would shed light on linguistic choices that corporations make in order to persuade, dissuade and manipulate audiences to believe in "goodness" and the appropriateness of corporate actions. This, in turn, could raise consumers' awareness of corporate discourse spins and help them become more vigilant and thus empowered. Yet, discourse studies on corporate engagement with audiences are rare (cf. Creelman 2015).

30.3 Issues

Despite the importance and growing interest in corporate discourse, the area presents a niche in discourse analysis and there are several reasons for this, including practical, epistemological and ethical issues. Firstly, corporate discourses, especially discourses produced within corporations, are not easily accessible. Even if access is granted, which is rare, companies put strict legal requirements in place to control that access and restrict the ways in which data can be used and presented, which can be a daunting experience for academic researchers. Companies prioritize commercial and promotional needs and will be willing to engage in research only if it is likely to foster these needs and enhance their corporate credibility. My own research experience with a UK food retailer supports that companies will try to shape a research project in such a way as to suit them, insisting on quick delivery of results. We were repeatedly told that five months is, on a corporate timescale, "a million years!". The industry also has a certain degree of distrust in academia in that academic work is often perceived as being too abstract and disconnected from real-world problems (Koller 2018). For a critical academic researcher/discourse analyst, doing research with a corporate partner might feel simply uncomfortable on epistemological and practical grounds. However, I would not discourage discourse analysts from trying to engage with the industry, as any kind of involvement can bring us closer to the inner world of corporations that remains otherwise hidden.

Secondly, research using CDA does not sit comfortably with corporate ethos and goals. The aim of CDA is to uncover discourse practices that are grounded in unequal power relations and are persuasive or manipulative, in short, the kind of practices that do not present corporations in the best

---

[3] www.bbc.co.uk/news/technology-44642569.

light and could "stain" their positive self-image. This partially explains why companies are less willing to grant access to internal communications, because this could be seen as a potential "infiltration." Researchers interested in corporate practices tend to revert then to documents that companies publish for wider audiences, such as annual and CSR reports. These are, however, carefully composed, "controlled" and polished text types written to boost the collective corporate identity and a positive self-image. Even texts that are written from a personal perspective such as the CEO letter or a testimony are carefully composed to strengthen the collective ethos and positive self-representation (Breeze 2013). We may then reasonably ask what new aspects an analysis of such texts would bring to our understanding of corporate discourses? Despite the uniformity of the corporate voice that permeates such texts, they give corporations "ample opportunities for reality construction" (Pollach 2018: 2) including around social and environmental issues. Writers of such texts have a wide pool of linguistic and discursive choices at their disposal. Yet, they "prefer" certain choices over others and, in doing so, construct the issues in a way that reflects practices and ideologies established in the corporate world working to serve the needs of that world (cf. van Dijk 1995). Studying corporate "reality constructions" can shed light on the ideologies underpinning corporate attitudes toward critical societal and environmental matters with the possibility of generating some accountability (Jaworska 2018).

Thirdly, there is the issue of crossing to the "dark side." Discourse analytical research into, for example, branding can shed light on a range of linguistic features that make a brand successful or less successful. Thus, this research might unintentionally engage in "reverse engineering" (Beattie 2014: 128) and deliver "tools" that could contribute to the perpetuation of problematic business-as-usual practices and be implicitly involved in their legitimization (Fairclough 1992; Koller 2018). On the other hand, the professional field of branding and advertising can be an attractive career option for linguists; linguistic expertise is increasingly sought by corporations looking to enhance their corporate communication, PR and branding (Koller 2018). Increasingly, departments of (applied) linguistics flag these areas as important employment opportunities for graduates in their own PR activities such as open days. We need to remember that, in such settings, discourse is essentially seen as an instrument that needs to bring about effects that contribute to operational and commercial goals. Again, this raises an ethical dilemma specifically for (critical) discourse analysts who see this use of discourse as an ideological "abuse" and write and teach about the need for critical language awareness (Mautner 2010). Being too critical and challenging corporate beliefs can have unpleasant consequences for an employee, and it is also unlikely to dramatically change the modus operandi of corporations. Should we then stop teaching students, that is, future professionals about the importance of criticality and critical language awareness? The answer is no; if anything, we should increase our efforts to show them how using discourse can "convey empathy, courtesy and professionalism without mimicking the customer-service discourse of the commercial sector" (Mautner 2010: 184).

30.4 Implications

The question of what the implications of investigating corporate discourses are goes back to the question of why to do this kind of research. I hope that this chapter has shown that exploring corporate discourses is necessary if we want to understand how powerful corporate organizations are and how they maintain and exercise that power. This is important not only from a purely discursive point of view; it has much more fundamental implications. The principles that corporations endorse, such as individualism, competition, utilitarianism and promotionalism, are not just integral to corporate organizations; they are becoming all-encompassing and "accepted" values that are increasingly colonizing public and private spheres. CDA research by Mautner (2010), Zhang and O'Halloran (2013) and Ledin and Machin (2015) provides strong evidence for this corporate colonization of public institutions and spaces, as manifested in their discursive practices being gradually "copied" from the corporate world. Studying corporate discourse will show us what the tendencies of this discourse are and alert us to the ways in which corporate values increasingly attempt to govern us and society at large. Why is this important? As Breeze (2013: 190) concludes, the principles which underlie corporate modus operandi, such as utilitarianism and consumerism, reduce "the human being to the economic sphere, where having is more than being." The human begin itself turns into a (human) resource and commodity. As Fromm reminds us (1978), life is not a business deal; it is a being, and as such nothing other than a form of self-realization and actualization of potentiality. Work assumes an important part in our life in that it helps us achieve some of that potentiality together with others, which, in turn, gives us dignity and satisfaction. Studying corporate discourse from a discourse-analytical perspective can help us learn to read the corporate text and talk in order to reveal the mechanics of corporate persuasion or dissuasion. Adding a critical understanding could help position our values and beliefs against the corporate rhetoric and, when necessary, help us challenge or reject it, so that we are not that easily turned into a mere resource. As Koller (2018: 17) stresses, "while intervening in a company's discourse does not change the broad economic structures in which it operates, any increase in respect towards, and agency for, stakeholders is to be welcomed."

In more practical terms, discourse analytical investigations of corporate text and talk can offer insights contributing to the creation of a more positive, collegial and balanced work environment. Research by Baxter (2010) on female leadership, which led her to formulate recommendations on how female managers could communicate to overcome certain gender barriers and stereotypes, is an indicative example of such practical and highly relevant implications.

30.5 Future Directions

This overview of the topic has shown that discourse analysts exploring corporate discourses have studied a range of talk and text types including internal and external communications. They have also approached the topic with a variety of research methods established in discourse analysis, including conversation analysis, genre analysis, interactional sociolinguistics, CDA and corpus linguistics. Nonetheless, future research on corporate discourses would benefit from expanding its portfolio of methods and data sources.

First, multimodality is a pervasive aspect of corporate discourse and yet, studies on corporate discourses that combine textual and visual analysis are few and far between. Multimodal discourse analysis has been adopted to study advertising. However, other corporate branding activities and even texts such as annual reports that originally were just compilations of words and numbers are increasingly becoming multimodal. Taking multimodality as an analytical framework would enrich future research on corporate discourse, showing how both the visual and the textual elements work together as means of corporate persuasion. Research by Ledin and Machin (2015, 2017) offers useful directions here.

Most research on corporate discourse has focused on the ways in which corporations engage with stakeholders, including internal and external audiences. It is now time to explore how the audiences engage with and respond to this kind of discourse. Investigating users' responses on social media could provide ample opportunities for researching such engagements. As the example of the *Let's Go* campaign by Greenpeace has shown, social media users do not necessarily "buy" into the corporate propaganda. What is more, they recontextualize it in creative and critical ways that can actually instigate a change in corporate practices. We need to expand the research agenda by exploring such online grassroot practices in more depth. The notions of entextualization (Bauman and Briggs 1990) and intertextuality (Bakhtin 1986) can offer useful analytical anchors here. Finally, experimental studies into readers' responses to corporate discourse could offer further cognitive insights into the ways in which corporate discourse persuades or dissuades. Fuoli and Hart's (2018) work on readers' responses to corporate trust-building strategies is an indicative step in this direction.

30.6 Summary

Corporations are powerful entities whose values and beliefs are increasingly encroaching on and enveloping public and private spheres, defining the roles and identities within these spheres. It is in our interest and in the interest of our students (future professionals) that we critically scrutinize the kinds of discourse that corporations produce, challenge them and, if possible, create a counterdiscourse to empower individuals. We also need to show how discourse can be used not just for the purpose of self-praise or persuasion but also as a means of creating a professional, equal and collegial workplace in which people can realize their individual potential.

Further Reading

Breeze, R. (2013). *Corporate Discourse*. London: Bloomsbury.

Using a combination of CDA and corpus linguistics, this volume offers comprehensive insights into the ways in which discourse constructs and maintains corporate identity and relationships with internal and external audiences. A wide range of written genres produced by corporations are explored in depth.

Darics, E. and Koller, V. (2018). *Language in Business, Language at Work*. London: Palgrave Higher Education.

This book presents an excellent introduction to the role of language in many facets of business communication including stakeholder communication, brand narratives and management of conflict and self-branding. Each topic is discussed in an engaging way by drawing on a range of authentic examples.

References

Alexander, R. J. (1999). Ecological Commitments in Business: A Computer-Corpus-Based Critical Discourse Analysis. In J. Verschueren (ed.) *Language and Ideology: Selected Papers from the 6th International Pragmatics Conference*. Antwerp: International Pragmatics Association. 14–24.

(2009). *Framing Discourse on the Environment*. New York: Routledge.

Alvesson, M. and Kärreman, D. (2000). Varieties of Discourse: On the Study of Organizations through Discourse Analysis. *Human Relations* 53(9): 1125–49.

Anderson, B. (1991). *Imagined Communities*, 2nd ed. London: Verso.

Austin, L. and Yin, J. (2018). *Social Media and Crisis Communication*. New York/London: Routledge.

Bakhtin, M. (1986). *Speech Genres and Other Late Essays*. Austin: University of Texas Press.

Bargiela-Chiappini, F., Nickerson, C. and Planken, B. (2007). *Business Discourse*. Basingstoke: Palgrave Macmillan.

Bauman, R. and Briggs, C. (1990). Poetics and Performance as Critical Perspectives on Language and Social Life. *Annual Review of Anthropology* 19: 59–88.

Baxter. J. (2010). *The Language of Female Leadership*. Basingstoke: Palgrave Macmillan.

Beattie, V. (2014). Accounting Narratives and the Narrative Turn in Accounting Research: Issues, Theory, Methodology, Methods and a Research Framework. *British Accounting Review* 46: 111–34.

Beattie, V., Dhanani, A. and Jones, M. J. (2008). Investigating Presentational Change in UK Annual Reports. *Journal of Business Communication* 45(2): 181–222.

Benoit, W. L. (1997). Image Repair Discourse and Crisis Communication. *Public Relations Review* 23(2): 177–86.

Bhatia, A. (2012). The Corporate Social Responsibility Report: The Hybridization of a "Confused" Genre (2007–2011). *IEEE Transactions on Professional Communication* 55(3): 221–38.

Boden, D. (1994). *The Business of Talk: Organizations in Action*. London: Polity Press.

Breeze, R. (2012). Legitimation in Corporate Discourse: Oil Corporations after Deepwater Horizon. *Discourse & Society* 23(1): 3–18.

(2013). *Corporate Discourse*. London: Bloomsbury.

Chaika, E. (1982). *Language: The Social Mirror*. Rowley, MA: Newbury House.

Coombs, W. T. (1998). An Analytic Framework for Crisis Situations: Better Responses from a Better Understanding of the Situation. *Journal of Public Relations Research* 10(3): 177–91.

Creelman, V. (2015). Sheer Outrage: Negotiating Customer Dissatisfaction and Interaction in the Blogosphere. In E. Darics (ed.) *Digital Business Discourse*. Basingstoke: Palgrave Macmillan. 160–85.

Darics, E. (2013). Non-verbal Signalling in Digital Discourse: The Case of Letter Repetition. *Discourse, Context & Media* 2(3): 141–8.

(2015). *Digital Business Discourse*. Basingstoke: Palgrave Macmillan.

Davis, C. B., Glantz, M. and Novak, D. R. (2016). You Can't Run Your SUV on Cute. Let's Go!: Internet Memes as Delegitimizing Discourse. *Environmental Communication* 10(1): 62–83.

Dennis, A. R., Rennecker, J. A. and Hansen, S. (2010). Invisible Whispering: Restructuring Collaborative Decision Making with Instant Messaging. *Decision Sciences* 41(4): 845–86.

Ellsworth, R. (2002). *Leading with Purpose: The New Corporate Realities*. Stanford, CA: Stanford University Press.

Fairclough, N. (1992). Introduction. In N. Fairclough (ed.) *Critical Language Awareness*. Harlow: Longman. 1–29.

Fromm. E. (1978). *To Have or to Be?* London: Abacus.

Fuoli, M. and Hart, C. (2018). Trust-Building Strategies in Corporate Discourse: An Experimental Study. *Discourse & Society* 29(5). https://doi.org/10.1177/0957926518770264.

Fuoli, M. and Paradis, C. (2014). A Model of Trust-Repair Discourse. *Journal of Pragmatics* 74: 52–69.

Garrett, R. K. and Danziger, J. N. (2007). IM = Interruption Management? Instant Messaging and Disruption in the Workplace. *Journal of Computer-Mediated Communication* 13(1): 23–42.

Gee, J. P. (2014). *An Introduction to Discourse Analysis: Theory and Method*, 4th ed. London: Routledge.

Gimenez, J. (2000). Business E-mail Communication: Some Emerging Tendencies in Register. *English for Specific Purposes* 19(3): 237–51.

Goffman, E. (1971). *The Presentation of Self in Everyday Life*. Harmondsworth: Penguin.

Handford, M. (2010). *The Language of Business Meetings*. Cambridge: Cambridge University Press.

Holmes, J. (2000). Doing Collegiality and Keeping Control at Work: Small Talk in Government Departments. In J. Coupland (ed.) *Small Talk*. London: Longman. 32–61.

Holmes, J. and Marra, M. (2004). Relational Practice in the Workplace: Women's Talk or Gendered Discourse? *Language in Society* 33: 377–98.

Holmes, J. and Stubbe, M. (2003). *Power and Politeness in the Workplace*. Upper Saddle River, NJ: Pearson Education.

Hyland, K. (1998). Exploring Corporate Rhetoric: Metadiscourse in the CEO's Letter. *Journal of Business Communication* 35(2): 224–45.

Incelli, E. (2013). Managing Discourse in Intercultural Business Email Interactions: A Case Study of a British and Italian Business Transaction. *Journal of Multilingual and Multicultural Development* 34(6): 515–32.

Jaworska, S. (2018). Change but No Climate Change: Discourses of Climate Change in Corporate Social Responsibility Reporting in the Oil Industry. *International Journal of Business Communication* 55(2): 194–219.

Jaworska. S. and Nanda, A. (2018). Doing Well by Talking Good? A Topic Modelling-Assisted Discourse Study of Corporate Social Responsibility. *Applied Linguistics* 39(3): 373–99.

Jay, T. (2000). *Why We Curse: A Neuro-psycho-social Theory of Speech*. Philadelphia, PA: John Benjamins.

Koester, A. (2006). *Investigating Workplace Discourse*. London: Routledge.

Koller, V. (2018). Language Awareness and Language Workers. *Language Awareness* 27(1–2): 4–20.

Lampi, M. (1986). *Linguistic Components of Strategy in Business Negotiations*, Studies B-85. Helsinki: Helsinki School of Economics.

Ledin, P. and Machin, D. (2015). The Semiotics of Modernist Space in the Branding of Corporations: A Multimodal Critical Discourse Analytic Approach. *International Journal of Marketing Semiotics* 3: 19–38.

(2017). The Neoliberal Definition of "Elite Space" in IKEA Kitchens. *Social Semiotics* 27(3): 323–34.

Lischinsky, A. (2011). The Discursive Construction of a Responsible Corporate Self. In A. E. Sjölander and J. Gunnarson Payne (eds.) *Tracking Discourses: Politics, Identity and Social Change*. Lund: Nordic Academic Press. 257–85.

(2018). Critical Discourse Studies and Branding. In J. Flowerdew and J. Richardson (eds.) *The Routledge Handbook of Critical Discourse Analysis*. London: Routledge. 540–52.

Livesey, S. (2002). Global Warming Wars: Rhetorical and Discourse Analytic Approaches to Exxonmobil's Corporate Public Discourse. *Journal of Business Communication* 39(1): 117–48.

Livesey, S. and Kearins, K. (2002). Transparent and Caring Corporations? A Study of Sustainability Reports by the Body Shop and Royal Dutch/Shell. *Organisation and Environment* 15(3): 233–58.

Mak, B. C. N. and Lee, C. (2015). Swearing Is E-business: Expletives in Instant Messaging in Hong Kong Workplaces. In E. Darics (ed.) *Digital Business Discourse*. Basingstoke: Palgrave Macmillan. 122–41.

Mautner, G. (2010). *Language and the Market Society: Critical Reflections on Discourse and Dominance*. New York: Routledge.

Merkl-Davies, D. M. and Koller, V. (2012). "Metaphoring" People out of this World: A Critical Discourse Analysis of a Chairman's Statement of a Defence Firm. *Accounting Forum* 36(3): 178–93.

Mullany, J. L. (2007). *Gendered Discourse in Professional Communication*. Basingstoke: Palgrave Macmillan.

Neeley, T. (2012). Global Business Speaks English. *Harvard Business Review*, https://hbr.org/2012/05/global-business-speaks-english.

Nickerson, C. and de Groot, E. (2005). Dear Shareholder, Dear Stockholder, Dear Stakeholder: The Business Letter Genre in the Annual General Report. In P. Gillaerts and M. Gotti (eds.) *Genre Variation in Business Letters*. Bern: Peter Lang. 325–46.

Pollach, I. (2018). Issue Cycles in Corporate Sustainability Reporting: A Longitudinal Study. *Environmental Communication* 12(2): 247–60.

Quan-Haase, A., Cothrel, J. and Wellman, B. (2005). Instant Messaging for Collaboration: A Case Study of a High-Tech Firm. *Journal of Computer-Mediated Communication* 10(4): JCMC10413. https://doi.org/10.1111/j.1083-6101.2005.tb00277.x.

Rutherford, B. A. (2005). Genre Analysis of Corporate Annual Report Narratives: A Corpus Linguistics-Based Approach. *Journal of Business Communication* 42(4): 349–78.

Scollon, R., Scollon, S. and Jones, R. (2012). *Intercultural Communication*, 3rd ed. Malden, MA: Wiley-Blackwell.

Suchman, M. C. (1995). Managing Legitimacy: Strategic and Institutional Approaches. *Academy of Management Review* 20(3): 571–610.

Van Dijk, T. A. (1995). Discourse Semantics as Ideology. *Discourse & Society* 6(2): 243–89.

Vigneau, L., Humphreys, M. and Moon, J. (2014). How Do Firms Comply with International Sustainability Standards? Processes and Consequences of Adopting the Global Reporting Initiative. *Journal of Business Ethics* 131(2): 469–86.

Wenger, E. (1998). *Communities of Practice: Learning, Meaning, and Identity*. Cambridge: Cambridge University Press.

Zhang, Y. and O'Halloran, K. L. (2013). "Toward a Global Knowledge Enterprise": University Websites as Portals to the Ongoing Marketization of Higher Education. *Critical Discourse Studies* 10(4): 468–85.

31

Mediatized Communication and Linguistic Reflexivity in Contemporary Public and Political Life

Cedric Deschrijver

31.1 Introduction

In an age saturated with developments in communications technology, getting to grips with the most recent developments in online discourse, let alone predicting future ones, becomes a daunting task. From a discourse-analytical perspective, we need at our disposal a general framework to macroscopically investigate globally occurring technological shifts and innovations in communication, but one that is at the same time amenable to particular contexts and attentive to locally situated shifting linguistic features.

The concept of "mediatization" constitutes a good candidate for the task sketched above. At first sight, "mediatization" lends itself to a literal, albeit very general, gloss: a state resulting from becoming part of media communications. As this bare-bones definition would suggest, the necessary complementary parts have been conceptualized in various ways, emphasizing different aspects of (media) communication and its role in contemporary society. Indeed, across social sciences, "mediatization" is a concept with many understandings and applications, a situation that may partly be ascribed to the concept's ambitious scope, especially in communications studies. It has been suggested to denote an all-enveloping metaprocess (e.g. Krotz 2007; Krotz and Hepp 2013) that could initiate "a paradigmatic shift within media and communication research" (Hepp, Hjarvard and Lundby 2015: 315). At the same time, "mediatization" also "lacks … an exact definition" (Knoblauch 2013: 297), engendering debates on the concept's validity for academic research.

This chapter argues that a clear conceptualization of the concept makes it a highly suitable basis for discourse-analytical research. While it is beyond the current contribution to exhaustively discuss all conceptualizations of "mediatization," Section 31.2 will provide a bird's eye view of the most common conceptualizations, applications and their implications. It will also discuss how different traditions of mediatization research may be integrated to discourse-analytical investigations. Specifically, it argues there is a wide scope for discourse-analytical research to closely engage with the linguistic-anthropological tradition of mediatization research and its focus on linguistic reflexivity. Section 31.3 identifies unresolved issues in mediatization research, after which implications for future research are discussed in Section 31.4. As the subjects of mediatization frameworks are changing rapidly, Section 31.5 anticipates future trends in communications media and how discourse-analytical investigations should engage with them.

It should at the outset be noted that "mediatization" and "mediation" have at times been treated as synonymous (e.g. Couldry 2008). Yet it is worthwhile in a discourse-analytical context to maintain a conceptual separation. In contrast to "mediatization," "mediation" is a basic feature of communication, referring to the "dialogic process which involves the movement of meanings and ideas between people" (Jaffe 2011: 564). While modern media technologies may enter acts of mediation, they are by no means a prerequisite for them. Since "mediation" is valid in a wider variety of communicative contexts, the "mediation"–"mediatization" distinction should not be forfeited in a discourse-analytical tradition.

31.2 Mediatization: An Overview

31.2.1 Traditions of Mediatization Research

Hepp (2014) distinguishes institutional vs. social-constructionist conceptualizations of mediatization research. **Institutional mediatization research** conceptualizes media as "more or less independent social institutions with own sets of rules" (Hepp 2014: 51), exerting (material and discursive) influence on society, social domains or on everyday interaction and social relations (cf. Schrott 2009). These investigations often refer to the concept of "media logic," which denotes "the assumptions and processes for constructing messages within a particular medium" (Altheide 2004: 294), including choice of topic coverage and ways of presentation. Increasingly, social affairs would be influenced by, and shaped toward, the logic of media as a social institution (Hjarvard 2008b).

Though this "media logic" should not be conceived of as "deterministic" (Altheide and Snow 1992: 467), an institutional understanding of mediatization nevertheless implies causality, with media features (such as linguistic form, topic or interest) affecting, indeed "mediatizing," societal domains (cf. Couldry 2008: 376–7).

The causality implied in institutional understandings of mediatization constitutes the main difference with **social-constructionist approaches**, which embed the concept in "the process of a communicative construction of socio-cultural reality" (Hepp 2014: 51). Specifically, mediatization in this tradition refers to how processes of communicative construction manifest themselves in media representations, as well as the role of various media in the communicative construction. Compared to institutional understandings, the emphasis lies on the spread of various media platforms in everyday life, rather than on the influence of particular institutional media logics. Supplanting the media-society causal relation with a more complex network of interactions (cf. Krotz 2009), the focus of social-constructionist mediatization research shifts to the production and circulation of certain practices that are "specifically tied to the expansion and differentiation of communication media" (Androutsopoulos 2014: 12; cf. Couldry and Hepp 2013).

Despite the generally accepted distinction between institutional and social-constructionist understandings of mediatization, their difference is arguably one of focus, rather than one of incompatible theoretical positions. Hepp (2013, 2014) signals a renewed rapprochement between the two branches, and logically they share several assumptions. On the one hand, both understandings rely on the assumption that communicative action effectuates changes in society. Institutional mediatization research also acknowledges that the influence of media institutions is co-constructed through interaction with audiences in specific communicative configurations (cf. Altheide 2013; Lundby 2009). On the other hand, social-constructionist traditions of mediatization cannot fully escape integrating aspects of institutional understandings into their analysis. While their focus lies on the interrelation between changing media and sociocultural shifts, they attach significance to how (features of) media serve as "first-movers" in the complex web of interactions (cf. Hepp 2014: 52). The distinction between society/culture and media reflects the latter's analytical separation from the former, implying media's special status in the web of interactions at the basis of sociocultural reality. As such, both "approaches share a ... constructivist understanding of ... the media in creating social reality" (Adolf 2011: 167), and prioritize various forms of media as an analytical site.

A third and final tradition of mediatization research may be termed a **linguistic-anthropological** or **sociolinguistic** tradition of mediatization research. Compared to the institutional and social-constructionist approaches, works in this tradition place a more sustained emphasis on localized potentials for meaning-making. This makes them especially amenable to investigate mediatization in varying local and shifting contexts.

In Agha's definition, mediatization refers to "institutional practices that reflexively link processes of communication to processes of commoditization" (2011c: 163).[1] As Androutsopoulos explains, both social-constructionist approaches to mediatization and that of Agha are "interested in the interface between mediation ... and the mass dissemination of standardi[z]ed messages" (2014: 12). The main difference lies in that the former formulates mediatization as a social theory, and the latter as a more general account of language use and semiotic processes. In this sense, the link between communication and commoditization, though highly salient in new and social media, counts on a long precedent. Agha situates the rising importance of mediatization in fifteenth to sixteenth-century Europe with the emergence of mass-produced printed books, though examples of mediatization may be found far before this moment. In contrast to institutional mediatization research, consequently, the linguistic-anthropological tradition sees mass media as constituting only one set of influential institutional practices.

A second difference with social-constructionist understandings of mediatization lies in the linguistic-anthropological strand's emphasis on the *reflexive* linking of communication to commoditization (cf. Section 31.2.3). This, it is argued, provokes a massive increase in the "scale of production and dissemination of messages across a population," which in turn inflates the number of possible stances and interpretations people can orient to in contemporary communicative encounters. Indeed, "mediatized moments provide massively parallel inputs to recontextualization" (Agha 2011c: 167). *Recontextualization* may be understood as the extraction of media fragments from their original contexts for use in another context, which may "involve formal, functional, and semantic modifications" (Androutsopoulos 2014: 20). Since the interpretation, uptake and recontextualization of (fragments of) one widely-spread message need not be homogeneous, this may in turn engender further recontextualizations and, thus, idiosyncratic, individualized or locally situated uptakes.

31.2.2 (Institutional) Mediatization and Critical Discourse Analysis

Research employing mediatization conceptualized through an institutional or social-constructionist focus has often investigated the mediatization of particular spheres in society. Varying between an exclusively institutional and a more social-constructionist focus, this research includes mediatization of consumption and tourism (Jansson 2002), of the military and their media output (Maltby 2012), of scientific output (Rödder and Schäfer 2010), of Israeli law (Peleg and Bogoch 2012), of

---

[1] Commoditization should be understood as the process by which "varieties of communicative action are treated as commodities" (Agha 2011b: 176). Commoditization may also apply to various artifacts or signs (cf. Agha 2011a).

fashion online (Skjulstad 2009), of religion (Hjarvard 2008a) and of journalism (Kammer 2013).

Insofar as these studies contain a focus on discourse, the focus is an uneven one and, with some exceptions, discourse-analytic methods are not particularly well-represented in research on the mediatization of particular societal domains. Instead, this type of mediatization research employs methods such as interviews, source interpretation, content analysis and sociological enquiry. Yet many of the questions that concern institutional mediatization research have been previously addressed by scholars in (critical) discourse studies. They also emphasized the influence of media representations and political speech on social life (in the promotion/reinforcement of ideologies), as well as connecting changing features of social and media landscapes to shifting linguistic features (e.g. marketization and conversationalization, Fairclough 1993). Other work, especially in the tradition of the discourse-historical approach, has systematically investigated allusions and (linguistic) presuppositions in political discourse (e.g. Wodak 2007), in order to draw attention to socially influential features of media discourse.

The theoretical position of much research in (critical) discourse studies approaches that of institutional mediatization research, but in comparison to the latter, discourse studies have been more systematic in analyzing linguistic features (such as passivizations or argumentation techniques) of the social trends they wish to analyze. Yet there are a number of exceptions in institutional mediatization research that further demonstrate the usefulness of discourse-analytical methodologies. Strömbäck and Dimitrova (2011), for instance, focus on linguistic indicators in assessing the mediatization of political news coverage. They identify the length of soundbites, the visibility of journalists in the reporting or how politics is linguistically framed as a strategic game or race. Falasca (2014), investigating journalistic frames employed in election coverage, shows that the framing of politics as a strategic game is connected to the extent of mediatization in reporting during election campaigns. It is not difficult to envisage further discourse-analytical support in researching these linguistic indicators. Conversation analysis, for instance, would be well-suited to investigate the role and interactional dominance of a reporter in certain coverage, while frameworks of (critical) metaphor analysis (cf. Charteris-Black 2004) are well-equipped to delve into the metaphorical portrayal of political events.

31.2.3 Linguistic-Anthropological Mediatization Research and Discourse Analysis

In conceptualizing mediatization as the reflexive linking of commoditization with communication, the analytical emphasis of linguistic-anthropological mediatization research will lie on ever-changing and ever-expanding media (in the sense of "mediums") rather than on merely one part of media communications (such as mass media). Of highest importance will be the rising complexity of mediation, engendering more complex forms of user engagement and uptake of mediatized communication.

Though this emphasis is also present in social-constructionist frameworks, linguistic-anthropological frameworks are better suited to incorporate discourse-analytical methods for two reasons. On the one hand, a linguistic-anthropological understanding extends the concept's applicability to a wider variety of contexts, as the framework is rooted in general processes of mediation rather than in a particular social theory.

On the other hand, the linguistic-anthropological view of mediatization has linguistic reflexivity at its heart. As detailed in works such as Lucy (1993), Silverstein (1993) and Verschueren (2000), all language use is characterized by linguistic reflexivity or, in an alternative formulation, it operates along a metapragmatic dimension. Both concepts denote that language (use) always refers to itself to varying degrees, from highly implicitly to highly explicitly. (For instance, the clause "your last mention of the term 'mediatization'" contains (i) an explicit metalinguistic reference to the term "mediatization," (ii) the explicitly metacommunicative "mention," (iii) the implicitly reflexive deictic relations engendered by "your" and "last," all of which are operating in dense relations of indexicality.) The related concept of metapragmatic awareness may rudimentarily be described as the fact that "language users know more or less what they are doing when using language" to different degrees (Verschueren 1999: 187 and cf. 2000).

In the current context of mediatization research, mediatization involves the "[reflexive linking] ... of communication to processes of commoditization" (Agha 2011c cf. Section 4.1). Much like language refers to itself to varying degrees of explicitness, mediatized communication similarly makes its (reflexive) links to "commodity formulations salient" to varying degrees (Agha 2011c: 163). If many people consistently orient to specific fragments and features of communication, this gives rise to persistent reflexive formulations. As an example, people may orient to a notion such as "media," where "*the media* is treated as a punctate agentive sender of messages whose audience is their *receiver*" (Agha 2011c: 164; emphasis in original). Though the accuracy of such a formulation is up for debate, the metapragmatic formulation of "media" constitutes an indicator of participants' experiences of mediatized communication, backgrounding other fragments in communication processes.

The link between (i) reflexive formulations about mediatized settings of communication and (ii) linguistic reflexivity as a feature of all language use makes linguistic-anthropological conceptualizations of mediatization especially relevant to discourse-analytical research. Indicators of metapragmatic awareness that come to the fore through discourse-analytical methods will provide an insight both into (i) how participants in semiotic/linguistic encounters conceive of their linguistic actions (such as their appropriateness to a particular setting) as well as into (ii) emic views on the potentially commoditized nature of the communication they are engaged in.

Briggs (2011), for instance, undertakes an analysis of how information about a (relatively harmless) virus is disseminated by health professionals through various mediatized channels. Specifically, his research, grounded in ethnography, analyses "how different participants culturally construct the game in which they see themselves as playing" (Briggs 2011: 218). He demonstrates how, in an attempt to reach a wider audience, health professionals adapt their messages according to their own knowledge and conception of media practices. This is a clear instance of mediatization at work, as the research demonstrates both language users' reflexive models of their communicative actions and their views on, and ideological norms about, achieving influence through mediatized communication.

Similar metapragmatic assessments are inevitably held by actors central to mass mediated communications, who will construct their own interpretations of media communication and its societal role and influence. Linguistic and discourse-analytical investigations focused on these interpretations and assessments, in turn, may reveal how shifting media constellations affect participants' own understandings of communication, as well as how they come to interpret, and orient to, the linguistic elements therein. Peng (2018), for instance, analyzes metapragmatic assessments of speech styles of Taiwanese vs. mainland China's Mandarin Chinese. The author identifies mutually interlocked trends of (i) shifting mainland China language ideologies about Taiwanese Chinese and (ii) Taiwanese television shows' changing use of particular speech styles in anticipating their mainland Chinese audiences and their (metapragmatic) expectations.

Van Hout and Burger (2017) discuss print news journalists' metapragmatic assessments of their own practices. The authors investigate "text bite news": short quotes of political figures that journalists reproduce alongside their own short (varyingly metapragmatic) comments. As the authors explain, "the [politicians'] quotes speak through recontextualization – that is, through the inflection of prior discourse with new meanings" (2017: 464), such as approval, irony or mockery on the part of the journalists. Yet the journalists' assessments of politicians' quotes are themselves revealing of underlying language-ideological and media-ideological assumptions. Where a political figure is critical of news media, for instance, their quotes are consistently negatively assessed by the commenting journalists, who also strictly demarcate their own practices from those alleged in the quote. As such, the "journalists impose [a media logic] on political actors seeking media attention or whose public discourse triggers media coverage" (2017: 481), recoverable through an analytical focus on metapragmatics.

In the same way, mediatization research may bring to light shifting assessments of varieties and genres of language use in a particular setting. Squires and Iorio (2014), for instance, analyze the extent that, and the way in which, tweets are quoted in news reports. In the timeframe between 2006 and 2011, they find that the perceived novelty of Twitter as a medium decreased. Concurrently, the presence of tweets in the news became more commonplace. At the same time, Twitter continued to be framed as a distinct medium of communication, whose language norms are metapragmatically judged to be distinct from those of the news outlet. In terms of journalists' assessments, while Twitter has generally become more accepted as a journalistic source, this is not the case for "acceptance of vernacular language practices 'native' to tweets" (Squires and Iorio 2014: 357). As mentioned earlier in this section, the metapragmatic focus of Squires and Iorio's (2014) study reveals both emic assessments of what constitutes "appropriate" language to certain participants and ideas about the utility and commoditized nature of communication (*in casu*, Twitter).

The same insights may be gained in offline contexts of media production through, for instance, analyzing news practitioners' statements about their own language use. By examining their navigation of linguistic choices, as Cotter (2014: 392) does, one gains "insight[s] into the news community's attitudes toward language use, the moral judgments that attend them, and the broader dimension of society's attitudes towards [news practitioners]." As consequences of processes of mediatization, these metapragmatic statements provide a first key to making sense of media developments and changing styles and modes of communication.

As these examples show, a linguistic-anthropological mediatization framework may highly fruitfully be applied to communicative contexts related to news media. Yet its relevance also lies beyond these contexts, as demonstrated by Cole and Pellicer (2012). These authors analyze the (metapragmatically informative) uptake formulations of a speech by Hillary Clinton in an Alabaman church during the 2007 US Democratic Primaries. The speech contained elements of "black preaching style" and was "favorably evaluated" by participants of the original communicative speech event (Cole and Pellicer 2012: 450). Subsequent to the speech, however, processes of mediatization allowed nonparticipants to recontextualize fragments of the event. These recontextualizations and re-evaluations rarely preserved elements of the original audience uptake; instead, they widely suggested that Clinton's use of the stylistic features was affected, mocking or fake. In turn, audiences were able not only to reinterpret the original communicative event and reassess its reception but also to produce normative guidelines on how any future uptake should (re)evaluate the original event (Cole and Pellicer 2012: 464).

Discourse-analytical attention to manifestations of metapragmatic awareness in a mediatization framework, then, "makes visible the multiple and varied forms, functions, and ideologies that continue to exist alongside their dominant counterparts" (Cole and Pellicer 2012: 465). It reveals potentially dominant language ideologies, yet also draws attention to multiple alternate forms of uptake. As Cole and Pellicer (2012) argue, though this increase in possible uptake formulations will not be free from the influence of societal power relations, nor will it be preordained or predictable.

Finally, a focus on metapragmatics is of especial importance in the context of online communication. As argued by, for instance, Thurlow and Poff (2013), the absence of nontextual contextualization cues in certain contexts of online communication may enhance language users' metapragmatic awareness. Textual cues and properties will also become more important in processes of alignment and identity formation (e.g. Georgakopoulou 1997) to make up for the lack of paralinguistic and embodied elements in text-based online discourse.

The same observation may also be extended to (more commonly occurring) multimodal electronic communication. Marshall (2015) draws attention to the "mediatization of the self" (based on a social-constructionist conceptualization of the term). Through this process, individuals will, to an ever-increasing extent, monitor their actions, online and offline, with the aim of creating a presentable, popular public persona through online means. They will do this by "constantly preening the various texts, images and media elements that [they] share with others" (Marshall 2015: 130). Not only does this imply that language users will adapt their texts and practices; it also implies that they will more markedly reflect on how their communicative actions might be taken up by other participants, thus further solidifying the link between mediatization and metapragmatic awareness.

31.3 Issues and Ongoing Debates

Debates about the validity or usefulness of "mediatization" as an analytical framework may, for current purposes, broadly be divided into two categories. Both relate distinctly to the different traditions of mediatization research (cf. Section 31.2). Firstly, institutional mediatization research, which has relied predominantly on the concept of "media logics" or on assumptions of media influence, has only been able to support its claims empirically to varying degrees of success. Conceptualizations of mediatization as a "historical shift" (Livingstone 2009: ix) have been said to overgeneralize localized, historically minor changes in media representation, which affects the validity of claims about media influence (e.g. Deacon and Stanyer 2014).

Indeed, certain investigations that attempt to empirically validate mediatization produce mixed results. Zeh and Hopmann (2013) carried out an investigation of twenty years (1990–2009) of Danish and German election coverage, taking as indicators of mediatization, inter alia, the amount of personalization and negativity in news coverage. While they report an increase for these indicators, the authors also note that most of the increase took place in the first half of their data set. This would indicate that either the "mediatization [of election coverage] peaked in the 1990s" (2013: 236) or that there is only "mixed evidence pointing to mediatization" (237) as a key factor, in favor of other factors specific to the elections and local circumstances such as a high unemployment rate. Alternatively, their investigation may have focused on flawed empirical indicators of institutional mediatization, yet at the same time it is unclear which indicators would demonstrate the societal shifts alleged by institutional mediatization research.

Secondly, and relatedly, a dearth of contrastive, historical research hampers the identification of diachronic links – or, alternatively, contrasts – that could illuminate how the contemporary interplay between media and society differs from earlier instantiations of this interface. In particular, more research is needed on how "media logics" themselves may be shifting, heterogeneously dispersed or reflexively/metapragmatically oriented to by participants. As Schulz (2004: 94) puts it, "[m]ediatization, media dependency and related hypotheses are products of the television era." The related twentieth-century concept of "media logic" would similarly lose its force in a twenty-first-century media configuration, due to it becoming more heterogeneously constructed. That is to say, while various media may still operate according to their own "media logic," the upshot will be combined or competing logics of a wide variety of platforms, interest groups and sectoral concerns. Tensions between "new" and "legacy" media, for instance, have been well documented, with traditional news media facing pressures to produce high-velocity "breaking news" updates, a decline in print readership and concomitant pressures on funding models (cf. Anderson 2011; Davies 2009).

In the author's view, this warrants a more decisive shift toward social-constructionist understandings of mediatization, as researchers will need to consider "a complex mix of economic, legal, technological, political, and cultural factors" that may affect media forms (Hepp, Hjarvard and Lundby 2015: 317). Similarly, Lundby (2009: 117) argues for mediatization research that emphasizes "how social and communicative forms are developed when media are taken into use in social interaction." Section 31.4 will discuss the implications of the overview of existing research and limitations discussed in the current section. After, Section 31.5 will present future directions of research that heed the calls of Hepp, Hjarvard and Lundby (2015) and Lundby (2009).

31.4 Implications: Mediatization and Prosumption

Mediatization as presented offers a solid basis for furthering research on the interface between society and mediated communication, especially by employing methods of discourse analysis. Further linkages between mediatization research and (socio)linguistic, discourse-analytical research may be developed in two ways: On the one hand, mediatization research may benefit from adopting discourse-analytical methods, in order to strengthen the empirical basis of its claims. On the other hand, much existing work in domains of (critical) discourse analysis, metaphor analysis and conversation analysis is amenable to employing the concept of mediatization as an interpretative lens. Indeed, as observed by Van Hout (2015), the large presence of "mediatization" in communications research has not been mirrored by an equally keen adoption in (socio)linguistics, yet not for lack of compatible interests. High on the agenda is the task of "carry[ing] out an interdisciplinary space for mediatization research" (Van Hout 2015: 715).

This chapter argues that linguistic-anthropological conceptualizations of mediatization permit a continued shift toward social-constructionist understandings. These are well-equipped to pay heed to, and potentially anticipate, technological developments in mediation (cf. Section 31.5). A key feature of contemporary communication media, for instance, are their inescapably interactive features, which rely on the input of a vast amount of individual (news) media consumers. Using Toffler and Toffler's (2006) term, contemporary news consumers may be characterized as "prosumers." No longer merely consumers of news coverage, they will be relatively more involved in its production. Additionally, as Jansson points out in his analysis of contemporary "image culture," "consumers/audiences" may themselves "think beyond the apparent logic of images, or to reflect upon the productive sources behind the image structure" (2002b: 24).

Indeed, the agenda-setting power of traditional media institutions has at the very least been limited, and the power to decide the topics and form of mass-mediated communication has been shared with, for example, bloggers or tweeters whose messages may go viral (cf. Wallsten 2010). Furthermore, the rise of the descriptor "the mainstream media" in everyday parlance may signal a declining trust in traditional media or at least a repositioning of it.[2] Along virtually all ideological positions, these traditional, mainstream media may be rejected in favor of more personalized and ideologically aligned outlets (e.g. Tewksbury 2005; Lelkes, Sood and Iyengar 2017).

These trends, too, may be analyzed in a mediatization framework, as they directly affect audience uptake of particular discourses. Research has shown, for instance, that the attribution of the same text to a different news source influences an audience's reaction to it. Specifically, the more

---

[2] Google's NGram Viewer, which searches for phrases in a large corpus of books, shows the phrase "mainstream media" starting to be used in the 1960s but ascending steeply in usage toward the second half of the 1980s. The ascent continues uninterruptedly until 2008, where the corpus ends.

partisan the reader, the more pronounced their disagreement with news texts when these are attributed to an ideologically disaligned source (Knight Foundation 2018: 8): "the 'brand' reputation of these sources affects perceived trustworthiness of the content more than the information presented." Opening up the research space to include individual(ized) uptake and voices, mediatization draws attention to the role of "prosumers" as contributors to mediatized discourse and its uptake. Additionally, a focus on metapragmatic formulations is well-equipped to investigate questions of audience orientations toward the media they engage with. It may also reveal how they orient to particular terms used in news communication (Deschrijver 2020).

All of the above does not mean that institutional mediatization frameworks have no place in future research. As mentioned in Section 31.2.2, critical discourse analysis approaches may benefit from employing an institutional understanding of mediatization as a research lens. At the same time, and keeping in mind the implications set out in this section, these investigations would benefit from more closely, and diachronically, attending to empirical indicators of mediatization, which could clarify how the effects of media institutions have shifted in the preceding decades. The chosen empirical indicators may be influenced by the topic of investigation. For instance, institutional mediatization research set in a broader discourse-analytical methodology could benefit from Jaffe's (2009) conceptualization of mediatization. She defines it as "all the representational choices involved in the production and editing of text, image, and talk in the creation of media products" (2011: 572; quoting Schmitz 2004 in Johnson and Ensslin 2007: 13), as well as media's role in promulgating points of views and normative social roles. For its part, her conceptualization continues to designate media as an important site for analysis, thus enhancing compatibility with institutional mediatization frameworks. Yet it also provides a grounded list of empirical criteria by which to judge mediatization, as it centers on specific linguistic features. These features include, amongst others, "selection, placement, sequencing, perspective-taking, stylistics-choices" as well as the highlighting of particular semiotic modes (Jaffe 2011: 572).

31.5 Future Directions: Multimodal, Global and Social Mediatization

The introduction to the current chapter emphasized the value of "mediatization" for investigating contemporary, fast-moving electronically mediated communication. Its main strength, it has been argued, lies in its versatility and adaptability, which anticipates future, as of yet unknown, changes. This section will attempt to sketch where these future changes are most likely to occur. In doing so, it provides a view of priority areas: multimodal, global, and social mediatization research.

Firstly, as flows of communication become increasingly complex, the theoretical relevance of "monomodal" texts will be affected. As observed by Schmitz (2014: 296), "the traditional prototypical notion of text (as a self-contained, co-written document dealing with one particular subject)" is severely affected by contemporary communications technologies, and the author argues that prototypical views of "text" are "guided by bygone times." Contemporary mediatized communication, in contrast, is characterized by "multimodal interactivity" (Knoblauch 2013: 310), making it more and more difficult to speak of a "text" as a basis of analysis. The semiotics roots of linguistic-anthropological mediatization frameworks make them well-equipped to investigate these multimodal features of contemporary communication, as well as an audience's orientation toward them.

Jensen (2013), in sketching updated conceptualizations of mediatization, identifies three key points that merit attention: (1) novel ways in which a medium may be embedded into another, especially by digital computer devices; (2) "a further embedding of media and communicative practices" into ordinary activities and daily tasks, such as using a GPS for navigation; and (3) the embedding of communication in the "natural environment and the human body" through, for example, mobile phones (Jensen 2013: 216ff and cf. Miller 2014). Jensen rightly concludes that, even though future developments here may be difficult to predict, they imply a retheorizing of how "[d]igital technologies ... affect social structuration in radically new ways" (2013: 218). These lines of argument are in many ways foreshadowed by McLuhan (1964), who drew attention to the social, cognitive and cultural consequences of the format, rather than the message, of communication (and cf. Knight Foundation 2018).

As Krotz also notes, "our media environment is becoming more and more complex, as the variety of devices that can take over communicative functions for people increases" (2009: 31), and many potential future complexities may not yet be apparent. Further integrating these developments into mediatization research should be a high priority.

Secondly, mediatization research has so far largely researched European and North American (media) contexts. This is especially the case for institutional mediatization research, which has accentuated media's role in enabling an "audience-oriented market logic in politics" (Landerer 2013: 253) with potentially corrosive effects on developed democracies. Yet this may obscure the role and localized consequences of similar mediatization processes in societies with entirely different sociopolitical structures. These societies may not share similar political ideologies, or their media constellations may more accurately be characterized as, for instance, a politicization of (mass) media rather than an institutional mediatization of politics.

Yet in spite of these sociopolitical differences, virtually all contemporary societies will see a rapid, locally contextualized transformation of their media configurations and technologies (e.g. Block 2013; Graber 2012; Hou 2018). A social-constructionist/sociolinguistic understanding of mediatization, as set out in Sections 31.3.2 and 31.4, highlights the emergence of new/social media formats and concomitant shifting modes of participation, the great expansion of source material available for recontextualization, and the intensification and diversification of ways for people to communicate with one another. In doing so, it initially backgrounds institutional context, enhancing its worldwide applicability. In contrastively researching different settings around the globe, "global mediatization" research may provide more empirical evidence of the precise effects of mediatization processes on communication, by enlarging the empirical basis upon which its claims are made. It will also acknowledge the globalized level at which much of contemporary communication potentially plays out.

Finally, one may envisage mediatization research with a special focus on the role of social media in mediatization processes. This would move the emphasis from general media configurations to the role, functions and consequences of social media in it. Specifically, social mediatization research may focus on "social media features of mediatization" such as participation cultures that "further heighten participatory modes and potentials for expression and/or contestation" (Georgakopoulou and Deschrijver 2018: para. 5). This occurs on various online platforms. Commenters on *The Guardian Online* may employ fragments of economic discourse to create an expert persona (Lampropoulou 2018). Alternatively, users on a mobile news apps may engage in "bashing" the news: attempting to most eloquently express dissatisfaction with news articles and socioeconomic context (Hou 2018). Interdisciplinary endeavors linking discourse studies and social media studies may also focus on the algorithmic logic behind many social network interactions, and the specific affordances for participants in social mediatization (cf. Gehl 2014).

31.6 Summary

As Landerer argues, "a broad conceptualization of mediatization is necessary to do justice to the complexity of the concept and its interdependencies with other social processes," yet one should avoid the "risk of inflating mediatization into a catch-all label" (Landerer 2013: 239).

The current chapter has attempted to provide starting points for this task in a discourse-analytical context. It provided, in Section 31.2, an overview of the main traditions of mediatization research. Aside from an institutional tradition (emphasizing the effects of media institutions on social life) and a social-constructionist tradition (emphasizing the complex network of mediated interactions underlying mediatization), the section identified the linguistic-anthropological tradition of mediatization research to be of particular relevance to discourse studies. While institutional mediatization research constitutes a natural fit with branches of critical discourse studies, linguistic-anthropological ones were argued to be better-equipped to deal with ever-changing media constellations and more complex networks of interactions that constitute mediatization.

Section 31.2.3 presented existing works in this tradition, which followed Briggs in arguing that "mediatization ... should be studied in terms of its everyday metapragmatics" (2011: 226). By doing so, analysts will be able to gain emic insights about both language use and participants' experience with and conceptualizations of media(tized) networks of communication. Additionally, the focus allows for a large degree of validity in various contexts – global or technological – where the concept is applied.

After presenting existing issues with mediatization as a research framework, Section 31.4 argued that discourse-analytical research of mediatization phenomena will be at its strongest when attending to empirical indicators. This will allow for contrastive research that illuminates how contemporary (or future) effects of mediatization differ from earlier ones. As for anticipating future trends, Section 31.5 suggests three main avenues for research: (1) multimodal mediatization research, (2) global mediatization research and (3) social mediatization research.

Since it is amenable to various discourse-analytical methods and contexts, the view on mediatization as set out here would heed Ekström et al.'s (2016) call for "a spectrum of diverse theories and analyses focusing on media-related transformations in society" (Ekström et al. 2016: 1093). Metapragmatically-oriented discourse analysis is eminently placed to investigate the three priorities identified by these authors: (1) carrying out historically contrastive research, (2) investigating differences between media types and contexts and (3) establishing a manner to measure and quantify aspects of mediatization to facilitate the first two priorities. Indeed, the understanding presented here is broad enough to engage in historically and/or contextually contrastive research, with linguistic reflexivity informing the measurement and quantification of aspects of mediatization.

Further Reading

Agha, A. (2011c). Meet Mediatization. *Language & Communication* 31: 163–70.

Agha's linguistic-anthropological approach to mediatization emphasizes the importance of commoditized features of communication and their influence in the recontextualization of parts of discourse. It is recommended further reading, especially for a theory of how language/discourse travels across different communication media (cf. Briggs, 2011).

Altheide, D. L. (2013). Media Logic, Social Control, and Fear. *Communication Theory* 23: 223–38.

This revised account of the notion of "media logic" underpins (institutional) mediatization research and discusses the discourses of fear as developed and sustained by media logic.

Androutsopoulos, J. (2014). Mediatization and Sociolinguistic Change: Key Concepts, Research Traditions, Open Issues. In J. Androutsopoulos (ed.) *Mediatization and Sociolinguistic Change*. Berlin: Mouton de Gruyter. 3–48.

The introduction to this edited volume offers a rich and comprehensive overview of mediatization research, its potential applications and its links with sociolinguistics. The volume overall is an indispensable tool for familiarizing oneself with mediatization research.

Georgakopoulou, A. and Deschrijver, C. (2018). Introduction to the Special Issue: The Social Mediatization of the Economy: Texts, Discourses, and Participation. *Language@Internet* 16: article 1.

This social-constructionist account of mediatization in online discourses on economic affairs proposes the concept of "social mediatization" to account for the ever-growing importance of social media interactions in influencing and shifting modes of participation. It also illuminates the spread and recontextualization of elite terms/discourse in public settings.

Schmitz, U. (2014). Semiotic Economy, Growth of Mass Media Discourse, and Change of Written Language through Multimodal Techniques: The Case of Newspapers (Printed and Online) and Web Services. In J. Androutsopoulos (ed.) *Mediatization and Sociolinguistic Change*. Berlin: Mouton de Gruyter. 279–304.

The author provides a comprehensive overview of the ways in which technological change in communication has affected newspaper communication and how processes of communication may continue to be changed by technological developments.

References

Adolf, M. (2011). Clarifying Mediatization: Sorting through a Current Debate. *Empedocles: European Journal for the Philosophy of Communication* 3(2): 153–75.

Agha, A. (2011a). Commodity Registers. *Journal of Linguistic Anthropology* 21 (1): 22–53.
  (2011b). Large and Small Scale Forms of Personhood. *Language & Communication* 31: 171–80.
  (2011c). Meet Mediatization. *Language & Communication* 31: 163–70.
Altheide, D. L. (2004). Media Logic and Political Communication. *Political Communication* 21: 293–6.
  (2013). Media Logic, Social Control, and Fear. *Communication Theory* 23: 223–38.
Altheide, D. L. and Snow, R. P. (1992). Media Logic and Culture: Reply to Oakes. *International Journal of Politics, Culture, and Society* 5(3): 465–72.
Anderson, C. W. (2011). Deliberative, Agonistic, and Algorithmic Audiences: Journalism's Vision of Its Public in an Age of Audience Transparency. *International Journal of Communication* 5: 529–47.
Androutsopoulos, J. (2014). Mediatization and Sociolinguistic Change: Key Concepts, Research Traditions, Open Issues. In J. Androutsopoulos (ed.) *Mediatization and Sociolinguistic Change*. Berlin: Mouton de Gruyter. 3–48.
Block, E. (2013). A Culturalist Approach to the Concept of the Mediatization of Politics: The Age of "Media Hegemony." *Communication Theory* 23: 259–78.
Briggs, C. L. (2011). On Virtual Epidemics and the Mediatization of Public Health. *Language & Communication* 31: 217–28.
Charteris-Black, J. (2004). *Corpus Approaches to Critical Metaphor Analysis*. Basingstoke: Palgrave Macmillan.
Cole, D. and Pellicer, R. (2012). Uptake (Un)limited: The Mediatization of Register Shifting in US Public Discourse. *Language in Society* 41: 449–70.
Cotter, C. (2014). Revising the "Journalist's Bible": How News Practitioners Respond to Language and Social Change. In J. Androutsopoulos (ed.) *Mediatization and Sociolinguistic Change*. Berlin: Mouton de Gruyter. 371–94.
Couldry, N. (2008). Mediatization or Mediation? Alternative Understandings of the Emergent Space of Digital Storytelling. *New Media & Society* 10(3): 373–91.
Couldry, N. and Hepp, A. (2013). Conceptualizing Mediatization: Contexts, Traditions, Arguments. *Communication Theory* 23: 191–202.
Davies, N. (2009). *Flat Earth News*. London: Vintage.
Deacon, D. and Stanyer, J. (2014). Mediatization: Key Concept or Conceptual Bandwagon? *Media, Culture & Society* 36(7): 1032–44.
Deschrijver, C. (2020). Metalinguistic Density as an Indicator of Sharedness: Economic and Financial Terms in Online Interaction. *Language & Communication* 71: 123–35.
Ekström, M., Fornäs, J., Jansson, A. and Jerslev, A. (2016). Three Tasks for Mediatization Research: Contributions to an Open Agenda. *Media, Culture & Society* 38(7): 1090–108.

Fairclough, N. (1993). Critical Discourse Analysis and the Marketization of Public Discourse: The Universities. *Discourse & Society* 4(2): 133–68.

Falasca, K. (2014). Political News Journalism: Mediatization across Three News Reporting Contexts. *European Journal of Communication* 29(5): 583–97.

Gehl, R. W. (2014). *Reverse Engineering Social Media: Software, Culture, and Political Economy in New Media Capitalism*. Philadelphia, PA: Temple University Press.

Georgakopoulou, A. (1997). Self-Presentation and Interactional Alliances in E-mail Discourse: The Style- and Code-Switches of Greek Messages. *International Journal of Applied Linguistics* 7(2): 141–64.

Georgakopoulou, A. and Deschrijver, C. (2018). Introduction to the Special Issue: The Social Mediatization of the Economy: Texts, Discourses, and Participation. *Language@Internet* 16: article 1. www.languageatinternet.org/articles/2018si/georgakopoulou.

Graber, K. (2012). Public Information: The Shifting Roles of Minority Language News Media in the Buryat Territories of Russia. *Language & Communication* 32: 124–36.

Hepp, A. (2013). The Communicative Figurations of Mediatized Worlds: Mediatization Research in Times of the "Mediation of Everything." *European Journal of Communication* 28(6): 615–29.

(2014). Mediatization: A Panorama of Media and Communication Research. In J. Androutsopoulos (ed.) *Mediatization and Sociolinguistic Change*. Berlin: Mouton de Gruyter. 49–66.

Hepp, A., Hjarvard, S. and Lundby, K. (2015). Mediatization: Theorizing the Interplay between Media, Culture and Society. *Media, Culture & Society* 37(2): 314–24.

Hjarvard, S. (2008a). The Mediatization of Religion: A Theory of the Media as Agents of Religious Change. *Northern Lights* 6(1): 9–26.

(2008b). The Mediatization of Society: A Theory of the Media as Agents of Social and Cultural Change. *Nordicom Review* 29(2): 105–34.

Hou, M. (2018). Economic News Comments on a Mobile News App: An Emerging Genre of Bashing. *Language@Internet* 16: article 4. www.languageatinternet.org/articles/2018si/hou.

Jaffe, A. (2009). Entextualization, Mediatization and Authentication: Orthographic Choice in Media Transcripts. *Text & Talk* 29(5): 571–94.

(2011). Sociolinguistic Diversity in Mainstream Media: Authenticity, Authority and Processes of Mediation and Mediatization. *Journal of Language and Politics* 10(4): 562–86.

Jansson, A. (2002). The Mediatization of Consumption: Towards an Analytical Framework of Image Culture. *Journal of Consumer Culture* 2(1): 5–31.

Jensen, K. B. (2013). Definitive and Sensitizing Conceptualizations of Mediatization. *Communication Theory* 23: 203–22.

Johnson, S. and Ensslin, A. (2007). Language in the Media: Theory and Practice. In S. Johnson and A. Ensslin (eds.) *Language in the Media: Representation, Identities, Ideologies*. London: Continuum. 3–24.

Kammer, A. (2013). The Mediatization of Journalism. *MedieKultur* 54: 141–58.

Knight Foundation. (2018). *An Online Experimental Platform to Assess Trust in the Media*. https://knightfoundation.org/wp-content/uploads/2020/02/KnightFoundation_NewsLens1_Client_Report_070918_ab.pdf

Knoblauch, H. (2013). Communicative Constructivism and Mediatization. *Communication Theory* 23: 97–315.

Krotz, F. (2007). The Meta-process of "Mediatization" as a Conceptual Frame. *Global Media and Communication* 3(3): 256–60.

(2009). Mediatization: A Concept with which to Grasp Media and Societal Change. In K. Lundby (ed.) *Mediatization: Concept, Changes, Consequences*. New York: Peter Lang. 21–40.

Krotz, F. and Hepp, A. (2013). A Concretization of Mediatization: How Mediatization Works and Why "Mediatized Worlds" Are a Helpful Concept for Empirical Mediatization Research. *Empedocles: European Journal for the Philosophy of Communication* 3(2): 119–34.

Lampropoulou, S. (2018). Economy Talk as Blaming Strategy: Crisis Framings in *The Guardian* News Stories and Recontextualizations in User Comments during the Greek Bailout Referendum. *Language@Internet* 16: article 5. www.languageatinternet.org/articles/2018si/lampropoulou.

Landerer, N. (2013). Rethinking the Logics: A Conceptual Framework for the Mediatization of Politics. *Communication Theory* 23: 239–58.

Lelkes, Y., Sood, G. and Iyengar, S. (2017). The Hostile Audience: The Effect of Access to Broadband Internet on Partisan Affect. *American Journal of Political Science* 61(1): 5–20.

Livingstone, S. (2009). Foreword: Coming to Terms with "Mediatization." In K. Lundby (ed.) *Mediatization: Concept, Changes, Consequences*. New York: Peter Lang. ix–xi.

Lucy, J. A. (ed.) (1993). *Reflexive Language: Reported Speech and Metapragmatics*. Cambridge: Cambridge University Press.

Lundby, K. (2009). Media Logic: Looking for Social Interaction. In K. Lundby (ed.) *Mediatization: Concept, Changes, Consequences*. New York: Peter Lang. 101–119.

Maltby, S. (2012). The Mediatization of the Military. *Media, War & Conflict* 5 (3): 255–68.

Marshall, P. D. (2015). Monitoring Persona: Mediatized Identity and the Edited Public Self. *Frame: Journal of Literary Studies* 28(1): 115–33.

McLuhan, M. (1964). *Understanding Media: The Extensions of Man*. New York: McGraw-Hill.

Miller, J. (2014). The Fourth Screen: Mediatization and the Smartphone. *Mobile Media & Communication* 2(2): 209–26.

Peleg, A. and Bogoch, B. (2012). Removing Justitia's Blindfold: The Mediatization of Law in Israel. *Media, Culture & Society* 34(8): 961–78.

Peng, C.-Y. (2018). Mediatized Taiwan Mandarin: Social Perceptions and Language Ideologies. *Chinese Language and Discourse* 9(2): 162–83.

Rödder, S. and Schäfer, M. S. (2010). Repercussion and Resistance: An Empirical Study on the Interrelation between Science and Mass Media. *Communications* 35: 249–67.

Schmitz, U. (2004). *Sprache in modernen Medien*. Berlin: E. Schmidt.

—— (2014). Semiotic Economy, Growth of Mass Media Discourse, and Change of Written Language through Multimodal Techniques: The Case of Newspapers (Printed and Online) and Web Services. In J. Androutsopoulous (ed.) *Mediatization and Sociolinguistic Change*. Berlin: Mouton de Gruyter. 279–304.

Schrott, A. (2009). Dimensions: Catch-All Label or Technical Term. In K. Lundby (ed.) *Mediatization: Concept, Changes, Consequences*. New York: Peter Lang. 41–61.

Schulz, W. (2004). Reconstructing Mediatisation as an Analytical Concept. *European Journal of Communication* 19(1): 87–101.

Silverstein, M. (1993). Metapragmatic Discourse and Metapragmatic Function. In J. A. Lucy (ed.) *Reflexive Language: Reported Speech and Metapragmatics*. Cambridge: Cambridge University Press. 33–58.

Skjulstad, S. (2009). Dressing Up: The Mediatization of Fashion Online. In K. Lundby (ed.) *Mediatization: Concept, Changes, Consequences*. New York: Peter Lang. 179–202.

Squires, L. and Iorio, J. (2014). Tweets in the News: Legitimizing Medium, Standardizing Form. In J. Androutsopoulos (ed.) *Mediatization and Sociolinguistic Change*. Berlin: Mouton de Gruyter. 331–60.

Strömbäck, J. and Dimitrova, D. V. (2011). Mediatization and Media Interventionism: A Comparative Analysis of Sweden and the United States. *International Journal of Press/Politics* 16(1): 30–49.

Tewksbury, D. (2005). The Seeds of Audience Fragmentation: Specialization in the Use of Online News Sites. *Journal of Broadcasting & Electronic Media* 49(3): 332–48.

Thurlow, C. and Poff, M. (2013). Text Messaging. In S. C. Herring, D. Stein and T. Virtanen (eds.) *Pragmatics of Computer-Mediated Communication*. Berlin: Mouton de Gruyter. 163–89.

Toffler, A. and Toffler, H. (2006). *Revolutionary Wealth*. New York: Knopf.

Van Hout, T. (2015). Review of the book *Mediatization and Sociolinguistic Change*. *Journal of Sociolinguistics* 19(5): 714–18.

Van Hout, T. and Burger, P. (2017). Text Bite News: The Metapragmatics of Feature News. *Text & Talk* 37(4): 461–84.

Verschueren, J. (1999). *Understanding Pragmatics*. London: Edward Arnold.

—— (2000). Notes on the Role of Metapragmatic Awareness in Language Use. *Pragmatics* 10(4): 439–56.

Wallsten, K. (2010). "Yes We Can": How Online Viewership, Blog Discussion, Campaign Statements, and Mainstream Media Coverage Produced a Viral Video Phenomenon. *Journal of Information Technology & Politics* 7(2–3): 163–81.

Wodak, R. (2007). Pragmatics and Critical Discourse Analysis: A Cross-Disciplinary Enquiry. *Pragmatics & Cognition* 15(1): 203–25.

Zeh, R. and Hopmann, D. N. (2013). Indicating Mediatization? Two Decades of Election Campaign Television Coverage. *European Journal of Communication* 28(3): 225–40.

32

Discourse Analysis and Digital Surveillance

Rodney H. Jones

32.1 Introduction

Some time ago I found a post on my Facebook newsfeed asking, "Which Friends Are Actually Your Mom and Dad?" (Figure 32.1). Despite the underlying creepiness of the question, I was curious. So, I clicked on the link and was brought to a dialogue window asking me if I would like to "Continue as Rodney?" What it meant was not did I want to continue being myself, but was I willing to share with a company called "Meaww World" my "friends list, timeline posts, and photos." Undeterred, I clicked "Okay," and was immediately taken to a page with a pulsing progress bar and the words: "*Calculating result* ..." along with an advertisement for a sofa, which was useful given that I had just spent almost an hour browsing online furniture shops. Finally, the answer was revealed on a new page, framed by an array of additional advertisements for furniture, an online supermarket and other fun quizzes I could take: based presumably on some algorithmic analysis of my personal information, Meaww World had determined that my two friends who could have been my parents were Simon (who could have been my mom), and Dino (who could have been my dad). Amused, I immediately posted the result on Facebook, When I did, of course, Simon and Dino, equally amused, shared it on their newsfeeds, and then went on to take the quiz themselves, giving Meaww World access to their data and that of their friends.

When we think of digital surveillance, we usually think of intelligence gathering by shadowy government agencies of the type uncovered by Edward Snowden. But most digital surveillance is more pedestrian, tied up with our everyday practices of searching the Internet, engaging with friends on social media, shopping and showing off. In fact, as Snowden's revelations chillingly revealed, government surveillance programs like Prism and Mystic are intimately tied to our use of search engines, social media sites and smartphones, through which we produce vast stores of

Figure 32.1 Quiz prompt from Nametest.com

data that can be exploited by advertisers, government agencies and more unsavory actors such as identity thieves and Russian hackers. The "Cambridge Analytica scandal," for example, that may have contributed to the 2016 election of Donald Trump, actually started when researchers convinced Facebook users to take an online quiz called "This is Your Digital Life," through which the company was eventually able to gain access to the data of over 87 million Facebook users (Grassenger and Krogerus 2017).

This short narrative does not just demonstrate the ubiquitous nature of digital surveillance; it also highlights a number of key questions about digital surveillance that are relevant to the work of discourse analysts. The first is obviously the role of discourse in making the whole sequence of actions that resulted in me relinquishing my data possible, from the garish scrawl of the original invitation, to the oblique way in which Meaww World asked for my consent, to the language and layout of the barrage of advertisements that accompanied this process. When we think of digital surveillance, we are accustomed to thinking in terms of complex code, algorithms and metadata – and, as I will discuss, these new forms of "language" are indeed central to these processes – but much of what makes digital surveillance possible has to do with the more traditional ways in which discourse is deployed to lure users into making compromising decisions. Secondly, there are fundamental questions about "speakership" and "listenership": who exactly is the "author" of the various texts involved here, including the original invitation, the resulting text which I shared with my friends on Facebook and even the advertisements, which were in part the result of my own internet activities in the hour before I clicked on this quiz? And who is the audience: is it me, Simon and Dino, our various friends who are subjected to this unusual post showing up on their newsfeeds, or Meaww World, who, after all, is the recipient of all of the information we have disclosed? Thirdly, there are questions about "meaning": how did Meaww World come to the conclusion that Simon and Dino could have been my parents? What was I trying to "say" by reposting this text on my timeline, and, most importantly, what kinds of meanings are Meaww World and the third parties it might sell my data to able to infer about me based on the data it has gathered? Finally, why did I fall for this scam in the first place? What is it about the discursive strategies of this company, my relationships with my friends on social media, the social practices associated with this medium and my own experiences of creating and interpreting texts online that made me decide to hand over all of the posts and pictures I have ever sent or received on Facebook to a company that I had never heard of?

In this chapter, I will discuss how tools from discourse analysis can contribute to our understanding of digital surveillance, exploring how the interaction among social relationships, discourse practices and technological tools in contemporary digital and physical spaces has created a "communicative ecology" (Foth and Hearn 2007) in which nearly all of our social interactions are engineered to produce data of maximal value for internet companies, advertisers and governments. While much of this new communicative ecology is made possible by digital technologies and the sophisticated patterns of participation and methods of discourse processing they make available, much of it also depends on more fundamental practices of human communication that stretch back to the birth of human language itself (Dunbar 1996), practices like gossip and boasting, and our seemingly insatiable desire to "see" and "be seen."

In what follows, I will first explore what insights from discourse analysis can contribute to our understanding of surveillance more generally. Then I will discuss the *mediated* nature of all surveillance and the different affordances and constraints different media bring to it. In Section 32.2, I will give an overview of the main discursive processes involved in digital surveillance, including participation, pretexting, entextualization, recontextualization and inferencing, showing how they occur differently when mediated through digital technologies. Next, I will identify some of the key issues and ongoing debates around digital surveillance related to discourse analysis, specifically identity, agency and power. I will then go onto discuss the implications of a discourse analytical approach to digital surveillance for the professional practices of applied and sociolinguists. Finally, I will lay out some future directions in which research on discourse and digital surveillance can move.

32.2 Information Games

To take a discourse analytical approach to surveillance means taking as a starting point the fact that surveillance is a pervasive fact of everyday life and always has been, even before the advent of social media sites and internet quizzes. Participation in social life is a matter of constantly being watched and "watching out" for others either to protect them or to protect ourselves from them. As Trottier (2012: 18) observes: "Surveillance is ubiquitous, not just because of ubiquitous technologies, but because watching and assessing pervade nearly every social relationship."

This observation is at the heart of much of the work in psychology, sociology and linguistics which informs contemporary approaches to discourse analysis, from Ruesch and Bateson's (1951: 15) observation that the basis of human communication is the "perception of (being) perceived," to Goffman's (1964: 135) definition of the social situation as "an environment of mutual monitoring possibilities." For Goffman, social interaction is essentially a series of "information games" involving "potentially infinite cycle(s) of concealment, discovery, false revelation and rediscovery" (1959: 13) through which we negotiate access to various "territories of the self" (1972: 28), ranging from how visible our bodies and physical actions are to the degree to which we make available the "preserve" of secrets that we hold inside our heads (or, nowadays, inside our digital devices). What is at issue for most people, says Goffman (1972: 60), "is not whether a preserve is exclusively maintained or shared, or given up, but rather (that) the individual is allowed (to determine) what happens to his claim." What makes surveillance, in the usual sense of the word, so unnerving for us is the fact that this claim is not being respected, that the information game is not being played "fairly." In the word surveillance (Fr. "looking from above") is an implication of *information asymmetry*, the notion that one party has the upper hand. But for Goffman, the need to address constant potential asymmetries in interaction and to negotiate the balance between what we know about others and what is known about us is an inescapable fact of social life.

All surveillance, then, cannot be regarded as necessarily nefarious or untoward. It is our ability to monitor others, and to negotiate how we are monitored by them, that is to a large degree responsible for our ability to "take action, seek information and communicate" (Albrechtslund 2008: 7). Both surveillance and secrecy help produce the social world – they are at the heart of how we interact, manage our relationships and organize our societies. And, in many situations, such as the one I described at the start of the chapter, we willingly make ourselves available for surveillance, perceiving certain psychological or social benefits from being visible to others. "The negotiation of social identity," says Phillips (2002: 416), "is not only about the construction and maintenance of boundaries, regions, and performances. It is also about negotiating the permeability of those boundaries."

32.2.1 Surveillance as Mediated Action

So how do media alter the ways in which these negotiations are accomplished? In order to answer this question, it is good to remember that all surveillance is mediated, that is, it is made possible by "technologies" of one kind or another, be they windows, keyholes, binoculars, cameras, electronic listening devices, digital media or just our own eyes and ears, and different media come with different affordances and constraints on who can be surveilled by whom, what kind of information can be gathered and what can be done with that information (Jones 2017a).

It is also good to remember that surveillance is never a single action – it always involves a chain of actions, each with explicit goals. Marx (2016), for example, lists seven discrete actions that are usually involved in surveillance: (1) tool selection, (2) subject selection, (3) data collection, (4) data processing/analysis, (5) data interpretation, (6) data use and (7) data fate. Each of these actions may involve the same or different mediational means with the same or different affordances and constraints on how that particular action can be executed.

A range of scholars from sociology, media studies, information sciences and the burgeoning field of surveillance studies have commented on how digital technologies have changed the information game in regard to the different surveillance-related actions delineated by Marx. One of the chief ways in which digital media have changed how surveillance is carried out, for example, is that they make the first two steps almost superfluous – there is no need to make choices about tools and subjects when the tools nearly all subjects are using (such as smartphones and social media accounts) make possible the surveillance of nearly everybody. As Haggerty and Ericson (2000: 606) point out, digital media have brought about "a rhizomatic levelling of the hierarchy of surveillance, such that groups which were previously exempt from routine surveillance are now increasingly being monitored." Just as it is no longer a matter of targeting specific people, it is also no longer a matter of utilizing specific technologies. With the rise of "ubiquitous computing" has come ubiquitous surveillance where wireless sensors are hidden inside of ordinary objects such as cars, kitchen appliances, toilets, buildings and clothes (Marx 2016), and information gathering is increasingly indiscriminate and automated. As Barnard-Willis (2012: 22) notes, "contemporary surveillance is driven by connections between seemingly disparate and previously discrete surveillance technologies, sites, practices and agents," what Haggerty and Ericson (2000) have famously referred to as "surveillant assemblages."

The second important effect of digital technologies that scholars have observed has been on the *kinds* of data that can be collected. In 1988, Roger

Clarke coined the term "dataveillance" to describe the "systematic use of personal data systems in the monitoring of people's actions and communications" (Clarke 1988: 498). Intelligence experts talk about the difference between surveillance engaged in through the actual observation of people (known as "human intelligence" of "humint") and that engaged in through the gathering of the "signals" people give off from their use of technologies (known as "signals intelligence" or "sigint"). Digital technologies have made possible a switch in surveillance techniques from the observation of actual persons to the observation of the "data trails" they leave as they interact with technologies, the incidental "exhaust" of their mediated actions. This results in an increased focus on information that is, in Goffman's (1963) terms, "given off," gleaned from actions like clicking, swiping, searching, "liking" and traveling from one physical location to another, actions that are usually not even regarded as particularly "meaningful" by those who produce them. In other words, they are not part of the traditional "preserves" that Goffman says social actors typically guard access to.

What digital technologies make possible are the capture and recording of these manifold incidental actions in digital format, accumulated and aggregated into "big data" sets that can be operated on by algorithms, which brings me to the third way in which digital technologies have changed the information game by introducing new and powerful ways of analyzing and interpreting data. This introduces yet another level of asymmetry between the surveillers and the surveilled: not only are the surveilled unaware that information they produce might be rendered meaningful, but they are also (for the most part) unequipped to interrogate the processes through which this information is interpreted. Tene and Polonetsky (2013: 255) compare the relationship between internet platforms and their users to a "game of poker where one of the players has his hand open and the other keeps his cards close."

The final way in which digital technologies have been seen to effect surveillance has to do with the "use" and ultimate "fate" of the data collected. While the effects of much digital surveillance, especially of the commercial kind, seem relatively innocuous, resulting in things like targeted advertising and discount offers, in reality the "social sorting" (Lyon 2003) that underpins these uses can act to reinforce social and economic inequalities and even lead to dangerous political polarization in the pursuit of profit (Lanier 2018). Surveillance of any type has the consequences of exasperating the kinds of power asymmetries that made it possible in the first place (Graham 1998), but the efficiency with which digital technologies are able to "sort" the subjects of surveillance results in a pervasive prioritization of "certain people's mobilities, service quality and life chances, while simultaneously reducing those of less favored groups" (such as lower-income people and minorities) (Graham and Wood 2003: 232).

While all of these observations are certainly true, they do not sufficiently capture the *discursive* and *interactive* dimensions of digital surveillance that are so conspicuous in the example with which I began this chapter: the way digital surveillance is made possible both through various kinds of semiconsensual transactions between users and companies and through myriad transactions between users themselves who post, like, share and otherwise circulate information about one another in a digitized version of Goffman's information game. They also do not sufficiently highlight how surveillance is crucially supported by complex, chained processes of text production and consumption in which information is continually transformed and recontextualized, its meaning potential changing along the way. Finally, they do not sufficiently address the pragmatic aspects of digital surveillance, the ways in which technologies are transforming not just how data are "interpreted" but also how meanings are *inferred* more generally. These are aspects of digital surveillance that only an approach informed by discourse analysis can address. While discourse analysis has had some place in surveillance studies, it has mostly been used to critique the way that surveillance is represented and justified in texts like newspaper articles and political speeches and through genres such as reality television (e.g. McGrath2004; Tiainen, 2017) rather than to examine the actual communicative processes that surveillance entails (Barnard-Wills 2012). The framework outlined in this chapter is intended to highlight those aspects of digital surveillance that are amenable to interrogation by discourse analysts.

32.2.2 Overview: Discourse and Digital Surveillance

A discourse analytical perspective on digital surveillance involves asking what *discursive processes* it entails: what possibilities for interaction, what sorts of interactional roles and what forms of meaning-making. These processes can be divided up into (1) participation: the way digital media create different possibilities for mutual monitoring and different interactional roles and responsibilities; (2) pretexting: the strategies used to compel people to disclose information about themselves; (3) entextualization: the ways digital media facilitate the transformation of actions into text/code and the kinds of meanings that are preserved, lost and changed through these processes; (4) recontextualization: the way information gathered through digital surveillance is transported into different textual contexts and combined with other information to produce new meanings and new possibilities for action; and (5) inferencing: the ways in which meanings are inferred from data and used to determine the subsequent kinds of texts and interactions to which users are exposed. Although these processes sometimes happen in succession, as in Marx's (2016) more "analogue" account of "surveillance strips," they more often constitute recursive moves in a complex system of feedback loops in which, for example, inferences arrived at through the analysis of data from multiple sources feed into the formulation of pretexts for the gathering of yet more data. In the following sections I will discuss these processes in more detail.

32.3 Participation

The meaning of participation from a discourse analytical perspective has to do not just with who is included in a particular interaction but also with what communicative rights and responsibilities different participants have. When it comes to surveillance, the key question about participation is: *who is watching whom?* Most models imagine rather static, dyadic participant roles of, as Marx (2012: xxv) puts it, a "surveillance agent (watcher/observer/seeker/inspector/auditor/tester)" and the "surveillance subject": "the person about whom information is sought." Marx does go on, however, to imagine other kinds of participants associated with the "watcher" role, for example, "sponsors, data collectors, and initial and secondary users of the data" (2012: xxv). Digital security experts have a slightly more elaborate scheme of participants, each with a conventionalized nickname: "Alice" and "Bob" for sender and receiver of communications which might be intercepted by "Eve" (for eavesdropper), "Carol" (for third person), "Chuck" (for malicious participant), "Mallet" (for active intruder), "Trent" (for trusted third party) and "Grace" (for government agent) (Rivest, Shamir and Adleman 1978). But even this more elaborate model of participation is constructed along the binary poles of "watcher" and "watched." In networked interactions of the kind described at the beginning of this chapter, however, the distinction between the monitor and the monitored is not so clear-cut. In many ways, in fact, this particular transaction is based upon different actors taking on *multiple* roles as different kinds of "watcher" and different kinds of "watched." One of the main reasons digital media have such a profound impact on the way that surveillance is carried out is that they have a profound impact on the way that social interaction is carried out more generally, making available more flexible frameworks for participation and creating ways for different kinds of participation frameworks to articulate with one another. As Haggerty (2006: 26) puts it, "the multiplication of sites of surveillance" made possible through new technologies "ruptures the unidirectional nature of the gaze, transforming surveillance from a dynamic microscope to one where knowledge and images of unexpected intensity and assorted distortions cascade from viewer to viewer and across institutions, emerging in unpredictable configurations and combinations, while undermining the neat distinction between watchers and watched through a proliferation of criss-crossing, overlapping and intersecting scrutiny."

This view of participation is, in fact, much more in line with what sociolinguists and discourse analysts have long noted, that, as Hymes

(1974: 54) put it, "the common dyadic model of speaker-hearer specifies... too many, sometimes too few, sometimes the wrong participants." All social interactions involve the possibilities for multiple modes of production and participation among participants, some ratified and some unratified (Goffman 1981). Face-to-face conversations also sometimes have auditors, bystanders and even eavesdroppers. What technology does is shift the opportunities that different participants have for "mutual monitoring."

Media in general contribute to the formation of participation frameworks by enabling and limiting how communication takes place, how it circulates and who has access to it (Hutchby 2001). In my previous work (Jones 2009), I compared the affordances of new media to architectural features like walls and windows which make both surveillance and privacy possible in physical environments. Digital media, I noted, give users tools to negotiate and modulate their visibility. Since then, however, fueled by advances in mobile technologies and the rise of platforms whose main business model is extracting data from users, digital environments have become more like a house of mirrors (Johnson and Regan 2014). Negotiations of surveillance and privacy are bound up in a web of multiple tiny acts of people watching each other and offering themselves up to be watched, all driven by algorithmic feedback loops which drive them deeper and deeper into interactions in which they are more likely to disclose more and more information.

These complex new participation frameworks create challenges for people as they try to regulate flows of information and maintain privacy. They also create challenges for discourse analysts, as they attempt to adapt analogue models of speakership and listenership to digital environments (also see Chapter 3 in this volume). Just as in our analogue interactions, the selves that we construct online are largely a result of "a tacit negotiation between ourselves and our imagined auditors" (Bowker 2005: 7). On the one hand, people use social media to "be seen," motivated to engage in consensual surveillance by a competition for social status, while, on the other, they employ a range of strategies to avoid "overexposure" such as self-censorship, producing polysemic performances that contain different messages for different audiences (boyd 2012), using contextualization strategies to negotiate the appropriateness of different messages (Tagg, Seargeant and Brown 2017) and alternately disclosing and withdrawing information in a form of "virtual identity hide and seek" (Papacharissi and Gibson 2011: 81).

Where older models of participation and audience design are less useful is in understanding the increased role of auditors, bystanders and eavesdroppers in nearly *all* of the interactions we have online. Although Bell (1984) talked about the "auditor effect" in social interactions, auditors in his model are secondary participants, and eavesdroppers are hardly considered participants at all. For most social media users, however, some awareness of the presence of eavesdroppers is a given, whether they be unratified human participants or faceless corporations mining their data, and a means needs to be developed to measure the degree to which this awareness changes their communication.

Another issue that older models of participation do not address is the presence of what Latour (2007) calls "new unexpected actors," audiences composed not of humans but of software programs and algorithms who participate in communicative exchanges as "(inter)active co-conspirators" with *both* agents and subjects of surveillance (Hess 2014). Some people, for example, report altering the way they communicate online based on how they believe algorithms might process and act upon their words, while, at the same time, certain interfaces are designed to inspire almost unabashed honesty. As a recent editorial in the IEEE newsletter *Technology & Society* noted: "We don't lie to our search engine. We're more intimate with it than with our friends" (ieeessit 2017).

Finally, what is perhaps most striking about the forms of participation enabled by digital media is that they are almost entirely driven by economic imperatives. On the one hand, internet companies design interfaces that favor certain kinds of interaction over others, offering, for example, the low-cost conviviality of the "like" button (Jones and Hafner 2012) because it has the effect of generating more useful data about people's preferences and personalities. On the other hand, users constantly find themselves engaging in cost–benefit analyses in which the benefits of participation in the network are measured against the costs of exposure of their "information preserves." Information has increasingly become the currency we must expend to engage in social life.

32.4 Pretextuality

The forms of participation that digital media make possible, however, are not enough to make the scale of surveillance which internet companies engage in possible, particularly in contexts like the European Union where regulations such as the General Data Protection Regulations (GDPR) require agents of surveillance to make their processes of data collection more transparent (European Commission 2017). In fact, most surveillance through digital technologies (even much of that conducted by government agents) is carried out within a framework of "consent" or, at least, "semi-consent," in which subjects of surveillance are asked to voluntarily relinquish their data. In these circumstances, surveillers must formulate "pretexts" in order to get people to open their information preserves to scrutiny.

The notion of "pretexting" comes from the field of social engineering, where it is defined as "the act of creating an invented scenario to persuade a targeted victim to release information or perform some action" (Hadnagy 2010: chapter 4). In this context, it is usually associated with conmen or online scammers like "Nigerian princes" (Blommaert and Omoniyi 2006). For discourse analysts, the idea of the pretext is much broader. Pretexts are seen as necessary conditions for all communication, sets of expectations that text producers and text consumers bring to interaction as a way of negotiating common ground. As Widdowson (2004: 79) puts it: "All texts are designed to be understood pre-textually ... it is the pretextual purpose that we bring to texts that controls how we engage with them." Another way of understanding pretexts from the discourse analytical perspective is Maryns and Blommaert's (2002: 11) definition of them as "conditions of sayability" – the practices, competencies and contextual frames that make it possible for certain people to credibly engage in certain kinds of interaction. From this perspective, pretexts always involve issues of power as different people bring different pretextual resources to communication. When it comes to pretexts for digital surveillance, both perspectives are relevant: digital pretextuality creates both the contexts for people to disclose personal information and what Maryns and Blommaert (2002: 11) call "pretextual gaps," characterized by increasing asymmetries in pretextual resources between surveillers and surveilled.

Internet companies create pretexts for us to surrender information in three ways. First are what might be called "paradigmatic pretexts" in which scenarios and genres are created to give us reasons to disclose information. These include scenarios like calling a taxi or playing an online game. Palen and Dourish (2003) note that digital media have given rise to a new range of genres which they call "genres of disclosure," genres like status updates and internet quizzes that are designed to compel users to share information. These genres are embedded in platforms whose "default settings" are designed to encourage maximum visibility. While users are usually given the opportunity to change default privacy settings, the power of genres and default settings to channel people into certain kinds of behavior is strong, partially because of the "transaction costs" involved in changing default settings or resisting the norms associated with particular genres.

The second form of pretexting common in digital environments might be called "syntagmatic pretexts," those that operate as a result of the ways in which utterances and actions are sequenced. Widdowson (2004), drawing on the work of Garfinkel (1986), argues that pretexts are not a matter of static identities and situations; they are about dynamically negotiating identities and situations as "ongoing accomplishments" through the moment by moment application of "practical reasoning." This kind of sequential reasoning comes into play in the design of "click wraps" and other permission dialogues to gain consent for information gathering which are presented to users at strategic points in ongoing processes (such as right when users want to take a picture with their phone or locate a place in a map app), so that users are inclined to "agree" to what's being asked of them, just to get on with the process.

Finally, there are what might be called "emergent pretexts" that arise from interfaces' incessant requests for disclosure that cause users to become "habituated" to giving consent (Longford 2005). One example of this is the way that the constant requests by websites for permission to use cookies required by laws such as Europe's GDPR has resulted in the routinization of consent, an emergent environment in which giving up personal data is seen as a necessary and unremarkable part of accessing information (see Section 32.8; also Jones 2018, Kim 2013).

32.5 Entextualization

Surveillance has always been about the production and circulation of texts. It is not enough to monitor someone – the results of that monitoring must somehow be "documented." As Gitelman (2014) notes, in his treatise on "paperwork" and modern bureaucracies, the "knowing-showing" dimension of documentation is not just about recording information but about controlling the way people understand the social orders that they inhabit. What makes this possible is the process of *entextualization*, the transformation of messages, actions and identities into texts. What is "known" and "shown" about subjects of surveillance is largely determined by how the modes and media employed to document their actions make them "legible" (Scott 1999).

Bauman and Briggs (1990: 73) define entextualization as "the process of rendering discourse extractable, of making a stretch of linguistic production into a unit-a *text*-that can be lifted out of its interactional setting." This process, they say, is always, to some degree, an exercise of power, since those who entextualize reality are able to decide what aspects of reality are captured and how they are represented. They write:

> To decontextualize and recontextualize a text is thus an act of control, and in regard to the differential exercise of such control the issue of social power arises. More specifically, we may recognize differential access to texts, differential legitimacy in claims to and use of texts, differential competence in the use of texts, and differential values attaching to various types of texts.   (Bauman and Briggs 1990: 76)

Digital media have fundamentally changed how entextualization is carried out in practices of surveillance in terms of *what* is entextualized, the *way* it is encoded and the way these coded artifacts are *circulated*. Whereas, in the past, surveillance produced analogue documents and sometimes images which operated within the epistemological boundaries of human language, digital surveillance produces digital documents which operate within a very different epistemology, the logic of code. And what can be "known/shown" through code is very different from what can be "known/shown" through language.

Dodge and Kitchin (2005) make a useful distinction between "data," all possible information about something, and "capta," the information that a system is able to record and store. For computer systems, "capta" consists primarily of streams of gestures – clicks, swipes, "likes," etc. – that people perform through interfaces – referred to as "click-streams." The mistake many people make when it comes to digital surveillance is being vigilant about what they "say" online, not about what they *do*: those thousands of tiny actions that produce what Battelle (2005: 6) calls "a massive click-stream database of desires, needs, wants, and preferences." The fact is that digital surveillance systems are not yet very good at dealing with the "content" of our communication. They are much better at recording binary actions in the form of "metadata." In the case of surveillance, however, this can actually be an advantage. While too much data can overwhelm surveillance systems and sometimes distort perceptions due to "noise," more metadata can make analysis more accurate (Blaze 2013). Collecting metadata is often discounted as less intrusive than actually "reading people's emails" or "listening to people's phone calls": as Reilly (2014) puts it, "metadata is the envelope, not the letter." Numerous studies (see, for example, Kosinski, Stillwell and Graepel 2013; MIT Media Lab n.d.), however, have shown that a great deal about people's psychology, personal habits, desires, intentions and even future behaviors can be inferred through metadata. "Metadata," writes Blaze (2013), "can reveal far more about us, both individually and as groups, than the words we speak." As General Michael Hayden, former head of the CIA, more bluntly puts it: "We kill people based on metadata" (Cole 2014).

32.6 Recontextualization

The flip side of entextualization is recontextualization, the ways in which documents of surveillance are transported and embedded into different contexts, and the ways these different contexts change the meanings of texts and what they can be used for. For some privacy scholars, the main way that surveillance violates privacy is not through the collection of information but though the introduction of that information into contexts for which it was not intended, violating what Nissenbaum (2009) calls "contextual integrity."

A central characteristic of digital media is the fact that they facilitate recontextualization; they are built upon a logic of "data flows" that encourages social norms of sharing, linking, embedding and recirculating texts. In daily social interactions, this constant "disembedding" (Giddens 1991) of actions and utterances from their contexts creates multiple challenges for communication. When it comes to digital surveillance, however, the key aspect of recontextualization is not the way information is transported into different social contexts as much as it is the way it is transported into different *informational* contexts. The emergence of data management platforms allows surveillers to combine information collected about users not just with information collected about the same users from different sources but also with information from millions of other users.

Furthermore, this flow of information from data set to data set is constant and dynamic. Rather than using the term recontextualization, Haggerty and Ericson (2000) borrow from Deleuze and Guattari (1987) the notions of "deterritorialization" and "reterritorialization," which involve not just inserting information into new contexts but reshaping abstracted content into different forms through combining it with other content. A key aspect of Deleuze and Guattari's notions of "deterritorialization" and "reterritorialization" is what they call "lines of flight," the different trajectories that information takes and how these trajectories develop their own momentum. With the speed and efficiency of digital networks, it is not just a matter of information being transported from one context to another; rather, it is about information moving along *trajectories* of recontextualization.

32.7 Inferencing

The final way in which digital surveillance differs from analogue surveillance from a discourse analytical perspective is in how information is *processed* and what is done with it. All surveillance involves a certain amount of "inferencing" – the data that is gathered is always to some degree incomplete and ultimately has to be "pieced together" to produce theories about the significance of what subjects of surveillance have said or done. In digital surveillance, these inferences are formed by algorithms working on the kinds of large sets of data already described. But the way that algorithms make inferences is very different from the way people do. While humans form inferences through a logic of causation in which we try to discern why someone said what they did by testing it against some mutually agreed upon theory of communication such as Grice's (1989) cooperative principle, algorithms form inferences based on a logic of *correlation* in which "[m]eaning is constructed mathematically, probabilistically, based on correlations between pieces of input" (Jones 2020; see also Anderson 2008; Ayres 2008). Although these associations are often made based on assumptions about communication and identity held by the people who have written and trained these algorithms, inferences themselves are based on decontextualized Bayesian probabilities rather than on situated human reasoning. This can often result in startlingly accurate inferences, such as when algorithms are able to predict with a high degree of probability a Facebook user's skin color, political affiliation, sexuality, religion, alcohol, cigarette and drug use, and even whether their parents were divorced on the basis of as few as sixty-eight "likes" (Kosinski, Stillwell and Graepel 2013), not because of human assumptions about the kinds of things people of a certain ethnicity or political persuasion might "like," but because of the ability of algorithms to detect patterns in the past "liking" behavior of millions of other users. On the other hand, inferences based on big data correlations do sometimes get it wrong, and when they do, there is no mutually accepted norm of reasoning or theory of communication to appeal to for victims.

Another characteristic of algorithmic inferencing is that it is less about understanding the past as it is about predicting the future. In his book on search, John Battelle (2005) calls the stores of information that companies gather about internet users a "database of intention," an apt phrase because what this database is chiefly used for is making judgments about the probability of future behavior – what people intend to do next. Moreover, the generation of predictive models based on information gathered from present interactions ends up determining the kinds of interaction that will be available to people in the future. In other words, predictive inferencing ends up creating feedback loops that often end up *causing* the very actions or attitudes that they predict, as, for example, when an algorithm infers that a user is a Donald Trump supporter and so feeds her increasing quantities of pro-Trump content, giving her the impression that pro-Trump sentiments are more widespread than they actually are. Magnet and Gates (2009: 3) see this "cybernetic quality of [digital] surveillance – the capacity to feed personal data about individuals back into the mechanisms of social control" as one of the main things that "distinguish newer techniques from earlier, less interactive forms of monitoring."

32.8 Key Issues and Ongoing Debates

These discursive changes in the way that surveillance is carried out due to the introduction of digital technologies do not just impact the way we understand surveillance; they also force us to rethink a number of key issues in discourse analysis such as identity, agency and power (also see Chapter 5 in this volume). It has become axiomatic, for example, in discourse analytical circles to regard identity as socially constructed and dynamically negotiated in interaction (see, for example, Bucholtz and Hall 2005). The forms of participation, entextualization and inferencing that support digital surveillance, however, promote a way of understanding identity that assumes that it is "based upon probabilistic and actuarial logics" (Barnard-Wills 2012: 153) rather than interactional dynamics. This does not mean that the "data doubles" (Haggerty and Ericson 2000: 614) that are constructed of us as a result of digital surveillance are static – like analogue identities, they are also contingent and negotiated – but what they are contingent on is not the social contexts in which we act but the informational contexts through which our data flows. In his book *We Are Data*, Cheney-Lippold (2017: 5) notes how algorithmically produced categories like man, woman, Asian and wealthy have little to do with the actual social categories of gender, race and class, and more to do with "a proprietary vocabulary" intended for "marketers, political campaigns (and) government dragnets." "Who we are in the face of algorithmic interpretation," he writes, "is who we are computationally calculated to be … composed of an almost innumerable collection of interpretive layers, of hundreds of different companies and agencies identifying us in thousands of competing ways. At this very moment, Google may algorithmically think I'm male, whereas digital advertising company Quantcast could say I'm female, and web-analytic firm Alexa might be unsure" (Cheney-Lippold 2017: 6).

Second is the issue of agency and the degree of control we are able to exercise over our actions. In a situation where software allows an increasingly greater degree of mental processes to be delegated to computational systems (Berry 2011), agency, in the words of Introna (2011: 118) "becomes increasingly encapsulated, nested as codes within codes within codes." It is not just that many of the information games we play in our social lives are becoming automated, but also that software might be "training" us to surrender our agency. A good example of this is the issue of consent, where the form and volume of dialogue boxes asking us to grant consent give rise to what Rock calls "tick box consent" (2016). Consent-gathering processes are often engineered "to skew individual decision-making, in effect creating an illusion of free choice that helps to legitimatize surveillance practices" (Kerr, Lucock and Steeves 2009: 2). Unfortunately, most technical and legislative solutions which aim to help people regain control of their data are based on the flawed assumption that the more we are asked to give our consent for data gathering, the more control we have over it. On the contrary, the deluge of permission dialogues that are required by such laws as Europe's GDPR likely results in a kind of "consent fatigue," with users more and more likely to suspend judgment and just click "agree" (Jones 2018).

Perhaps the most important task of discourse analysts, however, is understanding how electronic surveillance changes the way that power is discursively constituted and exercised. What has been called the "information revolution," says Andrejevic (2015: x), is better conceptualized as a surveillance revolution in which exercises of power are increasingly "informatic." This power operates both on the macro-level, as large platforms hoard vast stores of data which allow them to dictate the parameters of communication, commerce and, increasingly, governance, and on the micro-level, as the surveillance agendas of the platforms dictate the kinds of social interactions and the kinds of life chances that individuals can have. What has been missing from critiques of power in digital surveillance is a thorough understanding of how power is enabled and exercised through the discursive dimensions of surveillance, how, for example, the "encoding of human experience" forces users of digital media to "submit to particular ways of categorizing and conceptualizing the world" (Duranti 2011: 29), how asymmetries in information processing capabilities create "pretextual gaps" (Maryns and Blommaert 2002) and how, through the transformation of bodies into information, individuals are fragmented, disciplined and denied authentic opportunities for communication in which identities are situated, relational and mutually negotiated (Anthamatten 2015).

32.9 Implications for Professional Practice

Whether we like it or not, linguists are deeply implicated in the creation and maintenance of the modern surveillance apparatus. There is, for example, a long history of linguists cooperating with intelligence services in areas like language teaching and cryptology. Linguists contribute to the monitoring and disciplining of migrants through lending their forensic expertise to the evaluation of claims for refugee status and developing language tests which operate as tools of normalization and control (Shohamy 2014). Linguists write the natural language processing algorithms used to capture and analyze both intelligence data and data on consumer behavior, and even in our teaching we submit our students to a wide array of surveillance practices, many enabled by digital media such as plagiarism detection software and learning analytics platforms.

At the same time, applied linguists and discourse analysts can also be part of the solution, contributing to a robust critique of digital surveillance and helping citizens to regain agency and control over their information. Discourse analysts, for example, can help to formulate design solutions such as interfaces that more effectively elicit genuine consent from users when their data is being collected or enable them to monitor the data they are giving to others (Nguyen and Mynatt 2002). They can also help to design and implement curricula that alert students to the discursive aspects of digital surveillance and give them opportunities to productively reflect upon how they interact with both human and nonhuman actors within surveillant assemblages (see, for example, Jones 2017b). Finally, applied linguists and discourse analysts can make a contribution to policy and critique, both in the workplace, by, for example, raising ethical issues about the use of digital platforms to gather data about students and staff (Slade and Prinsloo 2013) and outside the classroom, by calling attention to policies that allow governments and private entities to gather data about citizens and helping to document and critique how digital surveillance affects the experiences and rights of migrants and refugees (see, for example, Khan 2019).

32.10 Future Directions

The main aim of this chapter has been to make a case for the application of tools from discourse analysis to understanding and critiquing digital surveillance. Future work in this area will need to respond both to rapid technological changes which introduce increasingly sophisticated ways to gather information about people and to theoretical and methodological advances in the field of discourse analysis.

One key development that will need to be addressed is the rise of biometric technologies, which present challenges to the way we understand how bodies and information are interconnected (van der Ploeg 2003), challenges which dovetail with trends in sociolinguistics that advocate for more attention to the embodied dimensions of communication (see, for example, Bucholtz and Hall 2016). As Hayles (1993: 162) writes: "[E]mbodiment mediates between technology and discourse by creating new experiential frameworks that serve as boundary markers for the creation of corresponding discursive systems."

Another important challenge will be the increasing sophistication of intelligent agents embedded in all sorts of mundane objects like toothbrushes, television sets and automobiles. Here the recent turn in applied linguistics toward posthuman theory (Pennycook 2017) holds the promise of helping us to understand how the "agency" of objects affects how we play the information game (also see Chapter 16 in this volume). Increased interest in the role of "affect" in digital communication (Bucher 2017; Wee 2015) will also contribute to future research on the discursive and interactive dimensions of digital surveillance, addressing how the new "affective economies" (Ahmed 2004) online might change how people communicate (also see Chapter 14 in this volume).

The most important thing for discourse analysts tackling the issue of digital surveillance will be to avoid beginning with a priori assumptions about the roles and identities of "surveillers" and "surveilled" and to focus on the complex and contingent nature of online surveillance in which both humans and nonhuman actors assume multiple positions, construct multiple identities and engage in myriad micro-strategies of compliance or resistance moment by moment though the medium of discourse (Barnard-Wills 2012).

32.11 Summary

This chapter has presented an overview of the discursive dimensions of digital surveillance. It began with an account of the ways in which other disciplines have seen the relationship between surveillance and digital media. It then went on to argue that surveillance is, to some degree, part of all interactions, as individuals and institutions employ different discursive strategies to conceal or disclose information about themselves and gather and process information about others. The chapter explained five aspects of digital surveillance relevant to discourse analysts: (1) participation (the way digital media make available unique opportunities for "mutual monitoring"); (2) pretexting (the strategies used to get users of digital media to surrender their data); (3) entextualization (the way digital media facilitate the capture and encoding of data); (4) recontextualization (the way digital media affect the way data are circulated); and (5) inferencing (the way inferences are made based on data sets). The chapter then went on to identify some key issues in discourse analysis impacted by digital surveillance as well as some implications for the professional practices of discourse analysts and other scholars of language. The chapter ended by considering how more recent trends in discourse analysis around such notions as embodiment (see Chapter 15 in this volume), posthumanism and affect might inform future work on discourse and digital surveillance.

Further Reading

Barnard-Wills, D. (2012). *Surveillance and Identity: Discourse, Subjectivity and the State*. Farnham: Ashgate.

This is one of the few examples in surveillance studies to seriously engage with theories of discourse analysis, exploring how regimes of surveillance discursively construct social identities and relationships between citizens/customers and the state and corporations.

Jones, R. (2017). Surveillant Media: Technology, Language and Control. In C. Cotter and D. Perrin (eds.) *The Routledge Handbook of Language and Media*. London: Routledge. 244–61.

This chapter gives a comprehensive explanation of the impact of different kinds of media on the discursive processes involved in surveillance.

Jones, R. (2019). The Text Is Reading You: Teaching Language in the Age of the Algorithm. *Linguistics and Education*. (available online at https://doi.org/10.1016/j.linged.2019.100750)

This article looks at digital surveillance from the point of view of *users* of digital media, reporting on a research project in which participants described their "folk theories" of how algorithms work and reflected on how these theories affect the way they communicate.

References

Ahmed, S. (2004). Affective Economies. *Social Text* 22(2): 117–39.

Albrechtslund, A. (2008). Online Social Networking as Participatory Surveillance. *First Monday* 13(3).

Anderson, C. (2008). The End of Theory: The Data Deluge Makes the Scientific Method Obsolete. *Wired Magazine*, June 23. www.wired.com/2008/06/pb-theory.

Andrejevic, M. (2015). Foreword. In R. E. Dubrofsky and S. A. Magnet (eds.) *Feminist Surveillance Studies*. Durham, NC: Duke University Press. ix–xviii.

Anthamatten, E. (2015). Visibility Is a Trap: Body Cameras and the Panopticon of Police Power. The Mantle, March, 23. www.mantlethought.org/philosophy/visibility-trap.

Ayres, I. (2008). *Super Crunchers: How Anything Can Be Predicted*. London: Hachette.

Barnard-Wills, D. (2012). *Surveillance and Identity: Discourse, Subjectivity and the State*. Farnham: Ashgate.

Battelle, J. (2005). *The Search: How Google and Its Rivals Rewrote the Rules of Business and Transformed Our Culture*. New York: Portfolio.

Bauman, R. and Briggs, C. L. (1990). Poetics and Performance as Critical Perspectives on Language and Social Life. *Annual Review of Anthropology* 19: 59–88.

Bell, A. (1984). Language Style as Audience Design. *Language in Society* 13: 145–204.

Berry, D. (2011). *The Philosophy of Software: Code and Mediation in the Digital Age*. Basingstoke: Palgrave Macmillan.

Blaze, M. (2013). Phew, NSA Is Just Collecting Metadata (You Should Still Worry). *Wired*, June 19. www.wired.com/2013/06/phew-it-was-just-metadata-not-think-again.

Blommaert, J. and Omoniyi, T. (2006). Email Fraud: Language, Technology, and the Indexicals of Globalisation. *Social Semiotics* 16(4): 573–605.

Bowker, G. C. (2005). *Memory Practices in the Sciences*. Cambridge, MA: MIT Press.

Boyd, D. (2012). Networked Privacy. *Surveillance & Society* 10(3/4): 348–50.

Bucher, T. (2017). The Algorithmic Imaginary: Exploring the Ordinary Affects of Facebook Algorithms. *Information, Communication & Society* 20(1): 30–44. https://doi.org/10.1080/1369118X.2016.1154086.

Bucholtz, M. and Hall, K. (2005). Identity and Interaction: A Sociocultural Linguistic Approach. *Discourse Studies* 7(4–5): 585–614. https://doi.org/10.1177/1461445605054407.

(2016). Embodied Sociolinguistics. In N. Coupland (ed.) *Sociolinguistics*. Cambridge: Cambridge University Press. 173–98.

Cheney-Lippold, J. (2017). *We Are Data: Algorithms and the Making of Our Digital Selves*. New York: New York University Press.

Clarke, R. (1988). Information Technology and Dataveillance. *Communications of the ACM* 31(5): 498–512.

Cole, D. (2014). "We Kill People Based on Metadata." *New York Review of Books*, May 10. www.nybooks.com/daily/2014/05/10/we-kill-people-based-metadata.

Deleuze, G., Guattari, F. and Massumi, B. (1987). *A Thousand Plateaus: Capitalism and Schizophrenia*. Minneapolis: University of Minnesota Press.

Dodge, M. and Kitchin, R. (2005). Codes of Life: Identification Codes and the Machine-Readable World. *Environment and Planning D: Society and Space* 23(6): 851–81.

Dunbar, R. (1996). *Grooming, Gossip and the Evolution of Language*. Cambridge, MA: Harvard University Press.

Duranti, A. (2011). Linguistic Anthropology: The Study of Language as a Non-neutral Medium. In R. Mesthrie (ed.) *The Cambridge Handbook of Sociolinguistics*. Cambridge: Cambridge University Press. 28–46.

European Commission. (2017). 2018 Reform of EU Data Protection Rules. https://ec.europa.eu/commission/priorities/justice-and-fundamental-rights/data-protection/2018-reform-eu-data-protection-rules_en.

Foth, M. and Hearn, G. (2007). Networked Individualism of Urban Residents: Discovering the Communicative Ecology in Inner-City Apartment Buildings. *Information, Communication & Society* 10(5): 749–72.

Garfinkel, H. (1986). Remarks on Ethnomethodology. In J. J. Gumperz and D. Hymes (eds.) *Directions in Sociolinguistics: The Ethnography of Communication*, 2nd ed. New York: John Wiley & Sons. 301–45.

Giddens, A. (1991). *The Consequences of Modernity*. Cambridge: Polity Press.

Gitelman, L. (2014). *Paper Knowledge: Toward a Media History of Documents*. Durham, NC: Duke University Press.

Goffman, E. (1959). *The Presentation of Self in Everyday Life*. New York: Doubleday.

(1963). *Stigma: Notes on the Management of Spoiled Identity*. Englewood Cliffs, NJ: Prentice Hall.

(1964). The Neglected Situation. *American Anthropologist* 66(6_PART2): 133–6.

(1972). *Relations in Public: Microstudies of the Public Order*. New York: Harper & Row.

(1981). *Forms of Talk*. Oxford: Blackwell.

Graham, S. (1998). Spaces of Surveillant Simulation: New Technologies, Digital Representations, and Material Geographies. *Environment and Planning D: Society and Space* 16(4): 483–504.

Graham, S. and Wood, D. (2003). Digitizing Surveillance: Categorization, Space, Inequality. *Critical Social Policy* 23(2): 227–48.

Grassenger, H. and Krogerus, M. (2017). The Data that Turned the World Upside Down. Vice, January 28. https://motherboard.vice.com/en_us/article/mg9vvn/how-our-likes-helped-trump-win.

Grice, H. P. (1989). *Studies in the Way of Words*. Cambridge, MA: Harvard University Press.

Hadnagy, C. (2010). *Social Engineering: The Art of Human Hacking*. Indianapolis, IN: Wiley.

Haggerty, K. D. (2006). Tear Down the Walls: On Demolishing the Panopticon. In D. Lyon (ed.) *Theorizing Surveillance*. London: Routledge. 23–45.

Haggerty, K. D. and Ericson, R. V. (2000). The Surveillant Assemblage. *British Journal of Sociology* 51(4): 605–22.
Hayles, N. K. (1993). The Materiality of Informatics. *Configurations* 1(1): 147–70.
Hess, A. (2014). You Are What You Compute (and What Is Computed for You): Considerations of Digital Rhetorical Identification. *Journal of Contemporary Rhetoric* 4(1/2): 1–18.
Hutchby, I. (2001). *Conversation and Technology: From the Telephone to the Internet*. Cambridge, UK/Malden, MA: Polity.
Hymes, D. (1974). *Foundations in Sociolinguistics: An Ethnographic Approach*. Philadelphia: University of Pennsylvania Press.
ieeessit. (2017). Ubiquitous Surveillance and Security. Technology and Society, June 29. http://technologyandsociety.org/ubiquitous-surveillance-and-security/.
Introna, L. D. (2011). The Enframing of Code Agency, Originality and the Plagiarist. *Theory, Culture & Society* 28(6): 113–41.
Johnson, D. G. and Regan, P. M. (2014). *Transparency and Surveillance as Sociotechnical Accountability: A House of Mirrors*. London: Routledge.
Jones, R. H. (2009). Inter-activity: How New Media Can Help Us Understand Old Media. In C. Rowe and E. Wyss (eds.) *New Media and Linguistic Change*. Cresskill, NJ: Hampton Press. 11–29.
   (2017a). Surveillant Media: Technology, Language and Control. In C. Colleen and D. Perrin (eds.) *Routledge Handbook of Language and Media*. London: Routledge. 244–61.
   (2017b). "The Text Is Reading You": Language Teaching in the Age of the Algorithm. Presented at the 18th World Congress of Applied Linguistics, Rio de Janeiro.
   (2018). GDPR and the Discursive Coercion of Consent. A plenary address presented at the "What's Up, Switzerland?" Conference: Language, Individuals and Ideologies in Mobile Messaging, University of Zurich, October 18–20.
   (2020). The Rise of the Pragmatic Web: Implications for Rethinking Meaning and Interaction. In C. Tagg and M. Evans (eds.) *Historicising the Digital*. Amsterdam: Mouton de Gruyter 17–37.
Jones, R. H. and Hafner, C. A. (2012). *Understanding Digital Literacies: A Practical Introduction*. London: Routledge.
Kerr, I., Lucock, C. and Steeves, V. (2009). *Lessons from the Identity Trail: Anonymity, Privacy and Identity in a Networked Society*. Oxford/New York: Oxford University Press.
Khan, K. (2019). *Becoming a Citizen: Linguistic Trials and Negotiations in the UK*. London/New York: Bloomsbury Academic.
Kim, N. S. (2013). *Wrap Contracts: Foundations and Ramifications*. Oxford: Oxford University Press.

Kosinski, M., Stillwell, D. and Graepel, T. (2013). Private Traits and Attributes Are Predictable from Digital Records of Human Behavior. *Proceedings of the National Academy of Sciences* 110(15): 5802–5.

Lanier, J. (2018). *Ten Arguments for Deleting Your Social Media Accounts Right Now*. New York: Henry Holt and Company.

Latour, B. (2007). *Reassembling the Social: An Introduction to Actor-Network-Theory*. Oxford/New York: Oxford University Press.

Longford, G. (2005). Pedagogies of Digital Citizenship and the Politics of Code. *Techné: Research in Philosophy and Technology* 9(1): 68–96.

Lyon, D. (2003). *Surveillance as Social Sorting: Privacy, Risk, and Digital Discrimination*. New York: Psychology Press.

Magnet, S. and Gates, K. (2009). Communicating Surveillance: Examining the Intersections. In K. Gates and S. Magnet (eds.) *The New Media of Surveillance*. London: Routledge.

Marx, G. T. (2012). "Your Papers Please": Personal and Professional Encounters with Surveillance. In D. Lyon, K. Ball and K. D. Haggerty (eds.) *The Routledge Handbook of Surveillance Studies*. London: Routledge. xx–xxxi.

(2016). *Windows into the Soul: Surveillance and Society in an Age of High Technology*. Chicago, IL: University of Chicago Press.

Maryns, K. and Blommaert, J. (2002). Pretextuality and Pretextual Gaps: On Re/defining Linguistic Inequality. *Journal of Pragmatics* 12(1): 11–30.

McGrath, J. (2004). *Loving Big Brother: Surveillance Culture and Performance Space*. London/New York: Routledge.

MIT Media Lab. (n.d.). Project Overview: On the Re-identifiability of Credit Card Metadata. www.media.mit.edu/projects/on-the-reidentifiability-of-credit-card-metadata/overview.

Nguyen, D. H. and Mynatt, E. D. (2002). *Privacy Mirrors: Understanding and Shaping Socio-technical Ubiquitous Computing Systems* (Technical Report). Georgia Institute of Technology. https://smartech.gatech.edu/handle/1853/3268.

Nissenbaum, H. (2009). *Privacy in Context: Technology, Policy, and the Integrity of Social Life*. Palo Alto, CA: Stanford University Press.

Palen, L. and Dourish, P. (2003). Unpacking "Privacy" for a Networked World. In Proceedings of the SIGCHI Conference on Human Factors in Computing Systems. New York: ACM. 129–36.

Papacharissi, Z. and Gibson, P. L. (2011). Fifteen Minutes of Privacy: Privacy, Sociality, and Publicity on Social Network Sites. In S. Trepte and L. Reinecke (eds.) *Privacy Online: Perspectives on Privacy and Self-Disclosure in the Social Web*. Berlin/Heidelberg: Springer. 75–89.

Pennycook, A. (2017). *Posthumanist Applied Linguistics*. London: Routledge.

Phillips, D. J. (2002). Negotiating the Digital Closet: Online Pseudonymity and the Politics of Sexual Identity. *Information, Communication & Society* 5(3): 406–24.

Reilly, C. (2014). The Metadata Debate: What You Need to Know about Data Retention. CNet, August 13. www.cnet.com/news/what-you-need-to-know-about-data-retention.

Rivest, R. L., Shamir, A. and Adleman, L. (1978). A Method for Obtaining Digital Signatures and Public-Key Cryptosystems. *Communication of the ACM* 21(2): 120–6.

Rock, F. (2016). Talking the Ethical Turn: Drawing on Tick-Box Consent in Policing. In S. Ehrlich, D. Eades and J. Ainsworth (eds.) *Discursive Constructions of Consent in the Legal Process*. Oxford: Oxford University Press. 93–117.

Ruesch, J. and Bateson, G. (1951). *Communication: The Social Matrix of Psychiatry*. New York: W.W. Norton.

Scott, J. (1999). *Seeing Like a State: How Certain Schemes to Improve the Human Condition Have Failed*. New Haven, CT: Yale University Press.

Shohamy, E. (2014). *The Power of Tests: A Critical Perspective on the Uses of Language Tests*. London: Routledge.

Slade, S. and Prinsloo, P. (2013). Learning Analytics: Ethical Issues and Dilemmas. *American Behavioral Scientist* 57(10): 1510–29.

Tagg, C., Seargeant, P. and Brown, A. A. (2017). *Taking Offence on Social Media: Conviviality and Communication on Facebook*. New York: Palgrave Macmillan.

Tene, O. and Polonetsky, J. (2013). Big Data for All: Privacy and User Control in the Age of Analytics. *Northwestern Journal of Technology and Intellectual Property* 11(5): 239.

Tiainen, M. (2017). (De)legitimating Electronic Surveillance: A Critical Discourse Analysis of the Finnish News Coverage of the Edward Snowden Revelations. *Critical Discourse Studies* 14(4): 402–19.

Trottier, D. (2012). *Social Media as Surveillance: Rethinking Visibility in a Converging World*. Farnham: Ashgate.

Van der Ploeg, I. (2003). Biometrics and Privacy: A Note on the Politics of Theorizing Technology. *Information, Communication & Society* 6(1): 85–104. https://doi.org/10.1080/1369118032000068741.

Wee, L. (2015). Mobilizing Affect in the Linguistic Cyberlandscape: The R-Word Campaign. In R. Rudby and S. Ben Said (eds.) *Conflict, Exclusion and Dissent in the Linguistic Landscape*. Basingstoke: Palgrave Macmillan. 185–203.

Widdowson, H. G. (2004). *Text, Context, Pretext: Critical Issues in Discourse Analysis*. Hoboken, NJ: Wiley-Blackwell.

Index

academic literacy, 441, 583
accountability, 628, 652, 679
activity, 11, 12, 14, 23, 54, 64, 73, 76, 78, 80, 82, 83, 84, 106, 116, 132–4, 136, 137, 241, 242, 296, 310, 358, 360, 361–3, 365, 372, 375, 378, 396, 424, 440–1, 446, 448, 468, 471, 475, 557, 560, 573, 583, 651, 654, 655, 656
affect, 83, 86, 223, 257–8, 260, 313, 321, 329–31, 332–4, 340, 343–5, 352, 357, 374, 384, 418, 420–1, 429–30, 475, 571, 693, 696, 697, 699, 725
agency, 54, 74, 77, 84, 99, 115, 227, 239, 245, 257, 261, 294, 340, 351, 355–6, 358–9, 360, 361–2, 364–6, 374, 420, 448, 458, 460, 461, 497, 500, 505, 507, 510–11, 513–15, 519, 538, 541, 596, 601, 622, 646–9, 650, 652–3, 675, 680, 710, 722–3, 724–5
assemblage, 74, 257, 317, 333, 354, 356–7, 358, 359–60, 362–4, 365, 371, 373, 396, 407, 409, 429, 442, 447, 712, 724
asylum, 98, 101, 102, 103, 190, 195, 336, 382, 383, 430, 458, 461, 475, 531, 548–58, 560, 562, 563–6
audience uptake, 694, 697
austerity, 194, 597, 645, 651, 655–7, 661
automated techniques, 257, 263, 274

Bakhtin, Mikhail M., 32, 41, 43–4, 45–6, 48, 58, 71–2, 77, 80, 100, 342, 429, 541, 606, 681
big data approaches, 263, 275
bottom-up, 308, 312
branding, 383, 384, 593, 597, 645, 671–3, 679, 681
breaking news, 96, 104–5, 696

CA. *See* conversation analysis
care homes, 117, 149, 150–1, 158
CDA. *See* critical discourse analysis
CGA. *See* critical genre analysis
chronotope, 3, 5, 6, 33, 46–7, 48, 57–9, 62, 71, 84–5, 94, 100–1, 102, 108, 388, 541
CL-CDS. *See* critical discourse studies: cognitive linguistic
code-meshing, 446
cognitive grammar, 187

cognitive linguistics, 116, 118, 186–9, 201–3, 207, 271, 336, 337
commoditization, 598, 690, 691–2
competence, 33–4, 71, 74, 121, 151, 336, 360, 375, 384, 388, 409, 447, 449, 719
complexity, 85, 97–8, 99, 175, 217, 221, 256, 263, 264, 271, 272, 273, 275, 313, 383, 449, 461, 462, 518, 551, 563, 580, 626, 644, 657, 692, 700
consequentialism, 470
construal, 14, 16, 188, 190–1, 194, 196, 198–201, 205, 207
contextualization, 1, 3–5, 25, 32, 36, 52–3, 54, 57, 58, 63, 64–5, 84, 258, 332, 457, 549, 595, 695, 716
conversation analysis, 3, 65, 92, 94, 115–18, 121, 123, 125–6, 129, 131, 135, 136, 144, 151, 159, 167, 176, 256, 259, 263, 266, 270, 275, 331–2, 339, 373, 385, 442, 449, 507, 509, 510, 514–15, 530, 537, 681, 691, 697
corporate
    discourse, 597, 666–8, 678–9, 680–2
    identity, 668, 671–3, 679
    social responsibility, 675
    talk, 597, 667
corpus linguistics, 115, 118, 165–6, 173–4, 175, 176–7, 178–82, 201–3, 239, 586, 681
corpus-assisted discourse studies (CADS), 118, 165–6, 167, 173–82
credibility, 418, 548, 550, 552–3, 560, 564, 566, 672, 676, 678
crisis communication, 676
critical approaches, 595, 660
critical discourse analysis, 80, 81, 115–16, 119, 165, 173, 178, 240, 241, 242, 256, 259, 260, 261, 263, 265, 268, 269–70, 274–5, 322, 352, 359, 420, 449, 457, 469, 508, 515, 530, 537–8, 586, 594–6, 598, 601–2, 603, 606, 608–9, 610, 611–12, 613–14, 616–17, 631, 644, 645, 651, 659, 660, 674, 675, 678, 680–1, 698
critical discourse studies, 186, 207, 236, 240, 241, 248, 601, 659, 701
    cognitive linguistic, 119, 186–9, 193, 195, 198, 199, 201–3, 207, 271

critical genre analysis, 595–6, 604, 606, 608, 610–11, 612, 613, 615, 616, 617, See also genre

deixis, 198, 199, 259, 300, 333
desire, 137, 200, 330, 352, 424–7, 430, 446, 467, 576, 710, 720
discursive formation, 75, 76–9, 81, 241, 243, 245, 366
distributed language, 396
diversity, 81, 83, 261, 318, 373, 378, 380, 383–4, 396, 439, 441, 444–6, 450, 460, 477, 502, 505–6, 507–10, 514, 518, 520, 578, 583, 625, 634

Eckert, Penelope, 9, 19, 21–2, 425, 427, 476, 477
economics, 147, 195, 446, 597, 622–3, 627, 646, 647–8, 649, 650, 651, 658–9, 660
embodiment, 101, 158, 257–8, 259–60, 287, 309, 328, 329–31, 332, 339, 340, 344, 365, 636, 725, 726
emotion, 41, 98, 103, 169, 187, 214, 222–3, 227, 258, 260, 327–31, 334, 336–45, 358, 373, 374, 387, 409, 410, 418, 420–1, 424, 429, 461, 538, 647, 654, 673
entextualization, 6, 82, 598, 710, 714, 719, 720, 722, 726
ethical regulation, 465–6, 472, 481, 482
ethics, 457–9, 465–6, 469–70, 472, 476, 481–2, 594, 602–3, 609, 614, 615, 616, 659, 660
ethnic minority, 479, 488, 495, 561
ethnicity, 93, 97, 377, 380, 420, 488, 496, 508, 509, 519, 541, 581, 584, 722
ethnography, 1, 5, 10, 17, 19, 22, 103, 117, 258, 309, 331, 358, 363, 373, 379, 385, 442, 449, 506, 512, 538, 578, 594, 693
events, 1, 13, 23, 37, 39, 42, 43, 47, 55, 58, 61, 74–5, 80, 81, 84, 85, 92, 94–5, 96, 101, 105, 137, 153, 174, 191, 195, 196, 200–1, 207, 222, 258, 263, 268, 270, 274, 294, 307, 313, 316, 317, 321–2, 330, 331, 332, 337, 340, 342, 344, 351, 357, 362, 373, 374, 377, 381, 386, 388, 396, 411, 417, 467, 500, 548, 551, 552–3, 557, 558, 580, 597, 609, 623, 648, 651, 652, 660–1, 666, 691
everyday settings, 117, 151, 462
evidence, 15, 121, 125, 131, 132–3, 134, 136, 147, 157, 174–5, 178, 179, 187, 202, 205–8, 217, 219, 223, 224, 269, 273, 318, 466, 475, 517, 518, 548–9, 550, 551, 552, 553–4, 556, 560–1, 562, 634, 636, 646, 657–8, 680, 696, 700

far-right, 431, 630
financial crisis, 596, 644, 650, 651, 653
  global, 596, 644, 647–8, 650–2, 653–4, 655, 660
footing, 33, 36–7, 48, 65
formats, 5, 36, 58–9, 60, 63–5, 98, 99, 670, 700
frame, 2, 5, 7, 14, 24, 35–7, 41–2, 45, 55, 56, 57–9, 62, 100–1, 116, 187, 193–8, 203, 205, 206, 214, 215–16, 219–20, 221–2, 225, 227–8, 406, 407, 428, 509, 536, 539, 548, 572, 584, 602, 613, 648, 658, 691
framing, 5, 14, 57, 84, 117, 118–19, 158, 166, 193, 194, 205, 206, 213, 215–20, 222–30, 351, 445, 572, 597, 613–14, 657–8, 691
French School, 119, 235–6, 240–1, 248

gender, 34, 37, 39, 85, 93, 107, 220, 244, 248, 260, 314–15, 317–18, 327, 335–6, 338, 341, 344, 353, 357, 380, 418, 419, 420, 422–3, 425, 426, 428, 430, 462, 488, 509, 515, 519, 529, 538, 539, 571, 573, 581, 601, 669, 681, 723
genre, 2, 5, 33, 41–3, 48, 77–81, 91, 93, 165, 186, 229, 268, 366, 371, 374, 424, 439–40, 443, 444–5, 450, 461, 548, 594, 595–6, 601–2, 603–17, 632, 656, 674, 681, 694, 714, 718
globalization, 24, 37, 81, 102, 371, 373, 377, 379–82, 383, 385, 387–8, 437, 443, 489
Goffman, Erving, 3, 5, 11, 32, 35–6, 37–8, 41, 43, 48, 53, 55, 56–8, 59, 222, 265, 271, 328, 331–2, 385, 671, 711, 713, 714, 716
Gumperz, John J., 3, 15–16, 18, 52–3, 65, 332, 342, 359, 372, 381, 383, 385, 457

hate, 336, 374, 422, 423, 425, 431, 628
historicity, 70–3, 74–6, 82, 83, 85
hope, 130, 320, 380, 430, 431, 574, 646, 659, 680

identity
  community identity, 314
  identities-in-interaction, 92–4, 95
ideology, 76, 188, 194, 207, 259–60, 269, 271, 287, 288, 307, 397, 477, 513, 528, 541, 596, 603, 612, 617, 632–3, 635, 644, 651, 653, 656, 659, 660
  neoliberalism, 244, 489, 630, 651, 652, 655–6, 659
image schema, 189–90, 193, 203
inclusion, 261, 294, 295, 321, 352, 460, 478, 492, 505–6, 507–10, 511–12, 513–14, 518, 520, 575, 586, 674
indexicality, 3–5, 10–11, 13–14, 16, 17, 22, 23–4, 40, 53, 57, 60, 64, 84, 94, 341, 382, 387, 388, 534, 538, 692
inferencing, 598, 710, 714, 721–2, 726
informed consent, 459, 474, 475–7, 482
inscription, 73, 78, 265, 294
interaction, 3–4, 5, 9–11, 14, 15, 16–17, 22, 23, 24–5, 33, 34–6, 38, 40, 53–4, 56–61, 62, 63, 64–5, 72–3, 80, 82, 84–5, 92–4, 96, 99, 117–18, 121–3, 125, 130, 131–5, 136–7, 143–5, 148–51, 155–9, 172, 177, 190–2, 197, 217, 221, 222, 229–30, 256, 258, 259, 260, 263, 264, 265, 268, 270, 274, 298, 300, 320, 328–34, 336, 337–42, 343–5, 351, 353, 358–9, 361, 362–3, 364, 366–7, 372–3, 374, 375, 378, 384–6, 396, 398, 407, 408, 410, 411, 423, 444, 457, 458, 461, 506–11, 512–14, 515, 518–20, 532–3, 536, 537–8, 539, 541, 551, 554, 565, 579, 585, 598, 612, 645, 654, 668, 669–70, 671, 676, 688, 689, 710, 711, 714–18, 722
interaction analysis, 263, 265, 275
  multimodal, 259, 270
interdisciplinarity, 85, 461
interdiscursivity, 6, 70, 76–8, 79, 80, 82, 85, 595, 610–11
interpellation, 335
  ideological, 77
interrogation, 108, 239, 248, 552, 553, 558, 564, 714
intersectionality, 374, 418–20, 421, 529, 580

intertextuality, 5, 6, 33, 36, 43, 44, 46, 47, 48, 71, 76, 77, 78–9, 80–2, 85, 440, 441, 512, 558, 681
interview, 19–20, 21, 35, 46, 61, 62, 91, 93, 95, 97, 103, 116, 131, 135, 148, 151, 156, 157, 159, 181, 243, 309, 378, 382, 385–6, 411, 440, 475–7, 512, 516, 552, 554, 576, 577, 612, 613, 623, 666, 691

Jakobson, Roman, 4, 10, 12–13, 25, 286, 328

Kongish, 402–4

language socialization, 581
language teaching and learning, 578, 581, 582
laughter, 144, 145, 151–3, 155
legitimacy, 207, 493, 516, 549, 552, 580, 614, 672, 676, 719
linguistic anthropology, 9–10, 17, 19, 82, 94, 95, 331, 332, 363, 508, 530, 536, 538–9, 598
linguistic diversity, 308, 338, 477
lived experience, 260, 261, 330, 337–8, 339, 340, 341, 344, 394, 397, 419, 420, 461, 513

marginalization, 386, 510, 512, 518
MDA. *See* multimodal discourse analysis
media
    digital, 103, 272, 712, 714, 715–16, 717, 718, 719, 720, 724, 725
    logic, 688–9, 693, 695–6
    social, 24, 44, 58, 62, 63, 91, 96, 98, 104, 108, 157, 167, 181, 258, 260, 307, 313, 316–17, 320–1, 322, 358, 365, 385, 402, 425, 468, 519, 585, 593, 596, 597–8, 623, 628, 632, 667, 676–8, 681, 690, 700, 701, 708–11, 712, 716
mediated discourse analysis, 256, 270, 362
mediatization, 105, 595, 597–8, 623, 624, 627, 633, 687–701
memorials, 319–21
metaphor, 63–4, 95, 115–17, 118–19, 193–5, 205–7, 213–15, 216–30, 271, 315, 318, 328, 336, 356, 360, 399, 576–7, 614, 644, 646–51, 652, 653–4, 656, 657, 660, 669, 674, 675, 691, 697
    and the economy, 596, 647
    Conceptual Metaphor Theory, 119, 187, 206, 213, 215, 216, 221–2, 223, 224–5, 226, 228, 271, 646
    linguistic metaphors, 222, 225
    systematic metaphors, 222, 225, 228
metapragmatics, 14, 24, 693–5, 701
methodology
    mixed methods, 118, 174, 179, 182, 257, 259, 263, 274, 275
metonymy, 119, 213, 215, 217–18, 229–30, 653
micro (discourse) analysis, 115–17, 143, 148, 155–6, 157–8, 159, 261, 330, 512, 513–14
micro–macro dichotomy, 4–6, 55–6, 81, 82–3, 84, 100, 115, 137, 177, 258, 352, 519, 541
migrants, 83, 99, 101–4, 190, 196, 372, 378, 379, 380, 383, 386, 388, 430, 459, 487–92, 494–6, 498, 499–500, 501, 554, 563, 724
minimizing harm, 469, 470–1, 482
mobility, 6–7, 83, 85, 92, 99, 102–4, 309, 352, 363, 371, 373, 379, 380, 381, 394, 443, 458, 490, 496

modality, 195, 199, 201, 288, 309, 310, 332
money, 218, 224, 318, 562, 594, 596, 644–6, 649, 650–1, 654–5, 658, 659–60
multimodal analysis, 116, 119, 125, 165, 263, 272, 273, 275, 653–4
multimodal discourse, 269, 274, 413
multimodal discourse analysis, 198, 202, 256, 258, 267–8, 271, 272, 274, 364, 428, 631, 681
    systemic functional, 268
multimodality, 116, 207, 258, 263–7, 268, 270, 271–2, 275, 333, 421, 441, 442, 595, 596, 616, 617, 623, 633, 674, 681
multi-semioticity, 256, 257

narration, 19–20, 549, 551, 559
narrative, 6, 42, 46, 83, 91–2, 93–104, 105, 108, 152, 158, 221, 257, 258, 260, 313, 317, 320–1, 338–40, 354, 364, 387, 421, 461, 482, 513, 547–54, 555–8, 559–60, 561–6, 581, 646, 658, 709
nationalism, 377
neoliberal capitalism, 651, 653, 656
new materialism, 354, 357
next turn proof procedure, 117, 121, 125
nexus
    analysis, 85, 256, 270, 339, 360, 519
    of practice, 52
    online–offline, 52, 53–4, 55, 365

online
    communication, 695
    discourse, 687, 695
    platforms, 25, 423, 449, 519, 700
ontology, 70, 257, 354–5, 361, 363, 365–6
organizational discourse, 97, 519, 602, 606, 611, 617, 675

participant roles, 5, 9, 33, 35, 36, 37, 41, 45, 48, 100, 715
participation frameworks, 35, 58, 65, 100, 101, 552, 715–16
Peirce, Charles Sanders, 10, 11–12, 13, 264, 282, 283, 285, 288–94, 297–8, 300, 301
performativity, 6, 92, 335, 357
permanent resident, 488
phenomenology, 65, 330, 337, 339
point of view, 93, 165, 173, 198–9, 202, 203–5, 228, 256, 259, 286, 470, 480, 548, 563, 676, 680
political discourse, 76, 108, 194, 220, 691
political identity, 92, 315
populism, 248, 594, 596, 622–5, 626–30, 631–6
positioning, 39, 94, 96–7, 103, 106, 108, 118, 120, 146, 197, 198, 199, 201, 243, 257, 330, 338, 339–40, 344, 351, 362, 461, 491, 513, 533, 538, 540, 563, 593, 612, 636, 652, 654
posthumanism, 261, 351, 353–5, 363, 364, 366
postmultilingualism, 395
poststructuralism, 119, 235–40, 241–3, 246, 247–8, 264, 421, 466, 515
poverty porn, 597, 645, 656, 657
power, 4, 6, 11, 18, 22, 32–3, 34, 35, 38, 44, 59, 75, 85, 98, 102, 104, 119, 155, 186, 207, 215, 217, 222, 223, 235–7, 238–40, 242, 243, 245, 246, 248, 257, 258, 289, 306, 310–11, 314, 318, 330, 334, 335, 338, 339, 341, 344, 350–1, 357, 362, 366, 373, 374, 381, 383, 398, 417–18, 419, 420, 421, 423, 428, 430,

444, 457, 458, 460-1, 479-81, 493, 505, 507, 508, 511, 514-16, 518, 520, 527-8, 537-40, 541-2, 572, 577, 593, 601, 607, 609, 612, 615, 616, 617, 624-5, 626, 630, 634, 635, 647, 652, 657, 658, 669, 671, 672, 678, 680, 695, 697, 710, 713, 718, 719, 722, 723
  soft, 614, 615, 616
pragmatics, 14, 17, 71, 73, 74, 79, 84, 92, 120, 165, 223, 240-1, 246, 270-1
progressivity, 122
project, 10, 17, 75, 76, 77, 94, 99, 125, 133-4, 136, 143, 155, 168, 169, 172, 176, 178, 215, 245, 315, 354, 474, 476-8, 576, 597, 655, 657-8, 669, 674, 678
public image, 628
public signs, 310, 313
purpose-built software, 257, 259, 263, 272

quality interaction, 117, 143, 144, 145-6, 148, 150, 158, 159

race, 34, 39, 41, 258, 336, 341, 344, 357, 377, 417, 419-20, 422, 423, 425, 426, 461, 509, 512, 515, 519, 527-30, 531-3, 534, 535-42, 555, 571, 581, 691, 723
racialization, 458, 461, 527, 528, 529, 535, 536-7, 538, 540, 541
racism, 247, 260, 327, 420, 422, 424, 426, 458, 461, 508, 528, 529, 530, 532, 533, 537-8, 539-41, 574, 612
reality, 5, 42, 59, 76, 83, 92, 94, 101, 170, 179, 194, 201, 216, 237, 239, 242, 248, 287, 288, 290, 296, 301, 307, 327, 374, 399, 498, 527, 530, 533, 536, 539, 551, 598, 601, 633, 654, 655, 658, 679, 689, 714, 719
reciprocity, 466, 470, 478-9, 482, 672
recontextualization, 44, 81, 101, 595, 598, 625, 631, 632, 690, 693, 700, 710, 714, 720-1, 726
reflexivity, 82, 248, 515, 520, 598, 688, 692, 701
refugees, 98, 102, 103, 462, 475, 497, 507, 552, 623, 625, 724
register, 4-5, 9-11, 13, 15-18, 22, 23-5, 33, 39-41, 44, 46-7, 48, 58, 237, 255, 268, 269, 287, 295, 301, 373, 387, 394-5, 405-6, 407, 410, 413, 497, 536, 572, 670
religious
  identity, 573, 579, 580, 583, 584
  literacy, 462, 572, 578-9, 580-4
  socialization, 580
repertoire, 3-4, 9, 16-19, 24, 39-41, 46, 82, 84, 94, 264, 342-3, 365, 372, 395, 396, 398, 399, 407, 408, 410, 412-13, 447, 460, 497, 498, 507, 512, 579, 633, 651, 669-70
  spatial, 361, 448
representation, 2, 11, 23, 94, 107, 148, 157, 186-8, 190, 202, 204, 207, 224, 235-6, 239, 243, 256, 258, 264, 269, 271, 289, 290, 301, 307, 315, 332, 338, 341, 344, 354-5, 357, 358, 365, 366, 385, 397, 466, 468, 531, 532-3, 540, 547, 574, 586, 601-2, 609, 625, 636, 648, 649, 651, 652, 657, 660, 673-4, 689, 691, 695
respecting autonomy, 469, 470, 475, 482
response relevance, 122, 124, 132
rhetorics, 596, 622-3, 624, 628-9, 631, 634, 635-6

selfie, 105-6
semiotics, 13, 207, 264, 265-6, 267, 268, 270, 310, 351, 352, 361, 397, 646, 654, 699
  social, 256, 259, 263, 265-7, 268-9, 274, 275, 401, 535, 631
shame, 337, 340, 343-4, 374, 427-8, 429, 431, 533
signature, 79, 294-6, 352
silence, 123-4, 131, 133, 320, 428, 595
Silverstein, Michael, 4, 10, 13, 21, 25, 82
Singlish, 402, 404-6
small stories, 6, 95-7, 106, 120, 257
  research, 92, 95, 97, 104, 108, 120
social action, 53, 54, 56, 59, 60, 64, 65, 76, 84-5, 93, 186, 188, 194, 201, 256, 257, 264, 269, 339, 447, 595, 601-7, 609, 611, 612-14, 616, 617
social interaction, 34, 46, 52, 115, 157, 264, 270, 328, 331, 394, 395, 399, 407, 409, 411, 442, 448, 474, 477, 507, 539, 541, 609, 696, 710, 711, 715-16, 720, 724
social practice, 17, 40, 75, 242, 244, 260, 261, 269, 310, 319, 327, 334, 358-9, 374, 408, 420, 461, 489, 498, 516, 527, 534, 537, 538, 542, 594, 597, 601, 608, 609-10, 611, 612-13, 616, 617, 631, 636, 655, 666, 710
sociolinguistics, 1, 3, 9-10, 17, 19, 20-1, 24, 82, 91-2, 94, 95, 239, 242, 261, 270, 306, 309, 328, 331, 340, 359, 362-3, 366, 372, 377, 381, 385-6, 387, 388, 397, 457, 468, 539, 598, 681, 725
space, 7, 11, 19, 42, 46, 54, 63-4, 71, 73, 76, 78, 79, 83, 84, 91-2, 99-100, 101-2, 103, 104, 125, 131, 189, 195, 200, 236, 242-3, 245, 246, 248, 256, 259, 263, 272, 296-8, 299, 306-8, 310-11, 313-15, 317, 319-20, 332-4, 341, 350, 372, 379, 395, 397, 398, 401, 408, 410, 421, 489-90, 497, 500, 507, 518, 531-2, 535, 540, 541, 555, 572, 573, 577, 578-9, 580, 582-3, 585, 596, 598, 609, 625, 629, 649, 653, 673, 697-8
spatiality, 614
stance, 5, 33, 36, 37-9, 41, 44, 48, 78, 94, 127, 131, 166, 201, 236, 257, 316, 332, 338-40, 355, 362, 367, 374, 406, 419, 424, 461, 515, 533, 573, 613, 634-5
statelessness, 488
strategy, 5, 33, 35, 37, 46, 75, 93, 98, 103, 107, 126, 188-9, 193, 196, 198, 199-201, 207, 244, 245, 271, 375, 429-30, 443-4, 446, 448-50, 461, 462, 469, 470, 493-4, 507, 508, 529, 535, 551, 593-4, 596, 597, 602, 603, 610, 611, 613-14, 623, 624, 629, 631-3, 635, 653, 655, 657, 658, 667, 670-1, 673, 675-7, 682, 710, 714, 716, 726
stylization, 4, 23, 461, 509
superdiversity, 83-4, 239, 309, 373, 377, 381, 383-5, 387-8, 496
surveillance, 7, 75, 365, 598, 678, 708-26
suspicion, 98, 216, 467, 549, 550, 558, 562-3, 565
systemic functional linguistics, 256, 263, 265-6, 275, 607

top-down, 246, 248, 308, 312, 395, 409, 673
translanguaging, 239, 309, 372, 373, 384, 388, 395-402, 404-13, 444, 505, 512, 516-18
translingual approaches, 445, 446

transnationalism, 373, 377–80, 381–2, 385, 386, 387–8
troubles-telling, 133, 144, 155
truth, 73, 173, 174, 245, 421, 466, 467–8, 470, 552, 564–5, 577
  post-truth, 593, 627

value, 3, 13, 15, 22, 35, 40, 53, 58, 73, 78, 105, 115, 116, 118, 147, 175, 180, 199, 200, 222–3, 247, 283–6, 287, 311, 315, 335, 351, 381–2, 387, 397, 406, 407, 425, 428, 446, 459, 465–71, 472–4, 478, 481, 482, 488, 492, 502, 509, 515, 534, 576–7, 578–9, 581–2, 584, 593–4, 596, 598, 608, 613–16, 617, 623, 629, 645, 658, 659–60, 671, 673, 680, 682, 698, 710, 719
  texts, 615–16, 617
variationism, 9, 19, 21
voicing, 5, 33, 39, 45–6, 48

World Englishes, 438, 445
writing, 41, 47, 57, 64, 101, 147, 218, 266, 294–5, 307, 318, 363, 377, 384, 397, 399, 403, 404–6, 408, 437, 439–41, 444, 445–6, 447, 448, 449, 498, 501, 512, 536–7, 549, 572, 576, 583, 677